THE ANNUAL DIRECTORY OF

American Bed & Breakfasts

1991 Edition

THE ANNUAL DIRECTORY OF

American Bed & Breakfasts

1991 Edition

Toni Sortor, *Editor*

RUTLEDGE HILL PRESS

NASHVILLE, TENNESSEE

Published in Nashville, Tennessee, by Rutledge Hill Press, Inc.
513 Third Avenue South, Nashville, Tennessee 37210

Cover design and Book design by Harriette Bateman
Maps and selected illustrations by Tonya Pitkin Presley, Studio III Productions

Photograph on front cover courtesy of Fearrington House Inn, Chapel Hill, North Carolina, © 1989 Bob Donnan Photography and used by permission.

Photograph on back cover courtesy of Chalet Suzanne Country Inn & Restaurant, Lake Wales, Florida, and used by permission.

Manufactured in the United States of America
1 2 3 4 5 6 — 92 91 90

Contents

THE ANNUAL DIRECTORY OF

American Bed & Breakfasts

1991 Edition

Introduction

Welcome to the world of B&Bs! As you can see, there's a B&B close to almost anywhere you want to go in the U.S., whether you're on vacation, stealing a getaway weekend, or traveling on business. There are certain advantages to staying at a B&B, too. Your hosts will generally be delighted to help you with sightseeing plans – or they'll leave you alone if you prefer. Your room will be clean and comfortable, sometimes simple, but sometimes downright luxurious – at a price lower than you would find in a local motel. And you'll have breakfast right there when you wake up, so you don't have to risk a diner or find a fast-food chain.

Most of all, B&B hosts are friendly, likeable people who enjoy having company and treating their guests with every consideration. It's a pretty good deal!

How to Use This Guide

Below is a sample listing. Let's walk through it. The B&B's town is listed first, alphabetically within the state. If there's more than one B&B in town, they'll be listed alphabetically by B&B name. The B&B's address follows the B&B name, if you want to write to make reservations or obtain a brochure. The descriptions that follow the address are meant to give you some idea of the town, the house, activities and amenities available.

NOTE: These descriptions were written by the B&B hosts themselves. The publisher has not visited these B&Bs and can't be responsible for any inaccuracies in the descriptions.

ANYWHEREVILLE

Hometown B&B

151 Front Street
Anywhereville, NY, 10000
(800) 123-4567

A true B&B, where your comfort is the major concern. Filled with antiques, this gracious Victorian home offers private baths, many stained-glass windows, wraparound veranda, and duck pond. All rooms are air-conditioned, and a huge breakfast is served. Near colleges, historic sites, and local attractions. Good family vacation spot.

Hosts: Sue & Jim Smith
Rooms: 4 (PB) $55-65
Full Breakfast
Closed January
Credit Cards: A, B, C
Notes: 2, 7, 8, 10, 11, 12, 13, 14

Following the descriptions are more specific notes: the hosts' names, private or shared baths, type of breakfast served, and so forth. In these notes, "PB" means private bath, "SB" means shared bath. Some entries may say "S2B," which means guests share two baths. Rates are for two people sharing one room, unless noted otherwise. The last line of the notes is made up of numbers that are explained at the bottom of each page. A 3 or 4 means lunch or dinner is available on the premises. For the sports entries – 10, 11, 12, 13 – the activity is within ten miles, not necessarily on the premises. If a B&B has note 14, you may book your stay through a travel agent.

You'll note that some entries have numbers or letters instead of house names, or don't list the hosts' names. These houses are booked through reservation service organizations that handle bookings for more than one house. Think of them as B&B travel agents. The advantage of booking through a service is that they have a wide variety of homes and generally do quality control. They can match your needs to the best house for you, but they do generally charge for this service.

To see where a given house is located in a state, turn to the state map and look for the name of the town the house is listed under. Some are quite rural; others are in large cities.

Inns vs. B&Bs

This book lists inns as well as B&Bs, but the inns serve breakfast as part of the room rate. Most of these inns are small, family-run places, although some are larger, with more available activities. You often have a choice between a homestay and a small inn in a given town, and may want to try both during your vacation.

How to Make a Reservation

You may either call or write to the B&B you've chosen. When you do, don't be afraid to ask questions! Will you have a private bath? If not, how many people share a bath? Is there a set time for breakfast? Does the house have all the facilities you need? Will they let you bring your children or Fido? Ask more questions than you'd ask of a hotel or motel. Your hosts will be happy to answer your questions, and many B&Bs have brochures they'll send if you request one.

Be sure to ask about payment and cancellation policies, too. Some B&Bs take credit cards, others take checks, but most prefer cash. Avoid unpleasant surprises.

When You Arrive

Plan to arrive at your B&B during their normal check-in hours, which you should ask about when you call. Arrive with the same number of people you booked for and no extraneous pets. The most important thing to remember is that you are a guest in someone's home, even though you're paying for a room and breakfast, and your hosts deserve common courtesy. If you'll be sharing a bath, remember to bring a robe and slippers. Staying at a B&B can be one of the most rewarding travel experiences you'll ever have, as Europeans who have been doing it for years will tell you, but it does take a little work on your part.

So, are you ready to go to Lawai, on the island of Kauai, Hawaii? It's in here. Have to take a high-school senior to visit Cornell? How about a family vacation on a ranch in Montana? No problem. Business trip to Des Moines? It's covered. Give B&Bs a try the next time you're traveling. Have fun!

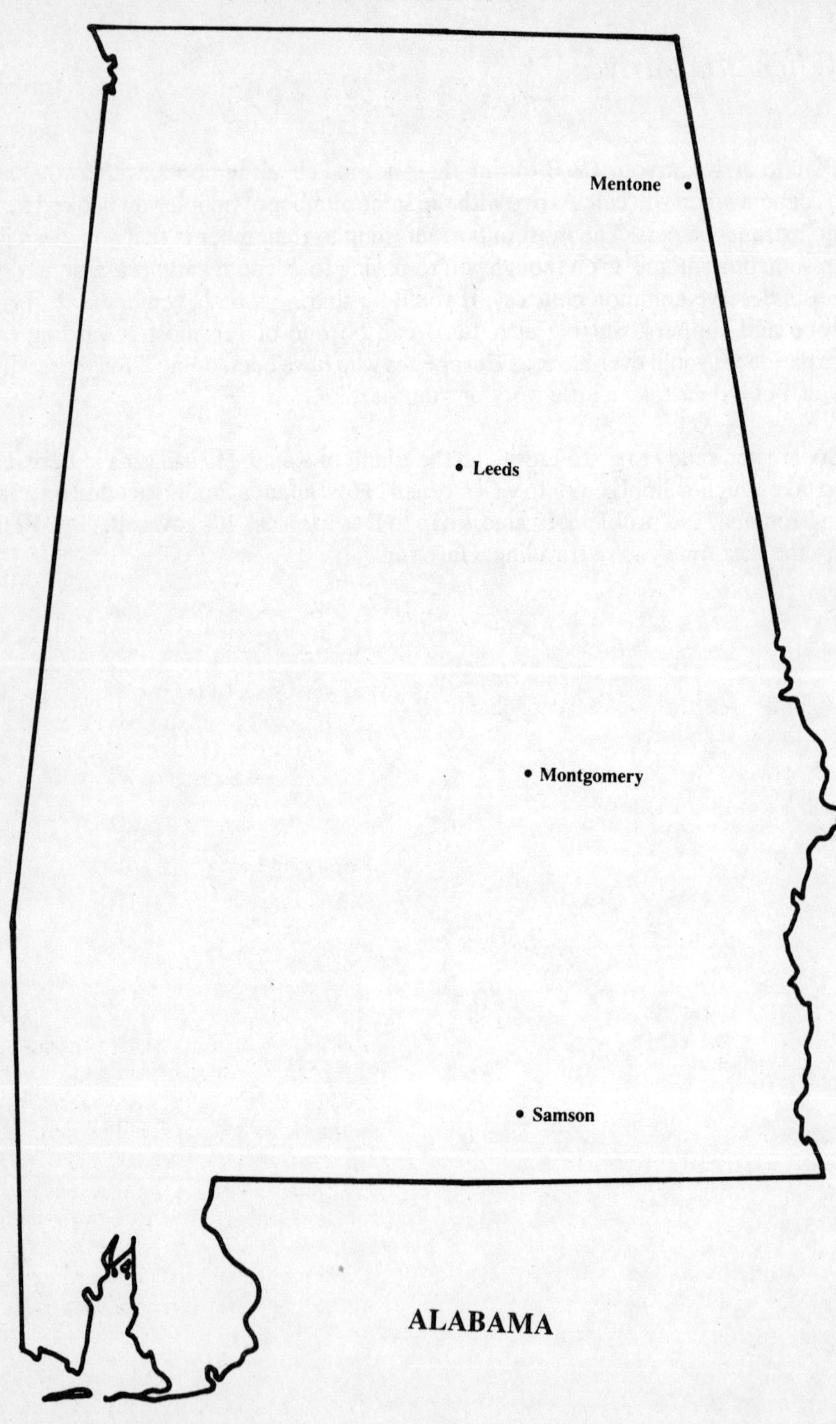
Mentone
Leeds
Montgomery
Samson
ALABAMA

Alabama

LEEDS

Country Sunshine

Route 2, Box 275
Leeds, AL, 35094
(205) 699-9841

A 4.5-acre secluded retreat with a quiet country atmosphere. Barn and pasture to board your horses. Ranch-style house with four bedrooms and four baths, TV den, fireplace, formal dining room, country dining room, outside screened patio. Guided fishing and camping is available in the area, as is horseback riding. Twenty minutes south of Birmingham, near the Botanical Gardens, Vulcan Park, and Oak Mountain State Park.

Host: Kay Rice
Rooms: 4 (PB and SB) $50-65
Full Breakfast
Credit Cards: No
Notes: 2, 3, 4, 5, 8 (over 13), 14

MENTONE

Mentone Inn

Highway 117, Box 284
Mentone, AL, 35984
(205) 634-4836

In an old-fashioned, relaxing, quaint old town near DeSoto Falls. Good hospitality; rock on the front porch and watch the world go by.

Host: Amelia Kirk
Rooms: 12 (PB) $55-65
Full Breakfast
Credit Cards: No
Notes: 2, 3, 4, 9, 14

MONTGOMERY

East Fork Farm

B&B Montgomery
P.O. Box 886
Millbrook, AL, 36054
(205) 285-5421

A beautifully designed country contemporary on 60 acres east of Montgomery, two minutes from I-85 and convenient to the Alabama Shakespeare Festival. Six bedrooms with private entrances opening onto a covered terrace and pool. Private baths and kitchenettes. The home features an oversized keeping room with large stone fireplace and a video room for movies and TV. Hearty Southern breakfasts. Honeymooners are especially welcome. $48.

Inverrary

B&B Montgomery
P.O. Box 886
Millbrook, AL, 36054
(205) 285-5421

A classic older restored farm home on 60 acres east of Montgomery and only a few minutes from I-85, convenient to the Alabama Shakespeare Festival. Great breakfasts, pastoral scenes, large red barn will delight you. A nearby antebellum country Episcopal church with English garden to explore. There are two private bedrooms with shared bath for families, or one bedroom with a private bath. $40.

NOTES: Credit cards accepted: A Master Card; B Visa; C American Express; D Discover Card; E Diners Club; F Other: 2 Personal checks accepted: 3 Lunch available: 4 Dinner available: 5 Open all year: 6 Pets welcome: 7 Smoking allowed: 8 Children welcome: 9 Social drinking allowed: 10 Tennis available: 11 Swimming available: 12 Golf available: 13 Skiing available: 14 May be booked through travel agents

Old Parsonage Lot

B&B Montgomery
P.O. Box 886
Millbrook, AL, 36054
(205) 285-5421

A restored c. 1840 raised cottage filled with antiques and charm, minutes from I-65N and fifteen minutes from downtown, located near an original antebellum country church built in the late 1830s. Share experiences with this well-traveled retired military officer and his wife, who are also musicians and antique lovers. They serve hearty country breakfasts and lots of hospitality. One bedroom with private bath. $40.

Red Bluff Cottage

B&B Montgomery
P.O. Box 886
Millbrook, AL, 36054
(205) 285-5421

A raised cottage reminiscent of days gone by, high above the Alabama River plain in Montgomery's historic Cottage Hill district. A deep upstairs porch provides a great view, and, weather permitting, a delightful place for a full, home-cooked breakfast. Guests can enjoy family antiques, a music room with harpsichord, four spacious bedrooms with private baths on the ground floor. Fireplace, terraces, gazebo. Conveniently located minutes from downtown, I-65 N, and I-85. $50.

SAMSON

Jola Bama Guest Home

201 South East Street
Samson, AL, 36477
(205) 898-2478

This comfortable clapboard Victorian boasts a collection of interesting antiques. Located eighty-five miles south of Montgomery, "The Cradle of the Confederacy." North Florida beaches and the Ft. Rucker Army Aviation Museum are nearby. Your host, a tree farmer and cattle rancher, looks forward to welcoming you.

Host: Jewel M. Armstrong
Rooms: 2 (PB or SB) $20-29
Continental Breakfast
Credit Cards: No
Notes: 5, 6, 7, 8 (16 and over), 9, 14

Alaska

ANCHORAGE

Accommodations Alaska Style 1D

3605 Arctic Blvd., No. 173
Anchorage, AK, 99503
(406) 259-7993

As close as you can get to Cook Inlet on land, by a small park and in view of the scenic coastal walking/bike trail, only a minute from excellent restaurants. Two rooms share one bath; family room with TV and hideabed. Glorious views of Mt. Susitna and the Alaska Range with Mt. McKinley some 250 road miles away. Full breakfast, no smoking. $50-60.

Accommodations Alaska Style 2D

3605 Arctic Blvd. No. 173
Anchorage, AK, 99503
(907) 344-4006

View Cook Inlet and majestic Sleeping Lady from the large picture windows of this home in a quiet neighborhood within two blocks of major hotels and restaurants. Two units, each equipped with full kitchen, color TV, telephone. Full breakfast, or may be self-serve from stocked kitchens.

Accommodations Alaska Style 5D

3605 Arctic Blvd. No. 173
Anchorage, AK, 99503
(907) 344-4006

Nicely decorated room on ground level of a modern home two blocks from Cook Inlet and fourteen blocks from city center. Twin beds, private bath, color TV, telephone. Enjoy the water view when you breakfast upstairs, or hostess will provide a continental breakfast in your room. $65.

Accommodations Alaska Style 6D

3605 Arctic Blvd. No. 173
Anchorage, AK, 99503
(907) 344-4006

Apartment suite in Anchorage's premier neighborhood, right on Cook Inlet. Two bedrooms, full bath, living room, and kitchen. Serve yourself breakfast from the stocked refrigerator. $70.

Accommodations Alaska Style 7D

3605 Arctic Blvd. No. 173
Anchorage, AK, 99503
(907) 344-4006

This large home in Bootlegger Cove neighborhood has a three-bedroom apartment with separate guest entrance. Your hostess is wild about fishing and has been known to share her catch with guests. Full bath, color TV, telephone, and kitchen stocked for breakfast. $70.

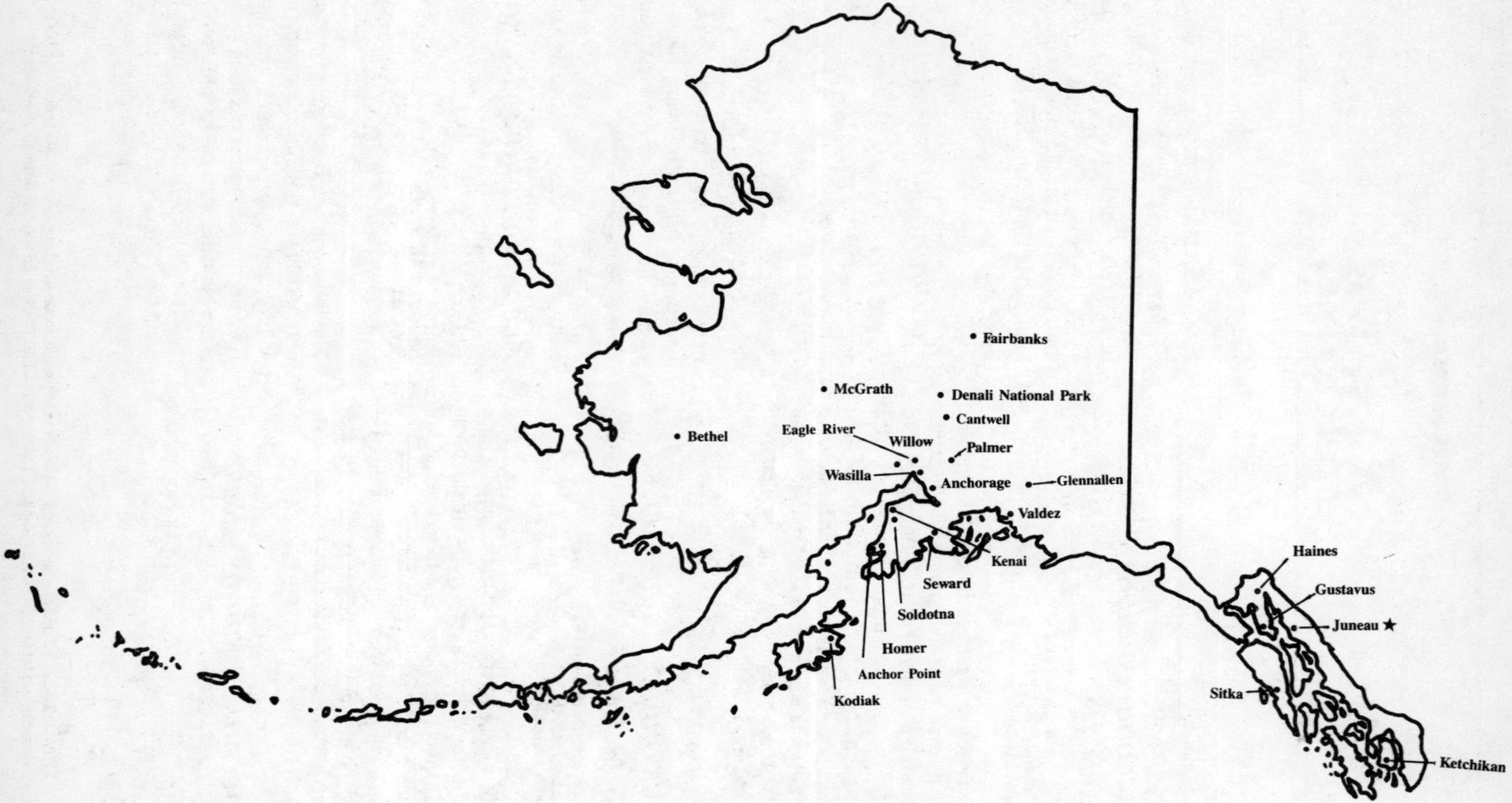

Fairbanks
McGrath
Denali National Park
Cantwell
Bethel
Eagle River
Willow
Palmer
Wasilla
Anchorage
Glennallen
Valdez
Kenai
Seward
Soldotna
Homer
Anchor Point
Kodiak
Haines
Gustavus
Juneau ★
Sitka
Ketchikan

ALASKA

Accommodations Alaska Style 20A

3605 Arctic Blvd., No. 173
Anchorage, AK, 99503
(406) 259-7993

Dutch charm, including hand-crocheted curtains, interesting collectibles, colorful flower gardens. Two rooms share a full bath and cozy family room on the ground level. Breakfast European style upstairs with your hosts, who are pioneers in international aviation in Alaska. Quiet neighborhood. Dutch and German are spoken. $50-60.

Accommodations Alaska Style 21A

3605 Arctic Blvd., No. 173
Anchorage, AK, 99503
(406) 259-7993

This charming split-level home has two pleasant guest rooms with double beds and a shared bath. Resident cat and dog assist hostess in the welcome. Hostess is a genealogy buff and will prepare a full breakfast of pancakes, omelets, or your choice. On a city bus route. $45-55.

Accommodations Alaska Style 30E

3605 Arctic Blvd. No. 173
Anchorage, AK, 99503
(907) 344-4006

This B&B offers a downstairs suite with two bedrooms, a full bath, and a family room. Feel free to explore the wonderful Alaskana collections on the premises. A full breakfast is served in the upstairs sun room, and French is spoken here. $55.

Accommodations Alaska Style 31E

3605 Arctic Blvd., No. 173
Anchorage, AK, 99503
(406) 259-7993

Large split-level family home with many fascinating collectibles. Beautiful mountain view from dining room, where you may enjoy a full breakfast with fresh strawberry or raspberry jam from the garden. Upstairs room has two double beds and a half bath. Downstairs, a room with a king bed shares a bath with a third room. All are welcome in the large family room with TV, refrigerator, telephone. Wheelchair access can be arranged. Resident cat. $40-50.

Accommodations Alaska Style 32E

3605 Arctic Blvd. No. 173
Anchorage, AK, 99503
(907) 344-4006

Two blocks from Humana Hospital, with a Chugach Mountain view, this ranch home has a beautiful garden, king room with private bath and sitting rooms with TV. Old Doberman enjoys guests and will accept guest pets in fenced yard. Breakfast of your choice is served on the garden patio if you wish. Guest passes at nearby athletic club available. $65.

Accommodations Alaska Style 35E

3605 Arctic Blvd. No. 173
Anchorage, AK, 99503
(907) 344-4006

Sunny home one block from bus line, with large downstairs suite including a queen bedroom, futon bed for third person, full bath. Family room for relaxing has TV and double bed. Gigantic breakfasts are served upstairs by the hosts. $55.

Accommodations Alaska Style 50M

3605 Arctic Blvd., No. 173
Anchorage, AK, 99503
(406) 259-7993

Cozy red house, about a twenty-minute walk to city center. There is a small room with double bed and half bath and another room that shares a bath with the hostess. Guests have own sitting room for TV and reading. Small dog in residence. Breakfast is made to order with fruit, juice, croissants, muffins, cereal. Two blocks to city bus line. $40-50.

Accommodations Alaska Style 51M

3605 Arctic Blvd. No. 173
Anchorage, AK, 99503
(907) 344-4006

A few blocks from the University Shopping Mall in a quiet subdivision, this split-level home has two guest rooms sharing bath and recreation room with TV on the lower level. Continental breakfast. Close to city bus line; no smoking. $50.

Accommodations Alaska Style 53M

3605 Arctic Blvd. No. 173
Anchorage, AK, 99503
(907) 344-4006

Picturesque tiny log cabin—one room with a corner kitchen, bath, and cozy sitting area with TV and double bed. Prepare your own breakfast or enjoy it in the main house with pioneer Alaskan hostess. A few blocks from restaurants and Coastal Trail. $50.

Accommodations Alaska Style 81H

3605 Arctic Blvd., No. 173
Anchorage, AK, 99503
(406) 259-7993

A very special tri-level home with a private suite decorated with antiques and country collectibles. Sitting room has wood-burning fireplace and writing nook; queen bedroom has private atrium bath with step-down tile shower. Outdoor hot tub on a deck overlooking the Chugach State Forest. Two children and two small dogs in residence. $90.

Accommodations Alaska Style 82H

3605 Arctic Blvd. No. 173
Anchorage, AK, 99503
(907) 344-4006

Separate apartment in beautiful home with a panoramic view of the city, Cook Inlet, the Alaska Range, and Mt. McKinley. Unit has a small herb and flower garden, deck, and lots of privacy. Both king and double beds in the bedroom, full kitchen with stocked refrigerator, or hostess will cook for you. Guests may use full gymnasium. $90.

Accommodations Alaska Style 83H

3605 Arctic Blvd., No. 173
Anchorage, AK, 99503
(406) 259-7993

Country home for animal lovers located twenty-five minutes from city center. Two gorgeous hybrid wolves live on a deck above the garage, and an aviary occupies the lower part of the house. Guest room with double bed shares a bath with a room with a single bed. Full or continental breakfast. Nice area for wooded trail hikes or bike riding. $40-50.

Accommodations Alaska Style 84H

3605 Arctic Blvd. No. 173
Anchorage, AK, 99503
(907) 344-4006

Suite in multi-level hillside home. Ground-floor twin bedroom and sitting room with double daybed. Full breakfast with your hosts or serve yourself from the stocked kitchen. Two large decks for north and south mountain and inlet views. Outdoor dog, inside bird. $65.

Accommodations Alaska Style 85H

3605 Arctic Blvd. No. 173
Anchorage, AK, 99503
(907) 344-4006

Modern home on Cook Inlet waterfront has an elegant sitting room and large decks for enjoying the beautiful view and midnight sun. Main-level room with queen bed and private bath. Upper room has a superb view, queen bed, shared bath. Continental breakfast. Swedish and some Japanese are spoken. $75-95.

All the Comforts of Home

Accommodations Alaska Style 88S

3605 Arctic Blvd. No. 173
Anchorage, AK, 99503
(907) 344-4006

Massive home at the foot of the ski slopes about 45 minutes from city center has six rooms. One has king bed, private bath. A variety of beds in other rooms, shared baths and Jacuzzi tub. Full breakfast; no smoking. $65-85.

All the Comforts of Home

12531 Turk's Turn
Anchorage, AK, 99516
(907) 345-4279

A rustic establishment with a quiet adult atmosphere. Although the "Alaskan mystique" may be intangible, our guests depart with a greater understanding of this beautiful land. Enjoy full country breakfasts while seated at an antique table in our bay window that really does overlook the bay. Year-round sauna and hot tub.

Hosts: Sydnee Mae Stiver & Frank J. McCurley
Rooms: 3 (1 PB; 2 SB) $60-125
Full Breakfast
Credit Cards: A, B, C
Notes: 2, 5, 8, 9, 10, 11, 12, 13, 14

ANCHOR POINT

Accommodations Alaska Style 91S

3605 Arctic Blvd. No. 173
Anchorage, AK, 99503
(907) 344-4006

This beautiful home on a bluff overlooks Cook Inlet and offers views of Mt. Redoubt and others. All rooms share a full bath on the ground level or another one flight up. Delicious full breakfast while you watch eagles soaring from the huge evergreens or feed popcorn to the jays on the outside deck.

Host is a retired Alaska fish and game officer, and knows all the great fishing holes. $50-60.

Accommodations Alaska Style 92S

3605 Arctic Blvd. No. 173
Anchorage, AK, 99503
(907) 344-4006

Inviting country home with spectacular scenery. Three horses and a friendly dog will keep you company while you relax, picnic, or play games. Can accommodate seven guests. Full breakfast; no smoking. Also available are two cabins with stocked refrigerators. $65.

BETHEL

Bentley's Porterhouse B&B

624 First Avenue
Box 529
Bethel, AK, 99559
(907) 543-3552

Located on the beautiful Kuskokwim River in southwest Alaska, offering comfortable rooms with cable TV. Full elegant breakfast is served on fine china—great sourdough waffles and bread! Special dietary accommodations on advance notice. Reservations advisable; brochure available.

Hosts: Bette Goodwine & Millie Bentley
Rooms: 9 (SB) $90
Full Breakfast
Credit Cards: A, B (for reservations)
Notes: 2, 5, 7, 8, 9

CANTWELL

Adventures Unlimited Lodge

Mile 100, Denali Highway
P.O. Box 89
Cantwell, AK, 99729
No telephone

Adventures Unlimited Lodge, remotely located in the heart of Alaska's Denali Valley, is situated among timbered valleys, rolling tundra, glaciers, and towering snowcapped mountains. The closest neighbor is thirty-five miles away. Trout and grayling fishing is abundant; one commonly sees caribou, moose, wolves, foxes, grizzly bears, and varied species of birds.

Hosts: Doug & Michelle Hamrick
Rooms: 5 (2 PB; 3 SB) $50
Full Breakfast
Credit Cards: No
Notes: 2, 3, 4, 5, 7, 8, 11, 13 (XC), 14

DENALI NATIONAL PARK

Camp Denali

Denali National Park
AK, 99755
(907) 683-2290

Cozy cabins in the heart of Denali National Park with spectacular views of Mt. McKinley. All-inclusive package: all meals, lodging, round-trip transportation from park entrance (180 miles), hiking, canoeing, fishing, wildlife observation, photography, cycling, rafting, gold panning, evening natural history programs. Naturalists on staff.

Hosts: Wallace & Jerryne Cole
Double Cabins: 12 (SB) $195/person; youth $147
Family Cabins (sleep 3-6): 6 (SB) $195/person; youth $147. Ten percent discount for 3 or more family members in same cabin.
Minimum stay 3, 4, or 5 nights; fixed arrival & departure dates
Credit Cards: No
Closed early Sept.-early June
Notes: 2, 3, 4, 8, 14

Kantishna Roadhouse

P.O. Box 130
Denali, AK, 99755
(907) 733-2535

Kantishna Roadhouse is a modern full-service lodge with all the amenities you would expect from a first-class wilderness resort. Our packages include transportation to and from Kantishna, three gourmet meals a day, and a wide range of activities. Call or write for plans and rates.

Host: Roberta L. Wilson
Rooms: 28 (PB)
Full Breakfast
Credit Cards: No
Open June 5-Sept. 10
Notes: 2, 3, 4, 7, 8, 9, 14

North Face Lodge

Denali National Park
AK, 99755
(907) 683-2290

Country inn located in the heart of Denali National Park, with view of Mt. McKinley. Vacation price includes: all meals, lodging, round-trip transportation from park entrance (180 miles), hiking, canoeing, fishing, cycling, nature photography, wildlife observation, rafting, gold panning, and evening natural-history programs. Naturalists on staff.

Hosts: Wallace & Jerryne Cole
Doubles: 13 (PB) $225-275/person; youth $169-219. Ten percent discount for 3 or more family members in same room.
Triples: 1 (PB)
Family Suite (sleeps 4) (PB)
Full Breakfast
Minimum stay: 2-3; fixed arrival & departure dates
Credit Cards: No
Closed early Sept.-early June
Notes: 2, 3, 4, 8, 14

EAGLE RIVER

Accommodations Alaska Style 50N

3605 Arctic Blvd. No. 173
Anchorage, AK, 99503
(907) 344-4006

Located fourteen miles north of Anchorage, this home contains a small museum for your pleasure with a variety of collections. Upstairs room with double bed has private bath. Two other rooms have single beds and shared bath. Complete European continental breakfast. Outdoor ducks and geese, indoor cats. $50.

FAIRBANKS

Accommodations Alaska Style 61N

3605 Arctic Blvd. No. 173
Anchorage, AK, 99503
(907) 344-4006

Natural log home three miles from the airport. Two country bedrooms with shared bath. Master bedroom has queen bed, private bath. Full breakfast is served on the large backyard deck. Two small dogs in residence. No smoking. $50-58.

Accommodations Alaska Style 62N

3605 Arctic Blvd. No. 173
Anchorage, AK, 99503
(907) 344-4006

Friendly home within walking distance of downtown attractions, close to the Chena River. One bedroom has a queen bed, private bath, and TV. Another with twin beds shares a bath with the hostess. A large basement room has a queen, single, two rollaways, TV, refrigerator, and private bath. Full breakfast. $36-58.

Accommodations Alaska Style 65N

3605 Arctic Blvd. No. 173
Anchorage, AK, 99503
(907) 344-4006

Modern home on the Ft. Wainwright side of town, on the Chena River, about two miles from downtown. Room with double bed and private bath. Two other rooms share a bath. Full or continental breakfast. Friendly cocker spaniel. $40-55.

Accommodations Alaska Style 66N

3605 Arctic Blvd. No. 173
Anchorage, AK, 99503
(907) 344-4006

Relax on the deck overlooking the Chena River and watch the riverboats cruise by, or walk to one of the most popular restaurants in Fairbanks. Bike paths and scenic hikes are also within walking distance; canoe rental nearby. One river-view room with queen bed, private bath with double Jacuzzi tub, TV, VCR. Another room has twin beds, shared bath. Airport pickup can be arranged. $48-60.

Accommodations Alaska Style 67N

3605 Arctic Blvd. No. 173
Anchorage, AK, 99503
(907) 344-4006

Country apartment with 2 acres of lawn and views of Fairbanks, Mt. McKinley, and the rest of the Alaska Range. Ten minutes from town or the airport. Completely equipped with queen bed, fireplace, TV, telephone, full kitchen stocked for breakfast. $65.

GLENNALLEN

Accommodations Alaska Style 91N

3605 Arctic Blvd. No. 173
Anchorage, AK, 99503
(907) 344-4006

Country home in a quiet subdivision with garden and tall trees has a spacious room on the second floor with queen bed, private bath, and sitting area. Family-style full breakfast. $55.

Accommodations Alaska Style 99N

3605 Arctic Blvd. No. 173
Anchorage, AK, 99503
(907) 344-4006

Ranch house with casual family atmosphere is home to longtime Alaskans. King bedroom shares a full bath with a twin room. Smoking is allowed. Full breakfast featuring Alaskan specialties; freezer space for fish. Host and hostess gladly help you with fishing plans and spin tales of the far north. $45-95.

Glacier Bay Country Inn

GUSTAVUS

Glacier Bay Country Inn

Box 5-ND
Gustavus, AK, 99826
(907) 697-2288

Peaceful storybook accommodations away from the crowds in a wilderness setting. Cozy comforters, warm flannel sheets. Superb dining features local seafood, garden-fresh produce, home-baked breads, spectacular desserts. Whale watching, sightseeing, and fishing aboard our deluxe 42-foot yacht. Glacier Bay boat/plane tours. All meals, transfers, use of bikes included in rate.

NOTES: Credit cards accepted: A Master Card; B Visa; C American Express; D Discover Card; E Diners Club; F Other: 2 Personal checks accepted: 3 Lunch available: 4 Dinner available: 5 Open all year

Hosts: Al & Annie Unrein
Rooms: 9 (7 PB; 2 SB) $168-184 AP
Full Breakfast
Credit Cards: No
Dinner included in daily rate
Notes: 2, 3, 4, 5, 8, 9, 13, 14

Gustavus Inn

Box 60, Gustavus, AK, 99826
(907) 697-2254

Glacier Bay's historic homestead, newly renovated, full-service inn accommodates twenty-six. Family-style meals, seafood, garden produce, wild edibles. Boat tours of Glacier Bay, charter fishing, and air transportation from Juneau arranged. Bikes and airport transfers included in the daily rates. American Plan only.

Hosts: David & Jo Ann Lesh
Rooms: 12 (7 PB; 5 SB) $110
Full Breakfast
Credit Cards: A, B, C
Closed Sept. 20-May 1
Notes: 2, 3, 4, 7, 8, 9, 14

Gustavus Inn

Puffin's Bed & Breakfast

1/4 Mile Logging Road, Box 3
Gustavus, AK, 99826
(907) 697-2260; winter: (907) 789-9787

Your own modern cottage on a 5-acre, partially wooded homestead carpeted in wildflowers and berries. Special diets accommodated. Hike beaches or bicycle miles of country roads. See marine life from a charter cruiser or kayak. Courtesy transportation; Glacier Bay tours, travel services available.

Hosts: Chuck & Sandy Schroth
Cottages: 3 (PB) $35-55; children under 12: $5; under 2: free
Full Breakfast
Credit Cards: A, B, C
Closed Oct. 15-April 15
Notes: 3, 4, 6, 7, 8, 9, 14

HAINES

The Summer Inn B&B

247 Second Ave., Box 1198
Haines, AK, 99827
(907) 766-2970

The Summer Inn B&B is a five-bedroom historic house with a live-in innkeeper. Located near the heart of downtown, it is within walking distance of the sights of Haines and close to the Chilkat Bald Eagle Preserve.

Hosts: Mary Ellen & Bob Summer
Rooms: 5.5 (SB) $63
Full Breakfast
Credit Cards: A, B
Notes: 2, 5, 8, 10, 11, 12, 14

HOMER

Brass Ring B&B

987 Hillfair Court
Homer, AK, 99603
(907) 235-5450

Our traditional log home offers a country atmosphere with seven individually decorated rooms. We feature a full Alaskan breakfast each morning, including sourdough blueberry pancakes and reindeer sausage. Guests will enjoy the convenient location near the airport, waterfront, and downtown shops and restaurants. We are only minutes from some of the best salmon and halibut fishing in the world. Laundry facilities; winter discount.

Hosts: Joyce & Vince Porte
Rooms: 7 (S3B) $55-65
Full Breakfast
Credit Cards: No
Notes: 2 (in advance), 5, 7 (outdoors), 8 (6 and over), 10, 11, 12, 13, 14

JUNEAU

Accommodations Alaska Style 110P

3605 Arctic Blvd. No. 173
Anchorage, AK, 99503
(907) 344-4006

Free pickup from ferry or airport any hour of the day or night is just part of the friendly service here. Minimum two-night stay. Full breakfast and guest kitchen for storing fish or preparing a meal. Five large rooms share a living room with a view of the Gastineau Channel. City or Mendenhall Glacier tours can be arranged. $48-55 + tax.

The Lost Chord

2200 Fritz Cove Road
Juneau, AK, 99801
(907) 789-7296

Our music business has expanded to become a homey B&B on an exquisite private beach. Breakfast is with the proprietors, who have been in Alaska from 1946. Located in the country twelve miles from Juneau; a car is suggested.

Hosts: Jesse & Ellen Jones
Rooms: 4 (1 PB; 3 SB) $35-65
Full Breakfast
Credit Cards: No
Notes: 2, 5, 6 (by arrangement), 7 (outside on deck), 8, 9, 10, 11, 12, 13, 14

KENAI

Accommodations Alaska Style 77S

3605 Arctic Blvd. No. 173
Anchorage, AK, 99503
(907) 344-4006

Cedar lodge-style B&B centrally located close to the Kenai River has three guest rooms: one with private bath and two sharing a bath. Guests have use of a full kitchen, private sitting room, and freezer to store fish. Full country breakfast served as early as 5:00 A.M. by hosts who understand fishermen. Transportation arranged from Kenai Airport. $65-70.

KETCHIKAN

North Tongass B&B

Box 684
Ketchikan, AK, 99928
(907) 247-2467

Friendly Alaskan hospitality, just minutes from Ketchikan. Near fine restaurants, grocery stores, and boat harbors. Lovely beach home with private guest quarters, entry, deck, and sitting room. Also quaint two-bedroom apartment nestled in the woods. Freezers available for your catch.

Hosts: Doug & Lynda Ruhl, Daryle & Wanda Vandergriff
Rooms: 10 (SB) $60
Continental Breakfast
Credit Cards: No
Notes: 2, 5, 8, 9, 11, 14

KODIAK

Kalsin Bay Inn

Box 1696, Kodiak, AK, 99615
(907) 486-2659

We are centrally located in the heart of fishing and hunting territory, near fossil beds and World War II bunkers. Satellite TV, laundry facilities, package store, and restaurant.

Hosts: Virginia Sargent & Wayne Sargent
Rooms: 10 (SB) $40-55
Full Breakfast
Credit Cards: No
Notes: 2, 3, 4, 5, 6, 7, 8

Kodiak B&B

308 Cope Street
Kodiak, AK, 99616
(907) 486-5367

Visitors will enjoy a spectacular view of Kodiak's busy fishing fleet in a location just above the boat harbor. Mary's home is easy walking distance from a historic Russian church, art galleries, Baronof Museum, and downtown restaurants. Enjoy the magic of this little fishing city with its Russian heritage, stunning beaches and cliffs, and abundant fish and bird life. Fresh local fish is often a breakfast option.

Host: Mary A. Neouroe
Rooms: 16 (13 PB; 3 SB) $66
Full Breakfast
Credit Cards: A, B
Notes: 2, 5, 6, 8, 9, 10, 12, 14

PALMER

Accommodations Alaska Style 92N

3605 Arctic Blvd. No. 173
Anchorage, AK, 99503
(907) 344-4006

Modern house 38 miles from Anchorage with farm hospitality. Two twin rooms, one queen, and one with a queen hideabed; shared baths. Full breakfast featuring farm-fresh ingredients, other meals on request. The sun room has a wonderful view of Pioneer Peak. Pastries at 9:00 P.M. under the midnight sun. Close to the University of Alaska agricultural farm. $50.

Accommodations Alaska Style 93N

3605 Arctic Blvd., No. 173
Anchorage, AK, 99503
(406) 259-7993

Beautifully decorated traditional European country home tucked in a quiet pine forest with friendly llamas to gaze on from your guest room windows. Flowers and quiet paths. One room with a queen and another with twins share a bath. Jacuzzi tub available. Full continental breakfast is served; German spoken, and Dutch is understood. Llama pack trips and day hikes can be arranged. $65-75.

SEWARD

Accommodations Alaska Style 71S

3605 Arctic Blvd. No. 173
Anchorage, AK, 99503
(907) 344-4006

Bungalow conveniently located within walking distance of the harbor has ground-level room with bay window, queen bed, TV, private shower. Upstairs room has a double bed, full shared bath with Jacuzzi. Full breakfast; children over twelve are welcome. Usually available weekdays only. $45-60.

Accommodations Alaska Style 72S

3605 Arctic Blvd. No. 173
Anchorage, AK, 99503
(907) 344-4006

Rural, casual neighborhood ten minutes from the city on the road to Exit Glacier. Modular home has a queen bedroom with private bath and room with double bed. Host is a commercial fisherman; hostess cooks a full breakfast for guests leaving on early boat tours. $40-60.

SITKA

Bed Inn 518

518 Monastery
Sitka, AK, 99835
(907) 747-3305

Spacious, comfortable, friendly, and affordable. Conveniently located within walking distance of shopping, restaurants, museums, and an abundance of interesting sites of Alaskan, Russian, and local history. Hiking trails. Nestled in the foothills of the Sitka Mountains. You'll enjoy the spectacular view of Alaska's natural beauty, from breathtaking mountains to soaring eagles.

Hosts: Margaret & Fred Hope
Rooms: 2 (1 PB; 1 SB) From $43
Continental Breakfast
Credit Cards: No
Notes: 2, 5, 7, 8, 9, 10, 11, 14

Helga's Bed & Breakfast

Box 1885
Sitka, AK, 99835
(907) 747-5497

Helga's B&B is located directly on Sitka Sound, on the bus route to the ferry. Outside barbecue is available for guests, and some rooms have mini-kitchens. Our two-bedroom apartment is perfect for families or two couples traveling together. Joe will take you out on a fishing charter in the evenings or weekends, or on a photo or sightseeing trip, if you prefer.

Hosts: Helga Garrison & family
Rooms: 5 (2 PB; 3 SB) $40-50
Full Breakfast
Credit Cards: A, B
Notes: 2, 5, 7, 8, 9

Karras Bed & Breakfast

230 Kogwanton Street
Sitka, AK, 99835
(907) 747-3978

Centrally located, overlooking Sitka Sound, the fishing fleet, and the Pacific Ocean. Walk to Sitka's main historic attractions, restaurants, and shopping. Telescope-equipped family room for lounging, reading, visiting, and watching the endlessly fascinating marine traffic. No smoking or alcoholic beverages allowed in the house.

Hosts: Pete & Bertha Karras
Rooms: $54-64.50
Full Breakfast
Credit Cards: C
Notes: 2, 5

SOLDOTNA

Accommodations Alaska Style 75S

3605 Arctic Blvd. No. 173
Anchorage, AK, 99503
(907) 344-4006

Large log house on the edge of a small lake with loons. Friendly hospitality and big breakfasts. Variety of bed sizes and rooms share bath with one or two other rooms. Lunches can be ordered for fishing or hiking trips. All meals available, as are guided fishing trips and transportation from Kenai or Soldotna airports. $55-75.

VALDEZ

Johnson House B&B

P.O. Box 364
Valdez, AK, 99686
(907) 835-5289

Five rooms share three baths. Cable TV in rooms; sauna; large-screen TV. Tennis, indoor swimming pool nearby. Free airport and ferry transfers.

Host: Brian K. Johnson
Rooms: 5 (PB) $55-75
Continental Breakfast
Credit Cards: No
Notes: 2, 5, 8, 9

WASILLA

Yukon Don's

HC 315086
Wasilla, AK, 99687
(907) 376-7472

Yukon Don's is an extraordinary B&B inn. Each room is decorated in a specific Alaskan theme (Iditarod, fishing, hunting, Klondike, etc.). Our 900-square-foot Alaska room is the guest lounge, furnished with an Alaskana collection, pool table, darts, Alaska video library, and more. The 270-degree view of the Chugach and Talkectna Mountains is unequaled.

Hosts: Aaron, Jesse, Kristi, Zach
Rooms: 6 (1 PB; 5 SB) $65
Suite: 1 (PB) $75
Continental Breakfast Bar
Credit Cards: No
Notes: 2, 5, 11, 12, 13, 14

WILLOW

Accommodations Alaska Style 94N

3605 Arctic Blvd., No. 173
Anchorage, AK, 99503
(406) 259-7993

Cabins can sleep up to six or eight, and some have modern conveniences; others use a central washhouse. Great fishing, hiking, berry picking, and the friendliest hostesses serve continental breakfast in the adjoining small lodge. Ski, skate, or canoe, depending on the season. Near small lake with a view of Mt. McKinley. Cabins are immaculate, charming, warm. Train depot is just a wave away. $40-125.

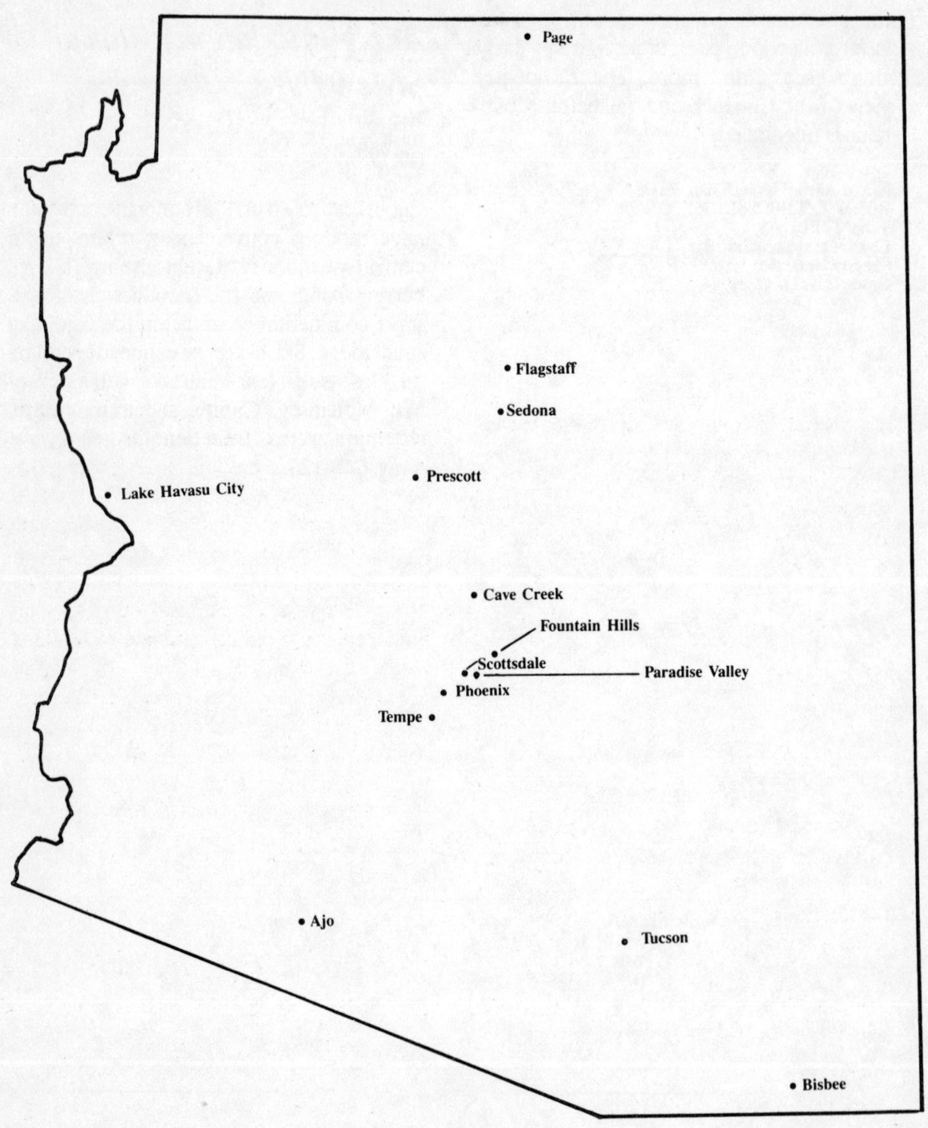
Page
Flagstaff
Sedona
Prescott
Lake Havasu City
Cave Creek
Fountain Hills
Scottsdale
Paradise Valley
Phoenix
Tempe
Ajo
Tucson
Bisbee

ARIZONA

Arizona

AJO

B&B Scottsdale & The West 104

P.O. Box 3999
Prescott, AZ, 86302
(602) 776-1102

Renovated 1925 mining corporation executive home near Organ Pipe Cactus National Monument, fifty minutes from Mexico. Three rooms, full breakfast, private baths. $59-69 + tax.

The Mine Manager's House Inn

1 Greenway
Ajo, AZ, 85321
(602) 387-6505; (800) TREADWAY

The Mine Manager's House B&B Inn is situated atop the highest hill in Ajo and was built in 1919. Each bedroom is decorated in a different motif and has its own bath. A birder's dream by day, with dark skies for the astronomer by night. Nearby, the Organ Pipe Cactus National Monument offers 300,000 acres of nature trails, rare Organ Pipe and Senila Cacti.

Hosts: Jean & Micheline Fournier
Rooms: 6 (PB) $49-99
Full Breakfast
Credit Cards: A, B
Notes: 5, 7 (limited), 10, 12, 14

BISBEE

The Greenway House

401 Cole Avenue
Bisbee, AZ, 85603
(602) 432-7170

Fully restored 1906 mansion of thirty-eight rooms, furnished with antiques. AAA approved, three diamonds. Eight guest suites with private baths and kitchens. Air conditioned; guest barbecue and patio area; game and billiard room. Located in turn-of-the-century copper mining town in the Mule Mountains of southeast Arizona. Art galleries, historic buildings and homes, walking tours, bicycling, bus tours. Chiricahua Mountains with scenic rock formations, lakes, hiking trails, renowned worldwide for number of bird varieties.

Hosts: Joy O'Clock & Dr. George S. Knox
Rooms: 8 (PB) $75-125
Continental Breakfast
Credit Cards: A, B, C
Notes: 2, 5, 9, 10, 11, 12

The Inn at Castle Rock

112 Tombstone Canyon Road
P.O. Box 1161
Bisbee, AZ, 85603
(602) 432-7195

Centrally located historic building with unusual decor, friendly ambience, an acre of gardens, two parlors, art gallery, antiques, and memorabilia. Bisbee is a historic mining camp, nestled in the mountains at 5,400-feet elevation. Shops, art galleries, and a mine tour are local attractions.

Host: Jim Babcock
Rooms: 14 (PB) $40-50 + tax
Continental Breakfast
Credit Cards: A, B
Notes: 2, 5, 7, 8, 9, 10, 11, 12, 14

CAVE CREEK

B&B Scottsdale & The West 72

P.O. Box 3999
Prescott, AZ, 86302
(602) 776-1102

Hike to old Indian sites from this house on 10 acres of lush desert with cactus and trees. Hostess is an archaeologist and jewelry designer. Continental breakfast, private entrance, queen bed. $50.

FLAGSTAFF

Arizona Mountain Inn

685 Lake Mary Road
Flagstaff, AZ, 86001
(602) 774-8959

Our Old English Tudor-style inn and cottages are located about three miles from Flagstaff. We have 13 wooded acres surrounded by national forest. Our rooms are decorated in antiques, crystal, and lace in a beautiful mix of European charm and classic Southwestern elegance.

Hosts: The Wanek Family
Rooms: 5 (1 PB; 4 SB) $50-100
Credit Cards: A, B, D
Notes: 2, 5, 9, 10, 11, 12, 13

B&B Scottsdale & The West 107

P.O. Box 3999
Prescott, AZ, 86302
(602) 776-1102

Located in a quiet neighborhood backing onto forest, this suite offers a king bed, family room, kitchenette, and private bath. Continental breakfast, private entrance, spa. Pet in residence. $65.

Dierker House

423 West Cherry Street
Flagstaff, AZ, 86001
(602) 774-3249

Charming old house with spacious, antique-filled rooms, private entrance, sitting room, and guest kitchen. An excellent breakfast is served at 8:00 A.M. in the downstairs dining room; continental breakfast for late risers.

Host: Dorothea Dierker
Rooms: 3 (SB) $40
Full Breakfast
Credit Cards: No
Notes: 2, 5, 9, 10, 11, 12, 14

Dierker House

FOUNTAIN HILLS

B&B Scottsdale & The West 70

P.O. Box 3999
Prescott, AZ, 86302
(602) 776-1102

Magnificent three-level Spanish contemporary house with tennis court. Lush tropical courtyard with forty-foot pool and gazebo. Full breakfast, private baths, private entrance, fireplace. Pet in home. $110.

B&B Scottsdale & The West 71

P.O. Box 3999
Prescott, AZ, 86302
(602) 776-1102

Extra large suite with desert and mountain views. Near F.L. Wright's Taliesin and Mayo Clinic West. Continental breakfast, private baths, private entrance. Pool. $65.

LAKE HAVASU CITY

B&B in Arizona LH101

P.O. Box 8628
Scottsdale, AZ, 85252
(602) 995-2831

Your host here will go out of his way to orient you and make you comfortable. Master suite with two twin beds that can be made into a king, full kitchen, private connecting bath, and private entrance. Other accommodations for four more people are available. Full breakfast; pool in backyard. $50-75.

LAKESIDE

B&B in Arizona LS101

P.O. Box 8628
Scottsdale, AZ, 85252
(602) 995-2831

This house is on the Fort Apache Indian Reservation boundary, one-half mile from Zane Grey's famous Mogollon rim. Hiking and cross-country ski trails are right out the door; the ski slopes of Sunrise are thirty miles away. Queen room with private connecting bath and double and queen rooms with a shared bath. Children are welcome; resident pets. A full breakfast is served that will knock your socks off. $45-70.

PAGE

B&B in Arizona PG102

P.O. Box 8628
Scottsdale, AZ, 85252
(602) 995-2831

This Southwestern home offers views of Lake Powell and the high desert of the neighboring Navajo reservation. The home sits on a cliff overlooking the lake, about seven miles from Wahweap Marina on the outskirts of Page. Two rooms share a pool, Jacuzzi, and private patio where a full breakfast is served. Shared bath. Adults only, no pets; resident dog. $55-65.

B&B Scottsdale & The West 111

P.O. Box 3999
Prescott, AZ, 86302
(602) 776-1102

Ninety minutes to the north rim of the Grand Canyon. Large suite with private entrance, cable TV, private bath. Close to all Lake Powell's attractions. Smoking is allowed; near golf and tennis. $40-60.

PARADISE VALLEY

B&B in Arizona PV106

P.O. Box 8628
Scottsdale, AZ, 85252
(602) 995-2831

A stunning private residence that has been transformed into a mini-resort. Breakfast is served on patio tables overlooking a croquet lawn, putting green, and view of Mummy Mountain, next to the pool. All rooms have private connecting baths, TV, ceiling fans, and phone. Resident cat. $65-85.

B&B in Arizona PV107

P.O. Box 8628
Scottsdale, AZ, 85252
(602) 995-2831

This home boasts a downstairs suite with large, comfortable den, brick fireplace, library, king room with private bath. A second bedroom has a twin bed. Full breakfast. Sun on the patio near the pool or practice your golf swing with the host's driving net. A word processor, copier, and FAX are available. $75-80.

B&B Scottsdale & The West 58

P.O. Box 3999
Prescott, AZ, 86302
(602) 776-1102

Elegant luxury Spanish home with magnificent landscaped pool and lawn area. Full breakfast, private baths. Pet in home. $85.

PHOENIX

B&B in Arizona PX110

P.O. Box 8628
Scottsdale, AZ, 85252
(602) 995-2831

Guest house with citrus trees on the slopes of Camelback Mountain with a complete kitchen. Pool and sunny patio, shuffleboard and badminton courts. Private connecting bath. Double hideabed and two twins. First day breakfast only; two-day minimum stay. $40-65.

B&B in Arizona PX115

P.O. Box 8628
Scottsdale, AZ, 85252
(602) 995-2831

This home has been featured in a number of articles on interior design and B&B. Breakfast of choice. Backyard with gazebo, open-pit fireplace, and Jacuzzi. Located between the downtown area and the Biltmore area. Double room with private hall bath. $45-55.

B&B in Arizona PX117

P.O. Box 8628
Scottsdale, AZ, 85252
(602) 995-2831

Quiet desert landscaped home in the midst of the Phoenix North Mountain Area. Well-traveled hostess does B&B in the English style with a full breakfast. Several golf courses and a horse track are only minutes away. Double bed and single bedrooms share a hall bath. Resident dog and cat. $30-40.

B&B in Arizona PX118

P.O. Box 8628
Scottsdale, AZ, 85252
(602) 995-2831

A rambling Southwestern home on the north slopes of the Phoenix Mountain Preserve, in horse country. Easy drive to Mayo Clinic, Paradise Valley Mall. Lovely pool and patio area for sunning and eating out when the weather is nice. Master suite with queen bed and connecting other bath. Three other rooms with private hall bath. Not available in midsummer. $45-55.

B&B in Arizona PX123

P.O. Box 8628
Scottsdale, AZ, 85252
(602) 995-2831

This home has a common park and large pool guests may use. Near the American Graduate School of International Management, Metrocenter, several golf courses. Double room with shared bath. Married couples or single women only. $35-40.

B&B in Arizona PX125

P.O. Box 8628
Scottsdale, AZ, 85252
(602) 995-2831

Quiet, immaculate home with a hostess who bakes homemade cinnamon and pecan rolls to go with her full breakfast. One bedroom with twin beds, one with double bed; shared bath. Sunny yard with a water fountain. $25-40.

B&B in Arizona PX134

P.O. Box 8628
Scottsdale, AZ, 85252
(602) 995-2831

Located near Metrocenter, North Mountain Park, and the bus line. Guest suite with king bed and private connecting bath. Private entrance. The kitchen is stocked for breakfast; hosts fix breakfast on weekends. $30-45.

B&B in Arizona PX136

P.O. Box 8628
Scottsdale, AZ, 85252
(602) 995-2831

Welcoming refreshments, a full breakfast, pool, heated Jacuzzi, even a small exercise gym are available at this Spanish Mediterranean inn with six rooms. Smoking is permitted; two resident cats. $100-115.

B&B in Arizona PX138

P.O. Box 8628
Scottsdale, AZ, 85252
(602) 995-2831

This beautifully decorated home on the north edge of downtown is ideal for the business traveler. Lovely king room with wicker furniture and private connecting bath and a second room with king bed, private bath. Terry robes for guests to use with the pool, deck area for sunbathing. Continental breakfast weekdays and full on weekends. $45-55.

B&B in Arizona PX140

P.O. Box 8628
Scottsdale, AZ, 85252
(602) 995-2831

A secluded enclave in the midst of an old date grove, with a great view of Camelback Mountain. Enjoy a continental breakfast, then lounge by the pool or Jacuzzi, or jog down the path by the canal. Master bedroom with queen bed and private hall bath. $55-60.

B&B Scottsdale & The West 51

P.O. Box 3999
Prescott, AZ, 86302
(602) 776-1102

Town home in a guarded community near Biltmore Fashion Plaza, Biltmore Golf Club, and the Ritz-Carlton Hotel. Continental breakfast, private bath, queen bed. $48.

B&B Scottsdale & The West 53

P.O. Box 3999
Prescott, AZ, 86302
(602) 776-1102

This large home is in the prime Arcadia area near 56th and Lafayette Blvd. north of the Arizona Country Club. Four rooms, pool, pet in home. $40-65.

B&B Scottsdale & The West 77

P.O. Box 3999
Prescott, AZ, 86302
(602) 776-1102

Award-winning resort-type home on 1 acre, frequently used for executive meetings, offers two guest room with private baths and full breakfast. Pool on premises; near golf and tennis. Resident pet; smoking allowed. $78-102 + tax.

B&B Scottsdale & The West 78

P.O. Box 3999
Prescott, AZ, 86302
(602) 776-1102

Located between the Arizona Biltmore Golf Club and Arizona Country Club, close to shopping on a quiet street. Continental breakfast, private bath. Pool. $45.

B&B Scottsdale & The West 81

P.O. Box 3999
Prescott, AZ, 86302
(602) 776-1102

Very good value. Cozy home near Camelback corridor, the Biltmore Fashion Plaza, and the Ritz-Carlton. One queen room with private bath, continental breakfast. Near golf. $40-45.

B&B Scottsdale & The West 82

P.O. Box 3999
Prescott, AZ, 86302
(602) 776-1102

North-central location, near West Thunderbird and 35th Avenue, three miles north of Metro Center Mall and the American Graduate School of International Management. Queen bed, continental breakfast, private bath, pool. Pet in home. $45.

B&B Scottsdale & The West 93

P.O. Box 3999
Prescott, AZ, 86302
(602) 776-1102

Convenient access to freeways. Near Metro Center Mall, off Freeway 17 at Union Hills. Deer Valley Park one block away. Double bed, private bath, continental breakfast, pool. Pet in home. $40.

B&B Scottsdale & The West 105

P.O. Box 3999
Prescott, AZ, 86302
(602) 776-1102

This very popular home was featured in *Arizona Highways* magazine in August 1989. Highlighted by antiques and stained glass. One double room with private bath and full breakfast. Spa, near golf and tennis, no smoking. $55-60.

Westways "Private" Resort Inn

Valley of the Sun
Box 41624
Phoenix, AZ, 85080
(602) 582-3868

Located in northwest Phoenix, Westways is adjacent to Thunderbird Park and Arrowhead Country Club. Arizona room with large-screen TV, VCR, games, library, and fireplace; guest wet bar/refrigerator and microwave available. Radio, TV, and sitting area in each deluxe queen-bedded guest room; diving pool, whirlpool, courtyard for guest use. Use of country club facilities.

Hosts: Darren Trapp & Brian Curran
Rooms: 6 (PB) $49-122; special rates available
Full or Continental Breakfast
Reservations necessary
Credit Cards: A, B, C
Notes: 2, 4, 5, 9, 10, 11, 12, 14

PINETOP

B&B in Arizona PT101

P.O. Box 8628
Scottsdale, AZ, 85252
(602) 995-2831

Piney woods surround this cabin with decks on which to watch the birds while you breakfast. Fireplace in the living room. Full breakfast. One bedroom with twin beds, and a hall bath with shower. Loft with extra beds for children ($10 each). Open summer months only. $50-70.

B&B in Arizona PT102

P.O. Box 8628
Scottsdale, AZ, 85252
(602) 995-2831

Sit in the country kitchen of this log cabin and watch the Albert's squirrels and Stallar jays or admire the rustic antique pine furniture. Room with king bed shares a hall bath with a double room; only one guest party at a time. Enjoy a full breakfast on the sun decks. For ski parties, there's a sofa sleeper in the living room. Wood-burning stove, cable TV, and vaulted ceilings. Available by appointment during the winter. $45-60.

PRESCOTT

B&B in Arizona PR103

P.O. Box 8628
Scottsdale, AZ, 85252
(602) 995-2831

Charming Victorian home on the National Register offers two upstairs rooms and shared hall bath. Crackling fires in the fireplaces warm you in winter. In the summer, relax on the porch swing or walk to the courthouse square. Resident cats. $35-50.

B&B in Arizona PR104

P.O. Box 8628
Scottsdale, AZ, 85252
(602) 995-2831

This restored lodging house is located near courthouse square. Bedrooms with twin or queen beds, private baths, and ceiling fans. Continental breakfast. Smoking is permitted. There are also two-room suites available. $45-75.

B&B in Arizona PR105

P.O. Box 8628
Scottsdale, AZ, 85252
(602) 995-2831

Magnificent house on a hill, a Queen Anne masterpiece. Full breakfast, hors d'oeuvres in the evening. First-floor two-room suite with two queen beds and private connecting bath. Three upstairs rooms with private baths, plus a wicker sitting area in a turret. Cats in residence; no children under twelve. $75-110.

B&B in Arizona PR106

P.O. Box 8628
Scottsdale, AZ, 85252
(602) 995-2831

A stunning modern home built on, and actually into, a mountain above Prescott. The twin-bed master bedroom has a private bath, floor-to-ceiling windows with a breathtaking view of Prescott and the hillside. Second room incorporates the rock of the hillside as a design feature and has a queen bed and private bath. Breakfast is served on the second-floor deck. Children eight or older are welcome. $45-60.

B&B in Arizona PR107

P.O. Box 8628
Scottsdale, AZ, 85252
(602) 995-2831

A classic log cabin in the pines with loft beds and sun decks with hummingbirds. There is a fireplace in the main room and TV sets in each guest room. A full breakfast and afternoon snacks are served. The loft room has a king bed, private bath. A second room offers twin beds. A downstairs room has a queen bed, deck, and shared bath. Resident dogs and cats. $70-100.

B&B Scottsdale & The West 83

P.O. Box 3999
Prescott, AZ, 86302
(602) 776-1102

Rural luxury on 25 acres with decks, spa, and volleyball. Full gourmet breakfast, private baths, private entrance. Pet in home. $55-65.

B&B Scottsdale & The West 84

P.O. Box 3999
Prescott, AZ, 86302
(602) 776-1102

Magnificent restored registered historic home on Nob Hill. Near Court House Plaza and Whiskey Row. Full breakfast. $110.

B&B Scottsdale & The West 86

P.O. Box 3999
Prescott, AZ, 86302
(602) 776-1102

Charming restored Queen Anne home just north of Courthouse Plaza. Two rooms, shared bath, no smoking, continental breakfast. Near golf. Pet in home. $45-50.

B&B Scottsdale & The West 87

P.O. Box 3999
Prescott, AZ, 86302
(602) 776-1102

Restored registered historic home in a convenient downtown location. Walk to Courthouse Plaza. Full breakfast, shared bath. Pet in home. $45.

Prescott Country Inn B&B

503 South Montezuma
Prescott, AZ, 86303
(602) 445-7991; (602) 445-7998

An atypical B&B with eleven charming country cottages, each with private bath. Twin or queen beds in two-bedrooms, one-bedroom, or studio cottages surround you with collectibles, quilted comforters, works of art, and plants. Your breakfast is brought to you, to be enjoyed in the privacy of your cottage or patio. Free access to a complete health club with swimming, sauna, spa, gym, racquetball and tennis.

Hosts: Sue & Morris Faulkner
Cottages: 11 (PB) $49-89
Continental-plus Breakfast
Credit Cards: A, B
Notes: 2, 5, 6, 7, 8, 9, 10, 11, 12, 14

SCOTTSDALE

B&B in Arizona SD126

P.O. Box 8628
Scottsdale, AZ, 85252
(602) 995-2831

Handcrafted Southwest adobe home on 2 acres of landscaped desert with a cactus garden, located in the Pinnacle Peak area of town. Twin beds in a room with private entrance overlooking the pool; private bath. Desert vistas from your bedroom window or next to the pool on the patio. Enjoy a gourmet breakfast with your hosts. Located fifteen minutes from the Mayo Clinic or downtown Scottsdale; near Princess Resort, Rawhide, Troon golf course, and Horseworld. $65.

B&B in Arizona SD133

P.O. Box 8628
Scottsdale, AZ, 85252
(602) 995-2831

A 1920s home on the slopes of Camelback Mountain, this classic adobe hacienda will make you feel welcome from the first moment. Relax and enjoy spectacular sunsets from the roof deck; visit nearby downtown Scottsdale or Phoenix and the many local golf courses. Two-story living room with fireplace. Continental breakfast is served weekdays; full on weekends. One bedroom has twin antique hand-carved Mexican bedsteads and a private half-bath. A second room has a queen bed and private connecting half-bath. Children eight and older are welcome; resident cat. $65.

B&B Scottsdale & The West 57

P.O. Box 3999
Prescott, AZ, 86302
(602) 776-1102

Very spacious accommodations on the second floor of a central Scottsdale office building near the Civic Center. Two rooms, private bath, private entrance, continental breakfast. $125.

B&B Scottsdale & The West 60

P.O. Box 3999
Prescott, AZ, 86302
(602) 776-1102

Charming guest house near Camelback Country Club and Gainey Ranch Golf Club. Hosts raise Arabians and beagles. Twin beds, continental breakfast, private bath, private entry, pool. Pet in home. $50.

B&B Scottsdale & The West 62

P.O. Box 3999
Prescott, AZ, 86302
(602) 776-1102

Bright, spacious suite located near McCormick Ranch, the Borgata Mall, and Hilton Village. Queen bed, full breakfast, private bath, private entry, pool. $55.

B&B Scottsdale & The West 63

P.O. Box 3999
Prescott, AZ, 86302
(602) 776-1102

Three miles east of Paradise Valley Mall, between Orange Tree Golf Club and the Scottsdale Country Club. King water bed, continental breakfast, pool. Pet in home. $50.

B&B Scottsdale & The West 66

P.O. Box 3999
Prescott, AZ, 86302
(602) 776-1102

This three-year-old contemporary home off Shea Blvd. is very popular. Close to Wright's Tallesin and Mayo Clinic West. Full breakfast; no smoking; private bath. Pool. $55-65.

B&B Scottsdale & The West 67

P.O. Box 3999
Prescott, AZ, 86302
(602) 776-1102

Large living space, private entrance in this two-level contemporary home in northeast Scottsdale near bike/jogging tract. Private upper deck over pool, large pool table. Two rooms, private baths. $55-68.

B&B Scottsdale & The West 68

P.O. Box 3999
Prescott, AZ, 86302
(602) 776-1102

Plenty of living space in this large Spanish-style home in north Scottsdale. The entry to this guest house is from the pool patio. Queen bed, continental breakfast, private bath. $55.

B&B Scottsdale & The West 69

P.O. Box 3999
Prescott, AZ, 86302
(602) 776-1102

For that special occasion, visit this luxury split-level guest house with mountain views near Pinnacle Peak Village. Solar pool; near golf. Smoking is allowed. Continental breakfast. One room with private bath and entrance, fireplace. $125.

B&B Scottsdale & The West 79

P.O. Box 3999
Prescott, AZ, 86302
(602) 776-1102

Spacious contemporary townhome in a gated community in a good central location near Hayden and Chaparral. One double room with private bath, continental breakfast. Near golf. Pet in home. $60-65.

B&B Scottsdale & The West 80

P.O. Box 3999
Prescott, AZ, 86302
(602) 776-1102

This home is located in the desert in far north Scottsdale. Ideal for nature lovers: peace, quiet, and stars. One double room with private bath. Pets in home. $45-65.

B&B Scottsdale & The West 95

P.O. Box 3999
Prescott, AZ, 86302
(602) 776-1102

Large four-poster canopy bed, continental breakfast, private bath, private entry. French doors to pool. Near Scottsdale Fashion Square and Phoenician Golf Club. $50-70.

B&B Scottsdale & The West 110

P.O. Box 3999
Prescott, AZ, 86302
(602) 776-1102

Great value for a guest house. Located near Scottsdale and Lincoln. Walk to The Borgata, Hilton Village, and new Crazy Golf center. Two rooms, private baths and entrance, continental breakfast, pool. Near golf and tennis. $75-85.

SEDONA

A Touch of Sedona B&B

595 Jordan Road
Sedona, AZ, 86336
(602) 282-6462

Eclectic elegance . . . furnished with stained-glass lamps, antiques, but with a mix of contemporary. Generous hospitality and old-fashioned breakfasts with home-baked bread await you in our lavish accommodations within walking distance of uptown.

Hosts: Dick & Doris Stevenson
Rooms: 4 (PB) $70-85
Full Breakfast
Credit Cards: A, B
Notes: 5, 7 (limited), 9, 10, 11, 12, 14

B&B in Arizona SE112

P.O. Box 8628
Scottsdale, AZ, 85252
(602) 995-2831

This house offers a full breakfast on the patio, with vistas across the valley to the ghost town of Jeroma. Twin beds and a queen bed are in The Studio, with private hall bath. A second room offers a queen bed and private bath. Two horse stalls and a corral on the premises for guest horses. Dog and cat in residence. Available weekends only. $45-60.

B&B in Arizona SE114

P.O. Box 8628
Scottsdale, AZ, 85252
(602) 995-2831

An artist's and photographer's delight, this old historic ranch has magnificent red rock views, gardens with spa and pool, and deer on the property. Lavish continental breakfast and late-afternoon refreshments. $90-120.

B&B in Arizona SE115

P.O. Box 8628
Scottsdale, AZ, 85252
(602) 995-2831

A ranch-style home in the shadows of the red rock country of Sedona. The lower level has a private entrance and is entirely for guests. Large living room with wood-burning stove, game table, TV/VCR. Kitchenette with small refrigerator and coffee maker. One room has queen and daybeds and private hall bath. Full breakfast and afternoon snack. The upstairs patio and Jacuzzi make starry evenings especially nice. Children over ten are welcome. $70-85.

B&B Scottsdale & The West 75

P.O. Box 3999
Prescott, AZ, 86302
(602) 776-1102

Popular home with friendly hosts on west highway 89A. Hosts collect huge music boxes and phonographs. Three rooms, private baths, full breakfast, private entrance. $40-50 + tax.

B&B Scottsdale & The West 97

P.O. Box 3999
Prescott, AZ, 86302
(602) 776-1102

Large home offering choice of four rooms or a private suite. Large buffet breakfast. Pet in home. $60-80 + tax.

B&B Scottsdale & The West 98

P.O. Box 3999
Prescott, AZ, 86302
(602) 776-1102

Peaceful location in West Sedona with red rock views. The suite sleeps four and has a private entrance. Full breakfast, private bath. Pet in home. $65-90 + tax.

Briar Patch Inn

Star Rt. 3, Box 1002
Sedona, AZ, 86336
(602) 282-2342

Eight acres of beautiful grounds along Oak Creek in spectacular Oak Creek Canyon. Rooms and cottages are all delightfully furnished with Southwest charm. A haven for those who appreciate nature amid the wonders of Sedona's mystical beauty. Suitable for small workshops.

Hosts: JoAnn & Ike Olson
Rooms: 15 (PB) $98-143
Continental-plus Breakfast
Credit Cards: A, B
Notes: 2, 5, 7, 8, 9, 11, 12, 14

Garland's Oak Creek Lodge

Box 152
Sedona, AZ, 86336
(602) 282-3343

What a delightful surprise this lodge is, tucked away in Oak Creek Canyon eight miles north of Sedona. An oasis of green lawns, gardens, and fruit trees, with fifteen log cabins. Fabulous fresh food graces the tables of the elegant, rustic dining room. Dinner and breakfast are included in the daily rate.

Hosts: Gary & Mary Garland
Cabins: 15 (PB) $134-154 MAP
Full Breakfast
Credit Cards: A, B
Closed Nov. 15-March 30
Notes: 2, 4, 7, 8, 9, 10

Graham's B&B Inn

Graham's B&B Inn

150 Canyon Circle Drive
P.O. Box 912
Sedona, AZ, 86336
(602) 284-1425

Graham's Bed & Breakfast Inn was built specifically as a B&B inn, in the modified Southwest style. Fine paintings and sculpture created by local artists are on display throughout the house. Large, spacious living room with games, books, TV, stereo, etc. Inviting pool and spa in beautifully landscaped grounds. Five guest rooms, each of which has a private bath and private balcony with a view of the spectacular red rock formations that have made Sedona famous. Excellent local restaurants, art galleries, and shops.

Hosts: Bill & Marni Graham
Rooms: 5 (PB) $95-140
Full Breakfast
Minimum stay weekends: 2 ; holidays: 2-3
Credit Cards: A, B
Closed Jan.
Notes: 2, 8, 9, 10, 11, 12, 14

Rose Tree Inn

376 Cedar Street
Sedona, AZ, 86336
(602) 282-2065

Small, quaint, private, quiet. Three units with fully furnished kitchenettes. Beautiful property situated in a lovely English garden environment. Within walking distance of "Old Town" Sedona. One hundred miles north of Phoenix; 2.5 hours to the Grand Canyon. Reservations a must.

Host: Rachel Gillespie
Rooms: 4 (PB) $59-89
Coffee and tea in room
Credit Cards: A, B
Notes: 2, 5, 7, 8, 9, 10, 11, 12, 14

TEMPE

B&B Scottsdale & The West 96

P.O. Box 3999
Prescott, AZ, 86302
(602) 776-1102

Very comfortable home near Superstition Freeway, close to Fiesta Mall and Shalimar Golf Course. King bed, full breakfast, private bath, pool. $50.

Valley O' the Sun B&B

Box 2214
Scottsdale, AZ, 85252
(602) 941-1281

Located on the Scottsdale-Tempe border, within walking distance of Arizona State University. Near restaurants, theaters, and shopping. Swimming, golf, horseback riding, and tennis nearby. Within minutes are the Phoenix Zoo, Desert Botanical Gardens, greyhound dog racing, ASU campus, and the Fiesta Bowl.

Host: Kay Curtis
Rooms: 2 (SB) $25-35
Full or Continental Breakfast
Credit Cards: No
Notes: 5, 7 (limited), 8 (over 12), 9, 10, 11, 12, 14

TUCSON

B&B in Arizona TU109

P.O. Box 8628
Scottsdale, AZ, 85252
(602) 995-2831

Get away to Tucson's surrounding desert while within range of the city. Enjoy mountain views while soaking in the Jacuzzi or pool. Close to golf, shopping, horseback riding. Two suites. The first has a kitchen stocked with groceries, private entrance, hall bath, bedroom with king bed, twin bed in the Arizona room, and queen hideabed in the living room. Children over sixteen and smoking are allowed in this suite. The second suite offers continental breakfast, private entrance, two rooms with double beds, hall bath. $60-80.

B&B in Arizona TU110

P.O. Box 8628
Scottsdale, AZ, 85252
(602) 995-2831

Adobe inn. Every room has its own entrance and private connecting bath. Continental breakfast weekdays, full weekends. $85-105.

B&B in Arizona TU114

P.O. Box 8628
Scottsdale, AZ, 85252
(602) 995-2831

This small ranch high in the Sonoran Desert foothills offers a full ranch breakfast featuring their own fresh eggs. Private guest house with stove, bath, twin and double bed. Jacuzzi and pool available. Children and pets are welcome; resident cat. $55.

B&B in Arizona TU116

P.O. Box 8628
Scottsdale, AZ, 85252
(602) 995-2831

Located in a quiet neighborhood in central Tucson, within walking distance of the University of Arizona and the medical center. Continental breakfast with homemade goodies. Guests are invited to enjoy the pool. Three rooms with private baths. Children sixteen and over are welcome; two-night minimum. $55-65.

B&B Scottsdale & The West 73

P.O. Box 3999
Prescott, AZ, 86302
(602) 776-1102

Very stylish living in a luxury 1929 Santa Fe adobe inn with five custom-designed suites, gourmet breakfast, and afternoon tea. No smoking. Near golf and tennis. $75-110 + tax.

B&B Scottsdale & The West 88

P.O. Box 3999
Prescott, AZ, 86302
(602) 776-1102

Gracious Southwest living in this lovingly restored 1870s home in El Presidio historic district. Garden courtyard with fountains. Four rooms, private baths, continental breakfast, private entry. $65-75 + tax.

B&B Scottsdale & The West 89

P.O. Box 3999
Prescott, AZ, 86302
(602) 776-1102

Fine private home in residential northeast Tucson features garden patio and private guest entrance. Two rooms, private baths, continental breakfast. Pet in home. $35-45 + tax.

B&B Scottsdale & The West 102

P.O. Box 3999
Prescott, AZ, 86302
(602) 776-1102

Several room choices and pool. Spacious hacienda-style home with central courtyard, near the University of Arizona three miles northeast of city center. Continental breakfast, private baths, pool. Pet in home. $65.

Desert Dream

825 Via Lucitas
Tucson, AZ, 85718
(602) 297-1220

Designed to complement its Catalina Mountain setting, this adobe ranch-style home commands a spectacular view of the city in the valley below. Your hostess will gladly furnish information on the many local attractions such as the desert museum, Sabino Canyon, Kitt Peak, churches, golf courses, restaurants, and shopping area. You are welcome to use the patio for your relaxing pleasure.

Host: Nell Putnam
Rooms: 1 (PB) $40
Continental Breakfast
Credit Cards: No
Notes: 2, 5, 9, 10, 11, 12, 13

El Presidio B&B Inn

297 North Main Street
Tucson, AZ, 85701
(602) 623-6151

A Victorian adobe, the inn is a splendid example of American-Territorial style, and on the National Register of Historic Places. Located downtown, within walking distance of the best restaurants, museums, and shopping. Guests enjoy a true Southwestern experience in spacious accommodations that open to large courtyards and gardens, fountains, lush floral displays. The ambience of Old Mexico.

Host: Patti Toci
Rooms: 4 (PB) $85-105
Full Breakfast
Credit Cards: No
Closed July
Notes: 2, 9, 10, 11, 12, 14

La Posade Del Valle

1640 North Campbell Avenue
Tucson, AZ, 85719
(602) 795-3840

An elegant 1920s inn nestled in the heart of the city with five guest rooms with private baths and outside entrances. Mature orange trees perfume the air as guests enjoy a gourmet breakfast and sip tea each afternoon on the patio overlooking the gardens.

Hosts: Charles & Debbi Bryant
Rooms: 5 (PB) $85-105
Full breakfast weekends; continental weekdays
Credit Cards: A, B
Notes: 2, 4, 5, 8 (over 12), 9, 10, 11, 12, 14

The Lodge on the Desert

306 North Alvernon
Tucson, AZ, 85711
(800) 456-5634; (602) 325-3366

A small in-town resort hotel providing the finest in food and accommodations. The lodge has been under the same family ownership for over fifty years. Close to golf, tennis, and shopping. One-half hour from Arizona-Sonora Living Desert Museum, Old Tucson movie location, Coronado National Forest. Three miles from the University of Arizona.

Host: Schuyler W. Lininger
Rooms: 40 (PB) $48-135
Continental Breakfast
Credit Cards: A, B, C, E, F
Notes: 2, 3, 4, 5, 6 (call), 7, 8, 9, 10, 11, 12, 14

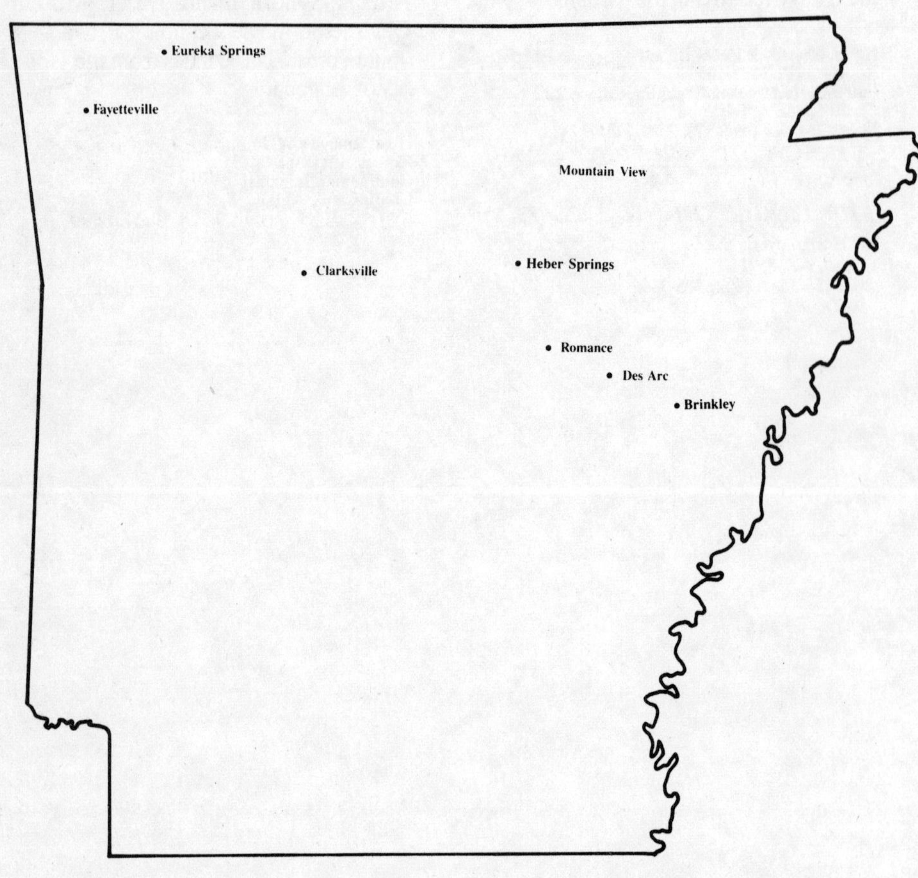
Eureka Springs
Fayetteville
Mountain View
Clarksville
Heber Springs
Romance
Des Arc
Brinkley

ARKANSAS

Arkansas

BRINKLEY

The Great Southern Hotel

127 West Cedar
Brinkley, AR, 72021
(501) 734-4955

Grand times and true Southern hospitality await you at the Great Southern Hotel. Restored in true Victorian elegance, with rooms that reflect a quaint, homey atmosphere reminiscent of bygone days. Fine dining in the award-winning Victorian Tearoom.

Hosts: Stanley & Dorcas Prince
Rooms: 4 (PB) $38-44
Full Breakfast
Credit Cards: A, B, C, D, F
Notes: 2 (deposit), 3, 4, 5, 8, 9

The May House Inn

CLARKSVILLE

The May House Inn

101 Railroad Avenue
Clarksville, AR, 72830
(501) 754-6851

Lovely Victorian home overlooking downtown historic Clarksville, offering turn-of-the-century charm. Features spacious bedrooms with beautiful antiques, finest amenities, and the Ozark Ritz Tea Room. Located on I-40 at Highway 64 and scenic Highway 21 (the gateway to the Ozarks), the area is a mountain lovers paradise.

Host: Pat Moody
Rooms: 4 (2 PB; 2 SB) $55-65
Full Breakfast
Credit Cards: A, B
Notes: 2, 3, 4, 5, 8, 10, 11, 12

DES ARC

The 5-B's

210 South Second Street
P.O. Box 364
Des Arc, AR, 72040
(501) 256-4789

Located in a rural setting on the Grand Prairie of central Arkansas; two blocks from Main Street in historic Des Arc, on the banks of White River, approximately fifteen miles north of I-40. Large colonial revival constructed in 1912 by Bedford Brown Bethel. Furnished with antiques and collectibles. The 5-B's: Bedford Brown Bethel Bed and Breakfast.

Hosts: Ann & Roy Hille
Rooms: 4 (2 PB; 2 SB) $37.50-45
Full Breakfast
Credit Cards: No
Notes: 2, 5, 8, 9, 10, 14

EUREKA SPRINGS

Bridgeford Cottage B&B

263 Spring Street

Eureka Springs, AR, 72632
(501) 253-7853

Nestled in the heart of Eureka Springs' historic residential district, Bridgeford Cottage is an 1884 Victorian delight. Outside are shady porches that invite you to pull up a chair and watch the world go by on Spring Street. Each room has a private entrance, antique furnishings, and private bath. Fresh coffee in your suite, a selection of fine teas, color TV, air-conditioning, and a mouthwatering breakfast.

Hosts: Michael & Denise McDonald
Rooms: 4 (PB) $65-85
Full Breakfast
Credit Cards: A, B
Notes: 2, 5, 7 (outside), 9, 10, 11, 12, 14

Dairy Hollow House

515 Spring Street
Eureka Springs, AR, 72632
(501) 253-7444

Welcome to Dairy Hollow House, a tiny, irresistible country inn and restaurant nestled in a serene, wooded valley. Just one mile from Eureka's historic downtown, we offer two houses, each with the prettiest rooms and suites imaginable. Waiting for you are fireplaces, landscaped hot tub, fresh flowers, regional antiques, and our own Ozark wildflower soaps. Best Inn of the Year, 1989, Uncle Ben's. We also offer murder mystery weekends each month during the season.

Hosts: Crescent Dragonwagon & Ned Shank
Rooms: 6 (PB) $105-165
Full Breakfast
Credit Cards: A, B, C, D, E
Notes: 2, 4, 5, 8, 9, 10, 11, 12, 14

Four Winds B&B

3 Echols Street
Eureka Springs, AR, 72632
(501) 253-9169

This turn-of-the-century cottage is privately located within the historic district of Eureka Springs—a quaint Victorian village in the Ozarks. Whimsically furnished in antiques, plants, and artwork. Enjoy the private deck in the trees and the hammock. Complimentary beverages, a delicious breakfast, and friendly atmosphere await you.

Host: Laura Menees
Rooms: 3 (2 PB; 1 SB) $45-65
Continental-plus Breakfast
Credit Cards: A, B
Notes: 2, 5, 6, 7, 8 (limited), 9, 10, 11, 12, 13, 14

Heartstone Inn B&B and Cottages

Heart of the Hills Inn

5 Summit Street
Eureka Springs, AR, 72632
(501) 253-7468

This historic home was built in the 1800s and offers three rooms with air-conditioning, refrigerator, TV, and private baths. There is also one completely equipped cottage with deck overlooking the woods. Eureka Springs is noted for its Passion Play, outstanding restaurants, fine museums, and trolley system.

Host: Jan Jacobs Weber
Rooms: 3 (PB) $55-75
Full Breakfast
Credit Cards: A, B
Closed Jan.
Notes: 2, 8, 9, 10, 11, 14

Heartstone Inn B&B and Cottages

35 Kings Highway
Eureka Springs, AR, 72632
(501) 253-8916

Nine rooms plus two charming guest cottages in the historic district of Eureka Springs. Turn-of-the-century charm, plus modern conveniences. Antiques, air-conditioning, private entrances, limited smoking.

Hosts: Iris & Bill Simantel
Rooms: 9 (PB) $52-89 plus tax
Cottages: 2 (PB)
Full Breakfast
Minimum stay holidays: 3; weekends: 2
Credit Cards: A, B, C
Closed Christmas
Notes: 2, 8, 9, 11, 12, 14

Redbud Manor

7 Kings Highway
Eureka Springs, AR, 72632
(501) 253-9649

This is indeed a Victorian B&B built by Grover Cleveland in 1891 and furnished with antiques. An elegant breakfast, air-conditioning, and private baths. Located on the Historic Loop and three blocks from the large convention center.

Hosts: Evelyn & Arthur Kintz
Rooms: 3 (PB) $65 + tax
Full Breakfast
Credit Cards: A, B, C, F
Notes: 2, 5, 7 (restricted), 9, 14

Scandia B&B Inn

P.O. Box 166, Hwy. 62 West
Eureka Springs, AR, 72632
(501) 253-8922; (800) 523-8922

We are a B&B in the finest tradition: charming furnishings, elegant breakfasts, and attentive service. Each cottage has its own individual decor with designer linens, private bath, and cable TV. A newly installed hot tub in a gazebo setting is nestled in the pines and is available 24 hours for your convenience.

Hosts: Cynthia Barnes & Marty Lavine
Rooms: 7 (PB) $65-95
Full Breakfast
Credit Cards: A, B, C, D
Closed Nov.-April 15
Notes: 2, 9, 11, 12

Singleton House

11 Singleton Street
Eureka Springs, AR, 72632
(501) 253-9111

This country Victorian home is an old-fashioned place with a touch of magic. Each guest room is whimsically decorated with a delightful collection of antiques and folk art. Breakfast is served on the balcony overlooking the fantasy wildflower garden below, with its goldfish pond and curious birdhouse collection. Located in the historic district. Guests park and walk a secret pathway to Eureka's shops and cafes.

Host: Barbara Gavron
Rooms: 5 (4 PB; 1 SB) $55-65
Full Breakfast
Credit Cards: A, B, C, D
Notes: 2, 5, 8, 9, 11, 12, 14

FAYETTEVILLE

Oaks Manor

945 Oaks Manor Drive
Fayetteville, AR, 72703
(501) 443-5481

Oaks Manor is a brick ranch with white columns, shutters, porches, and a beautiful patio overlooking woodland where squirrels and rabbits play. There is antique English colonial furniture in two bedrooms and the breakfast/dining area, where old china, handmade linens, and silver pieces are used. There is also a private parlor with piano, decorated in Victorian decor. The hostess provides Southern hospitality that makes guests feel welcome and comfortable.

Host: Clara Griffith
Rooms: 3 (PB) $40-45
Continental Breakfast
Credit Cards: No
Notes: 5, 7 (limited), 9, 12, 14

Oak Tree Inn

HEBER SPRINGS

Oak Tree Inn

Vinegar Hill and 110 West
Heber Springs, AR, 72543
(501) 362-7731

An inn for nonsmoking adults, each room with its own private whirlpool bath; five have wood-burning fireplaces. Located near 45,000-acre Greers Ferry Lake. Dessert and a full breakfast are served daily. Tennis courts, swimming pool, and hot tub. Lakeside condos and river cottage also available; children and smokers are welcome in these units.

Host: Freddie Lou Lodge
Rooms: 6 (PB) $65-75
Full Breakfast
Credit Cards: No
Notes: 2, 5, 10, 11, 12, 14

MOUNTAIN VIEW

The Inn at Mountain View

West Washington Street
Mountain View, AR, 72560
(800) 535-1301

On the National Registry of Historic Places. The Inn at Mountain View has been a traditional stopping place for folks since 1886. The inn has eleven guest suites, each with private bath. All rooms are furnished with antiques and air-conditioned. Breakfast is a hearty meal of homemade biscuits, sausage, gravy, eggs, Belgian waffles, fresh fruit compote, raspberry ambrosia, bacon, sausage, homemade peach and apple butters, juice, and lots of coffee. Mountain View is the world capitol of folk music, with the National Folk Center located one mile from the inn. The caverns at Blanchard Springs are about nine miles from the inn. White River trout fishing is five miles away, and the Buffalo River, noted for its canoe and float trips, is a short drive.

Hosts: Bob & Jenny Williams
Rooms: 11 (PB) $37-49
Full Breakfast
Credit Cards: A, B, C, D
Closed Dec. 10-March 15
Notes: 2, 8, 9, 10, 14

ROMANCE

Hammons Chapel Farm

271 Hammons Chapel Road
Romance, AR, 72136
(501) 849-2819

This working cattle farm features American Brahman cattle (origin: the sacred cows of

India) and Hereford cattle. Located in the foothills of the Ozarks, a short drive from beautiful 45,000-acre Greers Ferry Lake. This attractive white stucco ranch home reflects John's love of reading, writing, and painting, and Susan's love of cooking and gardening. There are no stairs to climb, and some of the antiques date back for generations.

Hosts: John & Susan Hammons
Rooms: 1 (PB) $45
Full Breakfast
Credit Cards: No
Notes: 2, 3, 4, 5, 6, 9

CALIFORNIA
Klamath
Mt. Shasta
McCloud
Trinidad
Arcata
Eureka
Ferndale
Round Mountain
Redding
Red Bluff
Leggett
Orland
Chico
Portola
Loyalton
Westport
Fort Bragg
Mendocino
Willitis
Princeton
Little River
Albion
Philo
Elk
Ukiah
Clear Lake
Lower Lake
Hopland
Boonville
Anchor Bay
Gualala
Cloverdale
Freestone
Geyserville
Davis
Coloma
Sacramento
Sutter Creek
Ione
Jackson
Healdsburg
Windsor
Cazadero
Guerneville
Jenner
Santa Rosa
Occidental
Valley Ford
Olema
El Cerrito
Inverness
Point Reyes Station
Bolinas
San Anselmo
San Raphael
Mill Valley
Sausalito
San Francisco
Burlingame
Montara
Half Moon Bay
Palo Alto
Muir Beach
Angwin
Calistoga
St. Helena
Yountville
Glen Ellen
Napa
Sonoma
Lodi
Angels Camp
Murphys
Jamestown
Brentwood
Tahoe City
Homewood
Georgetown
Tahoma
San Andreas
Mammoth Lakes
Twain Harte
Sonora
Columbia
Benicia
Fremont
Los Altos
Santa Clara
San Jose
Ben Lomond
San Gregorio
Soquel
Aptos
Capitola
Monterey
Pacific Grove
Carmel
Berkeley
Alameda
Oakland
Santa Cruz
Davenport
Stanford
Mariposa
Bishop
Oakhurst
Lemon Cove
Nipton
San Miguel
Cambria
Templeton
Los Osos
Pismo Beach
Arroyo Grande
Studio City
West Covina
Hollywood
Los Feliz
Lake Arrowhead
Los Alamos
Tarzana
Beverly Hills
Big Bear Lake
Ojai
Belair
Rancho Cucamonga
Santa Barbara
Ventura
Pacific Palisades
Torrance
Whittier
Idyllwild
Malibu
Anaheim
Palm Springs
Santa Monica
Los Angeles
Orange
Santa Ana
Hermosa Beach
Redondo Beach
Newport Beach
San Pedro
Laguna Beach
Dana Point
Seal Beach
San Clemente
Carlsbad
Julian (St. Julian)
Avalon
Garden Grove
Leucadia
Palos Verdes
Del Mar
Escondido
La Jolla
San Diego
Dulzura

California

ALAMEDA

Garratt Mansion

900 Union Street
Alameda, CA, 94501
(415) 521-4779

This 1893 Victorian makes time stand still on the tranquil island of Alameda. Only ten miles to Berkeley or downtown San Francisco. We will help maximize your vacation plans or leave you alone to regroup. Our rooms are large and comfortable, and our breakfasts are nutritious and filling.

Hosts: Royce & Betty Gladden
Rooms: 6 (3 PB; 3 SB) $75-125
Full Breakfast
Credit Cards: C
Notes: 2, 5, 8, 10, 12, 14

Garratt Mansion

Webster House

1238 Versailles Avenue
Alameda, CA, 94501
(415) 523-9697

Webster House is the twenty-second historical monument in the city. Quaint, enchanting 1854 Gothic Revival cottage is the oldest house on the island of Alameda. Nestled in coastal redwoods and scrub oaks, with a large deck, waterfall, fountain, Irish cream liqueur or champagne available, afternoon tea, and evening snack. Near beach, golf, tennis, fishing, shopping, and bicycling. Twenty minutes from San Francisco.

Hosts: Andrew & Susan McCormack
Rooms: 4 (SB) $75-105
Continental-plus Breakfast
Credit Cards: No
Notes: 2, 3, 5, 7(restricted), 8, 9, 10, 11, 12, 14

ALBION

Fensalden Inn

Box 99
Albion, CA, 95410
(707) 937-4042

A restored 1860s stagecoach way station with antique furnishings; several units with fireplaces. Quiet country setting with pastoral and ocean views. Enjoy strolling country lanes where grazing deer share the crisp morning air, or the evening panorama of the setting sun over a crimson-stained ocean.

Hosts: Frances & Scott Brazil
Rooms: 10 (PB) $80-135
Full Breakfast
Minimum stay weekends: 2; holidays: 3
Credit Cards: A, B
Notes: 2, 5, 8 (over 11), 9, 10, 11, 12, 14

ANAHEIM

Anaheim Country Inn

856 South Walnut
Anaheim, CA, 92802
(714) 778-0150

A 1910 Princess Anne-style home with spacious grounds and gardens in a quiet neighborhood about one mile from Disneyland and the Anaheim Convention Center. Easy access to beaches, Knotts Berry Farm, the *Queen Mary,* and the *Spruce Goose.* We can accommodate executive seminars, small family reunions, and small weddings.

Hosts: Lois Ramont & Marily Watson
Rooms: 8 (6 PB; 2 SB) $55-80
Full Breakfast
Credit Cards: A, B, C, D
Notes: 2, 5, 8 (12 and over), 9, 10, 11, 12, 14

Anaheim Country Inn

CoHost, America's B&B 14

P.O. Box 9302
Whittier, CA, 90608
(213) 699-8427

Comfortably furnished in country antiques, this comfortable home includes a suite with complete privacy, a queen bed and queen sofabed, and facilities for light cooking. A large country breakfast is served on antique china. Guests are welcome to use the fireplace in the living room with color TV. Located halfway between Disneyland and Knott's Berry Farm, near the Anaheim Convention Center and all Orange County attractions. $55.

Southern Comfort

B&B of Los Angeles
32074 Waterside Lane
Westlake Village, CA, 91361
(818) 889-8870

Retired couple with a spacious home near tourist attractions offer two downstairs guest rooms sharing a bath as well as an upstairs suite with living room, fireplace, balcony, TV, and bedroom with queen bed and minikitchen. Private bath. Nicely decorated in country antiques. Spa in yard. Full country breakfast. $35-50.

ANCHOR BAYN

NW Bed & Breakfast 500

610 SW Broadway
Portland, OR, 97205
(503) 243-7616

A splendid home in an area of incomparable beauty. Charming hosts enjoy photography, tennis, fishing, beachcombing, and Chinese cooking. They offer a private suite with a deck overlooking the woods and ocean. Two dogs and one cat in residence. $75.

ANGELS CAMP

Cooper House Bed & Breakfast Inn

Box 1388
Angels Camp, CA, 95222
(209) 736-2145

Beautiful turn-of-the-century home in California's historic gold country. Quiet location surrounded by manicured gardens. Spacious rooms with private baths and air-conditioning. Sumptuous full breakfast. Near caverns, wineries, giant sequoias, Columbia State Park, gourmet dining.

Host: Chris Sears
Rooms: 3 (PB) $81.12-88.40
Full Breakfast
Credit Cards: A, B
Notes: 2, 5, 7 (limited), 8, 9, 10, 11, 12, 13

ANGWIN

Big Yellow Sunflower B&B

235 Sky Oaks
Angwin, CA, 94508
(707) 965-3885

In the heart of the Napa Valley wine country, this home offers a fireplace, private entrance and deck, piano, kitchenette. Home-baked goodies and a bountiful full breakfast. Cozy and romantic, with some of the lowest rates in the area.

Hosts: Dale & Betty Clement
Rooms: 2 (PB) $45-85
Full and Continental Breakfast
Credit Cards: No
Notes: 2, 5, 6, 7 (outdoors), 8, 9, 10, 11, 12, 14

Forest Manor

415 Cold Springs Road
Angwin, CA, 94508
(707) 965-3538

Secluded 20-acre English Tudor estate tucked among forest and vineyards in famous Napa Wine country. Described as "one of the most romantic country inns . . . A small exclusive resort." Fireplaces, verandas, 53-foot pool, spas, spacious suites (one with Jacuzzi), refrigerators, coffee makers, home-baked breakfast. Close to over 200 wineries, ballooning, hot springs, and a lake.

Hosts: Harold & Corlene Lambeth
Rooms: 3 (PB) $95-175
Continental-plus Breakfast
Credit Cards: A, B
Notes: 2, 5, 9, 10, 11, 12, 14

APTOS

Apple Lane Inn

6265 Soquel Drive
Aptos, CA, 95003-3117
(408) 475-6868

Apple Lane Inn is a historic Victorian farmhouse restored to the charm and tranquility of an earlier age. It's located just south of Santa Cruz on 2.5 acres of grounds, with gardens, a romantic gazebo, and fields. Explore the many miles of beaches within walking distance. Golf, hiking, fishing, shopping, and dining are all close by.

Hosts: Doug & Diana Groom
Rooms: 5 (3 PB; 2 SB) $70-125
Full Breakfast
Credit Cards: A, B, D
Notes: 2, 5, 7 (limited), 9, 10, 11, 12, 14

Bayview Hotel B&B Inn

Bayview Hotel B&B Inn

8041 Soquel Drive
Aptos, CA, 95003
(408) 688-8654

Vintage California Victorian, in the heart of Aptos Village, built in 1878 and furnished with original antiques. Near golf, tennis, fishing, state beaches, and antique shops. Only one block from the entrance to the 10,000-acre forest of Nisene Marks State Park, with thirty-five miles of hiking trails. Fine restaurant, the Veranda, on the premises.

Hosts: Katya & James Duncan
Rooms: 8 (PB) $75-100
Continental-plus Breakfast
Credit Cards: A, B
Notes: 2, 3, 4, 5, 8 (over 5), 10, 11, 12, 14

Mangels House

570 Aptos Creek Road
Box 302
Aptos, CA, 95001
(408) 688-7982

A large Southern colonial situated on 4 acres of lawn and orchard, Mangels House is bounded by a 10,000-acre redwood forest and is only 3/4 mile from the beach. The five large, airy rooms are eclectic in decor and European in feel, reflecting the owners' background.

Hosts: Jacqueline & Ronald Fisher
Rooms: 5 (3 PB; 2 SB) $89-115
Full Breakfast
Credit Cards: A, B
Closed Dec. 24-26
Notes: 2, 5, 6 (outside), 7 (limited), 8 (over 12), 9, 10, 11, 12, 14

ARCATA

The Plough and the Stars Country Inn

1800 27th Street
Arcata, CA, 95521
(707) 822-8236

The Plough and Stars is an 1860s farmhouse on 2 pastoral acres at the edge of the coastal university town of Arcata. The inn and hosts welcome you to the pleasures of country living and the pampering of home-style hospitality. Quiet, spacious, comfortable, and warm. Outdoor hot tub available.

Hosts: Bill & Melissa Hans
Rooms: 3 (1 PB; 2 SB) $75-105
Full Breakfast
Credit Cards: A, B
Closed Dec. 15-Feb. 15
Notes: 2, 7 (limited), 8 (over 12), 9, 11, 12

ARROYO GRANDE

The Guest House

120 Hart Lane
Arroyo Grande, CA, 93420
(805) 481-9304

A charming colonial home built in 1865 and furnished with many rare antiques of that era. Beautiful, old-fashioned gardens, in which a hearty breakfast and afternoon libations are enjoyed. A short walk to the interesting shops and restaurants in the old village of Arroyo Grande.

Hosts: Mark Miller & Jim Cunningham
Rooms: 2 (SB) $45-60
Full Breakfast
Credit Cards: No
Notes: 2, 5, 7 (restricted), 9, 10, 11, 12

The Village Inn

407 El Camino Real
Arroyo Grande, CA, 93420
(805) 489-5926; (800) 767-0083

The Village Inn is a 1984 Victorian farm-style house featuring charming English country decor; antiques, and Laura Ashley prints and wall coverings. Seven spacious suites with private baths and a full gourmet breakfast. Arroyo Grande is in the heart of California's central coast, halfway between Los Angeles and San Francisco. Near several wineries, San Luis Obispo, Pismo Beach, Lake Lopez; less than one hour to Hearst Castle and San Simeon. Late afternoon beverages and hors d'oeuvres are served in the parlor.

Hosts: John & Gina Glass
Rooms: 7 (PB) $85-135
Full Gourmet Breakfast
Minimum stay holidays: 2
Credit Cards: A, B, C, D, E
Notes: 2, 5, 8 (over 10), 9, 10, 11, 12, 14

AUBURN

Power's Mansion Inn

164 Cleveland Avenue
Auburn, CA, 95603
(916) 885-1166

This magnificent mansion was built from a gold fortune in the late 1800s. It has easy access from I-80 and off-street parking. Close to water sports, hiking, horseback riding, skiing, ballooning, and restaurants.

Host: Anthony Verhaart
Rooms: 15 (PB) $75-160
Full Breakfast
Credit Cards: A, B, C
Notes: 2, 3, 4, 5, 6, 8, 9, 10, 11, 12, 13, 14

Gull House

AVALON

Gull House

344 Whittley Avenue
Box 1381
Avalon, CA, 90704
(800) 442-4884; (213) 510-2547

For honeymooners and those celebrating anniversaries. AAA-approved contemporary house with swimming pool, spa, barbecue, gas-log fireplaces, morning room with refrigerator, color TV. Close to bay beaches and all water activities. Deposit or full payment in advance reserves taxi pickup and return.

Hosts: Bob & Hattie Michalis
Suites: 2 (PB) $110-125
Continental Breakfast
Minimum stay: 2
Credit Cards: No
Notes: 2, 7, 9, 12

Zane Grey Pueblo Hotel

199 Chimes Tower Road
Box 216
Avalon, CA, 90704
(213) 510-0966

Hopi Indian style pueblo built in 1926 as the private home of author Zane Grey. Panoramic ocean and mountain views from the guest rooms, each of which has a queen bed and private bath. Pool and view decks are surrounded by natural gardens. Original living room with fireplace, piano, and TV. Courtesy taxi. Romantic atmosphere.

Hosts: Karen Baker & Kevin Anderson
Rooms: 17 (PB) $48-125
Continental Breakfast
Credit Cards: A, B, C
Notes: 2, 5, 7, 8, 9, 10, 11, 12, 14

BELAIR

El Camino Real B&B

P.O. Box 7155
Northridge, CA, 91327-7155
(818) 363-6753

Prestigious area, ten minutes from UCLA. Room with queen bed overlooks mountains and valley; shared bath. Swimming pool. Babies welcome. Continental breakfast. $55.

BENICIA

Captain Dillingham's Inn

145 East "D" Street
Benicia, CA, 94510
(707) 746-7164; (800) 544-2278 (CA only)

1850s Cape Cod-style house surrounded by a country garden, decks, gazebo, and plenty of outdoor seating. There are nine and one-half rooms—one is a two-bedroom suite. All rooms have private baths and feature whirlpool tubs, TV, phones, and beverage coolers. Full hot-and-cold buffet breakfast included. One-half block from the marina and easy walking distance to many shops and restaurants.

Hosts: Dennison & Roger Steck, Debbie Simas
Rooms: 9.5 (PB) $75-170
Full Breakfast
Credit Cards: A, B, C, E, F
Notes: 2, 5, 6, 7, 8, 9, 10, 11, 12, 14

Union Hotel

Union Hotel

401 First Street
Benicia, CA, 94510
(707) 746-0100

Built in 1882 and active as a twenty-room bordello until the early 1950s. The Union Hotel was completely renovated in 1981 into a twelve-room hotel and B&B. Each of the twelve rooms is decorated with a theme and named accordingly. Each room has a queen or king bed, individual room-temperature controls, Jacuzzi bathtub, and television. The superb stained-glass picture windows in the bar and dining room are worth a trip on their own. Restaurant on premises. Ideally located for visiting the wine country (20 minutes); 45 minutes from San Francisco; 20 minutes from the ferry to Fisherman's Wharf.

Host: Stephen Lipworth
Rooms: 12 (PB) $75-$135
Continental Breakfast
Credit Cards: A, B, C, D, E
Notes: 2, 3, 4, 5, 7, 8, 9, 14

BEN LOMOND

Fairview Manor

245 Fairview Avenue
P.O. Box 74
Ben Lomond, CA, 95005
(408) 336-3355

Nestled in the heart of the San Lorenzo Valley, Fairview Manor offers 3 acres of privacy on landscaped grounds. Near the Santa Cruz boardwalk; Big Basin State Park, with its redwood trees; Roaring Camp Narrow Gauge railroad rides.

Hosts: Frank Feely & Nancy Glasson
Rooms: 5 (PB) $89-99
Full Breakfast
Credit Cards: A, B
Notes: 2, 5, 9, 10, 11, 12, 14

BERKELEY

B&B International—San Francisco 1

1181-B Solano Avenue
Albany, CA, 94706
(415) 525-4569

This large Mediterranean-style house was built in 1938, and the garden is featured in several architectural publications. The house is two blocks from Kensington shops and restaurants and on the bus route to downtown and the campus. By car, it is ten minutes to UC Berkeley. The main-floor Casablanca Suite has a queen bed, private bath, and adjacent sitting room. The second-floor Spinnaker Room has twin beds and private bath. Both these suites have a view of San Francisco Bay. The Garden Room has a double bed and private half-bath. There is a hot tub for guest use, and smoking is permitted on the decks outside. $60.

Gramma's Inn Hotel & Gardens

2740 Telegraph Avenue
Berkeley, CA, 94705
(415) 549-2145

Two turn-of-the-century Tudor-style mansions, garden, and carriage houses set amid English country gardens. Rooms furnished with antiques; many have fireplaces, decks, porches, and/or views. Near the University of California, Berkeley shops, parks, and museums. Available for weddings, parties, and meetings, as well. Gourmet catering available.

Hosts: Barry Cleveland
Rooms: 30 (28 PB; 2 SB) $85-175
Full Breakfast
Credit Cards: A, B
Notes: 2, 5, 7 (limited), 8, 9, 10, 11, 12, 14

BEVERLY HILLS

Beverly Hills Guest House

B&B of Los Angeles
32074 Waterside Lane
Westlake Village, CA, 91361
(818) 889-8870

A small cottage to the rear of the main house with twin beds, private bath, small refrigerator, and TV. Doors open to a grassy sitting area. Bus line two blocks away. Two-night minimum. $45-50.

Canyon Cottage

B&B of Los Angeles
32074 Waterside Lane
Westlake Village, CA, 91361
(818) 889-8870

English country atmosphere with antique furnishings and a massive fireplace are offered by this writer host. Two bedrooms, each with private bath, queen bed, and TV. Just a mile downhill to Sunset Boulevard. Adults only; two-night minimum. $50-65.

CoHost, America's B&B 16

P.O. Box 9302
Whittier, CA, 90608
(213) 699-8427

Cozy home owned by a writer with a hot tub overlooking the backyard. Guests will enjoy talking with their host about movies of the past. The inviting fireplace offers a place to plan the next day's outing. Two doubles, one with queen bed. Private bath. $65-75.

El Camino Real B&B

P.O. Box 7155
Northridge, CA, 91327-7155
(818) 363-6753

Two fabulous three-room guest houses, separate from mansion, each consisting of a living room, kitchen, bed, and bath. Hot tub, swimming pool. Minutes to Rodeo Drive and Beverly Hills shopping and restaurants. Continental breakfast. $115.

BIG BEAR LAKE

Eagle's Nest Bed & Breakfast

Box 1003
Big Bear Lake, CA, 92315
(714) 866-6465

The Eagle's Nest B&B is ideally situated in the heart of a four-seasons resort. The lodge offers elegance in a rustic setting. The main house is a recently built two-story log cabin lodge. Five cozily decorated rooms all have private baths, queen beds, and warm goose-down comforters. Three new cottage suites with fireplaces; two with Jacuzzis.

Hosts: James Joyce & Jack Draper
Rooms: 8 (PB) $70-130
Continental-plus Breakfast
Credit Cards: No
Notes: 2, 5, 8, 9, 10, 11, 12, 13, 14

Knickerbocker Mansion

Box 3661
Big Bear Lake, CA, 92315
(714) 866-8221

A turn-of-the-century vertical log mansion on 2 acres surrounded by national forest. Warm, peaceful retreat for fun or business. Country and antique furnishings, hearty breakfast, and "Grandma's Kitchen" for snacks during the day. Indoor and outdoor Jacuzzis. Close to skiing, horseback riding, and all water sports; member of local athletic club. Honeymoon suite with Jacuzzi tub available.

Host: Phyllis M. Knight
Rooms: 10 (5 PB; 5 S3B) $85-150
Full Breakfast
Credit Cards: A, B
Notes: 2, 5, 8, 9, 10, 11, 12, 13, 14

BISHOP

The Matlick House

1313 Rowan Lane
Bishop, CA, 93514
(619) 873-3133

A 1906 ranch house, completely renovated, nestled at the base of the eastern Sierra Nevada Mountains. Close to year-round fishing, hiking, skiing, trail rides. Telephones available, air-conditioning, wine and hors d'oeuvres; antiques throughout.

Host: Nanette Robedaix
Rooms: 5 (PB) $55-75
Full Breakfast
Notes: 2, 5, 7 (limited), 8 (over 14), 9, 10, 11, 12, 13

BOLINES

Thomas' White House Inn

118 Kale Road
P.O. Box 132
Bolines, CA, 94924
(415) 868-0279

A New England-style inn near Pt. Reyes National Seashore in West Marin. Located in one of the most beautiful areas on the California coast. Two lovely rooms with window seats offer panoramic views of the mountains and the Pacific Ocean.

Host: Jacqueline Thomas
Rooms: 2 (SB) $91.80-102.60
Continental Breakfast
Credit Cards: No
Notes: 2, 4, 5, 7, 8, 9, 10

Thomas' White House Inn

BOONVILLE

Anderson Creek Inn

P.O. Box 217
12050 Anderson Valley Way
Boonville, CA, 95415
(707) 895-3091

The Anderson Valley is truly a peaceful setting for this spacious ranch-style B&B that affords ultimate privacy and lush views. Guests are treated to appetizers each eve-

NOTES: Credit cards accepted: A Master Card; B Visa; C American Express; D Discover Card; E Diners Club; F Other: 2 Personal checks accepted: 3 Lunch available: 4 Dinner available: 5 Open all year

ning and an elegant full breakfast in bed or in the dining room. Stroll through the gardens, sip wine by the pool, or enjoy our gentle llamas and rare lambs.

Hosts: Rod & Nancy Graham
Rooms: 4 (PB) $85-105
Full Breakfast
Credit Cards: A, B
Notes: 2, 5, 8, 9, 10, 11, 14

Toll House

15301 Highway 253
P.O. Box 268
Boonville, CA, 95415
(707) 895-3630

A secluded 360-acre ranch offering you quiet surroundings for relaxing and taking in the scenery, while providing for a variety of activities. Stroll through the lovely gardens, hike over dramatic hills, picnic among magnificent black oaks. The Toll House Restaurant features exquisite cuisine and the best of wines and champagnes. In the area you will enjoy wine tasting, swimming, fishing, cycling, hunting, redwood viewing, scenic drives, and many other activities.

Hosts: Barbara McGuinness & Betty Ingram
Rooms: 5 (PB) $95-145
Full Breakfast
Credit Cards: A, B, D
Notes: 2, 3, 4, 5, 9, 10, 12, 14

BRENTWOOD

The Woods

B&B of Los Angeles
32074 Waterside Lane
Westlake Village, CA, 91361
(818) 889-8870

Two-story redwood townhouse looking out to acres of eucalyptus and wildlife, yet only ten minutes from Beverly Hills and Santa Monica. Charmingly decorated with Early American furniture, with a patio, underground parking, and great bus transportation nearby. The house is only four miles to the beach. The upstairs guest room has a double bed, private bath, and TV. The master bedroom has a queen bed, fireplace, TV, and private bath with Jacuzzi tub. Children over twelve welcome. $45-80.

BURLINGAME

Burlingame B&B

1021 Balboa Avenue
Burlingame, CA, 94010
(415) 344-5815

Boating, swimming, fishing (bay and ocean), running, golf, hiking, art, entertainment, sports. Near Stanford, colleges, junior colleges, and transportation.

Hosts: Joe & Elnora Fernandez
Rooms: 1 (PB) $50
Continental Breakfast
Credit Cards: No
Notes: 2, 3, 5, 8, 10, 11, 12

Brannan Cottage Inn

CALISTOGA

Brannan Cottage Inn

109 Wapoo Avenue
Calistoga, CA, 94515
(707) 942-4200

Six guest rooms, all with private baths, central air and heat, and private entrances. Rates include a full breakfast and complimentary evening beverages. Mud baths, glider rides, champagne, wine tasting, and bike rentals are all within a five-minute drive.

Hosts: Pam & Jack Osborn
Rooms: 6 (PB) $110-145
Full Breakfast
Credit Cards: A, B, C
Notes: 2 (in advance), 5, 10, 11, 12, 14

Brannan's Loft

1436 Lincoln Avenue
P.O. Box 561
Calistoga, CA, 94515
(707) 963-2181

Located upstairs in a historic building in downtown Calistoga, overlooking busy Lincoln Avenue, with a spectacular view of towering Mount St. Helena. The loft offers three large units, beautifully decorated and comfortably furnished. Each is equipped with cable color TV, air-conditioning, and its own kitchenette. We offer complimentary wine, a smoke-free environment, and breakfast coupons for use at the restaurant downstairs.

Host: Inge Meinzer
Rooms: 3 (PB) $75-105 + tax
Credit Cards: A, B
Notes: 2, 3, 4, 5, 8, 9, 10, 11, 12, 14

Calistoga's Wishing Well Inn

2653 Foothill Blvd.
Calistoga, CA, 94515
(707) 942-5534

A country estate among vineyards, with elegant period interiors. Situated on 4 acres in a historical setting. Enjoy your country breakfast featuring homegrown fruits and preserves, and complimentary wine and hor d'oeuvres poolside with a magnificent view of Mt. St. Helena or on your private sun deck. Fireplace in the common parlor; Jacuzzi under the stars; all private baths. Near mud baths, balloon rides, wineries.

Hosts: Marina & Keith Dinsmoor
Rooms: 3 (PB) $100-120 + tax
Full Breakfast
Credit Cards: A, B
Notes: 2, 5, 8, 9, 10, 11, 12, 14

Calistoga Wayside Inn

1523 Foothill Blvd.
Calistoga, CA, 94515
(707) 942-0645

Enjoy cozy down comforters, the gentle music of water fountains, and wind chimes. Gourmet breakfast served on the patio in summer and in front of an open fire in winter. Hot tub and picnic baskets also available at this 70-year-old Spanish hacienda.

Hosts: Deborah & Leonard Flaherty
Rooms: 3 (PB) $90-115
Full Breakfast
Children welcome on weekdays
Credit Cards: A, B, C
Notes: 2, 8, 9, 10, 11, 12, 14

"Culvers," A Country Inn

1805 Foothill Blvd.
Calistoga, CA, 94515
(707) 942-4535

A lovely Victorian residence built in 1875, filled with antiques and offering a full country breakfast. Jacuzzi and seasonal pool, indoor sauna. Within minutes of wineries, mud baths, and downtown Calistoga. Lovely view of St. Helena mountain range from the veranda. Sherry is offered in the afternoon.

Hosts: Meg & Tony Wheatley
Rooms: 6 (SB) $105-115 + tax
Full Breakfast
Credit Cards: As deposit
Closed Dec. 24-Dec. 26
Notes: 2, 9, 10, 11, 12, 14

Foothill House

3037 Foothill Blvd.
Calistoga, CA, 94515
(707) 942-6933

"The most romantic inn of the Napa Valley," according to the *Chicago Tribune* travel editor. In a country setting, Foothill House offers spacious suites individually decorated with antiques, each with private bath and entrance, fireplace, and small refrigerator. Private cottage also available.

Hosts: Susan & Michael Clow
Rooms: 3 (PB) $95-210
Continental-plus Breakfast
Credit Cards: A, B, C
Notes: 2, 5, 9, 10, 11, 12, 14

Mountain Home Ranch

3400 Mountain Home Ranch Road
Calistoga, CA, 94515
(707) 942-6616

Located in the hills above the Napa Valley, our 300-acre vacation facility has been in the same family since 1913. Quiet, restful, rejuvenating. Pool, tennis, lake fishing, wilderness walking trails. Fifteen minutes to the heart of the wine country with its hot air ballooning, spas, and golf.

Hosts: George & Joey Fouts
Rooms: 14 (PB) $42-65
Continental Breakfast
Credit Cards: A, B
Closed mid-Dec.-end Jan.
Notes: 2, 7, 8, 9, 10, 11, 12, 14

The Pink Mansion

1415 Foothill Blvd.
Calistoga, CA, 94515
(707) 942-0558

A 115-year-old Victorian in the heart of the Napa Valley wine country. Within biking distance to several wineries; walking distance to Calistoga's many spas and restaurants. Fully air-conditioned; indoor pool; complimentary wine and cheese. Each room has a wonderful view and private bath.

Hosts: Jeff Seyfried
Rooms: 5 (PB) $72-$154
Full Breakfast
Minimum Stay Weekends & Holidays: 2
Credit Cards: A, B
Notes: 2, 5, 8 (over 12), 9, 10, 11, 12

Quail Mountain Bed & Breakfast

4455 North St. Helena Highway
Calistoga, CA, 94515
(707) 942-0316; (707) 942-0315

Quail Mountain is a secluded luxury B&B located on 26 wooded and vineyard acres. Three guest rooms, each with king bed, private bath, and private deck. Complimentary wine, pool, spa. Lovely breakfast. Close to Napa Valley tourist attractions.

Hosts: Don & Alma Swiers
Rooms: 3 (PB) $98-130
Full Breakfast
Minimum stay weekends & holidays: 2
Credit Cards: A, B
Notes: 2, 5, 7 (limited), 9, 10, 11, 12, 14

Scarlett's Country Inn

3918 Silverado Trail
Calistoga, CA, 94515
(707) 942-6669

Secluded 1890 farmhouse, set in the quiet of green lawns and tall pines, overlooking the vineyards. Three exquisitely appointed suites, one with fireplace and wet bar. Breakfast in your room or by the woodland swimming pool. Close to wineries, spas.

Hosts: Scarlett & Derek Dwyer
Rooms: 3 (PB) $85-125
Continental-plus Breakfast
Credit Cards: No
Closed Thanksgiving & Christmas
Notes: 2, 5, 7, 8, 9, 10, 11, 12, 14

Trailside Inn

4201 Silverado Trail
Calistoga, CA, 94515
(707) 942-4106

A charming 1930s farmhouse, centrally located in the country, with three very private suites. Each suite has its own entrance, porch or deck, bedroom, bath, fireplace, and air-conditioning. Fresh home-baked breads provided in your fully equipped kitchen.

Hosts: Randy & Lani Gray
Suites: 3 (PB) $85-110
Continental Breakfast
Credit Cards: C, D
Notes: 2, 5, 7, 8, 9, 10, 11, 12, 14

Washington Street Lodging

1605 Washington Street
Calistoga, CA, 94515
(707) 942-6968

Washington Street Lodging offers private cottages in a secluded river setting. Enjoy cozy country decor and many extra touches that make you feel at home. Each cottage has a private bath and full or partial kitchen. Within walking distance of downtown Calistoga spas, shopping, and restaurants. Short drive to the wineries.

Host: Joan Ranieri
Rooms: 5 (PB) From $80
Continental Breakfast
Credit Cards: No
Notes: 2, 5, 6, 7, 8, 9, 10, 11, 12, 14

Wine Way Inn

1019 Foothill Blvd.
Calistoga, CA, 94515
(707) 942-0680

A California Craftsman-style home built in 1915. Six guest rooms, all with private bath, all individually decorated in English and American antiques. There is an expansive multilevel deck surrounded by trees for sipping wine and enjoying the hosts' hospitality.

Hosts: Moye & Cecile Stephens
Rooms: 6 (PB) $75-110
Full Breakfast
Credit Cards: A, B
Notes: 2, 5, 9, 10, 11, 12, 14

Zinfandel House

1253 Summit Drive
Calistoga, CA, 94515
(707) 942-0733

Zinfandel House is in a wooded setting on a western hillside with a spectacular view of the famous Napa Valley vineyards. Halfway between St. Helena and Calistoga. Choose among three tastefully decorated rooms with a private or shared bath. Lovely breakfasts served on the deck or in the solarium.

Hosts: Bette & George Starke
Rooms: 3 (PB or SB) $65-$90
Full Breakfast
Credit Cards: No
Notes: 2, 5, 9, 10, 11, 12, 14

CAMBRIA

B&B International—San Francisco 2

1181-B Solano Avenue
Albany, CA, 94706
(415) 525-4569

This home is located among pine and oak trees and has a view of the ocean. Close to the Sea Otter Preserve and picturesque Cambria Village, with its interesting shops and fine restaurants. Two guest rooms. The first room has a double bed. If two rooms are needed, the second room has twin beds. Each room has a private bath. $70.

Beach House

6360 Moonstone Beach Drive
Cambria, CA, 93428
(805) 927-3136

The Beach House is located on the ocean front, with beautiful views, decks, and patios.

Some rooms have fireplaces. Large common room with large deck facing the ocean; watch our gorgeous sunsets. Hearst Castle six miles away. Complimentary bicycles.

Hosts: Penny Hitch & Tigg Morales
Rooms: 7 (PB) $111.30-143.10
Extended Continental Breakfast
Credit Cards: No
Notes: 2, 5, 8 (over 12), 9, 10, 11, 12, 14

Olallieberry Inn

2476 Main Street
Cambria, CA, 93428
(805) 927-3222

Located 1.5 miles from the beach and 6 miles from Hearst Castle, within walking distance of fine restaurants and delightful shops, in the heart of wine country.

Host: Linda Boyers
Rooms: 6 (PB) $80-100 + tax
Continental-plus Breakfast
Credit Cards: A, B
Notes: 2, 5, 8 (over 13), 10, 11, 12, 14

The Pickford House Bed & Breakfast

2555 MacLeod Way
Cambria, CA, 93428
(805) 927-8619

Only eight miles from Hearst Castle, Pickford House is decorated with antiques reminiscent of the golden age of film. Three rooms have fireplaces and a view of the mountains. Parlor with an 1860 bar is used for wine and tea bread at 5:00 P.M. TV in rooms. All have clawfoot tubs and showers in rooms. Children welcome.

Host: Anna Larsen
Rooms: 8 (PB) $65-110 plus tax
Full Breakfast
Credit Cards: A, B
Notes: 5, 7 (limited), 8, 9, 14

CAPITOLA

Summer House

216 Monterey Avenue
Capitola, CA, 95010
(408) 475-8474

A rustic summer house located on Depot Hill overlooking Capitola Village and beautiful Monterey Bay. A short walk to the beach, restaurants, theater, and unique shopping. Enjoy a redwood-paneled suite with its own private entrance opening onto a sun deck where your continental breakfast is served.

Host: Patricia M. Dooling
Rooms: 3 (SB) $54
Continental Breakfast
Credit Cards: No
Closed 9/15-10/15
Notes: 2, 6, 8, 9, 10, 11, 12

CARLSBAD

El Camino Real B&B

P.O. Box 7155
Northridge, CA, 91327-7155
(818) 363-6753

Gated community. Room with double bed and private bath. Small den with convertible double sofa and private half-bath great for two couples traveling together or a couple with children. Walk to beach. Pool, hot tub, full American breakfast. Five minutes from Snug Harbor Lagoon, with water and jet skiing available. $65.

Pelican Cove Inn

320 Walnut Avenue
Carlsbad, CA, 92008
(619) 434-5995

Pelican Cove Inn features: Jacuzzis, feather beds, fireplaces, private entries, private baths, lovely antiques, a sun deck, balconies, and a gazebo. Walk to the beach and restaurants. Palomar Airport and Amtrak pick up. Beach chairs, towels, picnic baskets available. Afternoon refreshments, flowers, fruit, and candy provided. New and beautiful.

Hosts: Bob & Celeste Hale
Rooms: 8 (PB) $85-150
Continental Breakfast
Minimum stay weekends & holidays: 2
Credit Cards: A, B, C
Notes: 2, 5, 7, 8 (over 12), 9, 10, 11, 12, 14

Pelican Cove Inn

CARMEL

B&B International—San Francisco 3

1181-B Solano Avenue
Albany, CA, 94706
(415) 525-4569

This spacious modern home has four fireplaces and a grand piano. It is a five-minute drive to Carmel Village and a short distance to other points of interest on the Monterey Peninsula. The guest room has a private entrance, queen bed, private bath, gas fireplace, cable TV, and a view of Point Lobos. Guest privileges for tennis, pool, and spa can be arranged at the Pebble Beach Club. Guests may smoke outside. $85.

Carriage House Inn

Junipero between 7th & 8th
Carmel, CA, 93921
(800) 433-4732; (800) 422-4732 (CA only)

Fresh flowers and country-inn flavor. Continental breakfast and newspaper delivered to your room each morning. Wood-burning fireplaces, down comforters. Spacious rooms, many with open-beam ceilings and sunken tubs. Wine and hors d'oeuvres each evening in the library. Carmel's only AAA-rated four-diamond inn. A very romantic getaway!

Host: Larry Hoover
Rooms: 13 (PB) $120-225
Continental Breakfast
Minimum stay weekends & holidays: 2
Credit Cards: All Major
Notes: 2, 5, 7, 10, 11, 12, 14

Cobblestone Inn

Junipero between 7th & 8th
Carmel, CA, 93921
(408) 625-5222

Situated in the heart of Carmel, the Cobblestone is an English country inn with a flowering garden and central courtyard. Each room is individually decorated with print wallpaper, fluffy comforters, pine furniture, fireplace, bathrobes, and fresh fruit. Enjoy a full breakfast and afternoon wine and hors d'oeuvres.

Host: Ms. Charlie Aldinger
Rooms: 24 (PB) $99-187
Full Breakfast
Credit Cards: A, B, C
Notes: 2, 5, 8, 9, 10, 11, 12, 14

Happy Landing Inn

Box 2619
Carmel, CA, 93921
(408) 624-7917

Delightful little B&B inn in the heart of downtown Carmel. Beautiful antiques, stained-glass windows, fresh flowers. Breakfast served in your room. This inn looks like a page out of a Beatrix Potter book; you'll love it.

Hosts: Robert & Carol Ballard
Rooms: 7 (PB) $90-135
European Breakfast
Minimum stay weekends: 2
Credit Cards: A, B
Notes: 2, 5, 8 (over 12), 9, 10, 12

Cobblestone Inn

Monte Verde Inn

Box 3373
Carmel, CA, 93921
(408) 624-6046

A charming country inn nestled in the heart of Carmel. Ten warmly furnished rooms with a lovely garden neatly tucked away for guests to enjoy. Wonderful continental breakfast. All rooms are nonsmoking.

Host: John Nahas
Rooms: 10 (PB) $75-145
Continental Breakfast
Credit Cards: A, B, C
Notes: 2, 5, 9, 10, 11, 12, 14

The Sandpiper Inn-at-the-Beach

2408 Bay View Avenue
Carmel, CA, 93923
(408) 624-6433

Within sight and sound of beautiful Carmel Beach. Quiet comfort and luxury in a relaxed atmosphere. Rooms and cottages are filled with antiques and fresh flowers; all have private baths. Some have glorious ocean views, others have fireplaces. Breakfast and complimentary sherry are served in the comfortable lounge. Perfect for anniversaries and special occasions.

Hosts: Graeme & Irene Mackenzie
Rooms: 16 (PB) $90-150
Continental Breakfast
Credit Cards: A, B, C
Notes: 2, 5, 10, 11, 12

Stonehouse Inn

P.O. Box 2517
Carmel, CA, 93921
(408) 624-4569

Victorian house (1906), furnished with antiques, within walking distance of the beach, shops, restaurants. Living room with large fireplace is the gathering spot for guests to enjoy spirits and snacks before dinner. Breakfast is served in the bright and cheery dining room each morning.

Hosts: Karin & Craig Fraki
Rooms: 6 (SB) $90-125
Full Breakfast
Credit Cards: A, B
Notes: 2, 5, 8 (14 and over), 9, 10, 12, 14

Tally Ho Inn

P.O. Box 3726
Carmel, CA, 93921
(408) 624-2232

The Tally Ho is located conveniently three blocks from a white sandy beach, in the heart of the village, close to superb restaurants and shopping. A delightful buffet breakfast is served in the dining room overlooking beautiful Carmel Bay. In the evenings, an aged French brandy awaits your return from dinner. Five minutes from seventeen-mile drive, championship golf, and the Monterey Aquarium.

Hosts: Barbara & Erven Torell
Rooms: 14 (PB) $105-250
Continental-plus Breakfast
Credit Cards: A, B, C
Notes: 2, 5, 7, 8, 9, 10, 11, 12, 14

Tally Ho Inn

Vagabond's House Inn

P.O. Box 2747
Carmel, CA, 93921
(408) 624-7738; (800) 262-1262

Situated in the heart of Carmel village, Vagabond's House Inn surrounds a Carmel-stone courtyard that is dominated by large oak trees, plants, ferns, and flowers in profusion. The eleven unique guest rooms are appointed with a combination of collectibles and antiques in a mixture of European elegance and country tradition.

Hosts: Honey Jones & Jewell Brown
Rooms: 11 (PB) $79-135
Continental Breakfast
Credit Cards: A, B, C
Notes: 2, 5, 6, 7, 9, 10, 11, 12, 14

Valley Lodge

Box 93
Carmel, CA, 93924
(408) 659-2261; (800) 641-4646

A quiet country inn nestled on 3 lovely acres in peaceful Carmel Valley, the sunbelt of the Monterey Peninsula. Relax and unwind in a garden patio room or a cozy fireplace cottage. Enjoy our heated pool, hot spa, sauna, game area, and fitness center. Walk to fine restaurants and quaint shops.

Hosts: Peter & Sherry Coakley
Rooms: 31 (PB) $85-125
Cottages: $160-230
Type of Beds: 4 Twin; 33 Queen; 3 King
Continental-plus Breakfast
Credit Cards: A, B, C
Notes: 2, 5, 6, 7, 8, 9, 10, 11, 12, 14

CAZADERO

Cazanoma Lodge

100 Kidd CR RD
Cazadero, CA, 95421-0037
(707) 632-5255

Old-world lodge located on 147 acres of redwood and fir forest with waterfall and trout pond. All suites and cabins have private baths. Located near the ocean and the Russian River wine country. Fine dining—German and American menu—full bar.

Hosts: Randy & Gretchen Neuman
Rooms: 5 (PB) $70-95
Continental Breakfast
Credit Cards: A, B, C
Closed Dec. 1-Feb. 20
Notes: 2, 4, 6 (cabins), 7, 8, 9, 10, 11, 12, 14

House of a Thousand Flowers

11 Mosswood Circle
Cazadero, CA, 95421
(707) 632-5571

A quiet bed and breakfast house hidden away in a redwood forest. Spectacular vistas from every window; shoji screens; a bubbling spa, and an abundance of flowers make this a perfect secluded getaway.

Hosts: Dave Silva
Rooms: 2 (SB) $74
Full Breakfast
Credit Cards: A, B
Notes: 2, 5, 8 (with prior arrangement), 9

CHICO

Bullard House B&B

256 East First Avenue
Chico, CA, 95926
(916) 342-5912

Bullard House is a charming country Victorian in a university town, centrally located to downtown. Tree-lined streets for wonderful biking; close to hunting and fishing areas.

Hosts: Patrick & Patricia Macarthy
Rooms: 5 (SB) $50-60
Continental Breakfast
Credit Cards: No
Notes: 2, 5, 9, 10, 11, 12, 14

NW Bed & Breakfast 509

610 SW Broadway
Portland, OR, 97205
(503) 243-7616

Attractive new home with pool. The host, a fisherman, is knowledgeable about the area. His wife is a musician. Hosts play bridge. Pickup at train and airport is available. Two rooms, shared bath. $50.

CLEAR LAKE

Muktip Manor

12540 Lakeshore Drive
Clear Lake, CA, 95422
(707) 994-9571

Suite consisting of bedroom, bath, kitchenette, sitting room, TV, and deck. Private beach on the largest lake in California, with canoe and bicycles available. Several golf courses are in the county. Hiking, biking, rock hounding. Located 110 miles north of San Francisco, near five wineries.

Hosts: Elisabeth St. Davids & Jerry Schiffman
Suite: 1 (PB) $50
Full Breakfast
Credit Cards: No
Notes: 2, 5, 6, 7, 9, 10, 11

CLOVERDALE

Vintage Towers B&B Inn

302 North Main Street
Cloverdale, CA, 95425
(707) 894-4535

This lovely Queen Anne Victorian mansion was built in 1901 with three architectually unique towers that now house some of the guest suites. Located near 52 wineries in the serene Sonoma Valley and the Russian River Basin. Gourmet breakfast prepared by a French pastry chef.

Hosts: Jim Mees & Garret Hall
Rooms: 7 (5 PB; 2 SB) $70-115
Full Breakfast
Credit Cards: A, B, C, D
Notes: 2, 7 (restricted), 8, 9, 10, 11, 12, 14

Ye Olde' Shelford House

29955 River Road
Cloverdale, CA, 95425
(707) 894-5956

An 1885 country Victorian in the wine country. The inn is surrounded by vineyards and hills and has a hot tub, bikes, and pool. All rooms are decorated with homemade quilts, family antiques, and fresh flowers. Full breakfast, refreshments, and beverages. Enjoy a vintage car ride with a delicious picnic lunch after sipping wine at local wineries ($60 extra a couple, by reservation).

Hosts: Ina & Al Sauder
Rooms: 6 (4 PB; 2 SB) $95-110 + tax

Full Breakfast
Credit Cards: A, B, D
Notes: 2, 5, 8, 9, 10, 11, 14

COLOMA

Coloma Country Inn

2 High Street, Box 502
Coloma, CA, 95613
(916) 622-6919

Surrounded by the 300-acre Gold Discovery State Park, this 1852 farmhouse provides quiet comfort and close access to Sutter's Mill, museum, and attractions. White-water raft and balloon with hosts. Featured in the June 1988 issue of *Country Living* magazine.

Hosts: Cindi & Alan Ehrgott
Rooms: 5 (3 PB; 2 SB) $69-79
Continental-plus Breakfast
Credit Cards: No
Notes: 2, 5, 8 (over 6), 9

Columbia City Hotel

COLUMBIA

Columbia City Hotel

Box 1870
Columbia, CA, 95310
(209) 532-1479

Centrally located in Columbia, a historic Gold Rush town preserved and protected by the State of California, this impeccable inn is surrounded by relics of the past. All rooms have been restored to reflect the 1850s. Downstairs, the highly acclaimed restaurant and always inviting What Cheer Saloon provide a haven for travelers seeking comfort and gracious hospitality. All rooms have half baths; hall showers.

Host: Tom Bender
Rooms: 9 (PB) $70-85
Continental Breakfast
Credit Cards: A, B, C
Closed Dec. 24-25, mid-week in Jan.
Notes: 2, 3, 4, 7 (limited), 8, 9, 10, 11, 12, 14

DANA POINT

Blue Lantern Inn

34343 Street of the Blue Lantern
Dana Point, CA, 92629
(714) 661-1304

The Blue Lantern Inn is a Cape Cod style country inn perched atop a bluff overlooking Dana Point Harbor and the Pacific. Each room is individually decorated with traditional furniture, pastel colors, and a fireplace, Jacuzzi tub, sun deck, and private bath.

Host: Tom Taylor
Rooms: 29 (PB) $125-275
Full Breakfast
Credit Cards: A, B, C
Notes: 2, 5, 7, 8, 9, 10, 11, 12, 14

DAVENPORT

New Davenport B&B

31 Davenport Avenue
Davenport, CA, 95017
(408) 425-1818; (408) 426-4122

Halfway between Carmel-Monterey and San Francisco, on Coast Highway 1. Small, rural, coastal town noted for whale watching, wind-surfing, Ano Nuevo Elephant Seal State Reserve, hiking, bicycling, and beach exploration. Wonderful restaurant and gift store with unusual treasures and jewelry. Artist owners; interesting ambience and location.

Hosts: Bruce & Marcia McDougal
Rooms: 12 (PB) $55-105
Full Breakfast
Credit Cards: C
Notes: 2, 3, 4, 5, 8, 9, 10, 11, 12

DAVIS

University Inn B&B

340 A Street
Davis, CA, 95616
(916) 756-8648

Directly adjacent to the University of California at Davis, this country inn offers a charming escape from a busy college town in a homelike setting. Each room has a private bath, phone, TV, and refrigerator. There are complimentary chocolates, beverages, and flowers, and a generous breakfast is served.

Hosts: Lynda & Ross Yancher
Rooms: 4 (PB) From $47
Full Breakfast
Credit Cards: All
Notes: 2, 5, 6 (limited), 7 (outside), 8, 9, 10, 11, 12, 14

DEL MAR

The Blue Door

13707 Durango Drive
Del Mar, CA, 92014
(619) 755-3819

Enjoy New England charm in a quiet Southern California setting. Lower-level two-room suite with king bed, private bath, and cozy sitting-room opening onto bougainvillea-splashed patio with open vista of Torrey Pines Reserve Canyon. Twenty miles north of San Diego. Creative full breakfast.

Hosts: Bob & Anna Belle Schock
Suite: (PB) $50-60
Full Breakfast
Credit Cards: No
Notes: 2, 5, 8 (over 16), 9, 10, 11, 12

Gull's Nest

12930 Via Esperia
P.O. Box 1056
Del Mar, CA, 92014
(619) 259-4863

Gull's Nest rustic hideaway is a contemporary wood home surrounded by pines with a beautiful ocean and bird sanctuary view from two upper decks. Home is decorated with many paintings, mosaics, and wood carvings. Five minutes from La Jolla and Del Mar. Close to I-5, and just twenty minutes from the San Diego Zoo and airport. One cat in residence.

Hosts: Michael & Constance Segel
Rooms: 2 (PB) $50-65
Full Breakfast
Credit Cards: No
Notes: 2, 5, 7 (outside), 8 (6 and up), 9, 11, 12

Rock Haus Inn

410 15th Street
Del Mar, CA, 92014
(619) 481-3764

This California-style bungalow is a historic landmark in the quaint village of Del Mar, overlooking the ocean and the town. Everything is within walking distance. Two blocks to the beach; one block to the town. Tennis is within one mile, and golf within ten miles.

Host: Doris Holmes
Rooms: 10 (4 PB; 6 SB) $75-135
Continental Breakfast
Minimum stay May 15-Oct. 15
Credit Cards: A, B, C
Notes: 2, 5, 9, 10, 11, 12, 14

DULZURA

Brookside Farm B&B Inn

1373 Marron Valley Road
Dulzura, CA, 92017
(619) 468-3043

A country farmhouse furnished with collectibles, handmade quilts, and stained glass. Tree-shaded terraces by a stream; farm animals; gardens; hot tub in the grape arbor. Perfect for country walks. Close to Tecate, Mexico, and thirty-five minutes from San Diego.

Hosts: Ed Guishard & Sally Smyth
Rooms: 9 (7 PB; 2 SB) $48.60-81
Full Breakfast
Minimum stay holidays and some rooms: 2
Credit Cards: No
Closed Christmas
Notes: 2, 4 (weekends), 9, 14

EL CERRITO

Dolphin Charters

1007 Leneve Place
El Cerrito, CA, 94530
(415) 527-9622

Luxury cruising yacht available for romantic water interludes during the midweek. Three guest cabins plus one large master bed make the boat ideal for one couple or family. Evening cruise and/or full meal service available with prior arrangement. The boat is available May 20-October 20.

Rooms: 3 (SB) $75
Continental Breakfast
Credit Cards: C
Notes: 2, 3, 4, 8, 9, 10, 11, 12, 14

ELK

Elk Cove Inn

6300 South Highway One
Elk, CA, 95432
(707) 877-3321

An 1883 Victorian atop a bluff with spectacular ocean views—some cabins with fireplaces. Full gourmet breakfast is served in our ocean-view dining room. Ready access to an expansive, driftwood-strewn beach. Beds have the subtle luxury of sun-dried linens. Relaxed, romantic atmosphere in a rural coastal village.

Host: Hildrun-Uta Triebess
Rooms: 7 (PB) $88-138
Full Breakfast
Credit Cards: No
Notes: 2, 5, 8 (over 12), 9, 11, 12

Greenwood Lodge

Box 172
Elk, CA, 95432
(707) 877-3422

1920s coastal cottages, four with private decks and three with spectacular ocean views. All with private entrances, private baths, sitting rooms with wood-burning stoves. About three hours and a century away from San Francisco. Rugged coastline, beaches, flower gardens, hiking, fishing, horseback riding, whale watching. Breakfast is delivered to each cottage on a tray.

Hosts: Bill & Kathleen Erwin
Oceanfront: 3 (PB) $125
Garden: 4 (PB) $95-110
Full Breakfast
Credit Cards: No
Notes: 2, 5, 7 (outside), 9, 10, 11, 12

ESCONDIDO

Halbig's Hacienda

432 South Citrus Avenue
Escondido, CA, 92027
(619) 745-1296

The Hacienda is a large, family-built adobe ranch house on a knoll, with fruit trees, patios, and garden. Valley and hills surround the property. The acreage provides a country atmosphere, but we are located on the edge of town.

Hosts: George & Mary Jane Halbig
Rooms: 2 (SB) $35-40

Continental Breakfast
Credit Cards: No
Notes: 2, 5, 6, 7 (restricted), 8, 9, 10, 11, 12, 14

EUREKA

"An Elegant Victorian Mansion"

1406 C Street
Eureka, CA, 95501
(707) 444-3144; (707) 443-6512

"Victorian opulence, grace, grandeur—the most elegant house in Eureka"—*New York Times.* A State Historic Landmark, on the National Register of Historic Places. Features hot tub, sauna, massage, croquet, mystery weekends, bicycles, antique cars. Near redwood parks, fishing, boating, tennis, cultural events, carriage rides, train rides, bay cruises. Corporate rates.

Hosts: Doug & Lily Vieyra
Rooms: 5 (2 PB; 3 SB) $85-105
Full Breakfast
Credit Cards: A, B
Notes: 2, 5, 9, 10, 11, 12, 14

An Elegant Victorian Mansion

Carter House & Hotel Carter

301 L Street
Eureka, CA, 95501
(707) 444-8062

Spectacularly re-created landmark Victorians in scenic Old Town Eureka, near the famed Carson Mansion. Original art and antique appointments. Bay and marina vistas, fireplaces, whirlpool baths, featherbeds, truly elegant dining. Dinners featured in *Bon Appetit.* "Best breakfast in California"—*California* Magazine.

Hosts: Mark & Christi Carter
Rooms: 27 (24 PB; 3 SB) $75-350
Full and Continental Breakfast
Credit Cards: A, B, C, E, F
Notes: 2 (on approved credit), 4, 5, 8 (over 8), 9, 10, 11, 12, 14

Heuer's Victorian Inn

1302 E Street
Eureka, CA, 95501
(707) 442-7334

A Queen Anne Victorian built in 1893 and restored to its present splendor in 1980. Just like being transported back in time to an earlier era. For that quiet, relaxing time, it's a must.

Hosts: Charles & Ausbern Heuer
Rooms: 3 (1 PB; 2 SB) $65
Continental Breakfast
Credit Cards: A, B, C, D, E, F
Notes: 2, 5, 9, 10, 12, 14

Iris Inn B&B

1134 H Street
Eureka, CA, 95501
(707) 445-0307

The Iris Inn is located just ten blocks from Eureka's restored Victorian Old Town. Our Queen Anne Victorian was built in 1900 for Humboldt County's first county clerk, William Haw. Humboldt County is the heart of California's redwood country, with Redwood National Park to the north and Humboldt State Park to the south.

Hosts: Sharon & Joe Bonino
Rooms: 4 (1 PB; 3 SB) $65-90
Full Breakfast
Credit Cards: A, B
Notes: 2, 5, 7, 8, 10, 11, 12, 14

Old Town B&B Inn

1521 Third Street
Eureka, CA, 95501
(707) 445-3951

Built in 1871 in the Redwood Empire, this historic Victorian home features a uniquely warm atmosphere, Teddy Bears, Rubber Duckies. Guests write: "The best....Breakfast to die for....Like Grandma's house." Corporate discount.

Hosts: Leigh & Diane Benson
Rooms: 5 (3 PB; 2 SB) $70-100
Full Breakfast
Credit Cards: A, B
Notes: 2, 5, 8 (over 10), 9, 10, 11, 12, 14

The Gingerbread Mansion

FERNDALE

The Ferndale Inn

619 Main Street
Ferndale, CA, 95536
(707) 786-4307

Classic Victorian home built in 1859, with intimate accommodations and antiques in a cozy country atmosphere. Located in the Victorian village of Ferndale, close to the ocean, the Eel River, Redwood National Park, and downtown shopping.

Hosts: Danielle & Jim McManamon
Rooms: 5 (2.5 PB; 2.5 SB) $65-115
Full Breakfast
Credit Cards: A, B, C
Closed Jan.
Notes: 2

The Gingerbread Mansion

400 Berding Street
P.O. Box 40
Ferndale, CA, 95536
(707) 786-4000

The West Coast's most photographed inn, located in northern California's Victorian village of Ferndale — a state historic landmark near redwood parks and Eureka — offers fireplaces, bicycles, English gardens. Four parlors, spectacular baths with "his and her" clawfoot tubs — unsurpassed elegance and hospitality.

Hosts: Wendy Hatfield & Ken Torbert
Rooms: 9 (PB) $85-175
Expanded Continental Breakfast
Minimum stay weekends & holidays: 2
Credit Cards: A, B
Notes: 2, 5, 8 (over 10), 9, 10, 11, 12, 14

Shaw House Inn

703 Main Street
P.O. Box 1125
Ferndale, CA, 95536
(707) 786-9958

This 1854 Carpenter Gothic is cottage-like in design, very cozy and bright. Like sleeping in Grandma's attic. We have lots of antiques and good reading in our library for our guests to enjoy. This is an all-redwood/one-wall-construction home. Afternoon tea at check-in, 3:00 to 6:00 P.M.

Hosts: Ken & Norma Bessingpas
Rooms: 5 (1 PB; 4 SB) $65-115
Continental-plus Breakfast
Credit Cards: A, B, C
Notes: 2, 5, 7 (limited), 8 (over 8), 10, 14

FORT BRAGG

Grey Whale Inn

615 North Main Street
Fort Bragg, CA, 95437
(707) 964-0640; (800) 382-7244 (CA only)

Stately four-story Mendocino coast landmark since 1915. Fourteen spacious rooms; two rooms have fireplaces; four have ocean views; two with private sun decks; one with private patio; one has a whirlpool tub; one has wheel chair access. Lounge with fireplace; TV room with VCR; recreation room with pool table. Mini-conference facilities. Whale watching (Dec.-March), fishing party boats, Skunk Train trips arranged.

Hosts: John & Colette Bailey
Rooms: 14 (PB) $70-140
Full Buffet Breakfast
Minimum stay weekends: 2; holidays: 3-4
Credit Cards: A, B, C
Notes: 2, 5, 8 (over 12), 9, 10, 11, 12, 14

Grey Whale Inn

Pudding Creek Inn

700 North Main Street
Fort Bragg, CA, 95437
(707) 964-9529

Two Victorian homes, built in 1884 by a Russian count, connected by a lush enclosed garden. Ten captivating rooms furnished in comfortable country or Victorian decor, with private baths. Two rooms have fireplaces; two have old-fashioned bathtubs. Within walking distance of Glass Beach, Pudding Creek, downtown shops and restaurants, logging museum, Skunk Train depot.

Hosts: Eugene & Marilyn Gundersen
Rooms: 10 (PB) $55-90
Full Breakfast
Credit Cards: A, B, C
Closed Jan.
Notes: 2, 8, 9, 10, 11, 12, 14

FREESTONE

Green Apple Inn

520 Bohemia Highway
Freestone, CA, 95472
(707) 874-2526

An 1860s New England-style farmhouse set in a meadow backed by redwoods. Located on 5 acres in the designated historic district of Freestone, between Bodega Bay and the Russian River. There are several excellent restaurants and small family wineries in the area. In the village itself are several unique shops.

Hosts: Rogers & Rosemary Hoffman
Rooms: 4 (PB) $78
Full Breakfast
Credit Cards: A, B
Notes: 2, 5, 8 (over 6), 9, 11, 12, 14

FREMONT

Lord Bradley's Inn

43344 Mission Blvd.
Fremont, CA, 94539
(415) 490-0520

This Victorian is nestled below Mission Peak, adjacent to the Mission San Jose. Numerous olive trees on the property were planted by the Ohlone Indians. Common room; garden, patio. Parking in rear. Take the bus or Bay Area Rapid Transit to San Francisco for a day.

Hosts: Keith & Anne Bradley Medeiros
Rooms: 8 (PB) $55-$65
Continental Breakfast
Credit Cards: A, B, E, F
Notes: 2, 5, 6, 8, 9, 14

GARDEN GROVE

Dream Weavers

B&B of Los Angeles
32074 Waterside Lane
Westlake Village, CA, 91361
(818) 889-8870

Beautiful older home in quiet neighborhood offers a large upstairs suite of two bedrooms and bath. One room has a king brass bed, fireplace, and balcony; the other, a queen bed, small refrigerator, and TV. Downstairs is a guest room with a double bed and private bath. Retired couple enjoy guests; hostess is a weaver and doll collector. Children are welcome. $45-80.

GEORGETOWN

American River Inn

Orleans Street, Box 43
Georgetown, CA, 95634
(916) 333-4499; (800) 245-6566 (CA only)

This "Jewel of the Mother Lode" is a totally restored 1853 miners' boarding house. Each room is individually decorated with Victorian and turn-of-the-century antiques. Gorgeous natural gardens; a refreshing mountain stream; pool with Jacuzzi; a dove aviary; bicycles. Enjoy a full breakfast in the morning, local wines and treats in the evening. Antique shop on the premises. Facilities for the handicapped. Georgetown is a Sierra foothills village with real flavor and six historic buildings to explore.

Hosts: Will & Maria
Rooms: 25 (12 PB; 13 SB) $74-98
Full Breakfast
Credit Cards: A, B, C
Notes: 2, 5, 7, 8 (over 8) 9, 11, 12, 13

GEYSERVILLE

Campbell Ranch Inn

1475 Canyon Road
Geyserville, CA, 95441
(707) 857-3476

Thirty-five-acre country setting in the heart of Sonoma County wine country. Spectacular view, beautiful gardens, tennis court, swimming pool, hot tub, bicycles. Full breakfast served on the terrace; homemade evening dessert. Color brochure available.

Hosts: Mary Jane & Jerry Campbell
Rooms: 5 (PB) $90-125
Full Breakfast
Minimum stay weekends Mar-Nov: 2; major holiday weekends: 3
Teenagers welcome
Credit Cards: A, B, D
Notes: 2, 5, 7 (limited), 9, 10, 11, 14

American River Inn

The Hope-Merrill House/The Hope-Bosworth House

Box 42, Geyserville, CA, 95441
(707) 857-3356

NOTES: Credit cards accepted: A Master Card; B Visa; C American Express; D Discover Card; E Diners Club; F Other: 2 Personal checks accepted: 3 Lunch available: 4 Dinner available: 5 Open all year

Vintage Victorian turn-of-the-century inns welcome travelers in grand style to the California wine country. Twelve rooms with private baths (two with Jacuzzi tubs), beautiful gardens, gazebo, vineyards, and swimming pool will make your stay a memorable experience. Featured in *Country Homes, Sunset, House Beautiful* magazines.

Hosts: Bob & Rosalie Hope
Rooms: 12 (10 PB; 2 SB) $60-115
Full Breakfast
Credit Cards: A, B
Notes: 2, 3, 5, 8, 9, 10, 11, 12, 14

GLEN ELLEN

Glenelly Inn

5131 Warm Springs Road
Glen Ellen, CA, 95442
(707) 996-6720

Charming country inn located in the Sonoma wine country near Jack London Park. Restored turn-of-the-century inn with with spacious lawn and oak trees. Boutique wineries and good restaurants nearby. One hour north of San Francisco.

Host: Kristi Hallamore Grove
Rooms: 8 (PB) $75-120
Full Breakfast
Credit Cards: A, B
Notes: 5, 7 (outside), 8 (by arrangement), 9, 10, 11, 12, 14

JVB Vineyard

14335 Sonoma Hwy.
P.O. Box 997
Glen Ellen, CA, 95442
(707) 996-4533

Two private little Spanish-style adobe haciendas overlooking our vineyard. Thirty-seven wineries and champagne cellars in historic Sonoma Valley. Site of raising of the Bear Flag, author Jack London's Wolf House, last mission on the California trail, and home of General Vallejo. Great waffles for breakfast.

Hosts: Beverly & Jack Babb
Rooms: 2 (PB) $85
Full Breakfast
Credit Cards: No
Notes: 2, 5, 9, 11, 12, 14

Tanglewood House

250 Bonnie Way
Glen Ellen, CA, 95442
(707) 996-5021

Tanglewood House is located in a secluded parklike setting near Jack London State Park. Our luxury suite with private entrance overlooks the swimming pool and has a large sitting room with fireplace, antiques, color TV, and refrigerator. The bedroom is furnished in antique pine.

Hosts: John & Mary Field
Rooms: 1 (PB) $95
Full Breakfast
Credit Cards: No
Notes: 2, 5, 11, 12, 14

North Coast Country Inn

GUALALA

North Coast Country Inn

34591 South Highway 1
Gualala, CA, 95445
(707) 884-4537

6 Pets welcome: 7 Smoking allowed: 8 Children welcome: 9 Social drinking allowed: 10 Tennis available: 11 Swimming available: 12 Golf available: 13 Skiing available: 14 May be booked through travel agents

A cluster of rustic redwood buildings with ocean views. Our rooms feature queen beds, fireplaces, kitchenettes, private baths, decks, and private entries. The inn has a hot tub and gazebo. Full breakfast is served in guest rooms. Nearby golf, hiking, horseback riding, fishing, and beaches.

Hosts: Loren & Nancy Flanagan
Rooms: 4 (PB) $102.60-124.20
Full Breakfast
Minimum stay weekends: 2; holidays: 3
Credit Cards: A, B
Notes: 2, 5, 9, 10, 11, 12, 14

The Old Milano Hotel & Restaurant

38300 Highway One
Gualala, CA, 95445
(707) 884-3256

Listed in the National Registry of Historic Places, this 1905 building is an example of early California architecture with interior Victorian appointments. Located on a 3-acre oceanfront estate with flowering gardens. Restaurant featuring gourmet dining Wednesday to Sunday. Cliffside hot tub overlooking the Pacific. Certified staff massage practitioner.

Host: Leslie Linscheid
Rooms: 9 (3 PB; 6 SB) $75-160
Full Breakfast
Credit Cards: A, B, C
Notes: 2, 4, 5, 10, 12, 14

Whale Watch Inn

35100 Highway 1
Gualala, CA, 95445
(707) 884-3667

Serene oceanside retreat consisting of eighteen rooms, some with two-person whirlpool tubs, most with fireplaces, some with kitchens. All have ocean views. Breakfast is served in your room. Beach access.

Rooms: 18 (PB) $150-225
Full Breakfast
Minimum stay weekends: 2; holidays: 3
Credit Cards: A, B, C
Notes: 2, 5, 8 (over 15), 10, 12

GUERNEVILLE

The Estate Inn

13555 Highway 116
Guerneville, CA, 95446
(707) 869-9093

A Sonoma County historic landmark reborn as an elegant B&B inn, the Estate is ideally located in the beautiful Russian River Valley, just minutes from award-winning wineries. Armstrong State Redwood Reserve, and the dramatic Pacific Coast. Saturday evening dinners.

Host: Jim Caron
Rooms: 10 (PB) $100-150
Full Breakfast
Credit Cards: A, B, C
Notes: 5, 9, 10, 11, 12, 14

Ridenhour Ranch House Inn

Ridenhour Ranch House Inn

12850 River Road
Guerneville, CA, 95446
(707) 887-1033

A 1906 inn on 2.25 acres of trees, gardens, and meadow situated in the Russian River area of Northern California. Each room is decorated in country English and American antiques, quilts, plants, and fresh flowers. The area provides numerous restaurants, and dinner can also be arranged at the inn.

Hosts: Diane & Fritz Rechberger
Rooms: 8 (5 PB; 3 SB) $65-115
Full Breakfast
Credit Cards: A, B
Notes: 2, 4, 5, 8 (over 10), 12, 14

Santa Nella House

12130 Highway 116
Guerneville, CA, 95446
(707) 869-9488

In the heart of the redwood, Russian River, and champagne country. Located in a redwood forest with a quiet, comfortable, homelike atmosphere. Wood-burning fireplaces, private baths, large, delicious breakfasts. Only eighteen miles from the ocean. Reservations suggested.

Hosts: Ed & Joyce Ferrington
Rooms: 4 (PB) $75-90
Full Breakfast
Credit Cards: A, B
Closed Jan. & Feb.
Notes: 2, 9, 10, 11, 12, 14

Old Thyme Inn

The Willows

15905 River Road
P.O. Box 465
Guerneville, CA, 95446
(707) 869-2824; (707) 869-3279

Five-acre country estate on the Russian River with sauna, hot tub, community kitchen, private dock with canoes. Summer camping and RV access. Quiet seclusion among the redwoods. Near wineries and the beautiful northern California coast.

Hosts: Bill & Rick
Rooms: 12 (6 PB; 6 SB) $40-100
Continental Breakfast
Credit Cards: A, B, C, D
Notes: 5, 9, 10, 11, 12, 14

HALF MOON BAY

Old Thyme Inn

779 Main Street
Half Moon Bay, CA, 94019
(415) 726-1616

This 1890s Victorian is on historic Main Street, and has an herbal theme. Guests are invited to stroll in Anne's English herb garden and take cuttings. Everybody loves Simon's buttermilk scones with herb tea for breakfast. Some rooms have double-size whirlpool tubs; fireplaces and antiques are everywhere.

Hosts: Anne & Simon Lowings
Rooms: 7 (PB) $70-205
Full Breakfast
Credit Cards: A, B, C
Notes: 2, 5, 6, 8, 9, 10, 11, 12, 14

Zaballa House

324 Main Street
Half Moon Bay, CA, 94019
(415) 726-9123

The first house built in Half Moon Bay (1859), standing at the entrance to historic Main Street, has been carefully restored into a B&B. The inn is set in a garden across the street from two fine restaurants and shopping. Guests enjoy the Victorian decor in rooms with high ceilings and antiques, some with double-wide whirlpool tubs and fireplaces. The friendly innkeeper provides an "all you can eat" buffet breakfast in the morning.

Host: Patricia Lee
Rooms: 9 (PB) $70-146
Full Breakfast
Credit Cards: A, B, C
Notes: 2, 5, 8, 9, 10, 11, 12, 14

HEALDSBURG

Calderwood

25 West Grant Street
P.O. Box 967
Healdsburg, CA, 95448
(707) 431-1110

Turn-of-the-century Victorian inn near over thirty wineries, rafting and fishing on the Russian River.

Hosts: Bob & Chris Maxwell
Rooms: 5 (PB) $80-95
Full Breakfast
Credit Cards: No
Notes: 5

Frampton House

489 Powell Avenue
Healdsburg, CA, 95448
(707) 433-5084

A stately 1908 Victorian located in the heart of Sonoma wine country, Frampton House offers personalized service and privacy. All-terrain bikes, Ping-Pong, exercycle, pool, spa, sauna, fireplace, wine. Custom-made tubs for two. Relax in any season.

Host: Paula Bogle
Rooms: 3 (PB) $75.60-97.20
Full Breakfast
Credit Cards: A, B
Notes: 2, 5, 7 (limited), 8 (over 14), 9, 10, 11, 12, 14

Grape Leaf Inn

539 Johnson Street
Healdsburg, CA, 95448
(707) 433-8140

A magnificently restored 1900 Queen Anne Victorian home with seven bedrooms, each with private bath (four with whirlpools and skylights). All rooms are air-conditioned and have king or queen beds. A full country breakfast is served each morning. Afternoon complimentary premium local wines and cheeses. Conveniently situated near Healdsburg town center, the Russian River, Lake Sonoma, and 53 wineries.

Hosts: Terry & Karen Sweet
Rooms: 7 (PB) $75-120
Full Breakfast
Credit Cards: A, B
Notes: 2, 5, 9, 10, 11, 12, 14

Haydon House

321 Haydon Street
Healdsburg, CA, 95448
(707) 433-5228

Located in a quiet residential area within walking distance of the historic plaza, many fine shops and restaurants. Minutes away from 59 wineries. Beautifully restored Victorian furnished in antiques. Separate Gothic cottage with two rooms and private baths with whirlpool tubs.

Hosts: Richard & Joanne Claus
Rooms: 8 (4 PB; 4 SB) $75-125
Full Breakfast
Credit Cards: A, B
Closed Dec. 15-31
Notes: 2, 9, 10, 11, 12, 14

Healdsburg Inn on the Plaza

116 Matheson Street
P.O. Box 1196
Healdsburg, CA, 95448
(707) 433-6991

A 1900 brick Victorian, formerly a Wells Fargo stagecoach express, now restored and elegantly furnished as a B&B. Bay windows view old town plaza; fireplaces; air-conditioned. Solarium/roof garden for afternoon party snacks, popcorn, wine, music. Desserts, coffee, and cookies available all day. Champagne breakfasts. TV, VCR. Family owned and operated, close to everything.

Hosts: Genny Jenkins & Dyanne Celi
Rooms: 9 (PB) $75-145
Full Breakfast
Credit Cards: A, B
Notes: 2, 5, 9, 10, 11, 12

Madrona Manor

1001 Westside Road
Healdsburg, CA, 95448
(707) 433-4231; FAX: (707) 433-0703

A National Historic District with four distinctive buildings, each distinguished by a sense of country elegance. Here is the graciousness one might feel at a friend's home, with luxurious European amenities: thick terry robes, expansive breakfast buffet, colorful grounds, and a nationally acclaimed restaurant.

Hosts: John & Carol Muir
Rooms: 21 (PB) $124-185
Full Breakfast
Credit Cards: A, B, C, E
Notes: 2, 4, 5, 6, 8, 10, 11, 12, 14

Madrona Manor

The Raford House

10630 Wohler Road
Healdsburg, CA, 95448
(707) 887-9573

A Victorian farmhouse sitting among the vineyards in a country setting that offers seven guest rooms, most with private baths, two with fireplaces. County historic landmark.

Innkeepers: The Villeneuves
Rooms: 7 (5 PB; 2 SB)
Full Breakfast
Credit Cards: A, B
Notes: 2, 5, 7 (outside), 8 (over 12), 9, 10, 11, 12, 14

HEALDSBURG/WINDSOR

Country Meadow Inn

11360 Old Redwood Highway
Windsor, CA, 95492
(707) 431-1276

This restored 1890 Victorian farmhouse sits on 6.5 acres in the heart of Sonoma County's wine country. Guest rooms are decorated with carefully selected antiques that add to the warm, welcoming atmosphere. Fireplaces, whirlpool tubs, terraced gardens, swimming pool, and a gourmet breakfast enhance the peaceful country setting.

Hosts: Sandy & Barry
Rooms: 5 (PB) $80.80-124.03
Full Breakfast
Credit Cards: A, B
Notes: 2, 5, 8, 9, 10, 11, 12, 14

HERMOSA BEACH

El Camino Real B&B

P.O. Box 7155
Northridge, CA, 91327-7155
(818) 363-6753

Second house from the beach. Three rooms available, two baths. Sit by the fireplace in the family room after a swim in the ocean. Hostess serves a full breakfast. Children and babies are welcome. $70-75.

HOLLYWOOD

El Camino Real B&B

P.O. Box 7155
Northridge, CA, 91327-7155
(818) 363-6753

Lovely English hostess has a hideaway room with queen bed and private bath, sun deck. Continental breakfast. Children and babies are welcome. $40.

HOMEWOOD

Rockwood Lodge

5295 West Lake Blvd.
Homewood, CA, 95718-0226
(916) 525-5273; FAX: (916) 525-5949

Old Tahoe-style home, made of rock, knotty pine, and hand-hewn timbers. The lodge has been completely renovated for the enjoyment of those who appreciate fine appointments and luxury combined with the warm, friendly atmosphere of Lake Tahoe's magical west shore.

Host: Louis Reinkens
Rooms: 4 (2 PB; 2 SB) $100-150 + tax
Continental Breakfast
Credit Cards: No
Notes: 2, 5, 9, 10, 11, 12, 13, 14

HOPLAND

Thatcher Inn

13401 South Highway 101
Hopland, CA, 95449
(744) 744-1890

This twenty-room Victorian country inn was established in 1890 and remodeled in 1989. Full bar and restaurant open to the public. Fireside library of 4,000 volumes. One of the largest single-malt Scotch whiskey collections in the U.S. All rooms have private baths. Swimming pool and outdoor dining.

Host: Ron Hooper
Rooms: 20 (PB) $85-140
Full breakfast weekends; continental weekdays
Credit Cards: A, B, C
Notes: 3, 4, 5, 9, 10, 11, 12, 14

IDYLLWILD

Wilkum Inn

Box 1115
Idyllwild, CA, 92349
(714) 659-4087

Nestled among the pines in a rustic mountain village, this two-story shingle-sided inn offers rooms that are individually furnished with the innkeepers' antiques and collectibles. Knotty-pine paneling and a river-rock fireplace enhance the hospitality of the common room.

Hosts: Annamae Chambers & Barbara Jones
Rooms: 5 (2 PB; 3 SB) $55-75
Continental-plus Breakfast
Credit Cards: No
Notes: 2, 5, 9, 11, 14

INVERNESS

Alder House

105 Vision Road
P.O. Box 644
Inverness, CA, 94937
(415) 669-7218

Located 48 miles north of San Francisco, on the border of Point Reyes National Seashore. Close to ocean beaches, 200 miles of hiking trails. One private cottage, surrounded by alder and willow trees, with views of Mt. Vision. Spacious, architect-designed interior with a wood stove, TV, kitchen, sun room, and deck.

Host: Susan Brayton
Cottage: 1 (PB) $135
Continental Breakfast
Credit Cards: No
Notes: 2, 5, 6, 8, 9, 10, 11, 12, 14

Ten Inverness Way

10 Inverness Way, Box 63
Inverness, CA, 94937
(415) 669-1648

The *L.A. Times* calls it "one of the niftiest inns in Northern California." Hearty breakfasts, private baths, ebullient garden, handmade quilts, Oriental rugs, stone fireplace, and private hot tub. A redwood-shingled haven for hikers and rainy-day bookworms.

Host: Mary Davies
Rooms: 4 (PB) $90-120 + tax
Full Breakfast
Credit Cards: A, B
Notes: 2, 5, 9, 11, 12, 14

The Heirloom

IONE

The Heirloom

214 Shakeley Lane
Ione, CA, 95640
(209) 274-4468

Travel down a country lane to our romantic English garden. Our petite colonial mansion (circa 1863) is shaded by century-old trees and scented by magnolias and gardenias. Furnished with heirloom antiques, fireplaces, and balconies. Breakfast has a French flair. Come enjoy gracious hospitality.

Hosts: Patricia Cross & Melisande Hubbs
Rooms: 6 (4 PB; 2 SB) $50-80
Full Breakfast
Credit Cards: No
Closed Thanksgiving, Dec. 24 & 25
Notes: 2, 8 (over 10), 9, 10, 11, 12, 14

JACKSON

Court Street Inn

215 Court Street
Jackson, CA, 95642
(209) 223-0416

An 1872 Victorian inn with five rooms and a two-room cottage: queen and double beds. Three rooms with private bath, four with semi-private. Full breakfast. Fireplace in one room, plus parlor and cottage. Patio with rose garden, front porch with swing, spa. Complimentary hors d'oeuvres. Near wineries, restaurants, shopping, and walking tours.

Hosts: Janet & Lee Hammond, Gia & Scott Anderson
Rooms: 7 (3 PB; 4 SB) $75-125
Full Breakfast
Credit Cards: A, B
Notes: 2, 5, 10, 11, 14

Gate House Inn

1330 Jackson Gate Road
Jackson, CA, 95642
(209) 223-3500

Charming turn-of-the-century Victorian in the country on an acre of garden property with a swimming pool. Rooms are decorated with Victorian and country furnishings. One has a fireplace, and the private cottage has a wood stove. Walk to fine restaurants and historic sites. Mobil rated, three stars.

Hosts: Stan & Bev Smith
Rooms: 5 (PB) $75-105
Full Breakfast
Credit Cards: A, B, D
Notes: 2, 5, 8 (over 12), 9, 10, 11, 12, 14

The Wedgewood Inn

11941 Narcissus Road
Jackson, CA, 95642
(209) 296-4300; (800) 933-4393

Charming Victorian replica tucked away on wooded acreage. Antique decor, afternoon refreshments, porch swing, balcony, woodburning stoves, full gourmet breakfast. In the heart of the gold country, close to excellent dining, shopping, and sight-seeing. Gazebo and terraced English gardens.

Hosts: Vic & Jeannine Beltz
Rooms: 6 (PB) $84.80-116.60
Full Breakfast
Credit Cards: A, B, D
Notes: 2, 5, 7 (limited), 8 (over 12), 9

JAMESTOWN

The Jamestown Hotel

18153 Main Street
P.O. Box 539
Jamestown, CA, 95327
(209) 984-3902

A unique opportunity to sample the flavor of early California living. From its old brick exterior to the cheerful, romantic dining room and cozy lounge, the hotel has been restored to the elegance of the Gold Rush days. Each room features antiques and private Victorian bath.

Hosts: Michael & Marcia Walsh
Rooms: 8 (PB) $55-100
Continental Breakfast
Credit Cards: A, B, C
Notes: 2, 3, 4, 5, 7, 9, 10, 11, 12, 14

Murphys Jenner Inn

The National Hotel

Box 502
Jamestown, CA, 95327
(209) 984-3446

Historic National Hotel B&B, an eleven-room Gold Rush hotel (1859). Fully restored, with an outstanding restaurant and the original saloon. Classic cuisine and gracious service are only part of our charm.

Hosts: Stephen and Pamela Willey
Rooms: 11 (5 PB; 6 SB) $45-75
Continental Breakfast
Credit Cards: A, B
Notes: 2, 3, 4, 5, 6 (by prior arrangement), 7, 8 (under 10 by arrangement), 9, 10, 11, 12, 13, 14

JENNER

Murphys Jenner Inn

10400 Coast Highway One
P.O. Box 69
Jenner, CA, 95450
(707) 865-2377

Our lovingly and quaintly furnished accommodations all have private entrances and baths. Most offer restful river, ocean, or coastal views. The absence of TV and telephones in the rooms sets the mood for relaxing amid one of nature's most wonderfully abundant and harmonious settings. Just a short walk to the rugged coastline and restaurants with fine California cuisine.

Hosts: Richard & Sheldon Murphy
Rooms: 10 (PB) $60-150
Continental Breakfast
Credit Cards: A, B, C
Notes: 2, 3, 4, 5, 7 (outside), 8, 9, 10, 11, 12

JULIAN

Julian Lodge

2427 "C" Street
P.O. Box 1930
Julian, CA, 92036
(619) 765-1420

A B&B mountain inn located sixty miles northeast of San Diego in the gold-mining town of Julian. Furnished with antiques in the 1885 style, with modern conveniences.

Situated in town, close to shops, museums, and restaurants.

Hosts: Jim & Linda Huie
Rooms: 23 (PB) $69-79
Full Breakfast
Credit Cards: A, B, C
Notes: 5, 8, 10, 14

Hosts: Vern, Dee, & Tom Taylor
Suites: 6 (PB) $95-150
Continental Breakfast
Minimum stay weekends: 2; holidays: 3
Credit Cards: No
Notes: 2, 5, 7, 8, 9, 10, 11, 12

KLAMATH

Requa Inn

451 Requa Road
Klamath, CA, 95548
(707) 482-8205

The Requa Inn is located on the majestic Klamath River just sixty miles north of Eureka. Bask in the sunshine at nearby sandy beaches, paddle a canoe upstream, or take sport in a river that boasts some of the best fishing in the northwest United States. The inn, originally built in the early 1880s, was moved to its present site in 1885 and rebuilt after a fire in 1914. Take pleasure in our spacious front parlor overlooking the river, or treat yourself to an unforgettable dinner in our dining room.

Hosts: Paul & Donna Hamby
Rooms: 12 (PB) $45-65
Full Breakfast
Credit Cards: A, B, C
Closed Jan. & Feb.
Notes: 2, 4, 7, 8 (10 and over), 9, 11, 14

LAGUNA BEACH

The Carriage House

1322 Catalina Street
Laguna Beach, CA, 92651
(714) 494-8945

The Carriage House features all private suites with living room, bedroom, bath, and some kitchen facilities. Some two-bedroom suites available. All surround a courtyard of plants and flowers, two blocks from the ocean. Close to art galleries, restaurants, and shops.

The Carriage House

Casa Laguna Inn

2510 South Coast Highway
Laguna Beach, CA, 92651
(714) 494-2996

A Spanish mission-style inn in an ocean-view hillside setting with tropical gardens and courtyards, heated pool, aviary, observation bell tower, and cozy library. Complimentary afternoon tea with wine, pates, cheeses, caviar, and hors d'oeuvres. Near Los Angeles and Disneyland.

Hosts: Larry & Joline Terry
Rooms: 20 (PB) $90-225 + tax
Continental Breakfast
Credit Cards: A, B, C, D, E
Notes: 2, 5, 7, 8, 9, 10, 11, 12, 14

Eiler's Inn

741 South Coast Highway
Laguna Beach, CA, 92651
(714) 494-3004

Located in the heart of Laguna, just a few steps from the Pacific Ocean. Tennis, shops, and restaurants are within walking distance. The inn offers elegant yet casual sophistication, with all rooms furnished in antiques, ocean views from the sun deck, fireplaces, and a flower-scented brick courtyard with bubbling fountain.

Hosts: Henk & Annette Wirtz
Rooms: 12 (PB) $100-175
Full Breakfast
Credit Cards: A, B, C
Notes: 2, 5, 7, 8, 9, 10, 11, 12, 14

LA JOLLA

B&B International—San Francisco 4

1181-B Solano Avenue
Albany, CA, 94706
(415) 525-4569

This four-bedroom, four-bath house is furnished in antiques. It has three fireplaces and a lovely garden patio and is within walking distance of the ocean, a park, and restaurants. Room one is a twin room with private bath and garden view. It has a TV. Room two is a separate cottage with a queen bed, fireplace, private bath, and TV. French doors lead into a flower-filled patio. Breakfast may be served on the patio, weather permitting. $65.

El Camino Real B&B

P.O. Box 7155
Northridge, CA, 91327-7155
(818) 363-6753

Three beautiful rooms available with shared and private baths. One block to the ocean. Hostess serves an expanded continental breakfast and afternoon snack in the dining room. $70-125.

Prospect Park Inn

1110 Prospect Street
La Jolla, CA, 92037
(619) 454-0133; (800) 433-1609; FAX: (619) 454-2056

Overlooking scenic La Jolla Cove, a block from beaches, restaurants, and shops. Delightful small hotel in the European tradition. Balconies, ocean-view rooms, penthouse suites, and studios with kitchen facilities. All modern amenities, continental breakfast, and afternoon tea. Close to all San Diego attractions. Weekly and monthly rates available.

Host: Brigitte Schmidt
Rooms: 23 (PB) $75-115
Continental Breakfast
Credit Cards: A, B, C, E
Notes: 2, 5, 8, 9, 10, 11, 12, 14

Bluebelle House B&B

NOTES: Credit cards accepted: A Master Card; B Visa; C American Express; D Discover Card; E Diners Club; F Other: 2 Personal checks accepted: 3 Lunch available: 4 Dinner available: 5 Open all year

LAKE ARROWHEAD

Bluebelle House B&B

Box 2177
Lake Arrowhead, CA, 92352
(714) 336-3292

Enjoy cozy elegance in an alpine setting. Five rooms, decorated in themes from European travels or favorite things. Walk to lake, village, beach, shops, restaurants. Three-star AAA rating. Your hosts love to pamper their guests. Evening refreshments.

Hosts: Rick & Lila Peiffer
Rooms: 5 (3 PB; 2 SB) $75-110
Continental-plus Breakfast
Credit Cards: A, B
Closed Dec. 24-27
Notes: 2, 5, 10, 11, 12, 13

Eagle's Landing

P.O. Box 1510
Blue Jay, CA, 92317
(714) 336-2642

Eagle's Landing is a contemporary mountain home furnished with antiques and arts and crafts from around the world, featuring an emphasis on hospitality, scrumptious breakfasts, a view of beautiful Lake Arrowhead, and an alpine forest. Chosen the number one B&B in Southern California by KABC's radio travel show in 1987.

Hosts: Dorothy & Jack Stone
Rooms: 4 (PB) $85-155
Full Breakfast
Credit Cards: A, B
Closed Dec. 24-29
Notes: 2, 5, 9, 10, 11, 12, 13, 14

Romantique Lakeview Lodge

28051 Hwy 189
Lake Arrowhead, CA, 92352
(714) 337-6633

Romance in the mountains, one and one-half hours from Los Angeles. High Victorian splendor, located at the famous Lake Arrowhead shopping village and lake. Quietly nestled among the tall pines and featuring breathtaking panoramic views. All rooms have color TV, VCR with a free library of silver-screen classics, fireplaces, and private luxury baths. Continental breakfast features our "sinful cinnamon rolls."

Hosts: Kurt & Bonnie Campbell
Rooms: 8 (PB) $75-210
Continental Breakfast
Credit Cards: A, B, C, D
Notes: 2, 5, 10, 11, 12, 13, 14

Saddleback Inn/Arrowhead

P.O. Box 1890
Lake Arrowhead, CA, 92352
(714) 336-3571

Originally constructed as the Raven Hotel in 1917, the Saddleback Inn is now a totally restored historic landmark. The property features 34 guest rooms and cottages, most with stone fireplaces and double whirlpool tubs. Varieties of suite combinations afford excellent accommodations for groups and families as well as couples. Full-service restaurant. Located ninety miles east of Los Angeles.

Hosts: Liza Colton & Donald Giota
Rooms: 34 (PB) $100-325
Full Breakfast weekends; continental weekdays
Credit Cards: A, B, C, D, E, F
Notes: 2, 3, 4, 5, 7, 8, 9, 10, 11, 13, 14

LEGGETT

Bell Glen Resort

70400 Hwy 101
Leggett, CA, 95455
(707) 925-6425

A world-class resort in California's redwood country. Individual deluxe B&B cottages on the banks of the Eel River, nestled under giant trees. Antiques, four-poster beds, bathtubs for two, teddy bears, bubble baths, rose gardens. Gourmet restaurant and historic stage stop saloon.

Hosts: Gene & Sandra Barnett
Rooms: 6 (PB) $65-90 + tax
Continental Breakfast
Credit Cards: A, B
Open May 1-Dec. 8
Notes: 2, 4, 7, 8, 9, 11, 14

LEMON COVE

Lemon Cove B&B

33038 Hwy 198
Lemon Cove, CA, 93244
(209) 597-2555

Located near the Sequoia National Park, the Lemon Cove B&B is nestled at the Sierra foothills, just one mile below Lake Kaweah. A bridal suite with fireplace, whirlpool bath, and balcony is one of six romantic rooms tastefully decorated with antiques and quilts. Awaken to the aroma of a luscious plantation breakfast.

Hosts: Pat & Kay Bonette
Rooms: 6 (4 PB; 2 SB) $55-89
Full Breakfast
Credit Cards: A, B
Notes: 2, 5, 8, 9, 11, 12

LEUCADIA

El Camino Real B&B

P.O. Box 7155
Northridge, CA, 91327-7155
(818) 363-6753

Twenty-seven miles from San Diego, this rustic home in the countryside overlooks the Pacific Ocean. You can walk in the country or stroll on the beach. Hosts can direct you to all that is interesting in San Diego. Full American breakfast. Two rooms share a bath. $50.

LITTLE RIVER

Glendeven

8221 North Highway One
Little River, CA, 95456
(707) 937-0083

Glendeven is a delightful small country inn located on a meadow headland overlooking Little River Bay. Tucked into the rural setting are the 1867 Maine-style farmhouse, the old water tower, the restored barn that holds a two-story guest suite, Gallery Glendeven, and Stevenscroft, with four elegant accommodations.

Hosts: Jan & Janet deVries
Rooms: 10 (8 PB; 2 SB) $70-140
Continental-plus Breakfast
Credit Cards: A, B
Notes: 2, 5, 8, 9, 10, 11, 12, 14

Victorian Farmhouse

7001 North Highway One
P.O. Box 357
Little River, CA, 95456
(707) 937-0697

A completely renovated 1877 inn, furnished in period antiques and located on the coast just two miles south of Mendocino, with its many art galleries, boutiques, and restaurants. Enjoy our apple orchard, flower gardens, and School House Creek. The ocean is a short walk for picnicking or whale watching in the winter months. All rooms have either king or queen beds, private baths. Some have fireplaces. Sherry is offered in the parlor each evening, and breakfast is brought to your room each morning.

Hosts: George & Carole Molnar
Rooms: 10 (PB) $80-95
Continental-plus Breakfast
Credit Cards: No
Notes: 2, 5, 8, 9, 10, 11, 12, 14

LODI

Wine & Roses Country Inn

2505 West Turner Road
Lodi, CA, 95242
(209) 334-6988

Converted to a charming romantic country inn with nine elegant suites filled with handmade comforters, antiques, and fresh flowers, our 1902 estate is secluded on 5 acres of towering trees and old-fashioned flower gardens. Afternoon tea and cookies, wine, delightful breakfast. Walk to lake with swimming, boating, and fishing. Five minutes to wine tasting, golf, tennis, health club. Delta waterways, Gold Country, and Sacramento are close by.

Hosts: Kris Cromwell, Del & Sherri Smith
Rooms: 9 (PB) From $85-115
Full Breakfast
Credit Cards: A, B, C
Notes: 2, 5, 9, 10, 11, 12, 14

Wine & Roses Country Inn

LOS ALAMOS

Union Hotel & Annex

362 Bell Street
P.O. Box 616
Los Alamos, CA, 93440
(805) 344-2744; (805) 964-0680

Staying in the Union Hotel is like stepping back in time, surrounded by nostalgia, history, and wonderful old-fashioned ambience of a bygone era. Swimming pool, Jacuzzi, pool room. Six theme suites available in addition to hotel rooms; each decorated as a fantasy world of its own.

Host: Dick Langdon
Rooms: 20 (9 PB; 11 SB) $110-200
Full Breakfast
Credit Cards: Yes
Notes: 2, 4, 5, 7, 9, 11, 12

LOS ALTOS

B&B International—San Francisco 5

1181-B Solano Avenue
Albany, CA, 94706
(415) 525-4569

This country-style home is located in a pleasant residential neighborhood within walking distance of downtown. There is nearby public transport. One guest room has a king bed; the second has a double. They share a bath, but it can be private. A third room with a single bed can also be made available. $60.

LOS ANGELES

B&B International—San Francisco 6

1181-B Solano Avenue
Albany, CA, 94706
(415) 525-4569

This home is in an exclusive neighborhood just south of Century City, close to Beverly Hills and UCLA. It is a three-bedroom, 2.5 bath, modern ranch home with a secluded rear garden. The guest room has twin beds that can be converted to a king, and a private bath. Guests may use the washer and dryer and keep snacks in the refrigerator. $65.

Eastlake Victorian Inn

1442 Kellam Avenue
Los Angeles, CA, 90026
(213) 250-1620

Beautifully restored and furnished historic monument located in L.A.'s first preservation district. Situated on a residential hilltop, we have views and the best central location near downtown, theaters, shopping, restaurants, Dodger Stadium, and Universal Studios. Close to Disneyland and the beaches. "Incomparably romantic," says the *L.A. Times.*

Hosts: Planaria Price & Murray Burns
Rooms: 9 (4 PB; 5 SB) $65-150
Full Breakfast
Credit Cards: A, B, C
Notes: 2, 4, 5, 8 (over 10), 9, 10, 11, 12, 14

LOS FELIZ

El Camino Real B&B

P.O. Box 7155
Northridge, CA, 91327-7155
(818) 363-6753

English nanny has an antique-filled home high in the hills. Two rooms available with a shared bath. Continental breakfast. Fifteen minutes to downtown, Music Center, Chinatown, Little Tokyo, and Pasadena. $45.

LOS OSOS

CoHost, America's B&B 17

P.O. Box 9302
Whittier, CA, 90608
(213) 699-8427

Lovely contemporary home with an exciting view of the ocean and bay. This home is two miles from the beaches and Montana De Oro State Park. Near golf courses, boating, and whale watching. This home is only thirty-five minutes from the Hearst Castle. Three bedrooms with king, queen, or twin beds and private and shared baths. Children welcome. $57.

Gerarda's B&B

1056 Bay Oaks Drive
Los Osos, CA, 93402
(805) 528-3973

The ideal place to stop between San Francisco and Los Angeles. On the coast with ocean and mountain views. Close to Hearst Castle, Morro Bay, and San Luis Obispo; golf, tennis, hiking, and shopping. Dutch hospitality; your host speaks several languages.

Host: Gerarda Ondang
Rooms: 3 (1 PB; 2 SB) $42
Full Breakfast
Credit Cards: No
Notes: 2, 4, 5, 6, 8, 9, 10, 11, 12

LOWER LAKE

The Swiss Chalet

5128 Swedberg Road
Lower Lake, CA, 95457
(707) 994-7313

Wood carvings, heavy beam ceilings, stained-glass windows in a chalet built entirely of redwood. Tole painting by stone fireplace. Private beach.

Hosts: Robert & Ingrid Hansen
Rooms: 2 (1 PB; 1 SB) $65
Full Breakfast
Credit Cards: No
Notes: 2, 5, 7, 8 (infants), 9, 10, 11, 12

LOYALTON

Clover Valley Mill House

Box 928
Loyalton, CA, 96118
(916) 993-4819

Heirlooms, Irish lace, comfortable antiques, and a fireplace in one of Sierra County's fine old residences. Located in a pioneer sawmill town in the heart of cowboy country. Explore a hundred lakes and a thousand miles of streams, or just curl up with a favorite book or an old-time movie. Located 42 miles northwest of Reno, Nevada. Corral for horses; volleyball; horseshoes.

Host: Leslie Hernandez
Rooms: 4 (1 PB; 3 SB) $60-75
Full Breakfast
Credit Cards: A, B
Notes: 2, 5, 9, 10, 11, 14

MALIBU

Casa Larronde

Box 86
Malibu, CA, 90265
(213) 456-9333

This is a private home on a private beach one mile from famous Surfers' Beach and the sport-fishing pier. The ocean suite has kitchenette, fireplace, ceiling fan, TV, phone, and 40 feet of glass overlooking its private deck. The locals call this beach Millionaires' Row.

Host: Charlou Larronde
One ocean suite w/bath: $100
Full Breakfast
Credit Cards: No
Notes: 2, 7, 8, 9, 10, 11

El Camino Real B&B

P.O. Box 7155
Northridge, CA, 91327-7155
(818) 363-6753

High on a hill, with a breathtaking panoramic view of the Pacific Ocean and artwork throughout. Minutes to beach; near the Getty Museum. Three rooms are available: upstairs suite with king bed and private bath; two rooms on the first floor with a shared bath. Children over five welcome. Continental breakfast. $40-50.

Malibu Guest House

B&B of Los Angeles
32074 Waterside Lane
Westlake Village, CA, 91361
(818) 889-8870

Enter down the path from the driveway to this cute cottage built behind the garage with views out through the canyon to the ocean. Living room with hideabed couch, TV, large balcony, full bath, bedroom with queen bed. Children welcome. Car essential. Two-night minimum on weekends. $65.

MAMMOTH LAKES

Snow Goose B&B Inn

Box 946
Mammoth Lakes, CA, 93546
(619) 934-2660

Home away from home in the European tradition. Enjoy a full breakfast each morning. Sierra Mountains winter ski resort and summer getaway. Ice skating, snowmobiling, hot-air ballooning, fishing, hiking, wind surfing. Walk to restaurants, shops, and entertainment.

Hosts: Wes & Laurie Johnson
Rooms: 15 (PB) $58-98
Suites: 3 (PB) $88-148
Full Breakfast
Minimum stay weekends: 1-2; holidays: 3
Credit Cards: A, B, C, D, E
Notes: 2, 5, 7, 8, 9, 10, 11, 12, 13, 14

MARIPOSA

Oak Meadows, too

5263 Highway 140N, Box 619
Mariposa, CA, 95338
(209) 742-6161

Located in the historic gold-rush town of Mariposa, this B&B has turn-of-the-century charm. New England architecture: rooms decorated with handmade quilts, wallpaper, and brass headboards. Close to Yosemite. Home of the California State Mining & Mineral Museum.

Hosts: Bill & Delcie Loucks
Rooms: 6 (PB) $49-59
Continental-plus Breakfast
Credit Cards: A, B
Notes: 2, 5, 14

The Pelennor

3871 Highway 49 South
Mariposa, CA, 95338
(209) 966-2832

Country atmosphere about 45 minutes from Yosemite National Park. After a day of sight-seeing, you may want to take a few laps in our lap pool, unwind in the spa, enjoy the available games, and listen to an occasional tune played on the bagpipes.

Hosts: Dick & Gwen Foster
Singles: $40; Doubles: $45
Type of Beds: 2 Twin; 1 Double; 2 Queen
Full Breakfast
Credit Cards: No
Notes: 2, 5, 6, 8, 9, 10, 11

McCLOUD

McCloud Guest House

606 West Colombero Drive
McCloud, CA, 96057
(916) 964-3160

Built in 1907, this beautiful old country home is nestled among stately oaks and lofty pines on the lower slopes of majestic Mt. Shasta. On the first floor is one of Siskiyou County's finer dining establishments. The second floor has a large parlor surrounded by our five guest rooms, each individually decorated.

Hosts: Bill & Patti Leigh, Dennis & Pat Abreu
Rooms: 5 (PB) $75-90
Continental Breakfast
Minimum stay holidays: 2
Credit Cards: A, B
Closed Thanksgiving & Christmas
Notes: 2, 4, 5, 11, 12, 13

MENDOCINO

Agate Cove Inn

11201 Lansing Street, Box 1150
Mendocino, CA, 95460
(707) 937-0551

Agate Cove Inn is located on an ocean bluff with the most dramatic view of the ocean and rugged coastline. There are individual cottages, each with an ocean view, a Franklin fireplace, and a private bath. Included is a full country breakfast served in the main 1860s farmhouse. Hiking, golf, and tennis are close by.

Hosts: Sallie McConnell & Jake Zahavi
Rooms: 10 (PB) $69-155
Full Breakfast
Credit Cards: A, B, C, D
Notes: 2, 5, 9, 10, 12, 14

Blue Heron Inn

390 Kasten Street
P.O. Box 1142
Mendocino, CA, 95460
(707) 937-4323

Located in the village of Mendocino, we offer European country charm and simple elegance. All rooms have beautiful ocean views. Our rates are modest. Mendocino has beautiful areas to hike, canoe, fish, swim, bike, and picnic.

Host: Linda Friedman
Rooms: 3 (1 PB; 2 SB) $58-90
Continental Breakfast
Credit Cards: No
Notes: 2, 3, 4, 5, 8, 9, 10, 11

Brewery Gulch Inn

9350 Coast Highway One
Mendocino, CA, 95460
(707) 937-4752

An authentic country B&B farm located on the rugged coast just one mile from the village of Mendocino. The lovely old white farmhouse is furnished in the Victorian style with queen beds, homemade quilts, and down pillows. Each guest room window provides views of the gardens and meadows beyond.

Hosts: Leo & Gen Pallanck
Rooms: 5 (3 PB; 2 SB) $75-115
Full Breakfast
Credit Cards: A, B
Notes: 2, 5, 10, 11, 12

Cypress House

Box 303
Mendocino, CA, 95460
(707) 937-1456

A private romantic garden cottage just for two, overlooking Mendocino Bay and village. Adjacent to an 80-acre oceanfront state park. All the special touches for a special getaway: fireplace, fresh flowers, down comforter, stereo, private hot tub, and much more. Country quiet, yet only five minutes to Mendocino Village.

Hosts: Roger & Pamela Weerts
Cabin: 1 (PB) $135
Continental Breakfast
Credit Cards: No
Notes: 2, 5, 9, 10, 11, 12

The Headlands Inn

The Headlands Inn

Box 132
Mendocino, CA, 95460
(707) 937-4431

The Headlands Inn is an 1868 Victorian, centrally located within Mendocino Village on California's scenic north coast, minutes from redwoods and wineries. Gourmet breakfasts are served to your room. All rooms have wood-burning fireplaces; spectacular ocean views overlooking an English-style garden. Two parlors, many unusual antiques.

Hosts: Pat & Rod Stofle
Rooms: 5 (PB) $95-138
Full Breakfast
Minimum stay weekends: 2; holidays: 3-4
Credit Cards: No
Notes: 2, 5, 8 (16 and over), 9, 10, 11, 12

Joshua Grindle Inn

44800 Little Lake Road
P.O. Box 647
Mendocino, CA, 95460
(707) 937-4143

Located on 2 acres in the historic village of Mendocino overlooking the ocean, the Joshua Grindle Inn is a short walk to the beach, Art Center, shops, and fine restaurants. Stay in the lovely two-story Victorian farmhouse, a New England-style cottage, or a three-story water tower. Six rooms have fireplaces; all have private baths, antiques, and comfortable reading areas. Enjoy a full breakfast served around a ten-foot refrectory table.

Hosts: Jim & Arlene Moorehead
Rooms: 10 (PB) $75-110
Full Breakfast
Credit Cards: A, B, C, D
Notes: 2, 5, 9, 10, 12, 14

Judge Tou Velle House B&B

455 North Oregon
Mendocino, CA, 95430
(503) 899-8938

Elegant historic home within walking distance to Britt, near white-water rafting, ballooning. Business travelers welcome. Five miles to Medord; near Ashland Shakespeare.

Hosts: John & Patricia Valletta
Rooms: 5 (PB)
Full Breakfast
Credit Cards: A, B
Notes: 2, 9, 10, 11, 12, 13, 14

MacCallum House Inn

45020 Albion Street
P.O. Box 206
Mendocino, CA, 95437
(707) 937-0289

Unique accommodations that include the Victorian home of Daisy MacCallum, water tower, greenhouse, barn, and English gardens. In the center of the village; walk to shops, restaurants, and beach.

Hosts: Melanie & Joe Reding
Rooms: 20 (7 PB; 13 SB) $45-135
Continental Breakfast
Minimum stay May-Dec. weekends: 2; holidays: 2-3
Credit Cards: A, B
Notes: 2, 4, 5, 8, 9, 10, 11, 12, 14

Mendocino Village Inn

Mendocino Farmhouse

Box 247
Mendocino, CA, 95460
(707) 937-0241

Mendocino Farmhouse is a small B&B with all the comforts of home. We are surrounded by redwood forest, beautiful gardens, a pond, and meadow. Choose among our comfortable rooms decorated with country antiques for a quiet night's rest and enjoy a sumptuous farmhouse breakfast in the morning.

Hosts: Margie & Bud Kamb
Rooms: 5 (PB) $75-95
Full Breakfast
Credit Cards: No
Notes: 2, 5, 6 (call), 8 (call), 10, 11, 12

Mendocino Village Inn

Main Street, Box 626
Mendocino, CA, 95460
(707) 937-0246

A well-done bed and breakfast inn characterized by hummingbirds, Picassos, French roast coffee, fuchsias, fireplaces, Vivaldi. This 1882 Victorian is filled with everything necessary for charm and gracious living, including four-poster beds, Bokharas, fresh blackberries, and complimentary wine.

Hosts: Sue & Tom Allen
Rooms: 12 (10 PB; 2 SB) $59-130
Full Breakfast
Minimum stay weekends: 2; holidays: 3
Credit Cards: A, B
Notes: 2, 5, 8 (over 10), 9, 10, 11, 12

Rachel's Inn

P.O. Box 134
Mendocino, CA, 95460
(707) 937-0088

Comfort with style in an elegantly restored 1860s house and new companion "barn." Ocean, garden, and meadow views. Wheel chair access. Adjoins state park with beaches, deer meadows, and forests. Whale and seal watching from ocean cliffs, hiking, nearby golf. Two miles from Mendocino village. Lavish breakfast.

Host: Rachel Binah
Rooms: 8 (PB) $96-165 + tax
Full Breakfast
Credit Cards: No
Notes: 2, 5, 7, 8, 9, 10, 12, 14

Whitegate Inn

Box 150
Mendocino, CA 95460
(707) 937-4892

Everything you look for in a B&B experience: antiques, fireplaces, ocean views, and all private baths. Elegant 1880 Victorian, located in the center of the historic preservation village of Mendocino. Shops, galleries, and nationally acclaimed restaurants are just steps away. A perfect setting for romantic trysts, weddings, or rest and relaxation.

Hosts: Patricia & John Valletta
Rooms: 5 (PB) $65-110
Full Breakfast
Credit Cards: No
Notes: 2, 5, 9, 10, 11, 12

MILL VALLEY

Mountain Home Inn

810 Panoramic Highway
Mill Valley, CA, 94941
(415) 381-9000

A romantic country inn high atop Mt. Tamalpais, offering spectacular views of the Marin Hills and San Francisco Bay. Ten cozy guest rooms await you. Some offer Jacuzzi baths, private decks, and fireplaces. Just outside our front door is Mt. Tamalpais State Park, offering miles of hiking trails. Muir Woods National Monument, Muir Beach, and Stinson Beach are just a short drive away. Twenty-five minutes from downtown San Francisco. Restaurant on premises.

Rooms: 10 (PB) $112-178
Full Breakfast weekends; continental weekdays
Credit Cards: A, B
Notes: 2, 3, 4, 5, 7, 8, 9, 10, 11, 12, 14

MONTARA

The Goose & Turrets

835 George Street
Box 937
Montara, CA, 94037
(415) 728-5451

A 1908 Italian villa in a quiet garden offers creature comforts and splendid breakfasts. Thirty minutes to San Francisco; half a mile to the beach. Near restaurants, horseback riding, tide pools, antiques, golf. We pick up at local harbor and airport. *Nous parlons Francais.*

Hosts: Raymond & Emily Hoche-Mong
Rooms: 5 (2 PB; 3 S2B) $70-90
Full Breakfast
Credit Cards: A, B, C, D
Notes: 2, 8, 9, 10, 11, 12, 14

Montara B & B

1125 Tamarind Street
Montara, CA, 94037
(415) 728-3946

Just twenty miles south of San Francisco on the scenic California coast. Semi-rural area with nearby hiking, beaches, and horseback riding. Private entrance, private bath, ocean view, fireplace, TV, stereo, telephone, sun deck. Business travelers welcome.

Hosts: Bill & Peggy Bechtell
Rooms: 1 (PB) $60-70
Full Breakfast
Minimum stay weekends & holidays: 2
Credit Cards: A, B
Notes: 2, 4, 5, 9, 10, 11, 12, 14

MONTEREY

The Jabberwock

598 Laine Street
Monterey, CA, 93940
(408) 372-4777

Alice's Wonderland, just four blocks above Cannery Row and the Monterey Bay Aquarium. The Jabberwock has a half acre of lush gardens and waterfalls overlooking Monterey Bay. Each room has down pillows and comforters. Hors d'oeuvres at 5:00 P.M. and cookies and milk at bedtime.

Hosts: Jim & Barbara Allen
Rooms: 7 (3 PB; 4 S2B) $90-165
Full Breakfast
Credit Cards: No
Notes: 2, 5, 9, 10, 11, 12, 14

The Jabberwock

Mt. Shasta, CA, 96067
(916) 926-5170

A delightful secluded hideaway surrounded by forest with an unparalleled view of majestic Mt. Shasta. A truly unique setting complete with hospitality, serenity, and charm. Located near ski areas, lakes, hiking trails, excellent restaurants, and a friendly, warm community. Our home is your home.

Hosts: Barbara & Phil Ward
Rooms: 2 (SB) $45
Cottage: Sleeps 6 (PB) $85
Full Breakfast
Credit Cards: No
Notes: 2, 8, 9, 10, 11, 12, 13

MT. SHASTA

Mt. Shasta Ranch

1008 W.A. Barr Road
Mt. Shasta, CA, 96067
(916) 926-3870

This Northern California historic two-story ranch house offers affordable elegance. There are four spacious guest rooms in the main house, each with private bath. Carriage house accommodations include five rooms. Two-bedroom vacation cottage available year-round. Guests are invited to enjoy our rec room with Ping-Pong, pool tables, and piano. Relax in our hot-spring spa. Close to lake, town, and ski slopes. Full country-style breakfasts each morning.

Hosts: Bill & Mary Larsen
Rooms: 9 (4 PB; 5 SB) $55-75
Full Breakfast
Credit Cards: A, B, C
Notes: 2, 5, 7, 8, 9, 10, 11, 12, 13, 14

Ward's Big Foot Ranch

1530 Hill Road
P.O. Box 585

MUIR BEACH

Muir Beach B&B

B&B of Los Angeles
32074 Waterside Lane
Westlake Village, CA, 91361
(818) 889-8870

Located seventeen miles north of San Francisco, overlooking the ocean, this contemporary country home offers large windows, open beams, and a balcony overlooking the water. The guest quarters overlook San Francisco and the Pacific. Fireplace, private entrance, and private bath. Sitting room with trundle beds for two, and bedroom with single bed. Muir Woods five minutes away. Dog in residence. Full breakfast. $95.

MURPHYS

Dunbar House, 1880

271 Jones Street
Box 1375
Murphys, CA, 95247
(209) 728-2897

You can explore the Gold Country during the day and enjoy a glass of lemonade or local wine on the wide porches in the afternoon. Inviting fireplaces and down com-

NOTES: Credit cards accepted: A Master Card; B Visa; C American Express; D Discover Card; E Diners Club; F Other: 2 Personal checks accepted: 3 Lunch available: 4 Dinner available: 5 Open all year

forters in your antique-filled room. Breakfast may be served in your room, the dining room, or in the century-old gardens.

Hosts: Bob & Barbara Costa
Rooms: 4 (PB) $95-135
Full Breakfast
Minimum stay weekends: 2
Credit Cards: A, B
Notes: 2, 5, 8 (over 10), 9, 10, 11, 12, 13, 14

Dunbar House, 1880

NAPA

Arbor Guest House

1436 G Street
Napa, CA, 94559
(707) 252-8144

This 1906 home and carriage house are furnished with period antiques and located in a quiet garden setting. The inn is a lovely retreat where you are pampered by thoughtful innkeepers. Fresh baked breads, seasonal fruits, juice, egg dishes, and beverages are served in the dining room or at patio tables.

Hosts: Bruce & Rosemary Logan
Rooms: 5 (PB) $85-125
Full Breakfast
Credit Cards: A, B, C
Notes: 2, 5, 9, 10, 12, 14

Beazley House

1910 First Street
Napa, CA, 94559
(707) 257-1649

You'll sense the hospitality as you stroll the walk past verdant lawns and bright flowers. The mansion is a chocolate brown masterpiece. You'll feel instantly welcome as you're greeted by a smiling innkeeper. There's a beautiful garden. And all rooms have a private bath; some a private spa and fireplace. A delicious full breakfast is included.

Hosts: Carol & Jim Beazley
Rooms: 10 (PB) $90-160
Full Breakfast
Credit Cards: A, B, D
Notes: 2, 5, 9, 10, 11, 12, 14

Churchill Manor B&B Inn

485 Brown Street
Napa, CA, 94559
(707) 253-7733

An 1889 grand mansion on a beautifully landscaped acre. Carved wood ceilings and columns, leaded-glass windows, and seven fireplaces. Furnished with antiques, Oriental rugs, and a grand piano. Buffet breakfast includes homemade breads, muffins, croissants, quiches, cheeses, and fresh fruits. Evening Napa varietal wine. Play croquet or ride our complimentary tandem bicycles.

Host: Joanna Guidotti
Rooms: 8 (PB) $70-145
Continental-plus Breakfast
Credit Cards: A, B, C
Notes: 2, 5, 9, 10, 11, 12, 14

Coombs Residence Inn on the Park

720 Seminary Street
Napa, CA, 94559
(707) 257-0789

An 1852 restored Victorian, elegantly furnished with European and American antiques. Down comforters, terry robes provided. Afternoon refreshments, wine, and sherry available. Swimming pool, whirlpool, bicycles available. No smoking.

Hosts: Pearl & Dave Campbell
Rooms: 4 (1 PB; 3 SB) $88.40-110.50
Continental Breakfast
Credit Cards: A, B
Notes: 2, 5, 9, 10, 11, 12, 14

Country Garden Inn

1815 Silverado Trail
Napa, CA, 94558
(707) 255-1197

The Country Garden is an 1860s carriage house decorated in English pine antiques and family heirlooms. Riverside setting on 1.5 acres of gardens. Afternoon tea, happy hour, wine in rooms, and dessert.

Hosts: George & Lisa Smith
Rooms: 10 (PB) $105-155
Full Breakfast
Credit Cards: A, B, C
Notes: 2, 5, 8 (over 16), 9, 10, 12, 14

The Crossroads Inn

6380 Silverado Trail
Napa Valley, CA, 94558
(707) 944-0646

Luxury, privacy, and sweeping Napa Valley views are yours at the Crossroads Inn, a singular retreat for appreciating the beauty and life-style of the wine country. Its commanding view of vineyards and mountains has no equal. Three spacious guest suites provide visitors with every amenity, including private spas.

Hosts: The Scott-Maxwell Family
Rooms: 3 (PB) $175-200
Continental Breakfast
Credit Cards: A, B
Notes: 2, 5, 7 (outside), 8 (over 16), 9, 10, 11, 12, 14

Goodman House

1225 Division Street
Napa, CA, 94559
(707) 257-1166

Located in California wine country, the Goodman House reflects an elegant and prestigious past as one of Napa's stately Victorian homes. Rooms are tastefully decorated with antiques, fireplaces, and spa tub. Morning brings a sumptuous country breakfast. Arrangements gladly made for ballooning, mud baths, etc. Midweek rates available.

Hosts: Bill Ormond & Susan Marie
Rooms: 4 (PB) $95-130
Full Breakfast
Credit Cards: A, B, F
Notes: 2, 5, 8, 9, 10, 11, 12, 14

La Belle Epoque

1386 Calistoga Avenue
Napa, CA, 94558
(707) 257-2161

Historic Queen Anne Victorian, bejeweled in stained glass. Six guest rooms furnished in period antiques, each with private bath. Charming wine-tasting room/cellar. Within walking distance of the Wine Train Depot, restaurants, shops, and riverfront. Wineries nearby, as well as hot-air ballooning, mud baths, tennis, swimming, and golf.

Hosts: Merlin & Claudia
Rooms: 6 (PB) $90-135
Full Breakfast
Credit Cards: A, B, C
Notes: 2, 5, 9, 10, 11, 12, 14

La Residence Country Inn

4066 St. Helena Highway
Napa, CA, 94558
(707) 253-0337

Accommodations, most with fireplaces, are in two structures: a Gothic revival home, decorated in traditional American antiques, and the "French barn," decorated with European pine antiques. Two acres of grounds with hot tub and a heated swimming pool surrounded by a gazebo and trellis. Complimentary wine is served each evening.

Hosts: David Jackson & Craig Claussen
Rooms: 20 (18 PB; 2 SB) $65-150
Full Breakfast
Credit Cards: A, B
Notes: 5, 8, 9, 10, 11, 12, 14

Napa Inn

Napa Inn

1137 Warren Street
Napa, CA, 94559
(707) 257-1444

The Napa Inn is a beautiful Queen Anne Victorian located on a quiet tree-lined street in the historic section of the town of Napa. The inn is furnished in turn-of-the-century antiques in the five guest rooms, large parlor, and formal dining room. The inn is conveniently located to the Napa, Sonoma, and Los Carneros wine regions. Also many other activities: hot-air ballooning, gliders, biking, hiking, golf, tennis, many fine restaurants, and the Napa Valley Wine Train.

Hosts: Doug & Carol Morales
Rooms: 5 (PB) $90-135
Full Breakfast
Credit Cards: A, B, D
Closed Christmas
Notes: 2, 10, 12, 14

The Old World Inn

1301 Jefferson Street
Napa, CA, 94559
(707) 257-0112

Elegant Victorian built in 1906. Eight rooms with private bath, one with private Jacuzzi, feature decor inspired by the colors of Swedish artist Carl Larsson. Enjoy afternoon tea and cookies, complimentary wine, international cheese board, dessert buffet, a gourmet breakfast, and our custom-built Jacuzzi.

Host: Diane Dumaine
Rooms: 8 (PB) $92-132
Continental-plus Breakfast
Credit Cards: A, B, C
Notes: 2, 5, 9, 10, 12, 14

Sybron House

7400 St. Helena Hwy.
Napa, CA, 94558
(707) 944-2785

Victorian inn situated on a hill in the middle of the Napa Valley, with magnificent views of surrounding wineries and vineyards. Excellent restaurants nearby, as well as ballooning, biking, hiking, golf, and mud baths.

Hosts: Sybil & Ron Maddox
Rooms: 4 (2 PB; 2 SB) $90-150
Continental Breakfast
Credit Cards: A, B, C
Notes: 2, 5, 9, 10, 12, 14

NEVADA CITY

Downey House B&B

517 West Broad Street
Nevada City, CA, 95959
(916) 265-2815

Eastlake Victorian, c. 1870, restored to its original elegance with lovely garden and water falling into a lily pond by umbrella tables where guests may eat breakfast. Located one block from fine shops and restaurants, live theater, museums, art galleries, and horse-drawn carriages. Near historic gold mines, lakes, streams, tennis, golf, skiing, horseback riding, etc.

Host: Miriam Wright
Rooms: 6 (PB) $70-90
Full Breakfast
Credit Cards: A, B
Notes: 2, 5, 8, 9, 10, 11, 12, 14

Grandmere's

449 Broad Street
Nevada City, CA, 95959
(916) 265-4660

Beautiful garden, suitable for weddings or receptions. All rooms are very well decorated, and the three suites have sofa sleepers and tubs in addition to showers.

Host: Louise Jones
Rooms: 7 (PB) $95-145
Full Breakfast
Credit Cards: A, B
Notes: 2, 5, 8, 9, 10, 11, 12

Piety Hill Inn

523 Sacramento Street
Nevada City, CA, 95959
(916) 265-2245

The inn consists of eight cottages surrounding a lush garden, which includes a gazebo-crowned hot tub. Featured are pre-Civil War to early twentieth-century furnishings, king beds, refrigerators, wet bars, TV, and breakfast in bed. Nearby are quaint shops, theater, music, excellent restaurants, hiking, swimming, and winter sports.

Hosts: Trieve & Barbara Tanner
Rooms: 8 (PB) $65-80
Full Breakfast
Credit Cards: A, B
Notes: 2, 5, 8, 9, 10, 11, 12, 13, 14

The Red Castle Inn

109 Prospect Street
Nevada City, CA, 95959
(916) 265-5135

High on a forested hillside, breezes linger on wide verandas, strains of Mozart echo through lofty hallways, chandeliers sparkle, the aura of another time prevails. In Gold Country, the four-story Gothic Revival inn "would top my list of places to stay. Nothing else quite compares with it"—*Gourmet.*

Hosts: Mary Louise & Conley Weaver
Rooms: 8 (6 PB; 2 SB) $75.60-118.80
Full Breakfast
Credit Cards: A, B
Notes: 2, 5, 7 (outside), 8 (over 10), 9, 10, 11, 12, 13 (XC), 14

The Red Castle Inn

NEWPORT BEACH

CoHost, America's B&B 11

P.O. Box 9302
Whittier, CA, 90608
(213) 699-8427

Charming contemporary home just a short walk from the beach. Two bedrooms, each with private bath. Hosts are caterers; the full breakfast is always a treat. Children are welcome. Complimentary hors d'oeuvres and beverages are served with a spectacular ocean view. $60.

The Dahl House

B&B of Los Angeles
32074 Waterside Lane
Westlake Village, CA, 91361
(818) 889-8870

Stained glass and a lot of wood and brick add to the charm of this unusual home minutes from the beach. The upstairs guest room, in a loft overlooking the living room, has a queen bed. There is a private bath, and stairs lead to a roof deck. A second guest room on the first floor has a double bed and private bath. Children over six are welcome. $50.

El Camino Real B&B

P.O. Box 7155
Northridge, CA, 91327-7155
(818) 363-6753

Schoolteacher's townhouse with a queen room and shared bath; swimming pool. Five minutes to Newport Harbor and boating. Fabulous Fashion Isle shopping. Children and babies are welcome. Continental breakfast. $45.

Portofino Beach Hotel

2306 West Oceanfront
Newport Beach, CA, 92663
(714) 673-7030

Luxurious oceanfront hotel with European decor and antiques. Each room individually decorated with marble baths, color TV, direct-dial phone. Some with double jetted spas, fireplaces, private sun decks. Wine and champagne bar in lounge. European hospitality by the sea.

Host: Christine Luetto
Rooms: 18 (PB) $100-235
Continental Breakfast
Credit Cards: A, B, C, E, F
Notes: 5, 7, 9, 10, 11, 12, 14

NIPTON

Hotel Nipton

72 Nipton Road
Nipton, CA, 92364
(619) 856-2335

Hotel Nipton, originally built in 1904, was completely restored in 1986. Located in the east Mojave National Scenic Area 65 miles south of Las Vegas. The hotel offers a panoramic view of the New York Mountains, outside Jacuzzi for star gazing, and is thirty minutes from Lake Mojave.

Hosts: Jerry & Roxanne Freeman
Rooms: 4 (SB) $48.15
Continental Breakfast
Credit Cards: A, B
Notes: 5, 7, 8, 9

NORTHRIDGE

El Camino Real B&B

P.O. Box 7155
Northridge, CA, 91327-7155
(818) 363-6753

Fabulous guest cottage behind a country home decorated in Victorian antiques. King bed, private bath, refrigerator, microwave, private eating area. Swimming pool and hot tub. Continental breakfast. $70.

OAKHURST

B&B International—San Francisco 8

1181-B Solano Avenue
Albany, CA, 94706
(415) 525-4569

6 Pets welcome: 7 Smoking allowed: 8 Children welcome: 9 Social drinking allowed: 10 Tennis available: 11 Swimming available: 12 Golf available: 13 Skiing available: 14 May be booked through travel agents

This contemporary rock and wood house overlooks a stream. It has a swimming pool, large garden, and a recreation room with pool table. Located close to Bass Lake and twenty minutes from the south gate to Yosemite, with a nearby golf course. One room has twin beds and a private bath. The second has a double bed with private bath. An additional hideabed in a sitting room could be used for children or adults in the same party. $55.

OAKLAND

B&B International—San Francisco 9

1181-B Solano Avenue
Albany, CA, 94706
(415) 525-4569

This Spanish classical home is situated on a hill overlooking Lake Merritt, in a neighborhood of estate homes. It has been featured in *Sunset* magazine and is a historic preservation residence. There are three guest rooms, two with queen beds and one with a single bed. Portable TVs are available. $68.

OCCIDENTAL

Heart's Desire Inn

3657 Church Street
Occidental, CA, 95465
(707) 874-1311

In the redwoods near the spectacular Sonoma coast and wine country, Heart's Desire Inn is a completely renovated 1867 Victorian with European ambience. With antique furnishings and goose-down comforters, each room features fresh flowers and a private bath. A courtyard garden, the parlor's fireplace, and a sumptuous breakfast are all for your enjoyment.

Hosts: Justina & Howard Selinger
Rooms: 8 (PB) $78-98; Suite $138
Expanded Continental Breakfast
Minimum Stay weekends & holidays: 2
Credit Cards: A, B, C, D
Notes: 2, 3, 4, 5, 9, 10, 11, 12, 14

OJAI

El Camino Real B&B

P.O. Box 7155
Northridge, CA, 91327-7155
(818) 363-6753

Nestled in the art colony of the Ojai Valley with a lovely mountain view, this B&B's hostess makes homemade muffins served with jam and jelly made from the fruit grown in her yard. Two rooms share a bath. Continental breakfast. $70.

The Theodore Woolsey House

1484 East Ojai Avenue
Ojai, CA, 93023
(805) 646-9779

A country inn built in 1887, with a charming living room with beamed ceiling and stone fireplace. Continental buffet breakfast in the spacious dining room or peaceful garden room. Sun with sun tea or fresh-squeezed lemonade by our oversized kidney-shaped pool overlooking the Topa Topa Mountains. An intimate, romantic atmosphere beckons you.

Host: Ana Cross
Rooms: 7 (4 PB; 3 SB) $50-125
Continental Breakfast
Credit Cards: No
Notes: 2, 5, 8, 9, 10, 11, 12, 14

OLEMA

Point Reyes Seashore Lodge

10,021 Coastal Highway One
Olema, CA, 94950
(415) 663-9000

An elegantly re-created turn-of-the-century lodge with eighteen rooms and three suites, many with whirlpool tubs and fireplaces. All with views of the adjacent Point Reyes Seashore National Park and Olema Creek. Only one hour's drive to San Francisco along Scenic Highway One. Many outdoor activities and fine local restaurants nearby.

Hosts: Judi & John Burkes
Rooms: 21 (PB) $95-175
Continental Breakfast
Credit Cards: A, B, C
Notes: 2, 5, 9, 10, 11, 12, 14

ORANGE

Country Comfort B&B

5104 East Valencia Drive
Orange, CA, 92669
(714) 532-2802

Located in a quiet residential area, this house has been furnished with your comfort and pleasure in mind. It is handicapped accessible with adaptive equipment available. Amenities include a swimming pool, cable TV and VCR, atrium, fireplace, piano, and the use of bicycles, one built for two. Breakfast often features delicious Scotch eggs, stuffed French toast, and hash, as well as fruits and assorted beverages. Vegetarian selections also available. Disneyland and Knotts Berry Farm are less than seven miles.

Hosts: Geri Lopker & Joanne Angell
Rooms: 4 (2 PB; 2 SB) $50-60
Full Breakfast
Credit Cards: No
Notes: 2, 5, 7 (outside), 8, 9, 10, 11, 12, 14

ORLAND

The Inn at Shallow Creek Farm

Route 3, Box 3176
Orland, CA, 95963
(916) 865-4093

A gracious two-story farmhouse offering spacious rooms furnished with antiques — a blend of nostalgia and comfortable country living. Three miles off Interstate 5. The inn is known for its orchard and fresh garden produce. Breakfast features old-fashioned baked goods and local fruits and juices.

Hosts: Kurt & Mary Glaeseman
Rooms: 4 (2 PB; 2 SB) $45-$75
Full Breakfast
Credit Cards: No
Notes: 2, 4, 5, 9, 11, 12, 14

Gosby House Inn

PACIFIC GROVE

Centrella B&B Inn

612 Central Avenue
Pacific Grove, CA, 93950
(408) 372-3372

Century-old Victorian, completely restored and furnished with antiques, Laura Ashley decor. Main house has eighteen rooms and three suites; all except two have private baths. Four adjacent cottages with five suites. Near ocean and convenient to all attractions. Continental-plus breakfast and evening wine and cheese are served.

Rooms: 26 (24 PB; 2 SB) $80-165
Continental-plus Breakfast
Credit Cards: A, B
Notes: 2, 5, 9, 10, 11, 12, 14

Gosby House Inn

643 Lighthouse Avenue
Pacific Grove, CA, 93950
(408) 375-1287

The Gosby House Inn sits in the heart of the quaint town of Pacific Grove. Its magnificent Queen Anne Victorian architecture will enchant you, as will its individually decorated sleeping rooms, antique doll collection, and gracious staff. A bountiful breakfast and afternoon wine and hors d'oeuvres are served. Fluffy robes, complimentary beverages, and a heaping cookie jar.

Host: Shelley Post Claudel
Rooms: 22 (20 PB; 2 SB) $85-130
Full Breakfast
Credit Cards: A, B, C
Notes: 2, 5, 8, 9, 10, 11, 12, 14

The Old St. Angela Inn

321 Central Avenue
Pacific Grove, CA, 93950
(408) 372-3246; (800) 873-6523

A 1910 Cape Cod style Victorian home overlooking Monterey Bay. Full breakfast is served daily, wine and cheese are served in front of the fireplace, and home-baked cookies and port are served after dinner. Truly an experience in comfort. Monterey Bay Aquarium, Cannery Row, Fisherman's Wharf, and restaurants are within walking distance.

Hosts: Marshall Simone & Curtis Brown IV
Rooms: 9 (6 PB; 3 SB) $75-135 + tax
Full Breakfast
Credit Cards: A, B
Notes: 5, 9, 10, 11, 12, 14

Roserox Country Inn By-The-Sea

557 Ocean View Boulevard
Pacific Grove, CA, 93950
(408) 373-7673

Historic country mansion set on the edge of the Pacific shoreline. Built at the turn of the century, the inn is an intimate four-story inn with original patterned oak floors, high ceilings, high brass beds, imported soaps and French water, designer linens, ocean sounds, and a special gift for each guest. A full country breakfast and wine and cheer hour. The Shoreline Trail to Cannery Row, Monterey Bay Aquarium, world-known shops and restaurants, as well as the swimming beach, bicycling, and fishing, are within thirty feet of the inn.

Host: Dawn Vyette Browncroft
Rooms: 8 (S4B) $85-135
Full Breakfast
Credit Cards: No
Notes: 2, 5, 9, 10, 11, 12, 14

Seven Gables Inn

555 Ocean View Blvd.
Pacific Grove, CA, 93950
(408) 372-4341

Seven Gables Inn is a century-old Victorian mansion situated on a rocky promontory overlooking scenic Monterey Bay. Furnished throughout with elegant, fine Victorian antiques. All rooms have panoramic ocean views and private baths. A very generous light breakfast and four o'clock high tea are included. Smoking in the garden only. Seven Gables provides easy access to the Monterey Aquarium, Cannery Row, Seventeen-Mile Drive, Carmel, and numerous other scenic sites in the Monterey area.

Hosts: The Flatley Family
Rooms: 14 (PB) $95-175
Continental-plus Breakfast

Credit Cards: A, B
Notes: 2, 5, 8, 9, 10, 11, 12, 14

PACIFIC PALISADES

Garden House

B&B of Los Angeles
32074 Waterside Lane
Westlake Village, CA, 91361
(818) 889-8870

Traditional home in a most exclusive neighborhood, with a delightful yard filled with flowers. Two guest rooms with shared bath. Separate entrance to rear yard. Recreation room with fireplace and refrigerator; TV. Beach one-half mile downhill. Children are welcome. $55.

PALM SPRINGS

B&B International—San Francisco 10

1181-B Solano Avenue
Albany, CA, 94706
(415) 525-4569

This contemporary single-story condo opens onto patios and a sweeping lawn area that leads to the pool and tennis courts. Less than a mile to the main street of Palm Springs. The guest room has twin beds and a private bath. There is an adjacent room with TV for guests to use. When the hostess goes to work early, guests serve themselves breakfast. $54.

Casa Cody B&B Country Inn

175 South Cahuilla
Palm Springs, CA, 92262
(619) 320-9346

Romantic, historic hideaway in the heart of Palm Springs village. Beautifully redecorated in Santa Fe decor, with kitchens, wood-burning fireplaces, patios, two pools and a spa. Close to the Desert Museum, Heritage Center, and Moorten Botanical Gardens. Nearby hiking in indian canyons, horseback riding, tennis, golf, water sports on Salton Sea. Polo, ballooning, helicopter and desert Jeep tours. Near celebrity homes, date gardens, and Joshua Tree National Monument.

Hosts: Therese Hayes & Frank Tysen
Rooms: 17 (PB) $35-160
Continental Breakfast
Credit Cards: A, B, C
Notes: 2, 5, 6, 7, 8, 9, 10, 11, 12, 13, 14

Villa Royale Inn

1620 South Indian Trail
Palm Springs, CA, 92264
(619) 327-2314

This European-style country inn is an oasis in the desert, with a series of interior courtyards framed with pillars, cascading bougainvillaea, and hovering shade trees. Around a beer and wine bar there is an outdoor living room with fireplace and comfortable Italian wicker chairs. Two large swimming pools, bicycles, gourmet picnic lunches, and dinner available.

Hosts: C. Murawski & Robert E. Lee
Rooms: 34 (PB) $69-270
Continental Breakfast
Credit Cards: A, B, C
Closed Aug.
Notes: 3, 4, 7, 9, 10, 11, 12, 13, 14

PALO ALTO

Adella Villa

Box 4528
Stanford, CA, 94309
(415) 321-5195; FAX: (415) 325-5121

A 1920s Tyrolean estate on one parklike acre just twenty-five minutes from San Francisco. Four lovely guest rooms with private baths and Jacuzzi tubs. Color TV and sherry in each room. Our music room features a Steinway grand piano. Full breakfast, swimming pool, security gates; very quiet.

Hosts: Allen & Ann Young
Rooms: 3 (PB) $99
Full Breakfast
Credit Cards: A, B, C
Notes: 2, 5, 8 (over 12), 9, 10, 11, 12, 14

The Victorian on Lytton

555 Lytton Avenue
Palo Alto, CA, 94301
(415) 322-8555

Special amenities include down comforters, Battenberg lace canopies, botanical prints, Blue Willow china, and clawfoot tubs. Wander through the English country garden with over 1,200 perennial plants. Relax with a picture book or novel in the parlor with a cup of tea while listening to classical music.

Hosts: Maxwell & Susan Hall
Rooms: 10 (PB) $99-148.50
Continental Breakfast
Credit Cards: A, B, C
Notes: 2, 5, 9, 10, 11, 12, 14

PALOS VERDES

CoHost, America's B&B 10

P.O. Box 9302
Whittier, CA, 90608
(213) 699-8427

Cozy oceanfront home with a private beach. Two guest rooms, each with private bath. TV in all rooms, full gourmet breakfast. Children are welcome. $60-70.

PHILO

The Philo Pottery Inn

8550 Hwy. 128
P.O. Box 166
Philo, CA, 95466
(707) 895-3069

Located in the Anderson Valley in Mendocino County, the inn was once a stagecoach stop on the way to the north coast. Visit the tasting rooms of the local wineries, bicycle through the valley, or picnic among the redwoods. A drive to the spectacular Mendocino coast is only twenty minutes away.

Hosts: Sue & Barry Chiverton
Rooms: 5 (3 PB; 2 SB) $75-92
Full Breakfast
Credit Cards: A, B
Closed Jan.
Notes: 2, 8 (over 8), 9

POINT REYES STATION

Horseshoe Farm B&B Cottage & Cabin

39 Drake's Summit
P.O. Box 332
Point Reyes Station, CA, 94956
(415) 663-9401

Private, cozy, charming cottage and cabin, both with sunny decks and fireplaces, in the peaceful, quiet woods of Inverness Ridge, adjacent to scenic wonders of 65,000-acre Point Reyes National Seashore. Private spas. Ocean beaches, hiking trails, whale watching, year-round bird watching. Great restaurants nearby.

Host: Paki Stedwell-Wright
Rooms: 2 (PB) $90-125
Full Breakfast
Credit Cards: No
Notes: 2, 5, 6, 7

Marsh Cottage B&B

Jasmine Cottage

11561 Coast Route One
Point Reyes Station, CA, 94956
(415) 663-1166

This charming guest cottage was built in 1879 for the original Point Reyes schoolhouse. Secluded, romantic cottage sleeps four, has a library, woodstove, full kitchen, beautiful pastoral views, private patios, and gardens. Five-minute walk down the hill to town; five-minute drive to spectacular Point Reyes National Seashore. A crib and high chair are available.

Host: Karen Gray
Cottage: 1 (PB) From $115 + tax
Full Breakfast
Credit Cards: No
Notes: 2, 4, 5, 6, 8, 9, 11

Marsh Cottage B&B

Box 1121
Point Reyes Station, CA, 94956
(415) 669-7168

The privacy of your own peaceful bayside retreat near Inverness and spectacular Point Reyes National Seashore. Exceptional location and views, tasteful interior, fireplace, fully equipped kitchen, complete bath. Breakfast provided in the cottage. Ideal for romantics and naturalists. Hiking and other sports nearby.

Host: Wendy Schwartz
Rooms: 1 (PB) $95-110
Full Breakfast
Minimum stay weekends & holidays: 2
Credit Cards: No
Notes: 2, 5, 8, 9, 11

Point Reyes Seashore Lodge

10021 Highway One
P.O. Box 39
Point Reyes Station, CA, 94950
(415) 663-9000

A re-creation of a turn-of-the-century lodge. Eighteen designer coordinated rooms and three suites, many with whirlpool tubs and fireplaces. A great base for exploring the Point Reyes National Seashore Park, bird or whale watching, and hiking and biking.

Hosts: Judi & John Burkes
Rooms: 21 (PB) $85-175
Continental-plus Breakfast
Credit Cards: A, B, C
Notes: 2, 5, 7, 8, 9, 10, 11, 12, 14

Thirty-nine Cypress

39 Cypress Street
Point Reyes Station, CA, 94956
(415) 663-1709

This redwood house on 3.5 acres has been furnished with family antiques, original art, and an eclectic library. It has an English country garden for guests to enjoy, plus a state-of-the-art spa with massaging jets. Spectacular view of Point Reyes peninsula and the upper reaches of Tomales Bay. Near beaches.

Host: Julia Bartlett
Rooms: 3 (SB) $85-95
Full Breakfast
Credit Cards: No
Notes: 2, 5

PORTOLA

Upper Feather B&B

256 Commercial Street
Portola, CA, 96122
(916) 832-0107

Small-town comfort and hospitality in casual country comfort style. No TV or radio, but we have board games, puzzles, and popcorn for relaxing. Walk to the railroad museum, restaurants, wild and scenic river, and national forest lands. Only one hour from Reno entertainment.

Hosts: Jon & Lynne Haman
Rooms: 5 (SB) $42.40
Suites: 1 (SB) $63.60
Full Breakfast
Credit Cards: No
Notes: 2, 5, 6, 8, 10, 11, 12, 13

PRINCETON

Pillar Point Inn

Mail to: P.O. Box 388
El Granada, CA, 94018
(415) 728-7377

Cape Cod-style inn, built in 1985, overlooking Pillar Point Harbor and the ocean. Adjacent to beaches, trails, marine activities. King and queen rooms, all with water views, gas fireplaces, feather beds, window seats, refrigerators, private baths (some with steam baths).

Host: Dick Anderton
Rooms: 11 (PB) $125-160
Full Breakfast
Credit Cards: A, B, C
Notes: 2, 5, 8, 9, 10, 11, 12, 14

Christmas House B&B Inn

RANCHO CUCAMONGA

Christmas House B&B Inn

9240 Archibald Avenue
Rancho Cucamonga, CA, 91730
(714) 980-6450

A 1904 Victorian mansion with seven fireplaces, intricate woodwork, and stained glass throughout. Located 40 miles east of Los Angeles, close to Ontario International Airport and freeway close to all of Southern California's attractions. Gracious turn-of-the-century surroundings and hospitality.

Hosts: Jay & Janice Ilsley
Rooms: 7 (4 PB; 3 SB) $66-138
Full Breakfast
Credit Cards: A, B, C, D
Notes: 2, 4, 5, 8 (over 12), 9, 10, 11, 12, 13, 14

RED BLUFF

The Faulkner House

1029 Jefferson Street
Red Bluff, CA, 96080
(916) 529-0520

An 1890s Queen Anne Victorian, furnished in antiques. Screened porch looks out on a quiet, tree-lined street for relaxing, or let us help you discover our area. Go hiking and skiing at Lassen National Park, visit Ide Adobe or a Victorian museum, enjoy Sacramento River fishing.

Hosts: Harvey & Mary Klinger
Rooms: 4 (1 PB; 3 SB) $55-80
Full Breakfast
Credit Cards: No
Notes: 2, 5, 7 (restricted), 9, 12, 13, 14

REDDING

Palisades Paradise B&B

1200 Palisades Avenue
Redding, CA, 96003
(916) 223-5305

You'll love the breathtaking view of the Sacramento River, city, and surrounding mountains from this beautiful contemporary home with its garden spa, fireplace, wide-screen TV-VCR, and homelike atmosphere. Palisades Paradise is a serene setting for a quiet hideaway, yet conveniently located one mile from shopping and Interstate 5, with water skiing and river rafting nearby.

Host: Gail Goetz
Rooms: 2 (SB) $50-$60
Continental-plus Breakfast weekdays, Full on weekends

Credit Cards: A, B, C
Notes: 2, 5, 7 (restricted), 8, 9, 10, 11, 12, 13, 14

REDONDO BEACH

Ocean Breeze B&B

122 South Juanita Avenue
Redondo Beach, CA, 90277
(213) 316-5123

Near the beach, between Los Angeles and Long Beach, close to all freeways and attractions. Private entry, spa bathtub, and hospital beds with heated mattress covers. Remote TV, microwave oven, toaster, coffee maker in large rooms. Rooms are new and luxurious, but cost one-third to one-half of local hotels.

Hosts: Norris & Betty Binding
Rooms: 2 (PB) $30-50
Continental Breakfast
Credit Cards: No
Notes: 2, 5, 7, 8 (over 5), 9, 10, 11, 12

ROUND MOUNTAIN

NW Bed & Breakfast 578

610 SW Broadway
Portland, OR, 97205
(503) 243-7616

Large log home, formerly a hunting lodge, in the foothills of the Cascades between Mt. Shasta and Mt. Lassen. Just one mile off Highway 299E and 33, east of Redding. Lovely retreat in the woods with mountain views. On their 30 acres, this couple raise cattle, turkeys, and peacocks. Hosts speak Spanish. Three rooms, shared baths. $55.

SACRAMENTO

Amber House B&B

1315 22nd Street
Sacramento, CA, 95816
(916) 444-8085

This 1905 mansion is elegantly appointed with antiques, original art, Oriental rugs, and fresh flowers. Relax in front of the fireplace or enjoy the cozy library. Guest rooms feature private baths (five with Jacuzzi tubs) private telephones, radios, TVs. Full gourmet breakfast.

Hosts: Michael & Jane Richardson
Rooms: 9 (PB) $77-195
Full Breakfast
Credit Cards: A, B, C, E, F
Notes: 2, 5, 9, 10, 11, 14

Amber House B&B

B&B International—San Francisco 12

1181-B Solano Avenue
Albany, CA, 94706
(415) 525-4569

This historic Victorian is eighty years old and is on the Sacramento Old House Tour. It is tastefully furnished with antiques. There is a piano in the living room and inviting front and back sun porches. In an ideal midtown location close to the Capitol, Old Town, museums, and restaurants. One guest room has a double bed; a second has twins. They share a bath and a view of the garden. $60.

ST. HELENA

Asplund Conn Valley Inn

726 Rossi Road
St. Helena, CA, 94574
(707) 963-4614

Nestled in lush garden surroundings with views of vineyards and rolling hills—peaceful, quiet, and romantic. In-room refrigerators, air-conditioning, antiques. Common room with fireplace, library, TV, piano. Complimentary wine, fruit, cheese and crackers. Lots of country roads for strolling or jogging. Volleyball, badminton. Close to wineries, restaurants, tennis, golf, swimming, spas, balloon rides, and glider rides.

Host: Elsie Asplund Hudak
Rooms: 3 (1 PB; 2 SB) $75-95
Expanded Breakfast
Credit Cards: A, B, C
Notes: 2, 5, 8, 9, 10, 11, 12, 14

Bartels Ranch & Country Inn

1200 Conn Valley Road
St. Helena, CA, 94574
(707) 963-4001; FAX: (707) 963-5100

Located in the heart of the world-famous Napa Valley wine country. Secluded, romantic, elegant country estate overlooking a "100 acre valley with a 10,000 acre view." Award-winning accommodations, expansive entertainment room, pool table, fireplace, library, and terraces overlooking the vineyard. Peaceful star-studded sky, bicycles, refrigerator, TV, and phone available. Well-planned itineraries and warm hospitality. Nearby wineries, lake, golf, tennis, fishing, boating, and mineral spas.

Host: Jami Bartels
Rooms: 3 (PB) $135-275
Continental-plus Breakfast
Credit Cards: A, B, C
Notes: 2, 3, 4, 5, 9, 10, 11, 12, 14

Cinnamon Bear B&B

1407 Kearney Street
St. Helena, CA, 94574
(707) 963-4653

Classic arts and craft house, built in 1910 and furnished in that style with lots of bears. Close to downtown shops and restaurants; air-conditioned. Afternoon socializing with snacks, desserts, beverages. TV, phone. Family owned and operated. Full breakfast.

Hosts: Genny Jenkins & Brenda Cream
Rooms: 4 (PB) $75-130
Full Breakfast
Credit Cards: A, B
Notes: 2, 5, 9, 10, 11, 12

Deer Run Inn

3995 Spring Mt. Road
St. Helena, CA, 94574
(707) 963-3794

A lovely cedar shake clapboard-style gem on 4 acres. There are two antique furnished guest units in the main house, each with private bath and entrance, one with fireplace. A third unit, a spacious carriage room in a separate building with private bath, entrance, and deck, offers the advantage of breakfast delivered each morning. Swimming pool, Ping-Pong, horseshoes, and tranquility are just a few of the amenities. Brandy, TV, library, garden walk. Close to restaurants, spas, wineries, balloon rides, and glider rides.

Hosts: Tom & Carol Wilson
Rooms: 3 (PB) $85-105
Continental-plus Breakfast
Credit Cards: No
Notes: 2, 5, 9, 10, 11, 12, 14

Erika's Hillside

285 Fawn Park
St. Helena, CA, 94574
(707) 963-2887

NOTES: Credit cards accepted: A Master Card; B Visa; C American Express; D Discover Card; E Diners Club; F Other: 2 Personal checks accepted: 3 Lunch available: 4 Dinner available: 5 Open all year

You will be welcomes with warm "European hospitality" when you arrive at this hillside chalet. Just two miles from St. Helena you will find a peaceful, wooded country setting and its view of the vineyards and wineries. The grounds (3 acres) are nicely landscaped. The rooms are spacious, bright, and airy, with private entrances and bath, fireplace and hot tub. Continental breakfast and German specialties are served on the patio or in the Gardenroom. The structure, more than 100 years old, has been remodeled and personally decorated by German-born innkeeper Erika Cunningham.

Host: Erika Cunningham
Rooms: 3 (PB) $65-165
Continental Breakfast
Credit Cards: No
Notes: 2, 5, 8, 9, 10, 11, 12, 14

Harvest Inn

1 Main Street
St. Helena, CA, 94574
(707) 963-WINE; (800) 950-8466

Situated in the heart of the Napa Valley wine country, this renaissance of courtly English Tudor architecture is surrounded by lovely gardens and a 14-acre working vineyard. Rooms are furnished with antiques, and most include fireplaces, wet bars, refrigerators, color TV, air conditioning, and telephones. A wine bar, two pools, and Jacuzzis are also available for guests of the inn.

Rooms: 55 (PB) $95-300
Continental Breakfast
Credit Cards: A, B, D
Notes: 5, 6, 8, 10, 11, 12, 14

Hilltop House B&B

9550 St. Helena Road
St. Helena, CA, 94574
(707) 944-0880

Romantic and restful, Hilltop House is only ninety minutes from San Francisco and is set high atop the Mayacamus Mountains on 135 acres of unspoiled, pristine wilderness. You will enjoy spectacular views, a hot tub under the stars, a full breakfast, plus hiking trails. Nearby are the wineries, great restaurants, balloon rides, and mud baths.

Hosts: Annette & Bill Gevanter
Rooms: 3 (PB) $85-145
Full Breakfast
Credit Cards: A, B
Notes: 2, 5, 8, 9, 10, 11, 12, 14

The Ink House B&B

1575 St. Helena Hwy.
St. Helena, CA, 94574
(707) 963-3890

Lovely Italianate Victorian farmhouse built by Theron H. Ink. Antiques, private baths. Observatory overlooking the vineyards. In the heart of the Napa Valley, close to world-famous wineries, spas, ballooning, and soaring.

Host: Lois Clark
Rooms: 4 (PB) $95-150
Continental Breakfast
Credit Cards: No
Notes: 2, 5, 9, 10, 11, 12, 14 (Sun.-Thurs.)

Harvest Inn

Villa St. Helena

2727 Sulphur Springs Avenue
St. Helena, CA, 94574
(707) 963-2514

6 Pets welcome: 7 Smoking allowed: 8 Children welcome: 9 Social drinking allowed: 10 Tennis available: 11 Swimming available: 12 Golf available: 13 Skiing available: 14 May be booked through travel agents

Secluded hilltop Mediterranean villa that combines quiet country elegance with panoramic views of the Napa Valley. Romantic, antique-filled rooms with private entrances, private baths; some with fireplaces. Twenty-acre estate with walking trails and a spacious courtyard pool. Complimentary wine is served.

Hosts: Ralph & Carolyn Cotton
Rooms: 3 (PB) $145-225
Continental Breakfast
Minimum stay weekends & holidays: 2
Credit Cards: A, B
Notes: 2, 5, 7, 8 (over 12), 9, 10, 11, 12, 14

The Wine Country Inn

The Wine Country Inn

1152 Lodi Lane
St. Helena, CA, 94574
(707) 963-7077

Perched on a knoll overlooking manicured vineyards and the nearby hills, this country inn offers twenty-five individually decorated guest rooms. The Smiths used family-made quilts, local antiques, fireplaces, and balconies to create an atmosphere of unparalleled comfort.

Hosts: Jim Smith & Diane Horkheimer
Doubles: 25 (PB) $116-139
Continental Breakfast
Credit Cards: A, B
Closed Christmas
Notes: 2, 5, 7, 9, 10, 11, 12, 14

ST. JULIAN

Julian Hotel

P.O. Box 1856
2032 Main Street
St. Julian, CA, 92036
(619) 765-0201

Built nearly one hundred years ago by a freed slave and his wife, the Julian Hotel still reflects the dream and tradition of genteel hospitality of the Victorian era for its overnight guests. The "Queen of the Back Country" has the distinction of being the oldest continuously operating hotel in Southern California.

Hosts: Steve & Gig Ballinger
Rooms: 18 (5 PB; 13 SB) $64-145
Full Breakfast
Credit Cards: A, B, C
Notes: 2, 5, 7, 8, 9, 10, 11, 14

SAN ANDREAS

Robin's Nest

P.O. Box 1408
San Andreas, CA, 95249
(209) 754-1076

This Victorian, built in 1895, retains its dramatic character and old-world charm with modern conveniences. The inn features seminars, weddings, family reunions, club and group events. Nearby activities include California Caverns, art and antique shops, Big Trees State Park, wine tasting, boating, fishing, water- and cross-country skiing. Come stay with us.

Host: Bryan Cannon
Rooms: 9 (7 PB; 2 SB) $55-95
Full Breakfast
Credit Cards: A, B
Notes: 2, 5, 8 (12 and over), 10, 11, 12, 14

SAN ANSELMO

B&B San Francisco 16

P.O. Box 349
San Francisco, CA, 94101
(415) 931-3083

Located in the wonderful town of San Anselmo in Marin County. A wonderful private suite with a deck overlooking Mt. Tampalpias has a double bed as well as a twin for a third party, and a kitchen. There is a hot tub and swimming pool. Full breakfast. $75.

Casa de Flores B&B

SAN CLEMENTE

Casa de Flores B&B

184 Avenue La Cuesta
San Clemente, CA, 92672
(714) 498-1344

San Clemente's best-kept secret. Midway between Los Angeles and San Diego sits a beautiful 6,000-square-foot Spanish home offering three two-room suites and a spectacular view of the Pacific Ocean and Dana Point Harbor. One suite features a fireplace in the bedroom and a spa in its own private enclosed patio. The other two suites each feature double sofabeds in the sitting rooms for two additional people at an extra charge. All suites offer TV/VCRs and in-room coffee. Beach chairs and towels, over one hundred videos, pool table, washer, dryer, and iron available. All beverages complimentary any time of day. Turn-down service with chocolate mint and an orchid bloom picked from over one thousand orchids on property. Beautiful beaches and fine restaurants are within a mile.

Hosts: Marilee & Robert Arsenault
Suites: 3 (PB) $85-125
Full Breakfast
Minimum stay holidays and weekends: 2
Credit Cards: No
Notes: 2, 5, 7, 8, 9, 10, 11, 12, 14

SAN DIEGO

The Balboa Park Inn

3402 Park Blvd.
San Diego, CA, 92103
(619) 298-0823

One of San Diego's most romantic settings. A San Diego guest house in the heart of the city. The affordable difference . . . a suite for the price of a room. Within walking distance of the San Diego Zoo, Old Globe Theatre, museums, restaurants, and ten minutes from the beach.

Host: Ed Wilcox
Suites: 25 (PB)
Continental Breakfast
Credit Cards: A, B, C, E, F
Notes: 2, 5, 7, 8, 9, 10, 11, 12, 14

B&B International—San Francisco 13

1181-B Solano Avenue
Albany, CA, 94706
(415) 525-4569

A Spanish-style home in a beautiful old residential area within walking distance of Old Town and restaurants on Mission Hill. Conveniently located for the zoo, beach, and airport. The guest room has a queen bed and semi-private bath. An additional twin room is sometimes available for members of the same party. $55.

Britt House 1887

406 Maple Street
San Diego, CA, 92103
(619) 234-2926

This Queen Anne Victorian has been lovingly restored. Located close to Balboa Park and zoo, beaches, airport, downtown. Full breakfasts and afternoon tea are served. Complimentary tennis and health club facilities at a nearby resort.

Host: Elizabeth L. Lord
Rooms: 9 (1 PB; 8 SB) $100-115
Full Breakfast
Credit Cards: A, B, C, F
Notes: 2, 3, 5, 8, 10, 11, 12, 14

Carole's B&B

3227 Grim Avenue
San Diego, CA, 92104
(619) 280-5258

A friendly, congenial home close to all major attractions. Only 1.5 miles to the San Diego Zoo and Balboa Park. This house, built in 1904, is decorated with antiques and has a large swimming pool. Complimentary wine and cheese are also served.

Hosts: Carole Dugdale & Michael O'Brien
Rooms: 8 (SB) $50
Continental Breakfast
Credit Cards: No
Notes: 5, 7, 9, 10, 11, 12, 14

The Cottage

3829 Albatross Street
San Diego, CA, 92103
(619) 299-1564

Located between the zoo and Sea World, The Cottage is a quiet retreat in the heart of a downtown residential neighborhood. The turn-of-the-century furnishings throughout evoke visions of a bygone era. Each morning you will be served a breakfast of freshly baked bread, fruit, and beverage.

Hosts: Robert & Carol Emerick
Rooms: 2 (PB) $45-70
Continental Breakfast
Credit Cards: A, B
Notes: 2, 5, 8, 10, 11, 12, 14

Harbor Hill Guest House

2330 Albatross Street
San Diego, CA, 92101
(619) 233-0638

Each room has a private bath, and each level a private entrance and kitchen. Harbor views. Close to the zoo, Balboa Park, Seaport Village, old town, downtown. Families welcome.

Host: Dorothy A. Miltourn
Rooms: 5 (PB) $60-75
Continental Breakfast
Credit Cards: No
Notes: 2, 5, 7, 8, 9, 10, 11, 12, 14

Keating House Inn

2331 Second Avenue
San Diego, CA, 92101
(619) 239-8585

An elegant antique-filled historic Queen Anne Victorian residence three blocks west of Balboa Park with its museums, theaters, and the San Diego Zoo. Sun and shade patios provide relaxing settings. Also enjoy our fresh flowers and complimentary wine and sherry.

Host: John Martin
Rooms: 8 (2 PB; 6 SB) $70-90
Continental Breakfast
Credit Cards: A, B, C
Notes: 2, 5, 7 (limited), 8 (over 12), 9, 10, 11, 12, 14

San Diego Condo

B&B of Los Angeles
32074 Waterside Lane
Westlake Village, CA, 91361
(818) 889-8870

NOTES: Credit cards accepted: A Master Card; B Visa; C American Express; D Discover Card; E Diners Club; F Other: 2 Personal checks accepted: 3 Lunch available: 4 Dinner available: 5 Open all year

First-floor unit with trundle beds (twin or king) in the bedroom and a double sofabed in the living room. Full kitchen and bath; TV; parking. Children welcome. Pool, Jacuzzi, and barbecue area. $60-75.

Vera's Cozy Corner

2810 Albatross Street
San Diego, CA, 92103
(619) 296-1938

This crisp white colonial with black shutters sits on a quiet cul-de-sac overlooking San Diego Bay. Comfortable guest quarters consist of a separate cottage with private entrance across a flower-filled patio. Vera offers fresh-squeezed orange juice from her own fruit trees in season as a prelude to breakfast, which is served in the dining room. The house is convenient to local shops and restaurants, beaches, and is a mile from the San Diego Zoo.

Host: Vera V. Warden
Rooms: 1 (PB) $45
Continental Breakfast
Credit Cards: No
Notes: 2, 5, 9, 10, 11, 12, 14

SAN FRANCISCO

Albion House Inn

135 Gough Street
San Francisco, CA, 94102
(415) 621-0896

A comfortable stop in a busy city. A large fireplace on a foggy morning, a great full breakfast daily, and then with a few minutes walk you are on Union Square.

Hosts: Jan & Robert de Gier
Rooms: 8 (PB) $65-110
Full Breakfast
Credit Cards: A, B, C
Notes: 2, 4, 5, 7, 9

Amsterdam Hotel

749 Taylor Street
San Francisco, CA, 94108
(415) 673-3277; (800) 637-3444

The Amsterdam Hotel reflects the charm of a small European hotel. From the spacious lobby and cozy sitting room to the beautifully decorated guest rooms, this 1909 B&B inn offers every modern convenience to the most discriminating business or pleasure traveler. All rooms feature color cable TV, radio, telephone, and completely remodeled bathrooms. The Amsterdam Hotel is just minutes away from San Francisco's historic cable cars, Union Square shopping, theaters, Chinatown, and the financial district.

Host: Harry
Rooms: 31 (26 PB; 5 SB) $45-65
Continental Breakfast
Credit Cards: A, B, C
Notes: 5, 7, 8, 9, 10, 11, 12, 14

Archbishops Mansion Inn

1000 Fulton Street
San Francisco, CA, 94117
(415) 563-7872

Centrally located on a beautiful park surrounded by much-photographed Victorian homes. All the interesting areas of the city are only minutes away. Every guest room is custom designed to create a personalized atmosphere reminiscent of the last century. Amenities include exquisite antiques, embroidered linens, and comfortable sitting area. Most rooms have fireplaces. Lovely private baths, stacks of towels, French-milled soaps, and private phones.

Hosts: Kathleen Austin, Jonathan Shannon, Jeffrey Ross
Rooms: 15 (PB) $139-285
Continental-plus Breakfast
Credit Cards: A, B, C
Notes: 2, 5, 7, 8, 9, 10, 11, 12, 14

Art Center & B&B Suites, Wamsley

1902 Filbert Street
San Francisco, CA, 94123
(415) 567-1526

The best residential area—Marina Cow Hollow—where history stands still. Twenty-minute walk to Fisherman's Wharf. A French-New Orleans inn, with privacy and kitchens, queen beds, and fireplaces. Shopping on Union Street, jogging at the marina. Day tours of Northern California's charms, theater, music, cruising, and dancing on the bay—all within easy reach. Business travelers and families welcome. Commercial discounts, art classes.

Hosts: George & Helvi Wamsley
Rooms: 4 (PB) $65-85
Full Breakfast
Credit Cards: All
Notes: 2, 5, 8, 9, 10, 12, 14

The Bed & Breakfast Inn

Four Charlton Court
San Francisco, CA, 94123
(415) 921-9784

Located on a quiet mews in the fashionable Union Street area, near parking and public transportation. There are four "pension" rooms with shared baths, four with private baths, and a private apartment with living room, kitchen, balcony, and spiral staircase to the bedroom loft. Each flower-filled room is decorated with family furniture and cherished antiques. Your door or window may open onto the garden.

Hosts: Bob & Marily Kavanaugh
Rooms: 10 (6 PB; 4 SB) $70-140
Continental Breakfast
Credit Cards: No
Notes: 2, 5, 7, 8, 9, 10, 11

B&B International—San Francisco 14

1181-B Solano Avenue
Albany, CA, 94706
(415) 525-4569

A fine Mediterranean-style home in Monterey Heights, with a panoramic view of the Pacific from the guest-suite deck. The suite has a large living/dining area, microwave, refrigerator, and coffee maker. The bedroom has a queen bed, private bath, and private entrance. Ample street parking. Restaurants are within five blocks. $66.

B&B International—San Francisco 15

1181-B Solano Avenue
Albany, CA, 94706
(415) 525-4569

This stately Victorian home was built in 1876 and is one of the fine houses that survived the 1906 earthquake. It contains one of the largest collections of miniatures in the world. The guest room has a queen bed, TV, and dressing room with wash basin. There is a full bath adjacent to the room and a half-bath on the first floor. $80.

B&B International—San Francisco 16

1181-B Solano Avenue
Albany, CA, 94706
(415) 525-4569

Located on Nob Hill, in an elegant turn-of-the-century building, this condo offers a queen guest room with private bath and antiques. Garage parking is available in the neighborhood. Smoking on the balcony. $90.

B&B International—San Francisco 17

1181-B Solano Avenue
Albany, CA, 94706
(415) 525-4569

A three-story, turn-of-the-century house located three miles from Union Square, Fisherman's Wharf, and Ocean Beach. Shops and restaurants are close by. Walkers will enjoy nearby Golden Gate Park and the Presidio jogging paths. There is a grand piano in the living room, a back garden, and a dog in residence. The bedroom/sitting room on the second floor is furnished with antiques and has a private bath. The double bed is extra long, and there is a TV and telephone. Two sunny rooms on the third floor share a bath. Both have extra-long double beds, and one has sleeping space for an additional person. They also have TV, stereos, sitting areas, and telephone hookup. $60.

B&B San Francisco 3

P.O. Box 349
San Francisco, CA, 94101
(415) 931-3083

Fisherman's Wharf area. Quiet, spacious, tastefully decorated room with fireplace, fresh flowers, and fruit basket. A full breakfast is served by the bay window. King bed and TV, shared bath. Second room has an antique double bed. Fisherman's Wharf is only two blocks away. $55-65.

B&B San Francisco 4

P.O. Box 349
San Francisco, CA, 94101
(415) 931-3083

Golden Gate Park is just a couple of blocks away. Entire loft with a great ocean view from the deck. Fireplace, king bed, and queen sofabed, plus kitchenette. This house is wonderful for a family. Near UC Medical Center. Full breakfast. $75.

B&B San Francisco 6

P.O. Box 349
San Francisco, CA, 94101
(415) 931-3083

Russian Hill, one of San Francisco's most beautiful neighborhoods, with wonderful views of the bay and bridge. It's a wonderful walk down the hill to Fisherman's Wharf and North Beach. Cable cars are just one block away. Two guest rooms, one with a king and one with a double, both with bay views. Full breakfast. $75.

B&B San Francisco 8

P.O. Box 349
San Francisco, CA, 94101
(415) 931-3083

A romantic Victorian suite atop famous Nob Hill. For the conventioneer, the Fairmont and Mark Hopkins hotels are just a few steps away. The guest room has a queen bed, and the living room has a fireplace. There is also a small kitchen. Full breakfast. $125.

B&B San Francisco 9

P.O. Box 349
San Francisco, CA, 94101
(415) 931-3083

Built in the late 1800s, the Nolan House offers real Victorian charm. The two guest rooms share a split-marble bath. One room has a fireplace. Full breakfast is served in the formal dining room. $85-95.

B&B San Francisco 10

P.O. Box 349
San Francisco, CA, 94101
(415) 931-3083

A scenic location in San Francisco with a panoramic view. Three guest rooms, each facing west, provide a lovely sunset overlooking the Glen Canyon Park, with its beautiful eucalyptus grove. View of Mt. Davidson from each guest room. One room has twin beds, another a queen; or a large family room can accommodate up to four. Two shared baths. Outstanding full breakfast. $60.

B&B San Francisco 11

P.O. Box 349
San Francisco, CA, 94101
(415) 931-3083

The Marina near the San Francisco Yacht Club is one of San Francisco's most popular areas. Fisherman's Wharf, the Yacht Club, the Palace of Fine Arts, and the Marina Green are only a short walk away. One guest room with an antique brass double bed. Full breakfast. $60.

Casa Arguello

225 Arguello Blvd.
San Francisco, CA, 94118
(419) 752-9482

Comfortable rooms in a cheerful, spacious flat ten minutes from the center of town. Located in a desirable residential neighborhood near Golden Gate Park and the Presidio. Restaurants and shops within walking distance. Excellent public transportation.

Host: Emma Baires
Rooms: 5 (3 PB; 2 SB) $50-73
Continental Breakfast
Credit Cards: No
Notes: 2, 5, 8, 9, 10, 11, 12, 14

Casita Blanca

330 Edgehill Way
San Francisco, CA, 94127
(415) 564-9339

Casita Blanca is a guest cottage high on a hill, close to Golden Gate Park. A delightful studio nestled in the trees, it has its own bath, kitchen, and fireplace.

Host: Joan Bard
Rooms: 1 (PB) $80
Continental Breakfast
Minimum stay: 2
Credit Cards: No
Notes: 2, 5

Chateau Tivoli

1057 Steiner Street
San Francisco, CA, 94115
(415) 776-5462; (800) 228-1647; FAX: (415) 776-0505

The Chateau Tivoli is a Landmark Mansion which was the residence of the owners of San Francisco's world-famous Tivoli Opera House. Guests experience a time-travel journey back to San Francisco's golden age of opulence, the 1890s. The chateau is furnished with antiques from Cornelius Vanderbilt, Charles de Gaulle, J. Paul Getty, and famous San Francisco madame Sally Stanford.

Hosts: Rodney Karr & Bill Gersbach
Rooms: 5 (PB) $100-125
Suites: 2 (PB) $200-300
Continental-plus Breakfast
Credit Cards: A, B, C
Notes: 2, 3, 4, 5, 8, 9, 10, 11, 12, 14

CoHost, America's B&B 20

P.O. Box 9302
Whittier, CA, 90608
(213) 699-8427

Delightful home near bus transportation to most of the delights of this famous city. Bedrooms are comfortable, and the hostess offers laundry facilities. Complete breakfast. $55.

Country Cottage B&B

5 Dolores Terrace
San Francisco, CA, 94110
(415) 931-3083

A cozy country-style B&B in the heart of San Francisco. The three guest rooms are comfortably furnished in antiques and brass beds. The house is located at the end of a quiet street, away from the city noise. There is a small patio with trees and birds. A full breakfast is served in the sunny kitchen.

Hosts: Susan & Richard Kreibich
Rooms: 3 (S2B) $65
Full Breakfast
Credit Cards: A, B, C
Notes: 2, 5, 8, 9, 10, 11, 12, 14

Dolores Park Inn

3641 17th Street
San Francisco, CA, 94114
(415) 621-0482

This 1874 Italianate Victorian inn is located in the sunny part of the city near international restaurants and transportation. A lush subtropical garden and patio with birds and a fountain give this charming and much-photographed home a special flair. Three rooms have fireplaces.

Hosts: Bernie & Leslie
Rooms: 6 (2 PB; 4 SB) $50-75
Continental or Full Breakfast
Minimum stay weekends & holidays: 2
Credit Cards: A, B
Notes: 2, 5, 7 (restricted), 8 (over 12), 9, 10, 14

The Golden Gate Hotel

775 Bush Street
San Francisco, CA, 94108
(415) 392-3702

The ambience, location, and price make the Golden Gate Hotel an extraordinary find in the heart of San Francisco. Dedicated to a high standard of quality and personal attention, Renate keeps fresh flowers in all the rooms, and her continental breakfast includes fresh croissants and the city's strongest coffee.

Hosts: John & Renate Kenaston
Rooms: 23 (14 PB; 9 SB) $50-79
Continental Breakfast
Credit Cards: A, B, C, E, F
Notes: 2 (prior arrangement), 5, 6 (prior arrangement), 7, 8, 9, 10, 11, 12, 14

The Grove Inn

890 Grove Street
San Francisco, CA, 94117
(415) 929-0780; (800) 829-0780

The Grove Inn is a charming, intimate, and affordable B&B. Centrally located and convenient to public transportation, it has two suites for the convenience of families with children. The owners and managers are always available for information, help in renting cars, booking shuttles to the airport, and city tours.

Hosts: Klaus & Rosetta Zimmermann
Rooms: 18 (14 PB; 4 SB) $45-65
Continental Breakfast
Credit Cards: A, B, C
Closed Dec.
Notes: 2, 5, 8, 9, 10, 11, 12, 14

The Inn San Francisco

943 South Van Ness Avenue
San Francisco, CA, 94110
(415) 641-0188; (800) 359-0913

Restored historic 27-room Italianate Victorian mansion, circa 1872. Ornate woodwork, Oriental carpets, marble fireplaces, and period antiques combined with modern hotel conveniences. Relax in the redwood hot tub in the garden or reserve a room with a private spa tub — the perfect romantic escape!

Hosts: Marty Neely & Connie Wu
Rooms: 21 (16 PB; 5 SB) $75.03-177.15
Continental-plus Breakfast
Minimum stay weekends & holidays: 2-4
Credit Cards: A, B, C
Notes: 2 (in advance), 5, 7 (limited), 8, 10, 11, 12, 14

Jackson Court

2198 Jackson Street
San Francisco, CA, 94115
(415) 929-7670

Jackson Court is situated in Pacific Heights, a prestigious residential area. Only fifteen minutes from downtown, Union Square, Chinatown, and the financial district. Fisherman's Wharf and other major attractions are only minutes away by cable car. Jackson Court maintains the tradition of San Francisco with elegance and style.

Host: Patricia Cremer
Rooms: 10 (PB) $95-140
Continental Breakfast
Credit Cards: A, B, C
Notes: 2, 5, 7, 9, 12, 14

The Inn San Francisco

Lore's Haus

22051 Betlen Way
Castro Valley, CA, 94546
(415) 881-1533

Located twenty-five minutes from San Francisco City Center off 580 West, Castro Valley, Redwood Road Exit. Guests say, "This is a must for people who enjoy the better things in life." Large, parklike garden, European ambience, sterling flatware, Rosenthal crystal, Arzberg china, eiderdowns. German spoken.

Host: Lore Bergman
Rooms: 2 (1 PB; 1 SB) $60
Full Breakfast
Credit Cards: No
Notes: 5, 7, 9, 10, 11, 12

The Mansions Hotel

2220 Sacramento Street
San Francisco, CA, 94115
(415) 929-9444

Two connected historic mansions in San Francisco's most prestigious neighborhood, Pacific Heights. Hideaway for the stars, guests have included Barbra Striesand, Eddie Fisher, Andre Sakharov, and others. Rates include sumptuous breakfast, fresh flowers, nightly concerts, sculpture gardens, billiard room. "Elegance to the Nth degree"—*San Francisco Examiner.* "Marvelous hospitality"—Barbra Striesand.

Host: Bob Pritikin
Rooms: 29 (PB) $89-225
Full Breakfast
Credit Cards: All major
Notes: 2, 3, 4, 5, 6, 7, 8, 9, 10, 11, 12, 14

Monica & Ed Widburg

2007 15th Street
San Francisco, CA, 914116
(415) 564-1751

This charming home in a quiet residential area has an ocean view and ample parking. There is one B&B room, but for groups up to four guests, additional accommodations are available in an adjacent room. Queen beds in both rooms. The park, museums, and zoo are close by. Public transportation is easily available to downtown and Fisherman's Wharf. Reservations required.

Hosts: Monica & Ed Widburg
Rooms: 1 (PB) $65
Full Breakfast
Credit Cards: No
Notes: 2, 5, 11, 12

The Monte Cristo

600 Presidio Avenue
San Francisco, CA, 94115
(415) 931-1875

The elegantly restored Monte Cristo was originally built in 1875 as a saloon and hotel. It has served as a bordello, a refuge after the 1906 earthquake, and a speakeasy. Only two blocks from Victorian shops, restaurants, and antique stores on Sacramento Street; ten minutes to any other point in the city.

Host: George
Rooms: 14 (11 PB; 3 SB) $63-108
Expanded Breakfast
Minimum stay weekends & holidays: 2-3
Credit Cards: A, B, C, D, E
Notes: 5, 7, 8, 10, 11, 12, 14

No Name Victorian B&B

847 Fillmore Street
San Francisco, CA, 94117
(415) 346-5182; (415) 931-3083; FAX: (415) 921-2273

Located in one of the most-photographed areas of San Francisco, the historic district of Alamo Square, the No Name B&B sits close to the civic center, opera house, Davies Symphony Hall, Union Square, and all the sights that make our city famous. In the evening, help yourself to wine and relax in the hot tub, where many a guest has had a surprise visit from our neighborhood resident, Nosey the Racoon. Three of the guest rooms have fireplaces.

Hosts: Susan & Richard Kreibich
Rooms: 5 (3 PB; 2 SB) $75-85
Full Breakfast
Credit Cards: A, B, C
Notes: 2, 5, 8, 9, 10, 11, 12, 14

Obrero Hotel & Basque Restaurant

1208 Stockton Street
San Francisco, CA, 94133
(415) 989-3960

Small, cheerful pension in the heart of San Francisco, in Chinatown, on the edge of North Beach, within walking distance of Union Square and Fisherman's Wharf. Great breakfasts and atmosphere.

Host: Bambi McDonald
Rooms: 12 (SB) $38.85-57.75
Full Breakfast
Credit Cards: No
Notes: 2 (in advance), 4, 5, 8, 9, 10, 11, 12

Petite Auberge

863 Bush Street
San Francisco, CA, 94108
(415) 928-6000

A French country inn in the heart of San Francisco. Each room is individually decorated; many have fireplaces. Guests enjoy a full buffet breakfast, afternoon wine and hors d'oeuvres, valet parking, fresh fruit, and homemade cookies. Truly romantic ambience.

Host: Rich Revaz
Rooms: 26 (PB) $116.55-172
Full Breakfast
Credit Cards: A, B, C
Notes: 2, 5, 7 (limited), 8, 9, 10, 12, 14

Red Victorian B&B Inn

1665 Haight Street
San Francisco, CA, 94117
(415) 864-1978

Built at the turn of the century as a country resort hotel serving nearby Golden Gate Park, the Red Victorian now enjoys an international clientele of globally minded, friendly people. From the aquarium bathroom to the Flower Child Room to the Redwood Forest Room to the Peace Gallery where breakfast is served among Transformational paintings, the Red Victorian exudes color and joy to its global family.

Hosts: Sami Sunchild, Michael Lach, Barbara Cooke & Jeffrey Hirsch
Suite: 1 (PB) $120-125
Rooms: 13 (3 PB; 10 SB) $55-100
Continental-plus Breakfast
Credit Cards: A, B, C
Notes: 2, 5, 10, 11, 12, 14

Petite Auberge

Union Street Inn

2229 Union Street
San Francisco, CA, 94117
(415) 346-0424

The Union Street Inn combines the charm and elegance of a nineteenth-century Edwardian home with the friendly, personal attention of a fine European-style pension. Just a short walk from our door you will find Fisherman's Wharf, Ghiradelli Square, the cannery, Pier 39, and fabulous restaurants.

Hosts: Helen Stewart & Joanne Bailey
Rooms: 6 (PB) $125-225
Continental-plus Breakfast
Credit Cards: A, B, C
Notes: 2, 5, 8, 9, 10, 11, 12, 14

Victorian Inn on the Park

301 Lyon Street
San Francisco, CA, 94117
(415) 931-1830

Queen Anne Victorian located near Golden Gate Park and decorated with Victorian antiques. Many rooms have fireplaces, and the Belvedere Room features a private balcony overlooking the park. The inn features fireplaces, dining room with oak paneling, and a parlor with fireplace. Complimentary wine served nightly; fresh breads baked daily.

Hosts: Lisa & William Benau
Rooms: 12 (PB) $81-138
Continental-plus Breakfast
Credit Cards: A, B, C
Notes: 2, 5, 7, 8, 9, 10, 11, 12, 14

White Swan Inn

845 Bush Street
San Francisco, CA, 94108
(415) 775-1755

In the heart of San Francisco, a bit of London resides. Each oversized guest room has a fireplace, wet bar, sitting area, color TV, radio, bathrobes, fresh fruit, and soft drinks. Enjoy a full breakfast, afternoon wine and hors d'oeuvres, newspaper, valet parking, concierge, laundry, FAX machine, living room, library, and gracious service.

Host: Rich Revaz
Rooms: 26 (PB) $161-177.60

Full Breakfast
Credit Cards: A, B, C
Notes: 2, 5, 7 (limited), 8, 9, 10, 12, 14

White Swan Inn

The Willows B&B Inn

710 14th Street
San Francisco, CA, 94114
(415) 431-4770

The warmth and comfort of an English country inn awaits you at The Willows. Begin your day with the pampered touch of breakfast in bed. Afternoon cheese and bed turn down. Castro neighborhood location with shops, restaurants, and subway surrounding the inn. Limited off-street parking.

Hosts: Brad Goessler & Tim Farquhar
Rooms: 11 (SB) $60-88
Continental Breakfast
Credit Cards: A, B, C
Notes: 5, 7

SAN GREGORIO

Rancho San Gregorio

5086 San Gregorio Road, Box 21
San Gregorio, CA, 94074
(415) 747-0722

Five miles inland from the Pacific off Highway 1 is an idyllic rural valley where Rancho San Gregorio welcomes travelers to share relaxed hospitality. Picnic, hike, or bike in wooded parks or ocean beaches. Country breakfast. Located forty-five minutes from San Francisco, Santa Cruz, and the Bay Area.

Hosts: Bud & Lee Raynor
Rooms: 4 (PB) $60-95
Full Breakfast
Credit Cards: A, B
Notes: 2, 5, 7 (restricted), 8, 9, 12, 14

SAN JOSE

B&B International—San Francisco 19

1181-B Solano Avenue
Albany, CA, 94706
(415) 525-4569

Located on the west side of town, in an area of established homes five miles from downtown and the airport. Bus service two blocks away; restaurant four blocks. Easy access to the highway to San Francisco or Santa Cruz and the beach. Two guest rooms on the second floor share one bath. Each room has a TV, but guests are welcome to share the amenities on the first floor. Breakfast is served in the dining room or lovely country kitchen. $50.

The Briar Rose B&B Inn

897 East Jackson Street
San Jose, CA, 95112
(408) 279-5999

An 1875 Victorian, fabulously restored to its former grandeur. Large rooms, appointed with period furnishings. Wraparound porch overlooking the delightful gardens, a pond, and arbor. Quaint cottage. Quiet neighborhood setting with a good central location. Ten minutes from San Jose Airport.

Hosts: James & Cheryl Fuhring
Rooms: 6 (4 PB; 2 SB) $65-110
Full Breakfast
Credit Cards: A, B, C
Notes: 2, 5, 8, 9, 11, 14

Country Rose Inn B&B

P.O. Box 1804
Gilroy, CA, 95021-1804
(408) 842-0441

An oasis thirty miles south of San Jose, twenty minutes from historic San Juan Bautista, and forty-five minutes from Monterey. Experience rural grandeur. Nestled in the heart of the south Santa Clara Valley wine region. Ancient oak lofts above the bridal suite, and four other lovely rooms offer views of rural repose. Ballooning, hiking, golf. Savor a fanciful breakfast in pastoral grace.

Host: Rose Hernandez
Rooms: 5 (PB) $85-149
Full Breakfast
Credit Cards: A, B, C
Notes: 2, 5, 9, 10, 11, 12, 14

SAN MIGUEL

Victorian Manor B&B

3200 North Mission, Box 8
San Miguel, CA, 93451
(805) 467-3306

Victorian Manor is located in California's central coast wine-growing area. Enjoy our full library and game room with its pool table and TV. Breakfast is served in the formal dining room.

Hosts: Catherine & Ed Allen
Rooms: 5 (1 PB; 4 SB), $50
Continental Breakfast
Credit Cards: No
Notes: 2, 5, 7 (restricted), 8, 9

SAN PEDRO

San Pedro B&B

B&B of Los Angeles
32074 Waterside Lane
Westlake Village, CA, 91361
(818) 889-8870

Sprawling contemporary home set on a hillside with a large deck across the rear of the house. Views of Catalina and the ocean in the distance. Three guest rooms in the guest wing share a bath. Double, twin, and trundle beds. Beach with tide pools three blocks downhill; restaurants and transportation three blocks uphill. Children welcome. $45.

SAN RAPHAEL

Casa Soldavini

531 C Street
San Rafael, CA, 94901
(415) 454-3140

A 1932 charming Spanish home, filled with many family antiques. Quiet and relaxing, within walking distance of the mission, museums, parks, shopping, and recreation. Each room uniquely decorated and private. Large sitting room with piano, TV, VCR, and library. Hearty, scrumptious homemade breakfasts, fresh ice-cold ice tea, snacks, and freshly squeezed lemonade daily.

Hosts: Dan Cassidy & Linda Soldavini
Rooms: 3 (1 PB; 2 SB) $65-75
Continental-plus Breakfast
Credit Cards: No
Notes: 2, 5, 6 (limited), 9, 10, 11, 14

SANTA ANA

CoHost, America's B&B 15

P.O. Box 9302
Whittier, CA, 90608
(213) 699-8427

NOTES: Credit cards accepted: A Master Card; B Visa; C American Express; D Discover Card; E Diners Club; F Other: 2 Personal checks accepted: 3 Lunch available: 4 Dinner available: 5 Open all year

Two-story Craftsman-style home, each room redecorated in the style of the era and furnished in American and Danish antiques. Near Disneyland, Knott's Berry Farm, South Coast Plaza, and Bowers Museum, this home features two large first-floor rooms with shared bath. $60.

SANTA BARBARA

The Arlington Inn

1136 De LaVina Street
Santa Barbara, CA, 93101
(805) 965-6532

A restored 1926 Victorian hotel with a rich history of royal guests. Offering European hospitality in the Santa Barbara tradition, we serve a full breakfast and early evening wine and cheese. Many of our individually decorated rooms have kitchens.

Host: Ronald D. Lopez
Rooms: 42 (39 PB; 3 SB) $80-90
Full Breakfast
Credit Cards: A, B, C
Notes: 2, 5, 7, 8 (under 12 free), 9, 10, 11, 12, 14

B&B International—San Francisco 20

1181-B Solano Avenue
Albany, CA, 94706
(415) 525-4569

A spacious ranch located on a hilltop in the Santa Barbara suburbs, with a view of the ocean and mountains, six miles from downtown Santa Barbara.The two guest rooms each open onto a patio, and guests can enter without going through the house. Room one has a double bed, and room two has twins. Full bath plus a half-bath for guest use. Outside smoking only. $65.

Bath Street Inn

1720 Bath Street
Santa Barbara, CA, 93101
(805) 682-9680

An 1873 Queen Anne Victorian, located in the heart of historic Santa Barbara. Scenic downtown is within walking distance. Rooms have views, balconies, and private baths. Breakfast is served in the dining room or garden; bikes are available; evening refreshments.

Host: Susan Brown
Rooms: 7 (PB) $90-115
Full Breakfast
Credit Cards: A, B, C
Notes: 2, 5, 7 (limited), 8, 9, 10, 11, 12, 14

The Bayberry Inn

111 West Valerio Street
Santa Barbara, CA, 93101
(805) 682-3199

Enjoy a stroll on our spacious grounds; play croquet or badminton; retreat from the world in our beautifully appointed in-town inn. Experience the comfort and splendor of another era. Gourmet breakfast. Many guest rooms have fireplaces.

Host: Keith Pomeroy
Rooms: 8 (PB) $85-135
Full Breakfast
Minimum stay weekends: 2
Credit Cards: A, B, C, D
Closed Dec. 24-26
Notes: 2, 6 (call), 9, 10, 11, 12, 14

Blue Quail Inn & Cottages

1908 Bath Street
Santa Barbara, CA, 93101
(805) 687-2300

Relax and enjoy the quiet country atmosphere of the Blue Quail Inn and Cottages, just three blocks to Sansum Clinic and Cottage Hospital. Linger over a delicious full breakfast including home-baked goods served on the patio or in the main house dining room. Let us pack a picnic lunch for your day of adventure on our bicycles, then return for afternoon wine and light hors d'oeuvres. Sip hot spiced apple cider in the evening before enjoying a very restful sleep in your cottage, suite, or guest room.

Host: Jeanise Suding Eaton
Rooms: 8 (6 PB; 2 SB), $74.25-110
Full Breakfast
Credit Cards: A, B, D
Closed Dec. 24 & 25
Notes: 2, 9, 10, 11, 12, 14

Cheshire Cat Inn

36 West Valerio Street
Santa Barbara, CA, 93101
(805) 569-1610

Victorian elegance in a Southern California seaside village. The Cheshire Cat is conveniently located near theaters, restaurants, and shops. Decorated exclusively in Laura Ashley papers and linens, the sunny guest rooms have private baths; some with fireplaces, spas, and balconies. Collectibles, English antiques, and fresh flowers enhance your stay in beautiful Santa Barbara.

Host: Midge Goeden & Christine Dunstan
Rooms: 11 (PB) $79-179
Continental-plus Breakfast
Credit Cards: No
Notes: 2, 5, 7 (outside), 9, 10, 11, 12, 14

Glenborough Inn

1327 Bath Street
Santa Barbara, CA, 93101
(805) 966-0589

Experience the "ultimate in romance." Enjoy gourmet breakfast in bed. Elegant fireplace suites, secluded garden hot tub, bicycles, evening hors d'oeuvres and cookies.

Host: Laurie O'Hanlon
Rooms: 9 (5 PB; 4 SB), $60-155
Full Breakfast
Credit Cards: A, B, C
Notes: 2, 5, 7, 10, 11, 12, 14

Harbour Carriage House

420 West Montecito
Santa Barbara, CA, 93101
(805) 962-8447

A renovated 1895 house, tastefully decorated in French and English antiques. Breakfast is served in the sunny solarium, and evening refreshments are served fireside. Two blocks from the harbor, the house adjoins the gardens of two historic homes.

Host: Vida-Marie McIsaac
Rooms: 9 (PB) $76.50-175
Full Breakfast
Credit Cards: A, B
Closed Christmas Eve & Day
Notes: 2, 8, 9, 10, 11, 12, 14

Ocean View House

Box 20065
Santa Barbara, CA, 93102
(805) 966-6659

A wonderful location in Santa Barbara in a quiet private home within walking distance of the ocean. Two rooms with antique charm, TV, interesting books, and collections. Oranges, apples, and melons are presented from our garden with breakfast on the patio.

Host: Carolyn Canfield
Rooms: 2 (PB) $50
Continental-plus Breakfast
Credit Cards: No
Notes: 2, 5, 7 (limited), 8, 9, 10, 11, 12, 14

Old Mission House

435 East Pedregosa
Santa Barbara, CA, 93103
(805) 569-1914

This is a Craftsman house, built in 1895, with fireplaces in all rooms. Within walking distance of the Santa Barbara Mission, parks, downtown stores, museums, and ten minutes by car to the beach.

Host: Marie Miller
Rooms: 3 (1 PB; 2 SB) $45-65 (suite)
Continental Breakfast
Credit Cards: No
Notes: 2, 5, 8, 9, 10, 11, 12

The Old Yacht Club Inn

431 Corona Del Mar Drive
Santa Barbara, CA, 93103
(805) 962-1277

The Old Yacht Club Inn has nine guest rooms in two houses: a 1912 California Craftsman and a 1920s Early California Style building. The inn opened as Santa Barbara's first B&B in 1980 and is now world renowned for its hospitality and warmth in comfortable surroundings and fine food. The inn is within a block of the beach and close to tennis, swimming, boating, fishing, and golf.

Hosts: Nancy Donaldson, Lu Caruso, Sandy Hunt
Rooms: 9 (PB) $70-130
Full Breakfast
Credit Cards: A, B, C, D
Notes: 2, 4 (Sat.), 5, 8, 9, 10, 11, 12, 14

The Old Yacht Club Inn

The Olive House

1604 Olive Street
Santa Barbara, CA, 93101
(805) 962-4902

Enjoy quiet comfort and gracious hospitality in a lovingly restored 1904 Craftsman-style house replete with redwood paneling, bay windows, window seats, coffered ceilings, and a fireplace in the living room. Richly refurbished in 1990. Breakfast is served in the large, sunny dining room that also houses a studio grand piano. Enjoy mountain and ocean views from the sun deck and several guest rooms.

Hosts: Lois & Bob Poire
Rooms: 6 (PB) $80-120
Continental-plus Breakfast
Credit Cards: A, B
Notes: 2, 5, 10, 11, 12, 14

The Parsonage

1600 Olive Street
Santa Barbara, CA, 93101
(805) 962-9336

Charming 1892 Victorian, furnished beautifully with antiques and Oriental rugs. Romantic honeymoon suite with city and ocean views. Enjoy breakfast on the spacious sun deck with its cozy gazebo. Centrally located within walking distance of the mission, shops, restaurants, and theaters.

Host: Hilde Michelmore
Rooms: 6 (PB) $85-150
Full Breakfast
Credit Cards: A, B
Notes: 2, 5, 10, 11, 12, 14

Simpson House Inn

121 East Arrellaga
Santa Barbara, CA, 93101
(805) 963-7067

Elegant 1874 Victorian home, secluded in an acre of English gardens, only a five-minute walk to downtown historic sights, theaters, restaurants, and shops. Furnished with antiques, fine art, Oriental carpets, and

English lace. Complimentary wine and bikes.

Hosts: Gillean Wilson, Glyn & Linda Davies
Rooms: 6 (5 PB; 1 SB) $76-150
Full Breakfast
Minimum stay weekends & holidays: 2
Credit Cards: A, B
Notes: 2, 5, 7 (restricted), 8 (over 12), 9, 10, 11, 12, 14

Simpson House Inn

The Upham Hotel & Garden Cottages

1404 De la Vina Street
Santa Barbara, CA, 93101
(800) 727-0876

Established in 1871, this beautifully restored Victorian hotel is situated on an acre of gardens. Guest rooms and suites are decorated with period furnishings and antiques. Continental breakfast and afternoon wine and cheese. Walk to museums, galleries, historic attractions, shops, and restaurants in downtown Santa Barbara.

Host: Andrea Gallant
Rooms: 49 (PB) $110-300
Continental Breakfast
Credit Cards: A, B, C, D, E, F
Notes: 2, 3, 4, 5, 7, 8, 9, 10, 11, 12, 14

Valli's View

340 North Sierra Vista
Santa Barbara, CA, 93108
(805) 969-1272

Just three miles from the center of Santa Barbara in the Monecito foothills, this lovely private home, with its garden setting, deck, patios, and ever-changing mountain views, has an ambience of tranquility and comfort. Enjoy lounges for sunning, a porch swing for relaxing, and all nearby tourist attractions. In the evening, enjoy a cup of cafe mocha or a glass of wine in the spacious living room that overlooks the mountains.

Hosts: Valli & Larry Stevens
Rooms: 3 (PB) $45-95
Full Breakfast
Minimum stay weekends: 2
Credit Cards: No
Notes: 2, 5, 6 (outside), 7 (outside), 8, 9, 10, 11, 12, 14

SANTA CLARA

Madison Street Inn

1390 Madison Street
Santa Clara, CA, 95050
(408) 249-5541

Just ten minutes from San Jose Airport and five minutes from Santa Clara University, this elegant Victorian sits peacefully in the heart of Silicon Valley. Telephones in rooms.

Hosts: Ralph & Theresa Wigginton
Rooms: 7 (3 PB; 4 SB) $55-75
Full Breakfast
Credit Cards: A, B, C, E
Notes: 2, 5, 8, 9, 10, 11, 12, 14

SANTA CRUZ

Babbling Brook Inn

1025 Laurel Street
Santa Cruz, CA, 95060
(408) 427-2437; FAX: (408) 427-2457

Waterfalls and a brook meander through the gardens of this twelve-room inn with French decor. Each room has a private bath, telephone, TV, fireplace, private deck, private entrance. Two have deep soaking bathtubs. Walk to beaches, the boardwalk, a garden mall, or tennis. Full breakfast and complimentary wine and cheese. Romantic garden gazebo for weddings.

Host: Helen King
Rooms: 12 (PB) $85-125
Full Breakfast
Minimum stay weekends: 2
Credit Cards: A, B, C, D, E
Notes: 2, 5, 8 (over 12), 9, 10, 11, 12, 14

Pleasure Point Inn

2-3665 East Cliff Drive
Santa Cruz, CA, 95062
(408) 475-4657

Enjoy a warm welcome from the innkeepers, who enjoy sharing their beachfront home with others. Boat charters daily on their forty-foot motor yacht.

Hosts: Margaret & Sal Margo
Rooms: 3 (PB) $95-125
Continental-plus Breakfast
Credit Cards: A, B
Notes: 2, 5, 8 (12 and over), 9, 10, 11, 12, 14

Valley View

Box 66593
Santa Cruz, CA, 95066
(415) 321-5195; FAX: (415) 325-5121

Magnificent forest/glass house with hot spa on the large deck that overlooks the 20,000-acre redwood valley below. Barbecue, stereo, cable TV, beautiful stone fireplace, piano. Unhosted for total privacy. Very peaceful. Only ten minutes to beaches.

Hosts: Scott & Tricia Young
Rooms: 2 (PB) $110
Full Breakfast
Credit Cards: A, B, C, E
Notes: 2, 5, 8 (over 12), 9, 10, 11, 12, 14

SANTA MONICA

B&B International—San Francisco 21

1181-B Solano Avenue
Albany, CA, 94706
(415) 525-4569

This 1931 Spanish revival home is close to UCLA and Wilshire Boulevard, in a quiet neighborhood. Within walking distance of public transportation . The guest room has a double bed and private bath, plus a small refrigerator. Three windows open onto a landscaped garden with patio. Restaurants are within a half mile. $65.

Channel Road Inn

219 West Channel Road
Santa Monica, CA, 90402
(213) 459-1920

Elegant inn one block from the beach in Santa Monica. "One of the most romantic places in Los Angeles"—*L.A. Magazine.* Views, bicycles, picnics available. Two miles from the J. Paul Getty Museum.

Hosts: Kathy Jensen & Susan Zolla
Rooms: 14 (PB) $85-175
Continental Breakfast
Credit Cards: A, B, C
Notes: 2, 5, 8, 9, 10, 11, 12, 14

SANTA ROSA

The Gables

4257 Petalume Hill Road
Santa Rosa, CA, 95404
(707) 585-7777

Historic landmark, architecturally classic Gothic, just one hour from San Francisco. Gateway to the redwoods, Sonoma/Napa Valley wineries, and the marvelous California north coast. Three sculptured marble fireplaces, spiral stairs. Honeymooners' favorite, with country elegance and good taste. Afternoon refreshments.

Hosts: Judith & Michael Ogne
Rooms: 5 (PB) $80-95
Full Breakfast
Credit Cards: A, B, C, D
Notes: 2, 5, 9, 14

Gee-Gee's

7810 Sonoma Highway
Santa Rosa, CA, 95409
(707) 833-6667

Lovely remodeled farmhouse on 1 acre in a parklike setting in the Valley of the Moon, surrounded by fine wineries, mountains, and orchards. Very pleasant guest rooms, gourmet breakfasts, sitting room with TV and fireplace, decks, swimming pool, complimentary bicycles. Free RV parking for B&B guests. Gift certificates available. French and German spoken.

Rooms: 4 (S2B) $70-85
Full Breakfast
Credit Cards: No
Notes: 2, 5, 10, 11, 12, 14

Melitta Station Inn

5850 Melitta Road
Santa Rosa, CA, 95409
(707) 538-7712

Rustic American country B&B on a country road in the Valley of the Moon near everything. Next to three state parks, hiking, biking, horseback riding, boating, fishing, hot-air balloons, gliders, hot baths, and massages. Within minutes of many fine restaurants and wineries.

Hosts: Vic Amstadter & Diane Crandon
Rooms: 6 (4 PB; 2 SB) $75-90
Full Breakfast
Credit Cards: A, B
Notes: 2, 5, 8 (10 and over), 9, 10, 11, 12, 14

Pygmalion House B&B

331 Orange Street
Santa Rosa, CA, 95407
(707) 526-3407

Pygmalion House, one of Santa Rosa's historic landmarks, is a fine example of Victorian Queen Anne architecture. Each morning a bountiful breakfast is served in the country kitchen. Throughout the day, complimentary bottled spring water and soft drinks are available. In the evening, guests may enjoy cheese, nuts, coffee, or tea while relaxing around the fireplace.

Host: Lola L. Wright
Rooms: 5 (PB) $50-70
Full Breakfast
Credit Cards: A, B, C
Notes: 2, 5, 9, 10, 11, 12, 14

Vintners Inn

4350 Barnes Road
Santa Rosa, CA, 95403
(707) 575-7350

A European-style inn, located in the middle of our own 50-acre vineyard, with the highly acclaimed John Ash & Co. restaurant on the premises. Just sixty miles north of San Francisco, in the heart of the Sonoma wine country.

Hosts: John & Francisca Duffy
Rooms: 44 (PB) $116.64-199.80
Continental Breakfast
Credit Cards: A, B, C, E
Notes: 2, 3, 4, 5, 8, 9, 10, 11, 12, 14

SAUSALITO

The Butterfly Tree

P.O. Box 790
Sausalito, CA, 94966
(415) 383-8447

At Muir Beach, you are in easy walking distance of the Pacific Ocean, Muir Woods, and the Golden Gate National Recreation Area. A secluded, fragile environment good for nature buffs, lovers, hikers, and bird watchers. Only thirty minutes from San Francisco; twenty minutes to the Sausalito ferry, shopping, and excellent dining. Complimentary afternoon wine or juice.

Host: Karla Andersdatter
Rooms: 3 (PB) $95-115 + tax
Full Breakfast
Credit Cards: No
Notes: 2, 5, 7 (restricted), 8 (under 6 months or over 6 years), 11, 14

Casa Madrona Hotel

801 Bridgeway
Sausalito, CA, 94965
(415) 332-0502; (800) 288-0502

Nestled in the hills of Sausalito, the Casa Madrona is truly a nineteenth-century reminder of a less hurried time. Rooms cascade down the hillside, offering enchanting views of the harbor. Each room is individually designed and decorated. An unforgettable haven of romance and retreat.

Host: John W. Mays
Rooms: 34 (PB) $95-195
Continental Breakfast
Credit Cards: A, B, C
Notes: 2, 3, 4, 5, 7, 8, 9, 10, 11, 12, 14

SEAL BEACH

The Seal Beach Inn & Gardens

212 5th Street
Seal Beach, CA, 90740
(213) 493-2416

The Seal Beach Inn and Gardens is a French Mediterranean-style B&B country inn located in the quaint seaside village of Seal Beach. A lavish gourmet breakfast is served.

Host: Marjorie Bettenhausen
Rooms: 23 (PB) $96-160
Full Breakfast
Credit Cards: A, B, C, E
Notes: 2, 5, 10, 11, 12, 14

Villa Pacifica

204 Ocean Avenue
Seal Beach, CA, 90740
(213) 594-0397

A winding walk out our private rear gate, past our greenhouses and grape arbor, puts you right on the sand and the last remaining California dunes. Jacuzzi, fireplace, all water sports available. Close to Disneyland, Knott's Berry Farm, the *Queen Mary,* and the *Spruce Goose.*

Hosts: Bruce Stark & Michelle Brendel
Rooms: 2 (PB) $110-125
Full Breakfast
Credit Cards: No
Notes: 2, 5, 10, 11, 12, 14

SEQUOIA NATIONAL PARK/LINDSAY

El Camino Real B&B

P.O. Box 7155
Northridge, CA, 91327-7155
(818) 363-6753

Restored 1902 Victorian home. Free nine holes of golf Monday-Thursday, fishing on Lake Success. Rates include a homemade breakfast, evening snack, and wine. Five rooms with shared baths, pool. $55-60.

SONOMA

B&B International—San Francisco 24

1181-B Solano Avenue
Albany, CA, 94706
(415) 525-4569

A beautifully restored farmhouse that has historical status and has been photographed for magazines. An old stonecutter's cottage has been renovated for guests. It has a king bed, private bath, and large deck. There is a Franklin stove as well as electric heat. A short walk to the Sonoma Plaza and gourmet restaurants. There are wineries within walking distance and hot springs nearby. $98.

El Dorado Hotel

405 First Street West
Sonoma, CA, 95476
(707) 996-3030

Situated in the heart of the wine country, just sixty miles north of San Francisco, the El Dorado overlooks Sonoma's historic Spanish Square. Rates include complimentary wine at check-in and a European breakfast. The El Dorado features fine Italian cuisine at Ristorante Platti. The hotel's central location makes it the perfect spot to embark on an afternoon in the tasting rooms or stroll through boutique-studded streets.

Rooms: 27 (PB) $120-140
Continental Breakfast
Credit Cards: A, B
Notes: 3, 4, 5, 7, 8, 9, 10, 11, 12, 14

The Hidden Oak

214 East Napa Street
Sonoma, CA, 95476
(707) 996-9863

The Hidden Oak is a large, two-story Craftsman bungalow in the historic neighborhood of Sonoma, one block from the Plaza. We have three exquisitely decorated rooms with queen beds and private baths. We include full breakfast and have complimentary bicycles. Located near the wineries, shopping, restaurants, art galleries, and historic sites.

Host: Catherine Cotchett
Rooms: 3 (PB) $85-160
Full Breakfast
Credit Cards: C
Notes: 2, 5, 10, 11, 12, 14

Thistle Dew Inn

171 West Spain Street
Sonoma, CA, 95476
(707) 938-2909

Two turn-of-the-century Victorians only one-half block from historic Sonoma Plaza. Six rooms, each with queen bed and private bath. Extensive collection of original Gustav Stickley furniture. Bikes, hot tub, and gardens for relaxation. Full breakfast, wine and hors d'ourvres in the afternoon.

Hosts: Norma & Larry Barnett
Rooms: 6 (PB) $85-95 + tax
Full Breakfast
Credit Cards: A, B, C
Notes: 2, 5, 8, 9

Victorian Garden Inn

316 East Napa Street
Sonoma, CA, 95476
(707) 996-5339

The Hidden Oak

Lush gardens with private nooks; classic rooms from storybooks; private entrances, private baths; rooms overlooking garden paths; gourmet breakfast, lunch, and breaks; midweek conferences at competitive rates; romantic getaways, excursions, and tours; all of these and more are yours. Just one and one-half blocks from the historic Sonoma Plaza and Sebastiani Winery.

Host: Donna Lewis
Rooms: 4 (3 PB; 1 SB) $79-135
California Breakfast
Credit Cards: A, B, C
Notes: 2, 5, 7, 8 (over 13), 9, 10, 11, 12, 14

SONORA

Lavender Hill B&B

683 South Barretta Street
Sonora, CA, 95370
(209) 532-9024

Delightfully restored 1900 Victorian with three lovely guest rooms, two with private baths. Formal parlor, dining room, antiques, porch swing, and beautiful grounds. Within walking distance of shops and restaurants in the heart of the Gold Country. Old-time charm with modern convenience.

Host: Alice Byrnes
Rooms: 4 (2 PB; 2 SB) $60-70
Full Breakfast
Credit Cards: No
Notes: 2, 5, 7 (restricted), 9, 10, 12

The Ryan House

153 South Shepherd Street
Sonora, CA, 95370
(209) 533-3445

Footsteps from town, a century removed. Gold-rush home, built in 1855, restored to become a B&B inn. Spacious gardens; near Yosemite, Columbia State Park, hunting, fishing, river rafting, antiquing, and wineries. Queen beds, antiques, handmade quilts. Theater packages arranged. Gift certificates available.

Hosts: Nancy & Guy Hoffman
Rooms: 3 (PB) $75-80
Full Breakfast
Credit Cards: A, B, D
Notes: 2, 5, 9, 10, 11, 12, 14

Serenity

15305 Bear Cub Drive
Sonora, CA, 95370
(209) 533-1441

Listen to the wind through the pines as you relax on the veranda. Appreciate the nicety of ironed, lace-trimmed linens and handmade comforters. Waken to enticing aromas from the kitchen refreshed and ready to explore nearby gold-rush towns, caverns, or Yosemite. Golf, quaint shops, theater, and dining are close.

Hosts: Fred & Charlotte Hoover
Rooms: 4 (PB) $75
Full Breakfast
Credit Cards: A, B, C
Notes: 2, 5, 7, 9, 10, 11, 12, 14

SOQUEL

B&B International—San Francisco 23

1181-B Solano Avenue
Albany, CA, 94706
(415) 525-4569

This redwood Victorian was built in 1875 and completely refurbished last year. It has six bedrooms and five baths. Two of the rooms are in the carriage house in the rear patio. The home is furnished in antiques, with handmade quilts, full tile baths, a hot tub, and gardens. All guest rooms have private baths. Smoking outside only. $95.

STANFORD

Adella Villa

P.O. Box 4523
Stanford, CA, 94309
(415) 321-5195; FAX: (415) 325-5121

Exclusive luxury villa on a secluded acre. Electronic gates, pool, fountains, BBQ. The 4,000 square-foot residence has four bedrooms, four private baths (two with Jacuzzi tubs), grand piano in the music foyer. Full breakfast cooked to order. Complimentary sherry and white wine, bicycles, and airport pickup.

Hosts: Scott & Tricia Young
Rooms: 4 (PB) $99
Full Breakfast
Credit Cards: All major
Notes: 2, 5, 8 (over 12), 9, 10, 11, 12, 14

STUDIO CITY

El Camino Real B&B

P.O. Box 7155
Northridge, CA, 91327-7155
(818) 363-6753

Five minutes from Universal Studios. Guest room contains one queen bed and one single bed, private bath. TV; air-conditioning; pool, hot tub; kitchen privileges. Children over fourteen are welcome. Continental breakfast. Close to freeway. $50-70.

Fig Cottage

B&B of Los Angeles
32074 Waterside Lane
Westlake Village, CA, 91361
(818) 889-8870

Stained glass, skylights, and country charm in every room. Enclosed garden patio with pool; sauna at additional cost. Guest room has twin beds, private bath, and TV. Adults only. Shopping, restaurants, and bus lines only two blocks away. $50.

SUTTER CREEK

The Foxes in Sutter Creek

Box 159
Sutter Creek, CA, 95685
(209) 267-5882

In the heart of historic Gold Rush country, this inn has six large, elegant suites with private baths, queen beds, air-conditioning, wood-burning fireplaces, and covered parking. Breakfast, cooked to your order, is delivered on silver service to your room. Beautiful gardens and a gazebo. Walk to shops and restaurants. Three-star Mobil rating. Hospitality is our specialty.

Hosts: Pete & Min Fox
Rooms: 6 (PB) $90-130
Full Breakfast
Credit Cards: A, B, D
Notes: 2, 5, 7 (outside), 9, 10, 11, 14

TAHOE CITY

Mayfield House

236 Grove Street
P.O. Box 5999
Tahoe City, CA, 95730
(916) 583-1001

Snug and cozy 1930s Tahoe home, half a block from the beach. Premium skiing within ten miles. Full breakfast, homemade baked goods. Within walking distance of shops and restaurants in Tahoe City. Off-street parking.

Hosts: Cynthia & Bruce Knauss
Rooms: 6 (SB) $70-105
Full Breakfast
Credit Cards: A, B
Notes: 2, 5, 7 (limited), 8, 9, 10, 11, 12, 13, 14

TAHOMA

The Captain's Alpenhaus

6941 West Lake Blvd.
Tahoma, CA, 95733
(916) 525-5000; 525-5266

A European-style country inn and gourmet restaurant with an Alpine bar, stone fireplace, B&B rooms, and cottages with fireplaces nestled in pine woods. Cozy and quaint resort on Lake Tahoe's unspoiled west shore, five minutes from Emerald Bay, one of the scenic wonders of the world.

Hosts: Joel & Phyllis Butler
Rooms: 7 (PB) $55-115
Suites: 2
Cottages: 6
Full Breakfast
Minimum stay holidays: 2
Credit Cards: A, B, C
Notes: 2, 3, 4, 5, 6, 7, 8, 9, 10, 11, 12, 13, 14

TARZANA

El Camino Real B&B

P.O. Box 7155
Northridge, CA, 91327-7155
(818) 363-6753

Large, sprawling home with two rooms available. The first has a king bed (or two twins), private bath, and large sitting room. The second room has a twin bed. Swimming pool, paddle court, air-conditioning. Children over twelve are welcome. Continental breakfast. $50.

TEMECULA

Loma Vista B&B

33350 La Serena Way
Temecula, CA, 92390
(714) 676-7047

Loma Vista is conveniently located to any spot in Southern California, right in the heart of the Temecula wine country. This beautiful new mission-style home is surrounded by lush citrus groves and premium vineyards. All six rooms have private baths; most have balconies; all are named after wines and so decorated.

Hosts: Betty & Dick Ryan
Rooms: 6 (PB) $85-115
Full Breakfast
Credit Cards: A, B
Closed Thanksgiving, Christmas, New Year's
Notes: 2, 9, 10, 11, 12, 14

TEMPLETON

Country House Inn

91 Main Street
Templeton, CA, 93465
(805) 434-1598

An 1886 Victorian farmhouse — designated historic site — in an old western town with many restored buildings. Quiet country setting with wine tasting and tour nearby. Full breakfast features crepes, quiches, souffles, homebaked breads, and fresh fruit. Perfect spot for weddings, showers, and parties.

Host: Dianne Garth
Rooms: 7 (4 PB; 3 SB) $68-83
Full Breakfast
Credit Cards: A, B
Notes: 2, 5, 8, 10, 11, 12, 14

Country House Inn

TORRANCE

CoHost, America's B&B 12

P.O. Box 9302
Whittier, CA, 90608
(213) 699-8427

Charming contemporary home with a lovely courtyard entrance. The house has a light, open feeling with an atrium that demonstrates the hostess's love of gardening. Near LAX and sights. A full breakfast is served. Children are welcome, and pickup is available at the airport with prior arrangement. Four miles to the beach. $65.

TRINIDAD

Trinidad Bed & Breakfast

Box 849
Trinidad, CA, 95570
(707) 677-0840

Welcome to our Cape Cod-style home overlooking beautiful Trinidad Bay. The inn offers spectacular views of the rugged coastline and fishing harbor below from two suites, one with a fireplace, and two upstairs bedrooms, all with private baths. Surrounded by dozens of beaches, trails, and redwood parks. Within walking distance of restaurants and shops. Our suites enjoy the luxury of breakfast delivered. The other two rooms enjoy breakfast at a family-style table.

Hosts: Paul & Carol Kirk
Rooms: (PB) $90-145
Continental-plus Breakfast
Credit Cards: A, B, D
Notes: 2, 5, 8 (over 10), 9, 10, 11, 12

TWAIN HARTE

Twain Harte's B&B

Box 1718
Twain Harte, CA, 95383
(209) 586-3311

Welcome to a vacation hideaway in a quaint mountain village offering a wooded setting, large decks, and walkways, recreation room, and antiques. One honeymoon suite and one family suite with private baths. Four rooms with queen beds share two full baths. Excellent dining within walking distance.

Hosts: Gene & Barbara Morales
Rooms: 6 (2 PB; 4 SB) $55-80
Full Breakfast
Credit Cards: A, B, C
Notes: 2, 5, 8, 9, 10, 11, 12, 13, 14

Twain Harte's B&B

UKIAH

Oak Knoll B&B

858 Sanel Drive
Ukiah, CA, 95482
(707) 468-5646

A large redwood contemporary home with spectacular views of hills, valleys, vineyards, and sheep. Spacious deck. Lovely furnishings of Orientals and chandeliers. Two rooms with shared bath, adjacent sitting

NOTES: Credit cards accepted: A Master Card; B Visa; C American Express; D Discover Card; E Diners Club; F Other: 2 Personal checks accepted: 3 Lunch available: 4 Dinner available: 5 Open all year

room, TV and movies on a 40" screen in the family room. Full breakfast in the dining room or on the deck in summer. Hiking, golf, and boating are nearby.

Host: Shirley Wadley
Rooms: 2 (SB) $60
Full Breakfast
Credit Cards: No
Notes: 2, 5, 9, 10, 11, 12, 14

VALLEY FORD

The Inn at Valley Ford

Box 439
Valley Ford, CA, 94972
(707) 876-3182

The inn is a 120-year-old farmhouse furnished with antiques. Each room commemorates an author and includes a collection of his work. Valley Ford, located in the pastoral hills of western Sonoma County, is just minutes from the Pacific. Nearby are galleries, antiques, wineries, restaurants, bird watching, bicycling, and hiking.

Hosts: Nicholas Balashov & Sandra Nicholls
Rooms: 5 (SB) $68-78
Continental-plus Breakfast
Credit Cards: A, B
Notes: 2, 5, 7 (outside), 9, 10, 11, 12, 14

VENTURA

Bella Maggiore Inn

67 South California Street
Ventura, CA, 93001
(805) 652-0277

One hour north of Los Angeles and three blocks to the ocean promenade and beaches. Within easy walking distance to fine restaurants, shops, the old mission, and the fairgrounds. We have a garden coutyard with flowers and a fountain, a lobby with fireplace and piano, complimentary appetizers, full breakfast, and scenic trolley tour.

Host: Thomas J. Wood
Rooms: 3 (PB) $50-60
Full Breakfast
Credit Cards: A, B, C, D, E
Notes: 2, 5, 7, 8 (13 and over), 9, 10, 11, 12, 14

La Mer

411 Poli Street
Ventura, CA, 93001
(805) 643-3600

Nestled in a green hillside, this Cape Cod-style Victorian overlooks the heart of historic San Buena Ventura and the California coastline. Originally built in 1890, a historical landmark, La Mer has individually decorated, antique-filled rooms furnished to capture a specific European country, all with private baths and entrances, plus ocean view.

Host: Gisela Flender Baida
Rooms: 5 (PB) $100-155
Full Breakfast
Minimum stay weekends & holidays: 2
Credit Cards: A, B
Closed Christmas
Notes: 2, 7 (limited), 8 (over 13), 9, 10, 11, 12, 14

WEST COVINA

Hendrick Inn

2124 East Mercer Avenue
West Covina, CA, 91791
(810) 919-2125

This large, rambling house will give you a real taste of the California life-style with its gorgeous deck, swimming pool, Jacuzzi. Centrally located for visiting Disneyland, L.A., the mountains, and the desert. Forty-five minutes to LAX; 20 to Ontario Airport.

Hosts: Mary & George Hendrick
Rooms: 3 (SB) $40-45
Suite: 1 (PB) $50
Full Breakfast
Credit Cards: No
Notes: 2, 4 (with notice), 5, 7, 8 (5 and over), 9, 10, 11, 12

WESTPORT

Bowen's Pelican Lodge & Inn

38921 North Highway One
Westport, CA, 95488
(707) 964-5588

A Victorian western inn reminiscent of the 1890s. In a remote location with the sea in its front yard, the mountain in back, and miles of virtually untouched wilderness all around. The nearest town, Fort Bragg, is fifteen miles away. A place to get away from it all, hike secluded beaches, explore the hills, or just unwind. Full bar & restaurant, home cooking.

Host: Velma Bowen
Rooms: 6 (4 PB; 2 SB) $48.60-81
Continental Breakfast
Minimum stay holidays: 2
Credit Cards: A, B
Notes: 2, 3, 4, 5, 7, 9, 14

Howard Creek Ranch

DeHaven Valley Farm

39247 North Highway One
Westport, CA, 95488
(707) 961-1660

The inn, a Victorian farmhouse built in 1875, is located on 20 acres of meadows, hills, and streams, across from the Pacific Ocean. Guests enjoy various farm animals, exploring tide pools, and soaking in the hot tub. Restaurant serves delicious four-course dinners complemented by home-grown herbs and vegetables. The inn is ideally located to visit the gigantic redwoods twenty-five miles to the north or the artist colony of Mendocino twenty-five miles to the south.

Hosts: Jim & Kathy Tobin
Rooms: 8 (6 PB; 2 SB) $85-125
Full Breakfast
Credit Cards: A, B, C
Closed Jan.
Notes: 2, 4, 8, 9, 10, 11, 12

Howard Creek Ranch

Box 121
Westport, CA, 95488
(707) 964-6725

A historic 1867 farm on 20 acres, only 100 yards from the beach. A rural retreat adjoining wilderness. Suite and cabins; views of ocean, mountains, creek, or gardens; fireplace/wood stoves; period furnishings; wood-heated hot tub, sauna, pool; horseback riding nearby. Gift certificates available.

Hosts: Charles (Sunny) & Sally Grigg
Rooms: 6 (3 PB; 3 SB) $54-$91.80
Full Breakfast
Credit Cards: A, B
Notes: 2, 5, 7 (limited), 8 (reservations requested), 9, 11

WHITTIER

Coleen's California Casa

Box 9302
Whittier, CA, 90601
(213) 699-8427

Take your children to Disneyland, Knott's Berry Farm, and Universal Studios, then come back to a luxurious home. Bedrooms are decorator designed with elegant private baths, one with Jacuzzi tub. From the deck you can see L.A., Long Beach, and Catalina Island. Hosts will help you plan your tours, provide baby-sitting, and pick you up at the airport for a charge.

Host: Coleen Davis
Singles: 1 (PB) $45-55
Rooms: 4 (PB) $55-70
Full Breakfast
Minimum stay: 2; holidays: 3
Credit Cards: No
Notes: 2, 3, 4, 5, 7(conditional), 8, 9, 10, 11, 12, 14

WILLITS

The Doll House B&B

118 School Street
Willits, CA, 95490
(707) 459-4055

The Doll House B&B houses a collection of 600 dolls. Located within walking distance of the terminus of the Skunk Train and Northcoast Daylight. Restored Victorian with country elegance. Located on the scenic Redwood Highway, Willits adjoins the wine country, lakes, and resorts along the Russian River.

Host: Laura Le Clear
Rooms: 3 (1 PB; 2 SB) $68 + tax
Full Breakfast
Credit Cards: No
Notes: 2, 9, 10, 11

YOUNTVILLE

Oleander House

7433 St. Helena Highway
Yountville, CA, 94599
(707) 944-8315

Country French charm, located at the very entrance of the wine country. Spacious, high-ceiling rooms done in Laura Ashley fabric and wallpaper and antiques. Breakfast is served in the large dining room on the main floor. All rooms have fireplaces, private baths, and their own decks.

Hosts: The Packards
Rooms: 4 (PB) $105-135
Full Breakfast
Credit Cards: A, B
Notes: 2, 9, 10, 11, 12, 14

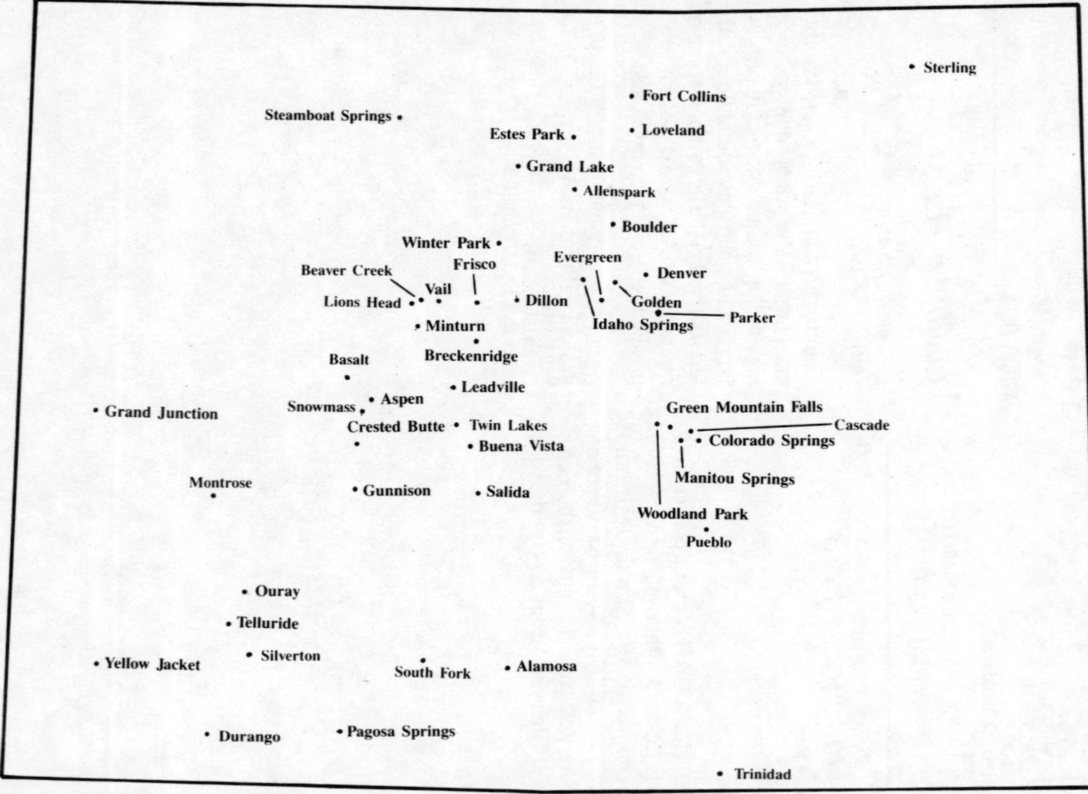
Sterling
Fort Collins
Steamboat Springs
Estes Park
Loveland
Grand Lake
Allenspark
Boulder
Winter Park
Evergreen
Frisco
Beaver Creek
Denver
Vail
Lions Head
Dillon
Golden
Parker
Idaho Springs
Minturn
Breckenridge
Basalt
Leadville
Aspen
Snowmass
Grand Junction
Green Mountain Falls
Cascade
Crested Butte
Twin Lakes
Colorado Springs
Buena Vista
Manitou Springs
Montrose
Gunnison
Salida
Woodland Park
Pueblo
Ouray
Telluride
Yellow Jacket
Silverton
South Fork
Alamosa
Durango
Pagosa Springs
Trinidad

COLORADO

Colorado

ALAMOSA

Cottonwood Inn B&B & Gallery

123 San Juan Avenue
Alamosa, CO, 81101
(719) 589-3882

Lovely turn-of-the-century Craftsman-style inn, decorated with antiques and local artwork. Near the Cumbres-Toltec Scenic Railway, Great Sand Dunes, wildlife refuges, Adams State College, cross-country skiing, llama trekking. Massages available. Delicious breakfasts featuring fresh-ground coffee, homemade baked goods, and fresh fruit. Complimentary wine in the evening.

Hosts: Julie Mordecai & George Sellman
Rooms: 5 (2 PB; 3 SB) $40-56
Full Breakfast
Credit Cards: A, B
Notes: 2, 5, 8, 9, 10, 11, 12, 14

ALLENSPARK

Allenspark Lodge

P.O. Box 247
Allenspark, CO, 80510
(303) 747-2552

A 1933 three-story, hand-hewn log lodge with a great room, game and reception room, hot tub, and the Wilderquest Room, with a selection of beverages and hors d'oeuvres. Fourteen rooms, some with private bath and deep bearclaw tubs. Horseback riding, hiking, galleries. Minutes from Rocky Mountain National Park.

Hosts: Mike & Becky Osmun
Rooms: 14 (5 PB; 9 SB) $28.95-69.95
Continental Breakfast
Credit Cards: A, B
Notes: 2, 3, 4, 5, 8, 9, 13, 14

ASPEN

Contemporary Lodge

B&B Rocky Mountains 42
P.O. Box 804
Colorado Springs, CO, 80901
(719) 630-3433

You will long remember this tastefully decorated 38-room contemporary lodge that has been made into a B&B. All doors enter from the spacious atrium/lounge. Each room has a queen bed and double fold-out, wet bar, refrigerator. Some balcony rooms have a Jacuzzi tub. Thirty-foot river-rock fireplace, apres ski wine and cheese, outdoor heated pool. Light buffet breakfast. $54-175, seasonal.

The Gingerbread House

B&B Colorado
P.O. Box 12206
Boulder, CO, 80303
(303) 494-4994

Located four blocks from Aspen Mountain and 2.5 blocks from the downtown mall, this little house has the perfect location for those without a car. After a day of skiing, hiking, or enjoying the music festival, you can soak in the indoor hot tub or relax on the deck. Two second-floor rooms with double beds share one bath. No smoking; resident dog. $55-65.

Little Red Ski Haus

118 East Cooper Street
Aspen, CO, 81611
(303) 925-3333

Charming 100-year-old Victorian three blocks from the center of town. No TV, but always interesting conversation. One could travel the world just sitting in our living room. The house is very popular with Australians. Exceptionally clean and friendly, especially suited to those traveling alone. Dinner is available on Wednesdays for $5.

Hosts: Marge Riley & Irene Zydek
Rooms: 16 (3 PB; 13 SB) $20-100
Full Breakfast winter; continental summer
Credit Cards: A, B
Closed April 10-May 31
Notes: 8, 9, 10, 11, 12, 13, 14

Little Red Ski Haus

Main Street

Bed & Breakfast Vail
P.O. Box 491
Vail, CO, 81658
(800) 748-2666

Located in downtown Aspen. All 22 rooms open to a center lounge. They have private baths, queen beds, wet bars, refrigerators, cable TV, and phones. On the premises are a heated pool, Jacuzzi, and parking lot. Continental breakfast and wine and cheese are served in the lounge daily. Smoking is allowed. $54-150 seasonal.

Mountain Lodge

B&B Rocky Mountains 83
P.O. Box 804
Colorado Springs, CO, 80901
(719) 630-3433

Enjoy exceptional quality and service at this 24-room B&B inn with beautifully appointed rooms. King suites with queen sleeper sofa and TV, wet bar, refrigerator, and private bath. Small queen bedrooms available. Within easy walking distance of the mall and four blocks from the gondola. Jacuzzi, telephones; balcony or deck on most rooms. Full breakfast during ski season, continental during other seasons. $40-140 seasonal.

Slice of Heaven

Bed & Breakfast Vail
P.O. Box 491
Vail, CO, 81658
(800) 748-2666

This host offers it all: hot tub, snowmobile rentals, snowmobile tours atop Aspen Mountain. Four guest rooms, one with private bath, full breakfast. Smoking is permitted. $120.

Snow Queen Victorian Lodge

124 East Cooper Street
Aspen, CO, 81611
(303) 925-8455; (303) 925-6971

The Snow Queen is a quaint family-operated Victorian ski lodge built in the 1880s. The charming parlor has a fireplace and color TV for guests. We have a variety of rooms with private baths, plus one kitchen unit. We are located in town, within walking distance of restaurants, shops, and the ski area. We also have a nice outdoor hot tub.

Hosts: Norma Dolle & Larry Ledingham
Rooms: 5 (PB) $65-135
Continental Breakfast
Credit Cards: A, B, C
Closed April 15 - May 15
Notes: 2, 8, 9, 10, 11, 12, 13, 14

What a View

Bed & Breakfast Vail
P.O. Box 491
Vail, CO, 81658
(800) 748-2666

Located within walking distance of downtown, your room offers plenty of privacy with a sunken Japanese tub. Continental breakfast; no smoking. $75.

BASALT

Altamira Ranch

B&B Colorado
P.O. Box 12206
Boulder, CO, 80303
(303) 494-4994

This contemporary, two-story brick home is located on a 167-acre working ranch. There is excellent cross-country skiing and hiking. The Roaring Fork River borders the ranch and offers great trout fishing and river sports. Your full breakfast may include fresh trout and raspberries. Two rooms on the second floor with double beds share a bath. Children and horses welcome; one resident dog. No smoking. $50-60.

BEAVER CREEK

In the Pines

Bed & Breakfast Vail
P.O. Box 491
Vail, CO, 81658
(800) 748-2666

Located five miles west of Beaver Creek, with cross-country skiing just outside the door. Wildlife is abundant. Two rooms with shared bath; continental breakfast; resident dog. No smoking. $65.

Whiskey Hill

Bed & Breakfast Vail
P.O. Box 491
Vail, CO, 81658
(800) 748-2666

Located one mile east of Beaver Creek and seven miles west of Vail, this home offers one queen room with private bath and continental breakfast. Private entrance, fireplace, TV. No smoking. $80.

BOULDER

The Bluebell

B&B Colorado
P.O. Box 12206
Boulder, CO, 80303
(303) 494-4994

This bright, airy contemporary home is furnished with antiques. The neighborhood is quiet but near the bus line, a bike path, mountain trails, and within walking distance of the CU stadium and the events center. The large bedroom with queen bed upstairs has a TV sitting room. Two smaller bedrooms are available for additional guests. Children are welcome; no smoking. $35-45.

Briar Rose B&B Inn

2151 Arapahoe
Boulder, CO, 80302
(303) 442-3007

Genuine comfort at Boulder's original guest house. The guest rooms are comfortable, with period furniture and flowers. Sit back and enjoy tea with homemade shortbread cookies while watching the antics at the bird feeder, or sit by a crackling fire.

Hosts: Linda McClure & Emily Hunter
Rooms: 11 (6 PB; 5 SB) $49-106.98
Continental Breakfast
Credit Cards: A, B, C, E
Notes: 2, 4, 5, 6, 7, 8, 9, 10, 11, 12

Creekside

B&B Colorado
P.O. Box 12206
Boulder, CO, 80303
(303) 494-4994

This is a lovely English-style cottage just below the CU campus and above Boulder Creek. There are two guest rooms, one with a double bed and the other with twins. Shared bath. Full breakfast includes freshly ground coffee and homemade breads. There is one resident cat. $35-40.

English Country Inn

B&B Rocky Mountains 159
P.O. Box 804
Colorado Springs, CO, 80901
(719) 630-3422

This beautiful English country-style inn, located in the central area of Boulder, offers genuine comfort and hospitality. Eleven rooms with private and shared baths, some with fireplaces and patios. Continental-plus breakfast. $68-98.

The Flatirons

B&B Colorado
P.O. Box 12206
Boulder, CO, 80303
(303) 494-4994

Situated just below the Flatirons, on a cul-de-sac bordering the greenbelt, this contemporary home offers a very quiet setting, yet is only minutes to downtown Boulder. There is a moss rock fireplace in the family room, which has a lovely view of the city. Continental breakfast, resident dog. Garden-level room with extra-long twin beds, full private bath; family room with fireplace, and private patio. $35-45.

Pearl Street Inn

1820 Pearl Street
Boulder, CO, 80302
(303) 444-5584

The Pearl Street Inn, Boulder's only downtown inn, blends the privacy and service of a country B&B with the amenities of a luxury hotel. The rooms, which encircle a garden courtyard, each have antique furniture, full bath, fireplace, and TV. The inn is located three blocks from a famous pedestrian mall and only a few minutes from the University of Colorado.

Host: Yossi Shem-Avi
Rooms: 7 (PB) $78-98
Continental Breakfast
Credit Cards: A, B, C
Notes: 2, 5, 6, 7, 8, 9, 10, 11, 12, 14

Pearl Street Inn

BRECKENRIDGE

Hummingbird House

B&B Rocky Mountains
P.O. Box 804

NOTES: Credit cards accepted: A Master Card; B Visa; C American Express; D Discover Card; E Diners Club; F Other: 2 Personal checks accepted: 3 Lunch available: 4 Dinner available: 5 Open all year

Colorado Springs, CO, 80901
(719) 630-3433

This cozy English Tudor house features two queen rooms with private baths. A third room with twins could be used for two children (shared bath). Large common sitting room with TV and stereo. One and one-half miles to base of ski area; transportation necessary. Private entrance, wood stove, wet bar, small refrigerator, hot tub. Golf, tennis, and bicycling nearby. Full breakfast. $45-69 seasonal.

Mountain Crest

Bed & Breakfast Vail
P.O. Box 491
Vail, CO, 81658
(800) 748-2666

This lovely contemporary cedar home sits in a large forest 1.5 miles south of Breckenridge Ski area. With your own private entrance, you have a large sitting room with pool table, color TV, and wood-burning stove. Your bedroom has a double bed and private bath. A full breakfast is served weekends; continental on weekdays. Backcountry cross-country skiing is available from the front door. No smoking. $80-85.

Victorian Log Home

B&B Rocky Mountains 86
P.O. Box 804
Colorado Springs, CO, 80901
(719) 630-3433

A three-story log Victorian home in the heart of the historic district. Master room with private bath has a queen bed and sitting room. A second room is available with a twin Victorian wicker daybed that makes two twins or one king bed. Within easy walking distance of downtown, one block from free ski shuttle. Apres ski refreshments, and cookies anytime. Complimentary pass to the health club with sauna and hot tub. Continental breakfast with fresh-baked goodies. No smoking; children twelve and over welcome. $77-97 seasonal.

Williams House B&B

303 North Main Street
P.O. Box 2454
Breckenridge, CO, 80424
(303) 453-2975

Step back in time as Breckenridge was just beginning and enjoy this charming restored historic home, circa 1885, decorated in antiques and lace curtains, complete with parlor and romantic fireplace. A hearty breakfast and homemade baked goods are served. An apres ski treat awaits guests daily. Within walking distance of shuttles, shops, restaurants, and bike path. The hosts will help make your stay special. Approved by Bed & Breakfast Innkeepers of Colorado.

Hosts: Diane Jaynes & Fred Kinat
Rooms: 4 (2 PB; 2 SB) $49-105
Full Breakfast
Credit Cards: C
Closed May & Oct.
Notes: 2, 9, 10, 11, 12, 13, 14

BUENA VISTA

Scenic Mountain Inn

B&B Rocky Mountains 3
P.O. Box 804
Colorado Springs, CO, 80901
(719) 630-3433

A small, cozy, quiet inn located in a scenic mountain area on the river. Catering to cross-country skiers in winter and wonderful for hiking and fishing in the summer. Stroll by the river bordering the property or enjoy the library with fireplace. Hostess will fix you a picnic lunch, and dogs can be accommodated in an outside run. Full breakfast; restricted smoking. $59.50-69.50.

CASCADE

Rocky Mt. Dream

B&B Rocky Mountains 167
P.O. Box 804
Colorado Springs, CO, 80901
(719) 630-3433

Awesome mountain setting in quaint Cascade. This 105-year-old Victorian has a breathtaking view with rooms, suites, and cozy cabins. Marvelous front porch and balcony, guest parlor, kitchen, and library. VCR and TV available. Full country breakfast in rooms; none in cabins. No smoking or pets; children ten and over in the inn, any age in cabins. Shared and private baths. $35-72.

COLORADO SPRINGS

Aspenglow

B&B Colorado
P.O. Box 12206
Boulder, CO, 80303
(303) 494-4994

At 9,500 feet, Aspenglow provides a casual and restful stay in some of the world's most beautiful scenery. Relax and enjoy the view or take in the historic Cripple Creek-Victor mining area. Enjoy a full breakfast around the winter fire, walk in the forest, and sit on the deck and watch the sun go down over the Continental Divide. Ground-level suite has two bedrooms, one with a queen and one with a single; private bath, living room, and breakfast area. $60.

Brownswalk

B&B Rocky Mountains
P.O. Box 804
Colorado Springs, CO, 80901
(719) 630-3422

This home features a three-room suite, private bath, and sitting room with TV. Fifteen miles from the Air Force Academy, twelve from the airport. Full breakfast. No pets, no smoking. $39.

Delft Haven

B&B Rocky Mountains
P.O. Box 804
Colorado Springs, CO, 80901
(719) 630-3433

This elegantly furnished home boasts a hillside view of Colorado Springs and the Garden of the Gods in the distance. One bedroom with canopy double bed, private bath. In an exclusive neighborhood just fifteen minutes south of city center, at the base of Cheyenna Mountain. Five minutes from Broadmoor Hotel and shops. There is a quiet balcony off the living room, large back deck in the garden, fireplace, TV, and piano. Full breakfast. No smoking, no pets; children six and over are welcome. $65.

1894 Victorian

P.O. Box 804
Colorado Springs, CO, 80901
(719) 630-3322

A quaint two-story yellow Victorian on the corner of a quiet residential area only one mile from downtown. Front porch for quietly sipping that cup of coffee or tea, private guest entrance, and private living room with stereo. On bus line. Resident friendly dog. Queen bed with private bath and Jacuzzi tub or double bed with semi-private bath available.

Host: Katie Robertson
Rooms: 2 (1 PB; 1 SB) $45-63
Full Breakfast
Credit Cards: A, B
Closed Nov.-April
Notes: 8 (8 and over), 9, 10, 11, 12, 14

El Shadmeir

B&B Rocky Mountains
P.O. Box 804
Colorado Springs, CO, 80901
(719) 630-3422

Delight in this wonderful, homey, passive solar home overlooking the Air Force Academy and Pikes Peak with Colorado Springs nestled at its base. Located twenty minutes north of the city, near the Black Forest in Monument. Hot tub, patio, barbecue, full breakfast with homebaked bread. No smoking, pets, or unmarried couples. Two queen rooms, each with private bath, and adjacent guest living room. $48.

Griffin's Hospitality House

4222 North Chestnut Street
Colorado Springs, CO, 80907
(719) 599-3035

The Griffins welcome singles, couples, and families. We are close to a park with tennis courts and on a bus line. Relax on our deck or in our spacious family room. Pikes Peak is right out the back door. Guests are encouraged to stay for at least three days, as there are so many sights to see. Extended-stay discounts available. Places to visit include the Air Force Academy, United States Olympic Training Center, Garden of the Gods, and more.

Hosts: Diane & John Griffin
Rooms: 3 (SB) $40
Full Breakfast
Minimum stay: 2
Credit Cards: No
Notes: 2, 5, 8, 9, 10, 11, 12, 13, 14

Holden House — 1902 B&B Inn

1102 West Pikes Peak Avenue
Colorado Springs, CO, 80904
(719) 471-3980

Storybook Victorian filled with antiques and heirlooms. Near historic district and central to the Pikes Peak area. Guest rooms boast quilts, down pillows, and private baths. Enjoy the parlor, living room with fireplace, or veranda with mountain views. Honeymoon suite with "tub for two"! Complimentary refreshments. Discount for two or more nights. A romantic's delight and business traveler's "Home Away From Home." Friendly resident cat "Mingtoy." BBIC approved.

Hosts: Sallie & Welling Clark
Rooms: 3 (PB) $57-65
Suites: 2 (PB) $75-85
Full Gourmet Breakfast
Minimum stay holidays & special events: 2-3
Credit Cards: A, B, C, D
Notes: 2, 5, 9, 10, 11, 12, 13, 14

Holden House--1902 B&B Inn

Tudor Manor

B&B Colorado
P.O. Box 12206
Boulder, CO, 80303
(303) 494-4994

This ivy-covered English Tudor home is located in the historic district and offers a unique blend of privacy and quiet. Each evening guests are served Colorado mineral water and fresh fruit. Complimentary wine and cheese are available upon request. Breakfast specialties include fresh baked bread and homemade preserves served in the cozy dining room or on the patio. Four guest rooms share two baths. Two rooms have twin beds, one has a double, and one a queen. Two of the rooms have sun decks. No smoking. $59-79.

CRESTED BUTTE

Purple Mountain Lodge

Box 897
Crested Butte, CO, 81224
(303) 349-5888

Our guests often enjoy sharing their adventures and discussing plans in the living room by a fire in the massive stone fireplace. If conversation slows, cable TV is available. Our spa, in the sun room, offers welcome relief to tired muscles. Crested Butte is located in a high (8,885 feet) open valley, surrounded by the Elk Mountains. It has many trails and roads to explore by foot, mountain bike, horseback, or four-wheel drive automobile. Nearby mountain lakes and streams provide canoeing, kayaking, rafting, and fishing.

Hosts: Walter & Sherron Green
Rooms: 7 (SB) $35-55
Full breakfast in ski season; continental in summer
Credit Cards: A, B
Closed April, May, Oct. & Nov.
Notes: 2, 7 (restricted), 8, 9, 10, 12, 13, 14

DENVER

Castle Marne

1572 Race Street
Denver, CO, 80206
(303) 331-0621; (800) 92-MARNE

Come fall under the spell of one of Denver's grandest historic mansions. Built in 1889, the Marne is on both the local and national historic registers. Your stay is a unique experience in pampered luxury. Minutes from the finest cultural, shopping, sightseeing attractions and the Convention Center. Twelve minutes from Stapleton International Airport.

Hosts: The Peiker Family
Rooms: 9 (PB) $75-145
Full Breakfast
Credit Cards: A, B, C
Notes: 2, 5, 9, 10, 11, 12, 14

Ferguson Manor

B&B Rocky Mountains 160
P.O. Box 804
Colorado Springs, CO, 80901
(719) 630-3433

An inn close to downtown, the capitol, Botanical Gardens, Denver University, and wonderful restaurants and shops. Bicycle available; wonderful jogging area. Four bedrooms, two suites available; continental-plus breakfast. Children are welcome; no pets, no smoking. $65-150.

The Gourmet

B&B Colorado
P.O. Box 12206
Boulder, CO, 80303
(303) 494-4994

This large English Tudor home in Lakewood is located on the quiet west side of Denver, yet is less than a fifteen-minute drive to downtown and historic Larimer Square. The home has an unusual antique collection and a thriving greenhouse. Your hostess serves a full gourmet breakfast. The first-floor room has a king bed and private bath. The second-floor room has a double brass bed and private bath. No pets, no smoking. $40-45.

Queen Anne Inn

2147 Tremont Place
Denver, CO, 80205
(303) 296-6666

Award-winning 1879 Victorian in downtown historic district. The luxurious, designer-quality surroundings and upscale amenities are among the most elegant anywhere. Already named "Best B&B in Town" and "Colorado Company of the Year." Listed by several editors as one of "America's Top Ten." Horse-drawn carriage rides, museums, art galleries, shopping, restaurants, cultural events, historic districts, lakes, streams, bike paths, and parks are available.

Hosts: Ann & Chuck Hillestad
Rooms: 10 (PB) $74-119 + tax
Continental-plus Breakfast
Credit Cards: A, B, C
Notes: 2, 4 (with advance notice), 5, 9, 10, 11, 12, 14

Victoria Oaks Inn

1575 Race Street
Denver, CO, 80206
(303) 355-1818

The warmth and hospitality of Victoria Oaks Inn is apparent the moment you enter this historic restored 1896 mansion. Elegant original oak woodwork, tile fireplaces, and dramatic hanging staircase replete with ornate brass chandelier set the mood for a delightful visit.

Hosts: Clyde & Ric
Rooms: 9 (1 PB; 8 SB) $49-79
Continental Breakfast
Credit Cards: A, B, C, E, F
Notes: 2, 5, 6, 7, 8, 9, 10, 11, 12, 14

The Walter House

B&B Rocky Mountains
P.O. Box 804
Colorado Springs, CO, 80901
(719) 630-3422

This home was built by Colorado pioneers in 1888. Lovely commons area and formal private garden. Three unique rooms on the second floor plus a penthouse suite available in the summer. Within walking distance of restaurants, the Denver Zoo, Natural History Museum, golf courses, hospitals. Continental breakfast with homebaked goodies. No pets, no smoking, children ten and over welcome. $45-50.

Zel's Soda Bar

B&B Colorado
P.O. Box 12206
Boulder, CO, 80303
(303) 494-4994

A lovely tri-level ranch home in Englewood that boasts a full soda fountain. The large patio is a wonderful place to enjoy the full country breakfast on spring mornings. The location is ideal for those attending meetings in the Denver Tech area. Two rooms (one with twins, one with a double bed), two private baths, TV, resident singing canary. No pets; children welcome; no smoking. $35-40.

DILLON

Continental Divide Overlook

B&B Rocky Mountains 133
P.O. Box 804
Colorado Springs, CO, 80901
(719) 630-3433

A wonderful log lodge in a secluded 37-acre alpine location overlooking the continental divide. Located close to various summer and winter activities, the lodge has four bedrooms that share two baths. A continental breakfast is served. No smoking; children five and over are welcome. $40-80.

DURANGO

Country Estate

B&B Rocky Mountains 44
P.O. Box 804
Colorado Springs, CO, 80901
(719) 630-3422

Homestead in the early 1900s by Swedish immigrants, this ranch evolved into a luxurious, European estate. The main house has four rooms with a view of the mountains, lake, and grazing herds of sheep. Not another house in sight. A cabin overlooking the lake has three rooms. Located fifteen minutes from Durango, close to Mesa Verde and the San Juan Mountains. Full breakfast. Available May 1-October 15. $70-135.

Gable House

B&B Rocky Mountains
P.O. Box 804
Colorado Springs, CO, 80901
(719) 630-3433

A wonderful spot for families. This large three-story Queen Anne Victorian home has spacious rooms, antique furnishings, double and single rooms that share two baths. Located near the Durango-Silverton Narrow Gauge Train and within walking distance of downtown restaurants and shops. No pets; children welcome. Open May to September. $60.

Penny's Place

B&B Rocky Mountains
P.O. Box 804
Colorado Springs, CO, 80901
(719) 630-3433

A remodeled Cape Cod house with a great view, located in a farmland area. Large main bedroom with king bed, private bath, and kitchenette. Two other rooms share a bath. Hot tub, pond, and stream on 26 acres. TV in room, crib and high chair available. No smoking inside the house. $40-50.

ESTES PARK

Emerald Manor

441 Chiquita Lane
P.O. Box 3592
Estes Park, CO, 80517
(303) 586-8050

Our elegant estate home is located in the Rocky Mountains, within easy walking distance of downtown Estes Park. The home is approximately 8,000 square feet, with indoor pool and sauna, game room with pool table. We serve full gourmet breakfast and look forward to meeting all our guests.

Hosts: Reggie & Moira Fowler
Rooms: 5 (S3B) $55-65
Full Breakfast
Credit Cards: For deposit only
Notes: 2, 5, 8 (over 15), 9, 10, 11, 12, 13

Rocky Pines B&B

B&B Colorado
P.O. Box 12206
Boulder, CO, 80303
(303) 494-4994

A contemporary mountain home nestled on 4.5 acres of rock outcroppings, ponderosa, and fir. Ideally situated within two miles of excellent hiking in Rocky Mountain National Park. Hearty full breakfasts are served on the deck. Your hosts are happy to provide trail lunches for hikers at no additional charge. There is one double room and one twin with a shared bath on the first floor. Children are welcome, no smoking, no pets; one resident dog. $35-45.

Turn of the Century Home

B&B Rocky Mountains 91
P.O. Box 804
Colorado Springs, CO, 80901
(719) 630-3433

This home has been completely redecorated and furnished with antiques and quilts to make you feel at home. There is also a log cabin and cottage in the back of the property, with kitchen and dining room. Your host is a chef, and will provide private gourmet dinners by prior arrangement. Breakfast is full. No pets or smoking; children twelve or older in the inn. $55-85.

Wanek's Lodge at Estes

Box 898
Estes Park, CO, 80517
(303) 586-5851

A modern mountain inn on a ponderosa-pine-covered hillside just a few miles from Rocky Mountain National Park. There is a resident cat, clean, cozy rooms, fireplace, plants, beautiful vistas from picture windows. Hosts are former teachers and very much interested in the environment.

Hosts: Jim & Pat Wanek
Rooms: 3 (SB) $47-52.50
Continental Breakfast
Credit Cards: No
Notes: 2, 4 (weekends), 5, 8 (over 10), 9, 10, 11, 12, 13

EVERGREEN

Hide-Away Inn

B&B Rocky Mountains 136
P.O. Box 804
Colorado Springs, CO, 80901
(719) 630-3433

Drive 45 minutes west of Denver and enjoy this lovely country setting. Five rooms share two baths and two common areas, one with a fireplace. Second-floor patio for outside breakfasts in nice weather. Two resident and one outside dog. A full breakfast is served. $45-55.

FORT COLLINS

Country Charm

B&B Rocky Mountains 138
P.O. Box 804
Colorado Springs, CO, 80901
(719) 630-3433

Lovely country home near Colorado State University with four guest rooms with shared bath, heirloom furniture, and collectibles from around the world. Large friendly dog, two cats, and ducks on premises. Sun porch on the second floor offers a sitting area with TV and large selection of books. The living room offers a piano, cable TV, and VCR. Full breakfast, restricted smoking. Children and small pets are welcome. $34.

FRISCO

Finn Inn

B&B Rocky Mountains
P.O. Box 804
Colorado Springs, CO, 80901
(719) 630-3433

This Frisco country home welcomes you with a beautiful mountain view from the large, open living room and wraparound deck. The rooms can be used as a suite that sleeps six, or as two separate rooms with semi-private bath. A third bedroom upstairs has a double bed, a twin, and a private half-bath. Hot tub on outside deck, antique pump organ, large moss rock fireplace. Breakfast is full. $57-66 seasonal.

Romantic Summit County Inn

B&B Rocky Mountains 109
P.O. Box 804
Colorado Springs, CO, 80901
(719) 630-3433

Step into comfort and enjoy this three-story, twelve-room inn in the heart of Summit County. Private or shared baths, double or queen beds. Hot tub, steam room, common area with TV and games, wood-burning stove, continental buffet breakfast. Located on the free shuttle route. $59-83 seasonal.

Willow Creek

Bed & Breakfast Vail
P.O. Box 491
Vail, CO, 81658
(800) 748-2666

Delightful summer breakfasts are served by the backyard creek. On the bike path and free local shuttle, the home is easily accessible to all areas of Summit County. Many antiques, Jacuzzi bath. One room with a queen and twin, private bath. $75.

GOLDEN

The Dove Inn

711 14th Street
Golden, CO, 80401
(303) 278-2209

Charming Victorian inn located in the foothills of west Denver, yet in the small-town atmosphere of Golden. Close to Coors tours, Rocky Mountain National Park; one hour to ski areas. No unmarried couples, please.

Hosts: Sue & Guy Beals
Rooms: 6 (4 PB; 2 SB) $41-59
Full Breakfast
Credit Cards: A, B, C, E
Notes: 2, 5, 8, 9, 10, 11, 12, 13, 14

GRAND JUNCTION

Spectacular Views

B&B Rocky Mountains 87
P.O. Box 804
Colorado Springs, CO, 80901
(719) 630-3433

Relax on the porch, with its spectacular views of Mount Garfield, Lincoln, and the Grand Mesa, as well as the beautiful orchards. Private entrance, king room upstairs, living area, bedroom with twin beds, full bath, and kitchen downstairs. Dinner is available. A full gourmet breakfast is served. No pets; children and smokers welcome. $50.

Turn of the Century Grace

B&B Rocky Mountains 89
P.O. Box 804
Colorado Springs, CO, 80901
(719) 630-3433

This charming four-bedroom B&B is nestled in the heart of Grand Junction. Each room has a queen bed; some rooms share a bath. There is a large front porch, and the house is near rafting, skiing, gold prospecting, hunting, and fishing. Airport or Amtrak pickup is available. Picnic hampers and other meals are available at an additional charge; full breakfast, cider, and refreshments in the evening. Children and smokers allowed; no pets. $38-42.

GRAND LAKE

Onahu Lodge

B&B Rocky Mountains
P.O. Box 804
Colorado Springs, CO, 80901
(719) 630-3433

This home is made of hand-hewn logs and has a spectacular view of Rocky Mountain National Park land. Watch elk at the salt lick from your patio overlooking the river. Two bedrooms, one with a double bed and the other with twins. Private and shared baths. There are nearby stables for horseback riding, excellent hiking, fishing, boating on the lake; golf and tennis are nearby. Horses may be boarded. Breakfast is continental-plus. No smoking; children over five are welcome. $45-55.

GREEN MOUNTAIN FALLS

Outlook Lodge

Box 5
Green Mt. Falls, CO, 80819
(719) 684-2303

This house was originally the parsonage for The Little Church in the Wildwood. Restored in 1989 to celebrate its centennial. Near Colorado Springs, with many major attractions within five miles. Enjoy hiking, horseback riding, swimming, tennis, fishing, sightseeing — or relax on our large veranda. Outlook Lodge provides nostalgia with German-American atmosphere.

Hosts: Tom & Ilka Fremin
Rooms: 9 (6 PB; 3 SB) $40-65
Full Gourmet Breakfast
Credit Cards: A, B
Notes: 2, 5, 8, 9, 10, 11, 12, 13(XC), 14

GUNNISON

Mary Lawrence Inn

601 North Taylor Street
Gunnison, CO, 81230
(303) 641-3343

Make our Victorian home the center of your excursions through Gunnison Country. The mountains, rivers, and lakes are extraordinary. Golf, swimming, rafting are accessible. Our inn is furnished with antiques and collectibles. Breakfasts are bountiful and imaginative. Special event weekends: fly fishing, crafts, mystery. Great ski package offered for Crested Butte skiing.

Hosts: Tom & Les Bushman
Rooms: 4 (2 PB; 2 SB) $48-55
Suite: (PB) $68
Full Breakfast
Credit Cards: A, B, D
Notes: 2, 5, 8, 10, 11, 12, 13, 14

Mary Lawrence Inn

IDAHO SPRINGS

St. Mary's Glacier B&B

B&B Colorado
P.O. Box 12206
Boulder, CO, 80303
(303) 494-4994

From the deck of this mountain retreat you will enjoy majestic views of the Continental Divide, a waterfall, and a lake. In the evening, return to your suite to be greeted by a teddy bear nestled in a down comforter on a queen brass bed. Relax in a private hot tub surrounded by hearts and bears, or enjoy a roaring fire in a wood-burning stove in the living room. Hike the glacier or enjoy the view from the deck with a telescope. Complimentary sherry; full breakfast. One bedroom suite with private bath and hot tub. Children over twelve welcome. No smoking. $48.

LAKE CITY

El Tesoro Escondido

B&B Rocky Mountains
P.O. Box 804
Colorado Springs, CO, 80901
(719) 630-3433

A unique, custom-designed adobe home with two bedrooms. Located on a hillside overlooking the quaint mining town of Lake City. The rooms share a full bath and half-bath. Both rooms have fireplaces; one has a double bed, the other twin bunk beds. There is a hot tub in the solarium; hiking and fishing are within walking distance. Breakfast is gourmet continental to full. No smoking or pets; children ten and over are welcome. $42-47.

The Moss Rose B&B

P.O. Box 910
Lake City, CO, 81235
(303) 366-4069

A remote, secluded retreat nestled in a high mountain valley at 9,700 feet. Fishing, hunting, biking, Jeeping, and just plain relaxing. Great breakfasts, queen beds, and a spectacular mountain setting.

Hosts: Dan & Joan Moss
Rooms: 3 (1 PB; 2 SB) $45-55
Full Breakfast
Credit Cards: A, B
Open June 1-Nov. 1
Notes: 2, 3, 4, 8, 9

LEADVILLE

Historic Delaware Hotel

700 Harrison Avenue
Leadville, CO, 80461
(719) 486-1418; (800) 748-2004

The Delaware Hotel was built in 1886. Each of the 36 rooms and suites features antique furnishing. All rooms have private baths and TV. On the premises we have a deli, ice cream parlor, old-time photo shop, gift shop, and sport and ski shop. Group rates available.

Rooms: 36 (PB) From $35
Continental Breakfast
Credit Cards: A, B, C, E
Notes: 2, 5, 6, 7, 8, 9, 11, 12, 13, 14

LIONS HEAD

Bird's Nest

Bed & Breakfast Vail
P.O. Box 491
Vail, CO, 81658
(800) 748-2666

This completely private guest accommodation is great for two traveling couples, a family of four, or those who like privacy. A fully stocked kitchen, two bedrooms, one bath, living room with fireplace, and outdoor Jacuzzi. A hearty breakfast including fresh-baked goodies and smoked meats from the family smokehouse is served in your quarters. Smoking is permitted. $150-225.

Guesthouse

Bed & Breakfast Vail
P.O. Box 491
Vail, CO, 81658
(800) 748-2666

This contemporary skylit home is in a great location for privacy. Four rooms with private baths, plus one suite with private entrance, sitting room with fireplace, and bath. European continental breakfast. $75-180.

LOVELAND

The Lovelander B&B

217 West Fourth Street
Loveland, CO, 80537
(303) 669-0798

Nestled against the Rocky Mountain foothills minutes from Rocky Mountain National Park, the Lovelander is a rambling Victorian-style inn. Its beauty and elegance are characteristic of the turn of the century, when the home was built. Near restaurants, shops, museums, and art galleries, the Lovelander is a haven for business and recreational travelers and romantics.

Hosts: Marilyn & Bob Wiltgen
Rooms: 9 (PB) $54-98
Full Breakfast
Credit Cards: A, B, C, E
Notes: 2, 5, 8 (over 10), 9, 10, 11, 12, 14

MANITOU SPRINGS

Historic Victorian Hotel

B&B Rocky Mountains 29
P.O. Box 804
Colorado Springs, CO, 80901
(719) 630-3422

Feel right at home in this three-story Queen Anne Victorian, one of the original seven hotels in town. Within walking distance of antique stores, restaurants, and shops. Nine rooms, full breakfast. Children ten and over are welcome. $45-70.

Manitou Inn & Cottages

B&B Rocky Mountains 163
P.O. Box 804
Colorado Springs, CO, 80901
(719) 630-3422

Enjoy Victorian elegance, walk to the town square and the shops, or visit the many attractions in the Pikes Peak region. Guest rooms at the inn include a lovely suite as well as a second room, each with queen bed and private bath. Afternoon tea or wine and dessert are served; full gourmet breakfast for those in the main house. No smoking. $65-90.

Onaledge B&B Inn

336 El Paso Blvd.
Manitou Springs, CO, 80829
(719) 685-4265

Built on a hill overlooking Manitou Springs, this 1912 rock English Tudor home speaks of romance. At the foot of Pikes Peak; near all attractions. Lovely honeymoon suite, gardens, and patios. Although within walking distance of the Garden of the Gods and downtown Manitou, Onaledge retains the seclusion of an English country inn.

Hosts: Mel & Shirley Podell
Rooms: 4 (PB) $70-90
Full Breakfast
Credit Cards: A, B, C, D
Notes: 2, 5, 7 (limited), 8 (limited), 9, 10, 11, 12, 13, 14

Small Victorian Castle

B&B Rocky Mountains 127
P.O. Box 804
Colorado Springs, CO, 80901
(719) 630-3433

This spectacular castle structure sits on a 20-acre estate overlooking the historic district, with commanding views of the Garden of the Gods, Iron and Red Mountains, and area attractions in Colorado Springs. Third-floor suite features two rooms with queen beds (one waterbed), private bath, telephone, TV, wet bar, and refrigerator. Continental breakfast. No smoking or pets; children four and over welcome. $110.

MINTURN

Eagle River Inn

145 North Main Street
Box 100
Minturn, CO, 81645
(303) 827-5761; (800) 344-1750

Lovely twelve-room inn decorated in the Southwestern style. All guest rooms have private baths. Enjoy a gourmet continental breakfast in our sunny breakfast room; in the evenings, relax in front of the fireplace while you enjoy wine, cheese, and classical music, or enjoy our outdoor hot tub overlooking the Eagle River. Located seven miles from the Vail ski resort.

Hosts: Beverly Rude and Richard Galloway
Rooms: 12 (PB) $69-120
Continental Breakfast
Minimum stay holidays: 2
Credit Cards: A, B, C
Closed May and October
Notes: 2, 8 (over 12), 9, 10, 11, 12, 13, 14

MONTROSE

Turn of the Century Inn

B&B Rocky Mountains 121
P.O. Box 804
Colorado Springs, CO, 80901
(719) 630-3433

Two bedrooms on the second floor of this lovely home share a bath. Enjoy comfort and relaxation on the old-fashioned front porch, walk to restaurants and shops. There is a large sitting room with TV, books, and games on the third floor. Picnic hampers are available on request, and coffee and cold drinks are available during the day. A hearty continental buffet breakfast is served. No smoking; no pets. $40.

OURAY

St. Elmo Hotel

426 Main Street
P.O. Box 667
Ouray, CO, 81427
(303) 325-4951

Listed in the National Registry of Historical Buildings, established in 1898 as a miners' hotel, and now fully renovated with stained glass, antiques, polished wood and brass trim throughout. An outdoor hot tub and an aspen-lined sauna are available for guests, as well as a cozy parlor and a breakfast room.

Hosts: Sandy & Dan Lingenfelter
Rooms: 9 (PB) $48-75
Full Breakfast
Credit Cards: A, B
Notes: 2, 3, 4, 5, 7 (restricted), 9, 10, 11, 13 (XC), 14

PAGOSA SPRINGS

Davidson's Country Inn B&B

Box 87
Pagosa Springs, CO, 81147
(303) 264-5863

A three-story log inn decorated in antiques and family heirlooms, located on a 32-acre ranch on Highway 160 in the foothills of the Rocky Mountains. Game room, outdoor activities, children's corner. Full country breakfast. Hiking, stream and lake fishing, rafting, skiing, and beautiful scenic drives are all nearby.

Hosts: Gilbert & Evelyn Davidson
Rooms: 9 (PB and SB) $43.50-55
Full Breakfast
Credit Cards: A, B
Notes: 2, 5, 6, 8, 10, 12, 13, 14

PAONIA

Agape Inn

B&B Colorado
P.O. Box 12206
Boulder, CO, 80303
(303) 494-4994

This inn incorporates turn-of-the-century charm in a beautiful setting on the north fork of the Gunnison River. Excellent stream and lake fishing; deer and elk hunting in the area. Cross-country skiing and snowmobiling are close by. Enjoy day trips to the Black Canyon of the Gunnison, Grand Mesa, historic Marble, Silverton, and Tulluride. Full country breakfast. Three second-floor rooms share 2.5 baths. No pets; no smoking; no alcoholic beverages. $30-45.

PARKER

Noel House B&B

B&B Colorado
P.O. Box 12206
Boulder, CO, 80303
(303) 494-4994

This large c. 1910 home boasts antique-filled rooms and heirloom quilts. It is located on the original Colorado Springs to Denver stagecoach line, and still maintains its Old West atmosphere. Full country breakfast. On weekends, a champagne breakfast is featured. Afternoon tea and wine are available, as well as evening dessert. Four rooms share two full baths; hot tub. No children, no pets, restricted smoking. $45.

PUEBLO

Abriendo Inn

300 West Abriendo Avenue
Pueblo, CO, 81004
(719) 544-2703

A classic B&B on the National Register of Historic Places, located in the heart of Pueblo and one mile off the interstate. Enjoy the comfort, style, and luxury of the past in rooms delightfully decorated with antiques, crocheted bedspreads, brass and four-poster beds. Restaurants, shops, galleries, golf, tennis, and other attractions are all within five minutes of the inn.

Host: Kerrelyn Trent
Rooms: 7 (5 PB; 2 SB) $48-85
Full Breakfast
Credit Cards: A, B, C, E
Notes: 2, 5, 7 (restricted), 8 (over 7), 9, 10, 11, 12, 13, 14

SALIDA

Historic Register Inn

B&B Rocky Mountains 7
P.O. Box 804
Colorado Springs, CO, 80901
(719) 630-3433

This lovely inn with Victorian furnishings was recently restored and boasts a 100-year-old library lounge. Excellent river rafting is available in the summer, hot springs, fishing on the Arkansas River, boating, golf, and good skiing. Rooms and dorm available. A full breakfast is served in the rooms; continental in the dorm. $39-49.

SILVERTON

Christopher House B&B

821 Empire Street
P.O. Box 241
Silverton, CO, 81433
(303) 387-5857 (June-Sept.); (904) 567-7549 (Oct.-May)

Traditional Irish B&B hospitality amid the scenic splendor of the Rocky Mountains. The charming 1894 Victorian home features original woodwork and fireplace, sturdy antiques. Comfortable carpeted rooms with mountain view and fresh flowers. Within walking distance of shops, restaurants, riding stable, stage coach, and narrow-gauge train station. Reasonable rates.

Hosts: Eileen & Howard Swonger
Rooms: 3 (SB) $39
Full Breakfast
Credit Cards: No
Closed Sept. 16-May 30
Notes: 2, 8, 9, 10, 14

SNOWMASS

C.C.'s

Bed & Breakfast Vail
P.O. Box 491
Vail, CO, 81658
(800) 748-2666

Outside hot tub to warm you after a long day on the slopes. Five minutes to Snowmass Mountain and fifteen to downtown Aspen. Located on bus route. Two rooms with private bath; full or continental breakfast. Two dogs in residence; no smoking. $65.

SOUTH FORK

Spruce Retreat

B&B Rocky Mountains 166
P.O. Box 804
Colorado Springs, CO, 80901
(719) 630-3433

This unique ski lodge was built from local spruce in 1926. The South Fork area has activities for all seasons: sleigh rides, ice skating, river rafting, fishing, hunting, Jeep tours, and much more. This lodge features eight rooms with shared baths, a hot tub, fireplace, game room. Sack lunches are available. In winter a full breakfast is served; continental in summer. $26-35. Ask about winter ski packages.

STEAMBOAT SPRINGS

Aspen Tree Cottage

B&B Colorado
P.O. Box 12206
Boulder, CO, 80303
(303) 494-4994

Located on a spacious corner lot in Old Steamboat, Aspen Tree is a small, sunny, bright residence that has been recently renovated. Antiques, a wood-burning stove, and magnificent breakfasts. The shuttle line is right outside, and it's only a ten-minute walk to town or wilderness trails. One room with a queen bed and adjacent private bath. No smoking. $35-50.

Cozy European Inn

B&B Rocky Mountains 154
P.O. Box 804
Colorado Springs, CO, 80901
(719) 630-3422

This European-style inn offers twenty-two rooms in the center of Steamboat Springs, within walking distance of many shops and restaurants. Each room shares a bath. Two resident cats. Large indoor hot tub, ski lockers and free bus pass to ski area and town. Full breakfast. Children welcome; pets with prior approval. $55-80.

Homestead Lodge

B&B Rocky Mountains 105
P.O. Box 804
Colorado Springs, CO, 80901
(719) 630-3422

Enjoy this rustic log lodge built of native spruce and furnished with antiques. This ranch sits on 400 acres adjacent to national forest. Three rooms, shared baths. Dogs in residence. Cabins with two bedrooms, bath, and living area are also available. Full breakfast and dinner are included in the rate. $110.

Inn Town

Bed & Breakfast Vail
P.O. Box 491
Vail, CO, 81658
(800) 748-2666

Situated in the heart of downtown, with restaurants, shops, hot mineral springs within walking distance. Each of 25 rooms has a private bath, TV, phone, and HBO. No charge for children. Continental breakfast. $57-119.

Iris House

B&B Colorado
P.O. Box 12206
Boulder, CO, 80303
(303) 494-4994

An artist's home, this rugged post-and-beam house is set in an aspen grove overlooking Steamboat and the Yampa Valley. It is furnished with heirlooms, art, lots of books, and comfortable furniture. The bath features an unusual shower and Japanese soaking tub. Full breakfast is served family style in the kitchen-great room or on the outside deck. Hiking trails, cross-country and downhill skiing nearby. One large room with a four-poster queen bed and adjacent private bath. No smoking. $65-85.

Old Town Elegance

B&B Rocky Mountains 155
P.O. Box 804
Colorado Springs, CO, 80901
(719) 630-3422

This comfortable B&B is centrally located downtown, two miles from the ski resort. Outside decks overlook the colorful gardens and quaint old town. Four guest rooms with private bath. Full breakfast. No children, no smoking. $50-70.

Sunny Cottage Inn

B&B Rocky Mountains 97
P.O. Box 804
Colorado Springs, CO, 80901
(719) 630-3422

This small family residence is located in old town, five blocks from downtown on the shuttle line to the ski area. One cozy room with queen bed and private bath. Full breakfast. No smoking. $40-50.

STERLING

The Crest House B&B

516 South Division Avenue
Sterling, CO, 80751
(303) 522-3753

This 1912 Victorian home must be seen to be appreciated. Experience small-town friendliness in an atmosphere of hand-beveled glass, early 1900 fixtures, and carved oak and cherry. Visit a bygone era in Centennial Country. Meet our multilingual green Amazon parrot, Gus. Close to downtown.

Hosts: Julius & Barbara Rico
Rooms: 5 (1 PB; 4 S2B) $45-65
Full Breakfast

NOTES: Credit cards accepted: A Master Card; B Visa; C American Express; D Discover Card; E Diners Club; F Other: 2 Personal checks accepted: 3 Lunch available: 4 Dinner available: 5 Open all year

Credit Cards: A, B
Notes: 2, 5, 6 (limited), 7 (limited), 8 (limited), 9, 10, 11, 12

TELLURIDE

Bear Creek B&B

221 East Colorado
P.O. Box 1797
Telluride, CO, 81435
(303) 728-6681

A contemporary B&B offering affordable charm and gracious service. Located on Main Street, providing easy access to dining, shopping, ski slopes, nordic track, ice skating, and ski shuttles. Rooms have queen beds, phones, private baths, cable and HBO, and daily maid service. Enjoy the large sauna and steam room, fireplace, and roof deck.

Hosts: Ralph & Norma Packard
Rooms: 8 (PB) $45-110
Full Breakfast
Credit Cards: A, B, C
Closed April 15-May 21 & Oct. 25-Nov. 20
Notes: 2, 8 (3 and over), 9, 10, 11, 12, 13, 14

French Style B&B

B&B Rocky Mountains 119
P.O. Box 804
Colorado Springs, CO, 80901
(719) 630-3433

A romantic inn, filled with antiques and reproductions, with twelve rooms, all with private balconies and views. Each room has separate vanity with bath/shower areas. Free shuttle to ski area, Jacuzzi and steam room, game room, pool table, mountain bikes, cable TV and stereo in all rooms. Full breakfast. No pets; children welcome. $100-235.

San Sophia

330 West Pacific Avenue
P.O. Box 1825
Telluride, CO, 81435
(800) 537-4781

Elegant, luxurious accommodations for the discriminating traveler. Indoor and outdoor dining areas, huge bathtubs for two, brass beds, handmade quilts, dramatic views of the surrounding 13,000-foot mountains. Common areas include an observatory, library, and gazebo with Jacuzzi. ". . . one of the most luxurious and romantic inns in America"—*Inside America.* Complimentary wine, beer, soft drinks, and cheese each afternoon.

Hosts: Dianne & Gary Eschman
Rooms: 16 (PB) $80-175
Full Breakfast
Credit Cards: A, B, C
Closed April 8-May 4 & Oct. 25-Nov. 24
Notes: 2, 8 (10 and over), 9, 10, 11, 12, 13, 14

TRINIDAD

My Wild Dutch Rose

B&B Colorado
P.O. Box 12206
Boulder, CO, 80303
(303) 494-4994

Make Trinidad a stop on your trip to and from New Mexico, or make it your home base. This lovely 1920s in-town home offers a spacious suite with queen bed, private bath, and sitting room. Trinidad has a quiet beauty, situated at the confluence of the Purgatoire River and Raton Creek. Full breakfast; children over ten welcome, pets allowed. $39-49.

TWIN LAKES

Frontier Lodge

B&B Rocky Mountains 142
P.O. Box 804
Colorado Springs, CO, 80901
(719) 630-3422

This historic lodge combines country charm with American frontier tradition. Located on the other side of Independence Pass from Aspen, surrounded by Mt. Albert, Mt. Massive, French and La Plata peaks. Hiking, fishing in the stream out back, cross-country skiing. Six rooms share two full baths. Hearty continental breakfast. No pets; restricted smoking; children welcome. $48.

VAIL

Alpen Haus

Bed & Breakfast Vail
P.O. Box 491
Vail, CO, 81658
(800) 748-2666

This home is one bus stop from Vail Village, on the golf course. Great views from each of the two guest rooms, one of which overlooks the Gore range and Vail village. The other looks out on tall pines and aspens. Private baths, hearty continental breakfast; no smoking. $105-115.

Annie's Place

B&B Vail Valley
P.O. Box 491
Vail, CO, 81658
(800) 748-2666

Located approximately one mile from Vail Village and near the free bus route, this home offers two bedrooms. Each room has a private bath and color TV. Outside, overlooking the creek, guests may relax in the hot tub. A full gourmet breakfast is served. Resident pets; no smoking. $125.

Away From It All

Bed & Breakfast Vail
P.O. Box 491
Vail, CO, 81658
(800) 748-2666

Located in West Vail, this newly decorated home offers a spacious guest room with private sauna and bath, a nice view, TV, and plenty of charm. In the summer, enjoy breakfast on the sunny deck overlooking the local golf course. One guest room with private bath and queen bed. No smoking; full breakfast. $85.

Brown Palace

Bed & Breakfast Vail
P.O. Box 491
Vail, CO, 81658
(800) 748-2666

Local skiing family that has lived in the valley for 27 years offers one bedroom with a shared hall bath and two twin beds. A full breakfast is served, and smoking and pets are allowed. $65-75.

Casita Baroloche

B&B Vail Valley
P.O. Box 491
Vail, CO, 81658
(800) 748-2666

This little mountain house of rough wood and antique country decor with a wood-burning fireplace has a magnificent mountain view. Your hostess will provide you with a selection of healthy vegetarian breakfasts. One king room with shared bath. Located on the free bus route. No smoking. $70.

Centennial House

Bed & Breakfast Vail
P.O. Box 491
Vail, CO, 81658
(800) 748-2666

Located in East Vail, this home offers two rooms with private or shared baths and a full breakfast. Hot tub is available for guest use. No smoking. $85.

Cottonwood Falls

B&B Vail Valley
P.O. Box 491
Vail, CO, 81658
(800) 748-2666

If you are looking for privacy, this home is for you. Minutes from Vail, this mountain hideaway is surrounded by aspen trees, mountain creeks, and waterfalls. Guests have a private apartment with private bath, queen bed. You may join your hosts for gourmet breakfasts or prepare your own from your stocked kitchen. Resident dog; smoking allowed. $125-150.

Deer Trail

B&B Vail Valley
P.O. Box 491
Vail, CO, 81658
(800) 748-2666

Located on the golf course, with free cross-country skiing right outside your door. The guest room has a nice view with vaulted ceiling, brass bed, and private bath. The general living area has a marble fireplace, big-screen TV, and huge video library. You can ski both Beaver Creek and Vail on the same day's ski pass. Continental breakfast; resident dog; no smoking. $85.

Fairway House

Bed & Breakfast Vail
P.O. Box 491
Vail, CO, 81658
(800) 748-2666

Located one-half mile east of the ski slopes, this beautiful rustic mountain home offers a stucco fireplace, king four-poster bed, and magnificent view of the Gore Range. There is an adjoining living room with fireplace, TV, VCR, wet bar, and pool table. Continental breakfast; no smoking. $100.

Game Creek House

Bed & Breakfast Vail
P.O. Box 491
Vail, CO, 81658
(800) 748-2666

Located seven miles from both Vail and Beaver Creek, on 9 acres surrounded on three sides by national forest. Breakfast is served in the kitchen overlooking the beautiful mountains. Bird watching, summer hiking, mountain biking, and cross-country skiing are abundant. In summer, Game Creek, with its many small falls, meanders through the yard. One room with double and twin beds, shared bath. Full breakfast; no smoking. $75.

Golden Solarium

Bed & Breakfast Vail
P.O. Box 491
Vail, CO, 81658
(800) 748-2666

Located ten minutes west of Vail, close to Beaver Creek Ski area and golf course. Indoor hot tub, one bedroom, private bath. Full or continental breakfast; resident dog and cat; no smoking. $80.

Hi Country Auberge

B&B Vail Valley
P.O. Box 491
Vail, CO, 81658
(800) 748-2666

A luxury mountain retreat overlooking Vail Mountain. Completely private lower level with two gorgeous bedrooms, each with private bath. Large first-floor living area has a fireplace, TV, cozy kitchen, and lovely dining area. Pool and hot tub are just outside the door. Garage parking is available in the condo complex. Full breakfast; no smoking. $100-125.

Hideaway House

Bed & Breakfast Vail
P.O. Box 491
Vail, CO, 81658
(800) 748-2666

This self-contained apartment has all the comforts of home. Fireplace, TV, private entrance. One-bedroom suite with queen bed and pullout double sofa, private bath. Self-serve breakfast; no smoking. $130-150.

Kay's Corner

B&B Vail Valley
P.O. Box 491
Vail, CO, 81658
(800) 748-2666

This brand-new home offers a great view and serenity. Your host is a ski instructor who knows the town and mountain inside out. One bedroom with twin beds and a private bath, TV, and refrigerator. Continental breakfast; no smoking. $80.

Matterhorn

Bed & Breakfast Vail
P.O. Box 491
Vail, CO, 81658
(800) 748-2666

Located five miles west of Vail Village, with a magnificent view of the Gore Valley. This German family offers a comfortable home. Two rooms. Smoking is allowed; resident cat. $60-75.

Minturn Meadows

Bed & Breakfast Vail
P.O. Box 491
Vail, CO, 81658
(800) 748-2666

Located west of downtown Vail, this home offers one room with twin beds and shared bath. A full breakfast is served. No smoking. Resident cats and dog. $60-65.

Moonshine Inn

Bed & Breakfast Vail
P.O. Box 491
Vail, CO, 81658
(800) 748-2666

One bedroom with private bath in this conveniently located home near the bus stop. The decor has a Southwestern flair, and full gourmet breakfast is served each morning. Resident dog; no smoking. $100.

Mountain Chalet

Bed & Breakfast Vail
P.O. Box 491
Vail, CO, 81658
(800) 748-2666

Ski out your front door to cross-country terrain; in the summer, walk onto the Vail Golf Course. This beautiful Bavarian chalet is decorated with antiques. There are an old-fashioned pool table, a large fireplace, and a sitting room with TV and stereo that opens to a beautiful view of the golf course. Two-room suite with a shared bath. Full breakfast; smoking allowed. $185.

Mountain View

B&B Vail Valley
P.O. Box 491
Vail, CO, 81658
(800) 748-2666

This mountain chalet is nestled on the side of a hillside with a magnificent view of Vail Mountain. There's a brick fireplace in the kitchen, wood-burning fireplace in the living room, and one double room with a shared bath. Full breakfast; on bus route; resident dog; no smoking. $85.

Outdoorsmen

Bed & Breakfast Vail
P.O. Box 491
Vail, CO, 81658
(800) 748-2666

Overlooking a lake and the majestic mountains, this condo is decorated by the hostess, an interior designer. One room with twin beds and private bath. Full breakfast; resident dog; no smoking. $65-75.

Pepperhouse

B&B Vail Valley
P.O. Box 491
Vail, CO, 81658
(800) 748-2666

This glassed-in A-frame home is located on the free bus route and surrounded by open land with aspen and pines. A full breakfast is served by your hostess, who has been in the restaurant business. Three guest rooms with private or shared baths. $85.

Plum House

B&B Vail Valley
P.O. Box 491
Vail, CO, 81658
(800) 748-2666

Located ten miles from Vail, this mountain home is in a small mountain town at the base of Shrine Mt. Pass. An upstairs room has a king bed, shared bath, and down comforter. Relax in the indoor hot tub or a good book in the library by the wood-burning stove. A full breakfast is served, and you may make arrangements for other meals. No smoking. $60.

Sandstone Sleeper

Bed & Breakfast Vail
P.O. Box 491
Vail, CO, 81658
(800) 748-2666

This private apartment is perfect for a couple looking for privacy. Full kitchen, private entrance, athletic club facilities, and baby-sitting are available. One bedroom with king bed, private bath; full breakfast. $125-150.

Ski Stop

B&B Vail Valley
P.O. Box 491
Vail, CO, 81658
(800) 748-2666

Surrounded with pine trees and nestled near a creek, this is a spacious mountain home with two guest rooms, one with private bath and one with shared bath. The downstairs room has a sauna, an adjoining family room with TV, pool table, and fireplace. Within easy walking distance to the free shuttle. Continental breakfast, no smoking, resident cat. $85.

Westview

Bed & Breakfast Vail
P.O. Box 491
Vail, CO, 81658
(800) 748-2666

Great location overlooking Vail Mountain. Snuggle by the brick fireplace or go out to the deck and listen to the winter creek. This two-bedroom unit sleeps four guests. Fully stocked kitchen; washer and dryer. The front bedroom has a great mountain view. Queen beds; no smoking; private bath. $150-175.

Village Artist

Bed & Breakfast Vail
P.O. Box 491
Vail, CO, 81658
(800) 748-2666

Centrally located on the free bus route in the heart of Vail. The general living area, TV, fireplace, and kitchen are shared with the hostess. Two rooms with shared bath, full or continental breakfast. Smoking is permitted.$75.

WINTER PARK

Cozy Ski Lodge

B&B Rocky Mountains 22
P.O. Box 804
Colorado Springs, CO, 80901
(719) 630-3422

Feel right at home in this homey ski lodge located in the heart of Winter Park. All rooms have two beds and private bath. Modified American Plan during ski season and B&B at other times. Indoor pool and sauna, free transportation to and from Winter Park slopes. Spa, restaurant, lounge, TV in common area. Full breakfast. B&B: $45-56.

Walden

B&B Rocky Mountains
P.O. Box 804
Colorado Springs, CO, 80901
(719) 630-3422

A beautiful solar home nestled in a wooded area with lovely view outside a small town near Winter Park. Two second-floor rooms, each with a balcony opening into the solar greenhouse and hot tub below. Queen beds, semi-private bath. Resident cat and dog. Near golf, hiking, and cross-country skiing. Gourmet breakfast; dinner available with advance notice. Children twelve and up; no smoking. $56-65.

Wildflower Meadows

B&B Rocky Mountains 17
P.O. Box 804
Colorado Springs, CO, 80901
(719) 630-3422

This inn is surrounded by pine forest and wildflower meadows. Modified American Plan is available in the winter. Don't miss the hot tub or the llamas. Seven rooms with private baths. No TV. Snacks and hot beverages. Dog, cat, and llamas on the premises. Shuttle available to ski areas. Full breakfast. $50-77.

WOODLAND PARK

Georgian Hide-away

B&B Rocky Mountains 107
P.O. Box 804
Colorado Springs, CO, 80901
(719) 630-3422

Each room of this Georgian Hideaway has an incredible view, private entrance, and pleasant decor. Located thirty miles west of Colorado Springs. Resident dog, full breakfast, no smoking. Children twelve and older are welcome. $60-75.

YELLOW JACKET

Wilson's Pinto Bean Farm

House No. 21434
Road 16
Yellow Jacket, CO, 81335
(303) 562-4476

Our farm is located in Montezume County, forty miles from the 4-Corners where the four western states join. Waving wheat, fragrant alfalfa, pinto beans, and mountains are visible in every direction. The farmhouse sits among elm trees, with orchards and gardens around. There are farm animals to enjoy, home-cooked meals, eggs to hunt, and fruits to pick in season. We can show children of all ages the delights of farm animals and country living.

Hosts: Arthur & Esther M. Wilson
Rooms: 2 (SB) $33
Full Breakfast
Credit Cards: No
Notes: 2, 4, 6, 7, 8, 9

Connecticut

AVON

Nutmeg B&B 414

P.O. Box 1117
West Hartford, CT, 06107
(203) 236-6698

Close to the area's private schools, this spacious contemporary offers a solarium, deck, and lovely grounds with a Japanese garden. The second-floor room has a cathedral ceiling, skylight, queen bed, and private bath. There is an adjacent studio with single bed for an extra person. Afternoon tea is served, and baby-sitting is available at an additional charge. Ping-Pong table, exercise bike, and swing set. Continental breakfast; no smoking; children welcome; resident pets. $60-85.

Nutmeg B&B 447

P.O. Box 1117
West Hartford, CT, 06107
(203) 236-6698

This contemporary home is filled with interesting collections and antiques and sits on a 2-acre mountaintop lot in the woods. The rooms have a breathtaking view of the valley. The two upstairs guest rooms are doubles and share a bath. Continental breakfast; smoking allowed; children welcome; resident pets. $60-85.

BETHLEHEM

Covered Bridge 1 BET

P.O. Box 447A
Norfolk, CT, 06058
(203) 542-5944

Nestled in the foothills of the Berkshires on 70 acres of hills and fields with grazing cows, this home was built in 1773. You can still see an original large stone fireplace, complete with baking oven, crane, and pot hooks. A total of five fireplaces, a tennis court, guest cottage, flagstone terrace, and glassed-in porches are yours to enjoy. Near antique shops, ski areas, White Memorial Park, White Flower Farm. One single with shared bath, six doubles, two with private baths, four with shared. Continental breakfast. $55-85.

BLOOMFIELD

Nutmeg B&B 407

P.O. Box 1117
West Hartford, CT, 06107
(203) 236-6698

A rambling 1920s farmhouse with its own duck pond. The first floor has a large country living room with a deck leading out to the pond. There are three guest rooms that share one full bath and two half baths. Continental breakfast; children ten and over are welcome; resident pets. $60-85.

Nutmeg B&B 450

P.O. Box 1117
West Hartford, CT, 06107
(203) 236-6698

A truly lovely B&B with parklike surroundings including nine pet goats. TV, refrigerator, and ice for guests' use. Convenient to West Hartford and Hartford, but just across the road from a state park for

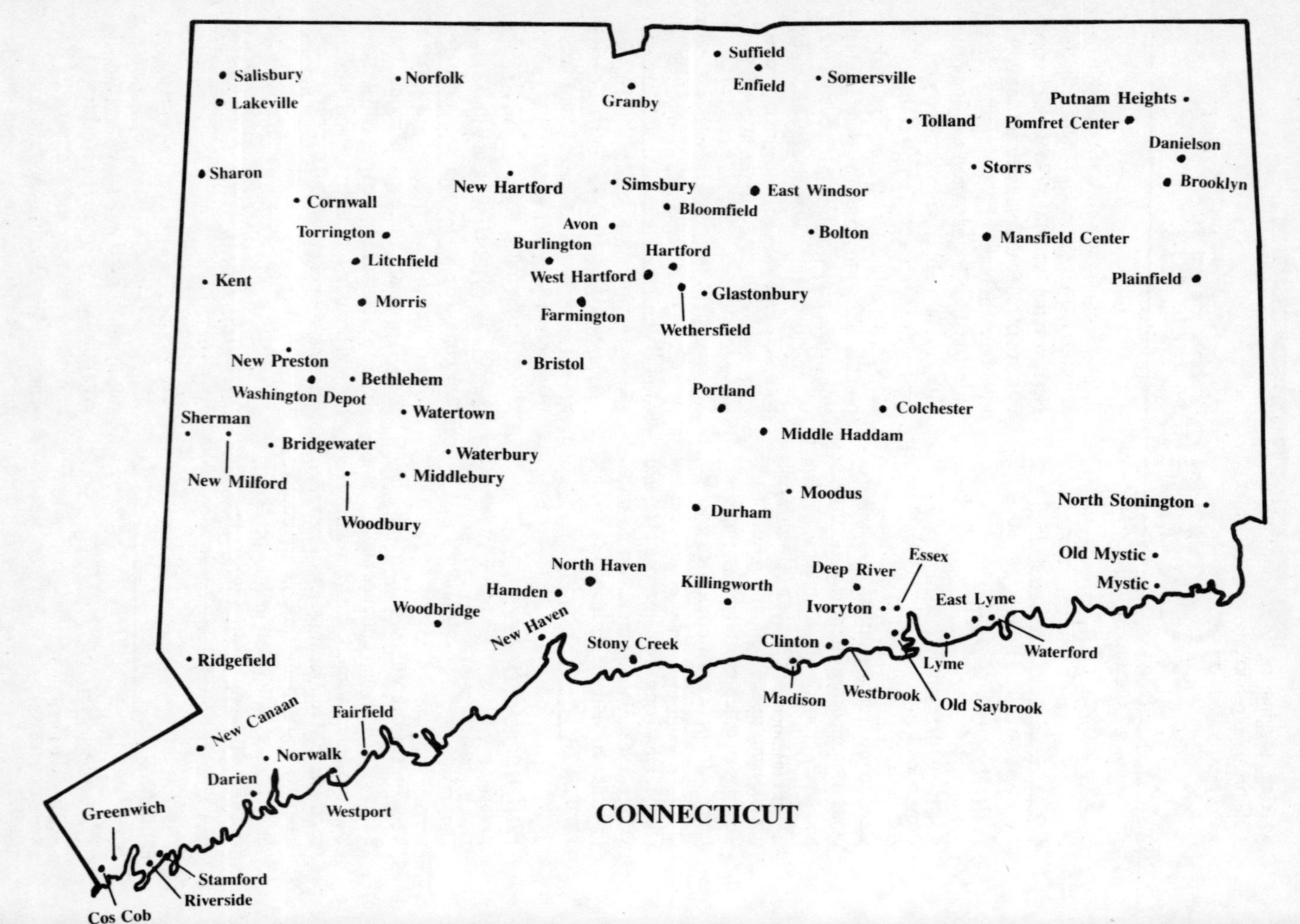
CONNECTICUT
Salisbury
Lakeville
Norfolk
Granby
Suffield
Enfield
Somersville
Tolland
Putnam Heights
Pomfret Center
Danielson
Brooklyn
Storrs
Sharon
Cornwall
New Hartford
Simsbury
East Windsor
Bloomfield
Avon
Torrington
Burlington
Bolton
Mansfield Center
Hartford
Litchfield
West Hartford
Kent
Glastonbury
Plainfield
Morris
Farmington
Wethersfield
New Preston
Bristol
Bethlehem
Washington Depot
Portland
Colchester
Sherman
Watertown
Middle Haddam
Bridgewater
Waterbury
New Milford
Middlebury
Moodus
Durham
North Stonington
Woodbury
Old Mystic
North Haven
Deep River
Essex
Hamden
Killingworth
Mystic
East Lyme
Ivoryton
Woodbridge
New Haven
Stony Creek
Clinton
Ridgefield
Waterford
Lyme
Madison
Westbrook
Old Saybrook
New Canaan
Fairfield
Norwalk
Darien
Westport
Greenwich
Stamford
Riverside
Cos Cob

walking, jogging, or cross-country skiing. Full breakfast; smoking allowed; children welcome; resident pets. $60-85.

BOLTON

Jared Cone House

25 Hebron Road
Bolton, CT, 06043
(203) 643-8538

Enjoy the charm of our historic country home. We have spacious bedrooms with queen beds and scenic views of the countryside. Bicycle and canoe available. We serve a full breakfast featuring our own maple syrup. Fine dining nearby, and we're a short distance from berry farms, antiques, herb farms, and parks.

Hosts: Jeff & Cinde Smith
Rooms: 3 (SB) $45-70
Full Breakfast
Credit Cards: No
Notes: 2, 5, 8, 10, 11, 12

BRIDGEWATER

Sanford/Pond House

Box 306
Bridgewater, CT, 06752
(203) 355-4677

A gracious Federal Greek revival mansion with stately, uniquely decorated bedrooms with sitting rooms or sitting areas and private baths. Relax in elegant style. "The Versailles of the region's B&Bs"—*Travel & Leisure* magazine. Excellent restaurants, antique shops, art galleries, and boutiques in the area.

Hosts: George & Charlotte Pond
Rooms: 5 (PB) $85-115
Continental-plus Breakfast
Credit Cards: A, B
Notes: 2, 5, 8, 10, 11, 12, 13, 14

BRISTOL

Chimney Crest Manor

5 Founders Drive
Bristol, CT, 06010
(203) 582-4219

English Tudor mansion with four suites—two with fireplace, two with kitchen. Twenty minutes from Hartford or Waterbury, three miles from Lake Compounce.

Hosts: Dan & Cynthia Cimadamore
Rooms: 4 (PB) $69.89-112
Full Breakfast
Credit Cards: A, B
Notes: 5, 7 (limited), 8, 10, 11, 12, 13

Nutmeg B&B 433

P.O. Box 1117
West Hartford, CT, 06107
(203) 236-6698

Visitors to Bristol's clock museum and history lovers would especially enjoy a stay in this Dutch colonial home owned by the city historian. The house has large lawns and gardens and is in an excellent residential area. The second-floor guest room has its own private bath. Full breakfast; no smoking; no children. $60-85.

BROOKLYN

Tannerbrook

329 Pomfret Road (Rt. 169)
Brooklyn, CT, 06234
(203) 774-4822

Restored 1750 colonial saltbox with 12 beautiful acres, including private spring-fed fishing lake, towering sugar maples, and hiking paths. Brooklyn is central for touring New England by way of nearby expressways. Boston and Hartford, onc hour; Cape Cod, one and one-half hours; New York, two and one-half hours.

Hosts: Jean & Wendell Burgess
Rooms: 2 (PB) $65

Full Breakfast
Credit Cards: A, B
Notes: 2, 5, 7, 8, 9, 10, 11, 12

BURLINGTON

Nutmeg B&B 403

P.O. Box 1117
West Hartford, CT, 06107
(203) 236-6698

This comfortable country Victorian is located close to the medical center. The back porch overlooks the surrounding woods. Three bedrooms, one with a single bed, one with twins, and one with a queen bed, share a bath. Continental breakfast; smoking permitted; children allowed. $60-85.

Captain Dibbell House

CLINTON

Captain Dibbell House

21 Commerce Street
Clinton, CT, 06413
(203) 669-1646

Our 1866 Victorian, located on a historic residential street, is two blocks from the harbor, and features a century-old wisteria-covered iron truss bridge. Our rooms are furnished with a comfortable mix of heirlooms, antiques, auction finds, and our growing collection of original art by New England artists. Bicycles are available.

Hosts: Helen & Ellis Adams
Rooms: 3 (PB) $75 + tax
Full Breakfast
Credit Cards: A, B
Closed Jan.
Notes: 2, 8 (over 14), 9, 10, 11, 12, 13, 14

COLCHESTER

The Hayward House Inn

35 Hayward Avenue
Colchester, CT, 06415
(203) 537-5772

A 1767 home on the National Historic Register; a Federal colonial furnished with antiques. All rooms have private bath. The Goodspeede Opera House, shops, beaches, golf, biking, and tennis are all within a short distance. Come experience small-town New England at its best. Tea room on premises.

Hosts: Bettyann & Stephen Possidento
Rooms: 6 (PB) $75-95
Continental-plus Breakfast
Credit Cards: No
Notes: 2, 3, 5, 8, 9, 10, 11, 12, 13 (XC), 14

Nutmeg B&B 401

P.O. Box 1117
West Hartford, CT, 06107
(203) 236-6698

Built in 1792, this fourteen-room house has been furnished in country French antiques. There are two large guest rooms, one with an antique queen bed, and the other with a double bed. There is also a single room off the hall bath that is shared among the guest rooms. Your hostess speaks fluent French. All antiques on the premises are for sale. Continental breakfast; no smoking; no children. $60-85.

CORNWALL

Hilltop Haven

Covered Bridge
Box 447, Norfolk, CT, 06058
(203) 542-5944

Enjoy panoramic views from this secluded 64-acre wooded hilltop estate close to the village of West Cornwall and the Housatonic River. The house is furnished throughout with Victorian and Oriental antiques. A cheery conservatory overlooking the Housatonic Valley, and a library with a five-foot stone fireplace are available for guests. Two rooms, private baths; full breakfast. $95.

COS COB

Nutmeg B&B 101

P.O. Box 1117
West Hartford, CT, 06107
(203) 236-6698

Built in 1830, this charming colonial is on the Greenwich historical register. Your hostess, who speaks French fluently, has decorated the entire home in American antiques. A library and three fireplaces add to the ambience. The guest room has a double bed and private bath. Full breakfast; children welcome. $60-85.

DANIELSON

Nutmeg B&B 417

P.O. Box 1117
West Hartford, CT, 06107
(203) 236-6698

Situated on 32 acres, including a spring-fed pond, this home is in a quiet country setting. Three B&B rooms share one large bath. Two of the rooms have twins and the third has a high-rise double bed. Spacious living room and family room with picture windows overlooking the pond. Full breakfast; no smoking; children welcome; resident pets. $60-85.

DARIEN

Nutmeg B&B 103

P.O. Box 1117
West Hartford, CT, 06107
(203) 236-6698

This unique home was built in the late 1800s as a stable for horses and cows and converted to a home in the late 1920s. Two rooms with twin beds share a bath. There is another room with a queen bed and private bath, and another twin-bedded room with a private bath. The views of Long Island Sound are breathtaking. Continental breakfast. $60-85.

DEEP RIVER

Riverwind Inn

209 Main Street
Deep River, CT, 06417
(203) 526-2014

With its eight wonderfully appointed guest rooms, rambling common areas, and informal country atmosphere, Riverwind is more than just a place to stay; it's a destination. Relax, step back in time, and enjoy a stay amid an enchanting collection of New England and Southern country antiques. Each morning starts with the inn's complimentary Southern buffet breakfast.

Hosts: Barbara Barlow & Bob Bucknall
Rooms: 8 (PB) $85-145
Full Breakfast
Credit Cards: A, B, C
Notes: 2, 5, 7, 9, 10, 11, 12, 14

DURHAM

Nutmeg B&B 516

P.O. Box 1117
West Hartford, CT, 06107
(203) 236-6698

Enjoy the swimming pool and the rural setting of this two-story colonial. Three upstairs bedrooms, two with double beds and the third with a single bed. All the rooms share a bath. Continental breakfast; no smoking; children welcome; resident pets. $60-85.

EAST LYME

Nutmeg B&B 517

P.O. Box 1117
West Hartford, CT, 06107
(203) 236-6698

This 1760 colonial has exposed beams, wide oak floorboards, seven fireplaces, and a hostess who bakes her own bread. In good weather breakfast is served on the outdoor deck, and there is a fireplaced living room. A guest room on the first floor has a king bed and private bath. A large second-floor room has a double bed and shared bath. Afternoon tea or apple cider is served in season. Full breakfast. $60-85.

EAST WINDSOR

Nutmeg B&B 410

P.O. Box 1117
West Hartford, CT, 06107
(203) 236-6698

This beautifully restored 1837 home has a pond and two goats. Stenciled walls and floors, antiques, family art, and personal collections. Four guest rooms have private or shared baths; one has a Jacuzzi tub. Afternoon tea and breakfast on the enclosed porch or in the dining room. Full breakfast. $60-85.

ENFIELD

Nutmeg B&B 409

P.O. Box 1117
West Hartford, CT, 06107
(203) 236-6698

This new Williamsburg Colonial is on 2 acres near the Enfield Mall. There is a lovely formal living room and a solarium. On the first floor, the master room has a double canopy bed and private bath with Jacuzzi. Also on the first floor is a smaller room with a private half bath. A second-floor double room has a shared bath. Continental breakfast; no smoking; children welcome; resident pets. $60-85.

ESSEX

Nutmeg B&B 508

P.O. Box 1117
West Hartford, CT, 06107
(203) 236-6698

If you're a boating enthusiast, your hostess would love to trade sailing stories with you. This home is right on the bank of the Connecticut River twenty miles from Mystic and close to Hammonasset public beach in Madison. Theaters and restaurants nearby. One room has a double canopy bed, and another has twin beds. Both rooms have a view of the water and share a bath. Breakfast can be served on the glass-enclosed porch overlooking the river. Full breakfast; smoking allowed; children welcome; resident pets. $60-85.

FAIRFIELD

Nutmeg B&B 110

P.O. Box 1117
West Hartford, CT, 06107
(203) 236-6698

Nestled in 2 acres of woods, this English cottage is the perfect spot for a cozy getaway. The guest room is furnished with a blend of country English and antiques. The room has a private bath and double antique iron and brass bed. In nice weather, breakfast can be served on the patio overlooking a pond.

Continental breakfast; no smoking or children. $60-85.

FARMINGTON

B&B Service 1

11 Bridlepath Road
W. Simsbury, CT, 06092
(203) 658-2181

An architect-designed modern contemporary in a wooded location within five feet of the highway, yet isolated from the bustle of the city in the historic town of Farmington near Miss Porter's School. $50-85.

Nutmeg B&B 405

P.O. Box 1117
West Hartford, CT, 06107
(203) 236-6698

A gracious New England estate built in 1762 has two of its twelve bedrooms for B&B. Close to everything in the Farmington Valley. Linger in the drawing room, relax on the screen solarium porch. Two rooms have antique furnishings, double beds, and private baths. Continental breakfast; no smoking; children welcome; resident pets. $60-85.

Nutmeg B&B 406

P.O. Box 1117
West Hartford, CT, 06107
(203) 236-6698

This elegant estate is now a gracious small inn with beautifully landscaped grounds, pool, tennis court, conference room, and lounge. There are six twin rooms and one double, all with color TV, telephone, and private baths. Convenient to the University of Connecticut Health Center and Hillstead Museum; short drive from Hartford. Continental breakfast; smoking allowed; children allowed. $60-85.

Nutmeg B&B 415

P.O. Box 1117
West Hartford, CT, 06107
(203) 236-6698

This is a luxurious new inn with 56 one- and two-bedroom suites. Each suite includes a bedroom with queen bed and sleeper sofa, kitchen, cable TV, telephone, fireplace, and bath. Complimentary privileges at the Farmington Farms Racquet Club. Extra services such as shopping, newspaper delivery, and nonsmoking rooms are available. Pets are accepted for an additional charge. Continental breakfast; smoking allowed; children welcome. $60-85.

Nutmeg B&B 445

P.O. Box 1117
West Hartford, CT, 06107
(203) 236-6698

This contemporary home on a 3-acre estate has two first-floor guest rooms. There is a large room with double bed, twin beds, and private bath. A second room has twin beds and a private bath and adjoins a den with one twin bed, TV, telephone, and fireplace. Full breakfast; smoking allowed; no children; resident pets. $60-85.

GLASTONBURY

Butternut Farm

1654 Main Street
Glastonbury, CT, 06033
(203) 633-7197

An eighteenth-century architectural jewel that is furnished in museum-quality period antiques. Estate setting with ancient trees, herb gardens, prize dairy goats, barnyard chickens, and pigeons. Ten minutes from Hartford. All Connecticut is within one and one-half hours.

Host: Don Reid
Rooms: 4 (2 PB; 2 S2B) $70.20-89.64

Full Breakfast
Credit Cards: A, B, C
Notes: 2, 5, 8, 9, 10, 11, 12, 13

Nutmeg B&B 444

P.O. Box 1117
West Hartford, CT, 06107
(203) 236-6698

Guests can enjoy the fireplace or a good book from the host's wide assortment. Two bedrooms, one with a double bed and one with twins, share a hall bath. Breakfast is served in the sunny, cheerful dining room. Full breakfast; no smoking; no children; resident pets. $60-85.

GRANBY

Nutmeg B&B 442

P.O. Box 1117
West Hartford, CT, 06107
(203) 236-6698

This stone house has a sophisticated country atmosphere, including horses out in the barn. The hostess will serve breakfast in your room, the dining room, or on the deck. Guests enjoy wine, cheese, and crackers in the late afternoon. The guest wing is totally separate and includes a sitting room with TV. Continental breakfast; no smoking; children welcome; resident pets. $60-85.

Nutmeg B&B 437

P.O. Box 1117
West Hartford, CT, 06107
(203) 236-6698

Located fifteen minutes from Bradley International Airport, this is a private B&B silo suite with a sitting area, queen bed, private bath, cable TV, mini-kitchen. Continental breakfast; smoking allowed; no children; resident pets. $60-85.

GREENWICH

The Stanton House Inn

76 Maple Avenue
Greenwich, CT, 06830
(203) 869-2110

This inn has thirty rooms and is situated in the heart of Greenwich on nearly 2.5 acres. The building is a Stanford White-designed turn-of-the-century mansion with original moldings and craftsmanship preserved wherever possible. Fireplaces (nonworking) and high ceilings prevail. Decorated in a Laura Ashley English inn motif with period antique reproductions.

Hosts: Tog & Doreen Pearson
Rooms: 27 (22 PB; 5 SB) $45-60/person
Continental Breakfast
Minimum stay holidays: 2
Credit Cards: A, B, C
Notes: 5, 8 (over 8), 9, 10, 11, 12

HAMDEN

Nutmeg B&B 203

P.O. Box 1117
West Hartford, CT, 06107
(203) 236-6698

This carriage house affords total privacy and is located at the foot of Sleeping Giant Mountain, so it is perfect for nature lovers, hikers, bikers, and lovers of quiet elegance. The house contains a complete kitchen, bedroom with double bed, unique bath with sunken tub, large patio, and private entrance and driveway. Continental breakfast; smoking allowed; children welcome. $60-85.

Nutmeg B&B 205

P.O. Box 1117
West Hartford, CT, 06107
(203) 236-6698

Come home to this two-story colonial located just outside New Haven. Decorated in Early American furnishings, there is a first-floor bedroom with double bed and private baths. Near public transportation. Continental breakfast; no smoking; children welcome. $60-85.

Nutmeg B&B 207

P.O. Box 1117
West Hartford, CT, 06107
(203) 236-6698

A pool and lovely deck add to your enjoyment in this comfortable home. Situated right outside New Haven, this house has a single room with shared bath. Continental breakfast; no smoking; resident pets. $60-85.

HARTFORD

B&B Service 2

11 Bridlepath Road
W. Simsbury, CT, 06092
(203) 658-2181

A historic Victorian, elegant farm mansion overlooking a ski run about forty-five minutes from Hartford. $50-85.

Nutmeg B&B 428

P.O. Box 1117
West Hartford, CT, 06107
(203) 236-6698

Classical musician husband and wife host this elegant late Victorian-style B&B. The authentic stained glass and hand-done stenciling add special charm to this city home. The cozy double room on the second floor has a shared bath. A pullout bed is available for children. Guests may eat with the hosts in the cheerful kitchen or alone. Only a few minutes' walk to Trinity, the Bushnell, and the Civic Center. Continental breakfast; no smoking; children welcome; resident pets. $60-85.

IVORYTON

The Copper Beech Inn

46 Main Street
Ivoryton, CT, 06442
(203) 767-0330

Gracious gardens and rustic woodlands set the stage for this handsome inn. A gallery offers antique Oriental porcelain, and the dining room is noted for fine country French cuisine. Beautiful countryside, quaint villages, museums, antique shops, theater, and water sports distinguish the area.

Hosts: Eldon & Sally Senner
Rooms: 13 (PB) $108-172.80
Buffet Breakfast
Minimum stay weekends & holidays: 2
Credit Cards: A, B, C, E
Closed Mondays, Christmas, New Year's Day
Notes: 2, 4, 8 (over 8), 10, 11, 12

The Copper Beech Inn

KENT

Covered Bridge 1 K

P.O. Box 447A
Norfolk, CT, 06058
(203) 542-5944

Charming eighteenth-century house is one of the oldest in Kent and is a splendid example of Federal architecture and decor.

Living room with fireplace is available for guests; upstairs suite has an ornately carved four-poster canopy bed. Two rooms, private baths, continental breakfast. $85-120.

Nutmeg B&B 306

P.O. Box 1117
West Hartford, CT, 06107
(203) 236-6698

Located just one mile from Lake Waramaug in the middle of 200 acres of fields and woods, this 1790s farmhouse offers four B&B rooms. Guests can enjoy their own living room and dining room. The first-floor rooms each have private baths. The larger rooms on the second floor each have a double and single bed. One shared bath upstairs. Continental breakfast; smoking allowed; children three and older are welcome; resident pets. $60-85.

Nutmeg B&B 310

P.O. Box 1117
West Hartford, CT, 06107
(203) 236-6698

Located just off scenic Route 7, this family B&B is convenient to the many private schools in the northwestern Connecticut hills. The entire second floor of this large Cape Cod home is open to guests. Two of the rooms have double beds, and one room has twins. Shared bath. Full breakfast; smoking allowed; children welcome; resident pets. $60-85.

KILLINGWORTH

Nutmeg B&B 502

P.O. Box 1117
West Hartford, CT, 06107
(203) 236-6698

This 200-year-old inn has a Victorian restaurant. Situated near Mystic Seaport, Gillette Castle, and Hammonasset State Park, the inn is convenient to all coastal attractions. There is a first-floor library, TV room, conference room, and sun porch for guests to enjoy. On the second-floor wing are three large rooms, one with twins and two with doubles, sharing a bath. Another wing has two doubles and one single room, all sharing a bath. All of the rooms are furnished with antiques. Continental breakfast; smoking allowed; children twelve and older welcome; resident pets. $60-85.

LAKEVILLE

Wake Robin Inn

Route 41
Lakeville, CT, 06039
(203) 435-2515

Newly renovated elegant country inn on 15 wooded acres overlooking the Connecticut Berkshires. Individually decorated rooms with private baths. Antiquing, golf, tennis, canoeing, and lake fishing nearby. Famous "Savarin" restaurant.

Host: Henri J.P. Manassero
Rooms: 41 (PB) $85-200
Continental Breakfast
Credit Cards: A, B, C
Notes: 2, 4, 5, 7, 8, 9, 10, 11, 12, 13, 14

LITCHFIELD

Covered Bridge 1 Litchfield

P.O. Box 447A
Norfolk, CT, 06058
(203) 542-5944

Eighteenth-century colonial farmhouse set on 200 acres with brook, barns, and a meadow where six horses pasture. This B&B is close to the center of the historic town of Litchfield and to White Flower Farm, wineries, skiing, and swimming. Three rooms, one private bath, two shared. Full breakfast. $85.

Tollgate Hill Inn & Restaurant

Route 202
Litchfield, CT, 06098
(203) 567-4545

A 1745 inn, listed on the National Register of Historic Places. Luncheon, cocktails, and dinner from a kitchen voted Best American Restaurant in Litchfield by *Connecticut Magazine* February,1990. Twenty beautifully decorated guest rooms and suites, all air-conditioned, with direct-dial telephone, private baths, cable TV. Some also have VCR, private bar, and fireplaces. Two hours from New York City. Closed most of March and Tuesdays, November-June.

Host: Frederick J. Zivic
Rooms: 20 (PB) $165-275 MAP
Full Breakfast
Credit Cards: A, B, C, E
Notes: 2, 3, 4, 6, 7, 8, 9, 10, 11, 12, 13

LYME

Nutmeg B&B 512

P.O. Box 1117
West Hartford, CT, 06107
(203) 236-6698

This new center-chimney colonial is located on several acres of woods and has its own walking trail and horseshoe court. Two comfortable guest rooms each have a private bath. The first room has a queen canopy bed, and the second has antique twins. Convenient to the Old Lyme Art Center, all shoreline attractions, and many outstanding restaurants. Full breakfast; no smoking; no children. $60-85.

Old Lyme Inn

85 Lyme Street
Lyme, CT, 06371
(203) 434-2600

Outside, wild flowers bloom all summer; inside, fireplaces burn all winter, beckoning you to enjoy the romance and charm of this thirteen-room Victorian country inn with an award-winning, 3-star *New York Times* dining room. Within easy reach of the state's attractions, yet tucked away in an old New England art colony.

Host: Diana Field Atwood
Rooms: 13 (PB) $95-125
Continental Breakfast
Credit Cards: A, B, C, D, E
Closed first two weeks of January
Notes: 2, 3, 4, 6, 7, 8, 9, 10, 11, 12, 14

MADISON

Madison Beach Hotel

94 West Wharf Road
Madison, CT, 06443
(203) 245-1404

Built in the early 1800s, the Madison Beach Hotel is nestled on a private beach on Long Island Sound. Distinctly Victorian in style and decor. Many rooms have private balconies overlooking the water. Antique oak bureaus, wainscotting, wicker and rattan furniture, along with old-fashioned wallpaper, complete the Victorian feeling. Restaurant serves lunch and dinner.

Hosts: Betty & Henry Cooney, Roben & Kathy Bagdasarian
Rooms: 35 (PB) $50-195
Continental Breakfast
Credit Cards: A, B, C, E
Closed Jan. & Feb.
Notes: 2, 3, 4, 7, 8, 9, 10, 11, 14

MANSFIELD CENTER

Nutmeg B&B 402

P.O. Box 1117
West Hartford, CT, 06107
(203) 236-6698

This lovely home sits on 5 acres of woods five miles from the University of Connecticut and Storrs and close to Caprilands Herb Farm. One large air-conditioned room has a double bed, fireplace, private bath. There are two smaller rooms, one with a single bed and one with a double bed, which share a bath. Four fireplaces to enjoy in the winter. Continental breakfast; no smoking; children are welcome; resident pets. $60-85.

MIDDLEBURY

Tucker Hill Inn

96 Tucker Hill Road
Middlebury, CT, 06762
(203) 758-8334

Tucker Hill Inn is a large center-hall colonial just down from the village green in Middlebury. It was built around 1920 and was a restaurant and catering house for almost forty years. Our period rooms are large and spacious. Nearby are antiques, country drives, music and theater, golf, tennis, water sports, fishing, hiking, and cross-country skiing.

Hosts: Richard & Susan Cabelenski
Rooms: 4 (2 PB; 2 SB) $55-75
Full Breakfast
Credit Cards: A, B
Closed Christmas Day
Notes: 2, 7 (restricted) 8, 9, 11, 12, 14

MIDDLE HADDAM

Nutmeg B&B 425

P.O. Box 1117
West Hartford, CT, 06107
(203) 236-6698

A late eighteenth-century barn about a quarter of a mile from the Connecticut River has been converted into a comfortable saltbox home. The guest cottage is a separate dwelling next door to the main house. It has a bedroom with double bed and couch that opens into a double bed for small children. Private bath and small kitchen. Guests have use of an eight-person hot tub, and, for a slight additional charge, canoe equipment. Continental breakfast; no smoking; children welcome; pets in residence. $60-85.

MOODUS

The Fowler House

Plains Road, Box 432
Moodus, CT, 06469
(203) 873-8906

The Fowler House is an exquisite example of 1890 Victorian architecture, set on the town green. It has original stained-glass windows, eight working Italian ceramic fireplaces, hand-carved woodwork, elegant wallcoverings. Afternoon tea is served on the wraparound porch or in the library or parlor. Concierge service, dinner and theater reservations, complimentary arrival beverage, romantic turn-down service. Fine dining, antiquing, and shops are nearby.

Hosts: Barbara Ally & Paul Seals
Rooms: 6 (4 PB; 2 SB) $70.20-97.20
Continental-plus Breakfast
Credit Cards: A, B
Notes: 2, 4, 5, 7, 8 (over 12), 9, 10, 11, 12, 13, 14

MORRIS

Nutmeg B&B 308

P.O. Box 1117
West Hartford, CT, 06107
(203) 236-6698

A 1750 farmhouse on 2.9 acres. The farm has horses, sheep, ducks, geese, and chickens. There are two rooms on the second floor that share one full bath. There is also a studio apartment on the second floor with private entrance, private bath, and kitchen facilities. Continental breakfast. $60-85.

MYSTIC

The Adams House

382 Cowhill Road
Mystic, CT, 06355
(203) 572-9551

This circa 1790 inn is situated in a quaint country setting less than two miles from Mystic drawbridge. Homey colonial atmosphere is enhanced by three old-fashioned fireplaces, lush greenery, and flower gardens. Guests may choose from six bedrooms with private baths in the main house or a completely private guest suite in an adjacent building that features private bath, sauna, refrigerator, and wet bar.

Hosts: Ron & Maureen Adams
Rooms: 6 (PB) $60-125
Continental Breakfast
Minimum stay weekdays & weekends: 2; holidays: 3
Credit Cards: A, B
Notes: 2, 5, 10, 11, 12

Comolli's House

36 Bruggeman Place
Mystic, CT, 06355
(203) 536-8723

Ideal for vacationers touring historic Mystic or the businessperson who desires a homey respite while traveling. This immaculate home, situated on a quiet hill overlooking the Mystic Seaport complex, is convenient to Olde Mistick Village and the Aquarium. Sight-seeing, sporting activities, shopping, and restaurant information is provided by your hosts. Off-season rates are available.

Host: Dorothy M. Comolli
Rooms: 2 (PB) $85
Continental Breakfast
Credit Cards: No
Notes: 2, 5

Red Brook Inn

Box 237
Old Mystic, CT, 06372
(203) 572-0349

Beautiful country inn on 7 acres of woods. Lovely rooms, furnished with antiques. Many working fireplaces throughout the inn and guest rooms. A quiet colonial atmosphere within 1.5 miles of Mystic Seaport Museum. Private baths.

Host: Ruth Keyes
Rooms: 11 (PB) $120-150 + tax
Full Breakfast
Minimum stay weekends & holidays: 2
Credit Cards: A, B
Notes: 2 (in advance), 5, 8, 9, 10, 11, 12

NEW CANAAN

Nutmeg B&B Agency 108

P.O. Box 1117
West Hartford, CT, 06107
(203) 236-6698

Located across from the nature center walks and trails, this inn is less than one mile from town and the railroad station. There are eighteen rooms, furnished with antiques and reproductions. Also on the property are eight apartments. This cheerful Victorian has the beautiful gingerbread woodwork and front porch characteristic of this period's homes. Continental breakfast; smoking allowed; children allowed. $60-85.

NEW HARTFORD

Highland Farm B&B

107 Highland Avenue
New Hartford, CT, 06057
(203) 379-6029

Built in 1879, Highland Farm B&B is a grand old Victorian with fourteen gables and is filled with rooms of antiques with an Oriental flair. Highland Farm is located in the quaint village of New Hartford on a secluded hilltop, yet minutes from nearby Litchfield and Hartford counties. The area offers a variety of year-round activities, including boating, camping, skiing, antique shops, and scenic area.

Hosts: Jim & Marion Kavanaugh
Rooms: 4 (1 PB; 3 SB) $75-95
Full Breakfast
Credit Cards: No
Notes: 2, 5, 7, 8 (over 12), 9, 10, 11, 12, 13, 14

Nutmeg B&B 435

P.O. Box 1117
West Hartford, CT, 06107
(203) 236-6698

An Early American farmhouse on 40 acres with a garden, pond, and animals. Each guest room has a sitting area, and the rooms may be used singly or as suites. Private baths. Breakfast includes fresh farm eggs and wonderful baked goods. Full breakfast; restricted smoking; children twelve and over welcome; resident pets. $60-85.

Nutmeg B&B 446

P.O. Box 1117
West Hartford, CT, 06107
(203) 236-6698

This large colonial is a perfect example of a New England home, with huge rooms, a mix of traditional and antique furnishings, and a beautiful view of the Litchfield Hills. The second-floor guest area has a private sitting room, picture windows, fireplace. There are two guest rooms, one with a queen bed, sun room. The second room has antiques, a double pullout bed, a fireplace. Both rooms have private baths. Continental breakfast; no smoking; children are welcome; resident pets. $60-85.

NEW HAVEN

The Inn at Chapel West

1201 Chapel Street
New Haven, CT, 06511
(203) 777-1201

Ten exquisite rooms, each with private bath, telephone, TV, air-conditioning. Near Yale University campus, New Haven Green, dining, shopping, art, and entertainment. Conference and meeting facilities. Catered private parties.

Host: Steven Schneider
Rooms: 10 (PB) $125-175
Continental Breakfast
Credit Cards: A, B, C, D
Notes: 2, 5, 7, 8, 9, 10, 12, 14

Nutmeg B&B 204

P.O. Box 1117
West Hartford, CT, 06107
(203) 236-6698

This 1921 colonial still has the original woodwork and wood-burning stove. Located in a residential section of New Haven, this home is ideal for the business traveler. There are three rooms available, two doubles and one single, all sharing two baths. Full breakfast; no smoking; children three and over are welcome; resident pets. $60-85.

Nutmeg B&B 208

P.O. Box 1117
West Hartford, CT, 06107
(203) 236-6698

Catch a game at the Yale Bowl or the bus downtown from this B&B in the Westville section of town. This beautiful English Tudor has two guest rooms, both with double beds and shared bath. Help yourself to a continental breakfast; children welcome; resident pets. $60-85.

Nutmeg B&B 210

P.O. Box 1117
West Hartford, CT, 06107
(203) 236-6698

Walk to Yale from this gracious Victorian home set in the residential section of New Haven. A newly decorated third-floor suite consists of a bedroom with antique iron double bed, a large private bath, and a smaller bedroom with a single bed. A guest room on the second floor offers a double bed and shared bath. Continental breakfast; smoking permitted; children permitted; resident pets. $60-85.

Nutmeg B&B 211

P.O. Box 1117
West Hartford, CT, 06107
(203) 236-6698

Built in 1902, this Federalist Georgian home is only a ten-minute walk from the Yale campus. A separate entrance leads to the three guest rooms, one with a king bed, one with a queen, and one with twins. There are two baths for the three rooms. Guests are invited to enjoy tennis or swimming at a nearby club. Full breakfast; smoking allowed; children welcome; resident pets. $60-85.

NEW MILFORD

Covered Bridge 1 NM

P.O. Box 447A
Norfolk, CT, 06058
(203) 542-5944

Vistas for viewing, woods for walking, hills for cross-country skiing, streams for fishing, flower gardens, a tennis court, and a pool are some of the attractions of this sprawling estate three miles outside town. On the first floor there is a large guest room with private deck. Upstairs there is another guest room. One has a private bath. Full breakfast. $55-95.

The Homestead Inn

5 Elm Street
New Milford, CT, 06776
(203) 354-4080

Enjoy warm hospitality in our charming Victorian inn located near the village green in the heart of the Litchfield Hills. Stroll to the village and enjoy the shops, restaurants, and movie theater. We have eight inn rooms and six motel rooms, all recently redecorated. Most have country antiques, private bath, color TV, air-conditioning, and phone. AAA approved.

Hosts: Rolf & Peggy Hammer
Rooms: 14 (PB) $65-85
Continental-plus Breakfast
Credit Cards: A, B, C, D
Notes: 2, 5, 7, 8, 9, 10, 11, 12, 13 (XC), 14

The Homestead Inn

Nutmeg B&B 315

P.O. Box 1117
West Hartford, CT, 06107
(203) 236-6698

A delightfully restored reverse-wood tobacco barn, this B&B is beautifully landscaped with a pool and tennis court. The first-floor room has a separate entrance to the deck, two twins or a king bed, and private bath. There is also a twin room with shared bath on the second floor. Unbelievable views, rare birds, and wild flowers. Breakfast includes your host's own berries, homemade jams, popovers, and muffins. Children welcome; resident pets. $60-85.

NEW PRESTON

Boulders Inn

Route 45
New Preston, CT, 06777
(203) 868-0541

An 1895 Victorian inn, carriage house, and guest houses located at the foot of Pinnacle

Mountain in northwest Connecticut, overlooking Lake Waramaug. Spectacular sunsets may be enjoyed from the exquisitely appointed living room, most guest rooms, dining room, or outside dining terraces. Eleven rooms have fireplaces. Three-star restaurant, private beach, boating, tennis, biking, and skiing.

Hosts: Ulla & Kees Adema
Rooms: 17 (PB) $145-225 MAP
Full Breakfast
Credit Cards: A, B, C
Notes: 2, 3 (Sun.), 4, 5, 7, 9, 10, 11, 12, 13, 14

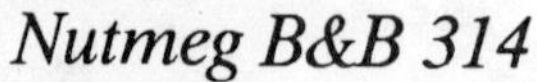

Nutmeg B&B 314

P.O. Box 1117
West Hartford, CT, 06107
(203) 236-6698

If you're looking for a B&B with a view, this is it. A lovely colonial with expansive lawns, this home overlooks Lake Warmaug. Both guest rooms face the lake. One has twin beds, the other has a double bed, and both have private baths. Lake Waramaug is ideal for water sports, and the nearby park allows boating, swimming, fishing, and dining. Minutes from Mohawk Mountain ski area. Continental breakfast; no smoking; no children. $60-85.

NORFOLK

Blackberry River Inn

Route 44, Norfolk, CT, 06058
(203) 542-5100

A 225-year-old colonial inn located in rural northwestern Connecticut. Eighteen guest rooms, some with working fireplaces. Cross-country skiing, swimming, trout fishing, tennis, the Norfolk Chamber Music Festival, Lime Rock Race Track, antiques nearby.

Hosts: Kim & Bob Zuckerman
Rooms: 18 (10 PB; 8 SB) $65-150
Continental-plus Breakfast
Credit Cards: A, B, C, E, F
Notes: 2, 3, 4, 5, 7, 8, 9, 10, 11, 12, 13 (XC), 14

Manor House

Manor House

Maple Avenue, Box 447
Norfolk, CT, 06058
(203) 542-5690

Victorian elegance awaits you at our historic Tudor/Bavarian estate. Antique-decorated guest rooms, several with fireplaces, canopies, and balconies, offer a romantic retreat. Enjoy a sumptuous breakfast in our Tiffany-windowed dining rooms or treat yourself to breakfast in bed. Designated Connecticut's Most Romantic Hideaway. Included in *50 Best B&Bs in the USA*.

Hosts: Hank & Diane Tremblay
Rooms: 9 (7 PB; 2 SB) $70-160
Full Breakfast
Credit Cards: A, B, C
Notes: 2, 5, 8 (over 12), 9, 10, 11, 12, 13, 14

Mountain View Inn

Route 272
Norfolk, CT, 06058
(203) 542-5595; (203) 542-6991

Tucked away in the village of Norfolk, with its bell towers and postcard landscapes, Mountain View Inn offers eleven charming guest rooms, full dining and bar service, recreational, musical, and cultural attractions. Mountain View is the perfect location for a country vacation at its best.

NOTES: Credit cards accepted: A Master Card; B Visa; C American Express; D Discover Card; E Diners Club; F Other: 2 Personal checks accepted: 3 Lunch available: 4 Dinner available: 5 Open all year

Host: Michele Sloane
Rooms: 11 (8 PB; 3 SB) $53.75-107.50
Full Breakfast
Minimum stay holidays: 2
Credit Cards: A, B
Notes: 2, 4, 5, 7, 8, 9, 10, 11, 12, 13

Weaver's House

Weaver's House

Route 44
Norfolk, CT, 06058
(203) 542-5108

An 1898 house overlooking the estate of the Norfolk Summer Chamber Music Festival. Simple hospitality in a village of forested hills, with four mapped areas of hiking trails. Village woodland pond for swimming. Cross-country skiers may warm themselves by the coal stove in the sitting room.

Hosts: Judy & Arnold Tsukroff
Rooms: 4 (S2B) $48-58
Full Breakfast
Credit Cards: A, B
Notes: 2, 5, 11, 13, 14

NORTH HAVEN

Nutmeg B&B Agency 202

P.O. Box 1117
West Hartford, CT, 06107
(203) 236-6698

Golfers will love this two-story frame home with a six-hole putting green on the grounds. Your hostess speaks French and Spanish. There are two guest rooms, one with twins that shares a bath with the hostess, and one that is a double-bedded suite with private bath and study. Continental breakfast; smoking allowed; children welcome; resident pets. $60-85.

NORTH STONINGTON

Covered Bridge 1 NS

P.O. Box 447A
Norfolk, CT, 06058
(203) 542-5944

An 1861 Victorian set in a charming, historic seacoast town close to Mystic. Fond memories of years spent traveling in England inspired the hosts to furnish their home in the Georgian manner, with formal antiques and accessories, many of which are for sale. The three guest rooms have four-poster canopy beds. A full English breakfast is served in the elegant dining room. Two rooms share a bath, one is private. Full breakfast. $90-120.

NORWALK

Nutmeg B&B Agency 107

P.O. Box 1117
West Hartford, CT, 06107
(203) 236-6698

Nestled into the woods, this inn is only an hour away from New York. There are five spacious rooms and suites. Three of the rooms have double beds, and two have king beds. All have elaborate private baths. Each room has a distinctive theme; one even has five skylights. Continental breakfast; smoking allowed; resident pets; no children. $60-85.

OLD MYSTIC

Covered Bridge 1 OM

P.O. Box 447A
Norfolk, CT, 06058
(203) 542-5944

An 1825 colonial set in the center of this historic whaling, ship-building, and fishing village. The inn has recently been renovated to include all modern conveniences. Each room is decorated with antiques, and several have fireplaces. The common rooms include a parlor, keeping room with fireplace, and breakfast room. Eight rooms, private baths. Full breakfast. $95-115.

Old Mystic Inn

58 Main Street
Old Mystic, CT, 06372
(203) 572-9422

Historic 1800s inn and carriage house in a quiet country setting, minutes from Mystic Seaport and vineyard/winery tours. Private baths and fireplaces, air-conditioning, and whirlpool baths. Lovely decorative stenciling throughout. Scrumptious country breakfasts. Small groups and weddings.

Hosts: Sandra & Preston Jump
Rooms: 12 (PB) $75-125
Full Breakfast
Minimum stay weekends & holidays: 2
Credit Cards: A, B, C
Notes: 2, 5, 8, 9, 10, 11, 12, 13

OLD SAYBROOK

Nutmeg B&B 503

P.O. Box 1117
West Hartford, CT, 06107
(203) 236-6698

A lovely Southern hostess greets guests at this 1740 colonial on the historic register. Situated on a very quiet private road, this house is seven blocks from Long Island Sound. There are two guest rooms on the second floor that share a bath and a suite with private entrance, double and single beds, private bath, and kitchenette. Continental breakfast; no smoking; children welcome; resident pets. $60-85.

OXFORD

Nutmeg B&B 303

P.O. Box 1117
West Hartford, CT, 06107
(203) 236-6698

Everything you come to the country for. A 1711 saltbox colonial on 4 acres of land with a pond for swimming and a brook for fishing. Guests enjoy a suite with private entrance, double bed, sitting room with TV/VCR, phone, and private bath. Breakfast includes fresh picked produce, strawberries, melons, or raspberries grown on the farm. Supper available on request. Full breakfast; no smoking; children welcome; resident pets. $60-85.

PLAINFIELD

French Renaissance House

550 Norwich Road
Plainfield, CT, 06374
(203) 564-3277

Our lovely historic home was built in 1871 by a wealthy Victorian gentleman. The house is one of the finest examples of French Renaissance Second Empire architecture in Connecticut. It is near Plainfield Greyhound Park, within reasonable driving distance of Mystic Seaport, Hartford, Providence and Newport, Rhode Island, and Sturbridge Village, Massachusetts.

Hosts: Ted & Lucile Melber
Rooms: 4 (1 PB; 3 S2B) $50 + tax
Full Breakfast
Credit Cards: A, B, E
Notes: 2, 5, 8, 9, 10, 11, 12

POMFRET CENTER

Nutmeg B&B 421

P.O. Box 1117
West Hartford, CT, 06107
(203) 236-6698

When visiting Pomfret and Rectory schools, try this large Victorian B&B. Overlooking the valley, the house is on about 6 acres with flower and vegetable gardens. The formal dining room and sitting room with TV have fireplaces. There are two guest rooms with king beds and private baths. One room has twin beds, and another with a queen shares a bath. Afternoon tea or dinner on request at an additional charge. Full breakfast; children welcome; resident pets. $60-85.

The Croft

PORTLAND

The Croft

7 Penny Corner Road
Portland, CT, 06480
(203) 342-1856

An 1822 colonial located in central Connecticut, convenient to Wesleyan University. The guest suite, which has a private entrance, has one or two bedrooms, according to your needs. Living room/dining area, kitchen, private bath. Pleasant surroundings include open fields, barns, and an herb garden. Golf and skiing are nearby.

Host: Elaine Hinze
Suite: 1 (PB) $60-105
Full Breakfast
Credit Cards: No
Notes: 2, 5, 8, 9, 10, 11, 12, 13, 14

PUTMAN HEIGHTS

The Felshaw Tavern

Five Mile River Road
Putman Heights, CT, 06260
(203) 928-3467

A noble center-chimney colonial, built in 1742 as a tavern and restored in the 1980s. Frequented by Revolutionary militia, including Israel Putman, of Bunker Hill fame. Furnished in antiques with working fireplaces in guest rooms and a beehive oven in the keeping room. Peaceful setting, perfect for walking, bicycling, and unwinding. One-half hour from Worcester and Providence; one hour to Boston and Hartford; two and one-half hours to New York City.

Hosts: Herb & Terry Kinsman
Rooms: 2 (PB) $75
Full Breakfast
Credit Cards: No
Notes: 2, 5, 7 (limited), 11, 12, 13, 14

RIDGEFIELD

Epenetus Howe House

91 North Salem Road
Ridgefield, CT, 06877
(203) 438-HOWE

Step back in time to colonial New England, just 1.5 hours from New York City and 35 minutes from Stamford, Connecticut. We welcome you to our 264-year-old historic home. Many fine restaurants, antique shops, contemporary museum, and outdoor activities are located nearby.

Hosts: John & Diane Armato
Rooms: 2 (SB) $55-85
Continental Breakfast
Credit Cards: A, B, C
Notes: 2, 5, 8, 9, 10, 11, 12, 13, 14

West Lane Inn

22 West Lane, Route 35
Ridgefield, CT, 06877
(203) 438-7323

The West Lane Inn offers colonial elegance in overnight accommodations. Also close to museum, points of interest, and shopping.

Host: M.M. Mayer
Rooms: 20 (PB) $120-160
Continental Breakfast
Credit Cards: A, B, C, E
Notes: 3, 5, 7, 8, 9, 10, 11, 12, 13, 14

RIVERSIDE

Nutmeg B&B Agency 105

P.O. Box 1117
West Hartford, CT, 06107
(203) 236-6698

These active hosts have decided to share their lovely country-style Cape home. One room off the living room has a double bed and private bath. For city-goers, New York is only one hour away. Full breakfast; no smoking; children welcome; resident pets. $60-85.

SALISBURY

Yesterday's Yankee

Route 44 East
Salisbury, CT, 06068
(203) 435-9539

A restored 1744 home with period furnishings sets the scene for comfortable air-conditioned guest rooms, complete gourmet breakfasts featuring home baking, and warm hospitality. Summer theater, auto racing, music centers, hiking, independent schools, antique shops, boating, swimming, and skiing are nearby.

Hosts: Doris & Dick Alexander
Rooms: 3 (SB) $65-75
Full Breakfast
Credit Cards: A, B, C
Notes: 2, 5, 8, 9, 10, 11, 12, 13, 14

SHARON

Covered Bridge 3 SHA

P.O. Box 447A
Norfolk, CT, 06058
(203) 542-5944

Enjoy the comfort of this 1890 colonial on 3 acres close to a pristine lake. In addition to several guest rooms, there is also an efficiency apartment available. The host will help you plan your stay in northwestern Connecticut. One single with shared bath, three doubles with private bath. $50-90.

SHERMAN

Covered Bridge 1 SH

P.O. Box 447A
Norfolk, CT, 06058
(203) 542-5944

Circa 1835, this B&B was a rest stop for travelers throughout the 1800s and has been restored for that purpose. All three rooms are decorated with antiques and special country accents. Private baths, full breakfast. $85.

SIMSBURY

B&B Service 3

11 Bridlepath Road
W. Simsbury, CT, 06092
(203) 658-2181

A restored schoolhouse in Simsbury at the foot of the mountain in a lovely, pastoral setting. Full breakfast. $50-85.

Nutmeg B&B 434

P.O. Box 1117
West Hartford, CT, 06107
(203) 236-6698

Stay in this lovely country home and enjoy the serene, quiet neighborhood. The house is a contemporary, decorated with traditional furnishings. The guest room has a double bed and private hall bath. Guests are invited to join the family in the spacious family room or on the deck. Breakfast in the country kitchen includes a wonderful woodland view. Continental breakfast; no smoking; children welcome; resident pets. $60-85.

Nutmeg B&B 436

P.O. Box 1117
West Hartford, CT, 06107
(203) 236-6698

This colonial is perfect for visitors to private schools in Avon and Simsbury. The house mixes traditional furniture and antiques with warmth and good taste. Guests are welcome throughout the house, including the comfortable den with fireplace and TV. On the second floor, one twin bedroom and one double room share a bath. Continental breakfast; smoking allowed; children welcome. $60-85.

Simsbury 1820 House

731 Hopmeadow Street
Simsbury, CT, 06070
(203) 658-7658

An authentic early nineteenth-century country inn with thirty-four individually designed guest rooms with private baths. Fine dining daily in our restaurant. Within walking distance of the charming town of Simsbury; twenty minutes to downtown Hartford and Bradley International Airport.

Host: Kelly Hohengarten
Rooms: 34 (PB) $85-125
Suite: 1 (PB) $135
Continental Breakfast
Credit Cards: A, B, C, D, E
Notes: 2, 3, 4, 5, 7, 8, 9, 10, 11, 12, 14

SOMERSVILLE

The Old Mill Inn

63 Maple Street
Box 443
Somersville, CT, 06072
(203) 763-1473

Originally built in the mid-eighteen hundreds, the house was enlarged and renovated in the mid-nineteen hundreds by the mill owner. Antique shops, boutiques, and restaurants are only minutes away. Two golf courses are only five minutes away; polo, theater, museums, and historic houses are also close. Only twenty minutes from Bradley International Airport and Hartford.

Hosts: Ralph & Phyllis Lumb
Rooms: 4 (2 PB; 2 SB) $48.60-54
Continental Breakfast
Credit Cards: No
Notes: 2, 5, 8 (over 5), 9, 10, 11, 12, 14

STAMFORD

Nutmeg B&B Agency 109

P.O. Box 1117
West Hartford, CT, 06107
(203) 236-6698

This house feels like country, but is located in the heart of the city. A private apartment has two bedrooms, one with twins and the other with a single bed, one bath, a fully equipped kitchenette, a living room with cable TV. Just off the living room is a private patio that overlooks a wooded yard and small creek. Continental breakfast. $60-85

STONY CREEK

Nutmeg B&B Agency 201

P.O. Box 1117
West Hartford, CT, 06107
(203) 236-6698

You will love having your own log cabin with a large double-bedded bedroom, living room with queen sofabed, large bath, and a kitchenette stocked for breakfast. The host built this charming retreat, and you can still smell the fresh pine. It has a wood-burning stove, stereo, TV, and all the amenities you need for a perfect getaway weekend. Continental breakfast; smoking allowed; children allowed. $60-85.

Nutmeg B&B 209

P.O. Box 1117
West Hartford, CT, 06107
(203) 236-6698

Breathtakingly set overlooking Long Island Sound and the Thimble Islands, the beautifully restored four-story Victorian is a special treat. Three guest rooms. Two have double beds, and the third has twins. The three rooms share one and one-half baths and a fourth-floor sitting room with double windows on each wall. View the rose garden with over 150 bushes from the double porches surrounding the home. Full breakfast; no smoking; children twelve and up are welcome; resident pets. $60-85.

STORRS

Farmhouse on the Hill Above Gurleyville

418 Gurleyville Road
Storrs, CT, 06268
(203) 429-1400

An elegant farmhouse located near the University of Connecticut. The Kollets raise Columbia sheep. Sturbridge, Mass., Worcester, Mass., Mystic, Hartford, and New London, Conn. are less than an hour away. Don't forget to try Elaine's muffins! Cribs, high chairs, and carriages available for children. Hot tub and exercise equipment in the new addition.

Hosts: Bill & Elaine Kollet
Rooms: 5 (PB) and 1 apartment, $35 and up + tax
Full Breakfast
Credit Cards: No
Notes: 2, 4 (by arrangement), 5, 7, 8, 9, 10, 11, 12, 13

SUFFIELD

Nutmeg B&B 427

P.O. Box 1117
West Hartford, CT, 06107
(203) 236-6698

This large custom-built ranch house is immaculate and quiet. It has a very private, spacious first-floor bedroom with its own entrance, bath, TV, and telephone. Queen bed. Fruit and snacks are always available. Full breakfast; smoking allowed; no children. $60-85.

TOLLAND

The Tolland Inn

63 Tolland Green
Tolland, CT, 06084-0717
(203) 872-0800

Built in 1800, The Tolland Inn stands in the northwest corner of the Tolland village green, a half-mile from I-84. Located midway between Boston and New York City, the inn is convenient to the University of Connecticut, Old Sturbridge, Caprilands, Hartford, and Brimfield Fair.

Hosts: Susan & Stephen Beeching
Rooms: 7 (5 PB; 2 SB) $54-64.80
Continental Breakfast
Credit Cards: A, B, C
Notes: 2, 5, 8 (over 10) 9, 10, 11, 12

TORRINGTON

Yankee Pedlar Inn

93 Main Street
Torrington, CT, 06790
(800) 777-1891

Escape to the Yankee Pedlar Inn, located in downtown Torrington's historic district, minutes from Litchfield County attractions. Newly renovated, air-conditioned guest rooms feature Hitchcock furnishings, color cable TV, and phones. Full dining and lounge with weekend entertainment. Write or call for free brochure.

Host: Christopher Bolan
Rooms: 60 (PB) From $34.50/person
Full Breakfast
Credit Cards: A, B, C, E, F
Notes: 2, 3, 4, 5, 7, 8, 9, 10, 11, 12, 13, 14

WASHINGTON DEPOT

Nutmeg B&B 313

P.O. Box 1117
West Hartford, CT, 06107
(203) 236-6698

This serene B&B is a true working farm with a brook, a small lake, a pool, and cross-country skiing on the property. Nearby you'll find canoeing, hiking, and good biking trails. Relax over a glass of wine before retiring to one of three guest rooms. All guest rooms share two baths. The perfect stopover for visiting the many private schools in the northwest of the state. Full breakfast; no smoking; children allowed; resident pets. $60-85.

WATERBURY

Covered Bridge 1 WA

P.O. Box 447A
Norfolk, CT, 06058
(203) 542-5944

This 1888 Victorian is on the National Register of Historic Places and sits on an acre in the historic district. There are several common rooms, including an antique-decorated living room with fireplace. A full breakfast and high tea are served in the paneled dining room. Five rooms, three with private baths. $85-125.

Nutmeg B&B 302

P.O. Box 1117
West Hartford, CT, 06107
(203) 236-6698

This beautifully restored Victorian was once a parsonage for the adjacent church. Guests have a choice of rooms with shared baths on the second floor or a three-room suite with private bath on the third floor. Special care is given to the breakfast, which is served in the dining room with linens and colorful garnishes. Full breakfast is available on request. No smoking; children welcome. $60-85.

Nutmeg B&B 305

P.O. Box 1117
West Hartford, CT, 06107
(203) 236-6698

Minutes from the business district, this spacious contemporary has a 20' by 40' in-ground pool. Your thoughtful hosts provide complimentary beverages, toiletries, robes, phones, and cable TV for your comfort. The guest rooms have double beds and private baths. One is on the main floor, and one is downstairs. A crib and bassinet are available on request. The downstairs room is equipped for a handicapped guest, and there is closed-captioned TV for the hearing impaired. Continental breakfast. $60-85.

WATERFORD

Nutmeg B&B 510

P.O. Box 1117
West Hartford, CT, 06107
(203) 236-6698

Located 500 feet from the river, this charming Cape is the perfect spot for a family getaway. There are three guest rooms, two with double beds and one with twins. One of the double rooms has a private full bath, and the other has a private half bath. Full breakfast; no smoking; children welcome. $60-85.

WATERTOWN

Covered Bridge 1 WAT

P.O. Box 447A
Norfolk, CT, 06058
(203) 542-5944

A nineteenth-century New England home less than a mile from Taft School, secluded at the end of a long driveway and surrounded by old maples, willows, and pines. This fourteen-room white colonial is warmly furnished with antiques and a varied art collection. Four guest rooms with shared baths. $50-75.

WESTBROOK

The Captain Stannard House

138 South Main Street
Westbrook, CT, 06498
(203) 399-7565

A charming 1850 Georgian Federal, where you can relax among the herb and perennial gardens or stroll to the beach. Bicycles are here for your use, as well as an antique and gift shop. Mystic Seaport, Gillette Castle, Essex Steam Train, riverboat cruises, and Goodspeede Opera House are nearby.

Hosts: Ray & Elaine Grandmaison
Rooms: 9 (PB) $65-85
Continental-plus Breakfast
Credit Cards: A, B, C
Notes: 2, 5, 9, 10, 11

WEST HARTFORD

Nutmeg B&B 404

P.O. Box 1117
West Hartford, CT, 06107
(203) 236-6698

This Tudor home on a quiet residential street offers a twin room with private bath on the second floor. Just minutes from downtown Hartford, St. Joseph's College, and the West Hartford branch of the University of Connecticut. Complimentary coffee or tea is available at any hour. Full breakfast; no smoking; no children. $60-85.

Nutmeg B&B 441

P.O. Box 1117
West Hartford, CT, 06107
(203) 236-6698

A lovely single-story home, furnished with a comfortable blend of modern, traditional, and antique furnishings. The guest room has twin beds and a private bath. There is TV in the room, but guests are welcome to join the hosts in the family room. Coffee and tea are always available. Continental breakfast; no smoking; children welcome. $60-85.

WESTPORT

Nutmeg B&B Agency 111

P.O. Box 1117
West Hartford, CT, 06107
(203) 236-6698

Breathtakingly set overlooking Long Island Sound, this stunning home combines rural beauty with metropolitan sophistication. The guest wing is totally private, with its own sitting room, fireplace, and entrance. There are three B&B rooms available, two with single beds and the third with a double spool bed. One of the singles has a private bath, and the other two rooms share a bath. For the summer season, guests can enjoy the beach, which is only one-quarter mile from the home, and the central air-conditioning. Continental breakfast; no smoking; children welcome; resident pets. $60-85.

WETHERSFIELD

Nutmeg B&B 408

P.O. Box 1117
West Hartford, CT, 06107
(203) 236-6698

Nestled in the historic village of Old Wethersfield, this classic Greek Revival brick house has been lovingly restored. Built in 1830, it boasts five airy guest rooms furnished with period antiques. Two rooms share a hall bath; the rest have private baths. Continental breakfast; children twelve and over are welcome. $60-85.

Nutmeg B&B 429

P.O. Box 1117
West Hartford, CT, 06107
(203) 236-6698

This attractive colonial home is rich in history. There is a lovely twin room with private hall bath, plus a small room with a single bed for a child. A park is nearby. Full breakfast; children welcome. $60-85.

WOODBRIDGE

Nutmeg B&B Agency 102

P.O. Box 1117
West Hartford, CT, 06107
(203) 236-6698

Looking for a leisurely, private spot only minutes from New Haven? This bi-level contemporary may be the answer. Situated on over 2 acres of land, the house offers a bedroom with double bed, cable color TV, adjacent sitting room, private bath, refrigerator, telephone, air conditioning, and a fireplaced living room that opens out onto a patio. Music lovers can enjoy the spinet piano in the sitting room. Continental breakfast; smoking allowed; children allowed; resident pets. $60-85.

WOODBURY

Curtis House

506 Main Street
Woodbury, CT, 06798
(203) 263-2101

Connecticut's oldest inn, in operation since 1754, in a quaint New England town famous for antique shops. The inn features canopied beds and a popular restaurant serving regional American fare, amply portioned and moderately priced.

Hosts: The Hardisty Family
Rooms: 18 (12 PB; 6 SB) $30-70
Continental Breakfast
Credit Cards: A, B
Closed Christmas Day
Notes: 2, 3, 4, 5, 7, 9, 10, 11, 12, 13

Nutmeg B&B 312

P.O. Box 1117
West Hartford, CT, 06107
(203) 236-6698

Antiquers, take notice: Here's a 1730 colonial that has been restored in period furniture. Two second-floor rooms have double beds and shared bath. A hearty breakfast includes homemade breads. Full breakfast. $60-85.

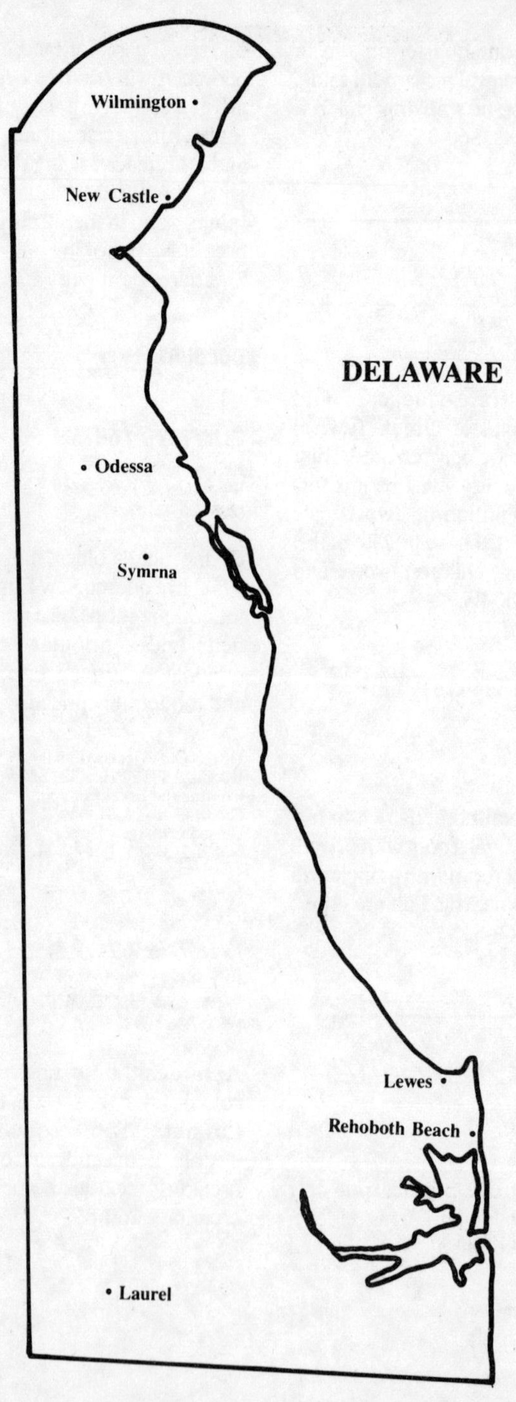
DELAWARE
Wilmington
New Castle
Odessa
Symrna
Lewes
Rehoboth Beach
Laurel

Delaware

LAUREL

Amanda's B&B Service 21

1428 Park Avenue
Baltimore, MD, 21217
(301) 225-0001

A convenient location for exploring the Eastern Shore area, this home, on the National Historic Register, offers very nice accommodations and breakfast. Nearby are antiques, shopping, flea markets, a state park, hunting, and wildlife. $65-75.

Savannah Inn B&B

LEWES

Savannah Inn B&B

330 Savannah Road
Lewes, DE, 19958
(302) 645-5592

Quaint village location; ocean and bay beaches, state park, resorts nearby. Casual, comfortable bedrooms with fans, books, piano, backyard, airy porch. Delicious vegetarian breakfasts; resident cat in owners' quarters. Hosts enjoy nature, outdoor sports, organic gardening.

Hosts: Dick & Susan Stafursky
Rooms: 7 (SB) $38-54
Continental Breakfast
Minimum stay weekends: 2; holidays:3
Credit Cards: No
Weekly Discount of 15%
Breakfast served Memorial Day-Sept. 30
Notes: 2, 7 (limited), 8, 9, 10, 11

NEW CASTLE

Jefferson House B&B

The Strand at the Wharf
New Castle, DE, 19720
(302) 323-0999; (302) 322-8944

Packed with charm and history, Jefferson House is an elegant 200-year-old riverfront hotel-residence. Located in the center of New Castle's historic district, just a few feet from all the historic buildings, museums, and parks. Antique furnishings, hot tub, air conditioning, fireplace, screened porch, efficiencies (long/short term). Brochure available.

Host: Chris Bechstein
Rooms: 3 (PB) $65-85
Full Breakfast
Credit Cards: A, B
Notes: 2, 5, 7, 8, 9, 10, 11, 12

William Penn Guest House

206 Delaware Street
New Castle, DE, 19720
(302) 328-7736

Choose one of three rooms in our beautifully restored 1682 guest house in the center of historic New Castle. Twenty minutes from museum and public gardens.

Hosts: Richard & Irma Burwell
Rooms: 3 (SB) $40
Continental Breakfast
Credit Cards: A, B
Notes: 2, 5, 8 (10 and over), 9, 10

ODESSA

Cantwell House

107 High Street
Odessa, DE, 19730
(302) 378-4179

Odessa was an important trading port on the Delaware River until the 1890s. The town contains fine examples of colonial, Federal, and Victorian architecture, including three museums owned by Winterthur. Cantwell House (circa 1840) has been completely restored and furnished in country antiques.

Host: Carole F. Coleman
Rooms: 3 (1 PB; 2 SB) $50-75
Continental Breakfast
Credit Cards: No
Notes: 2, 5, 7 (restricted), 8, 9, 10, 14

REHOBOTH BEACH

Tembo B&B

100 Laurel Street
Rehoboth Beach, DE, 19971
(302) 227-3360

Tembo, located 750 feet from the beach, offers a casual atmosphere with warm hospitality. Relax among Early American furnishings, antiques, oil paintings, waterfowl carvings, and Gerry's elephant collection. Immaculately clean bedrooms are bright and airy, with firm beds.

Hosts: Don & Gerry Cooper
Rooms: 6 (1 PB; 5 SB) $58.30-97.20
Continental Breakfast
Minimum stay weekends: 2; holidays: 3
Credit Cards: No
Notes: 2, 5, 6 (off-season), 8 (6 and over), 9, 10, 11, 12

SMYRNA

The Main Stay

41 South Main Street
Smyrna, DE, 19977
(302) 653-4293

The state capital of Dover is twelve miles; Wilmington forty, where you may visit Winterthur, the Dupont Estate, and Longwood Gardens.

Host: Phyllis E. Howarth
Rooms: 3 (SB) $40
Continental Breakfast
Credit Cards: No
Closed June 1-Nov. 1
Notes: 7 (restricted), 8, 9, 10, 12

WILMINGTON

The Boulevard B&B

1909 Baynard Blvd.
Wilmington, DE, 19802
(302) 656-9700

Beautifully restored city mansion, originally built in 1913. Impressive foyer and magnificent staircase leading to a landing complete with window seat and large leaded-glass windows flanked by fifteen-foot columns. Breakfast is served on the screened porch, weather permitting. Close to the business district and all area attractions. Brochure on request.

Hosts: Charles & Judy Powell
Rooms: 6 (4 PB; 2 SB) $55-70
Full Breakfast
Credit Cards: A, B, C
Notes: 2, 5, 7, 8, 9, 10, 11, 12, 14

Small Wonder B&B

213 West Crest Road
Wilmington, DE, 19803
(302) 764-0789

At I-95 exit 9. Convenient to duPont mansions and gardens (Hagley, Eleutherian Mills, Longwood, Winterthur, Nemours, Bellevue) and historic New Castle, Brandywine River Museum, Rockwood, and more. Air-conditioning, pool, hot tub.

Hosts: Dot & Art Brill
Rooms: 2 (PB) $55-70
Full Breakfast
Credit Cards: A, B, C
Notes: 2, 5, 8 (over 9), 9, 10, 11, 12, 14

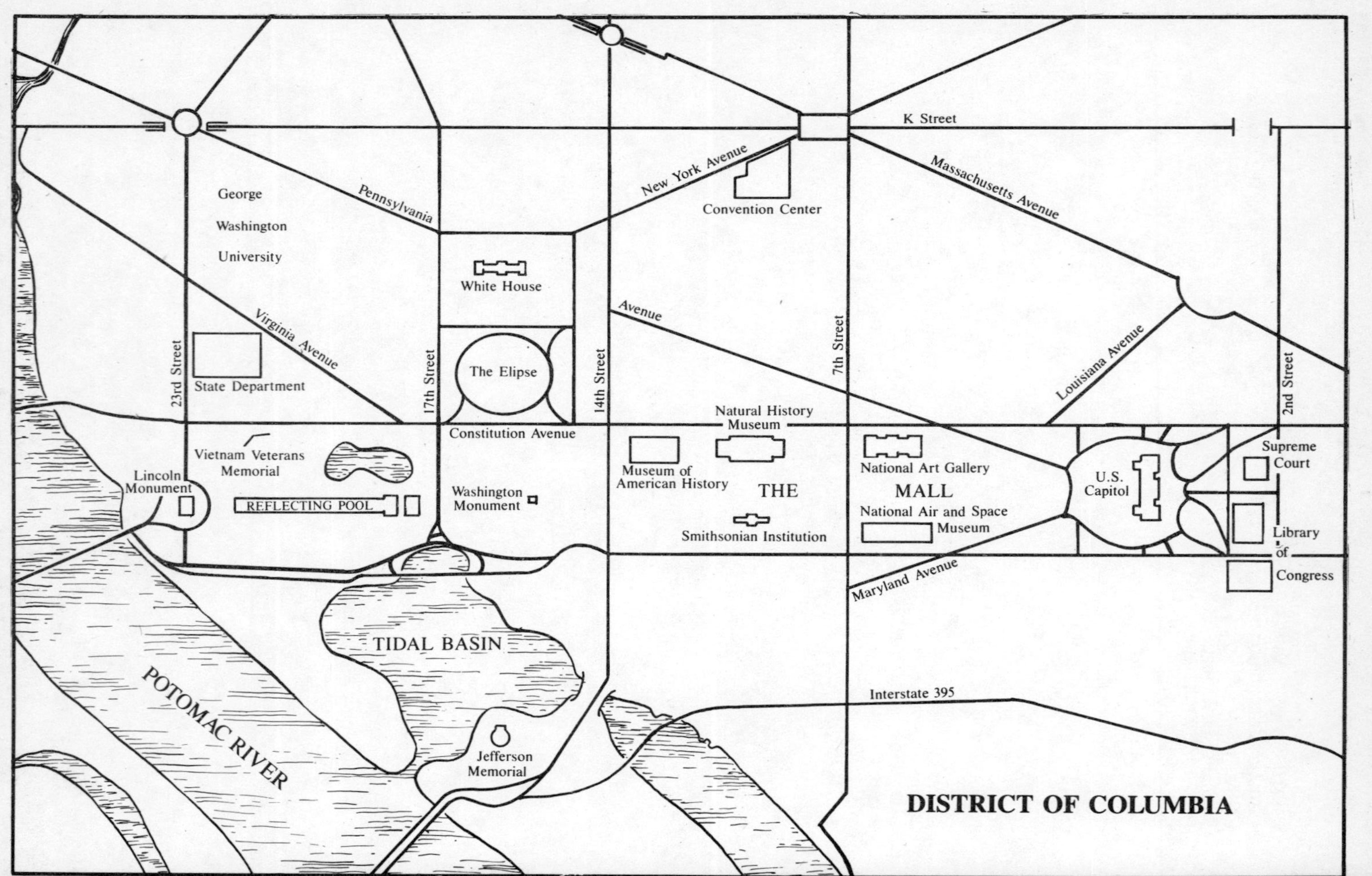
K Street
New York Avenue
Massachusetts Avenue
Convention Center
Pennsylvania
George
Washington
University
White House
Avenue
Virginia Avenue
23rd Street
State Department
17th Street
The Elipse
14th Street
7th Street
Louisiana Avenue
2nd Street
Constitution Avenue
Natural History
Museum
Supreme
Court
Vietnam Veterans
Memorial
Museum of
American History
National Art Gallery
U.S.
Capitol
Lincoln
Monument
REFLECTING POOL
Washington
Monument
THE
MALL
National Air and Space
Museum
Smithsonian Institution
Library
of
Congress
Maryland Avenue
TIDAL BASIN
POTOMAC RIVER
Interstate 395
Jefferson
Memorial
DISTRICT OF COLUMBIA

District of Columbia

Bed'n'Breakfast of Washington, D.C. 100

P.O. Box 12011
Washington, DC, 20005
(202) 328-3510

A 100-year-old Victorian home, carefully restored by its present owners. Original wood paneling, stained glass, chandeliers, lattice porch. Central air-conditioning, color TV and phones in each room, player piano. Adjoins Logan Circle Historic District, with excellent transportation and easy parking. Five rooms. $50-150.

Bed'n'Breakfast of Washington, D.C. 103

P.O. Box 12011
Washington, DC, 20005
(202) 328-3510

This house, built in 1932, is in Foxhall Village, an eight-square-block area constructed in the image of Bath, England. The house is on a quiet street away from heavy traffic. One room with a double bed and shared bath has French doors leading to the porch. An English basement apartment with double bed has a private bath, kitchen, TV, private phone, air-conditioning, separate entrance, and parking. $50-150.

Bed'n'Breakfast of Washington, D.C. 119

P.O. Box 12011
Washington, DC, 20005
(202) 328-3510

A spacious frame/stucco in one of Washington's most distinguished neighborhoods. Breakfast is served on an outdoor porch overlooking the gardens, weather permitting. One large room with twin beds, private bath, air-conditioning, and color TV. Located in Cleaveland Park, midway between Wisconsin and Connecticut Avenues. $50-150.

Bed'n'Breakfast of Washington, D.C. 126

P.O. Box 12011
Washington, DC, 20005
(202) 328-3510

A Georgian brick colonial with slate roof, located on a wide, tree-lined avenue in a residential neighborhood. Parking is available, and older children are welcome. There are two large guest rooms, each with color TV, private bath, and tiled shower. One has a four-poster double bed with canopy, fireplace, and access to a patio and garden. The second features a queen bed and its own balcony overlooking the garden. Located at Tenley Circle, between Georgetown and Chevy Chase, Maryland. $50-150.

Bed'n'Breakfast of Washington, D.C. 134

P.O. Box 12011
Washington, DC, 20005
(202) 328-3510

A large Federal brick townhouse designed and built in 1911 by Harry Wardman. Breakfast may be served in the cheery breakfast room or on the terrace overlooking the garden. An eclectic blend of antique and contemporary furnishings. Located in Woodley Park, a tree-lined neighborhood just across the Connecticut Avenue "Lion" Bridge from Dupont Circle and the downtown area. One room with queen bed, adjoining sitting room, and private bath. A second room with twin beds and a single room share a bath. $50-150.

Bed'n'Breakfast of Washington, D.C. 145

Bed'n'Breakfast of Washington, D.C. 145

P.O. Box 12011
Washington, DC, 20005
(202) 328-3510

A quintessential Washington townhouse in a prestigious tree-lined district on Capitol Hill. The elegantly restored thirteen-room residence is renowned among preservationists as by far the earliest (1891) and finest local example of Colonial Revival architecture. Three guest rooms with shared baths and a one-bedroom apartment. All rooms have color TV and telephone. $50-150.

Bed'n'Breakfast of Washington, D.C. 171

P.O. Box 12011
Washington, DC, 20005
(202) 328-3510

This split-level home is located in a country setting in Arlington, Virginia, a ten-minute drive from downtown Washington and National Airport. Two bedrooms each have a double bed and share a bath. Laundry facilities, parking, telephone, and color TV with VCR and cable are available. Smoking is permitted, and children are welcome. $50-150.

Bed'n'Breakfast of Washington, D.C. 173

P.O. Box 12011
Washington, DC, 20005
(202) 328-3510

Built in 1912, this house was one of the early row houses in the Mt. Pleasant area. On the third floor, there are two spacious guest rooms sharing a bath, one with a double iron post bed, the other with a double futon bed. Each room has a sitting area and desk. One room has a wonderful view of the Washington Monument; the other of the National Cathedral. Both have TV. $50-150.

Bed'n'Breakfast of Washington, D.C. 188

P.O. Box 12011
Washington, DC, 20005
(202) 328-3510

This custom-built brick home is located in a wooded country setting minutes from Washington, in Alexandria, Virginia. The drive to Washington takes ten to fifteen minutes. One bedroom with queen bed, private bath, TV, portable phone, air-conditioning. Use of private living room if desired. Children are welcome, and smoking is allowed. $50-150.

Bed'n'Breakfast of Washington, D.C. 196

P.O. Box 12011
Washington, DC, 20005
(202) 328-3510

This house was formerly the residence of the ambassador of Cambodia. It is filled with political mementos and works of art by such celebrated artists as David Hockney and Robert Motherwell. The house offers three sitting rooms, one with piano, and an up-to-date office in the basement with a FAX machine and computer. Two guest rooms with double beds, private baths, and TV. $50-150.

Crystal Bed & Breakfast

2620 South Fern Street
Arlington, VA, 22202
(703) 548-7652

Dutch colonial home with large, sunny rooms and lovely gardens. Minutes by subway from downtown museum area of D. C. Handmade quilts, antique furnishings, gourmet muffins, and large breakfasts. Recommended in nationwide travel column.

Host: Susan Swain
Rooms: 3 (SB) $65
Full Breakfast Weekends; continental weekdays
Credit Cards: B
Notes: 2, 5, 7, 8, 9, 10, 12, 14

Embassy Inn

1627 16th Street, NW
Washington, DC, 20009
(202) 234-7800; (800) 423-9111

A European-style inn located nine blocks north of the White House and within short walking distance to Metro subway transportation. Features a charming and relaxed atmosphere, personalized service, and extras such as continental breakfast, afternoon tea, and evening sherry and snacks each day.

Host: Susan Stiles
Rooms: 39 (PB) $78.09-100.29
Continental Breakfast
Credit Cards: A, B, C, E, F
Notes: 5, 7, 8, 9, 14

Kalorama Guest House at Woodley Park

2700 Cathedral Avenue, NW
Washington, DC, 20008
(202) 328-0860

This turn-of-the-century Victorian townhouse offers you a downtown residential home away from home. Decorated in period antiques, the guest house is a short walk to the underground Metro, restaurants, and shops. Only ten minutes from the Smithsonian and White House, yet offering you the relaxation and hospitality of a country inn. Enjoy our complimentary continental breakfast and evening aperitif.

Hosts: Michael Gallagher & Richard Lay
Rooms: 19 (12 PB; 7 SB) $40-85
Continental Breakfast
Credit Cards: A, B, C, E
Notes: 5, 7, 8, 9, 10, 11, 12, 14

The Reeds

P.O. Box 12011
Washington, DC, 20005
(202) 328-3510

A 100-year-old Victorian mansion that has been carefully and extensively restored. Original wood paneling, stained glass, chandeliers, porch. Each room has a color TV and phone; laundry facilities are available. Adjoins Logan Circle Historic District, with excellent transportation and easy parking. Ten blocks from the White House. Your hosts speak English and French.

Hosts: Charles & Jackie Reed
Rooms: 5 (SB) $55-82.50
Continental Breakfast
Credit Cards: A, B, C, E
Notes: 2 (two weeks before), 5, 8, 9

Van Ness Inn

3941 Van Ness Street, NW
Washington, DC, 20016
(703) 418-3629

The best part about this charming old Queen Anne is its spectacular upper Northwest location. Furnished in antiques, it is steps away from the subway, shops, National Cathedral, American University, embassies, and other monuments. The innkeeper is a lawyer and artist.

Host: Joel Odum
Rooms: 2 (SB) $55
Continental Breakfast
Credit Cards: A, B
Notes: 5, 6, 7, 8, 9, 10, 11, 12, 14

Windsor Inn

1842 16th Street, NW
Washington, DC, 20009
(202) 667-0300; (800) 423-9111

A charming art deco inn located eleven blocks from the White House in the heart of Washington, D.C. Features a relaxing and friendly atmosphere as well as personalized service from our staff. Complimentary continental breakfast, afternoon tea, and evening sherry and snacks are available daily.

Host: Susan Stiles
Rooms: 46 (PB) $89.19-111.39
Continental Breakfast
Credit Cards: A, B, C, E, F
Notes: 5, 7, 8, 9, 14

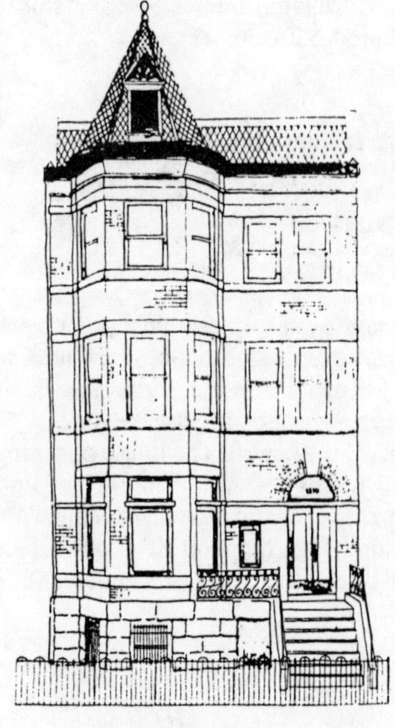

The Reeds

NOTES: Credit cards accepted: A Master Card; B Visa; C American Express; D Discover Card; E Diners Club; F Other: 2 Personal checks accepted: 3 Lunch available: 4 Dinner available: 5 Open all year

Florida

AMELIA ISLAND

Florida House Inn—1857

20-22 South Third Street
P.O. Box 688
Amelia Island, FL, 32034
(904) 261-3300

Located on Amelia Island in the heart of the fifty-block historic district of Fernandina. Built in 1857 as a tourist hotel; today's guests can enjoy the same large porches and twelve rooms, some with fireplaces, all with private baths. Country pine and oak antiques, cheerful handmade rugs and quilts found in each room. Airport pickup available; bikes, FAX machine; handicapped access.

Hosts: Bob & Karen Warner
Rooms: 12 (PB) $55-120
Full Breakfast
Credit Cards: All major
Notes: 2, 3, 4, 5, 7 (outside), 8, 9, 10, 11, 12, 14

The 1735 House

584 South Fletcher Avenue
Amelia Island, FL, 32034
(904) 261-5878; (800) 872-8531

An oceanfront country inn on a Florida beach. Antique nautical decorations enhance your private ocean view. Full suites, private bath, fresh-baked pastries, and morning newspaper. One suite located in a lighthouse, with two bedrooms, bath, galley, working light, and observation deck.

Hosts: Gary & Emily Grable
Suites: 6 (PB) $55-125
Continental Breakfast
Credit Cards: A, B, C
Notes: 2, 5, 7, 8, 9, 10, 11, 12, 14

APALACHICOLA

The Gibson Inn

P.O. Box 221
Apalachicola, FL, 32320
(904) 653-2191

All rooms are decorated with period furnishings: four-poster beds, ceiling fans, antique armoires, and pedestal lavatories with wide basins and porcelain fixtures. Shelling, boating, and fishing are close, plus four barrier islands to explore. Apalachicola is a seafood lover's paradise.

Hosts: Michael Koun & Ross Hewitt
Rooms: 30 (PB) $60-80
Full Breakfast
Credit Cards: A, B, C
Notes: 2, 4, 5, 6, 7, 8, 9, 14

The 1735 House

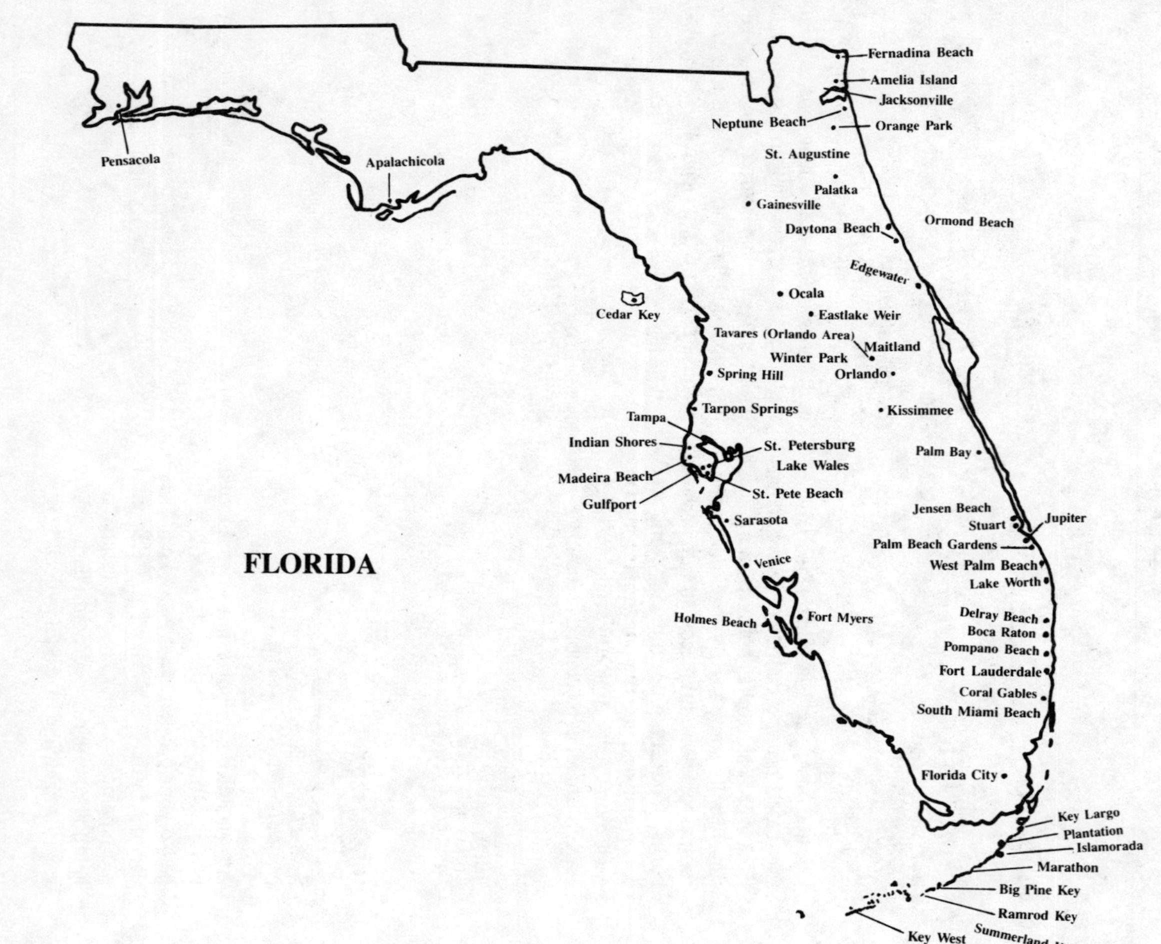
FLORIDA
Pensacola
Apalachicola
Fernadina Beach
Amelia Island
Jacksonville
Neptune Beach
Orange Park
St. Augustine
Palatka
Gainesville
Daytona Beach
Ormond Beach
Edgewater
Ocala
Eastlake Weir
Cedar Key
Tavares (Orlando Area)
Maitland
Winter Park
Orlando
Spring Hill
Tarpon Springs
Kissimmee
Tampa
Indian Shores
St. Petersburg
Lake Wales
Madeira Beach
St. Pete Beach
Gulfport
Sarasota
Palm Bay
Jensen Beach
Stuart
Jupiter
Palm Beach Gardens
West Palm Beach
Lake Worth
Venice
Holmes Beach
Fort Myers
Delray Beach
Boca Raton
Pompano Beach
Fort Lauderdale
Coral Gables
South Miami Beach
Florida City
Key Largo
Plantation
Islamorada
Marathon
Big Pine Key
Ramrod Key
Key West
Summerland Key

BIG PINE KEY

The Barnacle

Route 1, Box 780A
Big Pine Key, FL, 33043
(305) 872-3298

Enjoy the ambience of a home-stay bed and breakfast, along with every amenity. A unique experience on the ocean, surrounded by lush, verdant foliage, where you can enjoy peace and quiet, yet be only thirty miles from the attractions of Key West.

Hosts: Wood & Joan Cornell
Rooms: 4 (PB) $70-100
Full Breakfast
Credit Cards: No
Notes: 2, 5, 7, 9, 11

The Barnacle

Bed & Breakfast Co. FK265

P.O. Box 262
Miami, FL, 33243
(305) 661-3270

Unusual three-story frame home on the ocean. Rustic, with numerous skylights giving a sense of openness. Central living space with windows and balcony overlooking the water. Third level has two large guest rooms with private baths, separated by a large central hall for privacy. Private balconies off each room. Canoe, bikes, and rubber raft available. $75-80.

Canal Cottage

P.O. Box 266
Big Pine Key, FL, 33043
(305) 872-3881

Relax in the private apartment of this quaint, natural wood stilt home. Nestled in the treetops, cooled by island breezes and Bahama fans. Enjoy the bicycles, cable TV, gas grill, and fully furnished kitchen. Near a nature trail and the Key Deer Refuge.

Hosts: Dean & Patti Nickless
Rooms: 1 (PB) $75
Continental Breakfast
Credit Cards: No
Notes: 2, 5, 7, 8, 9, 11, 14

Deer Run

Long Beach Road
Box 431
Big Pine Key, FL, 33043
(305) 872-2015; (305) 872-2800

Deer Run is a Florida-cracker-style house nestled among lush native trees on the ocean. Breakfast is served on the large veranda overlooking the ocean. Dive at Looe Key National Marine Sanctuary, fish the Gulf Stream, or lie on the beach.

Host: Sue Abbott
Rooms: 2 (PB) $75-85
Full Breakfast
Minimum stay: 2
Credit Cards: No
Notes: 2, 5, 9, 11

BOCA RATON

Bed & Breakfast Co. BR75

P.O. Box 262
Miami, FL, 33243
(305) 661-3270

Pool-house cottage behind the main home, located one block from the Atlantic. Excellent neighborhood; one block to a five-star restaurant and other shops. Cottage has a king bed, refrigerator, microwave, cable TV. $70-80.

Bed & Breakfast Co. BR64

P.O. Box 262
Miami, FL, 33243
(305) 661-3270

Suburban ranch home with a variety of personal touches reflecting the hostess's interest in needlework, gardening, and flowers. Pleasant neighborhood, near ten golf courses; two miles to large mall; seven to beach. Two comfortable rooms with double beds share a bath. $35-45.

The Historic Island Hotel

CEDAR KEY

The Historic Island Hotel

P.O. Box 460
Cedar Key, FL, 32625
(904) 543-5111

Pre-Civil War Jamaican-style architecture, rustic "tabby-walled" building on the National Register of Historic Places. Award-winning hotel and gourmet natural foods dining room. Like staying in a museum: muraled walls, paddle fans, antiques, French doors, verandas, and gulf breezes make this a popular wedding and honeymoon retreat.

Host: Marcia Rogers
Rooms: 10 (6 PB; 4 S2B) $70-80 + tax
Full Breakfast
Credit Cards: A, B, D
Notes: 2, 4, 5, 8, 9, 10, 11

CORAL GABLES

Bed & Breakfast Co. MI022

P.O. Box 262
Miami, FL, 33243
(305) 661-3270

Two-room cottage behind a luxury Coral Gables home. Series of windows in living room/bedroom make it light and pleasant. Efficiency kitchen. Twin beds in bedroom and queen convertible in the living room. Excellent location close to Venetian Pool, Miracle Mile restaurants, shops, movie, bus station, golf. About four miles from downtown and four miles from airport. $60-70.

DAYTONA BEACH

Bed & Breakfast Co. DB263

P.O. Box 262
Miami, FL, 33243
(305) 661-3270

Charming studio room off the upper balcony of a new townhouse in a golf-course community. Close to everything. Guest room has queen convertible bed and private bath. $35-45.

Captains Quarters Inn

3711 South Atlantic Avenue
Daytona Beach, FL, 32127
(904) 767-3119

The inn features new oceanfront suites with private balconies overlooking the Atlantic Ocean and our swimming pool. Daily maid service, old English charm with poster beds.

Only minutes from Disney World. Enjoy our old-fashioned coffee shoppe and Rebecca's Place, full of gifts and antiques. We welcome you with wine and cheese, and deliver a daily newspaper to your door. AAA rated excellent.

Hosts: Beckey Sue Morgan & family
Rooms: 25 (PB) $75-110
Full Breakfast
Credit Cards: A, B, C, D
Notes: 2, 3, 5, 7, 8, 9, 10, 11, 12

DELRAY BEACH

Bed & Breakfast Co. DB45

P.O. Box 262
Miami, FL, 33243
(305) 661-3270

Ranch/pool home about three miles from the ocean. Contemporary, attractive, quality furnishing throughout. Bedroom with twins offers excellent privacy in one wing of the home. Three dogs in residence. $45-55.

Bed & Breakfast Co. DB211

P.O. Box 262
Miami, FL, 33243
(305) 661-3270

Two-story frame home in the historic area, built in 1921 and restored as a B&B. Three guest rooms with private baths. Across from the cultural arts center, museum, and park. Walk the short distance to the shops, center of town, and restaurants. $45-55.

EASTLAKE WEIR

Lakeside Inn B&B

P.O. Box 71
Eastlake Weir, FL, 32133
(904) 288-1396

Silver Springs and Ocala National Forest are within easy reach. We are located twenty-five miles south of Ocala, which is known for its horse-breeding facilities and farms.

Hosts: Sandy & Bill Bodner
Rooms: 5 (1 PB; 4 SB) $40-50
Full Breakfast
Credit Cards: No
Notes: 2, 5, 7 (outside), 8 (over 5), 9, 10, 11, 14

EDGEWATER

The Colonial House

110 East Yelkca Terrace
Edgewater, FL, 32132
(904) 427-4570

We are situated on Florida's east coast, between Daytona Beach and Cape Canaveral. Our guests will enjoy fine European hospitality in a quiet family atmosphere. Rooms have air conditioning, TV, refrigerator, and private bath. Enjoy our solar-heated swimming pool and Jacuzzi. Nearby beaches, golf, deep-sea fishing, the Space Center, Disney World.

Host: Eva Brandner
Rooms: 3 (PB) $45
Two-night minimum stay
Full Breakfast
Credit Cards: No
Notes: 2, 5, 8 (over 4), 9, 10, 11, 12, 14

FERNANDINA BEACH

The Bailey House

28 South Seventh Street
Fernandina Beach, FL, 32034
(904) 261-5390

Elegant 1895 Victorian filled with antiques; air-conditioning, private baths. On National Historic Register in the center of town, a short walk to restaurants, shops, marina, lighted tennis. Five minutes to Ft. Clinch, the beach, golf, and horseback riding. Bicycles available. Transportation available from the marina and municipal airport, with advance notice.

Hosts: Tom & Diane Hay
Rooms: 4 (PB) $65-$95

Expanded Continental Breakfast
Credit Cards: C
Notes: 2, 5, 7 (veranda only), 8 (over 10), 9, 10, 11, 12, 14

B&B Suncoast Accommodations

8690 Gulf Street
St. Petersburg Beach, FL, 33706
(813) 360-1753

Ocean view from your balcony. This efficiency sleeps four on the ground floor with a double room upstairs. VCR available on request. Bikes, fishing gear also available. Only 150 steps to the beach. Continental breakfast; two-night minimum stay. $50-110.

The Phoenix' Nest

619 South Fletcher Avenue
Fernandina Beach, FL, 32034
(904) 277-2129

On Amelia Island, a seaside retreat in the B&B tradition. Suites two hundred feet from the Atlantic. Beautiful, private, gracious, rich in color and texture. Fascinating books and magazines spanning 250 years are so enthralling you may hope it rains. Bikes, hammock, surf fishing gear, videos from Chaplin to Napolean, Koko to O'Keefe.

Host: Harriett Johnston Fortenberry
Suites: 4 (PB) $75-85
Continental Breakfast
Credit Cards: A, B
Notes: 2, 5, 7, 9, 10, 11, 12, 14

FLORIDA CITY

Grandma Newtons B&B

40 N.W. Fifth Avenue
Florida City, FL, 33034
(305) 247-4413

Visit Grandma and the relaxed country atmosphere of her historic 1914 two-story renovated country home. Minutes from national parks, the Florida Keys, and Miami. Spacious rooms with air-conditioning insure a peaceful rest that sets your appetite for our huge country breakfast.

Host: Mildred T. Newton
Rooms: 8 (4 PB; 4 SB) $39.95-$61.50
Full Breakfast
Minimum stay holidays: 2
Credit Cards: No
Notes: 2 (for deposit only), 5, 7, 8, 9, 10, 11, 12, 14

FORT LAUDERDALE

Bed & Breakfast Co. FL49

P.O. Box 262
Miami, FL, 33243
(305) 661-3270

Waterfront home in Wilton Manor with a large pool and sun deck. Guest room with two twins and a private bath is in a separate wing for privacy. One mile to the beach; five minutes to bus, shopping, restaurants. $45-55.

Bed & Breakfast Co. FL53

P.O. Box 262
Miami, FL, 33243
(305) 661-3270

In an older residential area of Wilton Manor, on a waterway. Bedroom is off an enclosed porch, private from the hosts' quarters. Contour queen bed with assorted controls; private bath. Convertible sofa could accommodate extra guests. Fruit trees and tropical plantings in the garden; spa. $45-55.

Bed & Breakfast Co. FL70

P.O. Box 262
Miami, FL, 33243
(305) 661-3270

One-story older home only one block from the Atlantic. Bedrooms are located at the rear of the home with private entry from driveway. Two twins and one double share a bath. $35-45.

Bed & Breakfast Co. FL72

P.O. Box 262
Miami, FL, 33243
(305) 661-3270

Ranch home on a waterway just off the Intercoastal. Exceptionally attractive home. Bedroom with two twins, private bath; large pool area with chickee-bar at one end. $55-65.

The Dolan House

1401 N.E. 5 Court
Fort Lauderdale, FL, 33301
(305) 462-8430

We are centrally located for the beach, shopping, businesses, and full park exercise facilities. Each room is equipped with ceiling fans and individual air-conditioners. Our garden and patio areas are great for enjoying the Florida sun, or you may want to slip into the hot tub spa. Twenty percent discount during June and July.

Hosts: Tom & Sandra Dolan
Rooms: 4 (2 PB; 2 SB) $59.95-65.40
Continental Breakfast
Minimum stay: 2
Credit Cards: No
Closed Aug. & Sept.
Notes: 2, 7 (restricted), 9, 10, 11

FORT MYERS

Bed & Breakfast Co. FM199

P.O. Box 262
Miami, FL, 33243
(305) 661-3270

Two-story colonial home in the rural setting of Alva, nine miles east of Ft. Myers. Off the main road, along a navigable creek. Farm animals nearby. $35-45.

Embe's Hobby House

5570-4 Woodrose Court
Fort Myers, FL, 33907
(813) 936-6378

This townhouse-type home is designed to be your home away from home during your stay. The bright, spacious suite is cheery and comfortable, with combined sleeping and living areas, including private bath with dressing room. There is a resident cat. Located just fifteen minutes from the beaches, Sanibel and Captiva islands, fine shopping, good restaurants, and the Edison and Ford homes.

Host: Embe Burdick
Rooms: 1 (PB) $55
Continental Breakfast
Credit Cards: No
Notes: 2, 5, 9, 10, 11, 12

GAINESVILLE

Bed & Breakfast Co. GA206

P.O. Box 262
Miami, FL, 33243
(305) 661-3270

Two-story country home just five miles off I-75 with easy access to the University of Florida and the city. Close to Silver Springs. Ideal for a weekend in the country, a football weekend, or longer visits. Two rooms, king or double bed, private baths. $35-45.

GULFPORT

B&B Suncoast Accommodations

8690 Gulf Street
Saint Petersburg Beach, FL, 33706
(813) 360-1753

Double room upstairs with TV room, private bath. Pool. Public beaches ten minutes away. Continental breakfast; two-night minimum stay. $45-60.

HAVANA

Gaver's B&B

301 East Sixth Avenue
Havana, FL, 32333
(904) 539-5611

Circa 1907 restored house with a large screened porch, cable TV, central air conditioning, ceiling fans, twelve-foot ceilings. Licensed by the State of Florida and the town of Havana. Off-street, lighted parking. Located in the center of town, two blocks from ten antique stores. Twelve miles north of I-10 and Tallahassee on US 27. Exit 29 off I-10.

Hosts: Shirley & Bruce Gaver
Rooms: 1 (PB) $55 + tax
Continental Breakfast
Credit Cards: No
Notes: 2, 5, 8, 9, 10, 11, 12, 14

HOLMES BEACH

Bed & Breakfast Co. HB201

P.O. Box 262
Miami, FL, 33243
(305) 661-3270

Lovely three-story beach house, completely renovated for B&B. Pool and patio in front; located on the beach. One bedroom downstairs, two on the second floor, and two on the third floor that open onto a deck overlooking the Gulf of Mexico. All private baths. Located on Anna Marie Island, just north of Sarasota. $75-95.

INDIAN SHORES

Meeks B&B on the Gulf Beaches

19506 Gulf Blvd.
Indian Shores, FL, 34635
(813) 596-5424

Our luxurious beach condo overlooks the pool and Gulf beaches. Sumptuous breakfast served. Nearby shopping and restaurants; easy drive to Busch Gardens and Disney World.

Hosts: Bob & Greta Meeks
Rooms: 3 (PB & SB) $50
Full Breakfast
Credit Cards: No
Notes: 2, 5, 7 (limited), 8, 9, 10, 11, 12

ISLAMORADA

Bed & Breakfast Co. FK44

P.O. Box 262
Miami, FL, 33243
(305) 661-3270

Ranch home with two guest rooms, private baths. Located twenty minutes from Pennekamp, the Coral Reef State Park, and Upper Keys attractions. Public beach is nearby. The hostess is a long-time Keys resident and is exceptionally helpful and friendly. $40-55.

JACKSONVILLE

House on Cherry Street

1844 Cherry Street
Jacksonville, FL, 32205
(904) 384-1999

Historic restored home on the St. John's River near downtown Jacksonville featuring antiques, elegant breakfasts, wine, snacks, and bicycles for guest use.

Host: Carol Anderson
Rooms: 4 (PB) $66.40-88.52
Full Breakfast
Credit Cards: A, B
Notes: 2, 5, 8 (6 and over), 9, 10, 12, 14

JENSEN BEACH

Bed & Breakfast Co. JB233

P.O. Box 262
Miami, FL, 33243
(305) 661-3270

Rambling ranch home in a development several miles from the ocean. Shops and commerce are nearby. Two guest rooms. One with two twins and private bath; second with a queen waterbed and shared bath. Pool available. $35-55.

JUPITER

Bed & Breakfast Co. JU248

P.O. Box 262
Miami, FL, 33243
(305) 661-3270

In a suburban area of Jupiter, about nine miles west of the ocean, close to the Burt Reynolds ranch with its country store and petting farm. The hostess makes many craft items and thoroughly enjoys having guests. Three bedrooms, one bath. Airport pickup and other transportation available. $30-40.

KEY LARGO

Bed & Breakfast Co. LK260

P.O. Box 262
Miami, FL, 33243
(305) 661-3270

Romantic one-bedroom apartment on the Atlantic, on first level of large two-story home. A well-maintained sand beach is in front; protected patio and above-ground pool. Double bed, with extra space for one child in the sitting area. Full kitchen. Two night minimum. Two miles to Pennekamp Park. $100.

Bed & Breakfast Co. LK264

P.O. Box 262
Miami, FL, 33243
(305) 661-3270

Two one-bedroom apartments on an open waterway. Spacious, with complete kitchen, cable TV, queen bed, plus sofa or cots for two extra guests. Large windows overlook front garden, deck, and water. Swim and fish from the dock. No charge for snorkeling gear, fish poles, bikes. Two-night minimum. $60-65.

KEY WEST

Colours Key West—The Guest Mansion

410 Fleming Street
Key West, FL, 33040
(305) 294-6977

Circa 1889. This Victorian mansion has been renovated and has maintained all the original architectural detail, including fourteen-foot ceilings, chandeliers, polished wood floors, and graceful verandas. The host states the mansion is for the liberal-minded adult only.

Host: James Remes
Rooms: 12 (10 PB; 2 SB) $72-150
Continental Breakfast
Credit Cards: A, B, C, D, F
Notes: 5, 7, 9, 10, 11, 12, 14

Duval House

Duval House

815 Duval Street
Key West, FL, 33040
(305) 294-1666

6 Pets welcome: 7 Smoking allowed: 8 Children welcome: 9 Social drinking allowed: 10 Tennis available: 11 Swimming available: 12 Golf available: 13 Skiing available: 14 May be booked through travel agents

Restored century-old Victorian houses with charm and deluxe amenities. Large swimming pool and quiet tropical gardens. Walk to restaurants and all attractions. AAA and Mobil Travel Guide approved.

Host: Richard Kamradt
Rooms: 28 (25 PB; 3 SB) $64-145
Continental Breakfast
Credit Cards: A, B, C
Notes: 5, 7, 9, 10, 11, 12

Eaton Lodge, Traditional Inn

511 Eaton Street
Key West, FL, 33040
(305) 294-3800

Designed for those who appreciate personal attention, dignified comfort, and the unique atmosphere of a nineteenth-century residence on the National Register of Historic Places. All rooms feature antique furnishings from England, refrigerator, air-conditioning, and a patio or veranda overlooking the lush tropical grounds.

Host: Mark Anderson
Rooms: 10 (PB) $75-145
Full Breakfast
Credit Cards: A, B
Notes: 2, 5, 7, 9, 10, 11, 12, 14

Heron House

512 Simonton Street
Key West, FL, 33040
(305) 294-9227

Heron House consists of three homes. One, built in 1856, represents the few remaining classic "Conch" houses. Location is in the very heart of the historic district, one block from the main tourist street and three blocks from the nearest beach.

Rooms: 17 (PB) $49.95-194.25
Continental Breakfast
Credit Cards: A, B, C
Notes: 2 (for deposit), 5, 7, 9, 10, 11, 12, 14

The Marquesa Hotel

600 Fleming Street
Key West, FL, 33040
(305) 292-1919

Exquisitely restored Victorian home—located in Old Town, Key West—six blocks from Gulf of Mexico, three miles from airport. All rooms with private bath, air-conditioning, remote-control cable TV, phone, and security safe. Small gourmet restaurant, pool, concierge. AAA four-star award.

Host: Carol Wightman
Rooms: 15 (PB) $105-275 seasonal
Credit Cards: A, B, C
Notes: 4, 5, 7, 8, 9, 10, 11, 12, 14

Merlinn Guest House

811 Simonton Street
Key West, FL, 33040
(305) 296-3336

Lush tropical pool, sun decks, and gardens in the heart of Old Town. Complimentary quiche breakfast and sunset cocktails. Eighteen cathedral-ceilinged rooms with private baths, air-conditioning, and TV. You'll never want to leave!

Host: Pat Hoffman
Rooms: 18 (PB) $59-110
Full Breakfast
Minimum stay holidays: 3
Credit Cards: A, B, C
Notes: 2 (deposit only), 5, 6, 7, 8, 9, 11, 14

The Popular House

415 William Street
Key West, FL, 33040

A 100-year-old Victorian located in the heart of Old Town Key West, the Popular House is within walking distance of the sights and sounds that have made the city famous. Air-conditioning, Jacuzzi, sauna, sun decks and porches for your immediate relaxation. Classic Caribbean casual. Continental breakfast at your leisure.

Host: Jody Carlson
Rooms: 7 (2 PB; 5 SB) $45-135
Continental Breakfast
Credit Cards: A, B, C
Notes: 2, 5, 7, 9, 10, 11, 12, 14

Whispers B&B Inn

The Watson House

525 Simonton Street
Key West, FL, 33040
(305) 294-6712

The Watson House, c. 1860, a distinctively furnished small inn/guest house in the historic preservation district. Received 1986 award for excellence in rehabilitation from Historical Florida Keys Preservation Board. Swimming pool, heated Jacuzzi, patio, decks, and gardens. All units have their own distinct style, private baths, color TV, air-conditioning, and telephone; larger suites have fully equipped kitchens. Privacy prevails; adults only; no pets. Brochure available.

Hosts: Joe Beres & Ed Czaplicki
Suites: 3 (PB) $85-295
Continental Breakfast
Credit Cards: A, B, C
Notes: 5, 7, 9, 10, 11, 12, 14

Whispers B&B Inn

409 William Street
Key West, FL, 33040
(305) 294-5969

As owner-managers, we take great pride in our service, hospitality, and the romance of our historic 1866 inn. Each room is unique and appointed with antiques. Included in the room rate is a full breakfast served in our tropical gardens.

Hosts: Les & Marilyn Tipton
Rooms: 12 (S3B) $75-110
Full Breakfast
Credit Cards: A, B, C
Notes: 5, 7 (limited), 9, 10, 11, 12, 14

Wicker Guesthouse

913 Duval Street
Key West, FL, 33040
(305) 296-4275

The Wicker Guesthouse, a compound of restored Conch homes, is ideally located on colorful Duval Street, within easy walking distance of beaches, restaurants, shops, and attractions. A 41' sailboat and 26' power boat are available for day trips to the coral reef.

Hosts: Mark & Libby Curtis
Rooms: 16 (2 PB; 14 SB) $49.95-94.35
Full Breakfast
Credit Cards: A, B, C
Notes: 2 (advance deposit), 5, 7, 8, 9, 10, 11, 12, 14

Chalet Suzanne Country Inn & Restaurant

KISSIMMEE

The Unicorn Inn English B&B

8 South Orlando Avenue
Kissimmee, FL, 32741
(407) 846-1200

Beautifully restored 1900 Victorian house in downtown Kissimmee. This unique English B&B hotel is in a quiet setting, but close to Disney and Epcot. Also very close to Lake Toho, with some of the best fishing in Florida. Enjoy some English hospitality.

Host: Janet Timbrell
Rooms: 4 (PB) $55-65
Apartments: 2 (PB) $75
Full Breakfast
Credit Cards: A, B
Notes: 2, 5, 7, 14

LAKE WALES

Chalet Suzanne Country Inn & Restaurant

P.O. Drawer AC
Lake Wales, FL, 33859-9003
(800) 676-6011; (800) 288-6011

Discover Europe in the heart of Florida. This historic country inn is located on 70 acres surrounded by orange groves. Thirty charming guest rooms with private baths. Award-winning dining overlooking Lake Suzanne. Forty-five minutes southwest of the Orlando area.

Hosts: Carl & Vita Hinshaw
Rooms: 30 (PB) $85-185
Full Breakfast
Credit Cards: A, B, C, D, E
Notes: 2, 3, 4, 5, 6, 7, 8, 9, 10, 11, 12, 14

LAKE WORTH

Bed & Breakfast Co. LW188

P.O. Box 262
Miami, FL, 33243
(305) 661-3270

Large five-bedroom frame home on a 5-acre working nursery with four B&B rooms. Family room with pool table, screened porches, living room with two-story fireplace. Two double rooms with private baths and two single rooms that share a bath. Fifteen minutes from the airport, twenty to West Palm Beach. $35-45.

MADEIRA BEACH

B&B Suncoast Accommodations

8690 Gulf Street
Saint Petersburg Beach, FL, 33706
(813) 360-1753

This home is on the bay, with a dock and swimming pool. Two double rooms are available with private bath. No smoking. Continental breakfast; two-night minimum stay. $50-70.

MAITLAND

A&A B&B of Florida 8

P.O. Box 1316
Winter Park, FL, 32790
(407) 628-3233

Large two-story home by Lake Sybelia. Accommodations are on the first floor. Lovely hostess, good with children, can accommodate a party of four. Private bath; full breakfast; air-conditioning. $55.

Hopp-Inn Guest House

MARATHON

Hopp-Inn Guest House

5 Man-O-War Drive
Marathon, FL, 33050
(305) 743-4118

We are located in the heart of the Florida Keys. Every room has a water view. Charter fishing on premises aboard the *Sea Wolf*. Families welcome in villas.

Hosts: The Hopp Family
Rooms: 5 (PB) $55-125
Villas: 4 (PB)
Full Breakfast
Credit Cards: A, B
Notes: 2 (for deposit), 5, 7 (limited), 8, 10, 11, 12

MIAMI

Bed & Breakfast Co. MI8

P.O. Box 262
Miami, FL, 33243
(305) 661-3270

Spacious ranch home in a choice residential area of Key Biscayne. Private entrance to guest room, king bed, entrance to screened pool area. Walk to the beach, shops, restaurants of this famous island. The hosts' talking parrot will amuse you. Two rooms, private baths. $35-45.

Bed & Breakfast Co. MI16

P.O. Box 262
Miami, FL, 33243
(305) 661-3270

Spacious estate in "horse country," southwest Dade County. Large ranch home where horses are boarded. Equestrian school is across the street; horse rentals nearby. Located ten to twenty minutes from the city, this house offers three bedrooms, one with a private deck and bath with whirlpool. All three have private baths. Cats on premises. $35-65.

Bed & Breakfast Co. MI18

P.O. Box 262
Miami, FL, 33243
(305) 661-3270

Delightful home designed by a landscape architect to bring the outside in. Excellent views and access to back patio and garden. Casual, comfortable, attractive furnishings. Close to bus, metrorail; walk to shops, restaurants, the University of Miami. Queen bedroom shares bath with hostess. Single occupancy only. $30-35.

Bed & Breakfast Co. MI24

P.O. Box 262
Miami, FL, 33243
(305) 661-3270

Two-room suite in Coconut Grove with private entry. In desirable section of North Grove, three blocks from the bay. Walk to village restaurants, shops, marinas; take the trolley to the village and bayside. Gazebo in large landscaped garden with fruit trees and hibiscus. Double bed, private bath. Double sofa in living room for extra guests. Handicapped equipped. $50-60.

Bed & Breakfast Co. MI25

P.O. Box 262
Miami, FL, 33243
(305) 661-3270

Exceptionally interesting rustic contemporary two-story home in a choice residential area of Coconut Grove. Spiral stairway goes from ground level to third level crow's nest for a view of Biscayne Bay and Miami. Guest room on first level with open deck on the waterway. $60-70.

Bed & Breakfast Co. MI26

P.O. Box 262
Miami, FL, 33243
(305) 661-3270

Moorish/Mediterranean architecture in a luxury home listed in the Historic Registry. Many exquisite antique furnishings, charming garden area, walled patio with swimming pool. Close to historic Plymouth Congregational Church; walk to Coconut Grove Village, restaurants, sidewalk cafes, marinas, boutiques. One block to twenty-mile bike path. One guest room with queen bed, private bath. $65-75.

Bed & Breakfast Co. MI27

P.O. Box 262
Miami, FL, 33243
(305) 661-3270

Beautiful two-story home with historic designation. Formerly used as an inn. Large rooms, great fireplace. The kitchen has been modernized, but retains its huge antique stove and icebox. Upstairs bedroom with king bed and bath with antique decor. Walk to village along tree-canopied streets to shop, eat, rent sailboats or fishing charters. Macrobiotic breakfast served on request. $50-60.

Bed & Breakfast Co. MI31

P.O. Box 262
Miami, FL, 33243
(305) 661-3270

Convenience and charm in a North Miami townhouse. On a canal and a bus line, with shops and restaurants across the street. Walk to the ocean and Bal Harbor, with its exclusive shops, in twenty minutes. Upstairs bedroom, private bath, twin beds. $40-50.

Bed & Breakfast Co. MI34

P.O. Box 262
Miami, FL, 33243
(305) 661-3270

A mansion on a private residential island in Biscayne Bay with two guest rooms and private baths. Furnishings reflect the Old World charm of the Danish hosts. Near golf course. Five-minute ride to the ocean, Theatre of Performing Arts, Art Deco District. Ecologically balanced pool, with no chemicals, and hot tub. $70-80.

Bed & Breakfast Co. MI215

P.O. Box 262
Miami, FL, 33243
(305) 661-3270

Luxury contemporary pool home. Living room, dining room, kitchen, and bedroom wing open onto oversized screened pool with patio and garden. Two bedrooms with private baths, spa, and queen beds. Close to shopping malls, Parrot Jungle, southwest Miami attractions. $45-55.

Bed & Breakfast Co. MI219

P.O. Box 262
Miami, FL, 33243
(305) 661-3270

Enjoy the view of the bay and Miami Beach from your bedroom in this luxury waterfront home in Miami Shores. Pool and hot tub border the bay. Two bedrooms, one with a king bed and the other with two twins; private baths. $70-80.

Bed & Breakfast Co. MI226

P.O. Box 262
Miami, FL, 33243
(305) 661-3270

Large one-story sprawling home on several lots in choice Coconut Grove area. Private entry to large bedroom/bath, two single beds, with windows on three sides and good views. Pool with many native trees and tropical plantings. Room with shared bath and convertible sofa also available. $45-70.

Bed & Breakfast Co. MI235

P.O. Box 262
Miami, FL, 33243
(305) 661-3270

Carriage house on estate grounds within walking distance of Coconut Grove Village. Tree-top sitting room/bedroom suite is pleasantly furnished. Attractively landscaped property in an area of luxury homes. $55-65.

Bed & Breakfast Co. MI246

P.O. Box 262
Miami, FL, 33243
(305) 661-3270

Luxury cottage in a tropical setting. Walk to shops, restaurants, cafes, and marinas. Walled estate with main house and cottage, landscaped with specimen tropical plantings, natural pool, and fountain. Completely equipped with microwave, dishwasher, cable TV/VCR. Double bed, sofa for one extra guest, private bath. $85-90.

Bed & Breakfast Co. MI247

P.O. Box 262
Miami, FL, 33243
(305) 661-3270

Cottage in Moorish-Mediterranean architecture of the 1920s. Sitting room, bedroom with queen bed, full kitchen, patio in a formal garden. Furnishings are antiques or excellent reproductions. Located on one of Coconut Grove's most beautiful streets. Three-night minimum. $95-100.

NEPTUNE BEACH

B&B Suncoast Accommodations

8690 Gulf Street
Saint Petersburg Beach, FL, 33706
(813) 360-1753

Twin room and single room available. Private baths. Located eighteen miles from Jacksonville, on the Atlantic Ocean. Continental breakfast; two-night minimum stay. $50-90.

Seven Sisters Inn

OCALA

Central Florida B&B

719 SE Fourth Street
Ocala, FL, 32671
(904) 351-1167

An 1899 Victorian in the historic district of downtown Ocala. Oriental rugs decorate the house, as well as an extensive doll collection. Homemade Irish scones come with breakfast. Close to Gainesville; ninety minutes to Disney/Epcot. Near Silver Springs (glass-bottom boats), Cross Creek, and historic McIntosh and Micanopy for antique buffs. Our white Angora cat, Ashley, lives on the premises.

Host: Marcie Gauntlett
Rooms: 1 (PB) $35-40
Full Breakfast
Credit Cards: No
Notes: 2, 4, 8 (over 12), 9, 12

Seven Sisters Inn

820 SE Fort King Street
Ocala, FL, 32671
(904) 867-1170

"One of the 12 best inns in America," says *Country Inns* Magazine. Queen Anne Victorian mansion won Best Restoration Award in State of Florida for 1986. "Impeccable, one of a kind," says travel guides. Tour local horse farms, visit Silver Springs Park, or Jeep Safari. Full gourmet breakfast served in surroundings of flowering walkways and large wicker-filled porches. Come create a memory.

Hosts: Jerry & Norma Johnson
Rooms: 5 (PB) $75-105
Full Breakfast
Credit Cards: A, B, C
Notes: 2, 5, 7 (limited), 8 (limited), 9, 10, 11, 12, 14

ORANGE PARK

The Club Continental

2143 Astor Street
Orange Park, FL, 32073
(904) 264-6070

The Inn at Club Continental offers superb French and American cuisine and cocktails in an elegant lounge. Enjoy the "good-time" atmosphere down the path by the river at the Riverhouse Pub. A restored pre-Civil War cottage is now a favorite local gathering place. The club also offers seven tennis courts, three swimming pools, and an 85-slip marina. Club Continental is close to charter fishing, St. Augustine, Marineland, Amelia Island, Kennedy Space Center, and Disney World.

Host: Caleb Massee, Jr.
Suites: 7 (PB) $55-70
Continental Breakfast
Credit Cards: C
Notes: 2, 3, 4, 5, 7, 8, 9, 10, 11, 12, 14

ORLANDO

A&A B&B of Florida 1

P.O. Box 1316
Winter Park, FL, 32790
(407) 628-3233

Beautiful large four-bedroom home with lots of flowers. Screened-in patio with exercise bike and other workout items. Sunning area. Only minutes to Disney and Epcot. Airport pickup available for a fee. One double room. Full breakfast; air-conditioning. $45-55.

A&A B&B of Florida 3

P.O. Box 1316
Winter Park, FL, 32790
(407) 628-3233

Contemporary home located in "Isle of Catalina" on a wide canal with a view of Orlando's beautiful lakes. You may use the pool for a morning or afternoon swim. One double room. Full breakfast; air-conditioning. $35-45.

A&A B&B of Florida 4

P.O. Box 1316
Winter Park, FL, 32790
(407) 628-3233

A smaller home in a nice area with lakefront property and a beautiful garden. Room with twin beds and private shower. Full breakfast is served on the patio when weather permits. $40.

A&A B&B of Florida 7

P.O. Box 1316
Winter Park, FL, 32790
(407) 628-3233

Ten minutes away from Disney and Epcot, this home offers a king bed and sitting room with TV and private bath. Near shopping area. Pool, full breakfast, air-conditioning. $55.

A&A B&B of Florida 11

P.O. Box 1316
Winter Park, FL, 32790
(407) 628-3233

Lovely rooms in an Old English home with lots of antiques. The blue room has Laura Ashley furnishings, private bath, private entrance, sunning area, and ample parking. The pink room has small kitchen facilities. Continental breakfast, air conditioning. $55-65.

Bed & Breakfast Co. OR65

P.O. Box 262
Miami, FL, 33243
(305) 661-3270

Comfortable, attractive twin room with private bath in good residential area ten minutes from the airport and twenty to major attractions. $35-45.

The Courtyard at Lake Lucerne

211 North Lucerne Circle East
Orlando, FL, 32801
(407) 648-5188

Victorian and Art Deco elegance in a tropical setting in the heart of downtown Orlando. Consisting of three separate buildings, each with its own distinctive style, surrounding a luxuriously landscaped courtyard with fountains. Complimentary bottle of wine on arrival and extended continental breakfast each morning.

Hosts: Charles, Sam, & Paula Meiner
Rooms: 23 (PB) $85
Continental-plus Breakfast
Credit Cards: A, B, C
Notes: 2, 5, 7, 8, 9, 10, 11, 12, 14

Esther's Bed & Breakfast

2411 Virginia Drive
Orlando, FL, 32803
(407) 896-9916

Located near Epcot Center and Disney World. A continental breakfast of homemade coffee cake or muffins, cheese, fruit, and coffee is served, plus evening wine or homemade ice cream in the midst of Esther's needlepoints of old masters' paintings. Swimming pool.

Host: Esther M. Allen
Rooms: 2 (SB) $37.10-$47.70
Continental Breakfast
Credit Cards: No
Notes: 2 (deposit only), 5, 8 (over 10), 9, 10, 11, 12

The Rio Pinar House

532 Pinar Drive
Orlando, FL, 32825
(407) 277-4903

A quiet, spacious, private home, furnished with antiques, featuring a breakfast porch overlooking a yard of trees and flowers. Located in a golf course community, convenient to the airport, downtown Church Street Station, Disney and Epcot, the Space Center, and Expressway exits.

Hosts: Delores & Vic Freudenburg
Rooms: 3 (PB) $45-55
Full Breakfast
Credit Cards: No
Notes: 2 (if sent in advance), 5, 8, 9, 12

The Spencer Home B&B

313 Spencer Street
Orlando, Fl, 32809
(407) 855-5603

Our suite with private entrance consists of one or two bedrooms with a queen and double bed and living room with queen sofabed. TV, swimming pool, kitchen, laundry are all available. Convention Center and most of Central Florida's attractions are within fifteen to thirty minutes away. Brochure available.

Hosts: Neal & Eunice Schattauer
Rooms: 1-2 (PB) $50-100
Continental-plus Breakfast
Credit Cards: No
Minimum stay: 2
Notes: 5, 8, 9, 11

ORMOND BEACH

Bed & Breakfast Co. OB247

P.O. Box 262
Miami, FL, 33243
(305) 661-3270

Stay two blocks from the ocean and an excellent beach, in a spacious ranch with a pool. Two bedrooms with private baths. One opens onto the pool area. Contemporary furnishings, queen beds. Good restaurants and shops a short drive. $40-55.

PALATKA

Bed & Breakfast Co. PA196

P.O. Box 262
Miami, FL, 33243
(305) 661-3270

Fifteen miles west of St. Augustine on the river. One-bedroom apartment is attached to ranch home. Large yard, dock for fishing and boats, relaxing atmosphere. Catch shrimp and fish off the dock. Double bed and convertible sofa in the living room. $45-55.

PALM BAY

Casa Del Sol

Country Estates
232 Rheine Road NW
Palm Bay, FL, 32907
(407) 728-4676

An award-winning home of Florida's Central East Coast. Breakfast is served from the lanai with breathtaking foliage. You can see a spaceship orbit. Enjoy the luxury of a Roman tub. Minutes away from the Space Pad and all Disney attractions.

Host: Stanley Finkelstein
Rooms: 3 (1 PB; 2 SB) $55-125
Full Breakfast
Credit Cards: No
Closed May 6-Oct. 15
Notes: 3, 4, 6, 7, 8, 9, 10, 11, 12, 14

PALM BEACH GARDENS

Bed & Breakfast Co. WP190

P.O. Box 262
Miami, FL, 33243
(305) 661-3270

Nestled amid pine and citrus trees is a cottage with pool and hot tub. The bedroom has two twins; dining area; bath. Formerly a tack room for the hostess's riding horses. In the morning you may feed the horses carrots and greet the country dogs. Riding stables are nearby. $50-60.

PENSACOLA

The Homestead Inn

7830 Pine Forest Road
Pensacola, FL, 32506
(904) 944-4816

This beautiful Victorian bed-and-breakfast inn combines the charm and grace of yesteryear with modern comfort and convenience. Personal attention is the order of the day in an atmosphere of intimate elegance. Guest rooms are individually appointed with private bath, color TV, and telephone. Some come with skylight and fireplace, and one extra-special honeymoon suite boasts a king canopy bed and fireplace. Guests enjoy complimentary homemade desserts each evening and awake to a six-course gourmet breakfast. A hot tub, billiard table, large-screen TV, and complete workout center are available to our guests.

Hosts: Neil & Jeanne Liechty
Rooms: 5 (PB) $69-79
Suites: 2 (PB) $79
Full Breakfast
Credit Cards: A, B, C
Notes: 2, 5, 8, 9, 12, 14

PLANTATION

Bed & Breakfast Co. PL68

P.O. Box 262
Miami, FL, 33243
(305) 661-3270

Comfortable ranch home in an upscale suburban community adjoining Ft. Lauderdale. The bedroom has two twins and private bath. Attractive, nicely maintained furnishings and grounds. Across the street from a community pool and tennis courts. Close to Nova University. $35-45.

POMPANO BEACH

Bed & Breakfast Co. PB1

P.O. Box 262
Miami, FL, 33243
(305) 661-3270

A ranch home at the north end of Pompano Beach, on the waterway about a ten-minute walk from the ocean. Guest bedrooms are in a separate wing of the home. One has a twin and a double bed, the other a queen. Refrigerators, private baths. Solar-heated pool, resident dogs. $45-55.

RAMROD KEY

Bed & Breakfast Co. LK63

P.O. Box 262
Miami, FL, 33243
(305) 661-3270

Roomy one-bedroom apartment in a separate building facing canal across from the Gulf of Mexico. Living room, bath, complete kitchen. Swim, snorkel, fish. Five-minute drive to Loo Key for the best snorkeling in the Keys. Property located in Key Deer Refuge. Large pool, deck, hot tub, play area for children. $75-80.

Bed & Breakfast Co. LK256

P.O. Box 262
Miami, FL, 33243
(305) 661-3270

Upper level of a large two-story building next to host home, on waterway, with view of the Gulf of Mexico. Newly built and furnished with a double and single bed, full kitchen, large dining/sitting space. Easy access to small beach. Use of paddle boat and pool across the way; dock for swimming and fishing. Close to Loo Key for excellent snorkeling. $75-80.

ST. AUGUSTINE

Carriage Way B&B

70 Cuna Street
St. Augustine, FL, 32084
(904) 829-2467

An 1883 Victorian in the historic district, within walking distance of the waterfront, shops, restaurants, and historic sites. Complimentary cordials, newspaper, cookies, bicycles, and breakfast. The atmosphere here is leisurely and casual.

Hosts: Karen Burkley-Kovacik & Frank Kovacik
Rooms: 7 (PB) $49-97
Continental Breakfast
Credit Cards: A, B
Notes: 2, 3, 4, 5, 8, 9, 10, 11, 12, 14

Casa de Solana B&B Inn

21 Aviles Street
St. Augustine, FL, 32084
(904) 824-3555

Circa 1763. Four antique-filled suites with cable TV, private bath, enclosed courtyard. Full breakfast is served in the formal dining room; a decanter of sherry is presented on arrival. The inn is downtown, with all the quaint shops, museums, restaurants, and horse and buggies to help you in your tour of Saint Augustine, our oldest city.

Hosts: Jim & Faye McMurry
Rooms: 4 (PB) $100-125
Full Breakfast
Minimum stay weekends & holidays: 2
Credit Cards: A, B, C
Notes: 2, 5, 9

Casa de Solana B&B Inn

The Kenwood Inn

38 Marine Street
St. Augustine, FL, 32084
(904) 824-2116

Local maps and early records show the inn was built between 1865 and 1885 and was functioning as a private boarding house as early as 1886. Located in the historic district, the inn is within walking distance of many fine restaurants and all historic sights. One block from the Intracoastal Waterway, with its passing fishing trawlers, yachts at anchor, and the classic Bridge of Lions. Beautiful ocean beaches are just across the bridge.

Hosts: Mark, Kerrianne & Caitlin Constant
Rooms: 12 (PB) $55-85
Continental Breakfast
Credit Cards: A, B, D
Notes: 2, 5, 9, 10, 11, 12

St. Francis Inn

279 St. George Street
St. Augustine, FL, 32084
(904) 824-6068

The qualities that make the St. Francis special include the varied selection of accommodations, the warmth and peacefulness of the inn, the ideal location, and the quality of guests it attracts. Its architectural charm and modern amenities also contribute to its overall appeal and comfort.

Host: Marie Register
Rooms: 14 (PB) $50-110
Continental Breakfast
Credit Cards: A, B
Notes: 2, 5, 8, 9, 10, 11, 12, 14

The Kenwood Inn

Westcott House

146 Avenida Menendez
St. Augustine, FL, 32084
(904) 824-4301

Circa 1890, restored in 1983, in the historic district within walking distance to historic sights. All rooms have private baths, king-sized beds, cable television, private telephone, and are furnished in antiques. Year-round climate control. On Matanzaz Bayfront, one-half block from the city's yacht pier.

Hosts: Ruth & Fred Erminelli
Rooms: 8 (PB) $75-135
Continental Breakfast
Credit Cards: A, B
Notes: 2, 5, 8, 9, 10, 11, 12, 14

ST. PETERSBURG

B&B Suncoast Accommodations

8690 Gulf Street
Saint Petersburg Beach, FL, 33706
(813) 360-1753

Private entrance to this clean twin-bedded room with cable TV. Ten minutes from the beach or downtown St. Petersburg. Pick fruit off the trees in season. Continental breakfast; two-night minimum stay. $45-55.

Bayboro House B&B

1719 Beach Drive SE
St. Petersburg, FL, 33701
(813) 823-4955

Turn-of-the-century Queen Anne home furnished in antiques. Old-fashioned porch swing to enjoy sea gulls and sailboats on Old Tampa Bay. Minutes from the Dali Museum, pier, Bayfront Center, Al Lange Stadium. Many fine restaurants in the area. Personal apartment available on request.

Hosts: Gordon & Antonia Powers
Rooms: 3 (PB) $60.50-71.50
Continental Breakfast
Credit Cards: A, B
Notes: 2, 5, 7 (limited), 9, 10, 11, 12

ST. PETERSBURG BEACH

B&B Suncoast Accommodations

8690 Gulf Street
Saint Petersburg Beach, FL, 33706
(813) 360-1753

Waterfront home with dock, kitchen, and laundry privileges. Heated spa. Located one-half mile to the Gulf of Mexico; tennis and golf nearby. Accommodations include one queen room with private bath and two double rooms with shared bath. Continental breakfast is served; two-night minimum stay. $40-70.

SARASOTA-SIESTA KEY

Bed & Breakfast Co. SK200

P.O. Box 262
Miami, FL, 33243
(305) 661-3270

Casual beach house on Siesta Key, a luxury residential community accessed from downtown Sarasota. Scottish and French hosts live in a cottage in the rear. Sun or relax on the deck or the wide sand beach just across the street. Rent sailboards, sailboats, bicycles in the nearby village. Three rooms, private baths. $65-90.

SOUTH MIAMI BEACH

Avalon Hotel

700 Ocean Drive
South Miami Beach, FL, 33139
(305) 538-0133; (800) 933-3306

A newly restored Art Deco hotel commanding a magnificent beachfront location. Our restored rooms feature all amenities, including cable TV, compact refrigerators, high-quality linens, and complimentary continental breakfast. Just minutes from Miami International Airport, Port of Miami, and I-95.

Host: Beth Hoban
Rooms: 60 (PB) $55-150
Continental Breakfast
Credit Cards: A, B, D
Notes: 2, 3, 4, 5, 7, 8, 9, 10, 11, 12, 14

SPRING HILL

B&B Suncoast Accommodations

8690 Gulf Street
Saint Petersburg Beach, FL, 33706
(813) 360-1753

Double bed, private bath. Located eight miles from the beach, near I-75. No smoking. Continental breakfast; two-night minimum stay. $40-50.

STUART

Stone Henge

Open House B&B
P.O. Box 3025
Palm Beach, FL, 33480
(407) 842-5190

From the rustic lakeside lodge, stroll across the foot bridge, past the fountains, and enjoy your morning coffee at the island gazebo. Later, look forward to wine and cheese or afternoon tea served in the vast cathedral-ceilinged living room. A piano invites you. Your cozy bedroom has a private entrance off the swimming pool and Jacuzzi. Beautiful beaches are a short drive away. $75.

SUMMERLAND KEY

Bed & Breakfast Co. LK207

P.O. Box 262
Miami, FL, 33243
(305) 661-3270

Sleep aboard a moored luxury 53-foot sailboat with all modern conveniences and an intricate electronic system. Master stateroom has double and single bed, private bath. A second stateroom has two singles and a hall bath. Moored at the dock of a lovely Keys home or offshore at low tide. $75-80.

Knightswood

Box 151
Summerland Key, FL, 33042
(305) 872-2246

Knightswood overlooks one of the loveliest views in the Keys. Guest room with private bath or apartment with bedroom, bath, kitchenette, rec room, and screened porch. Guests enjoy private dock, swimming pool, and separate spa. Located 27.5 miles from Key West.

Hosts: Chris & Herb Pontin
Rooms: 2 (PB) $72.15-83.25
Full Breakfast
Credit Cards: No
Notes: 2, 5, 9, 10, 11, 12

TAMPA

Bed & Breakfast Co. TA204

P.O. Box 262
Miami, FL, 33243
(305) 661-3270

Cozy older home in the heart of Tampa in a residential area that borders commercial properties, medical offices, Tampa Stadium, and a shopping mall. Guest room has twin beds, private bath. $35-45.

TARPON SPRINGS

East Lake Bed & Breakfast

421 Old East Lake Road
Tarpon Springs, FL, 34689
(813) 937-5487

Private home on 2.5 acres, located on a quiet road along Lake Tarpon. Your hosts are retired business people who enjoy new friends and are well informed about the area. A full home-cooked breakfast is served. Brochure available.

Hosts: Marie & Dick Fiorito
Rooms: 1 (PB) $35-40
Full Breakfast
Credit Cards: No
Notes: 2, 5, 9, 10, 11, 12, 14

Spring Bayou Inn

32 West Tarpon Avenue
Tarpon Springs, FL, 34689
(813) 938-9333

A large, comfortable home built around the turn of the century. Unique in architectural detail, reflecting the elegance of the past with modern-day conveniences. Located in historic district within walking distance of downtown and Spring Bayou.

Hosts: Ron & Cher Morrick
Rooms: 5 (PB) $55-82.50
Continental-plus Breakfast
Minimum stay weekends & holidays: 2
Credit Cards: No
Notes: 2, 5, 9, 10, 11, 12

TAVARES (ORLANDO AREA)

Bed & Breakfast Co. TV186

P.O. Box 262
Miami, FL, 33243
(305) 661-3270

Majestic colonial mansion on a lake in a small town famous for its antique shops. Leaded-glass windows, hand-carved newel posts, winding staircase reminiscent of the grand Southern era. Two large upstairs bedrooms with twin beds share a bath and adjoining sun room. Suite could accommodate six. Downstairs room with private bath. Pool and dock. $45-55.

VENICE

The Banyan House

519 South Harbor Drive
Venice, FL, 34285
(813) 484-1385

Experience the old-world charm of one of Venice's historic Mediterranean homes (c. 1926) on Florida's Gulf Coast. Our fully-equipped efficiencies are tastefully decorated, each with its own character. Large shaded courtyard with pool and

Jacuzzi. Close to beaches, restaurants, golf, and fishing. Complimentary bicycles.

Hosts: Church & Susan McCormick
Rooms: 9 (7 PB; 2 SB) $45-79
Continental Breakfast
Credit Cards: No
Notes: 2, 5, 8 (over 12), 10, 11, 12

WEST PALM BEACH

Bed & Breakfast Co. WP60

P.O. Box 262
Miami, FL, 33243
(305) 661-3270

Close to town attractions and the causeway to Palm Beach, with good access to the bus, restaurants, Norton Art Gallery, etc. Comfortable room with double bed, shared bath. Single women guests only. $35-38.

Bed & Breakfast Co. WP249

P.O. Box 262
Miami, FL, 33243
(305) 661-3270

One-story rambling home in the historic district, one block from the Intercoastal Waterway and ten minutes from exclusive Palm Beach. Open, airy rooms with contemporary furnishings and many tropical plants. Bicycles are provided at no charge. Pool in landscaped yard. Two bedrooms with private baths. $45-55.

WINTER PARK

A&A B&B of Florida 5

P.O. Box 1316
Winter Park, FL, 32790
(407) 628-3233

Inviting contemporary two-story home on a quiet cul-de-sac. Very close to downtown, with its famous Park Avenue shops. Lushly landscaped lakefront home with pool. Two spacious rooms with small refrigerator. Close to Disney and Epcot, Sea World, and the Convention Center. $55.

A&A B&B of Florida 6

P.O. Box 1316
Winter Park, FL, 32790
(407) 628-3233

Contemporary brick home in downtown Winter Park by the golf course. Two bright bedrooms upstairs have private baths. Queen and twin beds. The home has a pool and is one block from the fourth fairway. Full breakfast; air-conditioned. $55.

A&A B&B of Florida 10

P.O. Box 1316
Winter Park, FL, 32790
(407) 628-3233

Deluxe accommodations, with swimming, fishing, and horseback riding. Recently built colonial with circular staircase has beautifully appointed guest rooms with private baths. A dip in the pool is very inviting in the morning or evening. One king room; one queen. Full breakfast; air-conditioned. $55-65.

A&A B&B of Florida 12

P.O. Box 1316
Winter Park, FL, 32790
(407) 628-3233

Accommodations right by the Winter Park Pines Golf Course. You can watch the golfers from your room or sit on the spacious patio. Two rooms with private baths; air-conditioned. $55-60.

A&A B&B of Florida 13

P.O. Box 1316
Winter Park, FL, 32790
(407) 628-3233

Located west of I-4, the Whitaker Inn is only minutes away from the Interstate that takes you to Disney and Epcot. There is a pool and hot tub overlooking the lake, which is good for fishing. Continental breakfast; air-conditioning. $55.

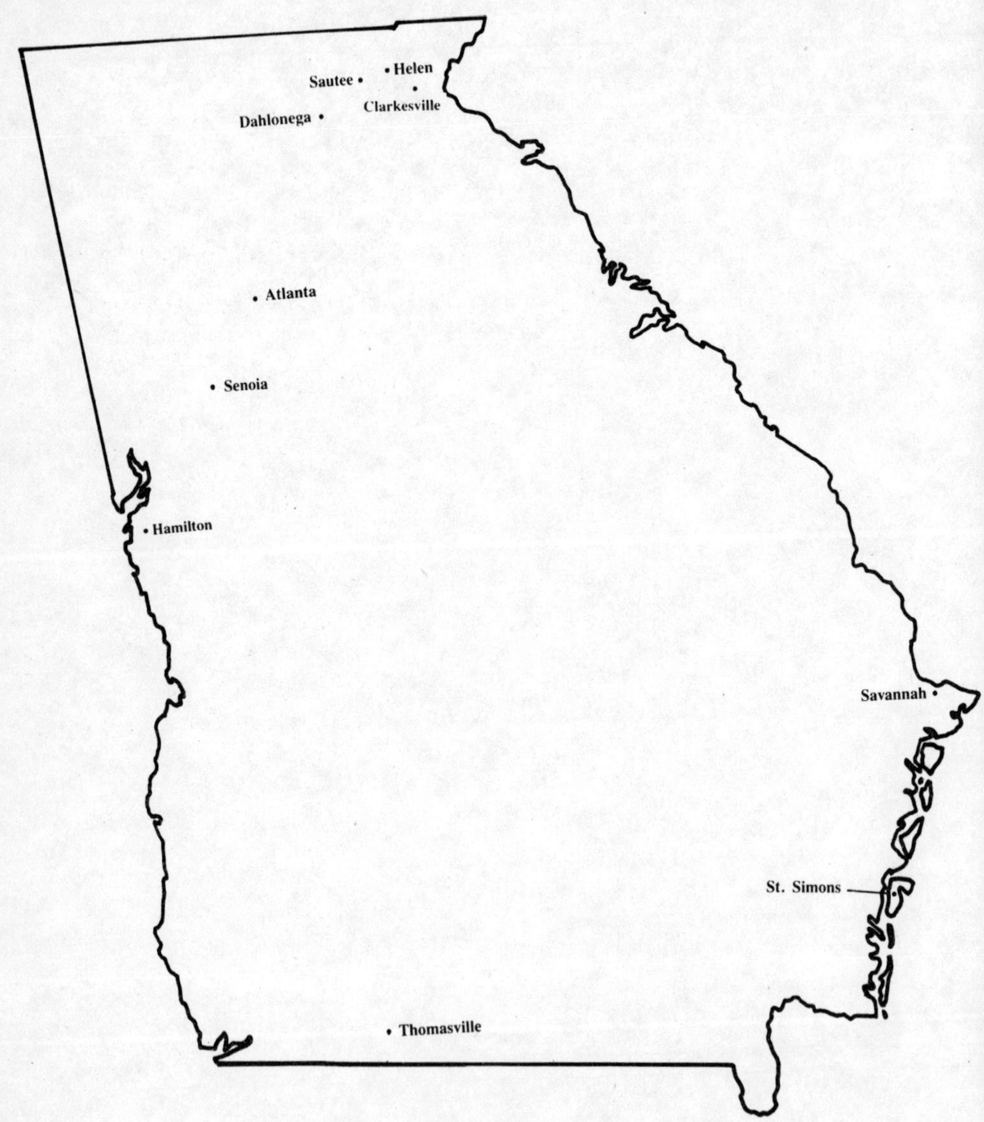
Helen
Sautee
Clarkesville
Dahlonega
Atlanta
Senoia
Hamilton
Savannah
St. Simons
Thomasville

GEORGIA

Georgia

ATLANTA

Atlanta's Woodruff Inn

223 Ponce de Leon Avenue
Atlanta, GA, 30308
(404) 875-9449

Southern hospitality and charm await you in this historic, beautifully restored B&B inn. Located in midtown Atlanta and convenient to everything. Lots of antiques. A full Southern breakfast cooked by the on-site owners is a real treat. Ya'll come.

Hosts: Joan & Douglas Jones
Rooms: 12 (8 PB; 4 SB) $65
Full Breakfast
Credit Cards: A, B, C
Notes: 2, 3, 5, 7 (limited), 8, 9, 10, 11, 12, 14

Beverly Hills Inn

65 Sheridan Drive
Atlanta, GA, 30305
(404) 233-8520

A charming city retreat located one-half block from public transportation, 1.5 miles from Lenox Square, and 5 minutes from the Atlanta Historical Society. Full kitchens, library, free parking, color TV, continental breakfast.

Hosts: Bonnie & Lyle Kleinhans
Rooms: 18 (PB) $59-74
Continental Breakfast
Credit Cards: A, B, C
Notes: 2, 5, 7, 8, 9, 10, 11, 12, 14

Woodruff Cottage

100 Waverly Way NE
Atlanta, GA, 30307
(404) 688-9498

The "Honeymoon Cottage" of Robert Woodruff, Atlanta's famous anonymous donor and soft-drink magnate. Totally restored Victorian located in historic Inman Park. One block from the subway station, close to dining. Twelve-foot ceilings, heart-pine woodwork, fireplaces, antiques, a screened porch, and private garden are yours to enjoy.

Host: Eleanor Matthews
Rooms: 3 (PB) $60-70
Full Breakfast
Credit Cards: No
Notes: 2 (deposit), 5, 7, 8, 9, 10, 11

CLARKESVILLE

The Charm House Inn

108 North Washington Street
P.O. Box 392
Clarkesville, GA, 30523
(404) 754-9347

A beautiful old Southern mansion with large, cheerfully decorated rooms, air conditioning, private baths, and working fireplaces. There is something for every age to enjoy here in the foothills of the Blue Ridge Mountains: white-water rafting, panning for gold, antique hunting, shopping, sightseeing. Near Helen, Dahlonega, Clayton, Dillard, or the Highlands.

Hosts: Mabel Fry & Rhea Allen
Rooms: 5 (PB) Call for rates
Full Breakfast
Credit Cards: A, B
Notes: 2, 5, 7, 8, 9, 10, 11, 14

DAHLONEGA

Mountain Top Lodge at Dahlonega

Route 7, Box 150
Dahlonega, GA, 30533
(404) 864-5257

Share the magic of a secluded country inn surrounded by towering trees and spectacular views. Enjoy antique-filled rooms, cathedral-ceiling great room, spacious decks, heated outdoor spa, some rooms with fireplaces, and porches. Generous country breakfast with homemade biscuits.

Host: David Middleton
Rooms: 10 (PB) $71.50-82.50
Suites: 1 (PB) $88-137.50
Full Breakfast
Minimum stay holidays: 2
Credit Cards: A, B, C, D
Notes: 2, 5, 7, 8 (12 and over), 9

The Smith House

The Smith House

202 South Chestatee
Dahlonega, GA, 30533
(404) 864-3566

Experience country hospitality in an 1884 inn. Old-time charm combined with newfangled comforts. All rooms have TV and private baths. Enjoy our famous family-style meals: three meats and nine to ten vegetables served daily.

Hosts: Fred, Shirley, Chris & Freida Welch
Rooms: 18 (PB) $52-75
Continental Breakfast
Credit Cards: A, B, C, D
Closed Christmas Day
Notes: 3, 4, 5, 7, 8, 10, 11, 14

HAMILTON

Wedgwood B&B

P.O. Box 115
Hamilton, GA, 31811
(404) 628-5659

Located six miles south of Callaway Gardens. Beautiful 1850 home decorated in Wedgwood blue with white stenciling. Enjoy the piano in the living room, a classic movie on the VCR in the den, read in the library, swing on the screened porch, or doze in a hammock in the gazebo under pecan trees. Roosevelt's Little White House is nearby.

Host: Janice Neuffer
Rooms: 3 (1 PB; 2 SB) $55-58
Full Breakfast
Credit Cards: No
Notes: 2, 5, 9, 10, 11, 12, 14

HELEN

Hilltop Haus

Chattahoochee Street
Box 154
Helen, GA, 30545
(404) 878-2388

Contemporary split-level overlooking alpine Helen and the Chattahoochee River. Near the foothills of the Smoky Mountains, six miles from the Appalachian Trail. Rich wood paneling and fireplaces create a homey atmosphere for the traveler. Homemade biscuits and preserves.

Host: Ms. Frankie Tysor
Rooms: 5 (3 PB; 2 SB) $50-60
Full Breakfast
Credit Cards: A, B
Notes: 2, 5, 7, 8 (over 10), 9, 10, 11, 12, 13, 14

ST. SIMONS

Little St. Simons Island

P.O. Box 1078
St. Simons, GA, 31522
(912) 638-7472

Privately owned 10,000-acre barrier island retreat with six miles of pristine beaches. Comfortable accommodations, bountiful regional meals with hors d'oeuvres and wine, horseback riding, fishing, boating, canoeing, bird watching, naturalist expeditions. A very unique experience in an unspoiled, natural environment.

Host: Debbie McIntyre
Rooms: 12 (10 PB; 2 SB) $235-375
Full Breakfast
Credit Cards: A, B, C
Closed Nov. 15-Feb. 15
Notes: 2, 3, 4, 7, 8 (5 and over), 9, 11, 14

SAUTEE

The Stovall House

Route 1, Box 1476
Sautee, GA, 30571
(404) 878-3355

Our 1837 farmhouse beckons you for a country experience in the historic Sautee Valley near Helen. The award-winning restoration and personal touches here will make you feel at home. Enjoy mountain views in all directions. Our restaurant, recognized as one of the top fifty in Georgia, features regional cuisine with a fresh difference.

Host: Ham Schwartz
Rooms: 5 (PB) $70
Continental Breakfast
Credit Cards: A, B
Notes: 2, 3, 4, 5, 7 (limited), 8, 9, 10, 11, 12

Woodhaven Chalet

Covered Bridge Road
Route 1, Box 1086
Sautee, GA, 30571
(404) 878-2580

A charming chalet located in a secluded mountain setting nestled only a few minutes' drive from the alpine village of Helen, Georgia. Deluxe continental breakfast includes fruit in season, juice, natural cereals, homemade breads, and beverages. Nearby hiking trails, horseback riding, fishing, and swimming. Original paintings in each room for sale. One unit has color TV, cooking facilities, and private deck and bath.

Hosts: Van & Ginger Wunderlich
Rooms: 3 (1 PB; 2 SB) $50-65
Continental-plus Breakfast
Credit Cards: No
Notes: 2, 5, 8 (over 10), 9, 11, 12

Ballastone Inn

SAVANNAH

Ballastone Inn

14 East Oglethorpe Avenue
Savannah, GA, 31401
(912) 236-1484; (800) 822-4553

A beautifully restored Victorian mansion dating from 1853 in the heart of the city's historic district, the Ballastone Inn is the epitome of gracious Southern hospitality. The eighteen guest rooms reflect a distinct Victorian flavor. Added touches include flowers and fresh fruit, terrycloth robes, fireplaces, TV with VCR, some Jacuzzis. There is a beautifully landscaped courtyard and a full-service bar. In the mornings, a continental breakfast is served in your room, the parlor, or the courtyard. Sherry, coffee or tea, fruit, and pastries are available in the front parlor. Nightly turndown service includes robes, chocolates, and brandy. We have been recommended by the *New York Times, Brides, Glamour, Atlantic,* and *Gourmet* magazines.

Hosts: Richard Carlson & Tim Hargus
Rooms: 18 (PB) $95-175
Continental Breakfast
Credit Cards: A, B, C
Notes: 2, 5, 7, 9, 10, 11, 12, 13, 14

Bed and Breakfast Inn

117 West Gordon Street at Chatham Sq.
Savannah, GA, 31401
(912) 238-0518

We are located in a restored 1853 townhouse in the historic district, amid old mansions, museums, restaurants, churches, and antique shops. Within easy walking distance to most major attractions and River Street.

Host: Robert T. McAlister
Rooms: 12 (4 PB; 8 SB) $33-71.50
Full Breakfast
Credit Cards: A, B, C, D
Notes: 2, 5, 7, 8, 9, 14

Comer House

Savannah Historic Inns
147 Bull Street
Savannah, GA, 31401
(800) 262-4667

Share the quiet beauty of Monterey Square in this elegant Victorian townhouse named for its original owner. Within a walled garden and Savannah gray-brick courtyard, private one- and two-bedroom garden suites reflect careful attention to historic detail retained in the restoration. Each has polished pine floors, period furnishings, and comfortable, cozy rooms. $65-85.

The Forsyth Park Inn

102 West Hall Street
Savannah, GA, 31401
(912) 233-6800

Circa 1893 Victorian Queen Anne mansion with sixteen-foot ceilings, fourteen-foot doors. Ornate woodwork, floors, stairways, fireplaces, antiques. Whirlpool baths, courtyard cottage. Faces 23-acre park in large historic district. Complimentary wine, social hour; fine dining, tours, beaches all nearby.

Hosts: Virginia & Hal Sullivan
Rooms: 10 (PB) $82-161
Continental Breakfast
Credit Cards: A, B, C
Notes: 2 (deposit), 5, 7, 8, 9, 10, 11, 12, 14

The Haslam/Fort House

Harris House

Savannah Historic Inns
147 Bull Street
Savannah, GA, 31401
(800) 262-4667

Newly and impeccably restored, this distinctive 1848 townhouse was home to a wealthy cotton merchant. Serene, relaxing, its garden apartment offers spacious bedrooms with queen bed and adjoining modern bath, living room with queen sofa-sleeper, equipped kitchen, and dining area adjoining a private garden. Continental breakfast. $85.

The Haslam/Fort House

417 East Charlton Street
Savannah, GA, 31401
(912) 233-6380; (800) 729-7787

Savannah's earliest B&B since 1979. This is an 1872 brick Victorian townhouse offering guests one entire suite of rooms (garden level) consisting of a living room with fireplace, king-sized bedroom, queen-sized bedroom, full private bath, and eat-in country kitchen. Guests have private entrances, off-street parking, full use of garden patio and terraces. Breakfast fully stocked for guests to prepare themselves. Ideal for two to four persons. TV, VCR, phone. Handicapped accessible. Children and pets welcome (one-time charge, $10). Central historic district location. Guests staying two nights or more are offered a tour of the house and evening cocktails. Advance reservations required.

Hosts: Alan Fort & Richard McClellan
Suite: 1 (PB) $65-90
Self-serve Breakfast
Credit Cards: No
Notes: 2, 5, 6, 7, 8, 9, 10, 11, 12

Jesse Mount House

209 West Jones Street
Savannah, GA, 31401
(912) 236-1774

The Jesse Mount House, built in 1854, is in the historic district of Savannah. There are two three-bedroom suites accommodating from one to six people in a party. The house and suites have many rare antiques and reproductions. The garden suite has a full kitchen and access to the walled rose garden. The upper suite has high, four-poster beds with canopies. Gilded harps are in the parlor and dining room, since your hostess is a concert harpist. Both suites have gas-log fireplaces, complimentary wine, fruit, and candy. Bicycles available.

Hosts: Howard Crawford & Lois Bannerman
Suites: 2-3 (PB) $90
Continental-plus Breakfast
Credit Cards: No
Notes: 2, 5, 6 (limited), 7, 8, 9, 10, 11, 12, 14

The Liberty Inn--1834

Liberty Inn—1834

128 West Liberty Street
Savannah, GA, 31401
(912) 233-1007; (800) 637-1007

One and two bedroom suites with adjoining baths. Family room, sun deck, parking. Period/antique furnishings, phone, cable TV, VCRs, and movies. Reservations arranged for dining, carriage, bus tours. In the heart of Savannah's historic district.

Hosts: Frank & Janie Harris
Suites: 5 (PB) $95-140
Continental Breakfast
Credit Cards: A, B, C
Notes: 2, 5, 7, 8, 9, 10, 11, 12, 14

Presidents' Quarters

225 East President Street
Savannah, GA, 31401
(912) 233-1600

A premier historic inn in the heart of the historic district, offering deluxe accommodations at affordable prices. Amenities include a full afternoon tea, complimentary continental-plus breakfast, Georgia wine. Suites feature Jacuzzi bathtubs, color cable TV with VCRs, gas-log fireplaces, ceiling fans. Balconies overlook our secluded courtyard and private walled parking. AAA four diamond rated.

Host: Muril L. Broy
Rooms: 16 (7 PB; 9 SB) $87-147
Continental-plus Breakfast
Credit Cards: A, B, C, D, E
Notes: 2, 5, 7, 8, 9, 12, 14

Pulaski Square Inn

203 West Charlton Street
Savannah, GA, 31401
(800) 227-0650

This elegant home, built in 1853, is located in Savannah's historic district, only a fifteen-minute walk from the Savannah River. It is completely restored with original wide pine floors, chandeliers, and marble mantles. It is furnished with antiques and traditional furniture throughout. Modern luxury baths with gold-plated fixtures.

Hosts: Hilda & J.B. Smith
Rooms: 8 (4 PB; 4 SB) From $48
Continental Breakfast
Credit Cards: A, B, C
Notes: 2, 5, 7, 8, 9, 10, 11, 12, 14

Remshart-Brooks House

Savannah Historic Inns
147 Bull Street
Savannah, GA, 31401
(800) 262-4667

Enjoy the casual Southern hospitality of this 1853 home of famous Savannah gray brick. Guest accommodations are furnished with country antiques. A sumptuous queen bed welcomes you, while the relaxing living room with fireplace, color TV, and sofabed assures a pleasurable stay. Continental breakfast of homemade breads and jam. Private entrances and off-street parking. $65.

Timmons House

Savannah Historic Inns
147 Bull Street
Savannah, GA, 31401
(800) 262-4667

Be a guest in the garden apartment of this classic home. This restored 1876 townhouse faces Troup Square and is in the heart of the historic district. The furnishings, complete with two fireplaces, provide every comfort, while the private walled garden offers a convenient respite for relaxation. Well-equipped kitchen, cable TV, laundry facilities, telephone. Continental breakfast and fruit are offered. $65.

SENOIA

The Culpepper House

35 Broad Street
Senoia, GA, 30276
(404) 599-8182

Treat yourself to a whimsical Victorian adventure in this restored home located in a picturesque country town just thirty minutes south of Atlanta's airport.

Host: Mary A. Brown
Rooms: 4 (1 PB; 3 SB) $50-60
Continental or Full Breakfast
Credit Cards: No
Notes: 2, 5, 7 (limited), 8 (infants or over 10), 9, 10, 12

The Veranda

252 Seavy Street
P.O. Box 177
Senoia, GA, 30276-0177
(404) 599-3905

Beautifully restored spacious Victorian rooms in a 1907 hotel on the National Register. Just thirty miles south of Atlanta airport. Freshly prepared Southern gourmet meals by reservation. Unusual gift shop featuring kaleidoscopes. Memorabilia and 1930 Wurlitzer player piano pipe organ. One room has a whirlpool bath; all have private baths.

Hosts: Jan & Bobby Boal
Rooms: 9 (PB) $65-95
Full Breakfast
Credit Cards: A, B, C
Notes: 2, 3, 4, 5, 8, 10, 11, 12, 14

THOMASVILLE

Deer Creek

1304 South Broad Street
Thomasville, GA, 31792
(912) 226-7294

Relax in comfort in this modern cedar home on 2 acres offering exquisite views from all rooms, deck, and terrace. Walking distance from plantation tours. Thomasville is a historic town that was a winter resort area in the 1800s. Fine restaurants and points of interest nearby.

Hosts: Gladys & Bill Muggridge
Rooms: 2 (PB) $48-70
Full Breakfast
Credit Cards: No
Notes: 2, 5, 7, 8, 9, 10, 12, 14

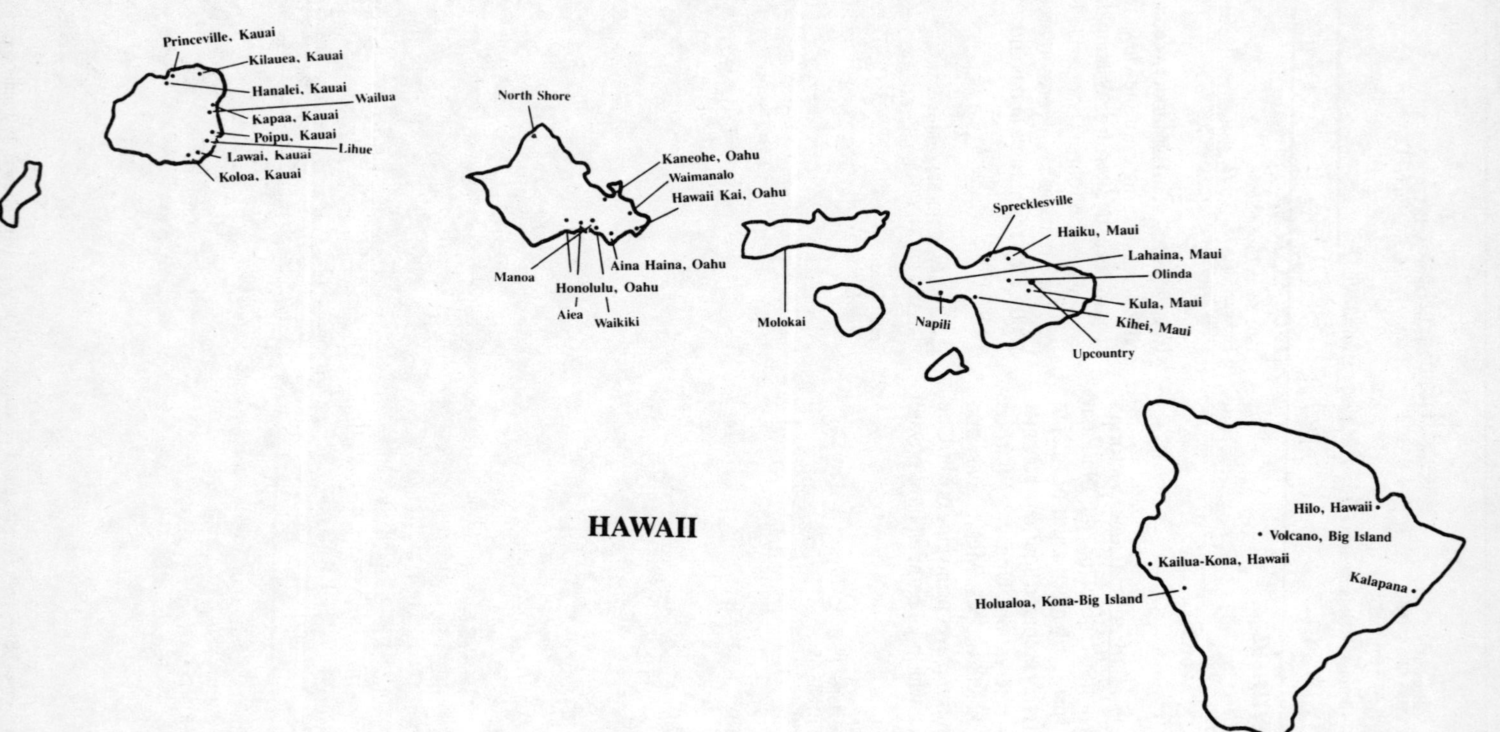
Princeville, Kauai
Kilauea, Kauai
Hanalei, Kauai
Wailua
Kapaa, Kauai
Poipu, Kauai
Lihue
Lawai, Kauai
Koloa, Kauai
North Shore
Kaneohe, Oahu
Waimanalo
Hawaii Kai, Oahu
Aina Haina, Oahu
Manoa
Honolulu, Oahu
Aiea
Waikiki
Molokai
Sprecklesville
Haiku, Maui
Lahaina, Maui
Olinda
Kula, Maui
Kihei, Maui
Napili
Upcountry
HAWAII
Hilo, Hawaii
Volcano, Big Island
Kailua-Kona, Hawaii
Kalapana
Holualoa, Kona-Big Island

Hawaii

AIEA, OAHU

B&B Honolulu (Statewide) NEESB

3242 Kaohinani Drive
Honolulu, HI, 96817
(800) 288-4666; FAX: (808) 595-2030

This Oahu home is about two miles from Pearl Harbor and the *Arizona* Memorial. Two rooms, one with double bed, the other with twin beds. Kitchen privileges with microwave and regular ovens, freezer, refrigerators, range, laundry facilities, and color TV. Car advisable. Children and smokers accepted. From $35 single; $45 double.

HAIKU, MAUI

Hamakualoa B&B

Go Native . . . Hawaii
65 Halaulani Place, P.O. Box 11418
Hilo, HI, 96721

A tea-house cottage in a peaceful, unspoiled environment on the lush north shore of Maui. Here in the center of a tropical jungle is a pleasant B&B with views of both the ocean and mighty Haleakala. The cottage is tastefully furnished with antiques and Oriental rugs. Features bedroom, living room, kitchenette, and screened lanai. Free-standing bathhouse and outhouse, both modern. Hostess is an artist. $50-55.

HANALEI, KAUAI

B&B Honolulu (Statewide) BARNC

3242 Kaohinani Drive
Honolulu, HI, 96817
(800) 288-4666; FAX: (808) 595-2030

This lovely home has three units. One has a private bath and queen bed. A downstairs one-bedroom apartment has a queen bed, TV, private patio, and garden with ocean view. The third-floor unit sleeps four (queen and twins) and has a view of Hanalei Bay. Cathedral windows offer sunset and waterfall views. The living room TV is available for all to enjoy. The beach is only one hundred yards away. Children over twelve welcome; restricted smoking; three-night minimum. From $70.

Haena Hideaway

Go Native . . . Hawaii
65 Halaulani Place, P.O. Box 11418
Hilo, HI, 96721

Luxuriate in this lovely tropical home only one block from a sandy beach. The spacious home sits in a garden of lush vegetation and flora. There is a cozy queen room with private bath in the main home or a charming studio cottage on the grounds. The cottage has a stove and refrigerator. Located within walking distance of the famous Charo's restaurant. Continental breakfast. $50-65.

HAWAII KAI, OAHU

B&B Honolulu (Statewide) ABEB

3242 Kaohinani Drive
Honolulu, HI, 96817
(800) 288-4666; FAX: (808) 595-2030

The hosts are originally from England, where B&B started. They have two guest rooms, one with a private bath, queen bed, TV, and refrigerator. The other has a double bed, TV, and shared bath. A hearty continental breakfast is served in the dining room. On a bus line, or a seven-minute drive to sandy white swimming beaches and Hanauma Bay. The host invites you to enjoy the pool. No smoking; adults only; two-night minimum. Resident dog. From $45.

B&B Honolulu (Statewide) HARRR

3242 Kaohinani Drive
Honolulu, HI, 96817
(800) 288-4666; FAX: (808) 595-2030

Located on a high ridge about fifteen minutes from Waikiki by car. The bedrooms in this home offer a beautiful view of the ocean and Koko Marina. Hanauma Bay (Oahu's best beach for snorkeling), two shopping centers, and other tourist attractions are within a five-minute drive. The rooms are large and have private baths. Coffee and doughnuts on weekday mornings; a special breakfast on weekends. From $55.

HILO, HAWAII

B&B Honolulu (Statewide) COOPJ

3242 Kaohinani Drive
Honolulu, HI, 96817
(800) 288-4666; FAX: (808) 595-2030

Two-story "sugar plantation camp" house. Private bath and entrance. The guest room is furnished with twin beds, fridge, hotpot, and TV. The host serves a homemade continental breakfast on the large lanai, where you can comfortably view the whole coast. At 1,000 feet, you will sleep comfortably during the cool nights. On the road to the home, you will see Rainbow Falls, the pools below, and their boiling pots. Very country—very quiet. Children welcome; restricted smoking. From $45.

B&B Honolulu (Statewide) LANNA

3242 Kaohinani Drive
Honolulu, HI, 96817
(800) 288-4666; FAX: (808) 595-2030

Located two miles out of Hilo on a cliff overlooking Hilo Bay, this Hawaiian-type home has a private yard with lovely pool. Two bedrooms are available, each with twin beds. One full bath and one half-bath are reserved for guests. The yard is beautifully landscaped, and there's a charming tea house on the grounds. Children and smokers welcome. From $50.

HOLUALOA, KONA-BIG ISLAND

Holualoa Inn

Box 222N
Holualoa, HI, 96725
(808) 324-1121

This architectural masterpiece features a spectacular view of the Kona coast. Located in the Kona coffee district on a 40-acre estate, the inn is a peaceful retreat, yet within a short drive of Kailua Village and many activities.

Host: Desmond
Rooms: 4 (PB) $75-125
Continental Breakfast
Credit Cards: A, B, C
Notes: 2, 5, 8 (12 and over), 9, 10, 11, 12, 14

HONOLULU, OAHU

B&B Hawaii O50

P.O. Box 449
Kappa, HI, 96746
(808) 822-7771; (800) 733-1632;
FAX: (808) 822-2723

Nestled in Nuuanu Valley, this is a beautiful, lush, private tropical setting with the sounds of the stream and singing birds. The view of the stream and tropical rain forests, as well as lovely landscaped garden, are yours to enjoy. Accommodations consist of a large one-bedroom queen suite with private entrance and sitting room, private bath, and two private decks. Smoking outside only. Three-night minimum. $65.

Hawaii Kai B&B

876 Kaahue Street
Honolulu, HI, 96825
(808) 395-5706

Single-family home with panoramic ocean and marina view. Private entrance and bath, large lanai and yard. TV, refrigerator, toaster; breakfast will be provided, but not served. Five minutes to snorkeling bay and sandy beaches. Large room with glass door opening to the view and lanai.

Host: C.R. Gerlich
Rooms: 1 (PB) $60
Full Breakfast
Credit Cards: No
Notes: 5, 7, 9, 10, 11, 12, 14

The Manoa Valley Inn

2001 Vancouver Drive
Honolulu, HI, 96822
(800) 634-5115

An intimate country inn located in lush Manoa Valley, just two miles from Waikiki Beach. Furnished in antiques, each room is individually decorated to enhance its charm and personality. Continental breakfast buffet, wine and cheese tasting served daily on the shady lanai.

Host: Marianne Schultz
Rooms: 6 (SB) $93.01-169.60
Continental Breakfast
Credit Cards: A, B, C
Notes: 2, 8 (14 and over), 9, 10, 11, 12

Rainbow B&B

Go Native . . . Hawaii
65 Halaulani Place, P.O. Box 11418
Hilo, HI, 96721

A large five-bedroom B&B home in the Pacific Heights area of Honolulu. The breathtaking view of the city and ocean is magnificent. Huge common living room for guests. Four doubles and one single room; three private baths, two shared. Continental breakfast. $30-45.

KAILUA, KONA, HAWAII

B&B Hawaii H34

P.O. Box 449
Kappa, HI, 96746
(808) 822-7771; (800) 733-1632;
FAX: (808) 822-2723

Located just twelve minutes from the airport and fifteen minutes from Kailua Village in the cool Kaloko Mauka area is this beautiful new home on 5 acres. It offers an attractive separate apartment at garden level with two bedrooms, bath, sitting room with TV and limited cooking facilities. Guests may choose to breakfast with their hosts or on their own. No smoking. After a busy day of sports, shopping, or sight-seeing, come to cool Kaloko, sit on your lanai high above the Kona coast, watch the magnificent sunset, and listen to the quiet humming of your hosts' llamas. Two-night minimum. $55.

B&B Honolulu (Statewide) PRICS

3242 Kaohinani Drive
Honolulu, HI, 96817
(800) 288-4666; FAX: (808) 595-2030

Windward Oahu is away from the bustle of Waikiki. This host offers two queen rooms with TV and refrigerator. For larger parties, a small twin room can be made available. Five-minute walk to the beach, or you may enjoy the pool. Enjoy the serenity of the golf-course view, or stroll to the boat dock on the quiet canal that runs just beyond the lawn. Continental breakfast. Smokers and children over nine (swimmers) welcome. Resident cats. From $45.

B&B Honolulu (Statewide) SASAE

3242 Kaohinani Drive
Honolulu, HI, 96817
(800) 288-4666

This one-bedroom detached cottage is only a five-minute walk to Kailua Beach, and next door to a park. Cool, lush, tropical area. The bedroom has a king bed and is air-conditioned. The living room has twin beds. Full kitchen, phone, cable TV, radio, and tape recorder. Children welcome. From $65.

B&B Honolulu (Statewide) WOODL

3242 Kaohinani Drive
Honolulu, HI, 96817
(800) 288-4666; FAX: (808) 595-2030

This is a single-family home with two rooms for guests. One room has twin beds; the other a single. A rollaway is also available to accommodate a family with children. Shared bath. Limited kitchen and refrigerator privileges. A car is not essential, since the host is helpful and the bus close by. Smokers accepted. From $35 single; $45 double.

Kailua B&B

Go Native . . . Hawaii
65 Halaulani Place, P.O. Box 11418
Hilo, HI, 96721

Beautiful home with swimming pool beside a quiet stream and golf course and within walking distance of Kailua Beach Park. Two units are available. One is a master bedroom with private bath and separate entrance, double bed and futon. No smoking. The other is a lovely cottage featuring a living room, bedroom, and kitchenette. Queen and trundle bed (sleeps 4). Large whirlpool bath, delightful hosts, continental breakfast. $40-65.

Luna Kai B&B

Go Native . . . Hawaii
65 Halaulani Place, P.O. Box 11418
Hilo, HI, 96721

Located in popular Kailua-Kona, these choice B&B accommodations include either a self-contained cottage or a delightful studio. The cottage is nestled in a tropical garden and has king or twin beds and an outside lanai. The studio is below the main house. A wonderful continental breakfast is served on a carpeted open lanai overlooking Kailua Bay and the Kona coastline. $70.

Pacific-Hawaii B&B

970 North Kalaheo Avenue
Suite A-218
Kailua, Oahu, HI, 96734
(800) 999-6026; FAX: (808) 261-6573

White sand beachfront home with a two-room suite, private bath, and private entrance. One room has a king bed and TV; the other features a double and single bed. There is a kitchenette, and sliding glass doors open to a small patio with table and chairs. Wonderful swimming right in front of the house. Our dog loves guests and will walk the two miles of beach with you.

Host: Doris Epp
Suite: 1 (PB) From $85
Continental Breakfast
Credit Cards: No
Notes: 2, 5, 8, 9, 10, 11, 12, 14

Seaside Plantation

Go Native . . . Hawaii
65 Halaulani Place, P.O. Box 11418
Hilo, HI, 96721

A beautiful, new (1990) plantation-style home especially designed for B&B guests. Conveniently located on Alii Drive, the main oceanside highway in Kailua-Kona, on the west of the island of Hawaii. Four guest rooms, three with queen beds, one with twins. Three have private lanais, and all have use of a complete kitchen and large dining lanai overlooking the ocean. Continental breakfast. $55.

KAIWA, OAHU

B&B Honolulu (Statewide) FINEV

3242 Kaohinani Drive
Honolulu, HI, 96817
(800) 288-4666; FAX: (808) 595-2030

On the windward side of Oahu, this attached studio is on the grounds of an estate. It has its own entrance, will sleep four, and has light cooking facilities. You're also welcome to use the pool. The host is a long-time resident and is glad to provide tips to help plan your time. A car is necessary; children and smokers accepted. From $40 single; $50 double.

KALAPANA

Kalani Honua by the Sea

RR. 2, Box 4500
Kalapana, HI, 96778
Reservations (800) 367-8047, ext. 669
Information (808) 965-7828

Kalani Honua welcomes guests to a pleasant country retreat. Four cedar lodges provide simple, comfortable accommodations on 20 secluded, oceanfront, landscaped acres of paradise on the Big Island. Our cafe serves delicious, healthy cuisine at reasonable rates. The spirit of aloha awaits you!

Host: Richard Koob
Rooms: 35 (9 PB; 26 SB) $20-72
Full Breakfast
Credit Cards: A, B, C, E
Notes: 3, 4, 5, 7, 8, 9, 10, 11, 14

KANEOHE, OAHU

B&B Honolulu (Statewide) RAYB

3242 Kaohinani Drive
Honolulu, HI, 96817
(800) 288-4666; FAX: (808) 595-2030

On the quiet, peaceful side of Oahu, this beautiful Japanese/Hawaiian home has a pool and two guest rooms with king beds and private garden baths with dressing rooms. The cabana by the pool has a guest refrigerator. Only two miles from the beach, shopping, and restaurants. Guests are welcome to enjoy the TV in the den. Adults only; smoking outside. Cheese and wine served poolside between 5:00 and 6:00 P.M. From $65.

House of Blue Ginger

Go Native . . . Hawaii
65 Halaulani Place, P.O. Box 11418
Hilo, HI, 96721

A lovely island-style home on Oahu's windward side with panoramic view of the majestic Koolau mountains and Kaneohe Bay. The home features lots of windows, three guest rooms and two baths, one private, one shared. The hostess serves continental breakfast and afternoon tea. $40-50.

Queen Emma's B&B

Go Native . . . Hawaii
65 Halaulani Place, P.O. Box 11418
Hilo, HI, 96721

A modern, spacious island home featuring five guest bedrooms, continental breakfast, and access to kitchen facilities, dining area, color TV, and lounge. Located in beautiful Temple Valley, on the windward side of Oahu, approximately twenty-five minutes from Waikiki Beach. Private entrance, gracious hosts. $35-45.

Windward B&B

Go Native . . . Hawaii
65 Halaulani Place, P.O. Box 11418
Hilo, HI, 96721

A spacious and delightful tropical home with continental ambience. Located in the suburb of Kaneohe, it features two guest bedrooms with private baths. Beautifully furnished with antiques, swimming pool, and library, the house overlooks Kaneohe Bay and ancient Heeia Fish pond. Afternoon tea and continental breakfast. $45-55.

KAPAA, KAUAI

Kay Barker's B&B

P.O. Box 740
Kapaa, HI, 96746
(808) 822-3073

The home is in a lovely garden setting, in a quiet rural area, with pastoral and mountain views. There is a large living room, TV room, extensive library, and lanai for you to enjoy. Brochures are available.

Host: Gordon Barker
Rooms: 5 (PB) $49.05-70.85
Continental Breakfast
Credit Cards: A, B
Notes: 2, 5, 7, 8, 9, 10, 11, 12, 14

Wailua B&B

Go Native . . . Hawaii
65 Halaulani Place, P.O. Box 11418
Hilo, HI, 96721

In a beautiful residential neighborhood looking down on the lovely Wailua River. Attached to the main home are two complete studio suites built of Koa wood. Impressive views from each apartment. Each unit has a small kitchen and full bath. There is also a charming courtyard. No smoking, continental breakfast. $45-55.

KIHEI, MAUI

B&B Honolulu (Statewide) FEKEJ

3242 Kaohinani Drive
Honolulu, HI, 96817
(800) 288-4666; FAX: (808) 595-2030

This host has a B&B with a private bath and entrance. The large studio has light cooking facilities, refrigerator, coffee maker, and microwave. The host serves a full breakfast with meat. There is an ocean view from the unit. Just six blocks to the beach; wheel-chair accessible. From $45.

B&B Honolulu (Statewide) SVENC

3242 Kaohinani Drive
Honolulu, HI, 96817
(800) 288-4666

This single-family Hawaiian-style pole home offers a panoramic view of the ocean and the slopes of Haleakala from the lanai. It has two identical rooms for guests on the ground floor. Cable TV, ceiling fan, twin or king bed, private bath, and refrigerator. There are many shops and restaurants in Kihei, and the ocean is only a mile from the house. Smokers accepted. From $50.

B & B "Maui Style" 2

P.O. Box 98
Puunene, HI, 96784
(800) 879-7865; (800) 848-5567

The view here is breathtaking. Lanai, Molokai, and Kahoolawe dot the ocean before you while fresh trade winds cool the afternoons. A separate guest room and bath are located on the garden level of this beautifully appointed home. Breakfast is served on the lanai, or a picnic can be prepared for an early start. On the same property is a guest home with two bedrooms, kitchen, living room, tiled bath, and large covered lanai. Continental breakfast. $50-100.

KILAUEA, KAUAI

Hale Ho'o Maha B&B

Go Native . . . Hawaii
65 Halaulani Place, P.O. Box 11418
Hilo, HI, 96721

Located on the north shore at Kilihiwai Bay, in a tropical garden, this home is ten steps from one of Hawaii's most beautiful beaches. Hike or boat up the river to waterfalls with lovely pools for swimming. Only minutes from riding stables, golf, shopping, and good restaurants. The home is a cozy one-bedroom with a seven-foot round bed and fully equipped kitchen. Twin beds in front living area. Boats, gas grill, clothes washer, and cable TV. Maximum two people; continental breakfast. $50-65.

Slippery Slide B&B

Go Native . . . Hawaii
65 Halaulani Place, P.O. Box 11418
Hilo, HI, 96721

A marvelous tropical-style redwood home strategically located on the north shore for breathtaking views of Kauai's mountains, valleys, and oceanscapes. Adjacent to "Slipper Slide" estate and within sound of tranquil waterfalls. Home features three bedrooms with shared baths. Private entrances, portable Jacuzzi, continental breakfast. $40.

KOLOA, KAUAI

Koloa B&B

Go Native . . . Hawaii
65 Halaulani Place, P.O. Box 11418
Hilo, HI, 96721

A delightful Japanese-hosted guest home in the countryside two miles from Poipu Beach. Bedroom with private entrance, twin beds, refrigerator, TV, and a small patio. Lush tropical yard with stream. Three-night minimum, continental breakfast. $40.

Poipu B&B Inn & Vacation Cottages

2720 Hoonani Road
Koloa, Kauai, HI, 96756
(808) 742-1146, Hawaii; (800) 552-0095

In Poipu, set amid almost one-half acre of lush tropical gardens and a short walk to the white sands of Poipu Beach, Kiahuna Tennis Club and pool (free to guests), restaurants and shops. All rooms have garden views, private baths (some whirlpools), color cable TV/VCR, clock radios, ceiling fans; most have king beds. The main house is a gracious plantation house built in 1933 and exquisitely renovated. The cottages also have kitchenettes, telephones, up to three beadrooms; some have ocean views. A secluded, tin-roofed cottage is ideal for honeymooners or those who want to get away. There is also a luxury suite right on the ocean with a two-person Jacuzzi and spectacular sunsets.

Rooms: 7; suites, cottages (PB) From $77-225
Continental Breakfast
Credit Cards: A, B, C, E, F
Notes: 2, 5, 8, 9, 10, 11, 12, 14

KONA, HAWAII

B&B Honolulu (Statewide) BOONW

3242 Kaohinani Drive
Honolulu, HI, 96817
(800) 288-4666; FAX: (808) 595-2030

This home is an expanse of emerald lawn with palms and numerous exotic fruit trees. It's fenced along the road with head-high poinsettias, surrounded by a wall of banana trees among groves of coffee and macadamias. Take a swim in the pool, play tennis nearby, or go to one of the nearby beaches. Three rooms, shared bath. Generous continental breakfast includes homemade breads. Enjoy bicycling, Ping-Pong, or hiking with the hosts, who have a dog. From $55.

KULA, MAUI

Bloom Cottage B&B

RR 2, Box 229
Kula, Maui, HI, 96790
(808) 878-1425

A perfectly romantic getaway spot, located one-third of the way up Haleakala Crater. Spectacular view; cool mountain climate; surrounded by herb and flower gardens. There is an antique Hawaiian quilt on four-poster bamboo bed, old wicker in breakfast nook, original art on the walls. The two-bedroom cottage has a fully stocked kitchen, large living room with fireplace, breakfast nook, bathroom. Hosts stock your refrigerator; you fix your own breakfast.

Hosts: Herb & Lynne Horner
Cottage: $87.20-98.10
Continental Breakfast
Credit Cards: No
Notes: 2, 5, 9, 14

Kula Lodge

Go Native . . . Hawaii
65 Halaulani Place, P.O. Box 11418
Hilo, HI, 96721

A marvelous rustic retreat that hugs the mountainside and blends with the astonishing ambience of Upcountry Maui. At 3,200 feet, the lodge sits in a garden of flowers as nearby flower farms color the area. Accommodations are five chalet-type cabins affording a panoramic view of the West Maui mountains, distant towns, and the Pacific. Fine dining at restaurant on the grounds. $80-125.

LAHAINA, MAUI

B&B Honolulu (Statewide) SWANT

3242 Kaohinani Drive
Honolulu, HI, 96817
(800) 288-4666; FAX: (808) 595-2030

Each of the three guest rooms and the family suite has a private entrance, bath, and lanai. Located only minutes from the old whaling village and the resort area of Kaanapali. A generous continental breakfast is served. Beach mats, umbrellas, boogie boards, surf boards, coolers, snorkeling gear, and beach chairs are available. Rooms are air-conditioned and have a small fridge. From $65.

Lahaina Guesthouse

Go Native . . . Hawaii
65 Halaulani Place, P.O. Box 11418
Hilo, HI, 96721

In the heart of Lahaina, only one block from the beach, this is an elegant tropical-style home with delightful living appointments. Five personalized guest rooms, three with private bath, a spacious family room, and relaxing living room. Full use of kitchenette stocked with gourmet cooking utensils and spices. Prepare your own snacks, picnics, or meals. From $55.

The Lahaina Hotel

127 Lahainaluna Road
Lahaina, Maui, HI, 96761
(808) 661-0577; (800) 669-3444; FAX: (808) 667-9480

Located in the heart of Lahaina Town, the Lahaina Hotel is convenient to natural and recreational attractions as well as fine restaurants and shops. The small hotel is lavishly furnished with turn-of-the-century antiques for a look and feel of the period's elegance. Guests enjoy breakfast on the balconies overlooking the bustle of activity on the street below.

Doubles: 13 (PB) $110-170
Type of Beds: 11 Double; 1 Queen; 1 King
Continental Breakfast
Credit Cards: A, B, C
Notes: 2, 4, 5, 8 (14 and over), 9, 10, 11, 12, 14

Laha 'Ole B&B

Go Native . . . Hawaii
65 Halaulani Place, P.O. Box 11418
Hilo, HI, 96721

A wonderful new oceanfront home in Lahaina, right at the water's edge. Hosts offer one bedroom in the main house and a self-contained guest wing. The bedroom has a queen bed, day bed, TV, private bath, and ocean view. The guest wing has private bath, kitchen and bedroom (no breakfast). Within walking distance of shops, restaurants, and entertainment. $55-75.

Plantation Inn

174 Lahainaluna Road
Lahaina, HI, 96761
(808) 667-9225; (800) 433-6815

This unique country inn blends an elegant turn-of-the-century ambience with the amenities of the finest hotels. Home of Gerard's, a fine French restaurant, rated as one of Hawaii's top ten by *Who's Who in America's Restaurants.*

Host: Jim Follett
Rooms: 17 (PB) $99-159
Full Breakfast
Credit Cards: A, B, C, D
Notes: 2, 4, 5, 7, 9, 10, 11, 12, 14

LAWAI, KAUAI

Victoria Place

Go Native . . . Hawaii
65 Halaulani Place, P.O. Box 11418
Hilo, HI, 96721

In a lovely, spacious skylit home perched high in the lush hills of southern Kauai, overlooking thick jungle, whispering cane fields, and the Pacific. Guests may choose from three bedrooms that open directly through glass doors onto a pool surrounded by flowering walls of hibiscus, gardenia, ginger, and bougainvillaea. On the pool deck is a small refrigerator for drinks. Indoor parlor with library and board games; continental breakfast. $55-75.

LIHUE, KAUAIA

B&B Honolulu (Statewide) ZAIML

3242 Kaohinani Drive
Honolulu, HI, 96817
(800) 288-4666

This lovely cottage is only two minutes from the airport. It has a private entrance and full bath, queen bed and queen hideabed in the living room. Color TV, piano. Twenty minutes to sunny Poipu beaches. No children or smokers. From $40.

MANOA, OAHU

B&B Honolulu (Statewide) CADEM

3242 Kaohinani Drive
Honolulu, HI, 96817
(800) 288-4666; FAX: (808) 595-2030

Manoa Valley, home of the state university, is a ten-minute drive from Waikiki and the beaches. The valley is cool and blessed with passing showers; the trade winds blow most of the time. This host offers a master bedroom with private bath, queen bed, TV, and a beautiful view of Diamond Head from the sun deck. The second room has twin beds and a half-bath with shared shower. Continental breakfast. Nonsmoking home; resident cat; children welcome. From $55.

MOLOKAI

B&B Honolulu (Statewide) NEWHJ

3242 Kaohinani Drive
Honolulu, HI, 96817
(800) 288-4666; FAX: (808) 595-2030

Surrounded by lush native plants and within easy walking distance to the beach, this house offers a unique Hawaiian holiday. The cottage is nestled in a tropical garden and lulled by the sound of the surf. Prawns and native freshwater fish can be seen in nearby streams. Waterfalls and refreshing pools await the ambitious hiker. From $62.

B&B Honolulu (Statewide) PHILJ

3242 Kaohinani Drive
Honolulu, HI, 96817
(800) 288-4666

This cedar home is next to a park in Kaunakakai. The host offers a continental breakfast on the deck overlooking the seas to the island of Lanai. The guest room has TV, double bed, couch, and private bath. Thirty feet to the ocean, three miles from town, and thirteen miles to the closest swimming beach. From $55.

NAPILI, MAUI

Coconut Inn

Go Native . . . Hawaii
65 Halaulani Place, P.O. Box 11418
Hilo, HI, 96721

Tucked in by pineapple-covered hills and surrounded by open space, this 41-unit retreat is located on Maui's Napili coast. Early Hawaiian architecture recreates the past of the island. The cozy accommodations range from studios and one-bedroom apartments to several special loft units. Each has a completely equipped kitchen and full bath. $65-80.

NORTH SHORE, OAHU

B&B Honolulu (Statewide) RICHN

3242 Kaohinani Drive
Honolulu, HI, 96817
(800) 288-4666; FAX: (808) 595-2030

This warm hostess has two large guest rooms only five minutes from the famous beaches of the North Shore of Oahu and forty minutes to the airport. The master bedroom has a queen bed, air- conditioning, and TV. The other room has twins and a shared bath. Guests are welcome to watch the living room TV or enjoy a swim in the pool. Continental breakfast on the patio with a view of the mountains and valleys. From $65.

OLINDA, MAUI

B & B "Maui Style" 1

P.O. Box 98
Puunene, HI, 96784
(800) 879-7865; (800) 848-5567

All of Maui is beneath you from the slopes of Haleakala when you stay at this B&B. This one-bedroom, open-beam cottage offers a fully equipped kitchen, king bed, and working fireplace. A breakfast of fresh tropical fruits and more is left in the refrigerator. Your hosts will invite you to the main house for cocktails and show you the protea they cultivate. In the main house there is another B&B room featuring antique twin beds, private bath, and dressing room. $65.

PAIA, MAUI

Huelo Point Flower Farm

Go Native . . . Hawaii
65 Halaulani Place, P.O. Box 11418
Hilo, HI, 96721

B&B on a 2-acre stunning oceanfront estate set high on the edge of a cliff overlooking Waipio Bay on Maui's rugged north shore. Only a half hour from Kahului, this breathtaking site offers B&B in the marvelous "gazebo" with queen futon, wicker furnishings, color TV, small fridge, hot plate, and other amenities. The cliffside views from the outside hot tub are unforgettable. $75-85.

POIPU, KAUAI

B&B Hawaii K-22

P.O. Box 449
Kappa, HI, 96746
(808) 822-7771; (800) 733-1632;
FAX: (808) 822-2723

Just across the street and about 1.5 blocks to famous Poipu park, a lovely plantation-style home offers three rooms, each with private bath. The largest has a king bed with dressing room and full bath. The other two rooms each have a bath with shower. Lots of room to relax in the screened-in lanai area or in the TV room. Tropical continental breakfast is served in the formal dining room. Two-night minimum; smoking outside only. $65-75.

B&B Honolulu (Statewide) NAKAS

3242 Kaohinani Drive
Honolulu, HI, 96817
(800) 288-4666

Located for easy sightseeing, this lovely guest room has twin beds, private bath and entrance. Small refrigerator, color TV, private patio in a tropical setting with running steam. The sandy beaches of Poipu are only a couple of miles away. Three-night minimum. From $35.

Spouting Horn B&B

Go Native . . . Hawaii
65 Halaulani Place, P.O. Box 11418
Hilo, HI, 96721

An intimate oceanfront retreat offering the paradise you've always dreamed about. This B&B is nestled beside lush green fields of sugarcane, only one mile from sunny Poipu Beach and convenient to all Kauai's attractions and activities. Five guest rooms, common dining and living room. Rooms have color cable TV, refrigerators, ceiling fan. Most have private baths. Continental breakfast is served on English china, crystal, silver, and fine linen. From $65.

PRINCEVILLE, KAUAI

Hale 'Aha Hospitality House

Box 3370
Princeville, Kauai, HI, 96722
(808) 826-6733; (800) 826-6733

Elite! Newly built on 1.5 acres of golf resort property, this gracious home offers the serenity of 480 feet of fabulous fairway frontage overlooking the ocean and lush mountains of Kauai. Hale 'Aha hospitality also offers honeymoon privacy with separate decks and entrances. Our 1,000-square-foot "Penthouse Suite" has its own balcony, with open beams and 360-degree views (including "Bali Hai"). Most exceptional.

Hosts: Herb & Ruth Bockelman
Rooms: 4 (PB) $80-180
Continental Breakfast
Credit Cards: A, B
Notes: 5, 10, 11, 12, 14

SPRECKLESVILLE, MAUI

B&B Hawaii M12

P.O. Box 449
Kappa, HI, 96746
(808) 822-7771; (800) 733-1632;
FAX: (808) 822-2723

This large older home is located on Baldwin Beach, in an exclusive neighborhood adjacent to the Maui Country Club and Golf Course. While shrubbery hides the beach from the home, it's an easy walk with the hosts' friendly dog. There is a large guest room with private bath and queen bed, private entrance. Off the bedroom is a large sitting room and the sunny kitchen where breakfast is served. Centrally located for touring Maui. No smoking in the house; two-night minimum. $60.

UPCOUNTRY, MAUI

B&B Honolulu (Statewide) BALDJ

3242 Kaohinani Drive
Honolulu, HI, 96817
(800) 288-4666; FAX: (808) 595-2030

Two wonderful upstairs suites furnished in antiques and collectibles with shared bath. Guests have full use of a living room with fireplace. The sprawling grounds have a panoramic view of the islands, small vineyards, macadamia nut, avocado, loquat trees. Pick their fruit at a moment's whim. Breakfast is served buffet style with fresh island fruit, tropical breads, Kona coffee, and exotic teas. From $65.

B&B Honolulu (Statewide) CHAMD

3242 Kaohinani Drive
Honolulu, HI, 96817
(800) 288-4666; FAX: (808) 595-2030

This host offers two rooms with a shared bath between them. Located only two miles from the beach and wind-surfing. A plantation house with true Hawaiian-style country living, including chickens. Five miles to town; two blocks to store. Restricted smoking. From $65.

B&B Honolulu (Statewide) HOPKJ

3242 Kaohinani Drive
Honolulu, HI, 96817
(800) 288-4666

This homestay offers two B&B guest rooms, one with king bed and another with twins. All have private bath and entrance. The home offers a panoramic view of Mt. Haleakala and the ocean. It sits on 2 secluded acres. Eight minutes to wind-surfing and beaches. From $50.

B&B Honolulu (Statewide) HORNH

3242 Kaohinani Drive
Honolulu, HI, 96817
(800) 288-4666; FAX: (808) 595-2030

Two guest rooms; one with a queen and one twin. Enjoy the fireplace or watch TV in the living room. Watch beautiful sunsets from your own private front porch. Smell the fresh-brewed Kona coffee, and enjoy the homemade muffins, fresh fruit, and juice. From $65.

B&B Honolulu (Statewide) POWEN

3242 Kaohinani Drive
Honolulu, HI, 96817
(800) 288-4666

Modern cedar chalet in cowboy country with two rooms, one with a queen bed and one with twins. The two rooms share the bath. The host provides beach mats, towels, and picnic supplies for the beach and warm clothing for trips to the Haleakala crater. From $55.

VOLCANO, BIG ISLAND

B&B Honolulu (Statewide) MORSG

3242 Kaohinani Drive
Honolulu, HI, 96817
(800) 288-4666; FAX: (808) 595-2030

Historic three-story home on a 7-acre estate. Hawaii Volcanos National Park, golf, hiking, museum, art, and helicopter tours nearby. The main house was built before 1889. There are rooms on each of the three floors, with queen and single beds; all shared baths. The host serves a full, hearty breakfast. Enjoy the fireplace on the cool mountain nights. From $30.

WAIKIKI, OAHU

B&B Honolulu (Statewide) SHEAR

3242 Kaohinani Drive
Honolulu, HI, 96817
(800) 288-4666; FAX: (808) 595-2030

Only two blocks from Waikiki Beach, this tasteful condo offers two guest rooms. The master bedroom has a king bed and private bath. The second room has a king or two twins with a shared bath. Enjoy the view of downtown Waikiki and the beach in the day and the stars and sunsets in the evening. Continental breakfast. Easy walking to shopping, restaurants, shows, and all the local tour agencies. From $40.

WAILUA, KAUAI

B&B Honolulu (Statewide) AKRES

3242 Kaohinani Drive
Honolulu, HI, 96817
(800) 288-4666

This separate guest house is located on the green pasture lands of Wailua. One bedroom with queen bed, living room with queen hideabed, completely equipped kitchen, private bath. Enjoy the mountain view from your private deck. A similar unit sleeping two is also available. Three miles to golf, shopping, beaches, and dining. From $60.

WAIMANALO, OAHU

Orchid Row B&B

Go Native . . . Hawaii
65 Halaulani Place, P.O. Box 11418
Hilo, HI, 96721

A charming hideaway bordered by the majestic Koolau Mountain Range at the foot of Mt. Olomana in the quiet countryside of Waimanalo (14 miles out of Waikiki). Located on an orchid farm, this marvelous apartment/studio features a private bath, queen bed, cable TV, cozy kitchenette. Only minutes from the best beaches on Oahu. Continental breakfast. $65.

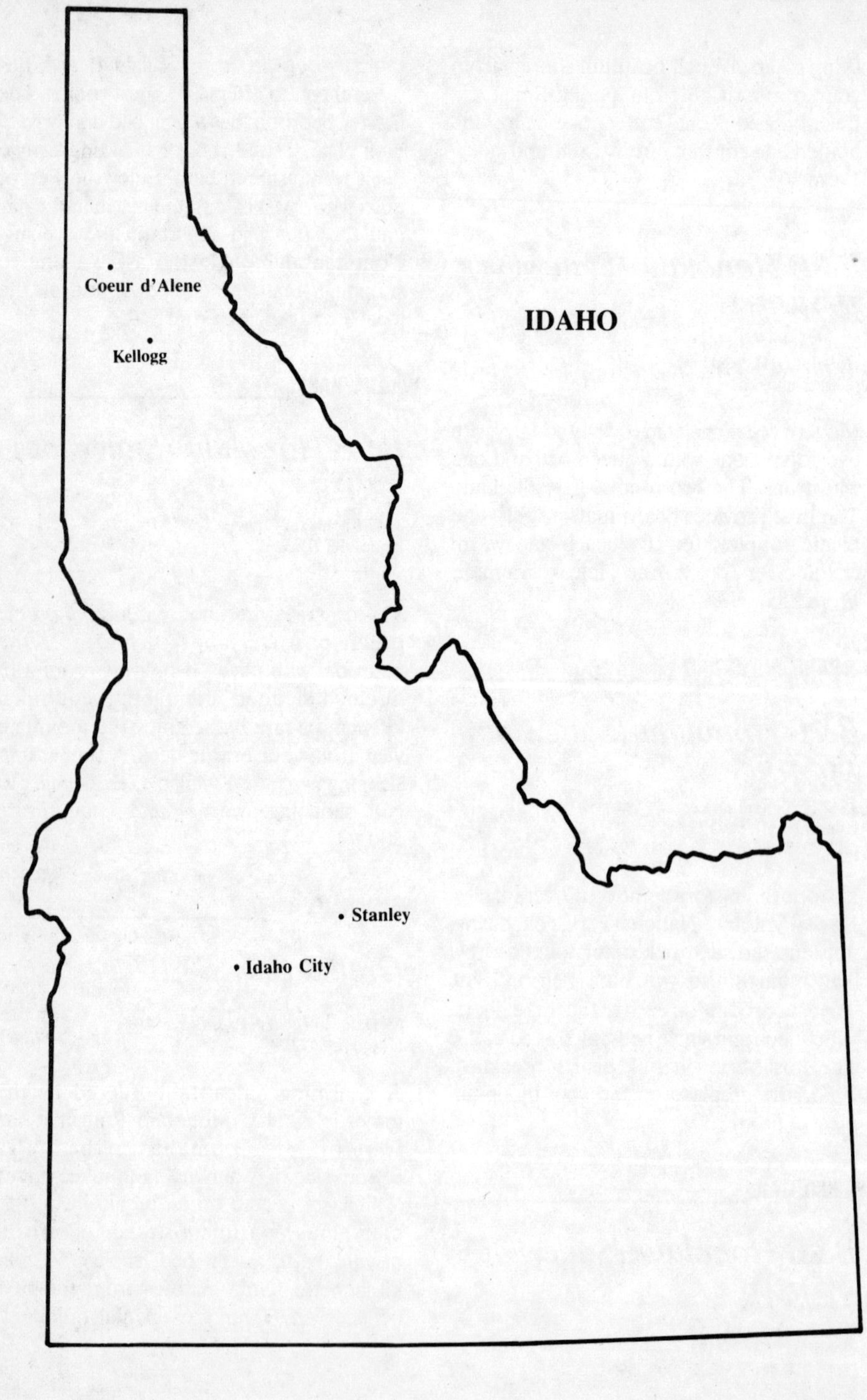
IDAHO
Coeur d'Alene
Kellogg
Stanley
Idaho City

Idaho

COEUR D'ALENE

Cricket on the Hearth

1521 Lakeside Avenue
Coeur d'Alene, ID, 83814
(208) 664-6926

Al and Karen Hutson have brought the beauty of Coeur d'Alene indoors and added a touch of country living, giving the inn an aura of "down home." The four guest rooms, two with private baths, are delightfully decorated to carry out a theme, setting the mood for a perfect getaway.

Hosts: Al & Karen Hutson
Rooms: 4 (2 PB; 2 SB) $40-55
Full Breakfast
Credit Cards: No
Notes: 2, 5, 9, 10, 11, 12, 13, 14

Greenbriar B&B Inn

315 Wallace
Coeur d'Alene, ID, 83814
(208) 667-9660

A three-story brick mansion built in 1908 and furnished with eclectic antiques. Easy walk to Lake Coeur d'Alene. Year-round outdoor spa, gourmet dinners. Catering available for weddings and receptions.

Host: Kris McIlvenna
Rooms: 7 (4 PB; 3 SB) $35-59
Full Breakfast
Credit Cards: A, B, C, D
Notes: 2, 4 (Fri. & Sat.), 5, 8, 9, 10, 11, 12, 13, 14

Inn the First Place

509 North 15th Street
Coeur d'Alene, ID, 83814
(208) 667-3346

An ex-grocery store? Yes, but now a cozy home. Lots of books, artwork, magazines, and wonderful breakfasts insure a delightful stay. Close to the freeway, downtown shopping, restaurants, and two swimming beaches. Two cats in residence. Reservations suggested.

Hosts: Tom & Lois Knox
Rooms: 3 (S2B) $37.45
Full Breakfast
Credit Cards: A, B
Notes: 2, 5, 7 (limited), 8 (over 10), 9, 10, 11, 12

IDAHO CITY

Idaho City Hotel

Box 70
Idaho City, ID, 83631
(208) 392-4290

Located in a historic gold-mining town, the hotel is furnished with antiques, phones, cable TV and HBO in each room. Near warm springs pool, hiking, fishing, skiing, and snowmobiling.

Host: Don Campbell
Rooms: 5 (PB) $28-36
Full Breakfast
Credit Cards: A, B, C, D
Notes: 2, 5, 6, 7, 8, 9, 10, 11, 13, 14

KELLOGG

The Montgomery House

305 South Division Street
Kellogg, ID, 83837
(208) 786-2311

Local activities include fishing, hiking, boating, rafting, gold-panning, golf, swimming, downhill and cross-country skiing. Many interesting attractions in the area: Mining Museum, Melo-drama theater, Silver Mine tour, Old Mission Church of Cataldo. Or just sit back and enjoy the scenery of the nearby mountains and valley or the quiet atmosphere of the Montgomery House. Ski packages available.

Hosts: Mary Terry & Robert Montgomery
Rooms: 8 (S3B) $22-28
Full Breakfast
Credit Cards: A, B
Notes: 2, 5, 6, 7, 8, 9, 10, 11, 12, 13, 14

STANLEY

Idaho Rocky Mountain Ranch

HC 64, Box 9934
Stanley, ID, 83278
(208) 774-3544

One of Idaho's oldest and finest guest ranches, offering comfortably decorated lodge and cabin accommodations. Beautiful mountain vistas from your front porch. Delightful meals served by a friendly staff. Hiking, fishing, horseback riding, mountain biking, rafting, cross-country skiing, wildlife viewing, and much more, both on and off the ranch. Located fifty miles north of Sun Valley on Highway 75. Brochure available; weekly rates available.

Hosts: Bill & Jeana Leavell
Rooms: 21 (PB) $80-105
Full Breakfast
Credit Cards: A, B
Closed April 15-May 31 & Sept. 15-Nov. 25
Notes: 2, 3, 4, 8, 9, 11, 13

Illinois

BISHOP HILL

Holden's Guest House

East Main Street
Bishop Hill, IL, 61419
(309) 927-3500

Opened in 1988, this restored 1869 farmstead is situated on 1.5 acres adjacent to your hosts and within blocks of the Bishop Hill historic district. Originally a commune, the village is a national landmark, offering five museums, restaurants, and over two dozen shops. It's truly a Utopia on the prairie.

Hosts: Linda & Steve Holden
Single suite: 1 (SB) $125
Rooms: 3 (1 PB; 2 SB) $50-60
Full Breakfast
Credit Cards: A, B
Notes: 2, 4, 5, 6, 7, 8, 9

CARLINVILLE

Courthouse Inn

307 East First South Street
Carlinville, IL, 62626
(217) 854-6566

Three-story brick colonial revival home, built in 1904. Each of our four rooms is provided with a queen bed, plump pillows, fluffy bath towels, and delightfully scented soaps. Central air conditioning, Jacuzzi; beautiful yard.

Hosts: Helene Gregor & Kim Brand
Rooms: 4 (2 PB; 2 SB) $55
Full Breakfast weekends; continental weekdays
Credit Cards: A, B, C
Notes: 2, 5, 7, 9, 10, 11, 12, 14

CARTHAGE

The Wright Farmhouse

RR 3
Carthage, IL, 62321
(217) 357-2421

Comfortable, quiet rooms with period furnishings in a restored nineteenth-century home on a working farm. Country charm plus private baths, air-conditioning, and private guest entrance. Nearby attractions include historic town square and courthouse and the scenic Mississippi River.

Hosts: John & Connie Wright
Rooms: 4 (PB) $26.50-37.10
Continental Breakfast
Credit Cards: A, B
Notes: 5, 8, 9, 10, 11, 12

CHAMPAIGN

Grandma Joan's Homestay

2204 Brett Drive
Champaign, IL, 61821
(217) 356-5828

This comfortable contemporary home with two fireplaces, multilevel decks, Jacuzzi, screened-in porch, and collection of modern and folk art, is located ten minutes from the University of Illinois. Grandma pampers you with cookies and milk at bedtime and a healthy breakfast. Let this be your home away from home.

Host: Joan Erickson
Rooms: 3 (SB) $45
Full Breakfast
Credit Cards: No
Closed Dec. 20-Jan. 10
Notes: 2, 7, 9, 10, 11, 12, 14

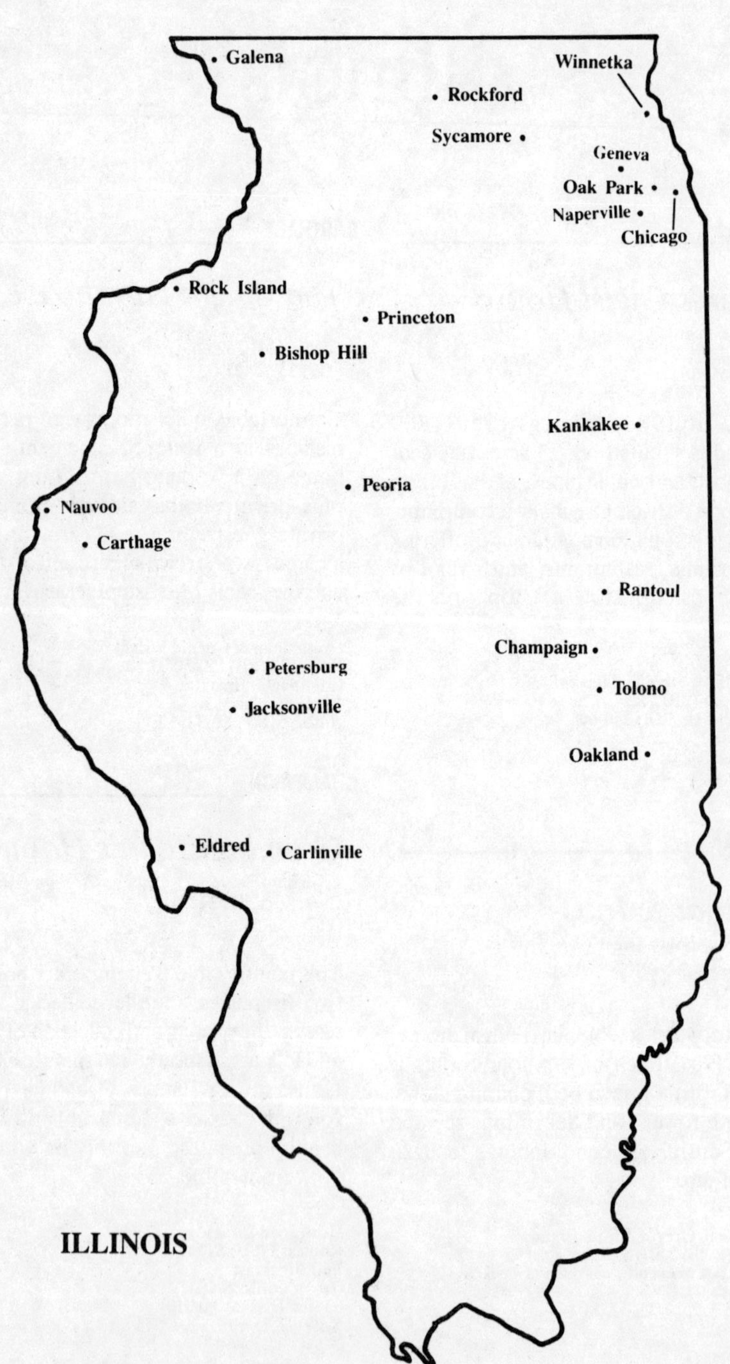
Galena
Winnetka
Rockford
Sycamore
Geneva
Oak Park
Naperville
Chicago
Rock Island
Princeton
Bishop Hill
Kankakee
Peoria
Nauvoo
Carthage
Rantoul
Champaign
Petersburg
Jacksonville
Tolono
Oakland
Eldred
Carlinville
ILLINOIS

CHICAGO

Hyde Park House

5210 South Kenwood Avenue
Chicago, IL, 60615
(312) 363-4595

Ours is a Victorian house with a veranda, porch swing, rear deck, two Steinways, attic greenhouse. Near the University of Chicago, Museum of Science and Industry, and twenty minutes from downtown by bus along the Lake Michigan shore. Also within walking distance are excellent sushi, Thai, Cantonese, Greek, Italian, and continental restaurants, gift shops, and art galleries.

Host: Irene Custer
Rooms: 3 (1 PB; 2 SB) $45-60
Continental Breakfast
Credit Cards: No
Notes: 2, 5, 7, 8, 9, 10, 11, 12, 13

ELDRED

Hobson's Bluffdale

RR 1
Eldred, IL, 62027
(217) 983-2854

Our ancestral farm has been in the family for eight generations. On 320 acres of beautiful bluffs near the Illinois River. Built of rock, the home is one of the oldest in the state. Six fireplaces, beehive oven, working farm with animals, horseback riding, pool, hot tub, hay rides. Scenic and restful, with bountiful meals.

Hosts: Bill & Lindy Hobson
Rooms: 9 (PB) $55
Full Breakfast
Credit Cards: A, B
Notes: 2, 3, 4, 8, 9, 11, 12, 14

GALENA

Aldrich Guest House

900 Third Street
Galena, IL, 61036
(815) 777-3323

The Aldrich combines the elegance of the nineteenth century with the amenities of the twentieth. Antique furnishings and period decor; central air-conditioning; queen and twin beds; full gourmet breakfast. Double parlor with grand piano and screened-in porch available to guests. Historic Galena is within walking distance. Golf, swimming, and skiing are nearby.

Host: Judy Green
Rooms: 5 (3 PB; 2 SB) $59-89
Full Breakfast
Credit Cards: A, B, C, D
Notes: 2, 5, 7 (restricted), 8 (6 and over), 9, 10, 11, 12, 13, 14

Aldrich Guest House

Avery Guest House

606 South Prospect Street
Galena, IL, 61036
(815) 777-3883

Located within Galena's historic district, this pre-Civil War home is a short walk from antique shops and historic buildings. Enjoy the scenic view from our porch swing; feel free to play the piano or just visit. Breakfast is served in the sunny dining room with a bay window overlooking the Galena River valley.

Hosts: Flo & Roger Jensen
Rooms: 4 (S2B) $40-60
Continental-plus Breakfast
Minimum stay weekends & holidays: 2
Credit Cards: A, B
Notes: 2, 5, 8, 9, 10, 11, 12, 13

Belle Aire Mansion Guest House

11410 Route 20 West
Galena, IL, 61036
(815) 777-0893

Belle Aire Mansion is a pre-Civil War home set on 16 beautiful acres only minutes from historic Galena. Our rooms are large and comfortable. Our guests say, "It's just like visiting friends." We say, " Welcome home — to our home."

Hosts: Jan & Lorraine Svec
Rooms: 4 (2 PB; 2 SB) $59.95-87.20
Credit Cards: A, B
Minimum stay holidays & special weekends: 2
Closed Christmas
Notes: 2, 8, 9, 11, 12, 13

Colonial Guest House

1004 Park One
Galena, IL, 61036
(815) 777-0336

Red brick guest house with large white pillars, built in 1826. Twenty-one rooms—seven guest rooms with baths and private entrances, cable TV, all antique furnishings. Located 1.5 blocks from town. In the summer, breakfast is served on the porches.

Host: Mary C. Keller
Rooms: 7 (PB) $50-55
Continental Breakfast
Credit Cards: No
Notes: 2, 5, 6, 7, 9, 10, 11, 12, 14

The Comfort Guest House

1000 Third Street
Galena, IL, 61036
(815) 777-3062

An 1856 Greek Revival brick home now serving as a European-style bed and breakfast. Rooms are furnished in antiques, with hand-tied quilts. Guests enjoy the living room, where there is a marble fireplace; play cribbage in the front parlor; or enjoy the front porch swing, TV, VCR. Breakfast is served on antique dishes in the formal dining room. The hostess is a master gardener and will share perennial gardening tips.

Host: Connie Sola
Rooms: 3 (S2B) $60-65
Continental-plus Breakfast
Credit Cards: A, B
Notes: 2, 5, 7 (restricted), 9, 10, 11, 12, 13, 14

DeSoto House Hotel

230 South Main Street
Galena, IL, 61036
(815) 777-0090; reservation: (800) 343-6562; FAX: (815) 777-9529

Legendary 135-year-old hotel in historic Galena that is noted for its deluxe accommodations and superior service. Enter and ascend our grand staircase, as did General Grant, Abraham Lincoln, and many other famous people have been guests of the DeSoto House Hotel. For a minimal charge, arrangements can be made to meet with a General Grant look-alike dressed in authentic Civil War general's uniform.

Host: Peter Schnabel
Rooms: 55 (PB) $79-150
Credit Cards: A, B, C, D
Notes: 3, 4, 5, 7, 8, 9, 14

Farster's Executive Inn

305 North Main Street
Galena, IL, 61036
(815) 777-9125

Farster's Executive Inn is located on Galena's historic Main Street, close to many major sites and restaurants. Originally an 1845 general store, the inn has been restored to its turn-of-the-century elegance, with today's conveniences. Jacuzzi, game room, and private off-street parking.

Hosts: Bob & Sandy Farster
Singles: 2 (SB) $55
Suites: 5 (SB) From $90
Continental Breakfast
Credit Cards: A, B, C, D
Notes: 2, 5, 6, 7, 8, 9, 10, 11, 12, 13, 14

The Goldmoor

9001 Sand Hill Road
Galena, IL, 61036-9341
(800) 397-6667; (BIS) 777-3425

The Goldmoor is located south of Galena on a bluff overlooking the Mississippi River. Deluxe suites with whirlpools and fireplaces, all private baths, TV, VCRs. Full scrumptious breakfast served overlooking the river. Honeymoon, anniversary, and romantic getaway packages are special at the Goldmoor.

Host: James C. Goldthorpe
Rooms: 5 (PB) $80-175
Full Breakfast
Credit Cards: A, B, C, D
Notes: 5, 6, 7, 8, 9, 10, 11, 12, 13, 14

Grandview Guest Home

113 South Prospect Street
Galena, IL, 61036
(815) 777-1387; (800) 373-0732

A 120-year-old brick traditional on "Quality Hill" overlooking the city and countryside. Victorian furnishings. Hearty continental breakfast featuring all home-baked goods and European coffees. Two blocks from Main Street shops, museums, and restaurants.

Hosts: Harry & Marjorie Dugan
Rooms: 3 (1 PB; 2 SB) $60-75
Continental-plus Breakfast
Credit Cards: A, B, C, D
Notes: 2, 5, 7, 8, 9, 10, 11, 12, 13, 14

Hellman Guest House

318 Hill Street
Galena, IL, 61036
(815) 777-3638

The Hellman Guest House, a brick Queen Anne built in 1895, reflects the beauty and elegance of the nineteenth century. Enjoy an inviting parlor, library, patio, and porch. Nestled on the hill, the Hellman provides an aura of seclusion and a breathtaking view of Galena. The shops and restaurants of the downtown historic district are just three short blocks down the hill.

Hosts: Merilyn Tommaro & Rachel Stilson
Rooms: 4 (PB) $69-95
Continental Breakfast
Credit Cards: A, B, C
Notes: 2, 5, 7 (limited), 8 (over 12), 9, 11, 12, 13

Ryan Mansion Inn

11383 Route 20W
Galena, IL, 61036
(815) 777-2043

Built in 1876, this 24-room mansion displays the finest in Italianate architecture that Galena has to offer. Crystal chandeliers, wood parquet flooring, Bohemian glass, Italian marble fireplaces, and period furnishing. Indoor whirlpool, parklike setting close to historic Galena, walking trails, and hayrides.

Host: Linda Pluiz
Rooms: 5 (PB) $75-99
Continental Breakfast
Credit Cards: C
Notes: 2, 4, 5, 7, 8, 9, 10, 11, 12, 13, 14

GENEVA

Oscar Swan Country Inn

1800 West State Street
Geneva, IL, 60134
(708) 232-0173

Experience gracious B&B hospitality in a 1902 colonial revival Williamsburg estate surrounded by 7 beautiful acres of country in the heart of the Fox Valley, near antique shopping. For your comfort, there are seven spacious rooms, quilts, and goose-down pillows. Antique furnishings and old-fashioned comfort grace the bedrooms, the parlor, and sitting areas that await you with fireplaces, carved swans, and novelties.

Hosts: Nina & Hans Heymann
Rooms: 8 (4 PB; 4 SB) $70-125

Full Breakfast
Credit Cards: A, B, C
Notes: 2, 5, 8, 9, 10, 11, 12, 14

Harrison House B&B

JACKSONVILLE

The 258 Inn B&B

Monton at Church Street
Jacksonville, IL, 62650
(217) 245-2588; 245-6665

184-year-old Victorian home, decorated with quilts and antiques, featuring home-baked breads and delicious breakfasts. Shop on site: antiques, quilts, bath shop, wicker store. Thirty miles west of Springfield. Near fishing, lakes, and boating. Very unique.

Hosts: Rosalee & Ray McKinley
Rooms: 2 (PB) $55-60
Full Breakfast
Credit Cards: No
Notes: 2, 5, 8 (over 12), 9, 10, 11, 12, 14

KANKAKEE

Norma's B&B

429 South Fourth Avenue
Kankakee, IL, 60901
(815) 937-1533

A clean, friendly, homey atmosphere away from home. Enjoy our front porch for visiting and relaxing. Located one and one-half blocks from the Kankakee River, with waterskiing, canoeing, and fishing for the sportsman. Parks, hospitals, and tennis courts are within walking distance.

Host: Norma Gall
Rooms: 5 (PB and SB) $25-40
Continental Breakfast
Credit Cards: No
Notes: 2, 3, 4, 5, 9, 10

NAPERVILLE

Harrison House B&B

26 North Eagle Street
Naperville, IL, 60540
(708) 420-1117

Harrison House B&B (c. 1911) is located twenty-five miles west of Chicago in historic Naperville. Five antique-filled, air-conditioned guest rooms with private baths, one with Jacuzzi. Walk to downtown restaurants, historic sites, quaint shops, and Centennial Beach. Homemade chocolate chip cookies, fresh flowers, gourmet coffee, and scrumptious breakfast. Friendly atmosphere. Relax and let us pamper you.

Hosts: Lynn Harrison & Dawn Dau
Rooms: 5 (3 PB; 2 SB) $38-98
Full Breakfast
Credit Cards: A, B, C
Notes: 2, 5, 9, 10, 11, 12, 13

NAUVOO

Mississippi Memories

Box 291, RR 1
Nauvoo, IL, 62354
(217) 453-2771

Gracious lodging on the Mississippi riverbank. Elegantly served full breakfasts, quiet wooded setting. Five minutes from restored Mormon City, "the Williamsburg of the Midwest." Watch spectacular sunsets, abundant wildlife, and barges drifting by from two decks. Excellent geode hunting; air-conditioning; fireplaces; piano; fruit and flowers in rooms.

Hosts: Marge & Dean Starr
Rooms: 5 (3 PB; 2 SB) From $45
Full Breakfast
Credit Cards: No
Notes: 2, 5, 8, 10, 11, 12, 13, 14

OAKLAND

Inn-on-the-Square

3 Montgomery
Oakland, IL, 61943
(217) 346-2289; 346-2653

Restored colonial inn offering a potpourri of the "village experience." Antiques, gifts, flowers, crafts, and ladies' apparel shop to pique your curiosity. Our Tea Room offers simple but elegant luncheons. Golf, swimming, conservation park, Amish settlement, and historic sites nearby.

Hosts: Max & Caroline Coon
Rooms: 4 (3 PB; 1 SB) $48.15
Full Breakfast
Credit Cards: A, B
Closed major holidays only
Notes: 2, 3, 5, 7 (limited), 8 (over 2), 9 (served by hosts), 10, 11, 12, 13 (XC)

OAK PARK

Toad Hall

301 North Scoville Avenue
Oak Park, IL, 60302
(708) 386-8623

A 1909 colonial five miles from downtown Chicago in the Frank Lloyd Wright Historic District. Old-world atmosphere and service. Antiques, Oriental rugs, Laura Ashley furnishings, telephones, TV, air-conditioning. Walk to twenty-five Wright masterpieces, lovely shops, restaurants, public transportation.

Hosts: Cynthia & Jerry Mungerson
Suites: 1 (PB) $65
Rooms: 2 (PB) $50-55
Full Breakfast
Credit Cards: No
Notes: 2, 9, 10, 11, 12

PEORIA

Eagle's Nest

11125 North Trigger Road
Dunlap, IL, 61525
(309) 243-7376

Country Georgian home, filled with interesting antiques, situated in a tranquil rural setting on 2.5 wooded acres. Swimming pool on premises; hiking, cross-country skiing. Continental breakfast is served on the screened porch in nice weather. Jubilee College and Wildlife Prairie Park are readily accessible. Ten minutes from Peoria.

Hosts: John & Lou Ann Williams
Rooms: 2 (PB) $30-35
Continental Breakfast
Credit Cards: No
Notes: 2, 5, 8, 9, 10, 11, 12

PETERSBURG

Carmody's Clare Inn

207 South 12th Street
Petersburg, IL, 62675
(217) 632-2350

Built in 1874 and lovingly restored. Antiques re-create the ambience of yesteryear. Petersburg is adjacent to New Salem, where Lincoln served as postmaster and wooed Ann Rutledge. Lincoln's home, law office, and tomb are twenty miles away in Springfield.

Hosts: Mike & Pat Carmody
Rooms: 3 (SB) $50 + tax
Full Breakfast
Credit Cards: No
Notes: 2, 5, 8 (10 and over), 9, 10, 12, 14

PRINCETON

Yesterday's Memories

303 East Peru Street
Princeton, IL, 61356
(815) 872-7753

Comfortable and homelike, the house is located one mile from I-80 in central Illinois. Within walking distance of most points of interest and excellent shopping. Free pickup from Amtrak. Uniquely furnished; organic gardens; country breakfasts with home-grown food.

Hosts: Marilyn & Robert Haslam
Rooms: 2 (SB) $40 + tax
Full Breakfast
Credit Cards: No
Notes: 2, 5, 8 (by arrangement), 11, 12

Yesterday's Memories

RANTOUL

Better 'N Grandma's Overniters

102 South Meyers Street
Rantoul, IL, 61866
(217) 893-0469

This 110-year-old Victorian has a varied decor: Mexican hallway, a touch of country, and the Orient in other areas. At $10 per person per night, Better 'N Grandma's is an economical B&B in downtown Rantoul. Nearby is Chanute Air Force Base, with its Air Park. Fifteen miles to Champaign-Urbana and the University of Illinois.

Host: Janet Anderson
Rooms: 3 (SB) $20
Continental Breakfast
Credit Cards: No
Notes: 2, 5, 10, 11, 12

ROCKFORD

Victoria's B&B Inn

201 North Sixth Street
Rockford, IL, 61107
(815) 963-3232

Opulence, elegance, and generous hospitality await you in this turn-of-the-century mansion. Walk out the door and enter "Victorian Village," seventy unique stores and eateries. Return and enjoy a cozy fire in a Victorian parlor or retire to your suite, with its heart-shaped Jacuzzi.

Hosts: Carol & Marty Lewis
Rooms: 4 (PB) $74.52-172.80
Continental Breakfast
Credit Cards: A, B
Notes: 2, 5, 9, 10, 11, 12, 13

ROCK ISLAND

Top O' the Morning

1505 Nineteenth Avenue
Rock Island, IL, 61201
(309) 786-3513

Sam and Peggy welcome you to their brick mansion on the bluffs overlooking the Mississippi River. Fantastic view, day or night. Three-acre wooded estate with winding drive, orchard, and gardens. Air-conditioned bedrooms, whirlpool tub, natural fireplaces.

Hosts: Sam & Peggy Doak
Rooms: 2 (PB) $40-50
Full Breakfast
Credit Cards: No
Notes: 2, 5, 7, 8, 9, 10, 11, 12, 13

SYCAMORE

Country Charm Inn

Route 2, Box 154
Quigley Road
Sycamore, IL, 60178
(815) 895-5386

Understated elegance is the hallmark of our three-story country farm home. Pit fireplace, 2,000-book library, mini petting zoo, trick horse (Champ), breakfast on the cozy front porch. Howard and Donna are former AFS hosts, and Donna, the oldest of fourteen children, loves people!

Hosts: Howard & Donna Petersen
Rooms: 3 (PB) $35-45
Full Breakfast
Minimum stay holidays: 2
Credit Cards: No
Closed Dec. 20-April 1
Notes: 2, 8, 9, 10, 11, 12

TOLONO

Aunt Zelma's Country Guest House

RR 1, Box 129
Tolono, IL, 61880
(217) 485-5101; 485-8925

Located near Champaign and the University of Illinois. Just three miles from Willard Airport. This one-story country home is furnished with family antiques, and quilts are displayed as bedspreads.

Host: Zelma Weibel
Rooms: 3 (1 PB; 2 SB) $36.10-42.40
Full Breakfast
Credit Cards: No
Notes: 2, 5, 8, 12

WINNETKA

Chateau des Fleurs

552 Ridge Road
Winnetka, IL, 60093
(312) 256-7272

Chateau des Fleurs is an elegant respite from the world that welcomes you with light, beauty, warmth, and lovely views of magnificent trees, gardens, and a swimming pool. A French country home filled with antiques, four fireplaces, fifty-inch television, and a grand piano. Located by a private road for jogging or walking, it is only four blocks from shops and restaurants and a thirty-minute train ride to Chicago's Loop. Ten minutes from Northwestern University.

Host: Sally H. Ward
Rooms: 3 (PB) $80-90
Continental-plus Breakfast
Minimum stay weekends & holidays: 2
Credit Cards: A, B
Notes: 2, 5, 8 (over 16), 9, 10, 11, 12, 14

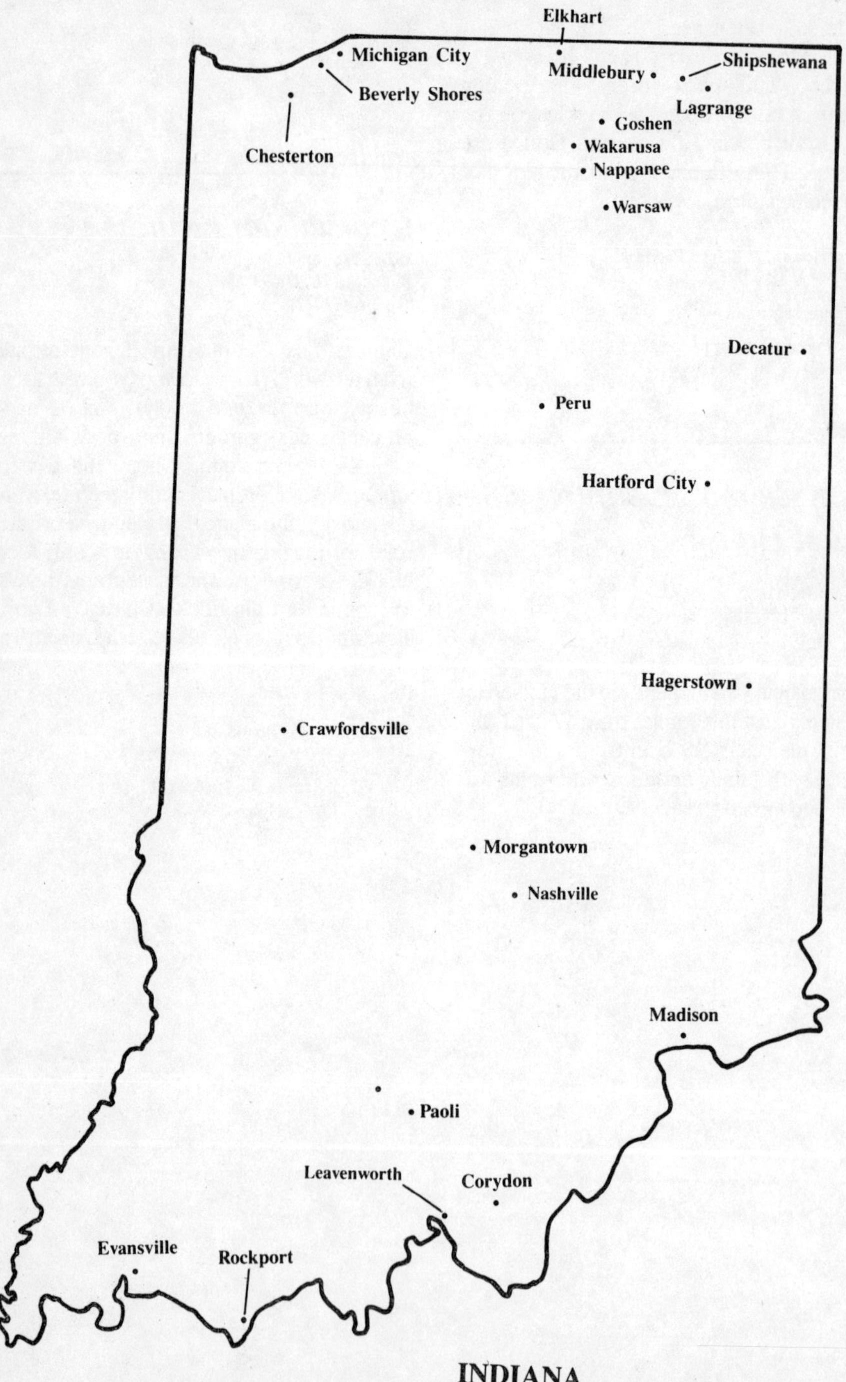

Elkhart
Michigan City
Beverly Shores
Chesterton
Middlebury
Shipshewana
Lagrange
Goshen
Wakarusa
Nappanee
Warsaw
Decatur
Peru
Hartford City
Hagerstown
Crawfordsville
Morgantown
Nashville
Madison
Paoli
Leavenworth
Corydon
Evansville
Rockport

INDIANA

Indiana

BEVERLY SHORES

Dunes Shore Inn

Lake Shore County Road
Box 807
Beverly Shores, IN, 46301
(219) 879-9029

A B&B in the Gasthof tradition; quiet, informal. One block to Lake Michigan. A four-season oasis for those who wish to relax in the natural beauty of the Indiana Dunes. Ideal stopping-off place for exploring this unique area.

Hosts: Rosemary & Fred Braun
Rooms: 12 (S4B) $43-50
Continental Breakfast
Minimum stay weekends & holidays: 2
Credit Cards: A, B
Notes: 2, 8, 9, 10, 11, 12, 13

CHESTERTON

Gray Goose Inn

350 Indian Boundary Road
Chesterton, IN, 46304
(219) 926-5781

English-style country house located on 100 wooded acres overlooking a private lake. Walking trails, paddle boat, rowboat, bikes are available for guests. Minutes from Dunes State and National Lakeshore; fifty minutes from Chicago.

Hosts: Tim Wilk & Chuck Ramsey
Rooms: 5 (PB) $60-75
Full Breakfast
Credit Cards: A, B, C, D
Notes: 2, 5, 7, 8 (12 and over), 9, 10, 11, 12, 13, 14

CORYDON

Kintner House Inn

101 South Capitol Avenue
Corydon, IN, 47112
(812) 738-2020

Completely restored inn (circa 1873), a National Historic Landmark. Fifteen rooms, each with private bath, furnished in Victorian and country antiques. Serves full breakfast. Also three apartment suites adjacent to inn, completely furnished and decorated, that are ideal for families. Unique shops, fine restaurants, antique malls, horse-drawn carriage, and excursion train all within walking distance of the inn. Sports available at the Corydon Country Club. Rated AAA and Mobil.

Host: Mary Jane Bridgwater
Rooms: 18 (PB) $61-95
Full Breakfast
Credit Cards: A, B, C, D, E
Notes: 2, 5, 8, 9, 10, 11, 12

Gray Goose Inn

6 Pets welcome: 7 Smoking allowed: 8 Children welcome: 9 Social drinking allowed: 10 Tennis available: 11 Swimming available: 12 Golf available: 13 Skiing available: 14 May be booked through travel agents

CRAWFORDSVILLE

Davis House

1010 West Wabash
Crawfordsville, IN, 47933
(317) 364-0461

Davis House is a Victorian mansion built of bricks manufactured on the site and furnished with antique and country pieces. Guest rooms have private baths and telephones. A convenience center is available to guests. Crawfordsville has several museums, many antique shops, good restaurants.

Hosts: Jan Stearns & Terry Wilson
Rooms: 4 (PB) $40-60
Continental Breakfast
Credit Cards: A, B, C, D
Notes: 2, 5, 7, 8, 9, 10, 11, 12, 14

DECATUR

Cragwood Inn B&B

303 North Second Street
Decatur, IN, 46733
(219) 728-2000

Enjoy the ambience of the past with the convenience of the present in this beautiful Queen Anne home. Magnificent woodwork and beveled glass windows reflect the craftsmanship of a bygone era. Several mystery parties are held during the year. Decatur is a delightful small town just minutes south of Ft. Wayne in Swiss Amish country. Commercial rates available.

Hosts: George & Nancy Craig
Rooms: 4 (2 PB; 2 SB) $45-55
Suite: 1 (PB) $75
Continental-plus Breakfast
Credit Cards: A, B
Notes: 2, 5, 9, 10, 11, 12, 14

ELKHART

Amish Acres B&B 501

1600 West Market Street
Nappanee, IN, 46550
(219) 773-4188

Older Mennonite couple lives in a new ranch-style house in the middle of farmland. Children have taken over the adjacent family farm, which guests can tour. Two rooms, each with double bed and private bath, both located on the first floor. Air-conditioning and TV available. Continental breakfast or more. $45.

EVANSVILLE

Brigadoon B&B Inn

1201 SE Second Street
Evansville, IN, 47713
(812) 422-9635

Romantic white-frame Victorian with 1892 parquet floors, four fireplaces, and stained glass. Enjoy the rainbows cast every sunny morning in the lace-curtained parlor. Large antique-furnished guest rooms are Scottish, English, Irish, and Welsh.

Host: Katelin Forbes
Rooms: 4 (2 PB; 2 SB) $40-45
Full Breakfast
Credit Cards: A, B
Notes: 2, 5, 6, 7, 8, 9, 10, 11, 12, 14

GOSHEN

Amish Acres B&B 301

1600 West Market Street
Nappanee, IN, 46550
(219) 773-4188

Located near Wakarusa, the hosts of this 100-acre working dairy farm still drive a horse and buggy. Two upstairs rooms with quilt-covered beds, and one downstairs room with a hideabed. Typical farm household with lots of activity; hosts have four children. $45.

Amish Acres B&B 302

1600 West Market Street
Nappanee, IN, 46550
(219) 773-4188

Newly built ranch-style house located on a 70-acre farm. Ideal for long quiet walks down the lane. Two rooms on the first floor, each with a double bed and private bath between the rooms. Air conditioned, wheelchair accessible. $45.

Amish Acres B&B 304

1600 West Market Street
Nappanee, IN, 46550
(219) 773-4188

Two-story new house. Mennonite hosts are retired but still own the large dairy farm next door. Very quiet, private bath with quilts on the beds. One double with twin on the second floor. One double with crib on second floor. $45.

Amish Acres B&B 305

1600 West Market Street
Nappanee, IN, 46550
(219) 773-4188

Eighty-acre Mennonite farm has a maple sugar camp you can tour. Two-story house with four rooms, one with an outside deck. Four double beds, shared bath. Continental breakfast or more. $45.

Amish Acres B&B 307

1600 West Market Street
Nappanee, IN, 46550
(219) 773-4188

This 36-acre property is surrounded by trees and wildlife. Mennonite hosts built this split-level house in 1988. Wheel chair accessible, private entrance, private kitchen area attached to lower-level room containing one double bed and private bath. Upper-level room contains one double bed and private bath. Hosts have numerous family heirlooms, craft items, and antiques throughout the house. $45.

The Checkerberry Inn

62644 CR37
Goshen, IN, 46526
(219) 642-4445

At the Checkerberry Inn you will find a unique atmosphere, unlike anywhere else in the Midwest. Each individually decorated room has breathtaking views of the unspoiled countryside. Outdoor pool, tennis court, and croquet green. Cycling, jogging, and walking area. Shopping and golf all within ten to fifteen minutes.

Hosts: John & Susan Graff
Rooms: 12 (PB) $115-165
Continental Breakfast
Credit Cards: A, B, C
Closed January
Notes: 2, 3, 4, 8, 9, 10, 11, 12, 14

HAGERSTOWN

Teetor House

300 West Main Street
Hagerstown, IN, 47346
(317) 489-4422

An elegant converted home with historic significance in the automotive industry on 10 landscaped acres with many unique amenities. Full breakfast included; excellent restaurants nearby. All rooms are fully air-conditioned, and some have TV.

Hosts: Jack & Joanne Warmoth
Rooms: 4 (PB) $66-93.50
Full Breakfast
Credit Cards: A, B
Notes: 2, 5, 7 (limited), 8, 9, 10, 11, 12, 14

HARTFORD CITY

De'Coy's Bed & Breakfast

1546 West 100N
Hartford City, IN, 47348
(317) 348-2164

Recently restored country home, completely furnished with antiques. Relaxing rural setting close to three universities. Each room demonstrates its own character, comfortable and unique. There is a cat in residence. Experience a friendly, pleasant getaway.

Hosts: Chris & Tiann Coy
Rooms: 5 (1 PB; 4 SB) $32-48
Full Breakfast
Credit Cards: No
Notes: 2, 5, 8, 9, 12, 14

LAGRANGE

The 1886 Inn

212 Factory Street
Lagrange, IN, 46761
(219) 463-4227

The moment guests see the large red-brick exterior and walk through the wooden front door of this 1886 inn, they are surrounded by historic charm and elegance. The house was originally built in 1886 as the home of a Civil War veteran and prominent politician and features a raised stone foundation and high, arching windows. Your hosts are glad to share the history and many unusual aspects of their home over breakfast. Only ten minutes from Shipshewana auction and flea market.

Hosts: Duane & Gloria Billman
Rooms: 4 (PB) $59
Continental-plus Breakfast
Credit Cards: A, B
Notes: 2, 5, 8, 10, 11, 12, 13

LEAVENWORTH

Ye Olde Scotts Inn

Route 1, Box 5
Leavenworth, IN, 47137
(812) 739-4747

Leavenworth is an interesting old river port founded in 1819. Spectacular views of the river are available from the bluffs at Leavenworth Overlook and in Crawford-Harrison State Forest. There are boat ramps, fishing, and water skiing, as well as excellent camping sites nearby. For spelunkers, there are three caves in the area.

Hosts: Jack & Allinmai Ramshaw
Rooms: 4 (SB) $28-30
Continental Breakfast
Credit Cards: No
Closed Oct. 15-April
Notes: 2, 11, 12

MADISON

Cliff House B&B

122 Fairmount Drive
Madison, IN, 47250
(812) 265-5272

This outstanding Victorian home was built in 1885 and is furnished with lovely antiques. Located on a bluff high above the town of Madison and the mighty Ohio River. Guests can relax and watch the river roll by. There are canopy beds in the rooms, and a candlelight breakfast is served in the morning.

Host: Jae Breitweiser
Rooms: 6 (PB) $55-82.50
Continental-plus Breakfast
Credit Cards: A, B
Notes: 2, 4, 5, 7 (limited), 8, 9, 10, 11, 12, 13, 14

MICHIGAN CITY

Plantation Inn

651 East 1500 North
Michigan City, IN, 46360
(219) 874-2418

A luxury country inn on several landscaped acres near the Indiana Dunes National Lakeshore recreation area. Two miles to the beaches, sport-fishing marinas, bird and wildlife sanctuaries. Close to restaurants, shopping, golf, theater, and other entertainment.

Host: Ann C. Stephens
Rooms: 5 (PB) $55-85
Full Breakfast
Credit Cards: A, B, C
Notes: 2, 4, 5, 7, 8 (12 and over), 9, 10, 11, 12, 13, 14

MIDDLEBURY

Bee Hive B&B

Box 1191
Middlebury, IN, 46540
(219) 825-5023

Come home to the farm. Enjoy country life, snuggle under a handmade quilt, and wake to the smell of fresh-baked muffins. Located in the heart of Amish Country. Enjoy the shops, flea markets, and antique stores in the area. Right off the Indiana turnpike.

Hosts: Herb & Treva Swarm
Rooms: 4 (1 PB; 3 SB) $49.95-60
Full Breakfast
Credit Cards: A, B
Notes: 2, 5, 8, 10, 12, 13

Patchwork Quilt Country Inn

11748 CR 2
Middlebury, IN, 46540
(219) 825-2417

Patchwork Quilt is a centennial farm growing soy beans or corn. Restaurant and country gift shop on the premises, and the three bedrooms are decorated in quaint country style.

Hosts: Maxine Zook & Susan Thomas
Rooms: 3 (SB) $54.95
Continental Breakfast
Credit Cards: A, B
Closed Jan. 1-15 and Sundays
Notes: 2, 3, 4, 8 (5 and over), 12

MORGANTOWN

The Rock House

380 West Washington Street
Morgantown, IN, 46160
(812) 597-5100

An 1894 Victorian built of concrete block, each block decorated with rocks, geodes, dice, doorknobs, dishes — even the skull of a wild boar! Visitors to Nashville/Brown County, Indiana University, and Lake Monroe are served a full breakfast before taking a "binocular" tour of the home's exterior (the only way to find all the embedded treasures).

Hosts: Doug & Marcia Norton
Rooms: 6 (2 PB; 4 SB) $50-65
Full Breakfast
Credit Cards: No
Notes: 2, 5, 7 (limited), 8, 9, 12, 13

NAPPANEE

Amish Acres B&B 102

1600 West Market Street
Nappanee, IN, 46550
(219) 773-4188

Large white square house has eleven rooms. Guests will sleep on host's grandma's antique bed, under a Lone Star quilt. Recently renovated with a new private bath. Young hosts have four young children. $45.

Amish Acres B&B 103

1600 West Market Street
Nappanee, IN, 46550
(219) 773-4188

Apostolic Christian hosts with three small children offer guests a lovely country home in a peaceful setting. Ceiling fans in room. Large white colonial with a columned front porch was originally a church built in 1865. $45.

Amish Acres B&B 104

1600 West Market Street
Nappanee, IN, 46550
(219) 773-4188

Large two-story farmhouse that has been in the same family for six generations. Amish Mennonite hosts have three small children. Three rooms are located on the second floor with five double beds and a single among them. Private bath on the second floor; outdoor deck for lounging. $45.

Amish Acres B&B 105

1600 West Market Street
Nappanee, IN, 46550
(219) 773-4188

Two-story white frame farmhouse located next to a country greenhouse. Hostess provides excellent hospitality. $45.

Amish Acres B&B 106

1600 West Market Street
Nappanee, IN, 46550
(219) 773-4188

White square frame two-story house. Three rooms with double beds on the second floor with a private bath. A lovely farm home with a hostess who is a delight to all who visit. Lots of antiques. $45.

Amish Acres B&B 107

1600 West Market Street
Nappanee, IN, 46550
(219) 773-4188

Eighty-acre Old Order Amish farm. Large home, buggy shed, large yard, very quiet. No indoor electricity or phone. Hostess operates her own craft shop on the premises with handmade items for sale. Three rooms on the second floor with shared bath. $45.

Amish Acres B&B 109

1600 West Market Street
Nappanee, IN, 46550
(219) 773-4188

Mennonite hosts with newly built house located on a 50-acre hay and wheat farm. One double bed on the first floor with private bath. $45.

Amish Acres B&B 112

1600 West Market Street
Nappanee, IN, 46550
(219) 773-4188

Two-story house located on an 80-acre farm. Quilts on the beds. Mennonite hosts offer four double beds, three rooms, second floor, private bath. $45.

Amish Acres B&B 114

1600 West Market Street
Nappanee, IN, 46550
(219) 773-4188

Large tri-level brick house, nestled among the Indiana farmland. Non-Amish couple with grown children has prepared the bottom floor for their guests' convenience. Private entrance, private bath, air-conditioning, and TV make this home a treat. Three rooms available. $45.

Amish Acres B&B 115

1600 West Market Street
Nappanee, IN, 46550
(219) 773-4188

Large brick colonial house has been restored with thick, rich carpet and fine furnishings. This house dates back to the pre-Civil War days and was among the homes in the Underground Railroad. Guests can enjoy tea and muffins in their room or a continental breakfast on 1850s Haviland china downstairs. Six rooms, each with air-conditioning and color TV. Rates vary by season.

NASHVILLE

Story Inn

P.O. Box 64
Nashville, IN, 47448
(812) 988-2273

Located on the southern edge of the Brown County State Park, this European-style country inn was once an old general store. Today it features fine dining and lodging in a pristine rural environment. Rooms are furnished with period antiques, original

NOTES: Credit cards accepted: A Master Card; B Visa; C American Express; D Discover Card; E Diners Club; F Other: 2 Personal checks accepted: 3 Lunch available: 4 Dinner available: 5 Open all year

artwork, fresh flowers, and air conditioning. Reservations required.

Hosts: Benjamin & Cyndi Schultz
Rooms: 13 (PB) $65-85
Full Breakfast
Credit Cards: A, B, C
Notes: 3, 4, 5, 8, 9, 10, 11, 12, 13

Story Inn

PAOLI

Braxtan House Inn B&B

210 North Gospel
Paoli, IN, 47454
(812) 723-4677

Braxtan House is a twenty-one-room Queen Anne Victorian, lovingly restored and furnished in antiques. The inn overlooks the historic courthouse square and is near Paoli Peaks ski resort, Patoka Lake, and antique and craft shops in picturesque southern Indiana hill country.

Hosts: Terry & Brenda Cornwell
Rooms: 6 (PB) $42-63
Full Breakfast
Minimum stay holidays: 2
Credit Cards: A, B, D (with surcharge)
Notes: 2, 5, 7, 8 (12 and over), 9, 10, 11, 12, 13

PERU

Rosewood Mansion Inn

54 North Hood Street
Peru, IN, 46970
(317) 472-7151

A large mansion of 10,000 square feet. Guest area includes parlor, library, entertainment room, oval dining room, large grand hall with open staircase to third floor. All rooms have private baths, telephone, and TV. FAX service available. Tennis, swimming, boating, parks, restaurants, shops, and three golf courses all within walking distance.

Hosts: Zoyla & Carm
Rooms: 8 (PB) $55-68
Full Breakfast
Credit Cards: A, B, C, D, E
Notes: 2, 3, 4, 5, 6, 7 (limited), 8 (12 and over), 9, 10, 11, 12, 13, 14

Braxtan House Inn B&B

ROCKPORT

The Rockport Inn

Third at Walnut
Rockport, IN, 47635
(812) 649-2664

The Rockport Inn, built as a private residence in 1855, is now operated as a country inn with six guest rooms and four dining rooms. It is known for its turn-of-the-century ambience and excellent cuisine.

Hosts: Carolyn & Emil Ahnell
Rooms: 6 (PB) $36-46
Continental Breakfast
Credit Cards: No
Notes: 2, 3, 4, 5, 7, 8, 9

SHIPSHEWANA

Green Meadow Ranch

Route 2, Box 592
Shipshewana, IN, 46565
(219) 768-4221

You're a stranger only once at Green Meadow. Nestled in the center of Amish and Mennonite country, two miles from Shipshewana, home of the Amish-Mennonite Visitors Center, the Shipshewana Auction, and many shops and attractions. We offer tours of the Amish country.

Hosts: Paul & Ruth Miller
Rooms: 11 (8 PB; 3 SB) $25
Continental-plus Breakfast
Credit Cards: A, B
Closed Jan. & Feb.
Notes: 2, 8, 11, 12

WAKARUSA

Amish Acres B&B 201

1600 West Market Street
Nappanee, IN, 46550
(219) 773-4188

A 138-acre dairy farm with 90 head of Holstein cows. Brick farmhouse is located down a lane surrounded by beautiful maple and spruce trees. Pond with diving board and raft for swimming. Across the road from a country meat market; fruit market one mile away. Several rooms are available on the second floor; baths may be shared if all rooms are occupied. $45.

Amish Acres B&B 202

1600 West Market Street
Nappanee, IN, 46550
(219) 773-4188

White two-story farmhouse with black shutters. The farm features a large tile brick dairy barn with geranium-filled window boxes. Hosts are a non-Amish farm couple with grown children. Two rooms on the second floor with one double and two twins. One king room on the second floor, and one double on the first floor, all with shared bath. $45.

Amish Acres B&B 203

1600 West Market Street
Nappanee, IN, 46550
(219) 773-4188

White house situated on a wooded lot with a circular drive. Charming Mennonite hostess. Second-floor rooms with shared bath on the first floor. $45.

WARSAW

Candlelight Inn

503 East Ft. Wayne Street
Warsaw, IN, 46580
(219) 267-2906

The Candlelight Inn offers a gentle reminder of the past with the comforts and convenience of the present. In-room phones, TV, and private baths. Antiques return you to the 1860s. Many lakes and antique shops provide great relaxation and sport. We are close to Amish country.

Hosts: Bill & Debi Hambright
Rooms: 4 (PB) $57-67
Full Breakfast
Credit Cards: A, B, C
Notes: 2, 5, 8, 9, 10, 11, 12, 13 (XC), 14

Iowa

ALTA

Addie's Place B&B

121 Cherokee Street
Alta, IA, 51002
(712) 284-2509

Addie's Place is a turn-of-the-century Queen Anne Victorian, lovingly restored. Wraparound porches and English gardens welcome travelers. Our small-town charm includes fresh air, quiet streets, and friendly people. A gift shop on the premises features work by our talented area artists.

Hosts: Gary & Cindy Molgaard
Rooms: 4 (1 PB; 3 private 1/2 baths) $35 + tax
Full Breakfast
Credit Cards: No
Notes: 2, 3, 4, 5, 8, 9, 10, 11, 12, 13

The Shaw House

ANAMOSA

The Shaw House

509 South Oak
Anamosa, IA, 52205
(319) 462-4485

Enjoy a relaxing step back in time in this three-story 1872 Italianate mansion on a hilltop overlooking scenery immortalized in the paintings of native son Grant Wood. Special rooms include porch with panoramic countryside view, two-room tower suite, and ballroom. Located on a 45-acre farm within easy walking distance of town. State park, canoeing, antiques are nearby.

Hosts: Connie & Andy McKean
Rooms: 4 (3 PB; 1 SB) $35-50
Full Breakfast
Credit Cards: No
Notes: 2, 3, 4, 5, 8, 9, 10, 11, 12, 13, 14

CALMAR

Calmar Guesthouse

RR 1, Box 206
Calmar, IA, 52132
(319) 562-3851

Newly remodeled Victorian home with many antiques, located near Luther College and NITI Community College. Close to world-famous Bily Clocks in Spillville, Niagara Cave, Lake Meyer, and much more. Wake up to a fresh country breakfast. Air-conditioned. Good variety of restaurants in the area.

Hosts: Art & Lucille Kruse
Rooms: 5 (1 PB; 4 SB) $35-45
Full Breakfast
Credit Cards: A, B
Notes: 2, 5, 7 (restricted), 8, 9, 10, 11, 12, 13

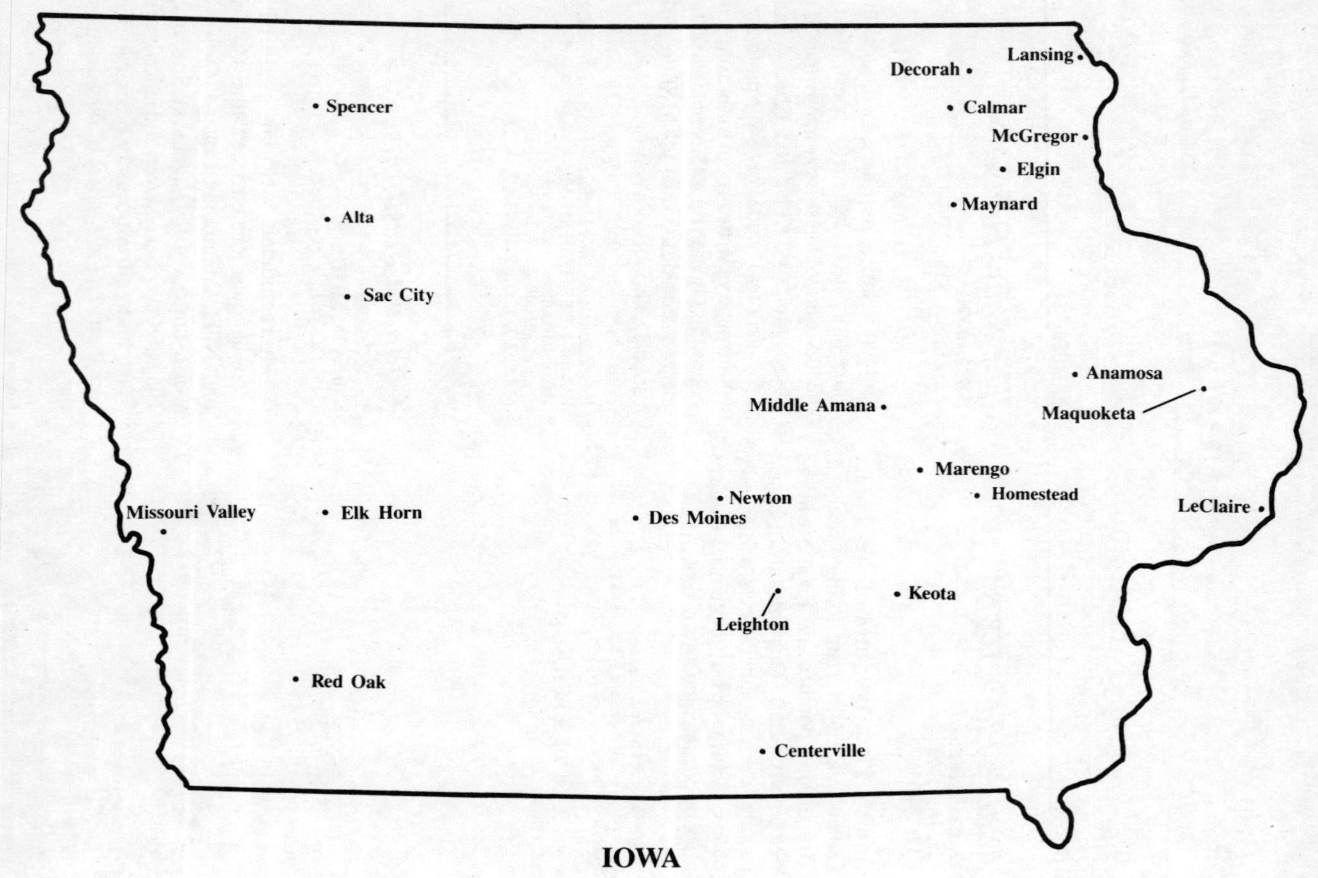
Lansing
Decorah
Calmar
McGregor
Elgin
Maynard
Spencer
Alta
Sac City
Anamosa
Maquoketa
Middle Amana
Marengo
Homestead
LeClaire
Newton
Des Moines
Missouri Valley
Elk Horn
Keota
Leighton
Red Oak
Centerville
IOWA

CENTERVILLE

Paint 'n Primitives

107 East Washington
Centerville, IA, 52544
(515) 856-8811

This Victorian-style home, located one block north of the world's largest square, houses an arts and crafts store and three charmingly decorated rooms. Near Lake Rathbun, boating, fishing, fish hatchery, museums. One whirlpool tub.

Hosts: Joe & Mary Murphy
Rooms: 3 (PB) $40-60
Full Breakfast
Credit Cards: A, B
Notes: 2, 5, 8, 11, 12

DECORAH

Montgomery Mansion B&B

812 Maple Avenue
Decorah, IA, 52101
(319) 382-5088

An 1877 restored brick Victorian located in a quiet residential neighborhood. Large, comfortable rooms, air-conditioning. Quiet sitting room upstairs with TV and library. Conveniently located for canoeing, tubing, trout fishing, hiking, shops, and museums.

Hosts: Bob & Diane Ward
Rooms: 4 (1 PB; 3 SB) $35-40
Full Breakfast
Credit Cards: A, B
Notes: 2, 5, 7 (limited), 8, 9, 10, 11, 12, 13, 14

DES MOINES

Brownswood B&B

5938 SW McKinley Avenue
Des Moines, IA, 50321
(515) 285-4135

On acreage with quiet country charm only minutes away from I-80 and I-35, with easy access to historic Valley Junction. Indoor and outdoor trampoline, ski/trim machine, air and water purification. Enjoy a full breakfast overlooking private yard of trees, flowers, and birds. Refreshments served on arrival and at bedtime. Adventureland, Living History Farms, art center, and nature walks through Brown's Woods.

Hosts: Elaine & John Walser
Rooms: 2 (SB) $46.80
Full Breakfast
Credit Cards: No
Notes: 2, 5, 6 (horses), 7, 8, 9, 10, 11, 12, 13 (XC)

ELGIN

Country Swiss Guest House

404 Mill Street
RR 2, Box 55
Elgin, IA, 52141
(319) 426-5796

Country Swiss Guest House is a classic home overlooking a Swiss setting with a river valley and streams stocked with trout. Nearby is a conservation park with skiing, canoe access, hiking trails for the blind, and deer, pheasant, and wild turkey hunting. Quaint Amish stores and antique shops also nearby.

Hosts: Sue & Ray Crammond
Rooms: 2 (1 PB; 1 SB) $45
Full Breakfast
Closed Christmas
Credit Cards: No
Notes: 2, 8 (over 12), 10, 11, 12, 13

ELK HORN

Rainbow H. Lodginghouse

RR 1, Box 89
Elk Horn, IA, 51531
(712) 764-8272

Visitors will enjoy the spacious setting of this grand brick home. Adults can enjoy a game of horseshoes or watch a crackling fire in the large recreation room. Children will enjoy having the room to explore outdoors and view the varied livestock, including some of the nation's finest Texas Longhorn cattle, which they may help feed. The house has air conditioning, private guest entrance, outdoor patio, color TV, and private guest bath. Choose a hearty breakfast or eat as light as you wish.

Hosts: Mark & Cherie Hensley
Rooms: 2 (PB) $26-36
Full Breakfast
Credit Cards: No
Notes: 2, 7, 8

The Travelling Companion

4314 Main Street
Elk Horn, IA, 51531
(712) 764-8932

Velkommen (Welcome) to The Travelling Companion. Delightful accommodations await you in this 1909 home nestled in the peaceful Danish town of Elk Horn. The Ortgies chose the house's name from one of Hans Christian Andersen's fairy-tale stories. Each guest room is named after a different fairy tale.

Hosts: Duane & Karolyn Ortgies
Rooms: 3 (SB) $40-50
Full Breakfast
Credit Cards: No
Notes: 2, 5, 8, 10, 11

HOMESTEAD

Die Heimat Country Inn

Main Street, Amana Colonies
Homestead, IA, 52236
(319) 622-3937

Die Heimat (German for "The Home Place") has nineteen rooms, all furnished with Amana walnut and cherry furniture, private baths, TVs, and air-conditioning. Colony heirlooms and antiques are found throughout the inn. Some rooms have Amana walnut canopy beds. Nature trail, golf course, wineries, woolen mills, and restaurants are all nearby.

Hosts: Don & Sheila Janda
Rooms: 19 (PB) $34.95-54.95
Continental-plus Breakfast
Credit Cards: A, B, D
Notes: 2, 5, 6, 7 (restricted), 8, 9, 10, 11, 12, 13 (XC), 14

KEOTA

Elmhurst

Route 1, Box 3
Keota, IA, 52248
(515) 636-3001

This 1905 Victorian mansion retains much of its original grandeur: stained-glass and curved windows, circular solarium, parquet floors, beamed ceilings, marble fireplace mantles, ballroom, two grand stairways, leather wall coverings, and more. Golf course, swimming, and nature trail across the road.

Host: Marjie Schantz-Koehler
Rooms: 4 (SB) $36.40
Full Breakfast
Credit Cards: No
Notes: 2, 3, 4, 5, 9, 10, 11, 12

Elmhurst

LANSING

FitzGerald's Inn

160 North Third Street
Box 157
Lansing, IA, 52151
(319) 538-4872

Century-old Victorian country home of unusual charm, situated on one of Lansing's

NOTES: Credit cards accepted: A Master Card; B Visa; C American Express; D Discover Card; E Diners Club; F Other: 2 Personal checks accepted: 3 Lunch available: 4 Dinner available: 5 Open all year

hilly residential streets. Terraced grounds rise dramatically to a bluff-top view of the Mississippi River at one of its most beautiful stretches. Ideal setting for relaxation, canoeing, boating, hiking, bird watching, skiing. Whole house rental available.

Hosts: Maire & Jeff FitzGerald
Rooms: 5 (3 PB; 2 SB) $52-67.60
Full Breakfast
Credit Cards: No
Notes: 2, 5, 7, 8, 9, 10, 11, 12, 13, 14

Lansing House

291 Front Street
Box 97
Lansing, IA, 52151
(319) 538-4263

Lansing House, a handsome riverfront home, is situated next to the picturesque Blackhawk Bridge and offers its guests an atmosphere of comfort and elegance — plus a picture-window view of the Great River. The area offers hikes in the woods and walks along the river. Rental boats are available for sight-seeing in the backwaters and fishing.

Hosts: Chris & Margaret Fitz Gerald
Rooms: 2 (SB) $60
Full Breakfast
Credit Cards: No
Notes: 2, 5, 10, 11, 13

LeCLAIRE

Latimer B&B

127 North Second Street
P.O. Box 417
LeClaire, IA, 52753
(319) 289-5747

A 1905 house that has been the home of the Latimer family since 1949. Warm and cozy large ten-room house, completely remodeled. Large porch with swing, and large yard to wander in. Conveniently located to several local attractions. A riverboat departs daily for a two-day trip up river. Buffalo Bill Museum one block away; Cody Homestead within ten miles. Quad-City Downs is a fifteen-minute drive. Other events in the Quad Cities area include the Bix Run and Hardee's Golf Classic.

Host: Darlene Nichols
Rooms: 4 (SB) $40 + tax
Full Breakfast
Credit Cards: No
Notes: 2, 5, 7, 8, 9, 10, 11, 12

The Monarch B&B Inn

303 Second Street
P.O. Box 227
LeClaire, IA, 52753
(319) 289-3011; (800) 772-7724

Overlooking the mighty Mississippi on the point where the rapids once began, in the historic town of LeClaire. Two miles north of I-80, Exit 306. The house was built c. 1860. Near riverboat cruises, French and Polish cuisine. Reservations required. High tea, lunch, and dinner. *Nous parlons Francais; Rozma wiam Po Polsku.*

Hosts: David & Emilie Oltman
Rooms: 5 (1 PB; 4 SB) $40-46
Full Breakfast
Credit Cards: A, B
Notes: 2, 3, 4, 5, 8, 12, 14

LEIGHTON

Heritage House

Route 1, Box 166
Leighton, IA, 50143
(515) 626-3092

A 1918 house that has been renovated, air-conditioned, and beautifully decorated. Over 2,600 acres nearby for hunting deer, quail, pheasant, and turkey, plus facilities to dress game and keep it refrigerated. Come for the Tulip Time Festival the second week in May, or visit Pella's historic village museum tours all year. For breakfast, enjoy homemade cinnamon rolls, scrambled eggs, bacon pie, or caramel French toast.

Loy's Bed & Breakfast

Host: Iola Vander Wilt
Rooms: 2 (SB) $28-35
Full Breakfast
Credit Cards: No
Closed Jan.
Notes: 2, 8, 9, 11, 12, 13

MARENGO

Loy's Bed & Breakfast

RR #1, Box 82
Marengo, IA, 52301
I80, Exit 216N
(319) 642-7787

Modern farm home on a large grain and hog farm. Recreation room and farm tour available. Close to the Amana Colonies and many other interesting places. Small conference retreat. Farm breakfast with hot breads.

Hosts: Loy & Robert Walker
Rooms: 3 (SB) $32.70-54.50
Full Breakfast
Credit Cards: No
Notes: 2, 4, 5, 8, 9, 10, 11, 12

MAYNARD

Boedeker's Bungalow/WestSide B&B & "Access" Annex

125 Seventh Street North
Maynard, IA, 50655
(319) 637-2711

Just off Highway 150, you'll have a hearty breakfast after a quiet rest and a country view from your private upstairs quarters. You're in the center of things in Fayette County, and right in northeast Iowa's famous hills and rivers territory. Air-conditioning and TV.

Host: Mrs. Margaret I. Boedeker
Rooms: 1 (PB) $36.40
Type of Beds: 2 Twin; 1 Double
Full Breakfast
Credit Cards: No
Notes: 2, 5, 7

McGREGOR

Little Switzerland Inn

Box 195
McGregor, IA, 52157
(319) 873-3670

The building housing the inn was constructed in 1862 as the home for Iowa's oldest weekly newspaper. Since then, it has undergone renovation. The newest addition to the inn is an authentic log cabin that was moved onto the property and furnished for guests with a large Jacuzzi and beautiful stone fireplace. The Mississippi River is less than a block away, and guests will enjoy watching its traffic from the balcony of the inn.

Hosts: Bud & Chris Jamesen
Rooms: 6 (5 PB; 1 SB) $20-55
Full Breakfast
Credit Cards: A, B
Notes: 2, 4, 5, 6, 7, 8, 10, 11, 13, 14

Little Switzerland Inn

Rivers Edge B&B

112 Main Street
McGregor, IA, 52157
(319) 873-3501

Beautiful river view, fully furnished kitchen, patio. Our second-story deck overlooks the river. Close to boating, fishing, hiking, hunting, skiing, golf.

Host: Rita Lange
Rooms: 3 (PB) $50
Continental Breakfast
Credit Cards: A, F
Notes: 2, 5, 8, 9, 10, 11, 12, 13

MIDDLE AMANA

Dusk to Dawn B&B

Box 124
Middle Amana, IA, 52307
(319) 622-3029

An invitation to relax in a peaceful, comfortable atmosphere, in a house decorated in beautiful Amana antiques. Located in historic Middle Amana, we have taken a touch of the past and accented it with a greenhouse, spacious deck, and Jacuzzi.

Hosts: Bradley & Lynn Hahn
Rooms: 4 (PB) $41.42
Continental Breakfast
Credit Cards: A, B
Notes: 2, 5, 7, 8, 9, 12

MISSOURI VALLEY

Apple Orchard Inn

RR 3, Box 129
Missouri Valley, IA, 51555
(712) 642-2418

A country retreat on a 26-acre apple orchard situated on a hill overlooking the beautiful Boyer Valley. Gourmet cooking, featuring homemade breads, apple butter, and jellies. Comfortable rooms, a keeping room, and a Jacuzzi room. German and Spanish spoken.

Hosts: Dr. Electa & John Strub
Rooms: 3 (SB) $55
Full Breakfast
Credit Cards: A, B
Notes: 2, 3, 4, 5, 8, 9, 10, 11, 12, 13, 14

NEWTON

La Corsette Maison Inn

629 First Avenue East
Newton, IA, 50208
(515) 792-6833

Historic turn-of-the-century Mission-style mansion. Charming French bedchambers; fireplaces; gourmet dining in a style of elegance. On I-80, thirty minutes from Des Moines. Close to horse track and Adventureland. Listed on the National Register of Historic Places.

Host: Kay Owen
Rooms: 4 (PB) $55-135
Full Breakfast
Credit Cards: A, B
Notes: 2, 4, 5, 6 (call), 8 (call), 9, 10, 11, 12, 14

La Corsette Maison Inn

RED OAK

Usher's Bed & Breakfast

711 Corning Street
Red Oak, IA, 51566
(712) 623-3222; (800) 373-5819

A restored turn-of-the-century home furnished with antiques. Two guest bedrooms, shared bath, private study, and home-cooked Iowa country breakfast served in a formal dining room, or on the sun deck. Located in the heart of town, surrounded by historic homes. Restaurants and shopping nearby. Reservations please.

Hosts: Marti & Denny Usher
Rooms: 2 (SB) $42-52
Full Breakfast
Credit Cards: A, B
Notes: 2, 3, 4, 5, 7 (limited), 10, 11, 12, 14

SAC CITY

Brick Bungalow B&B

1012 Early Street
Sac City, IA, 50583
(712) 662-7302

A warm welcome greets you in this brick house in a quiet neighborhood. This is a solid 1930s house with beautiful dark oak woodwork and beams. Guests are invited to use all of the house and spacious backyard. Families are especially welcome. Guest rooms have golden pine paneling, separate baths, electric blankets, and central air.

Host: Phyllis Hartman
Rooms: 2 (PB) $35
Full Breakfast
Credit Cards: No
Notes: 2, 5, 7 (limited), 8, 10, 11, 12

Hannah Marie Country Inn

SPENCER

Hannah Marie Country Inn

RR 1, Hwy. 71 South
Spencer, IA, 51301
(712) 262-1286; 332-7719

A lovingly restored farm home offering romantic country strolls, a good night's rest, and a hearty gourmet breakfast. Be pampered by our private baths, air-conditioning, afternoon hors d'oeuvres; relax in a whirlpool or hot shower. Afternoon theme teas Tues.-Sat. Iowa Great Lakes, twenty miles.

Hosts: Mary Nichols, Dave Nichols
Rooms: 3 (PB) $52-62.40
Full Breakfast
Credit Cards: A, B
Closed Dec.-April
Notes: 2, 6 (in barn), 7 (restricted), 8, 9 (limited), 10, 11, 12

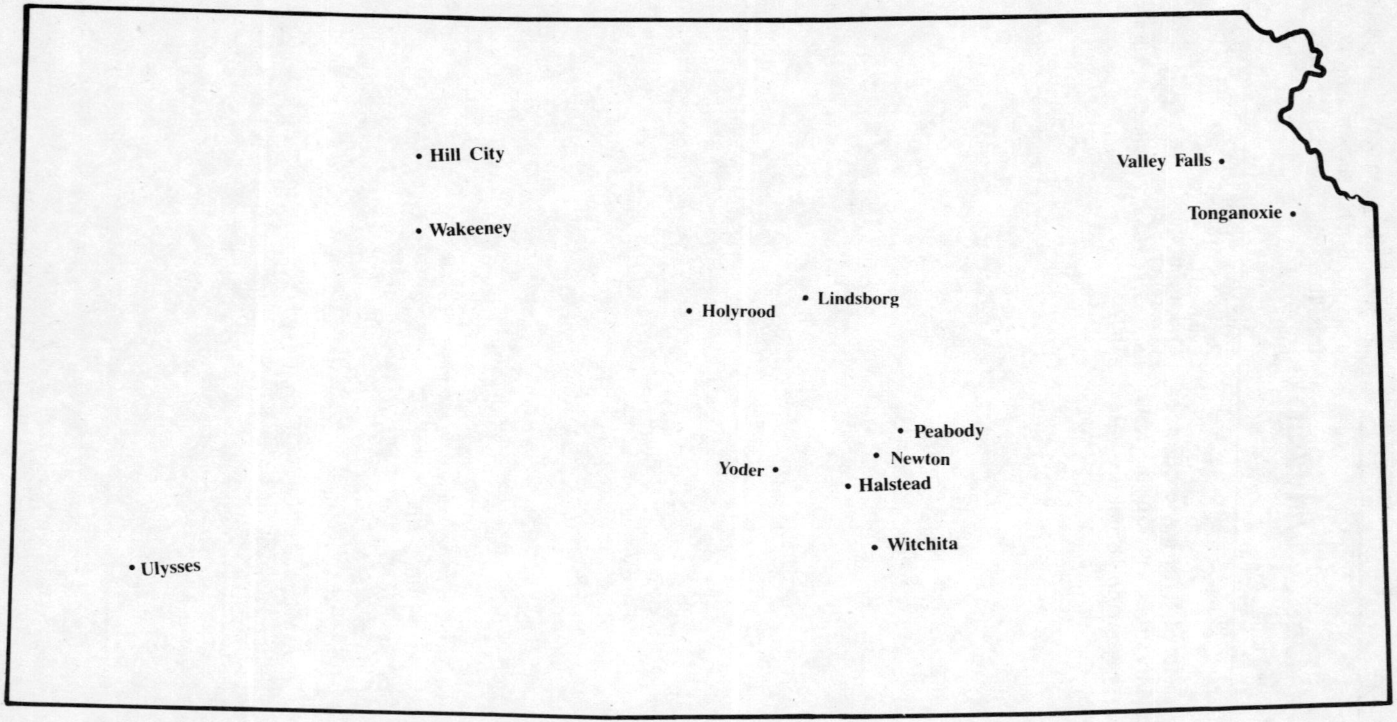

Hill City
Wakeeney
Valley Falls
Tonganoxie
Holyrood
Lindsborg
Peabody
Newton
Yoder
Halstead
Witchita
Ulysses

KANSAS

Kansas

HALSTEAD

Heritage Inn

300 Main Street
Halstead, KS, 67056
(316) 835-2118

Heritage Inn is an extraordinary 1922 bed and breakfast inn, located in the heart of Kansas. The moment you step through the doors of the Heritage Inn, you'll feel the comfort and relaxed charm of the 1920s, yet enjoy the convenience of the 1990s.

Hosts: Jim & Gery Hartong
Rooms: 4 (PB) $23
Full Breakfast
Credit Cards: A, B
Notes: 2, 3, 4, 5, 7, 8, 9, 10, 11, 12, 14

HILL CITY

Pomeroy Inn

224 West Main Street
Hill City, KS, 67642
(913) 674-2098

This two-story old limestone building was built in 1886 with walls that are twenty-six inches thick. We have a large lobby with two big picture windows; a big TV; couches, chairs, and tables for coffee and homemade Amarath and whole-wheat cinnamon rolls. Located on Highway 24, one block east of the intersection of Highways 24 & 283. Very comfortable; reasonable rates. Each room is unique, with handmade quilts. Phones available; cable TV.

Hosts: Don & Mary Worcester
Rooms: 9 (6 PB; 3 SB) $19.95-24.95
Continental Breakfast
Credit Cards: A, B, D
Notes: 2, 5, 6, 7, 8, 9, 10, 11, 12

HOLLYROOD

Hollyrood House

Route 1, Box 47
Hollyrood, KS, 67450
(913) 252-3678

Bird and other wildlife observation, Cheyenne Bottoms and Quirira Wildlife Refuges, also Wilson Lake, Kanopolis Lake. Hunting for pheasant, deer, and turkey. Bike riding, horseshoe pitching; buggy rides available. Or just sit under a tree and observe the lily ponds.

Host: Ron Schepmann
Rooms: 3 (1 PB; 2 SB) $30-45
Full Breakfast
Credit Cards: A, B
Notes: 2, 5, 6 (outside), 7 (restricted), 8, 9, 10, 11, 12, 14

LINDSBORG

Swedish Country Inn

112 West Lincoln Street
Lindsborg, KS, 67456
(913) 227-2985

Lindsborg is a Swedish community in the center of Kansas. Our inn is furnished in Swedish pine furniture, and beds have hand-quilted quilts. Full Scandinavian breakfast is served, and all rooms have private bath and TV. No smoking or pets. Near Bethany College, where Handel's *Messiah* is performed every Palm and Easter Sunday.

Host: Virginia Brunsell
Rooms: 19 (PB) $40-70

Full Breakfast
Credit Cards: A, B
Notes: 2, 3, 5, 8, 10, 11, 12

NEWTON

Hawk House B&B Inn

307 West Broadway
Newton, KS, 67114
(316) 283-2045

In the heart of wheat country. A three-story Victorian home with massive oak staircase and spacious common rooms punctuated with oak floors and stained glass. Each guest room is fully furnished with antiques, linens, and appointments. Guests are surrounded with elegance and hospitality. Air-conditioning.

Host: Norma Goering
Rooms: 4 (1 PB; 3 SB) $35-45
Full Breakfast
Credit Cards: A, B
Notes: 2, 5, 10, 11, 12

PEABODY

Jones Sheep Farm B&B

RR 2, Box 185
Peabody, KS, 66866
(316) 983-2815

Enjoy an entire turn-of-the-century home in a pastoral setting. Situated on a working sheep farm "at the end of the road," the house is furnished in 1930s style (no phone or TV). Quiet, private. Historic small town nearby.

Hosts: Gary & Marilyn Jones
Rooms: 2 (SB) $35
Credit Cards: No
Notes: 2, 5, 6, 10, 11, 12

TONGANOXIE

Almeda's B&B

220 South Main Street
Tonganoxie, KS, 66086
(913) 845-2295

Located in a picturesque small town made a historic site in 1983, the inn dates back to World War I. You are welcome to sip a cup of coffee at the stone bar once used as a bus stop in 1930. In fact, this room was the inspiration for the play *Bus Stop*.

Hosts: Almeda & Richard Tinberg
Rooms: 7 (PB and SB) $40
Continental Breakfast
Credit Cards: No
Notes: 2, 5, 9, 11, 12

ULYSSES

Fort's Cedar View

RR #3, Box 120B
Ulysses, KS, 67880
(316) 356-2570

Fort's Cedar View is located in the heart of the world's largest natural-gas field. We are on the Santa Fe Trail, eight miles north of famed Wagon Bed Springs, the first source of water after crossing the Cimarron River west of Dodge City, which is eighty miles northeast.

Host: Lynda Fort
Rooms: 4 (1 PB; 3 SB) $25-35
Full Breakfast
Credit Cards: No
Notes: 2, 5, 7 (limited), 10, 11, 12

VALLEY FALLS

The Barn B&B Inn

RR 2, Box 87
Valley Falls, KS, 66088
(913) 945-3225; (800) 869-7717

In the rolling hills of northeast Kansas you can sleep in a barn that is 98 years old. We serve you supper when you arrive and homemade bread made from the wheat raised on our farm, along with a full breakfast in the morning. There's also an exercise room and heated year-round pool for you to enjoy.

Hosts: Tom, Marcella & Patricia Ryan
Rooms: 18 (PB) $65
Full Breakfast
Credit Cards: A, B, C, D, E
Notes: 2, 3, 4, 5, 8, 9, 10, 11, 12, 14

WAKEENEY

Thistle Hill B&B

Route 1, Box 93
Wakeeney, KS, 67672
(913) 743-2644

Located halfway between Kansas City and Denver along I-70, this two-story country bed & breakfast has a large front porch and is decorated with antiques. An old-fashioned breakfast is served next to the brick fireplace in the oak-floored dining room.

Hosts: Dave & Mary Hendricks
Rooms: 3 (2 PB; 1 SB) $40
Full Breakfast
Credit Cards: No
Notes: 2, 5, 8, 9, 10, 11, 12,

WICHITA

Max Paul ... an inn

3910 East Kellogg
Wichita, KS, 67218
(316) 689-8101

Rooms are furnished with feather beds, European antiques, cable TV, and private baths. Executive suites have vaulted ceilings, wood-burning fireplaces, and features such as skylights and private balconies. There is a Jacuzzi/exercise room. Weekends, breakfast may be served to the room or in the garden. Centrally located for the airport, downtown, shopping, and local attractions.

Hosts: Jill & Roberta Eaton
Rooms: 14 (PB) $65-115
Full Breakfast
Credit Cards: A, B, C, D, E
Closed Christmas Day
Notes: 2, 5, 7, 9, 10, 11, 12

YODER

The Dauddy Haus

Route 2, Box 273
Yoder, KS, 67543
(No telephone)

Spend an evening back in time! Nice Amish farm with a variety of animals. A small harness shop is on the premises. Wake up to the roosters crowing or a buggy passing by, and eat a hearty breakfast like Gramma used to fix.

Hosts: Robert & Velma Schroek
Rooms: 5 (SB) $40
Full Breakfast
Credit Cards: No
No alcoholic beverages, cameras, or smoking in house
Notes: 2, 5, 8

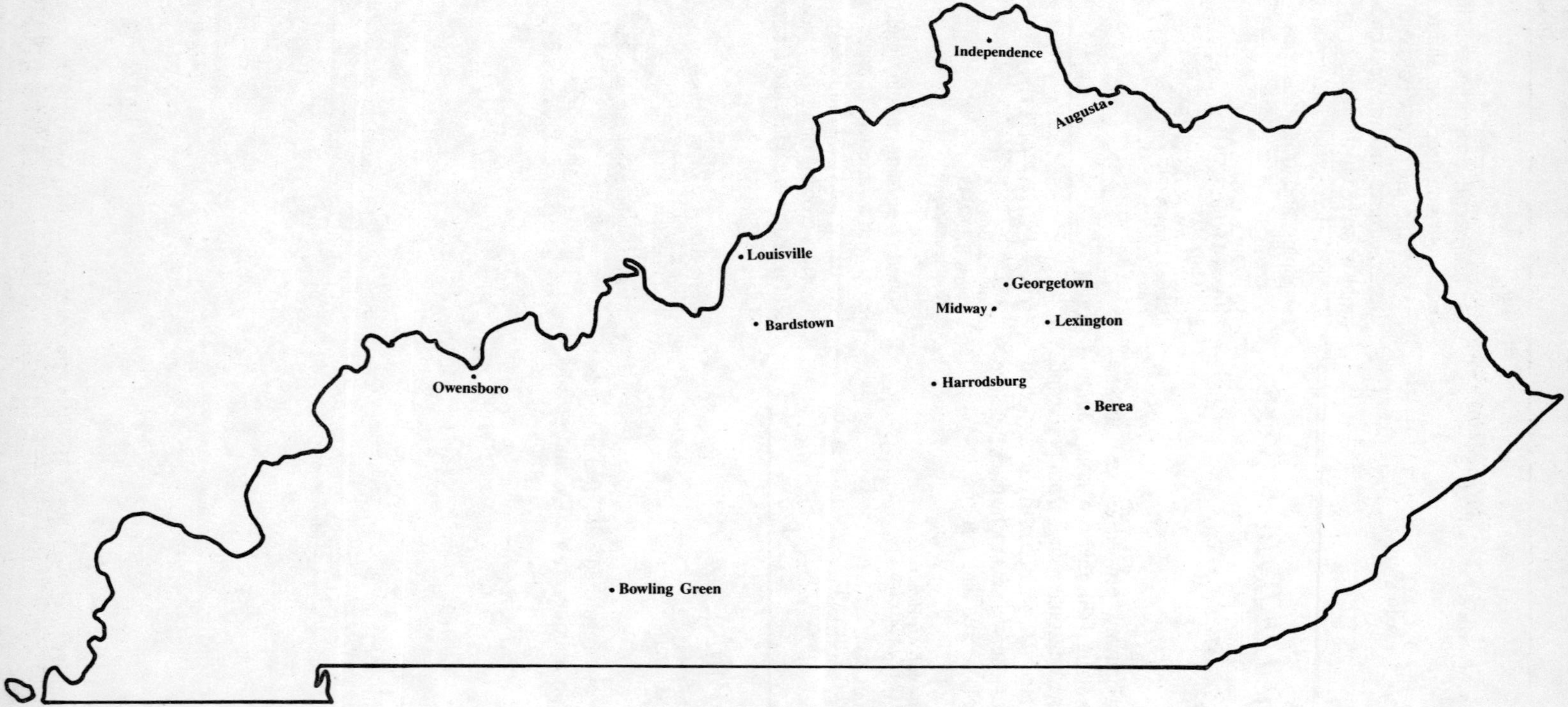

Independence
Augusta
Louisville
Georgetown
Midway
Lexington
Bardstown
Owensboro
Harrodsburg
Berea
Bowling Green

KENTUCKY

Kentucky

BARDSTOWN

Jailer's Inn

111 West Stephen Foster Avenue
Bardstown, KY, 40004
(502) 348-5551

The front building, now Jailer's Inn, was built in 1819 and used as a jail. In 1874 a new jail was built adjunct to the front building, which was then made into the jailer's residence. Listed in the National Register of Historic Places, the jailer's residence offers five rooms. Bardstown is famous for My Old Kentucky Home, the Stephen Foster Outdoor Drama, many famous distilleries, and is close to Lincoln's birthplace.

Hosts: Challen & Fran McCoy
Rooms: 5 (3 PB; 2 SB) $50-75
Continental Breakfast
Credit Cards: A, B, C
Closed Jan. & Feb.
Notes: 2, 9, 10, 11, 12, 14

BEREA

Bluegrass B&B 1

Route 1, Box 263
Versailles, KY, 40383
(606) 873-3208

Not every house can boast a 40-foot living room, but this one does. And three bedrooms from which to choose, as well; one with twin beds, one with a double, and the third with a queen. This 1890 edge-of-town home puts you next to the world-famous Berea craftsmen who produce everything from pottery to fine furniture. For those who enjoy antiques, this house is a real treat. No smoking, please. $50.

BOWLING GREEN

Bowling Green B&B

659 East 14th Avenue
Bowling Green, KY, 42101
(502) 781-3861

A 1939 gray shingled home on a shaded corner. A lounge, front porch, or picnic area help you relax in this comfortable family home near I-65. The restored town square and Western Kentucky University are nearby. Your hosts enjoy travel, photography, antiques, music, reading, and writing. They serve as foreign-exchange counselors and teach at Western Kentucky University. Mammoth Cave National Park is forty miles north; Opryland sixty minutes south.

Hosts: Ronna Lee & Norman Hunter
Rooms: 3 (1 PB; 2 SB) $30-40
Continental-plus Breakfast
Credit Cards: No
Notes: 2, 4 (advance reservations), 5, 9, 10, 11, 12

GEORGETOWN

Bluegrass B&B 2

Route 1, Box 263
Versailles, KY, 40383
(606) 873-3208

You'll have to see this huge canopied bed to believe it. It's seven feet square, with corkscrew posts nine feet high. It's one of the unusual items acquired by your hostess, who operates an antique shop as well as B&B. This suite has a full kitchen, private bath, and a second bed/sitting room. Upstairs are two more rooms, each with twin beds—a bath and a kitchen. $60.

Log Cabin B&B

350 North Broadway
Georgetown, KY, 40324
(502) 863-3514

Enjoy this Kentucky log cabin (c. 1809) with its shake roof, chinked logs, and period furnishings. Completely private. Two bedrooms, fireplace, fully equipped kitchen. Only five miles to Kentucky Horse Park and twelve miles north of Lexington. Children welcome.

Hosts: Clay & Janis McKnight
Cabin: (PB) $64
Continental-plus Breakfast
Credit Cards: No
Notes: 2, 5, 6, 7, 8, 9, 10, 11, 12

HARRODSBURG

Bluegrass B&B 3

Route 1, Box 263
Versailles, KY, 40383
(606) 873-3208

Your chance to stay in the house you've probably dreamed of. Large and luxurious, with sunken living room, library, and game room. Guests accommodated in newly redecorated second-floor room with private bath, double bed, and air-conditioning. Convenient to Shakertown, Old Fort Harrod, Danville, and Civil War battlefield at Perryville. Thirty minutes to Lexington and Keeneland. $60.

INDEPENDENCE

Cully's Country Home B&B

6876 Taylor Mill Road
Independence, KY, 41051
(606) 356-7865

Eighteen-acre mini farm in rural Kenton County. Fishing, swimming lakes, gardening, small animal reserve, ice skating in winter. A perfect retreat from the hustle and bustle of the city, yet only twenty minutes from downtown Cincinnati, Ohio, the hub of Reds baseball, Bengals football, famous historic music hall, Sawyer's Point, the Serpentine Wall, and spectacular Ohio riverboat restaurants.

Hosts: Nancy & Don Cully
Rooms: 2 (SB) $40
Full Breakfast
Credit Cards: A, B, D
Notes: 2, 5, 7, 8, 9, 10, 11, 12, 13, 14

LEXINGTON

Bluegrass B&B II

Route 1, Box 263
Versailles, KY, 40383
(606) 873-3208

In the 1880s, Lexington's largest and finest homes were being built along Broadway. Today these houses are enjoying a rebirth as dedicated couples restore their glories. Your hosts will be a professor of art and his wife, a government program manager. They offer a newly remodeled, large, air-conditioned bedroom with double bed, new private bath, and kitchenette. $45.

Bluegrass B&B III

Route 1, Box 263
Versailles, KY, 40383
(606) 873-3208

This is a lovely in-town house so surrounded by woods that you scarcely realize there are neighbors. Contemporary in style, its spacious feeling derives from its two-storied living room and generous use of glass. The guest room has twin mahogany four posters and attached private bath. Fully air-conditioned. $58.

Bluegrass B&B V

Route 1, Box 263
Versailles, KY, 40383
(606) 873-3208

"French on the outside; English inside." That's the way the owners describe their brand-new home with walled garden and graveled courtyard. Your accommodations will be a sitting room/bedroom suite with private bath and double bed. $60.

547

547 North Broadway
Lexington, KY, 40508
(606) 255-4152

One mini-suite with double bed, tile shower, kitchen, Victorian decor; in a private Victorian home. Plants, paintings, ceiling fans, and books. One-bedroom apartment with queen bed, bath, kitchenette, and living room. Additional bedroom available for family members.

Hosts: Joe & Ruth Fitzpatrick
Rooms: 3 (2 PB; 1 SB) $35-55
Full Breakfast
Credit Cards: No
Notes: 2, 5, 7, 8, 9, 10, 11, 12

Rokeby Hall B&B Inn

Rokeby Hall B&B Inn

318 South Mill Street
Lexington, KY, 40508
(606) 252-2368

Rokeby Hall is Lexington's only fully dedicated B&B inn, housed in an elegantly restored Victorian home in the historic South Hill district overlooking downtown Lexington. Complete with working fireplaces in the guest rooms, nineteenth-century furnishings and Oriental rugs, easy off-street parking, all modern amenities, and a full-time resident manager. Rokeby Hall makes a visit to Kentucky's beautiful Bluegrass region a memorable experience. Within easy walking distance of historic, shopping, and financial districts.

Host: Amy Hackett
Rooms: 4 (PB) $100-150 + tax
Full Breakfast
Credit Cards: A, B, C
Notes: 2, 3, 4, 5, 7, 8, 9, 10, 11, 12, 14

Sycamore Ridge

6855 Mt. Horeb Road
Lexington, KY, 40511
(606) 231-7714

Nestled on a ridge in horse country, surrounded by sycamore trees, this unique home affords our guests a peaceful retreat with a panoramic view of the Bluegrass. Complimentary wine and cheese awaits you. Our gourmet breakfast includes items such as fresh baked goods, fresh juice, whole-wheat banana pecan pancakes, and an assortment of flavored coffee and teas. Close to Kentucky Horse Park, downtown, and the airport.

Hosts: Debbie & Jon Demos
Rooms: 3 (PB) $90
Full Breakfast
Credit Cards: No
Notes: 2, 5, 9, 10, 11, 12, 14

LOUISVILLE

The Victorian Secret B&B

1132 South First Street
Louisville, KY, 40203.
(502) 581-1914

In historic Old Louisville you will find a three-story brick mansion appropriately named The Victorian Secret B&B. Its fourteen rooms offer spacious accommodations, high ceilings, eleven fireplaces, and original woodwork. Recently restored to its former elegance, the 110-year-old structure provides a peaceful setting for enjoying period furnishings and antiques.

Hosts: Nan & Steve Roosa
Rooms: 3 (1 PB; 2 SB) $53-58
Continental Breakfast
Credit Cards: No
Notes: 5, 7, 8, 9, 10, 11, 12

MIDWAY

Bluegrass B&B 7

Route 1, Box 263
Versailles, KY, 40383
(606) 873-3208

A small country inn located on a hill just outside Midway, close enough to the antique shops, yet with enough privacy for overnight guests to stroll the grounds. The inn has become a favorite dining place for travelers and natives alike. Two rooms, $54.

Louisiana

BATON ROUGE

Southern Comfort Reservations LBR01

2856 Hundred Oaks Avenue
Baton Rouge, LA, 70808
(504) 346-1928; (800) 749-1928

Centrally located conveniently to the university, hospitals, the interstate, shopping centers, government and financial districts. Two second-floor guest rooms, sitting area, large bath, double beds, refrigerator and microwave, HBO and VCR. Kitchenette available. Bath is private unless traveling with family or friends. $47.50-55.

Southern Comfort Reservations LBR07

2856 Hundred Oaks Avenue
Baton Rouge, LA, 70808
(504) 346-1928; (800) 749-1928

This lovely B&B is a tree-shaded Victorian in a centrally located residential area. One upstairs bedroom furnished with comfortable antiques has a private bath, its own entrance, TV, and phone. Adjoining living area is available as a sitting room. Full breakfast. No smoking; children welcome. $45.

COVINGTON

Southern Comfort Reservations LCOV1

2856 Hundred Oaks Avenue
Baton Rouge, LA, 70808
(504) 346-1928; (800) 749-1928

This is a delightful nonworking farm situated 35 miles across Lake Pontchartrain, north of New Orleans in the piney woods of St. Tammany Parish. Enjoy the landscaped gardens and dockside activities on the Tchefuncte River, including fishing and swimming. Comfortable guest cottage includes a living room with TV, full kitchen, twin, double, and king rooms, and one bath. Continental breakfast. $85.

FOLSOM

Southern Comfort Reservations LFOL1

2856 Hundred Oaks Avenue
Baton Rouge, LA, 70808
(504) 346-1928; (800) 749-1928

Roomy country house with plenty of space. Enjoy the country quiet and the sandy beach on the beautiful Tchefuncte River. Three guest rooms and two baths. Advance reservations necessary. $45-65.

JACKSON

Southern Comfort Reservations LJSN1

2856 Hundred Oaks Avenue
Baton Rouge, LA, 70808
(504) 346-1928; (800) 749-1928

Built in 1825-1836, this National Register property has been a home, a bank, was occupied by Union troops, and is now totally restored. Bedroom and private bath on the first floor. One two-bedroom and bath suite

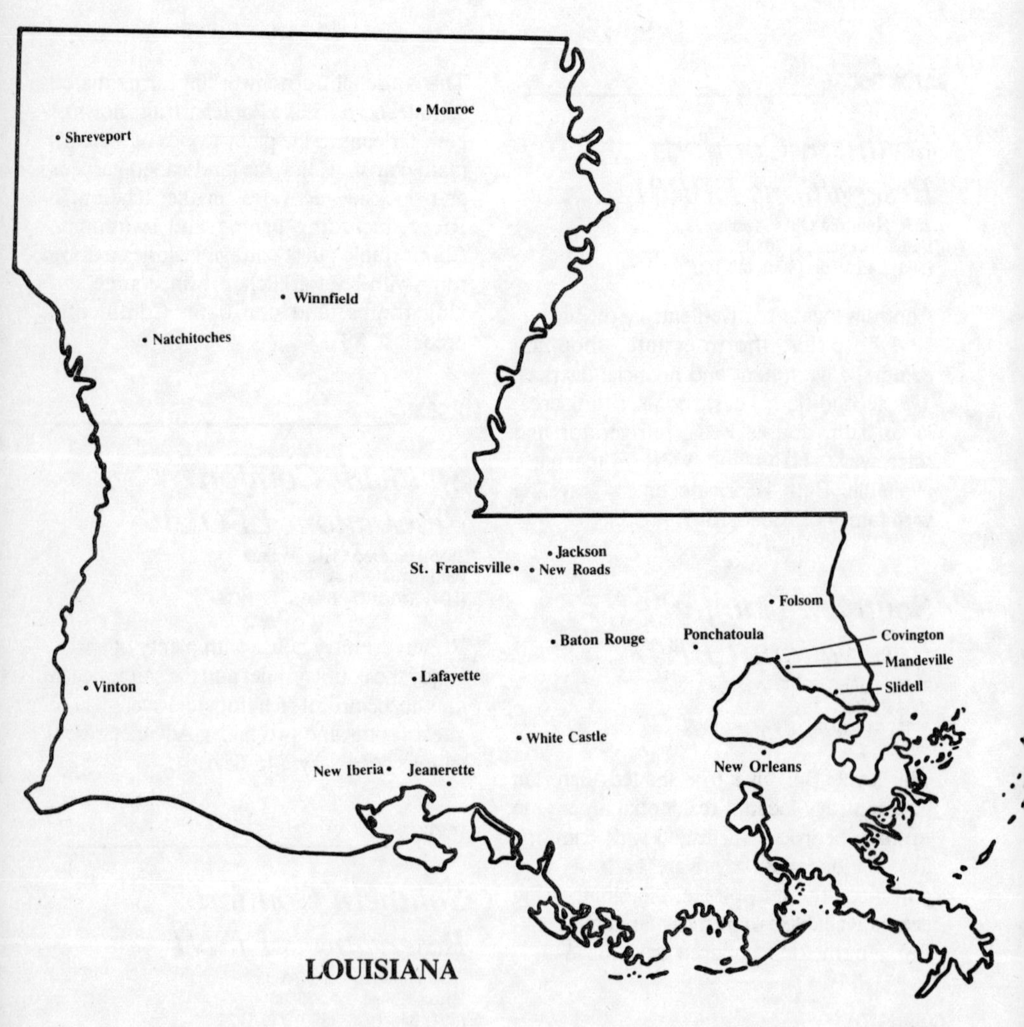
Shreveport
Monroe
Winnfield
Natchitoches
Jackson
St. Francisville
New Roads
Folsom
Ponchatoula
Covington
Baton Rouge
Mandeville
Vinton
Lafayette
Slidell
White Castle
New Iberia
Jeanerette
New Orleans
LOUISIANA

on the second floor. Children welcome. Full breakfast; restricted smoking; 10 percent senior citizen discount. Picnic lunches and private sight-seeing tours may be arranged. $65-130 + tax.

JEANERETTE

Bed & Breakfast on Bayou Teche

2148 1/2 West Main Street
Jeanerette, LA, 70544
(318) 276-5061

Located thirty miles southeast of Lafayette, on Highway 182. Contemporary residence with separate guest cottage containing one large room with three single beds, complete kitchen, TV, canoe, carport, use of washer, dryer, and barbecue pit. Minutes from Jungle Gardens, Tobasco pepper factory, Live Oak Gardens, and many other must-sees in Cajun Country.

Hosts: Warren & Barbara Patout
Rooms: 1 (PB) $45
Continental-plus Breakfast
Credit Cards: No
Notes: 2, 5, 7, 8, 9, 10, 12

LAFAYETTE

Southern Comfort Reservations LLF01

2856 Hundred Oaks Avenue
Baton Rouge, LA, 70808
(504) 346-1928; (800) 749-1928

This authentic Acadian raised mansion with its Victorian carriage house is furnished with a pleasant blend of Louisiana antiques. Breakfast is a Cajun feast served on a glassed-in porch overlooking the Old New Orleans style courtyard, or in the dining room, with its original fireplace. In the evening, after-dinner drinks and chocolates are offered. Pet kennel on the grounds. The suite will accommodate four; other rooms are available. Salt or freshwater fishing or duck hunting trips can be arranged. $75.

Southern Comfort Reservations LLF02

2856 Hundred Oaks Avenue
Baton Rouge, LA, 70808
(504) 346-1928; (800) 749-1928

This c. 1806 home on the outskirts of Lafayette is within easy distance of everything. Guest room has a separate entrance, private bath, a working fireplace, climate control, and antiques. The full breakfast may include meat, biscuits, fruit salad, grits, or a casserole. Resident cat and dog; smoking outside only. $65 + tax.

MADISONVILLE

Southern Comfort Reservations LMA01

2856 Hundred Oaks Avenue
Baton Rouge, LA, 70808
(504) 346-1928; (800) 749-1928

This one-year-old house is just 7 miles from the 26-mile Lake Pontchartrain Causeway leading to New Orleans. Its big porches, wide hallways, high ceilings, and bright rooms provide a casual atmosphere. Just steps to the beautiful river, where you can enjoy crabbing, fishing, and many water sports. Three bedrooms, shared bath. Full breakfast may include crab omelet or popover. $45.

MANDEVILLE

Southern Comfort Reservations LMAN2

2856 Hundred Oaks Avenue
Baton Rouge, LA, 70808
(504) 346-1928; (800) 749-1928

Lovely home facing Lake Pontchartrain, elegantly furnished, with a heated swimming pool and cabana greenhouse. One second-floor bedroom has a double bed and private hall bath. A second room has a double bed. Continental-plus breakfast; no smoking. $125.

MONROE

Southern Comfort Reservations LMON1

2856 Hundred Oaks Avenue
Baton Rouge, LA, 70808
(504) 346-1928; (800) 749-1928

Fifteen miles south of Monroe is this historic cottage, the only building remaining from a once-magnificent plantation. Its guest house has one large room with antique four-poster bed and a single sleigh bed, private bath and shower. There's a reading corner with TV and VCR. Enjoy the shade of the state's oldest and largest living pecan tree, fish from the levee, or play with the kittens and dogs. During cotton harvest (late Sept.-Oct.) you may visit the cotton gin. Rates include full breakfast and potluck dinner in the family dining room. $60.

NATCHITOCHES

Southern Comfort Reservations LNAT2

2856 Hundred Oaks Avenue
Baton Rouge, LA, 70808
(504) 346-1928; (800) 749-1928

This comfortable family home is located on the edge of town. There are two guest rooms, each with its own hall bath. Breakfast is a real treat, and the swimming pool and deck overlooking the former bed of the Red River add to your pleasure. Accessible to the handicapped. $55 + tax.

NEW IBERIA

Southern Comfort Reservations LNI02

2856 Hundred Oaks Avenue
Baton Rouge, LA, 70808
(504) 346-1928; (800) 749-1928

A contemporary home on a 3-acre estate overlooking Bayou Teche. The duck pond on the front lawn, unique house with glassed-in porch, large screened patio, and lighted tennis court combine to make your visit a delight. Two guest rooms, each with a bayou view, private bath, and queen bed, are connected by a large sitting room with TV and telephone. Continental breakfast; no smoking; children welcome. $65.

NEW ORLEANS

A Hotel—The Frenchmen

417 Frenchmen Street
New Orleans, LA, 70116
(504) 948-2166; (800) 831-1781

Two 1860s Creole townhouses, located across from the Old U.S. Mint at Esplanade and Decatur. Each room is individually decorated and climate controlled. Courtyard patio has pool and heated spa. Complimentary breakfast with daily changes in menu served in room or on the patio.

Host: Mark Soubie, Jr.
Rooms: 25 (PB) $84-124
Full Breakfast
Credit Cards: A, B, C
Notes: 2, 5, 7, 9, 11, 14

Artist's Guest Atelier

Bed & Breakfast, Inc.
Box 52257
New Orleans, LA, 70152
(800) 749-4640; (504) 525-4640

A cozy studio apartment with a balcony overlooking a walkway famous for fencing masters of the past, with natural brick walls and original artwork. The hostess, an artist, is just downstairs. Walk half a block to Royal Street's antique shops and art galleries. King bed, private bath, continental breakfast. $75-85.

Audubon Park Home

Bed & Breakfast, Inc.
Box 52257
New Orleans, LA, 70152
(800) 749-4640; (504) 525-4640

So convenient to the streetcar. Guests can ride to the interesting Riverbend area, with its specialty shops, and to French coffee houses, art galleries, antiques, famous restaurants, music clubs. The Audubon Zoological Garden, with its exciting walk-through Louisiana Swamp Exhibit, is also nearby. This is a 1950s brick home set in a lovely historic neighborhood. One room with double and twin beds, hall bath. Continental breakfast. $35-50.

Bellaire Home

Bed & Breakfast, Inc
1360 Moss Street
P.O. Box 52257
New Orleans, LA, 70152
(504) 525-4640

The hostess, a German teacher, offers a bedroom with private entrance opening onto a brick patio and pool. By car, it's ten minutes to downtown. Experience exotic Swampfari, ride in a piroque through moss-draped swamps, catching sight of native wildlife. One double room with private bath and continental breakfast. $30-45.

Bourbon Street Suite

Bed & Breakfast, Inc.
Box 52257
New Orleans, LA, 70152
(800) 749-4640; (504) 525-4640

Guests enjoy this private first-floor suite opening onto the residential section of world-famous Bourbon Street. The host is a landscape architect who has applied his talents to the many walled gardens of historic French Quarter homes. He is a New Orleans native and enjoys sharing his knowledge. One king room with private bath, continental breakfast. $65-100.

Bourbon Street Suite

The Columns Hotel

3811 Saint Charles Avenue
New Orleans, LA, 70115
(504) 899-9308

One of the stateliest remaining examples of turn-of-the-century Louisiana architecture, The Columns Hotel offers a return to old-age elegance and one of the best entrees into the New Orleans of today. Despite its elegance, The Columns is affordable and comfortable. Its nineteen rooms range from modest comfort to the very grand; each features some delight for the experienced traveler.

Hosts: Jacques & Claire Creppel
Rooms: 19 (9 PB; 10 SB) $50-105
Continental Breakfast
Credit Cards: A, B, C
Notes: 2 (in advance), 3, 4, 5, 7, 8, 9, 10, 11, 12, 14

Creole Cottage

Bed & Breakfast, Inc.
Box 52257
New Orleans, LA, 70152
(800) 749-4640; (504) 525-4640

As an architect, the host has been involved in many restorations, including his own, with some lovely antiques. His interest in native plants is reflected in his lush patio. French Quarter walking tours and Cajun dancing, even lessons, are available to guests. Just steps to the French Quarter and mini-bus. One double room with private bath. Continental breakfast. $50-70.

Creole Guest Cottage

Bed & Breakfast, Inc.
Box 52257
New Orleans, LA, 70152
(800) 749-4640; (504) 525-4640

Originally a slave quarter building, this private guest cottage has nice antique pieces, a balcony, and French doors opening onto a landscaped courtyard. Guests can easily stroll to the French Quarter and return to relax in the courtyard. Two rooms with double beds. Continental breakfast. $75-150.

Dauzat House

337 Burgundy Street
New Orleans, LA, 70130
(504) 524-2075

An historic oasis in the French Quarter offering townhouse suites, lush courtyard with pool, homemade amaretto, wood-burning fireplaces, superb antiques, and the personal attention you can't find in larger hotels.

Hosts: Richard L. Nicolais & Donald E. Dauzat
Suites: (PB) from $160
Credit Cards: No
Notes: 2, 5, 9, 11, 14

Designer Guest House

Bed & Breakfast, Inc.
Box 52257
New Orleans, LA, 70152
(800) 749-4640; (504) 525-4640

Originally the studio of a famous Southern sculptor, the cottage displays his artistic creativity while preserving its historic past. A short streetcar ride to galleries, antiques, restaurants, the French Quarter, and more. Hosts live in the 1876 main house. One room with queen bed and two twins in the living room; private bath. Continental breakfast. $95-135.

The Duvignaud House

Bed & Breakfast, Inc.
Box 52257
New Orleans, LA, 70152
(800) 749-4640; (504) 525-4640

Having just celebrated its 150th birthday, this house was once the plantation home of Louis Duvignaud. The historic neighborhood is called Faubourg St. John, named after Bayou St. John, which is nearby. It is an area of ongoing historic renovations, with several small French restaurants, a coffee shop, and gourmet grocery. One queen room (sofabed in living room), private bath. Continental breakfast. $50-100.

Garden District Building

Bed & Breakfast, Inc.
Box 52257
New Orleans, LA, 70152
(800) 749-4640; (504) 525-4640

Conveniently located right on the streetcar line; less than fifteen minutes from downtown. You will be sharing the host's lovely condominium and will have access to the swimming pool. Your host has lived in several cities around the world, where she has been involved in the hospitality industry.

One guest room with two twin beds, private bath. Continental breakfast. $45-70.

Garden District Building

Bed & Breakfast, Inc
1360 Moss Street
P.O. Box 52257
New Orleans, LA, 70152
(504) 525-4640

Conveniently located right on the streetcar line, the ride downtown or to the French Quarter is under fifteen minutes. You will be sharing the host's lovely condo and will have access to the swimming pool. One twin room with private bath and continental breakfast. $45-70.

Guest Suite

Bed & Breakfast, Inc.
Box 52257
New Orleans, LA, 70152
(800) 749-4640; (504) 525-4640

Greek Revival cottage offers a well-appointed guest apartment with its own private entrance and a view of the swimming pool. Hosts have tastefully decorated their home. The streetcar ride to downtown takes just ten minutes. A short walk takes guests to Magazine Street antique shops. In the Garden District. One king room with private bath (sofabed in living room), continental breakfast. $50-90.

Guest Suite in Greek Revival Home

Bed & Breakfast, Inc
1360 Moss Street
P.O. Box 52257
New Orleans, LA, 70152
(504) 525-4640

Nestled in an historic community just across the river from the French Quarter, this imposing Greek Revival home offers guests a private apartment overlooking the swimming pool. Walk or drive to the free ferry for a brief, romantic ride, or drive over the nearby bridge. One room, private bath, continental breakfast. $30-70.

Hawthorne Manor

926 Esplanade
New Orleans, LA, 70116
(504) 523-4131

The finest Greek Revival house, with priceless period antiques, exercise room, courtyards, limousine service. Located in the heart of the historic French Quarter, with the finest restaurants in the world, jazz, tour groups. The house is air-conditioned for your comfort.

Host: Kenny Hawthorne
Rooms: 8 (6 PB; 2 SB) $75-400
Continental Breakfast
Credit Cards: All major
Notes: 2, 5, 9, 10, 11, 12

Historic Home

Bed & Breakfast, Inc.
Box 52257
New Orleans, LA, 70152
(800) 749-4640; (504) 525-4640

Truly of national historic value, this home's title dates back to 1775. Guests occupy a well-appointed room with antiques. The hosts are longtime French Quarter residents and enjoy sharing their special knowledge with guests. One room with twin beds, private bath. Continental breakfast. $60-80.

Jensen's Bed & Breakfast

1631 Seventh Street
New Orleans, LA, 70115
(504) 897-1895

A 100-year-old Queen Anne Victorian beautifully decorated with antiques, stained glass, twelve-foot alcove ceilings, and cypress doors. Located across the street from the Garden District, an area famed for its lovely homes. The trolley is one block away and provides easy access to the French Quarter and Audubon Park and Zoo. All rooms are air-conditioned.

Hosts: Shirley, Bruce & Joni
Rooms: 4 (SB) $50-60
Continental Breakfast
Credit Cards: No
Notes: 2, 5, 8, 9, 10, 12

Lafitte Guest House

1003 Bourbon Street
New Orleans, LA, 70116
(504) 581-2678; (800) 331-7971

This elegant French manor house, in the heart of the French Quarter, is meticulously restored to its original splendor and furnished in fine antiques and reproductions. Every modern convenience, including air conditioning, is provided for your comfort. Complimentary continental breakfast, wine and hors d'oeuvres at cocktail hour, free parking, and a daily newspaper.

Host: Dr. Robert Guyton
Rooms: 14 (PB) $69-135
Continental Breakfast
Credit Cards: A, B, C, D
Notes: 5, 7, 8, 9, 10, 11, 12, 13

Lamothe House

621 Espladade Avenue
New Orleans, LA, 70116
(504) 947-1161

Elegantly restored Victorian mansion. All rooms have private baths, color TV, phones, and air-conditioning. Some have high ceilings. Jackson Square, French Market, many jazz clubs, and fine restaurants just a stroll away.

Rooms: 20 (PB) From $50
Continental Breakfast
Credit Cards: A, B, C
Notes: 5, 9, 10, 12, 14

Le Garconiere Guest Suite

Bed & Breakfast, Inc.
Box 52257
New Orleans, LA, 70152
(800) 749-4640; (504) 525-4640

A charming couple welcomes guests to their historic home in the French Quarter. Restaurants, antique shops, and jazz clubs are just a short walk from this quiet neighborhood. Private two-story guest cottage overlooking the tropical courtyard offers a balcony off the bedroom and a full kitchen. Guests can experience the streetcar along the Mississippi River, which travels past the French Quarter to riverboat cruise docks and the expansive Riverwalk Shopping Center. One king room, private bath. Continental breakfast. $75-100.

Lincoln, Ltd. 7

P.O. Box 3479
Meridian, MS, 39303
(601) 482-5483 for information
(800) 633-Miss for reservations

Lovely historic home furnished in antiques. Six beautifully appointed rooms with private baths. Located conveniently close to the Garden District and public transportation. Continental breakfast. $65-125.

Modern English Tudor

Bed & Breakfast, Inc
1360 Moss Street
P.O. Box 52257
New Orleans, LA, 70152
(504) 525-4640

In an exclusive subdivision neighborhood, this home is filled with collectibles. Venture forth along River Road into antebellum Louisiana plantation country to discover still-lingering traces of its rich past. Guests can drive to the French Quarter in twenty minutes. Two rooms with private baths, continental breakfast. $30-45.

Napoleon Avenue Home

Bed & Breakfast, Inc.
Box 52257
New Orleans, LA, 70152
(800) 749-4640; (504) 525-4640

Enjoy a light, tropical atmosphere in this home, recently and lovingly renovated by the hosts. After an exciting day of sight-seeing or conventioneering, guests relax on the wide front veranda. Host family is warm and inviting. The guest rooms are apart from the family's sleeping rooms. Downtown is five minutes away by car or fifteen by bus. Two bedrooms with private baths, continental breakfast. $40-70.

Queen Anne Victorian

Napoleon Avenue Home

Petit Guest Cottage

Bed & Breakfast, Inc.
Box 52257
New Orleans, LA, 70152
(800) 749-4640; (504) 525-4640

A darling private cottage just off Bourbon Street boasts a quiet residential neighborhood with jazz clubs and celebrated restaurants nearby. A walk to the riverfront streetcar offers a trip along the Mississippi, passing historic Jackson Square to the new Riverwalk Shopping Center. One queen room with private bath. Continental breakfast. $75-100.

Prytania Street Suite

Bed & Breakfast, Inc.
Box 52257
New Orleans, LA, 70152
(800) 749-4640; (504) 525-4640

The designer of this eighteenth-century home was in love with European architecture and modeled this building after an Austrian manse. Guests enjoy a lovely apartment that includes two bedrooms, full kitchen, and one and one-half baths. Just one block from the St. Charles streetcar line, this suite is convenient to everything. Continental breakfast. $76-126.

Quaint Guest Cottages

Bed & Breakfast, Inc.
Box 52257
New Orleans, LA, 70152
(800) 749-4640; (504) 525-4640

A special place filled with romance. Flavored with antiques and architectural details, the cottages look onto a patio and antique swing. The streetcar is downtown at the French Quarter in just fifteen minutes. Guests enjoy antiques, famous bistros, and music nearby.

Quaint Guest Cottages

Delightful hosts reside in the main house. Two cottages with private baths and continental breakfast. $50-95.

Queen Anne Victorian

Bed & Breakfast, Inc.
Box 52257
New Orleans, LA, 70152
(800) 749-4640; (504) 525-4640

Recently renovated, this home, with its original artwork and fabric-dressed walls, shows the special touches of the hostess, an interior designer. The Garden District mansions are just steps away, as are restaurants, antiques, and art galleries. So convenient to downtown and the French Quarter—ten minutes by streetcar. Three guest rooms, shared baths, continental breakfast. $40-70.

St. Charles Guest House B&B

1748 Prytania Street
New Orleans, LA, 70130
(504) 523-6556

A simple, cozy, affordable pension-style inn in hn the historic Lower Garden District. A favorite of university personnel, writers, performers, and seasoned travelers. On streetcar line, ten minutes from the French Quarter, zoo, aquarium. Complimentary bakery breakfast, pool, patio.

Hosts: Joanne & Dennis Hilton
Rooms: 30 (26 PB; 4 SB) $55
Continental Breakfast
Credit Cards: A, B, C
Notes: 5, 7, 8, 9, 10, 11, 12, 14

Southern Comfort Reservations LNO01

2856 Hundred Oaks Avenue
Baton Rouge, LA, 708086
(504) 346-1928; (800) 749-1928

Carrollton Cottage near universities, parks, museums. Easy access to all highways, French Quarter, downtown. Hostess speaks fluent Spanish. Small pets allowed; no children. Shared bath, double or twin beds; continental breakfast. $45-50.

Southern Comfort Reservations LNO04

2856 Hundred Oaks Avenue
Baton Rouge, LA, 708086
(504) 346-1928; (800) 749-1928

Late nineteenth-century Italianate mansion in the Lower Garden District with a central courtyard and balconies. Six rooms, private baths; four with nonworking fireplaces, all with TV. Continental breakfast. French and Spanish spoken. $65-135.

University Area Home

Bed & Breakfast, Inc.
Box 52257
New Orleans, LA, 70152
(800) 749-4640; (504) 525-4640

A comfortable, homey raised cottage. University campuses, restaurants, specialty shops, and music clubs are near. A pleasurable forty-minute streetcar ride will take you downtown (fifteen minutes by car). One room with double and twin beds, private bath. Continental breakfast. $30-70.

Uptown Home with Pool

Bed & Breakfast, Inc.
Box 52257
New Orleans, LA, 70152
(800) 749-4640; (504) 525-4640

In the shade of a magnificent live oak tree, guests relax in this turn-of-the-century home. The host is even willing to take guests canoeing through the swamps and bayous. Experience restaurants, shopping, historic homes, and jazz on your fifty-minute ride downtown (fifteen minutes by car or express bus). Two rooms with hall bath, continental breakfast. $25-40.

Victorian Cottage

Bed & Breakfast, Inc.
Box 52257
New Orleans, LA, 70152
(800) 749-4640; (504) 525-4640

A history buff, this host has lovingly restored his home. It offers peaceful, intimate guest rooms with private entrances onto the patio. Nearby is the old French Market and Mississippi Riverwalk. Continental breakfast on the patio, which has a wet bar for guests. Three guest rooms with private baths. $55-70.

NEW ROADS

Lincoln, Ltd. 38

P.O. Box 3479
Meridian, MS, 39303
(601) 482-5483 for information
(800) 633-Miss for reservations

This attractive Creole Cottage is wonderful for a weekend getaway or special fishing trip. Will accommodate groups by special request. The hostess is very knowledgeable about the history of the Mississippi River town and can offer many ideas about special places to see (plantation homes, fishing, etc.). A continental breakfast is served. $45.

PONCHATOULA

Southern Comfort Reservations LPNT1

2856 Hundred Oaks Avenue
Baton Rouge, LA, 70808
(504) 346-1928; (800) 749-1928

A touch of Europe, just 45 miles north of New Orleans and 45 miles east of Baton Rouge, this home operates as a German Gasthaus. Two bedrooms, each with antique double bed, share a bath. This charming home was built with all old wood and is furnished with unique antiques. True European breakfast; no smoking; 10 percent senior citizen discount. $50.

ST. FRANCISVILLE

Barrow House

524 Royal Street
Box 1461
St. Francisville, LA, 70775
(504) 635-4791

Sip wine in a wicker rocker on the front porch while you enjoy the ambience of a quiet neighborhood of antebellum homes. Rooms are all furnished in antiques from 1840-1870. Gourmet candlelight dinners are available, as is breakfast in bed. A cassette walking tour of the historic district is included for our guests.

Hosts: Shirley & Lyle Dittloff
Rooms: 3 (PB) $65
Suite: 1 (PB) $75
Continental Breakfast, Full Breakfast Available
Credit Cards: No
Closed Dec. 23-25
Notes: 2, 4, 5, 7, 8, 9, 12, 14

The Myrtles Plantation

Highway 61
St. Francisville, LA, 70775
(504) 635-6277

The Myrtles is known as "America's most haunted house." This twenty-room French Rococo mansion has elaborate plaster and ironwork throughout. Historic house tours and ghost tours; private parties welcome with reservations. Other plantation houses within a few miles.

Hosts: Mark Sowers & David Saling
Rooms: 10 (PB) $75-250.80
Full Breakfast
Credit Cards: A, B
Notes: 2, 4, 5, 8, 11

The St. Francisville Inn

118 North Commerce Street
St. Francisville, LA, 70775
(504) 635-6502

In the heart of Louisiana Plantation Country, the St. Francisville Inn has nine antique-furnished guest rooms opening onto a lovely New Orleans-style brick courtyard where guests may relax. The restored main house, c. 1880, has a restaurant, a sitting room for guests, porches, swings for rocking, and an original spectacular ceiling medallion with a Mardi Gras mask design. On the edge of the historic district.

Hosts: Florence & Dick Fillet
Rooms: 9 (PB) $42.90-64.90
Continental Breakfast
Credit Cards: A, B, C, D
Notes: 2, 3, 4, 5, 7, 8, 9, 12

The St. Francisville Inn

SHREVEPORT

Fairfield Place B&B

2221 Fairfield Avenue
Shreveport, LA, 71104
(318) 222-0048

Built before the turn of the century, Fairfield Place has been beautifully restored to bring you all the charm of a bygone era. Conveniently located near downtown, I-20, the medical centers, and Louisiana Downs. Within walking distance of fine restaurants and unique shops. Breakfast includes rich Cajun coffee and fresh-baked croissants, served in the privacy of your room, the balcony, porch, or courtyard.

Host: Jane Lipscomb
Rooms: 6 (PB) $65-145
Full Breakfast
Credit Cards: A, B, C
Notes: 2, 5, 9, 10, 11, 12

Fairfield Place B&B

SLIDELL

Southern Comfort Reservations LSDL1

2856 Hundred Oaks Avenue
Baton Rouge, LA, 70808
(504) 346-1928; (800) 749-1928

A beautiful contemporary house with deck overlooking the Pearl River and docks for three boats. One guest room has a king bed and private bath; one has a queen bed with private bath. Your choice of breakfast. No smoking. $75-85.

VINTON

Old Lyons House

1335 Horridge Street
Vinton, LA, 70668
(318) 589-2903

Queen Anne Victorian in the downtown area of a small rural town, restored and furnished with antiques. The hosts will make you welcome and do everything possible to insure that when you leave, you know the meaning of the words *Southern hospitality.* Horse racing, fishing, swimming, canoeing, nature, old homes, and more are all within a few minutes' drive. Massage therapist on premises.

Hosts: Danny Cooper & Ben Royal
Rooms: 2 (SB) $25-35
Full Breakfast
Credit Cards: No
Notes: 2, 5, 7, 8, 9, 10, 11

WHITE CASTLE

Nottoway Plantation Inn & Restaurant

P.O. Box 160, LA Hwy. 1
White Castle, LA, 70788
(504) 545-2730

Nottoway, c. 1859, is a Greek Revival and Italianate mansion built for a wealthy sugar cane planter just before the Civil War. The home is situated beside the Mississippi River and surrounded by large oak and pecan trees. Guest rooms are also available in a restored 150-year-old overseer's cottage.

Hosts: Cindy Hidalgo & Faye Russell
Rooms: 13 (PB) $125-250
Full Breakfast
Credit Cards: A, B, C, D
Notes: 2, 3, 4, 5, 7 (restricted), 8, 9, 10, 11, 14

WINNFIELD

Southern Comfort Reservations LWNF1

2856 Hundred Oaks Avenue
Baton Rouge, LA, 70808
(504) 346-1928; (800) 749-1928

There are three upstairs guest rooms and two baths, plus a large sitting room, common area, and wide veranda across the front of the house. Full breakfast. $45.

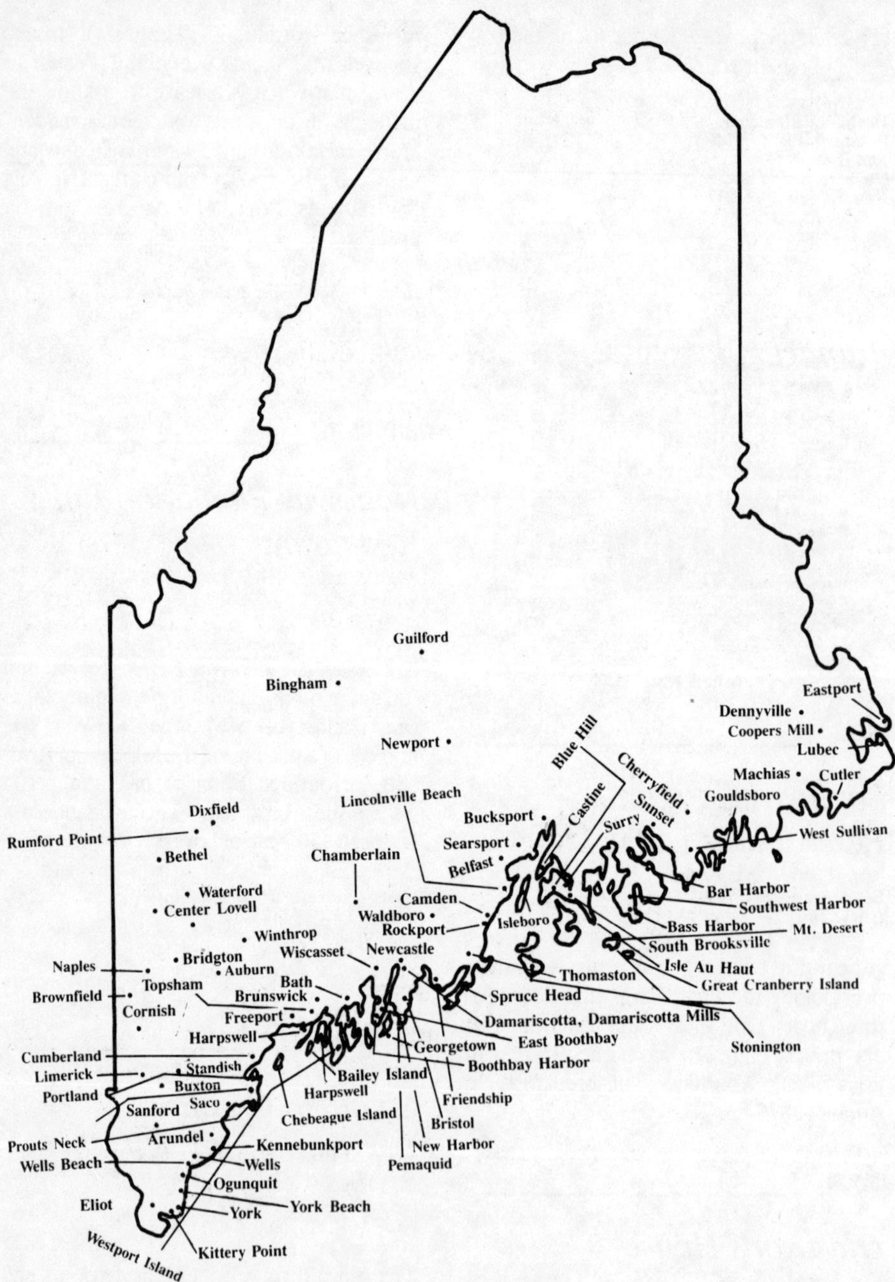
Guilford
Bingham
Eastport
Dennyville
Coopers Mill
Lubec
Newport
Blue Hill
Cherryfield
Machias
Cutler
Castine
Sunset
Gouldsboro
Lincolnville Beach
Bucksport
Surry
West Sullivan
Dixfield
Rumford Point
Searsport
Bethel
Chamberlain
Belfast
Bar Harbor
Waterford
Camden
Southwest Harbor
Center Lovell
Waldboro
Isleboro
Bass Harbor
Mt. Desert
Winthrop
Rockport
Wiscasset
Newcastle
South Brooksville
Naples
Bridgton
Auburn
Isle Au Haut
Thomaston
Topsham
Bath
Great Cranberry Island
Brownfield
Brunswick
Spruce Head
Cornish
Freeport
Damariscotta, Damariscotta Mills
Harpswell
East Boothbay
Stonington
Georgetown
Cumberland
Standish
Boothbay Harbor
Limerick
Buxton
Bailey Island
Portland
Harpswell
Friendship
Saco
Sanford
Chebeague Island
Bristol
Prouts Neck
Arundel
Kennebunkport
New Harbor
Wells Beach
Wells
Pemaquid
Ogunquit
Eliot
York
York Beach
Kittery Point
Westport Island

MAINE

Maine

ARUNDEL

Arundel Meadows Inn

Route One
Mail to: Box 1129
Kennebunk, ME, 04043
(207) 985-3770

This 165-year-old farmhouse features and extensive art collection and antiques in each of the seven uniquely decorated rooms. Several rooms feature working fireplaces. One owner was a professor at Boston University; the other is a professional chef. The inn is bordered by the Kennebunk River on the south and 3 acres of meadows to the east.

Hosts: Mark Bachelder & Murray Yaeger
Rooms: 7 (PB) $75-125
Full Breakfast, afternoon tea
Credit Cards: A, B
Notes: 2, 5, 7, 8 (12 and over), 9, 10, 11, 12

AUBURN

B&B of Maine 61

32 Colonial Village
Falmouth, ME, 04105
(207) 781-4528

A comfortable farmhouse on the rural outskirts of one of the larger cities in the state. Home of Bates College, near Lost Valley Ski area. Stroll through nature trails on the 80 acres of property. Restricted smoking; continental breakfast. One resident cat. Two comfortable guest rooms share one bath. $40-45.

BAILEY ISLAND

Katie's Ketch

Box 105
Bailey Island, ME, 04003
(207) 833-7785

Your host, Albert, is a retired lobsterman of forty years who hand carves duck decoys. Katie's plants abound in their Dutch colonial home. Bailey Island is a lobster-fishing community providing fishing, swimming, sailing, ferry rides, plus scrumptious fare from the sea that is served in nearby restaurants.

Hosts: Albert & Catherine Johnson
Rooms: 2 (SB) $60
Full Breakfast
Credit Cards: No
Notes: 2, 5, 7 (outside), 8, 9, 10, 11, 12

BAR HARBOR

Black Friar Inn

10 Summer Street
Bar Harbor, ME, 04609
(207) 288-5091

Comfortably restored and rebuilt Victorian with antiques. Six guest rooms with queen beds and private baths. Rates include full breakfast, late afternoon refreshments, and rainy-day teas. Easy access to Acadia National Park. Spring and fall salmon fishing trips with Maine guide can be arranged.

Hosts: Barbara & Jim Kelly
Rooms: 6 (PB) $75-95
Full Breakfast
Credit Cards: A, B
Open May-Oct.
Notes: 2, 8 (12 and over), 9, 10, 11, 12, 14

Canterbury Cottage

12 Roberts Avenue
Bar Harbor, ME, 04609
(207) 288-2112

A delightful Victorian shingled cottage built in 1900. Family owned and operated as a B&B. Guest rooms with private and shared baths; wholesome breakfast served in the country kitchen.

Hosts: Richard & Michele Suydam
Rooms: 4 (2 PB; 2 SB) $69.55-80.25
Continental-plus Breakfast
Credit Cards: No
Minimum stay holidays: 2
Notes: 2, 9, 10, 11, 12

Castlemaine Inn

39 Holland Avenue
Bar Harbor, ME, 04609
(207) 288-4563

Castlemaine Inn is nestled on a quiet side street in the village of Bar Harbor, which is surrounded by the magnificent Acadia National Park. Our rooms are well-appointed, with canopy beds and fireplaces. A delightful continental buffet-style breakfast is served.

Hosts: Terence O'Connell & Norah O'Brien
Rooms: 12 (PB) $75-125
Continental-plus Breakfast
Credit Cards: A, B
Notes: 2, 5, 8 (over 13), 9, 10, 11, 12

Cleftstone Manor

92 Eden Street
Bar Harbor, ME, 04609
(207) 288-4951

Cleftstone Manor is a distinguished thirty-three-room Victorian "cottage," set on a hill amid formal gardens, offering gracious accommodations in one of nature's magnificent meetings of land and sea, Mount Desert Island. We offer cozy fireside chats, a library, games, a lavish breakfast buffet, and the peacefulness of country living.

Hosts: Don & Pattie Reynolds, George & Carolee Moore
Rooms: 16 (14 PB; 2 SB) $85-175
Continental-plus Breakfast
Credit Cards: A, B
Closed Nov.-March
Notes: 2, 8 (8 and over), 10, 11, 12, 13 (XC), 14

Hearthside Bed & Breakfast

Hearthside Bed & Breakfast

7 High Street
Bar Harbor, ME, 04609
(207) 288-4533

Built as a private residence in 1907, Hearthside is now a beautiful and luxuriously appointed B&B. Our rooms feature a blend of country and Victorian furnishings; all have queen beds while most have private baths. We are conveniently located on a

NOTES: Credit cards accepted: A Master Card; B Visa; C American Express; D Discover Card; E Diners Club; F Other: 2 Personal checks accepted: 3 Lunch available: 4 Dinner available: 5 Open all year

quiet side street, within easy walking distance of shops, restaurants, and picturesque Frenchman's Bay. A short car ride from Acadia National Park.

Hosts: Susan & Barry Schwartz
Rooms: 9 (7 PB; 2 SB) $65-95
Continental Breakfast
Credit Cards: A, B
Notes: 2, 5, 8 (over 10), 9, 10, 11, 12, 13

Holbrook House

74 Mt. Desert Street
Bar Harbor, ME, 04609
(207) 288-4970

A nineteen-room Victorian inn with chintz, lace, and flowers. Full buffet breakfast. Just a five-minute walk to the ocean, shops, and restaurants; one mile to Acadia National Park. Sun room, library, and parlor.

Hosts: Dorothy & Mike Chester
Rooms: 10 (PB) $90-105
Full Breakfast
Minimum stay: 2
Credit Cards: A, B
Closed Oct. 15-June 10
Notes: 2, 8 (8 and over), 9, 10, 11, 12

Manor House Inn

106 West Street
Bar Harbor, ME, 04609
(207) 288-3759

Enjoy our 1887 Victorian summer cottage listed on the National Register of Historic Places. Located near Acadia National Park and within walking distance of downtown Bar Harbor.

Hosts: Mac Noyes
Rooms: 14 (PB) $85-150
Continental Breakfast
Minimum stay July, Aug., and holidays: 2
Credit Cards: A, B, C
Closed Nov.-mid April
Notes: 2, 8 (over 8), 9, 10, 11, 12

Maples Cottage Inn

16 Roberts Avenue
Bar Harbor, ME, 04609
(207) 288-3443

The Maples is located on a quiet residential side street, away from the traffic of Bar Harbor, yet within walking distance of shops, restaurants, and the sea. Acadia National Park is minutes away.

Host: Katy Wood
Rooms: 6 (PB) $45-120
Full Breakfast
Credit Cards: A, B
Notes: 2, 5, 9, 10, 11, 12, 13 (XC)

Manor House Inn

Mira Monte Inn

69 Mt. Desert Street
Bar Harbor, ME, 04609
(207) 288-4263

Built in 1864, this gracious eighteen-room Victorian mansion is renovated in the simpler style of Bar Harbor's elegance, featuring period furnishings, library, fireplaces, porches, and 1.5 acres of estate grounds. Friendly, informative staff.

Host: Marian Burns
Rooms: 11 (PB) $80-135
Continental-plus Breakfast
Minimum stay: 2
Credit Cards: A, B, C
Closed Oct. 25-May 10
Notes: 2, 7, 8, 9, 12, 14

Ridgeway Cottage Inn

11 High Street
Bar Harbor, ME, 04609
(207) 288-9682

The Ridgeway was built at the turn of the century and is decorated in an atmosphere reminiscent of the period. Acadia National Park and the sea are minutes away, offering a year-round wilderness playground. Our Wingwood Suite with fireplace is perfect for that special occasion.

Hosts: Peter Friend & Chris Hunt
Rooms: 6 (4 PB; 2 SB) $50-100
Full Breakfast
Credit Cards: A, B
Notes: 2, 5, 9, 10, 11, 12, 13 (XC)

The Tides

119 West Street
Bar Harbor, ME, 04609
(207) 288-4968

An 1887 Greek Revival, sixteen-room seaside estate within walking distance of the wharf and downtown Bar Harbor. Within two miles of Acadia National Park; ten minutes from the golf course; around the cove from the Blue Nose Ferry to Nova Scotia. Afternoon tea is served on the veranda overlooking the lawn and Frenchman's Bay.

Hosts: Tom & Bonnie Sawyer
Rooms: 3 (PB) $140-175
Full Breakfast
Credit Cards: A, B
Notes: 2, 5, 11, 12, 14

BASS HARBOR

B&B of Maine 56

32 Colonial Village
Falmouth, ME, 04105
(207) 781-4528

Refurbished old sea captain's home on a knoll, looking right at the ocean. Short stroll to the ferry landing for a trip to Swan's Island. Visit the Oceanarium or the Gilley Bird Museum. Hike the many nature trails, or just enjoy an unforgettable sunset from the front porch. Full breakfast; resident dog and cat; smoking outside only. All rooms share several baths. Two-night minimum preferred. $50-60.

The Bass Harbor Inn

Shore Road
Bass Harbor, ME, 04653
(207) 244-5157

On beautiful Mt. Desert Island, the Bass Harbor Inn offers you a lovely harbor view and choice of lodging ranging from rooms with private or half bath, fireplace, to suite with full kitchen and bath. Write for brochure.

Hosts: Alan & Barbara Graff
Rooms: 9 (PB and SB) $50-90
Continental Breakfast
Credit Cards: A, B

Glad II

60 Pearl Street
Bass Harbor, ME, 04530
(207) 443-1191

A comfortable 138-year-old Victorian home near the center of town and convenient to Maritime Museum, beaches, Freeport shopping, L.L. Bean, and Boothbay Harbor. Nicholas, my four-legged concierge, and I love to welcome new friends.

Host: Gladys Lansky
Rooms: 3 (SB) $42.80-48.15
Continental-plus Breakfast
Minimum stay weekends & holidays: 2
Credit Cards: A, B
Notes: 2, 5, 8 (over 12), 9, 10, 11, 12, 13, 14

Pointy Head Inn

Route 102A
Bass Harbor, ME, 04653
(207) 244-7261

Relax on the quiet side of Mount Desert Island near Acadia National Park, in an old sea captain's home on the shore of a picturesque harbor, where schooners anchor overnight. Haven for photographers and artists. Minutes to lighthouse, trails, restaurants, stores.

Hosts: Doris & Warren Townsend
Rooms: 6 (1 PB; 5 SB) $58.85-69.55
Full Breakfast
Minimum stay: 2
Credit Cards: No
Closed Nov.-mid May
Notes: 2, 8 (over 7), 9, 10, 11, 12

Elizabeth's B&B

BATH

B&B of Maine 20

32 Colonial Village
Falmouth, ME, 04105
(207) 781-4528

Comfortable, newly renovated B&B on a quiet street just a mile off Route 1. Short walk to the Maritime Museum. Guests are invited to enjoy the entire house: read or watch TV in the library, relax in the parlor, or use the grand piano in the music room. Resident dog; no smoking; no small children. Hostess will direct you to the beaches in the area and the many summer festivals. Comfortable guest rooms share a bath. $45.

Elizabeth's B&B

360 Front Street
Bath, ME, 04530
(207) 443-1146

Step into the warmth of yesteryear in a beautiful old home overlooking the Kennebec River. Choose from five guest rooms furnished with country antiques, two and one-half shared baths. Generous continental breakfast with home-baked breads. Guest living room with TV; limited smoking. Feline assistant, Mr. T, in residence.

Host: Elizabeth Lindsay
Rooms: 5 (S2.5B) $40-60 + tax
Continental Breakfast
Credit Cards: No
Open April 15-Jan. 1
Notes: 2, 7, 8 (over 10), 9, 10, 11, 12, 14

Fairhaven Inn

RR 2, Box 85
Bath, ME, 04530
(207) 443-4391

This classic, comfortable, quiet colonial, built in 1790, stands on the bank of the Kennebec River surrounded by 27 acres of meadows, lawns, and dark pine woods. Renowned for its breakfasts. Hiking and cross-country skiing on the premises; beaches nearby.

Hosts: George & Sallie Pollard
Rooms: 9 (PB and SB) $53.50-74.90
Full Breakfast
Credit Cards: A, B
Notes: 2, 5, 7 (limited), 8, 9, 10, 11, 12, 13, 14

BELFAST

B&B of Maine 38

32 Colonial Village
Falmouth, ME, 04105
(207) 781-4528

Just a few miles up the road, in an old fishing village known for its stunning Greek Revival houses. Enjoy the sights of this working harbor, or take a day cruise. The house, c. 1840, sits back from the street behind a sprawling lawn. Ornate tin ceilings and cherry spiral staircase leading to the second floor. Children are welcome, and a baby-sitting service is offered for a small fee. Full country breakfast. The hosts will also pack a lunch, if you like. Many guest rooms have their own marble sinks or an attached lavatory. All share several full baths. $45-50.

B&B of Maine 39

32 Colonial Village
Falmouth, ME, 04105
(207) 781-4528

A true Victorian home, built in 1905. Traditional antique furniture and a collectibles shop on the premises. Two guest parlors, one with TV. Plenty of reading material and comfortable chairs. Relax on one of several porches. The house is close to the village and harbor. Continental breakfast; no smoking inside; resident cat. Children over twelve only. All guest rooms have queen beds and private baths. $55.

Londonderry Inn

Belmont Avenue
Belfast, ME, 04915
(207) 338-3988

Restored 1803 farmhouse with four spacious guest rooms furnished with country charm. Besides the large country kitchen where a full breakfast is served, guests can enjoy two sitting rooms, a library with piano, and a sun porch. There are 2.5 shared baths. A quiet country setting with fields, woods, and pond for the connoisseur of life's simple pleasures.

Hosts: Suzanne & Buzz Smedley
Rooms: 4 (S2.5B) $45-50
Full Breakfast
Credit Cards: A, B
Minimum stay weekends & holidays: 2
Closed Nov. 1-Memorial Day
Notes: 2, 7 (limited), 8 (over 12), 9, 12, 14

Penobscot Meadows Inn

90 Northport Avenue
Belfast, ME, 04915
(207) 338-5320

Penobscot Meadows is a small, completely renovated, turn-of-the-century inn in quiet Belfast. Conveniently located for day trips to Acadia, Camden, Islesboro, Blue Hill, etc. Featuring four-star dining on our deck overlooking Penobscot Bay; extensive wine list.

Hosts: Dini & Bernie Chapnick
Rooms: 7 (PB) $41.73-105.93
Continental Breakfast
Credit Cards: A, B, D
Notes: 2, 4, 5, 6, 7, 8, 9, 10, 11, 12, 13 (XC)

BETHEL

B&B of Maine 50

32 Colonial Village
Falmouth, ME, 04105
(207) 781-4528

A 150-year-old farmhouse at the foot of a mountain range, with a river flowing by. There's bird watching, hiking, swimming, and canoeing right outside the door. Children are welcome and will enjoy the few goats, chickens, dogs, cat, and llama that call this farm home. Good trout fishing is just ten minutes away. Full breakfast; no smoking. Most rooms have queen beds; one has a double set of bunks; several have a single bed for a third member. All rooms share three baths. $50.

The Chapman Inn

Box 206
Bethel, ME, 04217
(207) 824-2657

An 1865 Federal in a National Historic District, facing the village common. Friendly, homelike atmosphere; large, sunny rooms. Delicious breakfasts feature fresh fruits, muffins, and a variety of main courses. Private saunas, game room, cable color TV in sitting room. Dorm accommodations also available.

Hosts: Doug & Robin Zinchuk
Rooms: 8 (3 PB; 5 SB) $55-65
Full Breakfast
Credit Cards: A, B, C
Notes: 2, 5, 6, 7, 8, 9, 10, 11, 12, 13, 14

The Chapman Inn

The Douglass Place

Star Route Box 90
Bethel, ME, 04217
(207) 824-2229

A four-season, nineteenth-century, Early American/Victorian home situated between two major ski areas and the White Mountains of New Hampshire. Marvelous location for antiquing, summer sports, and hiking. Gardens and gazebo in summer; game room, cozy fireplace in winter.

Hosts: Dana & Barbara Douglass
Rooms: 4 (SB) $37.45-48.15
Continental Breakfast
Minimum stay weekends & holidays: 2
Credit Cards: C
Closed Christmas & 2 weeks in April
Notes: 2, 6, 7, 8, 9, 10, 11, 12, 13

Sudbury Inn

Box 369, Main Street
Bethel, ME, 04217
(800) 395-7837; (800) 395-SUDS

Located near Sunday River ski area, the inn has fifteen rooms with private baths. Full breakfast; fine dining is available, as well as the famous Suds Pub, with entertainment on weekends. Area attractions include an eighteen-hole, 6,800-yard golf course, White Mountain National Forest, lakes, streams, and gorgeous landscapes.

Host: Jack Cronin
Rooms: 15 (PB) $50-90
Full Breakfast
Credit Cards: A, B, C
Notes: 2, 4, 5, 6, 8, 11, 12, 13

BINGHAM

Mrs. G's B&B

Box 389
Bingham, ME, 04920
(207) 672-4034

An old Victorian home on the picturesque Kennebec River, where white-water rafting is popular. Hiking on the Appalachian Trail, beautiful waterfalls, shopping, tennis, and golf are all nearby. Fifty miles from skiing at Sugarloaf.

Host: Frances M. Gibson
Rooms: 4 (SB) $25/person
Loft: Sleeps 9 (SB) $22/person
Full Breakfast
Credit Cards: No
Open May-Oct.
Notes: 2, 4 (with reservations), 7, 8, 9, 10, 11, 12, 13

BLUE HILL

Arcady Down East

South Street
Blue Hill, ME, 04614
(207) 374-5576

This Victorian mansion, listed on the National Register, is filled with period antiques. Coastal location on a ridge overlooking Blue Hill Bay, Mount Desert Island, and Acadia National Park. Sailing, fishing, hiking, biking, antiquing, crafts, and nearby historic attractions.

Hosts: Bertha & Gene Wiseman
Rooms: 7 (5 PB; 2 SB) $85-110

Arcady Down East

Full Breakfast
Credit Cards: A, B, C
Notes: 2, 5, 8, 10, 11, 12

The Blue Hill Inn

Union Street
P.O. Box 403
Blue Hill, ME, 04614
(207) 374-2844

Historic inn in continuous operation since 1840, located in a coastal village. Rooms with sitting rooms or fireplaces are available. Period furnishings, candlelight dining, six-course dinners. Biking, hiking, cross-country skiing, chamber music concerts. Within 45 minutes of Acadia National Park, Deer Isle, Castine. One hour from Bangor International Airport.

Hosts: Don & Mary Hartley
Rooms: 11 (PB) $80-130; MAP $120-160
Full Breakfast
Credit Cards: A, B
Notes: 2, 4, 5, 8 (over 13), 9, 13 (XC), 14

BOOTHBAY HARBOR

Admiral's Quarters Inn

105 Commercial Street
Boothbay Harbor, ME, 04538
(207) 633-2474

Commanding a view of the harbor waterfront, this early sea captain's mansion offers charming accommodations with private baths, a blend of antiques and white wicker, color cable TV. Morning coffee and light fare in the dining room or on the deck overlooking the waterfront.

Hosts: Jean & George Duffy
Rooms: 10 (PB) $65-90
Continental Breakfast
Credit Cards: A, B
Closed Nov.-through March
Notes: 2 (deposit), 7, 8 (over 12), 9, 10, 11, 12, 14

Anchor Watch

3 Eames Road
Boothbay Harbor, ME, 04538
(207) 633-2284

NOTES: Credit cards accepted: A Master Card; B Visa; C American Express; D Discover Card; E Diners Club; F Other: 2 Personal checks accepted: 3 Lunch available: 4 Dinner available: 5 Open all year

With a shorefront location on a scenic, quiet lane, the Anchor Watch is just a short walk to town for shopping, dining, and boat trips. From the breakfast room you will see lobstermen hauling their traps, lighthouses flashing, and ducks feeding along the shore.

Hosts: Diane & Bob Campbell
Rooms: 4 (PB) $62-75
Continental Breakfast
Credit Cards: No
Closed mid-Dec.-mid-Feb.
Notes: 2, 5, 9, 12

The Blue Hill Inn

Harbour Towne Inn

71 Townsend Avenue
Boothbay Harbor, ME, 04538
(207) 633-4300

Located on the waterfront, a short stroll from the historic coastal village, with scenic harbor views and outside decks in a quiet location. Walk to fascinating shops, art galleries, restaurants, churches, library, dinner theaters, boat trips, fishing, and much more. All rooms have private baths in this refurbished Victorian townhouse, which has been updated in traditional style. We also have a luxury penthouse that will sleep six in absolute privacy. Reservations recommended.

Hosts: Mr. & Mrs. Crisp
Rooms: 12 (PB) $42.90-165
Continental Breakfast
Credit Cards: A, B
Notes: 2, 5, 7, 8, 9, 10, 11, 12, 13 (XC), 14

Harbour Towne Inn

Hilltop Guest House

44 McKown Hill
Boothbay Harbor, ME, 04538
(207) 633-2941

This home is only a three-minute walk to all activities: boat trips, restaurant, dinner theater, and shops, and has ample parking facilities, a large porch, and a tree swing for the young and old. Family unit also available.

Hosts: Georgia Savory & Virginia Brewer
Rooms: 6 (2 PB; 4 SB) $32-42
Continental Breakfast
Credit Cards: No
Notes: 2, 5, 6, 7, 8, 9, 10, 11, 12, 14

The Howard House Motel

Route 27
Boothbay Harbor, ME, 04538
(207) 633-3933; (207) 633-6244

Each spacious room has a private bath, cable color TV, and its own balcony. Early American furnishings, high-beamed ceilings, and natural wood walls. Shopping, sight-seeing, boating, and fine restaurants are all nearby.

Hosts: The Farrins
Rooms: 15 (PB) $40-75
Full Buffet Breakfast
Credit Cards: No
Closed Dec.-Feb.
Notes: 2, 5, 7 (restricted), 8, 9, 10, 11, 12, 14

Topside—"The Inn on the Hill"

McKown Hill
Boothbay Harbor, ME, 04538
(207) 633-5404

Overlooking beautiful Boothbay Harbor on top of McKown Hill. Just a two-minute walk to all the activities on the waterfront, shops, restaurants, and dinner theater. Excellent accommodations. All rooms with private baths.

Hosts: Faye & Newell Wilson
Rooms: 30 (PB) $75-95
Continental Breakfast
Credit Cards: A, B
Closed Nov.-mid-May
Notes: 2, 7, 8, 9, 10, 11, 12

BRIDGTON

B&B of Maine 47

32 Colonial Village
Falmouth, ME, 04105
(207) 781-4528

This charming town sits at the foot of Pleasant Mountain and is surrounded by lakes. Swim off the hosts' own dock or use their canoe. Concerts, festivals, and summer theater are all nearby. The chairlift for skiers can be used in the fall to view the spectacular foliage. Large front porch, grand piano, guest living room. No smoking, no pets. Two-night minimum on summer weekends. $55-90.

The Noble House B&B

37 Highland Road, Box 180
Bridgton, ME, 04009
(207) 647-3733

Romantic turn-of-the-century manor, set amid stately old oaks and towering pines. Private lake frontage on scenic Highland Lake, with barbecue, canoe, and hammock. Cross-country and downhill skiing nearby. Sumptuous full breakfast, whirlpool baths, and family suites.

Hosts: Jane & Dick Starets
Rooms: 9 (6 PB; 3 SB) $58-110, plus tax
Full Breakfast
Minimum stay weekends & holidays: 2
Credit Cards: A, B, C
Closed Christmas
Notes: 2, 7 (limited), 8, 9, 10, 11, 12, 13, 14

Tarry-A-While B&B Resort

RD 2, Box 68
Highland Ridge Road
Bridgton, ME, 04009
(207) 647-2522

On Highland Lake, with three sandy beaches in a protected cove. Schloss-Victorian house and Gasthaus over 100 years old, where continental Swiss breakfast is served with a view of the lake. Cottages with four B&B units in each. Air- conditioned, with individually controlled heat. Large recreation hall. Free canoes, rowboats, pedal boats, tennis, and bicycles. Waterskiing, windsurfers, sailboats, and small motors are available for rent. Clean, quiet lake. Three housekeeping units are also available. Swiss cuisine restaurant on premises.

Hosts: Hans & Barbara Jenni
Rooms: 34 (26 PB; 8 SB) $80-120
Swiss Continental Breakfast
Credit Cards: No
Open mid-June to Labor Day
Notes: 2, 4, 7, 8, 9, 10, 11, 12

BRISTOL

B&B of Maine 29

32 Colonial Village
Falmouth, ME, 04105
(207) 781-4528

Attractively restored turn-of-the-century Victorian just a mile from a working harbor. Walk a short distance to rent a canoe for a leisurely paddle down a safe stream. This is a very unspoiled part of Maine, yet close to a lighthouse, museum, old fort, and sandy beach. Eat lobsters at the harbor deck restaurant and watch the fishermen come and go. All guest rooms have private baths. House not suitable for children; restricted smoking. Full breakfast. $55-65.

B&B of Maine 31

32 Colonial Village
Falmouth, ME, 04105
(207) 781-4528

This 1800 Federal home is at the end of a tree-shaded lane, surrounded by immaculately tended lawns and orchards. Thoroughbred horses romp in the rear; goats, sheep, and chickens greet you as you arrive. Dogs and cats outside. Paddle a guest canoe on the private lake just down from the house, or use the backyard barbecue. The hosts spin fleece from their own flock. Full, hearty breakfast. Rooms with queen bed and private bath. $70.

BROWNFIELD

B&B of Maine 66

32 Colonial Village
Falmouth, ME, 04105
(207) 781-4528

Contemporary country home nestled in a rural area surrounded by forests, located fourteen miles east of North Conway, NH. Parties, games, and even a sing-along often occur. Five guest rooms share three baths. Plenty of hiking, fishing, and hot springs for bathing. $50.

BRUNSWICK

The Samuel Newman House

7 South Street
Brunswick, ME, 04011
(207) 729-6959

Adjoining the Bowdoin College campus, this handsome Federal house was built in 1821 and is comfortably furnished in antiques. Hearty continental breakfast includes freshly baked muffins/pastry and homemade granola. Brunswick is a culturally rich college town just ten minutes north of Freeport.

Hosts: John & Jana Peirce
Rooms: 7 (SB) $53.50-58.85
Continental Breakfast
Credit Cards: A, B
Notes: 2, 5, 8, 9, 10, 11, 12, 13 (XC)

BUCKSPORT

B&B of Maine 48

32 Colonial Village
Falmouth, ME, 04105
(207) 781-4528

Located one block from the center of town, this Federal home offers guest rooms with private and shared baths. A full breakfast is served each morning; kitchenette is available. Restricted smoking. $40-45.

L'Ermitage

219 Main Street
Bucksport, ME, 04416
(207) 469-3361

All rooms are large and suitably furnished with antiques. The inn is an 1830 Victorian home facing the Penobscot River. Small, excellently rated restaurant features French cuisine for dinner only. Cocktails available; excellent wine list.

Hosts: Ginny & Jim Conklin
Rooms: 3(SB) $45-55
Full Breakfast
Credit Cards: A, B
Notes: 4, 5, 6, 7, 9, 11, 12

The Old Parsonage Inn

P.O. Box 1577
Bucksport, ME, 04416
(207) 469-6477

An 1809 Federal home, formerly the Methodist parsonage, located one-half mile from Route 1. Private guest entrance, winding staircase, and original architectural features. The third floor features the original meeting hall. Short walk to restaurants and the waterfront. Close to Ft. Knox, Acadia National Park, and Penobscot Bay.

Hosts: Brian & Judith Clough
Rooms: 3 (1 PB; 2 SB) $30-50
Full Breakfast
Credit Cards: A, B
Notes: 2, 5, 7 (limited), 8, 9, 10, 11, 12

BUXTON

B&B of Maine 27

32 Colonial Village
Falmouth, ME, 04105
(207) 781-4528

An impressive Federal house, c. 1805, set on 5 acres of sculpted and manicured grounds. The home has been meticulously maintained and restored as a B&B. Fireplaces in both living room and den. This home offers a very comfortable and homey atmosphere. A full breakfast is served on the sun porch overlooking the lawns and gardens. Four corner guest rooms are spacious and comfortable, with twin or full beds, and share two baths. Open May through October. $55-65.

CAMDEN

Blackberry Inn

82 Elm Street
Camden, ME, 04843
(207) 236-6060

Blackberry Inn is a restored Italianate Victorian with large, spacious rooms decorated in period style. Stroll to Camden's harbor and fine restaurants, or relax in our comfortable parlors. Wonderful full breakfasts in the formal dining room or sunny courtyard. Featured in *Daughters of Painted Ladies: America's Resplendent Victorians.*

Hosts: Vicki & Edward Doudera
Rooms: 8 (4 PB; 4 private half baths) $53.50-107
Full Breakfast
Credit Cards: A, B
Notes: 2, 5, 8, 9, 10, 11, 12, 13, 14

Blue Harbor House, A B&B

Blue Harbor House, A B&B

67 Elm Street
Camden, ME, 04843
(207) 236-3196; FAX (207) 236-3196

Overlooking Mount Battie and within walking distance of the village of Camden, Blue Harbor House offers guests a casual and comfortable country environment to relax and enjoy the beauty that is coastal Maine. Hearty breakfasts are served each morning on the sun porch. Picnic lunches and intimate candlelight dinners are available by reservation.

Hosts: Jody Schmoll & Dennis Hayden
Rooms: 9 (7 PB; 2 SB) $50-110
Full Breakfast
Credit Cards: A, B
Notes: 3, 4, 7 (restricted), 8, 9, 10, 11, 12, 13, 14

The Camden Maine Stay Inn

The Camden Maine Stay Inn

22 High Street
Camden, ME, 04843
(207) 236-9636

A comfortable bed, a hearty breakfast, and a friendly innkeeper will be found in this old colonial home. In Camden's historic district, a short walk to harbor, shops, restaurants, and state park. Recommended by the *Miami Herald; Lewiston Journal; Watterville Sentinel; Country Inns* magazine.

Hosts: Peter & Donny Smith, Diana Robson
Rooms: 8 (2 PB; 6 SB) $65-86
Full Breakfast
Credit Cards: A, B
Notes: 2, 5, 8 (over 10), 9, 10, 11, 12, 13, 14

Edgecombe-Coles House

HCR 60, Box 3010
Camden, ME, 04843
(207) 236-2336

Edgecombe-Coles House is a classic Maine summer home on a quiet hillside with magnificent views of Penobscot Bay. Each room is furnished with country antiques and has a private bath. Our generous breakfasts have been praised nationwide.

Hosts: Louise & Terry Price
Rooms: 6 (PB) $80.25-155.15
Full Breakfast
Credit Cards: A, B, C, E
Notes: 2, 5, 7, 8 (over 7), 9, 10, 11, 12, 13, 14

Hartstone Inn

41 Elm Street
Camden, ME, 04843
(207) 236-4259

A restored Victorian home in the heart of Camden, a stone's throw from the harbor. Sailing adventures arranged, picnic lunches, golf nearby, and tennis within a fifteen-minute drive. Music at the Bok amphitheater; plays at the "Opera House," and Christmas by the Sea Weekend.

Hosts: Sunny & Peter Simmons
Rooms: 7 (PB) $70-85
Full Breakfast
Credit Cards: A, B, C, D
Notes: 2, 4, 5, 7, 8, 9, 10, 11, 12, 13, 14

Hawthorn Inn

9 High Street
Camden, ME, 04843
(207) 236-8842

An elegant family-run Victorian inn with harbor view, spacious grounds, large deck. Walk through the back garden to shops and restaurants. Full breakfast and afternoon tea served. Carriage house bedrooms with private Jacuzzi and balconies.

Hosts: Pauline & Bradford Staub
Rooms: 11; 2 apartments (7 PB; 2 SB) $55-135
Full Breakfast
Minimum stay July & Aug.: 2
Credit Cards: A, B
Notes: 2, 5, 7, 8, 9, 10, 11, 12, 13

Hosmer House

Four Pleasant Street
Camden, ME, 04843
(207) 236-4012

An 1806 twin house on a quiet back street, just two blocks from the center of the village and harbor. Charming bedchambers, wallpapers, painted floors, antique furnishings, cozy common room with fireplace. Convenient to cafes and restaurants, galleries, shops, museums, hiking and ski trails, sailing, swimming.

Hosts: Richard & Dodie Schmidgall
Rooms: 3 (PB) $75-140
Full Breakfast
Credit Cards: A, B
Notes: 2, 5, 9, 10, 11, 12, 13, 14

Windward House

6 High Street
Camden, ME, 04843
(207) 236-9656

An historic 1854 Greek Revival on stately High Street above picturesque Camden Harbor. Our five tastefully appointed guest rooms are furnished with period antiques and have private baths. Several common rooms, gardens, full gourmet breakfast. Only a short walk to shops, restaurants, and the harbor.

Hosts: Jon & Mary Davis
Rooms: 6 (PB) $65-95
Full Gourmet Breakfast
Credit Cards: A, B
Notes: 2, 5, 7 (outside), 9, 10, 11, 12, 13, 14

CAPITOL ISLAND

Albonegon Inn

Capitol Island, ME, 04538
(207) 633-2521

Located on a private island four miles from Boothbay Harbor, the inn is perched on the edge of the rocks, with water views from every room. It is very simple, in the cottage style; the perfect place for quiet relaxation.

Hosts: Bob & Kin Peckham
Rooms: 15 (3 PB; 12 SB) $85.60
Continental Breakfast
Credit Cards: No
Closed Nov.-May
Notes: 2, 8, 10, 11, 12

CASTINE

The Manor

Battle Avenue
Castine, ME, 04421
(207) 326-4861

A romantic stone and shingle mansion located in what the *Washington Post* described as "Maine's most beautiful seaside village." Tranquil setting, spacious rooms with ocean views, private baths, candlelit fireside dining, marble-topped bar and fine wines. Near Acadia National Park.

Hosts: Paul & Sara Brouillard
Rooms: 12 (10 PB; 2 SB) $55-135
Cottage: $825/week
Continental Breakfast
Credit Cards: A, B
Closed Dec.-April
Notes: 2, 4, 6, 7, 8, 9, 10, 11, 12

CENTER LOVELL

Center Lovell Inn

Route 5, Box 261N
Center Lovell, ME, 04016
(207) 925-1575

Built in 1805, this house originally had two stories; a third was added in the mid-1800s. Center Lovell is situated in western Maine, within half an hour of four ski areas. Great fishing, canoeing, hiking, and bird watching area, with miles of quiet, unspoiled forest to explore.

Hosts: Bil & Susie Mosca
Rooms: 13 (9 PB; 4 SB) $63-97.50
Full Breakfast
Credit Cards: A, B, C
Closed Oct. 30-May 1
Notes: 2, 3, 7, 8, 9, 10, 11, 12, 13, 14

Center Lovell Inn

CHAMBERLAIN

Ocean Reefs on Long Cove

Route 32
Chamberlain, ME, 04541-3530
(207) 677-2386

Watch the waves break over the reefs, lobstermen hauling traps, or the shoreline between tides. Hike or bicycle roads along the rocky coast. Pemaquid Beach, Pemaquid lighthouse, Fort William Henry, and the boat to Monhegan Island are all within five miles.

Rooms: 4 (PB) $58
Continental Breakfast
Credit Cards: No
Closed Sept. 30-Memorial Day
Notes: 2, 7, 9, 10, 11, 12

CHEBEAGUE ISLAND

Chebeague Island Inn

P.O. Box 492
Chebeague Island, ME, 04017
(207) 846-5155; (207) 774-5891

Three-story inn high on a hill overlooking a golf course. The inn (c. 1926) offers no telephones or TV, but has a 117-foot long wraparound porch. Full of antiques and art. Enjoy litterless beaches; a great place for a family adventure. Baby-sitting service available. Access to island by ferry service only.

Hosts: Wendy & Kevin Bowden
Rooms: 21 (15 PB; 6 SB) $65-90
Full Breakfast
Credit Cards: All major
Open May-Oct.
Notes: 2, 3, 4, 6, 8, 9, 10, 11, 12, 14

CHERRYFIELD

Ricker House

Park Street, Box 256
Cherryfield, ME, 04622
(207) 546-2780

This comfortable 1802 Federal colonial borders the Narraguagus River and offers guests a central place for enjoying the many wonderful activities in Downeast Maine. Reasonably priced restaurants offer great menus, and all feature fabulous local lobster.

Hosts: William & Jean Conway
Rooms: 3 (SB) $48.15-53.50
Full Breakfast
Credit Cards: No
Notes: 2, 5, 8, 9, 10, 11, 12, 13 (XC)

COOPERS MILLS

Claryknoll Farm B&B

Route 215, Box 751
Coopers Mills, ME, 04341
(207) 549-5250

At Claryknoll, you can do all the sightseeing you want and still go home feeling rested. Three Corner Pond offers fishing, canoeing, swimming, picnicking, hiking, and wildlife observation. We're just thirty miles from the ocean. Lambs for children to pet, spacious rooms, shared bath. Small kitchen available for guest use.

Hosts: Bill & Lil Johnson
Rooms: 3 (SB) $40
Continental Breakfast
Credit Cards: No

Closed Nov.-April
Notes: 2, 8, 11

CORNISH

The Cornish Inn

Main Street
Cornish, ME, 04020
(207) 625-8501

Comfortable lodging in warm, informal surroundings. Located in an unspoiled Maine village amid mountain and river scenery. Seventeen hand-stenciled rooms, wraparound porch, comfortable library, and parlor available.

Hosts: Judie & Jim Lapak
Rooms: 17 (10 PB; 7 SB) $40-75
Full Breakfast
Credit Cards: A, B, C
Notes: 2, 4, 5, 7 (limited), 8, 9, 10, 11

CUMBERLAND

B&B of Maine 13

32 Colonial Village
Falmouth, ME, 04105
(207) 781-4528

Visit this traditional New England farmhouse built around 1900, with connecting sheds to a large barn. In a quaint country village just five miles from the coast. Fifteen minutes from Freeport shopping and Portland. Full breakfast; resident cat; restricted smoking. Two guest rooms, one with queen bed and one with twins, share a bath. $47-50.

B&B of Maine 17

32 Colonial Village
Falmouth, ME, 04105
(207) 781-4528

This 100-year-old colonial has a cozy breakfast room, guest parlor, and porch overlooking Casco Bay. Located in an affluent suburban neighborhood with easy access to Portland, just eight miles away. Near L.L. Bean and other Freeport shopping. Visit the nearby restaurant and marina with a view of the sailboat races on the bay. Continental breakfast. Three guest room share a bath. $35-55.

B&B of Maine 18

32 Colonial Village
Falmouth, ME, 04105
(207) 781-4528

Spacious, attractive farmhouse set on 144 acres of rolling fields and woods. Watch the sheep graze in the meadows. This is a working farm with Belgian draft horses, Dorset sheep, and Hereford cattle. The family room contains a grand piano that you are invited to use. Large game room and outdoor patio. Just three miles from I-95, eight from Portland, and twelve miles from Freeport. Full country breakfast is served. Two guest rooms have private baths; two others share a bath. Surcharge for one-night stay. $45.

CUTLER

B&B of Maine 59

32 Colonial Village
Falmouth, ME, 04105
(207) 781-4528

This big inn was built in 1870 to accommodate travelers from Boston to Canada via steamship. Located fifteen miles east of Machias, overlooking Cutler Harbor. Resident dog. No children; restricted smoking. Meals are offered here; hearty breakfast is included in the rates. All rooms share several baths. From $55.

DAMARISCOTTA

Brannon-Bunker Inn

HCR 64, Box 045X
Damariscotta, ME, 04543
(207) 563-5941

NOTES: Credit cards accepted: A Master Card; B Visa; C American Express; D Discover Card; E Diners Club; F Other: 2 Personal checks accepted: 3 Lunch available: 4 Dinner available: 5 Open all year

Intimate, relaxed country B&B located in a 1820 cape, 1880 converted barn, and 1900 carriage house. Seven rooms, furnished in themes reflecting the charm of yesterday with the comforts of today. Ten minutes to lighthouse, fort, beach, antique and craft shopping. Antique shop on the premises.

Hosts: Jeanne & Joe Hovance
Rooms: 7 (4 PB; 3 SB) $48.15-64.20
Continental Breakfast
Credit Cards: A, B, C
Notes: 2, 5, 8, 9, 10, 11, 12, 13, 14

DAMARISCOTTA MILLS

The Mill Pond Inn

Rt. 215
Damariscotta Mills, ME, 04553
(207) 563-8014

Whimsical and cozy 1780 home offering an excellent atmosphere for viewing the wonder of Maine's wildlife. The breakfast room with fireplace and deck faces a pond. Swim or canoe onto Damariscotta Lake across the street and see its loons and eagles. Near Pemaquid, Boothbay, and Camden. Artists welcome.

Hosts: Sherry & Bobby Whear
Rooms: 6 (PB) $55-65
Full Breakfast
Credit Cards: No
Notes: 2, 3, 4, 5, 6, 7, 8, 10, 11, 12, 14

DENNYSVILLE

Lincoln House Country Inn

Routes 1 & 86
Dennysville, ME, 04628
(207) 726-3953

The centerpiece of northeastern coastal Maine. A lovingly restored colonial on 95 acres bordering beautiful Cobsook Bay. Eagles, osprey, seals, whale watching. Choice accommodations. Rates include breakfast and dinner. Serves as a B&B only in the winter; reduced rates.

Hosts: Mary & Jerry Haggerty
Rooms: 10 (6 PB; 4 SB) $140-160
Full Breakfast
Credit Cards: A, B, C
Notes: 2, 4, 7, 8 (over 10), 9, 10, 11, 13

DIXFIELD

B&B of Maine 63

32 Colonial Village
Falmouth, ME, 04105
(207) 781-4528

This mid-1800s Victorian sits on the main street of a rural New England village. Fireplace in the living room with TV for guests' comfort. Full breakfast. Children over twelve are welcome. All beds are queens, and most rooms have private baths. There is also a bunk room with four bunks for small groups. $55.

EAST BOOTHBAY

Five Gables Inn

Murray Hill Road
East Boothbay, ME, 04544
(207) 633-4551

Five Gables Inn is a completely restored Victorian, circa 1865, located on Linekin Bay. All rooms have an ocean view and five have fireplaces. A gourmet breakfast is served in the large common room or on the spacious wraparound veranda.

Hosts: Ellen & Paul Morissette
Rooms: 15 (PB) $80-120
Full Breakfast
Minimum stay weekends: 2; holidays: 3
Credit Cards: A, B
Closed Nov. 16-May 15
Notes: 2, 8 (over 12), 9, 10, 11, 12

EASTPORT

Todd House

1 Caper Avenue
Eastport, ME, 04631
(207) 853-7232

Todd House, c. 1775, on Todd's Head, is a typical New England large cape with center chimney and a unique "good morning" staircase. Magnificent views of sunrises and sunsets over Passamaquoddy Bay; deck barbecue facilities. Well-behaved pets and children are welcome; handicapped accessible rooms.

Host: Ruth McInnis
Rooms: 7 (2 PB; 5 SB) $40-75 + tax
Continental-plus Breakfast
Credit Cards: No
Notes: 2, 5, 6, 8, 9, 10, 11, 14

Weston House

26 Boynton Street
Eastport, ME, 04631
(207) 853-2907

Built in 1810, this imposing Federal style house overlooks Passamaquoddy Bay across to Campobello Island. Listed on the National Register of Historic Places; located in a lovely downeast coastal village. Grounds include an expansive lawn suitable for croquet and a flower garden for quiet relaxation. Picnic lunches available.

Hosts: Jett & John Peterson
Rooms: $42.80-64.20
Full Breakfast
Credit Cards: No
Notes: 2, 5, 7 (restricted), 8, 9, 10

ELIOT

High Meadows B&B

Route 101
Eliot, ME, 03903
(207) 439-0590

A colonial house built in 1736 by a ship builder and captain. On 6 acres of land in the country, but only 4.5 miles to Route 1, fine restaurants, beaches, whale watching, and factory outlets.

Host: Elaine Raymond
Rooms: 5 (3 PB; 2 SB) $50-60
Full Breakfast
Credit Cards: No
Closed Nov. 1-April 1
Notes: 2, 9, 10, 11, 12

FREEPORT

The Bagley House

RR 3, Box 269C
Freeport, ME, 04032
(207) 865-6566

Peace, tranquility, and history abound in this magnificent 1772 country home. Six acres of fields and woods invite nature lovers, hikers, berry pickers, and cross-country skiers. The kitchen's hand-hewn beams and enormous free-standing fireplace with beehive oven inspire mouth-watering breakfasts. A warm welcome awaits you.

Host: Sig Knudsen
Rooms: 5 (PB) $80-100
Full Breakfast
Credit Cards: A, B, C, F
Notes: 2, 5, 8, 9, 10, 11, 12, 13, 14

Captain Josiah Mitchell House

188 Main Street
Freeport, ME, 04032
(207) 865-3289

Located in the town of Freeport just a five-minute walk from L.L. Bean on tree-shaded sidewalks, past beautiful old sea captains' homes. From the moment you arrive you'll know you've discovered a very special place. Furnished with antiques, four-posters, canopies; walls filled with oil paintings and floors covered with a large collection of Oriental rugs. Breakfast in the formal dining room with its magnificent chandelier. No smoking.

Hosts: Loretta & Alan Bradley
Rooms: 7 (PB) $58-72
Full Breakfast
Credit Cards: A, B
Notes: 5, 9, 11, 12, 13, 14

Harraseeket Inn

162 Main Street
Freeport, ME, 04032
(207) 865-9377

Luxury B&B inn two blocks north of L.L. Bean's. Antiques, fireplaces, Jacuzzi, steam or standard baths, cable TV, air-conditioning, tavern on premises. Afternoon tea served.

Hosts: Nancy & Paul Gray
Rooms: 54 (PB) $65-225
Full Breakfast
Credit Cards: A, B, C, D, E
Notes: 4, 5, 7, 8, 9, 10, 11, 12, 13 (XC)

Holbrook Inn

7 Holbrook Street
Freeport, ME, 04032
(207) 865-6693

Exceptionally comfortable and spacious accommodations. Each room has a queen bed, cable color TV, and private bath. Enjoy a hearty breakfast in our "Recipe Room." Just park your car and walk downtown to visit the many outlet shops.

Hosts: Ralph & Beatrice Routhier
Rooms: 3 (PB) $64.20-69.55
Full Breakfast
Credit Cards: No
Notes: 2, 5, 8 (over 10), 9, 11, 12, 13 (XC)

The Isaac Randall House

5 Independence Drive
Freeport, ME, 04032
(207) 865-9295

Comfortable, charming, antique-furnished, air-conditioned rooms in an 1823 farmhouse. Oriental rugs and lovely old quilts. Located on 5 wooded acres with a spring-fed pond. Just a few blocks from L.L. Bean and downtown Freeport. Hearty breakfasts and evening snacks. Resident cats. Smoking discouraged.

Hosts: Glynrose & Jim Friedlander
Rooms: 10 (8 PB; 2 SB) $48.15-107.00
Full Breakfast
Credit Cards: A, B, C
Notes: 2, 4, 5, 6, 8, 9, 11, 12

181 Main Street

181 Main Street
Freeport, ME, 04032
(207) 865-1226

Cozy, antique-filled 1840 cape just a five-minute walk to L.L. Bean and over 120 luxury outlets. In-ground pool, ample parking. On U.S. 1, a short drive from the beaches and rock-bound coast, Brunswick, and Bowdoin College. AAA approved.

Hosts: Ed Hassett & David Cates
Rooms: 7 (PB) $90
Full Breakfast
Credit Cards: A, B
Notes: 2, 5, 7 (limited), 9, 10, 11, 12, 13

White Cedar Inn

178 Main Street
Freeport, ME, 04032
(207) 865-9099

Quiet, unpretentious B&B just a short walk from Freeport's central outlet shopping district and L.L. Bean's famous retail store. Rooms are large, bright, and uncluttered. Quality reproductions and antiques throughout. Hearty breakfast is served in our sun room overlooking the town.

Hosts: Phil & Carla Kerber
Rooms: 6 (4 PB; 2 SB) $60-95
Full Breakfast
Credit Cards: A, B
Notes: 2, 5, 9, 10, 12, 13, 14

FRIENDSHIP

B&B of Maine 35

32 Colonial Village
Falmouth, ME, 04105
(207) 781-4528

Retreat to this oasis by the sea located on the mid-coast of Maine at the end of a peninsula in the Penobscot area. This historic home has been in the family for over a century. Watch the tides come and go as you swim in the unusually warm (for Maine) water in the cove near the house. Tennis courts are available for a nominal fee. Perfect area for bicycling, so bring yours along. Continental breakfast, restricted smoking. Three guest rooms share two baths. Open from Memorial Day through Labor Day weekend. $55.

GEORGETOWN

The Grey Havens

Box 308
Georgetown, ME, 04548
(207) 371-2616

"All you can see is sea and sky," wrote one guidebook. Listed on the National Register as "The last 'Shingle-style' hotel on the Maine coast." Turrets, veranda, 1904 interior. Peaceful and informal. Row to island sanctuary, walk long, quiet beaches, shop at Bean's and other famous outlets.

Hosts: The Hardcastle Family
Rooms: 14 (10 PB; 4 SB) $75-135
Full Breakfast
Credit Cards: No
Notes: 2, 4, 7, 8 (by arrangement), 9, 11, 14

GOULDSBORO

Sunset House

HCR 60, Box 62
Gouldsboro, ME, 04607
(207) 963-7156

This late Victorian home is a traditional B&B with views of both ocean and fresh water. Osprey, bald eagles, loons, and other wildlife can be observed in their natural environment. Schoodic Peninsula, considered the quiet side of Acadia National Park, is a short distance away.

Hosts: Carl & Kathy Johnson
Rooms: 7 (SB) $39-65
Full Breakfast
Credit Cards: A, B
Notes: 2, 5, 8 (over 10), 9, 11, 12, 13 (XC)

GREAT CRANBERRY ISLAND

The Red House

Great Cranberry Island, ME, 04625
(207) 244-5297

A charming shorefront saltwater farm of yesteryear with all the necessities of today. Traditionally decorated rooms with American-style home-cooked breakfast. Private or shared baths. Look from the island to Mt. Cadillac in Acadia National Park. Take the passenger ferry from Northeast Harbor, a lovely two-mile boat ride.

Hosts: Dorothy & John Towns
Rooms: 6 (3 PB; 3 SB) $40-75
Full Breakfast
Credit Cards: A, B
Closed Oct. 15-May 25
Notes: 2, 9, 10, 11, 12

GUILFORD

Guilford Bed & Breakfast

Elm & Prospect Streets
Guilford, ME, 04443
(207) 876-3477

A lovely 1905 post-Victorian with a half-wrap porch, situated high on a knoll within walking distance of the town and its shops. Hearty breakfast of homemade muffins, pancakes, eggs, and so forth. On the Appalachian Trail for hiking, or Squaw Mountain for skiing.

Hosts: Pat & John Selicious
Rooms: 4 (SB) $40-53.50
Full Breakfast
Credit Cards: A, B
Notes: 2, 3, 4 (upon request), 5, 8, 12, 13

HARPSWELL

Lookout Point House

141 Lookout Point Road
Harpswell, ME, 04079
(207) 833-5509

Fourteen gracious guest rooms overlooking the sea. Swimming, boating, bicycling; watch the lobster boats arriving daily. This 1761 house is on 5 acres of lush grounds and has a massive fireplace and piano for your enjoyment.

Hosts: Marilyn & Al Sewall
Singles: 1 (SB) $45
Rooms: 13 (2 PB; 11 SB) $55-90
Full Breakfast
Credit Cards: A, B
Notes: 2, 5, 7, 8 (over 8), 9, 10, 11, 12, 14

ISLE AU HAUT

The Keepers House

Isle au Haut, ME, 04645
(207) 367-2261

Remote island lighthouse station located in the undeveloped wilderness area of Acadia National Park. Guests arrive on the mail boat from Stonington. No phones, cars, TV, or crowds. Osprey, seal, deer, rugged trails, spectacular scenery, seclusion, peace, and inspiration. Three elegant meals included in rate.

Hosts: Jeff & Judi Burke
Rooms: 5 (SB) $175-220
All meals included in rate
Minimum stay July-Aug.:2
Credit Cards: No
Closed Nov. 1-April 30
Notes: 2, 8, 9, 11

ISLEBORO

B&B of Maine 36

32 Colonial Village
Falmouth, ME, 04105
(207) 781-4528

If you have ever wanted to visit an island, here's your chance. The ferry leaves every hour, eight times a day, from the harbor just north of Camden. It's a 25-minute scenic ride you will never forget. This delightful island retreat fronts on 900 feet of private beach. One large oceanfront room with double bed and private bath is separate from the main house, with its own entrance. Breakfast may be taken in your room, on the beach, or shared with the hosts on their screened porch. Open from July through September. Two-night minimum. $65.

KENNEBUNKPORT

B&B of Maine 9

32 Colonial Village
Falmouth, ME, 04105
(207) 781-4528

This hideaway B&B has been named for the Bufflehead Duck that inhabits the area. Nestled under a grove of trees on the bank of a tidal river, this Dutch colonial overlooks the port village. There are sun decks on several levels, a guest living room with stone fireplace, and plenty of windows to enjoy the view. A queen room has its own balcony and private bath. Two other rooms have private baths, and there is a two-room suite with private bath. Two-night minimum on summer and holiday weekends. $75-95.

B&B of Maine 11

32 Colonial Village
Falmouth, ME, 04105
(207) 781-4528

Large colonial home situated on a knoll overlooking a cove of the Kennebunk River. Built in 1793 and added to over the years, this home offers some solitude in this busy area. Ideal location for bikers, or a ten-minute walk to the village and beach. There is a rowboat available. Continental breakfast; resident cats and dog. Children are welcome. One double room has a private bath; two other rooms share a bath. Restricted smoking. $52-62.

The Breakwater Inn

Box 1160
Kennebunkport, ME, 04046
(207) 967-3118

A seaside inn at the mouth of the Kennebunk River offering views of the Atlantic. A short walk to Dock Square, close to beaches, and one mile from the "summer White House." Offering breakfast and dinner in a common dining room with fireplace and friendly faces.

Hosts: The Lambert Family
Rooms: 20 (PB) $65-125 seasonal
Full Breakfast
Credit Cards: A, B, C
Open April-Dec.
Notes: 2, 4, 7, 8, 9, 10, 11, 12, 14

The Captain Lord Mansion

Box 800
Kennebunkport, ME, 04046
(207) 967-3141; (800) 522-3141

An intimate Maine Coast inn featuring large, luxurious rooms, working fireplaces, private baths, queen four-poster beds, and antiques. Has received the coveted AAA four-diamond rating for eight consecutive years. Named in the top ten U.S. inns by *Country Inns Bed & Breakfast* magazine, January 1989.

Hosts: Bev Davis & Rick Litchfield
Rooms: 16 (PB) $125-200
Full Breakfast
Credit Cards: A, B, D
Notes: 2, 5, 9, 10, 11, 12

The Captain Lord Mansion

Cove House

South Maine Street
Kennebunkport, ME, 04046
(207) 967-3704

Cozy inn in an eighteenth-century colonial home, with spacious rooms decorated in country antiques. Full, hearty breakfast is served in the formal dining room. Short walk from village center and beach and near golf courses. Located in a quiet area on Chick's Cove.

Hosts: The Joneses
Rooms: 3 (1 PB; 2 SB) $52-62
Full Breakfast
Credit Cards: A, B, C
Notes: 2, 5, 7, 8, 9, 10, 11, 12

1802 House

Locke Street
Kennebunkport, ME, 04046
(207) 967-5632

A pleasant, cozy interlude that you will long remember.

Host: Patricia Ledda
Rooms: 6 (PB) $75-$123
Full Breakfast
Credit Cards: A, B, C
Notes: 2, 4, 5, 7, 9, 10, 11, 12, 14

English Meadows Inn

RR 3, Box 141
Kennebunk, ME, 04043
(207) 967-5766

English Meadows is an 1860 Victorian farmhouse that has been operating as an inn for more than eighty years. Located within a ten-minute stroll of the village of Kennebunkport, with its many unique shops, art galleries, and restaurants, English Meadows offers a friendly and comfortable place to visit.

Host: Charlie Doane
Rooms: 14 (10 PB; 4 SB) $70-85
Full Breakfast
Credit Cards: A, B
Notes: 2, 5, 8 (10 and over), 10, 11, 12

The Green Heron Inn

Ocean Avenue
Box 2578
Kennebunkport, ME, 04046
(207) 967-3315

This inn, with its inviting porch, is located between the river and the ocean in this colonial resort village. Ten guest rooms and a cottage all have private baths, air conditioning, color TV.

Hosts: Charles & Elizabeth Reid
Rooms: 10 (PB) $60-80
Cottage $82-90
Full Breakfast
Credit Cards: No
Notes: 2, 5, 6 (restricted), 7, 8, 9, 11, 12

The Inn at Harbor Head

RR 2, Box 1180, Pier Road
Kennebunkport, ME, 04046
(207) 967-5564

A waterfront inn nestled on the rocky shore of picturesque Cape Porpoise Harbor, a quiet fishing village a few miles east of bustling Kennebunkport. Luxuriate in the peace of changing tides and wheeling gulls. Lighthouses, lobster boats, luscious breakfasts.

Hosts: Joan & Dave Sutter
Rooms: 4 (PB) $95-150
Full Breakfast
Credit Cards: A, B, C
Notes: 2, 9, 11, 12, 14

The Inn on South Street

Box 478A
Kennebunkport, ME, 04046
(207) 967-5151

Enjoy the comfortable elegance of this nineteenth-century Greek Revival house. Three beautifully decorated guest rooms and one luxury suite. Private baths, fireplaces. A sumptuous breakfast is served each morning in the sunny kitchen with views of the water. Located on a quiet street, within walking distance of restaurants, shops, and water.

Hosts: Jacques & Eva Downs
Rooms: 4 (PB) $80-150
Full Breakfast
Credit Cards: C
Notes: 2, 5, 7 (restricted), 8 (over 12), 10, 11, 12, 13, 14

The Kennebunkport Inn

Dock Square
P.O. Box 111
Kennebunkport, ME, 04046
(207) 967-2621

The Kennebunkport Inn was originally built by a sea captain in the late 1800s. Today it has 33 rooms with private baths and colored TV. Located in the center of town, just a skip from Dock Square, but set back from the hubbub. Near shops, the historic district. A small outdoor pool overlooks the river, and there is a turn-of-the-century bar with a piano bar on weekends.

Hosts: Rick & Martha Griffin
Rooms: 33 (PB) $62-155
Full Breakfast May-Oct.; continental off-season
Credit Cards: A, B
Notes: 2, 4, 5, 7, 8, 9, 10, 11, 12, 14

Kilburn House

Chestnut Street
P.O. Box 1309
Kennebunkport, ME, 04046
(207) 967-4762

Kilburn House is an 1890s Victorian home located one block from the center of downtown Kennebunkport. Kennebunkport is a colonial New England village with many fine restaurants, beaches, and shops.

Hosts: Samuel A. Minier & Muriel Friend
Rooms: 4 (2 PB; 2 SB) $60-75 + tax
Suite: Two-bedroom (PB) $125 + tax
Continental Breakfast
Credit Cards: A, B, C
Notes: 2, 8, 9, 10, 11, 12

Kylemere House

South Street
Box 1333
Kennebunkport, ME, 04046
(207) 967-2780

Kylemere House, located in the historic district, is a quiet haven just a minute's walk from the beach, shops, galleries, and restaurants. Come and relax in a friendly atmosphere in our beautifully appointed rooms. Enjoy a Down East breakfast in our formal dining room overlooking the gardens.

Hosts: Bill & Mary Kyle
Rooms: 3 (2 PB; 1 SB) $65-90
Full Breakfast
Credit Cards: A, B, C
Closed Jan.-April
Notes: 2, 8 (over 12), 9, 10, 11, 12, 13, 14

Lake Brook Guest House B&B

Lower Harbour Village
57 Western Avenue
Kennebunk, ME, 04043
(207) 967-4069

Charming rooms with paddle fans, fresh-cut flowers, great full breakfasts. Lovely perennial garden. Rooms overlook a tidal marsh and brook. Lake Brook is centrally located only one-half mile from downtown, with its shops, restaurants, galleries. Just over one mile to the beach.

Host: Carolyn A. McAdams
Rooms: 4; (3 PB; 1 SB) $69.55-80.25
Full Breakfast
Credit Cards: No
Notes: 2, 5, 8, 9, 10, 11, 12

Maine Stay Inn & Cottages

Maine Stay Inn & Cottages

Box 500 A
Kennebunkport, ME, 04046
(207) 967-2117

Elegant inn rooms and delightful garden cottages located in the quiet surroundings of Kennebunkport's National Register of Historic Homes. Complimentary breakfast, afternoon tea, New England desserts. Color cable TV; private baths. Easy walking distance to restaurants, galleries, shops, and harbor. One mile to beach and golf.

Hosts: Lindsay & Carol Copeland
Rooms: 17 (PB) $85-170
Full Breakfast
Credit Cards: A, B, C

Closed Jan.; open weekends & holidays only from Nov.-March
Notes: 2, 7 (limited), 8, 9, 10, 11, 12, 14

Old Fort Inn & Resort

Box M-30
Kennebunkport, ME, 04046
(207) 967-5353; (800) 828-FORT

Discover the hospitality of a luxurious New England Inn that combines all yesterday's charm with today's conveniences, from the daily buffet breakfast to the comfort and privacy of our antique-appointed rooms. Includes pool, tennis court, color TV, telephones, and a charming antique shop, all in a secluded setting.

Hosts: David & Sheila Aldrich
Rooms: 16 (PB) $98-210
Full Breakfast
Credit Cards: A, B, C, D
Closed mid-Dec.-mid-April
Notes: 2, 7, 8 (over 12), 9, 10, 11, 12, 14

The White Barn Inn

RR 3, Box 387
Beech Street
Kennebunkport, ME, 04046
(207) 967-2321; FAX: (207) 967-2333

Main dining rooms are in two accurately restored barns; dining room in the inn serves daily breakfast and dinner on weekends from June to December. Living rooms are comfortably furnished, with fireplace, TV, an abundant library of periodicals and books. Piano bar in restaurant. Each guest room has been meticulously restored with period furnishings. Special touches include robes in each room, a welcome basket of fruit, fresh flowers, daily afternoon tea, and a home-baked breakfast. Member, Relais & Chateaus; four-diamond rated by the AAA.

Rooms: 25 (PB) $85-240
Continental Breakfast
Credit Cards: A, B, C

KITTERY POINT

Harbour Watch B&B

Follett Lane
Kittery Point, ME, 03905
(207) 439-3242

Colonial sea captain's house, in same family since 1797. Wonderful view, quiet atmosphere. Within five miles to outlet shops, theaters, beaches, fabulous restaurants, whale-watching excursions, harbor cruises. Evening musicales with harpsichord and baroque instruments. Just an hour's drive from Boston.

Hosts: Marian & Robert Craig
Rooms: 4 (S2B) $60
Continental Breakfast
Minimum stay weekends: 2; holidays: 2
Credit Cards: No
Closed Nov.-April
Notes: 2, 9, 10, 11, 12

Old Fort Inn

Whaleback Inn B&B

Box 162, Pepperrell Cove
Kittery Point, ME, 03905
(207) 439-9570

Located in the southernmost point in Maine, an hour's drive from both Portland, Maine, and Boston, Massachusetts. Three miles from Route 1 and the Kittery malls, in a quaint old house next to one of the area's best seafood restaurants.

Hosts: Ron Ames & Frank Frisbee
Rooms: 3 (SB) $55
Continental-plus Breakfast
Credit Cards: A, B, C
Closed Oct.-April
Notes: 2 ,9, 11, 12

LIMERICK

B&B of Maine 68

32 Colonial Village
Falmouth, ME, 04105
(207) 781-4528

Nestled in the rolling foothills of southwestern Maine, this eighteenth-century farmhouse has a spectacular view. The house is on the main street of a quiet country village, with many antique shops within a thirty-mile radius. Delightfully restored colonial village nearby. Full breakfast; no smoking. Nicely decorated guest rooms share a bath. $35-55.

LINCOLNVILLE BEACH

Longville Inn

P.O. Box 75
The Other Road
Lincolnville Beach, ME, 04849
(207) 236-3785

Lincolnville's finest inn, a restored century-old Victorian "cottage" by the sea. Flowering gardens, country setting. Fireplaces, soft flannel sheets, fluffy towels, cozy comforters, pampering. Enjoy an afternoon shopping, sight-seeing, walking the shore, or just relax in the gazebo. Sailing, hiking, museums, galleries, ferry service, fine dining, and lighthouses nearby.

Host: Lori Curren
Rooms: 5 (PB) $65-80
Full Breakfast
Credit Cards: No
Notes: 2, 4, 5, 7, 9, 10, 11, 12, 14

LUBEC

Breakers By The Bay

37 Washington
Lubec, ME, 04652
(207) 733-2487

One of the oldest houses in the 200-year-old town of Lubec, which is a small fishing village. Three blocks to Campobello Island, the home of Franklin D. Roosevelt. All rooms have hand-crocheted tablecloths and hand-quilted bedspreads. Four rooms have private decks for viewing the bay. All rooms that share a bath have their own washstands in them.

Host: E. M. Elg
Rooms: 5 (4 PB; 1 SB) $64.20
Full Breakfast
Credit Cards: No
Notes: 2, 12

MACHIAS

Clark Perry House

59 Court Street
Machias, ME, 04654
(207) 255-8458

An 1868 Victorian in a quiet coastal town. Within easy walking distance of shops, restaurants, places of worship, library, and historic sites. Rogue Bluffs State Park, Jasper Beach, and the University of Maine at Machias are nearby. On the National Register of Historic Places.

Hosts: Robin & David Rier
Rooms: 2 (SB) $50
Full Breakfast
Credit Cards: B
Notes: 2, 5, 8, 10, 11, 12, 13

MT. DESERT

B&B of Maine 44

32 Colonial Village
Falmouth, ME, 04105
(207) 781-4528

One-hundred-year-old farmhouse, newly renovated, overlooking a pond and the mountains of the park. A wonderful opportunity to watch the milking and feeding of a prize-winning goat herd, making cheese, tending the geese, ducks, chickens, and turkeys, collecting eggs, or gardening. One room with private bath. Queen room shares a bath. Twin room shares a bath. Several dogs and cats, and two small children, make up this household. $50-55.

NAPLES

Lamb's Mill Inn

Box 676, Lamb's Mill Road
Naples, ME, 04055
(207) 693-6253

Ewe hike, ewe bike, ewe ski, ewe zzz. . . . A charming inn located in the foothills of Maine's western mountain and lake region. Romantic country atmosphere on 20 acres of fields and woods. Four lovely rooms with private baths and full country breakfast. Near lakes, antique shops, skiing, canoeing. Hot tub.

Hosts: Laurie Tinkham & Sandy Long
Rooms: 4 (PB) $75-85
Full Breakfast
Credit Cards: No
Notes: 2, 5, 9, 10, 11, 12, 13, 14

NEWCASTLE

B&B of Maine 24

32 Colonial Village
Falmouth, ME, 04105
(207) 781-4528

This lovely old home retains its Victorian charm, with high ceilings and antiques throughout. A short stroll to the center of one of the prettiest village harbors on the coast. Front porch has a view of the water; rear patio surrounded by gardens. Dog and cat in residence. The airport limo and bus from Portland serve this community. Full gourmet breakfast. Spacious, attractive guest rooms may have private or shared baths. $40-55.

B&B of Maine 26

32 Colonial Village
Falmouth, ME, 04105
(207) 781-4528

A warm welcome will greet you at this c. 1860 colonial with a screened porch overlooking the harbor. Ten-minute walk to the village. Comfortable guest parlor with woodstove; antiques. Limited smoking; hearty gourmet breakfast. All guest rooms share a bath. $40-50.

The Captain's House B&B

P.O. Box 242
19 River Road
Newcastle, ME, 04553
(207) 563-1482

The Captain's House B&B is a Greek Revival home overlooking the Damariscotta River. On your arrival you will be overwhelmed with our river view, and inside you'll find our large, sunny rooms warm and inviting. Enjoy a leisurely walk to town for fine dining and carefree shopping. We serve homemade breads, blueberry pancakes, French toast, and farm-fresh eggs for a breakfast you'll never forget.

Hosts: Susan Rizzo & Joe Sullivan
Rooms: 5 (SB) $65
Full Breakfast
Credit Cards: No
Notes: 2, 5, 7, 8, 9, 10, 11, 12

Glidden House

RR 1, Box 740, Glidden Street
Newcastle, ME, 04553
(207) 563-1859

A lovely mansard-roofed Victorian (Second Empire) overlooking the Damariscotta River. A memorable house that's attractively furnished, comfortable, and quiet. Excellent breakfasts. Within walking distance of restaurants, shops, galleries, and historic sites.

Host: Doris E. Miller
Rooms: 3 (PB) $50-55
Full Breakfast
Credit Cards: B
Notes: 2, 5, 7 (restricted), 8, 9, 10, 11, 12, 13 (XC)

The Markert House

Glidden Street
Newcastle, ME, 04553
(207) 563-1309

Four rooms with two shared baths in a hillside 1900 Victorian overlooking the Damariscotta River. Your host is an artist, photographer, gourmet cook, and gardener. Reproduction Victorian veranda, antique furnishings, tasteful art gallery.

Host: William P. Markert
Rooms: 4 (SB) $40-55
Full Breakfast
Minimum stay weekends: 2
Credit Cards: A, B, C
Notes: 2, 5, 9, 12

The Newcastle Inn

River Road
Newcastle, ME, 04553
(207) 563-5685

A romantic country inn situated on the Damariscotta River — one of the longest-operating inns in the region. All fifteen rooms have private baths, and some have canopy beds. In the dining room, elegant candlelight dinners and multicourse breakfasts are served. The living room has a fireplace, and the porch overlooks the river.

Hosts: Ted & Chris Sprague
Rooms: 15 (PB) $75-95
Full Breakfast
Credit Cards: A, B
Notes: 2, 4, 5, 11, 12, 13 (XC), 14

NEW HARBOR

Gosnold Arms

HC 61, Box 161, Rt. 32
New Harbor, ME, 04554
(207) 677-3727

On the harbor, the Gosnold Arms Inn and cottages, all with private baths—most with water view. A glassed-in dining room overlooking the water is open for breakfast, dinner, and Sunday brunch. Within a ten-mile radius are lakes, beaches, lobster pounds, historic sites, boat trips, golf, antiques, shops, and restaurants.

Hosts: The Phinney Family
Rooms: 26 (PB)
Full Breakfast
Credit Cards: A, B
Open mid-May-Nov.
Notes: 2, 4, 7 (limited), 8, 9, 11, 12

NEWPORT

Lake Sebasticook B&B

8 Sebasticook Avenue
Box 502
Newport, ME, 04953
(207) 368-5507

Take a step back in history in our 1903 Victorian home located on a quiet street. Relax on the second-floor sun porch or comfortable wraparound porch and enjoy the sounds of ducks and loons on Lake Sebasticook. Take a short walk to the lake park, or play tennis at the city park a block away. In the morning, savor a full country breakfast including homemade breads.

Hosts: Bob & Trudy Zothner
Rooms: 3 (S2B) $37.45-53.50
Full Breakfast
Credit Cards: No
Closed Nov.-May 1
Notes: 2, 10, 11, 12, 13

NOTES: Credit cards accepted: A Master Card; B Visa; C American Express; D Discover Card; E Diners Club; F Other: 2 Personal checks accepted: 3 Lunch available: 4 Dinner available: 5 Open all year

OGUNQUIT

Beauport Inn

96 Shore Road
P.O. Box 1793
Ogunquit, ME, 03907
(207) 646-8680

A cozy nonsmoking B&B furnished with antiques, with private or semiprivate baths. Pine-paneled living room with fireplace and piano. Baked goods by the host. Antique shop on the premises.

Host: Dan Pender
Rooms: 4 (2 PB; 2 SB) $75-85
Continental Breakfast
Credit Cards: A, B, C
Closed Jan. & Feb.
Notes: 2, 8 (over 12), 9, 10, 11

Hartwell House

116 Shore Road
Ogunquit, ME, 03907
(207) 646-7210

In the tradition of fine European country inns, the Hartwell House offers its guests rooms and suites tastefully furnished with Early American and English antiques. Breakfast is included. Perkins Cove, Ogunquit Beach, and the Marginal Way are all within a few steps from the house.

Hosts: Jim & Trisha Hartwell
Rooms: 16 (PB) $65-175
Full or Continental Breakfast (seasonal)
Minimum stay weekends & holidays: 1-3
Credit Cards: A, B, C
Notes: 2, 5, 8 (14 or older), 9, 10, 11, 12, 14

The Morning Dove

30 Bourne Lane
Box 1940
Ogunquit, ME, 03907
(207) 646-3891

Elegant 1860s farmhouse featuring light, airy rooms with antiques, art, and European accents. Breakfast is served on the Victorian porch reminiscent of sidewalk cafes. Amenities include down comforters, air-conditioning, welcoming wine, chocolates, and plush towels. Short stroll to the beaches, cove, restaurants, and playhouse. Reservations appreciated.

Hosts: Peter & Eeta Sachon
Rooms: 8 (4 PB; 2 SB) $60-105
Continental-plus Breakfast
Minimum stay in season: 2
Credit Cards: A, B, C
Closed Nov. 1-May 1
Notes: 2, 7, 8 (12 and over), 9, 10, 11, 12, 13 (XC), 14

Seafair Inn

14 Shore Road
P.O. Box 1221
Ogunquit, ME, 03907
(207) 646-2181

A Victorian inn decorated with period antiques. Eighteen rooms, including efficiencies, most with private baths, air conditioning, and color cable TV. Ideally located on Ogunquit's famous trolley line, a block from the ocean, the Marginal Way, and the center of town. Continental breakfast is served on the glass-enclosed sun porch. Open April-October. Write or call for a brochure; reservations suggested.

Hosts: John & Susan Lesser
Rooms: 18 (14 PB; 4 SB) $40-93
Continental Breakfast
Credit Cards: A, B
Closed Nov.-March
Notes: 2, 7, 8, 10, 11, 12

The Trellis House

2 Beachmere Place
Ogunquit, ME, 03907
(207) 646-7909

A turn-of-the-century beach house, appointed with an eclectic blend of antiques. All rooms have private baths, and a full cottage breakfast is served. Walk to all that's special in Ogunquit.

Host: Jim Pontolilo
Rooms: 4 (PB) $90
Cottage Breakfast
Credit Cards: A, B
Notes: 2, 7 (limited), 9, 10, 11, 12

PEMAQUID

Little River Inn

Route 130
HC 62, Box 178
Pemaquid, ME, 04558
(207) 677-2845

Enjoy a relaxing vacation on the coast of Maine. Select a traditional room or one of our rustic gallery rooms. Minutes away from all the unique features that make Pemaquid special: lighthouse, beach, archaeological digs, New Harbor, galleries, antique shops, and great dining. Meet our sheep, explore the falls, fish on the river, or stroll through the forest. Canoe rentals and a golf course are within a few minutes. Adventure to Monhegan Island, or take a day trip to Camden or Boothbay.

Rooms: 4 (1 PB; 3 SB) $50-60
Full Breakfast
Credit Cards: A, B
Notes: 2, 4, 5, 7, 8, 10, 11, 12, 13

Little River Inn

PORTLAND

B&B of Maine 4

32 Colonial Village
Falmouth, ME, 04105
(207) 781-4528

This 1884 Italianate stucco house sits on a quiet street surrounded by carefully maintained historic homes. Business travelers will especially enjoy the convenience here, with phones and small TVs discreetly tucked into each room. There is a private sitting room upstairs and a larger common room on the first floor. Continental breakfast. All guest rooms have private baths, and there is a two-night minimum stay on weekends from May through October. $95.

B&B of Maine 16

32 Colonial Village
Falmouth, ME, 04105
(207) 781-4528

Charming, affordable guest house on an island just a seventeen-minute ferry ride from in-town Portland. The ferry leaves hourly during most of the day, and the inn is just .3 mile from the landing. Cars are permitted but not recommended; walking or cycling are the best ways to see the island. A continental breakfast is served every day except Monday and Friday; nearby coffee shop for those days. All guest rooms share three baths; surcharge for one-night stays. $40-60.

Inn at Park Spring

135 Spring Street
Portland, ME, 04101
(207) 774-1059

The smallest grand hotel in Portland. The Inn at Park Spring is a unique brick townhouse in the heart of downtown. Our location assures that you'll see the city at its best. Within walking distance of our charming Old Port district, with its one-of-a-kind shops and restaurants, art galleries and museum.

Hosts: Juli & Bob Riley
Rooms: 7 (5 PB; 2 SB) $80-90
Continental-plus Breakfast
Credit Cards: A, B, C
Notes: 2, 5, 7 (limited), 8 (off season), 9, 10, 11, 12, 14

NOTES: Credit cards accepted: A Master Card; B Visa; C American Express; D Discover Card; E Diners Club; F Other: 2 Personal checks accepted: 3 Lunch available: 4 Dinner available: 5 Open all year

Inn at Park Spring

PROUTS NECK

Pineapple Hospitality ME439

P.O. Box F821
New Bedford, MA, 02742-0821
(508) 990-1696

A 1779 home built on the site of an Indian fort. The suite consists of a large bedroom with a panoramic view and a full canopy bed. Comfortable chairs for reading, large private bath with adjoining dressing room, fireplaced living room, and glassed-in sun room with kitchen facilities. Upstairs bedroom has a king or twin beds with an ocean view and private bath. European breakfast is served. Closed November to March. Located six miles from Portland. Private beach across the street. $75-85.

RUMFORD POINT

The Last Resort

Box 12
Rumford Point, ME, 04279
(207) 364-4986

A colonial cape located in Rumford Corner, nestled in the foothills of western Maine. Country comfort and charm, and good old home cooking, are our specialty. Skiing within minutes; two state parks, and golf courses in the area. Fishing, hunting, hiking, and boating by the back door. Children are permitted. Plenty of wide-open space for outside activities.

Host: Joan Tucker
Rooms: 3 (PB) $50
Full Breakfast
Credit Cards: No
Notes: 2, 3 (picnic), 5, 7, 8, 9, 10, 11, 12, 13

SACO

B&B of Maine 19

32 Colonial Village
Falmouth, ME, 04105
(207) 781-4528

Watch the cows being milked or the cheese being made as you enjoy the hospitality of this farm family. Located on 165 acres of rolling hayfields and woods, this trim farmhouse is only twenty miles south of Portland and eight miles from Old Orchard Beach. Shaggy St. Bernard in residence. Cots and crib available for children. Two comfortable guest rooms share one bath; hearty farm breakfast. $45.

SANFORD

Oakwood Inn & Motel

279 Main Street
Sanford, ME, 04073
(207) 324-2160

Oakwood is located in the heart of Sanford, yet it is private, with a lovely courtyard and grounds. The inn boasts of many famous visitors. Handy to both ocean and mountains. At Oakwood you will find old-fashioned, turn-of-the-century charm.

Hosts: Sherri Biasin & Stephen Clark
Rooms: 7 (2 PB; 5 SB) $32-55
Continental Breakfast
Credit Cards: A, B, C, D
Notes: 5, 7, 8, 9, 10, 11, 12, 14

SCARBOROUGH

B&B of Maine 14

32 Colonial Village
Falmouth, ME, 04105
(207) 781-4528

Private access to an uncrowded sandy ocean beach from this comfortable family B&B. There is a sun deck and picnic area for guest use. Located about twenty minutes from Kennebunkport or Portland. There is a family dog and cat. No smoking; continental breakfast. Two guest rooms with private or shared baths. $55-70.

SEARSPORT

B&B of Maine 40

32 Colonial Village
Falmouth, ME, 04105
(207) 781-4528

An 1860 sea captain's mansion listed on the National Register of Historic Places, this home is an excellent example of Mansard architecture. Be sure to take time to visit the Penobscot Marine Museum and some of the many antique shops in the area. Open from May through October. No pets. Continental breakfast. All guest rooms have fireplaces, queen beds, and private baths. $45.

The Carriage House Inn

Box 238
Searsport, ME, 04974
(207) 548-2289

Built in 1874, this classic Victorian has been beautifully maintained, and the large, cheerful rooms offer a restful night's stay. Located in the center of the "Antique Capital of Maine," within walking distance of restaurants, flea markets, the museum, and oceanfront town park.

Hosts: Brad & Cathy Bradbury
Rooms: 4 (3 PB; 1 SB) $58.85-69.55
Continental Breakfast
Credit Cards: A, B
Closed March & April
Notes: 2, 8, 9, 10, 11, 12

The Carriage House Inn

SOUTH BROOKSVILLE

Breezemere Farm Inn

Box 290, Breezemere Farm Road
South Brooksville, ME, 04617
(207) 326-8628

Picturesque 1850 farmhouse plus seven cottages on 60 acres on Orcutt Harbor, East Penobscot Bay. Spruce to smell, islands to explore, water to sail, trails to hike, berries to pick, mussels to rake. Bikes, beach, boats. Friday night lobster clambakes, June through October. Free brochure.

Hosts: Joe & Linda Forest
Cottages: 6 (PB) $600-800/week
Rooms: 7 (S4.5B) $70-85
Full Breakfast
Credit Cards: A, B, C
Closed Nov. 1-May 15
Notes: 2, 4 (Fri. & Sat.), 8 (cottages), 9, 10, 11, 12, 14

SOUTH THOMASTON

Weskeag Inn

Route 73, Box 213
South Thomaston, ME, 04858
(207) 596-6676

The Weskeag Inn is a handsome 1800s shipbuilder's home in the village of South Thomaston. It is located on the Weskeag River, an estuary where one can fish, boat, watch lobstermen tend their traps. Nearby ferries to islands, state park with sandy beach.

Hosts: Gray & Lynne Smith
Rooms: 6 (2 PB; 4 S2B) $55-75
Full Breakfast
Credit Cards: A, B
Notes: 2, 5, 8, 9, 10, 11, 12, 13

SOUTH WATERFORD

B&B of Maine 53

32 Colonial Village
Falmouth, ME, 04105
(207) 781-4528

Since 1820, South Waterford has been a favorite all-season stopover for travelers. The farmhouse home has a wraparound porch for rocking and its very own lake with sandy beach, canoe, and rowboat for guests to use. Visit the White Mountains of NH or shop in North Conway, just 45 minutes away. Perfect area for cyclists. Full breakfast; no smoking inside. All guest rooms share several baths. $45-55.

SOUTHWEST HARBOR

B&B of Maine 43

32 Colonial Village
Falmouth, ME, 04105
(207) 781-4528

This traditional 1800s country home overlooks the harbor just a half mile down a country lane from Main Street. Your hostess has a piano available for guests, and often gets a songfest going. Wander across the street to watch the fishermen unload at the lobster pound. Rent a bike and discover some back roads. Just two miles to Bass Harbor and the Swan's Island ferry. Full breakfast; two shared baths. $55

B&B of Maine 55

32 Colonial Village
Falmouth, ME, 04105
(207) 781-4528

Cheery and comfortable classic Maine country home (c. 1857) with sunny deck for harbor viewing. Just one block from town. All rooms are decorated with antiques and colonial touches. Most rooms have queen beds; three rooms with private baths. Two rooms share a bath. Full breakfast. No children. $55-80.

B&B of Maine 57

32 Colonial Village
Falmouth, ME, 04105
(207) 781-4528

Sitting on a ridge with a spectacular view of the harbor, this contemporary home welcomes you to one of the prettiest spots on Mt. Desert Island. Enjoy the view from the glassed family room or the several decks. Since the property borders the southern side of Acadia National Park, there is ample opportunity for hiking, biking, or jogging right out the back door. Cycle and canoe rentals in the village. Resident dog; not suitable for children. Several rooms have private baths; others have queen beds and shared baths. Two-night stays preferred. $45-55.

Harbour Cottage Inn

P.O. Box 258
Southwest Harbor, ME, 04679-0258
(207) 244-5738

Our elegant but informal inn is located in the heart of Acadia National Park. Private baths offer either whirlpools or steam showers and hair dryers. Harbor-facing guest rooms have individual heat and ceiling fans. Hikers, bikers, boaters, skiers, and tourists are welcome to enjoy our warm, friendly hospitality.

Hosts: Ann & Mike Pedreschi
Rooms: 5 (PB) $50-90
Full Breakfast
Credit Cards: A, B, C
Notes: 2, 5, 7, 9, 10, 11, 12, 13, 14

The Island House

Box 1006
Southwest Harbor, ME, 04679
(207) 244-5180

Relax in a gracious, restful seacoast home on the quiet side of the island. We serve such Island House favorites as blueberry coffee cake and sausage/cheese casserole. Charming private loft apartment available. Acadia National Park is just a five-minute drive away. The house is located across the street from the harbor, with swimming, sailing, biking, and hiking nearby.

Host: Ann Gill
Rooms: 5 (1 PB; 4 SB) $55-100
Full Breakfast
Credit Cards: No
Closed Nov. 1-April 30
Notes: 2, 8 (over 12), 9, 10, 11, 12, 14

Island Watch B&B

Freeman Ridge Road
Southwest Harbor, ME, 04679
(207) 244-7229

Overlooking the great harbor of Mount Desert Island and the village of Southwest Harbor, Island Watch sits atop Freeman Ridge on the quiet side of the island. The finest panoramic views, privacy, and comfort. Walk to Acadia National Park and the fishing village of Southwest Harbor.

Host: Maxine M. Clark
Rooms: 7 (4 PB; 3 SB) $45-55
Full Breakfast
Credit Cards: No
Notes: 5, 8 (12 and over), 9, 10, 11, 12, 14

The Kingsleigh Inn

100 Main Street
Box 1426
Southwest Harbor, ME, 04679
(207) 244-5302

Located in the heart of Acadia National Park, overlooking the picturesque harbor. A romantic and intimate inn that will surround you with charm the moment you walk through the door. Many rooms enjoy spectacular harbor views, and all are very tastefully decorated.

Hosts: Tom & Nancy Cervelli
Rooms: 8 (PB) $55-145
Full Breakfast
Credit Cards: A, B
Notes: 2, 5, 8 (over 8), 9

The Kingsleigh Inn

Lindenwood Inn

Clark Point Road
Box 1328
Southwest Harbor, ME, 04679
(207) 244-5335

A lovely sea captain's home overlooking the harbor on the quiet side of Acadia National Park. Offers a warm, cozy atmosphere and full breakfast. Explore Mt. Desert Island, relax in the parlor, or play our harpsichord. Brochure available; open all year.

Hosts: Gardiner & Marilyn Brower
Rooms: 7 (3 PB; 4 SB) $42.80-123.05
Cottage: 1 (PB) $80.25-112.35
Full Breakfast
Children over 6 welcome in cottage; over 12 in inn
Notes: 2, 5, 8, 9, 10, 11, 12, 13, 14

Penury Hall

Main Street
P.O. Box 68
Southwest Harbor, ME, 04679
(207) 244-7102

On the quiet side of Mt. Desert, fourteen miles from more populous Bar Harbor, Penury Hall's guests enjoy breakfasts of eggs Benedict, blueberry pancakes, cinnamon waffles, or popovers. You're welcome to use the canoe or sail aboard *Abaco Rage,* a 21' daysailer. Our sauna can relax you after a hard day of hiking or cross-country skiing.

Hosts: Toby & Gretchen Strong
Rooms: 3 (SB) $40-55 + tax
Full Breakfast
Credit Cards: No
Notes: 2, 5, 7, 9, 10, 11, 12, 13

SPRUCE HEAD

Craignair Inn

Clark Island Road
Spruce Head, ME, 04859
(207) 594-7644

Craignair Inn is located on 4 acres of shorefront, set on a granite ledge rising from the sea. Miles of coastline to explore, clam flats, offshore islands, tidal pools. Short drive to the ferry for Monhegan Island; near Owls Head lighthouse and State Park. A nearby deep saltwater quarry pool surrounded by spruce and birch provides warm-water swimming for our guests.

Hosts: Terry & Norman Smith
Rooms: 21 (5 PB; 16 SB) $67.09-102.40
Full Breakfast
Credit Cards: A, B, C, D
Closed Feb.
Notes: 2, 4, 6, 7, 8, 9, 10, 11, 12, 13, 14

STANDISH

B&B of Maine 65

32 Colonial Village
Falmouth, ME, 04105
(207) 781-4528

A gracious colonial farmhouse, c. 1795, just twenty miles northwest of Portland. Private waterfront on lake just across the road with good swimming, fishing, and use of canoe or rowboat. Comfortably screened porch overlooks the lake. Ideal location for foliage viewing, and the 70 acres offer dozens of trails for cross-country skiing. Ski rental shop nearby. Full breakfast. Large first-floor room with double bed, private bath, and fireplace. Sunny second-floor room has twin beds, private bath, private entrance. Another single room adjoins this room for third person in party. Not suitable for children or pets. Two poodles in residence. $35-45.

STONINGTON

B&B of Maine 41

32 Colonial Village
Falmouth, ME, 04105
(207) 781-4528

Wonderful old house overlooking Penobscot Bay. Great spot to view the windjammers as they ply the coastal waters. Located on Deer Isle, which is reached by a two-lane bridge. Centrally located to the charming village, this B&B is open in the high summer months and available on a weekly basis other months of the year. Resident cat, continental breakfast buffet. There is a large guest room with water view and a smaller room. $40-50.

SUNSET

Goose Cove Lodge

Goose Cove Road
Sunset, ME, 04683
(207) 348-2508

Seventy acres of nature trails and one-half mile of ocean frontage with beaches. Cottages and rooms are rustic, with private baths, fireplaces, and sun decks overlooking the ocean. Modified American Plan mid-June to mid-September; B&B in the spring and fall. One-week minimum stay in July and August.

Hosts: George & Elli Pavloff
Rooms: 10 (PB) $80-90
Cottages: 11 (PB) $90-100
Full breakfast summer; continental spring & fall
Credit Cards: No
Closed Oct. 15-May 1
Notes: 2, 3, 4, 8, 9, 10, 11, 12

SURRY

The Surry Inn

P.O. Box 25
Surry, ME, 04684
(207) 667-5091

Two gracious buildings on sprawling grounds provide warmth, comfort, and exceptional dining. The main house, built in 1834, served as lodging for stage and steamship passengers in the last century. The expansive grounds have shore walks and a beach with the warmest saltwater bathing in the area. There is croquet, horseshoes, a canoe, and a rowboat. Located midway between Mt. Desert Island and lovely Deer Island.

Host: Peter Krinsky
Rooms: 13 (11 PB; 2 SB) $48-62
Full Breakfast
Credit Cards: A, B
Notes: 2, 4, 5, 7, 8 (over 5), 9, 10, 11, 12, 13, 14

THOMASTON

B&B of Maine 34

32 Colonial Village
Falmouth, ME, 04105
(207) 781-4528

This lovely midcoastal village on the outskirts of Camden and Rockland offers reasonable B&B accommodations. The large Cape Cod home rests among many historic homes once owned by sea captains. The genial hosts offer a hearty breakfast. Three comfortable rooms share two baths. $45.

TOPSHAM

Middaugh B & B

36 Elm Street
Topsham, ME, 04086
(207) 725-2562

Located in the historic district and listed on the National Register of Historic Places, this 150-year-old Federal Greek Revival home is ten minutes from L.L. Bean and Freeport. Centrally located between Camden, Boothbay Harbor, and Portland. A Maine coastal route home with a family atmosphere.

Hosts: Dewey & Mary Kay Nelson
Rooms: 2 (PB) $50-60
Full Breakfast
Closed Christmas
Credit Cards: No
Notes: 2, 8 (over 4), 10, 12

WALDOBORO

B&B of Maine 32

32 Colonial Village
Falmouth, ME, 04105
(207) 781-4528

Built in 1825, this Federal home sits on over 3 acres of nicely landscaped property. Beautifully restored woodwork, arched doorways, spiral staircase grace this spacious home. There is a 94-foot wraparound

Broad Bay Inn and Gallery & B&B

granite terrace where a hearty breakfast is served on good days. All guest rooms share several baths; three have working fireplaces. No children under twelve; restricted smoking; no pets. $45-64.

Broad Bay Inn and Gallery B&B

Box 607
Waldoboro, ME, 04572
(207) 832-6668

Lovingly restored 1830 inn, handsomely appointed with Victorian furnishings, canopy beds, paintings, candlelight dinner by reservation only. Breakfast banquet feasts and afternoon tea or sherry on the deck. Established art gallery in the barn. Walk down to the river, to tennis, theater, antique shops. A short drive to the lighthouse, Audubon sanctuary, and fishing villages. Send for your free brochure.

Hosts: Jim & Libby Hopkins
Rooms: 5 (S3B) $35-70
Full Breakfast
Credit Cards: A, B, C
Closed Jan.
Notes: 2, 4, 7 (limited), 8 (over 10), 9, 10, 11, 12, 13, 14

The Roaring Lion

Box 756
Waldoboro, ME, 04572
(207) 832-4038

A 1905 Victorian home with tin ceilings; elegant woodwork throughout. We cater to special diets and serve miso soup, sourdough bread, homemade jams and jellies. Hosts are well traveled and lived two years in West Africa. Their interests are books, gardening, art, and cooking.

Hosts: Bill & Robin Branigan
Rooms: 4 (1 PB; 3 SB) $53.50-64.20
Full Breakfast
Credit Cards: No
Notes: 2, 5, 8, 10, 11, 12, 13

WATERFORD

Lake House

Routes 35 & 37
Waterford, ME, 04088
(207) 583-4182

Lake House is one of 21 buildings in Waterford "Flat" listed on the National Historic Register. The inn was established in the 1790s. For much of the nineteenth century, it served as the Maine Hygienic Institute for Ladies. From the 1890s to 1940, it was operated as a hotel.

Hosts: Michael & Suzanne Uhl-Myers
Rooms: 4 (PB) $69-89
Full Breakfast
Credit Cards: A, B
Notes: 2, 4, 5, 9, 10, 12, 13, 14

The Parsonage House B&B and Wilderness Camping Area

Rice Road, P.O. Box 116
Waterford, ME, 04088
(207) 583-4115

The Parsonage, built in 1870 and elegantly restored, overlooks historic Waterford Village and Keoka Lake. It is surrounded by tranquil mountains and scenic beauty. Enjoy relaxing on the porch or engaging in a variety of local activities. Hearty breakfasts served.

Hosts: Joseph & Gail St-Hilaire
Rooms: 3 (1 PB; 2 SB) $42.80-53.50
Full Breakfast
Credit Cards: No
Notes: 2, 11, 12, 13

The Waterford Inne

Box 149
Waterford, ME, 04088
(207) 583-4037

Escape to country quiet in an inn offering the elegance of a fine country home. Ten uniquely decorated guest rooms and carefully furnished common rooms provide a fine setting for four-star dining in historic Waterford. Near mountains and coastline; water and woodland activities nearby.

Hosts: Barbara & Rosalie Vanderzanden
Rooms: 10 (7 PB; 3 SB) $60-100
Full Breakfast
Credit Cards: C
Closed March & April
Notes: 2, 4, 7, 8, 9, 10, 11, 12, 13 (XC), 14

WELLS

Purple Sandpiper Guest House

RR 3, Box 226C
Wells, ME, 04090
(207) 646-7990

We are located on Rt. 1, minutes from the beach. Our rooms are comfortably furnished with private baths, cable TV, and refrigerators. Continental breakfast includes fresh-baked muffins and coffeecakes. Miniature golf, tennis, and restaurants are within walking distance.

Hosts: Paul & Sandi Goodwin
Rooms: 6 (PB) $36-62
Continental Breakfast
Credit Cards: A, B, C
Closed mid-Oct.-mid-May
Notes: 2, 7, 8, 9, 10, 11, 12, 14

WELLS BEACH

B&B of Maine 6

32 Colonial Village
Falmouth, ME, 04105
(207) 781-4528

Located just a few hundred yards from the pounding surf and sandy beach in a secluded residential area. Near all resort attractions, this comfortable home is clean and inviting. Piano available to guests. Resident dog; outside picnic area. Full breakfast. All rooms share bath. Open June through October. $45-50.

WESTPORT ISLAND

B&B of Maine 49

32 Colonial Village
Falmouth, ME, 04105
(207) 781-4528

Complete privacy at the end of a dirt road. The island is reached by car over a causeway. This 1792 Federal farmhouse overlooks a huge expanse of water and has a private island that can be reached by a path at low tide. Artists, photographers, and writers will feel especially at home here. There are coves to explore and fields to roam. The spacious, comfortable home is on the National Register of Historic Places. Home not suitable for children or pets; smoking outside only. One double room has a private bath. A twin room shares a bath. Continental breakfast. Open through early fall. $50-60.

WEST SULLIVAN

B&B of Maine 45

32 Colonial Village
Falmouth, ME, 04105
(207) 781-4528

Fifty-year-old colonial home decorated with a European flair, conveniently located just off Route 1 only 27 miles east of Bar Harbor. Hosts are French-speaking and invite you to enjoy the peacefulness of this country home that overlooks Taunton Bay. Just a short drive from the coves and beaches of Winter and Prospect Harbor. Explore Schoodic Point. Good restaurants in the area. Bicycles are available for guests, and picnic lunches will be packed for a nominal fee with advance notice. A generous breakfast is served on the sun porch overlooking the bay. Resident cat and dog. No smoking. Guest rooms have private and shared baths. $55.

WINTHROP

B&B of Maine 64

32 Colonial Village
Falmouth, ME, 04105
(207) 781-4528

Watch the ducks and geese in the small pond in the backyard, or walk through to meadow to a large lake for a swim. Help gather eggs for breakfast, or watch cows being milked in the evening. The Shakespeare Theatre is only ten minutes away; the State Museum in Augusta is also worth a visit. Take a day for shopping in Freeport, which is only a half hour away. This farmhouse dates back to 1811. All rooms share a bath. Full country breakfast. $40.

The Squire Tarbox Inn

WISCASSET

The Squire Tarbox Inn

RR 2, Box 620
Wiscasset, ME, 04578
(207) 882-7693

A handsome antique farmhouse on a country road near midcoast Maine harbors, beaches, antique shops, and museums. The proper balance of history, quiet country, good food, and relaxation. Serves a delicious homemade goat cheese by the fire before dinner. Known primarily for rural privacy and five-course dinners. Daily rate includes breakfast and five-course dinner.

Hosts: Karen & Bill Mitman
Rooms: 11 (PB) $130-190
Continental-plus Breakfast
Credit Cards: A, B, C, D
Closed late Oct.-mid-May
Notes: 2, 4, 7 (limited), 8 (over 14), 9, 14

The Stacked Arms

RR2, Box 146
Wiscasset, ME, 04578
(207) 882-5436

All bedrooms decorated in different styles, each with a small refrigerator; ceiling fans in all upstairs rooms. Within thirty minutes of many day trips to museums, beaches, boat trips, shopping outlets, L.L. Bean, quaint fishing villages, and the Bath Iron Works, where naval vessels are built.

Hosts: Dee & Sean Maquire
Rooms: 5 (SB) $65-80
Full Breakfast
Credit Cards: A, B
Notes: 2, 4, 5, 7 (limited), 8 (over 5), 9, 10, 11, 12, 13, 14

Dockside Guest Quarters

YORK

Dockside Guest Quarters

Harris Island Road, Box 205
York, ME, 03909
(207) 363-2868

The Dockside Guest Quarters is a small resort on a private peninsula in York Harbor. Panorama of ocean and harbor activities. Spacious grounds with privacy and relaxing atmosphere. Accommodations are in an early seacoast lodge and modern, multiunit cottages.

Hosts: The Lusty Family
Rooms: 21 (19 PB: 2 SB) $48-117
Continental-plus Breakfast, lunch, cocktails, dinner
Minimum stay weekdays & weekends: 2; holidays: 3
Credit Cards: A, B
Closed Oct. 22-May 1
Notes: 2, 3, 4, 6, 7, 8, 9, 10, 11, 12, 14

Scotland Bridge Inn

One Scotland Bridge Road
York, ME, 03909
(207) 363-4432

The Scotland Bridge Inn is a place as special as Maine itself. A perfect place to stay during all four seasons. Relax in our living room, walk through our herbal English garden. Put your feet up on our veranda and watch the world go by. Full breakfast and afternoon tea are served.

Rooms: 3 (1 PB; 4 SB) $42.80-90.95
Full Breakfast
Credit Cards: A, B
Notes: 2, 4, 5, 8, 9, 10, 11, 12, 13 (XC)

The Wild Rose of York

78 Long Sands Road
York, ME, 03909
(207) 363-2532

An 1814 captain's house on a hill, with large porch and columns, very colonial, with a working fireplace in one room and a four-poster bed. Another room is smaller, with an attached sun porch, nonworking fireplace, and 100-year-old high-back oak bed. The third room is on the first floor with a queen bed and single bed. The house is located just over a mile from the beach.

Hosts: Fran & Frank Sullivan
Rooms: 3 (PB) $50-65
Full Breakfast
Credit Cards: No
Notes: 2, 8, 9, 10, 11, 12, 13 (XC)

YORK HARBOR

York Harbor Inn

Box 573, Route 1A
York Harbor, ME, 03911
(207) 363-5119; (800) 343-3869

Coastal country inn overlooking beautiful York Harbor, located in an exclusive residential neighborhood. Thirty-two air-conditioned rooms with antiques and ocean views, seven working fireplaces. Fine dining with ocean views year-round, and there's an English pub on the premises with entertainment. The beach is within walking distance, and boating, fishing, antique shops are all nearby.

Hosts: Joe, Jean, Garry & Nancy Dominguez
Rooms: 32 (PB) $55-120
Continental Breakfast
Credit Cards: A, B, C
Notes: 2, 3, 4, 5, 7, 8, 9, 10, 11, 12, 14

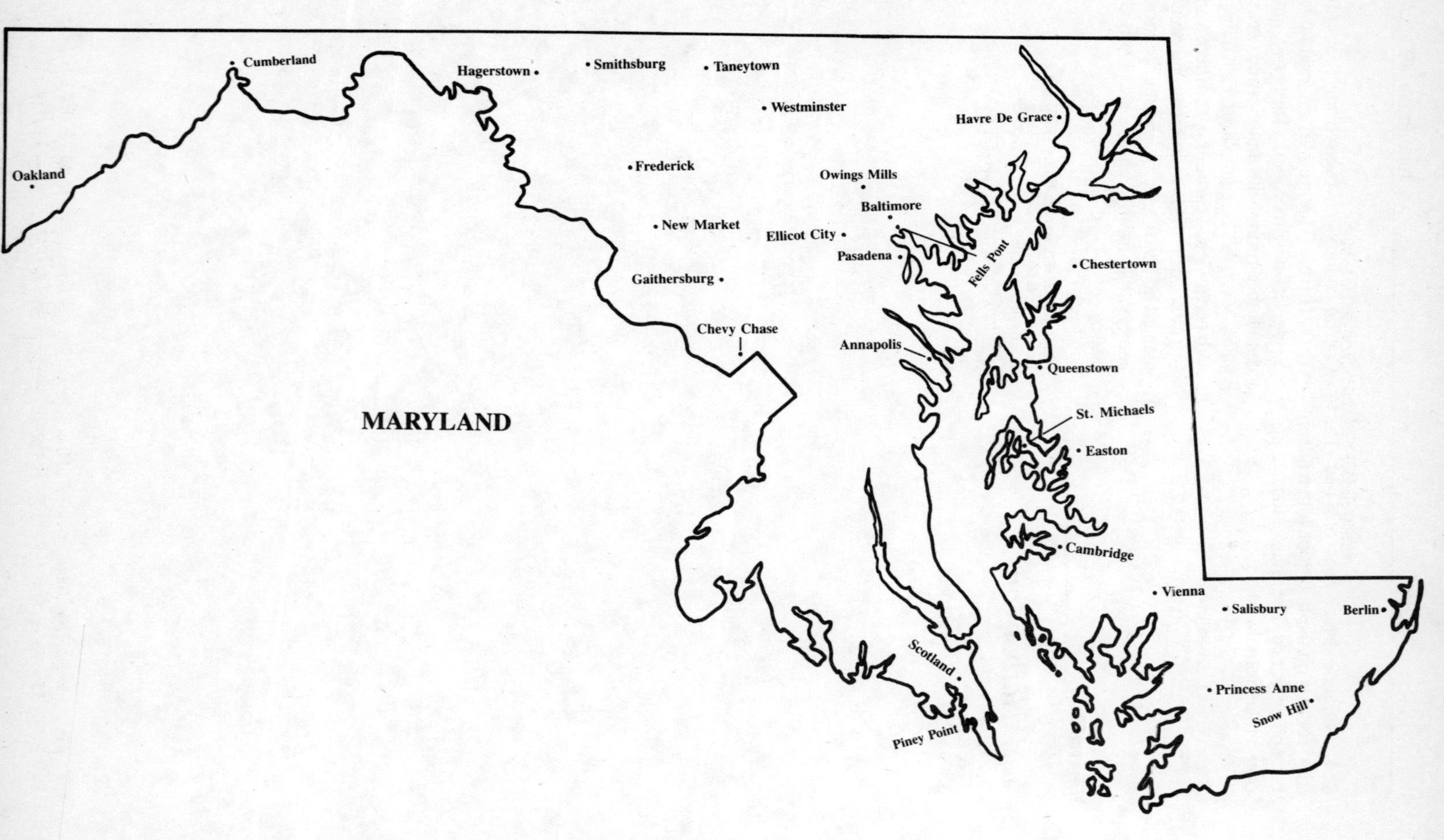
MARYLAND
Oakland
Cumberland
Hagerstown
Smithsburg
Taneytown
Westminster
Havre De Grace
Frederick
Owings Mills
Baltimore
New Market
Ellicot City
Pasadena
Fells Pont
Chestertown
Gaithersburg
Chevy Chase
Annapolis
Queenstown
St. Michaels
Easton
Cambridge
Vienna
Salisbury
Berlin
Scotland
Princess Anne
Snow Hill
Piney Point

Maryland

ANNAPOLIS

Amanda's B&B Service 1

1428 Park Avenue
Baltimore, MD, 21217
(301) 225-0001

On the water, with a boat dock, pool, and hot tub. Contemporary with two rooms just minutes from downtown Annapolis. Lovely setting, with sunsets to enjoy from the balcony overlooking the water. One room with a queen bed and private bath; another with a king bed and private bath. $65-75.

Amanda's B&B Service 2

1428 Park Avenue
Baltimore, MD, 21217
(301) 225-0001

In town, just a step from the Naval Academy, the docks, shops, restaurants, and historic sites. Elegant lodging with comfort and convenience for a relaxed, eventful trip to Annapolis. Private garden apartment with king bed and private bath; colonial suite with a double bed and private bath. $115-145.

Gibson's Lodgings

110 Prince George Street
Annapolis, MD, 21401
(301) 268-5555

Historic twenty-room inn with a conference room for business and private gatherings. A combination of charm and elegance. Located half a block from the city dock.

Host: Jeanne Schrift
Rooms: 20 (7 PB; 13 SB) $68-120
Continental Breakfast
Credit Cards: A, B, C
Notes: 2, 5, 8, 9, 12

The Jonah Williams House, 1830

101 Severn Avenue
Annapolis, MD, 21403
(301) 269-6020

Convenient to shopping, restaurants, and boating, just one block to the water taxi and two minutes to the city dock and the Naval Academy. Plenty of parking. A Laura Ashley historic environment.

Hosts: Dorothy & Hank Robbins
Rooms: 6 (1 PB; 5 SB) $70
Continental Breakfast
Credit Cards: No
Notes: 2, 5, 8 (10 and over), 9, 10, 11, 12

Murphy's B&B

125 Conduit Street
Annapolis, MD, 21401
(301) 974-9030

Three-story Victorian house in the heart of historic Annapolis. Comfortable, homelike accommodations. Lace curtains, hardwood floors, large living room with TV, brick courtyard. Two blocks from shops, restaurants, city dock, historic sites, Naval Academy.

Hosts: Dennis & Kerry Murphy
Rooms: 3 (SB) $65
Continental Breakfast
Credit Cards: No
Notes: 2, 5, 7 (restricted), 8, 9, 11, 12

Prince George Inn B&B

232 Prince George Street
Annapolis, MD, 21401
(301) 263-6418

This Victorian townhouse in the historic district offers antique-filled guest rooms and immaculate shared baths. A charming parlor with fireplace, sunny breakfast porches, and lovely garden are for guests' enjoyment. Easy walk to nearby shops, restaurants, dock, and Naval Academy.

Hosts: Norma & Bill Grovermann
Rooms: 4 (SB) $78.75
Buffet Breakfast
Credit Cards: A, B, C
Notes: 2, 7, 8 (12 and over), 9, 10, 12

Shaw's Fancy B&B

161 Green Street
Annapolis, MD, 21401
(301) 263-0320

Shaw's Fancy is located in the heart of historic Annapolis. Midweek, business, or romantic getaway packages available. The house is decorated in a mix of graceful Victorian furniture, lace, and fantasy art. Enjoy our garden and our hot tub.

Hosts: Jack House & Lilith Ren
Rooms: 3 (2 PB; 1 SB) $68.50-131.25
Suites available to sleep up to 4
Continental Breakfast
Credit Cards: No
Notes: 2, 5, 8 (over 10), 9

BALTIMORE

Admiral Fell Inn

888 South Broadway
Baltimore, MD, 21231
(301) 522-7377

Located on the waterfront, this charming historic inn houses 38 guest rooms that are uniquely appointed with antiques and fine reproductions. Our restaurant features New American cuisine and seafood specialties in an intimate atmosphere as well as light fare and spirits in our casual English-style pub.

Host: Dominike Eckenstein
Rooms: 40 (PB) $94-125
Continental Breakfast
Credit Cards: A, B, C
Notes: 2, 3, 4, 5, 7, 8, 9, 11, 12, 14

Amanda's B&B Service 5

1428 Park Avenue
Baltimore, MD, 21217
(301) 225-0001

Restored downtown Federal row house with courtyard, off-street parking. Within walking distance of the Inner Harbor. Spacious accommodations and delicious breakfast. Each room is decorated and coordinated in a different motif. Restaurants are within walking distance. Four rooms with double beds share two baths. $65.

Amanda's B&B Service 8

1428 Park Avenue
Baltimore, MD, 21217
(301) 225-0001

Located in Union Square, a historic neighborhood in downtown Baltimore, five minutes from the Inner Harbor. In an area of 1848 Victorian row houses, near the Mt. Clare Mansion, B&O Railroad Museum, Hollins Market, and H.L. Mencken House. The neighborhood is a mix of older families and young professionals. Two rooms, each with private bath; one with fireplace. $75.

Amanda's B&B Service 9

1428 Park Avenue
Baltimore, MD, 21217
(301) 225-0001

In Bolton Hill, a neighborhood on both the city and national historic registries. Primarily residential, just seven minutes from the Inner Harbor or a walk of just over a mile. A four-story row house with large rooms, interesting wall groupings, and an extensive collection of brass rubbings executed by the owner from original brasses in England. Queen room with private bath and king or twin room with shared bath. $60-65.

Amanda's B&B Service 12

1428 Park Avenue
Baltimore, MD, 21217
(301) 225-0001

Charming, quaint, nineteenth-century twelve-foot-wide row house in the Federal Hill/Cross Street Market Historic District. Eclectically rehabilitated to provide twentieth-century amenities. The Inner Harbor is an easy five to fifteen minute walk. Nearby commuter train service to Washington, DC. One room with queen bed and shared bath. $60.

Celie's Waterfront B&B

1714 Thames Street
Baltimore, MD, 21231
(301) 522-2323

Situated on Baltimore Harbor. Ideal for business or pleasure. Seven guest rooms with the charm of an antique-filled home. Some rooms have whirlpools, fireplaces, private balconies, and harbor views. All have access to a private garden and roof deck overlooking the harbor. Minutes to Harborplace and the central business district.

Host: Celie Ives
Rooms: 7 (PB) $95-140
Continental Breakfast
Credit Cards: A, B, C, D
Notes: 2 (with credit card), 5, 8 (over 10), 9, 10, 11, 12, 14

Mr. Mole

1601 Bolton Street
Baltimore, MD, 21217
(301) 728-1179

In the city on historic Bolton Hill, this 1840s townhouse offers tree-lined streets, period decor, and many antiques. Grand piano in music room. Suites, some with two bedrooms and sitting room. Garage parking. Walk to the symphony, opera, and metro; close to Johns Hopkins University and Inner Harbor, without the congestion.

Hosts: Collin Clarke & Paul Bragaw
Rooms: 5 (PB) $75-125
Continental Breakfast
Credit Cards: A, B
Notes: 2, 5, 9

Mulberry House

111 West Mulberry Street
Baltimore, MD, 21201
(301) 576-0111

An 1830 townhouse in downtown Baltimore with antiques, stained glass, crystal and brass chandeliers, Oriental rugs, Steinway grand piano, and fireplaces. Walk to most points of interest, including Harborplace, the convention center, the aquarium, and all the best restaurants.

Hosts: Charlotte & Curt Jeschke
Rooms: 4 (S2B) $65
Full Breakfast
Credit Cards: No
Notes: 2, 5, 8 (over 16), 9

Shirley Madison Inn

205 West Madison Street
Baltimore, MD, 21201
(301) 728-6550

Built in 1880, our historically registered urban inn re-creates the past with elegant antique furniture, fourteen-foot ceilings, original woodwork, and floor-to-ceiling windows. Our downtown location in Baltimore's historic Mt. Vernon residential district is a short walk to the Inner Harbor, "antique row," museums, and a host of dining alternatives. Enjoy our complimentary continental breakfast and evening aperitif.

Hosts: Rick Fenstemaker, Stanley Gondzar, Irene Borowicz
Rooms: 25 (PB) $55-105
Continental Breakfast
Credit Cards: A, B, C, E
Notes: 2, 4, 5, 7, 8, 9, 14

Society Hill Government House

1125 North Calvert Street
Baltimore, MD, 21202
(301) 752-7722

Eighteen spacious guest rooms, elegantly decorated with antiques and artwork. Complimentary continental breakfast, local telephone calls, parking, and city van service. Wine and coffee in the parlor.

Hosts: Linda Cooley
Rooms: 18 (PB) $100-120
Continental Breakfast
Credit Cards: A, B, C
Notes: 2, 5, 7, 8, 9, 10, 11, 12, 14

Society Hill Hopkins

3404 St. Paul Street
Baltimore, MD, 21218
(301) 235-8600

A beautiful 26-room urban inn located near Johns Hopkins University and the Baltimore Museum of Art. Only ten minutes from the Inner Harbour. Conference space available. Free parking, van service, local phone calls. Styles of rooms and suites varies—Federal, Art Deco, Contemporary—some with kitchenettes.

Hosts: Joanne Fritz & Douglas Pence
Rooms: 26 (PB) $90-135
Continental-plus Breakfast
Credit Cards: A, B
Notes: 2, 3, 4, 5, 7, 8, 9, 10, 12, 14

Society Hill Hotel

58 West Biddle Street
Baltimore, MD, 21201
(301) 837-3630; FAX: (301) 837-4654

A delightful converted townhouse within walking distance of the Meyerhoff Symphony Hall and Lyric Opera House, antique and boutique rows. This fifteen-room inn offers the exciting combination of a B&B and an American country inn. Brass beds, fresh flowers, rich Victorian furniture; breakfast served to your room. The hotel has a bar and restaurant on the premises, as well as a jazz piano bar.

Host: Kate Hopkins
Rooms: 15 (PB) $105-125
Continental Breakfast
Credit Cards: A, B
Notes: 2, 3, 4, 5, 7, 8, 9, 14

Twin Gates B&B Inn

Twin Gates B&B Inn

308 Morris Avenue
Baltimore, MD, 21093
(301) 252-3131; (800) 635-0370

Experience serene elegance in this Victorian mansion near the National Aquarium, Harborplace, and Maryland Hunt Country.

Friendly hosts, wine and cheese, and gourmet breakfasts.

Hosts: Gwen & Bob Vaughan
Rooms: 7 (3 PB; 4 SB) $85-95
Full Breakfast
Minimum stay weekends & holidays: 2
Credit Cards: A, B, C
Notes: 2, 5, 9, 10, 12, 14

BERLIN

Atlantic Hotel Inn & Restaurant

2 North Main Street
Berlin, MD, 21811
(301) 641-3589

Restored Victorian hotel with sixteen period-furnished rooms. A National Register building in the historic district. Elegant dining and piano lounge on the premises. Located eight miles west of Ocean City and Assateague Island National Seashore. Walk to nearby antique shops, gallery, and museum.

Host: Stephen T. Jacques
Rooms: 16 (PB) $55-90
Continental Breakfast
Credit Cards: A, B
Notes: 2, 3, 4, 5, 7, 8, 9, 10, 11, 12, 14

CAMBRIDGE

Sarke Plantation Inn

6033 Todd Point Road
Cambridge, MD, 21613
(301) 228-7020

An Eastern Shore waterfront property of 27 country acres with a spacious house that is furnished tastefully with many antiques. There is a large pool room with a regulation table, and the living room has a large fireplace, a good stereo system, and a grand piano for your enjoyment.

Host: Genevieve Finley
Rooms: 5 (3 PB; 2 SB) $50-90
Continental Breakfast
Credit Cards: A, B, C
Closed New Year's Eve
Notes: 2, 6, 7, 8 (over 10), 9, 11

CHESTERTOWN

The Inn at Mitchell House

RD 2, Box 329
Chestertown, MD, 21620
(301) 778-6500

Nestled on 10 rolling acres, surrounded by woods and overlooking a pond, this historic manor house, built in 1743, greets you with warmth and affords a touch of tranquility. A mere half mile from the Chesapeake, this six-bedroom inn, with parlors and numerous fireplaces, provides a casual, friendly atmosphere.

Hosts: Jim & Tracy Stone
Rooms: 6 (PB) $75-90
Full Breakfast
Credit Cards: A, B
Notes: 2, 5, 7, 8, 9, 10, 11, 12

The White Swan Tavern

The White Swan Tavern

231 High Street
Chestertown, MD, 21620
(301) 778-2300

The White Swan Inn has been a landmark in Chestertown since pre-Revolutionary days. A quiet, elegant place nestled on Maryland's Eastern Shore, with a history that goes back to before 1733, the White Swan was returned to its original purpose in 1978: "A comfortable tavern or Public House . . . situated in the center of business . . . with every attention given to render comfort and pleasure to such as favor it with their patronage."

Host: Mary Susan Maisel
Rooms: 6 (PB) $75-125
Continental Breakfast
Credit Cards: No
Notes: 2, 5, 7, 8, 9, 10, 11, 12, 14

CHEVY CHASE

Chevy Chase B&B

6815 Connecticut Avenue
Chevy Chase, MD, 20815
(301) 656-5867

Enjoy gracious hospitality and the convenience of being close to the sights of Washington, DC, in a charming beamed-ceiling, turn-of-the-century house and garden in historic Chevy Chase. Furnished with rare tapestries, Oriental rugs, and native crafts from around the world.

Host: S.C. Gotbaum
Rooms: 2 (PB) $55
Continental Breakfast
Credit Cards: No
Notes: 2, 5, 7, 8, 10, 11, 12

CUMBERLAND

Amanda's B&B Service 16

1428 Park Avenue
Baltimore, MD, 21217
(301) 225-0001

An 1820 Federal home, recently restored to a B&B. Cumberland is in western Maryland, with many scenic places to explore. Bicycle rentals, canoe trips arranged, day hikes, horseback riding, and rock climbing are available in the area. There are seven rooms with private and shared baths. $60-70.

EASTON

Amanda's B&B Service 10

1428 Park Avenue
Baltimore, MD, 21217
(301) 225-0001

Built in 1890, this large Victorian home has a wraparound porch, high octagonal tower, a roof hipped with dormers, and nicely appointed rooms. Located just a few minutes from St. Michael's. All rooms have air-conditioning, ceiling fans, and private baths. $75.

ELLICOTT CITY

Amanda's B&B Service 11

1428 Park Avenue
Baltimore, MD, 21217
(301) 225-0001

A picturesque little town with charming shops, old railroad stop, and antiques—resembles an old European mountain village. The stately Federal-period stone farmhouse sits on 2 acres with a pond. All rooms are air-conditioned. Four rooms, two with private bath, one with fireplace. $70-90.

FELLS POINT

Amanda's B&B Service 4

1428 Park Avenue
Baltimore, MD, 21217
(301) 225-0001

In the heart of Fells Point is a nicely decorated and furnished home with three rooms, each with private bath. Fells Point is a bustling area of the harbor with many restaurants and shops. In the summer you can ride the water taxi to the Inner Harbor or take the trolley. Two rooms with fireplaces for wintertime enjoyment, one without; all three rooms have double beds and private baths. $75-85.

FREDERICK

Middle Plantation Inn

9549 Liberty Road
Frederick, MD, 21701
(301) 898-7128

A rustic B&B built of stone and log. Drive through horse country to the village of Mt. Pleasant. Located several miles east of Frederick, on 25 acres. Each room has furnishings of antiques, with private bath, air-conditioning, and TV. Nearby are antique shops, museums, and many historic attractions.

Hosts: Shirley & Dwight Mullican
Rooms: 2 (PB) $75-85
Continental Breakfast
Credit Cards: No
Notes: 2, 5, 8 (15 and over), 9, 10, 11, 12, 14

"Spring Bank," A B&B Inn

7945 Worman's Mill Road
Frederick, MD, 21701
(301) 694-0440

An NRHP 1880 sixteen-room country house filled with antiques. Six spacious guest rooms, parlor with fireplace, and library of early books on Maryland history. Situated within 10 acres of lawn, walking paths, and crop land. Frederick's charming historic district, with its excellent restaurants, is within a ten-minute drive.

Hosts: Beverly & Ray Compton
Rooms: 6 (1 PB; 5 S2.5B) $70-85
Continental Breakfast
Credit Cards: A, B, C, D
Notes: 2, 5, 9, 10, 11, 12, 14

Turning Point Inn

3406 Urbana Pike
Frederick, MD, 21701
(301) 874-2421

Turning Point Inn is a lovely 1910 Edwardian estate home with Georgian features. Less than an hour from the Washington, DC, Baltimore, Gettysburg, and Antietam areas, this inn is situated for getaway weekends of sight-seeing, shopping, antiquing, hiking, or exploring nearby historic towns and battlefields.

Hosts: Charlie & Suzanne Seymour
Rooms: 5 (PB) $75-85
Full Breakfast
Credit Cards: A, B
Notes: 2, 3, (Tues.-Fri.), 4 (Tues.-Sun.), 5, 7 (limited), 8, 9, 10, 11, 12

Turning Point Inn

GAITHERSBURG

Gaithersburg Hospitality B&B

18908 Chimney Place
Gaithersburg, MD, 20879
(301) 977-7377

Located in Montgomery Village, near restaurants, shopping, and recreation, this luxury home is furnished in family pieces with your comfort and pleasure in mind. It offers all amenities and is convenient (30 minutes) to Washington, DC, via the Metro or your car. Home cooking!

Hosts: Joe & Suzanne Danilowicz
Doubles: (PB) $50 + tax
Singles: (PB) $40
Full Breakfast
Credit Cards: No
Closed Jan. 15-Feb. 15
Notes: 2, 8, 9, 10, 11, 12, 14

HAGERSTOWN

Lewrene Farm B&B

RD 3, Box 150
Hagerstown, MD, 21740
(301) 582-1735

Close to I-70 and I-81 on a quiet 125-acre farm near Antietam Battlefield, Harpers Ferry, the C&O Canal. Baltimore and Washington, DC, are only seventy miles away. Colonial-style home with antique furnishings, large living room, fireplace, deluxe bedrooms. Hostess speaks English and Spanish. Quilts for sale.

Hosts: Lewis & Irene Lehman
Rooms: 6 (3 PB; 3 SB) $45-70
Full Breakfast
Credit Cards: No
Notes: 2, 5, 8, 10, 11, 12

Lewrene Farm B&B

HAVRE DE GRACE

Vandiver Inn

301 South Union Avenue
Havre de Grace, MD, 21078
(301) 939-5200

Turn-of-the-century charm and Victorian hospitality await the visitor to historic Havre de Grace's only guest inn. Tastefully appointed rooms, fireplaces, and culinary delights designed to reward the overnight guest. Use the inn as a home base for walking to the decoy museum, the Concord Point Lighthouse, the historic Lockhouse, or Antique Row.

Hosts: Mark & Jill Traub
Rooms: 8 (6 PB; 2 SB) $65-85
Full Breakfast
Credit Cards: A, B, C
Notes: 2, 4, 5, 7, 8 (over 12), 9, 10, 11, 12, 14

NEW MARKET

National Pike Inn

9 West Main Street
Box 299
New Market, MD, 21774
(301) 865-5055

This Federal house, built in the early 1800s, offers a special charm that must be shared. Each guest room has its own special decor. Shop for antiques, dine in excellence, or simply stroll the streets of this quaint village fifteen minutes from Frederick and thirty minutes from Harpers Ferry. Small conference area available on request.

Hosts: Tom & Terry Rimel
Rooms: 5 (2 PB; 3 SB) $65-100
Continental-plus Breakfast
Credit Cards: A, B
Notes: 2, 5, 7, 8 (over 5), 10, 12, 13

The Strawberry Inn

17 Main Street
Box 237
New Market, MD, 21774
(301) 865-3318

An 1840 Maryland farmhouse that's completely restored. Each guest room has its own private bath, and rooms are tastefully furnished with comfortable antiques. Common room with wood-burning fireplace for wine or tea after a day of antique shopping in "The Antique Capital of Maryland." Restaurant across the street.

Hosts: Jane & Ed Rossig
Rooms: 5 (PB) $65-90
Continental Breakfast
Credit Cards: No
Notes: 2, 5, 7, 9, 10, 11, 12

OAKLAND

Red Run Inn

Route 5, Box 268
Oakland, MD, 21550
(301) 387-6606

Nestled in a natural wooded setting, Red Run overlooks the expansive blue waters of Deep Creek Lake. On 18 acres, with a large swimming pool, two tennis courts, cross-country ski trail, horseshoe pits, and dock facilities.

Host: Ruth M. Umbel
Rooms: 6 (PB) $65-100
Continental Breakfast
Credit Cards: A, B, C
Closed Nov. 15-May 1
Notes: 7, 8, 9, 10, 11, 12, 13, 14

OWINGS MILLS

Amanda's B&B Service 6

1428 Park Avenue
Baltimore, MD, 21217
(301) 225-0001

Northwest of Baltimore, this Victorian country colonial was originally built 150 years ago. Recently updated without losing the charm of the original house. Convenient to I-795, a large shopping mall, downtown, or activities in Baltimore County. One room with double bed and private bath. $65.

PASADENA

Amanda's B&B Service 3

1428 Park Avenue
Baltimore, MD, 21217
(301) 225-0001

Fifteen minutes from Annapolis, facing the water in a lovely setting that is quiet and peaceful. One double room with private bath and one queen room with private bath. $75-80.

PINEY POINT

Amanda's B&B Service 15

1428 Park Avenue
Baltimore, MD, 21217
(301) 225-0001

Enjoy the southern part of Maryland from this bayside bungalow with water in the front and back. Watch the sunset and listen to the water lap from the gazebo on the bayside. Minutes from St. Mary's and Solomon's. The house, a rambling ranch, offers three rooms. Breakfast may be on the porch facing the water or in the dining area. Private baths. $75.

Elmwood c. 1770 B&B

PRINCESS ANNE

Elmwood c. 1770 B&B

Locust Point Road
Box 220
Princess Anne, MD, 21853
(301) 651-1066

This historic manor house has a wonderful setting on 160 acres of fields, woods, and lawn, with a mile of waterfront and commanding view of the Manokin River. The goal of the innkeepers is to surround their guests with the life-style of the nineteenth century and tranquility.

Hosts: Helen & Steve Monick
Rooms: 4 (SB) $75-109.25
Cottages: 2 (PB) $95 two-night minimum
Full Breakfast
Credit Cards: A, B
Closed Christmas, New Year's & Easter weekends
Notes: 2, 7 (limited), 8 (12 and over), 9, 10, 14

QUEENSTOWN

Amanda's B&B Service 7

1428 Park Avenue
Baltimore, MD, 21217
(301) 225-0001

Get a jump start on a trip around the Eastern Shore by spending several nights in this quaint small town just across the Bay Bridge. Uniquely designed architecture, traditional furnishings, antiques, and wicker. Five rooms with private baths. $65.

ST. MICHAELS

Kemp House Inn

412 Talbot Street
St. Michaels, MD, 21663
(301) 745-2243

Built in 1805 by Col. Joseph Kemp, who commanded the local militia in the War of 1812 (Robert E. Lee was a guest in the house). Four-poster beds with trundle beds underneath, period furnishings, fireplaces, candlelight, tab curtains, and flannel nightshirts.

Hosts: Diane & Steve Cooper
Doubles: 7 (3 PB; 4 SB) $50-100
Type of Beds: 3 Twin; 4 Double; 3 Queen
Continental Breakfast
Minimum stay weekends: 2; holidays: 3
Credit Cards: A, B
Notes: 2, 5, 7, 8, 9, 12, 14

Wades Point Inn on the Bay

P.O. Box 7
St. Michaels, MD, 21663
(301) 745-2500

On the Eastern Shore of Chesapeake Bay, this historic country inn is ideal for those seeking country serenity and bay splendor. The main house (c. 1819) was built by a noted shipwright, and from 1890 to the present, the inn has provided a peaceful setting for relaxation and recreation such as fishing, crabbing, and a one-mile nature and jogging trail on the inn's 120 acres. Chesapeake Bay museum, cruises, and sailing charters are nearby.

Hosts: Betsy & John Feiler
Rooms: 24 (14 PB; 10 SB) $65-155
Continental Breakfast
Credit Cards: A, B
Closed major winter holidays & Feb.
Notes: 2, 8, 9, 10, 11, 12

SALISBURY

Amanda's B&B Service 14

1428 Park Avenue
Baltimore, MD, 21217
(301) 225-0001

Colonial home on 5 acres nestled among trees, some over 200 years old. Formerly the homestead of a journalist nominated for the Pulitzer Prize. The four beautifully decorated rooms encircle the center hall staircase and have private baths. $50-65.

SCOTLAND

St. Michael's Manor B&B

St. Michael's Manor & Vineyard
Scotland, MD, 20687
(301) 872-4025

St. Michael's Manor (1805) was originally patented to Leonard Calvert in 1637. The house, located on Long Neck Creek, is furnished with antiques. Boating, canoeing, bikes, swimming pool, and wine-tasting are available. Near Pt. Lookout State Park, Civil War monuments, and historic St. Mary's City.

Hosts: Joseph & Nancy Dick
Rooms: 3 (SB) $35-55
Full Breakfast
Credit Cards: No
Notes: 2, 5, 7 (limited), 8, 9, 10, 11

SMITHSBURG

Blue Bear B&B

Route 2, Box 378
Holiday Drive
Smithsburg, MD, 21783
(301) 824-2292

Country charm and warm, friendly hospitality await you at the Blue Bear. There are two beautifully decorated and air-conditioned rooms with a shared bath. Enjoy a delicious breakfast of fresh fruits, breads and pastries, and quiche. We want you to feel at home here.

Host: Ellen Panchula
Rooms: 2 (SB) $30-40
Continental Breakfast
Credit Cards: No
Notes: 2, 5, 8 (over 12), 10, 11, 12

SNOW HILL

Snow Hill Inn

104 East Market Street
Snow Hill, MD, 21863
(301) 632-2102

Five comfortable, air-conditioned guest rooms with private and semi-private baths. Inviting living room with fireplace for relaxing, reading, or socializing. On-site restaurant offers weekday lunches and weekend candlelight dining indoors and outdoors. Near golf, boat rides, canoeing, biking, and tennis.

Hosts: The Quillens
Rooms: 5 (2 PB; 3 SB) $50.20-70.20
Continental Breakfast
Credit Cards: A, B
Notes: 2, 3, 4, 5, 7, 8, 9, 10, 11, 12

TANEYTOWN

Amanda's B&B Service 13

1428 Park Avenue
Baltimore, MD, 21217
(301) 225-0001

An antebellum mansion on 24 acres, carefully restored and decorated with exquisite detail and period antiques. Clay tennis court, gardens, and croquet court. Four rooms, each with canopy bed, fireplace, and private bath. $125.

Glenburn

3515 Runnymede Road
Taneytown, MD, 21787
(301) 751-1187

Glenburn is a circa 1840 Georgian home with Victorian additions. Guest rooms overlook pasture, lawns, woods with creek. European and American antiques. Exceptional setting for a getaway. Close to Gettysburg; sixty miles from Washington, DC. Agricultural and recreational area with historic interest.

Hosts: Robert & Elizabeth Neal
Rooms: 5 (3 PB; 2 SB) $65-100
Full Breakfast
Credit Cards: No
Notes: 2, 5, 7 (restricted), 9, 10, 11, 12, 13

VIENNA

The Tavern House

Box 98
Vienna, MD, 21869
(301) 376-3347

A colonial tavern on the Nanticoke River featuring the simple elegance of colonial living and special breakfasts that are a social occasion. A glimpse into Michener's *Chesapeake* for those who love colonial homes, the peace of a small town, or watching osprey in flight.

Hosts: Harvey & Elise Altergott
Rooms: 4 (SB) $60-65
Full Breakfast
Credit Cards: A, B
Notes: 2, 5, 7, 8 (over 12), 9, 10, 14

WESTMINSTER

The Winchester Country Inn

430 South Bishop Street
Westminster, MD, 21157
(301) 876-7373

Built in the 1760s by the founder of Westminster, the Winchester Country Inn is one of Carroll County's oldest buildings. Various recreational facilities and historic points of interest abound around the inn, which is centrally located in Maryland. The refurbished interior makes this one of the most delightful and refreshing country inns open to the public.

Rooms: 5 (3 PB; 2 SB) $55-70
Full Breakfast
Credit Cards: A, B
Notes: 2, 5, 7 (limited), 8 (6 and over), 9, 10, 11, 12

The Winchester Country Inn

NOTES: Credit cards accepted: A Master Card; B Visa; C American Express; D Discover Card; E Diners Club; F Other: 2 Personal checks accepted: 3 Lunch available: 4 Dinner available: 5 Open all year

Massachusetts

ADAMS

Bascom Lodge

Box 1652
Lanesboro, MA, 02137
(413) 743-1591

A rustic stone-and-wood lodge on the summit of Mt. Greylock, fifty feet from the great Appalachian Trail, that features an all-you-can-eat breakfast and dinner, bunk-style dormitory, private accommodations, and 100-mile views.

Hosts: Appalachian Mountain Club
Rooms: 3 (SB) $55
Bunks: 26 (SB) $25
Full Breakfast
Credit Cards: A, B
Closed mid-Oct.-mid-May
Notes: 2, 4, 8, 11, 12

AMHERST

Berkshire B&B Homes PV17

P.O. Box 211
Williamsburg, MA, 01096
(413) 268-7244

A 1968 Garrison colonial with traditional and antique furnishings. Parlor for guest use. Two twin rooms, semiprivate bath. Continental breakfast, no smoking, children welcome. $45-55.

ASHFIELD

Ashfield Inn

Main Street, Box 129
Ashfield, MA, 01330
(413) 628-4571

An elegant Georgian mansion on over 9 acres of grounds boasting formal gardens, woods, and manicured lawns. Attractions include historic Deerfield Village, the Mohawk Trail, antique shopping, festivals, cross country and downhill skiing, maple sugaring, foliage.

Hosts: Craig & Colette Christian
Rooms: 8 (S4B) $79.28-100.42
Full Breakfast on weekends; Continental on weekdays; MAP available
Credit Cards: A, B, C
Notes: 2, 3, 4, 5, 6, 8, 9, 10, 11, 12, 13

ATTLEBORO

B&B Affiliates MA238

P.O. Box 3291
Newport, RI, 02840
(401) 849-1298

Comfortable country decor creates a homey atmosphere in this new colonial home. Relax in a traditional sitting room, an informal sitting room with wood stove, or a backyard deck. A swing set is available for children. Two double rooms with shared bath, full breakfast. Pets in residence; guest dog permitted. Children are welcome, and a portacrib is available. $55-65.

AUBURN

Capt. Samuel Eddy B&B Inn

609 Oxford Street South
Auburn, MA, 01501
(508) 832-5282

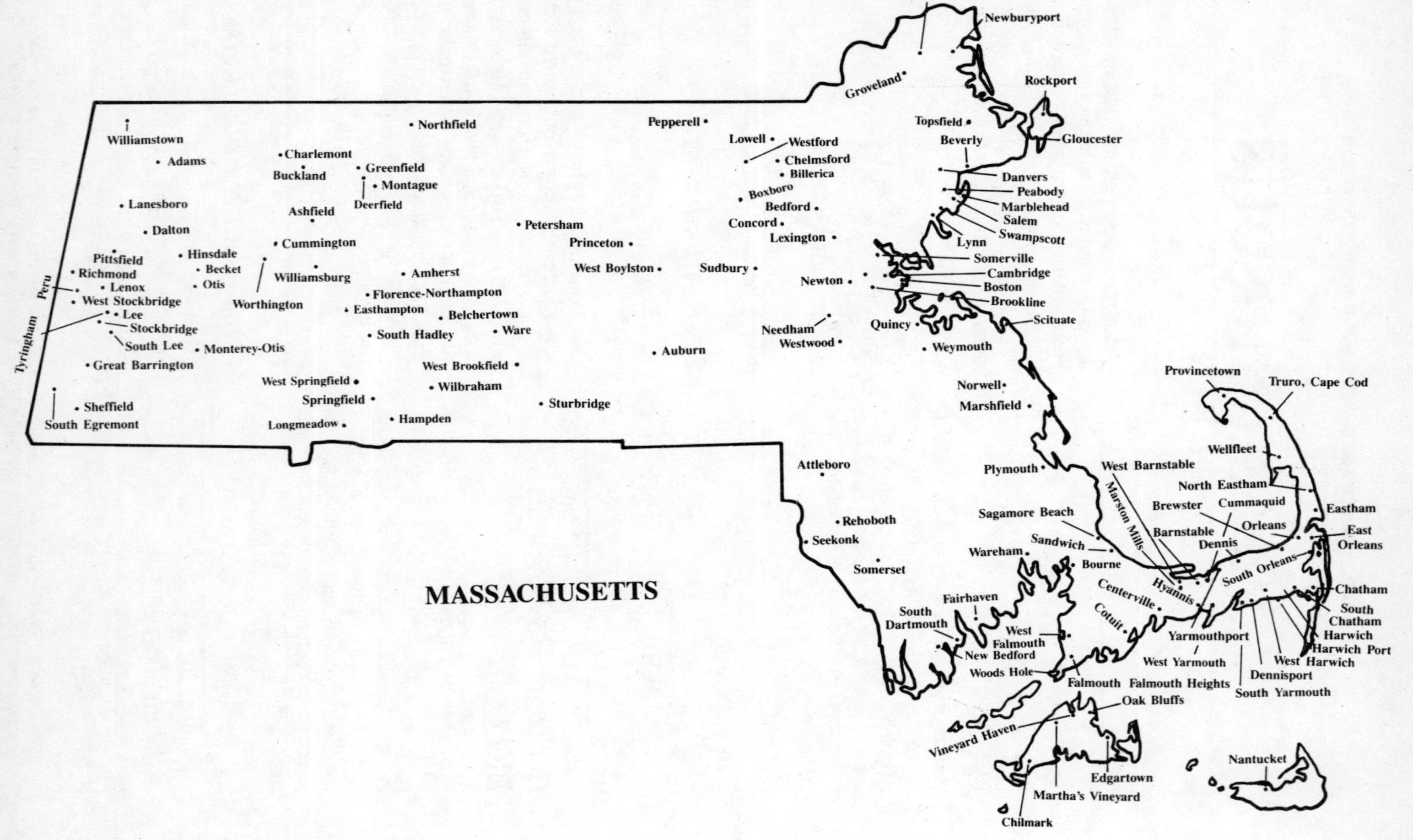
MASSACHUSETTS
Williamstown
Adams
Lanesboro
Dalton
Pittsfield
Richmond
Peru
Lenox
West Stockbridge
Lee
Stockbridge
South Lee
Tyringham
Great Barrington
Sheffield
South Egremont
Hinsdale
Becket
Otis
Monterey-Otis
Charlemont
Buckland
Ashfield
Cummington
Williamsburg
Worthington
Greenfield
Montague
Deerfield
Northfield
Amherst
Florence-Northampton
Easthampton
South Hadley
Belchertown
Ware
West Springfield
Springfield
Longmeadow
Hampden
West Brookfield
Wilbraham
Sturbridge
Petersham
Princeton
West Boylston
Auburn
Pepperell
Lowell
Westford
Chelmsford
Billerica
Boxboro
Bedford
Concord
Lexington
Sudbury
Newton
Needham
Westwood
Groveland
West Newbury
Newburyport
Rockport
Gloucester
Topsfield
Beverly
Danvers
Peabody
Marblehead
Salem
Swampscott
Lynn
Somerville
Cambridge
Boston
Brookline
Scituate
Quincy
Weymouth
Norwell
Marshfield
Attleboro
Rehoboth
Seekonk
Somerset
Plymouth
Sagamore Beach
Sandwich
Bourne
Wareham
Fairhaven
South Dartmouth
New Bedford
West Falmouth
Woods Hole
Falmouth
Falmouth Heights
Cotuit
Centerville
Hyannis
Marston Mills
West Barnstable
Barnstable
Brewster
Cummaquid
Dennis
Orleans
South Orleans
Yarmouthport
West Yarmouth
South Yarmouth
Dennisport
West Harwich
Harwich Port
Harwich
South Chatham
Chatham
East Orleans
Eastham
North Eastham
Wellfleet
Truro, Cape Cod
Provincetown
Oak Bluffs
Vineyard Haven
Edgartown
Martha's Vineyard
Chilmark
Nantucket

Come join us and step back in time to the warmth and charm of the eighteenth century in our 1765 inn. Antiques throughout, canopy beds, and common rooms with fireplaces. Breakfast is served in the sun room overlooking the herb gardens and pool area. Close to Sturbridge Village, thirteen colleges, and Boston. Visit our Country Shop.

Hosts: Jack & Carilyn O'Toole
Rooms: 5 (PB) $50-85
Full Breakfast
Credit Cards: A, B
Notes: 2, 3, 4, 5, 8, 9, 10, 11, 12, 14

Ashley Manor

BARNSTABLE (CAPE COD)

Ashley Manor

Box 856
Barnstable, MA, 02630
(508) 362-8044

Ashley Manor is a very special place, a gracious 1699 mansion on a 2-acre estate in Cape Cod's historic district. Romantic rooms and suites feature private baths and fireplaces. Elegant public rooms with antiques, Oriental rugs. Delicious full breakfast in formal dining room or on terrace overlooking parklike grounds and new tennis court. Walk to the beach and village.

Hosts: Donald & Fay Bain
Rooms: 6 (PB) $100-165
Full Breakfast
Minimum stay weekends: 2
Credit Cards: A, B, C
Notes: 2, 5, 7 (limited), 8 (over 14), 9, 10, 11, 12, 14

Beechwood

2839 Main Street
Barnstable, MA, 02630
(508) 362-6618

Beechwood is a carefully restored Queen Anne Victorian located in the heart of Cape Cod's north shore historic district. The rooms are furnished with unusual antique pieces. The wraparound veranda, shaded by ancient beech trees, is a perfect place to relax in the hammock or rockers. Short walk to town, harbor, or beach.

Hosts: Anne & Bob Livermoie
Rooms: 6 (PB) $95-135
Full Breakfast
Credit Cards: A, B, C
Notes: 5, 9, 10, 11, 12, 14

Charles Hinckley House

Box 723
Barnstable, MA, 02630
(508) 362-9924

Small, intimate country inn in historic Barnstable. Circa 1809 Federal gem listed on the National Register. Fireplace suites with private baths, four-poster beds, and English country breakfasts. A five-minute walk down a country lane to Cape Cod Bay; 1.5 miles to Barnstable harbor and all boating activities. Golf and tennis are within minutes, and museums, beaches, antique and craft shops are abundant.

Hosts: Les & Miya Patrick
Rooms: 4 (PB) $109-139
Full Breakfast
Credit Cards: No
Notes: 2, 3, 4, 5, 9, 10, 11, 12, 14

Cobb's Cove

Box 208
Barnstable, MA, 02630
(508) 362-9356

Our colonial timbered manor overlooks Barnstable Village, the harbor, and Cape Cod Bay. Walk to the beach and whale-watch boat. All rooms have a full bath with whirlpool tub and toweling robes. Enjoy our keeping room, with its huge Count Rumford fireplace, and breakfast on the peaceful garden patio.

Hosts: Evelyn Chester & Henri-Jean
Rooms: 6 (PB) $139-169
Full Breakfast
Credit Cards: A, B
Notes: 2, 5, 7, 9, 10, 11, 12, 14

Genny's B&B

B&B Cape Cod 27
P.O. Box 341
West Hyannisport, MA, 02672
(508) 775-2772

This 1852 renovated Victorian is a few steps off the Old Kings Highway. Each guest room has decorative wall coverings, period furnishings, and fresh flowers. All have private baths. Outside, a wraparound porch provides a place to relax after a day at the beach or shopping in nearby antique stores. $65-70.

Honeysuckle Inn

591 Main Street
Barnstable, MA, 02668
(508) 362-8418

Charming restored farmhouse, circa 1810, on the National Registry of Historic Places. Features feather beds, English country breakfast, afternoon tea on the screened porch. All rooms have private baths with fluffy terry-cloth robes and homemade cookies at bedside. Large great room with TV. Near beautiful Sandy Neck Beach. Bicycles and beach towels are available for guests.

Hosts: Barbara & Bob Rosenthal
Rooms: 3 (PB) $90-105
Full Breakfast
Credit Cards: A, B, C, D
Notes: 2, 5, 7, 9, 10, 11, 12, 14

Thomas Huckins House

2701 Main Street
P.O. Box 515
Barnstable, MA, 02630
(508) 362-6379

Experience the charm of old Cape Cod. Sleep in canopy beds next to working fireplaces in this restored 1705 house. Breakfast in the antique-filled keeping room; walk to the ocean and village through the historic district on the Cape's picturesque and less-crowded North Shore.

Hosts: Burt & Eleanor Eddy
Rooms: 3 (PB) $75-95
Full Breakfast
Credit Cards: A, B
Notes: 2, 5, 7, 8 (over 6), 9

BASS RIVER

Old Cape House

108 Old Main Street
Bass River, MA, 02664
(508) 398-1068

Enjoy warm hospitality in the English tradition in our circa 1815 Greek Revival house. All rooms are furnished New England style, with lacy curtains and quilts. Garden and porch for relaxation. Enjoy a plentiful breakfast of home-baked muffins and breads. Close to several fine beaches, golf, sailing, fishing, shops, and restaurants.

Hosts: George & Linda Arthur
Rooms: 4 (PB) $55-65
Continental Breakfast
Credit Cards: No
Closed Oct. 20-May 20
Notes: 2 (for deposits), 8 (over 15), 9, 10, 11, 12

BECKET

Canterbury Farm

Fred Snow Road
Becket, MA, 01223
(413) 623-8765

Seventeenth-century B&B, secluded on 200 acres, with cross-country skiing and summer gardens. A full breakfast with fresh bread and homemade maple syrup is served. Five minutes to Jacob's Pillow, lakes, trails, camps; Tanglewood is nearby. Children are welcome.

Hosts: Linda & David Bacon
Rooms: 4 (1 PB; 3 SB) $60-80
Full Breakfast
Credit Cards: No
Notes: 2, 3, 5, 8, 9, 10, 11, 12, 13, 14

Old Cape House

BEDFORD

Bed & Breakfast Folks BB3

48 Springs Road
Bedford, MA, 01730
(617) 275-9025

An old colonial home with fireplaces, wide-board pine floors, and exposed old brick and wood, in the historic district, close to the center of town. Convenient to Cambridge, Lexington, Boston, and Concord. From $50.

BELCHERTOWN

Berkshire B&B Homes PV5

P.O. Box 211
Williamsburg, MA, 01096
(413) 268-7244

1839 Victorian in a small New England town. Living room with fireplace. Double bed, private bath, double pullout, single bed. Shared bath. Continental breakfast, no smoking. Animal in residence. Children twelve and over are welcome. $30-60.

Berkshire B&B Homes PV23

P.O. Box 211
Williamsburg, MA, 01096
(413) 268-7244

1850 colonial with colonial furnishings. Large living room and book-filled library for guests' use. Double-bed room with private bath; single bedroom with shared bath. Full breakfast, no smoking, children welcome. Pet in residence. $30-60.

Berkshire B&B Homes PV29

P.O. Box 211
Williamsburg, MA, 01096
(413) 268-7244

1850 Federal Greek Revival on 13 acres. Antique furniture. Double bed and twin bed available; semiprivate bath. Full breakfast, no smoking, children welcome. $45-55.

BEVERLY

Beverly Cove B&B

B&B Marblehead & North Shore
P.O. Box 172
Beverly, MA, 01915
(508) 921-1336

Very attractive split level just a two-minute walk from a private beach in a quiet area close to Endicott College. Three rooms with shared baths. Restricted smoking, full breakfast. Children over nine are welcome; one resident cat. Each room has TV, and there is a refrigerator for guest use. $54.

Lady Slippers B&B

B&B Marblehead & North Shore
P.O. Box 172
Beverly, MA, 01915
(508) 921-1336

Dutch colonial, attractive family home facing the ocean. The hostess speaks some Spanish and Hebrew. Four rooms, one with a private bath. No smoking; children welcome; one dog in residence. Continental breakfast. $40-75.

Ryal Side B&B

B&B Marblehead & North Shore
P.O. Box 172
Beverly, MA, 01915
(508) 921-1336

An attractive colonial home close to Route 128 with three rooms, one of which has a private bath. No smoking, no pets; children are welcome. Continental breakfast. $55-65.

BILLERICA

Bed & Breakfast Folks BB6

48 Springs Road
Bedford, MA, 01730
(617) 275-9025

A lovely waterfront home with a separate king bedroom and bath on the second floor. Includes private balcony overlooking the river. From $50.

BOSTON

B&B Associates Bay Colony IW280

P.O. Box 57166
Babson Park Branch
Boston, MA, 02157-0166
(617) 449-5302

Located near the Mass. Turnpike (Route 90) just west of town, this twenty-five room Queen Anne home offers convenience and elegance. Breakfast is served in the second-floor sitting room, with its restored hand-painted ceiling. A small refrigerator and microwave are available for guests. Two rooms, shared bath. Continental breakfast, restricted smoking. Children are welcome. Two resident dogs. Hosts speak French. $75.

B&B Associates Bay Colony M104

P.O. Box 57166
Babson Park Branch
Boston, MA, 02157-0166
(617) 449-5302

Those seeking the charm of an old European hotel will enjoy this prestigious private club, with its elegant drawing room and gracious dining room. Convenient to Newbury Street shops, historic sites, and the Hynes Convention Center. Four rooms, two with private bath. Children welcome, smoking permitted, continental breakfast. $65.83-93.25.

B&B Associates Bay Colony M107

P.O. Box 57166
Babson Park Branch
Boston, MA, 02157-0166
(617) 449-5302

In Beacon Hill, just two blocks from the public gardens and the quaint shops and cafes that line Charles Street. An exquisitely furnished brick Federal townhouse with fine antiques. Three rooms with shared baths, continental breakfast, children over six are welcome, smoking permitted. $85.

B&B Associates Bay Colony M110

P.O. Box 57166
Babson Park Branch
Boston, MA, 02157-0166
(617) 449-5302

Stay in the heart of Old Boston on Beacon Street near Copley Square, the Hynes Convention Center, the Charles River, and Boston University. A three-story townhouse graced with high ceilings and large rooms. Five rooms, one with private bath. Continental breakfast, smoking allowed, children welcome. Two small dogs in residence. $75-85.

B&B Associates Bay Colony M314

P.O. Box 57166
Babson Park Branch
Boston, MA, 02157-0166
(617) 449-5302

Selected as one of the "100 Best B&Bs in America," this fine 1863 brick townhouse offers three guest rooms, each meticulously restored. Guests return often, so reservations are necessary. Private baths, full breakfast, no smoking. Children over ten are welcome. $97.

B&B Associates Bay Colony M319

P.O. Box 57166
Babson Park Branch
Boston, MA, 02157-0166
(617) 449-5302

This nineteenth-century brick townhouse is on a pretty, quiet street near Copley Square. Your hostess, an artist who restores antique needlework, has blended Victorian and contemporary furnishings. Three rooms, one with private bath. Continental breakfast, no smoking, resident cat. Children over six welcome. $65-78.

B&B Associates Bay Colony M480

P.O. Box 57166
Babson Park Branch
Boston, MA, 02157-0166
(617) 449-5302

This 1799 Charlestown landmark has recently been restored. Guests will enjoy this unique little stone house just five minutes away from downtown by public transit. Steep stairs to second-floor guest rooms. Two rooms, shared bath. Full breakfast. From $80.

B&B Associates Bay Colony M817

P.O. Box 57166
Babson Park Branch
Boston, MA, 02157-0166
(617) 449-5302

Located on the northern perimeter of Harvard, this spacious Victorian offers comfort and convenience. Your hosts are well-traveled and speak Italian, French, Spanish, German, Russian, Mandarin, Cantonese, and Japanese. Two rooms with shared bath. Generous continental breakfast. $60.

Greater Boston Hospitality 7

P.O. Box 1142
Brookline, MA, 02146
(617) 277-5430

This outstanding home offers four elegant "fantasy bedrooms." The British Officers Room has a double bed and private library. The French Dining Room offers a king bed with French antiques. A London drawing room has a queen canopy bed and sitting area. The China Trade Room has a queen four-poster bed. All rooms have private baths, air-conditioning, and telephones. Full breakfast is served in your room. High tea and refreshments are served in the library in the afternoon. Limited smoking. Minutes to Copley Square, Copley Place, and the Prudential Center. $125-135.

Greater Boston Hospitality 12

P.O. Box 1142
Brookline, MA, 02146
(617) 277-5430

A registered historic home erected in 1799. This petite gray quarry stone townhouse boasts pumpkin-pine floors and authentic Williamsburg colors. A brick guest room with fireplace and combed paneling overlooks the linden trees of a small city park. There is a double four-poster bed and private bath, air-conditioning, and TV. Continental breakfast; no smoking; children welcome. Within walking distance of Quincy Market, Faneuil Hall, and the Freedom Trail. $80.

Greater Boston Hospitality 14

P.O. Box 1142
Brookline, MA, 02146
(617) 277-5430

A turn-of-the-century brick townhouse located on a major street two miles from downtown. Nine double rooms with private baths and five with shared baths. Many of the rooms have an extra twin bed. Seven decorative fireplaces and high ceilings. Continental breakfast; washer and dryer available; parking included. All rooms with private baths are air-conditioned. $54-78.

Greater Boston Hospitality 16

P.O. Box 1142
Brookline, MA, 02146
(617) 277-5430

Located in the historic Back Bay area, this spacious condo offers a large double room with private connecting half bath. Full bath is off the hall. Enjoy relaxing in the living room overlooking Commonwealth Avenue. Built in 1900, this building was completely renovated in 1984. TV, air conditioning, garages nearby. Close to Boston University, Fenway Park, Copley Square, and Copley Place. $80.

Greater Boston Hospitality 19

P.O. Box 1142
Brookline, MA, 02146
(617) 277-5430

Beautiful 1940 custom-built home in a fine residential area. Set back on 2 acres of magnificent grounds. Close to Boston College, Boston University, Pine Manor, Harvard Medical area. Full breakfast. Smokers accepted. Large second-floor room with a double bed, single bed, and adjoining private bath. Lower-level library room has a queen sofabed, wood-burning stove, private half bath. $55-65.

Greater Boston Hospitality 20

P.O. Box 1142
Brookline, MA, 02146
(617) 277-5430

This B&B is at the foot of Beacon Hill, located across the street from Mass. General Hospital. It has a variety of twin and double rooms with shared baths. Kitchens on each floor. Children over five are welcome; full breakfast; parking not included. Private garage across street. Limited smoking. $52.

Greater Boston Hospitality 21

P.O. Box 1142
Brookline, MA, 02146
(617) 277-5430

In the Back Bay area, this classic 1890 brownstone is in one of Boston's finest residential areas, minutes from the Public Garden, fine shops, and scores of restaurants. Four large guest rooms with mahogany furniture and floors. Each room has twin beds and a private adjoining bath. Lunch and dinner are available with reservations. Children welcome, smoking permitted. $80.

Greater Boston Hospitality 22

P.O. Box 1142
Brookline, MA, 02146
(617) 277-5430

An elegant turn-of-the-century brownstone in Boston's Back Bay area includes two private single rooms with shared bath. High ceilings, nice appointments, in prime location. Lunch and dinner available by reservation. Parking extra. Continental breakfast. Adults only. $60.

Greater Boston Hospitality 23

P.O. Box 1142
Brookline, MA, 02146
(617) 277-5430

This 1847 Greek Revival is less than 100 yards from the Freedom Trail and across the street from the second oldest (1640) park in Boston, where Revolutionary War, and later Civil War, troops trained. Climb an impressive staircase to your bedroom and large deck overlooking a garden courtyard. A private bath is included. One cat in residence. Full breakfast on weekends; continental on weekdays. Children over fourteen welcome. Air conditioned. $80.

Greater Boston Hospitality 24

P.O. Box 1142
Brookline, MA, 02146
(617) 277-5430

Surrounded by Copley Place, the Prudential Center, elegant shops, galleries, and fine restaurants, this B&B is in one of Boston's luxury high-rise apartments in a premier locale. Large twin room with private adjoining bath. Air conditioned. Continental breakfast. Parking available in garage under building. $82.

Greater Boston Hospitality 26

P.O. Box 1142
Brookline, MA, 02146
(617) 277-5430

Modeled after a small European inn, these two renovated townhouses comprise an intimate fifteen-room B&B located in the heart of Boston's Back Bay area, minutes from the Prudential Center, Copley Square, and the Christian Science Center. Continental breakfast and refreshments and hors d'oeuvres on the outdoor deck or in the living room. Central air conditioning; private phones; color TV. Smoking permitted. Fifteen well-appointed rooms with private and shared baths. $60-87.

Greater Boston Hospitality 28

P.O. Box 1142
Brookline, MA, 02146
(617) 277-5430

Stunning brick Federal home with nine fireplaces, a small greenhouse, and three guest rooms on the third floor. Pickled strip oak floors, Laura Ashley and Pied Deux fabrics. A queen room with private bath overlooks a hidden garden. Two additional rooms, one with a double four-poster bed and the other with a single bed, share a bath. Continental-plus breakfast. One dog and three cats in residence. Children welcome. $78-98.

Greater Boston Hospitality 29

P.O. Box 1142
Brookline, MA, 02146
(617) 277-5430

Gorgeous 1790 townhouse in the historic district offers a separate B&B floor with a double room, dining room, kitchen, and bath, living room and connecting roof deck. Breakfast is either served or stocked in your kitchen. No smoking. No parking, but garages are close. $85.

Greater Boston Hospitality 32

P.O. Box 1142
Brookline, MA, 02146
(617) 277-5430

Built in 1928 by Crocker Snow, this red brick home is listed in the National Historic Commission. Three large guest rooms, two with queens and one with twins, share 1.5 baths. Excellent full breakfast. Piano. Children are welcome. One dog and two cats in residence; no smoking; parking included. Walk to Harvard Medical area and the Museum of Fine Arts. $55.

Greater Boston Hospitality 36

P.O. Box 1142
Brookline, MA, 02146
(617) 277-5430

Conveniently located for driving in or out of Boston, this fine brick colonial offers two guest rooms with shared bath on a separate B&B floor. Adjoining den and patio off each bedroom. Color TV in each room. Children over eighteen are welcome; no smoking; parking included. $62.

Greater Boston Hospitality 37

P.O. Box 1142
Brookline, MA, 02146
(617) 277-5430

This unusual B&B is in a converted Georgian carriage house on a cul-de-sac in an outstanding neighborhood. Twin or queen room with private bath and guest sitting room. Glass door opens to a large patio where breakfast is sometimes served in the summer. Full breakfast; adults only; parking included. $84.

Greater Boston Hospitality 40

P.O. Box 1142
Brookline, MA, 02146
(617) 277-5430

Your English hostess offers a very large white colonial situated on over an acre of beautiful grounds. There are two large rooms that share a bath; one with a queen bed and the other with twins. Full breakfast, parking. Children over eight are welcome. No smoking. $60-75.

Greater Boston Hospitality 44

P.O. Box 1142
Brookline, MA, 02146
(617) 277-5430

This 1894 Victorian guest house is located in a quiet, elegant neighborhood of Victorian homes in the Dorchester section of Boston. Six rooms on the second floor, some with private and some with shared baths. Children are welcome; crib available. Substantial continental buffet breakfast. Near the World Trade Center, Bayside Exposition Center, Kennedy Library, the University of Massachusetts, Milton Academy. $50-70.

Greater Boston Hospitality 47

P.O. Box 1142
Brookline, MA, 02146
(617) 277-5430

Attractive center entrance colonial in a quiet residential neighborhood minutes from the Longwood medical area and the Museum of Fine Arts. Three rooms. The first has a king bed and private adjoining bath. The second has twin beds and shared bath. A smaller single room is also available. Parking is included. Adults and older children are welcome. $45-57.

Greater Boston Hospitality 125

P.O. Box 1142
Brookline, MA, 02146
(617) 277-5430

One-hundred-year-old condominium that has been completely renovated, across the street from one of Boston's wharves. Walk to Quincy market, Faneuil Hall, the North End. Modern double room with private bath and continental breakfast. Balcony view to the water and downtown financial district. No smoking. $75.

Greater Boston Hospitality 181

P.O. Box 1142
Brookline, MA, 02146
(617) 277-5430

A 1868 brick townhouse just minutes from the Hynes Convention Center, Copley Place, and the Prudential Center. Large, well-appointed room has a double bed and private bath. There is a single room for additional family member. TV, refrigerator, toaster oven, coffee maker; continental breakfast. Guest den and telephone. Children are welcome. No smoking. $75.

Greater Boston Hospitality 185

P.O. Box 1142
Brookline, MA, 02146
(617) 277-5430

Beautiful 1916 stucco home with five fireplaces, located in an historic area, offers a large twin or king room with private bath and working fireplace. Continental-plus breakfast. Children over eight are welcome. No smoking; parking included. $75.

BOURNE

Canalside B&B

B&B Cape Cod 53
P.O. Box 341
West Hyannisport, MA, 02672
(508) 775-2772

A 1988 contemporary castle-style house nestled along the banks of the Cape Cod Canal. The entire first floor is for B&B guests, including a living room with cable TV and a fireplace. One room has two twin beds and shares a bath with a second room with a queen waterbed. A suite offers a king bed and private bath. The second room in the suite has a queen pull-out bed and water view. Continental breakfast, no smoking, children fourteen and over are welcome. $60-80.

BOXBORO

Bed & Breakfast Folks BB4

48 Springs Road
Bedford, MA, 01730
(617) 275-9025

A charming contemporary home on a secluded country road, yet close to Route 495. From $50.

BREWSTER (CAPE COD)

The Bramble Inn

2019 Main Street
P.O. Box 807
Brewster, MA, 02631
(508) 896-7644

Three antique houses in the heart of the historic district, featuring one of the top three restaurants on the Cape. Within walking distance of tennis, the beach, shops, and restaurants. Just a short drive from Cape Cod National Seashore, Museum of Natural History, Cape Cod Rail Trail (seventeen-mile bike path), and Nickerson State Park.

Hosts: Ruth & Cliff Manchester
Rooms: 12 (PB) $85-125
Full Breakfast
Credit Cards: A, B, C, D, E
Closed Jan. 1-March 31
Notes: 2, 4, 7, 8 (over 8), 9, 10, 11, 12, 14

Captain Freeman Inn

15 Breakwater Road
Brewster, MA, 02631
(508) 896-7481

Charming old sea captain's mansion offers luxury suites with balcony, private spa, fireplace, canopy bed, TV, air- conditioning. Spacious rooms with canopy beds and private baths and rooms with shared bath. Enjoy the wraparound porch, outdoor pool, bikes, and full breakfast. Centrally located on Cape Cod's historic north side, close to beaches, restaurants, and shopping.

Hosts: John & Barbara Mulkey
Rooms: 12 (9 PB; 3 SB) $50-185
Full Breakfast
Credit Cards: A, B, D
Notes: 2, 5, 8 (12 and over), 9, 10, 11, 12, 14

The Deck House

Orleans B&B Associates
P.O. Box 1312
Orleans, MA, 02653
(508) 255-3824

Enjoy your own deck for watching gorgeous sunsets on 250-acre Upper Mill Pond. Custom-designed house has two large guest rooms on the second floor. Sliders provide private entrances. Guests share a large bath. Continental breakfast served on one of the decks overlooking the water. Swimming, canoeing, sailing, and windsurfing all at your doorstep. $65.

Isaiah Clark House & Rose Cottage

1187 Main Street
Brewster, MA, 02631
(508) 896-2223

Built in 1780, this inn was once the mansion of a famous sea captain and is set on 5 acres of land. All guests enjoy a full American breakfast served on a deck overlooking a private pond. Many guest rooms have working fireplaces. breakfast on a deck overlooking a private pond. Host was formerly a Swiss-trained hotelier. Special welcome for honeymooners.

Host: Charles Phillipe DiCesare
Rooms: 12 (8 PB; 4 SB) $62-105
Full Breakfast
Credit Cards: A, B, C, D
Notes: 5, 7 (limited), 8, 9, 10, 11, 12, 14

Lois's B&B

B&B Cape Cod
P.O. Box 341
Hyannisport, MA, 02672
(508) 775-2772

This large Greek Revival house has wide, shaded porches, broad lawns, a nearby wooded area, and trails for hiking. Directly to the rear of the property is a state-owned fresh-water pond. There are three guest rooms: one with private bath, two with shared. A continental breakfast is left in the lounge on the first floor, and there is a refrigerator and TV available for guests. Smoking is restricted; children three and over are welcome; two-night minimum stay. $54.

Ocean Gold

74 Locust Lane
Brewster, MA, 02631
(508) 255-7045

We have a private fresh-water pond near bike trails, tennis, golf, bay and ocean beaches. Gourmet breakfasts, our own chickens, fresh eggs daily, homemade breads, jams. Lovely flower gardens. Located next to Nickerson State Park.

Hosts: Marge & Jim Geisler
Rooms: 3 (1 PB; 2 SB) $65
Full Breakfast
Credit Cards: No
Notes: 2, 5, 9, 10, 11, 12, 14

Old Sea Pines Inn

2553 Main Street
Brewster, MA, 02631
(508) 896-6114

Lovely old turn-of-the-century mansion, once the "Sea Pines School of Charm and Personality for Young Women," now a newly renovated and redecorated country inn. Furnished with antiques, some of the rooms have working fireplaces. Situated on 3.5 acres of land, with a wraparound porch looking out over the lawn, trees, and flowers. Complimentary beverage on arrival.

Hosts: Stephen & Michele Rowan
Rooms: 16 (PB) $45-90
Full Breakfast
Credit Cards: A, B, C, E
Notes: 2, 5, 7, 8 (over 8), 9, 10, 11, 12, 14

Quail Hollow

Orleans B&B Associates
P.O. Box 1312
Orleans, MA, 02653
(508) 255-3824

Spacious grounds surround this charming eighteenth-century Cape farmhouse situated between two ponds. Your second-floor room has a queen bed, cable TV, and private bath. Across the hall, a single room is available for another family member ($25). Both rooms have a water view. Light breakfasts are served on a large screened porch overlooking the water. Canoe over to the lakeside beach for swimming or walk there in ten minutes. $65.

The Skep Garden

Orleans B&B Associates
P.O. Box 1312
Orleans, MA, 02653
(508) 255-3824

Ideally located for exploring the unique charms of historic Route 6A, yet off the beaten path in quiet surroundings. Bike path, tennis, and golf are minutes away; a short walk takes you to a private Cape Cod Bay beach. Two upstairs bedrooms are available for guests;. bath is shared if both rooms are occupied. Full breakfast is served in the dining room. $50.

Stonybrook

Orleans B&B Associates
P.O. Box 1312
Orleans, MA, 02653
(508) 255-3824

A pre-1776 restored colonial with a storybook setting next to the old grist mill and famous Stony Brook Herring Run. Private entrance to upstairs bedroom with fireplace, double bed, private bath, and sitting room. Attractive sitting area outside overlooks the mill pond. $60.

BROOKLINE

The Pleasant Pheasant

296 Heath Street
Brookline, MA, 02167
(617) 566-4178

The Pleasant Pheasant is located on 2 secluded acres. It boasts comfortable accommodations, complete amenities with full breakfast, and a hostess happy to make your stay a pleasant one. Located five miles west of Boston, near Boston College, Pine Manor College, Longwood Hospital, Harvard Medical School, and Boston University.

Host: Marian Ferguson
Rooms: 2 (1 PB; 1 SB) $50-70
Full Breakfast
Credit Cards: No
Closed Christmas week
Notes: 2, 5, 7, 8, 9, 10, 11, 12

BUCKLAND

1797 House

Upper Street-Clarlemont Road
Buckland, MA, 01338
(413) 625-2975

Our eighteenth-century home is located in a peaceful rural area, yet is convenient to many attractions and all points in New England. Large rooms, private baths, down quilts, and a lovely screened porch insure your comfort. We offer a modicum of civilization in an increasingly uncivilized world.

Host: Janet Turley
Rooms: 3 (PB) $55-65
Full Breakfast
Credit Cards: No
Closed Dec.
Notes: 2, 9, 10, 11, 12, 13

CAMBRIDGE

A Cambridge House B&B Inn

2218 Massachusetts Avenue
Cambridge, MA, 02140
(617) 491-6300; (800) 232-9989

Featured on TV by the BBC in Europe, Evening Magazine's TV coverage of "Discover New England." "Breakfasts not to be missed"—*Glamour* Magazine. "Our vote goes to A Cambridge House"—*Los Angeles Times.* The enchantment of historic Boston and Cambridge, a major New England oceanfront area attracting millions of worldwide tourists annually.

Hosts: Ellen Riley & Tony Femmino
Rooms: 10 (1 PB; 9 SB) $85-165
Full Breakfast
Credit Cards: A, B, C
Notes: 2, 5, 14

B&B Associates Bay Colony M875

P.O. Box 57166
Babson Park Branch
Boston, MA, 02157-0166
(617) 449-5302

A lovely large home in a quiet neighborhood adjacent to jogging paths. The home is just a twenty-minute walk from Harvard Square and features skylights, sliding doors to a deck, a playroom and fenced yard for children. Three rooms with private baths. Full breakfast. $55.

Greater Boston Hospitality 38

P.O. Box 1142
Brookline, MA, 02146
(617) 277-5430

This lovely 1890 Victorian is in a fine residential area only a fifteen-minute walk from Harvard Square. There is a double room and a single room, shared bath, and use of a large den with working fireplace. Continental-plus breakfast. One Siamese cat in residence. Children over fourteen welcome; no smoking; air- conditioned. $68.

Greater Boston Hospitality 42

P.O. Box 1142
Brookline, MA, 02146
(617) 277-5430

This 1890 late colonial home with three working fireplaces is in the prime Harvard Square area. Two guest rooms, each with two twins pushed together and a shared bath. Family-style full breakfast and use of the whole house, including a piano. Children are welcome; two cats and one dog in residence. $65.

CENTERVILLE

Adam's Terrace Gardens Inn

539 Main Street
Centerville, MA, 02632
(508) 775-4707

An old sea captain's home built around 1830, Terrace Gardens Inn is located in the village of Centerville on Captain's Row, within walking distance of churches, shops, a country store, library, and world-famous Craigville Beach. It is an excellent location for touring all parts of old Cape Cod and the islands of Nantucket and Martha's Vineyard.

Hosts: Pat & John Veracka
Rooms: 8 (5 PB; 3 SB) $50-65 + tax
Full Breakfast
Credit Cards: No
Notes: 2, 5, 8, 9, 10, 11, 12, 14

Bednark's B&B

B&B Cape Cod 43
P.O. Box 341
West Hyannisport, MA, 02672
(508) 775-2772

This contemporary Cape Cod home overlooks Lake Wequaquet, a freshwater lake that provides excellent recreational activities. The second floor has been set aside for B&B guests. There are three rooms, one with a private bath. Continental breakfast is served in the dining room or on the deck. Children are welcome, and smoking is permitted. Bring your small boat, wind surfer, and fishing pole and enjoy the lake. Golf course is half a mile away. The home is near Craigville Beach and the warm-water beaches of Nantucket Sound. $55-65.

Carver House

638 Main Street
Centerville, MA, 02632
(508) 775-9414

Flowers decorate a picket fence in front of the Carver House. The inn, located one-half mile from Craigville Beach, has three rooms with twin beds and TV; two rooms have sinks. Carver House is centrally located for golf, biking, tennis, and the island ferries.

Hosts: Marguerite & Harold MacNeely
Rooms: 3 (SB) $45
Continental Breakfast
Credit Cards: No
Notes: 2, 5, 7, 9, 10, 11, 12

Copper Beech Inn

497 Main Street
Centerville, MA, 02632
(508) 771-5488

Built in 1830 by an intercoastal ship captain, this charmingly restored house is now in the National Register of Historic Places. It stands amid tall trees including the largest European beech tree on Cape Cod. Interior features include a parlor and a common room for guest use. Walk to Craigville Beach, one of the ten best beaches in the United States. Hyannis, the population center of the Cape, where the ferry to Nantucket and Martha's Vineyard are located, is four miles away. Air-conditioning.

Host: Joyce Diehl
Rooms: 3 (PB) $80-85
Full Breakfast
Minimum stay May 25-Oct. 10: 2
Credit Cards: A, B, C
Notes: 2, 5, 7 (restricted), 8 (12 and over), 9, 10, 11, 12

Copper Beech Inn

CHARLEMONT

Forest Way Farm

Jacksonville Stage Road
Charlemont, MA, 01337
(413) 337-8321

This carefully restored circa 1812 mountaintop country inn reflects the ambience of rural New England. Family heirlooms, nicely decorated rooms, and farm breakfasts with homemade fixin's and grits make your stay an unforgettable experience.

Hosts: Jimmie & Paul Snyder
Rooms: 3 (S2.5B) $45-65
Full Breakfast
Minimum stay holidays: 2
Credit Cards: C
Notes: 2, 5, 7, 12, 13, 14

CHATHAM (CAPE COD)

Blue Heron

Orleans B&B Associates
P.O. Box 1312
Orleans, MA, 02653
(508) 255-3824

This elegant contemporary house is located in the hilly area surrounding Pleasant Bay, only a short walk from the beach. Second-floor guest room with king waterbed and skylight, sitting area, and luxurious bath. Another twin room can accommodate another couple or adult children ($60). Both rooms have color TV. Breakfast is served on a sunny deck overlooking seasonal gardens, or in the dining room. Low cholesterol breakfast is one of their specialties. $70.

The Bradford Inn & Motel

26 Cross Street
P.O. Box 750
Chatham, MA, 02633
(508) 945-1030

The Bradford Inn and Motel is a unique complex of twenty-five rooms located in the quaint seaside village of Chatham. The location is within the historic district, a short stroll from charming shops, theaters, concerts, restaurants, beach, golf, and tennis. Yet the accommodations are in a secluded area away from the hustle of the village proper.

Hosts: William & Audrey Gray
Rooms: 25 (PB) $80-165
Full Breakfast
Credit Cards: A, B, C, D
Notes: 2, 4, 5, 7, 8 (over 8), 9, 10, 11, 12, 14

The Bronze Bell

Orleans B&B Associates
P.O. Box 1312
Orleans, MA, 02653
(508) 255-3824

The Bradford Inn & Motel

Enjoy the seashore ambience of Cape Cod's "Elbow Town," with it unrivalled 67 miles of shoreline. Gracious New England hospitality awaits you at this traditional Cape home in a quiet residential section. A short walk takes you to Chatham's charming quaint village. The second floor has a private bath and expansive bedroom with TV, double bed, and two singles. Generous continental breakfast is served in the country room or on the patio. $60.

Chatham Bow B&B

B&B Cape Cod
P.O. Box 341
Hyannisport, MA, 02672
(508) 775-2772

This is a Cape Cod bow-roof reproduction built twelve years ago by the present owner, designed after an old colonial home in the area. Wide board floors, braided rugs, skylights, and a huge fireplace. Three guest rooms: two with private baths. A continental breakfast is available for guests from 8:00-9:30 A.M. daily. No smoking or pets; children are welcome. $50.

Chatham Town House Inn

11 Library Lane
Chatham, MA, 02633
(508) 945-2180; (800) 242-2180

Fashionable hotel-country inn with all amenities in a central Cape Cod location features nonsmoking dining rooms, breakfast, swimming pool and spa, canopy beds, balconies for romance. A honeymooner's dream. Come and be enchanted with our sea captain's mansion. Walk to the sea and all activities.

Hosts: Russell & Svea Peterson
Rooms: 24 (PB) $98-175
Full Breakfast
Credit Cards: All major
Notes: 2, 3, 5, 9, 10, 11, 12, 13, 14

Cranberry Inn at Chatham

359 Main Street
Chatham, MA, 02633
(508) 945-9232; (800) 332-4667

A tradition of excellence. Meticulously restored landmark inn located in Chatham's historic village district. Antique furnishings, four-poster beds, private baths, air-conditioning, telephone, TV, continental breakfast. Tavern. Fireplaced suites. Excellent beaches, shops, and restaurants all just steps away.

Hosts: Richard Morris & Peggy DeHan
Rooms: 14 (PB) $90-160
Continental-plus Breakfast
Credit Cards: A, B, C
Closed Jan. & Feb.
Notes: 2, 7, 8 (over 12), 9, 10, 11, 12, 14

The Cyrus Kent House Inn

63 Cross Street
Chatham, MA, 02633
(800) 338-5368

Comfortably elegant, the inn is an award-winning restoration of a nineteenth-century sea captain's mansion. Rooms are large, bright, and airy, furnished with antiques. Private baths. Conveniently located on a quiet lane in the quaint seaside village of Chatham—a historic district. Excellent restaurants and beaches are within steps.

Host: Richard Morris
Rooms: 8 (PB) $90-145
Continental Breakfast
Credit Cards: A, B, C
Closed Jan., Feb., March
Notes: 2, 7, 8 (over 12), 9, 10, 11, 12, 14

Cyrus Kent House Inn

Harbor View

Orleans B&B Associates
P.O. Box 1312
Orleans, MA, 02653
(508) 255-3824

Quiet residential area overlooking Pleasant Bay. Full breakfast on glass-enclosed porch with view of the Atlantic and Chatham Bars Inn golf course. Sandy beach and busy Fish Pier at end of street. Five-minute walk to the beach, golf, tennis, and the center of town. Two bedrooms, each with private bath and TV. Gardens on two levels for sun bathing. This attractive home is furnished with treasures from the Far East and Europe. $75.

Moses Nickerson House Inn

364 Old Harbor Road
Chatham, MA, 02633
(508) 945-5859; (800) 628-6972

Where memories begin . . . A quiet, romantic country inn, built in 1839 for whaling captain Moses Nickerson. The seven light, airy guest rooms are furnished with fine period antiques, Oriental rugs, canopy beds; some with fireplaces. Flowers from the garden, fresh fruit, and sun-dried linens. Breakfast is served in the garden room.

Hosts: Elsie & Carl Piccola
Rooms: 7 (PB) $95-135 seasonal
Continental Breakfast
Credit Cards: A, B, C
Notes: 2, 3, 5, 9, 10, 11, 12, 14

Salt Marsh House

Orleans B&B Associates
P.O. Box 1312
Orleans, MA, 02653
(508) 255-3824

Fresh breezes ruffle the white curtains in this pristine house, to give you a real feeling of being at the seaside. Only a two-minute walk to Nantucket Sound beach with sailboat and windsurfer rentals and snack bar. Three rooms on the second floor. One spacious king has a private bath; two twin rooms share a large bath. Buffet breakfast is served from 7:30-noon, with fresh-baked breads and fruits. $55-65.

The Sleepy Whale

Orleans B&B Associates
P.O. Box 1312
Orleans, MA, 02653
(508) 255-3824

A separate entrance brings you into a huge ceilinged family room with many windows giving country views. Another door leads to your own spacious deck for sunning and relaxing. Private bath, wet bar with refrigerator; color TV. New double day bed for comfortable sleeping, plus a convertible couch, also double. Breakfast is served by sociable hosts on your deck or in the country kitchen. Only .4 mile walk to the warm waters of Nantucket Sound and a sandy beach. $65.

Sunny Hours

Orleans B&B Associates
P.O. Box 1312
Orleans, MA, 02653
(508) 255-3824

A charming Cape Cod cottage overlooking a salt marsh, with all its wildlife and changing vistas. Walk or bike to lovely Harding's Beach on Nantucket Sound. A large twin room with TV and private bath. An adjoining twin room is available for persons in the same party at $25 for one or $40 for two. Full breakfast on a sunny deck or screened porch. $50.

CHELMSFORD

Westview Landing

4 Westview Avenue
Box 4141
South Chelmsford, MA, 01824
(508) 256-0074

Large contemporary home overlooking Hart's Pond, located three miles from routes 495 and 3, and thirty miles north of Boston. Close to historic Lexington, Concord, and Lowell. Many recreational activities: swimming, boating, fishing, bicycling. Hot spa on premises.

Hosts: Lorraine & Robert Pinette
Rooms: 3 (SB) $40-50
Full Breakfast
Credit Cards: No
Closed Christmas & New Year's
Notes: 2, 4, 5, 8, 9, 10, 11, 12, 13, 14

Breakfast at Tiasquam

CHILMARK, MARTHA'S VINEYARD

Breakfast at Tiasquam

RR 1, Box 296
Chilmark, MA, 02535
(508) 645-3685

Breakfast at Tiasquam is set among the farms, ponds, woodlands, and rolling pastures of Martha's Vineyard, on the peak of a hill well off the beaten path. Just minutes away is one of the most beautiful beaches on the entire East Coast, Lucy Vincent. Delicious full country breakfast; beautifully decorated, smoke-free house; attention paid to craftsmanship, privacy, comfort, and quiet. Breakfast at Tiasquam will make your stay on Martha's Vineyard truly unforgettable.

Host: Ron & Julie Crowe
Rooms: 8 (2 PB; 6 SB) $75-160
Full Breakfast
Credit Cards: No
Notes: 2, 5, 8, 9, 10, 11, 12, 14

CONCORD

Anderson-Wheeler Homestead

154 Fitchburg Tpk.
Concord, MA, 01742
(508) 369-3756

An 1890 Victorian with wraparound veranda, tastefully decorated with antiques accentuated with window seats and fireplaces. A popular area for canoeing, bird watching, and cross-country skiing. Rural, but convenient to two restaurants and a grocery store. Only three miles from historic Concord center, Walden Pond, and the Audubon Center.

Hosts: David & Charlotte Anderson
Rooms: 5 (2 PB; 3 SB) $65-75
Continental-plus Breakfast
Credit Cards: A, B, C, E
Notes: 2, 5, 7 (limited), 8, 9, 10, 11, 12, 13 (XC), 14

Colonial Inn

48 Monument Square
Concord, MA, 01742
(508) 369-9200; (800) 370-9200

Located in the heart of Concord Center and host to guests since 1716, this inn offers charming accommodations with telephones, TV, and air-conditioning. Walk to many historic attractions and experience traditional New England fare in our dining room.

Host: Jurgen Demisch
Rooms: 55 (PB) $87.76-142.61
Full Breakfast
Credit Cards: A, B, C, E
Notes: 2, 3, 4, 5, 7, 8, 9, 11, 12, 13, 14

Colonel Roger Brown House

1694 Main Street
Concord, MA, 01742
(508) 369-9119

This 1775 colonial home is on the Historic Register and located close to the Concord and Lexington historic districts. Fifteen miles west of Boston and Cambridge. Five rooms with air conditioning, private baths, TV, and telephones. Continental breakfast and complimentary beverages at all times.

Host: Kate Williams
Rooms: 5 (PB) $65-75
Continental Breakfast
Credit Cards: A, B, C, D
Notes: 2, 5, 8 (over 12), 9, 10, 11, 12, 13, 14

Hawthorne Inn

462 Lexington Road
Concord, MA, 01742
(508) 369-5610

Built circa 1870 on land once owned by Ralph Waldo Emerson, Nathaniel Hawthorne, and the Alcotts. Located alongside the "Battle Road" of 1775 and within walking distance of authors' homes, battle sites, and Walden Pond. Furnished with antiques, handmade quilts, original artwork, Japanese prints, and sculpture.

Hosts: G. Burch & M. Mudry
Rooms: 7 (PB) $75-150
Continental Breakfast
Credit Cards: No
Notes: 2, 5, 6, 7 (limited), 8, 9, 10, 11, 12, 13 (XC), 14

COTUIT

Salty Dog Inn

451 Main Street
Cotuit, MA, 02635
(508) 428-5228

A circa 1850 house once owned by a cranberry farmer in quaint Cotuit on Cape Cod. Warm-water beaches are nearby and may be reached on one of our complimentary bikes. Enjoy the fine restaurants and theater at Hyannis or Falmouth. Island boats are a short drive away. Brochure available.

Hosts: Lynn & Jerry Goldstein
Rooms: 4 (1 PB; 3 SB) $45-65

Continental Breakfast
Minimum stay Memorial Day-Labor Day: 2
Credit Cards: A, B
Notes: 2, 8 (over 12), 10, 11, 12

CUMMAQUID

Anderson Acres

B&B Cape Cod 61
P.O. Box 341
West Hyannisport, MA, 02672
(508) 775-2772

Cummaquid is part of the village of Barnstable. A drive through shows you what the village may have been like 200 years ago, in whaling days. This Cape Cod house was built in 1950 on 2.5 acres in a parklike setting. Three rooms have private baths. A full breakfast is available from 8:00 to 9:30; continental for late risers. No smoking inside the house; no facilities for children. $75-85.

Salty Dog Inn

CUMMINGTON

Cumworth Farm

RR 1, Box 110
Route 112
Cummington, MA, 01026
(413) 634-5529

A 200-year-old house with a sugar house and blueberry and raspberry fields on the premises. Pick your own berries in season. The farm raises sheep and is close to Tanglewood, Smith College, the William Cullen Bryant Homestead, cross-country skiing, and hiking trails.

Hosts: Ed & Mary McColgan
Rooms: 8 (SB) $50
Full Breakfast
Credit Cards: No
Notes: 2, 5, 8, 10, 11, 12, 13, 14

Windfields Farm

Windsor Bush Road
RR 1, Box 170
Cummington, MA, 01026
(413) 684-3786

Secluded, spacious Federal homestead on a dirt road amid fields and forests. Guests have their own entrance, book-lined living room, fireplace, piano, dining room. Family antiques, paintings, flowers. Windfields organic produce, eggs, maple syrup, raspberries, wild blueberries enrich the hearty breakfasts. Near Tanglewood, six colleges.

Hosts: Carolyn & Arnold Westwood
Rooms: 2 (SB) $44-55
Full Breakfast
Minimum stay weekends & holidays: 2
Credit Cards: No
Closed March & April
Notes: 2, 8 (over 12), 9, 11, 13

DALTON

The Dalton House

955 Main Street
Dalton, MA, 01226
(413) 684-3854

The main house has five rooms plus a large sitting room with fireplace where breakfast is served. The carriage house has been restored and now has four rooms and two large suites. All rooms have private baths, air-conditioning, and thermostats. In the warm months, breakfast may be enjoyed outside on the deck. There is also a picnic area and swimming pool.

Hosts: Gary & Bernice Turetsky
Rooms: 11 (PB) $48-100

Full Breakfast
Credit Cards: A, B, C
Notes: 2, 5, 8 (over 7), 9, 10, 11, 12, 13, 14

DANVERS

B&B Associates Bay Colony CN150

P.O. Box 57166
Babson Park Branch
Boston, MA, 02157-0166
(617) 449-5302

This immaculate 200-year-old house has beamed ceilings, beehive fireplaces, a lovely in-ground pool, and private guest quarters. Your hostess serves a full homemade breakfast on antique pewter. Two rooms, shared bath. Restricted smoking; children welcome; resident cat. $65.

Greater Boston Hospitality 112

P.O. Box 1142
Brookline, MA, 02146
(617) 277-5430

This 1854 home is close to all North Shore attractions. Air- conditioned; color TV. Two fireplaces in the house, and interesting antiques. Guests may enjoy the family room or swim in a private swimming pool. Full breakfast. Two queen rooms with shared guest bath; also a canopied double room with shared bath. Cots, crib, and portacrib available. No charge for child under five. $70.

DEERFIELD-SOUTH

Deerfield B&B

The Yellow Gabled House
307 North Main Street
Deerfield-South, MA, 01373
(413) 665-4922

This old country house is located in the heart of a historic and cultural area and is the site of the Bloody Brook Massacre in 1675. Furnished with period antiques and promises of a comfortable stay with the ambience and personal attention unique to New England. Convenient to the five-college area, prep school, and easily accessible to splendid back-roading. Located one mile from the crossroads of I-91, Route 116 and Routes 5 and 10. Air-conditioned.

Host: Edna Julia Stahelek
Rooms: 3 (PB) $55
Full Breakfast
Credit Cards: No
Notes: 2, 5, 8 (10 and up), 9, 10, 11, 12, 13, 14

DENNIS

The Four Chimneys Inn

946 Main Street
Dennis, MA, 02638
(508) 385-6317

A comfortable, spacious 1881 Victorian home with lovely gardens, located on historic Rt. 6A across from Scargo Lake. Short walk to Cape Cod Bay, the playhouse, Fine Arts Museum, restaurants, shops. Golf, tennis, bike trails within two miles. Centrally located, convenient to all of Cape Cod.

Hosts: Christina Jervant & Diane Robinson
Rooms: 9 (7 PB; 2 SB) $39-90
Continental-plus Breakfast
Credit Cards: A, B, C, D
Closed Jan. & Feb.
Notes: 2, 7, 8 (over 8), 9, 10, 11, 12

Isaiah Hall B&B Inn

152 Whig Street
Dennis, MA, 02638
(508) 385-9928; (800) 736-0160

Enjoy country ambience and hospitality in the heart of Cape Cod. Lovely 1857 farmhouse quietly located within walking distance of the beach and village shops, restaurants, museums, cinema, and playhouse. Nearby bike trails, tennis, and golf.

Host: Marie Brophy
Rooms: 11 (10 PB; 1 SB) $50-90
Continental-plus Breakfast

Minimum stay in season & holidays: 2
Credit Cards: A, B, C
Closed end Oct.-mid-March
Notes: 2, 7, 8 (over 8), 9, 10, 11, 12, 14

Rita's B&B

B&B Cape Cod 24
P.O. Box 341
West Hyannisport, MA, 02672
(508) 775-2772

This Cape Cod house was built six years ago. It is a short distance from the old Congregational Church and the historic district. Located a few hundred feet from a saltwater cove inlet, it offers a first-floor living room with TV, a nice deck on the back of the house, and two guest rooms on the second floor with a shared bath. Continental breakfast; children twelve and over are welcome. No smoking inside. $55.

Isaiah Hall B&B Inn

Scargo's B&B

B&B Cape Cod 68
P.O. Box 341
West Hyannisport, MA, 02672
(508) 775-2772

Built in 1880 by a wealthy sea captain, the house has been renovated. There is a parlor on the first floor for guests, and access to the beautiful grounds. Scargo Lake is 150 feet from the house; fish and swim from the private dock. Four guest rooms, one with a private bath. Smoking is restricted; children twelve and over are welcome. One resident cat. $50-110.

DENNISPORT

The Rose Petal B&B

152 Sea Street
Box 974
Dennisport, MA, 02639
(508) 398-8470

Lovely accommodations and complete homemade breakfast in an attractively restored 1872 historic home in the heart of Cape Cod. Walk to beach, shops, dining, or relax in our guest parlor or beautifully landscaped yard. We are a short drive to the ferries to Nantucket and Martha's Vineyard. Enjoy the diverse recreation, beautiful scenery, and interesting history of Cape Cod. Brochures are available.

Hosts: Dan & Gayle Kelly
Rooms: 4 (SB) $40-55
Full Breakfast
Minimum stay holidays: 2
Credit Cards: A, B
Reservations preferred
Notes: 2, 5, 7 (restricted), 8, 9, 10, 11, 12, 14

1721 House

B&B Cape Cod 4
P.O. Box 341
West Hyannisport, MA, 02672
(508) 775-2772

The warm-water beach can be seen from two of the three king bedrooms on the second floor of this antique colonial. Characteristic low ceilings, nonworking fireplaces, and semi-private baths. A full breakfast is served on china in the dining room. Golf, tennis, and fine restaurants are a short walk. $60-85.

EASTHAM

Chester Woods

Orleans B&B Associates
P.O. Box 1312
Orleans, MA, 02653
(508) 255-3824

Half-Cape country house in a wooded area has charm, comfort, and convenience. First-floor suite with king bed and sitting area. Second-floor guest room has double bed. Guests share a bath. Lovable Springer Spaniel in residence. Breakfast is served in the country kitchen. Near National Seashore Visitor's Center, bike path, and ocean beaches. $50-60.

Crosshatch Haven

Orleans B&B Associates
P.O. Box 1312
Orleans, MA, 02653
(508) 255-3824

Cozy, sunlit, modern suite. Two skylighted rooms, one double and one twin, separated by reading room with color TV. Bath has stall shower. Moments from Rail Trail, bay beach, Visitor's Center, and library. Access to clean freshwater pond for swimming and canoeing. Breakfast is served in the dining area or on the sunny deck off the music room. Children are welcome; resident dog. $55.

Fort Hill House

Orleans B&B Associates
P.O. Box 1312
Orleans, MA, 02653
(508) 255-3824

In a superb location facing toward the Atlantic at historic Fort Hill, this new house combines Cape Cod heritage with contemporary design. You have your choice of a king room with private bath and separate entrance; queen with shared bath; large twin with shared bath. Watch the heron from wide decks overlooking the marsh. $50-70.

Great Oak

Orleans B&B Associates
P.O. Box 1312
Orleans, MA, 02653
(508) 255-3824

Charming Cape residence located on a pleasant, quiet street 1.5 miles from the National Seashore Beaches and Cape Cod Bay. Private ground-level entrance to fireplaced living room with TV, queen room, private bath with shower. Enjoy a continental breakfast served in your sitting room or on the sunny screened porch. The perfect spot for those seeking seclusion and privacy. $60.

Lakeside

Orleans B&B Associates
P.O. Box 1312
Orleans, MA, 02653
(508) 255-3824

This comfortable new house is wrapped with a wide deck overlooking spacious lawns and Great Pond. Two large double rooms on the first floor share a bath. Hearty breakfast in the sunny dining room with a water view or out on the deck. One and one-half mile to Kingsbury Beach. $60.

The Over Look Inn

Route 6, Box 771
Eastham, MA, 02642
(508) 255-1886; (800) 356-1121

Located on the beautiful outer cape, across from Cape Cod National Seashore. Full breakfast, afternoon tea. Victorian billiard room, library, parlour, porches. Near biking, hiking, fine dining. Scottish hospitality.

Hosts: Ian & Nan Aitchison
Rooms: 8 (PB) $60-100
Full Breakfast
Credit Cards: A, B, C
Notes: 2, 5, 7 (limited), 8 (12 and over), 9, 10, 11, 12, 14

Pilgrim's Place

Orleans B&B Associates
P.O. Box 1312
Orleans, MA, 02653
(508) 255-3824

In a quiet neighborhood just up from a secluded bay beach, within walking distance to paths circling two ponds and close to the bike trail. A restful home offering two rooms with shared full bath. Rooms on the ground floor offer either a queen bed or extra-long twins. Cable TV and VCR available in the sitting area. A full breakfast is served on the deck or in the breezeway. Continental breakfast on the days the host is off to play tennis. $60.

Soft Winds

Orleans B&B Associates
P.O. Box 1312
Orleans, MA, 02653
(508) 255-3824

Staying here is like having your own comfortable apartment. Private guest wing with living room, kitchen, bath, bedroom, and private deck. Cable TV with HBO. Continental breakfast foods are on hand. Next to bike path and convenient to beaches and ponds. $70.

Spindrift

Orleans B&B Associates
P.O. Box 1312
Orleans, MA, 02653
(508) 255-3824

Delightful wing on an old house just a five-minute walk from the Coast Guard Beach. Close to bike path. Private entrance into library/sitting room, with large window facing the ocean. Queen or twin room with private bath. Patio. Interesting hosts offer privacy or hospitality, as you wish. Bountiful breakfast is served on dishes made by your host, a potter who maintains a shop in Orleans. $140/two rooms.

Tory Hill

Orleans B&B Associates
P.O. Box 1312
Orleans, MA, 02653
(508) 255-3824

An old Cape house with a private entrance into its separate guest wing. Twin sitting room with vanity and fridge. Private bath. Your choice of continental or full breakfast. Enjoy the attractive parlor or patio. Owners have an interesting specialized antique business in an adjacent barn, and everything reflects their lively interests. You can walk to the ice cream parlor from here. Bay beach .75 mile; 2 miles to the ocean. $65.

The Whalewalk Inn

The Whalewalk Inn

220 Bridge Road
Eastham, MA, 02642
(508) 255-0617

On 3 acres of lawns and gardens on the unspoiled outer cape. Near National Seashore (27,000-acre beach preserve) and the Audubon sanctuary. Completely restored 1839 whaling captain's home with wide planked pine floors and common rooms with fireplaces. BYOB cocktail hour every night. Many fine restaurants are nearby.

Hosts: Carolyn & Dick Smith
Rooms: 12 (PB) $90-150
Full Breakfast
Credit Cards: No
Closed Dec. 15-April 1
Notes: 2, 9, 10, 11, 12, 14

Nauset House Inn

Windsong

Orleans B&B Associates
P.O. Box 1312
Orleans, MA, 02653
(508) 255-3824

Cape Cod Bay beckons from this wonderfully located small apartment wing with private deck. Living room with TV and fireplace, twin room, bath, and large kitchen. Hostess will bring breakfast tray to your suite, or you may breakfast in the main house as early as 7:00 A.M. Nice views of the bay and lovely short walk to uncrowded beach. Children are welcome. $80.

EASTHAMPTON

Berkshire B&B Homes PV7

P.O. Box 211
Williamsburg, MA, 01096
(413) 268-7244

1984 colonial on 1.5 acres. Parlor with fireplace. Pond with ducks on premises; fishing. Double room with private bath; extra daybed available. Continental breakfast, limited smoking, children welcome. $65-75.

EAST ORLEANS

The Farmhouse

163 Beach Road
East Orleans, MA, 02653
(508) 255-6654

This nineteenth-century farmhouse has been carefully restored and furnished to provide a unique blend of country life in a seashore setting. Short walk to Nauset Beach, close to sailing, golf, tennis, bike trails, theater, fishing, shopping, museums, and surfing. Some ocean view-rooms. Breakfast is served on an ocean view deck.

Hosts: The Standishes
Rooms: 8 (4 PB; 4 SB) $32-95
Continental-plus Breakfast
Credit Cards: A, B
Notes: 2, 5, 7 (restricted), 8, 9, 10, 11, 12, 14

Nauset House Inn

143 Beach Road
Box 774
East Orleans, MA, 02643
(508) 255-2195

The Nauset House Inn is a place where the gentle amenities of life are still observed, a quiet place removed from the cares of the workaday world, a place where sea and shore, orchard and field all combine to create a perfect setting for tranquil relaxation. The Nauset House Inn is ideally located near one of the world's great ocean beaches,

NOTES: Credit cards accepted: A Master Card; B Visa; C American Express; D Discover Card; E Diners Club; F Other: 2 Personal checks accepted: 3 Lunch available: 4 Dinner available: 5 Open all year

yet is close to antique and craft shops, restaurants, art galleries, scenic paths, and remote places for sunning, swimming, and picnicking.

Hosts: Diane & Al Johnson
Rooms: 14 (8 PB; 6 SB) $45-95
Full Breakfast
Credit Cards: A, B
Closed Nov. 1-March 31
Notes: 2, 7 (restricted), 8 (over 12), 9, 11, 12

The Red Geranium

Orleans B&B Associates
P.O. Box 1312
Orleans, MA, 02653
(508) 255-3824

From the moment you step into this lovely country cape, you will feel the warmth of home. Located in historic East Orleans, only a bike trip away from the pure waters of Nauset Beach and a short walk from village shopping and fine dining. Relax in comfortable bedrooms decorated with heirloom treasures, double or twin beds, individually controlled air conditioning, cable TV. Breakfast, a social event, is served in the colonial dining room at beautifully appointed tables with your choice of a light or full breakfast. $60-80.

Ship's Knees Inn

Ship's Knees Inn

186 Beach Road
P.O. Box 756
East Orleans, MA, 02643
(508) 255-1312

A 160-year-old restored sea captain's home; rooms individually appointed with their own colonial color schemes and authentic antiques. Only a short walk to popular sand-duned Nauset Beach. Pool and tennis on premises. Also available three miles away, overlooking Orleans Cove, are an efficiency and two heated cottages. Open all year.

Rooms: 21(8 PB; 13 SB) $40-100
Continental Breakfast
Minimum stay summer weekends: 2, with private baths
Credit Cards: Yes
Notes: 2, 5, 7, 8 (over 12), 9, 10, 11, 12, 14

Treehouse

Orleans B&B Associates
P.O. Box 1312
Orleans, MA, 02653
(508) 255-3824

You can easily bike the one mile to famous Nauset Beach from this house. Accommodations include an attractive queen bedroom and a second room with a carved double bed. Air conditioning; shared bath. Comfortable common TV room. Ideal for couples traveling together. Have a generous breakfast in the skylighted cathedral-ceilinged dining room. $70.

The White Rose

Orleans B&B Associates
P.O. Box 1312
Orleans, MA, 02653
(508) 255-3824

Memories of a happy childhood are evoked by the old-fashioned charm of this wonderful house. Set in beautifully landscaped, spacious grounds with a brick terrace for sun bathing and reading, it is close to shopping, restaurants, and beaches. Upstairs, a large double room makes you feel at home. Down the hall, there is a quiet twin room. TV in each room. Large shared bath. Your English host knows how to provide a good breakfast and make your stay memorable. $55.

EDGARTOWN, MARTHA'S VINEYARD

The Arbor

222 Upper Main Street
Box 1228
Edgartown, MA, 02539
(508) 627-8137

Circa 1890 turn-of-the-century guest house on the bicycle path in historic Edgartown. Short walk to downtown and the harbor. Guests may relax in the hammock, have tea in the courtyard, or walk the unspoiled beaches of Martha's Vineyard.

Host: Peggy Hall
Rooms: 10 (8 PB; 2 SB) $75-110 + tax
Continental Breakfast
Minimum stay in season: 3
Credit Cards: A, B
Closed Nov. 1-April 30
Notes: 2, 7, 8 (over 12), 9, 10, 11, 12, 14

Ashley Inn

Box 650
Edgartown, MA, 02539
(508) 627-9655

Among spacious lawns, rose gardens, and apple trees, the Ashley Inn offers an attractive 1860s captain's home with country charm. Conveniently located on Edgartown's historic Main Street, the inn is a leisurely stroll to shops, beaches, and fine foods. Each room is tastefully decorated with period antiques, brass, and wicker. Join us for breakfast and relax in our hammocks. We hope to make your visit to Martha's Vineyard a memorable one.

Hosts: Jude Cortese & Fred Hurley
Rooms: 10 (8 PB; 2 SB) $85-160
Continental Breakfast
Credit Cards: A, B, C
Notes: 2, 5, 7, 8 (over 12), 9, 14

The Captain Dexter House of Edgartown

35 Pease's Point Way
Box 2798
Edgartown, MA, 02539
(508) 627-7289

Built in 1840, the Captain Dexter House of Edgartown espouses a country-colonial atmosphere with its hardwood floors, original moldings, and New England-style dormers. The inn is decorated with period antiques, working fireplaces, canopied beds, and fresh flowers. Enjoy our complimentary continental breakfast and evening aperitif. Walk to the harbor, shops, and restaurants.

Host: Michael Maultz
Rooms: 11 (PB) $65-180
Continental Breakfast
Credit Cards: A, B, C
Notes: 5, 8, 9, 10, 11, 12, 14

Colonial Inn of Martha's Vineyard

38 North Water Street
P.O. Box 68
Edgartown, MA, 02539
(508) 627-4711

Located in the heart of historic Edgartown, overlooking the harbor, sits the Colonial Inn. The inn offers 42 newly renovated and lovingly refurbished rooms, all with heat, air-conditioning, color TV, and private bath. Continental breakfast is served daily in the solarium and garden courtyard.

Host: Linda Malcouranne
Rooms: 42 (PB) $50-185
Continental Breakfast
Credit Cards: A, B, C
Closed Jan., Feb., March
Notes: 2, 3, 4, 7, 8, 9, 10, 11, 12, 14

The Daggett House

54 N. Water Street
Box 1333
Edgartown, MA, 02539
(508) 627-4600

The Governor Bradford Inn

The only bed and breakfast in Edgartown that is on the water. The rooms in this circa 1660 home were all redecorated in 1988-1989. Open all year.

Host: Sue Cooper-Street
Rooms: 23 (PB) $153.58
Suites: 2 (PB) $246.83
Continental Breakfast
Credit Cards: A, B, C
Notes: 2, 5, 7, 8, 9, 10, 11, 12

The Governor Bradford Inn

128 Main Street
Edgartown, MA, 02539
(508) 627-9510

The atmosphere at this restored 1865 Edgartown captain's home is one of casual elegance. Guests can walk to the many shops and restaurants in Edgartown, bicycle to beaches, or simply relax. Freshly baked treats are served at breakfast and afternoon tea. Guest rooms are decorated with a mixture of antiques and reproductions. All have private bath.

Hosts: Bill & Kim Johnson
Rooms: 16 (PB) $60-195
Continental Breakfast
Credit Cards: A, B, C, E
Notes: 2, 5, 7, 8 (over 10), 9, 10, 11, 12, 14

Point Way Inn

Box 128
Edgartown, MA, 02539
(508) 627-8633

Our delightful country inn provides a warm, relaxed retreat, with working fireplaces in eleven rooms. Tea and scones are provided in the winter; in the summer, lemonade and oatmeal cookies are served in the gazebo overlooking the croquet court and gardens. Complimentary courtesy car available.

Hosts: Linda & Ben Smith
Rooms: 15 (PB) $70-205
Continental Breakfast
Minimum stay holidays: 2
Credit Cards: A, B, C
Notes: 2, 5, 7, 8, 9, 10, 11, 12, 14

EGREMONT

Berkshire B&B Homes SC8

P.O. Box 211
Williamsburg, MA, 01096
(413) 268-7244

1803 country farmhouse on 3 acres, furnished with country and antiques. Twenty-five minutes from Lenox. One queen bed, two doubles, one double and a single, twins. All rooms have private baths. Full breakfast, no smoking, children sixteen and over welcome; pet in residence. $75-100.

FAIRHAVEN

Edgewater B&B

2 Oxford Street
Fairhaven, MA, 02719
(508) 997-5512

A gracious waterfront house located in the early whale shipbuilding area of historic Fairhaven. Spectacular views of neighboring New Bedford Harbor, close to historic areas, beaches, factory outlets; five minutes from I-195. Five rooms, each with private bath (two with fireplaces and sitting rooms).

Host: Kathy Reed
Rooms: 5 (PB) $45-65
Continental Breakfast
Credit Cards: A, B, C
Notes: 2, 5, 7, 8, 9, 10, 11, 12, 14

FALMOUTH

Capt. Tom Lawrence House

75 Locust Street
Falmouth, MA, 02540
(508) 540-1445

An 1861 Victorian, former whaling captain's residence, in the historic village of Falmouth. Comfortable, spacious corner guest rooms. Firm beds — some with canopies. Steinway piano and working fireplace. Gourmet breakfast consists of fresh fruit, breads, pancakes made from freshly ground organic grain, and a variety of other delicious specialties. German spoken.

Rooms: 6 (PB) $69-89
Full Breakfast
Minimum stay: 2
Credit Cards: A, B
Notes: 2, 5, 7 (restricted), 8 (over 12), 9, 11, 12

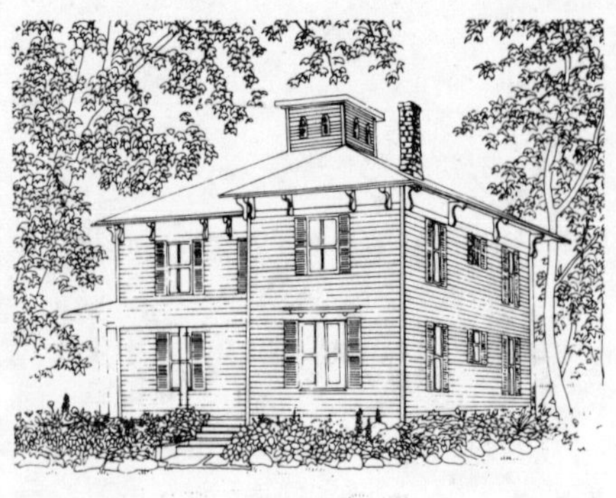

Capt. Tom Lawrence House

Gladstone Inn

219 Grand Avenue South
Falmouth, MA, 02540
(508) 548-9851

An oceanfront Victorian inn overlooking Martha's Vineyard. Established in 1910. Light, airy guest rooms have period furniture and their own wash stations. Buffet breakfast is served on our glassed-in porch that also provides a cozy place to read, watch cable TV, or relax. Refrigerators, bikes, and gas grill are provided for our guests to use.

Hosts: Jim & Gayle Carroll
Singles: 2 (SB) $30
Rooms: 16 (1 PB; 15 SB) $50-70
Full Breakfast
Credit Cards: No
Closed Oct. 15-May 15
Notes: 2, 7, 8 (12 and over), 9, 10, 11, 12

Grafton Inn

261 Grand Avenue South
Falmouth, MA, 02540
(508) 540-8688

Oceanfront Victorian inn with miles of beautiful beach and breathtaking views of Martha's Vineyard. Sumptuous breakfasts are served on a lovely enclosed porch. Private baths, airy, comfortable rooms furnished with period antiques, thoughtful amenities. Picnic lunches and bicycles are available, as is ample parking. Short walk to restaurant, shops, and ferry. Ask about off-season rates and package plans.

Hosts: Liz & Rudy Cvitan
Rooms: 11 (PB) $65-95
Full Breakfast
Credit Cards: A, B, D
Closed Dec. 15-Feb. 15
Notes: 2, 9, 10, 11, 12, 14

Grafton Inn

Mostly Hall B&B Inn

27 Main Street
Falmouth, MA, 02540
(508) 548-3786

Romantic 1849 Southern plantation-style Cape Cod home with wraparound veranda and widow's walk. Set back from the road on an acre of beautiful gardens with a gazebo. Close to restaurants, shops, beaches, island ferries. Spacious corner rooms, gourmet breakfast, bicycles, private baths.

Hosts: Caroline & Jim Lloyd
Rooms: 6 (PB) $75-110
Full Breakfast
Minimum stay Memorial Day-Columbus Day: 2; selected holidays: 2-3
Credit Cards: No
Closed Jan.-mid Feb.
Notes: 2, 8 (16 and over), 9, 10, 11, 12

The Palmer House Inn

81 Palmer Avenue
Falmouth, MA, 02540-2857
(508) 548-1230

Turn-of-the-century Victorian bed and breakfast located in the historic district. Antique furnishings return you to the romance of a bygone era. Full gourmet breakfast featuring Pain Perdue, Belgian waffles, Finnish pancakes. Close to island ferries, beaches, shops. Bicycles available.

Hosts: Ken & Joanne Baker
Rooms: 8 (PB) $75-110
Full Breakfast
Minimum stay: 2
Credit Cards: A, B
Notes: 2, 5, 8 (over 12), 10, 11, 12, 14

Village Green Inn

40 West Main Street
Falmouth, MA, 02540
(508) 548-5621

Gracious old Victorian, ideally located on historic Village Green. Walk to fine shops and restaurants, bike to beaches, tennis, and the picturesque bike path to Woods Hole. Enjoy nineteenth-century charm and warm hospitality in elegant surroundings. Four lovely guest rooms and one romantic suite all have private baths. Discounted rates from Nov.-May.

Hosts: Linda & Don Long
Rooms: 5 (PB) $70-100
Full Breakfast
Credit Cards: A, B, C
Notes: 2, 5, 7 (outside), 8 (16 and over), 9, 10, 11, 12

FALMOUTH HEIGHTS

The Moorings Lodge

207 Grand Avenue South
Falmouth Heights, MA, 02540
(508) 540-2370

A Victorian sea captain's home on the ocean, within walking distance of restaurants and island ferries. Complimentary homemade breakfast buffet served overlooking Vineyard Sound and the islands. Call us your home while you tour the Cape.

Hosts: The Benard Family
Rooms: 8 (6 PB; 2 SB) $45-65 + tax
Full Breakfast
Minimum stay weekdays & weekends: 2; holidays: 3
Credit Cards: No
Closed Columbus Day-May 15
Notes: 2, 7, 8 (over 10), 9, 10, 11, 12

FLORENCE

Berkshire B&B Homes PV10

P.O. Box 211
Williamsburg, MA, 01096
(413) 268-7244

Turn-of-the-century stucco home on 17 acres of land, near a local park. Guest rooms are furnished with antiques. Two double rooms, one twin; shared bath. Full breakfast; no smoking; children twelve and over welcome; pet in residence. $40-55.

GLOUCESTER

B&B Associates Bay Colony NS500

P.O. Box 57166
Babson Park Branch
Boston, MA, 02157-0166
(617) 449-5302

Just steps from the Atlantic, this white frame house is located in the little village of Lanesville five miles from Gloucester and Rockport. There are three guest rooms and a separate cottage, shared baths. Continental breakfast; no smoking; children over ten are welcome. Resident St. Bernard. $60.

Riverview B&B

B&B Marblehead & North Shore
P.O. Box 172
Beverly, MA, 01915
(508) 921-1336

Beautiful 1898 riverfront home on the Annisquam River with wonderful views of the boating and bird life. Four guest rooms share two full baths; two rooms have decks facing the river. Smoking is permitted. Continental breakfast; children over ten are welcome. $65-75.

GREAT BARRINGTON

Berkshire B&B Homes SC12

P.O. Box 211
Williamsburg, MA, 01096
(413) 268-7244

1890s Victorian in-town residence. Parlor available for guests' use. Fifteen minutes from Lexington. Two queen rooms with private baths. Full breakfast; no smoking; children ten and over are welcome. $95.

Covered Bridge 3 GB

P.O. Box 447A
Norfolk, CT, 06058
(203) 542-5944

Charming Victorian farmhouse in a rural setting. There are three large, comfortable rooms, each with private bath, cable TV, and air-conditioning. A barn on the grounds has also been converted into a two-bedroom cottage. Continental breakfast. $85-110.

Elling's B&B Guest House

RD 3, Box 6
Great Barrington, MA, 01230
(413) 528-4103

Our 1746 homestead, with porches, lawns, flower gardens with views of hills and cornfields, offers six charming guest rooms.

Large guest living room with fireplace, and a generous buffet breakfast. Our guests return to enjoy Tanglewood, ballet, the playhouses, and winter sports. We've been hosts for nineteen years now.

Hosts: Jo & Ray Elling
Rooms: 6 (2 PB; 4 SB) $55-80
Continental Breakfast
Credit Cards: No
Notes: 2, 5, 10, 11, 12, 13

Littlejohn Manor

1 Newsboy Monument Lane
Great Barrington, MA, 01230
(413) 528-2882

Victorian charm recaptured in this uniquely personable home. Antiques grace four warmly furnished air-conditioned guest rooms — two with fireplaces. Guest parlor with color TV and fireplace. Full English breakfast and afternoon tea. Set on spacious, landscaped grounds, with extensive herb and flower beds. Scenic views. Within five miles of Butternut Basin and Catamount.

Hosts: Herbert Littlejohn, Jr., & Paul A. DuFour
Rooms: 4 (SB) $60-80
Full Breakfast
Minimum stay weekends: 2; holidays: 3
Credit Cards: No
Notes: 2, 5, 7 (limited), 9, 10, 11, 12, 13

Round Hill Farm

17 Round Hill Road
Great Barrington, MA, 01230
(413) 528-3366

A haven for nonsmokers. Classic nineteenth-century hilltop horse farm overlooking 300 acres, on a dirt road 2.6 miles from town. Miles of tended fields, trails, trout stream, with panoramic views of the Berkshire Hills. Please call for our brochure.

Hosts: Thomas & Margaret Whitfield
Rooms: 9 (4 PB; 5 SB) $65-150
Full Breakfast
Horses welcome
Credit Cards: A, B, C
Nonsmokers only, please
Notes: 2, 5, 8 (over 16), 9, 10, 11, 12, 13, 14

Seekonk Pines Inn

142 Seekonk Cross Road
Great Barrington, MA, 01230
(413) 528-4192

Restored 1830s homestead, located in a rural Berkshire setting. Large guest living room with fireplace and grand piano. Full country breakfast changes daily. Special

Round Hill Farm

diets accommodated. Convenient to Tanglewood and other cultural events, museums, shops, hiking. Features antique quilts, stenciling, original watercolors, and gardens.

Hosts: Linda & Chris Best
Rooms: 6 (4 PB; 2 S2.5B) $49.37-99.67
Full Breakfast
Credit Cards: A, B
Notes: 2, 5, 8, 9, 10, 11, 12, 13

The Turning Point Inn

3 Lake Buel Road
Great Barrington, MA, 01230
(413) 528-4777

An eighteenth-century former stagecoach inn. Full, naturally delicious breakfast. Featured in the *New York Times, Boston Globe, L.A. Times.* Adjacent to Butternut Ski Basin; near Tanglewood and all Berkshire attractions. Hiking, cross-country ski trails. Sitting rooms with fireplaces, piano, cable TV. Groups and families welcome.

Hosts: The Yosts
Rooms: 9 (3 PB; 6 SB) $75-100
Full Breakfast
Minimum stay weekends: 1-2; holidays: 2-3
Credit Cards: No
Notes: 2, 5, 8, 9, 10, 11, 12, 13, 14

GREENFIELD

Berkshire B&B Homes PV32

P.O. Box 211
Williamsburg, MA, 01096
(413) 268-7244

Turn-of-the-century colonial revival on 3.5 acres. Living room and library with pool table for guest use. Three queen rooms, one double room, two twin rooms. Private and shared baths. Full breakfast; no smoking; children ten and over welcome; pet in residence. $75-95.

GROVELAND

Seven Acres Farm B&B

B&B Marblehead & North Shore
P.O. Box 172
Beverly, MA, 01915
(508) 921-1336

Unique converted barn B&B on an herb farm. The hosts speak Greek and have three children at home and live upstairs. A large first-floor room has a 3/4 bed, shared bath, and cot for a child. Restricted smoking; one dog and two cats on premises. Breakfast is full on the weekends and continental weekdays. $45.

HAMPDEN

Berkshire B&B Homes GS11

P.O. Box 211
Williamsburg, MA, 01096
(413) 268-7244

1987 Cape Cod home on 35 acres with contemporary and antique furnishings. Parlor and den for guest use. Two queen rooms with semi-private bath. Continental breakfast; restricted smoking; children welcome. $70.

HARWICH

Freshwater Whale

Orleans B&B Associates
P.O. Box 1312
Orleans, MA, 02653
(508) 255-3824

Charming antique-filled cottage has view from every room of a large, clear pond that's excellent for swimming. Two large rooms, one king, one twin. Private bath. Full breakfast with hot homemade breads on deck or in the country kitchen. On the lower level, there is a family room with fireplace and TV for guests that opens to a patio, old-fashioned garden, and sandy beach. Canoe and beach towels provided. Five minutes to ocean beach, bike path, golf, and tennis. $70.

Hank's B&B

B&B Cape Cod 7
P.O. Box 341
West Hyannisport, MA, 02672
(508) 775-2772

This Cape-style home sits 100 yards from a freshwater pond. It offers two second-story guest rooms: one with double bed, the other with two twins. The bath is shared. This very comfortable home features a full breakfast in the dining room, complete with fresh home-baked specialties. Located on the Cape Cod Bike Trail, it is great for bike riders. The pond is available for swimming and fishing. The beach is one mile away. $56.

The Larches

97 Chatham Road
Harwich, MA, 02645
(508) 432-0150

A charming 1835 Greek Revival with contemporary wing surrounded by flower and vegetable gardens. Close to swimming, bike trails, art galleries, little theater, and summer stock. Continental breakfast is served in gracious surroundings on the patio, if preferred.

Hosts: Dr. & Mrs. Edwin O. Hook
Rooms: 2 (1 PB; 1 SB) $50-60
Continental Breakfast
Credit Cards: No
Notes: 9, 10, 11, 12

Serendipity

Orleans B&B Associates
P.O. Box 1312
Orleans, MA, 02653
(508) 255-3824

Peace and quiet "on golden pond." Spacious deck overlooks a private sandy beach. All rooms have a water view. Upstairs, master room with king bed and full bath. Downstairs, there is a large room with double sofabed and full bath. Private entrance from patio. Adjacent single room on each floor for another family member ($30). Minutes to ocean, tennis, and golf. $60.

Windchimes

Orleans B&B Associates
P.O. Box 1312
Orleans, MA, 02653
(508) 255-3824

Central Cape location for all activities. Residential area with a three-to-four-minute walk to fine Nantucket Sound beach. Bicycle path nearby. New spacious guest suite with full private bath, queen bed, living room area with color TV, and front and rear private entrances. Enjoy your own nice yard. Full breakfast. $70.

HARWICH PORT

B&B Associates Bay Colony CC370

P.O. Box 57166
Babson Park Branch
Boston, MA, 02157-0166
(617) 449-5302

White wicker rocking chairs and hanging geraniums on the wraparound porch of this Victorian home beckon you. Located less than half a mile from the sandy beach, there are five large guest rooms with brass beds, period furnishings, and pastel wallpapers. Shops and restaurants are within easy walking distance. $95.

The Coach House

74 Sisson Road
Harwich Port, MA, 02646
(508) 432-9452

Delightful old cape home, once an estate barn, offering quiet, comfortable elegance. Conveniently located for day trips to Martha's Vineyard and Nantucket, whale watching, and 21-mile bike trail through woodlands and cranberry bogs to the National Seashore.

Hosts: Sara & Cal Ayer
Rooms: 3 (2 PB; 1 SB) $65-70
Continental Breakfast
Minimum stay weekends & holidays: 2
Credit Cards: A, B, C
Closed Nov.-April
Notes: 2, 7, 9, 10, 11, 12, 14

Eagles Nest B&B

B&B Cape Cod
P.O. Box 341
Hyannisport, MA, 02672
(508) 775-2772

Built in the 1860s and expanded at the end of the Victorian era, this house reflects the influence of the period. Guests have their own private entrance that leads to the second floor of the house where there are two bedrooms and a shared bath. A continental breakfast is served in the sitting room from 8:00-9:00 A.M. The house is near Bank Street beach, village shops, fine restaurants, two public golf courses. Tennis courts, a freshwater pond for swimming, and bike trails are within two miles of the house. Smoking is allowed; infants and children four and over are welcome. $60.

Harbor Breeze

Captain's Quarters & Bayberry Shores
326 Lower County Road
Harwich Port, MA, 02646
(800) 992-6550

Three distinct walk-to-the-beach B&Bs offering a choice of country casual, Victorian romantic, or traditional homestay settings in the beautiful coastal town of Harwich Port—the best central location for touring Cape Cod. Hearty continental breakfast, family suites, TVs, refrigerators, pool, tennis. Efficiency suite with fireplace and cottage also available.

Rooms: 18 (PB) $65-125
Continental Breakfast
Credit Cards: A, B, C
Notes: 2, 5, 7, 8, 9, 10, 11, 12, 14

Harborwalk Guest House

6 Freeman Street
Harwich Port, MA, 02646
(508) 432-1675

A rambling 1880 guest house just a short walk from one of the best seafood restaurants on the Cape. The beaches, village, shops, and recreational activities are a short distance away.

Hosts: Marilyn & Preston Barry
Rooms: 6 (4 PB; 2 SB) $45-60
Continental Buffet Breakfast
Credit Cards: No
Closed: Nov.-April
Notes: 2, 8 (over 4), 9, 10, 11, 12, 14

The Inn on Bank Street

88 Bank Street
Harwich Port, MA, 02646
(508) 432-3206

A B&B in the center of lovely Harwich Port. Five-minute walk to ocean beach. Close to good restaurants, quaint shops, picturesque harbors. Enjoy breakfast on the sun porch of a Cape Cod country inn.

Hosts: Janet & Arky Silverio
Rooms: 6 (PB) $62-77
Continental-plus Breakfast
Credit Cards: A, B (for deposit)
Notes: 2, 7 (restricted), 8, 9, 10, 11, 12, 14

HINSDALE

Berkshire B&B Homes NC7

P.O. Box 211
Williamsburg, MA, 01096
(413) 268-7244

One-hundred-year-old remodeled home on 10 acres. Private entrance for guests. One double bed with private bath. Full breakfast; restricted smoking; children welcome. $65.

Berkshire B&B Homes NC10

P.O. Box 211
Williamsburg, MA, 01096
(413) 268-7244

A center-hall colonial, built in 1770, on 6 acres. Furnished with antique and country furniture. Parlor for guest use. One queen room, two double rooms, one twin room. Private and shared baths. Full breakfast; no smoking; children welcome. Hot tub and family pet on premises. $50-65.

HYANNIS

Elegance By-The-Sea

162 Sea Street
Hyannis, MA, 02601
(508) 775-3595

Romantic 1880 Queen Anne Victorian home, furnished with antiques in the European style. Walk to beaches, restaurants, island ferries. Great location as a base for visiting all of Cape Cod. Many common areas available to guests: porch, breakfast greenhouse room, formal dining room with separate tables, fireplace and parlor with TV and piano.

Hosts: Clark & Mary Boydston
Rooms: 6 (PB) $59.80-80
Full Breakfast
Minimum stay weekends & holidays: 2
Credit Cards: A, B, C
Closed January
Notes: 2, 8 (over 16), 9, 10, 11, 12

The Inn On Sea Street

358 Sea Street
Hyannis, MA, 02601
(508) 775-8030

Victorian splendor steps from the beach and Kennedy compound. Six romantic guest rooms. Antiques, canopy beds, and Persian rugs abound in this hospitable atmosphere. Full gourmet breakfast of fruit and home-baked delights served at individual tables set with sterling silver, crystal, china, and fresh flowers. One-night stays always welcomed.

Hosts: Lois M. Nelson & J. B. Whitehead
Rooms: 6 (4 PB; 2 SB) $60.34-93.25
Full Breakfast
Credit Cards: A, B, C
Closed Nov. 1-April 1
Notes: 2, 9, 10, 11, 12, 14

Scudder Manor

B&B Cape Cod 32
P.O. Box 341
West Hyannisport, MA, 02672
(508) 775-2772

This 200-year-old colonial is conveniently located a mile from downtown Hyannis. It's a short walk to the Kennedy Compound, the yacht club, and beautiful warm-water beaches. Room one on the second floor has a double bed. It shares a full bath with room two, which features two four-poster twin beds. Continental breakfast. Restricted smoking; children twelve and over are welcome; one dog in residence. $55.

Sea Breeze Inn

397 Sea Street
Hyannis, MA, 02601
(508) 771-7213

Quaint fourteen-room inn just a three-minute walk from the beach and within walking distance of downtown Hyannis, where you will find shopping, restaurants, and nightclubs. All our rooms have private baths, and some have ocean views.

Hosts: Martin & Patricia Battle
Rooms: 14 (PB) $45-80
Continental Breakfast
Credit Cards: A, B, C
Notes: 2, 5, 7, 8, 9, 10, 11, 12, 14

HYANNISPORT

The Simmons Homestead Inn

288 Scudder Avenue
Hyannisport, MA, 02647
(508) 778-4999

An 1820 sea captain's estate that is now the nicest inn on Cape Cod. In the country, yet only one-half mile from Hyannis. Simply lovely rooms are all unique. A very pleasant inn with large porches, and huge common rooms; the perfect home base for enjoying the Cape.

Hosts: Bill & Peggy Putman
Rooms: 9 (PB) $100-140
Full Breakfast
Credit Cards: A, B, C
Notes: 2, 5, 7, 9, 10, 11, 12

The Simmons Homestead Inn

LANESBORO

Berkshire B&B Homes NC1

P.O. Box 211
Williamsburg, MA, 01096
(413) 268-7244

Two-hundred-year-old colonial farmhouse at the foot of Mt. Greylock. Working sheep farm and bakery on premises. Rooms furnished with country charm. Sitting area with TV for guests. One double room, two rooms with double and single beds. Shared baths. Continental breakfast; children welcome; pet in residence. $40-55.

Berkshire B&B Homes NC9

P.O. Box 211
Williamsburg, MA, 01096
(413) 268-7244

Late 1800s colonial farmhouse on 3 acres, close to town center. This home was a turkey farm in years past. Three double rooms with shared baths. Full breakfast; no smoking; children eight and up are welcome. Pet in residence. $55-65.

LEE

Berkshire B&B Homes SC13

P.O. Box 211
Williamsburg, MA, 01096
(413) 268-7244

1870 colonial revival with parlor and upstairs den for guest use. Ten minutes from Lenox; within walking distance of the town of Lee. Two queen rooms and one double room; private baths. Full breakfast; restricted smoking; children five and up are welcome. $70-80.

Haus Andreas

Stockbridge Road
Lee, MA, 01238
(413) 243-3298

Completely restored colonial mansion with heated pool, tennis, lawn sports, bicycles, air conditioning. Fireplaces in some rooms. Libraried living room with grand piano; TV room with VCR; guest pantry.

Hosts: Gerhard & Lilliane Schmid
Rooms: 8 (PB) $69-212
Continental-plus Breakfast
Credit Cards: A, B
Notes: 2, 5, 7 (restricted), 8 (over 10), 9, 10, 11, 12, 13

Blantyre

LENOX

American Country Collection 63

984 Gloucester Place
Schenectady, NY, 12309
(518) 370-4948

Spoil yourself at this casually elegant B&B inn in the heart of the Berkshires. Meticulously restored and on the National Register of Historic Places, this home features large rooms and six fireplaces. Nine guest rooms, seven with private baths. There are also two private suites in the carriage house. Resident dog. $65-185.

Blantyre

P.O. Box 995
Lenox, MA, 01240
(413) 637-3556 (413) 298-3806

A gracious country house hotel surrounded by 85 acres of grounds. The hotel has a European atmosphere and exceptional cuisine, offering tennis, croquet, and swimming.

Host: Roderick Anderson
Rooms: 23 (PB) $150-500
Continental Breakfast
Credit Cards: All major
Closed Nov. 1-May 21
Notes: 2, 3, 4, 7, 10, 11, 12, 14

Brook Farm Inn

15 Hawthorne Street
Lenox, MA, 01240
(413) 637-3013

There is poetry here. Large library, poets on tape. Near Tanglewood (Boston Symphony), theater, ballet, shops. Pool, gardens, fireplaces in winter. Cross-country and downhill skiing close in the winter. Relax and enjoy.

Hosts: Bob & Betty Jacob
Rooms: 12 (PB) $65-155
Full Breakfast
Minimum stay weekends & holidays: 2
Credit Cards: A, B
Notes: 2, 5, 7 (restricted), 8 (15 and over), 9, 10, 11, 12, 13

Cornell Inn

197 Main Street
Lenox, MA, 01240
(413) 637-0562

Warm and friendly 1880 Victorian inn with fireplaces, antique furnishings, private baths. The carriage house has been converted to four modern suites with fireplaces, kitchens, Jacuzzi tubs. Centrally located to all downhill skiing and free cross-country skiing.

Host: Davis Rolland
Rooms: 17 (PB) From $55-350
Continental Breakfast

Credit Cards: A, B
Notes: 2, 5, 7, 9, 10, 11, 12, 13, 14

Covered Bridge 1 LEN

P.O. Box 447A
Norfolk, CT, 06058
(203) 542-5944

An 1800s colonial within walking distance of the village center. There are several common rooms for the guests, including a living room with wood-burning stove. The seven guest rooms are decorated with the owner's collection of antique quilts. A continental breakfast is served in the pleasant dining room. Two rooms have private baths. $65-100.

Cornell Inn

East Country Berry Farm

830 East Street
Lenox, MA, 01240
(413) 442-2057

Historic colonial farmhouse on 20 acres with fireplace rooms, mountain views, and homemade goodies. Pool, berries. Near lakes, golf, tennis, hiking, horseback riding, Tanglewood, summer theater, and dance festivals. Canoe trip packages May-Sept. Afternoon tea. Friendly, relaxing, romantic. Excellent restaurants, galleries, museums, boutiques, and factory outlets. In the winter, enjoy cross-country and downhill skiing.

Host: Rita Fribosh Miller
Rooms: 6 (5 PB; 1 SB) $55-125
Continental-plus Breakfast
Credit Cards: A, B, C
Notes: 2, 5, 6 (prior approval), 7, 8, 9, 10, 11, 12, 13, 14

The Gables Inn

103 Walker Street
Lenox, MA, 01240
(413) 637-3416

Former home of authoress Edith Wharton. Queen Anne style with period furnishings, pool, tennis, fireplaces, and theme rooms.

Hosts: Mary & Frank Newton
Rooms: 14 (PB) $60-140
Continental Breakfast
Minimum stay weekends & holidays: 2-3
Notes: 2, 5, 7, 8 (over 12), 9, 10, 11, 12, 13

Garden Gables Inn

141 Main Street
Box 52
Lenox, MA, 01240
(413) 637-0193

A charming 200-year-old gabled inn located in the historic center of Lenox on 5 wooded acres dotted with gardens, maples, and fruit trees. A 72-foot outdoor swimming pool, fireplaces, Jacuzzi. Minutes away from Tanglewood and other attractions. Good skiing in winter. Reasonable rates with breakfast included.

Hosts: Mario & Lynn Mekinda
Rooms: 11 (PB) $60-145
Continental-plus Breakfast
Credit Cards: A, B
Notes: 2, 5, 9, 10, 11, 12, 13, 14

Gateways Inn & Restaurant

71 Walker Street
Lenox, MA, 01240
(413) 637-2532

NOTES: Credit cards accepted: A Master Card; B Visa; C American Express; D Discover Card; E Diners Club; F Other: 2 Personal checks accepted: 3 Lunch available: 4 Dinner available: 5 Open all year

Stay and dine in this elegantly restored inn located in the heart of Lenox. Close to Tanglewood and many cultural attractions. Mobil four-star rated.

Host: Vito Perulli
Rooms: 9 (PB) $90-295
Continental Breakfast
Minimum stay summer weekends: 3
Credit Cards: A, B, C, E
Notes: 2, 4, 5, 9, 10, 12, 13

Pine Acre

111 New Lenox Road
Lenox, MA, 01240
(413) 637-2292

We are nestled in the Berkshire Hills, near many cultural attractions: Tanglewood, Norman Rockwell Museum, ballet at Jacob's Pillow, summer playhouse. Pine Acre is a cozy B&B home with hiking, biking, canoeing, and both cross-country and downhill skiing right at the doorstep. Wood stove in the dining room. Super dining in the area.

Host: Karen Fulco
Rooms: 3 (2 PB; 1 SB) $65
Continental Breakfast
Credit Cards: No
Notes: 2, 5, 7, 8, 9, 10, 11, 12, 13, 14

Underledge Inn

76 Cliffwood Street
Lenox, MA, 01240
(413) 637-0236

Underledge offers elegance and country charm in a Victorian mansion. Large air-conditioned parlor bedrooms are decorated with an air of bygone days. Stroll down the street to discover Lenox Village's fine restaurants, boutiques, galleries, and quaint shops. Minutes from Tanglewood, Berkshire Theater, Jacob's Pillow, Edith Wharton, the opera, and Shakespeare.

Host: Cheryl Lanoue
Rooms: 9 (PB) $60-150
Continental Breakfast
Credit Cards: A, B, C
Notes: 5, 7, 8 (over 10), 9, 10, 11, 12, 13, 14

Walker House

74 Walker Street
Lenox, MA, 01240
(413) 637-1271

Reflecting the owners' tastes and passions, each guest room is named and decorated for a classical composer. The large parlor contains a piano that has been the focal point of many concerts and recitals and the inspiration for many visitors to return to, or try for the first time, the keyboard.

Hosts: Richard & Peggy Houdek
Rooms: 8 (PB) $54.85-153.58
Continental-plus Breakfast
Minimum stay weekends: 2-3; holidays: 3
Credit Cards: No
Notes: 2, 5, 6 (with approval), 8 (12 and over), 9, 10, 11, 12, 13

Walker House

Whistlers' Inn

5 Greenwood Street
Lenox, MA, 01240
(413) 637-0975

Historic 1820 Tudor mansion on 7 acres of woodland just three blocks from the town center. Antique-filled home has eight fireplaces, English library, baronial dining room, and Louis XVI music room with

Steinway and chandeliers. Home-baked breakfast, afternoon sherry/tea.

Hosts: Joan & Richard Mears
Rooms: 11 (PB) $80-190
Full Breakfast
Credit Cards: A, B, C
Notes: 2, 5, 7, 8, 9, 10, 11, 12, 13

LEXINGTON

Bed & Breakfast Folks BB5

48 Springs Road
Bedford, MA, 01730
(617) 275-9025

Enjoy a private three-room suite with separate entrance. Convenient to Cambridge. From $50.

Carol's B&B

B&B Marblehead & North Shore
P.O. Box 172
Beverly, MA, 01915
(508) 921-1336

A pretty Cape Cod home about two miles from the historic Battle Green and only a mile from Route 128/95. Three rooms, shared baths, no smoking. Expanded continental breakfast; children welcome. $55.

Greater Boston Hospitality 86

P.O. Box 1142
Brookline, MA, 02146
(617) 277-5430

Your charming host and hostess offer a twin room with private bath, a single room, and a twin-bedded room. Private and shared baths. One cat and one dog on the premises. Use of other rooms, washer and dryer; swimming available in nearby neighborhood pool. Excellent full breakfast; parking included. Smoking allowed. $55.

Halewood House

2 Larchmont Lane
Lexington, MA, 02173
(617) 862-5404

A quaint New England home. The two B&B rooms and bath are separate from the hostess's living area; well-decorated and beautifully appointed. One features a Laura Ashley print, the other a traditional decor. Large modern bath. Less than one mile from I-95 and downtown Lexington.

Host: Carol Halewood
Rooms: 2 (SB) $55
Continental Breakfast
Credit Cards: No
Notes: 5, 9, 10, 11, 12, 14

Red Cape B&B

61 Williams Road
Lexington, MA, 02173
(617) 862-4913

Historic area with easy access to public transportation to downtown Boston. B&B in a quiet neighborhood; bedroom with private bath is decorated with handmade quilts. Hostess is a retired secretary, interested in quilting and other handwork. Host semiretired engineer and golfer. Resident friendly cat.

Hosts: Ruby & Dick Transue
Rooms: 1 (PB) $50-60
Full Breakfast
Credit Cards: No
Notes: 2, 5, 7 (limited), 8, 9, 10

The Victorian B&B

B&B Marblehead & North Shore
P.O. Box 172
Beverly, MA, 01915
(508) 921-1336

A beautiful home close to many historic sites. Three rooms. The first has a double bed, private bath, and fireplace. The second has twin beds (or a king), private bath, and fireplace. On the second floor, there is a two-room suite with double bed, single studio couch in the sitting room, TV, and private bath. Smoking is permitted, and children are welcome. Continental breakfast. $65-70.

LONGMEADOW

Berkshire B&B Homes GS7

P.O. Box 211
Williamsburg, MA, 01096
(413) 268-7244

1920s Old English country home in a residential neighborhood with antique furniture. One double room with an additional single bed; private or semiprivate bath. Continental breakfast; no smoking; children twelve and over welcome. $50-65.

LOWELL

Bed & Breakfast Folks BB9

48 Springs Road
Bedford, MA, 01730
(617) 275-9025

A restored Victorian in the heart of the National Park district. From $50.

MARBLEHEAD

Greater Boston Hospitality 88

P.O. Box 1142
Brookline, MA, 02146
(617) 277-5430

A gorgeous 1910 English stone and stucco cottage-style mansion set high above the Atlantic, with views that extend forever. Six spacious rooms, each with private bath. Have coffee on a brick terrace nestled in lush flower gardens. Listen to the mewing of the gulls, or watch the black cormorants and eider ducks swimming in the cove. One-minute walk to a sandy beach and a five-minute drive into town, with its restaurants, boutiques, galleries, and shops. Limited smoking; children over twelve welcome. Some rooms have working fireplaces. $100-125.

Greater Boston Hospitality 89

P.O. Box 1142
Brookline, MA, 02146
(617) 277-5430

One hundred yards from the ocean, this mammoth 95-year-old Victorian is owned by a charming couple from New Zealand, a black labrador, and two cats. Full breakfast. Three rooms are available: one with twin beds and a large deck; one with a double bed, deck, and shared bath; one queen room with a private bath. Children over two are welcome. Smoking outside only. $64-69.

The Harbor Light Inn

58 Washington Street
Marblehead, MA, 01945
(617) 631-2186

Premier inn one block from the harbor, with rooms featuring air conditioning, TV, private baths, and working fireplaces. Two rooms have double Jacuzzis and sun decks. Beautiful eighteenth-century period mahogany furniture.

Rooms: 12 (PB) $75-95 + tax
Continental Breakfast
Credit Cards: A, B, C
Notes: 2, 5, 7, 8, 9, 10, 11, 12

Harborside House

23 Gregory Street
Marblehead, MA, 01945
(617) 631-1032

An 1840 colonial in the historic district overlooking Marblehead Harbor, the nation's yachting capital. Near quaint shops, historic sites, beach. Enjoy our breakfast porch, third-story sun deck, antique dining room, fireplaced living room, and resident cat. Hostess is a professional dressmaker and competitive swimmer.

Host: Susan Blake
Rooms: 2 (SB) $65
Continental Breakfast
Credit Cards: No
Notes: 2, 5, 8 (over 10), 10, 11

Harborview

B&B Marblehead & North Shore
P.O. Box 172
Beverly, MA, 01915
(508) 921-1336

This beautifully restored home in Marblehead Neck, built in the 1920s, commands spectacular views of the harbor and has a completely private guest suite. Only one of the two guest rooms is occupied at a time, unless two couples are traveling together. One room has a double bed; the second has two antique twin beds. Restricted smoking. Continental breakfast. Children are welcome; one cat in residence. $85-90.

Marblehead Cape

B&B Marblehead & North Shore
P.O. Box 172
Beverly, MA, 01915
(508) 921-1336

An attractive Cape Cod home in a pretty suburban area close to sandy beaches and the Salem line. Guest rooms are separate from the host's quarters. One room has a double bed and one twin, shared bath. The second room has two twins and a shared bath. No smoking; full or continental breakfast. Air conditioned. Children over six are welcome, and babies. $65.

Oceanfront Tudor

B&B Marblehead & North Shore
P.O. Box 172
Beverly, MA, 01915
(508) 921-1336

This house is on a cliff overlooking the Atlantic, three miles south of Old Town, and a short walk from a sandy beach. Five rooms have private baths. Smoking is permitted; children over six are welcome. Continental breakfast. $95-125.

Old Town Victorian

B&B Marblehead & North Shore
P.O. Box 172
Beverly, MA, 01915
(508) 921-1336

Attractive Victorian in historic Old Town, a quaint, well-manicured area across the street from the harbor above the Boston Yacht Club. The guest sitting room faces the harbor. Four rooms with private baths. Continental breakfast; children welcome; one dog in residence. $85-90.

1752 Antique Colonial

B&B Marblehead & North Shore
P.O. Box 172
Beverly, MA, 01915
(508) 921-1336

Attractive colonial in a quiet area, surrounded by seventeenth- and eighteenth-century colonials. A short walk from the shops and restaurants, with a view of Little Harbor and rooftops. A third-floor room has a queen bed, small private bath, one twin futon, plus a sofa suitable for a child. Continental breakfast; one dog and one cat in residence. $60-65.

Spray Cliff on the Ocean

25 Spray Avenue
Marblehead, MA, 01945
(800) 446-2995; (508) 741-0680

Spray Cliff on the Ocean is a marvelous Old English Tudor mansion set high above the Atlantic with views that extend forever. Six rooms with private baths, some with fireplaces, some with ocean views. Continental breakfast. Steps from a sandy beach.

Hosts: Richard & Diane Pabick
Rooms: 6 (PB) $90-130
Continental Breakfast
Credit Cards: A, B, C, D, E, F
Notes: 2, 5, 7, 8, 9, 10, 11, 12, 13 (XC), 14

Ten Mugford Street

Ten Mugford Street

10 Mugford Street
Marblehead, MA, 01945
(617) 639-0343; 631-5642

Located in the historic district, we offer five two-room suites with private baths, plus four double rooms with shared baths. Two units have kitchens, and three have private living rooms with king-size pull-out couches. Two antique buildings, newly renovated, allow for comfort and charm.

Hosts: Liz & Mike Mentuck
Rooms: 4 (SB) $65-75
Suites: 5 (PB) $75-95
Continental Breakfast
Credit Cards: A, B
Notes: 2, 5, 7, 8, 9, 10, 11, 12

MARSTONS MILLS

B&B Cape Cod 58

P.O. Box 341
West Hyannisport, MA, 02672
(508) 775-2772

This colonial house was built in 1790 and is situated on 3 acres of land overlooking a freshwater pond with swans and ducks. Original outbuildings include a carriage house with a water view. A porch with wicker furniture overlooks the nearby swimming pool. Room one has a double four-poster bed, a working fireplace, and an adjoining area with two twins and a private bath. Room two offers two twin canopy beds, a private bath, and a working fireplace. Rooms three and four have double beds with a bath. Restricted smoking; resident dog; children twelve and over are welcome. $80-110.

MEDFORD

B&B Associates Bay Colony IN210

P.O. Box 57166
Babson Park Branch
Boston, MA, 02157-0166
(617) 449-5302

Just twenty minutes from Concord and Lexington, fifteen from Boston, and 1.5 miles from Tufts University, this young family offers a charming third-floor guest room with antique quilt and brass bed. Bath is shared. Continental breakfast; restricted smoking; children welcome. Resident dog. $55.

MILL RIVER

Covered Bridge 1 MR

P.O. Box 447A
Norfolk, CT, 06058
(203) 542-5944

Circa 1830 colonial filled with country charm, located in a classic New England village amid the lovely Berkshire countryside. Spend your day strolling or cycling, swimming or fishing in the nearby river—or just relax in the hammock. Two rooms, shared bath. Continental-plus breakfast. $65-75.

MONTAGUE

Berkshire B&B Homes PV34

P.O. Box 211
Williamsburg, MA, 01096
(413) 268-7244

Country Victorian on 2 acres, with antique and country furniture. Parlor and den for guest use. One double room, one twin room, shared bath. Full breakfast; restricted smoking, children twelve and over welcome. $50-55.

NAHANT

Nahant Victorian

B&B Marblehead & North Shore
P.O. Box 172
Beverly, MA, 01915
(508) 921-1336

This Victorian home is one block from a sandy beach and has a large porch facing the ocean. Nahant is only fifteen minutes from Logan Airport and twenty minutes from Boston, yet secluded. A third-floor two-room suite has a brass double bed and sitting room. Private bath. Continental breakfast; two cats in residence. $60.

NANTUCKET

Carlisle House Inn

26 North Water Street
Nantucket, MA, 02554
(508) 228-0720

Built in 1765, the Carlisle House has been a quality inn for more than 100 years. Located just off the center of town, the inn has been carefully restored. Hand-stenciled wallpapers, working fireplaces, inlaid pine paneling, wide board floor, rich Oriental carpets.

Hosts: Peter Conway & Sue Arnold
Rooms: 14 (8 PB; 6 SB) $125
Minimum Stay: 2
Continental Breakfast
Credit Cards: C
Notes: 2, 5, 7, 8 (over 10), 9, 14

The Cliff Lodge

The Centerboard Guest House

8 Chester Street
Nantucket, MA, 02554
(508) 228-9696

"Possibly the most elegant and certainly the most romantic of Nantucket's small inns"—*Inn Spots and Special Places in New England,* 1989 edition. A newly restored Victorian guest house close to historic cobblestone Main Street and the beach. Most noteworthy is the handsome suite with Jacuzzi and fireplace.

Hosts: Marcia Wasserman & Reggie Reid
Rooms: 6 (PB) $85-225
Continental Breakfast
Credit Cards: A, B, C
Notes: 2, 5, 7, 11, 12, 14

The Cliff Lodge

9 Cliff Road
Nantucket, MA, 02554
(508) 228-9480

Enjoy bed and breakfast accommodations in a 1771 sea captain's home. Overlooking scenic Nantucket town and harbor, a short walk from the many fine restaurants, art galleries, and shops on Main Street. Beautiful English country decor! See us in *Country Homes* Magazine, August 1988. Cocktail snack served at 5:00 P.M.

Host: Gerrie Miller
Rooms: 12 (PB) $50-150
Continental Breakfast
Credit Cards: A, B, C
Notes: 2, 5, 7, 8 (over 7), 9, 10, 11, 12, 14

Cobblestone Inn

5 Ash Street
Nantucket, MA, 02554
(508) 228-1987

This 1725 home is located on a quiet street in Nantucket's historic district. Just a few minutes' walk from the steamboat wharf, museums, shops, and restaurants. Guests can walk to nearby beaches or explore others by taking a bike path. Relax in the yard, sun porch, and living room.

Hosts: Robin Hammer-Yankow & Keith Yankow
Rooms: 5 (PB) $50-120
Continental Breakfast
Credit Cards: No
Notes: 2, 5, 8, 9, 10, 11, 12

Corner House, Circa 1790

49 Centre Street
Nantucket, MA, 02554
(508) 228-1530

In the heart of Nantucket's old historic district. Experience the spirit of a romantic past in this especially attractive and comfortable eighteenth-century inn. All rooms are furnished in charming detail with antiques, canopy beds, down comforters, pretty sheets. Some rooms have TV. Other joys include the keeping room, screened porch, English garden terrace, afternoon tea, and friendly service. Walking distance to all Nantucket's shops, restaurants, museums, galleries, and beaches. No car needed.

Hosts: John & Sandy Knox-Johnston
Rooms: 14 (PB) $55-130
Continental-plus Breakfast
Credit Cards: A, B
Closed Jan. 4-mid Feb.
Notes: 2 (for deposit), 7, 8 (over 8), 9, 10, 11, 12

Corner House, Circa 1790

Country Island Inn

57 Easton Street
Nantucket, MA, 02554
(508) 228-7461

Recently restored, we offer quiet country elegance and gracious hospitality. Six comfortable guest rooms with private baths, antique furnishings, and distinctive floral papers make each room unique. Short walk to town, ferry, beaches, tennis, shopping, galleries, and restaurants. Open every season; we look forward to your stay.

Hosts: Cheryl Matsubara & Joe Grannan
Rooms: 6 (PB) $75-135
Continental Breakfast
Credit Cards: A, B, C
Notes: 5, 9, 10, 11, 12, 14

The Four Chimneys

The Four Chimneys

38 Orange Street
Nantucket, MA, 02554
(508) 228-1912

155-year-old sea captain's mansion, with canopy beds, ten fireplaces, harbor views, fine antiques, and porches. In the historic district. Continental breakfast is served in your room; cocktail snack at 5:00 P.M.

Host: Bernadette Mannix
Rooms: 10 (PB) $98-155
Continental Breakfast
Minimum stay weekends & holidays: 3
Credit Cards: A, B, C
Closed Dec. 15-April 15
Notes: 2, 8, 9, 10, 11

Grieder Guest House

43 Orange Street
Nantucket, MA, 02554
(508) 228-1399

House built in the early 1700s on the "street of whaling captains." Rooms with four-poster beds, antiques, exposed beams made from ships' knees. Only several minutes' walk from Main Street. Parking permits and refrigerators provided. Large off-street yard.

Hosts: Ruth & Bill Grieder
Rooms: 2 (SB) $55-80
Continental Breakfast
Credit Cards: No
Notes: 2, 7, 8 (over 3), 9, 10, 11, 12

House of Seven Gables

32 Cliff Road
Nantucket, MA, 02554
(508) 228-4706

Located in the old historic district of Nantucket. A continental breakfast is served to your room. Most rooms in this 100-year-old Victorian have a view of Nantucket Sound.

Hosts: Sue & Ed Walton
Rooms: 10 (8 PB; 2 SB) $80-140
Continental Breakfast
Credit Cards: A, B, C
Notes: 2, 5, 7, 8 (over 16), 9, 10, 11, 12

House of Seven Gables

La Petite Maison

132 Main Street
Nantucket, MA, 02554
(508) 228-9242

An owner-managed European inn quietly located five minutes from the center of town. Breakfast on the sun porch with homemade baked goods, stimulating conversation, and new friends from all over the world. Relax in our yard and experience this year's vegetable garden.

Host: Holli Martin
Rooms: 12 (SB) $55-95
Suite: 1 (PB) $150-200
Apartment: $150-200
Continental Breakfast
Credit Cards: No
Closed Dec. 10-April 30
Notes: 2, 6, 7, 8 (over 10), 9, 10, 11, 12, 14

The Periwinkle Guest House

7-9 North Water Street
Nantucket, MA, 02554
(508) 228-9267

The Periwinkle comprises two adjacent nineteenth-century homes in the heart of Nantucket Town. Several top-floor rooms command a harbor view with private, detached private, and shared baths, and suites suitable for families. Double backyard with picnic tables and chairs.

Host: Sara Shlosser-O'Reilly
Rooms: 18 (8 PB; 10 SB) $40-120
Continental Breakfast
Credit Cards: A, B, C
Notes: 2, 5, 7, 8, 9, 10, 11, 12, 14

Seven Sea Street Inn

7 Sea Street
Nantucket, MA, 02554
(508) 228-3577

Seven Sea Street is a red oak, post-and-beam country inn newly constructed with an authentic Nantucket ambience. All guest rooms come with a queen canopy bed, cable TV, small refrigerator, and private bath. Additional amenities include a full-size indoor Jacuzzi whirlpool and widow's walk deck with view of Nantucket Harbor. Ideally located in the historic district.

Hosts: Matthew & Mary Parker
Rooms: 8 (PB) $85-165
Continental Breakfast
Minimum stay weekends: 2; holidays: 3
Credit Cards: A, B, C
Notes: 2, 4, 5, 8 (over 8), 9, 10, 11, 12

76 Main Street

76 Main Street
Nantucket, MA, 02554
(508) 228-2533

All the quiet and subtle beauty of Nantucket is yours to explore while you make yourself comfortable in our 1883 Victorian home in the historic district, on elm-shaded and cobblestone Main Street. We are dedicated to your enjoyment of the island and look forward to accommodating you.

Hosts: Mitch Blake & Shirley Peters
Rooms: 18 (PB) $100-130
Continental Breakfast
Credit Cards: A, B, C
Notes: 2, 5, 8 (in annex), 9, 10, 11, 12, 14

The Summerhouse

South Bluff, Box 313
Siasconset, Nantucket
MA, 02564
(508) 257-9976

The Summerhouse is a romantic hideaway on the ocean on the southeast tip of Nantucket Island. All rooms are in individual antique-filled whaling cottages with private marble baths and Jacuzzi tubs. The property boasts lavish gardens, beachside swimming pool, and gourmet restaurant.

Host: Peter G. Karlson
Rooms: 14 (PB) $175-365
Continental Breakfast
Credit Cards: A, B, C
Open May 15-Nov. 1
Notes: 2, 3, 4, 6, 7, 8, 9, 10, 11, 14

The Woodbox Inn

29 Fair Street
Nantucket, MA, 02554
(508) 228-0587

Nantucket's oldest inn, built in 1709. Located one and one-half blocks from the center of town, the Woodbox offers three double rooms and six suites, all with private bath. Candlelight gourmet dinner available.

Host: Dexter Tutein
Rooms: 9 (PB) $110-175
Full Breakfast
Credit Cards: No
Closed mid-Oct.-June 1
Notes: 2, 4, 7, 8, 9, 10, 11, 12

NEEDHAM

Greater Boston Hospitality 100

P.O. Box 1142
Brookline, MA, 02146
(617) 277-5430

This suburban Williamsburg Cape is minutes from Wellesley or Babson colleges, close to I-95, and within a three-minute walk to the bus to Boston. Beautiful king or twin room with private bath. Parking included. Children welcome. $55.

Greater Boston Hospitality 101

P.O. Box 1142
Brookline, MA, 02146
(617) 277-5430

Beautiful 66-year-old Royal Barry Wills home full of nooks and crannies. Close to Wellesley, Babson, and Mt. Ida colleges, Glover Hospital, and the Route 128 Industrial Park. Three guest rooms, one with queen bed, one with a double, and one with twins. Shared 1.5 baths. Full New England breakfasts are served in the dining room or on the sun deck. No smoking; children over twelve are welcome. $55.

Greater Boston Hospitality 102

P.O. Box 1142
Brookline, MA, 02146
(617) 277-5430

Close to Dedham, West Roxbury, and Wellesley, this large Williamsburg Cape offers a double room with private bath and an extra twin room with crib for other family members. A continental-plus breakfast is served in the lovely dining room. $55.

NEW BEDFORD

B&B Affiliates MA276

P.O. Box 3291
Newport, RI, 02840
(401) 849-1298

Located in the historic district, this 1880s Victorian is walking distance to all attractions. An upstairs sleeping room is tucked under the eaves with private sitting area. On the main floor, the guest room has comfortable furnishings. Both rooms have private baths. Hearty continental breakfast, cats in residence. Children are welcome; restricted smoking. $50.

Pineapple Hospitality MA1041

P.O. Box F821
New Bedford, MA, 02742-0821
(508) 990-1696

This beautifully restored 1860s Gothic Revival cottage is within six blocks of downtown. Two guest rooms are appointed with antique queen bed and headboard or double sleigh bed. Private baths. Continental breakfast is served in the elegant dining room. Smoking is allowed, and children are welcome. $65-75.

NEWBURYPORT

The Morrill Place Inn

B&B Marblehead & North Shore
P.O. Box 172
Beverly, MA, 01915
(508) 921-1336

This beautiful Federal mansion was built in 1806 and is featured in many books because of its stenciled walls and Trompe l'oeil effects. It has twelve fireplaces. Located near the historic downtown harbor area. Nine rooms with antique beds, private and shared baths. No smoking; continental breakfast; children over twelve are welcome. Two cats in residence. $57.75-73.

The Windsor House in Newburyport

38 Federal Street
Newburyport, MA, 01950
(508) 462-3778

This eighteenth-century Federal mansion offers a rare blend of Yankee hospitality and the English bed and breakfast tradition. Spacious rooms recall the spirit of the English country house. Located in an historic seaport near a wildlife refuge, whale watching, and antiques.

Hosts: Judith Alison & John Royston Harris
Rooms: 6 (3 PB; 3 SB) $85-130
Full Breakfast
Minimum stay weekends & holidays: 2
Credit Cards: A, B, D
Notes: 2, 5, 6, 8, 10, 11, 12, 13, 14 (for 3 or more days)

NEWTON

The English Tudor B&B

B&B Marblehead & North Shore
P.O. Box 172
Beverly, MA, 01915
(508) 921-1336

A large home close to Boston College and exclusive shopping malls. Second-floor double room with shared bath; second room with twins and shared bath. On the third floor there is a room with a 3/4 bed, small study, and private bath. Continental breakfast; no smoking; children welcome. $65-85.

Greater Boston Hospitality 107

P.O. Box 1142
Brookline, MA, 02146
(617) 277-5430

This large, beautifully furnished late Victorian has a handsome double room with private adjoining bath. There is also a daybed in a sitting area within the room. Handicapped accessible. Parking included; full breakfast. $65.

Greater Boston Hospitality 108

P.O. Box 1142
Brookline, MA, 02146
(617) 277-5430

Excellent suburban B&B. This custom-built home offers a double room with private bath. Attentive hostess offers a full breakfast and makes homemade peach preserves. Air-conditioned; no smoking; parking included. $70.

Greater Boston Hospitality 109

P.O. Box 1142
Brookline, MA, 02146
(617) 277-5430

Spacious 1898 Queen Anne Victorian offers a double room and a single room with shared bath on the second floor and a small third-floor apartment. Two cats in residence. The second-floor rooms are air conditioned. Fireplace in library and dining room. $55-83.

Nina's Victorian B&B

B&B Marblehead & North Shore
P.O. Box 172
Beverly, MA, 01915
(508) 921-1336

An attractive home in an exclusive area very near public transportation to Boston and Route 128. Four rooms with shared and private baths. Smoking outside only. Continental breakfast. $55-80.

NORTH EASTHAM

Penny House Inn

4885 State Highway
Box 238, Route 6
North Eastham, MA, 02651
(508) 255-6632

Captain Isaiah Horton built the Penny House in 1751. Traditional wide-planked pine floors grace each room of the main house, and 200-year-old beams buttress the ceiling of the public room, where breakfast is served. Only five minutes from the majestic dunes and unspoiled Atlantic beaches of the National Seashore Park and five minutes to the warm waters of Cape Cod Bay. Near the bird sanctuary, miles of bicycle paths, nature trails, and sport fishing.

Hosts: Bill & Margaret Keith
Rooms: 12 (6 PB; 6 S3.5B) $60-110
Full Breakfast
Credit Cards: A, B, C
Notes: 2, 5, 7 (restricted), 8 (over 12), 9, 10, 11, 12, 14

NORTHFIELD

Centennial House B&B

94 Main Street
Northfield, MA, 01360
(413) 498-5921

In its ten years as a bed and breakfast, this lovely old colonial, built in 1811, has hosted guests from throughout the country and the world. Located in one of New England's lovely villages and near the fine independent school, Northfield Mount Hermon, Centennial House looks forward to welcoming you.

Host: Marguerite Linsert Lentz
Rooms: 5 (2 PB; 3 SB) $50-70
Hearty Continental Breakfast
Credit Cards: A, B
Notes: 2, 5, 10, 11, 12, 13

The Squakheag House B&B

RR 2, Box 6
Northfield, MA, 01360
(413) 498-5749

Lovely Federal-period home built in 1824. Four fireplaces, close to cross-country skiing, biking, canoeing, swimming, golf. Set right in the heart of antique country. There's something for every season. Located just four miles from the beautiful Mohawk Trail.

Hosts: David & Cindy Abbe
Rooms: 2 (SB) $50
Full Breakfast
Credit Cards: A, B
Notes: 2, 5, 8, 9, 10, 11, 12, 13

NORTHAMPTON (FLORENCE)

The Knoll

230 North Main Street
Northampton (Florence), MA, 01060
(413) 584-8164

The Knoll is situated on 17 acres overlooking farmland and forest. It is in town and yet in a rural setting with an acre of lawn and large circular driveway. This is the five-college area of western Massachusetts: Smith, Amherst, Mt. Holyoke, the University of Massachusetts, and Hampshire.

Host: Mrs. Lee Lesko
Rooms: 3 (SB) $40-50 + tax
Full Breakfast
Credit Cards: No
Notes: 2, 5, 10, 11, 12, 13

OAK BLUFFS, MARTHA'S VINEYARD

Arend's Samoset on the Sound

Box 847
Oak Bluffs, MA, 02557
(508) 693-5148

Charming Victorian beach house, built in 1873, on the waterfront. Five minutes' walk to the ferries, shops, restaurants, parks, tennis, bike rentals, and so forth. The house offers a living room, piano nook, dining room, sun porch, open porch, widow's walk, and an unobstructed view of the sunrise over Martha's Vineyard Sound.

Hosts: Valgerd & Stanley Arend
Rooms: 8 (3 PB; 5 S3B) $60-100
Continental Breakfast
Credit Cards: A, B, C
Closed Columbus Day-Memorial Day
Notes: 2 (deposit), 7, 8, 9, 10, 11, 12, 14

King's B&B

B&B Cape Cod 201
P.O. Box 341
West Hyannisport, MA, 02672
(508) 775-2772

Built in the eighteen hundreds as a summer cottage, this home is a small B&B inn. It offers six bedrooms with private or shared bath. A full continental breakfast is served in the Victorian antique-filled dining room. The house overlooks a park, with the ocean and beach beyond. The ferry, five blocks away, is an easy walk. Close to the village shops, restaurants, and stores. $75-120.

The Nashua House

P.O. Box 803
Oak Bluffs, MA, 02557
(508) 693-0043

A holiday on Martha's Vineyard on a budget. Clean rooms, continental breakfast in July and August, shared baths, steps to the beach, ferries, harbor, shuttle buses, bike rentals, restaurants, movies, the historic gingerbread campgrounds, and antique carousel by the sea.

Hosts: Harry & son
Rooms: 15 (SB) $25-65
Continental Breakfast
Credit Cards: A, B, C
Closed Oct.-April
Notes: 8 (over 10), 10, 11, 12

The Oak House

Seaview Avenue, Box 299AB
Oak Bluffs, MA, 02557
(508) 693-4187

Enjoy a romantic seaside Victorian holiday. Elegant oak interior in restored 1876 summer home of Governor Claflin. Furnished with antiques; most rooms have ocean view. Wide porches and stained glass sun porch. Daily maid service; afternoon tea; lovely beach; walk to ferry and downtown.

Host: Betsi Convery-Luce
Rooms: 10 (PB) $95-140
Two-room Suite: (PB) $190
Continental Breakfast
Minimum stay weekdays & weekends: 3; holidays: 3
Credit Cards: A, B
Closed Oct. 16-May 10
Notes: 2, 7, 8 (10 and over), 9, 10, 11, 14

ORLEANS

Arey's Pond Relais

Orleans B&B Associates
P.O. Box 1312
Orleans, MA, 02653
(508) 255-3824

A very special house filled with warmth, a myriad of delightful details, and intriguing, unusual collections. Your spacious guest room opens onto a flower-filled patio for your own private use and may serve as a private entrance. Queen bed with white wicker headboard invites rest. Private bath, small guest refrigerator. Walk to freshwater sandy beach. Gourmet breakfast on an expansive deck overlooking Arey's Pond, a saltwater inlet leading to Little Pleasant Bay. $70.

Bird Nest

Orleans B&B Associates
P.O. Box 1312
Orleans, MA, 02653
(508) 255-3824

Large, airy bed/sitting room with king bed, color TV, private bath. A nice feature is the private guest entrance through the front garden and farmer's porch. Breakfast varies daily from continental to full, and is served in the solar garden room. A bird lover and gardener's delight. Ocean, bay, freshwater ponds, and shopping are just minutes away. Ideal spot for walkers or joggers; tandem bike available. $65.

Capt. Doane House

Orleans B&B Associates
P.O. Box 1312
Orleans, MA, 02653
(508) 255-3824

Seafaring Captain Doane built this house in 1810 for his family in the old Rock Harbor area of town, on a quiet lane. The house offers large rooms that speak of years gone by. Upstairs, two double rooms share a brand-new bath. An extra person can be accommodated on a daybed in one room. Adjacent single room. Guest living room with TV and screened porch. Host offers warm Irish hospitality in this old Cape setting. On bike trail; walk to historic Rock Harbor. $50.

1840 House

B&B Cape Cod 69
P.O. Box 341
West Hyannisport, MA, 02672
(508) 775-2772

This 1840 Greek Revival is located in the historic district in the center of Orleans. The first-floor parlor has a fireplace and comfortable furnishings for relaxing at the end of a day at the beach. Four rooms, all with private baths. Continental breakfast. Children over twelve and nonwalking infants are welcome. Restricted smoking; resident dog. An easy walk to fine restaurants, galleries, theater, and the harbor. $65-85.

Gray Gables

Orleans B&B Associates
P.O. Box 1312
Orleans, MA, 02653
(508) 255-3824

An enormous old elm shades a secluded yard with lawn furniture set out for your pleasure. A private entrance leads to the guest wing of a fine old house with plenty of charm and wonderfully warm hosts. Windows on three sides of the spacious guest room, king bed, refrigerator, TV, air conditioning. Bath has huge tiled shower. Full breakfast is served on Limoges china in your room at 8:30, or a continental breakfast will be set out for you if you should care to sleep late. Quiet elegance. $65.

Guest House

Orleans B&B Associates
P.O. Box 1312
Orleans, MA, 02653
(508) 255-3824

This new half-Cape is located off the beaten path, midway between Orleans and Chatham. A private guest area on the second floor has a double room with private bath. A twin room can accommodate another couple or family member. Lovely garden in which birds and wildlife abound. One-half mile to Pleasant Bay beach, continental breakfast. $50.

High Tide (Lan Mara)

Orleans B&B Associates
P.O. Box 1312
Orleans, MA, 02653
(508) 255-3824

Guest wing in traditional Cape house situated near historic Rock Harbor on 7 acres of beautiful marsh and upland. Quiet twin room with private bath. Living room with fireplace. One-half mile to bike trail, and .8 mile to Bay beach. Delicious breakfasts and warm hospitality. $50.

Long View

Orleans B&B Associates
P.O. Box 1312
Orleans, MA, 02653
(508) 255-3824

High above the Town Cove, with sweeping vistas as far as the Atlantic, this house offers a large second-floor king room with sliders opening onto its own private deck. Private bath. Another large twin room can accommodate another couple or adult children. Wonderful for walking or biking, this is an ideal location. Generous continental breakfast. $70.

Maison du Mer

Orleans B&B Associates
P.O. Box 1312
Orleans, MA, 02653
(508) 255-3824

This lovely country contemporary home overlooks Cape Cod Bay, with it sparkling water and brilliant sunsets. Walk down a short, sandy lane lined with wild roses and cranberry bogs to a quiet beach. The guest entrance leads into a large, airy living room, twin room, and modern bath. A sunny dining area for breakfast overlooks pretty seaside garden—or enjoy your meal on the deck. $70.

Mayflower House

Orleans B&B Associates
P.O. Box 1312
Orleans, MA, 02653
(508) 255-3824

This handsome reproduction bow-roof house stands on land that has been in the host's family for generations. A town landing on Pleasant Bay is just a short walk. Breakfast is served in the attractive first-floor parlor. Spacious first-floor room has queen bed. Upstairs, a large second room has two double beds. Both have private baths, color TV, and air-conditioning. Friendly resident Doberman. $60.

Morningside

Orleans B&B Associates
P.O. Box 1312
Orleans, MA, 02653
(508) 255-3824

Waterfront suite with private entrance in a gracious home overlooking Nauset Harbor and the Atlantic, with private beach. Huge room with king bed and sitting area faces the ocean. Private bath, full breakfast. $90.

Roseland Cottage

Orleans B&B Associates
P.O. Box 1312
Orleans, MA, 02653
(508) 255-3824

Old-fashioned charm awaits you as you enter this 1840 Federal house. Guests enjoy the short stroll to the beach via the shaded back road. Continental breakfast with fresh seasonal fruits is served on the lovely screened porch. Picture-book room with double bed, and rustic twin room share modern bath. Three-tenths of a mile to Skaket Beach, 4.5 miles to Nauset Beach. Off the beaten path, but close to everything. $55.

Salty Ridge

Orleans B&B Associates
P.O. Box 1312
Orleans, MA, 02653
(508) 255-3824

A handsome new Cape house with a terrific breezeway that guests love. Right on the Cape Cod Rail Trail for easy access to biking. Large, comfortable rooms on second floor, each with private bath. One king and one with double and twin beds. The atmosphere in this house is relaxed and cordial. Full breakfast with careful attention to special-needs diets. Fine dining within walking distance. One mile to Skaket Beach. $60.

1700 House

Orleans B&B Associates
P.O. Box 1312
Orleans, MA, 02653
(508) 255-3824

A weathered quarterboard marks this historic house. Tender, loving care and sensitive planning has made all the old features gleam, and the mellow country furnishings and collections provide interest at every turn. The subject of many house tours and articles on antique homes, this house is said to be the second oldest in Orleans. First-floor room with high four-poster bed and private bath. Second-floor room has a choice of king or twin beds and private bath. Walk to Academy Playhouse and shops. Swim in Crystal Lake. $65-75.

Sweet Retreat

Orleans B&B Associates
P.O. Box 1312
Orleans, MA, 02653
(508) 255-3824

A delightful in-town studio. Outside stairs lead to a private deck made comfortable with attractive garden furniture. Enter into kitchenette area with breakfast table. A step down into comfortable bedroom with queen bed and private bath. Host owns a patisserie and imaginative catering business. Count on good things being provided for breakfast. Bike to beaches and walk to village art shows, craft fairs, ball games, restaurants, and shops. $65.

Taffrail

Orleans B&B Associates
P.O. Box 1312
Orleans, MA, 02653
(508) 255-3824

Located in one of the choicest areas of Orleans and owned by a delightful couple. Separate entrance leads upstairs to a large room overlooking Nauset Harbor and the Atlantic. Double bed, private bath, and small kitchenette. Living/sitting area with fireplace and TV. Breakfast is available in your own private guest quarters or on the main house patio facing the ocean. Just a short walk to saltwater beach. $85.

Vollerwasser

Orleans B&B Associates
P.O. Box 1312
Orleans, MA, 02653
(508) 255-3824

A private entrance leads to a second-level apartment with large living room overlooking the water. TV and refrigerator. Twin room with full bath. Enjoy the company of your hosts while breakfasting on their handsome waterfront deck at the main house. Observe fascinating bird life and boating activities on Town Cove. Choice secluded area, yet close to beaches, shopping, and restaurants. $75.

Winterwell

Orleans B&B Associates
P.O. Box 1312
Orleans, MA, 02653
(508) 255-3824

Restored eighteenth-century Cape Cod farmhouse just a .3 mile stroll to Skaket Beach. In the main house, a separate entrance leads to a first-floor guest room with double bed and twin bed. Full private bath. Living room for reading or TV. Spacious guest wing with separate entrance offers a bedroom with queen bed, private bath, sitting room, and kitchen/dining area. Continental breakfast is served on the enclosed porch. $60-75.

OTIS

Berkshire B&B Homes SC6

P.O. Box 211
Williamsburg, MA, 01096
(413) 268-7244

One-hundred-year-old country farmhouse on 15 acres with antiques, wraparound screen porch, and glass porch. Very close to private schools; twenty minutes to Lenox. Three rooms with kings (or twins); one queen room; attic with double and twin beds. Attic has a private bath. Others have semiprivate. Full breakfast; no smoking; children ten and over are welcome. Pets in residence. $75-130.

PEABODY

1660 Antique Colonial

B&B Marblehead & North Shore
P.O. Box 172
Beverly, MA, 01915
(508) 921-1336

A beautifully restored historic home, one of the oldest frame homes still standing. It is furnished with antiques throughout and has exquisite decor. The second-floor two-room suite has an antique double bed and fireplace in the bedroom and twin sofabed in the sitting room. Close to Route 128 and Route 95. No smoking. Expanded continental breakfast. Children welcome; resident dog. $75.

PEPPERELL

Bed & Breakfast Folks BB2

48 Springs Road
Bedford, MA, 01730
(617) 275-9025

A lovely restored 200-year-old colonial with a barn full of sheep and horses. Help make maple syrup or enjoy some with your breakfast. A warm, comfortable home with fireplaces in some rooms and lovely antiques in others. From $50.

PERU

American Country Collection 69

984 Gloucester Place
Schenectady, NY, 12309
(518) 370-4948

Built in 1830 as the town parsonage, this private homestay features original wide-plank floor and floor-to-ceiling windows that look out onto old stone walls and 13 acres of woods. Guests dine in a sun room with bay windows and French doors that open onto a patio. Three excellent cross-country centers and one downhill ski area are within eight miles. Excellent hiking, biking, and state forests, two lakes for canoeing, fishing, and swimming are within a mile. Two guest rooms with private bath. One resident cat. Continental-plus breakfast. $55-60.

Chalet d'Alicia

East Windsor Road
Peru, MA, 01235
(413) 655-8292

This Swiss chalet-style home offers a private, casual atmosphere. Set in the Berkshire Mountains, it overlooks the beautiful countryside. Fresh homemade breads and muffins round off the full country breakfasts. Four resident cats and one dog make everyone welcome. Tanglewood, Jacob's Pillow, Williamstown theater, and lots of cross-country skiing are nearby.

Hosts: Alice & Richard Halvorsen
Rooms: 3 (1 PB; 2 SB) $55
Full Breakfast
Credit Cards: No
Notes: 2, 5, 6 (inquire), 7, 8, 9, 10, 11, 12, 13

PETERSHAM

Winterwood at Petersham

North Main Street
Petersham, MA, 01366
(508) 724-8885

An elegant sixteen-room Greek Revival mansion built in 1842, located just off the common of a classic New England town. The inn boasts numerous fireplaces and several porches for relaxing. Cocktails available. On the National Register of Historic Homes.

Hosts: Jean & Robert Day
Rooms: 5 (PB) $63.42-84.56
Continental Breakfast
Credit Cards: A, B, C
Notes: 2, 5, 7, 8, 9, 12

PITTSFIELD

Country Hearts Bed 'N' Breakfast

52 Broad Street
Pittsfield, MA, 01201
(413) 499-3201

Centrally located, Country Hearts is easily accessible to all Berkshire attractions. Nestled on a quiet residential street well known for its collection of beautifully restored "aristocrats," this lovely Painted Lady is waiting to open her doors to you.

Hosts: Jan & Steve Foose
Rooms: 3 (1 PB; 2 SB) $40-75
Full Breakfast
Credit Cards: A, B
Notes: 2, 8, 9, 10, 11, 12, 13

PLAINFIELD

Berkshire B&B Homes PV8

P.O. Box 211
Williamsburg, MA, 01096
(413) 268-7244

1987 chalet-style home with country and contemporary furniture. Den with wood stove. The hosts raise horses. Queen room, twin room; semiprivate bath. Full breakfast; no smoking; children twelve and over welcome. Resident pet. $50-65.

PLYMOUTH

Another Place Inn

240 Sandwich Street
Plymouth, MA, 02360
(508) 746-0126

Another Place is an inn with many facets of charm and convenience. Begin your stay in this antique half-cape with an authentic seventeenth-century breakfast. Plymouth's historic sites and the ocean are all in walking distance. Near Route 3, the Cape, Boston, and Newport.

Host: Carol A. Barnes
Rooms: 2 (SB) $55-60
Full Breakfast
Credit Cards: No
Notes: 2, 5, 8 (call), 11, 12, 14

The Little Inn

Be Our Guest B&B
P.O. Box 1333
Plymouth, MA, 02360
(617) 837-9867

This 200-year-old Federal colonial offers three guest rooms. One has a queen bed and private bath. The second has an antique double bed and shares a bath with the adjoining room with twin mahogany sleigh beds. Built in 1785, the home has fireplaces throughout and many antiques. Less than a mile to the beach, on a scenic road forty minutes south of Boston and twenty minutes north of Plymouth Center. A full breakfast is served. No smoking; children welcome. $60.

Pineapple Hospitality MA1060

P.O. Box F821
New Bedford, MA, 02742-0821
(508) 990-1696

150-year-old sea captain's house, with antiques, Oriental rugs, and heirloom collections. Delightful hostess serves a continental breakfast. Smoking is allowed. One resident Persian cat. $65-75.

Seawinds

Be Our Guest B&B
P.O. Box 1333
Plymouth, MA, 02360
(617) 837-9867

This cozy Cape-style home is located on Vineyard Sound. Walk to the beach or ten minutes to the ferry that takes you to the islands. Three guest rooms. One single and two with double beds share 1.5 baths. Outdoor shower available. Beautifully decorated to make you feel at home. Continental breakfast. $50.

Sycamore

Be Our Guest B&B
P.O. Box 1333
Plymouth, MA, 02360
(617) 837-9867

Conveniently located between Boston and Plymouth, this ranch-style home is within walking distance of the harbor. Beautifully decorated with a blend of contemporary and antiques. A guest room with queen bed, private bath, and deck, is lovely in lace. A second twin room shares a bath with the hosts. A full breakfast is served. Walk to shops and restaurants. $50.

PRINCETON

The Harrington Farm

178 Westminster Road
Princeton, MA, 01541
(508) 464-5600; (800) 736-3276

Located on the western slope of Mount Wachessett, this 1763 farmhouse has the charm and antiques of old and all the modern conveniences you want. Quiet and serene, with hiking and cross-country ski trails starting at our back door. Gourmet dining.

Hosts: Victoria Morgan & John Bomba
Rooms: 8 (3 PB; 4 SB) $57.50-100
Full Breakfast
Credit Cards: A, B
Notes: 2, 4, 5, 6 (limited), 8, 9, 11, 13, 14

PROVINCETOWN

Bed'n B'fast

44 Commercial Street
Provincetown, MA, 02657
(508) 487-9555

Greek Revival, circa 1850, between the town and beach in the quiet West End. Open year round. True bed 'n b'fast, serving full American b'fast till noon. BYOB Safari Bar. Fully equipped apartments also available. Predominately a gay operation, where all are welcome.

Hosts: Bill Gilbert & Dick B. Knudson
Rooms: 5 (2 PB; 3 SB) $42.96-140.16
Full Breakfast
Credit Cards: A, B, C
Notes: 5, 7, 9, 14

Elephant Walk Inn

156 Bradford Street
Provincetown, MA, 02657
(508) 487-2543

A romantic Edwardian inn near Provincetown's center. The spacious, well-appointed rooms offer an eclectic mixture of antique furnishings and decorations. All have private bath, color TV, refrigerators, and ceiling fans. Enjoy our large sun deck of lounge with your morning coffee. Free parking on the premises. Brochure available.

Host: Len Paoletti
Rooms: 8 (PB) $45-78
Continental Breakfast
Credit Cards: A, B, C
Closed Nov.-March
Notes: 2 (deposit), 7, 8 (off-season), 9, 10, 11

Elephant Walk Inn

The Fairbanks Inn

90 Bradford Street
Provincetown, MA, 02657
(508) 487-0386

The Fairbanks Inn is a lovingly restored 200-year-old ship captain's house filled with a collection of art, antiques, and reproductionfurnishings. Rooms have four-poster or canopy beds, Oriental rugs, wide pine-planked floors. Some have working fireplaces. In the summer, a continental breakfast is served on our glass-enclosed porch that overlooks the patio and private gardens.

Host: Don Graichen
Rooms: 14 (7 PB; 7 SB) $48-90
Continental Breakfast
Credit Cards: A, B, C
Notes: 7, 9, 10, 11, 12, 14

Land's End Inn

22 Commercial Street
Provincetown, MA, 02657
(508) 487-0706

High atop Gull Hill, Land's End Inn overlooks Provincetown and all of Cape Cod Bay. Large, airy, comfortably furnished living rooms, a large front porch, and lovely antique-filled rooms provide relaxation and visual pleasure to guests.

Host: David Schoolman
Rooms: 15 (11 PB; 4 SB) $70-200
Continental Breakfast
Minimum stay weekends: 2; holidays: 4; summer: 7
Credit Cards: No
Notes: 2, 5, 7, 8 (infants or over 12), 9, 10, 11, 12, 14

Rose and Crown Guest House

158 Commercial Street
Provincetown, MA, 02657
(508) 487-3332

The Rose and Crown is a classic Georgian "square rigger" built in the 1780s. The guest house sits behind an ornate iron fence, and a ship's figurehead greets visitors from her post above the paneled front door. During restoration, wide floorboards were uncovered and pegged posts and beams exposed. An appealing clutter of Victorian antiques and artwork fills every nook and cranny.

Host: Preston Babbitt, Jr.
Rooms: 8 (PB and SB) $60-100
Continental Breakfast
Credit Cards: C
Notes: 5, 7, 9, 10, 11, 12, 14

White Wind Inn

174 Commercial Street
Provincetown, MA, 02657
(508) 487-1526

A white Victorian, c. 1845, across the street from the beach and five minutes' walk from almost everything. Continental breakfast in season. Please write or call for brochure.

Host: Russell Dusablon
Rooms: 12 (10 PB; 2 SB) $45-110
Continental Breakfast in season
Credit Cards: A, B, C, D, F
Notes: 5, 6 (inquire), 10

Rose and Crown Guest House

REHOBOTH

B&B Affiliates MA159

P.O. Box 3291
Newport, RI, 02840
(401) 849-1298

Enjoy a taste of country life on this 100-acre tree farm. Hike or cross-country ski through the woodland trails out the back door. Farm animals include Shetland ponies, horses, chickens, and pigeons. Take a pony cart out for a slow tour of the area, or help with the chores. Three rooms with shared bath. Full country breakfast. Children over two are welcome; smoking outdoors only. Two box stalls are available for guest horses, and baby-sitting is available. $45.

Perryville Inn

157 Perryville Road
Rehoboth, MA, 02769
(508) 252-9239

This nineteenth-century restored Victorian on the National Register of Historic Places is located on 4.5 wooded acres featuring a quiet brook, mill pond, stone walls, and shaded paths. Bicycles are available for guests, including a tandem, to explore the unspoiled countryside. The inn overlooks an eighteen-hole public golf course. All rooms are furnished with antiques and accented with colorful handmade quilts. Nearby you will find antique stores, museums, Great Woods Performing Arts Center, fine seafood restaurants, and an old-fashioned New England clambake. Arrange for a horse-drawn hayride or a hot-air-balloon ride. Within one hour of Boston, Plymouth, Newport, and Mystic.

Hosts: Tom & Betsy Charnecki
Rooms: 5 (3 PB; 2 SB) $40-75
Continental Breakfast
Credit Cards: A, B, C, D
Notes: 2, 5, 8, 9, 10, 11, 12, 14

RICHMOND

Middlerise B&B

State Road
Richmond, MA, 01254-0017
(413) 698-2687

A charming country home six miles from Tanglewood in the heart of the Berkshires. Quiet, private, and congenial, with a guest living room. Convenient to all winter and summer activities.

Hosts: Carol & Carter White
Rooms: 3 (1 PB; 2 SB) $70-80
Continental Breakfast
Credit Cards: No
Closed Nov. 15-Jan. 31
Notes: 2, 6 (call), 7, 8 (call), 9, 10, 11, 12, 13

Host: Inge Sullivan
Rooms: 6 (PB) $95-115
Continental Breakfast
Credit Cards: A, B
Closed mid-Nov.-mid-May
Notes: 2, 9, 10, 11, 12

ROCKPORT

Bed & Breakfast Folks BB7

48 Springs Road
Bedford, MA, 01730
(617) 275-9025

A lovely separate apartment with windows and doors leading to a private deck overlooking the ocean. From $50.

Bide A Wee B&B

B&B Marblehead & North Shore
P.O. Box 172
Beverly, MA, 01915
(508) 921-1336

Ocean-view antique-furnished Cape Cod house across the road from Halibut Point State Park, a rocky promontory jutting into the ocean with a wonderful sunset view. Three rooms, with private and shared baths. Restricted smoking; resident dog and cat. Children are welcome. Full breakfast on weekends, continental on weekdays. $65-80

Eden Pines Inn

Eden Road
Rockport, MA, 01966
(508) 546-2505

Directly on the ocean in historic Rockport, an old fishing village filled with shops. The inn is within walking distance of two picturesque beaches and affords a most spectacular view of ocean activity — lobstermen, fishermen. Spacious sun deck; private baths and sitting areas in each room.

Eden Pines Inn

The Inn on Cove Hill

37 Mt. Pleasant Street
Rockport, MA, 01966
(508) 546-2701

Our 200-year-old house's ambience features canopy beds and antiques, continental breakfast at our umbrella tables in the garden. The picturesque harbor unfolds from the third-floor porch vista or at dockside one block away.

Hosts: Marjorie & John Pratt
Rooms: 11 (9 PB; 2 SB) $46-90
Continental Breakfast
Minimum stay: 2
Credit Cards: No
Closed late Oct.-March
Notes: 2, 8 (16 and over), 9, 10, 11, 12

Lantana House

22 Broadway
Rockport, MA, 01966
(508) 546-3535

An in-town Victorian guest house open year round in the historic district of Rockport —a classic, picturesque, seacoast village. A one- to five-minute walk takes you to the beaches, art galleries, restaurants, and gift shops. Rockport is an artists' haven.

Host: Cynthia Sewell
Rooms: 7 (5 PB; 2 SB) $60-70
Continental Breakfast
Minimum stay weekdays: 1-3; weekends: 2; holidays: 3
Credit Cards: No
Notes: 2, 5, 7 (restricted), 8, 9, 10, 11, 12

Mooringstone for Nonsmokers

12 Norwood Avenue
Rockport, MA, 01966
(508) 546-2479

Quiet, central location with home-baked muffins and breads at breakfast. Comfortable new ground-floor rooms with air-conditioning, cable TV, refrigerators. Park and walk to beach, restaurants, shops, headlands. Daily, weekly, and off- season rates available. No room tax; ask for our brochure.

Hosts: David & Mary Knowlton
Rooms: 3 (PB) $74-77
Continental Breakfast
Reservation in season: 2
Credit Cards: A, B, C
Closed mid-Oct.-mid-May
Notes: 2, 9, 10, 11, 12

Old Farm Inn

291 Granite Street, Route 127
Rockport, MA, 01966
(508) 546-3237

A country farmhouse inn in a seaside town. Surrounded by an oceanfront park, the inn has a warm, comfortable, peaceful setting, yet dining, shops, and beaches are only minutes away. We share our inn, knowledge of the area, and our hospitality with you.

Hosts: The Balzarini Family
Rooms: 8 (PB) $65-98
Continental-plus Breakfast
Minimum stay weekends: 2; holidays: 3
Credit Cards: A, B, C
Closed Jan.-March
Notes: 2, 7, 8, 9, 10, 11, 12, 14

Pleasant Street Inn

17 Pleasant Street
Rockport, MA, 01966.
(508) 546-3915

Pleasant Street Inn sits on a knoll overlooking Rockport, just one hour north of Boston. The inn has seven guest rooms, all with private baths. Pleasant Street Inn is conveniently located to shops, galleries, restaurants, and beaches. Ample parking.

Hosts: Roger & Lynne Norris
Rooms: 7 (PB) $70-90
Continental Breakfast
Credit Cards: A, B
Notes: 2, 5, 7, 8 (over 6), 9, 10, 11, 12, 14

Ralph Waldo Emerson Inn

Ralph Waldo Emerson Inn

Box 2369
Rockport, MA, 01966
(508) 546-6321

A traditional country inn with a wide front porch overlooking the ocean, the Emerson features Greek Revival architecture, spacious public rooms, heated salt-water pool, sauna and whirlpool, and a theater with an eight-foot screen projector TV and VCR.

Tennis, whale watching, and golf are available nearby. Dinner is served in season.

Host: Gary Wenyss
Rooms: 36 (PB) $83-118
Full Breakfast
Credit Cards: A, B, D
Closed Dec. 1-March 31
Notes: 2, 4, 7, 8, 9, 10, 11, 12

Rocky Shores Inn & Cottages

65 Eden Road
Rockport, MA, 01966
(508) 546-2823

Rocky Shores Inn sits on the easternmost point of Cape Ann, between the picturesque harbors of Rockport and Gloucester. The inn is a 1905 seaside mansion that overlooks the historic twin lights of Thacher Island and the open sea. Our guests enjoy our beautiful beaches, whale watching, sailing, fishing, shopping on famous Bearskin Neck, and having lobsters in harbor-front restaurants.

Hosts: Renate & Gunter Kostka
Rooms: 11 (PB) $78-97
Cottages: 11
Continental-plus Breakfast
Credit Cards: A, B, C
Closed Nov.-March
Notes: 2, 7, 8, 10, 11, 12, 14

Seven South Street—The Inn

7 South Street
Rockport, MA, 01966
(508) 546-6708

Built in 1750, the inn has a friendly, informal atmosphere. In a quiet setting, with gardens, deck, and pool. An ample continental breakfast is served each morning, after which the guest is free to explore the art galleries and shops within walking distance of the inn.

Host: Aileen Lamson
Rooms: 6 (3 PB; 3 SB) $55-72
Continental Breakfast
Credit Cards: No
Notes: 2, 7, 9, 10, 11, 12

SAGAMORE BEACH

B&B of Sagamore Beach

One Hawes Road
Sagamore Beach, MA, 02562
(508) 888-1559

A private, peaceful home overlooking Cape Cod Bay. Sixty miles to Provincetown or Boston. Relax in the casual atmosphere in front of the fireplace or on the large porches and decks that surround the house. Walk for miles on the quiet, sandy beach. Home has been featured in *Bon Appetit* and *Better Homes & Gardens.*

Host: John F. Carafoli
Rooms: 3 (SB) $85
Continental Breakfast
Credit Cards: No
Notes: 2, 5, 9, 10, 11, 12, 14

Sea Cliff B&B

B&B Cape Cod 19
P.O. Box 341
West Hyannisport, MA, 02672
(508) 775-2772

This three-level contemporary Cape was built in 1989. In a quiet, secluded setting, with passive solar heating. The back of the house faces Cape Cod Bay. There are two guest rooms on the second floor. One has a queen bed and private bath. The second room has two twins. They share a bath. Room three is a suite with private entrance, ocean deck, parlor, fireplace, private bath, and small kitchen. A full breakfast is served in the dining room. Restricted smoking; children are welcome. $95-150.

SALEM

Amelia Payson House

16 Winter Street
Salem, MA, 01970
(508) 744-8304

Built in 1845, this fine example of Greek Revival architecture is located in the heart of Salem's historic district. Guest rooms are furnished with canopy or brass beds and antiques. A five-minute stroll to downtown shopping, historic houses, museums, Pickering Wharf's waterfront dining, and train station.

Hosts: Ada & Donald Roberts
Rooms: 4 (2 PB; 2 SB) $55-85
Continental Breakfast
Credit Cards: A, B, C
Notes: 5, 8 (over 12), 9, 10, 11, 12

Antique Colonial Guest House

B&B Marblehead & North Shore
P.O. Box 172
Beverly, MA, 01915
(508) 921-1336

An attractive antique-furnished home one block from the harbor and the Peabody Museum and half a block from the Salem Common. Four rooms with private baths. Smoking is permitted. Continental breakfast; air-conditioning. Children are welcome. $80.

Coach House Inn

284 Lafayette Street
Salem, MA, 01970
(508) 744-4092

Return to the elegance of an earlier time. Enjoy the intimacy of a small European-type hotel. Cozy, comfortable rooms with private baths retain the charm of this Victorian mansion. Complimentary continental breakfast. Air-conditioning, off-street parking. Only sixteen miles from Boston.

Host: Patricia Kessler
Rooms: 11 (9 PB; 2 SB) $74-86
Continental Breakfast
Credit Cards: A, B, C
Notes: 5, 7, 8, 9, 10, 11, 12, 13

1845 Antique Colonial

B&B Marblehead & North Shore
P.O. Box 172
Beverly, MA, 01915
(508) 921-1336

Beautifully restored Greek Revival house decorated in antiques. Just around the corner from the Witch Museum and the Essex Institute. Four rooms with shared and private baths. No smoking; children over eight are welcome. Continental breakfast. $65-95.

Hammond-Osgood-Dodge House

B&B Marblehead & North Shore
P.O. Box 172
Beverly, MA, 01915
(508) 921-1336

An 1830 Federal row house in the historic district of Salem, beautifully furnished with many antiques. There is a third-floor room with antique four-poster French Twist double canopy bed, private bath, and working fireplace. A second room offers twin beds and a shared bath. Smoking is permitted. Full breakfast; children welcome. $65-67.

The Inn at Seven Winter St.

7 Winter Street
Salem, MA, 01970
(508) 745-9520

The inn is an impeccably restored French Victorian home, with each room finely appointed with antiques and period furniture. Private baths, cable TV, phone, air-conditioning in every room. Some have fireplaces; others have a large sun deck. Excellent location in the historic district. Please write or call for our brochure. We offer a smoke-free environment.

Hosts: Sally Flint, Jill & Dee L. Cote
Rooms: 9 (PB) $65-85
Suite (PB) $110
Continental Breakfast
Credit Cards: A, B, C
Notes: 2, 5, 8, 9, 10, 11, 12, 13, 14

The Salem Inn

7 Summer Street
Salem, MA, 01970
(508) 741-0680; (800) 446-2995

Elegantly restored 1834 Federal townhouse, located in the heart of Salem's historic district. Twenty-one luxuriously appointed rooms with private baths and some working fireplaces. Direct-dial phones, TVs, and air-conditioning. Hearty continental breakfast and lovely rose garden Courtyard Cafe.

Hosts: Richard & Diane Pabich
Rooms: 22 (PB) $80-100
Continental Breakfast
Credit Cards: A, B, C, D, E, F
Notes: 2, 3, 4, 5, 7, 8, 9, 10, 11, 12, 13 (XC), 14

The Schoolhouse B&B

B&B Marblehead & North Shore
P.O. Box 172
Beverly, MA, 01915
(508) 921-1336

A beautifully decorated home in a turn-of-the-century schoolhouse converted to a condo. There are skylights and cathedral ceilings to enjoy. A short walk from the Salem commuter rail station. The large second-floor room has twin beds, private bath, TV. No smoking; continental breakfast; air conditioning. Babies and children over five are welcome. $60. Minimum two nights.

Stephen Daniels House

1 Daniels Street
Salem, MA, 01970
(508) 744-5709

Built by a sea captain in 1667 and enlarged in 1756. The house is beautifully restored and furnished with antiques. Wood-burning fireplaces in the bedrooms with charming canopy beds. Continental breakfast is served before two huge fireplaces. Walk to all points of interest in Salem.

Host: Mrs. Catherine Gill
Rooms: 5 (3 PB; 2 SB) $50-95
Continental Breakfast
Credit Cards: C
Notes: 2, 5, 6, 7, 8, 9, 10, 11, 12, 13

SANDWICH

Academy Hill B&B

B&B Cape Cod 15
P.O. Box 341
West Hyannisport, MA, 02672
(508) 775-2772

High on Academy Hill, this sixty-year-old Cape overlooks the village of Sandwich. A spacious queen room and twin room with private baths are available. Continental breakfast in the dining area or on the porch. Walk to all town facilities. $65-70.

Capt. Ezra Nye House

152 Main Street
Sandwich, MA, 02563
(508) 888-6142; (800) 388-2278

A sense of history and romance fills this 1829 Federal home, built by the distinguished clipper ship captain Ezra Nye. Located in the heart of the oldest town on Cape Cod, the inn is near many famous attractions.

Hosts: Elaine & Harry Dickson
Rooms: 6 (4 PB; 2 SB) $50-80
Continental-plus Breakfast
Minimum stay holidays: 2
Credit Cards: A, B, C
Notes: 2, 5, 8 (6 and over), 9, 10, 11, 12, 14

Hawthorn Hill

Box 777
Sandwich, MA, 02563
(508) 888-3333; 3336

Rambling English country house with continental hospitality. Quiet and serene, yet close to all attractions. Situated on Shawme Pond, adjacent to Heritage Plantation. Large, sunny breakfast and living room, deck, woods to roam in, rowboat for exercise. Short distance to beaches.

Host: Maxime Caron
Rooms: 2 (PB) $70
Full Breakfast
Credit Cards: C
Notes: 2, 7, 8, 9, 10, 11, 12

Isaiah Jones Homestead

Isaiah Jones Homestead

165 Main Street
Sandwich, MA, 02563
(508) 888-9115

An intimate Victorian bed and breakfast inn with beautiful antiques, fresh flowers, and candlelight. Homemade, freshly baked breakfast and afternoon tea. Walk to most points of interest. "Superior in every respect—a trip into the past."

Hosts: Kathy & Steven Catania
Rooms: 4 (PB) $71.31-120.47
Continental Breakfast
Minimum stay weekends & holidays: 2
Credit Cards: A, B, C, D
Closed Christmas Eve & Christmas Day
Notes: 2, 10, 11, 12, 14

SCITUATE

Christine's B&B

B&B Cape Cod 64
P.O. Box 341
West Hyannisport, MA, 02672
(508) 775-2772

This lovely Victorian home built in 1905 has a commanding view of Scituate Harbor. Bedrooms have a water view from one or more windows. It is a few hundred feet to the harbor. Four rooms, two with private baths, are decorated in Victorian style. A gourmet breakfast is served in the dining room or on the porch overlooking the harbor. Children sixteen and over are welcome; smoking outside only. Two resident cats. $74.74-80.42.

Rasberry Ink

748 Country Way
North Scituate, MA, 02066
(617) 545-6624

Coastal Scituate is 350 years old, located 25 miles southeast of Boston, midway between Boston and Plymouth. Scituate was the home of Thomas Lawson—an early 1900s copper king—Lawson estate is close by. Raspberry Ink is an early Victorian farmhouse furnished in lace and antiques, located in the village. Lots of antique shops nearby; ocean and historical sites.

Hosts: Fran Honkonen & Carol Hoban
Rooms: 2 (SB) $65
Continental Breakfast
Credit Cards: No
Closed Christmas, New Year's, Thanksgiving
Notes: 2, 10, 11, 12, 13 (XC)

SEEKONK

B&B Affiliates MA225

P.O. Box 3291
Newport, RI, 02840
(401) 849-1298

This 1799 Federal house is a National Historic Property nestled on a 9-acre knoll overlooking the fields and banks of the Palmer River. Breakfast is served in the original kitchen with its massive cooking fireplace. Three rooms with shared baths. Full country breakfast. Children are welcome; smoking outdoors only. $45.

SHEFFIELD

A Unique Bed & Breakfast Inn

Box 729
Sheffield, MA, 01257
(413) 229-3363

A most relaxing B&B. Cozy, attractively furnished and decorated. Central air-conditioning. Lounge/dining room with fireplace. Full buffet country breakfast. Twenty minutes to Tanglewood Music Festival; fifteen to Lime Rock; ten to skiing. Hand-ironed percale sheets, fresh flowers in rooms. Antique shops galore.

Host: May Stendardi
Rooms: 3 (PB) $95-110
Full Breakfast
Minimum stay weekends & holidays: 2-3
Credit Cards: A, B (for reservations only)
Notes: 5, 8 (15 and over), 9, 10, 11, 12, 13

Covered Bridge 1 SH

P.O. Box 447A
Norfolk, CT, 06058
(203) 542-5944

This charming log home, commanding a sweeping view of the Berkshires, is the perfect spot for an idyllic pastoral retreat. A horse grazes nearby, and it's a short walk across the fields to the swimming pond. Two rooms, shared bath, full breakfast. $85.

Covered Bridge 2 SH

P.O. Box 447A
Norfolk, CT, 06058
(203) 542-5944

1771 colonial set in the village of Sheffield, surrounded by antique shops and close to Tanglewood. There are several common rooms for guests to enjoy, as well as a tree-shaded terrace. The four guest rooms are decorated with antiques; one has a canopy bed. One private bath, three shared, full breakfast. $80-90.

Staveleigh House

South Main Street
Sheffield, MA, 01257
(413) 229-2129

Renovated 1821 Georgian colonial in the center of the historic district. Five guest rooms furnished for maximum comfort. Full breakfast, afternoon tea. Close to all Berkshire cultural and scenic attractions. Sheffield is well-known as a center for antiques, with more than thirty shops.

Hosts: Marion Whitman & Dorothy Marosy
Rooms: 5 (2 PB; 3 SB) $63.42-89.85
Full Breakfast
Minimum stay weekends: 2
Credit Cards: No
Notes: 2, 5, 8 (over 12), 9, 10, 11, 12, 13

Staveleigh House

SOMERSET

B&B Affiliates MA267

P.O. Box 3291
Newport, RI, 02840
(401) 849-1298

This beautiful Greek Revival house, built in 1845 on gardens that date back to the 1700s, once served as a sea captain's home. There is a large dining room with fireplace, where a gourmet breakfast is served. Guests may also use the spacious living room with fireplace and stereo. Two second-floor rooms with shared bath and a suite with balcony and fireplace. Pets in residence; children welcome; outdoor smoking only. $45-70.

SOMERVILLE

Greater Boston Hospitality 131

P.O. Box 1142
Brookline, MA, 02146
(617) 277-5430

Immaculately maintained mansard Victorian with twin and king rooms with private half-bath or shared bath and deck. Full breakfast on weekends, continental-plus during the week. Minutes to Tufts University. No smoking; children welcome; parking included. $63.

SOUTH CHATHAM

Ye Olde Nantucket House

Box 468
South Chatham, MA, 02659
(508) 432-5641

Built on Nantucket in 1840 and later moved to its present location, the inn has five rooms with private baths and Victorian decor. Shopping, the Chatham lighthouse, recreational activities, and a Nantucket Sound beach are all nearby.

Host: Norm Anderton
Rooms: 5 (PB) $62-75
Continental-plus Breakfast
Credit Cards: A, B
Notes: 2 (deposit), 5, 8 (over 8), 9, 10, 11, 12, 14

SOUTH DARTMOUTH

B&B Affiliates MA293

P.O. Box 3291
Newport, RI, 02840
(401) 849-1298

Located in a lovely coastal area overlooking horse and cow pasture close to the harbor and historic sites. Two second-floor guest rooms are tastefully appointed with many antiques. Hearty continental breakfast; cat in residence; no children; smoking outside only. $50.

SOUTH EGREMONT

The Egremont Inn

Old Sheffield Road
South Egremont, MA, 01258
(413) 528-2111; (800) 255-7213

Located in the historic district, this 1780 inn has several dining rooms, public sitting areas, bar, tavern, swimming pool, tennis courts, and 22 guest rooms. Breakfast and dinner included.

Host: John Black
Rooms: 22 (PB) $90-175
Continental Breakfast
Credit Cards: A, B, C, D
Minimum stay summer weekends: 3
Notes: 2, 4, 5, 6, 7, 8, 9, 10, 11, 12, 13, 14

SOUTH HADLEY

Berkshire B&B Homes PV4

P.O. Box 211
Williamsburg, MA, 01096
(413) 268-7244

This 1794 colonial is tastefully furnished with antiques and offers a sitting room for guests' use. Two double rooms and two single rooms, continental breakfast, restricted smoking. Children ten and over are welcome. Shared baths. $35-55.

Berkshire B&B Homes PV 13

P.O. Box 211
Williamsburg, MA, 01096
(413) 268-7244

1920 Garrison Colonial on .75 acre of land. Traditional furniture; parlor for guest use. Twin beds, shared bath. Continental breakfast, restricted smoking, children welcome. $45-55.

Merrell Tavern Inn

SOUTH LEE

Merrell Tavern Inn

Route 102, Main Street
South Lee, MA, 01260
(413) 243-1794

This 200-year-old brick stagecoach inn is listed on the National Register and located in a small New England village along the banks of the Housatonic River. Rooms with fireplaces, canopy beds, and antique furnishings. Full breakfast is served in the original tavern room. One mile to Norman Rockwell's beloved Stockbridge.

Hosts: Charles & Faith Reynolds
Rooms: 9 (PB) $55-130
Full Breakfast
Credit Cards: A, B, C
Notes: 5, 8, 9, 10, 11, 12, 13, 14

SOUTH ORLEANS

La Mouette (The Gull)

Orleans B&B Associates
P.O. Box 1312
Orleans, MA, 02653
(508) 255-3824

This beautiful house offers exceptional hospitality and comfort in any season. On the first floor, elegant, spacious rooms are inviting. Gourmet breakfast is served in the large, cheerful sun room. Upstairs are two guest rooms: a double room with sitting room facing the water, private bath; and a large twin room with water view and private bath with Jacuzzi. $90.

Lockwood House

Orleans B&B Associates
P.O. Box 1312
Orleans, MA, 02653
(508) 255-3824

Large ancestral home lovingly maintained by young hosts. Private dock on the waters of Pleasant Bay. Very old Cape feeling—nostalgic. One double room with full bath, private porch and entrance. Adjoining library. Continental breakfast is served on your porch or in the library. Animal lovers especially welcome, as hosts have two well-behaved dogs and a cat. Near famous Captains golf course. $70.

SOUTH YARMOUTH

Belvedere B&B

B&B Cape Cod 2
P.O. Box 341
West Hyannisport, MA, 02672
(508) 775-2772

This 1820 sea captain's house has wide board floors and a widow's walk. It is restored and in immaculate condition. Each of the three rooms is Victorian in decor. One has a private bath, and two share a bath. Walk to the beach and fine restaurants. This hostess serves a continental breakfast in the dining room. A carriage house is also available for four guests. $60-70.

SPRINGFIELD

Berkshire B&B Homes GS 3

P.O. Box 211
Williamsburg, MA, 01096
(413) 268-7244

1940s Tudor style home on .25 acre. Formal furniture. Living room and patio for guest use. Pond across the street. King and queen rooms share a bath. Full breakfast, restricted smoking, children welcome, pets in residence. $45-55.

Berkshire B&B Homes GS 4

P.O. Box 211
Williamsburg, MA, 01096
(413) 268-7244

1896 Victorian on .25 acre. Victorian and antique furniture. Formal parlor, library, and TV room for guest use. Queen bed, shared or private bath. Continental breakfast, no smoking, children welcome, animal in residence. $55-60.

Berkshire B&B Homes GS 5

P.O. Box 211
Williamsburg, MA, 01096
(413) 268-7244

1920s colonial revival home on .5 acre. American traditional furnishings. Double bed with pullout double; twin beds; single bed. Shared bath. Continental breakfast, no smoking, children welcome. $35-50.

Berkshire B&B Homes GS 6

P.O. Box 211
Williamsburg, MA, 01096
(413) 268-7244

1896 Greek Revival on .25 acre. Colonial and antique furniture. Parlor for guest use. View of Forest Park. Three twin rooms, shared bath. Continental breakfast, no smoking, children six and over welcome. $45-50.

STOCKBRIDGE

The Inn at Stockbridge

Route 7, Box 618
Stockbridge, MA, 01262
(413) 298-3337

An elegant Georgian colonial set on 12 acres. Each room is individually decorated with antiques and reproductions. Eight rooms, each with private bath, five with king beds. A scrumptious full breakfast is served in a formal dining room setting. In-ground pool. Complimentary wine and cheese. Near Tanglewood, Rockwell Museum, and all Berkshire attractions.

Hosts: Lee & Don Weitz
Rooms: 8 (PB) $75-160
Full Breakfast
Credit Cards: A, B, C
Notes: 2, 5, 7 (limited), 8 (over 12), 9, 10, 11, 12, 13, 14

Woodside B&B

Box 1096
Stockbridge, MA, 01262
(413) 298-4977

Enjoy comfort and hospitality in our contemporary country home located just one mile from the center of Stockbridge, home of the Norman Rockwell Museum. Close to Tanglewood, Chesterwood, Jacob's Pillow Dance Festival. In winter, enjoy skiing at nearby resorts. Handicapped access, special diets accommodated.

Hosts: Paula Schutzmann, R.N., Sarah & Katie Harvey
Rooms: 3 (1 PB; 2 SB) $55-85
Full Breakfast weekends, Continental on weekdays
Credit Cards: A, B
Notes: 2, 5, 6, 7 (restricted), 8, 9, 10, 11, 12, 13

STURBRIDGE

Berkshire B&B Homes ST 3

P.O. Box 211
Williamsburg, MA, 01096
(413) 268-7244

1971 Dutch gambrel home with country and antique furniture. Parlor for guest use. High English Tea by reservation. One double with private bath; another double and twin room with shared bath. Full breakfast, no smoking, children welcome. $55-65.

Berkshire B&B Homes ST 7

P.O. Box 211
Williamsburg, MA, 01096
(413) 268-7244

1988 English Tudor home on 3.5 acres. Modern and contemporary furniture. Parlor for guest use, FAX machine. Twin beds, private bath. Full room with futon and semi-private bath. Full breakfast, no smoking, children ten and over welcome, animals in residence. $50-60.

Berkshire B&B Homes ST 8

P.O. Box 211
Williamsburg, MA, 01096
(413) 268-7244

1987 contemporary post-and-beam home on 1.5 acres. Antique and contemporary furnishings. The house overlooks a lovely lake. Double room with private bath and a small sitting area with view of lake. Twin room with private bath has a view of the woods. Full breakfast, no smoking, children fourteen and older are welcome. $65-75.

Bethlehem Inn

72 Stallion Hill, Box 451
Sturbridge, MA, 01566
(508) 347-3013

Bethlehem Inn is operated to help defray the costs of operating Bethlehem in Sturbridge. Guests share the family living room and TV.

Host: Agnes Duquette
Rooms: 2 (1 PB; 1 SB) $40-60
Continental Breakfast
Credit Cards: No
Closed December
Notes: 2, 7, 9, 10, 11, 12, 13

Sturbridge Country Inn

530 Main Street
Sturbridge, MA, 01566
(508) 347-5503

Circa 1840 Greek Revival mansion, fully restored post-and-beam structure. Vaulted ceilings, sun porches. Each room has a fireplace and luxury bath, plus many amenities. Close to Old Sturbridge Village. Conveniently located in the heart of Sturbridge.

Host: Kevin MacConnell
Rooms: 9 (PB) $79-99
Continental Breakfast
Credit Cards: A, B, C, D
Notes: 2, 4, 5, 7, 8, 9, 10, 11, 12, 13

SUDBURY

Checkerberry Corner B&B

5 Checkerberry Circle
Sudbury, MA, 01776
(508) 443-8660

Located in a quiet residential neighborhood, we are only a short drive to Longfellow's Wayside Inn, the Old North Bridge, the Alcott, Emerson, Hawthorne, and Thoreau houses. Boston's Freedom Trail, Quincy Markets, and other attractions are easily reached within forty minutes.

Hosts: Stu & Irene MacDonald
Rooms: 3 (SB) $55-65
Full Breakfast
Credit Cards: No
Notes: 2, 5, 8, 9, 14

SWAMPSCOTT

The Maguire's

43 Hampden Street
Swampscott, MA, 01907
(617) 593-5732

Located two blocks from the Atlantic Ocean and public beaches, ten miles from historic Boston. Public transportation available. Horse and dog racing is held daily within eight miles, and there are famous restaurants along the North Shore. Twenty miles from Lexington and Concord; five from Salem; eighteen from Gloucester and Rockport.

Hosts: Tom & Arline Maguire
Rooms: 3 (SB) $50
Full breakfast weekends; continental weekdays
Credit Cards: No
Notes: 5, 7, 8, 9, 10, 11, 12

Oak Shores B&B

64 Fuller Avenue
Swampscott, MA, 01907
(617) 599-7677

This 60-year-old Dutch colonial is on Boston's lovely North Shore. Rooms are filled with fine restored furniture. Sleep in the comfort of old brass and iron beds, relax in our private garden, or stroll the two blocks to the beach. Near public transportation.

Host: Marjorie L. McClung
Rooms: 2 (SB) $60
Continental Breakfast
Credit Cards: No
Closed Dec. 2-March 31
Notes: 8 (9 and over), 10, 11

Oak Shores B&B

Oceanview Victorian

B&B Marblehead & North Shore
P.O. Box 172
Beverly, MA, 01915
(508) 921-1336

Beautiful Victorian with American country decor and hand-stenciled walls. Four guest rooms share two baths. No smoking; continental breakfast; air conditioned. Children over six are welcome. $60-70.

Vinnin Square

B&B Marblehead & North Shore
P.O. Box 172
Beverly, MA, 01915
(508) 921-1336

Attractive condo next to shopping mall close to Marblehead, Swampscott, and Salem.

The guest room offers a queen bed and shared bath. Smoking is permitted; continental breakfast; air conditioning. Children are welcome. Swimming pool and tennis courts on premises. $55-60.

TOPSFIELD

The Wild Berry B&B

B&B Marblehead & North Shore
P.O. Box 172
Beverly, MA, 01915
(508) 921-1336

A Greek Revival home close to Hood's Pond, where guests may swim. In winter, there are cross-country ski trails behind the house. This is an historic small town where you may expect riders on horseback to share the road with you. Visit the Ipswich River Audubon Sanctuary, where you may rent a canoe and paddle down the river. Two second-floor rooms; one with private bath and one with shared bath. Smoking outdoors only. Children are welcome; dogs in residence. Full breakfast. $60-75.

TRURO

Edgewood Farm

Orleans B&B Associates
P.O. Box 1312
Orleans, MA, 02653
(508) 255-3824

This is authentic rural Truro as our grandparents knew it. Private lane leads to a typical old Cape house and a long, low cottage. Surrounded by meadows, a trail up Great Hill overlooks the Atlantic. The cottage offers two studios, each with private bath. One has a fireplace and kitchenette, the other a nice sun room opening onto extensive lawns. There is also one double room with bath on the second floor of the main house. Breakfast is served in the dining room adjacent to a comfortable lounge. Fine collection of early Provincetown paintings. $65-70.

The Parker House

P.O. Box 1111
Truro, MA, 02666
(508) 349-3358

The Parker House is a warm, charming, classic 1820s full Cape, overlooking the center of Truro. Located midway between the bay and ocean, with both beaches within walking distance. Restaurants and quaint streets of Provincetown and Wellfleet are ten minutes away by car.

Host: Stephen Williams
Rooms: 2 (SB) $55
Continental Breakfast
Credit Cards: No
Notes: 2, 5, 10, 11, 12

The Golden Goose

TYRINGHAM

The Golden Goose

Main Road
Tyringham, MA, 01264
(413) 243-3008

Small, friendly 1800 country inn, nestled in Tyringham Valley in the Berkshires. Victorian antiques, sitting rooms with fireplaces, homemade breakfast fare. Within a half hour are Tanglewood, Stockbridge, Jacob's Pillow, Hancock Shaker Village, the Norman Rockwell Museum, Berkshire Theater Festival, skiing, golf, tennis. The inn is a mile off the Appalachian Trail.

Hosts: Lilja & Joe Rizzo
Rooms: 6 (4 PB; 2 SB) $60-110
Continental-plus Breakfast
Credit Cards: No
Notes: 2, 5, 7, 8 (in apartment), 9, 10, 11, 12, 13, 14

VINEYARD HAVEN, MARTHA'S VINEYARD

The Bayberry

RFD 1, Box 546
Vineyard Haven, MA, 02568
(508) 693-1984

The Bayberry is a charming Cape Cod-style home with brick chimneys and silver-gray weathered shingles. Each of the five guest rooms features antique furnishings. Breakfast of hot, homemade bread, freshly brewed coffee, and a special main dish is served before the fireplace or out on the terrace. We can pack a picnic basket for your day or arrange a game of golf or tennis for you. After a busy day, relax with other guests on the terrace and enjoy the complimentary tea, wine, and delicious hors d'oeuvres.

Host: Rosalie Powell
Rooms: 5 (3 PB; 2 SB) $95-130
Full Breakfast
Credit Cards: A, B
Notes: 2, 5, 8 (over 12), 9, 10, 11, 12

Crocker House Inn

4 Crocker Avenue
P.O. Box 1658
Vineyard Haven, MA, 02568
(508) 693-1151

A charming turn-of-the-century Victorian home with eight spacious rooms, each with private bath. Three rooms feature private entrances and balconies. Our honeymoon suite is equipped with working fireplace. The inn is just a short walk from the beach, ferry landing, shops, and restaurants. Continental breakfast is included in the rate. A nonsmoking inn.

Host: Darlene Stavens
Rooms: 8 (PB) $70-160
Continental Breakfast
Credit Cards: A, B
Notes: 2, 9, 10, 11, 12, 14

High Haven House

P.O. Box 289
Vineyard Haven, MA, 02568
(508) 693-9204

On the island of Martha's Vineyard, a short walk from the shops and ferry. Pool, hot tub; beautiful beaches and nature trails are nearby, as well as fishing and boating. Third night free off season.

Hosts: Joe & Kathleen Schreck
Rooms: 11 (4 PB; 7 SB) $65-110
Continental Breakfast
Credit Cards: A, B, C
Notes: 2, 5, 7, 8, 9, 10, 11, 12, 14

Lothrop Merry House

Lothrop Merry House

Owen Park, Box 1939
Vineyard Haven, MA, 02568
(508) 693-1646

The Merry House, built in the 1790s, overlooks beautiful Vineyard Haven Harbor, has a private beach, expansive lawn, flower-bordered terrace. Most rooms have ocean view and fireplace. All are charming, furnished with antiques and fresh flowers. Complimentary canoe and sunfish for guests' use. Sailing also available on our 54' ketch, *Laissez Faire.* Close to ferry and shops. Open year round.

Hosts: John & Mary Clarke
Rooms: 7 (4 PB; 3 SB) $60-150
Continental Breakfast
Minimum stay weekends & holidays: 2-3
Credit Cards: A, B
Notes: 2 (for deposit), 5, 7, 8, 9, 10, 11, 12, 14

Thorncroft Inn

Box 1022
Vineyard Haven, MA, 02568
(508) 693-3333

Nineteen antique-appointed rooms in four restored buildings. Private baths, working fireplaces, air-conditioning, two-person Jacuzzis. Romantic and intimate, in a non-commercial environment. Located on 3.5 landscaped acres in an exclusive residential neighborhood one mile from the main ferry dock.

Hosts: Karl & Lynn Buder
Rooms: 19 (PB) $99-249
Full Breakfast
Minimum stay weekends & holidays in season: 3
Credit Cards: A, B, C, F
Notes: 2, 4, 5, 7 (limited), 8 (over 12), 9, 14

WARE

1880 Inn

14 Pleasant Street
Ware, MA, 01082
(413) 967-7847

A beautiful twelve-room colonial inn, complete with six fireplaces and rustic country beams. Each room is named. Enjoy afternoon tea before the cozy fireplace.

Host: Margaret Skutnik
Rooms: 5 (2 PB; 3 SB) $52.25-57.75
Full Breakfast
Minimum stay weekends & holidays: 2
Credit Cards: No
Notes: 5, 8, 9, 10, 11, 12, 14

WAREHAM

Little Harbor Guest House

20 Stockton Shortcut
Wareham, MA, 02571
(508) 295-6329

Surrounded by an eighteen-hole golf course, we are a short half-hour drive to Plymouth, New Bedford, or Hyannis. In-ground pool, or walk to the beach. There are many great restaurants and quaint shops only a few miles away.

Hosts: Dennis & Ken
Rooms: 5 (SB) $57
Continental Breakfast
Credit Cards: A, B
Notes: 2, 5, 7, 8, 9, 10, 11, 12

WELLFLEET

A Different Drummer

Orleans B&B Associates
P.O. Box 1312
Orleans, MA, 02653
(508) 255-3824

A spacious multilevel home located on a hill overlooking secluded Drummer's Cove. Four-minute walk to Bay beach; ocean only a mile away. Enjoy a sun deck on two levels, a screened-in porch, and light-filled living/dining area that looks out into the treetops. On a separate level are two bedrooms, one twin and one queen, that share a bath and adjacent TV and reading room. $60.

Captain Lewace House

Orleans B&B Associates
P.O. Box 1312
Orleans, MA, 02653
(508) 255-3824

Large, handsome, historic house restored to perfect condition. Walk to everything, including Wellfleet Harbor Beach. Pretty private porch for evening relaxation. Large room for breakfast or study, and an air-conditioned queen room with comfortable sitting area and private bath. Buffet continental breakfast. Hosts have a travel agency and are very knowledgeable about the Cape. $75.

Deep Denes

Orleans B&B Associates
P.O. Box 1312
Orleans, MA, 02653
(508) 255-3824

When you turn off Ocean View Drive and start up through the woods on a dirt road, you know you are headed for an exciting adventure. Overlooking the great Atlantic, set in unusual gardens, with lots of glass to take advantage of the views, this house offers peace and enrichment. Very talented hosts. For your comfort, serene double room, adjacent sitting room with fireplace, and private bath. Be sure to see the Japanese garden. Short distance to private beach. $60.

Inn at Duck Creek

Box 364, Wellfleet, MA, 02667
(508) 349-9333

Five-acre complex with duck pond and salt marsh. Two outstanding restaurants. Within walking distance of the village of Wellfleet and within the Cape Cod National Seashore. Antique shops, fine art galleries, ocean and bay beaches, fresh-water ponds, cycling, and boating all nearby.

Hosts: Robert Morrill & Judith Pihl
Rooms: 25 (17 PB; 8 SB) $55-90
Continental Breakfast
Minimum stay weekends: 2; holidays: 3
Credit Cards: A, B, C
Closed Oct. 15-May 15
Notes: 4, 7, 8, 9, 10, 11, 12

Inn at Duck Creek

Owl's Nest

Orleans B&B Associates
P.O. Box 1312
Orleans, MA, 02653
(508) 255-3824

Peace and quiet surrounds this Gothic contemporary home located on 6 acres known as Owl Woods. A charming cathedral-ceilinged living room and dining room, filled with antiques, are yours to enjoy. Upstairs, a skylighted sitting and writing area separates two queen rooms that share a large bath. Continental breakfast is served inside or on the 40-foot deck overlooking the perennial gardens and pine woods. Walk down a country lane to a picturesque bay beach. A short ride to ocean or pond swimming. $60.

Sunset Hill

Orleans B&B Associates
P.O. Box 1312
Orleans, MA, 02653
(508) 255-3824

Very clean, comfortable, inviting house with private guest entrance. Sit out on your patio and enjoy spectacular sunsets. Entrance

Honeysuckle Hill

foyer has cafe table where you may enjoy a nice continental breakfast. Large room with private bath, sitting area, and full double bed. On the ocean side of Wellfleet, close to beaches and convenient to town. $65.

The White Eagle

Orleans B&B Associates
P.O. Box 1312
Orleans, MA, 02653
(508) 255-3824

Located in South Wellfleet, a short walk to Bay beach or a short drive to the ocean. Ground-floor private entrance into a large room with sitting/dining area, queen bed, TV, and wet bar with refrigerator. Full private bath. Breakfast is delivered to your door in the morning. $70.

WEST BARNSTABLE

Honeysuckle Hill

591 Main Street
West Barnstable, MA, 02668
(508) 362-8418

Charming country inn near the dunes of Sandy Neck beach. Full country breakfast and afternoon tea. Feather beds, down comforters, and homemade cookies at bedside. English toiletries and terry-cloth robes in private baths. Wraparound screen porch filled with wicker, and a large great room for games and large-screen TV watching make this a perfect spot for any season.

Hosts: Bob & Barbara Rosenthal
Rooms: 3 (PB) $75-105
Full Breakfast
Minimum stay on seasonal weekends & holidays: 2
Credit Cards: A, B, C
Notes: 2, 5, 7, 8 (over 12), 9, 10, 11, 12, 14

WEST BOYLSTON

The Rose Cottage

24 Worcester Street
Routes 12 & 140
West Boylston, MA, 01583
(508) 835-4034

Enjoy the quiet elegance of a nineteenth-century cottage overlooking Wachusett Reservoir. Marble fireplaces, gaslight lamps, gabled roof, and gingerbread dormers.

Browse our antique shop filled with two floors of treasures.

Hosts: Michael & Loretta Kittredge
Rooms: 5 (1 PB; 4 S2B) $65
Apartment: 1 fully furnished; $350/week
Full Breakfast
Minimum stay holidays: 2
Reservations required
Credit Cards: No
Notes: 2, 5, 7 (limited), 8 (limited), 9, 10, 11, 12, 13

WEST BROOKFIELD

Berkshire B&B Homes ST6

P.O. Box 211
Williamsburg, MA, 01096
(413) 268-7244

1880 Victorian with country and Victorian furniture. Parlor for guest use. Air-conditioning. Two rooms with double beds share a bath. Full breakfast. $50-60.

WEST FALMOUTH

The Elms

P.O. Box 895
West Falmouth, MA, 02574
(508) 540-7232

Charming Victorian, built in the early 1800s, features nine beautifully appointed bedrooms, seven private baths, and antique decor throughout. A four-course gourmet breakfast is served each morning. Tour the manicured grounds to survey the flower and herb gardens, or relax in the gazebo. One-half mile from the ocean.

Hosts: Betty & Joe Mazzucchelli
Rooms: 9 (7 PB; 2 SB) $70-85
Full Breakfast
Credit Cards: No
Notes: 2, 5, 7, 8 (over 14), 9, 10, 11, 12

WESTFORD

Bed & Breakfast Folks BB3

48 Springs Road
Bedford, MA, 01730
(617) 275-9025

A restored colonial filled with antique quilts, a working fireplace or two, and an attached flower shop with many unique creations for sale. From $50.

WEST HARWICH

Cape Cod Sunny Pines B&B Inn

77 Main Street
West Harwich, MA, 02671
(508) 432-9628

Irish hospitality in a Victorian ambience. Family-style gourmet Irish breakfast by candlelight on bone china and crystal. All private, antique-decorated suites. Evening happy hour poolside or fireside. Walk to Nantucket Sound, fine restaurants, biking and hiking tails. Take day trips to the islands or go whale watching. New Jacuzzi overlooking pool and garden on wraparound Victorian porch.

Hosts: Eileen & Jack Connell
Rooms: 7 (PB) $75-95 + tax
Full Breakfast
Minimum stay weekdays & weekends: 2 ; holidays: 3
Credit Cards: A, B, C
Notes: 2, 5, 7, 9, 10, 11, 12, 14

Cape Cod Sunny Pines B&B Inn

Lion's Head Inn

186 Belmont Road
P.O. Box 444
West Harwich, MA, 02671
(508) 432-7766

The Lion's Head Inn is a former sea captain's house dating from the 1820s. Recently renovated, it combines the charm of yesteryear with modern amenities. Located on a private residential street with a Nantucket Sound beach one-half mile away. Swimming pool on premises. Some family-sized suites and cottages available.

Hosts: Bill & Kathleen Lockyer
Rooms: 6 (PB) $80-99
Full Breakfast
Credit Cards: A, B
Minimum stay July & Aug.: 2
Notes: 2, 5, 7, 8 (by arrangement), 9, 10, 11, 12

The Tern Inn

91 Chase Street
West Harwich, MA, 02671
(508) 432-3714

Prime mid-cape location near Nantucket Sound beaches. The inn presents a cheerful atmosphere in a nostalgic original Cape built two centuries ago. Wide board floors, "bean pot" cellar, and sparkling windows are complimented by antiques and hospitality. Housekeeping cottages, swimming pool, and basketball court on the spacious grounds.

Hosts: Bill & Jane Myers
Rooms: 5 (PB) $49.37-76.79
Full Breakfast
Minimum stay weekends & holidays: 2
Credit Cards: No
Closed Dec. 1-April 1
Notes: 2, 7, 8, 9, 10, 11, 12

WEST NEWBURY

West Newbury B&B

B&B Marblehead & North Shore
P.O. Box 172
Beverly, MA, 01915
(508) 921-1336

In a country setting, just ten minutes away from the Plum Island Wildlife Reserve and beach. Beautiful antique-furnished Cape Cod house. Two rooms share a bath. Smoking permitted; children over ten or babies with their own cribs are welcome. Guest living room with working fireplace and wet bar setup adjoining the guest rooms. Swimming pool, large deck. $65-75.

WEST SPRINGFIELD

Berkshire B&B Homes GS9

P.O. Box 211
Williamsburg, MA, 01096
(413) 268-7244

This brick colonial on 1 acre of land offers formal and colonial furniture. View of city park; jewelry shop on premises. Parlor for guest use. Three double bedrooms with shared and private baths. Full breakfast; no smoking; children welcome. Pet in residence. $50-60.

WEST STOCKBRIDGE

Card Lake Country Inn

Main Street
West Stockbridge, MA, 01266
(413) 232-7120

Our charmingly restored guest rooms all have antiques, and many have brass beds. The atmosphere is warm, comfortable, and casual. The restaurant and tavern on the premises serve excellent food with daily specials and homemade soups and desserts. The building dates back to 1803.

Hosts: Lynn & Larry Schiffman
Rooms: 8 (4 PB; 4 SB) $50-100
Full Breakfast
Credit Cards: A, B, C
Notes: 2, 3, 4, 5, 7, 8, 9, 10, 11, 12, 13, 14

WESTWOOD

B&B Associates Bay Colony IW725

P.O. Box 57166
Babson Park Branch
Boston, MA, 02157-0166
(617) 449-5302

This antique country house and barn are graced by an inviting brick patio with large in-ground pool. The first floor has been redesigned to provide a view of the grounds through walls of glass. Three rooms, shared baths. Full breakfast, smoking allowed, children welcome, resident cat. $55.

WEST YARMOUTH

The Manor House

57 Maine Avenue
West Yarmouth, MA, 02673
(508) 771-9211

Lovely romantic charm, located at mid-Cape. Quiet setting, near all Cape activities, five miles from ferry and airport. Clean, comfortable, large, sunny guest rooms, all with private baths. Within walking distance of beach on Lewis Bay.

Host: Kathy Henry
Rooms: 6 (PB) $50-65
Continental Breakfast
Credit Cards: A, B
Notes: 2, 5, 8 (over 7), 9, 10, 11, 12, 14

WILBRAHAM

B&B With Barbara and Bob

15 Three Rivers Road
Wilbraham, MA, 01095
(413) 596-6258

This lovely 1928 Dutch colonial is located in the country. Immaculate guest rooms are on the second floor with a shared bath and Jacuzzi. Sun porch, TV, swimming pool, and patio for guests' use. Your host, an artist whose works grace the home, is a former banker, while your hostess managed an insurance agency.

Hosts: Barbara & Bob Gliddene
Rooms: 3 (SB) $55
Continental Breakfast
Credit Cards: No
Notes: 2, 5, 6, 8, 9, 10, 11, 12, 13

WILLIAMSBURG

Berkshire B&B Homes PV2

P.O. Box 211
Williamsburg, MA, 01096
(413) 268-7244

One-hundred-year-old Victorian on 1 acre. Private sitting room for guests, with fireplace. Short walk to town center. One room with double beds; two with two twins; shared bath. Full breakfast; restricted smoking; children eight and over are welcome. $45-50.

Berkshire B&B Homes PV3

P.O. Box 211
Williamsburg, MA, 01096
(413) 268-7244

Two-hundred-year-old restored farmhouse on 27 acres of land. Bedrooms are furnished with antique brass and iron beds. Screened porch and sitting room with TV for guests. Two double rooms and a twin room share a bath. Full breakfast; no smoking; children welcome. Pet in residence. $40-50.

Berkshire B&B Homes PV18

P.O. Box 211
Williamsburg, MA, 01096
(413) 268-7244

Restored 1864 Victorian farmhouse with a living room for guest use. Short walk to town center. One double room and one single share a bath. Full breakfast; restricted smoking; children welcome. $45-50.

Berkshire B&B Homes PV28

P.O. Box 211
Williamsburg, MA, 01096
(413) 268-7244

A two-story 1945 Cape on 4 acres with parlor and breezeway for guests. Queen room with a private bath. A room with two double beds and another with twins share a bath. Continental breakfast; no smoking; children nine and up are welcome. $55-75.

WILLIAMSTOWN

American Country Collection 22

984 Gloucester Place
Schenectady, NY, 12309
(518) 370-4948

Set high on a knoll with a tri-state view of the mountains and valleys, this country home and the surrounding 52-acre farm is the perfect complement to a busy vacation. Swim, row, or fish for trout in the stocked 1.5-acre pond, walk or cross-country ski the 5 kilometers of trails. The children will enjoy the chicks, pigs, cows, and oxen in the barn and pasture. Each of the guest rooms is furnished with country treasures, marble-topped dressers, and antique oak beds. Shared bath. Children are welcome; resident pets. $60.

Berkshire B&B Homes NC4

P.O. Box 211
Williamsburg, MA, 01096
(413) 268-7244

An 1870s country farmhouse on 127 acres. Furnished with country and natural-wood furniture. Gazebo outdoors and sitting room indoors for guests. Queen bedroom with private bath and working fireplace; one room with one double bed; two rooms with two double beds; shared baths. Continental breakfast; restricted smoking; children six and over are welcome. Pet in residence. $65-85.

Berkshire B&B Homes NC11

P.O. Box 211
Williamsburg, MA, 01096
(413) 268-7244

Two-hundred-year-old farmhouse on a 600-acre dairy farm. Scenic farmland and view of mountains and fields. Antique furniture. Tours of farm, swimming in pond, fishing for bass. Open field for cross-country skiing and hiking. One double room and one twin room share a bath. Continental breakfast; restricted smoking; children six and over are welcome. Resident animals. $45.

Berkshire B&B Homes NC14

P.O. Box 211
Williamsburg, MA, 01096
(413) 268-7244

This 1985 solar contemporary home offers a den with TV. A twin room has a private bath. Another room with a hideaway bed shares a bath. Full breakfast; children welcome; no smoking; pets in residence. $65-75.

Steep Acres Farm B&B

520 White Oaks Road
Williamstown, MA, 01267
(413) 458-3774

Located two miles from Williams College and the Williamstown Theatre Festival. A country home on a high knoll with spectacular views of the Berkshire Hills and

One Centre Street Inn

Vermont's Green Mountains. Trout and swimming pond welcome guests on this working farm's 52 acres adjacent to both the Appalachian and Long Trails. Short distance to Tanglewood and Jacob's Pillow dance.

Hosts: Mary & Marvin Gangemi
Rooms: 4 (S3B) $40-60
Full Breakfast
Credit Cards: No
Notes: 2, 5, 9, 10, 11, 12, 13

WOODS HOLE

The Marlborough

320 Wood Hole Road
Woods Hole, MA, 02543
(508) 548-6218

The Marlborough is an intimate Cape Cod cottage of five guest rooms individually decorated with antiques and collectibles, each with private bath and air conditioning. the spacious wooded grounds include a pool and paddle tennis court. We have a private beach one mile away with life guard and free parking; 1.5 miles to the Martha's Vineyard ferry. Easy day trips to Boston, Newport, Plymouth, Provincetown, and Nantucket.

Host: Patricia Morris
Rooms: 5 (PB) $65-95
Full Breakfast
Credit Cards: No
Notes: 2, 5, 10, 11, 12, 14

WORTHINGTON

Country Cricket Village Inn

Route 112
Worthington, MA, 01098
(413) 238-5366

Colonial-style inn on 23 acres near the town common of a lovely New England village. The central location permits you to enjoy the many cultural activities of the Berkshires and the Hampshire Hills. Five country bedrooms, all with private bath. A common room offers visiting, reading, TV, or fireplace watching. Air-conditioned.

Hosts: Jacquie & Don Bridgeman
Rooms: 5 (PB) $80
Full Breakfast
Credit Cards: A, B, C
Notes: 2, 5, 8 (10 and over), 9, 10, 11, 12, 13 (XC), 14

Hill Gallery

HC65, Box 96
Worthington, MA, 01098
(413) 238-5914

Located on a mountaintop in the Hampshire Hills on 25 acres. Enjoy relaxed country living in an owner-built contemporary home with art gallery, fireplaces, and swimming pool. Self-contained cottage also available.

Hosts: Ellen & Walter Korzec
Rooms: 2 (PB) $55
Full Breakfast
Minimum stay holidays: 2
Credit Cards: No
Notes: 2, 5, 8 (over 5), 9, 10, 11, 12, 13

Inn Yesterday

Huntington Road
Worthington, MA, 01098
(413) 238-5529

In 1877 this restored Greek Revival home was known as Frissell's Inn. Today Inn Yesterday welcomes guests with many amenities of the past, including antiques throughout. In nice weather, a full country breakfast is served in the porch sun room.

Hosts: Janet & Robert Osborne
Rooms: 3 (SB) $60
Full Breakfast
Credit Cards: No
Notes: 2, 5, 7 (limited), 8 (over 5), 9, 10, 11, 12, 13

YARMOUTH PORT

Crook' Jaw Inn

186 Main Street, Route 6A
Yarmouth Port, MA, 02675
(508) 362-6111

The Crook' Jaw Inn is a 200-year-old former way station and sea captain's home, listed on the National Register of Historic Places. Route 6A is the Cape of 100 years ago. Choice of dinner menu and full breakfast are included in the nightly rate and may be enjoyed in our intimate dining room or on the patio. Picnic baskets available for day trips. Special weekly rates available.

Hosts: Don Spagnolia & Ed Shedlock
Rooms: 7 (PB) $80-99
Full Breakfast
Credit Cards: A, B, C
Notes: 2, 4, 5, 7, 8, 9, 10, 11, 12

Olde Captain's Inn

101 Main Street
Yarmouth Port, MA, 02675
(508) 362-4496

Charming restored captain's home, located in the historic district. Fine lodgings and superb continental breakfast. Cable TV. The inn has a truly friendly, elegant atmosphere. Walk to shops and restaurants. Stay two nights and your third night is free.

Hosts: Betsy O'Connor & Sven Tilly
Rooms: 3 (SB) $50-60
Continental Breakfast
Credit Cards: No
Notes: 2, 5, 7, 9, 10, 11, 12

Old Yarmouth Inn

Route 6A, P.O. Box 626
Yarmouth Port, MA, 02675
(508) 362-3191

The oldest inn on Cape Cod (built in 1696), on historic Route 6A. Charming antique homes, inns, and antique shops along the road, as well as golf, swimming, and other activities.

Host: Karl Manchon
Rooms: (PB) $80-90 in season; $60-70 out
Full Breakfast
Credit Cards: A, B, C
Notes: 2, 3, 4, 5, 7, 9, 10, 12

One Centre Street Inn

1 Centre Street
Yarmouth Port, MA, 02675
(508) 363-8910

This vintage colonial inn has been restored with a lot of care and is very comfortable, with country decor and antique furnishings throughout. The house boasts wide pine floors, old hutches and clocks, hook rugs, and fresh-cut flowers.

Hosts: Stefanie & Bill Wright
Rooms: 5 (3 PB; 2 SB) $50-85
Full Breakfast
Credit Cards: A, B, C
Notes: 2, 4, 5, 8, 9, 11, 12, 14

Wedgewood Inn

83 Main Street
Yarmouth Port, MA, 02675
(508) 362-5157

Located in the historic area of Cape Cod, the inn is in the National Register of Historic Places and has been featured in *Country Inns of America.* Near beaches, art galleries, antique shops, golf, boating, and fine restaurants. Fireplaces and private screened porches.

Rooms: 6 (PB) $105-145
Full Breakfast
Credit Cards: A, B, C, E
Notes: 2, 5, 7 (restricted), 8 (over 10), 9, 10, 11, 12, 14

MICHIGAN
Calumet
Big Bay
Wakefield
Michigamme
Marquette
McMillan
Blaney Park
Manistique
Crystal Falls
Sault Ste. Marie
St. Ignace
Mackinac Island
Stephenson
Garden
Petoskey
Bay View
Ellsworth
Eastport
Walloon Lake
Elk Rapids
Suttons Bay
Boyne Falls
Charlevoix
Glen Arbor
East Jordan
Northport
Central Lake
Cedar
Bellaire
Omena
Alden
Traverse City
Maple City-Leland
Frankfort
Harrisville
Port Austin
Manistee
Cadillac
Caseville
Ludington
Harbor Beach
Pentwater
Big Rapids
Midland
White Cloud
Bay City
Caro
Whitehall
Satinaw
Frankemuth
Grand Haven
Ithaca
Clio
Muskegon
Davison
Grand Rapids
Owosso
Port Huron
Metamora
Holland
East Lansing
St. Clair
Saugatuck
Douglas
Lansing
Detroit
Fennville
Allegan
Dimondale
South Haven
Battle Creek
Kalamazoo
Ann Arbor
Lawrence
Paw Paw
Homer
Coldwater
Brooklyn
Benton Harbor
Tecumseh
Adrian
Union Pier
Blissfield
Niles

Michigan

ADRIAN

Briar Oaks Inn

2980 North Adrian Hwy.
Adrian, MI, 49221
(517) 263-1659

Come enjoy the warmth and charm of our Williamsburg-style inn. Nestled among century-old oak trees, overlooking winding Beaver Creek, sits this completely renovated inn. It features private baths, air-conditioning, TV, phones, and a special guest room with canopy bed, whirlpool for two, and breakfast in your room.

Hosts: Connie & Dallas Marvin
Rooms: 4 (PB) $42-69
Full Breakfast

ALDEN

Torch Lake B&B

10601 Coy Street
Alden, MI, 49612
(616) 331-6424

Renovated nineteenth-century Victorian with period furniture, European laces, and stained glass. The hilltop setting provides exceptional views of magnificent Torch Lake. Alden offers gourmet dining, tiny boutiques. Located in the center of Michigan's Gold Coast of golf.

Hosts: Jack & Patti Findlay
Rooms: 3 $55-65

ALLEGAN

Delano Inn

302 Cutler
Allegan, MI, 49010
(616) 673-2609

Elegance and comfort with friendly small-town charm. Built in 1863, this national registered historic mansion is decorated in antiques and has beautiful landscaped gardens. Minutes from riverfront walk, antiquing, fishing, downhill and cross-country skiing. Twenty minutes from Saugatuck, Holland, and Lake Michigan. $45-85.

Winchester Inn

524 Marshall Street
Allegan, MI, 49010
(616) 673-3621

Historic elegance in an 1863 mansion steps from downtown riverfront shopping, antiquing; ten minutes to downhill and cross-country skiing, and 25 minutes to Lake Michigan beaches, Saugatuck, and Holland. Five rooms, private baths. $55-75.

ANN ARBOR

The Homestead B&B

9279 Macon Road
Saline, MI, 48176
(313) 429-9625

In the country, within fifteen minutes of Ann Arbor and Ypsilanti. Relax in the living room or parlor of our 1851 brick farmhouse furnished with comfortable antiques. Walk, cross-country ski on our 50 acres of woods, fields, and river.

Host: Shirley Grossman
Rooms: 5 (SB) $50-60
Full Breakfast
Credit Cards: A, B, E
Notes: 2, 5, 7, 9, 10, 12, 13, 14

Reynolds House at Stonefield Farm

5259 West Ellsworth Road
Ann Arbor, MI, 48103
(313) 995-0301

A cozy wood-frame cottage among pine trees on 10 acres of rolling farmland. Farm animals include sheep and chickens. The cottage has three bedrooms, bath, full living room, and kitchen. The main house, where a full breakfast is served, has a wood stove, piano, and sun deck. $50-60.

The Urban Retreat

2759 Canterbury Road
Ann Arbor, MI, 48104
(313) 971-8110

Comfortable 1950s ranch home on a quiet, tree-lined street, minutes from downtown and the University of Michigan campus. Rooms are furnished with antiques, old-fashioned wallpapers, and stained glass. Stretch your legs along the paths of the adjacent County Farm Park, 127 acres of meadowland. The Retreat has been designated a "Backyard Wildlife Habitat" by the National Wildlife Federation.

Hosts: Andre Rosalik & Gloria Krys
Rooms: 2 (SB) $50
Full Breakfast
Credit Cards: No
Notes: 2, 5, 7, 9, 10, 11, 12, 13, 14

Wood's Inn

2887 Newport Road
Ann Arbor, MI, 48103
(313) 665-8394

An 1859 Victorian, totally furnished with period furniture and accessories, on 2 acres. Just five minutes from downtown and the University of Michigan campus. The Huron River provides a quiet background for relaxation. Four rooms. $45-50.

BATTLE CREEK

Greencrest Manor

6174 Halbert Road
Battle Creek, MI, 49017
(616) 962-8633

This French Normandy mansion is situated on the highest elevation on St. Mary's lake and is constructed of sandstone, slate, and copper. Three levels of formal gardens include fountains, stone walls, iron rails, and cut sandstone urns. Five rooms. $70-120.

The Old Lamp-Lighter's

276 Capital Avenue NE
Battle Creek, MI, 49017
(616) 963-2603

Features of this magnificent Arts & Crafts-style home include: Fifteen-inch-thick walls, clear clay French tile roof, porch roofs and house gutters of copper, quarry tile porch floor. The two-floor foyer features the original stenciled canvas with its background restorėd, an elegant open oak staircase, and a large stained-glass window on the west wall. The library features a fireplace flanked by shelves covered with leaded glass doors depicting Aladdin's lamp. Close to the Y Center, Bailey Park, Kellogg Community College, McCamly Place, Civic Theatre, Kellogg Center Arena and Auditorium, shops, restaurants, and the linear parkway for walks and jogging.

Host: Roberta Stewart
Rooms: 7 (4 PB; 3 SB)
Full Breakfast
Credit Cards: A, B, C, D
Notes: 2, 5, 8, 10, 11, 12, 13 (XC), 14

BAY CITY

Stonehedge Inn

924 Center Avenue
Bay City, MI, 48708
(517) 894-4342

With stained-glass windows and nine fireplaces, this 1889 historic English Tudor home is an elegant journey into the past. The magnificent open foyer and staircase lead to eight guest rooms on the second and third floors. Many original features. Near downtown on M-25. $60-85.

William Clements Inn

1712 Center Avenue
Bay City, MI, 48708
(517) 894-4600

This 1886 Victorian mansion features six elaborately furnished guest rooms, all with private baths and telephones, six fireplaces, and an organ. Central air-conditioning, banquet and meeting rooms; catering available. $59-89.

BAY VIEW

The Florence

317 Park Avenue
P.O. Box 1031
Bay View, MI, 49770
(616) 348-3322

This charming Victorian cottage, built in 1878, is one of 450 historic cottages in Bay View, a National Historic Landmark. Guest rooms feature Victorian antiques and handmade quilts. Gourmet breakfasts are served in the original wood-paneled dining room or on the porch. Open May-Oct. Eight rooms. $50-70.

The Gingerbread House

205 Bluff Street
P.O. Box 1273
Bay View, MI, 49770
(616) 347-3538

This 1881 Victorian summer cottage offers spacious arrangements with ample views of Little Traverse Bay. Guests may enjoy easy access to a sandy beach. Deluxe continental breakfast. No smoking or pets. Open May 15-Oct. Five rooms. $50-80.

BELLAIRE

Bellaire B&B

212 Park Street
Bellaire, MI, 49615
(616) 533-6077

Enjoy the charm of our 1879 home overlooking a large shaded yard with tree-lined drive and shuffleboard court. Within short walking distance are parks with tennis and swimming, a theater, and quaint downtown shops. Surrounded by hills and lakes and adjacent to Shanty Creek-Schuss Mountain Golf and Ski Resort. Three rooms. $43-60.

The Richardi House

402 North Bridge Street
Bellaire, MI, 49615
(616) 533-6111

Grand eleven-room Victorian mansion with beautiful period antiques throughout. Built in 1895 and listed on the National Register. Located in downtown Bellaire, just minutes from championship golf and some of the Midwest's finest skiing. Full breakfast, no smoking. Four rooms. $50-70.

BENTON HARBOR

Bolins' B&B

576 Colfax Avenue
Benton Harbor, MI, 49022
(616) 925-9068

A 75-year-old English Tudor conveniently located near beaches, parks, events. Bountiful orchards and farms are nearby. Breakfast features home baking and area produce. Four rooms. $25-30.

BIG BAY

Big Bay Point Lighthouse

3 Lighthouse Road
Big Bay, MI, 49808
(906) 345-9957

A registered working lighthouse. Boasts one mile of Lake Superior shore, 100 wooded acres, groomed trails, 60-foot tower, 5-acre lawn, mountain views, Safari tours to waterfalls within the Huron Mountains, artisan center, hiking, skiing, and water sports.

Hosts: Marilyn & Buck Gotschall
Rooms: 6 (4 PB; 2 SB) $85-120
Continental Breakfast
Credit Cards: No
Notes: 2, 3, 4, 5, 9, 10, 11, 13, 14

BIG RAPIDS

Taggart House

321 Maple Street
Big Rapids, MI, 49307
(616) 796-1713

This historic Greek Revival mansion features a graciously curved staircase that divides at a landing and separates to form two stairways that lead to a suite and two bedrooms with private baths. A ground-floor wing offers a king bed and handicap entrance. Located in a quiet neighborhood near downtown. $45-65.

BLANEY PARK

Celibeth House

Blaney Park Road
Route 1, Box 58A
Blaney Park, MI, 49836
(906) 283-3409

The Celibeth House, built in 1895, offers eight lovely rooms. Each room is spacious, clean, and tastefully furnished. Guests may also enjoy the cozy living room, a guest reading room, enclosed quaint porch, and a lovely back porch overlooking 86 acres.

Host: Elsa Strom
Rooms: 8 (6 PB; 2 SB) $40-50
Continental Breakfast
Credit Cards: A, B
Open May 1-Dec. 1; By reservation only Dec. 1 - May 1
Notes: 2, 8, 9, 13

H.D. Ellis Inn

BLISSFIELD

H.D. Ellis Inn

415 West Adrian Street
Blissfield, MI, 49228
(517) 486-3155

A restored brick Victorian, circa 1883. Charming accommodations, period furniture. Across the street and adjacent to the well-known Hathaway House Restaurant (National Registered Historic Site), Main Street Stable & Tavern, and many specialty shops. Bicycles available, including a tandem.

Host: Donalta DeSoro
Rooms: 4 (2 PB; 2 SB) $40-65
Continental Breakfast
Credit Cards: A, B
Notes: 2, 3, 4, 5, 6, 7, 8, 9, 10, 11, 12, 13 (XC), 14

BOYNE CITY

Duley's State Street Inn

303 State Street
Boyne City, MI, 49712
(616) 582-7855

A charming turn-of-the-century home furnished with a combination of antiques and modern conveniences. Guests are invited to relax in the living room and parlor before a cozy fire or enjoy cable TV. Homemade baked goods are part of the full breakfast. Minutes from Boyne Country's famous golf and skiing, and a short walk from downtown and Lake Charlevoix. Three rooms. $65-80.

BOYNE FALLS

Arman House B&B

2571 Grove Street
P.O. Box 195
Boyne Falls, MI, 49713
(616) 549-2764

Located two minutes from the famous Boyne Mountain Ski Resort, near golf, many lakes and beaches, and fine dining. Accommodations include rooms with a shared bath and a country parlor with a stone fireplace. Chickens, horses, and resident cat. Three rooms. $45.

BROOKLYN

The Chicago Street Inn

219 Chicago Street
Brooklyn, MI, 49230
(517) 592-3888

An 1880s Queen Anne Victorian, located in the Heart of the Irish Hills. Furnished with family and area antiques. Antiquing, hiking, biking, shops, swimming, museums and more are available. Area of quaint villages.

Hosts: Karen & Bill Kerr
Rooms: 4 (PB) $55-65
Credit Cards: A, B
Continental-plus Breakfast
Notes: 2, 5, 7, 9, 10, 11, 12, 14

CADILLAC

American Inn B&B

312 East Cass Street
Cadillac, MI, 49601
(616) 779-9000

This turn-of-the-century home offers wood carving, stained-glass windows, and hardwood floors. Amenities include air-conditioning, private phones, private baths, cable, sauna, and hot tub. Five rooms and one suite with a view of Lake Cadillac. $55-150.

Essenmacher's B&B

204 Locust Lane
Cadillac, MI, 49601
(616) 775-3828

Contemporary home on beautiful Lake Mitchell. Quilts and crafts made by the hosts and other artisans. Lakeside guest rooms have private baths and are within walking distance of golf, bowling, and restaurants. Evening bonfires available. Two rooms. $55.

CALUMET

Calumet House

P.O. Box 126
1159 Calumet Avenue
Calumet, MI, 49913
(906) 337-1936

The Calumet House is located on the scenic, historic Keweenaw Peninsula. The house was built by the Calumet and Hecla Mining Company c. 1895. It features original woodwork and antique furniture. Breakfast is served in the formal dining room, which has the original butler's pantry. Near Michigan Technological University and Suomi College.

Hosts: George & Rose Chivses
Rooms: 2 (SB) $25
Full Breakfast
Credit Cards: No
Notes: 2, 5, 9, 10, 11, 12, 13

CARO

Garden Gate B&B

315 Pearl Street
Caro, MI, 48723
(517) 673-4823

Built with charm in the Cape Cod colonial style, Garden Gate B&B is a new home designed with its guests in mind. Antiques adorn every corner of its rooms. In a quiet residential area of Caro. In summer, the yard is full of flowers and shrubs, including a large planting of New England wild flowers. On cool evenings, guests can warm up by the fireplace that adds rustic charm to the living room.

Hosts: Jim & Evelyn White
Rooms: 5 (PB) $50 and up
Full Breakfast
Credit Cards: A, B
Notes: 2, 4, 5, 7 (discouraged), 8, 9, 10, 11, 12, 13 (XC)

CASEVILLE

Country Charm Farm

5048 Conkey Road
Caseville, MI, 48725
(517) 856-3110

Come experience a working farm with a variety of animals. Our newly decorated country home offers central air, a windmill, duck pond, and 40 acres. Continental breakfast. Five rooms. $45-75.

CEDAR

Hillside B&B

Route 1-A, West Lakeshore Road
Cedar, MI, 49621
(616) 228-6106

Enjoy a quiet, relaxing visit at this 1898 Victorian farmhouse. Two guest rooms share a bath, open to a sitting room, and may be rented as a suite. Breakfast is served in the dining room with a view of the lake. Hike, explore the barn, or climb the hill for a magnificent view. $45-50.

Jarrold Farm

Box 215A, County Road 643
Cedar, MI, 49621
(616) 228-6955

A turn-of-the-century farmhouse, barn, and granary with 10 acres of rolling hills to hike or cross-country ski. Relax by the fieldstone fireplace in a living room with high ceilings and antiques. Enjoy beautiful sunsets from the two-level deck overlooking the countryside. Cycling, golf, and skiing nearby. Two rooms. $50.

CENTRAL LAKE

Bridgewalk B&B

2287 South Main Street
P.O. Box 577
Central Lake, MI, 49622
(616) 544-8122

A footbridge leads to this completely restored turn-of-the-century Victorian on a large wooded site. Elegantly appointed with original woodwork, high ceilings, and large guest rooms. Nearby are golf courses, recreation sites on clear lakes, and gourmet dining. Open May-mid-Oct. Four rooms, private baths. $60-75.

Darmon Street B&B

7900 Darmon Street
P.O. Box 284
Central Lake, MI, 49622
(616) 544-3931

Set in the beautiful valley of Central Lake, with private frontage on Hanley Lake.

Come stay in this charming 1890s Michigan farmhouse. Three rooms. $55.

Twala's B&B

Route 1, Box 84B
Central Lake, MI, 49648
(616) 599-2864

Twala's faces the sunset over Torch Lake and Grand Traverse Bay, where on a typically clear evening you'll see the glow of distant Traverse City. Indoor swimming pool and Jacuzzi, private baths. Three rooms. $55-95.

CHARLEVOIX

Aaron's Windy Hill Guest Lodge

202 Michigan Street
Charlevoix, MI, 49720
(616) 547-2804

Aaron's Windy Hill is a three-story Victorian with a unique stucco exterior and riverstone front porch where guests enjoy a buffet breakfast. Each room has a sitting area, ceiling fan. Three rooms sleep up to five people. Three two-room suites, one with kitchenette. Open May-Oct. $65-85.

Bay B&B

Route 1, Box 136A
Charlevoix, MI, 49720
(616) 599-2570

On the shores of Lake Michigan, twelve miles south of Charlevoix, this lakeside home is peaceful, quiet, and secluded. Two rooms, private baths, resident pets. $60-80.

Bridge Street Inn

113 Michigan Avenue
Charlevoix, MI, 49720
(616) 547-6606

Beautiful three-story Colonial Revival with warm wooden floors, antique furnishings, plush beds, and the comfort and charm of days gone by. Located one block from the drawbridge on US 31, with spectacular lake views and a short walk from sandy beaches, shops, galleries, and fine restaurants. No smoking. Nine rooms. $58-105.

Charlevoix Country Inn

106 West Dixon
Charlevoix, MI, 49720
(616) 547-5134

Welcome to our 1896 country inn. Relax and get acquainted in the common room or out on the porch while watching boats and colorful sunsets on Lake Michigan. Breakfast and evening beverage wine and cheese social. Open May-Oct. 15. Ten rooms. $60-125.

Patchwork Parlour B&B

109 Petoskey Avenue
Charlevoix, MI, 49720
(616) 547-5788

Charming old Victorian on the north side, five doors from a sandy Lake Michigan beach. Easy walk to bridge, Round Lake yacht harbor, downtown shopping, Beaver Island Ferry. Private baths and continental-plus breakfast. Open May-Oct. Eight rooms. $58-78.

CLIO

Chandelier Guest House

1567 Morgan Road
Clio, MI, 48420
(313) 687-6061

Near Michigan's main attractions: Frankenmuth, Cross Road Village, Chesaning (show boat), Birch Run (marketplace). Relax in our country home. Your hosts, of German descent, provide a special treat on your arrival and will serve your breakfast in bed if you ask them to. One-half mile to plaza for shopping and meals. Reservations recommended.

Hosts: Al & Clara Bielert
Rooms: 2 (SB) $45-90
Full Breakfast
Credit Cards: No
Notes: 2, 5, 7, 8, 9, 10, 11, 12, 14

COLDWATER

Batavia Inn

1824 West Chicago Road
Coldwater, MI, 49036
(517) 278-5146

An 1872 Italianate country inn with original massive woodwork, high ceilings, and restful charm. Located near antique and outlet shopping, lakes, parks, museums, and recreation. In-ground pool in season. Five rooms. $49-69.

Chicago Pike Inn

215 East Chicago Street
Coldwater, MI, 49036
(517) 279-8744

Turn-of-the-century colonial mansion adorned with antiques from the Victorian era. Six guest rooms with private baths, formal dining room, library, and reception room featuring a sweeping cherry staircase and parquet floors. Full country breakfast. $75-130.

CRYSTAL FALLS

Crystal Inn B&B

600 Marquette Avenue
Crystal Falls, MI, 49920
(906) 875-6369

Enjoy casual elegance in Michigan's beautiful Upper Peninsula in our 1914 B&B. No matter what season, you'll find an abundance of wildlife and natural beauty. Walking distance to downtown. Three rooms. $36.

DAVISON

Oakbrook Inn

7256 East Court
Davison, MI, 48423
(313) 658-1546

Less than five minutes from Flint, on 20 acres with orchard and creek. Rooms feature antiques, handmade quilts and crafts. Guest lounge with pool table and TV, indoor pool, and hot tub. All rooms have private baths. Seven rooms. $50-90.

DETROIT

The Blanche House Inn

506 Parkview
Detroit, MI, 48214
(313) 822-7090

This 1905 colonial is located one block from the Detroit River. Classic oak woodwork and floors, ten-foot entrance doors of etched glass, antique furnishings, private baths, and suite with Jacuzzi. Eight rooms. $65-105.

DIMONDALE

Bannick's B&B

4608 Michigan Road
Dimondale, MI, 48821
(517) 646-0224

Large ranch-style home features attractive decor throughout with stained-glass entrances. Our 2.75 rural acres offer a quiet escape from the fast pace of the workaday world. Located on a main highway (M 99) only five miles from Lansing and close neighbor to Michigan State University.

Hosts: Pat & Jim Bannick
Rooms: 2 (SB) $20-30
Full Breakfast

Credit Cards: No
Notes: 5, 8, 11, 12, 13

DOUGLAS

Rosemont Inn

Box 857
Douglas, MI, 49406
(616) 857-2637

Our Victorian home, built in 1886, offers fourteen delightful rooms, each with private bath and air-conditioning. Nine rooms feature gas fireplaces; two of our three common rooms have wet bars and TV; one has a fireplace. We have a heated pool and are located across the street from a public beach on Lake Michigan. Unique shopping, charter fishing, golf, and cross-country skiing are nearby.

Hosts: Mike & Shelly Sajdak
Rooms: 14 (PB) $50-85
Continental Breakfast
Minimum stay weekends May 1-Oct. 31: 2
Credit Cards: A, B
Notes: 2, 5, 7, 8, 9, 10, 11, 12, 13

Rosemont Inn

EAST JORDAN

Easterly Inn

209 Easterly
P.O. Box 366
East Jordan, MI, 49727
(616) 536-3434

A recently restored three-story 1906 classic Queen Anne house located in a quiet historic town two blocks from Lake Charlevoix. Near dining and skiing. Four rooms. $60-70.

EAST LANSING

Coleman Corners B&B

7733 Old M-78
East Lansing, MI, 48823
(517) 339-9360

Our modern bi-level home was built on the original 80-acre Coleman family farm. Lounge on the deck overlooking the pool or get cozy next to a warm fire. Four rooms. $55.

EASTPORT

Torch Lake Sunrise B&B

Box 52
Eastport, MI, 49627
(616) 599-2706

A place to come home to on the shore of beautiful Torch Lake. A charming contemporary lakeshore home with two guest rooms, private baths. Close to Traverse City and Charlevoix. Open May 15-Oct. 15. $50-70.

ELK RAPIDS

Cairn House B&B

8160 Cairn Highway
Elk Rapids, MI, 49629
(616) 264-8994

Cairn house is an elegant 1800s southern-colonial located fifteen minutes north of Traverse City in a country setting. A full breakfast is served in the kitchen. Private baths, cable TV, three rooms. Open May 1-Oct. 1. $60.

Widows Walk

603 River Street
Elk Rapids, MI, 49629
(616) 264-5767

This 1868 Georgian home on Grand Traverse Bay is rich in history and elegance. Original hardwood floors, brass chandeliers, Persian rugs, and brass beds in each of four rooms. Private baths. $45-95.

ELLSWORTH

Ellsworth House

Route 1, 204 Lake Street
Ellsworth, MI, 49729
(616) 588-7001

Established as an inn in 1876, this is the oldest restored structure in Ellsworth. Relax on the full-length balcony overlooking Lake St. Clair. Three rooms, private baths. $55.

House on the Hill

Box 206
Ellsworth, MI, 49729
(616) 588-6304

A restored Victorian farmhouse furnished with beautiful antiques. The house sits on 53 acres overlooking St. Clair Lake. Guests are welcome to explore the grounds, relax in the parlor, or bask in the sun on our large veranda. Gourmet restaurants within walking distance. Open April 1-Feb. 1. Three rooms. $65.

Lavender Hill B&B

Route 1, Box 92
Ellsworth, MI, 49729
(616) 588-7755

Lovely renovated farmhouse atop 7 acres offering spectacular sunsets and a panoramic view of Grand Traverse Bay and Leelanau. Ideally located for year-round activities: boating, fishing, skiing, golf, gourmet dining, and antiquing. No smoking. Three rooms. $60.

FENNVILLE

The Crane House

6051 124th Avenue
Fennville, MI, 49408
(616) 561-6931

This restored farmhouse was built by the Cranes in the 1880s and is elegantly primitive, from its handmade quilts and stenciled rooms to its warm and inviting parlor with a 1900 parlor stove. Five rooms. $60-80.

Heritage Manor Inn

2253 Blue Star Highway
Fennville, MI, 49408
(616) 543-4384

Country hospitality in an English Tudor country inn furnished with antiques and country decor. Cozy logstone fireplace, indoor pool, large whirlpool, kiddy pool. Canoeing, horseback riding, cross-country packages. Antique shop on premises. Ten rooms, suites, and three townhouses. $70-95.

Hidden Pond Farm

P.O. Box 461
Fennville, MI, 49408
(616) 561-2491

Frommer's calls us one of the fifty best B&Bs in America. Five common rooms, 28 acres of wooded, ravine land with pond. Two rooms. $90-120.

J. Paules' Fenn Inn

2254 South 58th Street
Fennville, MI, 49408
(616) 561-2836

Nestled in the countryside, this stately inn was built in 1900. Private and shared baths, sun deck, fireplace, and air-conditioning. Quiet country living, yet minutes from Saugatuck, Holland, and South Haven. Eight rooms. $55-65.

The Kingsley House

The Kingsley House

626 West Main Street
Fennville, MI, 49408
(616) 561-6425

An elegant Victorian inn on the edge of Fennville, near Saugatuck, Holland, and South Haven. The five guest rooms with private baths are decorated in true Victorian elegance. Sandy beaches, specialty shops, fine dining, and a playhouse theater are nearby. The Allegan State Forest, with miles of nature trails, is enjoyable to explore. Bicycles available, as well as a picnic area. Country lovers delight. Featured in *Innsider Magazine* and *Great Lakes Getaway.*

Hosts: David & Shirley Witt
Rooms: 5 (PB) $65-125
Full Breakfast
Credit Cards: A, B
Notes: 2, 5, 8 (over 15), 9, 10, 11, 12, 13, 14

The Porches B&B

2297 Lakeshore Drive
Fennville, MI, 49408
(616) 543-4162

Built in 1897, the Porches offers five guest rooms with private baths. Located three miles south of Saugatuck, we have a private beach and hiking trails. Large common room with TV. Overlooking Lake Michigan, with beautiful sunsets from the front porch. Open May 1-Nov. 1. Five rooms. $55-64.

FRANKENMUTH

B&B at The Pines

327 Ardussi Street
Frankenmuth, MI, 48734
(517) 652-9019

Frankenmuth, a Bavarian village, is Michigan's number-one tourist attraction. Our ranch-style home is within walking distance of tourist area and famous restaurants. Bedrooms tastefully decorated with heirloom quilts, antique accents, and ceiling fans. Enjoy homemade breads and rolls.

Hosts: Richard & Donna Hodge
Rooms: 3 (1 PB; 2 SB) $37.80
Continental-plus Breakfast
Credit Cards: No
No smoking or drinking
Notes: 2, 5, 6, 8

Bavarian Town B&B

206 Beyerlein Street
Frankenmuth, MI, 48734
(517) 652-8057

A comfortable family dwelling with air-conditioning and private half baths. Your hosts are direct descendants of the first immigrants to Frankenmuth. Two rooms. $35-45.

Frankenmuth Bender Haus

337 Trinklein Street
Frankenmuth, MI, 48734
(517) 652-8897

Spacious home in a well-kept neighborhood. The host's family were original 1845 settlers to the area, and he speaks fluent German. Four rooms. $45-60.

Kueffner Haus B&B

176 Park Street
Frankenmuth, MI, 48734
(517) 652-6839

A 1920s bungalow in a quiet older neighborhood, within easy walking distance of Frankenmuth's major attractions. Two second-floor rooms with shared bath, living room, and kitchenette. Main-floor room with private bath. $35-45.

FRANKFORT

Morningside B&B

Box 411
Frankfort, MI, 49635
(616) 352-4008

Elegant fifteen-room Queen Anne Victorian furnished with antiques. Located near the southern entrance to Sleeping Bear Dunes; short walk to dune beach, fishing pier, lighthouse, shops, marinas, and fine dining. Full breakfast, four rooms. $75.

GARDEN

The Summer House

P.O. Box 107
Garden, MI, 49835
(906) 644-2457

Built in 1880, this two-story Colonial Revival has been restored and decorated in Victorian style. Located on the picturesque Garden Peninsula, just seven miles from Fayette State Historical Park. Enjoy swimming, hunting, fishing, hiking, and snowmobile trails. Five rooms. $40-65.

GLEN ARBOR

Sylvan Inn

6680 Western Avenue
Glen Arbor, MI, 49636
(616) 334-4333

The Sylvan Inn is a beautifully decorated historic landmark building situated in the heart of the Sleeping Bear Dunes National Lakeshore. Its easy access to Lake Michigan and other inland lakes makes a stay at the Sylvan Inn truly a unique experience.

Hosts: Jenny & Bill Olson
Rooms: 14 (7 PB; 7 SB) $50-110
Continental Breakfast
Credit Cards: A, B
Closed Nov., March, & April
Notes: 2, 8 (8 and over), 9, 10, 11, 12, 13, 14

GRAND HAVEN

Harbor House Inn

Harbor & Clinton Streets
Grand Haven, MI, 49417
(616) 846-0610

A charming, Victorian-style inn overlooking Grand Haven's historic Lake Michigan. The convenient location enables you to stroll the boardwalk and explore the many quaint shops and restaurants in the downtown area. A short walk from the wonderful white sandy beaches of the lake. Enjoy cross-country skiing on the rolling dunes in the winter, or take a fall color tour on the Harbor Steamer.

Host: Ann Jaenicke
Rooms: 15 (PB) $85-115
Continental Breakfast
Credit Cards: A, B
Notes: 2, 5, 9, 10, 11, 12, 13

Seascape B&B

20009 Breton Street
Spring Lake, MI, 49456
(616) 842-8409

On Lake Michigan shore, offering a private, sandy beach and panoramic view of Grand Haven Harbor. All lakefront rooms with private baths. Relaxing lodging in a nautical seashore cottage. Stroll or cross-country ski on duneland nature trails.

Host: Susan Meyer
Rooms: 3 (PB) $65-85
Full Breakfast
Credit Cards: A, B
Closed Dec. 22-26
Notes: 2, 5, 7 (restricted), 9, 10, 11, 12, 13, 14

GRAND RAPIDS

Fountain Hill B&B

222 Fountain NE
Grand Rapids, MI, 49503
(616) 458-6621

This 1874 classic Italianate home overlooking downtown Grand Rapids is in the historic Heritage Hill district. Walk to great restaurants, cultural centers, and entertainment. TV, telephones, air-conditioning. Two rooms, one with Jacuzzi tub; private baths. $45-65.

Heald-Lear House

455 College Avenue SE
Grand Rapids, MI, 49503
(616) 451-4849

This large 1893 Craftsman shingle home is part of the Heritage Hill historic district, located close to downtown and the expressways. Guest rooms have adjoining private baths. Continental breakfast is served overlooking the garden in a solarium with an Italian marble fountain. Two rooms. $55.

HARBOR BEACH

The Wellock Inn

404 South Huron Avenue
Harbor Beach, MI, 48441
(517) 479-3645

This restored "Dream House" of lumberman businessman John Wellock is filled with antique furniture from the early 1900 era, when it was built. Oak woodwork and beveled glass enhance the beauty and provide for a very relaxing atmosphere.

Hosts: Lavonne & Bill Cloutier
Rooms: 4 (2 PB; 2 SB) $40-45
Continental Breakfast
Credit Cards: A, B
Notes: 2, 5, 6, 7, 8, 9, 10, 11

HARRISVILLE

Red Geranium Inn B&B

Box 613, 508 East Main (M-72)
Harrisville, MI, 48740
(517) 724-6153

Guests will find a homey ambience in this home that was built in 1910. In a parklike setting, it overlooks both downtown and Lake Huron, and features a 38-foot glass-enclosed porch, plus rear deck. Within minutes of shopping, restaurants, and beautiful Harbor of Refuge, yet a quiet oasis for real relaxation.

Hosts: Mary & Jim Hamather
Rooms: 5 (SB) $45
Continental-plus Breakfast
Credit Cards: No
Notes: 2, 7 (restricted), 8, 9, 10, 11, 12, 13

HOLLAND

Dutch Colonial Inn

560 Central Avenue
Holland, MI, 49423
(616) 396-3664

Gracious Dutch colonial home build in 1930. This award-winning B&B features lovely heirloom antiques, 1930 furnishings, and elegant decor. Private baths with the optional use of whirlpool tub for two. Near excellent shopping, Hope College, bike paths, cross-country ski trails, and Michigan's finest beaches. Five rooms. $50-80.

McIntyre B&B

13 East Thirteenth Street
Holland, MI, 49423
(616) 392-9886

Lovely, spacious older home built in 1906 and completely modernized. Three sunny air-conditioned rooms, family antiques. Hearty continental breakfast in the dining room. No smoking, no pets. $50.

The Parsonage

6 East 24th Street
Holland, MI, 49423
(616) 396-1316

This elegant and historic B&B home is situated in a peaceful residential neighborhood close to Hope College, exceptional dining, summer theater, and Lake Michigan. We're proud of the superior rating we receive from our guests. Ten minutes to Traverse City, Bloomfield Hills area. Three hours from Chicago.

Host: Bonnie Verwys
Rooms: 4 (2 PB; 2 SB) $60-90
Full Breakfast
Credit Cards: No
Notes: 2, 8 (over 10), 9, 10, 11, 12, 14

HOMER

Grist Mill Inn

310 East Main Street
Homer, MI, 49245
(517) 568-4063

Historic home in Homer, lavishly decorated with antiques, vintage linens, and an array of turn-of-the-century collections. Close to Marshall and Allen, Michigan's antique capitol. Biking and canoeing packages available. Notes for sumptuous champagne breakfast on weekends. Six rooms. $50-65.

ITHACA

Chaffins Balmoral Farm Bed 'n Breakfast

1245 West Washington Road
Ithaca, MI, 48847
(517) 875-3410

Turn-of-the-century farmhouse located on cash-crop farm. Easily identified by its stone fence and large, hip-roofed barn. Your stay at Balmoral Farm consists of: agricultural information, overnight stay, and hot country breakfast featuring homemade blueberry muffins. Accommodations include one bedroom with two double beds and a bedroom with twin beds—bathroom is shared. The remodeled home, furnished with family antiques, had its kitchen featured in *Country Woman.* Central Michigan University and Alma College located nearby. Hiking, tennis, swimming, golf, bicycling, bowling, and roller skating are all nearby, in addition to antique and gift boutiques in neighboring towns.

Host: Sue Chaffin
Rooms: 3 (1 PB; 2 SB) $25-40
Full Breakfast
Credit Cards: No
Closed Nov. 15-April 15
Notes: 2, 8, 10, 11, 12

KALAMAZOO

Stuart Avenue Inn B&B

405 Stuart Avenue
Kalamazoo, MI, 49007
(616) 342-0230

A full-service inn in three meticulously restored Victorian buildings in a registered historic district. Beautiful antiques and handprinted wallpapers combine with modern amenities. Features over an acre of gardens. Evening meals available on request. Near downtown, Western Michigan University, Kalamazoo College; forty-five minutes from Lake Michigan. Ideal for business and pleasure travelers.

Hosts: The Casteels
Rooms: 20 (PB) $55-120
Continental Breakfast
Credit Cards: A, B, C, D, E
Notes: 2, 4, 5, 8, 9, 10, 11, 12, 13, 14

Stuart Avenue Inn B&B

Hall House

106 Thompson Street
Kalamazoo, MI, 49007
(616) 343-2500

This 1923 brick Georgian colonial showcases Honduran mahogany, Italian marble, and handmade tile. Located one-half block from Kalamazoo College and five blocks from the central business district. Four rooms, private baths, TV, air-conditioning. $75.

LANSING

Maplewood

15945 Wood Road
Lansing, MI, 48906
(517) 372-7775

Maplewood, a country home built in 1890, sits on 3 acres overlooking the countryside. Close to MSU, the state capital, I-127, golf courses, and other recreational facilities. Three rooms. $45-55.

LAWRENCE

Oak Cove Resort

58881 46th Street
Lawrence, MI, 49064
(616) 674-8228

Historic lodge and cottages nestled in woods overlooking a beautiful lake in Michigan wine country. Rowboats, canoes, paddleboats, golf, heated pool, trails, games, bicycles, winery tour, scenic wine train, and flea market nearby. Meal plan and full package available. Turn-of-the-century lodge.

Hosts: Susan & Bob Wojcik
Rooms: 14 (7 PB; 7 SB) $85 + tax
Full Breakfast
Credit Cards: No
Closed mid-Sept.-Memorial Day
Notes: 2, 3, 4, 8, 9, 10, 11, 12, 14

MACKINAC ISLAND

Metivier Inn

P.O. Box 285
Mackinac Island, MI, 49757
(616)-627-2055

This lovely country inn was originally built in 1877 as a private residence. Recently renovated, it offers rooms with queen beds and private baths, a large wicker-filled front porch, and a cozy living room with a wood burner. Deluxe continental breakfast. Open mid-May-mid-Oct. Seventeen rooms. $88-165.

MANISTEE

1879 E.E. Douville House

111 Pine Street
Manistee, MI, 49660
(616) 723-8654

Victorian home with ornate, hand-carved woodwork, interior shutters, a soaring staircase, and elaborate archways with pocket doors original to the house. Ceiling fans in every room. Lake Michigan beaches, fishing, golf, skiing, and historical buildings are nearby.

Hosts: Barbara & Bill Johnson
Rooms: 3 (SB) $40-45
Continental Breakfast
Credit Cards: No
Notes: 2, 5, 9, 10, 11, 12, 13

MANISTIQUE

Marina Guest House

230 Arbutus
Manistique, MI, 49854
(906) 341-5147

The 1905 house was rebuilt in 1922 and served as a B&B until 1936 for people summering in the Upper Peninsula. Most crossed Lake Michigan on car ferries that docked within view of this B&B. Located at the marina, one block from the business district, just off US 2 and M 94.

Host: Margaret A. Beach
Rooms: 7 (3 PB; 4 SB) $31.20-52
Full Breakfast
Credit Cards: No
Notes: 2, 5, 8 (with reservations), 9, 10, 11, 12, 13 (XC)

MAPLE CITY/LELAND

Country Cottage B&B

135 East Harbor Highway
Maple City/Leland, MI, 49664
(616) 228-5328; (616) 228-5672

Quiet country beauty near sandy beaches, winter skiing, golf, hiking, biking, and nature's best. Garden-fresh flowers with a continental buffet breakfast. Enjoy winery visits, fun shopping, and the quiet countryside.

Host: Karen Eitzen
Rooms: 4 (1 PB; 3 SB) $50-70
Continental-plus Breakfast
Credit Cards: A, B
Notes: 2, 5, 7, 8, 9, 10, 11, 12, 13

MARQUETTE

Michigamme Lake Lodge

2403 SW 41 West
Marquette, MI, 49855
(906) 225-1393

Exclusive two-story grand lodge, situated on the shore of Lake Michigamme. Built in 1934, log construction, surrounded by birch trees, flower gardens, and the Peshekee River. Large grand room to gather in with a two-and-one-half-story fireplace. Sandy beach, swimming, fishing, hiking trails, and biking. On State Register of History. All rooms decorated with down quilts and a little of the past. Gifts and antiques. Located thirty miles west of Marquette.

Hosts: Frank & Linda Stabile
Rooms: 9 (3 PB; 6 SB) $100-125
Continental Breakfast
Credit Cards: A, B
Open May 15-Nov. 1
Notes: 2, 8, 9, 10, 11

MCMILLAN

Helmer House Inn

Big Manistique Lake
County Road 417

McMillan, MI, 49853
(906) 586-3204

Helmer House is a Michigan historic site, once a general store and US post office, now renovated and furnished in antiques. Centrally located to several Upper Peninsula points of interest, including Sault Locks, Mackinac Island, Pictured Rocks, Kitchitikippi Tahquamenon Falls, and Fayette.

Hosts: Robert & Marge Goldthorpe
Rooms: 5 (SB) $30-50
Full Breakfast
Credit Cards: A, B
Open mid-May to mid-Oct.
Notes: 2, 4, 7, 8, 9, 10, 11

METAMORA

Arizona East

3528 Thornville Road
Metamore, MI, 48455
(313) 678-3107

Enjoy the drive through the woods to our rambling contemporary home. All guests have access to the formal dining room, cozy living rooms with fireplace, music room with player piano, and 12 acres for strolling. Five rooms. $50-65.

MICHIGAMME

Cottage on the Bay

HCR 1, Box 960
Michigamme, MI, 49861
(906) 323-6191

Nestled on a quiet bay on beautiful Lake Michigamme. Charming cottage offering privacy, quiet surroundings, private beach, tastefully decorated rooms, and country breakfast. Located in the heart of the Upper Peninsula forty miles west of Marquette. Twenty-five acres of dense woodlands. Open Memorial Day to mid-Oct. Two rooms. $55.

MIDLAND

Jay's B&B

4429 Bay City
Midland, MI, 48640
(517) 496-2498

If you rest better in a quiet, residential setting, want a home away from home, and find a summertime garden deck appealing, along with cable TV, phone service, and off-street parking, then Jay's is for you!

Host: Jay Hanes
Rooms: 2 (SB) $40
Continental-plus Breakfast
Credit Cards: No
Notes: 2, 5, 10, 11, 12, 13

MUSKEGON

Blue Country B&B

1415 Holton Road
Muskegon, MI, 49445
(616) 744-2555

Comfort is served with care year-round in our early 1900s homestay. Each of our four bedrooms is cozy, cheery, and ideal for families. A full breakfast is enjoyed, with many birds providing entertainment. Conveniently located by US-31, restaurants, Lake Michigan parks. $34.50-36.50.

NILES

Yesterdays Inn B&B

518 North Fourth
Niles, MI, 49120
(616) 683-6079

Elegant 1875 Italianate home with graceful porches, tall shuttered windows, and teardrop front door. Enjoy restful, relaxing evenings after sampling the year-round activities in the area. Golf, antique, canoe, or ski. Two blocks from shopping and restaurants.

Hosts: Elizabeth & Bob Baker
Rooms: 5 (3 PB; 2 SB) $50
Continental-plus Breakfast
Credit Cards: A, B
Notes: 2, 5, 8, 10, 11, 12, 13, 14

NORTHPORT

The Old Mill Pond Inn

202 West Third Street
Northport, MI, 49670
(616) 386-7341

An 1895 summer cottage filled with antiques, original art, and unusual collections, where the main objective is a relaxed, comfortable atmosphere, a good night's sleep, and a delicious breakfast.

Host: David Chrobak
Rooms: 5 (SB) $70
Full Breakfast
Credit Cards: A, B
Notes: 2, 5, 7, 9, 10, 11, 12, 13, 14

OMENA

Omena Shores B&B

P.O. Box 15.
Omena, MI, 49674
(616) 386-7311

Come enjoy Leelanau County's quiet beauty. Our home is a restored 1858 barn with original hand-hewn beams. Four beautiful guest rooms are furnished with antiques and wicker. Walk to Omena, the beach, winery, art gallery, and country store. Full country breakfast. Four rooms, three private baths. $50-85.

OWOSSO

Mulberry House B&B

1251 N. Shiawassee Street
Owosso, MI, 48867
(517) 723-4890

Lovely restored 1890 farm home with many antiques. Breakfast is served in the beautiful dining area with a bay window or on the deck. Enjoy the large porch with swing and wicker. Many historic areas to visit within an hour's drive. A wonderful getaway for that special occasion or just to treat yourself!

Host: Carol Holmes
Rooms: 3 (1 PB; 2 SB) $45-60
Continental-plus Breakfast
Credit Cards: A, B, D
Notes: 2, 5, 7, 8, 9, 10, 11, 12

PAW PAW

Carrington's Country House

43799 60th Avenue
Paw Paw, MI, 49079
(616) 657-5321

A 150-year-old farmhouse located amid fruit orchards and vineyards. Spacious guest rooms offer magnificent views of the surrounding sugar maple and tulip trees, orchards, and gardens. A glass-enclosed porch provides year-round comfort for eating, reading, or TV. Three rooms. $31.20-52.

PENTWATER

The Pentwater Inn

180 East Lowell
Box 98
Pentwater, MI, 49449
(616) 869-5909

We are located twenty minutes south of Ludington, two blocks from town with a beautiful beach, unique shopping, charter boats, excellent cross-country skiing, tennis, and golf. Two large decks, Ping-Pong, game table, cable TV, and tandem available for guests. 1880 home furnished with antiques.

Hosts: Sue & Dick Hand
Rooms: 5 (S2B) $45-55
Continental Breakfast
Credit Cards: A, B
Notes: 2, 5, 8 (over 12), 9, 10, 11, 12, 13

PETOSKEY

Terrace Inn

P.O. Box 266
Petoskey, MI, 49770
(616) 347-2410; (800) 530-9898

The Terrace Inn, a romantic Victorian hotel, was built in 1910 and retains its early twentieth-century charm. Each of the 44 rooms is furnished in original period furniture and has a private bath. The dining room, open for breakfast, lunch, and dinner in season, has a reputation for fine dining.

Hosts: Patrick & Mary Lou Barbour
Rooms: 44 (PB) $42-89
Continental Breakfast
Credit Cards: A, B, C
Notes: 2, 3, 4, 5, 7, 8, 9, 10, 11, 12, 13, 14

PORT AUSTIN

Questover Inn

8510 Lake Street
Port Austin, MI, 48467
(517) 738-5283

Beautiful three-story Greek Revival home that dates back to the 1850s. Antiques throughout the home, with some of the original furnishings. Located at the tip of the thumb, with miles of sandy beaches and parks for your enjoyment.

Hosts: Gary & Lori Babcock
Rooms: 4 (SB) $45-55
Continental Breakfast
Credit Cards: No
Notes: 2, 5, 7, 8, 9, 10, 11, 12, 13

PORT HURON

The Victorian Inn

1229 Seventh Street
Port Huron, MI, 48060
(313) 984-1437

Fine dining and guest rooms in an authentically restored Victorian. One hour north of metropolitan Detroit, this fine inn has a timeless ambience matched by its classic, creative cuisine, gracious service, and knowledgeable wine list. All food and beverages are prepared with utmost attention to detail. Cozy pub on the lower level.

Hosts: Lewand Lynne Secory, Ed & Vicki Peterson
Rooms: 4 (2 PB; 2 SB) $45-60
Continental Breakfast
Credit Cards: A, B, C, D, E, F
Notes: 2, 3, 4, 5, 7, 9, 10, 11, 12, 13

The Victorian Inn

SAGINAW

Brockway House B&B

1631 Brockway
Saginaw, MI, 48602
(517) 792-0746

This Southern colonial mansion has been an historic treasure for years. Primitive antiques, sun-dried linens, and gourmet breakfasts await you. Four rooms. $65-85.

The Heart House

419 North Michigan
Saginaw, MI, 48602
(517) 753-3145

Take a walk back in time. Nestled along the Saginaw River in historic Old Saginaw City.

Nine elegant guest rooms, decorated in antiques from the 1920s and 1930s. Private baths. Restaurant on premises. Quaint shops, pubs, and entertainment all within walking distance. $55-65.

ST. CLAIR

Murphy Inn

505 Clinton Street
St. Clair, MI, 48079
(313) 329-7118

A two-story white wood-frame building dating from 1836, only two blocks from the river. Seven guest rooms retain their old-fashioned charm and are furnished in country antiques and rich English wallpaper, with chenille bedspreads, ceiling fans, and in the bridal suite, a balcony overlooking the river.

Hosts: Ron & Cindy Sabotka
Rooms: 7 (PB) $42-75
Continental Breakfast
Credit Cards: A, B, C, D
Notes: 3, 4, 5, 7, 8, 9, 10, 11, 12, 13, 14

Murphy Inn

ST. IGNACE

Colonial House Inn & Motel

90 North State Street
St. Ignace, MI, 49781
(906) 643-6900

On the National Historic Register, the Colonial House Inn was built in 1870. Today the beautifully renovated inn houses unique antiques and gifts for sale. Just walk across the street to catch the ferry to Mackinaw Island.

Hosts: Elizabeth Brown & Jay Gunden
Rooms: 9 (PB) $35-75
Continental Breakfast
Credit Cards: A, B
Closed Nov. 15-April 15
Notes: 2, 7, 8, 9, 10, 11, 12, 13, 14

SAUGATUCK

The Kirby House

P.O. Box 1174
Saugatuck, MI, 49453
(616) 857-2904

An historic Victorian manor with eight beautifully appointed guest rooms, sumptuous breakfast buffet, pool in season, hot tub all year, complimentary skis in winter and bikes in summer. Fireplace rooms available, private baths.

Hosts: Loren & Marsha Kontio
Rooms: 8 (6 PB; 2 SB) $65-100
Full Breakfast
Credit Cards: A, B, C
Notes: 2, 5, 6, 7, 8, 9, 10, 11, 12, 13, 14

The Park House

888 Holland Street
Saugatuck, MI, 49453
(616) 857-4535

Saugatuck's oldest residence (1857) hosted Susan B. Anthony. Summer guests enjoy Lake Michigan, short walks to town, and air-conditioning. Winter guests relax fireside with our dog, Jimmy, curled at their feet. Tulip Festival, Victorian Christmases, Grand Escapes are favorites.

Hosts: Lynda & Joe Petty
Rooms: 10 (PB) $68.90-127.20
Continental Breakfast
Credit Cards: A, B, D
Notes: 2, 5, 7 (limited), 9, 10, 11, 12, 13, 14

Twin Gables Country Inn

900 Lake Street
Saugatuck, MI, 49453
(616) 857-4346

Built in 1865, this State Historic Inn is rich in history, having undergone several changes of function. Recently restored, it features fourteen charming guest rooms with private baths and antiques. Swimming pool, indoor hot tub, air-conditioning, fireplace.

Hosts: Michael & Denise Simcik
Rooms: 14 (PB) $44-94.34
Continental Breakfast
Minimum stay weekends: 2; holidays: 3
Credit Cards: A, B
Notes: 2, 5, 8 (over 5), 9, 10, 11, 12, 13

SAULT STE. MARIE

The Water Street Inn

140 East Water Street
Sault Ste. Marie, MI, 49783
(906) 632-1900

Built in 1904, this restored Queen Anne home overlooking the St. Mary's River features Tiffany windows, original woodwork, Italian marble fireplaces, and four antique-filled rooms with private baths. Just 1.5 blocks from the Soo Locks, with a wide wraparound porch for viewing the passing freighters. No smoking. $55-85.

SOUTH HAVEN

The Last Resort B&B Inn

86 North Shore Drive
South Haven, MI, 49090
(616) 637-8943

This historic inn is located on a picturesque peninsula between Lake Michigan and the Harbour . . . all rooms view water. Half a block to the beach, fishing, boating, and restaurants, a lovely stroll to town. Tennis, golf, wineries, and orchards are close by. The artist innkeepers share their original art and jewelry in The Inn Gallery.

Hosts: Wayne & Mary Babcock
Rooms: 12 (3 PB; 9 SB) $48-150
Continental Breakfast
Credit Cards: No
Closed Nov. 1-mid-April
Notes: 2, 7 (restricted), 9, 10, 11, 12, 14

Ross House B&B

229 Michigan Avenue
South Haven, MI, 49090
(616) 637-2256

The historic Ross House was built in 1886 by lumber tycoon Volney Ross. It sits on a quiet, tree-lined street on the south side of the Black River. Lake Michigan public beaches, downtown shopping area, and many fine restaurants are only blocks away.

Hosts: Cathy Hormann & Brad Wilcox
Rooms: 7 (1 PB; 6 S3B) $45-55
Full Breakfast
Credit Cards: No
Notes: 2, 5, 9, 10, 11, 12, 13 (XC)

STEPHENSON

Top O' the Hill

Center Street
Stephenson, MI, 49887
(906) 753-4757

Located in a small, quiet town in the southwest corner of the Upper Peninsula of Michigan, close to the Wisconsin border, away from the tourist traps of larger cities. There are nice restaurants, craft shops, and lots of natural beauty.

Hosts: Art & Phyllis Strohl
Rooms: 2 (1 PB; 1 SB) $30-35
Continental Breakfast
Credit Cards: No
Notes: 2, 5, 8, 9, 10, 11, 12, 13 (XC)

SUTTONS BAY

The Cottage B&B

503 St. Joseph Avenue
P.O. Box 653
Suttons Bay, MI, 49682
(616) 271-6348

Savor life in this small coastal village located on the beautiful Leelanau Peninsula fifteen miles north of Traverse City. Private baths, cable TV, air-conditioning, and full breakfast. Short walk to beach, marina, shops, restaurants, theater. Minutes from downhill and cross-country skiing. Three rooms. $55-60.

TECUMSEH

The Boulevard Inn

904 West Chicago Blvd.
Tecumseh, MI, 49286
(517) 423-5169

A Victorian inn in quaint Tecumseh. "The Inn the town helped build." Beautifully restored, warm, and inviting. Master suite has three rooms: bedroom, private sitting room, and bath with Jacuzzi. All rooms are elegant and unique. We look forward to being your getaway resting spot.

Host: Carol Thiede
Rooms: 7 (3 PB; 4 SB) $62.40-114.40
Full Breakfast
Credit Cards: A, B, C
Notes: 2, 5, 9, 10, 11, 12, 14

TRAVERSE CITY

Bass Lake Inn

61 Lakeside Street
Traverse City, MI, 49684
(616) 943-4790

New two-story waterfront inn located in the woods on 152 feet of beautiful Bass Lake, located halfway between Traverse City and Interlochen. Come and enjoy the fishing, canoeing, and beautiful sunsets. Cross-country and downhill skiing nearby. Sauna and Jacuzzi. Two rooms. $75.

Cherry Knoll Farm

2856 Hammond Road East
Traverse City, MI, 49684.
(616) 947-9806.

This lovely Victorian farmhouse, built c. 1885, has been recently remodeled and decorated in country style. Guest rooms are large, with air-conditioning, and share two baths. Family room with fireplace and TV. Full breakfast. Located just fifteen minutes from downtown Traverse City and five minutes from the bay. Three rooms. $60.

Cider House

5515 Barney Road
Traverse City, MI, 49684
(616) 947-2833

The emphasis here is on the simple, warm country life, as you awake to the smell of apple blossoms in the spring and juicy apples in the fall. Relax and enjoy cider or homemade Scottish shortbread and tea on the front porch of our contemporary "Bob Newhart Show" inn overlooking the orchard. Or relax in front of our fireplace in winter.

Hosts: Ron & Nan Tennant
Rooms: 5 (PB) $65 + tax
Full Breakfast
Credit Cards: No
Closed Christmas Day & Thanksgiving
Notes: 2, 9, 10, 11, 12, 13, 14

Warwickshire Inn B&B

5037 Barney Road
Traverse City, MI, 49684
(616) 946-7176

This stunning turn-of-the-century gem sits on a hill surrounded by large shade trees and overlooks Traverse City. Famous for the family-style breakfast that's elegantly served on fine Wedgewood china and sterling silver. Close to beaches, skiing, and the Interlochen Arts Academy. Air-conditioned.

Hosts: Patricia & Dan Warwick
Rooms: 3 (PB) $55-65
Full Breakfast
Credit Cards: No
Notes: 2, 5, 7 (limited), 9, 10, 11, 12, 13, 14

UNION PIER

The Inn at Union Pier

9708 Berrien Street
P.O. Box 222
Union Pier, MI, 49129
(616) 469-4700

An elegant refurbished inn that blends barefoot informality with all the comforts of a well-appointed country home. Across from Lake Michigan. Fifteen guest rooms have Swedish fireplaces; outdoor hot tub.

Hosts: Madeleine & Bill Reinke
Rooms: 15 (PB) $85-125
Full Breakfast
Credit Cards: A, B
Notes: 2, 5, 7, 8, 10, 11, 12, 13

WAKEFIELD

The Meford House

P.O. Box 149
Wakefield, MI, 49968
(906) 224-5151

The Medford House sits on a 20-acre hilltop, providing a spectacular view of the Porcupine Mountains and a secluded atmosphere. The spacious lounge features a fireplace, cable TV, stereo, and pool table. Queen beds. Four rooms. $43-79.

WALLOON LAKE

Masters House

P.O. Box 293
Walloon Lake, MI, 49796
(616) 535-2944

This large home was part of the tourist and logging history of Walloon Lake from the 1890s, serving as a lodging facility. Walloon Lake Village, beach, and gourmet dining are within walking distance. Ski and golf resorts are within seven miles; hunting, fishing, cross-country, and snowmobile trails are within four miles. Five rooms. $40-90.

WHITE CLOUD

The Shack Country Inn

2263 West Fourteenth Street
White Cloud, MI, 49349
(616) 924-6683

Built in 1945 and added to in 1989, this log structure has 26 guest rooms, five with private hot tubs. Air-conditioning, TV, telephone; two large fireplace rooms. Located on 100 acres on Robinson Lake, in an excellent area for swimming, fishing, snowmobiling, and cross-country skiing. $40-85.

WHITEHALL

Timepeekers Inn & Clock Shop

303 Mears Avenue
Whitehall, MI, 49461
(616) 894-5169

Beautiful century-old home with screened porch, spacious rooms, and antique furnishings. Comfortable, quiet atmosphere year-round. Two blocks from shops and restaurants; one block from White Lake; across from the summer theater. Four rooms. $35-60.

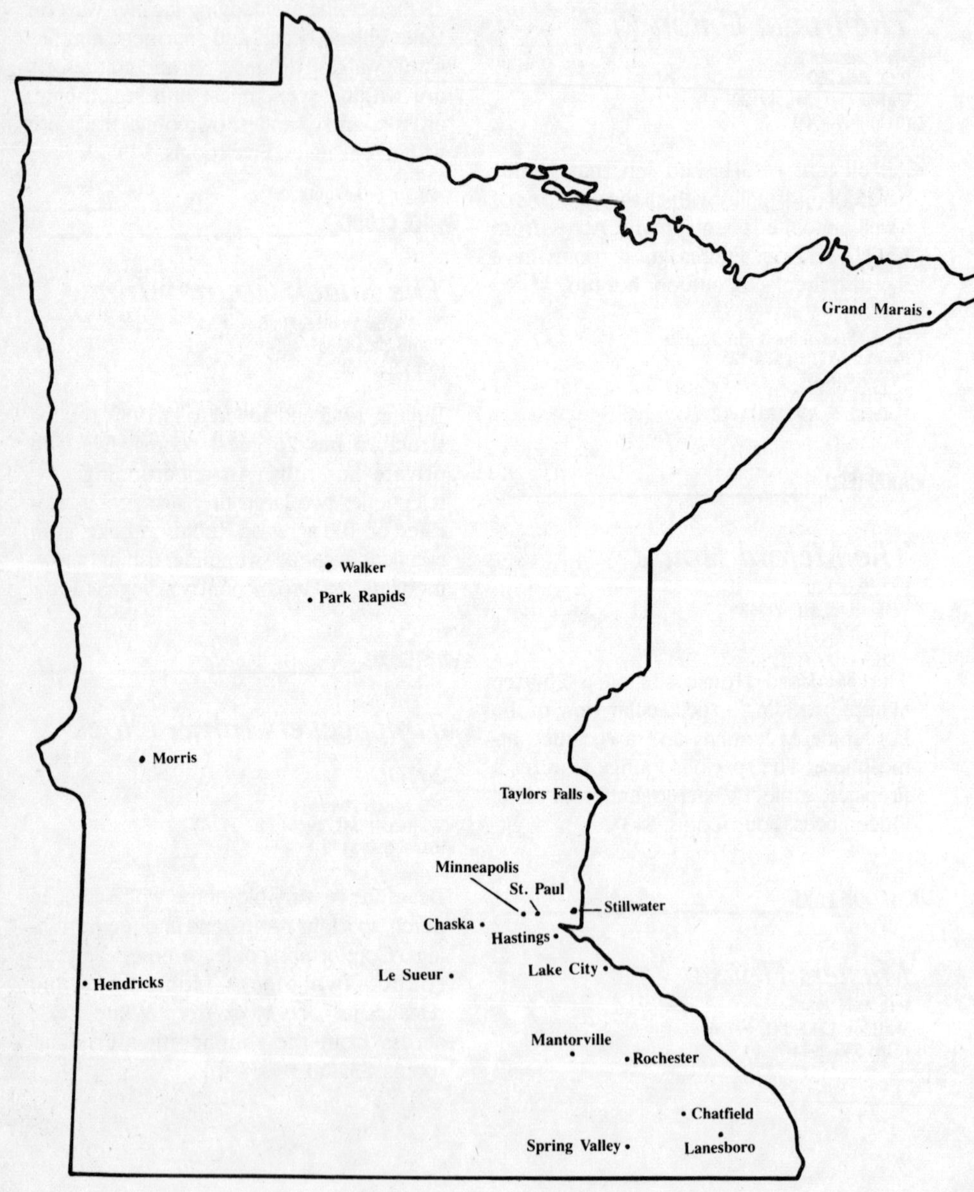
Grand Marais
Walker
Park Rapids
Morris
Taylors Falls
Minneapolis
St. Paul
Stillwater
Chaska
Hastings
Lake City
Le Sueur
Hendricks
Mantorville
Rochester
Chatfield
Lanesboro
Spring Valley

MINNESOTA

Minnesota

CHASKA

Bluff Creek Inn

1161 Bluff Creek Drive
Chaska, MN, 55318
(612) 445-2735

A Victorian brick farm home built in 1864, and decorated with country antiques, porch swings, and fireplaces. Lodgings include a full three-course breakfast plus wine and a snack in the evening. Nearby are hiking and biking trails, a dinner theater, arboretum, and race track. Thirty minutes from the Metro area.

Host: Anne Karels
Rooms: 4 (PB) $65-95
Full Breakfast
Credit Cards: A, B
Notes: 2, 5, 9, 13

CHATFIELD

Lunds' Guest House

500 Winona Street
Chatfield, MN, 55923
(507) 867-4003

Charming 1920 bungalow, furnished in 1920s and 1930s furniture. Quaint kitchen, dining room, living room with fireplace, TV, old electric organ. Large screened front porch and small screened back porch. A quiet escape just twenty miles from Rochester and 100 miles from Minneapolis.

Hosts: Shelby & Marion Lund
Rooms: 4 (PB) $45-50
Continental Breakfast
Credit Cards: No
Notes: 2, 5, 7 (outside), 8, 9, 10, 11, 12, 13

GRAND MARAIS

Pincushion Mountain B&B

P.O. Box 181
Gunflint Trail
Grand Marais, MN, 55604
(218) 387-1276; (800) 542-1226

This year-round B&B sits on a ridge of Minnesota's Sawtooth Mountains overlooking the north shore of Lake Superior 1,000 feet below. New, country decor. Hiking, biking, and cross-country ski trails are at our doorstep. Twenty minutes from BWCA canoe entry points; three miles from Grand Marais.

Hosts: Scott & Mary Beattie
Rooms: 4 (1 PB; 3 SB) $63-82
Full Breakfast
Credit Cards: A, B
Closed April
Notes: 2, 8 (over 10), 9, 10, 11, 12, 13, 14

Pincushion Mountain B&B

HASTINGS

Thorwood Inn

Fourth and Pine
Hastings, MN, 55033
(612) 437-3297

French Second Empire (1880) home with suite-sized rooms and private dining area in each. Private baths, some with double whirlpools, and fireplaces. Huge breakfast served to your schedule. Located one block from Mississippi River bluff and walking tour of historic downtown. Central air-conditioning; dining packages and limousine available.

Hosts: Dick & Pam Thorsen
Rooms: 13 (PB) $49-195
Full Breakfast
Credit Cards: A, B, C
Notes: 2, 4, 5, 9, 10, 11, 12, 13, 14

HENDRICKS

Triple L Farm B&B

Route 1, Box 141
Hendricks, MN, 56136
(507) 275-3740

The Triple L Farm is a working family farm with a large remodeled 1890 home. Guest rooms have antique furnishings and homemade quilts.

Hosts: Lanford & Joan Larson
Rooms: 2 (1 PB; 1 SB) $25-45
Full Breakfast
Credit Cards: A, B, C, D
Notes: 2, 3, 4, 7, 9, 10, 11, 12, 13 (XC)

LAKE CITY

Evergreen Knoll Acres B&B

RR 1, Box 145
Lake City, MN, 55041
(612) 345-2257

This B&B is located on a dairy farm with 65 milk cows, 160 acres of land 8.5 miles southwest of Lake City and 35 miles north of Rochester. Nearby Lake Pepin provides fishing, sailing, and waterskiing. The large, German-style country home was built in 1919 and is furnished with antiques, country crafts, air-conditioning, and a fireplace.

Hosts: Paul & Bev Meyer
Rooms: 3 (SB) $45-55
Full Breakfast
Credit Cards: No
Closed Christmas
Notes: 2, 5, 8, 9, 10, 11, 12, 13

Red Gables Inn

403 North High Street
Lake City, MN, 55041
(612) 345-2605

Red Gables Inn is in a quiet residential section of Lake City, home of the largest small-boat marina on the Mississippi. The red Victorian was built in 1865 and displays a mixture of Italianate and Greek Revival architecture. Formal Victorian antiques are in the parlor and dining room, while the guest rooms have floral wallpapers and iron, brass, and painted Victorian beds. In early evening, guests may join the innkeepers for wine and hors d'oeuvres.

Hosts: Mary & Doug De Roos
Rooms: 9 (5 PB; 4 SB) $48-68
Full Breakfast
Credit Cards: A, B
Notes: 2, 5, 7 (limited), 8 (13 and over), 9, 10, 11, 12, 13, 14

The Victorian B&B

620 South High Street
Lake City, MN, 55041
(612) 345-2167

An 1896 Victorian home where each room has a lake view. Carved woodwork, stained-glass windows, antique music boxes and furnishings. Air conditioned. Dinner cruises on Lake Pepin. Mayo Clinic thirty-five miles; Minneapolis-St. Paul sixty-five miles. Breakfast is served in your room, the formal dining room, or on the porches.

Hosts: Joel & Sandra Grettenberg
Rooms: 3 (1 PB; 2 private 1/2 baths) $50-65
Continental-plus Breakfast
Credit Cards: No
Notes: 2, 5, 8 (over 10), 9, 10, 11, 12, 13, 14

LANESBORO

Carrolton Country Inn

RR 2, Box 139
Lanesboro, MN, 55949
(507) 467-2257

Carrolton Country Inn is nestled among hills in an open valley near Lanesboro in SE Minnesota Historic Bluff Country. We're located on the Root River and Trail for hiking, biking, cross-country skiing, fishing, and canoeing year around. This private guest home with Victorian accents has accommodations for B&B, whole-house rental, and family reunions. Ask for our free brochure.

Hosts: Charles & Gloria Ruen
Rooms: 4 (2 PB; 2 SB) $50-75
Full Breakfast
Credit Cards: A, B
Notes: 2, 5, 8, 9, 10, 11, 12, 13

Carrolton Country Inn

Scanlan House B&B

708 Parkway Avenue South
Lanesboro, MN, 55949
(507) 467-2158

An 1889 Victorian home on the National Register of Historic Places. Five large bedroom suites appointed in period pieces. Original ornate woodwork and beautiful stained-glass windows. Two fireplaces and rooms with private and shared baths. Located four blocks from the Root River, with its canoeing, fishing, and tubing, and the 38-mile paved Root River Trail for biking, hiking, walking, and cross-country skiing. Eleven golf courses in the area. Tennis courts. An exquisite B&B; you'll have the feeling of home. Complimentary wine and imported chocolates; scented padded hangers in the closet.

Hosts: The Mensings
Rooms: 5 (2 PB; 3 SB) $65-90
Full Breakfast
Credit Cards: A, B, C
Notes: 2, 5, 8, 9, 10, 11, 12, 13, 14

LE SUEUR

The Cosgrove B&B

228 South Second Street
Le Sueur, MN, 56058
(612) 665-2763

Located in the heart of the beautiful Minnesota River Valley, the Cosgrove is a gracious Victorian home with four period rooms, two with fireplaces. A full breakfast is served in the formal wood-paneled dining room. A National Historic Register home.

Host: Pam Quist
Rooms: 4 (SB) $65
Full Breakfast
Credit Cards: No
Notes: 2, 5, 7, 8, 9, 10, 11, 12, 13 (XC)

MANTORVILLE

Grand Old Mansion

Box 185
Mantorville, MN, 55955
(507) 635-3231

Enjoy bed and breakfast in this lovely ornate Victorian that's filled with antiques and collectibles. Dine in an elegant atmosphere at Hubbell House, or visit the several antique and specialty shops.

Hosts: Irene & Clair Felker
Rooms: 4 (2 PB; 2 SB) $30-50
Full Breakfast
Credit Cards: No
Notes: 2, 5, 7 (limited), 9, 11, 12, 13, 14

MINNEAPOLIS

Nan's B&B

2304 Fremont Avenue South
Minneapolis, MN, 55405
(612) 377-5118

Comfortable urban 1890s Victorian family home with guest rooms furnished in antiques. Friendly, outgoing hosts will help you find your way around town. Near downtown, lakes, theaters, galleries, restaurants, and shopping. One block from buses.

Hosts: Nan & Jim Zosel
Rooms: 3 (SB) $45
Full Breakfast
Credit Cards: C
Notes: 2, 5, 6, 7, 8, 11, 12

Canterbury Inn B&B

MORRIS

The American House

410 East Third Street
Morris, MN, 56267
(612) 589-4054

Victorian home decorated with antiques and country charm. Ride our tandem bike on scenic trails. Within walking distance of area restaurants and shops. Located one block from the University of Minnesota, Morris campus.

Host: Karen Berget
Rooms: 3 (SB) $35-44
Full Breakfast
Credit Cards: No
Notes: 2, 5, 8, 9, 10, 11, 12, 14

PARK RAPIDS

Dickson Viking Huss B&B

202 East Fourth Street
Park Rapids, MN, 56470
(218) 732-8089

Aunt Helen invites you to her charming contemprary home with vaulted ceiling and fireplace in her living room that features a watercolor exhibit. Big continental breakfast. Bicycle or cross-country ski the Heartlant Trail. Visit Itasca Park, the source of the Mississippi. Unique shops and restaurants. MN inspected.

Host: Helen K. Dickson
Rooms: 3 (1 PB; 2 SB) $29.50-41.50
Continental-plus Breakfast
Credit Cards: A, B
Notes: 2, 5, 7 (limited), 8, 9, 10, 11, 12, 13 (XC), 14

ROCHESTER

Canterbury Inn B&B

723 Second Street SW
Rochester, MN, 55902
(507) 289-5553

Canterbury Inn combines the charm of an 1890 Victorian landmark with modern comforts and delightful cuisine. Gourmet breakfasts are served anytime (in bed on request), plus complimentary teatime hors d'oeuvres and libations. We have a city location near the Mayo Clinic, off-street parking, and central air-conditioning.

Hosts: Mary Martin & Jeffrey VanSant
Rooms: 4 (PB) $64.90-75.90
Full Breakfast
Credit Cards: A, B
Notes: 2, 5, 7 (limited), 8 (over 10), 9, 10, 11, 12, 13 (XC), 14

ST. PAUL

Chatsworth B&B

984 Ashland Avenue
St. Paul, MN, 55104
(612) 227-4288

Elegantly furnished Victorian home in a quiet residential neighborhood. Fifteen minutes from the airport. Near Governor's Mansion and numerous restaurants and shops. Easy access to both downtown St. Paul and Minneapolis. Two rooms with double whirlpool baths. Licensed; smoke-free.

Hosts: Donna & Earl Gustafson
Rooms: 5 (3 PB; 2 SB) $61.48-100.70
Continental-plus Breakfast
Credit Cards: No
Notes: 2, 5, 8, 9, 10, 11, 12, 13

SPRING VALLEY

Chase's

North Huron Avenue
Spring Valley, MN, 55975
(507) 346-2850

It's life in the slow lane at our Second Empire mansion. It's flowers, birds, stars, and exploring this unglaciated area. Step back in time with a tour: Amish, Laura Ingalls Wilder, caves—or enjoy our trails, trout streams, bike trail.

Hosts: Bob & Jeannine Chase
Rooms: 5 (PB) $60-75
Full Breakfast
Credit Cards: A, B
Closed Dec.-Feb.
Notes: 2, 8, 9, 10, 11, 12, 13

STILLWATER

The Rivertown Inn B&B

306 West Olive Street
Stillwater, MN, 55082
(612) 430-2955

Beautifully restored 1882 three-story lumberman's mansion. Nine charming guest rooms individually decorated with fine Victorian antiques; some with double whirlpools and fireplaces. Full breakfast is served. Overlooks Stillwater and the St. Croix River Valley. Four blocks from historic Main Street. Stillwater's oldest B&B.

Hosts: Chuck & Judy Dougherty
Rooms: 9 (PB) $49-139
Full Breakfast
Credit Cards: A, B
Notes: 2, 5, 8 (over 12), 9, 10, 11, 12, 13, 14

The Rivertown Inn B&B

TAYLORS FALLS

The Old Jail Company

100 Government Road, Box 203
Taylors Falls, MN, 55084
(612) 465-3112

The historic Taylors Falls Jail Guesthouse and the "Cave" and "Playhouse" suites in the Schottmuller Brewery building next door overlook the St. Croix River Valley, just a few yards from Interstate Park, with its ancient glacial potholes and dramatic black rock cliffs. Swim, fish, rent canoes and bikes, enjoy riverboat cruises, antiques, potteries, and much more.

Hosts: Julie & Al Kunz
Rooms: 3 (PB) $60-110
Full Breakfast
Credit Cards: No
Notes: 2, 5, 7, 9, 10, 11, 12, 13

WALKER

Chase on the Lake Lodge & Motor Inn

P.O. Box 206
Walker, MN, 56484
(218) 547-1531; (800) 533-2083

Beautiful Tudor-style lodge and motor inn on the lake in Walker, one block from downtown. Marine dining room and lounge with entertainment. Banquet facilities, fishing, golf, hiking, bicycling, and snowmobile trails nearby.

Hosts: Jim & Barb Aletto
Rooms: 32 (30 PB; 2 SB) $52-56
Full Breakfast
Credit Cards: A, B, C, D
Notes: 2, 3, 4, 5, 7, 8, 9, 10, 11, 12, 13, 14

Mississippi

ABERDEEN

Lincoln, Ltd. 43

P.O. Box 3479
Meridian, MS, 39303
(601) 482-5483 for information
(800) 633-Miss for reservations

This fine Victorian home is filled with antiques and decorated in a style typical of the period. The guest bedroom features an antique bed and is decorated in the Victorian manner. Other attractions include four historic churches and two c. 1830 cemeteries. $55.

BROOKHAVEN

Lincoln, Ltd. 1

P.O. Box 3479
Meridian, MS, 39303
(601) 482-5483 for information
(800) 633-Miss for reservations

A beautiful nineteenth-century home, completely restored and furnished in the Victorian style with antiques. The host is well-known as a decorator and architectural designer. Four large rooms, each with private bath. Dinner is available by special arrangement and reservation. A full breakfast is served in the dining room. $95-105.

CHATHAM (NEAR GREENVILLE)

Lincoln, Ltd. 48

P.O. Box 3479
Meridian, MS, 39303
(601) 482-5483 for information
(800) 633-Miss for reservations

This antebellum mansion, c. 1856, is one of the finest examples of Italianate-style architecture in Mississippi. It is located on historic Lake Washington and listed on the National Register of Historic Places. On the River Road just south of Greenville, the home is surrounded by several acres of beautiful river land. Sit on the front porch and enjoy a lake view, stroll the grounds. Four rooms; three with private baths, one with shared. $85.

COLUMBUS

Lincoln, Ltd. 5

P.O. Box 3479
Meridian, MS, 39303
(601) 482-5483 for information
(800) 633-Miss for reservations

This house is a Federal house and the oldest brick house in Columbus. It was built in 1828 and has been completely restored and furnished with antiques of the period. Three bedrooms, each with private bath and full breakfast. $65.

COMO

Lincoln, Ltd. 49

P.O. Box 3479
Meridian, MS, 39303
(601) 482-5483 for information
(800) 633-Miss for reservations

A very attractive guest cottage in a delightful small Mississippi town right on I-55, between Memphis and Jackson. There are also accommodations in the main house. Breakfast is continental in the guest cottage and

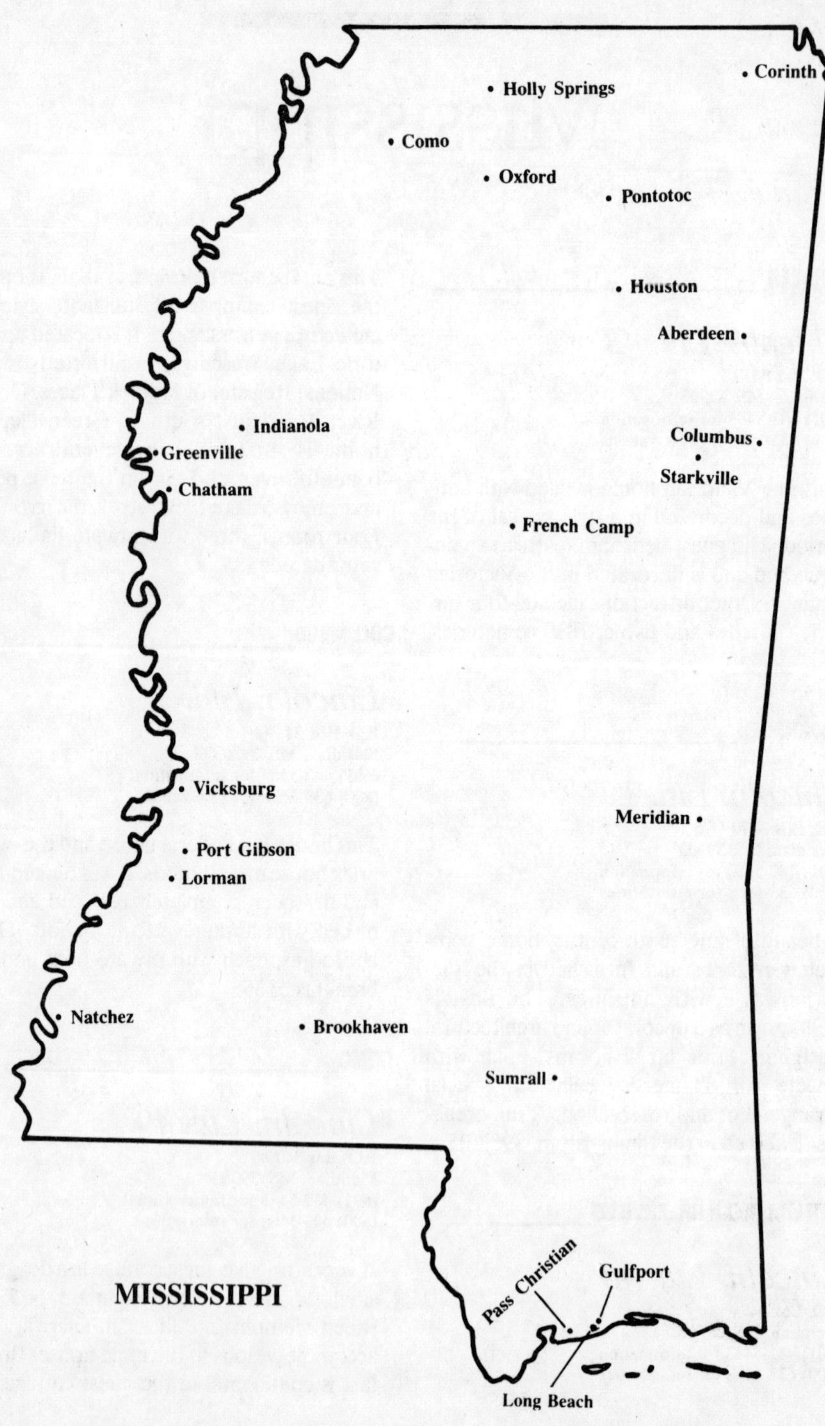
Corinth
Holly Springs
Como
Oxford
Pontotoc
Houston
Aberdeen
Indianola
Greenville
Chatham
Columbus
Starkville
French Camp
Vicksburg
Meridian
Port Gibson
Lorman
Natchez
Brookhaven
Sumrall
Pass Christian
Gulfport
Long Beach
MISSISSIPPI

full in the main house. Two rooms with private baths. $60-80.

CORINTH

Lincoln, Ltd. 37

P.O. Box 3479
Meridian, MS, 39303
(601) 482-5483 for information
(800) 633-Miss for reservations

A beautiful Victorian home, completely furnished with antiques. Convenient to Memphis and Shiloh National Park. A full Southern breakfast is served; lunch and dinner are also available. Four rooms with private bath. $70.

FRENCH CAMP

Lincoln, Ltd. 59

P.O. Box 3479
Meridian, MS, 39303
(601) 482-5483 for information
(800) 633-Miss for reservations

Enjoy the spacious view of forest and wildlife from the wide windows of this two-story log home. The home, constructed with chinked log walls, was reconstructed from two log cabins over 100 years old. Two rooms with private baths. $53.

GULFPORT

Lincoln, Ltd. 42

P.O. Box 3479
Meridian, MS, 39303
(601) 482-5483 for information
(800) 633-Miss for reservations

A nice contemporary home in a quiet neighborhood just two blocks from the beach and convenient to the Biloxi convention center. Private, nicely furnished bedroom with private bath. $45.

HOLLY SPRINGS

Hamilton Place

105 East Mason Avenue
Holly Springs, MS, 38635
(601) 252-4368

Antebellum home built in 1838 and listed on the National Register. All rooms furnished in antiques. There is an antique shop in the carriage house, seasonal pool, and year-round hot tub for guests to enjoy. Museum, art gallery, and other historic homes are within walking distance.

Hosts: Linda & Jack Stubbs
Rooms: 4 (PB) $55-68.90
Full Breakfast
Credit Cards: A, B
Notes: 2, 4, 5, 7, 8, 9, 10, 11, 12, 14

HOUSTON

Lincoln, Ltd. 39

P.O. Box 3479
Meridian, MS, 39303
(601) 482-5483 for information
(800) 633-Miss for reservations

A Victorian home, completely renovated in a small Mississippi town. Located just one block from the town square, there are five comfortable rooms, all with private bath and TV. Guests may relax and socialize in the downstairs sitting room. A full Southern breakfast is served. $45.

INDIANOLA

Lincoln, Ltd. 9

P.O. Box 3479
Meridian, MS, 39303
(601) 482-5483 for information
(800) 633-Miss for reservations

Enjoy a full breakfast of country ham and homemade biscuits at this extremely attractive two-story home in the heart of the Mississippi Delta. The hosts, known for their hospitality, will take guests on a tour of the area and direct them to well-known area restaurants. Four rooms with private baths. $45.

LONG BEACH

Lincoln, Ltd. 53

P.O. Box 3479
Meridian, MS, 39303
(601) 482-5483 for information
(800) 633-Miss for reservations

Three-story raised French cottage located 1.5 miles south of I-10 Long Beach, on 5 acres of live oaks and magnolias. Antiques, six fireplaces, and a 64-foot front porch with swings. Gardens, campsites, and cabins will soon be available. Four rooms, three with private baths and one with shared bath. $39-69.

Rosswood Plantation

LORMAN

Rosswood Plantation

Route 552, Lorman, MS, 39096
(601) 437-4215

An authentic antebellum mansion, close to Natchez and Vicksburg, offering luxury, comfort, charm, and hospitality on a serene country estate. Once a cotton plantation, Rosswood now grows Christmas trees. Ideal for honeymoons. A Mississippi landmark, National Register, AAA recommended.

Hosts: Jean & Walt Hylander
Rooms: 4 (PB) $90
Full Breakfast
Credit Cards: A, B
Notes: 2, 5, 7, 8, 9, 14

MERIDIAN

Lincoln, Ltd. 13

P.O. Box 3479
Meridian, MS, 39303
(601) 482-5483 for information
(800) 633-Miss for reservations

Restored Victorian home filled with antiques and located on 10 wooded acres within the city limits. Hostess is a noted gourmet cook and will, by special arrangement, prepare dinner for an additional charge. Full breakfast. $60-65.

Lincoln, Ltd. 15

P.O. Box 3479
Meridian, MS, 39303
(601) 482-5483 for information
(800) 633-Miss for reservations

This contemporary home has hosts who are active in both local and state affairs. Their home is filled with art and collections from their travels. One room with private bath and full bed. $45.

Lincoln, Ltd. 57

P.O. Box 3479
Meridian, MS, 39303
(601) 482-5483 for information
(800) 633-Miss for reservations

Nestled in the woods, this California-style home has a bedroom with private bath and a loft area that will sleep two additional people traveling with the same party. Wake up to the sound of birds, have breakfast on the patio, walk in the woods, or sun on the deck. $45-55.

Lincoln, Ltd. 58

P.O. Box 3479
Meridian, MS, 39303
(601) 482-5483 for information
(800) 633-Miss for reservations

A new contemporary inn convenient to I-59 and I-20. Beautiful spacious rooms. Meeting space for up to sixty people. Continental breakfast is served. Swimming pool and whirlpool on premises; weekly and monthly rates available. $39-45.

NATCHEZ

The Burn

712 North Union Street
Natchez, MS, 39120
(601) 442-1344

Circa 1834, three-story mansion especially noted for its semispiral stairway, unique gardens, and exquisite collection of antiques. Overnight guests are pampered with a seated plantation breakfast, tour of the home, and use of the swimming pool. Owner occupied.

Hosts: Loveta & Tony Byrne
Rooms: 6 (PB) $75-125
Full Breakfast
Credit Cards: A, B, C, D, E
Notes: 2, 5, 7, 9, 10, 11, 12, 14

The Burn

D'Evereux

Natchez Pilgrimage Tours
P.O. Box 347
Natchez, MS, 39120
(800) 647-6742

Circa 1840. Resembling a Greek temple, D'Evereux sits in the heart of a 7-acre manicured park near downtown Natchez. A broad gallery leads into the spacious home, which was designed by James Hardie. One room in the main house. Continental breakfast; children fourteen and over welcome. $100.

Elgin

Natchez Pilgrimage Tours
P.O. Box 347
Natchez, MS, 39120
(800) 647-6742

In a country setting just three miles from the city limits, Elgin offers accommodations in a separate 1853 building. Guests may relax in the downstairs living room or on their own upstairs gallery. Full Southern breakfast. The three-bedroom guest house offers a sitting room, kitchen; school-age children welcome. $75-120.

Hope Farm

Natchez Pilgrimage Tours
P.O. Box 347
Natchez, MS, 39120
(800) 647-6742

Hope Farm was built from 1775-1789 and is furnished with exquisite antiques and distinctive tester beds. Each room has a private bath. A full Southern breakfast is served in the formal dining room, followed by a complete tour of the house. Four bedrooms; children six and over are welcome. $80.

Linden

Natchez Pilgrimage Tours
P.O. Box 347

Natchez, MS, 39120
(800) 647-6742

C. 1800. Step through the magnificent doorway used in *Gone With the Wind* and be greeted by the sixth generation owners. All rooms are furnished with antique heirlooms; each has private bath. Freshly brewed coffee and a plantation breakfast start your day. Seven rooms in the main house; children ten and over are welcome. $80 + tax.

Linden

Monmouth

Natchez Pilgrimage Tours
P.O. Box 347
Natchez, MS, 39120
(800) 647-6742

C. 1818. Twelve luxurious guest rooms and two suites with genuine antiques, private baths, TV, telephone, air-conditioning. Situated on 26 beautiful acres. Rate includes a full Southern breakfast and tour of the house. Children fourteen and older are welcome. $85-160.

Mount Repose

Natchez Pilgrimage Tours
P.O. Box 347
Natchez, MS, 39120
(800) 647-6742

A lovely 1824 plantation home located on 250 acres of rolling hills, green pastures, tree-lined ponds, and magnificent live oaks. The two bedrooms are located in the main house, which is furnished in period family antiques. No smoking; children welcome. $75.

Ravenna

Natchez Pilgrimage Tours
P.O. Box 347
Natchez, MS, 39120
(800) 647-6742

Two bedrooms are available in the main house, and there is a one-bedroom guest house with sitting room and small kitchen. Full Southern breakfast is served; children are welcome. $85-120.

Shields Town House

Natchez Pilgrimage Tours
P.O. Box 347
Natchez, MS, 39120
(800) 647-6742

C. 1860. Located two blocks from Stanton Hall, this Greek Revival home was the last fine townhouse built in Natchez prior to the Civil War. Exquisitely furnished in eighteenth- and early nineteenth-century antiques. Two one-bedroom guest houses, sitting room, kitchen. Continental breakfast; children twelve and over are welcome. $75-85.

Texada

Natchez Pilgrimage Tours
P.O. Box 347
Natchez, MS, 39120
(800) 647-6742

Situated in the old Spanish Quarter, Texada, built in 1792, has served as a tavern, hotel, and territorial legislative hall. Four bedrooms in the main house with Southern breakfast. There is also a two-bedroom guest house with sitting room and kitchen. Children three and over are welcome. $75.

OXFORD

Lincoln, Ltd. 23

P.O. Box 3479
Meridian, MS, 39303
(601) 482-5483 for information
(800) 633-Miss for reservations

Built in 1838, this lovely antebellum home is made entirely of native timber and is on the National Register. In an attic, 150 years of fashion are displayed on mannequins. Guests can enjoy cakes that are still warm and have breakfast on the balcony. Conveniently located close to the University of Mississippi and the William Faulkner home. Downstairs suite filled with antiques, $65. Two upstairs rooms, one with a private bath and one shared, $50-70.

Lincoln, Ltd. 24

P.O. Box 3479
Meridian, MS, 39303
(601) 482-5483 for information
(800) 633-Miss for reservations

Charming small inn with five guest rooms with private baths. Convenient to the University of Mississippi and Faulkner residence. Continental breakfast; lunch available; dinner may be available on request. Five rooms, private baths. $45.

PASS CHRISTIAN

Lincoln, Ltd. 25

P.O. Box 3479
Meridian, MS, 39303
(601) 482-5483 for information
(800) 633-Miss for reservations

Enjoy staying in a log home on 40 acres of land just 2.5 miles north of I-20 and 2.5 miles from the beach. This home has a private bedroom and bath, a loft for families traveling with children, and a swimming pool. $55.

PONTOTOC

Lincoln, Ltd. 52

P.O. Box 3479
Meridian, MS, 39303
(601) 482-5483 for information
(800) 633-Miss for reservations

A very attractive historic Victorian with three guest roms, all with private baths. High ceilings in all the rooms. Rock on the front porch or use the lovely library with fireplace. Full continental breakfast is served. $45-55.

PORT GIBSON

Oak Square Plantation

1207 Church Street
Port Gibson, MS, 39150
(601) 437-4350 (800) 729-0240

Antebellum mansion in the town General U.S. Grant said was "too beautiful to burn." Heirloom antiques, canopied beds. On the National Register of Historic Places. AAA 4-diamond rated.

Hosts: Mr. & Mrs. William Lum
Rooms: 10(PB) $60-85
Full Breakfast
Credit Cards: A, B, C
Notes: 2, 5, 8, 9, 14

Southern Comfort Reservations MPG02

2856 Hundred Oaks Avenue
Baton Rouge, LA, 70808
(504) 346-1928: (800) 749-1928

A rural, 100-acre working plantation with a 125-year-old classic Greek Revival mansion. Relax and enjoy the antiques, spacious grounds, plantation tour. Fish in their well-stocked pond, read the first owner's journal, perhaps meet the friendly ghost. Plantation breakfast, a welcoming julep, and fresh fruit in your room. Smoking is restricted. Four rooms with private baths. Children are welcome; baby-sitting can be arranged. $90.

STARKVILLE

Lincoln, Ltd. 56

P.O. Box 3479
Meridian, MS, 39303
(601) 482-5483 for information
(800) 633-Miss for reservations

This 200-year-old, hand-hewn square log cabin has all the conveniences of today. Located in the middle of 35 acres overlooking a small lake and nestled in a grove of cedars. The guest suite on the second floor has a large sun deck, large living room, separate bedroom with fireplace, and a four-poster bed. Complimentary beverage, continental breakfast. $45-55.

Lincoln, Ltd. 60

P.O. Box 3479
Meridian, MS, 39303
(601) 482-5483 for information
(800) 633-Miss for reservations

This special country home is in a wonderful setting among a 15-acre Christmas tree farm with cows and horses. The guest suite is located on the second floor with a living/kitchen area, bedroom, and private bath. It can sleep up to four people. Convenient to Mississippi State University fifteen minutes away. $45-60.

SUMMRELL (HATTIESBURG)

Lincoln, Ltd. 61

P.O. Box 3479
Meridian, MS, 39303
(601) 482-5483 for information
(800) 633-Miss for reservations

Located on 48 acres, just twenty minutes from Hattiesburg and USM, this cottage offers one to three bedrooms, each with private bath, telephone, and TV. The central living room has a wood-burning fireplace, library, and VCR. Enjoy fishing or boating in the pond, watch the Australian swans, or picnic beside a mountain-laurel-lined creek. Full breakfast; Cajun dinner can be prepared with advance reservations. No smoking. 10% senior citizen discount. $45-50.

VICKSBURG

Anchuca

1010 First East Street
Vicksburg, MS, 39180
(601) 636-4931; (800) 262-4822

Anchuca is an 1830 Greek Revival mansion housing some of the most magnificent period antiques and artifacts, complete with gas-burning chandeliers. Beautiful brick courtyards completely surround the mansion and renovated slave quarters. Overnight guests are accommodated in the slave quarters, the guest cottage, and one room in the main house. A tour of the home, pool, and hot tub are available.

Hosts: May Burns & Kathy Tanner
Rooms: 9 (PB) $75-115
Full Breakfast
Credit Cards: A, B, C, D
Notes: 2, 5, 6, 7, 8, 9, 10, 11, 12, 14

Cedar Grove Mansion-Inn

2200 Washington Street
Vicksburg, MS, 39180
(800) 862-1300; (800) 448-2820 in Miss.

Relive *Gone With the Wind* in this 1840 magnificently furnished inn. Four acres of gardens, fountains, and courtyards. Gas lights, four-poster beds, period antiques. Pool, Jacuzzi, and the terrace has a view of the Mississippi River. Chosen by *Escape In Style* as one of the most romantic inns in the world. Four-diamond rated by AAA and a National Historic Property.

Host: Estelle Mackey
Rooms: 18 (PB) $75-140
Full Breakfast
Credit Cards: A, B, C
Notes: 2, 5, 7 (limited), 8 (6 and over), 9, 11, 14

The Corners

601 Klein Street
Vicksburg, MS, 39180
(800) 444-7421

The inn is the home of Bettye and Cliff Whitney, who will welcome you upon arrival with a refreshing drink on the veranda. *Food and Wine* magazine (Oct. 1990) says The Corners is the ultimate in understated elegance. Four-diamond rated by AAA and a national Historic Property. Built as a wedding present in 1872, the mansion has its original parterre gardens, a 68-foot long gallery with spectacular view of the Mississippi River and Delta. Architecture combines Greek Revival, Victorian, and Steamboat Gothic. Furnished with antiques. Comfort and hospitality emphasized.

Hosts: Cliff & Bettye Whitney
Rooms: 8 (PB) $65-95
Suite (PB) $140
Full Breakfast
Credit Cards: A, B, C
Notes: 2, 5, 8, 9, 14

The Duff Green Mansion

1114 First East Street
Vicksburg, MS, 39180
(601) 636-6968; (800) 992-0037

Exquisitely restored antebellum inn listed on the National Register of Historic Places. Built in 1856, it is considered one of Mississippi's finest architectural treasures. Duff Green Mansion played a prominent role as a hospital in the siege of Vicksburg. Luxurious accommodations with private baths and a swimming pool.

Hosts: Tim & Lucy DeRossette
Rooms: 7 (PB) $50-150
Full Breakfast
Credit Cards: A, B, C
Notes: 2, 3, 4, 5, 6, 7, 8, 9, 10, 11, 12, 14

Lincoln, Ltd. 27

P.O. Box 3479
Meridian, MS, 39303
(601) 482-5483 for information
(800) 633-Miss for reservations

True Southern hospitality in this Federal-style home. Here history combines with every modern amenity, including a hot tub and swimming pool. Sleep in an antique-filled bedroom and enjoy a full plantation-style breakfast in the formal dining room. A tour of the home and welcoming beverage are included. $75-110.

Lincoln, Ltd. 32

P.O. Box 3479
Meridian, MS, 39303
(601) 482-5483 for information
(800) 633-Miss for reservations

Situated on 6 landscaped acres, this outstanding home in the Federal style features exquisite milled woodwork, sterling silver doorknobs, French bronze chandeliers, and a lonely ghost. Three lovely guest rooms are furnished in antiques. A tour of the home, plantation breakfast, and mint juleps are included. $75.

Lincoln, Ltd. 35

P.O. Box 3479
Meridian, MS, 39303
(601) 482-5483 for information
(800) 633-Miss for reservations

Circa 1873, built as a wedding present from father to daughter, this house is an interesting mixture of Victorian and Greek Revival. All rooms are furnished with antiques and have private baths; some available with fireplaces and TV. Enjoy a spectacular view of the Mississippi River and Valley from a rocking chair on the front gallery. Plantation breakfast included. $65-85.

Lincoln, Ltd. 36

P.O. Box 3479
Meridian, MS, 39303

(601) 482-5483 for information
(800) 633-Miss for reservations

Lavish antebellum mansion built between 1840 and 1858. *Gone With the Wind* elegance you won't forget. Exquisitely furnished with many original antiques; formal gardens, gazebos, and fountains. Relax in the courtyard, or use the pool and spa. On the National Register of Historic Places. Fourteen rooms, all with private bath. $75-105.

Lincoln, Ltd. 41

P.O. Box 3479
Meridian, MS, 39303
(601) 482-5483 for information
(800) 633-Miss for reservations

Elegant antebellum mansion, c. 1856, located in Vicksburg's historic district. The best example of Paladian architecture in Mississippi. Used as a hospital during the Civil War, the house was shelled during the siege of Vicksburg. Eight rooms with private baths. $85-140.

Missouri

ARROW ROCK

Borgman's B&B

706 Van Buren
Arrow Rock, MO, 65320
(816) 837-3350

We invite you to experience the historic town of Arrow Rock in the warmth of our century-old home. Four rooms, shared bath, no smoking. Home-baked breakfast. Arrow Rock (1829) is a National Historic Landmark town at the beginning of the Santa Fe trail and was the home of artist George Caleb Bingham.

Hosts: Kathy & Helen Borgman
Rooms: 4 (SB) $40-45
Continental-plus Breakfast
Credit Cards: No
Notes: 2, 5, 8

Borgman's B&B

BONNE TERRE

Lamplight Inn B&B

207 East School Street
Bonne Terre, MO, 63628
(314) 358-4222; 358-3332

"The food at the Lamplight Inn and the antique-filled bedrooms provide a setting that could put you in several European countries. We enjoyed lovely sleeping accommodations at the Wibskov's Bed & Breakfast home. Our room was magnificent" —*St. Louis Post-Dispatch.*

Hosts: Jorgen & Krista Wibskov
Rooms: 4 (3 PB; 1 SB) $55-75
Full Breakfast
Credit Cards: A, B, C
Notes: 2, 3, 4, 5, 7 (restricted), 8, 9, 10, 11, 12, 14

BRANSON AREA

Ozark Mt. Country B&B 101-B

P.O. Box 295
Branson, MO, 65616
(800) 321-8594

This elegant early 1900 home in downtown Branson has been lovingly restored, redecorated, and air-conditioned. Spacious parlor available for guest use. The entire home is furnished with antiques, and a full breakfast is served in the formal dining room or on the large front porch. Two guest rooms are on the main floor, and five upstairs rooms have private baths. Available March-December; no preteenagers. $50-70.

MISSOURI
St. Joseph
Hannibal
Weston
Platte City
Parkville
Independence
Kansas City
Arrow Rock
Warrensburg
California
Hermann
Marthasville
St. Louis
Washington
Warsaw
Osage Beach
Camdenton
Bonne Terre
Ste. Genevieve
Springfield
Hartville
Joplin
Carthage
Mt. Vernon
Nixa
Marionville
Highlandville
Eminence
Vanzant
Indian Point
Branson
West Plains
Kimberling City
Gainsville

Ozark Mt. Country B&B 103-B

P.O. Box 295
Branson, MO, 65616
(800) 321-8594

On a clear day you can see forever from this lovely new home high on the bluff overlooking Lake Taneycomo. The home is located three miles from Branson, just around the corner from the School of the Ozarks. Two miles to boat launch on Lake Taneycomo. Hosts will cook, refrigerate, or freeze your catch. Guest area includes a large bedroom with queen bed, sitting area, and private entrance off the deck. There is cable color TV, a private bath, air conditioning. No preschool children; restricted smoking. $45.

Ozark Mountain Country B&B 106

P.O. Box 295
Branson, MO, 65616
(800) 321-8594

This home offers two guest rooms twelve miles from downtown Branson. View of Table Rock Lake. One-quarter mile to fishing and swimming area; one mile to boat launch, rentals, and picnic area. One room has a double bed and private hall bath. A downstairs room offers a double bed, adjoining sitting room with TV, and divan for extra person. Children welcome; no smoking. $35-40.

Ozark Mountain Country B&B 107-B

P.O. Box 295
Branson, MO, 65616
(800) 321-8594

Enjoy Ozark hospitality in a secluded area two blocks from Table Rock Lake. The dam, state park, marina, and Lake Taneycomo are just two miles away. Full breakfast on weekends and continental during the week. Children are welcome; no smoking. One room has a king bed, private entrance, private bath, color TV, and air conditioning. A second room has a private entrance, private bath, sitting area, and TV. $50.

Ozark Mountain Country B&B 108-B

P.O. Box 295
Branson, MO, 65616
(800) 321-8594

Located in a quiet area within five minutes of Branson. Hosts offer a recreation room with queen hideabed and sitting area. There is also a bedroom with twin beds. Children welcome; no smoking. During the school year, B&B is only available on weekends. $35.

Ozark Mt. Country B&B 112-B

P.O. Box 295
Branson, MO, 65616
(800) 321-8594

A delightful retreat on Lake Taneycomo, across the lake from Branson. All guests have access to swimming pool, fishing dock, charcoal grill, picnic table, and rental boats. The home offers three lakeview guest areas, each with private entrance, cable color TV, private bath, convenient parking. The heated pool is open from mid-May to mid-September. Children over twelve are welcome. $50-85.

Ozark Mt. Country B&B 118

P.O. Box 295
Branson, MO, 65616
(800) 321-8594

Contemporary home in Branson offers four guest areas, two upstairs and two on a lower level, including exclusive guest use of large sitting areas on each floor with fireplace, TV, and VCR. The lower level has large sliding doors opening onto a spacious patio, Jacuzzi spa, and swimming pool. Guests will be greeted with complimentary refreshments on arrival; a special gourmet or country breakfast is served in the formal dining room overlooking the pool and patio. $55.

Ozark Mountain Country B&B 119

P.O. Box 295
Branson, MO, 65616
(800) 321-8594

A new contemporary home on a hill above Table Rock Lake, about seven miles southwest of Branson and 1.5 miles from Silver Dollar City. One guest room with private bath. A second room has a single bed. Full breakfast will be served on the deck or in the dining room. Restricted smoking; adults only. $50.

Ozark Mountain Country B&B 120

P.O. Box 295
Branson, MO, 65616
(800) 321-8594

A charming contemporary home in Branson on a hill overlooking a wooded haven for birds and other wildlife and Roark Creek, near its entrance to Lake Taneycomo. Four guest rooms and two baths on the main floor. Guests are welcome to use the large great room with TV, fireplace, and picture window, and to sit on the screened porch overlooking the creek. Full breakfast with choice of entrees. $40.

Ozark Mt. Country B&B 122

P.O. Box 295
Branson, MO, 65616
(800) 321-8594

Private three-room cabin about one-half mile west of Silver Dollar City built in the early 1920s. The cabin offers a great room with double bed, a day bed for two, and a dining area. The kitchenette is well equipped, and the large bath includes an old-fashioned tub and separate shower. Not suitable for children. A hearty continental breakfast will be served in the privacy of your cottage. $60.

BRIGHTON

Ozark Mt. Country B&B 204-B

P.O. Box 295
Branson, MO, 65616
(800) 321-8594

Private guest cottage on a farm near Brighton. Surrounding the main residence and stone guest house are 258 acres of soft rolling, tree-covered hills, spring-fed pools, ponds and creeks. This country scene is complete with Arabian horses, burros, a pony, rare wood ducks, mallards, geese, cats, and a lovable Great Dane. The guest cottage offers a double bed with handmade hickory bedstead, complete kitchen area, bath, fireplace, and divan for one extra person. From $70.

CALIFORNIA

Ozark Mt. Country B&B 222

P.O. Box 295
Branson, MO, 65616
(800) 321-8594

This 1896 home, a few blocks from Highway 50, has been carefully renovated to retain its Victorian character. The three guest rooms feature antiques, shared bath. Antique lovers will enjoy talking on an authentic crank telephone, listening to a Thomas Edison crank phonograph, relaxing on the big front porch, and browsing through the antique shop on the premises. Restricted smoking, no pets. Three resident dogs and two cats. $35.

CAMDENTON

Ozark Mountain Country B&B 207-C

P.O. Box 295
Branson, MO, 65616
(800) 321-8594

This charming home is in a quiet neighborhood. The host serves a full, hearty breakfast in the dining room or on the shady deck. Adults only; no smoking. Small resident dog. Two rooms with hall bath. $40.

Ramblewood B&B

402 Panoramic Drive
Camdenton, MO, 65020
(314) 346-3410 after 5:00

This inviting cottage nestles in a grove of oak and dogwood. The decor is traditional, touched with Victorian. You'll be welcomed with tea or lemonade and homemade goodies. Your breakfast is special, beginning with a beautiful fruit plate, followed by tempting dishes and breads. You are minutes from the lake, state park, fine restaurants, music shows, and shops.

Host: Mary E. Massey
Rooms: 2 (SB) $40
Full Breakfast
Credit Cards: No
Notes: 2, 5, 9, 10, 11, 12

CARTHAGE

Brewer's Maple Lane Farms B&B

RR 1, Carthage, MO, 64836
(417) 358-6312

A National Register Historic Place with twenty rooms filled with family heirlooms. The 676-acre farm is ideal for hunting, fishing, or a family vacation. There's a barnyard full of animals, a playground for kids, and a 22-acre lake for fishermen. Church groups receive special discounts.

Hosts: Arch & Renee Brewer
Rooms: 4 (SB) $40-50
Cottage: 2 Bedrooms
Continental Breakfast
Notes: 2, 5, 6 (outside), 8, 10, 11, 12

Hill House

Hill House

1157 South Main
Carthage, MO, 64836
(417) 358-6145

Hill House is a c. 1887 brick Victorian mansion furnished in antiques. Rooms feature feather beds, tied comforters, and nonworking fireplaces. Breakfast is a full meal. Menus vary, but always include home-baked muffins and one-of-a-kind specialty jams.

Hosts: Dean & Ella Mae Scoville
Rooms: 4 (PB) $26.60-42.54
Credit Cards: No
Notes: 2, 5, 8, 10, 11, 12

EMINENCE

River's Edge B&B Resort

HCR 1, Box 11
Eminence, MO, 65466
(314) 226-3233

We've built a beautiful new building that's custom designed for your maximum enjoyment of the river. Each room has a private entrance that opens to a deck overlooking the river. There's also a big hot tub, campfires, floating, fishing, beach, Ping-Pong, hiking, endless sight-seeing, and giant springs.

Hosts: Lynett & Alan Peters
Rooms: 15 (14 PB; 1 SB) $39-69
Continental Breakfast
Credit Cards: No
Notes: 2, 5, 7, 8, 9, 10, 11, 14

GAINSVILLE

Ozark Mountain Country B&B 225

P.O. Box 295
Branson, MO, 65616
(800) 321-8594

This spacious colonial home is reminiscent of "Dallas's" Southfork Ranch. Located next to a family-owned grist mill and country store that date to the early 1900s, in a quiet valley overlooking a private lake ten miles from Gainsville. Three spacious guest rooms, four full baths, game room with pool table and Ping-Pong, indoor swimming pool and hot tub. Full country breakfast. Guests are welcome to fish the lake, hike the scenic areas of the working ranch, or take a swim in the pool. Float trips may be arranged on nearby streams. Adults only; restricted smoking. $55.

HANNIBAL

Fifth Street Mansion

213 South Fifth Street
Hannibal, MO, 63401
(314) 221-0445

Historic 1858 Italianate home of lifelong friends of Mark Twain combines Victorian charm with contemporary comforts. Period furnishings, original fireplaces, stained glass, and old-fashioned hospitality abound. Walk to historic sites, shops, restaurants. Inquire about special weekends.

Hosts: Donalene & Mike Andreotti
Rooms: 7 (PB) $55-85
Full Breakfast
Credit Cards: A, B, C
Notes: 2, 5, 7, 8, 9, 10, 11, 12, 14

Garth Woodside Mansion

RR 1, Hannibal, MO, 63401
(314) 221-2789

You'll be surrounded by Victorian splendor in our 1871 home that once hosted Mark Twain. Stroll our 39 acres or fish in our pond. Enjoy pampered elegance with afternoon tea and nightshirts for you to wear. One of the Midwest's best country inns.

Hosts: Irv & Diane Feinberg
Rooms: 8 (6 PB; 2 SB) $58-80
Full Breakfast
Credit Cards: A, B
Minimum stay holidays: 2
Notes: 2, 5, 7 (limited), 8 (over 12), 9, 10, 12

HARTVILLE

Frisco House

Box 118
Hartville, MO, 65667
(417) 741-7304; (417) 833-0650

Victorian home on the National Register, located in the noncommercial area of the Ozarks near the Laura Ingalls Wilder home and museum and an Amish community. The house has been completely restored and furnished with antiques, many third and fourth-generation heirlooms, including oil paintings, Oriental rugs, hanging lamps, china, brass, and wooden artifacts. Meals are served on railroad dining-car china and silver.

Hosts: Charley & Betty Roberts
Rooms: 4 (SB) $30-35
Full Breakfast
Credit Cards: No
Closed part of Jan. & Feb.
Notes: 2, 9, 14

HERMANN

Birk's Goethe Street Gasthaus

700 Goethe Street
Hermann, MO, 65041
(314) 486-2911

Bed & Breakfast in our romantic Victorian mansion daily, except for two weekends a month, when you can be Agatha Christie and try to solve the mystery of the month.

Hosts: Elmer & Gloria Birk
Rooms: 9 (7 PB; 2 SB) $51.05-72.54
Full Breakfast
Credit Cards: A, B, C
Closed Dec. 24-Jan. 1
Notes: 2, 7 (limited), 8 (over 16), 9, 10, 11, 12, 14

HIGHLANDVILLE

Ozark Mt. Country B&B 220

P.O. Box 295
Branson, MO, 65616
(800) 321-8594

A new log home with cathedral ceilings about halfway between Springfield and Branson, featuring hand-crafted accessories, art, collectibles, and rustic decor. Your party will be the exclusive guests. Hosts offer two guest rooms on the main floor, continental breakfast, exclusive use of family room with TV. Adults only. Resident dog. Two rooms, from $35.

INDEPENDENCE

Woodstock Inn B&B

1212 West Lexington
Independence, MO, 64050
(816) 833-2233

Located in the heart of historic Independence, close to the Truman Library and home, historic mansions, sports stadiums, theme parks, and Latter Day Saint centers. Eleven guest rooms, all with private bath, air-conditioning, tasteful furnishings. Two suites are handicap accessible. Excellent food, private parking, personalized touring directions. German language capability.

Hosts: Lane & Ruth Harold
Rooms: 11 (PB) $40-59
Full Breakfast
Credit Cards: A, B
Notes: 2 (deposit), 5, 8, 9, 10, 11, 12, 14

Woodstock Inn B&B

INDIAN POINT AREA

Ozark Mt. Country B&B 116

P.O. Box 295
Branson, MO, 65616
(800) 321-8594

This home on Indian Point, two miles from Silver Dollar City, is on Table Rock Lake. The home offers a large, carpeted, air-conditioned guest area that is great for families. Private entrance, patio overlooking the lake, large boat dock. Guests may secure a rental boat at the dock; public launch is less than a mile from the home. The guest area has a queen bed, sitting area, adjoining bath. Another small bedroom has a double bed. Full breakfast, children welcome, no smoking. From $50.

Ozark Mountain Country B&B 117

P.O. Box 295
Branson, MO, 65616
(800) 321-8594

A rustic contemporary executive lakefront home in the Indian Point area three miles from Silver Dollar City. The home is in a quiet, secluded area on Table Rock Lake and offers two guest areas with private baths. A gourmet continental breakfast is served at your leisure in the great room or on the deck overlooking the lake. Fish and swim in the lake, stroll along the beach, or watch the sunset from the deck. Children welcome; no smoking. $45-57.

JOPLIN

Ozark Mountain Country B&B 209

P.O. Box 295
Branson, MO, 65616
(800) 321-8594

Enjoy country living on a 676-acre farm eight miles northeast of Carthage. This marble home with red tile roof was built between 1900 and 1904 and is listed on the National Register of Historic Places. The farm features a 22-acre lake, three fishing ponds, one mile of creek frontage, kennels, playground, hunting, and game room. Four second-floor rooms share two baths. Two of the guest rooms have a single bed in addition to a double. One room has twin beds. Prices include a hearty continental breakfast and tour of the home and grounds. Children welcome. $50.

Ozark Mt. Country B&B 223

P.O. Box 295
Branson, MO, 65616
(800) 321-8594

This home in Joplin was built in 1898 and has been completely redone. Complete breakfast with choice of several entrees. Children are welcome; under the age of two, they are free. Crib available, TV available in sitting area. Three second-floor guest rooms. $30-50.

Doanleigh Wallagh Inn

KANSAS CITY

Doanleigh Wallagh Inn

217 East 37th Street
Kansas City, MO, 64111
(816) 753-2667

A turn-of-the-century mansion minutes from Crown Center, Country Club Plaza, and Westport. Antiques, telephone, and cable television with movie channels in each room. Also available for parties, weddings, and conferences. Hosts will help plan sightseeing and make restaurant reservations.

Hosts: Carolyn & Edward Litchfield
Rooms: 12 (PB) $60-110
Full Breakfast
Credit Cards: A, B, C
Notes: 2, 5, 7 (limited), 8, 9, 10, 12, 14

Ozark Mt. Country B&B 221

P.O. Box 295
Branson, MO, 65616
(800) 321-8594

A new home located on a private lake on the southeast side of Kansas City offers three guest rooms, an adjacent balcony library with TV. Guests are welcome to use the family room with fireplace, antiques, and a pipe organ. A full breakfast is served in the kitchen, sun room, or dining room. Adults only, no pets. $50-55.

Pridewell

600 West Fiftieth Street
Kansas City, MO, 64112
(816) 931-1642

A fine Tudor residence situated in a residential area on the Civil War battlefield of the battle of Westport. Near the Nelson Art Gallery, University of MO-KC, Missouri Repertory Theatre, Rockhurst College. Adjacent to Country Club Plaza Shopping District, including several four-star restaurants, public transportation, public tennis courts, and park.

Hosts: Edwin & Louann White
Rooms: 2 (1 PB; 1 SB) $58-65
Full Breakfast
Credit Cards: No
Notes: 4, 7, 8, 9, 10, 12, 14

KIMBERLING CITY AREA

Ozark Mt. Country B&B 102-B

P.O. Box 295
Branson, MO, 65616
(800) 321-8594

Charming new log home four miles south of Kimberling City on Highway 13. Guests are welcome to use living/dining room with TV and covered deck with beautiful view of Table Rock Lake. Hearty breakfast is served in dining area or on the deck. Boat launch, picnic area, and swimming in Table Rock Lake just two miles from home. Easy access to Silver Dollar City, Branson, music shows and entertainment, Swiss Villa Amphitheater, Springfield, and Eureka Springs, Arkansas. Two rooms share a bath. Not suitable for preteenagers; limited smoking. Log cabin also available for family groups. From $40.

Ozark Mountain Country B&B 105-B

P.O. Box 295
Branson, MO, 65616
(800) 321-8594

A gorgeous new home with a spectacular view of Table Rock Lake and the Ozark Mountains, located ten miles south of Kimberling City. Two bedrooms, each with a double bed and bath. Both rooms open to a private lakeside patio area. Exclusive guest use of sitting area with game room and TV. School-age children are welcome. Hearty country breakfast; air conditioned. $55.

Ozark Mountain Country B&B 121

P.O. Box 295
Branson, MO, 65616
(800) 321-8594

A quaint farm home about halfway between Silver Dollar City, Missouri, and Eureka Springs, Arkansas. The original home was built of hand-hewn limestone. Guests will enjoy the deck overlooking the woods and the special country breakfast. Children are welcome. Hosts offer a large guest room with double bed and three twins. Smoking on deck or porch only. $40.

MARIONVILLE

Ozark Mt. Country B&B 210

P.O. Box 295
Branson, MO, 65616
(800) 321-8594

White Squirrel Hollow Inn is a Victorian home built about 1896. Watch the rare white squirrel families at play on the grounds. Guests are welcome to use the parlor with fireplace and TV, library, formal dining room, upstairs sitting room with TV, and spacious front porch. The entire home has been lovingly restored. Hearty country breakfast is served in the dining room or on the screened porch. There are five upstairs guest rooms with private or semiprivate bath. Children over ten are welcome; limited smoking. Private cottage next to the main home is also available. $40-65.

MARTHASVILLE

Gramma's House B&B

Route 3, Box 410
Marthasville, MO, 63357
(314) 433-2675

Recall the good memories of your gramma's house when you stay in this 150-year-old farmhouse. Nearby attractions are the historic Daniel Boone Home, antique shopping in Washington, Augusta, and Hermann. A terrific country setting for picnics, hiking, playing horseshoes, or just relaxing on the porch swing.

Hosts: Judy & Jim Jones
Rooms: 3 (1 PB; 2 SB) $45-65
Full Breakfast
Credit Cards: A, B
Notes: 2, 5, 7, 8, 9, 14

Gramma's House B&B

MT. VERNON

Ozark Mt. Country B&B 226

P.O. Box 295
Branson, MO, 65616
(800) 321-8594

An 1890s farmhouse, completely restored, located 2.5 miles north of Mt. Vernon, near I-44. Located high on a limestone bluff overlooking the rural valley, where guests can enjoy the spectacular view and occasional glimpses of wildlife. Children welcome. Three air-conditioned upstairs rooms are available with TV, shared bath. Limited smoking. Breakfast includes homemade jams, jellies, bread, and pastries. $27.50-40.

NIXA

Ozark Mountain Country B&B 211

P.O. Box 295
Branson, MO, 65616
(800) 321-8594

A modern country home ten minutes from Springfield and thirty from Branson. Toast your toes and sip hot cider by the quaint fireplace, or relax on the deck and watch the sunset. Golf and tennis are available nearby. A hearty country breakfast is served in the dining room on antique china or on the deck overlooking the rolling hills. Two rooms with antique beds and private baths. Resident dog and cats. Restricted smoking; teenagers welcome. $55.

OSAGE BEACH

Ozark Mt. Country B&B 208

P.O. Box 295
Branson, MO, 65616
(800) 321-8594

New home on Lake of the Ozarks offers two guest rooms with queen bed and private bath. One room has a private entrance. Sitting room adjoining the guest room has two daybeds and kitchenette, sliding doors to a private lakeside patio. Children welcome; baby-sitting available. Pets are accepted with prior arrangement—they will be kept outside. From $40.

PARKVILLE

Down to Earth Lifestyles B&B

12500 North Crooked Road
Route 22, Parkville, MO, 64152
(816) 891-1018

Unique getaway haven offering the best of midwestern country and city living. Indoor heated pool, plus 86 acres with farm animals, fishing ponds, wildlife, walking, and jogging. Full special-order breakfast served at place and time of guest's choice.

Hosts: Lola & Bill Coons
Rooms: 4 (PB) $55-65
Full Breakfast
Credit Cards: No
Notes: 2, 5, 7, 8, 9, 10, 11, 12, 13, 14

PLATTE CITY

Basswood Country Inn B&B

15880 Interurban Road
Platte City, MO, 64079
(816) 431-5556

Ten minutes northeast of Kansas City International Airport. This 74-acre country estate has seven fishing lakes, wooded trails, four new country French suites, private entrances, and decks. A 1935 two-bedroom restored lakeside cottage sleeps six. Bess Truman entertained her bridge club at Basswood in the 1940s and 1950s.

Hosts: Don & Betty Soper
Rooms: 4 (PB) $54-59
Cottage (PB) $89
Continental Breakfast
Minimum stay holidays: 2
Children over 7 welcome; younger in cottage
Credit Cards: A, B
Notes: 2, 5, 7, 8, 9, 11, 12, 14

STE. GENEVIEVE

Inn St. Gemme Beauvais

78 North Main Street
Ste. Genevieve, MO, 63670
(314) 883-5744

The inn, located in the historic district of the oldest permanent settlement west of the Mississippi, has seven guest rooms furnished with antiques. A three-course breakfast is served in an elegant Victorian dining room, and there is a common room in what was once a moonshine tavern.

Hosts: Paul Swenson & Marcia Willson
Rooms: 7 (PB) $55-65
Full Breakfast
Credit Cards: A, B
Notes: 2, 5, 7, 8, 9, 10, 11, 12

ST. LOUIS

The Coachlight B&B

P.O. Box 8095
St. Louis, MO, 63156
(314) 367-5870

Three-story turn-of-the-century brick home situated in the historic central west end. Furnished in fine antiques, Laura Ashley fabrics, down comforters, antiques quilts. Mahogany four-poster bed, brass bed, white wicker furniture. Within walking distance of historic mansions, sidewalk cafes, unique shops, and galleries. Next to forest park, art museum, zoo. Minutes from the Arch and riverfront.

Hosts: Susan & Chuck Sundermeyer
Rooms: 3 (PB) $65-80
Full Breakfast
Credit Cards: A, B, C
Notes: 2, 5, 7 (limited), 8 (over 3), 9, 10, 12, 14

Lafayette House

Lafayette House

2156 Lafayette Avenue
St. Louis, MO, 63104
(314) 772-4429

An 1876 brick Queen Anne mansion in the center of things to do in St. Louis. Furnished with antiques, but with modern conveniences. Extensive library, many interesting collections. Complimentary soda, wine, cheese, crackers. Train, plane, and bus pickup for a small fee. Three cats in residence.

Hosts: Sarah & Jack Milligan
Rooms: 4 (1 PB; 3 SB) $40-65
Suite: 1 (PB) sleeps 6-8
Minimum stay in suite: 2
Full Breakfast
Credit Cards: No
Notes: 2, 5, 6 (by prior arrangement), 7 (limited), 8, 9, 10, 11, 12, 13, 14

The Winter House

3522 Arsenal Street
St. Louis, MO, 63118
(314) 664-4399

Victorian brick, c. 1897, with turret. Located near hospitals and universities and just a short walk to Tower Grove Park, a Victorian walking park adjacent to the Missouri Botanical Garden.

Hosts: Sarah & Kendall Winter
Rooms: 2 (1 PB; 1 SB) $48
Continental-plus Breakfast
Credit Cards: A, B, E
Notes: 2, 5, 8 (over 11), 9, 10, 11, 12, 14

SPRINGFIELD

Ozark Mountain Country B&B 201-B

P.O. Box 295
Branson, MO, 65616
(800) 321-8594

This old-fashioned country home is located about fifteen miles east of Springfield and four miles from Rogersville, Missouri, on a 1200-acre Arabian horse farm. A completely furnished kitchen, dining room, living room, and den with TV are available for guest use. Continental breakfast. There is a hot tub a short distance up the hill, in a summer house. You may bring your own horse ($5/day) and watch the working of the ranch, but cannot ride the ranch horses. Children are welcome. Three rooms, two with private bath. $40-50.

Ozark Mt. Country B&B 205-S

P.O. Box 295
Branson, MO, 65616
(800) 321-8594

A lovely two-story colonial in a quiet rural area in southeast Springfield. Sight-seeing trips and airport pickup can be arranged for an additional fee. All guests welcome to use upstairs game-exercise room with a Jacuzzi spa and gas grill available. Three guest rooms; full breakfast. $40-60.

Walnut Street Inn

900 East Walnut Street
Springfield, MO, 65806
(417) 864-6396

An 1894 beautifully restored Queen Anne Victorian featured as the Designers' Showcase home. Gorgeous antiques and charming rooms. Walk to fine restaurants, theaters, and antique shops. Relax with other guests while enjoying wine and cheese at check-in and a full gourmet breakfast in the morning.

Hosts: Karol & Nancy Brown
Rooms: 7 (PB) $60-95
Full Breakfast
Credit Cards: A, B, C
Notes: 2, 3, 5, 8, 9, 10, 11, 12, 13, 14

VANZANT

Ozark Mt. Country B&B 224

P.O. Box 295
Branson, MO, 65616
(800) 321-8594

A working ranch tucked away in the Mark Twain National Forest about seventy miles southeast of Springfield. The rustic ranch house features one king bed, two twin beds, private deck and entrance, private bath, and game table. Guests are welcome to help with daily chores, hike the area, or just enjoy the fresh country air. Full breakfast is served in the dining room, or a continental breakfast will be delivered to your room. Evening meals are available by reservation ($6/person). The ranch is close to several old grist mills, beautiful springs, and float streams. Special archery and firearm hunts for deer and wild turkey may be arranged. Limited smoking. From $40.

Cedarcroft Farm

WARRENSBURG

Cedarcroft Farm

Route 3, Box 130
Warrensburg, MO, 64093
(816) 747-5728

Cedarcroft Farm offers old-fashioned country hospitality, country comfort, and country cooking in an antique-filled 1867 family farmhouse. Guests may explore the 80 acres of secluded woods, meadows, and streams and enjoy a full country breakfast. Civil War re-enactor hosts demonstrate

1860s soldier's life. Modern amenities include central air conditioning.

Hosts: Sandra & Bill Wayne
Rooms: 2 (SB) $40
Full Breakfast
Credit Cards: A, B, D
Notes: 2, 4, 5, 7 (limited), 8, 9, 11, 12, 14

WARSAW

Ozark Mountain Country B&B 215

P.O. Box 295
Branson, MO, 65616
(800) 321-8594

A completely remodeled 1900 bungalow. A full breakfast features all you can eat of a variety of entrees. Cable TV in guest sitting room. Children welcome. Warsaw is on the headwaters of the Lake of the Ozarks, three miles from Truman Lake. $35-40.

WASHINGTON

Washington House B&B

3 Lafayette Street
P.O. Box 527
Washington, MO, 63090
(314) 239-2417; (314) 239-9834

Washington House, built c. 1837, is located in a National Register Historic District. This authentically restored inn on the Missouri River features river views, canopy beds, antiques, complimentary wine, and full breakfast. Washington House is located in the heart of Missouri's wine country, only 45 minutes west of St. Louis.

Hosts: Chuck & Kathy Davis
Rooms: 4 (PB) $65
Full Breakfast
Credit Cards: No
Notes: 2, 5, 8, 9, 10, 11, 12, 14

WEST PLAINS

Ozark Mountain Country B&B 212

P.O. Box 295
Branson, MO, 65616
(800) 321-8594

Relax on this 60-acre farm located six miles south of West Plains. The ranch-style home is air conditioned and offers a double bed and color TV. Continental breakfast. Well-behaved pets are welcome, and there is a stable for two horses, a shed for six horses, dog pens, and dog houses. One resident cat. Available weekends only. No pre-teenagers or smoking. $50.

Ozark Mt. Country B&B 219

P.O. Box 295
Branson, MO, 65616
(800) 321-8594

A 100-year-old colonial home two blocks from the town square, decorated in country and colonial furnishings and antiques. Guests may read in the library, watch cable TV in the parlor, stroll the garden area, or sit in the gazebo. Three upstairs rooms share two baths. A full county breakfast with home-baked breads is served in the dining room. Dinner is available by reservation. From $30.

Montana

ABSAROKEE

B&B Western Adventure 268

P.O. Box 20972
Billings, MT, 59104
(406) 259-7993

This 1900 colonial house has a wraparound porch for relaxing and enjoying the big yard. On Highway 78, about twenty minutes off I-90, fifty miles southeast of Billings. There are three bedrooms, one with private bath. Wagon train rides on the Bozeman trail nearby can be arranged. Hunting, fishing, and floating on nearby Stillwater River. Ninety miles from Yellowstone. A full Montana breakfast is served. Children over four are welcome. $45-50.

BIGFORK

O'Duachain Country Inn

675 Ferndale Drive
Bigfork, MT
(406) 837-6851

Luxurious log lodging with full gourmet breakfast. Located on 5 acres of landscaped solitude. Walking trails, ponds, and wildlife. One-day junkets include Glacier National Park, Flathead and Swan lakes and valleys, Jewel Basin hiking, National Bison Range. Golf, swimming, boating, and skiing areas abound.

Hosts: Margot & Tom Doohan
Rooms: 5 (2 PB; 3 SB) $60-85
Full Breakfast
Credit Cards: A, B, C
Notes: 2, 5, 8, 9, 10, 11, 12, 13

BIG SANDY

B&B Western Adventure 253

P.O. Box 20972
Billings, MT, 59104
(406) 259-7993

Charlie Russell Country in north central Montana is the setting for these two unique B&B accommodations. Participate in ranch life: feed and groom the horses, feed the chickens, gather eggs. Or go on a scenic tour to the Bear Paw Mountains and the Missouri Breaks. Game is abundant in the area. Just outside of Big Sandy are two log cabins with accommodations for four, each with its own bath. The second is a sprawling ranch lodge about forty miles south of Big Sandy, which has four bedrooms sharing two full baths. $26-40.

Lone Mountain Ranch

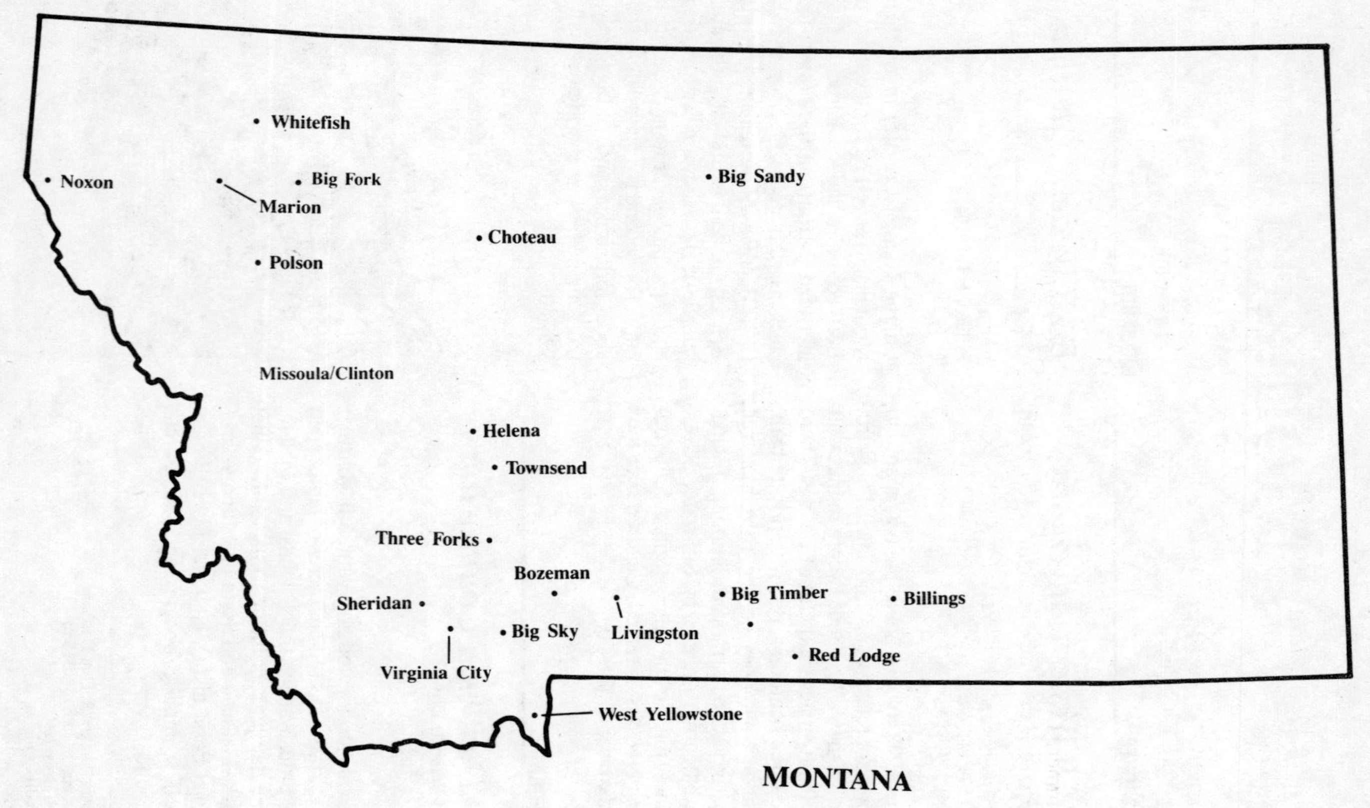

Whitefish
Noxon
Big Fork
Marion
Big Sandy
Choteau
Polson
Missoula/Clinton
Helena
Townsend
Three Forks
Bozeman
Sheridan
Big Timber
Billings
Big Sky
Livingston
Virginia City
Red Lodge
West Yellowstone
MONTANA

BIG SKY

Lone Mountain Ranch

Box 69, Big Sky, MT, 59716
(406) 995-4644

Comfortable ranch cabin accommodations nestled in a secluded valley. Horseback riding, Yellowstone National Park interpretive trips, Orvis-endorsed fly-fishing program, kids' activities, nature hikes in summer. Cross-country skiing, sleigh-ride dinners in winter. Nationally acclaimed cuisine in our spectacular new dining lodge. All meals are included in the weekly rate.

Hosts: Bob & Vivian Schaap
Cabin: 23 (PB) $798-1036/week
Type of Beds: 24 Twin; 2 Double; 23 Queen
Full Breakfast
Credit Cards: A, B
Notes: 2, 3, 4, 8, 9, 10, 11, 12, 13, 14

BIG TIMBER

B&B Western Adventure 233

P.O. Box 20972
Billings, MT, 59104
(406) 259-7993

This gracious country ranch home is tucked in the Absarokee National Forest beside gentle Deer Creek. Antelope and whitetail deer are always within view on this cattle and sheep ranch. In fall and spring, guests are welcome to witness lambing, shearing, and branding. Wildlife and scenic photographers will find this ranch a paradise. Six rooms share three baths. A guest house with its own bath can sleep six. Full breakfast. $45-60.

BILLINGS

B&B Western Adventure 254

P.O. Box 20972
Billings, MT, 59104
(406) 259-7993

This elegantly rustic cedar-sided ranch home is located on 5 acres overlooking beautiful Vermilion Ranch Valley. There is a private 2-acre lake stocked with rainbows and blue-gills. A large variety of migratory fowl and resident birds will be found in the area. Three bedrooms share a large bath, a family living room with TV, pool table, and private entrance. A fourth room has a private bath, TV, and king bed. Custer Battlefield is one hour away; golf, shopping, and other attractions are within twenty minutes. Full breakfast; smoking allowed; children welcome. $40-55.

B&B Western Adventure 267

P.O. Box 20972
Billings, MT, 59104
(406) 259-7993

This country home on the edge of town sits among stately pines and a large yard. A resident flock of wild ducks and geese have made the pond their home. Two fireplaces and antique furnishings give this home warmth and charm. Three bedrooms: one with queen bed and private bath. The other two have double beds and share a bath. Continental breakfast; no smoking inside; children over ten are welcome. $45-65.

BOZEMAN

B&B Western Adventure 202

P.O. Box 20972
Billings, MT, 59104
(406) 259-7993

A 1906 Colonial Revival home in the Bonton Historic District, with a large front porch and swing. This lovely home is comfortably furnished with turn-of-the-century antiques. Three bedrooms; two shared baths, one private. Full breakfast is served in front of the wood-burning fireplace or on the redwood deck in the summer. Located ninety minutes from Yellowstone Park, fifteen miles from Bridger Bowl skiing. $35-45.

B&B Western Adventure 203

P.O. Box 20972
Billings, MT, 59104
(406) 259-7993

This home is located on 11 acres in the beautiful Gallatin Valley, with a blue ribbon trout stream within walking distance. Hunt in fall, ski in winter, hike, raft, and swim in summer. Three bedrooms in the main house and three in the guest house. Heated pool in summer, rafting equipment for rent. Full breakfast served to those in the main house. Children are welcome to help feed the ducks and other animals. $60-100.

Hillard's B&B and Guest House

11521 Axtell Gateway Road
Bozeman, MT, 59715
(406) 763-4696

Located ten miles from Bozeman in a quiet setting close to the Gallatin River and excellent trout fishing. Close to the airport, twenty-five miles to Bridger Bowl or Big Sky for skiing. Big-game area; seventy-five miles to West Yellowstone.

Hosts: Larry & Doris Hillard
Rooms: 2 (SB) $62.40
Guest House: 3 bedrooms & private bath
Full Breakfast
Credit Cards: No
Notes: 2, 4, 5, 6, 7, 8, 9, 11, 12, 13

Voss Inn B&B

319 South Willson
Bozeman, MT, 59715
(406) 587-0982

Magnificently restored Victorian inn in the historic district with elegant guest rooms with private baths. A delightful gourmet breakfast is served in the privacy of your room. Bozeman is ninety miles north of Yellowstone Park, near skiing, fishing, hiking, snowmobiling. Guided day trips are conducted into Yellowstone and the surrounding area by your host.

Hosts: Bruce & Frankee Muller
Rooms: 6 (PB) $50-65
Full Breakfast
Credit Cards: A, B
Notes: 2, 5, 8 (over 5), 9, 10, 11, 12, 14

Voss Inn B&B

CHOTEAU

B&B Western Adventure 224

P.O. Box 20972
Billings, MT, 59104
(406) 259-7993

This two-story home is constructed of hand-hewn logs and stone and filled with antiques. Thick quilts, crisp linens, antiques, and original artwork grace each room. Gift shop on the premises. Two rooms with double beds share a bath. Located near the Bob Marshall Wilderness area and the Egg Mountain Fossil Beds. Bicycles and picnic baskets can be arranged with advance notice. Winter skiing at Teton Pass. Full breakfast; no smoking; children over six are welcome. $28-35.

HELENA

B&B Western Adventure 208

P.O. Box 20972
Billings, MT, 59104
(406) 259-7993

This elegant 1875 Victorian has been restored and filled with antiques and Oriental rugs. Seven spacious rooms all have private baths, telephones, and a city view. Located fifteen minutes from I-15. A full gourmet breakfast is served, smoking is allowed on the porch, and children are welcome. No pets. $40-60.

LIVINGSTON

B&B Western Adventure 234

P.O. Box 20972
Billings, MT, 59104
(406) 259-7993

This stately 1903 mansion is on the National Register of Historic Homes. Hosts live in a separate part of the home. Children are welcome. There are three blue ribbon trout streams within twenty miles, and the town has a rich railroad history with museums and fine art shops. Four bedrooms; one private bath, three share two baths. Full breakfast; no smoking. $50-65.

MARION

B&B Western Adventure 237

P.O. Box 20972
Billings, MT, 59104
(406) 259-7993

This working Charolais cattle ranch is in the upper Rocky Mountain range, between the Kootenai and Lolo National Forests near Kalispell. An ideal location for wildlife lovers, photographers, hikers, and sportsmen. The guest house with private bath sleeps six; two rooms in the house sleep four. Guided photography tours, day pack trips, horse boarding, guided hunting trips can all be arranged. Full ranch breakfast. $50-60.

MISSOULA/CLINTON

B&B Western Adventure 239

P.O. Box 20972
Billings, MT, 59104
(406) 259-7993

This two-story colonial is surrounded by 25 acres of woods and meadows. Located two miles off I-90, ten miles east of Missoula, the house has three spacious bedrooms and a shared bath. River rafting is available within one mile; twenty minutes to two ski areas. The University of Montana is just ten minutes away. A full breakfast with home-baked bread is served in the dining room or on the deck. No smoking or pets; children over sixteen are welcome. $50-65.

NOXON

B&B Western Adventure 151

P.O. Box 20972
Billings, MT, 59104
(406) 259-7993

A Southern plantation-style home with six huge columns and a porch across the front. Four guest rooms with private bath, full breakfast. trail rides, hiking, fishing, houseboat cruises, lake swimming, and rafting are all nearby. Family vacation packages;

laundry facilities. Pets and smoking are permitted with consideration of other guests. $45-55.

POLSON

Ruth's B&B

802 Seventh Avenue West
Polson, MT, 59860
(406) 883-2460

We have two separate guest rooms with portable facilities and one room in our home. Bath and shower facilities are shared in the home. Each room has a comfortable double bed, TV, and daveno that can be used for an extra bed. Each room will accommodate four people.

Host: Ruth Hunter
Rooms: 3 (SB) $25 + tax
Full Breakfast
Credit Cards: No
Notes: 2, 5, 8, 9, 10, 11, 12

RED LODGE

B&B Western Adventure 225

P.O. Box 20972
Billings, MT, 59104
(406) 259-7993

This charmingly restored 1896 historic home has been a saloon and hotel in the past. It is a combination of logs and dry wall, beautifully decorated with antique furniture and art. Two rooms with private baths, one with a queen bed and the other with a double. Private guest sitting room. Located on Highway 212, sixty-seven miles northeast of Yellowstone Park. Continental-plus breakfast with fresh baked goods is served on fine china. $45-50.

Willows Inn

224 South Platt Avenue
P.O. Box 886
Red Lodge, MT, 59068
(406) 446-3913

Charming 1903 Victorian with picket fence and porch swing. Beautiful rooms with four-poster, brass, and iron beds. Close to Yellowstone and skiing. Hiking, golf, whitewater rafting, music and folk festivals, and rodeos. Delicious home-baked pastries and afternoon refreshments. Video movies, books, games, and large sun deck. Housekeeping cottage also available.

Host: Elven Boggio
Rooms: 5 (3 PB; 2 SB) $45-60
Continental-plus Breakfast
Credit Cards: A, B
Notes: 2, 5, 7 (restricted), 8 (over 10), 9, 11, 12, 13, 14

SHERIDAN

B&B Western Adventure 222

P.O. Box 20972
Billings, MT, 59104
(406) 259-7993

A lovely new home in ranch country in the Ruby River Valley. The house has a fantastic mountain view in every direction and is the home of King's Arabian horses. Four fishing rivers within forty minutes. The home is open June to September and has three bedrooms that share two baths. An extra bath is available downstairs. Guided fishing trips available nearby. Full ranch breakfast; limited smoking. $30-40.

THREE FORKS

B&B Western Adventure 252

P.O. Box 20972
Billings, MT, 59104
(406) 259-7993

This stately three-story 1910 hotel has been refurbished and restored to its former elegance. A 120-foot veranda fronts the inn. Offering more than twenty rooms, some with private baths, some shared. Located in midwestern Montana, just minutes from I-90 west of Bozeman. A lavish continental breakfast is served in the dining room with fresh fruits, cheese, baked breads and rolls. No smoking or pets. $30-50.

TOWNSEND

Hidden Hollow Ranch

211 Flynn Lane
Townsend, MT, 59644
(406) 266-3580

Hidden Hollow is an 11,000-acre ranch/farm with meadows, mountains, creeks, fields with hay, grain, livestock. Beautiful gardens, farm museum. Modest large farmhouse with a homey atmosphere.

Hosts: Frank & Rose Flynn
Rooms: 7 (SB) $30-40
Suite: Two bedrooms, private bath $65
Full Breakfast
Credit Cards: No
Closed Nov.-April
Notes: 8, 11, 12

VIRGINIA CITY

B&B Western Adventure 238

P.O. Box 20972
Billings, MT, 59104
(406) 259-7993

This historic home was built in 1879 and has been totally restored inside and out. Big trees, rose gardens, and honeysuckle grace the large backyard with gazebo. Five bedrooms, all with handmade quilts and antique furnishings, share two baths. Resident dog. There is an antique and gift shop on the premises. Gold and garnet panning can be done nearby. Enjoy old-time melodrama at the town theater, and ride the historic train from Virginia City to Nevada City. Excellent fishing on the Madison River. Continental breakfast. $33-42.

B&B Western Adventure 251

P.O. Box 20972
Billings, MT, 59104
(406) 259-7993

A stately 1884 grey stone house with a large front porch. Furnished in antiques, with quilts, brass beds, and crafts throughout. Six rooms and a suite that sleeps five. Full sourdough breakfast; continental for late risers. Cross-country ski out the back door; snowmobile trails are nearby. $35-48.

WEST YELLOWSTONE

B&B Western Adventure 230

P.O. Box 20972
Billings, MT, 59104
(406) 259-7993

This lovely home is tucked into national forest land. Deer and moose are often at the salt lick in the backyard at dusk. Tie your own flies and view video tapes about fly fishing in the area. Just fifteen miles away is the famed Big Spring. Drift boating on the Madison and Gallatin Rivers and Hebgen Lake are all within twenty miles. Three bedrooms. One on the first floor has a private shower; two on the second floor share a full bath. Located ten miles from the west entrance of Yellowstone Park. $50.

WHITEFISH

B&B Western Adventure 232

P.O. Box 20972
Billings, MT, 59104
(406) 259-7993

This charming home, c. 1920, offers comfortable surroundings in one of Whitefish's finest old homes. The inn is tucked at the base of the Big Mountain Ski Resort in Flathead Valley and offers unlimited opportunities for recreation. Whitefish is located on Highway 93 in northwest Montana, less than thirty miles from Glacier National Park. Five rooms with private baths; restricted smoking. $55-65.

Kandahar Lodge

Box 1659
Whitefish, MT, 59937
(406) 862-6098

Kandahar is a beautiful mountain lodge in an alpine setting at Big Mountain Ski Resort village area, five miles above the town of Whitefish. Along with fifty rooms, we offer personal service and hospitality in a rustic yet elegant setting. There are a variety of summer activities, and you can ski to the backdoor during winter. We have two indoor sauna Jacuzzi spa areas, as well as an excellent cafe.

Hosts: Buck & Mary Pat Love
Rooms: 50 (PB) $68-98
Continental Breakfast
Credit Cards: A, B, C, D
Notes: 2, 4, 7, 8, 9, 10, 11, 12, 13, 14

Nebraska

DIXON

The George's

RR 1, Box 50
Dixon, NE, 68732
(402) 584-2625

You'll have an opportunity to see a modern farm operation, from crop growing to a small flock of chickens, and stay in a remodeled, air-conditioned home. Hearty breakfasts feature homemade jellies and jams. Pheasant hunting in season; bird watching anytime. Thirty-five miles west of Sioux City, Iowa; twelve from Laurel; Ponca State Park and Wayne State College within twenty miles. Lunch and dinner available with prior arrangement.

Hosts: Harold & Marie George
Rooms: 3 (SB) $35
Full Breakfast
Credit Cards: No
Notes: 2, 3, 4, 5, 7 (outside), 8, 9, 14

GRETNA

Bundy's B&B

16906 South 255
Gretna, NE, 68028
(402) 332-3616

Our bed and breakfast features antiques and collectibles and is an active farm home. A Christian atmosphere with a good farm breakfast is yours to enjoy. Close to Nebraska's only snow ski area and two blocks from swimming and dining.

Hosts: Bob & Dee Bundy
Rooms: 4 (SB) $15-25
Full Breakfast
Credit Cards: No
Notes: 2, 5, 11, 13

MADRID

Clown 'N Country

Box 115
Madrid, NE, 69150
(308) 326-4378

We have a ranch farm home, quiet and friendly, with a heated pool, hot tub, and many fun things to do. Our full breakfast and hospitality are qualities our guests remember.

Hosts: Ford & Lou Cornelius
Rooms: 2 (SB) $35
Full Breakfast
Credit Cards: No
Notes: 2, 3, 4, 5, 8, 10, 11

OMAHA

The Jones's

1617 South 90th Street
Omaha, NE, 68124
(402) 397-0721

Large private residence with large deck and gazebo in the back. Fresh homemade cinnamon rolls are served for breakfast. Horse racing nearby in summer, as well as several golf courses and Boys Town.

Hosts: Don & Theo Jones
Rooms: 3 (1 PB; 2 SB) $25
Continental Breakfast
Credit Cards: No
Notes: 2, 5, 6, 7, 8, 9, 10, 12

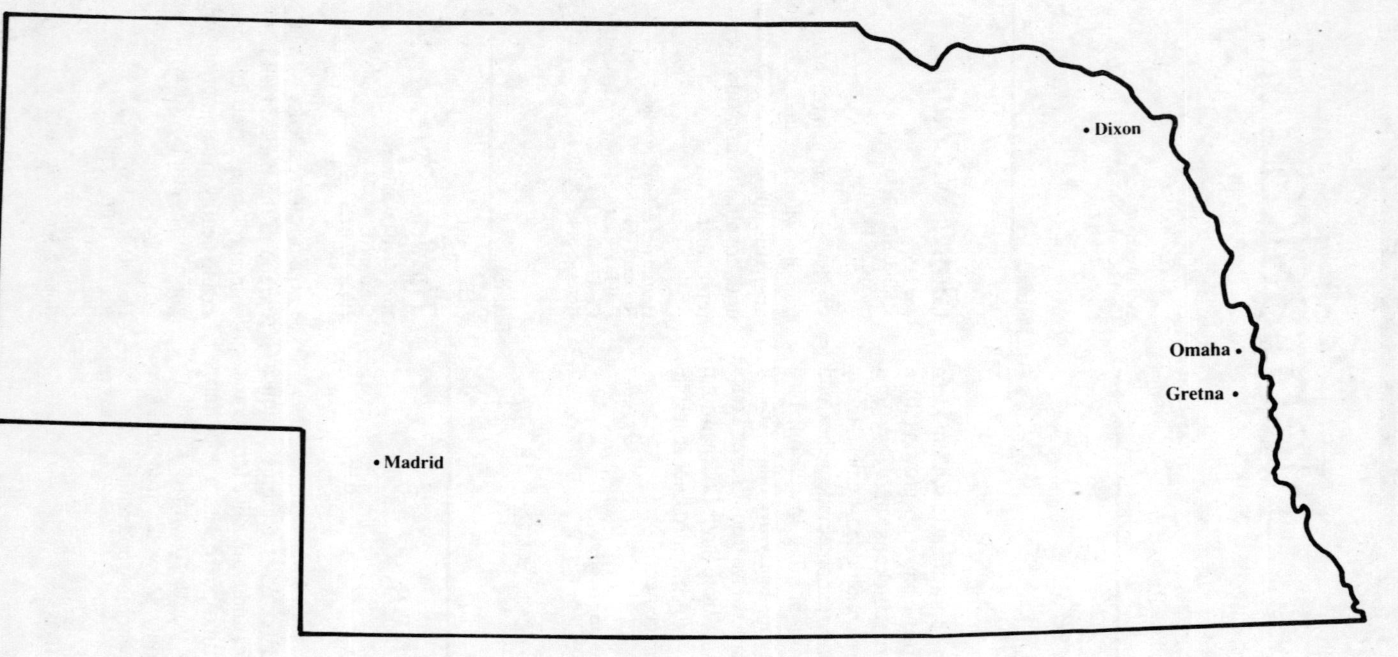

NEBRASKA

The Offutt House

140 North 39th Street
Omaha, NE, 68131
(402) 553-0951

This comfortable mansion, built in 1894, is part of the city's section of large homes built around the same time by Omaha's most wealthy residents. Rooms are comfortably spacious and furnished with antiques. Some feature fireplaces. The house is near downtown Omaha and the historic Old Market area, which offers many beautiful shops and excellent restaurants. Reservations, please.

Host: Jeannie K. Swoboda
Rooms: 7 (2 PB; 5 SB) $40-70
Continental Breakfast
Credit Cards: A, B, C
Notes: 2, 5, 7, 8 (over 12), 9, 10, 11, 12, 14

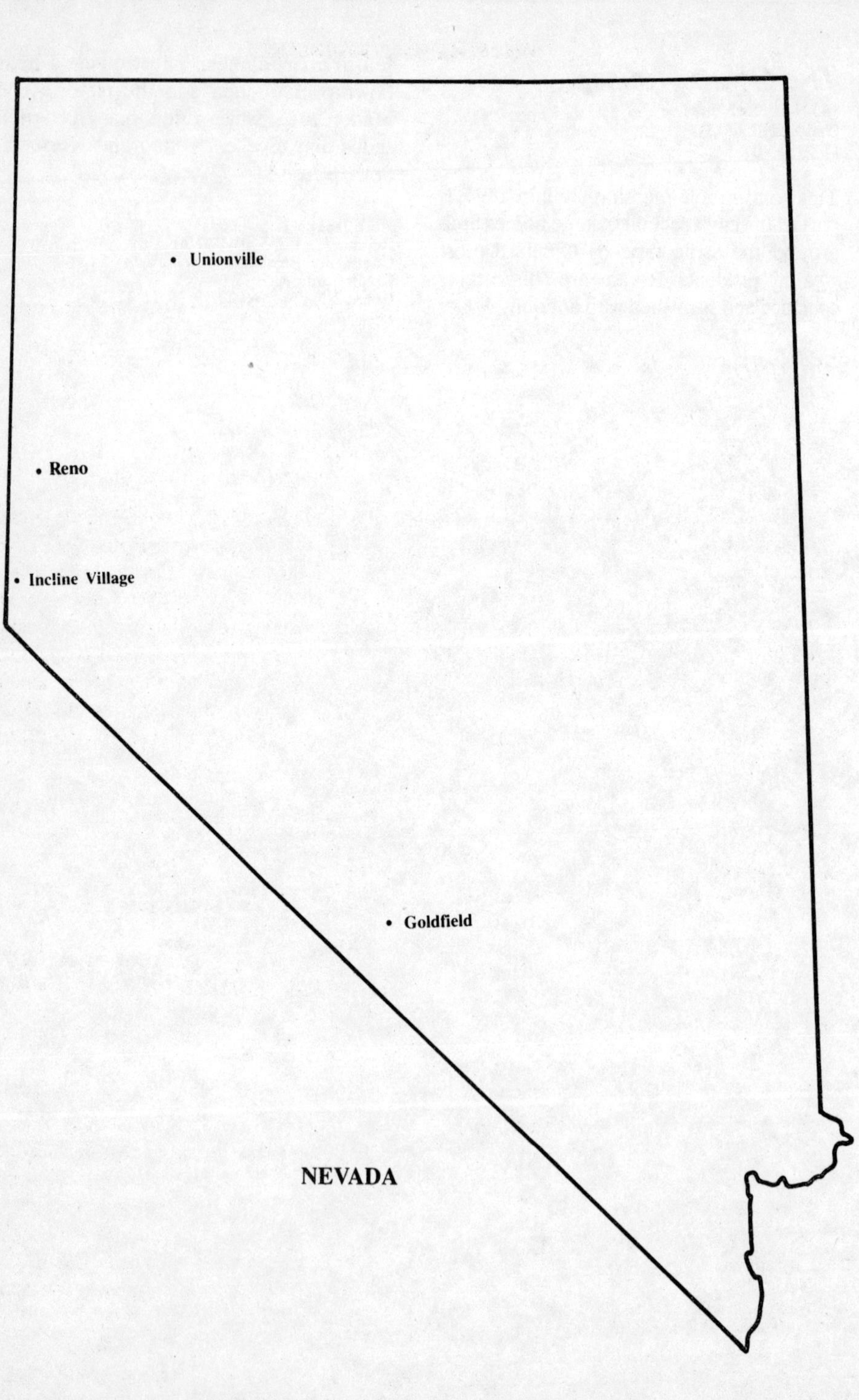
Unionville
Reno
Incline Village
Goldfield
NEVADA

Nevada

GOLDFIELD

Sundog B&B

211 Sundog Street
Goldfield, NV, 89013
(702) 485-3438

This historic (1906) home is within walking distance of downtown Goldfield, once Nevada's largest city. Eager to share their love of the desert, David and Maire are always willing to answer questions or give directions. This B&B has a European flair, as Maire hails from Ireland. Goldfield is a history buff or photographer's delight.

Hosts: David & Maire Hayes
Rooms: 3 (1 PB; 2 SB) $30-50
Full Breakfast
Credit Cards: A, B
Notes: 2, 5, 7, 8, 9, 14

INCLINE VILLAGE

Haus Bavaria

Box 3308
Incline Village, NV, 89450
(702) 831-6122

Haus Bavaria is located on the north shore of beautiful Lake Tahoe. It's a Bavarian style chalet, established in 1980, that offers comfortable home hospitality, including a full breakfast.

Host: Bick Hewitt
Rooms: 5 (PB) $70-80
Full Breakfast
Credit Cards: A, B
Notes: 2, 5, 9, 10, 11, 12, 13, 14

RENO

Bed & Breakfast—South Reno

136 Andrew Lane
Reno, NV, 89511
(702) 849-0772

Located just off Highway 395 in Steamboat Valley, ten miles south of Reno. The decor is Early American, which includes poster beds and beamed ceilings. Landscaped lawns, patios, and decks surround a heated swimming pool. Facing the B&B are ranch lands, Mt. Rose and Slide Mountain for hiking, sleigh riding and downhill skiing. Visit Lake Tahoe, Virginia City, or the many Reno casinos.

Hosts: Caroline S. Walters & Robert McNeill
Rooms: 3 (1 PB; 2 SB) $54-64
Full Breakfast
Credit Cards: No
Nov. 15-March 15, weekends only
Notes: 2, 7, 8, 9, 10, 11, 12, 13, 14

Lace & Linen

Suite 114, 4800 Kietzke Lane
P.O. Box 70401
Reno, NV, 89570-0401
(702) 826-3547

This B&B is furnished in pastels with antiques and Oriental rugs, white Victorian wicker, and European pieces. Guests may relax in the living room by the wood-burning fireplace and view the beautiful Sierra Nevadas or sit on the balcony to watch the sunset or the city lights at night.

Host: Patricia Parks
Doubles: 3 (PB) $45-70
Type of Beds: 4 Twin; 1 King
Continental Breakfast
Credit Cards: No
Notes: 3 (on request), 4 (on request), 5, 7 (limited), 9, 10, 11, 12, 13, 14

UNIONVILLE

Old Pioneer Garden

P.O. Box 79
Unionville, NV, 89418
(702) 538-7585

Located in an unspoiled corner of the world where there are more deer than people. Hiking, fishing, and exploring are favorite activities here. People have been known to spend their entire visit in our library, since we collect books. Rye Patch Lake, a half-hour away, is good for boating, fishing, and swimming.

Hosts: Len & Mitzi Jones
Rooms: 10 (3 PB; 7 S3B) $35-45
Full Breakfast
Credit Cards: No
Closed Jan. & Feb.
Notes: 2, 3, 4, 6, 8, 9, 14

New Hampshire

ALEXANDRIA

Stone Rest B&B

652 Fowler River Road
Alexandria, NH, 03222
(603) 744-6066

Contemporary home in a rural setting—great for R&R. Solar room with six-person hot tub and a Mt. Cardigan view. Close to Newfound Lake. Horseshoes, volleyball, etc., on premises. Close to hiking trails. Housekeeping cottages also available.

Hosts: Dick & Peg Clarke
Rooms: 3 (PB) From $38 + tax
Full Breakfast
Credit Cards: No
Notes: 2, 5, 9, 10, 11, 13

ANDOVER

The English House

Box 162
Andover, NH, 03216
(603) 735-5987

We have renovated, decorated, and furnished our home to recreate an English country house. We serve afternoon tea to our guests as well as a notable breakfast. All breads, muffins, cakes, jams, jellies, and marmalades are homemade.

Hosts: Gillian & Ken Smith
Rooms: 7 (PB) $54-75
Full Breakfast
Minimum stay foliage weekends & holidays: 2
Credit Cards: A, B
Closed one week in mid-March
Notes: 2, 5, 8 (8 and over), 9, 10, 11, 12, 13, 14

ASHLAND

Country Options

Box 736
Ashland, NH, 03217
(603) 968-7958

An 1893 homestead offering comfortable ambience and delicious hearty breakfasts. Large common room with wood stove for winter; light, airy sun porch for summer. "In the early 80's when the movie makers went looking for a place to be Golden Pond they found everything they wanted right here"—*Yankee*. We know you will, too.

Hosts: Sandra Ray & Nancy Puglisi
Rooms: 5 (SB) $54
Full Breakfast
Credit Cards: No
Notes: 2, 5, 9, 10, 11, 12

BARTLETT

The Country Inn at Bartlett

Route 302, P.O. Box 327
Bartlett, NH, 03812
(603) 374-2353

A B&B inn for hikers, skiers, and outdoor lovers in the White Mountains of New Hampshire. Inn and cottage rooms, fireplaces, hearty breakfasts, outdoor hot tub. The warmth and friendly atmosphere of our inn is here for you to enjoy. Come stay with us.

Host: Mark Dindorf
Rooms: 17 (11 PB; 6 SB) $28-48/person
Full Breakfast
Credit Cards: A, B, C
Notes: 2, 5, 6, 8, 9, 10, 11, 12, 13, 14

NEW HAMPSHIRE
Jefferson
Bethlehem
Franconia
Sugarhill
Jackson
Lincoln
Bartlett
Intervale
North Conway
Conway
Eaton Center
Campton
Chocorua
Lyme
Plymouth
Holderness
Ossipee
Ashland
Canaan
Meredith
Centre Harbor
Alexandria
Wolfeboro
Wakefield
Laconia
Winnisquam
Tilton
Andover
New London
Franklin
North Sutton
Loudon
Sutton Mills
Bradford
Henniker
Suncook
Walpole
Portsmouth
Rye
Hampton
Marlborough
Hampton Beach
Jaffrey
Greenfield
Rindge

The Notchland Inn

Hart's Location
Bartlett, NH, 03812
(603) 374-6131

A traditional country inn where hospitality hasn't been forgotten. We have eleven guest rooms, all with working fireplaces and private baths. Gourmet dining, spectacular mountain views, hiking, cross-country skiing, and swimming are offered at our secluded mountain estate.

Hosts: John & Pat Bernardin
Rooms: 11 (PB) $63-75/person
Full Breakfast
Credit Cards: A, B, C
Notes: 2, 4, 5, 10, 11, 12, 13, 14

The Bells

BETHLEHEM

The Bells

Strawberry Hill Street
Bethlehem, NH, 03574
(603) 869-2647

Situated in town, within walking distance of restaurants, antique shops, golf, and tennis; all White Mountain attractions close by. Unusual Victorian house named for the scores of bells hanging from the eaves. Inside, gracious suites and the romantic room-with-a-view cupola are furnished with four generations of heirlooms and mementos.

Hosts: Bill & Louise Sims
Rooms: 4 (PB) $60-70
Full Breakfast
Minimum stay some holidays
Credit Cards: A, B, C
Notes: 2, 5, 7, 8, 9, 10, 11, 12, 13, 14

The Mulburn Inn

Main Street
Bethlehem, NH, 03574
(603) 869-3389

A sprawling summer estate built in 1913 as a family retreat on the Woolworth Estate. Spacious, elegant rooms, stained-glass windows, and even an elevator are maintained in gracious style. Located in the heart of the White Mountains, minutes from Franconia Notch and the Mt. Washington Valley attractions.

Hosts: Bob & Cheryl Burns, Moe & Linda Mulkigian
Rooms: 7 (PB) $55-75
Full Breakfast
Credit Cards: A, B, C, D
Notes: 2, 5, 8, 9, 10, 11, 12, 13, 14

BRADFORD

The Bradford Inn

Main Street
Bradford, NH, 03221
(603) 938-5309

The Bradford Inn, a restored 1898 small country hotel, features comfortable lodging and J. Albert's Restaurant, which serves exceptional regional New England cuisine. Fireplaces, large parlors, wide halls with antiques and personal mementos. Four-season activity area.

Hosts: Connie & Tom Mazol
Rooms: 12 (PB) $59-79
Full Breakfast
Credit Cards: A, B, C, D, E
Notes: 2, 4, 5, 6, 7, 8, 9, 10, 11, 12, 13, 14

Mountain Lake Inn

P.O. Box 443
Bradford, NH, 03221
(603) 938-2136; (800) 662-6005

A true New England country inn, built in 1760 on the shores of Massaseusm Lake. Our private sandy beach provides summer enjoyment. In winter, our guests snowshoe on our 167 acres. The inn is tastefully decorated with antiques and period furniture, and our country cuisine will please the most delicate palate. Peace and tranquility abound.

Hosts: Carol & Phil Fullerton
Rooms: 9 (PB) $75-85
Full Breakfast
Credit Cards: A, B, D
Notes: 2, 4, 5, 7, 8, 9, 10, 11, 12, 13, 14

CAMPTON

Mountain Fare Inn

Mad River Road
Campton, NH, 03223
(603) 726-4283

Lovely 1840s farmhouse, truly country New Hampshire — simple and welcoming. Adjacent to the White Mountain National Forest. Two hours north of Boston, and a perfect stop between Vermont and Maine. Open year round for foliage, skiing, antiquing, hiking, or resting. Hearty full breakfasts. Guided hiking weekends available for groups on request. Candlelight dining.

Hosts: Susan & Nicholas Preston
Rooms: 8 (PB) $50-75
Full Breakfast
Credit Cards: No
Notes: 2, 4, 5, 8, 9, 10, 11, 12, 13, 14

CANAAN

The "Inn" on Canaan Street

Box 92
Canaan, NH, 03741
(603) 523-7310

On one of the most beautiful streets in New Hampshire, the inn is in a historic district on 14 lakefront acres just twenty-five minutes from Hanover. Fields, flowers, fireplaces, antiques, paintings—all combine to give an atmosphere of warmth and comfort.

Hosts: Lee & Louise Kremzner
Rooms: 4 (2 PB; 2 SB) $65-85
Full Breakfast
Credit Cards: A, B
Notes: 2, 3 (with reservations), 5, 9, 10, 11, 12, 13, 14

CENTRE HARBOR

Red Hill Inn

RFD 1, Box 99M
Centre Harbor, NH, 03226
(603) 279-7001

Restored country estate on 60 acres overlooking Squam Lake and the White Mountains. Twenty-one rooms, all with private baths, many with fireplaces and Jacuzzi. Country gourmet restaurant serving all meals, entertainment in the Runabout Lounge. Cross-country skiing (and rentals) on property. Two hours north of Boston.

Hosts: Rick Miller & Don Leavitt
Rooms: 21 (PB) $65-125
Full Breakfast
Credit Cards: A, B, C, E, F
Notes: 2, 3, 4, 5, 7, 8, 9, 10, 11, 12, 13, 14

CHOCORUA

Staffords-in-the-Field

Box 270
Chocorua, NH, 03817
(603) 323-7766

Federalist building, c. 1779, located at the base of the White Mountains and shaded by maples. The inn sits on a knoll, surrounded by acres of rolling fields. Antique-filled rooms, gourmet dining, walking trails, mountain climbing, swimming, boating, summer theater. Outlet shopping twenty miles north. This is our twenty-fifth year as innkeepers.

Hosts: Fred & Ramona Stafford
Rooms: 12 (6 PB; 6 SB) $45-70
Full Breakfast

Credit Cards: A, B, C, D, F
Closed April
Notes: 2, 4, 8, 9, 10, 11, 12, 13, 14

CONWAY

Darby Field Inn

Bald Hill Road
Conway, NH, 03818
(603) 447-2181

A charming, out-of-the-way country inn that offers excellent dining, a cozy atmosphere, and spectacular mountain views. We have an outdoor pool, cross-country ski trails, and a staff that is both friendly and courteous. Reservations recommended. Rate includes breakfast, dinner, tax, and gratuity.

Hosts: Marc & Marily Donaldson
Rooms: 16 (12 PB; 4 SB) $170.80
Full Breakfast
Minimum stay weekends: 2; holidays: 2-3
Credit Cards: A, B, C
Notes: 2, 4, 5, 7, 8 (2 to 12), 9, 10, 11, 12, 13

Valley Manner B&B

B&B Marblehead & North Shore
P.O. Box 172
Beverly, MA, 01915
(508) 921-1336

This Victorian B&B is located just steps from a covered bridge. The living room features an antique pump organ. Baby-sitting is available with advance notice. Four rooms on the second floor, private and shared baths. Restricted smoking. Full breakfast on weekends and continental-plus on weekdays. In the summer, you may enjoy the swimming pool, nearby tubing, fishing, tennis, golf, waterslides, and band concerts. $50-65.

EATON CENTER

The Inn at Crystal Lake

Route 153, Box 12
Eaton Center, NH, 03832
(603) 447-2120

Unwind in a restored 1884 inn in a quiet, scenic corner of the Mt. Washington Valley. Eleven guest rooms have Victorian antiques and private baths. There's a parlor, TV den/library, and cocktail lounge for your enjoyment. Swim, fish, sail, canoe, ski, skate, shop, or just relax! MAP available.

Hosts: Walter & Jacqueline Spink
Rooms: 11 (PB) $70-90
Type of Beds: 5 Double; 5 Queen; 1 Canopy
Full Breakfast
Credit Cards: A, B, C
Notes: 2, 4, 5, 7 (limited), 8, 9, 10, 11, 12, 13, 14

FRANCONIA

Blanche's B&B

Route 116, Easton Valley Road
Franconia, NH, 03580
(603) 823-7061

A Victorian farmhouse restored to a former glory it probably never had. Set in a meadow a half-mile beyond several working farms, the house looks up on Kinsman Ridge. Six miles from Franconia Notch. 100 percent cotton linens. Full breakfast.

Hosts: John Vail & Brenda Shannon
Rooms: 5 (SB) $55-60
Full Breakfast
Credit Cards: A, B, C
Notes: 2, 5, 8, 9, 10, 11, 12, 13

Bungay Jar B&B

Box 15, Easton Valley Road
Franconia, NH, 03580
(603) 823-7775

Built from an eighteenth-century barn and nestled among woodlands in Robert Frost's Easton Valley, this mountain home offers a relaxed country setting with garden walks to river. Secluded, yet convenient to all attractions in the White Mountain National Forest. Fireplaced, two-story living room, library, sauna, balconies, and large guest rooms with mountain views. Hosts are a practicing landscape architect and patent attorney who are avid hikers and skiers.

Hosts: Kate Kerivam & Lee Strimbeck
Rooms: 6 (4 PB; 2 SB) $60-100
Full Breakfast, afternoon tea or mulled cider
Credit Cards: A, B, C
Notes: 2, 5, 8 (over 6), 9, 10, 11, 12, 13, 14

Franconia Inn

Easton Road
Franconia, NH, 03580
(603) 823-5542

A charming inn situated on 107 acres in the Easton Valley, affording breathtaking views of the White Mountains. The inn's 34 rooms are decorated simply, yet beautifully. Elegant American cuisine highlights the inn's quiet country sophistication. Children welcome. Located on Route 116.

Hosts: The Morris Family
Rooms: 34 (30 PB; 4 SB) $75-110
Full Breakfast
Credit Cards: A, B, C
Closed April 1-May 15
Notes: 2, 4, 7, 8, 9, 10, 11, 12, 13, 14

FRANKLIN

Maria Atwood Inn

Route 3A
Franklin, NH, 03235
(603) 934-3666

Offering a charmingly romantic atmosphere, our brick federal colonial inn (circa 1830) is conveniently located for all seasonal activities. Enjoy a snack in front of the fireplace or in the television room before retiring to one of our seven spacious guest rooms; four with fireplaces, all with private baths and comfy beds. Awaken refreshed and with hearty appetite to a bountiful breakfast served in our library, or out-of-doors, weather permitting. If requested, we are happy to suggest activities and map out routes. We look forward to your visit.

Hosts: Irene & Philip Fournier
Rooms: 7 (PB) $65
Full Breakfast
Credit Cards: A, B, C, E, F
Notes: 2, 5, 8 (12 and over), 9, 10, 11, 12, 13, 14

GREENFIELD

Greenfield B&B Inn

Box 400
Greenfield, NH, 03047
(603) 547-6327

Laura Ashley-style Victorian mansion on 3 acres of lawn in the valley between Keene and Nashua. Enjoy the relaxing mountain view from the spacious veranda. Very close to skiing, swimming, hiking, tennis, golf, biking, and bargain antique shopping. A favorite of honeymooners of all ages. Senior citizen discount.

Hosts: Vic & Barbara Mangini
Rooms: 9 (5 PB; 4 SB) $45-60
Vacation apartment sleeps six
Full Breakfast
Credit Cards: A, B
Notes: 2, 5, 6 (limited), 7 (limited), 8 (limited), 9, 10, 11, 12, 13, 14

HAMPTON

The Curtis Field House

735 Exeter Road
Hampton, NH, 03842
(603) 929-0082

A restored custom Cape established in 1638, located on 5 country acres on Route 101-C, just over the Exeter line three miles from the center of Exeter. Seven miles from the ocean; fifty from Boston. Historic Portsmouth and Durham are nearby. A full breakfast is served. Our large bedrooms with private baths and air-conditioning are decorated with antiques and many lovely reproductions crafted by a descendant of Darby Field.

Hosts: Mary & Daniel Houston
Rooms: 3 (2 PB; 1 SB) $65
Full Breakfast
Credit Cards: A, B
Closed Dec.-March
Notes: 2, 9, 10, 11, 12

The Inn at Elmwood Corners

252 Winnacunnet Road
Hampton, NH, 03842
(603) 929-0443

The Elmwood is located in a seacoast NH village one mile from the ocean. Built in 1870, the inn is filled with country touches such as quilts, baskets, and stenciling. Guests share a sitting room with refrigerator, TV, books, and games. Two studios have kitchenettes as well as private baths. Memorable gourmet breakfasts await you.

Hosts: John & Mary Hornberger
Rooms: 7 (2 PB; 5 S2.5B) $40-90
Full Breakfast
Credit Cards: A, B
Notes: 2 (for deposits), 5, 7, 8, 9, 10, 11, 12, 13(XC)

The Inn at Elmwood Corners

The Roy Family B&B

473 Ocean Blvd.
Hampton, NH, 03842
(603) 926-7893; (800) 321-5505

Oceanfront accommodations in an immaculate New England home on the shores of the Atlantic. The house is decorated in a mix of traditional, Victorian, and casual pieces. Choose from two spacious sun decks to enjoy the sun and ocean views. On rainy days, relax in the cozy TV room furnished in white wicker or venture off to one of many nearby discount outlet malls and historic points of interest. Your hosts can provide picnic lunches or special dinners with advance reservations. The sandy beach is one and one-half miles long and includes boardwalk shops, boutiques, and restaurants.

Hosts: Matt & Cathie Roy
Rooms: 6 (SB) $45-65
Continental Breakfast
Credit Cards: A, B, D
Notes: 5, 7, 8 (12 and over), 9, 10, 11, 12, 13 (XC)

HAMPTON BEACH

The Oceanside

365 Ocean Blvd.
Hampton Beach, NH, 03842
(603) 926-3542

The Oceanside overlooks the Atlantic Ocean and its beautiful sandy beaches. Each of the ten rooms is tastefully and individually decorated, many with period antiques and all with private baths. The small intimate cafe is open for breakfast during July and August and features homemade bread and pastries. At other times a complimentary continental breakfast is available. This gracious inn is located in a less-congested part of Hampton Beach within easy walking distance of restaurants, shops, and other attractions.

Hosts: Skip & Debbie Windemiller
Rooms: 10 (PB) $83-98
Continental Breakfast
Credit Cards: A, B, C, D
Closed mid-Oct.-mid-May
Notes: 8 (limited), 9, 10, 11, 12

HENNIKER

Henniker House

2 Ramdsell Road
Box 191
Henniker, NH, 03242
(603) 428-3198

Henniker House, a nineteenth-century Victorian with wraparound porches, is bracketed by huge pine trees. The solarium/breakfast room overlooks the Contoocook River and opens to a fifty-foot deck overhanging the river. Henniker is the site of New England College, the heart of antiquing, arts, crafts, quilting, fiber weaving, music festivals. Biking expeditions, camping, hiking, skiing, fishing, and relaxing are available is this village of 2,500.

Host: Bertina Williams
Rooms: 4 (2 PB; 2 SB) $55-65
Full Breakfast
Credit Cards: A, B
Notes: 2, 3, 4, 5, 8, 9, 10, 11, 12, 13, 14

HOLDERNESS

The Inn on Golden Pond

Route 3
Holderness, NH, 03245
(603) 968-7269

An 1879 colonial home located on 55 wooded acres. Bright and cheerful sitting, breakfast, and game rooms. Close to major ski areas. Nearby is Squam Lake, the setting for the film *On Golden Pond.*

Host: Bill Webb
Rooms: 9 (7 PB; 2 SB) $81-91
Full Breakfast
Minimum stay holidays
Credit Cards: A, B, C
Notes: 2, 5, 8 (over 12), 9, 10, 11, 12, 13, 14

INTERVALE

Old Field House

Route 16A, P.O. Box 1
Intervale, NH, 03845
(603) 356-5478; (800) 444-9245

Colonial-style building with a stone facade, located just three miles north of North Conway on Route 16A. Choose from seventeen guest rooms, each with private bath, air conditioning, phone, TV. Living room with fireplace for get togethers or card games. On premises are clay tennis courts, outdoor heated pool, shuffleboard, and cross-country skiing. Area attractions include alpine ski resorts, hiking, fishing, canoeing, factory-outlet shopping. AAA and Mobil rated.

Hosts: Tim & Micki Merritt
Rooms: 17 (PB) $55-100
Continental Breakfast
Credit Cards: A, B, C
Notes: 2, 5, 7, 8, 9, 10, 11, 12, 13, 14

Wildflowers Guest House

Route 16
Intervale, NH, 03845
(603) 356-2224

Return to the simplicity and elegance of yesteryear. With our ideal location and gracefully decorated rooms, our small 1878 Victorian inn specializes in comfort and convenience for the modern-day traveler. We welcome you to enjoy and share our home.

Hosts: Dean Franke & Eileen Davies
Rooms: 6 (2 PB; 4 SB) $43.20-99.36
Continental Breakfast
Credit Cards: A, B
Closed Nov.-April
Notes: 2, 7, 8, 9, 10, 11, 12, 13

Ellis River House

JACKSON

Dana Place Inn

Box L
Jackson, NH, 03846
(603) 383-6822

Century-old inn located at the base of Mt. Washington on 300 acres along the Ellis River. Dana Place features cozy rooms, fine dining, indoor heated pool and river swimming, Jacuzzi, tennis, hiking, walking trails, fishing and cross-country skiing on the premises. Golf, attractions, outlet shopping nearby.

Hosts: Harris & Mary Lou Levine
Rooms: 33 (29 PB; 4 SB) $59-98
Full Breakfast
Credit Cards: A, B, C, D
Notes: 2, 3, 4, 5, 6, 7, 8, 10, 11, 12, 13, 14

Ellis River House

Route 16, Box 656
Jackson, NH, 03846
(603) 383-9339

A traditional B&B that boasts fine lodging and superb country dining in a turn-of-the-century farmhouse overlooking the spectacular Ellis River. Jacuzzi, antiques, minutes to all area attractions. Cross-country ski from our door. Enjoy hiking, canoeing, and outlet shopping.

Hosts: Barry & Barbara Lubao
Rooms: 5 (SB) $47.20-141.60
Cottage: 1 (PB)
Suites: 1 (PB)
Full Breakfast
Credit Cards: A, B, C
Notes: 2, 4, 5, 6, 7 (limited), 8, 9, 10, 11, 12, 13, 14

The Inn at Jackson

Box H, Thornhill Road
Jackson, NH, 03846
(800) 289-8600; (603) 383-4321

You'll find us on a knoll overlooking the peaceful village of Jackson. In summer you can enjoy golf, swimming, tennis, fishing, or just a walk on a quiet mountain trail. In winter enjoy cross-country skiing, alpine skiing, sleigh rides, or relax by our cozy fireplace. We offer spacious guest rooms with a relaxing atmosphere.

Hosts: Steve & Lori Tradewell
Rooms: 8 (PB) $56-78
Full Breakfast
Minimum stay weekends & holidays: 2
Credit Cards: A, B, C
Notes: 2, 5, 7, 8, 9, 10, 11, 12, 13, 14

The Inn at Jackson

The Village House

P.O. Box 359, Route 16A
Jackson, NH, 03846
(603) 383-6666

Just over the covered bridge is this charming colonial inn with wraparound porch facing the mountains. In summer enjoy tennis on our court, swimming in our pool, riding, golf, hiking, canoeing, and fine dining. Winter visitors ski from our door onto the 157 kilometers of cross-country trails. Downhill skiing is available at four major nearby mountains. Sleigh rides, ice skating, and snowshoeing are also available.

Host: Robin Crocker
Rooms: 10 (8 PB; 2 SB) $40-100
Full Breakfast in ski season; continental other seasons
Credit Cards: A, B
Notes: 2, 5, 7, 9, 10, 11, 12, 13, 14

JAFFREY

The Benjamin Prescott Inn

Route 124 East
Jaffrey, NH, 03452
(603) 532-6637

Come discover the charm of the past and the comforts of the present with true hospitality. Within a classic Greek Revival home furnished with antiques are ten charming guest rooms, each with private bath. Enjoy a full breakfast of hearty country fare. Relax, view to surrounding dairy farm, and walk the stone-wall lined lane.

Hosts: Jan & Barry Miller
Rooms: 10 (PB) $60-130
Full Breakfast
Credit Cards: A, B
Notes: 2, 5, 9, 11, 12, 13, 14

The Galway House B&B

247 Old Peterborough Road
Jaffrey, NH, 03452
(603) 532-8083

A traditional B&B operated like those in the Old Country. A great way to get to know the area and its people. Set on a quiet, woodland road in the heart of the Monadnock Region, the Currier & Ives corner of NH, this B&B makes an excellent point from which to enjoy the many attractions of this four-season area.

Hosts: Joe & Marie Manning
Rooms: 2 (SB) $45
Full Breakfast
Credit Cards: No
Notes: 2, 7 (restricted), 8, 9, 10, 11, 12, 13

Historic Woodbound Inn

Woodbound Road
Jaffrey, NH, 03452
(603) 532-8341; (800) 252-3033

Historic Woodbound Inn has been a year-round vacation resort since 1892, featuring a 1200-yard par 3 golf course, clay tennis courts, 36 Km. of cross-country ski trails, and nearby fishing. Our dining room serves three meals a day, with MAP rates available on request.

Host: Debbieanne Prussman
Rooms: 31 (26 PB; 5 SB) $90
Full Breakfast
Credit Cards: A, B, C
Notes: 2, 3, 4, 5, 9, 10, 11, 12, 13

Lilac Hill Acres B&B

5 Ingalls Road
Jaffrey, NH, 03452
(603) 532-7278

Five-star service in a beautiful 1840 home overlooking beautiful 115-acre Gilmore Pond. Surrounded by mountains. Hiking, skiing, summer playhouses, antiquing, and dining close by. Hearty breakfast served in the morning.

Hosts: Frank & Ellen McNeill
Rooms: 5 (2 PB; 3 S2B) $50-70 + tax
Full Breakfast
Credit Cards: No
Closed Christmas-New Year's & Easter
Notes: 2, 8 (14 and over), 9, 10, 11, 12, 13, 14

JEFFERSON

Applebrook B&B

Route 115A
Jefferson, NH, 03583-0178
(603) 586-7713

Comfortable, casual B&B in a Victorian farmhouse. Beautiful sunset views of Mt. Washington from our large sitting room with goldfish pool. Bike, hike, fish, ski, or go antique hunting. Near Santa's Village and Six-

The Jefferson Inn

Gun City. Group dinners available, brochure available.

Hosts: Sandra J. Conley & Martin M. Kelly
Rooms: 10 (2 PB; 8 SB) $40-60
Full Breakfast
Credit Cards: A, B, D
Notes: 2, 4, 5, 6, 8, 9, 11, 12, 13, 14

The Jefferson Inn

RFD 1, Box 68A
Jefferson, NH, 03583
(603) 586-7998

Situated among the White Mountain National Forest, the Jefferson Inn offers 360-degree views and nightly sunsets. With Mt. Washington nearby, the inn is an ideal location for hiking, cross-country and downhill skiing, and most outdoor activities. Afternoon tea, swimming pond; family suite available.

Hosts: Greg Brown & Bertie Koelewijn
Rooms: 10 (5 PB; 5 SB) $46-68
Full Breakfast
Minimum stay weekends & holidays: 2
Credit Cards: A, B, C
Closed Nov. & April
Notes: 2, 8, 9, 10, 11, 12, 13

LACONIA

Ferry Point House

R-1 Box 335
Laconia, NH, 03246
(603) 524-0087

Ferry Point House is a gracious country Victorian built in the early 1800s as a summer retreat on picturesque Lake Winnisquam. The gazebo on the point and sixty-foot veranda allow for comfortable, quiet moments with panoramic views. Each morning you will be treated to a very special breakfast that may include stuffed French toast, cheese baked apples, French breakfast crepes. We specialize in hospitality and warm service.

Hosts: Joe & Diane Damato
Rooms: 5 (3 PB; 2 SB) $55-65
Full Breakfast
Credit Cards: No
Open Memorial Day-Labor Day and weekends in Sept. & Oct.
Notes: 2, 8, 9, 10, 11, 12

Ferry Point House

Tin Whistle Inn

1047 Union Avenue
Laconia, NH, 03246
(603) 528-4185

Enjoy gracious hospitality at a charming post-Victorian home. Fireplaced living room, lead-glass windows, oak woodwork. Comfortable, spacious bedrooms. View memorable sunsets from the large veranda overlooking Paugus Bay. Minutes to Lake Winnipesaukee attractions and winter skiing facilities. Full, no-need-for-lunch breakfasts.

Host: Maureen C. Blazok
Rooms: 4 (1 PB; 3 SB) $45-60 + tax
Full Breakfast
Credit Cards: A, B, C, D, F
Closed Nov.
Notes: 2, 6, 7 (restricted), 8, 9, 10, 11, 12, 13

LINCOLN

Red Sleigh Inn

Pollard Road
P.O. Box 562
Lincoln, NH, 03251
(603) 745-8517

Family-run inn with mountain views. Just off the scenic Kancamagus Highway. One mile to Loon Mountains. Waterville, Cannon, and Bretton Woods nearby. Many summer attractions and superb fall foliage. Shopping, dining, and theater are minutes away. Hiking, swimming. golf, and train rides.

Hosts: Bill & Loretta
Rooms: 7 (1 PB; 6 SB) $55-65
Full Breakfast
Credit Cards: No
Notes: 2, 5, 11, 12, 13, 14

LOUDON

The Inn at Loudon Ridge

Box 195, Lower Ridge Road
Loudon, NH, 03301
(603) 267-8952

A rambling colonial Garrison-style home, surrounded by 33 wooded acres. The inn's rooms are large, airy, and punctuated with antiques. The cozy sitting room, with its piano and fireplace, invites socializing or quiet relaxation. Browse through dozens of local antique and craft shops; sample fresh maple syrup at the nearby sap house, or tour an historic Shaker village. Gunstock Ski Resort and the Lakes Region offer seasonal activities. In warm weather, you are welcome to use the inn's swimming pool and tennis court.

Hosts: Liz & Carol Early
Rooms: 5 (3 PB; 2 SB) $50-65 + tax
Full Breakfast
Credit Cards: A, B, C
Notes: 2, 5, 8 (12 and over), 9, 10, 11, 13

LYME

Loch Lyme Lodge

RFD 278, Route 10
Lyme, NH, 03768
(603) 795-2141

Loch Lyme Lodge has been hosting guests since 1924. From May through September, the twenty-five cabins and rooms in the main lodge are open for the enjoyment of summer vacationers. During the fall and winter months, the main lodge, a farmhouse built in 1784, is open. Children are welcome at any season, and the emphasis is always on comfortable, informal hospitality.

Hosts: Paul & Judy Barker
Rooms: 4 (SB) $24-36/person
Full Breakfast
Credit Cards: No
Notes: 2, 3 (summer), 4 (summer), 5, 6 (summer), 8, 9, 10, 11, 12, 13

MARLBOROUGH

Peep-Willow Farm

Bixby Street
Marlborough, NH, 03455
(603) 876-3807

Peep-Willow Farm is a working thoroughbred horse farm that also caters to humans. Situated on 20 acres with a view all the way to the Connecticut River Valley. Guests are welcome to help with chores or watch the young horses frolic in the fields, but there is no riding. Flexibility and serenity are the key ingredients to enjoying your stay.

Host: Noel Aderer
Rooms: 3 (SB) $25-40
Full Breakfast
Credit Cards: No
Notes: 2, 5, 6 (by arrangement), 8, 9, 13 (XC), 14

MEREDITH

The Nutmeg Inn

Pease Road, RFD 2
Meredith, NH, 03253
(603) 279-8811; (800) 642-9229

A restored 1763 stagecoach inn. Country decorated rooms with handmade quilts and crafts. Some rooms with fireplaces for added romance. Spend the day enjoying swimming, boating, fishing, skiing, antiquing. Relax in our graciously appointed parlor. As the sun sets, enjoy gourmet candlelight dining. On-site pool, central air-conditioning, full liquor license.

Hosts: Daryl & Cheri Lawrence
Rooms: 8 (6 PB; 2 SB) $60-85
Full Breakfast
Credit Cards: A, B, C, D, E, F
Notes: 4, 5, 8, 9, 10, 11, 12, 13, 14

NEW LONDON

New London Inn

Main Street
New London, NH, 03257
(603) 526-2791

Here you will find a classic New England inn with wide verandas overlooking this serene New Hampshire college town. The inn is comfortable and cozy, and the prize-winning gardens are glorious. "...spiffier and better known for its dining room than ever" — *Boston Globe.*

Hosts: Maureen & John Follansbee
Rooms: 30 (PB) $77-100
Full Breakfast
Minimum stay weekends: 2
Credit Cards: A, B
Notes: 2, 4, 5, 7, 8, 9, 10, 11, 12, 13, 14

NORTH CONWAY

The Buttonwood Inn

Box 1817AD
Mt. Surprise Road
North Conway, NH, 03860
(603) 356-2625; (800) 882-9928, NH & Canada

Built in thc 1820s as a farmhouse, the inn is tucked away on Mt. Surprise, where it's quiet and secluded, yet only two miles to the village and excellent dining and shopping. Minutes to Mt. Washington, skiing (cross-country from our door), hiking, fishing, and canoeing. Enjoy our outdoor pool.

Hosts: Ann & Hugh Begley
Rooms: 9 (PB and SB) $23-49/person
Full Breakfast
Credit Cards: A, B, C
Notes: 2, 3 (winter), 4 (winter), 5, 7, 8, 9, 10, 11, 12, 13, 14

The Buttonwood Inn

The Center Chimney—1787

P.O. Box 1120, River Road
North Conway, NH, 03860
(603) 356-6788

One of the earliest houses in North Conway—now a cozy, affordable B&B, just off Main Street and the Saco River (swim, fish, and canoe). Walk to shops, restaurants, summer theater, free ice skating and cross-country skiing. Rock and ice climbing on nearby Cathedral Ledge.

Host: Farley Ames Whitley
Rooms: 4 (SB) $44-55
Continental Breakfast
Credit Cards: No
Notes: 2, 5, 7, 8, 9, 10, 11, 12, 13

Cranmore Mt. Lodge

Box 1194, Kearsarge Road
North Conway, NH, 03860
(603) 356-2044

Cranmore Mt. Lodge, an historic New England country inn, is the perfect place to unwind. Our atmosphere is homey, and our accommodations and reasonable rates are ideal for families and groups. Formerly owned by Babe Ruth's daughter and visited by him many times. Hiking, rock climbing, skiing, kayaking, canoeing, bicycling, tennis, golf, riding, summer theater, and fine restaurants are just some of the area's attractions.

Hosts: Dennis & Judy Helfand
Rooms: 20 (5 PB; 15 SB) $67-99
Full Breakfast
Credit Cards: A, B, C, D
Notes: 2, 4, 5, 7, 8, 9, 10, 11, 12, 13

Merrill Farm Resort

RFD Box 151
North Conway, NH, 03860
(603) 447-3866; (800) 445-1017

Three-diamond AAA resort on the Saco River. 1790 inn with efficiencies, motel rooms, or spacious loft units. Outdoor pool, canoes on the river, in-room whirlpools, conference facilities. All rooms have cable TV and telephones. Tax-free outlet shopping in summer, and winter recreation area.

Hosts: Lee & Christine Gregory
Rooms: 60 (PB) $39-129
Continental Breakfast
Credit Cards: A, B, C, D, E
Notes: 2, 5, 7, 8, 9, 10, 11, 12, 13, 14

Peacock Inn

P.O. Box 1012
North Conway, NH, 03860
(603) 356-9041

The Peacock Inn is nestled in the heart of the Mount Washington Valley, near the quaint village of North Conway. Most of the eighteen guest rooms in this 200-year-old Victorian mansion have been restored with private baths and tastefully decorated. The room rate includes a fireside county breakfast, complimentary beverage, and cheese and crackers in the afternoon. Guests may use the facilities of the Mount Cranmore Racquet Club: indoor swimming, tennis, racquetball, exercise room, and sauna.

Hosts: Claire & Larry Jackson
Rooms: 18 (14 PB; 4 SB) $78-118
Full Breakfast
Credit Cards: A, B, C, D
Notes: 2, 5, 7, 8, 9, 10, 11, 12, 13, 14

The 1785 Inn

The 1785 Inn

Route 16
North Conway, NH, 03860
(603) 356-9025; (800) 421-1785

The 1785 Inn offers romantic accommodations, spectacular views of Mt. Washington, and award-winning dining. In the spring and summer, there are nature walks, hikes, swimming pool, fishing, lawn games, etc. In the fall, the best views of foliage anywhere. And in the winter, there are 60 Km. of cross-country trails and only two miles to downhill skiing.

Hosts: Becky & Charlie Mallar
Rooms: 16 (11 PB; 5 SB) $60-115
Full Breakfast
Credit Cards: A, B, C, D, E, F
Notes: 2, 4, 5, 7, 8, 9, 10, 11, 12, 13, 14

Sunny Side Inn

Seavey Street
North Conway, NH, 03860
(603) 356-6239

A casual, affordable country inn in a restored 1850s farmhouse. Short walk to North Conway Village and its many shops and restaurants. Enjoy mountain views from our flower-trimmed porches in summer or relax by the fireplace in winter.

Hosts: Chris & Marylee Uggerholt
Rooms: 10 (2 PB; 8 SB) $45-65
Full Breakfast
Minimum stay holidays: 2
Credit Cards: A, B
Notes: 2, 5, 7, 8, 9, 10, 11, 12, 13

Follansbee Inn

NORTH SUTTON

Follansbee Inn

P.O. Box 92
North Sutton, NH, 03260
(603) 927-4221

An authentic 1840 New England inn with white clapboard and green trim. Located on peaceful Kezar Lake, with an old-fashioned porch, comfortable sitting rooms, and charming antique furnishings. Nestled in a small country village, but convenient to all area activities. A healthy, no-smoking inn. Private pier with rowboat, canoe, paddle boat, and windsurfer for guests. Beautiful walk around the lake.

Hosts: Dick & Sandy Reilein
Rooms: 23 (11 PB; 12 SB) $70-90
Full Breakfast
Credit Cards: A, B
Closed parts of Nov. & April
Notes: 2, 4, 5, 8 (over 10), 9, 10, 11, 12, 13, 14

OSSIPEE

Acorn Lodge

Duncan Lake, Box 144
Ossipee, NH, 03864
(603) 539-2151

Once President Grover Cleveland's summer fishing camp, Acorn Lodge overlooks tranquil Duncan Lake. Breakfast is served on the veranda, then you may want to fish from our dock or use our rowboat or canoe. Enjoy a cool swim from our sandy beach or play lawn games. Close to Wolfeboro, summer theater, golf. Bicycle available.

Hosts: Julie & Ray Terry
Rooms: 6 (PB) $46
Continental Breakfast
Credit Cards: A, B
Closed Oct. 15-May 15
Notes: 2, 7, 8, 9, 10, 11, 12, 13

PLYMOUTH

Crab Apple Inn

RR 4, Box 1955
Plymouth, NH, 03264
(603) 536-4476

This inn is an 1835 brick Federal situated beside a brook at the foot of Tenney Mountain. The grounds are complemented by an English garden and brick courtyard. Located at the gateway to the White Mountains.

Hosts: Bill & Carolyn Crenson
Rooms: 4-5 (PB) $75-85
Full Breakfast
Credit Cards: A, B, C
Notes: 2, 5, 7, 8 (over 10), 9, 10, 11, 12, 13

The Hilltop Inn

PORTSMOUTH

The Inn at Strawberry Banke

314 Court Street
Portsmouth, NH, 03801
(603) 436-7242

A small, quiet, relaxing colonial inn with comfortable guest rooms and lounges for reading, conversation, or just sitting. Located in the heart of historic Portsmouth (originally Strawberry Banke, 1630) within a few short blocks of the working port, quaint shops, waterfront parks, historic homes, harbor cruises, and great dockside restaurants.

Host: Sarah Glover O'Donnell
Rooms: 7 (PB) $60-80
Full Breakfast
Credit Cards: A, B, C
Notes: 2, 5, 9, 10, 11, 12, 13 (XC)

RINDGE

Grassy Pond House

Rindge, NH, 03461
(603) 899-5166; 899-5167

An 1831 homestead nestled among 150 forested acres, overlooking water and gardens. Convenient to main roads, restaurants, antique marts, weekly local auctions, theater, music, and craft fairs. Hike the Grand Monadnock; ski cross-country and downhill. A retreat for all seasons.

Hosts: Carmen Linares & Bob Multer
Rooms: 4 (2 PB; 2 SB) $55-65
Full Breakfast
Minimum stay during foliage: 2
Credit Cards: No
Notes: 2, 5, 9, 10, 11, 12, 13, 14

RYE

Rock Ledge Manor B&B

1413 Ocean Blvd., Route 1A
Rye, NH, 03870
(603) 431-1413

Gracious traditional seaside manor home that's part of an old gingerbread colony begun 1840-1880. Six minutes to historic Portsmouth and Hampton, NH. Within a half hour of southern Maine's seacoast attractions; twenty minutes to the University of New Hampshire. After a brisk walk on the oceanside, a full memorable breakfast will be waiting for you.

Hosts: Norman & Janice Marineau
Rooms: 4 (2 PB; 2 SB) $65-75; add $5 for single night's stay
Full Breakfast
Credit Cards: No
Notes: 2, 5, 8 (12 and over), 9, 10, 11, 12, 13(XC)

SUGAR HILL

The Hilltop Inn

Main Street
Sugar Hill, NH, 03585
(603) 823-5695

An 1895 Victorian inn in the small village of Sugar Hill, which is nestled in the heart of the White Mountains. Near alpine and nordic skiing, hiking, Franconia Notch. Peaceful and homey, with beautiful sunsets and a large country breakfast. AAA approved.

Hosts: Meri & Mike Hern
Rooms: 4 (2 PB; 2 SB) $50-95
Suite: 1 (2 rooms, PB, sleeps 4)
Efficiency apartment: 1 (sleeps 2-8)
Full Breakfast
Minimum stay holidays and fall foliage: 2
Credit Cards: A, B, C
Notes: 2, 5, 6, 7, 8, 9, 10, 11, 12, 13

SUNCOOK

Suncook House

62 Main Street
Suncook, NH, 03275
(603) 485-8141

A brick Georgian home on 3 acres in the center of Suncook. The house has been recently renovated and is furnished in period pieces. You may relax in the formal living room, which has an organ, or in the sun parlor or den. Convenient to the White Mountains and the lakes area of New Hampshire; an easy walk to village restaurants, tennis courts. New Hampshire College and Bear Brook State Park are both a five-minute drive.

Hosts: Gerry & Evelyn Lavoie
Rooms: 4 (1 PB; 3 SB) $35-50 + tax
Full Breakfast
Credit Cards: No
Open mid-April-mid-Oct.
Notes: 2, 8, (over 13), 9, 10, 12, 14

SUTTON MILLS

The Quilt House

B&B Marblehead & North Shore
P.O. Box 172
Beverly, MA, 01915
(508) 921-1336

A 130-year-old Victorian country house overlooking a quaint village. The hostess runs workshops on quilting, and there are many fine quilts throughout the house. Three second-floor rooms with two shared baths. No smoking; full breakfast; children are welcome. $45.

TILTON

Black Swan Inn

308 West Main Street
Tilton, NH, 03276
(603) 286-4524

An 1880 restored Victorian located in the lakes region of 4 acres overlooking the Winnipesaukee River. Exceptional mahogany and oak woodwork and stained-glass windows. Two screened porches and formal gardens for guests' enjoyment. Refrigerators and sodas available for guests.

Hosts: Janet & Bob Foster
Rooms: 7 (3 PB; 4 SB) $55-65
Full Breakfast
Credit Cards: A, B, C, D, F
Closed March
Notes: 2, 7, 8 (12 and over), 9, 10, 11, 12, 13, 14

The Country Place

RFD 2, Box 342
Tilton, NH, 03276
(603) 286-8551

Our beautifully maintained 100-year-old home is located on 6 acres and has lovely mountain views. An open porch runs along two sides of the house. Hearty breakfasts are served in the country kitchen. Brochures available.

Hosts: Ed & Claire Tousignant
Rooms: 3 (S2B) $48.60-54
Full Breakfast
Credit Cards: No
Notes: 2, 5, 7, 8 (12 and over), 9, 10, 11, 12, 13

WAKEFIELD

The Wakefield Inn

RR 1, Box 2185
Wakefield, NH, 03872
(603) 522-8272

Located within the historic district of Wakefield Corner. Early travelers arrived by stagecoach. The majestic mountains and cool blue lakes offer unlimited outdoor activities. Or just relax and enjoy the ambience of days gone by.

Hosts: Lou & Harry Sisson
Rooms: 6 (PB) $65
Full Breakfast
Minimum stay holidays: 2
Credit Cards: A, B, C
Notes: 2, 4, 5, 7, 8 (over 10), 9

The Josiah Bellows House

WALPOLE

The Josiah Bellows House

North Main Street
Walpole, NH, 03608
(603) 756-4250

Experience the quiet dignity evident in each of the fourteen rooms. Canoe or fish in the Connecticut River, hike or picnic on Mt. Monadnock, or golf or tennis at the local country club. Currier & Ives loved this part of New England.

Hosts: Lois Ford & Lou Ciercielli
Rooms: 4 (2 PB; 2 SB) $55-65
Full Breakfast
Credit Cards: A, B
Notes: 2, 5, 11, 13, 14

WINNISQUAM

Tall Pines Inn

Old Route 3, Box 327
Winnisquam, NH, 03289
(603) 528-3632

A four seasons destination on Lake Winnisquam. Spectacular lake and mountain views; boat rental and sandy beach only yards away. Winter skiing within minutes of our wood stove. Special dinners by reservation. "Almost always open."

Hosts: Kent & Kate Kern
Rooms: 3 (1 PB; 2 SB) $48-70
Full Breakfast
Minimum stay weekends & holidays: 2
Credit Cards: A, B
Notes: 2, 4, 5, 7 (limited), 9, 10, 11, 12, 14

WOLFEBORO

The Wolfeboro Inn

44 North Main Street
P.O. Box 1270
Wolfeboro, NH, 03894
(800) 451-2389

With 43 guest rooms, a private beach on Lake Winnipesaukee, and two restaurants, the Wolfeboro Inn combines the charm, ambience, and decor of an authentic 1812 New England country inn with the privacy, amenities, and quality service that signifies the return of the grand hotel to the Lakes Region.

Host: Robin Schempp
Rooms: 43 (PB) $72-185
Continental Breakfast
Credit Cards: A, B, C, D
Notes: 2, 3, 4, 5, 7, 8, 10, 11, 12, 14

New Jersey

AVON-BY-THE-SEA

Cashelmara Inn

22 Lakeside Avenue
Avon-by-the-Sea, NJ, 07717
(201) 776-8727

Oceanside/lakefront Victorian inn where you can enjoy views of the Atlantic from your bed. Rooms decorated in beautiful Victorian antiques; wicker-filled veranda overlooking the ocean; suite with fireplace also available. Only fifty-five minutes from New York City and one hour from Philadelphia.

Host: Martin J. Mulligan
Rooms: 14 (PB) $60-150
Full Breakfast
Minimum stay summer weekends: 3; holidays: 4
Credit Cards: A, B, C
Notes: 2, 5, 8, 9, 10, 11, 12

BARNEGAT

The Dynasty

248 Edison Road
Pebble Beach
Barnegat, NJ, 08005
(609) 698-1566

A quiet, air-conditioned home on a peninsula with dock space, just minutes to Atlantic City. Filled with the ultimate in antiques collected from around the world. Breakfast is served at our award-winning pool, with foliage, a view of the sunset and wildlife reserve.

Host: Stanley Finkelstein
Rooms: 3 (1 PB; 2 SB) $53-125
Full Breakfast
Credit Cards: No
Closed Nov. 8-April 15
Notes: 3, 4, 6, 7, 8, 9, 10, 11, 12, 14

BEACH HAVEN

Bayberry Barque B&B Inn

117 Center Street
Beach Haven, NJ, 08008
(609) 492-5216

Our nineteenth-century Victorian is located one block from the ocean in historic Beach Haven. The Barque is tastefully restored to its past splendor, with the open staircase illuminated by an original stained-glass window, natural pine floors, and antique furniture. Walk to restaurants, shops, theaters, fishing, and charters to Atlantic City.

Hosts: Glenn, Pat & Gladys
Rooms: 9 (2 PB; 7 SB) $40-100
Continental-plus Breakfast
Credit Cards: A, B, C
Notes: 5, 8, 9, 10, 11

Magnolia House

215 Centre Street
Beach Haven, NJ, 08008
(609) 492-0398

Treat yourself to one of Long Beach Island's newly restored Victorian inns with twelve romantically decorated rooms, all with private bath, off-street parking, air conditioning, beach chairs, umbrella, and beach tags. A short walk to unique shops and restaurants. Live summer theater, fishing, tennis, and boat charters to Atlantic City.

Hosts: Gail & Tom Greenwald
Rooms: 12 (PB) $75-120
Full Breakfast
Credit Cards: No
Open May-Oct.
Notes: 2, 9, 10, 11, 12, 14

Stanhope
Lyndhurst
Frenchtown
Flemington
Princeton
Stockton
Avon-By-The-Sea
Belmar
Spring Lake
Sea Girt
Haddonfield
Barnegat
Salem
Beach Haven
Longport
Ocean City
North Wildwood
Cape May
NEW JERSEY

Magnolia House

decor is formal, the atmosphere is friendly and relaxed.

Hosts: Jay & Marianne Schatz
Rooms: 14 (PB) $85-150
Continental Breakfast (summer); Full (spring & fall)
Minimum stay June 15-Sept. 30 & major holidays: 3-4 and on most weekends
Closed Dec.-March
Credit Cards: A, B, C
Notes: 2 (as deposit), 8 (over 12), 9, 10, 11, 12

BELMAR

The Seaflower B&B Inn

110 Ninth Avenue
Belmar, NJ, 07719
(201) 681-6006

Our Dutch colonial home was built in 1907. Now with private baths, the flower-and-light-filled rooms make a perfect seashore getaway. Beach and boardwalk are one-half block away for sunning or moonlights strolls. Enjoy all the activities ocean and bay provide, great seafood, historic sites, and amusements.

Hosts: Pat O'Keefe & Knute Iwaszko
Rooms: 7 (5 PB; 2 SB) $50-80
Full Breakfast
Credit Cards: No
Notes: 2, 5, 7 (limited), 8 (over 10), 9, 10, 11, 12, 14

CAPE MAY

The Abbey

Columbia Avenue & Gurney Street
Cape May, NJ, 08204
(609) 884-4506

The Abbey consists of the main house, which is an 1869 Gothic revival villa built for a wealthy coal baron, and the cottage, which he built in 1873 for his son. Both houses are furnished with antiques, and although the decor is formal, the atmosphere is friendly and relaxed.

The Albert Stevens Inn

127 Myrtle Street
Cape May, NJ, 08204
(609) 884-4717

Restored 1889 Victorian Queen Anne classic, built as a wedding gift by a local physician for his wife, Bessie. Victorian elegance in the two large parlors allow guests the space to read and relax while enjoying afternoon tea and sherry. One parlor has the original mother-of-pearl inlay parlor suite presented by Dr. Stevens to his wife. The house is centered around a unique floating staircase that is suspended from the third-floor tower. Two formal dining rooms and a large wraparound veranda provide comfortable eating. The guest rooms reflect gracious Victorian tastes with period antiques and flowing lace. Just minutes from historic Cape May, shopping, and prime beachfront.

Hosts: Curt & Diane Rangen
Rooms: 7 (4 PB; 2 suites) $80-145
Full Breakfast
Credit Cards: A, B
Notes: 2, 3, 4, 5, 9, 10, 11, 12, 14

Barnard-Good House

238 Perry Street
Cape May, NJ, 08204
(609) 884-5381

We are known for our breakfast. Selected as number one by *New Jersey Monthly* magazine, we continue to make it even better. We serve four courses, all gourmet and homemade. Our purple house caters to happiness and comfort with Victorian restoration. All rooms have private baths and air-conditioning.

Hosts: Nan & Tom Hawkins
Rooms: 5 (PB) $90.10-116.60
Full Breakfast
Minimum stay weekdays & weekends in season: 3; holidays in season: 4
Credit Cards: A, B (for deposit only)
Closed Nov. 15-March 15
Notes: 2, 7 (restricted), 8 (14 and over), 9, 10, 11, 12

Bedford Inn

Bedford Inn

805 Stockton Avenue
Cape May, NJ, 08204
(609) 884-4158

Restored Italianate Victorian inn with an unusual double staircase to the third floor. Full-width first- and second-floor verandas have comfortable antique wicker furniture and old-fashioned porch rockers. Large buffet breakfast and afternoon tea by the parlor fireplace in the winter. All rooms are air-conditioned.

Hosts: Cindy & Al Schmucker
Rooms: 11 (PB) $79.50-137.50
Full Breakfast
Credit Cards: A, B, C
Notes: 2, 5, 7, 8 (7 and over), 9, 10, 11, 12

The Brass Bed Inn

719 Columbia Avenue
Cape May, NJ, 08204
(609) 884-8075

Our individually restored rooms boast a fine collection of nineteenth-century brass beds, antiques, lace curtains, and dramatic period wall coverings. In the fall and winter, full, hearty breakfasts are served by the hearth. Spring and summer features lighter fare. All year we serve tea and light refreshments in the afternoon. Two blocks to beaches. The house was built in 1872.

Hosts: John & Donna Dunwoody
Rooms: 8 (6 PB; 2 SB) $65-115
Full Breakfast
Credit Cards: A, B
Closed Thanksgiving & Christmas Day
Notes: 2, 5, 9 (moderate), 10, 11, 12, 14

Chalfonte Hotel

301 Howard Street
Cape May, NJ, 08204
(609) 884-8409

A rustic 1876 Victorian summer hotel with verandas, rocking chairs, and delicious Southern fare. Relaxing and comfortable — the pleasures of another era await you. Inquire about workshops, children's programs, classical and jazz concerts, historic programs, tours, and special discounts. Dinner is included in the daily rate.

Hosts: Anne LeDuc & Judy Bartella
Rooms: 72 (11 PB; 61 SB) $90-150
Full Breakfast
Credit Cards: A, B
Closed Nov.-April
Notes: 2, 4, 7 (limited), 8, 9, 10, 11, 12, 14

Cliveden Inn

709 Columbia Avenue
Cape May, NJ, 08204
(609) 884-4516

Enjoy the Cliveden's comfortable and attractive accommodations. All rooms are spacious and cozy, with period furniture.

Chalfonte Hotel

Centrally located on Cape May's popular Columbia Avenue in the historic district. Two blocks from the beach and within easy walking distance to the Victorian Mall and fine restaurants. Afternoon tea and continental breakfast.

Hosts: Sue & Al De Rosa
Rooms: 10 (8 PB; 2 SB) $70-80
Continental-plus Breakfast
Credit Cards: A, B, C
Closed Nov.-April 22
Notes: 2, 7 (restricted), 8, 9, 10, 11, 12, 14

Colvmns by the Sea

1513 Beach Drive
Cape May, NJ, 08204
(609) 884-2228

Elegant Victorian mansion overlooking the ocean in an historic landmark village. Large, airy rooms are decorated with antiques. Gourmet breakfast and snacks, complimentary bikes, beach towels, and badges. Relaxing, enjoyable retreat for history buffs, bird watchers, and seashore lovers. Great restaurants nearby.

Hosts: Barry & Cathy Rein
Rooms: 11 (PB) $95-155
Full Breakfast
Minimum stay summer weekends & holidays: 3
Credit Cards: A, B
Closed Jan.-April
Notes: 2, 7 (limited), 8 (over 12), 9, 10, 11, 12

Duke of Windsor B&B Inn

817 Washington Street
Cape May, NJ, 08204
(609) 884-1355

Queen Anne Victorian house with a forty-five-foot tower built in 1896 and restored with Victorian furnishings. Foyer with three-story carved oak open staircase, fireplace. Sitting room, parlor with fireplace, library, dining room. Beach tags provided, hot and cold outdoor showers, and off-street parking is available.

Hosts: Bruce & Fran Prichard
Rooms: 10 (8 PB; 2 SB) $65-105
Full Breakfast
Credit Cards: A, B
Notes: 2, 8 (over 12), 9, 10, 11, 12

Gingerbread House

28 Gurney Street
Cape May, NJ, 08204
(609) 884-0211

An elegantly restored 1869 Victorian cottage listed on the National Register. Enjoy the well-appointed guest rooms, listen to classical music by the fire in the parlor, or enjoy the porches in warm weather. Centrally located one-half block from the beach.

Hosts: Fred & Joan Echevarria
Rooms: 6 (3 PB; 3 SB) $65-130
Full Breakfast
Minimum stay summers: 4
Credit Cards: No
Notes: 2, 5, 7, 8 (7 and over), 9, 10, 11, 12

Duke of Windsor B&B Inn

The Humphrey Hughes House

29 Ocean Street
Cape May, NJ, 08204
(609) 884-4428

Nestled in the heart of Cape May's historic section is one of her most authentically restored inns—perhaps the most spacious and gracious of them all. Until 1980 it was the Hughes family home, and while the house is filled with magnificent antiques, it still feels more like a home than a museum.

Hosts: Lorraine & Terry Schmidt
Rooms: 7 (PB); 3 suites $85-120
Full Breakfast
Minimum stay weekends: holidays
Credit Cards: A, B
Notes: 5, 10, 11, 12

Mainstay Inn

635 Columbia Avenue
Cape May, NJ, 08204
(609) 884-8690

The Mainstay Inn and Cottage are two of Cape May's most beautiful Victorian structures, and are decorated and furnished to historic perfection. Tom and Sue welcome all visitors; community breakfast and afternoon tea are highlights of the day. All rooms are large, airy, well lighted, and very comfortable. The Mainstay is in its nineteenth season — one of the first B&Bs in America.

Hosts: Tom & Sue Carroll
Rooms: 12 (PB) $85-140 & tax
Full Breakfast
Minimum stay weekends: 3; holidays: 4
Credit Cards: No
Closed mid-Dec. to mid-March
Notes: 2, 9, 10, 11, 12

Mainstay Inn

The Mason Cottage

625 Columbia Avenue
Cape May, NJ, 08204
(609) 884-3358

The Mason Cottage was built in 1871 as the summer residence for a wealthy Philadelphia entrepreneur. Located in the historic district, the inn is French Second Empire, with a curved mansard roof. Within the inn, our guests discover elegance, meticulous restoration, and warm hospitality. Nearby activities include Victorian carriage rides, historic house tours, antique shops, beaches, and Victorian Shopping Mall.

Hosts: Dave & Joan Mason
Rooms: 5 (4 PB; 1 SB) $70-140
Continental-plus Breakfast
Credit Cards: A, B
Closed Nov.-May
Notes: 2, 7 (outside), 8 (12 and over), 9, 10, 11, 12, 14

Perry Street Inn

Perry Street Inn

29 Perry Street
Cape May, NJ, 08204.
(609) 884-4590

Historic location between the beach and the mall. Near fine restaurants, unique shopping, rich birding areas, all water sports. Tennis and golf close by. Victorian beach house with ocean views, period furniture, breakfast buffet, and parking. Also modern motel suites on same property.

Hosts: John & Cynthia Curtis
Rooms: 10 (5 PB; 5 SB) $40-90
Full Breakfast
Credit Cards: A, B
Notes: 2, 5, 7, 9, 10, 11, 12, 14

Poor Richard's Inn

17 Jackson Street
Cape May, NJ, 08204
(609) 884-3536

Run by two expatriate New York artists since 1977 and lovingly restored over time, Poor Richard's has been unhurriedly growing into its own persona, one where the hosts are helpful and knowledgeable but insistent on being unobtrusive; one where the personal touches of the present and the furnishings and architecture of the past ask more to be lived in than admired.

Hosts: Richard & Harriett Samuelson
Rooms: 9 (4 PB; 5 SB) $42-92
Continental Breakfast
Credit Cards: A, B
Closed Jan. 2-Feb. 12
Notes: 2, 3, 4, 6, 7, 8, 9, 10, 11, 12

The Queen Victoria

The Queen Victoria

102 Ocean Street
Cape May, NJ, 08204
(609) 884-8702

The Wells family welcomes you as friends and treats you royally with unpretentious service and attention to detail. Four restored buildings, furnished with antiques, are in the center of the historic district. Nationally recognized for special Christmas activities.

Hosts: Dane & Joan Wells
Rooms: 17 (13 PB; 4 SB) $49-175 plus tax
Suites: 7 (PB)
Full Breakfast
Credit Cards: A, B
Notes: 2, 5, 8, 9, 10, 11, 12

White Dove Cottage

619 Hughes Street
Cape May, NJ, 08204
(609) 884-0613

Elegant 1866 home located on a gas-lit street in the center of historic Cape May. Two blocks from the beach; near tennis and Victorian Shopping Mall. A delightful retreat, open year-round. Ask for details of our honeymoon, anniversary, or birthday specials.

Hosts: Frank Smith & Lorraine George
Rooms: 5 (PB) $75-125
Full Breakfast
Credit Cards: No
Notes: 2, 5, 8 (8 and over), 10, 11

Windward House

24 Jackson Street
Cape May, NJ, 08204
(609) 884-3368

Edwardian shingle-style cottage one-half block to beach and Victorian Mall. Completely decorated in elegant antiques plus vintage collectibles, paintings, and clothing. All rooms have private baths, mini-refrigerators, sitting areas, ceiling fans, and air-conditioners. Some have TV. Three sun and shade porches, plus three common rooms. Stained and leaded glass abound throughout.

Hosts: Sandy & Owen Miller
Rooms: 8 (PB) $90-135
Full Breakfast, afternoon tea
Minimum stay weekends: 2-3; holidays: 4
Credit Cards: A, B
Notes: 2, 5, 7, 8 (over 12), 9, 10, 11, 12

Woodleigh House

808 Washington Street
Cape May, NJ, 08204
(609) 884-7123

Victorian, but informal. Centrally located, with off-street parking, beach bikes, comfortable parlor, courtyard, and gardens. Walk to everything: marvelous restaurants, sights galore, nearby nature preserve, dinner theater, craft and antique shows.

Hosts: Jan & Buddy Wood
Rooms: 4 (PB) $80-100
Continental-plus Breakfast
Credit Cards: A, B
Notes: 2, 5, 8 (over 5), 10, 11, 12

CAPE MAY COUNTY

Henry Ludlam Inn

RD #3, Box 298
Woodbine, NJ, 08270
(609) 861-5847

Ludlam Inn is an historic circa 1804 home situated on a 55-acre lake, where you can nourish your senses and sustain your soul. Sip wine in front of the fireplace in your room; sleep on a featherbed; awake to a gourmet breakfast. Near beaches, state parks, and restaurants. Come and explore.

Rooms: 5 (3 PB; 2 SB) $65-95
Full Breakfast
Minimum stay holidays: 3
Credit Cards: A, B, C
Notes: 2, 4, 5, 7 (limited), 8 (over 12), 9, 10, 11, 12, 14

FLEMINGTON

Jerica Hill

96 Broad Street
Flemington, NJ 08822
(908) 782-8234

Be warmly welcomed at this gracious Victorian country home. The bright, airy guest rooms are furnished with canopy, brass, and four-poster beds, antiques, fresh flowers. Large living room with an open fire in the winter, and wicker-filled screened porch in the summer. Special adventures include champagne hot-air balloon flights and country winery tours.

Host: Judith Studer
Rooms: 5 (2 PB; 3 SB) $60-90
Continental Breakfast
Credit Cards: A, B, C
Notes: 2, 5, 9, 10, 11, 12

FRENCHTOWN

The Old Hunterdon House

12 Bridge Street
Frenchtown, NJ, 08825
(201) 996-3632

This Civil War era Italianate mansion in a small Delaware River village captures the ambience of the Victorian age. Distinctive architecture, period furnishings, and attention to detail and guest comfort all combine to make for a memorable stay. Convenient to excellent dining, antique and outlet shopping, and recreational activities in Bucks and Hunterdon counties.

Hosts: Tony & Gloria Cappiello
Rooms: 7 (PB) $90-150
Continental-plus Breakfast
Credit Cards: A, B, C
Notes: 2, 5, 9, 10, 11, 12

HADDONFIELD

The Queen Anne Inn

44 West End Avenue
Haddonfield, NJ, 08033
(609) 428-2195

The Queen Anne Inn boasts a thirty-foot turret, wraparound porch, loft ceilings, paneled doors, and country Victorian decor. We have a common living area with cable TV and large country kitchen. Walk to historic downtown Haddonfield to shops and restaurants. Historic Philadelphia is twenty minutes away by car.

Hosts: Jennifer & Andrew DeVos
Rooms: 10 (SB) $55-80
Continental Breakfast
Credit Cards: A, B, C
Notes: 2, 5, 8 (over 4), 9, 10, 11, 12, 14

LONGPORT

Winchester House

1 South 24th Avenue
Longport, NJ, 08403
(800) 628-4073

Located in a quiet residential seashore community overlooking Great Egg Harbor Bay. All rooms are spacious, air-conditioned, with private baths, cable TV, radio, and daily maid service. Atlantic City casinos and the boardwalk are less than five miles away. Tennis, golf, swimming, boating, fishing, and great restaurants are nearby.

Hosts: Jim & Mary Jane Kelly
Rooms: 14 (PB) $60-65
Continental Breakfast
Credit Cards: A, B
Closed Sept. 20-May 20
Notes: 2, 7, 8, 9, 10, 11, 12, 14

LYNDHURST

The Jeremiah J. Yereance House

410 Riverside Avenue
Lyndhurst, NJ, 07071
(201) 438-9457

This 1841 house, a state and national landmark, is five minutes from the Meadowlands complex and twenty minutes from New York City. The guest rooms in the south wing include a front parlor with fireplace, a central hall, and a small but comfortable bedroom that adjoins the parlor and private bath. The North Wing includes a common parlor with three bedrooms that share a bath.

Hosts: Evelyn & Frank Pezzolla
Rooms: 4 (1 PB; 3 SB) $55-75 + tax
Continental Breakfast
Credit Cards: C
Notes: 2, 5, 8 (over 12), 9, 10

NORTH WILDWOOD

Candlelight Inn

2310 Central Avenue
North Wildwood, NJ, 08260
(609) 522-6200

The Candlelight Inn is a beautifully restored B&B built at the turn of the century by Leaming Rice. This Queen Anne Victorian structure served as the family home for many years until it was purchased by its present innkeepers in 1985. Within minutes of Cape May and Atlantic City. Special touches and personalized service abound.

Hosts: Paul DiFilippo & Diane Buscham
Rooms: 9 (7 PB; 2 SB) $55-150
Full Breakfast
Credit Cards: A, B, C
Notes: 2, 5, 9, 10, 11, 12, 14

BarnaGate

OCEAN CITY

BarnaGate

637 Wesley Avenue
Ocean City, NJ, 08226
(609) 391-9366

We offer a warm welcome to share our five newly redone guest rooms with private and semiprivate baths. Enjoy our front porch in summer and our cozy living room all year. Located within easy reach of Atlantic City, historic attractions, and Cape May, we also have biking, walking, jogging, and swimming.

Hosts: Frank & Lois Barna
Rooms: 5 (1 PB; 4 SB) $50-70
Continental Breakfast
Credit Cards: A, B
Notes: 5, 8 (10 and over), 9, 10, 11, 12

The Enterprise B&B

1020 Central Avenue
Ocean City, NJ, 08226
(609) 398-1698

Our breakfast is just one of the reasons we were rated "One of the best Inns" between Atlantic City and Cape May. We cater to couples looking for that special getaway rendezvous at the shore. 25 percent savings Sept.-May. Open all year.

Hosts: Stephen & Patty Hydock
Rooms: 9 (7 PB; 2 SB) $80.25
Full Breakfast
Credit Cards: A, B
Notes: 2, 5, 7, 8 (over 12), 9, 10, 11, 12

New Brighton Inn

519 Fifth Street
Ocean City, NJ, 08226
(609) 399-2829

Magnificently restored 1880s seaside Queen Anne style Victorian. Premises comfortably furnished with antiques throughout. Breakfast on sun porch. A romantic, relaxing, charming hideaway close to the beach, boardwalk, tennis courts, restaurants, and fine shops.

Hosts: Daniel & Donna Hand
Rooms: 4 (2 PB; 2 SB) $55-75
Full Breakfast
Credit Cards: A, B, C
Notes: 2 (NJ), 5, 8 (over 10), 10, 11, 12

Top O' The Waves

5447 Central Avenue
Ocean City, NJ, 08226
(609) 399-0477

Come to Top O' The Waves. Located right on the beach, this private vacation complex features luxury ocean-front rentals. Cozy single units and a spacious duplex with all amenities. The hosts delight in making your R&R of surf, sun, and sand special, and give everyone privacy, luxury, and service. Special off-season rates for businesspersons and senior citizens. The only B&B on the beach in all Cape May County.

Hosts: Dolly & Des Nunan
Rooms: 14 (10 PB; 4 SB) $76-125
Continental Breakfast
Minimum stay summer single units: 3: duplexes 2 weeks
Credit Cards: A, B, C
Notes: 2 (2 weeks in advance), 5, 7, 8, 9, 10, 11, 12

New Brighton Inn

OCEAN GROVE

Cordova

26 Webb Avenue
Ocean Grove, NJ, 07756
(201) 774-3084; (212) 751-9577

The Cordova is a century-old Victorian located in a lovely, historic beach community with Old World charm. It's only 1.5 blocks from the white sand beach and wooden boardwalk. Selected by *NJ Magazine* as "one of the 7 best places on Jersey Shore." Family atmosphere. Many former presidents (Wilson, Cleveland, Roosevelt) have slept in Ocean Grove and spoken at the 7,000-seat "Great Auditorium"—the largest wooden structure in the US.

Host: Doris Chernik
Rooms: 15 (SB) $35-60
Continental-plus Breakfast
Credit Cards: No
Closed Labor Day-Memorial Day
Notes: 2, 7 (restricted), 8, 9, 10, 11, 14

PRINCETON

B&B of Princeton 1

P.O. Box 571
Princeton, NJ, 08540
(609) 924-3189

Large Victorian home with three double guest rooms a few minutes' walk from the university and center of town. The hostess, a long-time Princeton resident, will go out of her way to assure her guests comfort and to help them with problems of any nature. Continental to full breakfast is provided. Staying in this home is like visiting grandmother. $40-70.

B&B of Princeton 2

P.O. Box 571
Princeton, NJ, 08540
(609) 924-3189

Lovely home on a tree-shaded street a few minutes' walk from the university and town center. This home has two double and one single guest rooms. Continental breakfast. $40-70.

B&B of Princeton 3

P.O. Box 571
Princeton, NJ, 08540
(609) 924-3189

Large townhouse approximately one mile from the town center. This home has a variety of sleeping arrangements perfect for a family. Hostess will reduce rates for long-term guests. Continental breakfast. $40-70.

Ashling Cottage

SALEM

Ma' Bowman's B&B

156 Harmersville Pecks Corner Road
Salem, NJ, 08079
(609) 935-4913

Farm country seclusion in the middle of cultivate acres. Quiet, pleasant, congenial hosts, good homemade food and breads, and entertainment on the premises at no extra cost. Hosts like to play pinochle and other card and table games.

Hosts: Lou & Mickey Bowman
Rooms: 5 (SB) $25
Continental Breakfast
Credit Cards: No
Notes: 3, 4, 5, 6, 7, 8, 9, 10, 11, 12

SEA GIRT

Holly Harbor Guest House

112 Baltimore Blvd.
Sea Girt, NJ, 08750
(908) 449-9731

Sea Girt is a quiet residential town sixty miles south of New York City on the Jersey shore. Gracious cedar-shingled house is bordered by holly trees and has a spacious front porch. Only one block from the beach.

Hosts: Bill & Kim Walsh
Rooms: 12 (SB) $75-100
Full Breakfast
Credit Cards: A, B, C
Notes: 2, 5, 8, 9, 10, 11, 12

SPRING LAKE

Ashling Cottage

106 Sussex Avenue
Spring Lake, NJ, 07762
(201) 449-3553

Under sentinel sycamores since 1877 in a storybook setting, Ashling Cottage, a Victorian seaside inn, has long served as a portal to an earlier time. A block from the ocean and just half a block from a fresh-water lake.

Hosts: Goodi & Jack Stewart
Rooms: 10 (8 PB; 2 SB) $60-120
Continental-plus Breakfast
Credit Cards: No
Closed Jan. & Feb.
Notes: 2, 7 (limited), 8 (over 12), 9, 10, 11, 12

The Chateau

500 Warren Avenue
Spring Lake, NJ, 07762
(201) 974-2000

The house may be 101 years old, but it's brand-new inside: air-conditioning, color cable TV, HBO, phones, refrigerators. Suites and parlors have living rooms, wet bars, paddle fans. Some have fireplaces and facilities for FAX machines and personal computers. VCRs, private porches and balconies.

Host: Scott Smith
Rooms: (PB) $44-96
Suites: (PB) $70-142
Continental Breakfast
Credit Cards: A, B, C
Closed Nov. 1-March 29
Notes: 2, 7, 8, 9, 10, 11, 12, 14

The Grand Victorian

1505 Ocean Avenue
Spring Lake, NJ, 07762
(201) 449-5327

The Grand Victorian is a charming year-round hotel with history dating back to 1883. Located directly on the ocean. The comfortable and relaxing porches provide breathtaking views of the waves and the magnificent blue skies. Gracious hospitality. The individually decorated rooms are sure to provide you with rest and relaxation.

Hosts: Angele & Lisa Sarkar
Rooms: 23 (16 PB; 7 SB) $65-160
Full Breakfast
Credit Cards: A, C, F
Notes: 2, 3, 4, 5, 9, 10, 11, 12, 14

Normandy Inn

The Hewitt-Wellington Hotel

200 Monmouth Avenue
Spring Lake, NJ, 07762
(201) 974-1212

Winner of triple AAA Four Diamond award. Beautifully appointed rooms and two-room suites on the lake, overlooking the ocean. Private balconies and wraparound porches, air conditioning, ceiling fans, private marble baths, telephone, and cable TV. Refined dining in our intimate restaurant. On-site heated pool and provided beach passes. Ask for our free brochure.

Host: Patrick Barber
Rooms: 29 (PB) $70-230
Continental Breakfast
Credit Cards: A, B, C
Closed Nov. 16-March 31
Notes: 3, 4, 8, 9, 10, 11, 12, 14

Normandy Inn

21 Tuttle Avenue
Spring Lake, NJ, 07762
(201) 449-7172

Less than a block from the ocean, this 1888 Italianate villa has been authentically restored inside and out. Antique-filled guest rooms and parlors invite you to step back in time to nineteenth-century elegance. Our wide front porch with wicker furniture offers quiet conversation and cool breezes at sunset. A hearty country breakfast awaits you in the morning. Explore the wide, tree-lined streets, turn-of-the-century estates, quaint shops and boutiques. Golf, tennis, horseback riding, and historic villages are nearby.

Hosts: Michael & Susan Ingino
Rooms: 17 (PB) $93-131 (Sept.-June)
Apartment: 1 (PB) $115-160
Full Breakfast
Minimum stay March-Nov.: weekends: 2; holidays: 3; July & Aug. weekends: 4; July & Aug. midweek: 2
Credit Cards: A, B, C
Notes: 2, 5, 7, 8, 9, 10, 11, 12, 14

Victoria House

214 Monmouth Avenue
Spring Lake, NJ, 07762
(201) 974-1882

Nineteenth-century Victorian in a beautiful seaside resort. Within easy walk of the beach, churches, and center of town. Perfect for a honeymoon, birthday, reunion, or that special occasion. Enjoy the spacious porch, charming rooms with wicker and antiques, and a friendly atmosphere.

Host: Maggie Galisch
Rooms: 10 (2 PB; 8 SB) $50-95
Continental-plus Breakfast
Credit Cards: A, B, C, F
Notes: 2, 5, 7 (restricted), 8, 9, 10, 11, 12

STANHOPE

Whistling Swan Inn

110 Main Street
P.O. Box 791
Stanhope, NJ, 07874
(201) 347-6369

We are northwest New Jersey's finest Victorian B&B, located just off I-80 only 45 minutes west of the George Washington Bridge. Near Waterloo Village, International Trade Zone, skiing, antiques, shops, restaurants. "For those with more refined nesting instincts."

Hosts: Paula Williams & Joe Mulay
Rooms: 10 (PB) $65-95
Full Breakfast
Credit Cards: A, B, C
Notes: 2, 5, 9, 10, 11, 12, 13, 14

STOCKTON

The Stockton Inn, "Colligan's"

Main and Bridge Streets
Stockton, NJ, 08559
(609) 397-1250

1710. Inspiration for the Rodgers and Hart song, "There's a Small Hotel (With a Wishing Well)." Distinctive suites and rooms, many with fireplaces. American/Continental cuisine served fireside. In season, choose the garden with its waterfalls and trout pond. Three miles from galleries, theaters, and antiquing in Lambertville-New Hope.

Hosts: Andrew McDermott & Bruce Monti
Rooms: 11 (PB) $60-130
Continental Breakfast
Credit Cards: A, B, C
Closed Christmas
Notes: 3, 4, 5, 7, 9, 10, 12, 13

Woolverton Inn

6 Woolverton Road
Stockton, NJ, 08559
(609) 397-0802

A 10-acre estate with formal gardens, stately trees, and an elegant stone colonial Victorian manor house. Thirteen antique-filled rooms offer privacy with convenient access to many activities. We offer croquet, horseshoes, or bicycling. Museums, shopping, antiques, water sports, and golf are nearby.

Host: Louise Warsaw
Rooms: 13 (3 PB; 10 SB) $66-165
Full Breakfast
Credit Cards: A, B
Notes: 2, 5, 9, 10, 11, 12, 14

Whistling Swan Inn

New Mexico

ALBUQUERQUE

Adobe & Roses

1011 Ontega NW
Albuquerque, NM, 87114
(505) 898-0654

An adobe hacienda on 2 acres in Albuquerque's North Valley, featuring a casually elegant and spacious suite with private entrance, fireplace, piano, kitchen, big windows overlooking the gardens and horse pasture. Also a two-bedroom, two-bath adobe guest house. A quiet, romantic place to visit.

Host: Dorothy Morse
Rooms: 2 (1 PB; 1 SB) $50-100
Full Breakfast
Credit Cards: No
Notes: 2, 5, 6, 8, 9, 10, 12

B&B of New Mexico 402

P.O. Box 2805
Santa Fe, NM, 87504
(800) 648-0513

Beautiful, large, single-story adobe home with eighteen-inch-thick walls, brick floors, viga ceilings—very private. Surrounded by alfalfa fields, and yet close to Albuquerque. Children are welcome. Two rooms, private baths. $55.

Casa De Placitas

B&B Rocky Mountains
P.O. Box 804
Colorado Springs, CO, 80901
(719) 630-3422

Enjoy this unique passive solar adobe home with breathtaking views of the Sandia Mountains. King room features traditional Southwestern viga ceilings, brick floors, wood-burning stove, TV, and private Mexican tiled bath. Separate studio guest house is also available. Located in Placitas, twenty minutes north of Albuquerque. Full English breakfast. No children or pets. $40.

Trafalgar

B&B Rocky Mountains
P.O. Box 804
Colorado Springs, CO, 80901
(719) 630-3422

A touch of England in a home packed full of interesting English furnishings. One room with king bed, shared bath. Swimming pool. Near mountains and stables, close to golf, tennis, and hiking. No children or pets, please. $40.

W.E. Mauger Estate

701 Roma Avenue NW
Albuquerque, NM, 87102
(505) 242-8755

A wonderfully intimate restored Queen Anne residence whose high ceilings and rich brass appointments mark it singularly old-fashioned. We take great pride in offering comfortable Victorian accommodations for sixteen souls in a style reminiscent of an era when graciousness, thoughtfulness, and elegance were a way of life.

Hosts: Richard & Uta Carleno
Rooms: 6 (PB) $50-75

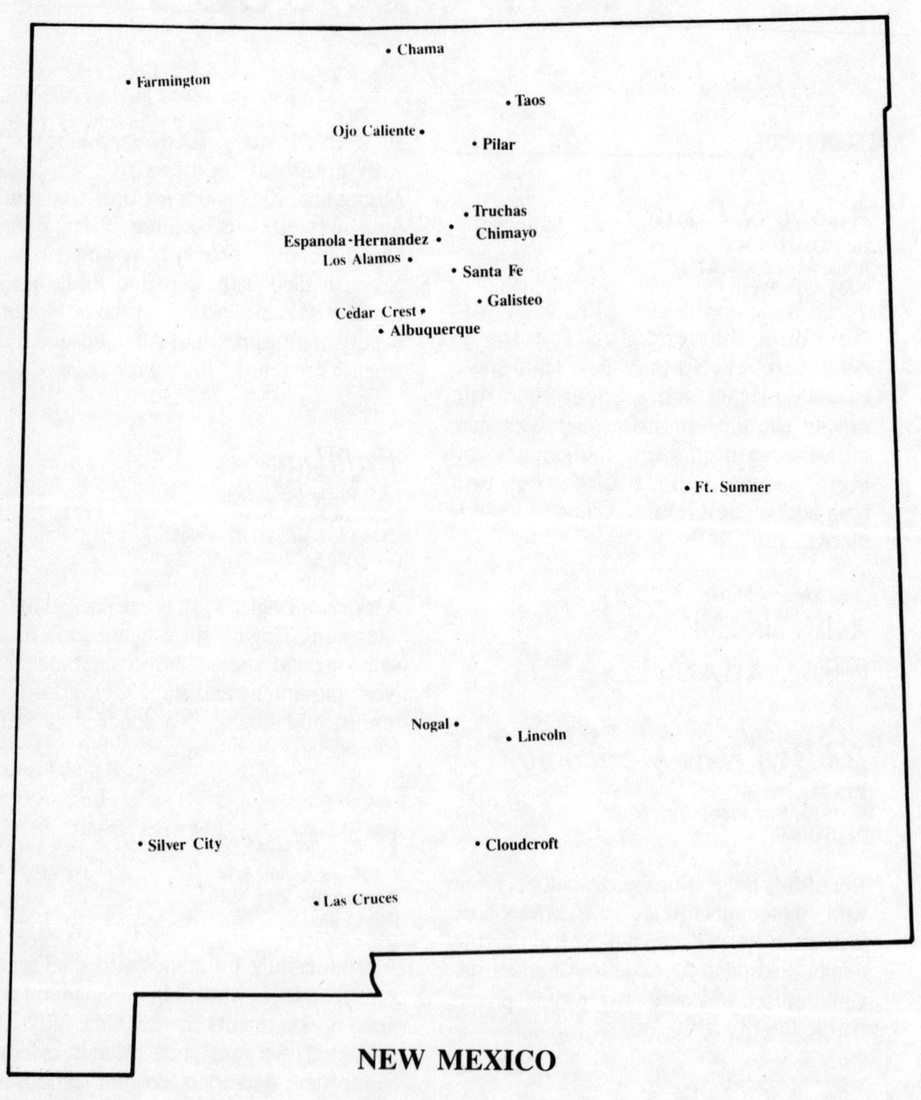

Chama
Farmington
Taos
Ojo Caliente
Pilar
Truchas
Chimayo
Espanola-Hernandez
Los Alamos
Santa Fe
Galisteo
Cedar Crest
Albuquerque
Ft. Sumner
Nogal
Lincoln
Silver City
Cloudcroft
Las Cruces
NEW MEXICO

Continental-plus Breakfast
Credit Cards: A, B, C, E, F
Notes: 2, 5, 6 (call), 7 (restricted), 8, 9, 10, 11, 12, 13, 14

CEDAR CREST

The Apple Tree

12050 Highway 14 N
P.O. Box 287
Cedar Crest, NM, 87008
(505) 281-3597

Authentic adobe casita with rustic brick floors, log-beamed ceiling, and kiva fireplace. Sleeps up to four. Seven miles from Albuquerque in the Sandia Mountains on the Turquoise Trail Scenic Byway (NM 14 North). Nearby: pueblo ruins, galleries, museums, hiking, skiing, horseback riding, rock climbing. Self-catered full breakfast brought to casita.

Hosts: Norma & Garland Curry
Rooms: 2 (PB) $65-95
Full Breakfast
Credit Cards: No
Notes: 2, 5, 6 (inquire), 7 (outside), 8, 9, 10, 11, 12, 13, 14

CHAMA

Historic Chama Adobe

B&B Rocky Mountains 132
P.O. Box 804
Colorado Springs, CO, 80901
(719) 630-3422

Just a few miles south of Chama, in northern New Mexico, near the Colorado border. This adobe dwelling dates back to 1869 and is located in the village of Brazos, with a view of the El Choro waterfall. One suite and six double rooms, three with private baths, one with balcony, one with fireplace. Dining room, two sitting rooms, den with TV, courtyard, water well, and flowers. Cross-country skiing, hunting, and fishing nearby. Wheelchair access. Full breakfast, restricted smoking. $53-63.

CHIMAYÓ

La Posada De Chimayó

Box 463
Chimayó, NM, 87522
(505) 351-4605

A cozy, comfortable adobe inn in a traditional northern New Mexico village famous for its tradition of fine Spanish weaving and its beautiful old church, El Santuario. Thirty miles north of Santa Fe on the High Road to Taos.

Host: Sue Farrington
Suites: (sitting room, bed, bath) $75-85
Full Breakfast
Minimum stay holidays: 2-4
Credit Cards: A, B
Notes: 2, 5, 6 (with advance notice), 8 (over 12), 9

CLOUDCROFT

B&B of New Mexico 504

P.O. Box 2805
Santa Fe, NM, 87504
(800) 648-0513

Large, comfortable log cabin in the Sacramento Mountains, close to Alamogordo, the Space Museum, and White Sands National Park. Within ten miles of local skiing, hunting, and fishing. Beautiful tall pine trees—quiet and cozy. Five rooms shared baths, full breakfast. $50-65.

The Pavilion at The Lodge

1 Corona Place
Cloudcroft, NM, 88317
(800) 842-4216; (505) 682-2566

Nestled in the pines at 9,200 feet in New Mexico's southern Rockies. Restored, historic lodge with eleven charmingly rustic rooms and suites: knotty-pine walls, down-stuffed comforters, and stone-laid fireplaces. Guests can enjoy all main Lodge amenities and facilities: golf course, swimming pool, beautiful dining room with Tiffany windows.

Hosts: Jerry & Carole Sanders
Rooms: 11 (PB) $49.95-150
Continental Breakfast
Credit Cards: A, B, C, D, E
Notes: 2, 3, 4, 5, 8, 9, 10, 11, 12, 13, 14

ESPANOLA

B&B of New Mexico 260

P.O. Box 2805
Santa Fe, NM, 87504
(800) 648-0513

This simply elegant adobe casita is nestled in the pine cliffs of northern New Mexico. It is filled with local handmade crafts and furniture. High beamed ceiling, Talavera tile, pine floors, and a fireplace in the bedroom. The sleeping arrangements can be either a king bed or two twins. Located near Espanola, halfway between Santa Fe and Taos, within a short walk of the Chama River. The room is detached from the main house for privacy; full breakfast is served. $70.

La Puebla House

Route 3, Box 172A
Espanola, NM, 87532
(505) 753-3981

Opened in 1981, this traditional adobe with flagstone floors, vigas, and latillas, is a lovely country setting from which to explore the many attractions of northern New Mexico. Nearby are Indian pueblos and ruins, the Santa Fe opera, and the many attractions of Santa Fe, Taos, Abiquiu, and the Espanola Valley.

Host: Elvira Bain
Rooms: 6 (SB) $45
Continental Breakfast
Credit Cards: A, B
Notes: 2, 5, 6 (outside), 8, 9

FARMINGTON

B&B of New Mexico 601

P.O. Box 2805
Santa Fe, NM, 87504
(800) 648-0513

Built in traditional northern New Mexico adobe, situated on the cliffside confluence of the San Juan and La Plate rivers, on the outskirts of Farmington. The newly constructed B&B suite consists of a bedroom with queen bed, living/dining room with two twin daybeds, bath with Mexican tile shower, kitchen, and hot tub. $65.

FT. SUMNER

B&B of New Mexico 301

P.O. Box 2805
Santa Fe, NM, 87504
(800) 648-0513

This small guest house has two rooms that can accommodate up to four people who share a bath. Located near Ft. Sumner, by the ghost town of Taiban, in Billy the Kid country. As a special treat, your hostess will grill a lamb for your dinner ($10/person extra), with tortillas and vegetables (reservations necessary). $60-90.

GALISTEO

The Galisteo Inn

Box 4, Galisteo, NM, 87540
(505) 982-1506

Visit our 240-year-old adobe hacienda in the beautiful countryside of northern New Mexico twenty-three miles southeast of Santa Fe; enjoy our hot tub, sauna, pool, bicycles, and horseback riding. Our dinners feature creative Southwestern cuisine nightly except for Monday and Tuesday. Reservations required.

Hosts: Joanna Kaufman & Wayne Agrniokoski
Rooms: 11 (7 PB; 2 SB) $60-150
Continental Breakfast
Credit Cards: A, B
Notes: 2, 4, 5, 9, 11

HERNANDEZ

Casa del Rio

Box 92
Hernandez, NM, 87532
(505) 753-2035

Casa del Rio is a private adobe guest house furnished with local handmade furniture and crafts, plus a beautiful Kiva fireplace. Set amid the pink cliffs of northern New Mexico, we are within a half hour of Santa Fe, Taos, and Los Alamos.

Hosts: Eileen & Mel Vigil
Rooms: 1 (PB) $70-80
Full Breakfast
Credit Cards: A, B, E
Notes: 2, 5, 6 (outside), 7 (limited), 8 (under 3), 9, 11, 13, 14

LAS CRUCES

Lundeen Inn of the Arts

618 South Alameda Blvd.
Las Cruces, NM, 88005
(505) 526-3327

The Inn of the Arts offers gracious hacienda living in a historic Mexican/Territorial adobe home. Works of fine art are provided by the adjoining Linda Lundeen Gallery. Each of the fifteen rooms (named after famous artists) displays original paintings and prints. A peaceful environment for an elegant, artistic retreat.

Hosts: Jerry & Linda Lundeen
Rooms: 15 (PB) $45-85
Full Breakfast weekends; continental weekdays
Credit Cards: A, B, C
Notes: 2, 5, 9, 10, 11, 12, 14

LINCOLN

B&B of New Mexico 505

P.O. Box 2805
Santa Fe, NM, 87504
(800) 648-0513

The most beautiful and unique home in this area, located on 2.2 acres on the Rio Bonito in historic Old Lincoln Town. The owner has bucks, peacocks, peahens, quail, pigeons, dogs, and cats, plus 350 feet of river frontage. The indoor garden simply must be seen to be believed! Two rooms with queen beds share a bath and a powder room down the hall. Just twelve miles from Ruidoso airport. Cats and dogs welcome. $50.

LOS ALAMOS

Casa del Rey

305 Rover Street
Los Alamos, NM, 87544
(505) 672-9401

Quiet residential area, friendly atmosphere. Located in White Rock, minutes from Los Alamos and forty minutes from Santa Fe. Excellent recreational facilities and restaurants nearby. The area is rich in Indian and Spanish history. Breakfast features homemade granola and breads served on the sun porch overlooking flower gardens and views of the mountains.

Host: Virginia King
Rooms: 2 (SB) $30
Continental-plus Breakfast
Credit Cards: No
Notes: 2, 5, 8 (8 and over), 9, 10, 11, 12, 13

NOGAL

Monjeau Shadows Country Inn

Bonito Route
Nogal, NM, 88341
(505) 336-4191

A charming Victorian farmhouse built in the 1980s, with each room decorated in antiques for the restful comforts of home. Near national forests with fishing, hiking, and skiing. Located on wooded acreage with formal flower gardens. Billy the Kid Country, just a few miles from the home of the world's richest horse race.

Hosts: Carolyn & Jim Cantrell
Rooms: 4 (PB) $50-80
Continental Breakfast
Credit Cards: A, B
Notes: 2, 4, 5, 7, 8, 9, 10, 11, 12, 13, 14

OJO CALIAENTE

B&B of New Mexico 270

P.O. Box 2805
Santa Fe, NM, 87504
(800) 648-0513

One hour from Santa Fe and forty minutes from Taos, Ojo Caliente is within easy reach of most of northern New Mexico's diverse cultural opportunities. Enjoy a hot soak and massage at the mineral springs just a four-minute walk away, or take guided horseback rides and pack trips. A very quiet, peaceful place. Each room has a bath with shower; some have kitchenettes. Continental breakfast. $26-32.

PILAR (NEAR TAOS)

The Plum Tree

Box 1-A
Pilar, NM, 87531
(800) 678-7586

Located in Pilar — a centuries-old village along the banks of the Rio Grande — between the cultural centers of Taos (15 mi.) and Santa Fe (50 mi.). Hike along the river in the Rio Grande Gorge or the mountains of Sangre de Cristo. We are centrally located for going to Indian Pueblos or natural hot springs. Join us for summer fine arts workshops, fall nature studies, and winter cross-country skiing and snow picnics.

Host: Dick Thibodeau
Rooms: 5 (3 PB; 2 SB) $22-45
Continental Breakfast
Credit Cards: A, B
Notes: 2, 5, 8, 9, 11, 13, 14

SANTA FE

Alexander's Inn

529 East Palace
Santa Fe, NM, 87501
(505) 986-1431

For a cozy, romantic stay in Santa Fe, nestle into a B&B featuring the best of American country charm. Located in a lovely residential neighborhood on the town's historic east side, the inn is within walking distance of the downtown plaza and Canyon Road. Afternoon tea and homemade cookies are served.

Host: Carolyn Delecluse & Mary Jo Schneider
Rooms: 5 (3 PB; 2 SB) $70-110
Continental-plus Breakfast
Credit Cards: A, B
Notes: 2, 5, 8 (6 and over), 9, 10, 11, 12, 13, 14

B&B of New Mexico 101

P.O. Box 2805
Santa Fe, NM, 87504
(800) 648-0513

Private residence with two rooms, one with queen bed and private bath, the other with twin beds and private bath. Both have their own telephone. The house is ideally located four blocks from downtown Santa Fe, close to galleries, shops, and museums, just fourteen miles from Santa Fe Ski Basin. One block from the municipal pool, sports complex, and tennis courts. $55-70.

B&B of New Mexico 104

P.O. Box 2805
Santa Fe, NM, 87504
(800) 648-0513

Large two-story home with a Spanish tile roof in the foothills of the Sangre de Cristo mountains. The master bedroom has a king waterbed, fireplace, sitting area, refrigerator, and private bath. A second room has a queen bed and shares a bath across the hall with a twin room. There is a pool table for guest use and an outside dog. $45-70.

B&B of New Mexico 105

P.O. Box 2805
Santa Fe, NM, 87504
(800) 648-0513

Beautiful two-story home within two miles of the plaza. Large downstairs room with queen bed, refrigerator, private bath. Twin upstairs room with private 3/4 bath. Breakfast upstairs in the dining room with a view of the hills. The living room has views of the Sangre de Cristo mountains, beamed ceiling, and kiva fireplace. $50-65.

B&B of New Mexico 106

P.O. Box 2805
Santa Fe, NM, 87504
(800) 648-0513

Beautiful home on the north side of town on top of a hill with 360-degree views. Large living room with beamed ceiling and fireplace. Nice bedroom with king bed, private bath with Mexican tile. Small bedroom with double bed has a woven rug and doll collection. Hot tub. Smoking allowed, as the owner smokes; resident pets. $60-135.

B&B of New Mexico 110

P.O. Box 2805
Santa Fe, NM, 87504
(800) 648-0513

Beautiful pueblo-style home in the foothills of the Sangre de Cristo Mountains. Gorgeous sunsets and views of the city lights at night. Jogging trails in back of the home. Very quiet; fifteen minutes to ski basin, ten to the plaza. Patio for sunning. The living room and dining room have high beamed ceilings with fireplace. the master bedroom has a king bed, dressing area, walk-in closet, private bath, and views of the foothills. A small room has twin beds and private bath. Resident cat. $55-65.

B&B of New Mexico 119

P.O. Box 2805
Santa Fe, NM, 87504
(800) 648-0513

This lovely old adobe used to be the Santa Fe Meat & Livestock headquarters (c. 1867-1890). Located in the heart of the historic district, five blocks from the plaza and one block south of Canyon Road. Parts of the home are believed to be dated prior to 1846. All of the outside and some of the inside walls are made of adobe—in some cases, thirty inches thick. The ceiling of the living room has six inches of dirt on tip, in spite of the pitched roof. The bunkhouse can sleep four in two queens sharing a bath. Queen bed and private bath in the main house. $60-70.

B&B of New Mexico 127

P.O. Box 2805
Santa Fe, NM, 87504
(800) 648-0513

Beautiful, spacious adobe-style home in fashionable northeast Santa Fe, only 1.25 miles from downtown. Situated on a ridge above the city, this home offers a lovely view, spectacular sunsets, and a walled backyard. Extensive decks; kiva fireplacc; bcamed ceiling in the den. Glass-enclosed hot tub. King room with private bath, and a twin room with private bath. $55-70.

B&B of New Mexico 128

P.O. Box 2805
Santa Fe, NM, 87504
(800) 648-0513

This is a delightful home on the east side of town only a half block from Canyon Road and within walking distance of town. Hardwood floors, sun porch, cable TV. There are two rooms to choose from, a master with queen bed and private bath, and a second with a full bed with private 3/4 bed. Resident cat is not allowed in the guest rooms. $55-70.

B&B of New Mexico 132

P.O. Box 2805
Santa Fe, NM, 87504
(800) 648-0513

Peaceful, artistic atmosphere with an eclectic mix of antiques, contemporary, and Southwest. Rough sawn and beamed ceilings. Patio for sunning, great views of the Sangre de Cristo and Jemez Mountains, sunsets, and city lights. Two kiva fireplaces, telephone, TV, antique bedroom with large private bath across hall. $55.

B&B Scottsdale & The West 108

P.O. Box 3999
Prescott, AZ, 86302
(602) 776-1102

An Adobe dwelling on the east side, within walking distance of galleries and the historic Plaza. Private baths, full breakfast, private entrance, fireplace. $85-125.

Casa De La Cuma B&B

105 Paseo De La Cuma
Santa Fe, NM, 87501
(505) 983-1717

Located on a hill with mountain views, we are close to the downtown plaza, shopping, restaurants, galleries, and museums. City sports facility across the street. A special continental breakfast awaits our guests in the sun room or the patio. A fireplace is in the guests' common room. Enjoy our Southwest sunsets, too. Bienvenidos!

Hosts: Norma & Al Tell
Singles: 1 (PB) $100
Rooms: 3 (1 PB; 2 SB) $75
Suite: $135
Continental-plus Breakfast
Credit Cards: No
Closed Dec. 15-Jan. 31
Notes: 2, 8 (12 and over), 9, 10, 11, 12, 13, 14

Dunshee's

986 Acequia Madre
Santa Fe, NM, 87501
(505) 982-0988

A romantic adobe getaway in the historic east side, about a mile from the plaza. Your suite includes a living room and bedroom with Kiva fireplaces, antiques, folk art, fresh flowers, homemade cookies, refrigerator, private bath, and patio. Gourmet breakfast. Brochure available.

Host: Susan Dunshee
Rooms: 1 (PB) $88-99
Full Breakfast
Minimum stay weekends & holidays: 2
Credit Cards: A, B
Closed Christmas
Notes: 2, 8, 9

El Paradero

200 West Manhattan
Santa Fe, NM, 87501
(505) 988-1177

Just a short walk from the busy plaza, this 200-year-old Spanish farmhouse was restored as a charming twelve-room Southwestern inn. Enjoy a full gourmet breakfast, caring service, and a relaxed friendly atmosphere. The inn offers lots of common space, and a patio for afternoon tea and snacks.

Hosts: Thom Allen & Onida MacGregor
Rooms: 14 (10 PB; 4 SB) $38-95
Full Breakfast
Credit Cards: No
Notes: 2, 5, 6, 8 (over 4), 9, 10, 11, 12, 13 (17 mi.), 14

Enchanting Inn

B&B Rocky Mountains 146
P.O. Box 804
Colorado Springs, CO, 80901
(719) 630-3422

This delightful inn is located two blocks from the Plaza. There are 38 rooms, all with a Southwest character, TV, refreshments. Continental breakfast; children welcome; restricted smoking. $105-180. Children under twelve free.

European-Santa Fe Mix

B&B Rocky Mountains 124
P.O. Box 804
Colorado Springs, CO, 80901
(719) 630-3422

This European-style B&B inn has authentic Southwestern charm. Two guest rooms in the main house, one with double brass bed and the other a queen four-poster. Private baths feature oversized showers. Shared guest living room with TV, fireplace. A twin detached guest house features its own brick patio. Resident cat. Full breakfast, complimentary fruit, sherry, cookies. Children ten and over are welcome; smoking is permitted. $75-90.

Grant Corner Inn

122 Grant Avenue
Santa Fe, NM, 87501
(505) 983-6678

An exquisite colonial manor home in downtown Santa Fe with an ideal location just two blocks from the historic plaza, the inn nestles among intriguing shops, restaurants, and galleries. Each room is appointed with antiques and treasures from around the world: antique quilts, brass and four-poster beds, armoires, and art work. Private phones, cable television, and ceiling fans. Complimentary wine is served in the evening.

Hosts: Louise Stewart & Pat Walter
Singles: 2 (1 PB; 2 SB) $50-60
Rooms: 13 (7 PB; 6 SB) $50-125
Full Breakfast
Credit Cards: A, B
Closed January
Notes: 2, 7, 8, 10, 11, 12, 13

Grant Corner Inn

Historic Hacienda

B&B Rocky Mountains 144
P.O. Box 804
Colorado Springs, CO, 80901
(719) 630-3422

Lots of land, beautiful view. This unique B&B invites you to come and share 380 years of history. It features two authentic adobe guest houses, one with the traditional Indian-made fireplace, handmade furniture, and the work of local artists. The second building features two rooms with private baths. Continental breakfast is brought to each house. Children twelve and over are welcome, and smoking is permitted. $65-75.

Inn on the Alameda

303 East Alameda
Santa Fe, NM, 87501
(505) 984-2121

This delightful 38-room European-style small hotel is a stone's throw from Canyon Road and the Plaza. Hancrafted rooms, splendid breakfast buffet, and intimate library with fireplace and full-service bar.

Host: Gil Martinez
Rooms: 38 (PB) $135-240
Continental Breakfast
Credit Cards: A, B, C, E, F
Notes: 2, 5, 6, 7, 8, 9, 10, 11, 12, 14

Intimate Santa Fe Casitas

B&B Rocky Mountains 111
P.O. Box 804
Colorado Springs, CO, 80901
(719) 630-3422

This B&B features a casita for two and a suite with two bedrooms and small kitchen, both surrounded by a quiet patio that lies behind adobe walls. The suite has a queen bed and fireplace. The casita has a queen bed, wood-burning stove, and private bath. Continental breakfast. No smoking or pets. $85-165.

Preston House

Preston House

106 Faithway Street
Santa Fe, NM, 87501
(505) 982-3465

Located downtown in a quiet garden setting, where guests may enjoy breakfast and afternoon tea on the flagstone patio among blooming lilacs or by the glowing pinon fire in the parlor. Antiques, stained-glass windows, fresh-baked breads, and personalized service complete the Preston House experience.

Host: Signe Bergman
Rooms: 15 (13 PB; 2 SB) $45-125
Continental Breakfast
Credit Cards: A, B, C
Notes: 2, 5, 8 (6 and over), 9, 10, 11, 12, 13, 14

Southwestern Casita

B&B Rocky Mountains 112
P.O. Box 804
Colorado Springs, CO, 80901
(719) 630-3422

A handsome one-room adobe guest house nestled in northern New Mexico. King bed, fireplace, Mexican tiled private bath. Arabian horses on the premises, and horse boarding is available. Full breakfast is served in the main house. No smoking, no pets, children with approval. $70.

Sunset House

436 Sunset
Santa Fe, NM, 87501
(505) 983-3523

Pueblo-style home located four blocks from downtown, close to galleries, shops, museums. The ambience is focused on warmth and friendliness in an artistic atmosphere of quiet and mountain views.

Hosts: Jack & Gloria Bennett
Rooms: 2 (PB) $55-70
Continental Breakfast
Credit Cards: A, B, C
Notes: 2, 5, 9, 10, 11, 12, 14

NOTES: Credit cards accepted: A Master Card; B Visa; C American Express; D Discover Card; E Diners Club; F Other: 2 Personal checks accepted: 3 Lunch available: 4 Dinner available: 5 Open all year

SILVER CITY

Bear Mountain Guest Ranch

Box 1163
Silver City, NM, 88062
(505) 538-2538

Two-story ranch house, two cottages, five-bedroom house available for guests. Elevation 6250 feet; air-conditioning unnecessary. Pinyon-juniper area. Ranch features home cooking, Lodge and Learn programs (6 days, 5 nights), tours for birdwatching, wild plant identification, ghost towns, archaeological sites, and prehistoric primitive pottery workshops. Rate includes breakfast, sack lunch, and dinner.

Host: Myra B. McCormick
Rooms: 16 (PB) $84.50
Credit Cards: No
Notes: 2, 3, 4, 5, 6, 7 (limited), 8, 9, 12, 14

TAOS

American Artists Gallery House

P.O. Box 584
Taos, NM, 87571
(505) 758-4446

Charming Southwestern hacienda filled with artwork by American artists. Adobe fireplaces, private baths, outdoor hot tub, and gardens. Magnificent view of mountains. Minutes from art galleries, museums, restaurants, St. Francis Assisi Church, and ski valley. Our home is your home with live-in guides. We enjoy visiting and will share our knowledge of the area.

Hosts: Benjamin & Myra Carp
Rooms: 5 (PB) $60-85
Full Breakfast
Credit Cards: No
Notes: 2, 5, 8, 9, 10, 11, 12, 13, 14

B&B of New Mexico 201

P.O. Box 2805
Santa Fe, NM, 87504
(800) 648-0513

Each room in this charming home features a kiva fireplace, private bath, private entrance, magnificent view of Taos mountains. There is a living room with fireplace, dining room and sun porch, all with beamed ceilings. You will enjoy the bricked portico, side gardens, and rear redwood deck with outdoor hot tub. A full breakfast is served. Four rooms. $55-80.

B&B of New Mexico 205

P.O. Box 2805
Santa Fe, NM, 87504
(800) 648-0513

Mountains and sagebrush delight the eye from this unique artist's home. Only three miles to the Taos Plaza. Choose from two rooms, one with a private bath and separate entrance, the other with an antique spindle bed, shared bath, and hand-sewn quilts. Both rooms have breathtaking views. $44-60.

The Brooks Street Inn

119 Brooks Street
Box 4954
Taos, NM, 87571
(505) 758-1489

Selected as one of the ten best inns of North America for 1988 by *Country Inns* magazine, we're casual, fun, and just a short walk from the plaza. Our rambling main house and charming guest house feature fireplaces, reading nooks, and private baths.

Hosts: Susan Stevens & John Testore
Rooms: 6 (PB) $65.47-98.21
Continental Breakfast
Credit Cards: A, B, C
Notes: 2, 5, 8 (over 5), 9, 13, 14

Hacienda del Sol

109 Mabel Dodge Lane
Box 177
Taos, NM, 87571
(505) 758-0287

Once part of art patroness Mabel Dodge Luhan's estate, this spacious adobe adjoins 95,000 acres of Taos Pueblo Indian Land, providing a majestic view of Taos Mountain. Just north of Taos Plaza. Most rooms feature kiva fireplaces and private baths.

Hosts: Carol & Randy Pelton
Rooms: 7 (5 PB; 2 SB) $54.69-120.18
Continental Breakfast
Credit Cards: A, B
Notes: 2, 5, 8, 9, 10, 11, 13, 14

Historic Adobe

B&B Rocky Mountains 153
P.O. Box 804
Colorado Springs, CO, 80901
(719) 630-3422

This charming adobe inn is located in the heart of the historic area. Each room has a private bath and TV; five have traditional fireplaces; one has a loft that sleeps four and a hot tub. Continental-plus breakfast served on the flower-filled patio in the summer or by the fireplace in the winter. $45-75.

La Posada de Taos

309 Juanita Lane
Box 1118
Taos, NM, 87571
(505) 758-8164

La Posada de Taos offers guests modern comforts in a provincial adobe inn with an atmosphere of friendliness that truly makes the word *guest* valid. The hospitality is highly personal, unique, and will bring you back to Taos again.

Host: Sue Smoot
Rooms: 5 (PB) $55-94
Full Breakfast
Minimum stay May-Oct. weekends: 2 ; holidays: 3
Credit Cards: No
Notes: 2, 5, 6, 7, 8, 9, 10, 12, 13, 14

Mabel Dodge Luhan House

Box 3400
Taos, NM, 87571
(505) 758-9456

A national and state historic site on 5 acres bordered by the Taos Pueblo Reservation on the north and east and well within walking distance of town. The house is sequestered behind an adobe wall whose gates are part of the original St. Francis Church in Ranchos de Taos. Huge cottonwood, beech, and elm trees shade the house and flagstone placita. All main rooms have ceilings of viga and latia construction, arched Pueblo-style doorways and fireplaces, hand-carved doors, and dark hardwood floors.

Host: Kitty Otero
Rooms: 18 (12 PB; 6 SB) $55-125
Full Breakfast
Credit Cards: A, B
Notes: 2, 3, 5, 6, 7 (limited), 8, 9, 10, 11, 12, 13

Sagebrush Inn

B&B Rocky Mountains 128
P.O. Box 804
Colorado Springs, CO, 80901
(719) 630-3422

This is a two-story adobe home in a quiet rural area just outside Taos. Enjoy 360-degree views of mountains, sunsets, rainbows, and stars. Large guest room has separate entrance, private bath, queen bed and two singles. A small second room has a double bed and shared bath. Families welcome, no pets. $44-60.

Salsa Del Salto B&B

P.O. Box 453
El Prado, NM, 87529
(505) 776-2422

Salsa del Salto is perfectly located between Taos and the world-famous Taos Ski Valley.

Our rooms are elegant, each with a king bed and full bath. To complete the setting, we have an outdoor hot tub, swimming pool, and tennis courts. We serve a full gourmet breakfast each morning.

Hosts: Mary Hockett & Dadou Mayer
Rooms: 6 (PB) $95-160
Full Breakfast
Credit Cards: A, B
Notes: 2, 5, 8, 9, 10, 11, 13, 14

Unique Retreat

B&B Rocky Mountains 46
P.O. Box 804
Colorado Springs, CO, 80901
(719) 630-3422

This two-bedroom suite includes a large living room, high viga ceiling, Persian rug, artwork, wood stove, and color cable TV. There is an enclosed sun room off the king room on the second floor. This room also has a kiva fireplace. The second room, downstairs, has a double bed. Located three blocks from La Loma Plaza. Gourmet breakfast. $80.

Whistling Waters

Talpa Route, Box 9
Ranchos de Taos, NM, 87557
(505) 758-7798

Old adobe hacienda and furniture/pottery gallery. Two courtyards, cottonwoods, stream, six fireplaces, vigas, arched doorways. Furnished in early Southwest-primitive antiques. Located in old, quiet Spanish community at the edge of Taos, with mountain views. Skiing, hunting, fishing near.

Hosts: Al & Jo Hutson
Rooms: 4 (PB) $45-75
Full Breakfast
Minimum stay holidays: 3
Credit Cards: No
Notes: 2, 5, 8 (over 10), 9, 10, 11, 12, 13, 14

The Willows Inn

P. O. Box 4558
Taos, NM, 87571
(505) 758-2558

We have two of the largest and oldest willows in North America. The former home and studio of E. Martin Hennings, member of the Taos Society of Artists. On the state historical registry. Near Taos Pueblo, Taos Ski Valley, Angel Fire, Eagle Nest, and Santa Fe.

Hosts: George Van de Kerckhove & Estella Enriquez
Rooms: 5 (PB) $75-120
Full Breakfast
Credit Cards: A, B
Notes: 2, 3 (on request), 4 (on request), 5, 7, 8, 9, 10, 11

TRUCHAS

Rancho Arriba

Box 338
Truchas, NM, 87578
(505) 689-2374

A European-style B&B with an informal and tranquil atmosphere. This traditional adobe hacienda is located on an historic Spanish land grant. Spectacular mountain view in every direction, amid colonial villages featuring traditional arts and architecture. Adobe churches, hand weaving, wood carving, quilting.

Host: Curtiss Frank
Rooms: 4 (SB) $35-50
Full Breakfast
Credit Cards: No
Notes: 2, 4, 5, 7 (outside), 8, 9, 13

NEW YORK
Ogdensburg
Niagara Falls
Lewiston
Watertown
Lake Placid
Elizabethtown
North Hudson
Crown Point
North River
Ticonderoga
Chestertown
Wevertown
Turin
Sandy Creek
Lake Pleasant
Bolton Landing
Warrensburg
Lake Luzerne
Queensbury
Penfield
Sodus Point
Sodus
Palmyra
Olcott Harbor
Youngstown
Queenston
Lockport
Buffalo
East Aurora
Colden
Syracuse
Jamesville
Fulton
LaFayette
Cazenovia
Durhamville
Vernon
Rome
Chittenango
Alder Creek
Dolgeville
Herkimer
Mumford
Avon
Canandaigua
Geneva
Waterloo
Geneseo
Penn Yan
Naples
Nunda
Canaseraga
Hammondsport
Gowanda
Westfield
Mayville
Chautauqua
Little Valley
Alfred
Corning
Burdett
Trumansburg
Ithaca
Lansing
Homer
Dryden
Candor
Binghamton
Oxford
Bainbridge
Afton
Waterville
Brookfield
West Winfield
Mohawk
Richfield Springs
Cooperstown
Nelliston
Johnstown
Galway
Schuylerville
Saratoga Springs
Ballston Spa
Charlton
Schenectady
Troy
Albany
Cobleskill
Rensselaer
Howes Cave
Jefferson
Stillwater
Cambridge
Pittstown
Cherry Plains
Burnt Hills
Rexford
Berlin
Altamont
East Greenbush
Averill Park
Castleton on Hudson
Niverville
New Baltimore
Canaan
Cairo
Spencertown
Old Chatham
Philmont
Austerlitz
Ghent
Hillsdale
Claverack
Palenville
Craryville
Margaretville
Mt. Tremper
Germantown
Rhinebeck
Saugerties
Roscoe
Kingston
Red Hook
Hancock
De Bruce
Livingston Manor
Amenia
West Shokan
New Paltz
High Falls
Fosterdale
Clintondale
Dover Plains
Forestburgh
Middletown/Slate Hill
Cold Springs
Chappaqua
Garrison
Manhasset
Glen Cove
Stony Brook
Oldfield
East Hampton
Setauket
Southold
Northport
Port Jefferson
Shelter Island
Greenville
New Rochelle
Watermill
Amagansett
Westbury
Hampton Bays
Southampton
New York
Westhampton Beach
East Islip
Sayville
Hempstead
Levittown
Long Beach
Massapequa

New York

AFTON

American Country Collection 88

984 Gloucester Place
Schenectady, NY, 12309
(518) 370-4948

This imposing 200-year-old pillared colonial is situated on over 6 parklike acres of riverfront property. A massive forty-foot common room serves as the breakfast room. Take a dip in the river, unwind in the Jacuzzi, or just relax and enjoy the view from the patio courtyard. Located twenty miles from Binghampton and twenty-five from Oneonta. A first-floor suite has a canopy bed and sofabed, working fireplace, private bath, private entrance, and patio. Three second-floor rooms share a first-floor bath. Smoking is permitted; children are welcome; breakfast buffet. $40-58.

ALBANY

American Country Collection 8

984 Gloucester Place
Schenectady, NY, 12309
(518) 370-4948

An antique-filled 1760 Dutch farmhouse just fifteen miles southwest of downtown Albany, set on 10 acres of woods with two streams and an old graveyard. Summer guests are welcome to use the in-ground pool. One two-bedroom guest suite on the second floor with private bath, woodstove, and air conditioning, as well as TV. Restricted smoking; children welcome; resident cat. $60.

American Country Collection 36

984 Gloucester Place
Schenectady, NY, 12309
(518) 370-4948

A fifty-year-old colonial in a quiet residential neighborhood just four miles north of the center of Albany. The separate guest wing contains two guest rooms, a guest bath, and a sitting room with TV. No smoking; infants and children over twelve welcome; full breakfast on weekends and continental-plus on weekdays. $55-60.

ALDER CREEK

Alder Creek Golf Club & Country Inn

B&B Connection NY
RD 1, Box 325
Vernon, NY, 13476
(315) 829-4888

This charming colonial gentleman's estate is located twenty miles north of Utica. Nautical antiques and ship models set a relaxed mood. Guests are invited to share their musical talents on the Steinway grand piano. A nine-hole golf course offers a challenging round with clubs, carts, and professional lessons available. Nearby lakes and streams offer outdoor recreation. $45-125.

ALFRED

Hitchcock House

15 South Main Street
Alfred, NY, 14802
(607) 587-9102

In the heart of Alfred's village historic district, Hitchcock House was built in 1932. Just a short walk from the many activities on the campuses of Alfred University and Alfred State College, Hitchcock House offers guests an opportunity to capture the distinctive character of the small upstate NY community.

Hosts: June & Bob Hitchcock
Rooms: 3 (1 PB; 2 SB) $40-48
Full Breakfast
Credit Cards: No
Notes: 2, 5, 7, 8, 9, 10, 11, 12, 13

Hitchcock House

Saxon Inn

One Park Street
Alfred, NY, 14802
(607) 871-2600

Twenty elegantly appointed guest rooms and six suites with working fireplaces. Richly furnished in deluxe cherry woods with a colonial style. Complimentary European breakfast in our fireside hospitality room; afternoon high tea. Nonsmoking rooms are available; handicapped accessible.

Host: Robert Nixon
Rooms: 26 (PB) $69-79
Continental Breakfast
Credit Cards: A, B, C, D, E
Notes: 2, 5, 7 (restricted), 8, 10, 11, 14

ALTAMONT

American Country Collection 20

984 Gloucester Place
Schenectady, NY, 12309
(518) 370-4948

This impressive home was built in 1765 and served as a tavern during colonial days. Wide-plank floors, crackling fires in mammoth fireplaces, antiques, clawfoot tubs, period wallpapers. Located at the base of the Helderburg Mountains on six acres of ground with a tennis court, gazebo, large barns, and flowing brook. Four guest rooms share two baths. Restricted smoking; children welcome; resident pets. $50-60.

American Country Collection 45

984 Gloucester Place
Schenectady, NY, 12309
(518) 370-4948

This 75-year-old refurbished colonial is just twenty miles from Albany, situated well back from the road on 15 acres that include barns, a swimming pool, patio, and orchards. One third-floor guest suite has two bedrooms, living room, private bath. One single room on the second floor shares a bath with the owner. Smoking outdoors; resident pets; children welcome. $45.

AMAGANSETT

B & B of Long Island AD

P.O. Box 392
Old Westbury, NY, 11568
(516) 334-6231

This exquisite little cottage is one block from the ocean beach. Two bedrooms, one queen, one double, separated by the bath. Kitchen with refrigerator, sink, electric coffee pot, and dining area. Step out of the house and into a swimming pool. Hosts have their own home adjacent to cottage and leave a sumptuous continental breakfast for you to enjoy at your leisure. Additional rooms also available in the hosts' home. $115.

AMENIA

Troutbeck

Box 26, Leedoville Road
Amenia, NY, 12501
(914) 373-9681

Troutbeck is a world-class country inn with a regional four-star rating for its cuisine. Indoor (covered and heated) and outdoor pools, tennis courts, 442 acres, and a reputation for relaxed, attentive service. Just 2.25 hours from midtown New York City. Open only on weekends. Room rate includes all meals and open bar from Friday evening to Sunday, 2:00 P.M.

Hosts: Jim Flaherty & Kathy Robinson
Rooms: 34 (PB) $575-790/couple
Full Breakfast Saturday; Continental on Sunday
Credit Cards: C
Closed Weekdays and Christmas weekend
Notes: 2, 3, 4, 7, 8 (over 12), 9, 10, 11, 12, 13

AUSTERLITZ

Pineapple Hospitality NY308

P.O. Box F821
New Bedford, MA, 02742-0821
(508) 990-1696

Located six miles from the NY Thruway, fifteen minutes from Tanglewood and other Berkshire attractions. The home is a ski chalet house with contemporary decor on 3 secluded acres of woodland. Cathedral ceilings, lots of windows and privacy. Two guest rooms with shared bath, private living room, wet bar. There is also a sleep sofa in the living room, so the whole floor could easily sleep six. $75-175.

AVERILL PARK

Ananas Hus B&B

Route 3, Box 301
Averill Park, NY, 12018
(518) 766-5035

The Tomlinsons' hillside ranch home, located in West Stephentown on thirty acres, offers a panoramic view of the Hudson River Valley, natural beauty, and tranquility, plus patio dining in summer and the warmth of a fireplace in winter. Skiing and culture abound in nearby western Mass. and the Capitol District of New York State.

Hosts: Thelma & Clyde Tomlinson
Rooms: 3 (SB) $42.80-53.50
Full Breakfast
Minimum stay weekend holidays: 2
Credit Cards: No
Closed Christmas Day
Notes: 2, 5, 8 (over 12), 9, 11, 12, 13

The Gregory House

Route 43, Box 401
Averill Park, NY, 12018
(518) 674-3774

A charming blend of old and new, this country inn is just minutes east of Albany. Four candlelit dining rooms offer gourmet dinners as well as your included continental breakfast. A common room with fireplace is available for socializing, and an in-ground pool and patio welcome visitors in the summer. Summer theater, mountain trails, golf, skiing, historic tours, and more are nearby.

Hosts: Bette & Bob Jewell
Rooms: 12 (PB) $60-80
Continental Breakfast
Credit Cards: A, B, C, E
Notes: 2, 4, 5, 7, 8 (over 6), 9, 10, 11, 12, 13, 14

AVON

Mulligan Farm B&B

5403 Barber Road
Avon, NY, 14414
(716) 226-6412

The house, barns, and farm are all listed on the National Register of Historic Places and overlook 1,200 acres of farmland along the Genesee River (*Genesee* is an Indian word meaning "pleasant valley"). A comfortable country atmosphere and rural hospitality await guests.

Hosts: Lesa & Jeff Mulligan
Rooms: 4 (2 PB; 2 SB) $50
Full Breakfast
Credit Cards: No
Notes: 2, 5, 11, 12, 14

BAINBRIDGE

Berry Hill Farm

B&B Connection NY
RD 1, Box 325
Vernon, NY, 13476
(315) 829-4888

Restored 1820s farmhouse on a hilltop surrounded by vegetable and flower gardens, with 180 acres for hiking, swimming, bird watching, berry picking, skating, cross-country skiing. The rooms are furnished with comfortable antiques. A ten-minute drive takes you to restaurants, golf, tennis, auctions, and antique centers. Cooperstown and several colleges—SUNY Binghamton, Cornell, Colgate, Ithaca—are only 45 minutes away. $45-125.

BALLSTON LAKE

American Country Collection 12

984 Gloucester Place
Schenectady, NY, 12309
(518) 370-4948

Early American artist William Bliss Baker chose this high outcrop of land, with its commanding view of the lake, for his summer home and studio in 1885. A separate entrance leads to the first-floor suite with bedroom, library, living room with fireplace, and private terrace. Ten miles from Saratoga; twenty to Albany. No smoking. European breakfast. $75-95.

BERLIN

The Sedgwick Inn

Route 22, Berlin, NY, 12022
(518) 658-2334

An historic colonial inn located on 12 acres in the scenic Taconic Valley, beautifully furnished with antiques. We are close to the Williamstown Theater, the Tanglewood Festival, other Berkshire attractions, and both downhill and cross-country skiing. We have a renowned restaurant and a small motel unit behind the main house.

Hosts: Robert & Edith Evans
Rooms: 10 (PB) $60-75
Suites: 1 (PB) $100
Full Breakfast
Credit Cards: A, B, C, E
Notes: 2, 3, 4, 5, 6 (motel only), 7, 8, (motel only), 9, 10, 11, 13

The Sedgwick Inn

BINGHAMTON

Pickle Hill B&B

B&B Connection NY
RD 1, Box 325
Vernon, NY, 13476
(315) 829-4888

From the natural woodwork and stained-glass windows to the rocking chairs on the front porch, Pickle Hill evokes the charm and simple pleasures of nineteenth-century living. There's a lounge for reading, listening to music, or playing board games. Within 1.5 hours are some of the historic, cultural, and scenic gems of upstate New York: Cooperstown, Baseball Hall of Fame, Ithaca, Mark Twain's home in Elmira, Watkins Glen, and the Finger Lakes wine country. $45-125.

BOLTON LANDING

American Country Collection 56

984 Gloucester Place
Schenectady, NY, 12309
(518) 370-4948

A comfortable, quiet, homelike atmosphere amid the hustle-bustle of a busy summer resort area. This in-town location has 3 acres of lawns and wooded areas. Farm buildings dot the property, including an ice house, greenhouse, and barns. An ample home-cooked breakfast is the specialty of the house. Eight miles from Lake George Village. Public beach within walking distance. Three second-floor rooms share one bath. Smoking permitted in common areas; resident pets. $45.

Hayes Guest House

7161 Lakeshore Drive
P.O. Box 537
Bolton Landing, NY, 12814
(518) 644-5941

Located at Lake George, this charming 1900s cottage gives you a flavor of the Adirondacks you will never forget. Relax in the sun across the street at Veteran's Beach or enjoy a scenic view of the mountains. Each room has its own private bath and air-conditioning. Great vacationland; fun for everyone.

Hosts: Cheryl & Dick Hayes
Rooms: 3 (PB) $80-95
Continental Breakfast
Credit Cards: A, B, C
Notes: 2, 3, 4, 5, 8 (over 8), 9, 10, 11, 12, 13

Hilltop Cottage B&B

Lakeshore Drive
P.O. Box 186
Bolton Landing, NY, 12814
(518) 644-2492

Clean, comfortable renovated farmhouse in the beautiful Lake George-eastern Adirondack region. Walk to restaurants, beach, marinas. Hearty breakfast, homey atmosphere, helpful hosts.

Hosts: Anita & Charlie Richards
Rooms: 4 (1 PB; 3 SB) $45-55
Full Breakfast
Credit Cards: No
Notes: 2, 5, 8 (over 4), 9, 10, 11, 12, 13

BROOKFIELD

Bivona Hill B&B

B&B Connection NY
RD 1, Box 325
Vernon, NY, 13476
(315) 829-4888

This multilevel home is nestled on a hillside with a panoramic view of beautiful Beaver Creek Valley. Each room affords a spectacular view, and the suite offers a queen bed with fireplace and private bath. Generous country breakfast. Overnight stabling facilities are available for horses if you would like to explore the 130 miles of state horse trails nearby. Centrally located from Routes 8, 12, and 20. Near Cooperstown,

Colgate University, and Madison-Bouckville antique district. $45-125.

BUFFALO

Bryant House

236 Bryant Street
Buffalo, NY, 14222
(716) 885-1540

Stay in a charming Victorian house — a pleasant alternative to commercial accommodations — five minutes to downtown Buffalo and the Canadian border; convenient to excellent theaters, boutiques, restaurants, and Niagara Falls. Our house features antiques and fireplaces and your breakfast may be served on our multilevel deck overlooking the garden.

Hosts: John & June Nolan
Rooms: 2 (PB) $39-59
Continental Breakfast
Credit Cards: No
Notes: 2 (deposit only), 5, 8, 9,

Rainbow Hospitality B116

466 Amherst Street
Buffalo, NY, 14207
(716) 874-8797

Second Empire house (c. 1870) in historic neighborhood. Complete breakfast served in parlor with fireplace and large, sunny plant-filled bay window. Horse and carriage rides can be arranged; tour the ships of Buffalo's Naval Park; take a ride on the *Miss Buffalo.* Located minutes from the rapid rail line to the waterfront and a national historic district with antique shops, art galleries, and restaurants. $35-45.

Rainbow Hospitality B117

466 Amherst Street
Buffalo, NY, 14207
(716) 874-8797

A sprawling brick ranch located in a prime suburban section of Buffalo. Elegantly furnished and air-conditioned, surrounded by parklike grounds. Guests have a separate bath. Approximately fifteen miles from Niagara Falls. $35-45.

Bryant House

Rainbow Hospitality B125

466 Amherst Street
Buffalo, NY, 14207
(716) 874-8797

Warm, friendly hosts welcome you to their charming home. Breakfast may be served in the dining or kitchen area. In warm weather, the rear deck, facing beautifully landscaped yard, is made available for guests. Great location near a large shopping mall, one-half hour from skiing, Chestnut Ridge Park, and just minutes from Buffalo and Chautauqua. $35-45.

Rainbow Hospitality B200

466 Amherst Street
Buffalo, NY, 14207
(716) 874-8797

Charming turn-of-the-century Victorian located in the heart of Buffalo's historic-preservation area. Your hosts will recommend excellent restaurants, boutiques, art galleries, and theaters. Minutes to downtown's revitalized cultural and entertainment centers, the waterfront, and the Peace Bridge leading to Canada. Niagara Falls is only eighteen miles north. Two resident cats. $35-45.

Rainbow Hospitality B220

466 Amherst Street
Buffalo, NY, 14207
(716) 874-8797

This former grist mill (1801) captures the charm of the past and the convenience of the present in its four picturesque guest rooms, each furnished with antiques and reproductions, private bath, and air-conditioning. Inviting fireplaces, tap room, and gift shop. Country dining and antique shops are at the doorstep. Just nine miles from the airport and eleven from Amtrak. From $70.

Rainbow Hospitality B300

466 Amherst Street
Buffalo, NY, 14207
(716) 874-8797

The guest quarters of this special B&B include an air-conditioned suite with bedroom, full bath, and living area. There is a refrigerator, cable TV, and access to a sauna. Guests may have breakfast in their suite, in the formal dining room, or on the outdoor patio. Convenient to colleges, museums, art galleries; minutes from Canada and Niagara Falls. $50-65.

Rainbow Hospitality B305

466 Amherst Street
Buffalo, NY, 14207
(716) 874-8797

Gracious Queen Anne historic home being restored to its former grandeur. Two rooms offer private and shared baths. The gardens and green glen are beautifully maintained and available for quiet relaxation and walking. Ideal for an outdoor summer wedding. $50-65.

Rainbow Hospitality B306

466 Amherst Street
Buffalo, NY, 14207
(716) 874-8797

Graceful 1910 English Tudor. Enjoy breakfast on the open porch of this historic home, take a leisurely stroll down Paradise Path through wooded acres, stopping along the way to watch the wildlife. Sandy creek awaits those who enjoy fishing, or gather around the antique player piano for an old-fashioned singalong. $35-45.

Rainbow Hospitality B310

466 Amherst Street
Buffalo, NY, 14207
(716) 874-8797

Charming colonial in quiet country setting, an antique lovers' delight. Hosts provide twin and double rooms. A short distance from the town of Clarence, Williamsville, and Buffalo Airport. $35-45.

Rainbow Hospitality CO107

466 Amherst Street
Buffalo, NY, 14207
(716) 874-8797

Charming country mini-estate, located in the Boston Hills and ski area twenty-five miles from Buffalo and fifty miles from Niagara Falls. Three guest rooms in a separate chalet include one bath and a full kitchen, dining/living room, piano, pool table, and fireplace. A large pond for swimming and lovely woods for hiking or skiing are on the premises. $35-45.

Rainbow Hospitality SP590

466 Amherst Street
Buffalo, NY, 14207
(716) 874-8797

Spacious split level in a rural country setting close to skiing, country auctions, and crafts. Double and twin rooms with shared bath. Hosts enjoy sharing their beautifully landscaped yard in summer and fireplace in winter. $35-45.

BURDETT

The Red House Country Inn

Finger Lakes National Forest Picnic Area Rd.
Burdett, NY, 14818
(607) 546-8566

The only residence within 13,000+ acre Finger Lakes National Forest. Twenty-eight miles of hiking and cross-country trails. Near Watkins Glen Gorge, wineries, swimming beach. The house is a completely restored 1840s farmstead with beautifully appointed rooms, a pool, and 5 acres of lawns and gardens. Large breakfast; guest kitchen. Goats and chickens on the property.

Hosts: Joan Martin & Sandy Schmanke
Rooms: 6 (S4B) $47-75
Full Breakfast
Minimum stay weekends & holidays: 2
Credit Cards: A, B, C
Closed Thanksgiving & Christmas
Notes: 2, 8 (over 12), 9, 11, 13, 14

BURNT HILLS

American Country Collection 114

984 Gloucester Place
Schenectady, NY, 12309
(518) 370-4948

In the heart of an historic village is this 150-year-old farm, surrounded by 12 acres of apple orchards. Several common rooms, TV, fireplaces, and a large patio and porch add to the charm of the home. Two guest rooms with private baths, plus additional space for a larger party. Full breakfast. Burnt Hills is convenient to the Capitol District, Saratoga Springs, and less than an hour from Lake George. Restricted smoking; school-age children welcome; guest pets welcome for additional charge. $60.

CAIRO

American Country Collection 13

984 Gloucester Place
Schenectady, NY, 12309
(518) 370-4948

Built in the late 1700s by Dutch and German settlers, this Shaker-style farmhouse offers old-fashioned country comforts. Nestled on 150 acres of woodland, hills, and meadows, this working horse farm includes a stable, tack shop, and sugar house. Fish in the three stocked ponds and learn how to sugar in the spring. Fifteen minutes from the Catskill Game Farm. Cross-country skiing on the property; downhill ten miles away at Windham. Two double rooms, one shared bath. No smoking; children welcome; full breakfast. $50.

CAMBRIDGE

American Country Collection 10

984 Gloucester Place
Schenectady, NY, 12309
(518) 370-4948

The main house was built from 1896-1903 and features stained-glass windows, ceiling murals, and an Otis brass cage elevator. The carriage house offers a variety of suites, each with one to three bedrooms, living room, color TV, and private bath. Twenty miles from Bennington, VT, twenty-five from Saratoga Springs, NY. Smoking is permitted; children welcome; continental breakfast. $55.

Maple Ridge Inn

RD 1, Box 391C
Cambridge, NY, 12816
(518) 677-3674

Grand large Victorian mansion furnished in fine antiques. All rooms have private baths. Located in country surroundings twenty-five minutes from Saratoga Springs and ten from the Vermont border.

Host: Ken Riney
Rooms: 4 (PB) $75-150
Continental Breakfast
Credit Cards: No
Notes: 2, 5, 7, 8, 9, 10, 11, 12, 13, 14

CANAAN

Berkshire B&B Homes NY 4

P.O. Box 211
Williamsburg, MA, 01096
(413) 268-7244

1806 Federal home on the historic register, furnished with Victorian and Federal furniture. Ten minutes from Lenox. Three rooms with double beds, two twin rooms, and two cozy double rooms. Shared baths. Full breakfast, restricted smoking, children six and over welcome. Pets in residence. $50-60.

CANANDAIGUA

Lakeview Farm B&B

4761 Route 364
Rushville, NY, 14544
(716) 554-6973

Hospitality and nature at its best in this country home located on the east side of Canandaigua Lake on 170 acres of woods, fields, and streams. Pond, ravine, and cross-country skiing on the premises; near a public beach. Only ten minutes from Canandaigua restaurants. Air-conditioned.

Hosts: Howard & Betty Freese
Rooms: 2 (SB) $45-50
Full Breakfast
Credit Cards: C
Notes: 2, 5, 7 (outdoors), 8, 10, 11, 14

Nottingham Lodge B&B

5741 Bristol Valley Road
Canandaigua, NY, 14424
(716) 374-5355

Rural and mountainous, located on Route 64 across from Bristol Mountain Ski Center. This English Tudor lodge has a common room two stories high, with balcony, barnwood walls, and a cobblestone fireplace. Casual elegance. Three guest rooms, one with private bath; full breakfast. Ski packages are available. Bicycle tours available May through October.

Hosts: Bonnie & Bill Robinson
Rooms: 3 (1 PB; 2 SB) $55 + tax
Full Breakfast
Credit Cards: A, B
Notes: 2, 5, 8, 12, 13

Oliver Phelps Country Inn

252 North Main Street
Canandaigua, NY, 14424
(716) 396-1650

An historic B&B located in the heart of beautiful Canandaigua. Federal-style home built in the 1800s is decorated in country charm. Each guest room has a private bath. Guests are treated to a full breakfast featuring fresh-from-the-oven muffins, breads, and sticky buns.

Hosts: John & Joanne Sciarratta
Rooms: 4 (PB) $65-85
Full Breakfast
Credit Cards: A, B
Notes: 2, 5, 8 (6 and over), 9, 10, 11, 12, 13

Wilder Tavern Country Inn

5648 North Bloomfield Road
Canandaigua, NY, 14425
(716) 394-8132

An 1829 brick stagecoach inn welcomes travelers to the beautiful Finger Lakes area. Second floor is air-conditioned. Superior breakfasts with homemade breads and preserves. Other meals available by prior arrangement. Summer music festival, winery tours, historic architecture, Sonnenberg Gardens, and antique shops nearby.

Host: Linda C. Swartout
Rooms: 4 (1 PB; 3 SB) $53.50-69.55
Full Breakfast
Credit Cards: A, B
Notes: 2, 3, 4, 8 (over 12), 9, 10, 11, 12, 13, 14

CANASERAGA

Rainbow Hospitality A701

466 Amherst Street
Buffalo, NY, 14207
(716) 874-8797

Gracious 100-year-old Queen Anne Victorian mansion minutes from Buffalo's downtown and cultural events. Near colleges, major hospital, Allentown antique shops, Elmwood Avenue restaurants and boutiques, and only twenty minutes from Niagara Falls. Four comfortable rooms, two shared baths, superb breakfast, and pleasant surroundings. No smoking. $35-45.

CANDOR

Edge of Thyme B&B

6 Main Street
Candor, NY, 13743
(607) 659-5155

Turn-of-the-century Georgian house with antiques, leaded-glass windowed porch, comfortable atmosphere, and outdoor gardens with pergola. Central to the Finger Lakes, Cornell University, Ithaca College, Watkins Glen, wineries, and Corning Glass.

Hosts: Eva Mae & Frank Musgrave
Rooms: 7 (2 PB; 5 SB) $50-65
Full Breakfast
Credit Cards: A, B
Notes: 2, 5, 8, 12, 13 (XC), 14

CASTLETON ON HUDSON

American Country Collection 71

984 Gloucester Place
Schenectady, NY, 12309
(518) 370-4948

Located just ten minutes east of Albany, an ideal location for the capital district, Saratoga, Lenox, or Stockbrige. In the evening, guests are invited to join the hosts for popcorn and refreshments by the fire in the living room or enjoy a movie on the VCR in the den. A running track and tennis court are just across the street. One first-floor guest room has a queen bed and private bath. Smoking outdoors only; children welcome; resident pets. $60.

CAZENOVIA

Brae Loch Inn

5 Albany Street, US Route 20
Cazenovia, NY, 13035
(315) 655-3431

Family owned and operated since 1946; originally built in 1805. As close to a Scottish

Inn as you will find this far west of Edinburgh! Victorian antiques, mellow tartan plaids, original stained glass, shop featuring Scottish wools and crystal on the premises. All rooms have their own private bath and shower, color TV, air-conditioning, and electric heat. Dinners available in the main-floor dining room.

Hosts: H. Grey & Doris Barr
Rooms: 12 (PB) $62.06-73.83
Continental Breakfast
Minimum stay holidays: 2
Credit Cards: A, B, C, E
Notes: 2, 4, 5, 7, 8, 9, 10, 11, 12, 13, 14

Maple Nook Farm

B&B Connection NY
RD 1, Box 325
Vernon, NY, 13476
(315) 829-4888

In the early 1940s, a small Early American farmhouse built in 1790 was joined to this Greek Revival, built in 1830. A federal-style music room was added to the house at the same time. The barns are also of interest, representing over a century of changing barn architecture, and should be seen with the house as a typical early Cazenovia farm complex. $45-125.

CHAPPAQUA

Crabtree's Kittle House

11 Kittle Road
Chappaqua, NY, 10514
(914) 666-8044

Built in 1790, Crabtree's Kittle House maintains a distinctive blend of country style and comfort. Only twenty miles from New York City, the inn is also a comfortable base from which to explore Van Cortlandt and Philipsburg Manors, Sunnyside, and Pocantico Hills. Not to be missed are the dinner specialties of the house, including crisp roast duckling and the freshest seafood available. Entertainment on weekends.

Hosts: John & Dick Crabtree
Rooms: 11, $75-85
Continental Breakfast
Credit Cards: A, B, C, E
Notes: 2, 4, 5, 7, 8, 9

Brae Loch Inn

CHARLTON

American Country Collection 87

984 Gloucester Place
Schenectady, NY, 12309
(518) 370-4948

A pre-revolutionary estate on 100 country acres just twelve miles west of Saratoga Springs. The brick home is constructed in the Federal Period style during the late 1700s. Stone patio, formal gardens, wooded paths to the private pond and pond house. One first-floor room with double bed and private bath. One second-floor room with double bed and private bath. Smoking is permitted; children are welcome. Full breakfast. $65-85.

CHAUTAUQUA

Rainbow Hospitality C100

466 Amherst Street
Buffalo, NY, 14207
(716) 874-8797

6 Pets welcome: 7 Smoking allowed: 8 Children welcome: 9 Social drinking allowed: 10 Tennis available: 11 Swimming available: 12 Golf available: 13 Skiing available: 14 May be booked through travel agents

Historic 1821 mansion with ten guest rooms, each with private bath and period furnishings. Beautifully located on a knoll overlooking Lake Erie, and minutes from Chautauqua Institute. Local wineries and antique shops combine with winter ski trails for seasonal enjoyment. Delicious gourmet breakfast. $50-65.

Rainbow Hospitality C102

466 Amherst Street
Buffalo, NY, 14207
(716) 874-8797

Nestled in the heart of western New York, this small rural village Victorian offers double bedrooms and a separate living room and kitchen. Fall and winter guests may enjoy cross-country skiing or bringing home fruit from area orchards and vineyards. $35-45.

Rainbow Hospitality C103

466 Amherst Street
Buffalo, NY, 14207
(716) 874-8797

An 1857 Victorian country villa, beautifully decorated. Convenient to Chautauqua Lake, fishing, hiking, and horseback riding. $35-45.

Rainbow Hospitality C104

466 Amherst Street
Buffalo, NY, 14207
(716) 874-8797

Charming lakeside Dutch colonial mansion, located on the east shore of Chautauqua Lake. Enjoy the Chautauqua Institute, where outstanding cultural programs are held during the summer, or hike and picnic on the 11-acre grounds that include a private beach and dock. Winter sports include skiing, snowmobiling, ice fishing, and sleigh rides. $35-45.

Rainbow Hospitality C105

466 Amherst Street
Buffalo, NY, 14207
(716) 874-8797

Private first-floor suite and deluxe one-bedroom apartment are available in this beautiful lakefront home. Antique and gift shops on the premises. Continental breakfast and bicycles are provided. From $70.

Rainbow Hospitality C106

466 Amherst Street
Buffalo, NY, 14207
(716) 874-8797

Colonial Revival house built in 1929, decorated with antiques and collectibles reminiscent of the relaxing country life-style. Freshly baked breads, seasonal fruits, and carefully prepared entrees greet guests at the harvest table. $35-45.

Rainbow Hospitality C107

466 Amherst Street
Buffalo, NY, 14207
(716) 874-8797

Fluffy eiderdown and an old armoire like the one you used at grandma's, together with an iron and brass bed, can be found at this historic Federal home built in 1832. This lovely inn is located on the shore of Lake Erie and has a full restaurant. All rooms have private baths. $35-45.

Rainbow Hospitality C108

466 Amherst Street
Buffalo, NY, 14207
(716) 874-8797

Private home in the village on Lakewood on Chautauqua Lake. Your hostess is a talented cook and offers a complete breakfast. Within walking distance of the lakeside village and beach. Comfortable driving distance to all ski areas and the Chautauqua Institute. $35-45.

Rainbow Hospitality C109

466 Amherst Street
Buffalo, NY, 14207
(716) 874-8797

Gracious lakefront home, tastefully furnished with antiques and Oriental rugs. Special features are central air and an inviting in-ground pool. Convenient to Chautauqua Institution and all summer and winter activities. $35-45.

Rainbow Hospitality C110

466 Amherst Street
Buffalo, NY, 14207
(716) 874-8797

Stagecoach colonial, c. 1800s, on a 7-acre farm with family room fireplace and 3,000-book library. Hosts offer three B&B rooms, two double and one twin. Meals are served in the family room, dining room, kitchen, or on the patio. $35-45.

Rainbow Hospitality C111

466 Amherst Street
Buffalo, NY, 14207
(716) 874-8797

Spectacular view of Lake Chautauqua from this lakefront home with all the amenities. Newly redone rooms have private guest bath, porches, and dock. Two double rooms. $35-45.

Rainbow Hospitality C112

466 Amherst Street
Buffalo, NY, 14207
(716) 874-8797

Historic 1890 two-story home on the grounds of Chautauqua, offering a third-floor apartment or suite. Just four short blocks to the kale. Tennis, golf, and sailing during the spring and summer, and cross-country skiing on the grounds. Call or write for details.

CHERRY PLAINS

Covered Bridge 1 CP

P.O. Box 447A
Norfolk, CT, 06058
(203) 542-5944

This 1790 colonial, nestled in the New York Bershires, is very secluded, yet minutes from Tanglewood and summer theaters. Hiking trails, cross-country skiing, and a pond for fishing and skating are available on the grounds. Enjoy a full breakfast and dinner, both made with natural foods. Four rooms with private baths. $110.

CHESTERTOWN

Friends Lake Inn

Friends Lake Road
Chestertown, NY, 12817
(518) 494-4751

Located in the Adirondacks, overlooking Friends Lake, the inn is located twenty minutes north of Lake George. Gore Mountain Ski Center is only fifteen minutes away. Breakfast and dinner are served daily. Built in the 1860s as a boarding house, the inn has been completely restored and refurbished.

Hosts: Sharon & Greg Taylor
Rooms: 11 (9 PB; 2 SB) $70-140
Full Breakfast
Minimum stay weekends:2; holidays: 3
Credit Cards: A, B, C,
Closed Mon. & Tues., Nov.-mid-Dec., April, May
Notes: 2, 4, 5, 7, 8, 9, 10, 11, 12, 13, 14

CHITTENANGO

Cherry Valley Ventures 4003

6119 Cherry Valley Turnpike
LaFayette, NY, 13084
(315) 677-9723

A large colonial with a screened porch that overlooks a splendid landscaped yard with flowers of all types. Near Green Lakes State Park, Cazenovia, Syracuse University, Oneida and Onondage lakes, LeMoyne College. One guest room has a double bed with private bath; a twin room on the second floor has a shared bath. One dog in residence. $45.

CLAVERACK

Meadowlark Manor

Box 588
Claverack, NY, 12513
(518) 851-9808

An 1860 Federal mansion with a traditional decor. The house has six large white pillars and has entertained many guests over the years. Located in Columbia County, it is central to many historic areas and recreational activities.

Host: Noreen Marcincuk
Rooms: 4 (2 PB; 2 SB) $40-77
Full Breakfast
Credit Cards: A, B
Notes: 2, 5, 7, 8, 9, 11, 12, 13, 14

CLINTONDALE

American Country Collection 117

984 Gloucester Place
Schenectady, NY, 12309
(518) 370-4948

An 1860s Victorian home with wraparound porch on about 2 acres in this small town. Rooms of European and Victorian decor with antiques and reproductions accented with the hostess's own needlework. Three attractive guest rooms, each with one queen bed. Two rooms share one bath. One room with private bath and indoor balcony that looks over the sun room. Full breakfast; no smoking; adults only; pets in residence. $65.

COBLESKILL

American Country Collection 28

984 Gloucester Place
Schenectady, NY, 12309
(518) 370-4948

Wicker and Eastlake antiques accent this family home that contains four guest rooms sharing two baths. There is a common room for games, relaxation, and TV. SUNY Cobleskill is within walking distance; Howe Caverns is five miles; Cooperstown thirty-five miles. Restricted smoking; children are welcome; continental breakfast. $45-65.

COLDEN

Back of the Beyond

7233 Lower East Hill Road
Colden, NY, 14033
(716) 652-0427

A charming country mini-estate located in the Boston Hills and ski area of western New York: twenty-five miles from Buffalo and fifty from Niagara Falls. Accommodations are in a separate chalet with three bedrooms, one and one-half baths, fully furnished kitchen, dining/living room, piano, pool table, and fireplace. Stroll through our organic herb, flower, and vegetable gardens, swim in the pond, or hike the woods. Cross-country ski trails on the premises; commercial downhill slopes are only one mile away.

Hosts: Bill and Shash Georgi
Rooms: 3 (S1.5B) $45-50
Full Breakfast
Credit Cards: No
Notes: 2, 5, 8, 9, 10, 11, 12, 13, 14

COLD SPRING

Pig Hill Inn

73 Main Street
Cold Spring, NY, 10516
(914) 265-9247

"Picture perfect, like a spread in *House Beautiful*" —*N.Y. Magazine*. "What makes Pig Hill different is . . . that everything is for sale"—*N.Y. Magazine*. Enjoy a gourmet breakfast in bed before hiking on the Appalachian Trail. Go antique hunting, or visit West Point. Stroll three blocks to the river to watch windsurfers. Then again, you could just curl up in front of the fire with a good book.

Host: Wendy O'Brien
Rooms: 8 (4 PB; 4 SB) $90-140
Full Breakfast
Credit Cards: A, B, C, E
Notes: 2, 5, 10, 12, 13, 14

COOPERSTOWN

Ängelholm

14 Elm Street, Box 705
Cooperstown, NY, 13326
(607) 547-2483

Leave your cars and cares behind and wander the lovely streets, parks, museums, and shops of Cooperstown from Ängelholm, one of Cooperstown's historic homes. Only a four-minute walk to Main Street and the Baseball Hall of Fame. A hearty breakfast in the formal dining room is a marvelous way to start a happy day of exploring the Leatherstocking Country, which is rich in history, scenic drives, recreation, antique shops, and colleges.

Hosts: George & Carolin Dempsey
Rooms: 4 (2 PB; 2 SB) $70-90
Full Breakfast
Credit Cards: A, B
Notes: 2, 5, 7 (limited), 8, 9, 10, 11, 12

The Inn at Brook Willow

RD 2, Box 514
Cooperstown, NY, 13326
(607) 547-9700

An 1885 Victorian country home on 14 acres, with a fine collection of antiques in the main house and three guest rooms in the "reborn barn." Fresh fruit, garden flowers, and a bountiful breakfast await each guest. Two fireplaces, fields, and meadows relax the traveler. Five minutes to the Baseball Hall of Fame and Otsego Lake.

Hosts: Joan & Jack Grimes
Rooms: (PB) $55-75 (Single rate upon request)
Minimum stay weekends & holidays: 2
Full Breakfast
Credit Cards: No
Notes: 2, 5, 9, 10, 11, 12, 13

Wynterholm

B&B Connection NY
RD 1, Box 325
Vernon, NY, 13476
(315) 829-4888

Located in the village of Cooperstown, Wynterholm is a three-story historic Second Empire home built c. 1868. Cherry staircase, stained-glass windows, tin ceilings, and original paintings. All rooms have color TV and air-conditioning. Enjoy a continental breakfast in the formal dining room with fireplace and chandeliers. Walk to Otsego Lake, the Baseball Hall of Fame, restaurants, golf course, and tennis. Adults over seventeen welcome. $45-125.

CORNING

DeLevan House

188 DeLevan Avenue
Corning, NY, 14830
(607) 962-2347

Southern Colonial home/hospitality. Overlooking Corning. Quiet surroundings, outstanding accommodations, complimentary wine.

Host: Mary M. DePumpo
Rooms: 3 (1 PB; 2 SB) $65.40-70.85
Full Breakfast
Credit Cards: No
Notes: 2, 5, 7, 8 (over 12), 9, 11, 12

1865 White Birch B&B

69 East First Street
Corning, NY, 14830
(607) 962-6355

Imagine a friendly, warm atmosphere in an 1865 Victorian setting. Cozy rooms await our guests; both private and shared baths. Awake to the tantalizing aromas of a full, home-baked breakfast. Walk to museums, historic Market Street, and the Glass Center. Experience it all at the White Birch.

Hosts: Kathy & Joe Donahue
Rooms: 4 (2 PB; 2 SB) $45-70
Full Breakfast
Credit Cards: A, B (deposit)
Notes: 2, 5, 7 (restricted), 8, 9, 12, 13 (XC)

Rosewood Inn

134 East First Street
Corning, NY, 14830
(607) 962-3253

Six elegantly appointed, air-conditioned Victorian guest rooms, four with private baths. Generous breakfast served in beautiful paneled dining room. Within walking distance of Corning Glass Center, museums, restored Market Street, restaurants, and shops.

Hosts: Dick & Winnie Peer
Rooms: 6 (4 PB; 2 SB) $68-100
Full Breakfast
Minimum stay on holidays
Credit Cards: A, B, C, E
Notes: 2, 5, 7, 8, 9, 14

West Wind Farm B&B

RD 3, Box 402A
Corning, NY, 14830
(607) 962-3979

Just ten minutes from Corning Painted Post area attractions: glass museum, Corning Glass corporate headquarters, Rockwell Museum, historic Market Street, Dresser Rand corporate headquarters. Conveniently located in the beautiful Finger Lakes region, near Watkins Glen, Ithaca, local wineries, and horseback riding.

Host: G. Lauriston Walsh, Jr.
Rooms: 4 (1 PB; 3 SB) $55-75
Full Breakfast
Credit Cards: A, B, C, E
Dog kennel on premises
Notes: 2, 4, 5, 6, 7, 8, 9, 10, 11, 12, 13 (XC)

CRARYVILLE

American Country Collection 51

984 Gloucester Place
Schenectady, NY, 12309
(518) 370-4948

This old 1870 colonial borders the main street in this tiny town just six miles from the Massachusetts border. Five guest rooms. One first-floor suite with private bath, and four rooms on the second floor, three of them with a shared bath. Restricted smoking; children are welcome; continental breakfast. $50-70.

CROWN POINT

American Country Collection 95

984 Gloucester Place
Schenectady, NY, 12309
(518) 370-4948

A magnificent Victorian mansion, c. 1887, with four fireplaces, high ceilings, carved woodwork. Enjoy refreshing summer breezes from one of the three porches or watch the sunrise over the Green Mountains. Located near Lake Champlain, near the Vermont border, the house offers five rooms, two with private baths, furnished with fine antiques. Continental-plus breakfast; smoking outdoors only; children welcome. $40-55.

DE BRUCE

De Bruce Country Inn

De Bruce Road
De Bruce, NY, 12758
(914) 439-3900

In a spectacular 1,000-acre natural setting within the Catskill Forest, overlooking the Willowemoc Trout Stream, the inn offers turn-of-the-century charm and hospitality. Terrace dining, wooded trails, wildlife, pool, sauna, fitness and health, fresh air and mountain water.

Hosts: Ron & Marilyn
Rooms: 15 (PB) From $70/person
Full Breakfast and Dinner
Credit Cards: A, B, C
Dec. 15-April 1 by special arrangement
Notes: 2 (deposit only), 4, 6 (call), 7, 8, 9, 10, 11, 12, 13

DOLGEVILLE

Adrianna Bed & Breakfast

44 Stewart Street
Dolgeville, NY, 13329
(315) 429-3249

Adrianna is located just off the New York Thruway at Exit 29A, amid glorious views of the Adirondack foothills. Just a short ride to Cooperstown, Saratoga, Syracuse, and Utica areas. A most cozy and hospitable B&B.

Host: Adrianna Naizby
Rooms: 3 (1 PB; 2 SB), $45
Full breakfast
Minimum stay weekends & holidays: 2
Credit Cards: A, B
Closed Christmas Eve & Day
Notes: 2, 5, 7, 13

DOVER PLAINS

The Mill Farm

66 Cricket Hill Road
Dover Plains, NY, 12522
(914) 832-9198

This 1850 rambling colonial makes you feel a welcomed guest. Guests enjoy panoramic views from the large sitting porch. The home is decorated with antique furniture and linens. The setting is real country, yet we are only one and one-half hours north of New York City near the Connecticut line.

Host: Margery Mill
Rooms: 4 (1 PB; 3 SB) $50-90
Full Breakfast
Minimum stay weekends and holidays: 2
Credit Cards: No
Married couples only, please
Closed Feb. & March
Notes: 2, 9, 10, 11, 12, 13

Sarah's Dream

DRYDEN

Sarah's Dream

49 West Main Street
Dryden, NY, 13053
(607) 844-4321

A place to be coddled. On the National Register of Historic Places, this 1828 homestead, furnished with antiques, is subtly elegant without being pretentious. The beds and breakfasts will make you sigh. Convenient to Ithaca, Cornell, wineries, and the

Finger Lakes. All rooms are air-conditioned; one with fireplace.

Hosts: Judi Williams & Ken Morusty
Rooms: 4 (PB) $40-85
Suites: 2 (PB)
Full Breakfast
Credit Cards: A, B, C
Notes: 2, 5, 8 (over 10), 9, 10, 11, 12, 13

Spruce Haven B&B

9 James Street
Box 119
Dryden, NY, 13053
(607) 844-8052

This log home surrounded by tall spruce trees gives you the feeling of being in the woods while still enjoying the advantages of the village. On a quiet street, this warm and friendly home is within twelve miles of Ithaca, Cortland, lakes, golf, skiing, colleges, museums. Restaurants nearby. One night's deposit holds reservations.

Host: Margaret Thatcher Brownell
Rooms: 2 (SB) prices on request
Full Breakfast
Credit Cards: No
Notes: 2, 5, 8, 10, 11, 12, 13

DURHAMVILLE

Towering Maples B&B

B&B Connection NY
RD 1, Box 325
Vernon, NY, 13476
(315) 829-4888

Completely renovated 1850s farmhouse and barn, situated on 3 acres on the banks of the historic Erie Canal. The home is tastefully decorated with a country motif and features solid cherry furnishings. $45-125.

EAST AURORA

Rainbow Hospitality EA780

466 Amherst Street
Buffalo, NY, 14207
(716) 874-8797

Spacious contemporary located on 70 acres with trails, creek, inground pool. Two spacious rooms include queen and king accommodations, shared bath. Minutes from the quaint village of East Aurora; twenty minutes from downtown Buffalo; fifty minutes from Niagara Falls. $50.

EAST CHATHAM

American Country Collection 83

984 Gloucester Place
Schenectady, NY, 12309
(518) 370-4948

This private home and barn incorporates a two-room B&B suite with private entrance. The building was recently constructed with interior walls of fieldstone and 200-year-old barn wood and beams. The house and barn sit atop 35 acres and have an idyllic view of rolling hills, grassy fields, and grazing horses. Full breakfast. $85.

EAST GREENBUSH

American Country Collection 65

984 Gloucester Place
Schenectady, NY, 12309
(518) 370-4948

Located only four miles from Albany, this home is in a quiet residential area. The guest suite offers a living room, two bedrooms that share a bath. Restricted smoking. $40.

EAST HAMPTON

Mill House Inn

33 North Main Street
East Hampton, NY, 11937
(516) 324-9766

A 1790 colonial located in "America's most beautiful village." Open all year so you can enjoy lemonade while overlooking the Old Hook windmill or a restful nap in our backyard hammock. In the off-season, enjoy hot cider by the fireplace or a brisk walk to the beach.

Hosts: Barbara & Kevin Flynn
Rooms: 8 (6 PB; 2 SB) $75-145
Full Breakfast
Minimum stay weekends in season: 3; holidays in season: 4; holidays off-season: 2-3
Credit Cards: A, B, C
Notes: 2, 5, 8 (12 and over), 10, 11, 12

EAST ISLIP

B & B of Long Island IL

P.O. Box 392
Old Westbury, NY, 11568
(516) 334-6231

Minutes from Hecksher State Park, this split-level home is furnished with some exquisite Victorian antiques. Two rooms, one with twin beds, the other double; TV in each room. Shared bath if both rooms are occupied. Full breakfast. Dog in residence. $62.

ELIZABETHTOWN

American Country Collection 72

984 Gloucester Place
Schenectady, NY, 12309
(518) 370-4948

This B&B, several cottages, and an art studio and gallery in the old barn, are on 2.5 acres bordered on two sides by the Boquet River, a favorite fishing and swimming hole. The main house, an early 1800s colonial, has a large living room with original pinc paneling, antique tables, and a carved rosewood Steinway Grand piano. In summer, breakfast is served on the covered stone patio that overlooks the grounds. Ten minutes from Lake Champlain, twenty from Ausable Chasm, just a few miles off I-87. There are five guest rooms, three with private baths. Restricted smoking; children welcome; resident pets. $64-76.

FORESTBURGH

Inn at Lake Joseph

RD 5, Box 81, Country Road 108
Forestburgh, NY, 12777
(914) 791-9506

A quiet, secluded 125-year-old Queen Anne mansion surrounded by 2,000 acres of wildlife preserve and forest, with a 250-acre private lake. Once the vacation estate of cardinals Hayes and Spellman, the house now offers swimming, boating, fishing, tennis, cross-country skiing and more on the premises. Both breakfast and dinner are included in the daily rate.

Host: Ivan Weinger
Rooms: 9 (PB) $108-198
Full Breakfast and Dinner
Credit Cards: A, B, C
Notes: 2, 3, 4, 5, 7, 8, 9, 10, 11, 12, 13, 14

FOSTERDALE

Fosterdale Heights House

RD 1, Box 198
Fosterdale, NY, 12726
(914) 482-3369

Circa 1840 country Victorian B&B, just two hours from New York City. Enjoy the parlor with its grand piano; pond; Christmas tree farm; enchanted forest; and bountiful country breakfast. Informal evenings of chamber music and parlor games break out frequently. Free brochure.

Hosts: Roy & Trish Singer
Rooms: 12 (3 PB; 9 SB) $52-103
Full Breakfast
Minimum stay holidays: 2
Credit Cards: A, B
Notes: 2, 4, 5, 7, 9, 10, 11, 12, 13

Battle Island Inn

This house was a stagecoach stop and tavern in the late 1700s. It is located twelve miles from Saratoga Springs, fifteen from Sacandaga Lake, near Skidmore and Union colleges. Three rooms, each with private bath, plus a summer cottage with two rooms and private baths. Restricted smoking; children welcome; resident pets; full breakfast. $45-85.

FULTON

Battle Island Inn

RD #1, Box 176
Fulton, NY, 13069
(315) 593-3699

Battle Island Inn is a pre-Civil War farm estate that has been restored and furnished with period antiques. The inn is across the road from a golf course that also provides cross-country skiing. Guest rooms are elegantly furnished with imposing high-back beds, TVs, phones, and private baths. Breakfast is always special in our 1840s dining room.

Hosts: Joyce & Richard Rice
Rooms: 7 (6 PB; 1 SB) $59-80
Full Breakfast
Credit Cards: A, B, D
Notes: 2, 5, 8, 9, 12, 13, 14

GALWAY

American Country Collection 49

984 Gloucester Place
Schenectady, NY, 12309
(518) 370-4948

GARRISON

The Bird & Bottle Inn

Route 9, Old Albany Post Road
Garrison, NY, 10524
(914) 424-3000

Originally known as Warren's Tavern in 1761, this building was a stagecoach stop along the Old Albany Post Road. In 1940 the inn was renamed The Bird & Bottle Inn. It's a perfect spot to stay overnight in one of the three rooms in the main building, each of which has a private bath, working fireplace, air conditioning, and canopied bed. A cottage steps away from the main building offers the same appointments. Located near West Point, Boscobel Restoration, antiquing, and hiking. Price includes gourmet dinner and breakfast Wednesdays through Sunday. On Mondays and Tuesdays, a continental breakfast is served to overnight guests.

Host: Ira Boyar
Rooms: 4 (PB) $195-215
Full Breakfast
Credit Cards: A, B, C, E
Closed first two weeks of Jan.
Notes: 4, 7 (restricted), 8, 9, 10, 11, 12, 13 (XC), 14

GENESEO

American House B&B Inn

39 Main Street
Geneseo, NY, 14454
(716) 243-5483

American House is a Victorian home in the heart of the historic village of Geneseo. Nearby attractions include Letchworth State Park, Genesee Country Museum, Conesus Lake, and the National Warplane Museum. The State University at Geneseo is one block away.

Hosts: Harry & Helen Wadsworth
Rooms: 6 (2 PB; 4 SB) $53.50-74.90
Continental Breakfast
Credit Cards: No
Notes: 2, 5, 7, 8, 9, 10, 11, 12, 13, 14

Virginia Deane's B&B

GENEVA

Geneva On The Lake

1001 Lochland Road
Geneva, NY, 14456
(315) 789-7190; (800) 3GENEVA

Geneva On The Lake is a small resort on Seneca Lake in the Finger Lakes wine district. An Italian Renaissance villa offering luxurious suites overlooking a furnished terrace, formal gardens, pool, and lake. "The food is extraordinarily good," writes *Bon Appetit.* Friendly, attentive staff. Awarded AAA four diamonds. Suite rates include continental breakfast, complimentary bottle of wine, fresh fruit, and flowers on arrival, a wine and cheese party on Friday evenings, and a daily copy of the *New York Times.*

Host: Norbert H. Schickel, Jr.
Suites: 29 (PB) $149-322
Type of Beds: 3 Twin; 4 Double; 22 Queen
Continental and Full Breakfast
Minimum stay weekends: 2 if Sat., May 15-Oct. 31
Credit Cards: A, B, C, D
Notes: 2, 4 (weekends only), 5, 7, 8, 9, 10, 11, 12, 14

Virginia Deane's B&B

168 Hamilton Street
Geneva, NY, 14456
(315) 789-6152

Located across from Hobart-William Smith College, with a public tennis court nearby, this home offers two rooms with private or shared bath.

Rooms: 2 (PB or SB) $42.80-48.15
Continental Breakfast
Credit Cards: No
Notes: 2, 5, 9, 10, 11, 12

GERMANTOWN

American Country Collection 102

984 Gloucester Place
Schenectady, NY, 12309
(518) 370-4948

This historic center-hall colonial, built c. 1807, is situated on 3.5 acres of trees and rolling farmland. Post-and-beam construction, with oak-pinned rafters, hand-hewn timbers, and poured-glass windows. Three air-conditioned windows share two baths. Full country breakfast, plus drinks anytime, late-night snacks, and use of refrigerator. Twenty miles from Hyde Park. Restricted smoking; children over ten welcome. $60.

American Country Collection 113

984 Gloucester Place
Schenectady, NY, 12309
(518) 370-4948

Mountain vistas highlight this raised ranch on a knoll facing the Catskills just 1.5 miles from the Hudson River and marina. Two guest rooms, a guest bath, and private guest family room with TV and fireplace are offered. Usually only one party at a time is accepted. Accessible to Olana, historic sites, shopping, and recreational activities. Smoking outdoors; children welcome; guest dogs welcome. $50-60.

GHENT

American Country Collection 82

984 Gloucester Place
Schenectady, NY, 12309
(518) 370-4948

This early nineteenth-century rural farmhouse sits on 10 scenic acres. There are open fields for walking and picnicking, a private pond for fishing and paddle boating, and a miniature horse farm. Guest wing with private living room. One room has private bath; one suite with two bedrooms and private bath. Children are welcome. Resident dog. Full breakfast. Located in the upper Hudson Valley, just a few miles from the Taconic Parkway. Skiing within fifteen miles; Tanglewood, twenty-four. $60.

GLEN COVE

B & B of Long Island GCP

P.O. Box 392
Old Westbury, NY, 11568
(516) 334-6231

This stunning Victorian home has been converted to a spectacular contemporary interior with atriums in the breakfast room so you can enjoy the landscaped gardens and swimming pool. Two upstairs bedrooms, one with old-world charm, brass double bed, Tiffany-style lamp, loveseat, and private bath. The other has a charming country look and private bath. Hosts are French, and breakfast is continental. Walk to village, Long Island railroad, and fabulous restaurants. $68-72.

GOWANDA

The Teepee

RD 1, Box 543
Gowanda, NY, 14070
(716) 532-2168

This bed and breakfast is operated by Seneca Indians on the Cattaraugus Indian Reservation near Gowanda, New York. Tours of the reservation and the Amish community nearby are available.

Hosts: Maxwell & Phyllis Lay
Rooms: 3 (SB) $30 single; $40 double
Full Breakfast
Credit Cards: No
Notes: 2, 5, 6, 7, 8, 9, 10, 11, 12

Greenville Arms

GREENVILLE

Greenville Arms

RD 1, Box 2
Greenville, NY, 12083
(518) 966-5219

A Victorian country inn in the northern Hudson River Valley on 6 acres of beautiful grounds with a swimming pool. Fine gourmet dining on premises.

Hosts: Eliot & Letitia Dalton
Rooms: 19 (13 PB; 6 SB) $75-110
Full Breakfast
Credit Cards: A, B
Notes: 2, 4, 5, 8, 9, 10, 11, 12, 13, 14

Blushing Rose B&B

HAMMONDSPORT

Blushing Rose B&B

11 William Street
Hammondsport, NY, 14840
(607) 569-3402; (607) 569-3483

Step back in time in a warm country house filled with antiques. Hammondsport is an historic village with shopping, dining, and great walking. Keuka Lake is just a few doors away; wineries are nearby, plus Corning Glass and Watkins Glen.

Hosts: The Laufersweilers
Rooms: 4 (PB) $55-75
Full Breakfast
Credit Cards: No
Closed Christmas & Easter
Minimum stay holiday weekends & special village events
Notes: 2, 5, 9, 10, 11, 12, 13

The Bowman House

61 Lake Street, Box 586
Hammondsport, NY, 14840
(607) 569-2516

Located in the heart of New York wine country. Pleasant experience in picturesque Hammondsport. Large 1880s Queen Anne Victorian home. Privacy, sitting rooms, library, welcoming touches enhance relaxation after village shopping, visiting wineries, museums, and Finger Lakes. Unique comfort, gracious hosts.

Hosts: Manita & Jack Bowman
Rooms: 4 (2 PB; 2 SB) $60-75
Continental-plus Breakfast
Minimum stay holidays: 2
Credit Cards: No
Notes: 2, 5, 9, 10, 12, 13

HAMPTON BAYS

House on the Water

Box 106, Hampton Bays, NY, 11946
(516) 728-3560

Ranch house on two acres of garden on Shinnecock Bay. Quiet location. One mile to village, train, and bus. Seven miles to Southampton and Westhampton. Two miles to ocean beaches. Bicycles, wind surfers, pedal boat, barbecue, beach lounges, and umbrellas. German, Spanish, and French spoken.

Host: Mrs. Ute
Rooms: 2 (PB) $75-95
Full Breakfast
Minimum stay weekdays: 2; weekends: 3; holidays: 4
Credit Cards: No
Closed Nov. 1-May 1
Notes: 2, 9, 10, 11, 12

HANCOCK

Sunrise Inn B&B

RD 1, Box 232B
Walton, NY, 13856
(607) 865-7254

At this nineteenth-century farmhouse nestled in the Catskills, you will enjoy homey comfort, country tranquility, a gazebo, wraparound porch, library, and wood stove. Awaken to the aroma of homemade soda bread. Browse through a quaint antique shop. Pets in residence. No smoking allowed.

Hosts: Jim & Adele Toth
Rooms: 3 (1 PB; 2 SB) $36.40-58
Continental Breakfast
Credit Cards: No
Notes: 5, 8, 9, 12

HEMPSTEAD (Garden City Line)

Duvall B&B

237 Cathedral Avenue
Hempstead, NY, 11550
(516) 292-9219

Charming old Dutch colonial near airports, railroad to New York City (40 minutes), beaches, Adelphi and Hofstra universities, Nassau Coliseum. Furnished with antiques, rooms have air conditioning and color TV. On-premises parking, complimentary wine. Many nearby tourist attractions.

Hosts: Richard & Wendy Duvall
Rooms: 4 (2PB; 2SB) $60-75 plus 8% tax
Full Breakfast
Minimum Stay weekends: 2; Holidays: 3
Credit Cards: No
Checks for deposit in advance only; cash or traveler's checks on arrival
Notes: 4, 5, 8, 9, 12

HERKIMER

Bellinger Woods B&B

B&B Connection NY
RD 1, Box 325
Vernon, NY, 13476
(315) 829-4888

This is a c. 1860 Victorian that has been carefully restored and furnished with antiques and traditional pieces. A full breakfast is served in the formal dining room. Located just down the hill from Herkimer County Community College and within walking distance of many fine stores. Easily accessible from I-90 (Exit 30) and minutes from downhill and cross-country skiing, the Herkimer Diamond Mines. Near Utica and Cooperstown. $45-125.

HIGH FALLS

Locktender Cottage

Route 213
High Falls, NY, 12440
(914) 687-7700

Step back in time to a quaint Victorian guest house for a romantic getaway in a charming canal town. Dine in the National Historic Landmark, the Dupuy Canal House Restaurant, serving imaginative culinary treats from regional and international food. One and one-half hours north of New York City in the Catskill foothills. Choice of fireplace or Jacuzzi suite.

Host: John Novi
Rooms: 2 (PB) $85-110
Full Breakfast
Credit Cards: All major
Closed Feb.
Notes: 2, 4, 7, 8, 9, 10, 11, 12, 13, 14

HILLSDALE

Berkshire B&B Homes NY 6

P.O. Box 211
Williamsburg, MA, 01096
(413) 268-7244

1830 colonial on 1 acre, with antique and Victorian furniture. Parlor and den with TV/VCR for guest use. Queen bed with private bath; double bed with private or semi-private bath; single room with semi-private bath. Continental breakfast, no smoking, children welcome. $50-90.

HOMER

David Harum House

80 South Main Street
Homer, NY, 13077
(607) 749-3548

Glendale Farm B&B

Famous Federal period house built circa 1815 located in the historic district. Eleven by thirty-four foot entrance foyer with beautiful spiral staircase. David Harum memorabilia on display. Half mile from I-81.

Hosts: Ed & Connie Stone
Rooms: 2 (PB) $35-55
Full Breakfast
Credit Cards: No
Notes: 2, 5, 8, 9, 10, 11, 12, 13

HOWE'S CAVE

American Country Collection 58

984 Gloucester Place
Schenectady, NY, 12309
(518) 370-4948

Conveniently located three miles from I-88, this 150-year-old Greek Revival sits high on a hill overlooking the scenic valley and tiny hamlet of Barnerville. Howe Caverns are just 1.5 miles away; Secret Caverns, 2 miles; Stone Fort and Iroquois Museum, 11 miles; Cooperstown and the Baseball Hall of Fame, 30 miles. Three rooms, one with private bath. Children over twelve are welcome. Resident Springer spaniel. Continental breakfast. $50.

ITHACA

Glendale Farm B&B

224 Bostwick Road
Ithaca, NY, 14850
(607) 272-8756

Our large, comfortable home is furnished with antiques, Oriental carpets, and beamed ceilings. During the winter there is always a fire burning in the fireplace. In the summer the large screened porch provides a place to relax with a book or pleasant conversation. Near Cornell University and Ithaca College, state parks, wineries, Corning Glass, Cayuga Lake. Close to Watkins Glen Racetrack.

Host: Jeanne Marie Tomlinson
Rooms: 12 (5 PB; 7 SB) $75
Full Breakfast
Credit Cards: A, B, C
Notes: 2, 4, 5, 8, 9, 10, 11, 12, 13

Log Country Inn

Box 581
Ithaca, NY, 14851
(607) 589-4771; (800) 274-4771

Enjoy the rustic charm of a log house at the edge of a 7,000-acre state forest. Modern accommodation in the spirit of international hospitality. European country breakfast, afternoon tea. Hiking, skiing, and sauna. Convenient to Ithaca College, Cornell,

Corning Glass, wineries, and antique shopping.

Host: Wanda Grunberg
Rooms: 3 (1 PB; 2 SB) $45-65
Full Breakfast
Credit Cards: A, B
Notes: 2, 3, 4, 5, 6, 8, 9, 10, 11, 12, 13

Peirce House B&B

218 South Albany Street
Ithaca, NY, 14850
(607) 273-0824

Willard Peirce built this turn-of-the-century downtown residence in a style befitting a proper Victorian family. Our lovingly restored home features period furniture, fireplaces, stained glass, fine woodwork, Oriental rugs, whirlpool baths, air- conditioning. Just three blocks to shops, galleries, restaurants, movies. One mile to Cornell, Ithaca College, Cayuga Lake. Special weekday rates.

Hosts: Cathy Emilian & Joe Daley
Rooms: 4 (PB) $70-100
Full Breakfast
Credit Cards: A, B, C
Notes: 2, 5, 9, 10, 11, 12, 13

Peregrine House Victorian Inn

140 College Avenue
Ithaca, NY, 14850
(607) 272-0919

An 1874 brick home with sloping lawns and pretty gardens, just three blocks from Cornell University. Down pillows, fine linens, and air-conditioned bedrooms with Victorian decor. In the center of Ithaca, one mile from Cayuga Lake with its boating, swimming, summer theater, and wineries. Wonderful breakfasts, free snacks.

Hosts: Nancy Falconer & Susan Vance
Rooms: 8 (PB) $69-99
Full Breakfast
Credit Cards: A, B
Notes: 2, 5, 7, 8 (over 8), 9, 10, 11, 12, 13, 14

Rose Inn

Box 6576
Ithaca, NY, 14851
(607) 533-7905

An elegant 1840s Italianate mansion on 20 landscaped acres. Fabulous circular staircase of Honduran mahogany. Prix fixe dinner served with advance reservations. Mobil 4-star rated; AAA 4 diamonds.

Hosts: Sherry & Charles Rosemann
Rooms: 15 (PB) $90-150
Suites: From $165
Full Breakfast
Minimum stay weekends & holidays: 2
Credit Cards: A, B, C
Notes: 2, 4, 5, 8 (over 12), 9, 10, 11, 12, 13, 14

JAMESVILLE

High Meadows B&B

B&B Connection NY
RD 1, Box 325
Vernon, NY, 13476
(315) 829-4888

High Meadows is just a ten-minute scenic drive from Syracuse and within two hours of The Thousand Islands, Alexandria Bay, the Adirondacks, wine country, Lake Ontario, and numerous ski areas. There are two guest rooms with a shared bath, air-conditioning, fireplace, plant-filled solarium, wraparound deck, and a magnificent forty-mile view. $45-125.

JEFFERSON

The Wind in the Willows

B&B Connection NY
RD 1, Box 325
Vernon, NY, 13476
(315) 829-4888

A spacious country home with a relaxed atmosphere on 4.5 acres in the quiet hamlet of Jefferson, located in the northern Catskills. Two guest rooms offer king beds, and two suites feature a kitchenette—all with private bath. Nearby activities include golf, horseback riding, hiking, hanggliding, swimming, boating, and fishing. $45-125.

JOHNSTOWN

American Country Collection 99

984 Gloucester Place
Schenectady, NY, 12309
(518) 370-4948

This 100-year-old Victorian is set on manicured lawns. Two bedrooms share a bath in the tastefully decorated home, complete with piano, organ, and two TV sets. Enjoy a full country breakfast in the morning. $40.

KINGSTON

Rondout B&B

88 West Chester Street
Kingston, NY, 12401
(914) 331-2369

Spacious and gracious 1905 mansion on 2 acres in a quiet neighborhood near the historic district, between the Hudson River and the Catskill Mountains. Hearty breakfasts, evening refreshments, hospitable and knowledgeable hosts. Excellent restaurants, cruises, antiques, museums, galleries, theaters, and five colleges are nearby. Kingston, rich in history and architectural variety, is an Urban Cultural Park.

Hosts: Adele & Ralph Calcavecchio
Rooms: 2 (SB) $60-75
Full Breakfast
Credit Cards: A, B
Notes: 2, 5, 8, 9, 10, 11, 12, 14

LAFAYETTE

Cherry Valley Ventures 3009

6119 Cherry Valley Turnpike
LaFayette, NY, 13084
(315) 677-9723

This California ranch provides a perfect country setting with a view of the valley below and herds of buffalo and dairy cattle on the adjacent hillside. Located ten minutes from Syracuse. One guest room has a draped canopy double bed. The second has a half-canopy queen bed. The third has a queen bed and large windows with a view. Continental breakfast. $45-95.

Cherry Valley Ventures 3019

6119 Cherry Valley Turnpike
LaFayette, NY, 13084
(315) 677-9723

Newly built contemporary on a hill with a panoramic view. The master bedroom has a private deck, king bed, private bath, and TV. Hot-air ballooning nearby; snowmobiling, and cross-country skiing right outside the door. Continental or full breakfast. $55.

LAKE LUZERNE

The Lamplight Inn

2129 Lake Avenue, Box 70
Lake Luzerne, NY, 12846
(518) 696-5294

Romantic 1890 Victorian inn. Warm, friendly atmosphere: fireplaces, country breakfasts, freshly ground coffee, antiques, Oriental rugs, chess. Perfect getaway for couples. One block from Lake Luzerne in the southern Adirondacks. Ten minutes to Lake George; twenty to Saratoga Springs.

Hosts: Gene & Linda Merlino
Rooms: 10 (PB) $65-95
Full Breakfast
Credit Cards: C
Notes: 2, 8 (over 12), 9, 10, 11, 12, 13, 14

LAKE PLACID

Blackberry Inn

59 Sentinel Road
Lake Placid, NY, 12946
(518) 523-3419

Colonial built in 1915 is located one mile from the center of the village, on Route 73. Five guest rooms offer country flair and are convenient to all major Olympic sites and surrounded by Adirondack Parks beauty. Nearby recreation includes skiing, skating, hiking, golf, and fishing. Home-baked breakfasts.

Hosts: Bill & Gail Billerman
Rooms: 5 (SB) $45-65
Continental-plus Breakfast
Credit Cards: No
Notes: 2, 5, 7, 8, 9, 10, 11, 12, 13

Interlaken Inn and Restaurant

Highland House Inn

3 Highland Place
Lake Placid, NY, 12946
(518) 523-2377

Peaceful central location in the village of Lake Placid. Each room is equally appealing, all having been recently redecorated. The full breakfast includes our special blueberry pancakes. Fully efficient country cottage also available adjacent to inn.

Hosts: Teddy & Cathy Blazer
Cottage: $70-85
Rooms: 7 (PB) $50-65
Full Breakfast
Minimum stay weekends: 2
Holidays: 3
Credit Cards: A, B
Notes: 2, 5, 7, 8, 9, 10, 11, 12, 13

Interlaken Inn and Restaurant

15 Interlaken Avenue
Lake Placid, NY, 12946
(518) 523-3180

A Victorian inn in the heart of Lake Placid featuring a gourmet restaurant and twelve uniquely decorated rooms. The inn has tin ceilings, a cozy fireplace in the living room, lots of lace and charm. Nearby you can enjoy golf, skiing, or any of the pleasures of the Adirondacks.

Hosts: Roy & Carol Johnson
Rooms: 12 (PB) $100-150/couple, MAP
Full Breakfast
Minimum stay weekends & holidays: 2
Credit Cards: A, B, C
Closed Nov. and April
Notes: 2, 4, 7, 8 (over 5), 9, 10, 11, 12, 13, 14

South Meadow Farm & Lodge

Cascade Road (Route 73)
Lake Placid, NY, 12946
(518) 523-9369

Small working farm on 130 acres, bordered by state land in the heart of the Adirondack High Peaks. Ski out the back door onto Olympic cross-country trails. Family-style lodging with full, hearty meals. Come join us all year and share our lodge, our view, and our Adirondack hospitality.

Host: Betty Eldridge
Rooms: 5 (1 PB; 4 SB) $40-90
Full Breakfast
Credit Cards: No
Notes: 2, 3, 4, 5, 8, 9, 10, 11, 12, 13

Spruce Lodge B&B

31 Sentinel Road
Lake Placid, NY, 12946
(518) 523-9350

A large private home owned by the Wescott family since 1949. Located in Lake Placid, within a ten-mile radius of all area activities.

Rooms: 7 (2 PB; 5 SB) $42.80-53.50
Continental Breakfast
Credit Cards: A, B
Notes: 2, 5, 8, 9, 10, 11, 12, 13

Stagecoach Inn

370 Old Military Road
Lake Placid, NY, 12946
(518) 523-9474

Built in 1833, this inn was the original stagecoach stop for travelers to the Adirondacks. In fact, Verplank Colvin stayed here when he conducted the survey of the Adirondacks in 1873. The interior of the inn is in original condition, wainscoting floor to ceiling, with birch-log trim. Only modern baths have been added.

Host: Lyn Witte
Rooms: 9 (5 PB; 4 SB) $55-80
Full Breakfast
Credit Cards: No
Notes: 2, 5, 7, 8, 9, 10, 11, 12, 13, 14

LAKE PLEASANT

Hummingbird Hill

B&B Connection NY
RD 1, Box 325
Vernon, NY, 13476
(315) 829-4888

Rustic lodge overlooking Oxbow Lake; a fieldstone fireplace covers one wall of the family room. Located just seven miles from Speculator and within driving distance of Gore Mountain, Indian Lake, or the Adirondack Museum. $45-125.

LANSING

The O.P. Townley House

304 Peruville Road
P.O. Box 297
Lansing, NY, 14882
(607) 533-4230

Elegant 1873 brick Italianate farmhouse with beautiful arched doorways. Located ten minutes from Cornell, Ithaca, and Cayuga Lake. Relaxed atmosphere. Enjoy a breakfast including homemade breads with jams made from our own fruit trees, grapes, and berries. Two rooms with private Jacuzzi baths; two share a bath. Great for cycling (tandem available); near parks and lakes. Two miles from airport; pickup available.

Host: Rick Palmer
Rooms: 4 (2 PB; 2 SB) $55-65
Full Breakfast
Credit Cards: No
Notes: 5, 9, 10, 11, 12

LEVITTOWN

B & B of Long Island LL

P.O. Box 392
Old Westbury, NY, 11568
(516) 334-6231

Close to Sunrise and Wantagh Highway, this pleasant home has a twin bedded room, TV, private bath, and air conditioning. Hosts have hosted students from all over the world. Continental breakfast. $58.

LEWISTON

Rainbow Hospitality L207

466 Amherst Street
Buffalo, NY, 14207
(716) 874-8797

Colonial home, convenient to the village of Lewiston and Artpark. Spacious master suite and private bath. Soft music, candles, and fine linen await you at the breakfast table in this comfortable family home. $50-65.

Rainbow Hospitality L208

466 Amherst Street
Buffalo, NY, 14207
(716) 874-8797

This 150-year-old Greek Revival is beautifully furnished according to the period of the home. Large, private guest rooms offer a veranda and fireplace. Lovely grounds and covered porches for relaxing before or after the theater. Artpark, New York State's performing arts complex, is just three blocks away. Fifteen-minute drive to Niagara Falls. Breakfast might include your host's homemade sausage among other family recipes and local specialties. $50-65.

Rainbow Hospitality L209

466 Amherst Street
Buffalo, NY, 14207
(716) 874-8797

One-hundred-year-old farmhouse in a quiet country setting surrounded by farmland. Your charming hostess relates the history of the home. Pets in residence include a poodle and cats. Easily accessible to the village of Lewiston and historic Fort Niagara. $35-45.

Rainbow Hospitality L210

466 Amherst Street
Buffalo, NY, 14207
(716) 874-8797

Charming, private, historic guest house in the heart of historic Lewiston. Master bedroom and private bath on the second floor. Walk to shops, restaurants, and Artpark. Ten-minute drive to Niagara Falls. A kitchenette and continental breakfast are included. From $70.

Rainbow Hospitality L211

466 Amherst Street
Buffalo, NY, 14207
(716) 874-8797

A gracious Victorian, minutes from the village of Lewiston and Artpark. Beautifully perched on the banks of the lower Niagara River, the inn provides guests a breathtaking view of the Canadian shoreline and sunset. Just seven miles north of Niagara Falls. Four guest rooms, including a brass-bedded queen, double, twin, and suite. Shared and private baths. Wraparound porches. $50-65.

Rainbow Hospitality L217

466 Amherst Street
Buffalo, NY, 14207
(716) 874-8797

Guests are invited to relax and enjoy the sunset from the beautiful wraparound porch of this late 1800s Victorian. The home is decorated with country and period antiques. There is a spacious suite with two bedrooms, full bath and half bath, full kitchen, and living room with antiques. Private entrance. The home sits on 3.5 acres of land. From $70.

Rainbow Hospitality L222

466 Amherst Street
Buffalo, NY, 14207
(716) 874-8797

An efficiency suite in a private home in a quiet residential neighborhood close to Lewiston, Artpark, Niagara Falls, and Niagara University. German hosts welcome you. A special treat often shared with guests are the hosts' delicious cookies. $50-65.

Rainbow Hospitality L223

466 Amherst Street
Buffalo, NY, 14207
(716) 874-8797

Restored farmhouse and former stagecoach stop, totally restored. Private bath and master bedroom suite overlook acres of grape vineyards. French doors open to a charming Victorian table set with continental breakfast and homebaked breads and muffins. $50-65.

Rainbow Hospitality L300

466 Amherst Street
Buffalo, NY, 14207
(716) 874-8797

A contemporary colonial, located in a prestigious residential setting convenient to Niagara Falls, Lewiston, and Niagara University. The hostess enjoys gardening and travel, and is knowledgeable on Niagara arts history. Breakfast is served in the lovely family room overlooking the beautifully landscaped gardens. One double and one single room, private baths. $35-45.

Rainbow Hospitality L305

466 Amherst Street
Buffalo, NY, 14207
(716) 874-8797

Contemporary colonial, located in a prestigious residential setting convenient to the falls, Lewiston, and Niagara University. Breakfast is served in the lovely family room overlooking landscaped gardens. A double and a single room are offered with private baths. $35-45.

Rainbow Hospitality L306

466 Amherst Street
Buffalo, NY, 14207
(716) 874-8797

This home provides beautiful views of Lewiston and the lights of Toronto on a clear evening. Tennis courts. Breakfast may be served in the formal dining room or glass-enclosed breakfast room overlooking the escarpment and historic Lewiston portage. $50-65.

Rainbow Hospitality L530

466 Amherst Street
Buffalo, NY, 14207
(716) 874-8797

Walk to Artpark and Lewiston. Two-bedroom ranch home, living room, dining room, and kitchen. Self-serve or kitchen privileges on request. One block from historic Center Street, restaurants, and gift shops. $35-45.

LITTLE VALLEY

Napoli Stagecoach Inn

Napoli Corners
Little Valley, NY, 14755
(716) 938-6735

A real stagecoach inn from 1830-1880. The family room has a fireplace, and the library contains 3,000 volumes. Comfort and easy hospitality are memorable, with access to skiing and golf at Holiday Valley, history at Seneca Indian Museum, culture at Chautaugua Institution, and nature at Allegheny State Park.

Hosts: Marion & Emmett Waite
Rooms: 3 (SB) $27-37.80
Full Breakfast
Credit Cards: No
Notes: 2, 4, 5, 8 (10 and over), 10, 11, 12, 13, 14

LIVINGSTON MANOR

Clarke's Place in the Country

RD 2, Box 465A
Livingston Manor, NY, 12758
(914) 439-5442

A unique contemporary rustic home on 3 acres in the heart of the Catskills. White pine interior throughout, with a great room that features a twenty-foot cathedral ceiling and wood-burning stove. Canoeing, swimming, and fishing on private lake nearby. Minutes from downhill and cross-country skiing. Guests enjoy a hearty country breakfast. Fine food and live entertainment, terrific antiques and auctions, unusual shops and attractions—and the world's best trout fishing.

Chestnut Ridge Inn

Hosts: The Clarkes
Rooms: 2 (PB) $55-65 + tax
Full Breakfast
Credit Cards: A, B
Notes: 5, 8, 11, 12, 13

Lanza's Country Inn

RD 2, Box 446
Livingston Manor, NY, 12758
(914) 439-5070

Catskill Mountain outdoor enjoyment: rivers, streams, lakes, woods, mountains, country roads, and quaint villages. Comfortable antique-filled rooms, great food. Invigorating, relaxing, with friendly, personal service. You'll love our "Covered Bridge Country."

Hosts: Dick, Pat, & Mickey Lanza
Rooms: 8 (PB) $52-80
Full Breakfast
Minimum stay holidays: 2
Credit Cards: A, B, C
Notes: 2, 4, 5, 7, 8, 9, 10, 11, 12, 13

LOCKPORT

Chestnut Ridge Inn

7205 Chestnut Ridge Road
Lockport, NY, 14094
(716) 439-9124

An 1826 Federal mansion with 8 acres of gardens and lawns, circular staircase, library, fireplaces, and antique furniture. On the historic Niagara frontier, within minutes of Niagara Falls, Canada, and Fort Niagara. Country auctions, lush fruit farms, fairs, summer theaters. Holidays are special occasions.

Hosts: Frank & Lucy Cervoni
Suite: 1 (PB) $75-95
Rooms: 2 (PB) $70-75
Full Breakfast
Credit Cards: No
Notes: 2, 3, 5, 8, 9, 10, 11, 12, 13

LONG BEACH

B & B of Long Island LBM

P.O. Box 392
Old Westbury, NY, 11568
(516) 334-6231

Built in 1906 as the summer home for Senator Reynolds, this was one of the first Mediterranean-style homes built in the area. Magnificent stained-glass windows and grand staircase leading to the two guest rooms. Private or semiprivate bath. Breakfast is served in the formal dining room. Perfect for those without a car, as it's only about three blocks to the beach or railroad station. $75.

MANHASSET

B & B of Long Island SM

P.O. Box 392
Old Westbury, NY, 11568
(516) 334-6231

This is the second oldest house in the area, built in 1840 and lovingly restored. The huge dining room has three chandeliers and a table that seats thirty. Several guest rooms with double or twin beds and sitting rooms with TV, plus a suite for families. Baths are private. Walk to the railroad for a quick trip to the city or to local restaurants and movies. $60.

Plumbush

MARGARETVILLE

American Country Collection 48

984 Gloucester Place
Schenectady, NY, 12309
(518) 370-4948

High atop a hill on 5.5 acres in the midst of the Catskills sits this completely restored historic Victorian with large front porch overlooking the mountains. Located near trout fishing, horseback riding, pond and lakes for swimming and canoeing, golf, cross-country skiing, antiquing, and downhill skiing. Five second-floor rooms, three with private baths. One suite has a double and one twin bed with private bath. $55-65.

MASSAPEQUA

B & B of Long Island MJ

P.O. Box 392
Old Westbury, NY, 11568
(516) 334-6231

Directly on the beach, this contemporary home is the perfect place to relax. Enjoy the water view from the king bed. Glass doors open to your private deck with stairs to the beach. Private bath, air-conditioning. Also twin-bedded room with shared bath. Enhanced continental breakfast is served in the spacious dining alcove overlooking the living room. Boat available for guests. Minutes to Bethpage State Park and Jones Beach. $80.

MAYVILLE

Plumbush

RD 2, Box 332
Mayville, NY, 14757
(716) 789-5309

Newly restored circa 1865 Italian villa hilltop country home surrounded by 125 acres. Just one mile from Chautauqua Institute. Bluebirds and wildlife abound. Bicycles available; cross-country ski trail. Sunny rooms, wicker, antiques, and a touch of elegant charm. As seen in *Insider Magazine,* May/June 1990 and *Victoria Magazine,* August 1989.

Hosts: George & Sandy Green
Rooms: 4 (PB) $55-85

Continental-plus Breakfast
Credit Cards: A, B
Notes: 2, 5, 8 (over 12), 9, 10, 11, 12, 13, 14

The Village Inn

111 South Erie Street
Route 394
Mayville, NY, 14757
(716) 753-3583

Spend restful nights in a turn-of-the-century Victorian located near the shores of lakes Chautauqua and Erie. The home is furnished with many antiques and trimmed in woodwork crafted by European artisans. Near the Chautauqua Institution, antique shops, wineries, swimming, golf, biking, arts and crafts, hang gliding, skiing.

Host: Dean Hanby
Rooms: 3 (SB) $50
Full Breakfast
Credit Cards: C
Notes: 2, 5, 7, 8, 9, 10, 11, 12, 13, 14

MIDDLETOWN/SLATE HILL

American Country Collection 64

984 Gloucester Place
Schenectady, NY, 12309
(518) 370-4948

Fall festivals, winery tours, canoeing, swimming, and skiing. Thoroughbred horses and tack shop on premises. Three rooms plus two suites, two shared baths and an extra first-floor bath. Full breakfast. Located five miles from I-84, 65 miles from New York City, 18 from New Paltz. Ski at Mt. Peter, Vernon Valley, or Big Vanilla. $65-75.

MOHAWK

Country Hills

B&B Connection NY
RD 1, Box 325
Vernon, NY, 13476
(315) 829-4888

This spacious 1860s farmhouse sits amid rolling lawns overlooking the Mohawk Valley. It is surrounded by barns, outbuildings, and acres of private woods traversed by cross-country ski trails, walking, and hiking trails. The suites have full baths and are ideal for honeymooners or family travelers. Near Remington Arms, Herkimer County Community College, the General Herkimer Home, Herkimer Diamond Mines, Jordanville Monastery, and many other attractions. Located three miles south of the New York State Thruway, Exit 30. $45-125.

MONTAUK

Greenhedges Oceanside Villa B & B

Essex Street, Box 122
Montauk, NY, 11954
(516) 668-5013

Two blocks from the public beach, this 1926 brick and stucco Tudor is on a private acre surrounded by green hedges. Sunken living room, cathedral ceilings, two fireplaces, lovely gardens, solarium, gazebo. One block to village. Tennis, restaurants, golf, surfing, fishing, horseback riding, and health spa nearby.

Hosts: Ellie & Warren Adams
Rooms: 3 (PB) $59-96.75
Continental Breakfast
Minimum stay weekends: 2; holidays: 3
Credit Cards: No
Closed mid-Nov.-mid-March
Notes: 2, 7, 8 (over 7), 9, 10, 11, 12, 14

MT. TREMPER

Mt. Tremper Inn

Box 51, Route 121 & Wittenberg Road
Mt. Tremper, NY, 12457
(914) 688-5329

Victorian hospitality and elegant antiques await you in this 1850, twenty-three-room mansion in the middle of the Catskill Mountains. Large parlor with fireplace, library/game room, classical music at breakfast. Outdoor dining in season. Near Woodstock, all ski slopes, historic Kingston and Rhinebeck.

Hosts: Lou Caselli & Peter LaScala
Rooms: 12 (2 PB; 10 SB) $60-90
Full Breakfast
Credit Cards: A, B
Notes: 2, 5, 7 (restricted), 9, 10, 11, 13, 14

Mt. Tremper Inn

MUMFORD

Genesee Country Inn

948 George Street
Box 340
Mumford, NY, 14511-0340
(716) 538-2500; FAX (716) 538-4565

This historic stone mill is located on 6 quiet acres of woods and waterfalls. Lovingly restored, with all timely conveniences, nine individually decorated guest rooms. Many oversized beds; balconies; rooms overlooking water; fireplaces; lots of historic stenciling. Tea and full breakfast are served. Nearby is a museum, fine restaurants, Rochester, NY, Letchworth State Park; Niagara Falls one hour. Trout fishing.

Rooms: 9 (PB) $80-115
Full Breakfast & Tea
Credit Cards: A, B, E
Notes: 2, 5, 7, 9, 11, 12, 13, 14

NAPLES

The Vagabond Inn

3300 Sliter Road
Naples, NY, 14512
(716) 554-6271

Contemporary, luxurious seclusion in the mountains. Large, elegant bedrooms with private or shared baths and spectacular views. Jacuzzi, swimming pool, a huge fieldstone fireplace, sixty-foot great room, and kitchen for guests' use only. Terrific winter ski packages, our own cross-country trails, and miles of hiking. Fifteen minutes to lakes and wineries.

Host: Celeste Stanhope-Wiley
Rooms: 4 (2 PB; 2 SB) $60-125
Continental Breakfast
Credit Cards: A, B
Notes: 2, 5, 7, 9, 11, 13, 14

NELLISTON

Historian B&B

B&B Connection NY
RD 1, Box 325
Vernon, NY, 13476
(315) 829-4888

This Victorian stone house, built in 1842, overlooks the Mohawk River and is listed in the National Register of Historic Homes. Guests may relax on a fifty-foot deck overlooking the river. Located on Route 5, three miles from Exit 29 on I-90. $45-125.

NEW BALTIMORE

American Country Collection 89

984 Gloucester Place
Schenectady, NY, 12309
(518) 370-4948

Located halfway between Albany and Catskill, within an hour of Saratoga, New Paltz, Lenox, and Stockbridge, this early

1800s farmhouse sits on a hillside overlooking the Hudson River, which is within walking distance. Three rooms with private baths. Smoking is permitted. $60.

NEW PALTZ

American Country Collection 116

984 Gloucester Place
Schenectady, NY, 12309
(518) 370-4948

Country Victorian farmhouse on 4.5 acres of orchards and fields. Rooms have fresh flowers, and some have cozy feather-beds. Three rooms share a bath. One room has a double bed and working fireplace. A well-balanced, healthy breakfast begins the day, as the hostess specializes in vegetarian gourmet cuisine. Smoking restricted; children welcome. $55-85.

Nana's

54 Old Ford Road
New Paltz, NY, 12561
(914) 255-5678

Nana's B&B is in the Hudson River fruit belt near two beautiful resorts. Enjoy the mountains, three lakes, swimming, boating, hiking, mountain climbing, cross-country skiing, etc. Nana's is in a country setting on 20 acres. Antique furnishings, full country breakfast.

Host: Kathleen Maloney
Rooms: 2 (SB) $40-50
Full Breakfast
Credit Cards: No
Notes: 2, 5, 8, 9, 10, 11, 12, 13

NEW ROCHELLE

Rose Hill Guest House

44 Rose Hill Avenue
New Rochelle, NY, 10804
(914) 632-6464

This beautiful and intimate French Normandy home's hostess is a real estate agent and bridge Life Master. Weather permitting, enjoy breakfast on the flowered patio or in the chandeliered library/dining room. Thirty minutes to Manhattan by train or car. Safe parking behind house.

Host: Marilou Mayetta
Rooms: 2 (SB) $48.50-64.65
Continental Breakfast
Minimum stay holidays: 2
Credit Cards: No
Notes: 2, 5, 7, 8, 9, 14

NEW YORK

Al B's B&B

B&B Network of NY
134 W. 32nd Street
Suite 602, NY, NY, 10001
(212) 645-8134

Luxury doorman building with courtyard in the heart of midtown on the east side. Minutes from Grand Central Station, United Nations, and Bloomingdale's. Air-conditioning, cable TV, laundry facilities.

Rooms: 1 (PB) $90
Continental Breakfast
Credit Cards: No
Notes: 5, 8

Alden's B&B

B&B Network of NY
Suite 602
134 W. 32nd Street, NY, NY, 10001
(212) 645-8134

Nicely furnished loft in an eighteenth-century warehouse. Original wooden beams and windows, cast-iron columns, exposed brick. TV, stereo, air-conditioning, ceiling fans, laundry facilities. Only one-half block from historic South Street Seaport. Near Wall Street, Battery Park, Statue of Liberty, and Chinatown.

Rooms: 1 (SB) $60-80
Continental Breakfast

Credit Cards: No
Notes: 5, 7, 8

Ariel's B&B

B&B Network of NY
Suite 602
134 W. 32nd Street, NY, NY, 10001
(212) 645-8134

Beautifully furnished penthouse apartment near Broadway theaters, Lincoln Center, Central Park, and Carnegie Hall. Unique jeweled canopy bed, terrace, telephone, air-conditioning. Laundry on premises.

Rooms: 2 (1 PB; 1 SB) $80
Continental Breakfast
Credit Cards: No
Notes: 5, 8

Bed & Breakfast (& Books) 1

35 West 92nd Street
New York, NY, 10025
(212) 865-8740

Beautifully renovated townhouse on quiet, tree-lined street near Central Park offers one double room with bath next door. A quiet sitting area nearby has TV and books. Convenient to museums, theaters, shopping, and all transportation. Children welcome in loft areas. Air-conditioned. $80.

Bed & Breakfast (& Books) 3

35 West 92nd Street
New York, NY, 10025
(212) 865-8740

Very large, sunny twin-bedded room with private bath in spacious seven-room apartment. On a high floor with lovely river views and sunsets. Art Deco; air conditioned; 24-hour doorman. $80.

Bed & Breakfast (& Books) 7

35 West 92nd Street
New York, NY, 10025
(212) 865-8740

Charming, bright, antique-filled apartment on the thirty-first floor has magnificent views of Manhattan and the Hudson River from every room. A plant-filled window garden with flowers in spring and summer. The hostess, a world traveler, can accommodate guests in her master room with queen bed. Air-conditioning; 24-hour security. $67.50.

Bed & Breakfast (& Books) 8

35 West 92nd Street
New York, NY, 10025
(212) 865-8740

Comfortably furnished apartment has twin room in a pre-World War II building with 24-hour elevator and doorman service. The hostess, a therapist, will make you very welcome. Close to Broadway restaurants and shops. Convenient transportation to theaters, midtown shopping, and all museums. Air-conditioned. $67.50.

Bed & Breakfast (& Books) 9

35 West 92nd Street
New York, NY, 10025
(212) 865-8740

Comfortable and beautifully decorated two-bedroom, two-bath apartment offers a twin guest room with bath next door. Guests are welcome to use the large dining room with TV and sofa as their sitting room. 24-hour elevator and doorman service; air-conditioning. Walk to all museums and Central Park. Children welcome. $72.50.

Bed & Breakfast (& Books) 10

35 West 92nd Street
New York, NY, 10025
(212) 865-8740

Attractively furnished old-world-style apartment with bright, sunny, twin room with TV, air conditioning, and bath next door. 24-hour doorman. $85.

Bed & Breakfast (& Books) 14

35 West 92nd Street
New York, NY, 10025
(212) 865-8740

Lovely apartment in older traditional building offers a twin room with private bath. This cozy and warm actress's home has antiques, paintings, and books. Continental breakfast, air- conditioning, TV, and 24-hour manned elevator service. Children over 14 are welcome. $80.

Bed & Breakfast (& Books) 15

35 West 92nd Street
New York, NY, 10025
(212) 865-8740

In a stylish townhouse. Spacious room with modern art, queen futon bed, shared bath, air-conditioning. Within walking distance of the theater district, Carnegie Hall, the U.N., Bloomingdale's, and great restaurants. Children welcome. $85.

Bed & Breakfast (& Books) 19

35 West 92nd Street
New York, NY, 10025
(212) 865-8740

Large, comfortable apartment in a small building in the Washington Square area. Room with double bed, own phone, and private bath. The building is surrounded by New York University, many modestly priced ethnic restaurants, and several off-Broadway theaters. Small room with twin bed also available. $72.50.

Bevy's B&B

B&B Network of NY
Suite 602
134 W. 32nd Street, NY, NY, 10001
(212) 645-8134

Large Soho artist's loft. Guest room on upper level. European feeling, nicely furnished. Near galleries, shops, restaurants. Cat on premises.

Rooms: 1 (PB) $60-80
Continental Breakfast
Credit Cards: No
Notes: 5, 7, 8

1845 Townhouse

B&B Network of NY
Suite 602
134 W. 32nd St.
New York, NY, NY, 10001
(212) 645-8134

Beautiful home on the upper east side with a backyard. Choice of two bedrooms, one with a four-poster bed, each with private bath. Library/sitting room with TV. No smoking. $90.

Eileen's B&B

B&B Network of NY
134 W. 32nd St., Suite 602
New York, NY, NY, 10001
(212) 645-8134

Doorman building apartment on the seventeenth floor overlooking Central Park and reservoir. Lovely room with queen bed, private bath. Two cats in residence. No smoking. $90.

Ginger's B&B

B&B Network of NY
134 W. 32nd St., Suite 602
New York, NY, NY, 10001
(212) 645-8134

Magnificent view overlooking Lincoln Center and the Hudson River. Beautifully furnished apartment in a doorman building. Air conditioning, piano, laundry on the floor. Choice of king bed or twins. $90.

James's B&B

B&B Network of NY
134 W. 32nd St., Suite 602
New York, NY, NY, 10001
(212) 645-8134

Four bedrooms, three baths, very friendly host. Five-minute walk to the Empire State Building. Lots of flexibility in bed types and sleeping arrangements. From $60 + tax.

Japanese Writer's B&B

B&B Network of NY
Suite 602
134 W. 32nd Street, NY, NY, 10001
(212) 645-8134

One-half block from Central Park on the upper west side. Private studio with TV, air-conditioning, ceiling fan. Full Japanese breakfast on request. Laundry on premises, garden. One dog and two cats in residence.

Rooms: 1 (PB) $120
Full Breakfast
Credit Cards: No
Notes: 7, 8

Jim R's B&B

B&B Network of NY
Suite 602
134 W. 32nd Street, NY, NY, 10001
(212) 645-8134

Seven-story mansion from 1899 overlooking the Hudson River and Riverside Park. Backyard with barbecue. Eight fireplaces, pool room, exercise room, Victorian furnishings, stained glass, roof garden, Jacuzzi, steam bath, elevator.

Rooms: 5 (3 PB; 2 SB) $135
Continental Breakfast
Credit Cards: No
Notes: 7, 8

Julius's B&B

B&B Network of NY
Suite 602
134 W. 32nd Street, NY, NY, 10001
(212) 645-8134

Luxury doorman building on the upper east side near Central Park, museums, shopping, express subway. TV and air conditioning, terrace. Health club with pool; laundry on premises. Host has NYC guide license.

Rooms: 1 (PB) $60-90
Continental Breakfast
Credit Cards: No
Notes: 5, 7, 8

Linda K's B&B

B&B Network of NY
Suite 602
134 W. 32nd Street, NY, NY, 10001
(212) 645-8134

Beautifully furnished home of an interior designer. One block from Bloomingdale's. Luxury highrise with doorman. TV, air conditioning, phones, garage, and laundry in building.

Rooms: 2 (1 PB; 1 SB) $60-90
Continental Breakfast
Credit Cards: No
Notes: 5, 7, 8

Mary G's B&B

B&B Network of NY
Suite 602
134 W. 32nd Street, NY, NY, 10001
(212) 645-8134

In the heart of Greenwich Village, this host has two rooms for guests. Air conditioning, TV, nicely furnished. Only 1.5 blocks from Washington Square Park.

Rooms: 2 (1 PB; 1 SB) $80
Continental Breakfast
Credit Cards: No
Notes: 5, 7, 8

Nan's B&B

B&B Network of NY
134 W. 32nd St., Suite 602
New York, NY, 10001
(212) 645-8134

Newly decorated studio in charming, vine-covered 100-year-old brownstone on the upper east side. Kitchen overlooks a sunny garden. Air conditioning, twin or double beds, cable TV, private entrance. No smoking. $120.

Robin's B&B

B&B Network of NY
134 W. 32nd St., Suite 602
New York, NY, 10001
(212) 645-8134

Incredible 4000-square-foot loft in the heart of midtown near Broadway theaters. Three bedrooms (two with queen antique beds with down quilts and pillows), two baths (one with sauna), stereo, TV, air conditioning, original artwork, pool table, copy and FAX machines, private telephone line. No smokers or children. $90.

Sheila's B&B

B&B Network of NY
134 W. 32nd St., Suite 602
New York, NY, 10001
(212) 645-8134

Two blocks from historic Gramercy Park, on a beautiful block, this large room with private bath has air conditioning, TV, lots of light and plants, original artwork. Two resident cats; no smoking. $90.

Victorian Townhouse

B&B Network of NY
134 W. 32nd St., Suite 602
New York, NY, 10001
(212) 645-8134

Two blocks from Bloomingdale's, this magnificent home has a garden, antique rugs and paintings, air conditioning, TV. Choice of rooms with either queen or twin beds. Private bath, continental breakfast. $90.

NIAGARA FALLS

Linen 'n Lace B&B Inn

659 Chilton Avenue
Niagara Falls, NY, 14301
(716) 285-3935

Built in 1906, this home boasts beautiful oak wainscoting and woodwork, stained-glass windows, antiques, and warm, friendly hospitality. A full breakfast is served daily. Relax on the large front porch after a day of sightseeing. Located downtown, near bus service and fine dining. Ample parking in a private lot. Near the US/Canadian border, Niagara Falls Convention Center, and all sightseeing attractions.

Host: Mary A. Martin
Rooms: 6 (2 PB; 4 SB) $55-75
Full Breakfast
Credit Cards: No
Notes: 5, 7, 8, 9, 10, 11, 12, 14

Rainbow Hospitality NF100

466 Amherst Street
Buffalo, NY, 14207
(716) 874-8797

Dutch colonial, located on a quiet residential street. Walk to Niagara Gorge and stone museum, state parks, and picnic areas. Spacious king bed, shared bath, and Victorian decor combine to bring guest a unique Niagara adventure. $35-45.

Rainbow Hospitality NF101

466 Amherst Street
Buffalo, NY, 14207
(716) 874-8797

Spectacular view of the Niagara River. This unique boat house is private and quiet, yet minutes from Niagara Falls and Buffalo. Knotty pine throughout, living room, kitchen, two bedrooms and private bath. Sofa in living room opens to double bed. On request, the main house has a double room with private bath. $35-45.

Rainbow Hospitality NF102

466 Amherst Street
Buffalo, NY, 14207
(716) 874-8797

Large Victorian home turned B&B by a most interesting, well-traveled hostess. Comfortable, homey accommodations, reasonable rates. Ten minutes from downtown Niagara. $35-45.

Rainbow Hospitality NF104

466 Amherst Street
Buffalo, NY, 14207
(716) 874-8797

Hosted studio apartment in the heart of the city. Guests have a separate entrance to this cozy first-floor studio apartment. The refrigerator will be stocked, or the hostess will deliver a continental breakfast to your door with home-made muffins, pastries, and cereals. $50-65.

Rainbow Hospitality NF110

466 Amherst Street
Buffalo, NY, 14207
(716) 874-8797

Stately home two blocks from the falls, on a quiet street of lovely older homes. Enjoy Southern hospitality and a full cooked breakfast. Front patio and two guest rooms, each having a double bed and shared bath. $35-45.

Rainbow Hospitality NF112

466 Amherst Street
Buffalo, NY, 14207
(716) 874-8797

Spacious private garden apartment with kitchenette in a residential neighborhood. Double bed with adjoining sitting area, private entrance, bath. Just five minutes from downtown, Convention Center, and parks. A first-floor double room with shared bath is also available on request. $35-45.

Rainbow Hospitality NF113

466 Amherst Street
Buffalo, NY, 14207
(716) 874-8797

Experience old Niagara. Walk to the falls, parks, bridges to Canada, and shopping. Spacious 1900s Tudor in an area of fine homes. Four rooms with private and shared baths. $35-45.

Rainbow Hospitality NF114

466 Amherst Street
Buffalo, NY, 14207
(716) 874-8797

Residential home on the Niagara River minutes from the falls and downtown Buffalo. Front suite with living room, dining room, and double bed rooms offers guests privacy and a beautiful view of the river from the screened front veranda. Additional rooms include twin and single rooms with shared bath. Full breakfast. $35-45.

NIVERVILLE

American Country Collection 79

984 Gloucester Place
Schenectady, NY, 12309
(518) 370-4948

Beautifully preserved gingerbread and an old oak door with Venetian glass inserts detail this Italianate home built in 1870 in this small town in the northern area of the Hudson Valley twenty minutes from Albany. Tanglewood is twelve miles away; the Shaker Museum is five. Two second-floor rooms share one bath. No smoking; adults only; full breakfast. $60-70.

Pine Tree Inn B&B

NORTH HUDSON

Pine Tree Inn B&B

Route 9
North Hudson, NY, 12855
(518) 532-9255

Small century-old classic Adirondack inn. Full breakfast served, featuring homemade breads, in the dining room with its original tin ceiling. Period furniture decorates the country-comfortable rooms. Centrally located for year-round activities.

Hosts: Peter & Patricia Schoch
Rooms: 5 (S2B) $35-55
Full Breakfast
Minimum stay holidays: 2-3
Credit Cards: No
Notes: 2, 4 (winter only), 5, 7, 8 (over 6), 9, 10, 11, 12, 13

NORTHPORT

B & B of Long Island NC

P.O. Box 392
Old Westbury, NY, 11568
(516) 334-6231

On a beautiful piece of property minutes from Cold Spring Harbor and Huntington. Two rooms, one with double bed, the other with two single beds. Bath is shared only if both rooms are occupied. Breakfast is continental, but hosts will serve eggs if desired. Guests are encouraged to relax in the family den and enjoy TV or the VCR, or just sit on the porch. Sunken Meadow Beach is close by, and Fire Island is just a short distance via the Robert Moses Causeway. $62.

B & B of Long Island NK

P.O. Box 392
Old Westbury, NY, 11568
(516) 334-6231

This house offers a completely private upstairs area with a double room, writing desk, easy chair, and dresser. The adjoining room has a couch, TV, coffee tables. Downstairs bathroom is shared. Also available at times is the master bedroom with double bed. Only three blocks from the Long Island railroad and a short distance to the beach and towns of Cold Spring Harbor and Northport. $62.

NORTH RIVER

Highwinds Inn

Barton Mines Road, P.O. Box 70
North River, NY, 12856
(518) 251-3760

Located at an elevation of 2,500 feet on 1,600 acres of land in the middle of a garnet mine. All rooms and the dining area have a spectacular view to the west. On the property we have mountain biking, canoeing, hiking to several peaks and ponds, garnet mine tours, gardens, cross-country ski touring, and workshops that might include watercolor painting, cooking, kayak clinics, yoga. Nearby spring rafting on the Hudson; Lake George; Octoberfest.

Host: Kim Repscha
Rooms: 4 (1 PB; 3 SB) $35/person
Full Breakfast
Credit Cards: A, B
Closed Nov.
Notes: 2, 3 (picnic), 4, 8 (over 12), 9, 10, 11, 12, 13, 14

NUNDA

Butternut B&B

44 East Street
Nunda, NY, 14517
(716) 468-5074

A stately Victorian situated in the Genesee Valley, five minutes from Letchworth Park. Picnic baskets packed and bikes provided. Skiing is minutes sway at Swain. Fireplaces, natural woodwork, bathrooms with clawfoot tubs, screened porches, gracious rooms with many antiques. Cozy, comfortable full and queen bedrooms.

Hosts: Barb & Bob Lloyd
Rooms: 4 (2 PB; 2 SB) $50-65
Full Breakfast
Credit Cards: No
Notes: 2, 3, 4, 5, 7 (restricted), 8, 9, 10, 11, 12, 13, 14

OLCOTT HARBOR

Rainbow Hospitality O105

466 Amherst Street
Buffalo, NY, 14207
(716) 874-8797

Stately Queen Anne Victorian, built in 1910, with four lovely guest rooms. One room is part of a circular turret with leaded windows surrounding an antique double bed. Shared bath. Breakfast includes fresh fruit from local orchards, Danish and coffee. Served on the large sandstone porch or in the formal dining room. Convenient to lake fishing and charters. From $70.

Rainbow Hospitality O201

466 Amherst Street
Buffalo, NY, 14207
(716) 874-8797

Inviting guest house overlooking the harbor, this 76-year-old Victorian has porches, turrets, stained and leaded glass windows, and is being restored. Guests enjoy a beautiful harbor view. Dog in residence. $35-45.

OLD CHATHAM

American Country Collection 37

984 Gloucester Place
Schenectady, NY, 12309
(518) 370-4948

This 175-year-old Greek Revival home features a collection of antiques from the late 1700s. Guests have the use of a comfortable private sitting room, bedroom and private bath. Located in the heart of Columbia Country, just west of Massachusetts. Tanglewood is eighteen miles away; Stockbridge twenty-five; Albany, twenty. One room with private hall bath, continental breakfast. $40.

OLDFIELD

B & B of Long Island OP

P.O. Box 392
Old Westbury, NY, 11568
(516) 334-6231

With a spectacular view of Long Island Sound, guests can watch the boats go by from a hammock or lounges on the landscaped lawn. Take a swim from the private beach of this rambling home. Twin-bedded room with private bath; full country breakfast served either in the plant-filled sun room overlooking the water or in the country kitchen. Room with double convertible couch also available. $75.

OXFORD

Whitegate B&B

B&B Connection NY
RD 1, Box 325
Vernon, NY, 13476
(315) 829-4888

This Greek Revival farmhouse has all the charm of the 1820s with the conveniences of today. Both the spacious kitchen and guest entertainment areas have fireplaces. A large solarium offers a picturesque view of the meadow and surrounding hills. The home is located on 136 acres on the Finger Lakes hiking trail, and is near swimming, biking, canoeing, fishing, cross-country skiing, and snowmobiling. $45-125.

PALENVILLE

American Country Collection 31

984 Gloucester Place
Schenectady, NY, 12309
(518) 370-4948

This large old Victorian is nestled in a tiny town along the creek, adjacent to the scenic mountain road that winds up to Tannersville. Skiers enjoy good proximity to ski areas. Built as a boarding house in 1864, the home is comfortable and informal. Five rooms with shared or private baths. Continental breakfast on weekdays; full on weekends. Located in the heart of the Catskill region one mile from the Catskill Game Farm, twelve from Woodstock; eight miles from Hunter Mountain. $40-55.

PALMYRA

Canaltown B&B

119 Canandaigua Street
Palmyra, NY, 14522
(315) 597-5553

Savor a delicious country breakfast in this 1850s historic Greek Revival home. Located close to antique stores and local museums. One hundred yards to the Erie Canal Hiking Trail; canoe rentals nearby.

Hosts: Robert & Barbara Leisten
Rooms: 2 (SB) $48.50
Full Breakfast
Credit Cards: No
Notes: 2, 5, 8, 9, 13, 14

PENN YAN

The Wagener Estate B&B

351 Elm Street
Penn Yan, NY, 14527
(315) 536-4591

Centrally located in the Finger Lakes, this bed & breakfast is in an historic 1796 home furnished with antiques and country charm and nestled on 4 acres. Hospitality, comfort, and an elegant breakfast await you.

Hosts: Norm & Evie Worth
Rooms: 5 (2 PB; 3 SB) $55-65
Full Breakfast
Credit Cards: A, B, C
Closed January
Notes: 2, 8 (over 5), 9, 10, 11, 12

PHILMONT

American Country Collection 66

984 Gloucester Place
Schenectady, NY, 12309
(518) 370-4948

This lodge-style contemporary B&B is set back from the country road on 8 acres of woods. Located in the Hudson River Valley between the river and Massachusetts, near Tanglewood, Ski Catamount, and the Shaker Museum. Four guest rooms, two with private baths. Limited smoking; children are welcome; resident cat; full breakfast. $55-65.

Hosts: Ned & Joyce Crislip
Rooms: 4 (2 PB; 2 SB) $65-75
Full Breakfast
Credit Cards: A, B
Notes: 2, 5, 6 (with prior approval), 8 (no infants), 9, 10, 11, 12, 13

PORT JEFFERSON

B & B of Long Island PJP

P.O. Box 392
Old Westbury, NY, 11568
(516) 334-6231

Situated right in this picturesque town with its harbor and quaint boutiques and craft shops. Guests can walk everywhere from this charming home (almost 100 years old) set in a glade. The unusual foyer is almost rotunda-like, with the dining room and living room on either side and a staircase that winds up to two bedrooms and shared bath. Full breakfast. $58.

QUEENSBURY

Crislip's B&B

RD 1, Box 57
Queensbury, NY, 12804
(518) 793-6869

Located just minutes from Saratoga Springs and Lake George, this landmark Federal home provides spacious accommodations complete with period antiques, four-poster beds, and down comforters. The country breakfast menu features buttermilk pancakes, scrambled eggs, and sausages. Your hosts invite you to relax on the porches and enjoy the mountain view of Vermont.

QUEENSTON

Rainbow Hospitality Q200

466 Amherst Street
Buffalo, NY, 14207
(716) 874-8797

German country inn, a short drive from Niagara Falls and overlooking the lower Niagara River. This charming, historic inn is filled with early Canadian furnishings. Ten minutes to Niagara-on-the-Lake and Lewiston. From $70.

RED HOOK

American Country Collection 115

984 Gloucester Place
Schenectady, NY, 12309
(518) 370-4948

Situated on 2 acres surrounded by stone walls and an old garden, this 170-year-old Federal home offers a lower level suite with beamed ceilings, wide-plank floors, and deep-set windows. There's a nonworking fireplace, beehive oven, double bed, and mini kitchen with microwave. A full breakfast is brought to the suite. Children are welcome. $65-75.

RENSSELAER

Tibbitts House Inn

100 Columbia Turnpike
Rensselaer, NY, 12144
(518) 472-1348

Tibbitts House Inn

We are a 135-year-old farmhouse acquainted with country living. The old house has an 84-foot windowed porch on which breakfast is served in season. Rooms are papered in cheerful patterns with braided and rag rugs on polished fir floors. Handmade quilts top crisp bed linens. Antiques abound. We are two miles from Albany and the state capitol, museums, and convention center. The newly opened Knickerbocker Arena hosts current stars of TV and movies, as well as rock groups and pop singers.

Host: Claire Rufleth
Rooms: 5 (1 PB; 4 SB) $46-50
Full Breakfast
Credit Cards: No
Notes: 2, 5, 7, 8, 10, 11

REXFORD

American Country Collection 42

984 Gloucester Place
Schenectady, NY, 12309
(518) 370-4948

This historic Queen Anne Victorian manor house began as a cabin in 1763 and grew to its present form in 1883. Schenectady is four miles away; Saratoga fifteen; Albany twenty. Near Union College, Skidmore, SUNY. Local cross-country skiing. There is one air-conditioned three-room suite on the second floor with two bedrooms and a sitting room with TV. Two first-floor rooms each have a TV and shared bath. Smoking permitted. $65-115.

RHINEBECK

Village Victorian Inn

31 Center Street
Rhinebeck, NY, 12572
(914) 878-8345

A seductive retreat filled with antiques, canopy beds, fine linens and laces. Located in the heart of historic Rhinebeck Village and close to fine dining, historic mansions, the Hudson River, and antiquing.

Hosts: Judy & Richard Kohler
Rooms: 7 (PB) $135-175
Full Breakfast
Credit Cards: A, B, C
Notes: 2, 5, 10, 11, 12, 13, 14

RICHFIELD SPRINGS

Jonathan House

39 East Main Street
P.O. Box 9

Richfield Springs, NY, 13439
(315) 858-2870

Jonathan House is a towering 1880s restored Victorian, richly furnished with English, French, and American antiques, Persian rugs, and works of art. Step back 100 years to an opulent, more gracious time for a memorable vacation experience. All rooms have queen beds with available rollaways. A full breakfast is served in the elegant dining room. Located on scenic Route 20, minutes from Cooperstown's Baseball Hall of Fame and convenient to other tourist attractions and I-90.

Hosts: John & Peter Parker
Rooms: 4 (2 PB; 2 SB) $55-75
Full Breakfast
Credit Cards: A, B, C
Notes: 2, 5, 8, 9, 10, 11, 12, 13, 14

Village Victorian Inn

Summerwood

72 East Main Street
P.O. Box 388
Richfield Springs, NY, 13439
(315) 858-2024

Graciously appointed Queen Anne Victorian on the National Registry, set on 3 acres of lawn and trees. Close to Cooperstown, Glimmerglass Opera, two lakes, good antiquing. TV and laundry facilities available. Breakfast is a special event.

Hosts: Lona & George Smith
Rooms: 5 (3 PB; 2 SB) $50-70 + tax
Full Breakfast
Credit Cards: No
Notes: 2, 4 (with reservations), 5, 7 (restricted), 8, 9, 11, 12, 14

ROCHESTER-PENFIELD

Strawberry Castle

1883 Penfield Road
Penfield, NY, 14526
(716) 385-3266

A suburban Rochester landmark Victorian Italianate on 3 acres with pool and patio. Brass or Empire beds in large, air-conditioned rooms. Fine restaurants and golf courses nearby. A relaxing retreat for your traveling pleasure.

Hosts: Cynthia & Charles Whited
Rooms: 3 (SB) $49.50-82.50
Continental Breakfast
Credit Cards: A, B, C
Notes: 2, 5, 7, 8 (12 and over), 9, 11, 14

ROME

Maplecrest B&B

B&B Connection NY
RD 1, Box 325
Vernon, NY, 13476
(315) 829-4888

Maplecrest is a modern split-level home three miles northwest of Rome, within minutes of Griffith Air Base and Fort Stanwix. Among the breakfast specialties served in the pleasant dining room or on the spacious deck are French toast, muffins, and hot oatmeal. Guests enjoy the comfort of a well-appointed family room with fireplace. $45-125.

ROSCOE

Huff House

RD #2, Roscoe, NY, 12776
(914) 482-4579

A 100-year-old B&B resort under fourth-generation ownership and management. Located on 180 acres in the scenic western Catskill mountains, with on-premise golf, tennis, heated pool, and stocked trout pond. Centrally located between the famous Beaverkill, Willowemac, and Delaware rivers. Excellent food and wine cellar.

Hosts: Joseph & Joanne Forness
Rooms: 24 (PB) $90
Full Breakfast
Credit Cards: C
Closed Nov.-April
Notes: 2, 3, 4, 6 (restricted), 7, 8, 9, 10, 11, 12, 14

SANDY CREEK

Evelyn's Pink House Inn

9125 South Main Street, Box 85
Sandy Creek, NY, 13145
(315) 387-3276

We're just 2.5 miles from Lake Ontario and 5 from the Salmon River, the greatest salmon, steelhead, and trout fishing area in the North Country. Wonderfully maintained cross-country skiing and snowmobile trails, and beautiful state parks are within ten miles.

Host: Evelyn Sadowski
Rooms: 5 (SB) $25 & tax/person
Full Breakfast
Credit Cards: No
Closed Jan. 11-March 15
Notes: 7, 8 (over 10), 9, 11, 12, 13

SARATOGA SPRINGS

American Country Collection 101

984 Gloucester Place
Schenectady, NY, 12309
(518) 370-4948

Located in Round Lake, NY, this unique cobblestone colonial is over 160 years old and is on 2 acres of land great for nature walks. Furnished with colonial decor, the B&B has five guest rooms with double beds that share two baths. Continental breakfast. Children over twelve are welcome. One dog and two cats in residence. Located five miles from Saratoga Performing Arts Center and seven miles from the racetrack. $45-75.

American Country Collection 103

984 Gloucester Place
Schenectady, NY, 12309
(518) 370-4948

Located in Stillwater, NY, twenty minutes from Saratoga Springs, on 1.5 acres along the Hudson River with a dock. Two-bedroom air-conditioned cottage with kitchen and private bath. Queen room with private bath in the main house. Full breakfast. Children welcome; one dog in residence. $75-95.

American Country Collection 105

984 Gloucester Place
Schenectady, NY, 12309
(518) 370-4948

This 150-year-old Victorian farmhouse sits amid a 9-acre organic farm, complete with barnyard animals. Seven guest rooms, three with private baths, are furnished in antiques. Full country breakfast; children welcome. Located two miles from Saratoga Springs. $90-100.

American Country Collection 112

984 Gloucester Place
Schenectady, NY, 12309
(518) 370-4948

Located in Greenfield, NY, just outside Saratoga Springs, this 200-year-old historic colonial farmhouse was used by the British during the War of 1812. It has also been a stagecoach stop and part of the Underground Railroad. Oriental rugs cover the floors. Three guest rooms, all with private baths; full breakfast. Children over twelve are welcome. Dogs, cats, and goats on premises. $90-100.

The Inn on Bacon Hill

200 Wall Street
Schuylerville, NY, 12871
(518) 695-3693

Relax in the peacefulness of elegant country living in this restored 1862 Victorian just twelve minutes from historic Saratoga Springs and its racetracks. Enjoy the inn's double parlors, each with marble fireplace, library of books, high ceilings, baby grand piano, original moldings, and antique chandeliers. Innkeeping course offered.

Host: Andrea Collins-Breslin
Rooms: 4 (2 SB; 2 PB) $60-125 seasonal
Full Breakfast
Minimum stay: 2 days during August
Credit Cards: A, B
Notes: 2, 5, 8 (over 16), 9, 10, 11, 12, 13, 14

The Inn on Bacon Hill

Six Sisters B&B

149 Union Avenue
Saratoga Springs, NY, 12866.
(518) 583-1173

Uniquely styled 1880s Victorian beckons you with its relaxing veranda. Conveniently located within walking distance of museums, city park, downtown specialty shops, antiques, and restaurants. Spacious rooms, all with private bath and luxurious beds, prepare you for a leisurely home-cooked breakfast. Mineral bath and massage package available Nov.-April.

Hosts: Kate Benton & Steve Ramirez
Rooms: 4 (PB) From $60-80
Full Breakfast
Credit Cards: No
Notes: 2, 5, 8 (over 10), 9, 10, 11, 12

The Westchester House

The Westchester House

102 Lincoln Avenue
Saratoga Springs, NY, 12866
(518) 587-7613

Gracious Queen Anne Victorian featuring elaborate fireplaces, beautiful wainscotting, antique furnishing, and modern comforts. All the charm and excitement of historic Saratoga Springs are at our doorstep. Walk to the museums, racetracks, shops, restaurants, and the springs that made Saratoga famous.

Hosts: Bob & Stephanie Melvin
Rooms: 7 (5 PB; 2 SB) $59.40-97.20
Continental Breakfast
Minimum stay weekends & holidays: 2
Credit Cards: A, B, C
Notes: 2, 5, 8 (over 12), 9, 10, 11, 12, 13, 14

SAUGERTIES

The House on the Quarry

7480 Fite Road
Saugerties, NY, 12477
(914) 246-8584

Enjoy beautiful walking trails and unlimited tennis; sit on the deck and watch the sun set behind Overlook Mountain; and on cool evenings, relax in the living room in front of a huge roaring fire. We are minutes from the galleries, shops, and restaurants of Woodstock. Cross-country skiing and tennis on premises.

Hosts: Pat & Tad Richards
Rooms: 2 (PB) $85
Full Breakfast
Credit Cards: No
Notes: 2, 5, 7, 9, 10, 13

SAYVILLE

B & B of Long Island SS

P.O. Box 392
Old Westbury, NY, 11568
(516) 334-6231

Spectacular waterfront contemporary furnished with antiques. Guests have their own private entrance, and the bath has a sauna-like decor. The hosts often take guests to Fire Island on their boat. Two golf courses are nearby, free tennis courts, hiking areas, and horseback riding. Short walk to excellent restaurants. $80.

SCHENECTADY

American Country Collection 43

984 Gloucester Place
Schenectady, NY, 12309
(518) 370-4948

Nestled in the heart of the city's historic Stockade district, this home served as a tavern in the late 1700s. Rooms have original wide-plank floors and are furnished with fine examples of period antiques. Each of the three guest rooms has a TV, and one has a working fireplace. Smoking is permitted; children are welcome. $85.

SETAUKET

B & B of Long Island SF

P.O. Box 392
Old Westbury, NY, 11568
(516) 334-6231

This beautifully restored c. 1800 farmhouse is furnished with antiques of every period. The owner is an antique dealer. Two guest rooms, one with a double bed, the other with two singles. Shared bath if both rooms are occupied. Three miles to the beach, minutes to the town of Stonybrook with its university. TV in each room. Continental buffet breakfast in the huge country kitchen with beamed ceilings. $68.

SHELTER ISLAND

Belle Crest Inn

163 North Ferry Road
Shelter Island, NY, 11965
(516) 749-2041

Spacious Dutch colonial in a lovely garden setting, convenient to Dering Harbor. All guest rooms are furnished in Early American collectibles and antiques. Romantic guest rooms, some with private baths, canopy beds, air-conditioning, and TV. A full breakfast is served in the dining room.

Hosts: Yvonne & Henry Loinig
Rooms: 8 (4 PB; 4 SB) $45-125
Full Breakfast
Credit Cards: A, B
Notes: 2, 4, 5, 7, 8, 9, 10, 11, 12, 13, 14

The Chequit Inn

Grand Avenue
Shelter Island, NY, 11965
(516) 749-0018

An 1870 Victorian clapboard house with a veranda overlooking Dering Harbor. Refurbished by new owners in 1990. Each room has its own personality and is decorated with antiques original to the inn, with an eclectic and often quirky concentration of accessories. Three-star restaurant on premises.

Hosts: Alice & Guy Gorelik, Mindy & Harry Chernoff
Rooms: 20 (15 PB; 5 SB) $75-150
Full Breakfast July & Aug.
Credit Cards: A, B, C
Closed Nov. 1-March 31
Notes: 3, 4, 7 (limited), 8, 9, 10, 11, 12

SODUS

Maxwell Creek Inn, Inc.

7563 Lake Road
Sodus, NY, 14551
(315) 483-2222

An 1840 cobblestone house decorated in antiques, with two sitting rooms with organ and player piano. Our rural setting offers apple blossoms in May, boating, swimming, sailing, golf in summer, apple picking and fall foliage, skiing in winter. Charter fishing from April to October. Separate stone cottage sleeps four to six. Tennis and fishing on premises.

Hosts: Joseph & Edythe Ann Long
Rooms: 8 (1 PB; 7 S4B) $50-75
Full Breakfast
Credit Cards: No
Notes: 2, 5, 7, 8, 9, 10, 11, 12, 13, 14

SODUS POINT

Carriage House Inn

8375 Wickham Blvd.
Sodus Point, NY, 14555
(315) 483-2100; (800) 292-2990

Stay in our 1870 Victorian house or our stone carriage house, built 1877. All rooms have private baths. Situated on 4 acres in a quiet residential area overlooking an historic lighthouse and Lake Ontario. Beach access. Suite and efficiency also available.

Host: James denDecker
Rooms: 8 (PB) $50-60
Full Breakfast
Credit Cards: A, B
Notes: 2, 3 (to go) 4, 5, 7, 8, 9, 10, 11, 12, 13, 14

Silver Waters Guesthouse B&B

8420 Bay Street
Sodus Point, NY, 14555
(315) 483-8098

This historic home, built after the War of 1812, was an inn at one time. Located in the heart of Sodus Point — a vacation and world-class fishing resort. Stroll the sandy beach, enjoy the sand bluffs and beautiful sunsets.

Host: Zaida Bruno
Rooms: 4 (SB) $55-75
Continental Breakfast
Credit Cards: No
Notes: 2, 5, 8, 9, 10, 11, 12, 13

SOUTHAMPTON

B & B of Long Island SB

P.O. Box 392
Old Westbury, NY, 11568
(516) 334-6231

Ideally located, this lovely Cape Cod is two blocks from Main Street and Jobs Lane and about one mile from the beach. Two twin rooms and one double share two baths. TV in each room. Enjoy a continental breakfast on the screened patio. $88.

B & B of Long Island SW

P.O. Box 392
Old Westbury, NY, 11568
(516) 334-6231

Magnificent home in luxurious community, one mile to beach and less to town. This huge new Cape Cod offers a choice of four rooms. The master has a queen bed, private bath, and doors leading out to the patio. Two upstairs rooms share a bath if both are occupied. An additional room has a single bed and private half-bath. There is a swimming pool, and a continental breakfast is served buffet style in the country kitchen or patio overlooking the pool. Bicycle available. $95-110.

The Old Post House Inn

136 Main Street
Southampton, NY, 11968
(516) 283-1717

The Old Post House is the only small, charming country inn in the village. Built in 1684, it is listed on the National Register. All rooms have private baths and air-conditioning. Continental breakfast is included. Next block to boutiques and two doors from Saks Fifth Avenue.

Hosts: Cecile & Ed Courville
Rooms: 7 (PB) $80-170
Continental Breakfast
Credit Cards: A, B, C
Notes: 5, 7, 8 (over 12), 9, 10, 11, 12, 14

Village Latch Inn

101 Hill Street
Southampton, NY, 11968
(516) 283-2160

Village Latch Inn is known internationally for its charming ambience. A 37-room mansion on 5 glorious acres, right in town, within walking distance of the famous Jobs Lane boutiques. Swimming and tennis; all rooms have private bath. Rent your own mansion for group celebrations, corporate outings, and weddings.

Hosts: Marta & Martin White
Rooms: 70 (PB) $79-175
Continental Breakfast
Minimum stay weekends: 2
Credit Cards: All major
Notes: 2, 5, 6, 7, 8, 9, 10, 11, 12, 14

SOUTHOLD

B & B of Long Island SB

P.O. Box 392
Old Westbury, NY, 11568
(516) 334-6231

Enjoy an intimate gourmet breakfast in your own room or with other guests in this lovely 1800s Dutch colonial a few miles from the beach and vineyards. Three rooms, each furnished with Victorian antiques, share a bath. Perfect for guests without a car, since the hosts will drive them to the beach or Greenport ferry for trips to Shelter Island. Nice walk to town for antiquing and restaurants. $60.

B & B of Long Island SD

P.O. Box 392
Old Westbury, NY, 11568
(516) 334-6231

This stunning contemporary home is right on the beach. Enjoy a great breakfast in the sunny dining room overlooking the water. Two rooms—one queen size, the other, twins that can be put together for a king—share a bath. Step out to the deck and relax after your swim. A marina a few yards away rents sailboats and wind surfers. Ferries to Shelter Island leave every fifteen minutes from Greenport, which is just a few minutes' drive. $75.

SPENCERTOWN

American Country Collection 90

984 Gloucester Place
Schenectady, NY, 12309
(518) 370-4948

This hilltop home on 8 acres overlooks a small picturesque lake just a few miles from the Massachusetts border, near Old Chatham, Stockbridge, Tanglewood, and skiing. Two second-floor rooms have private baths. A single room is available for an additional guest in the same party. Smoking outdoors; children welcome; continental-plus breakfast. $65-75.

STILLWATER

American Country Collection 5

984 Gloucester Place
Schenectady, NY, 12309
(518) 370-4948

A quiet pastoral retreat on 100 acres complete with mountain vistas, this B&B is a restored 1800 barn with barnboard and original beams. Located between Saratoga Lake and Saratoga National Historical Park. Two spacious suites with king beds and private baths; one first-floor room with queen bed and private bath; one second-floor room with queen bed and private bath. Smoking outdoors; children ten and over welcome; resident pet. $65-115.

STONY BROOK

Three Village Inn

150 Main Street
Stony Brook, NY, 11790
(516) 751-0555

The Three Village Inn is truly a unique location, offering historic colonial charm with magnificent views of Stony Brook Harbor on Long Island Sound. We offer the finest in food, service, and hospitality. Our dining rooms are open daily; weekend live music in our tap room. We have thirty-two guest rooms, ranging from rooms in the original 1751 inn to rooms in our country cottages— each with private bath, phone, and cable TV.

Hosts: Jim & Louis Miaritis
Rooms: 32 (PB) $85-110
Full Breakfast
Credit Cards: A, B, C
Closed Christmas
Notes: 3, 4, 5, 8, 9, 10, 11, 12, 14

SYRACUSE

Cherry Valley Ventures 3017

6119 Cherry Valley Turnpike
LaFayette, NY, 13084
(315) 677-9723

In an elite district of the city, easily accessible to business district, the estate is attractive to business and pleasure seekers. Seven guest rooms, furnished in antiques, many of which are for sale. Large living room with a tiled fireplace, Oriental carpets, and a baby grand piano. Library with fireplace; large dining room. A screen porch is also available for relaxing. Continental breakfast; dog in residence. $30-95.

TICONDEROGA

American Country Collection 46

984 Gloucester Place
Schenectady, NY, 12309
(518) 370-4948

Enjoy a horsedrawn sleigh ride along the wooded paths of this 52-acre farm, cross-country ski past pond and through pastures, visit the chickens, pigs, cow, four horses, dog, cats, and rooster. Near canoeing, fishing, swimming, Fort Ticonderoga, Lake George Village, and Shelburne Museum, VT. Three double rooms share a bath. Smoking outdoors; children welcome; full breakfast. $40.

TROY

American Country Collection 18

984 Gloucester Place
Schenectady, NY, 12309
(518) 370-4948

Built in 1810 as a farmhouse, this B&B still contains a cooking fireplace in the kitchen and original wide-plank flooring. Located just fifteen minutes from Albany, near RPI and Russell Sage colleges. One first-floor room with a double bed and private bath. There is also an efficiency apartment with private bath. Smoking outdoors only; children welcome; resident pets; full breakfast. $40-50.

Sage Cottage

TRUMANSBURG

Sage Cottage

112 East Main Street
Trumansburg, NY, 14886
(607) 387-6449

Unwind in the homey elegance of our Gothic Revival home. Savor a full breakfast complemented by homemade herb breads and jams. Explore our flourishing herb gardens and historic village. Four cozy guest rooms with private baths. Taughannock Falls, wineries, Ithaca are nearby.

Host: Dorry Norris
Rooms: 4 (PB) $45-55
Full Breakfast
Minimum stay holiday weekends: 2
Notes: 2, 5, 9, 11, 12, 13

TURIN

Towpath Inn

Box E, West Road
Turin, NY, 13473
(315) 348-8122

Originally a stagecoach stop, this charming country inn has a touch of Scandinavian decor. Located at the base of Snow Ridge Ski Area, Tug Hill Plateau, and across from an 18-hole golf course. We offer several room types, three cozy dining rooms, fireplace lounge, and bar facing the ski slopes. Game room, outdoor heated Jacuzzi, and sauna. Sport packages available.

Hosts: Roger & Ann Abbey
Rooms: 19 (15 PB; 4 SB) $91-106 + gratuity & tax
Full Breakfast
Credit Cards: A, B
Notes: 2, 4, 5, 7, 8, 9, 11, 12, 13, 14

VALLEY FALLS

Maggie Towne's B&B

RD 2, Box 82
Valley Falls, NY, 12185
(518) 663-8369; (518) 686-7331

An old colonial located amid beautiful lawns and trees fourteen miles east of Troy. Enjoy tea or wine before the fireplace in the family room. Use the music room or read on the screened porch. Your hostess will prepare lunch for you to take on tour or enjoy at the house. It's twenty miles to historic Bennington, Vermont, and thirty to Saratoga Springs, NY.

Host: Maggie Towne
Rooms: 3 (SB) $35-45
Full Breakfast

Credit Cards: No
Notes: 2, 3, 5, 8, 9

VESPER

Cherry Valley Ventures 3014

6119 Cherry Valley Turnpike
LaFayette, NY, 13084
(315) 677-9723

This countrified ranch was once part of a 300-acre Guernsey farm. Built by your hosts, its twelve rooms have natural paneling and fireplaces of stone. A private entrance, complete kitchen, large fireplace, and pool table. Three rooms have double beds and private baths. Breakfast is continental or full, with homemade butter and jelly. $45 + tax.

WARRENSBURG

American Country Collection 67

984 Gloucester Place
Schenectady, NY, 12309
(518) 370-4948

The guest house of this 1850 Greek Revival inn features ten rooms and a Jacuzzi in a plant-filled solarium. Crackling fireplaces, wide-plank floors, period wallpapers, and local antiques. The inn has a public restaurant, a fireplaced tavern, and a common room with TV. Located five miles from Lake George and twenty-five from Saratoga Springs. Within walking distance of cross-country skiing, tennis, fishing, antique shops, tobogganing, and nature trails. All ten rooms have private baths, air-conditioning, and fireplaces. $85-95.

Country Road Lodge

HCR 1, Box 227, Hickory Hill Road
Warrensburg, NY, 12885
(518) 623-2207

The Adirondack Mountain/Hudson River view hasn't changed since 1905, when the now-abandoned railroad bridge was built. Minutes from Lake George, we've offered seclusion and casual comfort since 1974. Homemade bread, hiking, skiing, horseshoes, badminton, books, board games. Fine restaurants and antiquing nearby.

Hosts: Steve & Sandi Parisi
Rooms: 4 (S2B) $52-65
Full Breakfast
Credit Cards: No
Notes: 2, 5, 7, 9, 10, 11, 12, 13, 14

White House Lodge

53 Main Street
Warrensburg, NY, 12885
(518) 623-3640

An 1847 Victorian in the heart of the Adirondacks — an antiquer's paradise! The home is furnished with many antiques. Only five minutes to Lake George Village, historic Fort William Henry, and Great Escape. Walk to restaurants, antique shops, and shopping areas. Enjoy the comfort of the air-conditioned TV lounge or rock on the front porch. Twenty minutes to Gore Mountain Ski Lodge and the Adirondack Balloon Festival. Smoking in TV lounge only.

Hosts: James & Ruth Gibson
Rooms: 5 (SB) $85
Continental Breakfast
Credit Cards: A, B
Notes: 5, 7 (restricted), 8 (over 7), 10, 11, 12, 13, 14

WATERLOO

Art Barn B&B

0089 Packwood Road
Waterloo, NY, 13165
(315) 789-2075

Charming country setting built by General Dobbin in 1823. Tennis court, meadow, and woods. Five miles to Seneca Lake. Suite with private bath and room with private bath. Located 3.5 miles south of Thruway Exit 42 off Rt. 14, within three miles of routes 5 and 20. Antique shop on premises.

Host: Betty Waldman
Rooms: 2 (PB) $55-65
Full Breakfast
Credit Cards: No
Notes: 2, 5, 9, 10, 12

Front Porch Antiques and B&B

1248 Routes 5 & 20
Waterloo, NY, 13165
(315) 539-8325

Inviting Victorian home in beautiful Finger Lakes region, between Seneca and Cayuga lakes, near Rochester and Syracuse. Comfortable rooms, private and shared baths. Full breakfast is served in the dining room or on the terrace. Antique/gift shop on premises. Museums, historic homes, antiquing, wineries, and more. Four seasons of recreation and scenic enjoyment.

Hosts: Carol & Paul Anderson
Rooms: 3 (2 PB; 1 SB) $50
Full Breakfast
Credit Cards: A, B, C
Notes: 2, 5, 7, 9, 10, 11, 12, 13

WATERMILL

B & B of Long Island WF

P.O. Box 392
Old Westbury, NY, 11568
(516) 334-6231

Beautifully restored c. 1870 home with several rooms to choose from. One twin, one double, and one king with private bath. The twin and double share a bath if both rooms are occupied. Continental breakfast. One mile to the beach and one block to the little town of Watermill. Cottage with two bedrooms, kitchen, living room, dining area, and bath also on the grounds. $95-125.

WATERTOWN

Starbuck House

253 Clinton Street
Watertown, NY, 13601
(315) 788-7324

Seventeen-room Italianate mansion built in 1869. Completely restored and updated, the inn offers accommodations for nine guests in five comfortable rooms, one of which is a suite. Breakfast is served in an elegant formal dining room; guests socialize in the living room.

Host: Marsha Brown
Rooms: $70-80
Full Breakfast
Credit Cards: A, B, C
Notes: 2

WATERVILLE

B&B of Waterville

211 White Street
Waterville, NY, 13480
(315) 841-8295

This Victorian home in a historic area is close to Utica, Hamilton College, Colgate University, antique shops. One block from Rt. 12 and one mile from Rt. 20. Accommodations include a triple with private bath, triple and double rooms with shared bath. Experienced, enthusiastic hosts are a retired utility manager and a quilt maker.

Hosts: Carol & Stanley Sambora
Rooms: 3 (1 PB; 2 SB) $35-65
Full Breakfast
Credit Cards: A, B, C
Notes: 2, 5, 8, 9, 10, 12, 13

WESTBURY

B & B of Long Island WR

P.O. Box 392
Old Westbury, NY, 11568
(516) 334-6231

Beautifully maintained Cape Cod with two huge upstairs pine-paneled bedrooms and half-bath. Each room has twin beds. Shower and bath are shared with host. Located in a lovely residential neighborhood close to the village and railroad. Full breakfast. $60.

B & B of Long Island WW

P.O. Box 392
Old Westbury, NY, 11568
(516) 334-6231

This home offers two large rooms with twin beds, private bath, full breakfast served in the big, homey country kitchen. Minutes from Nassau Coliseum, Hofstra and Adelphi universities, Nassau Community College, Winthrop University Hospital, and New York Technical Institute. $60.

WESTFIELD

William Seward Inn

RD 2, South Portage Road
Westfield, NY, 14787
(716) 326-4151

"A country inn well done." Formerly the home of Lincoln's secretary of state, this 1821 Greek Revival mansion features ten rooms with period antiques and private baths. Comfortable elegance close to Westfield's wineries and national antique center. Minutes from the world-famous Chautauqua Institution and both downhill and cross-country skiing.

Hosts: Peter & Joyce Wood
Rooms: 10 (PB) $58-92
Full Breakfast
Credit Cards: A, B
Notes: 2, 4 (winter), 5, 8 (over 12), 9, 10, 11, 12, 13, 14

WESTHAMPTON BEACH

Seafield House

2 Seafield Lane
Westhampton Beach, NY, 11978
(800) 346-3290

Seafield House, a one-hundred-year-old country retreat, is only ninety minutes from Manhattan on Westhampton Beach's exclusive Seafield Lane. A swimming pool and tennis court are on the premises, and it's only a short walk to the beach. The Hamptons offer numerous outstanding restaurants and shops. Indoor tennis is available locally, as is a health spa at Montauk Point.

Host: Elsie Pardee Collins
Rooms: 2 (PB) $100-200 (suites)
Full Breakfast
Minimum stay: 2
Credit Cards: C
Notes: 2, 5, 9, 10, 11

WEST SHOKAN

Glen Atty Farm

Box 188, Moonhaw Road
West Shokan, NY, 12494
(914) 657-8110

An 1840s farmhouse and working farm with horses, sheep, pigs, chickens, ducks, etc. Relaxing country atmosphere with many walking trails and stream. Two bedrooms, one with a fireplace and one with a king bed and two twins. Close to Woodstock and many fine restaurants. Two cats and one small dog in residence.

Hosts: Susan & Tom Kizis
Rooms: 2 (SB) $40-65
Full Breakfast
Minimum stay: 2
Credit Cards: No
Notes: 2, 5, 7, 8 (over 6), 9, 10, 11

WEST WINFIELD

Five Gables B&B

B&B Connection NY
RD 1, Box 325
Vernon, NY, 13476
(315) 829-4888

Victorian elegance in a century-old home with stenciling, Oriental rugs, and antiques. Four guest rooms, including a bridal suite with queen bed and private bath with Jacuzzi tub. Guests are invited to enjoy the comfortable parlor before an evening out. $45-125.

WEVERTOWN

Mountainaire Adventures

Route 28, Box A
Wevertown, NY, 12886
(518) 251-2194; (800) 950-2194

Newly renovated private lodge and chalet in the Adirondack Park near Lake George and Gore Mountain Ski Center. Jacuzzi, sauna, beer and wine, bikes and boats. Custom adventure trips, such as white-water rafting, are available. Ideal for private meetings, with audio-visual services available.

Host: Douglas Cole
Rooms: 8 (6 PB; 2 SB) $50-75
Full Breakfast
Credit Cards: A, B
Notes: 2, 4, 5, 6, 7, 8, 9, 10, 11, 12, 13

YOUNGSTOWN

Rainbow Hospitality Y106

466 Amherst Street
Buffalo, NY, 14207
(716) 874-8797

A 150-year-old country manor, beautifully furnished, in an idyllic setting just fifteen minutes north of Niagara Falls and thirty minutes to Buffalo. Spacious veranda overlooks the lower Niagara River and is the setting for leisurely morning meals. Guest rooms include Queen Anne furnishings and private suites. $50-65.

Rainbow Hospitality Y110

466 Amherst Street
Buffalo, NY, 14207
(716) 874-8797

Large villa overlooking the Niagara River and Canada. This beautiful home is surrounded by stately copper beech trees. Huge rooms with fireplaces for relaxing. Private baths and porch or patio adjacent to each room. $50-65.

Rainbow Hospitality Y111

466 Amherst Street
Buffalo, NY, 14207
(716) 874-8797

Country colonial, located in a quiet residential area just nine miles north of Niagara Falls. Blended Victorian and contemporary furnishings. Family pets in residence. $35-45.

North Carolina

ASHEVILLE

Aberdeen Country Inn

64 Linden Avenue
Asheville, NC, 28801
(704) 254-9336

A 1908 colonial with wraparound porch for summer eating and rocking. Antiques, working fireplaces, books, and large conservatory kitchen for winter dining. Private grounds with century-old trees. Six blocks to downtown and three miles to the Biltmore Estate. Welcome!

Hosts: Linda & Ross Willard
Rooms: 9 (PB) $65-75
Full Breakfast
Minimum stay holidays & fall weekends
Credit Cards: A, B
Notes: 2, 5, 8 (over 12), 9, 10, 11, 12, 14

Albemarle Inn

86 Edgemont Road
Asheville, NC, 28801
(704) 255-0027

With its carved oak staircase, massive oak doors, and fireplaces, the Albemarle provides spacious and gracious accommodations in a turn-of-the-century environment. King and queen beds, eleven-foot ceilings, and clawfoot bathtubs provide a unique and memorable lodging experience.

Hosts: John & Rosina Mellin
Rooms: 20 (PB) $58-74
Full Breakfast
Credit Cards: A, B
Notes: 2, 4, 5, 7 (restricted), 8 (14 and over), 9, 10, 11, 12, 14

Cairn Brae

217 Patton Mountain Road
Asheville, NC, 28804
(704) 252-9219

Cairn Brae is located in the mountains above Asheville. Very private, on 3 acres of woods, but only twelve minutes from downtown. Guests have private entrance to living room with fireplace. Complimentary snacks are served on the terrace overlooking Beaverdam Valley. Beautiful views from all rooms. Woodsy trails.

Hosts: Milli & Ed Adams
Rooms: 3 (PB) $65-80
Continental-plus Breakfast
Credit Cards: A, B
Closed Nov. 1-April
Notes: 2, 8 (over 6), 9, 10, 11, 12

Cairn Brae

Carolina B&B

177 Cumberland Avenue
Asheville, NC, 28801
(704) 254-3608

Lovingly restored turn-of-the-century home on an acre of beautiful gardens in the his-

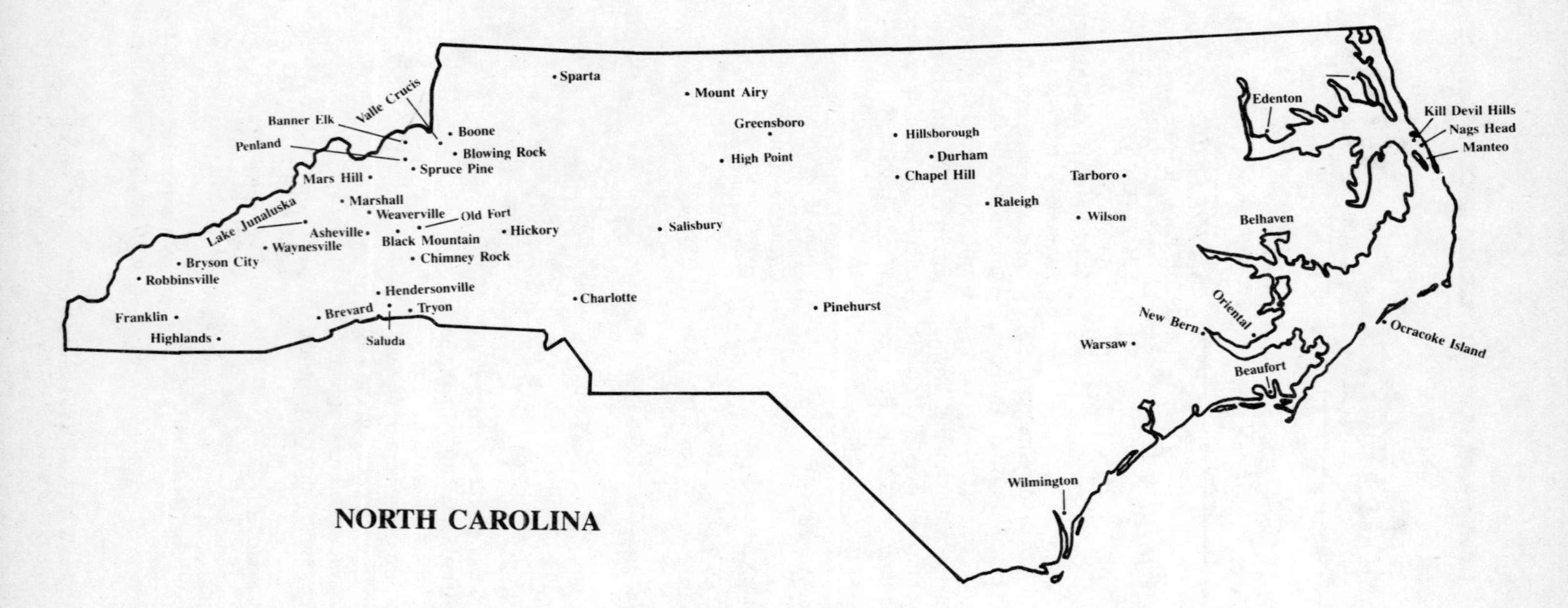
NORTH CAROLINA
Sparta
Mount Airy
Greensboro
High Point
Hillsborough
Durham
Chapel Hill
Raleigh
Tarboro
Wilson
Edenton
Kill Devil Hills
Nags Head
Manteo
Belhaven
Oriental
New Bern
Ocracoke Island
Warsaw
Beaufort
Wilmington
Pinehurst
Salisbury
Charlotte
Hickory
Boone
Blowing Rock
Valle Crucis
Banner Elk
Penland
Spruce Pine
Mars Hill
Marshall
Weaverville
Old Fort
Lake Junaluska
Asheville
Black Mountain
Chimney Rock
Waynesville
Bryson City
Robbinsville
Hendersonville
Brevard
Tryon
Saluda
Franklin
Highlands

toric Montford District. Charming guest rooms with fireplaces, antiques, and collectibles—private baths. Convenient to downtown shops and restaurants and Biltmore Estate. A quiet, relaxing getaway in the heart of the city.

Hosts: Karin, Sam & Regina Fain
Rooms: 5 (PB) $75 + tax
Full Breakfast
Credit Cards: A, B
Notes: 2, 5, 7 (limited), 8 (12 and over), 10, 12, 14

Cedar Crest Victorian Inn

674 Biltmore Avenue
Asheville, NC, 28803
(704) 252-1389

An 1890 Queen Anne mansion listed on the National Register of Historic Places. Lavish interior features carved oak paneling, ornate glasswork, authentic Victorian decor with period antiques and romantic guest rooms. Croquet pitch and English gardens. Located one-quarter mile from entrance to the Biltmore Estate and four miles from the Blue Ridge Parkway.

Hosts: Jack & Barbara McEwan
Rooms: 13 (9 PB; 4 SB) $65-105
Continental-plus Breakfast
Credit Cards: A, B, C, D
Notes: 2, 5, 7 (limited), 8 (over 12), 9, 10, 12, 14

Corner Oak Manor

53 Saint Dunstans Road
Asheville, NC, 28803
(704) 253-3525

This lovely English Tudor home is located minutes away from the famed Biltmore Estate and Gardens. Antiques, handmade wreaths, weavings, and stitchery compliment the restored elegance of this home. There is a full gourmet breakfast, living room with fireplace, baby grand piano, outdoor deck, and Jacuzzi for guest use.

Hosts: Karen & Andy Spradley
Rooms: 4 (PB) $75-95
Full Breakfast
Credit Cards: A, B
Notes: 2, 3, 5, 8, 9, 10, 11, 12, 14

Cornerstone Inn

230 Pearson Drive
Asheville, NC, 28801
(704) 253-5644

A restored c. 1924 Dutch Tudor home in the heart of the historic district. Furnished throughout with American and European antiques. All rooms have private baths and air-conditioning; full country breakfast. Minutes from downtown, the Biltmore Estate, Blue Ridge Parkway, and other points of interest.

Hosts: Lonnie & Evelyn Wyatt, Gary & Nancy Gaither
Rooms: 4 (PB) $65-75
Full Breakfast
Credit Cards: A, B
Notes: 2, 5, 9, 10, 12

Flint Street Inns

100 & 116 Flint Street
Asheville, NC, 28801
(704) 253-6723

Two lovely old homes on an acre lot with century-old trees. Comfortable walking distance to town. Guest rooms are furnished with antiques and collectibles, are air-conditioned, and some have fireplaces. The inns provide wine, bicycles, and restaurant menus. Breakfast is full Southern style, featuring home-baked breads and iron-skillet biscuits.

Hosts: Rick, Lynne & Marion Vogel
Rooms: 8 (PB) $75
Full Breakfast
Credit Cards: A, B, C, D
Notes: 2, 5, 7 (limited), 14

The Old Reynolds Mansion

100 Reynolds Heights
Asheville, NC, 28804
(704) 254-0496

Bed and breakfast in an antebellum mansion listed on the National Registry. Beautifully restored with furnishings from a bygone era. In a country setting with acres of trees, mountain views from all rooms. Wood-burning fireplaces, two-story verandas, pool.

Hosts: Fred & Helen Faber
Rooms: 10 (8 PB; 2 SB) $40-75 + tax
Continental Breakfast
Minimum stay weekends & holidays: 2
Credit Cards: No
Open weekends only Jan.-March
Notes: 2, 7, 8 (12 and over), 9, 10, 11, 12

Reed House

119 Dodge Street
Asheville, NC, 28803
(704) 274-1604

Come stay with us in our comfortable Victorian home built in 1892. Near Biltmore House. We have working fireplaces in every room. Breakfast, featuring home-made, low-sodium muffins, is served on the wraparound porch. Relaxing rocking chairs everywhere. Furnished in period decor.

Host: Marge Turcot
Rooms: 4 (1 PB; 3 SB) $45-60
Continental Breakfast
Credit Cards: A, B
Closed Nov. 1-May 1
Notes: 2, 7, 8, 9, 10, 11, 12

Richmond Hill Inn

87 Richmond Hill Drive
Asheville, NC, 28806
(800) 545-9238

Elegant historic Victorian mansion built in 1889 in Asheville's Blue Ridge Mountains, near Biltmore Estate. Listed on the National Register of Historic Places. Now magnificently renovated and elegantly furnished with twelve guest rooms with private baths. Fine dining and gracious service in gourmet restaurant. Interesting book collections in the library.

Host: Susan Michel
Rooms: 12 (PB) $95-200
Full Breakfast
Credit Cards: A, B, C
Notes: 2, 3, 4, 5, 7 (restricted), 8, 9, 10, 11, 12, 14

BANNER ELK

Archer's Inn

Route 2, Box 56-A
Banner Elk, NC, 28604
(704) 898-9004

Archer's Inn is perched on the side of Beech Mountain, NC (the highest city in the eastern US), with a beautiful view of the Elk River Valley and surrounding mountains. All the rooms have fireplaces and private baths. Just two miles to skiing and close to the Blue Ridge Parkway and Grandfather Mountain.

Hosts: Joe & Bonny Archer
Rooms: 14 (PB) $45-95
Full Breakfast
Credit Cards: A, B
Notes: 2 (for deposits), 4 (seasonally), 5, 7 (limited), 8, 9, 10, 11, 12, 13, 14

BEAUFORT

The Cedars Inn

305 Front Street
Beaufort, NC, 28516
(919) 728-7036

This lovingly restored eighteenth-century inn offers twelve elegantly appointed rooms with private baths and fireplaces. The dining room boasts the finest cuisine on the Carolina coast. Daily tours of historic Beaufort and the Outer Banks are available in season. Special weekly rate for Sunday night through Friday morning including breakfast—$275 plus tax.

Hosts: Bill & Pat Kwaak
Rooms: 12 (PB) $75-125
Full Breakfast
Minimum stay in-season weekends: 2 ; holidays: 3
Credit Cards: A, B
Notes: 2, 4, 5, 7, 8, 9, 10, 11, 12

Delamar Inn

217 Turner Street
Beaufort, NC, 28516
(919) 728-4300

Enjoy the Scottish hospitality of this Civil War home in the heart of Beaufort's historic district. The inn offers three antique-furnished guest rooms, each with its own private bath. After a delightful breakfast, enjoy your second cup of coffee and newspaper on the upper porch or take an easy stroll down to the waterfront, curiosity shops, or historic sites. If you're a bit more energetic, we suggest a short drive to the beaches at Fort Macon, or take the ferry to Ocracoke on the Outer Banks.

Hosts: Philip & Kay
Rooms: 3 (PB) $48-78
Continental-plus Breakfast
Credit Cards: A, B
Notes: 5, 7 (restricted), 8 (over 12), 10, 11, 12

1854 Shotgun House

406 Ann Street
Beaufort, NC, 28516
(919) 728-6248

A completely restored 1854 Greek Revival in the center of historic Beaufort, one block from the boardwalk, where you can see yachts and watch the wild ponies graze on Shackleford Shoals. Come and be pampered with designer sheets, antique furniture, down comforters, and clean, modern baths.

Host: Debra Wheeless
Rooms: 3 (PB) $75
Full Breakfast
Credit Cards: A, B
Notes: 2, 5, 7, 8, 9, 14

BEECH MOUNTAIN

Archers Inn

Route 2 Box 56A
Beech Mountain Parkway
Beech Mountain, NC, 28604
(704) 898-9004

A quaint country B&B perched on the side of Beech Mountain. There are private baths and fireplaces in every room, and most have a porch or deck. Most rooms and the great room have a panoramic view of the Elk River Valley and surrounding mountains. Carriage rides available.

Hosts: Bonny & Joe Archer
Rooms: 14 (PB) $45-95
Full Breakfast
Credit Cards: A, B
Notes: 2, 4 (summers), 5, 7, 8, 9, 10, 11, 12, 13, 14

River Forest Manor & Marina

BELHAVEN

River Forest Manor & Marina

600 East Main Street
Belhaven, NC, 27810
(919) 943-2151

An elegant mansion located on the Pungo River. Besides being a wonderful country inn with leaded cut-glass windows and crystal chandeliers, River Forest Manor is also a fully equipped marina. A famous smorgasbord is served nightly during the season; dinner from a menu the balance of the year. The grand old manor offers a carefully preserved feeling of Victorian times.

Hosts: Ms. Melba G. Smith & Axson Smith, Jr.
Rooms: 12 (PB) $40-75
Continental Breakfast
Credit Cards: A, B, C
Notes: 4, 5, 9, 10, 11, 12

BLACK MOUNTAIN

Bed & Breakfast Over Yonder

Route 1, Box 269
North Fork Road
Black Mountain, NC, 28711
(704) 669-6762

This comfortable old mountain home, furnished with antiques, has views of mountains and the surrounding woods from its landscaped decks and terrace. Secluded on 40 acres, it is two miles from I-40 and Black Mountain, which has antique and craft shopping. Close to the Blue Ridge Parkway and Asheville's Biltmore House. Our breakfast specialty is fresh mountain brown trout.

Host: Wilhelmina Headley
Rooms: 5 (PB) $36.75-52.50
Full Breakfast
Credit Cards: No
Closed Dec.-May
Notes: 2, 7 (limited), 8, 9, 10, 11, 12

BLOWING ROCK

Gideon Ridge Inn

P.O. Box 1929
Blowing Rock, NC, 28605
(704) 295-3644

With a sweeping view of mountains and foothills, guests are surrounded by antiques and family heirlooms. The library, with its massive stone fireplace, is the center of the inn, where guests relax after days spent hiking, browsing village shops, or driving the Blue Ridge Parkway.

Hosts: Jane & Cobb Milner
Rooms: 8 (PB) $80-120
Full Breakfast
Credit Cards: A, B, C
Notes: 2, 5, 8 (over 12), 9, 10, 11, 12, 13, 14

Ragged Garden Inn

Box 1927, Sunset Drive
Blowing Rock, NC, 28605
(704) 295-9703

A cozy, European, chestnut-bark-covered home with a romantic candlelit dining room downstairs. Located on 1 acre just half a block from the quaint village of Blowing Rock, near the Blue Ridge Parkway. Rooms are individually decorated with interesting artwork and artifacts.

Hosts: Joe & Joyce Villani
Rooms: 9 (PB) $60-85
Full Breakfast
Credit Cards: A, B, C
Closed Jan.
Notes: 2, 4, 7, 8 (over 12), 9, 10, 11, 12, 13, 14

BOONE

Overlook Lodge

Box 1327, Boone, NC, 28607
(704) 963-5785

Cozily secluded mountain house in the heart of the Blue Ridge Mountains. Spectacular view from two large decks. Adjacent to National Forest and the Blue Ridge Parkway. Great Room with fireplace. Golf, skiing, hiking, whitewater rafting, antique and craft shopping, outdoor drama all nearby.

Host: Nancy Garrett
Rooms: 5 (3 PB; 2 SB) $55-100
Full Breakfast
Credit Cards: A, B
Notes: 2, 5, 7, 8, 9, 10, 12, 13, 14

BREVARD

The Inn at Brevard

410 East Main Street
Brevard, NC, 28712
(704) 884-2105

Listed on the National Register of Historic Places, this inn hosted a reunion dinner for Stonewall Jackson's troops in 1911. Beautifully restored in 1984 with a European flavor throughout. Just minutes from Brevard Music Center, Blue Ridge Parkway, and Pisgah National Forest.

Hosts: Eileen & Bertrand Bourget
Rooms: 15 (14 PB; 1 SB) $55-65
Full Breakfast
Credit Cards: A, B
Closed Dec. 21-April 30
Notes: 2, 4, 9, 10, 12

The Red House Inn

412 West Probart Street
Brevard, NC, 28712
(704) 884-9349

The Red House was built in 1851 and has been lovingly restored and furnished in turn-of-the-century period antiques. Located in the Blue Ridge Mountains, with the wonderful Brevard Music Center every night during the summer.

Hosts: Lynne Ong & Mary MacGillycuddy
Rooms: 6 (PB and SB) $43-57
Full Breakfast
Credit Cards: No
Closed Nov. 15-April 1
Notes: 2, 9, 11, 12, 14

BRYSON CITY

Folkestone Inn

767 West Deep Creek Road
Bryson City, NC, 28713
(704) 488-2730

Enjoy the romance of an old world inn, the charm and nostalgia of the long-forgotten life-style of gracious country living. The inn is located in the Great Smoky Mountains, in Swain County, which is 86 percent parkland. You may hike, fish, sail, raft, or horseback ride.

Hosts: Norma & Peter Joyce
Rooms: 9 (PB) $59-79
Full Breakfast
Credit Cards: No
Notes: 2, 5, 10, 11

Fryemont Inn

Box 459
Bryson City, NC, 28713
(704) 488-2159

Overlooking the Great Smoky Mountains National Park. All rooms have private bath. Dinner and breakfast are included in the daily rate, and the inn is on the National Register of Historic Places. Featured in *Bon Appetit.*

Hosts: Sue & George Brown
Rooms: 39 (PB) $80-160
Full Breakfast
Credit Cards: A, B
Closed Nov.-mid-April
Notes: 2, 4, 7, 8, 9, 10, 11, 14

CHAPEL HILL

The Inn at Bingham School

P.O. Box 267
Chapel Hill, NC, 27514
(919) 563-5583

An award-winning restoration of a headmaster's home for a school that operated from 1845 to 1865. The inn has five large rooms with private baths and a three-room guest cottage with whirlpool bath. Located fifteen minutes from Chapel Hill on 10 acres of rolling farmland. Full breakfast, evening refreshments. Charter member of the NC B&B Association.

Hosts: Jane & Bob Kelly
Rooms: 6 (PB) $75-110 + tax
Full Breakfast
Credit Cards: No
Closed Dec. 18-Jan. 2
Notes: 2, 7, 8 (over 12), 9, 10, 12, 14

CHARLOTTE

The Homeplace

5901 Sardis Road
Charlotte, NC, 28270
(704) 365-1936

Restored 1902 Country/Victorian on 2.5 acres with garden gazebo and wraparound porch. Victorian elegance and old-fashioned charm with a full home-cooked breakfast. A quiet setting and unique experience for the traveler, business executive, or connoisseur of fine older homes.

Hosts: Peggy & Frank Dearien
Rooms: 3 (PB) $68-78
Full Breakfast
Minimum stay holidays: 2
Credit Cards: A, B, C
Notes: 2, 5, 8 (over 10) 14

Fearrington House Inn

Fearrington Village Center
Pittsboro, NC 27312
(919) 542-2121

Reminiscent of a small European inn, Fearrington House Inn maintains membership in Relais and Chateaux, an association of 350 deluxe hotels and gourmet restaurants in 37 countries. Guest enjoy attentive service unsurpassed. Each room is a unique blend of architecture, antiques, artwork, and fabrics. The inn is the result of a decade-long search for original artwork, English antiques, and hand-picked appointments. Even the beautiful pine plank flooring came from and old English workhouse.

Hosts: R. B. and Jenny Fitch
Rooms: 5 (PB) $125
Suites: 9 (PB) $155-$185
Full Breakfast
Credit Cards: A, B
Closed Dec. 23-27
Notes: 2, 4, 8 (over 12), 9, 10, 11, 12, 14

The New England Inn

3726 Providence Road
Charlotte, NC, 28211
(704) 362-0008

We offer four very attractive and comfortable rooms with quiet good taste of decor that enhances the charm of the inn. Located in one of the most attractive residential areas, guests enjoy carefully landscaped yards, which are spectacular in the spring and fall. Enjoy our library, game room, great shopping areas, and restaurants. A sumptuous breakfast with gourmet coffees is served each morning.

Hosts: Jeanne & Ken England
Rooms: 4 (3 PB; 1 SB) $50-70
Full Breakfast
Credit Cards: A, B
Notes: 2, 5, 8 (over 12), 10, 11, 12, 14

CHIMNEY ROCK

The Gingerbread Inn

Box 187
Chimney Rock, NC, 28720
(704) 625-4038

The Gingerbread Inn is located on the Rocky Broad River. The rooms are country finished — ruffled curtains, dust ruffles, quilts, etc. There are two decks located on the river with chairs for relaxing while listening to the flowing water.

Hosts: Tom & Janet Sherman
Rooms: 5 (2 PB; 3 SB) $40-55
Continental Breakfast
Credit Cards: No
Notes: 2, 5, 7, 8, 9

DURHAM

Arrowhead Inn

106 Mason Road
Durham, NC, 27712
(919) 477-8430

This restored 1775 manor house, on 4 rural acres, offers homey hospitality in an atmosphere that evokes colonial Carolina. But along with eighteenth-century architecture, decor, and furnishings, Arrowhead Inn features contemporary comfort, sparkling housekeeping, and bounteous, home-cooked breakfasts.

Hosts: Jerry & Barbara Ryan
Rooms: 9 (5 PB; 4 SB) $54-102.20
Full Breakfast
Credit Cards: A, B, C, E
Closed Dec. 22-Jan.1
Notes: 2, 5, 7, 8, 9, 10, 11, 12, 14

EDENTON

The Lords Proprietors' Inn

300 North Broad Street
Edenton, NC, 27932
(919) 482-3641

Establishing a reputation for the finest accommodations in North Carolina, the inn offers twenty elegantly appointed rooms with private baths and spacious parlors for gathering for afternoon tea by the fire. Inquire about special weekend programs that include dinner and tour.

Hosts: Arch & Jane Edwards
Rooms: 20 (PB) $80 + tax
Continental-plus Breakfast
Credit Cards: No
Notes: 2, 5, 7 (restricted), 8, 9, 10, 11, 12

The Trestle House Inn

Route 4, Box 370
Edenton, NC, 27932
(919) 482-2282

Located south of Albemarle's colonial capital, off Route 32 and Soundside Road. Luxurious, immaculate accommodations include private baths, HBO, exercise room with steam bath, game room with billiards and shuffleboard, sun deck, private stocked 15-acre fishing lake. Overlooks a 60-acre wildlife preserve.

Hosts: Fran & Rich Oliver
Rooms: 4 (PB) $110
Full Breakfast
Credit Cards: A, B, C
Notes: 2, 5, 7 (limited), 8, 9, 12, 14

FRANKLIN

Buttonwood Inn

190 Georgia Road
Franklin, NC, 28734
(704) 369-8985

A quaint, small mountain inn awaits those who prefer a cozy country atmosphere. Before hiking, golfing, gem mining, or horseback riding, enjoy a breakfast of puffy scrambled eggs and apple sausage ring or eggs Benedict, Dutch babies, blintz souffle, strawberry omelet, or stuffed French toast. Relax, enjoy, return!

Host: Liz Oehser
Doubles: 4 (2 PB; 2 SB) $50.76-64.80
Type of Beds: 2 Twin; 3 Double
Full Breakfast
Credit Cards: No
Closed Dec.-March
Notes: 2, 9, 10, 11, 12

The Franklin Terrace

67 Harrison Avenue
Franklin, NC, 28734
(704) 524-7907; (800) 633-2431

The Franklin Terrace, built as a school in 1887, is listed in the National Register of Historic Places. Wide porches and large guest rooms filled with period antiques will carry you to a time gone by, when Southern hospitality was at its best. Antiques, crafts, and gifts are for sale on the main floor. Within walking distance of Franklin's famous gem shops, clothing boutiques, and fine restaurants.

Hosts: Ed & Helen Henson
Rooms: 9 (PB) $44-65
Continental Breakfast
Credit Cards: A, B
Open April 1-Nov. 1
Notes: 2, 7, 8, 9, 10, 11, 12

GREENSBORO

Greenwood

205 North Park Drive
Greensboro, NC, 27401
(919) 274-6350

Enjoy the warm hospitality of our 1905 home on the park in the historic district of Greensboro. Three minutes from downtown; three miles from I-85 and I-40. Air-conditioning, two fireplaces in living rooms, swimming pool, TV room, guest kitchen. Hearty continental breakfast is served.

Host: Jo Anne Green
Rooms: 5 (3-4 PB; 2 SB) $54-75.60
Continental-plus Breakfast
Minimum stay Southern Furniture Market: 3
Credit Cards: A, B, C
Notes: 2, 5, 7, 8 (over 4), 9, 10, 11, 12, 14

HENDERSONVILLE

Claddagh Inn

755 North Main Street
Hendersonville, NC, 28792
(704) 697-7778; (800) 225-4700

The Claddagh Inn is located in downtown Hendersonville, just two blocks from the beautiful Main Street Shopping Promenade. The inn has undergone extensive remodeling. The guest rooms have private bath, telephone, air-conditioning, TV available. Our guests awake to a delicious full country breakfast. AAA approved. Listed on National Registry.

Hosts: Marie & Fred Carberry
Rooms: 14 (PB) $39-69 plus tax
Full Breakfast
Credit Cards: A, B, C, D
Notes: 2, 5, 7, 8, 9, 10, 11, 12, 14

The Waverly Inn

783 North Main Street
Hendersonville, NC, 28792
(800) 537-8195; (704) 693-9193

Listed in the National Register of Historic Places, this is the oldest surviving inn in Hendersonville. The newly renovated inn has something for everyone, including: claw-foot tubs, king and queen four-poster canopy beds. Convenient to restaurants, shopping, Biltmore Estate, Carl Sandburg home, Blue Ridge Parkway, and Flat Rock Playhouse. AAA approved.

Hosts: John & Diane Sheiry
Rooms: 16 (PB) $53-73
Full Breakfast
Credit Cards: A, B, C, D
Notes: 2, 5, 7, 8, 9, 10, 11, 12, 14

HICKORY

The Hickory B&B

464 Seventh Street SW
Hickory, NC, 28602
(704) 324-0548

Early turn-of-the-century space, with modern comfort. We offer more than hospitality. Major furniture sales, mountain sports, and a central location for this arts mecca lure visitors to Hickory. Antique and year-round flea markets nearby.

Hosts: Bill & Jane Mohney
Rooms: 4 (2 PB; 2 SB) $35-50
Full Breakfast
Credit Cards: No
Notes: 2, 5, 7, 8, 9

The Old Mill

Box 252
Hickory, NC, 28710
(704) 625-4256

1920s Bavarian chalet-style B&B perched on the banks of a rushing mountain stream in scenic Hickory Nut Gorge. Attractions within thirty minutes include Flat Rock, Hendersonville, Asheville, Biltmore House, Black Mountain, Green River, and the Blue Ridge Parkway.

Host: Walt Davis
Rooms: 4 (PB) $50-85

Full Breakfast
Credit Cards: A, B, C, D
Notes: 2, 9, 10, 11, 12

HIGHLANDS

Colonial Pines Inn

Route 1, Box 22B
Highlands, NC, 28741
(704) 526-2060

A quiet country guest house with lovely mountain view. Comfortably furnished with antiques and many nice accessories. Half a mile from Highlands' fine dining and shopping area. Full breakfast includes egg dishes, homemade breads, fresh fruit, coffee, juice. Separate guest house with fireplace.

Hosts: Chris & Donna Alley
Rooms: 6 (PB) $60-75
Apartment: 1 (PB, kitchen; sleeps 4)
Full Breakfast
Credit Cards: A, B
Notes: 2, 5, 8, 9, 10, 11, 12, 13

Colonial Pines Inn

HIGH POINT

The Premier B&B

1001 Johnson Street
High Point, NC, 27262
(919) 889-8349

No place like home. Enjoy a glass of wine by the fireplace or on the front porch. Relax by candlelight in a bubble bath. Mingle with folks from all over. Awaken to the smell of a magnificent breakfast. Shop for furniture conveniently. Business or pleasure, we provide the perfect mix.

Host: Peggy Burcham
Rooms: 6 (PB) $60-125
Full Breakfast
Credit Cards: A, B, C
Notes: 2, 4, 5, 7 (limited), 8, 9, 10, 12

HILLSBOROUGH

The Inn at Teardrops

175 West King Street
Hillsborough, NC, 27278
(919) 732-1120

The Inn at Teardrops is an old-fashioned B&B for those who enjoy quiet comfort in an elegant setting. The house is furnished with antiques and reproductions. Make yourself at home. Relax in the elegant splendor of our parlor, play the old baby grand, or stroll in our gardens. Many antique shops are nearby.

Rooms: 6 (4 PB; 2 SB) $50-85
Full Breakfast
Credit Cards: A, B
Notes: 2, 5, 7 (outside), 8, 9, 10, 11, 12, 14

KILL DEVIL HILLS

Ye Olde Cherokee Inn

500 North Virginia Dare Trail
Kill Devil Hills, NC, 27948
(919) 441-6127

Large pink beach house with cypress-wood interior five hundred feet from ocean beach. Quiet, restful. Ideal for relaxing and romance. Close to fine restaurants, golf, hang gliding, scuba diving, wind surfing, deep-sea fishing, and shopping. Be as active or inactive as you wish. Private baths.

Hosts: Bob & Phyllis Combs
Rooms: 6 (PB) $55-81
Continental Breakfast
Minimum stay holidays: 3
Credit Cards: A, B, C
Closed Nov.-March
Notes: 2, 9, 10, 11, 12, 14

LAKE JUNALUSKA

Providence Lodge

1 Atkins Loop
Lake Junaluska, NC, 28745
(704) 456-6486; (800) 733-6114

Providence Lodge is located near the Blue Ridge Parkway and is an easy drive from the Cherokee Indian Reservation, Great Smoky Mountain National Park, or the Biltmore Estate in Asheville. Rustic, with period furniture, comfortable beds, claw-foot tubs, and big porches. Delicious family-style meals feature the best in country cooking.

Hosts: Ben & Wilma Cato
Rooms: 16 (8 PB; 8 SB) $60
Full Breakfast
Credit Cards: No
Closed Sept.-May
Notes: 2, 4, 8, 9, 10, 11, 12

Sunset Inn

21 North Lakeshore Drive
Lake Junaluska, NC, 28745
(704) 456-6114; (800) 733-6114

This beautiful house has large porches with views of the lake and Smoky Mountains. The warm, friendly atmosphere contributes to a relaxing vacation or provides a restful stop between area attractions: Cherokee, Maggie Valley, Biltmore Estate, Blue Ridge Parkway. Scrumptious meals are just one reason guests keep coming back.

Hosts: Wilma Cato & Norma Wright
Rooms: 20 (16 PB; 4 SB) $36-45/person
Full Breakfast
Credit Cards: No
Closed Nov. 1-May 20
Notes: 2, 4, 7, 8, 9, 10, 11, 12, 13

MANTEO

Scarborough Inn

Box 1310
Manteo, NC, 27954
(919) 473-3979

The comforts of the present: private baths, TV, refrigerator, room telephone, and in-room coffee. Plus memorable touches from the past: family heirlooms, antiques, and collectibles, all carefully chosen and lovingly managed by natives Sally and Phil, of historic Roanoke Island.

Hosts: Phil & Sally Scarborough
Rooms: 10 (PB) $37.80-48.60
Continental Breakfast
Minimum stay holidays: 3
Credit Cards: A, B, C, E, F
Notes: 4, 5, 7, 8, 9, 10, 11, 12

The Tranquil House Inn

P.O. Box 2045
Manteo, NC, 27954
(919) 473-1404; (800) 458-7069

Only minutes from the Outer Banks beaches, this B&B waterfront inn is reminiscent of a bygone elegance. Tranquil House has twenty-eight individually decorated rooms, library with fireplace, wraparound porches lined with rockers. Wake up to complimentary breakfast; later enjoy your complimentary bottle of wine and snack tray.

Host: Margaret Buell
Rooms: 28 (PB) $55-125
Continental Breakfast
Credit Cards: A, B, C, E
Notes: 2, 5, 7, 8, 9, 10, 11, 12, 14

MARSHALL

Marshall House

5 Hill Street
Marshall, NC, 28753
(704) 649-9205; (800) 562-9258

Built in 1903, the inn overlooks the peaceful town of Marshall and the waters of the French Broad River. The house is a twenty-room country inn, decorated with fancy chandeliers, antiques, and pictures. It has been entered in the National Register of Historic Places under the name of the James H. White House.

First Colony Inn

Host: Ruth Boylan
Rooms: 8 (2 PB; 6 SB) $35-50
Continental Breakfast
Credit Cards: A, B, C, D, E
Notes: 2, 3, 4, 5, 6, 7, 8, 9, 10, 11, 12, 14

MARS HILL

Baird House, Ltd.

121 South Main Street
Mars Hill, NC, 28754
(704) 689-5722

Five guest rooms—two with a working fireplace two with private bath — are featured in an old brick, antique-filled bed and breakfast inn that once was the grandest house in this pastoral corner of the western North Carolina mountains. Eighteen miles north of Asheville.

Host: Mrs. Yvette Wessel
Rooms: 5 (2 PB; 3 SB) $42-52.50
Full Breakfast
Credit Cards: C
Closed Dec.
Notes: 2, 7, 8, 9, 10, 11, 12, 13, 14

MOUNT AIRY

Pine Ridge Inn

2893 West Pine Street
Mount Airy, NC, 27030
(919) 789-5034

Built in 1948, this Southern mansion offers private bedroom suites, swimming pool with sun deck, large indoor hot tub, exercise room. Lunch and dinner available Tuesday-Saturday.

Hosts: Ellen & Manford Haxton
Rooms: 7 (5 PB; 2 SB) $50-85
Continental Breakfast
Credit Cards: A, B, C
Notes: 2, 3, 4, 5, 7, 8, 9, 10, 11, 12, 14

NAGS HEAD

First Colony Inn

6721 South Virginia Dare Trail
Nags Head, NC, 27959
(919) 441-2343

Enjoy Southern hospitality in our historic inn with a boardwalk directly to our private, sandy ocean beach, ocean and sound views, and a cozy parlor. We are convenient to the Wright Brothers Memorial and other historic and natural attractions. Efficiencies, wet bars, luxury baths, two stories of wonderful wraparound verandas with rockers and hammocks; antique and reproduction furniture.

Hosts: Richard & Camille Lawrence
Rooms: 26 (PB) $100-200
Continental Breakfast
Credit Cards: A, B, C, D, E
Notes: 2, 5, 7 (limited), 8, 9, 10, 11, 12, 14

NEW BERN

The Aerie

509 Pollock Street
New Bern, NC, 28560
(919) 636-5553

A Victorian inn one block from Tryon Palace. Individually decorated rooms are furnished with antiques and reproductions; sitting room with player piano. Bicycles are available for guests who want to tour New Bern's historic district.

Hosts: Rick & Lois Cleveland
Rooms: 7 (PB) $80
Full Breakfast
Credit Cards: A, B
Notes: 2, 5, 7, 8, 9, 12, 14

Harmony House Inn

215 Pollock Street
New Bern, NC, 28560
(919) 636-3810

This circa 1850 Greek Revival inn provides comfortable elegance in the historic district. Unusual spaciousness, antiques, a guest parlor, rocking chairs and swings on the front porch, and a parking area add to guests' enjoyment. Near Tryon Palace, restaurants, and shops.

Hosts: A.E. & Diane Hansen
Rooms: 9 (PB) $70
Full Breakfast
Credit Cards: A, B, C
Notes: 2, 5, 7, 8, 9, 10, 12, 14

Kings Arms Inn

212 Pollock Street
New Bern, NC, 28560
(919) 638-4409

The King's Arms Inn, named for an old New Bern tavern reputed to have hosted members of the First Continental Congress, upholds a heritage of hospitality and graciousness as New Bern's "first and foremost" in bed and breakfast accommodations. Spacious rooms with comfortable four-poster, canopy, or brass beds, fireplaces, private baths, and elegant decor harbor travelers who want to escape the present and steep themselves in colonial history. Home-baked breakfasts include: banana or zucchini bread, blueberry, lemon ginger, apple streusel, or sweet potato muffins, Smithfield ham and biscuits, fresh fruit, juice, and cinnamon coffee or tea — all delivered to your room with the morning paper.

Hosts: David & Diana Parks
Rooms: 9 (PB) $55-75
Continental-plus Breakfast
Credit Cards: A, B, C
Notes: 2, 5, 7, 8, 9, 10, 11, 12, 14

New Berne House Inn

709 Broad Street
New Bern, NC, 28560
(800) 842-7688

An inn for the young and the young at heart. Particularly pleasing English Country decor in New Bern's authentically restored B&B. Hardwood floors, antiques, working fireplaces, and a friendly ghost. Guest rooms feature antique beds, converted to king and queen size, piles of pillows, and crisp eyelet sheets. Private vintage baths. Scrumptious breakfasts feature pralines and cream waffles, honey-glazed ham, and spiced apple crepes. Afternoon tea, complimentary beverages, and tandem bikes. Mystery weekends, tour packages. Closest accommodations to Tryon Palace.

Hosts: Shan & Joel Wilkins
Rooms: 6 (PB) $54-81
Full Breakfast
Credit Cards: A, B, C, D, E, F
Notes: 2, 5, 6, 8, 9, 10, 11, 12, 14

OCRACOKE ISLAND

Oscar's House

Route 12, Box 206
Ocracoke Island, NC, 27960
(919) 928-1311

Oscar's House offers friendly accommodations in a comfortable 1940s home on Ocracoke Island. The home is one block from the harbor and one mile from the Atlantic Ocean, within easy walking distance to shops, restaurants, and historic sites. The full breakfast is healthy, and special diets are catered to.

Host: Ann Ehringhaus
Rooms: 3 (1 PB; 2 SB) $50-55
Full Breakfast
Credit Cards: A, B
Closed Nov.-early April
Notes: 2, 7 (restricted), 8 (over 3), 9, 11

OLD FORT

The Inn at Old Fort

P.O. Box 1116
Old Fort, NC, 28762
(704) 668-9384

Two-story Gothic Revival-style Victorian cottage, c. 1880. Located on more than 3.5 acres overlooking the historic small town of Old Fort. Features rooms furnished with antiques; warm, friendly conversation; front-porch rockers; terraced lawn and gardens; and extended continental breakfasts featuring freshly baked breads and fresh fruits.

Hosts: Chuck & Debbie Aldridge
Rooms: 5 (3 PB; 2 SB) $35-45
Continental-plus Breakfast
Credit Cards: No
Notes: 2, 5, 7 (outside), 8, 9, 10, 11, 12, 14

ORIENTAL

The Tar Heel Inn

Box 176, Oriental, NC, 28571
(919) 249-1078

This quiet fishing village is located on the Neuse River and the Pamlico Sound and is known as the sailing capital of N.C. This quaint circa 1890 inn has been restored to capture the feeling of an old English-style country inn with comfortable common rooms. The patios and gardens are yours to enjoy, and you can even borrow bikes to pedal around town. Excellent restaurants and shops, sailing, golf, tennis, and fishing are within walking or biking distance.

Hosts: Dave & Patti Nelson
Rooms: 7 (PB) $55-75
Full Breakfast
Credit Cards: No
Closed: Dec., Jan., Feb.
Notes: 2, 8, 9, 10, 11, 12, 14

PENLAND

Chinquapin Inn

P.O. Box 145
Penland, NC, 28765
(704) 765-0064

Couched in tall pines, with a backdrop of Blue Ridge Mountain silhouettes, Chinquapin Inn is an intimate and hospitable B&B located within walking distance of Penland School of Crafts. Travelers interested in accommodations off the beaten path will find the inn a welcoming home away from home.

Hosts: Bill & Sue Ford
Rooms: 4 (SB) $35-45 + tax
Continental-plus Breakfast
Credit Cards: No
Notes: 2, 5, 6 (call), 7 (restricted), 8, 9, 10, 11, 12

PINEHURST

Magnolia Inn

P.O. Box 818
Pinehurst, NC, 28374
(800) 526-5562; (800) 526-5562

The Magnolia Inn was built in 1896. In 1990 it was completely renovated and refurbished with Victorian furnishings and accessories.

Located in the heart of the picturesque Village of Pinehurst, where shopping, dining, walking and carriage tours are available. There are more than thirty golf courses within fifteen miles of the inn.

Hosts: Ann & Gene Ballard
Rooms: 13 (PB) $90
Full Breakfast
Credit Cards: A, B
Notes: 2, 5, 10, 11, 12, 14

RALEIGH

The Oakwood Inn

411 North Bloodworth Street
Raleigh, NC, 27604
(919) 832-9712

The Oakwood Inn is an 1871 Victorian listed on the National Register and located in a downtown historic district. Its Victorian heritage is seen in the carefully restored decor, period architecture, and details such as names scratched on a windowpane in 1875.

Host: Diana Newton
Rooms: 6 (PB) $75-90
Full Breakfast
Credit Cards: A, B, C
Closed Christmas week
Notes: 2, 7, 8 (over 12), 14

ROBBINSVILLE

Blue Boar Lodge

200 Santeetlah Road
Robbinsville, NC, 28771KD
(704) 479-8126

Secluded mountain retreat cooled by mountain breezes. Hiking, fishing, hunting, bird watching, and canoeing are all very close by. Rustic but modern house. Meals served family style on our lazy Susan table. Located away from all city traffic, ten miles northwest of Robbinsville. Quiet and peaceful. Rate includes breakfast and dinner.

Hosts: Roy & Kathy Wilson
Rooms: 7 (PB) $90
Full Breakfast
Credit Cards: A, B
Open April 1-mid-Oct.
Notes: 4, 7

SALISBURY

The 1868 Stewart-Marsh House

220 South Ellis Street
Salisbury, NC, 28144
(704) 633-6841

Gracious 1868 Federal style home on quiet tree-lined street in the West Square Historic District. Cozy pine-paneled library, screened porch with wicker, spacious guest rooms with air-conditioning, antiques, heart pine floors. Delicious breakfast with home-baked muffins and breads plus entree. Warm, friendly, Southern hospitality. Historic sights, antebellum homes, shopping, and restaurants are within walking distance. Guided tours available. Easy access to I-85.

Hosts: Gerry & Chuck Webster
Rooms: 2 (PB) $45-50 + tax
Continental-plus Breakfast
Credit Cards: A, B
Notes: 2, 5, 7 (outdoors), 9, 10, 12, 14

Rowan Oak House

208 South Fulton Street
Salisbury, NC, 28144
(704) 633-2086

A romantic Victorian Queen Anne with high ceilings and big rooms, seven fireplaces, antique wallpaper. Filled with antiques, flowers, and goodwill. Stained glass in the front carries out the ribbon and leaf motif found on some mantles. The beautifully rounded cupola rises high above the 4,800-square-foot mansion.

Hosts: Bill & Ruth Ann Coffey
Rooms: 3 (PB) $65-75
Full Breakfast
Credit Cards: A, B
Notes: 2, 5, 7 (limited), 8 (over 12), 9, 10, 11, 12, 14

SALUDA

The Orchard Inn

P.O. Box 725
Saluda, NC, 28773
(704) 749-5471

A mountaintop inn offering outstanding hospitality and memorable dining. This turn-of-the-century country house has a touch of plantation elegance, with a large living room with fireplace, antiques, folk art, and masses of books for guests to enjoy.

Hosts: Ann & Ken Hough
Rooms: 12 (PB) $75-125
Full Breakfast
Credit Cards: No
Notes: 2, 4, 5, 9, 10, 11, 12

SPARTA

Turby-villa

East Whitehead Street
Sparta, NC, 28675
(919) 372-8490

This B&B is located on twenty acres of beautiful mountain farmland. Breakfast is selected from a menu and served on a glassed-in porch with a beautiful view of the mountains. We are ten miles from the Blue Ridge Parkway, which is maintained by the National Park Service. We are on Highway 18N two miles from Sparta.

Hosts: Maybelline & R.E. Turby Turbiville
Rooms: 3 (PB) $52
Full Breakfast
Credit Cards: No
Notes: 2, 5, 7, 8, 9, 10, 12

SPRUCE PINE

The Fairway Inn Bed & Breakfast

110 Henry Lane
Spruce Pine, NC, 28777
(704) 765-4917

Beautiful country home with a scenic view. Located on highway 226, three miles north of the Blue Ridge Parkway. Gourmet breakfast and homemade breads. Wine and cheese in the afternoon. Restaurants nearby.

Hosts: Margaret & John P. Stevens
Rooms: 6 (PB) $60-70
Full Breakfast
Credit Cards: No
Closed Jan.-April
Notes: 2, 7, 8, 9, 10, 12, 13, 14

TARBORO

Little Warren

304 East Park Avenue
Tarboro, NC, 27886
(919) 823-1314

Large, gracious, Edwardian family home, renovated and modernized, located within a quiet neighborhood in the historic district. Deeply set wraparound front porch overlooks the town common, which is one of two originally chartered commons remaining in the United States. Antiques available.

Hosts: Patsy & Tom Miller
Rooms: 3 (PB) $50.40-68.25
Continental and Full Breakfast
Credit Cards: A, B, C
Notes: 2, 5, 7, 8 (over 6), 9, 10

Mill Farm Inn

Mast Farm Inn

The inn consists of ten different buildings and cabins on 3 landscaped acres in the foothills of the Blue Ridge Mountains. Golf, tennis, swimming, antique shopping, and wonderful sight-seeing are close at hand. All this is complimented by a fine restaurant in which to start and end the day.

Hosts: Jeremy & Jennifer Wainwright
Rooms: 29 (PB) $85-95
Full Breakfast
Credit Cards: A, B
Notes: 2, 3, 4, 5, 7, 8, 9, 10, 11, 12, 14

TRYON

Mill Farm Inn

Box 1251
Tryon, NC, 28782
(800)-545-6992

The disappointments of travel are forgotten at Mill Farm Inn! Emphasis is on important amenities: a homelike atmosphere, the warmth of bedrooms with private baths, and cozy, relaxing living and dining rooms that make our special guests feel at home.

Hosts: Chip & Penny Kessler
Rooms: 10 (PB) $45-55
Continental Breakfast
Credit Cards: No
Notes: 2, 5, 8, 9, 12

Pine Crest Inn

P.O. Box 1030
200 Pine Crest Lane
Tryon, NC, 28782
(800) 633-3001; (704) 859-9135

Stone Hedge Inn

Box 366
Tryon, NC, 28782
(704) 859-9114

Grand old estate on 28 acres at the base of Tryon Mountain. Lodging in the main building, cottage, and guest house. Private baths, TV, antiques, and wonderful views. Some rooms have kitchens and some have fireplaces. A full breakfast is served in the dining room by the picture windows; our

NOTES: Credit cards accepted: A Master Card; B Visa; C American Express; D Discover Card; E Diners Club; F Other: 2 Personal checks accepted: 3 Lunch available: 4 Dinner available: 5 Open all year

restaurant serves fine continental country-inn cuisine.

Hosts: Ray & Anneliese Weingartner
Rooms: 6 (PB) $56-75
Full Breakfast
Credit Cards: A, B
Notes: 2, 4, 5, 7, 8 (over 6), 9, 10, 11, 12

VALLE CRUCIS

Mast Farm Inn

Box 704
Valle Crucis, NC, 28691
(704) 963-5857

Recently restored twelve-room inn on the National Register of Historic Places. Vegetables and berries for the dining room are grown on the 18-acre farm located in North Carolina's High Country near the Blue Ridge Parkway. Country cooking with a gourmet touch. Golf, hiking, swimming, fishing, and skiing are nearby. Breakfast and dinner are included in the daily rate.

Hosts: Sibyl & Francis Pressly
Rooms: 12 (10 PB; 2 SB) $46-124 MAP
Continental-plus Breakfast
Credit Cards: A, B
Closed March 6-April 25 & Nov. 6-Dec. 26
Notes: 2, 4, 9, 10, 11, 12, 13

WARSAW

The Squire's Vintage Inn

Route 2, Box 130R
Warsaw, NC, 28398
(919) 296-1831

The Squire's Vintage Inn is located in the heart of Duplin County, as is its companion restaurant, The Country Squire, noted for its delicious cuisine and good taste. The rural setting adds to the privacy, intimacy, and relaxation for an overall feeling of "getting away from it all." Located near historic Kenansville.

Host: Iris Lennon
Rooms: 12 (PB) $44.10-51.45
Continental Breakfast
Credit Cards: A, B, C, E
Notes: 2, 4, 5, 7, 8, 9, 12

WAYNESVILLE

Grandview Lodge

809 Valley View Circle Road
Waynesville, NC, 28786
(704) 456-5212; (800) 255-7826

A country inn in the western North Carolina mountains; open all year. Southern home cooking, with breakfast featuring homemade breads, jams, and jellies. Dinner includes fresh vegetables, freshly baked breads, and desserts. Meals served family style; included in the rates. Private bath and cable TV.

Hosts: Stan & Linda Arnold
Rooms: 15 (PB) $80-90
Full Breakfast
Credit Cards: No
Notes: 2, 4 (included), 5, 7, 8, 9, 10, 11, 12, 13, 14

Hallcrest Inn

299 Halltop Circle
Waynesville, NC, 28786
(704) 456-6457

The homelike atmosphere here encourages a relaxing stay at this 1880s farmhouse on a mountaintop. Southern-style meals are served around large, lazy Susan tables. All rooms have private baths. There's a beautiful view from the front porch, where rocking chairs await you. The daily rate includes both breakfast and dinner.

Hosts: Russell & Margaret Burson
Rooms: 12 (PB) $75
Full Breakfast
Credit Cards: No
Closed Nov.-late May
Notes: 2, 3 (by arrangement), 4, 7, 8, 9 (restricted), 10, 11, 12, 14

Heath Lodge

900 Dolan Road
Waynesville, NC, 28786
(704) 456-3333

Our mountain inn offers an appealing blend of past and present. Enjoy our wooded setting from a porch rocker or relax in our outdoor hot tub. Bountiful breakfasts and country gourmet dinners are included in our inviting rates.

Hosts: David & Bonnie Probst
Rooms: 22 (PB) $85-95 MAP
Full Breakfast
Credit Cards: No
Closed Nov.-April
Notes: 2, 4, 7, 8, 9, 10, 11, 12, 13

The Palmer House

108 Pigeon Street
Waynesville, NC, 28786
(704) 456-7521

Built before the turn of the century, The Palmer House is one of the last of Waynesville's once numerous tourist homes. Within one block of Main Street. Relaxing environment, beautiful mountains, good food; a home away from home.

Hosts: Jeff Minick & Kris Gillet
Rooms: 7 (PB) $45-55
Full Breakfast
Credit Cards: A, B
Notes: 2, 5, 8, 9, 10, 11, 12

WEAVERVILLE/ASHEVILLE

Dry Ridge Inn

26 Brown Street
Weaverville, NC, 28787
(704) 658-3899

Large comfortable farmhouse, circa 1849, furnished with many antiques and handmade quilts. We try to keep our home in the manner of the time it was built: no TV, but plenty of books, games, an old Victrola, and good conversation.

Hosts: John & Karen VanderElzen
Rooms: 5 (PB) $48.60-59.40
Full Breakfast
Minimum stay fall weekends and holidays: 2
Credit Cards: A, B
Notes: 2, 5, 8, 9, 11, 12, 13

WILMINGTON

Anderson Guest House

520 Orange Street
Wilmington, NC, 28401
(919) 343-8128

An 1851 Italianate townhouse with separate guest quarters overlooking our private garden. Furnished with antiques, ceiling fans, working fireplaces; drinks on arrival. A delightful gourmet breakfast is served.

Hosts: Landon & Connie Anderson
Rooms: 2 (1 PB; 1 SB) $50-65
Full Breakfast
Credit Cards: No
Notes: 2, 5, 6, 7 (limited), 8, 9, 10, 11, 12

Dry Ridge Inn

The Five Star Guest House

14 North Seventh Street
Wilmington, NC, 28401
(919) 763-7581

The Five Star Guest House was built in 1908 and is just minutes from beaches, restaurant, shops, and galleries. It features spacious bedrooms furnished with antiques and private baths with deep clawfoot tubs. Listed with AAA.

Hosts: Harvey & Ann Crowther
Rooms: 3 (PB) $50-75
Full Breakfast

NOTES: Credit cards accepted: A Master Card; B Visa; C American Express; D Discover Card; E Diners Club; F Other: 2 Personal checks accepted: 3 Lunch available: 4 Dinner available: 5 Open all year

Credit Cards: A, B, C
Notes: 2, 5, 7, 8 (over 12), 9, 10, 11, 12, 14

The Inn at St. Thomas Court

101 South Second Street
Wilmington, NC, 28401
(919) 343-1800; (800) 525-0909

Located in downtown historic Wilmington, within walking distance of all cultural and social points of interest. Features turn-of-the-century ambience, all suites, with hardwood floors, balconies, courtyards, and sun deck. Full business services, conference rooms, bar. Ten minutes from beaches. Forty-foot sailboat for charter to guests.

Host: Mike Compton
Rooms: 17 (PB) $85-125
Continental Breakfast
Credit Cards: A, B, C, E
Notes: 2, 5, 7, 8, 9, 10, 11, 12, 14

The Five Star Guest House

Murchison House

305 South Third Street
Wilmington, NC, 28401
(919) 343-8580

Located in the historic Wilmington residential district, this modified Victorian Gothic mansion features four spacious rooms with private baths, clawfoot tubs, four back verandas overlooking the enclosed formal garden and brick courtyard. Two blocks from Cape Fear River and numerous shops and restaurants. Horse-drawn carriage rides available.

Hosts: Mr. & Mrs. Joseph P. Curry
Rooms: 4 (PB) $60-65
Full Breakfast
Credit Cards: A, B, C, D
Notes: 2, 5, 7, 8, 9, 10, 11, 12

Worth House

412 South Third Street
Wilmington, NC, 28401
(919) 762-8562

The Worth House is an elegant old Queen Anne that looks like a beautifully decorated wedding cake. Be pampered with lush towels, fine linens, imported soaps, and attentive personal service. Enjoy a gourmet breakfast in bed, on a private veranda, or in our dining room. Delicious beach and fireside baskets available.

Hosts: Terry Meyer & Kate Walsh
Rooms: 4 (PB) $70-85
Full Breakfast
Credit Cards: No
Notes: 2, 3, 4, 5, 7, 8 (over 12), 10, 11, 12, 14

WILSON

Miss Betty's

600 West Nash Street
Wilson, NC, 27893
(919) 243-4447

Located in the historic section of downtown Wilson, the inn comprises two beautifully decorated historic structures. Guests may visit any of the more than fifteen antique shops that have given Wilson the title of "antique capital of North Carolina," attend local tobacco auctions from July to October, feast on Wilson's famous barbecue, or stroll leisurely through the historic district.

Hosts: Betty & Fred Spitz
Rooms: 8 (PB) $65-75
Full Breakfast
Credit Cards: A, B
Notes: 2, 5, 7, 9, 10, 11, 12

North Dakota

GOODRICH

Old West B&B Service 5

Box 211
Regent, ND, 58650

Warmly decorated frame home with handmade quilts and wall hangings. Horseback riding available. Duck and deer hunting in area. Limited German spoken. $25.

JAMESTOWN

Old West B&B Service 7

Box 211
Regent, ND, 58650

A 1920s country farm home with cozy rooms decorated with antiques, collectibles, and hand-crafted quilts. Two of the three rooms share a bath; the third has a private bath. $35.

KILLDEER

Old West B&B Service 6

Box 211
Regent, ND, 58650

Located in the foothills of the scenic Killdeer Mountains, twenty miles from Theodore Roosevelt National Park. There are Indian relics in the area, as well as a battlefield. Children are welcome. No smoking in guest rooms. $25.

LIDGERWOOD

Kaler B&B

Route 2, Box 151
Lidgerwood, ND, 58053
(701) 538-4848

Enjoy country living on this 640-acre small grain farm, situated in the pheasant heartland. This older farm home has five beautiful bedrooms upstairs. A delicious full breakfast is served, and children are most welcome.

Hosts: Mark & Dorothy Kaler
Rooms: 5 (SB) $25-30
Full Breakfast
Credit Cards: No
Notes: 2, 5, 7, 8, 9, 10, 11, 12

LUVERNE

Old West B&B Service 12

Box 211
Regent, ND, 58650

This B&B is a unique blend of an old 1926 farmhouse and a 1978 addition filled with antiques and collectibles. Located a mile from the Sheyenne River, it offers fishing, hunting, canoeing, hiking, biking, skiing. Two rooms with double beds and a bath in the old house. Scandinavian breakfast. Children welcome; no smoking; no credit cards. $35.

MINOT

Old West B&B Service 10

Box 211
Regent, ND, 58650

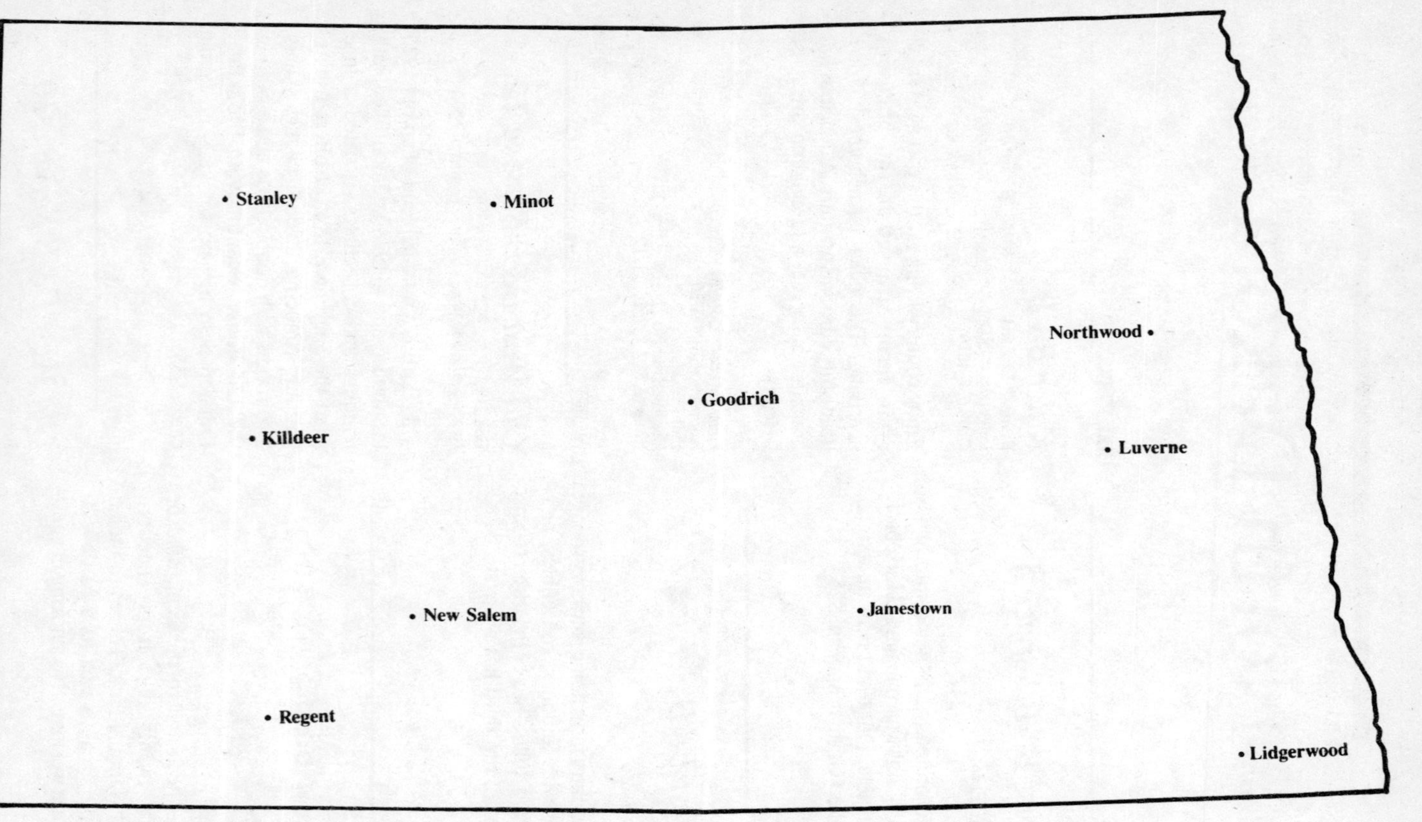

NORTH DAKOTA

Second-floor bedrooms offer complete privacy. Located a few blocks from Minot State College, the home is air-conditioned. Children are welcome, and smoking is permitted except for in the bedrooms. $35.

NEW SALEM

Old West B&B Service 11

Box 211
Regent, ND, 58650

Scandinavian-style log home built by Finnish craftsman in a quiet country setting. Located four miles off I-94, forty minutes from Bismarck and 100 miles from the Badlands. Guest rooms consist of one large bedroom with queen bed and private bath and a family room with fireplace, wet bar, refrigerator, TV, full bed, and private entrance. Ideal for two couples. Also, one large room upstairs with two full beds and a half bath. Children are welcome; smoking in the family room only. Continental breakfast. $35.

NORTHWOOD

Old West B&B Service 9

Box 211
Regent, ND, 58650

This is an opportunity to visit a diversified farm operation. Bring your binoculars for bird watching. Family members are craft oriented. Children over twelve are welcome. Norwegian is spoken. Riding horses available. $35.

REGENT

Old West B&B Service 3

Box 211
Regent, ND, 58650

Not far from Medora and the Badlands. Outdoor heated pool available in summer. Two bedrooms with double beds. No smoking or children under twelve. Seasonal rates during hunting season. Other times, $35.

STANLEY

Old West B&B Service 1

Box 211
Regent, ND, 58650

This ranch-style home is located in the Little Knife River Valley. Close to Lake Sakakawea, with swimming, fishing, and boating, and fifteen miles from Fort Berthold Indian Reservation. Rodeos and Indian powwows in the summer. The guest quarters consist of two large bedrooms, private bath, and family room with fireplace, pool table, games, and semiprivate entry. No smoking or pets. $30.

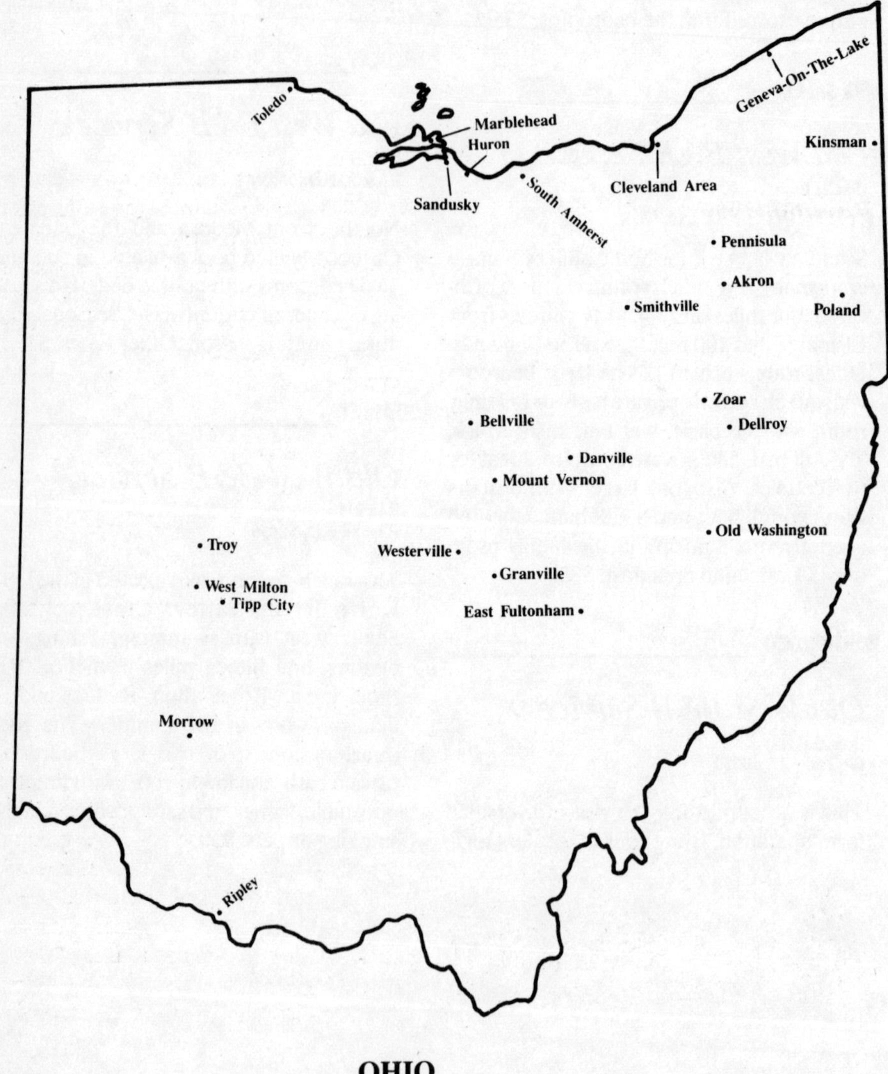
Toledo
Marblehead
Huron
Sandusky
South Amherst
Cleveland Area
Geneva-On-The-Lake
Kinsman
Pennisula
Akron
Smithville
Poland
Zoar
Dellroy
Bellville
Danville
Mount Vernon
Old Washington
Troy
Westerville
Granville
West Milton
Tipp City
East Fultonham
Morrow
Ripley

OHIO

Ohio

AKRON

Portage House

601 Copley Road
Akron, OH, 44320
(216) 535-1952

A large, gracious Tudor home in Portage, on the portage route between the Cuyahoga and Tuscarawas rivers. Five second-floor rooms and two baths, large living room. Breakfast is served in the formal dining room or at the large center island in the modern kitchen. Homemade breads and jams. Your host is a retired physics professor.

Hosts: Jeanne & Harry Pinnick
Rooms: 5 (1 PB; 4 SB) $30
Full Breakfast
Credit Cards: No
Closed Dec. & Jan.
Notes: 2, 6, 7 (limited), 8, 9, 10, 11, 12, 13

The Frederick Fitting House

BELLVILLE

The Frederick Fitting House

72 Fitting Avenue
Bellville, OH, 44813
(419) 886-2863

An 1863 Victorian home in a quaint country village between Columbus and Cleveland. Gourmet breakfast served in hand-stenciled dining room, garden gazebo, or country kitchen. Near Mohican and Malabar Farm state parks, downhill and cross-country skiing, canoeing, Kenyon and Wooster colleges.

Hosts: Ramon & Suzanne Wilson
Rooms: 3 (1 PB; 2 SB) $40-60
Full Breakfast
Credit Cards: No
Closed Thanksgiving & Christmas
Notes: 2, 4, 7, 8 (over 7), 9, 10, 11, 12, 13

CENTERVILLE

Yesterday B&B

39 South Main Street
Centerville, OH, 45458
(513) 433-0785

Located ten miles south of the center of Dayton, in the heart of the Centerville historic district, the house adjoins a group of fine antique shops and is near restaurants and two museums. The house was built in 1882 and is tastefully furnished with antiques. Within easy driving distance of the Air Force Museum in Dayton, Kings Island Amusement Park, historic Lebanon and Waynesville, a major antique center. The University of Dayton, Wright State University, and downtown Dayton are fifteen to twenty minutes away. Discount for stay of three or more nights.

Host: Barbara
Rooms: 3 (PB) $60-65
Continental-plus Breakfast

Credit Cards: No
Notes: 2, 5, 8 (12 and over), 9, 10, 12, 14

CLEVELAND

The Captain's House

Private Lodgings, Inc.
P.O. Box 18590
Cleveland, OH, 44118
(216) 321-3213

A wonderful Victorian on the National Register of Historic Places, the Captain's House is rich in local history and a delight to the eye. Two lovely rooms or a suite, continental breakfast, smoking outdoors only. Resident dog. $45-75.

Fairmount House

Private Lodgings, Inc.
P.O. Box 18590
Cleveland, OH, 44118
(216) 321-3213

A white brick home that is listed on the Historic Register. Should you wish to play pool, a regulation table is available. Double bed and private bath across the hall. A single suite is also available. Air-conditioned; driveway parking; smoking permitted. Continental breakfast. $52.50-62.50.

Little Maine

Private Lodgings, Inc.
P.O. Box 18590
Cleveland, OH, 44118
(216) 321-3213

Peninsula offers us Little Maine, a cabin in the woods. Total privacy is assured with a laid-in breakfast. There is a fireplace to laze in front of. $90.

Maxon House

Private Lodgings, Inc.
P.O. Box 18590
Cleveland, OH, 44118
(216) 321-3213

A large Victorian farmhouse in Olmsted Falls on 2 acres of land. Built in 1872 and lovingly restored. Two comfortable guest rooms, each with a double bed, share a bath. Off-street parking. Also in residence are a dog, cat, and goose. Continental breakfast. $45-50.

Notre Maison

Private Lodgings, Inc.
P.O. Box 18590
Cleveland, OH, 44118
(216) 321-3213

A French chateau in an eastern Cleveland suburb with two rooms with private baths. One room has twin beds, and the other has a double bed. The host is French and speaks nine languages. No smoking; driveway parking. A carriage house that sleeps three is also available. $59.50-75. Continental breakfast.

Speidle Farmhouse

Private Lodgings, Inc.
P.O. Box 18590
Cleveland, OH, 44118
(216) 321-3213

This century-old farmhouse has lovely details, wicker furniture, depression glass, and a delightful host couple. Double bed, private bathroom. No smoking; off-street parking; continental breakfast. $45-55.

Twinsburg Cottage

Private Lodgings, Inc.
P.O. Box 18590
Cleveland, OH, 44118
(216) 321-3213

This cottage has a contemporary look. Near a pond reached by a small bridge. Cross-country skiing or quiet walks in the woods. A laid-in breakfast assures complete privacy. $82.50.

DANVILLE

The White Oak Inn

29683 Walhonding Road
Danville, OH, 43014
(614) 599-6107

Turn-of-the-century farmhouse in a rolling wooded valley features restored antiques and hand-stitched quilts. Guests read, play board games, or socialize in the fireplaced common room or relax on the fifty-foot front porch. An outdoor enthusiast's haven. Near the world's largest Amish population and the historic Ohio-Erie canal town.

Hosts: Joyce & Jim Acton
Rooms: 7 (PB) $50-100
Full breakfast weekends; continental weekdays
Credit Cards: A, B
Notes: 2, 4, 5, 9, 10, 11, 12

DELLROY

Pleasant Journey Inn

4247 Roswell Road SW
Dellroy, OH, 44620
(216) 735-2987

An elegant fourteen-room post-Civil War mansion decorated in antiques and centrally located near Atwood Lake. Nearby horseback riding, golf, fishing, swimming, boating, and Amish country visits.

Hosts: Jim & Marie Etterman
Rooms: 4 (1 PB; 3 SB) $46-60
Continental-plus Breakfast
Credit Cards: A, B
Notes: 2, 5, 9, 10, 11, 12, 13, 14

EAST FULTONHAM

Hill View Acres

7320 Old Town Road
East Fultonham, OH, 43735
(614) 849-2728

Located ten miles southwest of Zanesville off US 22W. Large, spacious home on 21 acres with pond. Enjoy the pool, year-round spa, or relax in the family room by the fireplace. Country cooking is a specialty. The area is popular for antiquing, pottery, and outdoor activities.

Hosts: Jim & Dawn Graham
Rooms: 2 (SB) $27-32
Full Breakfast
Credit Cards: A, B
Notes: 2, 3, 4, 5, 7, 8, 9, 10, 11, 12

GENEVA-ON-THE-LAKE

The Otto Court B&B

5653 Lake Road
Geneva-on-the-Lake, OH, 44041
(216) 466-8668

Hotel and cottage complex overlooking Lake Erie. Within walking distance of the famous Geneva-on-the-Lake amusement center, Geneva State Park and Marina, and the Old Firehouse Winery. Conveniently located near the historic Ashtabula Harbor area and thirteen covered bridges.

Host: Mrs. C. Joyce Otto
Rooms: 12 (8 PB; 4 SB) $32-45
Full Breakfast
Minimum stay weekends & holidays: 2
Credit Cards: A, B
Notes: 2, 4, 5, 7, 8, 9, 10, 11, 12

GRANVILLE

Buxton Inn—1812

313 East Broadway
Granville, OH, 43023
(614) 587-0001

Quiet elegance and cozy charm describe Buxton Inn's four guest rooms, all authentically furnished in period antiques. We have five dining rooms, a tavern, and wine cellar. The adjacent Warner House—1815—houses eleven period rooms. Breakfast, lunch, and dinner are available daily.

Hosts: Orville & Audrey Orr
Rooms: 15 (PB) $59.95-87.20
Continental Breakfast
Credit Cards: A, B, C, E
Notes: 2, 3, 4, 5, 7, 8, 9, 10, 11, 12

HURON

Captain Montague's Guest House

229 Center Street
Huron, OH, 44839
(419) 433-4756

A memorable step back in time. Private baths, air-conditioning, swimming pool surrounded by lattice-fenced gardens. Adjacent gazebo with white wicker furniture; parlor with fireplace and player piano. Five to ten minutes from well-known golf courses, estuaries, Cedar Point and Outlet Mall. Walking distance to Lake Erie and restaurants.

Hosts: Shirley & Bob Reynolds
Rooms: 6 (PB) $58-75 + tax
Continental-plus Breaktast
Credit Cards: No
Closed Dec. 15-March 1
Notes: 2, 9, 10, 11, 12, 13 (XC)

KINSMAN

Hidden Hollow

9340 Route 5
Kinsman, OH, 44428
(216) 876-8686

We are built on a hillside, with an eighty-foot balcony up and down. Very country; very private. Breakfast by the pool or in the large kitchen. Lots of birds and wildlife.

Hosts: Bob & Rita White
Rooms: 4 (PB) $42-50
Full Breakfast
Credit Cards: 2, 5, 6, 7, 8, 9, 11, 12

MARBLEHEAD

Old Stone House on the Lake

133 Clemons Street
Marblehead, OH, 43440
(419) 798-5922

Stately stone mansion, built in 1861, gracing the shoreline of Lake Erie's western basin. Overlooks Kelleys Island and is located between the Kelleys ferry and Marblehead lighthouse. Patio on the water, library sitting room with cable TV, and games. Craft and gift shop in summer kitchen. Shopping, sight-seeing, marinas, and restaurants are all nearby. Seasonal executive fishing-charter service available.

Hosts: Pat Parks & Dorothy Bright
Rooms: 12 (SB) $55-85
Continental-plus Breakfast
Credit Cards: A, B, D
Notes: 2, 5, 7, 9, 10, 11, 12, 14

Old Stone House on the Lake

MORROW

Country Manor B & B

6315 Zoar Road
Morrow, OH, 45152
(513) 899-2440

Country Manor sits on a quiet 55 acres overlooking a valley, yet is conveniently located in an active area of southern Ohio that features Kings Island Amusement Park, Jack Nicklaus Golf Course, and Lebanon Raceway. Large, comfortable rooms feature 1868 elegance with modern conveniences.

Hosts: Rhea Hughes & Bobby Salyers
Doubles: 3 (1 PB; 2 SB) $50-60

NOTES: Credit cards accepted: A Master Card; B Visa; C American Express; D Discover Card; E Diners Club; F Other: 2 Personal checks accepted: 3 Lunch available: 4 Dinner available: 5 Open all year

Type of Beds: 2 Twin; 2 Double
Full Breakfast
Credit Cards: No
Closed Thanksgiving & Christmas
Notes: 2, 8 (over 12), 9, 10, 11, 12

Russell-Cooper House

MOUNT VERNON

The Russell-Cooper House

115 East Gambier Street
Mount Vernon, OH, 43050
(614) 397-8638

History lives! Landmark c. 1829 Victorian mansion restored to 1880s grandeur. Nestled in America's Hometown—Mount Vernon—central Ohio's vacation headquarters. Antiques abound. Luxurious guest rooms with baths, full breakfast, art gallery, and more. Don't miss this national award-winning B&B in the heart of it all—for a memory you'll always cherish.

Hosts: Tim & Maureen Tyler
Rooms: 6 (PB) $50-68
Full Breakfast
Credit Cards: A, B
Notes: 2, 3, 4, 5, 7, 8 (over 12), 9, 10, 11, 12, 13, 14

OLD WASHINGTON

Zane Trace B&B

Box 115, Old National Road
Old Washington, OH, 43768
(614) 489-5970

Brick Victorian built in 1859. In-ground swimming pool, extra-large rooms, beautiful woodwork with high ceilings, antique furnishings. The quaint, quiet village of Old Washington is seven miles east of Cambridge, Ohio, Exit 186 off I-70. Write for your free brochure.

Host: Ruth Wade-Wilson
Rooms: 4 (SB) $32-60
Continental Breakfast
Credit Cards: No
Closed Nov.-April
Notes: 2, 7, 8 (over 10), 9, 11, 12

Tolle House

PENINSULA

Tolle House

1856 Main Street
Peninsula, OH, 44264
(216) 657-2900

Restored Victorian century house, extensively decorated and furnished by hosts. Private parlor for guests with TV, games, easy chairs. Porches with swings and rockers. Full country breakfast; five o'clock tea. Historic village has shops, antiques, old stone sidewalks. Surrounded by national park. Bike, hike, fish, golf, ski, explore. Peaceful yesteryear atmosphere.

Hosts: Ina & Jerry Tolle
Rooms: 3 (SB) $45-50
Full Breakfast
Credit Cards: No
Notes: 2, 5, 7, 8 (over 10), 9, 10, 11, 12, 13

POLAND

Inn at the Green

500 South Main Street
Poland, OH, 44514
(216) 757-4688

A classically proportioned Victorian townhouse on the south end of the green in preserved Connecticut Western Reserve Village. Featuring large moldings, twelve-foot ceilings, five Italian marble fireplaces, original poplar floors, and interior-shuttered windows.

Hosts: Ginny & Steve Meloy
Rooms: 4 (2 PB; 2 SB) $35-50
Continental Breakfast
Credit Cards: A, B
Notes: 2, 5, 7, 8 (over 7), 9, 10, 11, 12, 14

RIPLEY

The Signal House

234 North Front Street
Ripley, OH, 45167
(513) 392-1640

Share historic charm and hospitality while visiting our 1830s home on the scenic Ohio River. View spectacular sunsets from our porches or elegant parlors. Enjoy spacious rooms furnished with family antiques in an air of yesteryear. The area offers antique and craft shops, restaurants, museums, wineries, herb farms, covered bridges, history, and friendly people.

Hosts: Vic & Betsy Billingsley
Rooms: 3 (SB) $58-68
Full Breakfast
Credit Cards: No
Notes: 2, 5, 7 (limited), 9, 10, 11, 12

SANDUSKY

Bogarts Corner B&B

1403 East Bogart Road
Sandusky, OH, 44870
(419) 627-2707

A home away from home. Relax in one of our many rocking chairs on the porch or in the rooms. Easy access to interstates 80, 90, and U.S. 2. We're in the center of Lake Erie vacationland and all the activities Lake Erie has to offer: dinner cruises, island hopping, swimming and sunning.

Hosts: Zendon & Davilee Willis
Rooms: 5 (2 PB; 3 SB) $35-45
Full Breakfast
Credit Cards: No
Closed Oct. 1-May 1
Notes: 2, 6, 7, 8, 10, 11, 12, 14

SMITHVILLE

The Smithville

171 West Main Street
P.O. Box 142
Smithville, OH, 44677
(216) 669-3333; (800) 869-6425

Conveniently located in the heart of Wayne County, five miles north of Wooster on SR 585. Ideal stopping place while visiting Amish country, the College of Wooster, ATI, or OARDC. Pro Football Hall of Fame in Canton is nearby, as are gift, craft, antique shops, and fine restaurants.

Hosts: Jim & Lori Kubik
Rooms: 3 (1 PB; 2 SB) $42-52
Full Breakfast
Credit Cards: A, B
Notes: 2, 5, 8, 10, 11, 12

SOUTH AMHERST

Birch Way Villa

111 White Birch Way
South Amherst, OH, 44001
(216) 986-2090

Birch Way Villa is located in a 30-acre wooded lot with a 10- acre spring-fed lake and tennis court. The hostess is a gourmet cook and serves excellent meals. Children are welcome. The home is fully air-conditioned, and many recreational facilities and historic sites are nearby. Tennis lessons and fishing in the summer.

Hosts: Simon & Marjorie Isaac
Rooms: 3 (S1.5B) $45
Full Breakfast
Credit Cards: No
Closed Nov. 21-26; Dec. 23-Jan. 2
Notes: 2, 3, 4, 7 (restricted), 8, 10, 11, 12, 13, 14

TIPP CITY

Willow Tree Inn

1900 West Street, Route 571
Tipp City, OH, 45371
(513) 667-2957

Restored 1830 Federal manor home with four fireplaces. Each room is a suite. Pond, ducks, original 1830 barn on the premises; working springhouse/smokehouse; beautiful gardens. Just minutes north of Dayton, in a quiet location with attentive, personal service.

Hosts: Tom & Peggy Nordquist
Rooms: 4 (1 PB; 3 SB) $65 + tax
Full Breakfast
Credit Cards: A, B
Notes: 2, 5, 7 (restricted), 8 (over 8), 9, 10, 11, 12

TOLEDO

Mansion View Inn B&B

2035 Collingwood Blvd.
Toledo, OH, 43630
(419) 244-5676

Mansion View Inn is located in the historic Old West End, near downtown, the Toledo Museum of Art, and the Toledo Zoological Gardens. On the National Register of Historic Places, the 101-year-old mansion was built in the Queen Anne style, with intricate displays of stone and glass. Each guest room is a showcase of art, antiques, and fanciful color.

Hosts: Matt Jasin, Tam Gagen & Tim Oller
Rooms: 4 (PB) $55-75 + tax
Full Breakfast
Credit Cards: A, B
Notes: 2, 5, 8, 9, 10, 11

Allen Villa B&B

TROY

Allen Villa B&B

434 South Market Street
Troy, OH, 45373
(513) 335-1181

This B&B has seven fireplaces and is decorated in period antiques. Each room has a private bath, TV, telephone, and central air-conditioning. There is a self-serve snack bar for your evening pleasure, and a bountiful breakfast is served on the fifteen-foot antique dining room table that seats twelve guests.

Hosts: Robert & June Smith
Rooms: 4 (PB) $40-60
Full Breakfast
Credit Cards: A, B, C
Notes: 2, 5, 7, 8, 9, 10, 11, 12, 14

WESTERVILLE

Priscilla's B&B

5 South-West Street
Westerville, OH, 43081
(614) 882-3910

Located in an historic area adjacent to Otterbein College, this 1854 New England style home is surrounded by a white picket fence. The interior abounds with antiques and collectibles. Guests are welcome to borrow bicycles, use the patio, enjoy concerts in the adjoining park, walk to the Benjamin Hanby Museum or the quaint shops. Miniature shop located on the premises

Host: Priscilla Haberman Curtiss
Rooms: 2 (SB) $40 + tax
Continental Breakfast
Credit Cards: No
Notes: 5, 7 (limited), 9, 12

WEST MILTON

Locust Lane Farm B&B

5590 Kessler Cowlesville Road
West Milton, OH, 45383
(513) 698-4743

Delightful old Cape Cod home in a rural setting. Air-conditioned bedrooms. Relax in the library or in front of the fireplace. Full breakfast served on the lovely screened porch in the summer. Browse through local antique shops, enjoy the nature center, golf, or canoeing.

Hosts: Ruth & Don Shoup
Rooms: 2 (1 PB; 1 SB) $40-50
Full Breakfast
Credit Cards: No
Notes: 2, 5, 8, 10, 12, 14

ZOAR

The Weaving Haus

Box 605
Zoar, OH, 44697
(216) 874-3318

Built in 1825 by German separatists for the purpose of weaving flax and wool for their fabrics. There are four levels to Weaving Haus, one being a vaulted fruit cellar. Conveniently located for strolling around the village and exploring other historic buildings. Just minutes from the Football Hall of Fame.

Hosts: Dan & Nancy Luther
Rooms: 2 (SB) $50-60
Full Breakfast
Credit Cards: A, B
Notes: 2, 5, 10, 11, 12, 13

Oklahoma

GUTHRIE

Harrison House Inn

124 West Harrison
Guthrie, OK, 73044
(405) 282-1000

Twenty-three rooms furnished in Victorian style with antiques and quilts. All have private baths. Central heat and air with thermostats in every room. Located next door to the theater in central downtown Guthrie. Featured in *Glamour, Insider,* and *Southern Living.*

Host: Phyllis Murray
Rooms: 23 (PB) $50-80
Continental-plus Breakfast
Credit Cards: A, B, C, D, E
Notes: 2, 5, 6, 7, 8, 9, 10, 11, 12, 14

Harrison House Inn

Stone Lion Inn

1016 West Warner
Guthrie, OK, 73044
(405) 282-0012

Our 8,000-square-foot elegantly restored Victorian mansion is centered in Guthrie, the largest historic preservation project in the U.S. Guthrie hosts the world's largest Masonic Temple, The Sand Plum restaurant (a four-star establishment), and wonderful antique stores and gift stores. Guthrie is thirty minutes from the airport, Remington Park, Frontier City, and several other points of interest.

Hosts: Becky Luker & Grant Aguirre
Rooms: 6 (PB) $50-75
Full Breakfast
Credit Cards: A, B
Notes: 2, 4, 5, 6, 8, 9, 12, 14

OKLAHOMA CITY

The Grandison Inn

1841 N.W. Fifteenth Street
Oklahoma City, OK, 73106
(405) 521-0011

Three stories furnished with antiques in the Victorian style. Built originally in 1896, the house has lots of windows, fruit-bearing trees, and a gazebo. Central heat and air. Convenient to downtown Oklahoma City and Interstates 40 and 35.

Hosts: Claudia & Bob Wright
Rooms: 5 (PB) $40-90
Continental Breakfast
Credit Cards: A, B, C
Notes: 2, 4 (by reservation), 5, 7, 8 (over 12), 9, 10, 11

Newton & Joann Flora

23312 West W46
Oklahoma City, OK, 73112
(405) 840-3157

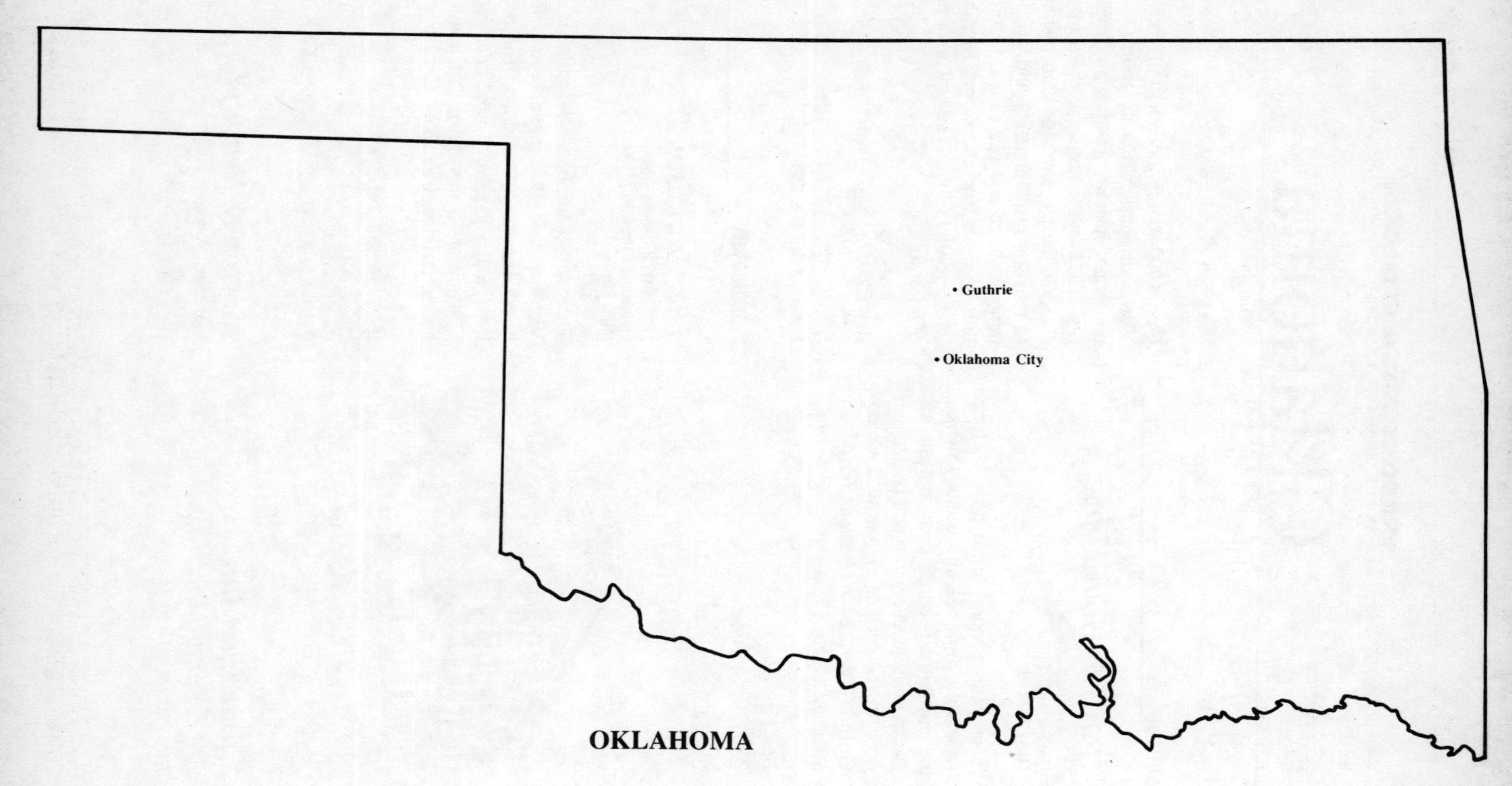
Guthrie
Oklahoma City
OKLAHOMA

This house, furnished with antiques and collectibles, has a large patio off the living-room area that overlooks downtown Oklahoma City. TV, radio, and library are available for guests. Easy access to the Cowboy Hall of Fame, Remington Park Race Track, Omniplex, and other points of interest. Many good eating places in the vicinity.

Hosts: Newton W. & Joann Flora
Rooms: 2 (PB) $40-45
Continental Breakfast
Credit Cards: No
Notes: 2, 5, 7, 8, 9 (light), 12

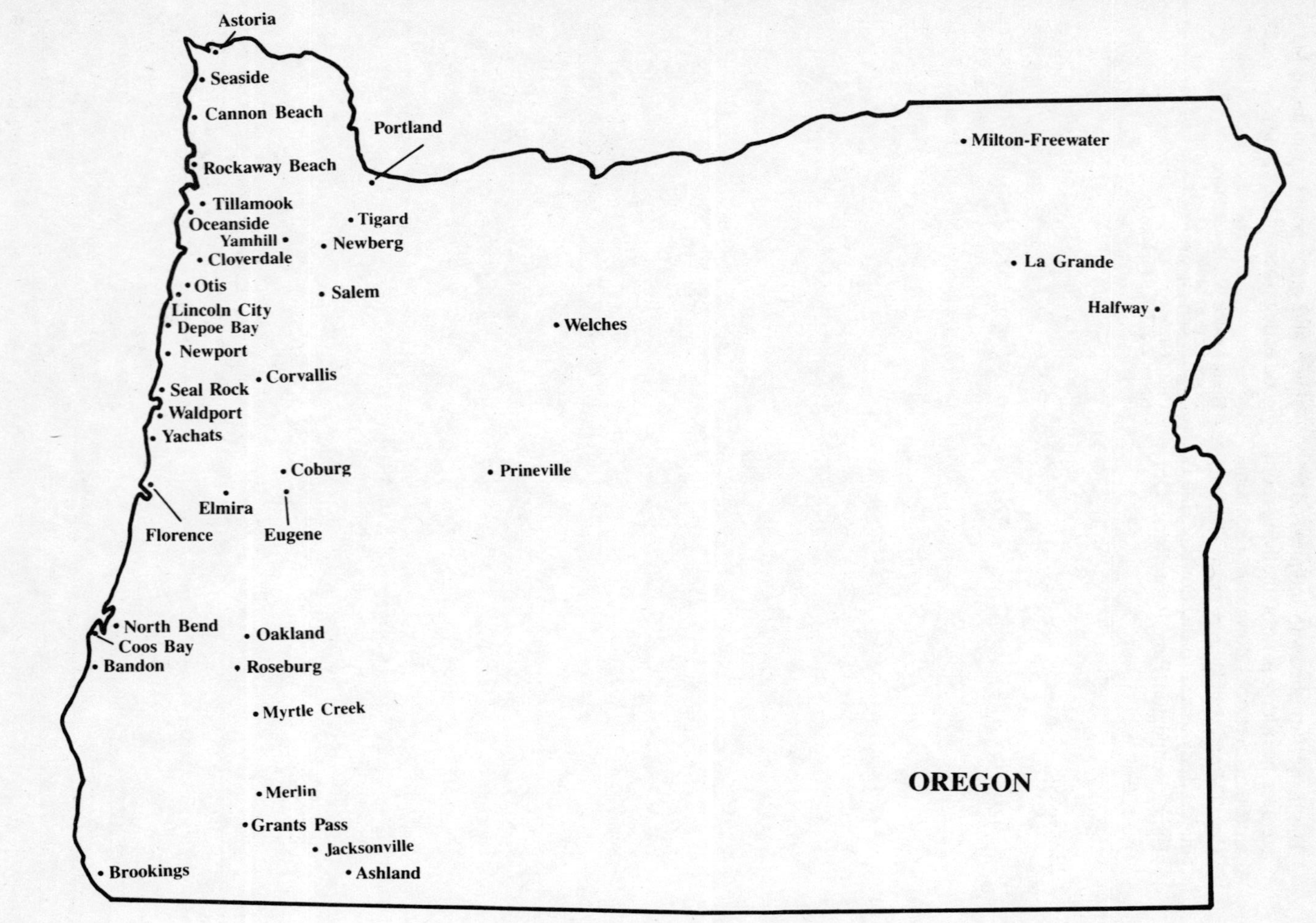

OREGON
Astoria
Seaside
Cannon Beach
Portland
Rockaway Beach
Tillamook
Oceanside
Yamhill
Tigard
Newberg
Cloverdale
Otis
Lincoln City
Depoe Bay
Salem
Newport
Corvallis
Seal Rock
Waldport
Yachats
Coburg
Elmira
Florence
Eugene
North Bend
Coos Bay
Bandon
Oakland
Roseburg
Myrtle Creek
Merlin
Grants Pass
Jacksonville
Ashland
Brookings
Welches
Prineville
Milton-Freewater
La Grande
Halfway

Oregon

ASHLAND

Chanticleer Inn

120 Gresham Street
Ashland, OR, 97520
(503) 482-1919

Seven-room guest house with all the charm of a French provincial inn. Magnificent gardens, beautiful views, and legendary breakfasts. Located within walking distance of the famous Oregon Shakespeare Festival, shopping, and fine dining.

Hosts: Jim & Nancy Beaver
Rooms: 7 (PB) $75-160
Full Breakfast
Credit Cards: A, B
Notes: 2, 5, 8, 9, 10, 11, 12, 13, 14

Country Willows

1313 Clay Street
Ashland, OR, 97520
(503) 488-1590

A quiet, relaxing hideaway on 5 white-fenced acres with a beautiful view of the Siskiyou Mountains. This 1905 house was elegantly rebuilt with your comfort in mind. Enjoy a full breakfast on the porch or relax by the pool and spa.

Hosts: Bill & Barbara Huntley
Suite: (PB) $75-130 off-season rates available
Full Breakfast
Credit Cards: A, B
Notes: 2, 5, 9, 10, 11, 12, 13, 14

Cowslip's Belle

159 North Main Street
Ashland, OR, 97520
(503) 488-2901

Just three blocks to theaters. The Cowslip's recipe is cozy down comforters, chocolate truffles and Teddy bears, 1913 craftsman, antiques, Maxfield Parrish, peach pandowdy, scrumptious breakfasts. Four queen/twin guest rooms, private baths, private entrances, air-conditioning.

Hosts: Jon & Carmen Reinhardt
Rooms: 4 (PB) $58-92
Full Breakfast
Credit Cards: A, B
Notes: 2, 5, 9, 10, 11, 12, 13, 14

Cowslip's Belle

Fadden's Inn

326 North Main Street
Ashland, OR, 97520
(503) 488-0025

An 1890s cedarwood country inn with multi-roomed suites. One suite has its own kitchen. All have private outside entrances, private baths, air conditioning, and their own coffee makers with daily homemade goody baskets. Each suite has redwood decking, fantastic views, and local artist's watercolor display. Only four blocks to the theaters and Lithia Park.

Host: David Fadden
Suites: 2 (PB) $70-95
Continental Breakfast
Credit Cards: A, B
Notes: 2, 5, 9, 10, 11, 12, 13

Hersey House

Hersey House

451 North Main Street
Ashland, OR, 97520
(503) 482-4563

Gracious living in an elegantly restored Victorian with a colorful English country garden. Sumptuous breakfasts. Central air-conditioning. Walk to Plaza and three Shakespeare theaters. Nearby: white-water rafting on the Rogue River, Jacksonville National Historic District, Britt Music Festival, Crater Lake National Park.

Hosts: K. Lynn Savage & Gail Orell
Rooms: 4 (PB) $73.10-89
Full Breakfast
Credit Cards: No
Closed Nov. 1-April 20
Notes: 2, 8 (12 and over), 10, 11, 12, 13, 14

The Iris Inn

59 Manzanita Street
Ashland, OR, 97520
(503) 488-2286

A 1905 Victorian furnished with antiques. Elegant breakfasts feature eggs benedict and cheese-baked eggs. Mountain views, quiet neighborhood. Nearby are the Oregon Shakespeare Theater and the Rogue River for rafting.

Host: Vicki Lamb
Rooms: 5 (1 PB; 4 SB) $72-82
Full Breakfast
Credit Cards: A, B
Notes: 2, 5, 8 (7 and over), 10, 11, 12, 13

The Morical House

668 North Main Street
Ashland, OR, 97520
(503) 482-2254

A superbly restored 1880s farmhouse on 1.5 acres of beautifully landscaped grounds, The Morical House offers nineteenth-century elegance and hospitality with twentieth-century comfort. Five gracious guest rooms with private baths, large complimentary breakfast, afternoon refreshments.

Hosts: Pat & Peter Dahl
Rooms: 5 (PB) $55-95
Full Breakfast
Credit Cards: A, B
Notes: 2, 5, 8 (over 12), 10, 11, 12, 13, 14

Mt. Ashland Inn

550 Mt. Ashland Road
Ashland, OR, 97520
(503) 482-8707

Situated on the crest of the Siskiyou Mountains, this beautiful handcrafted log inn commands spectacular mountain views, including 14,200-foot Mt. Shasta. Hand carvings, Oriental rugs, and antiques provide an atmosphere of comfortable elegance. Guests enjoy the sunny deck and large stone fireplace. Hiking and skiing at the door.

Hosts: Jerry & Elaine Shanafelt
Rooms: 5 (PB) $75-120
Full Breakfast
Credit Cards: A, B
Notes: 2, 5, 8 (over 10), 9, 12, 13, 14

Pinehurst Inn at Jenny Creek

17250 Highway 66
Ashland, OR, 97520
(503) 488-1002

Nestled in the heart of the southern Oregon Cascades, Pinehurst Inn is a nature-lover's paradise. Cross-country skiing, fishing, hiking, wagon or sleigh rides are at our front door. Nearby is world-class whitewater rafting, bird watching, and downhill skiing. Full restaurant with daily specials. Cozy, comfortable creekside accommodations.

Hosts: Craig Kircher & Barbara Grobert
Rooms: 5 (PB) $70-95
Full Breakfast
Credit Cards: A, B
Notes: 2, 4, 5, 6, 8, 9, 13 (XC), 14

Romeo Inn

295 Idaho Street
Ashland, OR, 97520
(503) 488-0884

Mobil gives us a three-star rating. A quiet, elegant, lovely Cape Cod amid pines with a valley view. Four spacious rooms with central air-conditioning; some rooms have fireplaces. Two luxurious suites with fireplaces; one has whirlpool tub. There's a beautiful spa and pool, gardens, and gourmet breakfast. Walk to the Oregon Shakespeare Theaters and town.

Hosts: Margaret & Bruce Halverson
Rooms: 6 (PB) $89-160
Full Breakfast
Credit Cards: A, B
Notes: 2, 5, 9, 10, 11, 12, 13, 14

ASTORIA

Franklin House B&B Inn

1681 Franklin Avenue
Box 804
Astoria, OR, 97103
(503) 325-5044

A five-star Victorian charmer. You'll note the feeling of elegance when you enter the Franklin House Bed & Breakfast Inn, built in the late 1800s. Nearby you will find the Columbia River Maritime Museum, Captain George Flavel House. The ocean is five miles away. Full breakfast and a gift shop on the premises; river view; off-street parking.

Host: Karen N. Nelson
Rooms: 5 (PB) $53-75
Full Breakfast
Minimum stay summer & holidays: 2
Credit Cards: A, B
Closed 2 days for Thanksgiving & Christmas
Notes: 2, 8

Romeo Inn

Franklin Street Station B&B

1140 Franklin Street
Astoria, OR, 97103
(503) 325-4314

1900 Victorian home built by shipbuilder Ferdinand Fisher. Five rooms (2 rooms are suites); two have views of the Columbia River. All rooms have queen beds, private baths. Full breakfast is served each morning. Ornate craftsmanship throughout the home expresses the rich history of Astoria. Three-star rating in *Northwest Best Places.* Close to downtown, and within walking distance of museums.

Hosts: Jim & Renee Caldwell
Rooms: 5 (PB) $50-85
Full Breakfast
Credit Cards: A, B
Notes: 2, 5, 8, 9, 10, 11, 12, 14

Franklin House B&B Inn

Grandview B&B

1574 Grand Avenue
Astoria, OR, 97103
(503) 325-0000; (503)325-5555

Wonderful views of the Columbia River; close to the best maritime museum on the West Coast and other museums, churches, and Victorian homes. Tour domestic and foreign ships in port. Light, airy, three-story Victorian with hardwood floors.

Host: Charleen Maxwell
Rooms: 3 (PB) $40.28-79.50
Suites: 3 (2 bedrooms, PB) $79.50-103.88
Continental-plus Breakfast
Credit Cards: A, B, D
Notes: 2, 5, 8 (over 10), 10, 11, 12, 14

BANDON

Lighthouse B&B

650 Jetty Road
Box 24
Bandon, OR, 97411
(503) 347-9316

Contemporary home located on the beach across from the historic Bandon lighthouse. Unequaled jetty, lighthouse, and ocean views. Walk to Old Town, shops, galleries, and fine restaurants. In-room Jacuzzi available; fireplace, wood stove.

Hosts: Bruce & Linda Sisson
Rooms: 4 (PB) $75-95
Continental-plus Breakfast
Credit Cards: A, B
Notes: 2, 5, 8 (over 12), 9, 10, 12, 14

Seabird Inn

3165 Beach Loop Drive
Bandon, OR, 97411
(503) 347-2056

A contemporary home located within easy walking distance of one of Oregon's most dramatic beaches. Spacious, well-appointed rooms with private baths adjoin a large, light-filled solarium — all tastefully decorated in soft pastels. Evening wine; full gourmet breakfast.

Hosts: Carol & Ollie Sapousek
Rooms: 2 (PB) $74
Full Breakfast
Credit Cards: No
Closed Christmas
Notes: 2, 9, 12

BROOKINGS

Holmes Sea Cove B&B

17350 Holmes Drive
Brookings, OR, 97415
(503) 469-3025

A delightful seacoast hideaway with a spectacular ocean view, private guest entrances, and a tasty continental breakfast served to your room. Enjoy beach-combing and whale watching.

Hosts: Jack & Lorene Holmes
Rooms: 3 (PB) $75-85
Continental-plus Breakfast
Credit Cards: A, B
Notes: 2, 5, 7 (limited), 9, 10, 11

The Ward House B&B

Box 86
Brookings, OR, 97415
(503) 469-5557

A 1917 vintage home built in the "craftsman style" architecture by William Ward. Restored and furnished with antiques and treasures. Large parlor, hot tub/sauna, spacious bedrooms upstairs. Ocean view; just a few blocks from the river and harbor. Gourmet breakfast, including Norwegian waffles.

Hosts: Sheldon & Gro
Rooms: 2 (PB) $65
Full Breakfast
Credit Cards: A, B
Notes: 2, 5, 8 (over 12), 9, 10, 11, 14

CANNON BEACH

Tern Inn

3663 South Hemlock
Box 952
Cannon Beach, OR, 97110
(503) 436-1528

European-style B&B with an ocean view. Light goose-down quilts for year-round comfort, private bath, and color TV. Fresh home-baked goods are served, including vegetarian and low cholesterol foods. Rooms are suitable for up to four adults or may be combined for seven adults. Special off-season and weekly rates; gift certificates. Five percent lodging tax.

Hosts: Chris & Enken Friedrichsen
Rooms: 2 (PB) $72.45-93.45
Full Breakfast
Minimum stay Memorial Day-Labor Day: 2-3
Credit Cards: No
Notes: 2, 9, 10, 11, 12, 14

CLOVERDALE

The Hudson House

37700 Highway 101 South
Cloverdale, OR, 97112
(503) 392-3533

An historic Victorian, built in 1906, surrounded by lush Tillamook Valley, yet less than three miles from the beach. Free golf, gourmet breakfasts, and evening tea and cookies. Rooms are graced with comforters, flowers, and robes (shared baths). Croquet lawn, nearby wine touring, and some of the best salmon and steelhead fishing on the Oregon coast. Truly grand and warmly romantic.

Hosts: Anne & Steve Kulju
Rooms: 6 (2 PB; 4 SB) $40-60
Full Breakfast
Credit Cards: A, B
Notes: 2, 5, 9, 11, 12, 14

Sandlake Country Inn

8505 Galloway Road
Cloverdale, OR, 97112
(503) 965-6745

This state historic registry 1894 farmhouse is the perfect hideaway for first or second honeymoons. Private garden spa, honeymoon suite (four rooms) with private luxury bath, deck, view of Cape Lookout, parlor, vintage movies. Full breakfast in bed. Just a mile to the beach; picnic baskets available.

Hosts: Margo & Charles Underwood
Rooms: 2 (PB) $60-75
Full Breakfast
Credit Cards: A, B
Notes: 2, 3, 4, 5, 14

COBURG

Wheeler's B&B

Box 8201
Coburg, OR, 97401
(503) 344-1366

Modern country home located one-half mile off I-5, seven miles north of Eugene and just a few minutes from Autzen Stadium. Guest quarters include the entire upstairs of the house. Hiking, swimming, antique shops, century-old homes are nearby. Children over ten are welcome, and small pets only with their own kennels.

Hosts: Joe & Isabel Wheeler
Rooms: 2 (SB) $34-39
Full Breakfast
Credit Cards: A, B
Closed Dec.-April
Notes: 2, 6 (dogs w/kennels), 7 (restricted), 8 (over 10), 9, 10, 11, 12

COOS BAY

Blackberry Inn B&B

843 Central
Coos Bay, OR, 97420
(503) 267-6951

Located on the southern Oregon coast, this charming B&B offers the elegant atmosphere of an old Victorian home. Since the inn is separate from the hosts' residence, the guests can enjoy the hospitality but have privacy, too. A quick walk takes you to several restaurants, stores, a theater, an art museum, and the city park with its lovely Japanese gardens, tennis courts, and picnic areas.

Hosts: John & Louise Duncan
Rooms: 4 (3 PB; 1 SB) $35-50
Continental Breakfast
Credit Cards: A, B
Notes: 2, 5, 8, 9, 10, 11, 12

Captain's Quarters B&B

265 South Empire Blvd.
Box 3231
Coos Bay, OR, 97420
(503) 888-6895

An 1892 Victorian lovingly restored to its original beauty. Former home of Captain McGenn of the *Breakwater.* Bedrooms face the colorful bay and North Spit. One can watch the ships come in. Close to beaches, parks, boat charters. No smoking. Full homemade breakfasts are served in the dining room or on the sun porch.

Hosts: John & Jean Griswold
Rooms: 2 (SB) $45
Full Breakfast
Credit Cards: No
Notes: 2, 8 (over 12), 9, 10, 11, 12

CORVALLIS

Huntington Manor

3555 NW Harrison Blvd.
Corvallis, OR, 97330
(503) 753-3735

Huntington Manor is a beautiful 65-year-old Williamsburg colonial that has been completely refurbished and is elegantly furnished with American and European antiques. Guest rooms feature down comforters and color TV.

Host: Ann Sink
Rooms: 3 (PB) $48 + tax
Full Breakfast
Credit Cards: A, B
Notes: 2, 5, 8 (over 12), 9, 10, 11, 12, 14

DEPOE BAY

Channel House B&B Inn

35 Ellingson Street
P.O. Box 56
Depoe Bay, OR, 97341
(503) 765-2140

Perched high on the rocks at the entrance of the channel to picturesque Depoe Bay you will find Channel House B&B Inn. One can almost reach out and touch the fishing boats passing through the narrow jaws of the channel.

Hosts: Bill & Rachael Smith
Rooms: 9 (PB) $52-150
Full Breakfast
Credit Cards: A, B
Notes: 2, 5, 7, 8, 9, 10, 11, 12, 14

ELMIRA

McGillivray's Log Home B&B

88680 Evers Road
Elmira, OR, 97437
(503) 935-3564

West of Eugene, Oregon, you will find the best of yesterday with the comforts of today. Situated on 5 wooded acres, this air-conditioned log home has wheel-chair access. The hearty breakfasts are often prepared on an antique wood cook stove.

Host: Evelyn R. McGillivray
Rooms: 2 (PB) $36.50-62.40
Full Breakfast
Credit Cards: A, B
Notes: 2, 5, 8, 9, 11

Kjaer's House in the Woods

EUGENE

Kjaer's House in the Woods

814 Lorane Highway
Eugene, OR, 97405
(503) 343-3234

A 1910 craftsman-style home in a peaceful setting on a quiet, country-like road ideal for walking, jogging, hiking, deer and bird watching. Antiques, Oriental carpets, fireplace, square grand piano available for guests. "Urban convenience/suburban tranquility."

Hosts: George & Eunice Kjaer
Rooms: 3 (SB) $55
Full Breakfast
Minimum stay weekends: 2
Children under 2 or over 12 welcome
Closed Dec. 22-Jan. 3
Credit Cards: No
Notes: 2, 8, 9, 10, 11, 12, 14

Lorane Valley B&B

86621 Lorane Highway
Eugene, OR, 97405
(503) 686-0241

Unique home on 22 acres of quiet wooded hillside and meadow. Nine Angus cows and Scottie dog in residence. Single party in a private suite, full breakfast with a varied menu. Spacious rooms, fresh flowers, complete kitchen with microwave, Jacuzzi in the private bath. Air-conditioned. Four and one-half miles from the Hult Center for the Performing Arts and downtown Eugene.

Hosts: Esther & George Ralph
Rooms: 1 (PB) $69 + tax
Full Breakfast
Credit Cards: A, B, C
Notes: 2, 3, 4, 5, 8, 9, 10, 11, 12

FLORENCE

The Johnson House

Box 1892
Florence, OR, 97439
(503) 997-8000

The Johnson House, the oldest house in Florence, was built in 1892. The structure and details in this splendid old Victorian are original. Antique furnishings in every room evoke the atmosphere of warm, plain living on the Oregon coast nearly a century ago.

Hosts: Jayne & Rom Fraese
Rooms: 5 (1 PB; 4 SB) $75-95

Full Breakfast
Credit Cards: A, B
Notes: 2, 5, 9, 10, 11, 12, 14

GRANTS PASS

AHLF House B&B

762 NW Sixth Street
Grants Pass, OR, 97526
(503) 474-1374

1902 Queen Anne Victorian, architecturally interesting. Largest historic residence in Grants Pass. Furnished with lovely antiques, this beautifully appointed home offers travelers pleasing accommodations. Featured on the walking tour of National Historic Buildings. A Victorian evening, with music and refreshments, is special.

Hosts: Herbert & Betty Buskirk, Rosemary Althaus
Rooms: 3 (SB) $65
Full Breakfast
Credit Cards: No
Notes: 2, 5, 9

Lawnridge House

1304 NW Lawnridge
Grants Pass, OR, 97526
(503) 476-8518

Restored, antique-furnished 1909 Craftsman, shaded by 200-year-old oaks. Beamed ceilings, fireplace, VCR in guest living room. One suite features queen canopy bed, balcony, closeted 'fridge full of goodies, TV, air conditioned, phone, sitting room, and bath. A second contains handmade canopied king bed, bay windows, TV, air conditioning, phone, private bath. A third room offers a queen bed, bay windows, TV. Dark wood floors, Oriental rugs. Full NW regional breakfasts.

Host: Barbara Head
Rooms: 3 (2 PB; 1 SB) $45-70
Full Breakfast
Credit Cards: No
Notes: 2, 5, 8, 9, 10, 11, 12, 14

HALFWAY

Birch Leaf Farm B&B

RR 1, Box 91
Halfway, OR, 97834
(503) 742-2990

Alpine lake and stream fishing, white-water rafting, jet-boat trips, hunting. Exceptional birding area, cross-country skiing, near 3 million acres of wilderness. Hells Canyon, a national recreational area, is nearby. Lovely historic home on a 42-acre farm, with natural wood floors, decks, and stream.

Hosts: Dave & Maryellen Olson
Rooms: 5 (1 PB; 4 SB) $55-65
Full Breakfast
Credit Cards: A, B
Notes: 2, 5, 6, 9, 11, 13, 14

JACKSONVILLE

Jacksonville Inn

175 East California Street
Jacksonville, OR, 97530
(503) 899-1900

Jacksonville Inn offers eight air-conditioned rooms furnished with restored antiques and a historic honeymoon cottage furnished with everything imaginable. A lovely breakfast is provided. An award-winning dinner house featuring gourmet dining and over 700 wines is located in an 1863 vintage building.

Hosts: Jerry & Linda Evans
Rooms: 9 (PB) $80-175
Full Breakfast
Credit Cards: A, B, C, D, E
Notes: 2, 3, 4, 5, 6 (small), 8, 9, 10, 11, 12

Livingston Mansion B&B Inn

4132 Livingston Road
P.O. Box 1476
Jacksonville, OR, 97530
(503) 899-7107

Built in 1915, this rambling Edwardian house looks over the valley and mountains.

Set on 4.5 wooded acres, Livingston Mansion offers a peaceful return to the early 1900s. Rooms are decorated in antiques. Family-owned and operated. We welcome guests with open arms.

Hosts: Bob & Elaine Grathwol
Rooms: 7 (3 PB; 4 SB) $85-110
Full Breakfast
Credit Cards: A, B, C
Notes: 2, 5, 7 (outside), 11, 12, 13, 14

McCully House Inn

240 East California Street
Jacksonville, OR, 97530
(503) 899-1942

Jacksonville's finest and oldest country inn. Historic home built in 1860 features three beautiful rooms with full baths and a full-service restaurant serving the Pacific Northwest's freshest ingredients. Chef/owners are CIA graduates. Outdoor garden patios, antiques. Within the shopping district, near Britt Music Theater.

Hosts: Patricia Groth & Philip Accetta
Rooms: 3 (PB) $65-75
Full Breakfast
Credit Cards: A, B, C
Notes: 2, 3, 4, 7 (outside), 8, 9, 10, 11, 13, 14

LA GRANDE

Stange Manor

1612 Walnut Street
La Grande, OR, 97850
(503) 963-2400

Large early 1920s Georgian colonial home on beautiful grounds with lovely views. The home has lovely furnishings and a comfortable atmosphere. Guest baths feature large, old-fashioned tubs. One suite available with a marvelous old fireplace.

Hosts: Steve & Gail Hart, Gene & Bernadine Curry
Rooms: 5 (3 PB; 2 SB) $35-60
Full Breakfast
Credit Cards: A, B, C
Notes: 2, 5, 9, 10, 11, 12, 13

LINCOLN CITY

Palmer House B&B Inn

646 N.W. Inlet
Lincoln City, OR, 97367
(503) 994-7932

Panoramic ocean view. Two bedrooms and one suite, all with private baths; one with fireplace. Two rooms have private entrances. Common room with fireplace and many amenities. Plus deck for relaxing and watching the ocean tides or sunsets. In the morning, a three-course gourmet breakfast is served. Many shops and restaurants are nearby. Members of PAII, Oregon B&B Guild.

Rooms: 3 (PB)
Full Breakfast
Credit Cards: A, B
Notes: 2, 5, 10, 11, 12, 14

MERLIN

Morrison's Rogue River Lodge

8500 Galice Road
Merlin, OR, 97532
(503) 476-3825; (800) 826-1963

A beautiful country inn is located on the banks of the Rogue River in southern Oregon. Enjoy gourmet and country cuisine. Facilities include a pool, tennis, and a putting green. White-water rafting in summer, steelhead and salmon fishing in the fall.

Hosts: B.A. & Elaine Hanten, Michelle Ryan
Rooms: 13 (PB) $75-120 American Plan
Full Breakfast
Credit Cards: A, B, C
Closed Nov. 15-May 1
Notes: 2, 4, 7, 8, 9, 10, 11, 14

MILTON-FREEWATER

Birch Tree Manor

615 South Main Street
Milton-Freewater, OR, 97862
(503) 938-6455

A handsome brick home surrounded by birch trees that offers guests pleasant, personable accommodations. Located at the foot of the Blue Mountains in eastern Oregon, where travelers can experience year-round outdoor activities. Full breakfast with local fruit and berries, along with homemade breads and pastries.

Hosts: Ken & Priscilla Dauble
Rooms: 3 (1 PB; 2 SB) $35-45
Full Breakfast
Minimum stay holidays: 2
Credit Cards: A, B
Notes: 2, 5, 8, 10, 11, 12, 13, 14

MYRTLE CREEK

Sonka's Sheep Station Inn

901 NW Chadwick Lane
Myrtle Creek, OR, 97457
(503) 863-5168

The Sonka Ranch covers 260 acres along the picturesque South Umpqua River. This working ranch raises purebred Dorset sheep and market fat lambs from 700 commercial ewes. Depending on the time of the year, guests can share ranch activities such as lambing, shearing, and haying. The working border collies always give demonstrations. Enjoy rural relaxing or visit local points of interest. More than just a B&B, we promise a memorable farmstay.

Hosts: Louis & Evelyn Sonka
Rooms: 4 (3 PB; 1 SB) $45-60
Full Breakfast
Credit Cards: A, B
Closed Christmas holidays
Notes: 2, 3, 4, 8, 9, 11, 14

NEWBERG

Secluded B&B

19719 NE Williamson Road
Newberg, OR, 97132
(503) 538-2635

Secluded beautiful country home located on 10 acres. The ideal retreat in the woods for hiking, country walks, and observing wildlife. Ten minutes' drive to several wineries; about one hour to the coast. Breakfast is a special occasion. Many antiques in the home. Located near George Fox College and Linfield College.

Hosts: Durell & Del Belanger
Rooms: 2 (1 PB; 1 SB) $35 & 50
Full Breakfast
Credit Cards: No
Closed January
Notes: 2, 8 (under 6 months or over 6 years), 10, 11, 12, 14

NEWPORT

Ocean House B&B

4920 NW Woody Way
Newport, OR, 97365
(503) 265-6158

Ocean House, overlooking beautiful gardens and surf at Agate Beach, is a special place to relax and enjoy the many coastal pleasures. Newport's historic bay front, restaurants, and shops are nearby, and magnificent scenery stretches north and south. No smoking, pets, or children.

Hosts: Bette & Bob Garrard
Rooms: 4 (PB) $52-83.50
Full Breakfast
Credit Cards: A, B
Closed Dec. 15-Jan. 7
Notes: 2, 9, 10, 11, 12

Sylvia Beach Hotel

267 NW Cliff
Newport, OR, 97365
(503) 265-5428

Oceanfront B&B for book lovers. No smoking. Each room is named after a different author and decorated individually. Some have fireplaces. Hot spiced wine is served in the library at 10:00 P.M. Dinner served nightly. Not suitable for young children.

Hosts: Goody Cable & Sally Ford
Rooms: 20 (PB) $50-120
Full Breakfast
Credit Cards: A, B, C
Notes: 2, 4, 5, 9

NORTH BEND

Sherman House

2380 Sherman Avenue
North Bend, OR, 97459
(503) 756-3496

This 1903 Pennsylvania Dutch home located two blocks from Highway 101 offers harbor and mountain views. Close to the rugged coast, sand dunes, botanical gardens, waterfalls, and recreational activities. Antique furnishings include an extensive toy collection.

Hosts: Phillip & Jennifer Williams
Rooms: 3 (2 PB; 1 SB) $55-60
Full Breakfast
Credit Cards: C
Notes: 2, 5, 7, 8, 9

The Pringle House B&B

OAKLAND

The Pringle House B&B

Locust & Seventh Streets
Box 578
Oakland, OR, 97462
(503) 459-5038

A gracious 1880 Queen Anne Victorian home, on National Register, overlooking historic town. Comfortable, quiet, charming rooms with antiques, quilts, and doll collection. Cozy common rooms. Near fine dining, antiques, fishing, boating, six wineries, wildlife park. Brochure available.

Hosts: Jim & Demay Pringle
Rooms: 2 (S2B) $45-55
Full Breakfast
Credit Cards: No
Notes: 2, 5, 8 (over 11), 9, 10, 11, 12

OCEANSIDE

Sea Haven Inn

Box 203
Oceanside, OR, 97134
(503) 842-3151; (800) 447-9708

Sea Haven Inn is a new inn with nine rooms, six suites, and an annex of seven ocean-front cabins. All accommodations have private baths and color TV. Suites have refrigerators. The inn is all ocean front, on a cliff 250 feet high.

Suites: 6 (PB) $60-75
Rooms: 3 (PB) $55
Full Breakfast
Credit Cards: A, B
Notes: 2, 3, 5, 7 (limited), 8, 9, 11, 14

OTIS (OREGON COAST)

Salmon River Lodge

5622 Salmon River Highway
Otis, OR, 97368
(503) 994-2639

We enjoy fixing large breakfasts such as huckleberry hotcakes with homemade fruit syrups. Nearby kite shops, beach access, mountain trails, horseback riding, boats for fishing or crabbing, factory outlet mall, shops and galleries, and excellent restaurants.

Hosts: Marvin & Paunee Pegg
Rooms: 4 (2 PB; 2 SB) $35-45
Full Breakfast
Credit Cards: A, B
Closed Dec. 24-25
Notes: 2, 5, 6 (outside), 7 (outside), 8, 9, 10, 11, 12, 14

PORTLAND

Cape Cod B&B

5733 SW Dickinson Street
Portland, OR, 97219
(503) 246-1839

We are conveniently located seven miles south of Portland off I-5. Our 1939 Cape Cod home is furnished with traditional and antique furniture collected over a forty-year period. An outdoor spa, in the ivy-hedged enclosed gardens, relaxes you for the next day's activities. Air-conditioned, cable TV, VCR.

Hosts: John & Marcelle Tebo
Rooms: 2 (SB) $40-50
Full Breakfast
Credit Cards: No
Closed Nov.-mid-March
Notes: 2 (one month in advance), 7 (outside), 8, 9, 10, 12, 14

General Hookers B&B

125 SW Hooker
Portland, OR, 97201
(503) 222-4435

Portland's premier Victorian B&B, a romantic Queen Anne, lovingly restored, in a quiet historic district near downtown. Preferred by business travelers for its superb location and amenities: air-conditioning, cable TVs, VCRs, use of a local fitness club. Call or write for illustrated brochure. Fully licensed.

Host: Lori Hall
Rooms: 4 (1 PB; 3 SB) $80-110
Continental Breakfast
Minimum stay holidays: 2
Credit Cards: A, B, C
Notes: 2, 5, 8 (over 10), 9, 10, 11, 12, 14

John Palmer House

4314 North Mississippi Avenue
Portland, OR, 97217
(503) 284-5893

Forty-five minutes from Columbia Gorge, Mt. Hood, wine country. One hour from the Pacific Ocean. Our beautiful historic Victorian can be your home away from home. Award-winning decor; gourmet chef. Your hosts delight in providing the extraordinary. Dinner available. Free color brochure.

Hosts: Mary & Richard Sauter
Rooms: 7 (3 PB; 4 SB) $112.65
Full Breakfast
Credit Cards: A, B (6% service charge)
Wine sold on premises
Notes: 2, 4 (with notice), 5, 8, 9, 14

NW Bed & Breakfast 359

610 SW Broadway
Portland, OR, 97205
(503) 243-7616

English-style home built fifty years ago in a central location. Furnished and decorated with casual elegance. Wooded setting, garden. Breakfast is served on the terrace when weather permits. Down pillows and comforters, air-conditioning in rooms. One king room with private bath and one double room with shared bath. $40-50.

NW Bed & Breakfast 367A

610 SW Broadway
Portland, OR, 97205
(503) 243-7616

Comfortable home with a secluded backyard in a countrylike neighborhood. Convenient west-side location, with easy access to all freeways. Heated pool and spa available. Hosts have lived in Japan and can help with translations. Two poodles in residence. Guest female dogs are welcome. One room with twin beds and private bath. $40.

NW Bed & Breakfast 374A

610 SW Broadway
Portland, OR, 97205
(503) 243-7616

NOTES: Credit cards accepted: A Master Card; B Visa; C American Express; D Discover Card; E Diners Club; F Other: 2 Personal checks accepted: 3 Lunch available: 4 Dinner available: 5 Open all year

Spacious western cedar home in Sylvan Hills, with original artwork and forested view. Baby grand piano for guests' use. Close to arboretum, science museum, zoo, city center, bus. Deck overlooks the valley and lovely garden. Hosts speak Japanese and serve a Japanese or American breakfast. If requested, hostess will serve Japanese ceremonial tea in tatami mat tearoom for a nominal fee. Separate guest quarters: two rooms with double beds, shared bath. $45.

Portland Guest House

Portland Guest House

1720 NE Fifteenth Street
Portland, OR, 97212
(503) 282-1402

Portland's most convenient address; a 100-year-old restored Victorian home with great beds, private phones, gourmet breakfasts. Adjacent to Lloyd Center Shopping Mall, ten-theater cinemaplex, and gourmet food market. Quick transit to the Coliseum, convention center, and downtown.

Host: Susan Gisvold
Rooms: 4 (2 PB; 2 SB) $40-65
Family Suite: (PB) $75-95
Full Breakfast
Credit Cards: A, B, C
No smoking
Notes: 2, 5, 9, 10, 14

Portland's White House

1914 NE 22nd Street
Portland, OR, 97212
(503) 287-7131

Turn-of-the-century lumber baron's mansion on the Historic Register that has been restored to its original splendor. Large Greek columns, circular driveway, and fountain in front.

Hosts: Mary & Larry Hough
Rooms: 6 (4 PB; 2 SB) $65-98
Full Breakfast
Credit Cards: A, B
Notes: 2, 5, 9, 10, 11, 12, 14

PRINEVILLE

The Elliott House

305 West First Street
Prineville, OR, 97754
(503) 447-7442

Queen Anne-style Victorian home built in 1908. Listed on the National Register of Historic Places, with period furnishings and decor. Badminton and croquet on the lawns. In a quiet neighborhood, yet within walking distance of town center. Afternoon tea is served in the parlor or on the veranda.

Hosts: Tuck & Carol Dunlap
Rooms: 3 (1 PB; 2 SB) $50-60
Full Breakfast
Credit Cards: No
Notes: 2, 5, 8, 9, 10, 11, 12

ROCKAWAY BEACH

Beach House B&B

115 North Miller
Rockaway Beach, OR, 97136
(503) 355-2411; (503) 355-8282

Portland's White House

Comfortable seventy-year-old home on the ocean, within walking distance of shops, restaurants, and recreational facilities. Breakfast served in owner's restaurant across the street any time of day. Fireplace, color TV, games, beach-combing, walking, or running on seven miles of beach.

Host: Margie Tiegs
Rooms: 2 (SB) $39.90-42
Full Breakfast
Minimum stay weekends & holidays: 2
Credit Cards: A, B
Notes: 2, 5, 10, 11, 12, 14

ROSEBURG

The Woods

428 Oakview Drive
Roseburg, OR, 97470
(503) 672-2927

The Woods is snuggled into 7 southwestern Oregon wooded acres. Fish, swim, or raft the scenic North Umpqua River; visit several famous boutique wineries; or unwind in a Douglas County park. Your world-traveling hosts will make you feel welcome. Brochure available.

Hosts: Wiley & Judy Wood
Rooms: 3 (PB) $50-60
Full Breakfast
Credit Cards: No
Closed Thanksgiving & Christmas
Notes: 2, 4, 5, 8, 9, 10, 11, 12

SALEM

NW Bed & Breakfast 411A

610 SW Broadway
Portland, OR, 97205
(503) 243-7616

Nicely furnished, comfortable B&B inn. Relaxing setting on the banks of a creek. Convenient location on State Street, with transportation right outside the door. Guest rooms are attractive, and one faces the creek. Suite has separate kitchen, TV, VCR. Full breakfast. Two queen rooms share a bath; suite has a private bath. $45-65.

NW Bed & Breakfast 453

610 SW Broadway
Portland, OR, 97205
(503) 243-7616

Large, charming home built in 1910, attractively decorated with antiques and collectibles. Located four blocks from the State Capitol Building and five minutes from downtown Salem Shopping Mall. Living room with fireplace, TV, VCR, stereo. Dog in residence. One room has a double antique bed and private bath. Second room has a queen bed and shared bath. $40-50.

SEAL ROCK

Blackberry Inn

6575 Pacific Coast Highway 101
Seal Rock, OR, 97376
(503) 563-2259

A 1930s Cape Cod in a wooded setting. Beach access, down comforters, fireplace, hot tub under the stars, breakfast in bed available. Body work: therapeutic massage, mud baths, herbal steams. Seal Rock is twelve miles south of Newport, near tide pools and uncrowded beach. A peaceful place for thoughtful moods of quiet simplicity.

Host: Barbara Tarter
Rooms: 4 (PB) $59-75
Full Breakfast
Credit Cards: A, B
Notes: 2, 9, 12

"Victoriana" B&B

SEASIDE

"Victoriana" B&B

606 12th Avenue
Seaside, OR, 97138
(503) 738-8449

"Victoriana" B&B offers country hospitality in the European tradition. Built in 1899, "Victoriana" is one of Seaside's oldest homes. Conveniently located one-half mile from downtown shopping; two and a half blocks to the beach and promenade. Riverview location, with easy access to fishing and crabbing. A relaxing, peaceful atmosphere.

Host: LaRee Johnson
Rooms: 2 (SB) $50
Full Continental Breakfast
Credit Cards: No
Notes: 2, 5, 8 (over 12), 9, 10, 11, 12, 14

TIGARD

NW Bed & Breakfast 381A

610 SW Broadway
Portland, OR, 97205
(503) 243-7616

Colonial French country home in a private peach orchard with sweeping views of mountains and valley. Private tennis court and solar-heated swimming pool. Located twelve freeway miles from downtown Portland. Guest's garden-level room is furnished with antiques. An adjacent sitting room has a fireplace, TV, VCR, and opens onto the pool area. Summer breakfasts feature seasonal orchard fruits. Guest suite has one room with queen bed and one with a double water bed. $50.

TILLAMOOK

Blue Haven Inn

3025 Gienger Road
Tillamook, OR, 97141
(503) 842-2265

Built in 1916, newly refurbished and decorated with antiques and collectibles. Blue Haven Inn is situated in a quiet country setting, surrounded by spacious gardens and tall evergreens. Each room is individually decorated, offering a distinctly unique atmosphere, with books, games, music, and television in the library.

Hosts: Ray & Joy Still
Rooms: 3 (1 PB; 2 SB) $45-60
Full Breakfast
Credit Cards: No
Notes: 2, 4, 5, 9, 10, 11, 12, 14

WALDPORT

Cliff House

Adahi Street-Yaquina John Point
Box 436
Waldport, OR, 97394
(503) 563-2506

Pampered elegance by the sea. Each room is uniquely decorated with antiques, chandeliers, carpeting, remote color TV; all have private cedar baths and balconies. Elegant lodging coupled with magnificent panoramic ocean view. Deep-sea fishing, river fishing, crabbing, golf club (half a mile), croquet. Horseback riding close by; massage by appointment.

Hosts: Gabrielle Duvall & Debra J. Novgrod
Rooms: 5 (PB) $95-225
Full Breakfast
Minimum stay weekends: 2; holidays, 3
Credit Cards: A, B
Closed Oct. 15-March 31
Notes: 2, 4, 9, 10, 11, 12, 14

WELCHES

Mountain Shadows B&B

20390 West Angelsey Road
Box 147
Welches, OR, 97067
(503) 622-4746

A log home built in 1978 by the owners. Situated in a wooded setting at the end of a country lane, with panoramic views of Mt. Hood and the surrounding foothills. In the heart of Mt. Hood Recreation Area: fishing, golf, hiking, skiing, tennis are all nearby. Featured in *Northwest Discoveries* Dec. 7, 1988; *This Week* magazine; *Northwest Best Places;* and *Best Places to Stay in the Pacific Northwest.*

Hosts: Juanita & Wes Post
Rooms: 3 (1 PB; 2 SB) $50-65
Full Breakfast
Credit Cards: A, B
Notes: 2, 5, 6 (call first), 8 (call first), 9, 10, 11, 12, 13, 14

YACHATS

Ziggurat

95330 Highway 101
Yachats, OR, 97498
(503) 547-3925

Ziggurat means terraced pyramid, and this one is a spectacular, contemporary, four-story sculpture by the sea. Guests have the privacy of the entire first floor, with a sauna, solarium, and library/living room. There are glass-enclosed decks on the second floor for ocean viewing, where superb food is served. Your hosts are world meanderers. Dunes, parks, and coastal activities are nearby.

Hosts: Mary Lou Cavendish & Irv Tebor
Rooms: 2 (SB) $75-110 + tax
Full Breakfast
Credit Cards: No
Closed Dec. 20-27
Notes: 2, 8 (over 14), 9, 14

YAMHILL

Flying M Ranch

23029 NW Flying M. Road
Yamhill, OR, 97148
(503) 662-3222; FAX: (503) 662-3202

The bounty of Yamhill County's wine country joins with the evergreen coastal mountains to harbor the Flying M's spectacular log lodge. Delectable cuisine, year-round horseback riding, limitless outdoor activities. Full service restaurant, lounge, airstrip, gift shop, primitive camping, fishing, and dancing on Friday and Saturday evenings.

Hosts: Bryce & Barbara Mitchell
Rooms: 35 (PB) $50-150
Full Breakfast
Credit Cards: A, B, C, E
Closed Dec. 24 & 25
Notes: 2, 3, 4, 5, 6, 7, 8, 9, 10, 11, 14

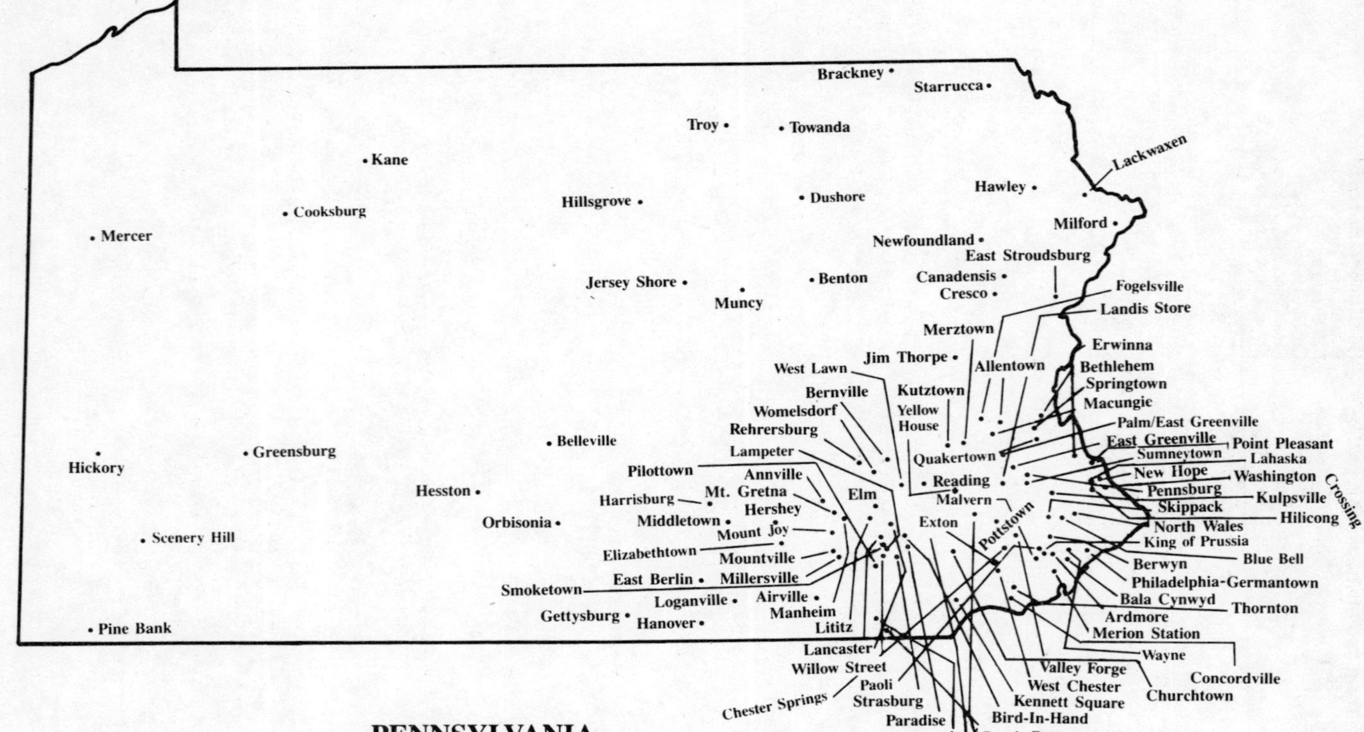
PENNSYLVANIA
Brackney
Starrucca
Troy
Towanda
Kane
Hawley
Lackwaxen
Dushore
Hillsgrove
Cooksburg
Milford
Mercer
Newfoundland
East Stroudsburg
Canadensis
Cresco
Jersey Shore
Benton
Muncy
Fogelsville
Landis Store
Merztown
Erwinna
Jim Thorpe
Allentown
Bethlehem
West Lawn
Springtown
Kutztown
Bernville
Macungie
Womelsdorf
Yellow House
Palm/East Greenville
Rehrersburg
East Greenville
Point Pleasant
Quakertown
Sumneytown
Lahaska
Belleville
Greensburg
Lampeter
New Hope
Washington Crossing
Hickory
Pilottown
Annville
Reading
Pennsburg
Kulpsville
Hesston
Mt. Gretna
Elm
Malvern
Skippack
Harrisburg
Hershey
Hilicong
Orbisonia
Middletown
Exton
North Wales
Scenery Hill
Mount Joy
Pottstown
King of Prussia
Elizabethtown
Mountville
Blue Bell
Berwyn
East Berlin
Millersville
Philadelphia-Germantown
Smoketown
Airville
Bala Cynwyd
Loganville
Thornton
Gettysburg
Manheim
Ardmore
Pine Bank
Hanover
Lititz
Merion Station
Lancaster
Wayne
Willow Street
Valley Forge
Concordville
Paoli
West Chester
Chester Springs
Churchtown
Strasburg
Kennett Square
Paradise
Bird-In-Hand
Holtwood
Peach Bottom
Gordonville
Kinzers

Pennsylvania

AIRVILLE

Spring House

Muddy Creek Forks
Airville, PA, 17302
(717) 927-6906

Built in 1798 of fieldstone, the house is named for the pure spring it protects in the tranquil pre-Revolutionary river valley village. Lovingly restored to stenciled whitewashed walls, furnished with antiques and art, the inn offers full breakfast of local specialties, wine by the fire or on the front porch, Amish-made cheese, and caring hospitality. Horseback riding, wineries, hiking, trout fishing in immediate area. Near Amish.

Host: Ray Constance Hearne
Rooms: 5 (3 PB; 2 SB) $52-85
Full Breakfast
Minimum stay weekends & holidays: 2
Credit Cards: No
Notes: 2, 5, 8, 9, 11, 12, 14

Spring House

ALLENTOWN

Coachaus

107-111 North Eighth Street
Allentown, PA, 18101
(215) 821-4854; (800) 762-8680

Five gracious, century-old, lovingly restored brownstones provide a center city oasis from which to explore shops, historic sites, museums, fine dining, golf, hiking, skiing, and professional theater. The rooms, apartments, and townhouses each have a unique charm and are fully equipped with the finest amenities for your relaxation.

Host: Barbara Kocher
Rooms: 24 (PB) $75-155 + tax
Full Breakfast
Credit Cards: A, B, C, E
Notes: 2, 5, 7, 8, 9, 10, 11, 12, 13, 14

Row Home on the Park

B&B of Southeast Pennsylvania
146 W. Philadelphia Avenue
Boyertown, PA, 19512
(215) 367-4688

The hostess offers a single room on the second floor and two on the third, one with a queen bed and the other with a double bed. There is a guest sitting room with TV on the second floor. The shared bath is on the second floor. Children five and older are welcome; small, well-behaved pets may be allowed. Close to downtown, minutes from Dorney Park and colleges. $45-50.

ANNIVILLE

Hershey Bed & Breakfast 8

P.O. Box 208
Hershey, PA, 17033
(717) 533-2928

Victorian mansion built in 1860, ten miles from Hershey, eighteen miles from Harrisburg, and two miles from Indiantown Gap. All queen beds in seven guest rooms, four of which can accommodate four people. Children are welcome. Air conditioned, full breakfast, private baths. $50-70.

ARDMORE

B&B Connections 205

P.O. Box 21
Devon, PA, 19333
(800) 448-3619; (215) 687-3565

This Main Line duplex will make you feel you've discovered a bit of Ireland. Two rooms on the second floor, one with double bed and the other with a single. Two third-floor rooms, each with a double bed. All rooms share a bath. Full breakfast. $55.

Bed & Breakfast Connections 206

P.O. Box 21
Devon, PA, 19333
(800) 448-3619

This Dutch colonial dates back to 1910 and has been tastefully decorated with a contemporary flair. The cozy third-floor guest room is attractively appointed, with a king or twin beds, private bath. Full breakfast.$50.

BALA CYNWYD

B&B Connections 224

P.O. Box 21
Devon, PA, 19333
(800) 448-3619; (215) 687-3565

Comfortable suburban home with easy access to Center City attractions and Main Line universities. Two second-floor accommodations offer a private suite arrangement for a family or may be reserved separately. One room features an antique brass bed and TV. Shared bath. Continental-plus breakfast. $55-60.

BALLY

Bally Spring Farm

B&B of Southeast Pennsylvania
146 W. Philadelphia Avenue
Boyertown, PA, 19512
(215) 367-4688

A unique 1734 stone house on 100 acres for that special getaway. The estate has a private 2,285-foot runway so guests can fly in. There is a 6-acre lake stocked with bass and a stream stocked with trout. Near antique shops, outlets, downhill skiing. Four rooms; one with private bath. $50-65.

Christman House

B&B of Southeast Pennsylvania
146 W. Philadelphia Avenue
Boyertown, PA, 19512
(215) 367-4688

Located in rural Montgomery County, Christmas House offers two rooms on the second floor. One room with a double bed has access to a second-floor balcony; the second has twin beds. Breakfast is served on the porch in the summer. Convenient for Gosherhoppen Folk Festival, Perkiomen School. About twenty minutes from Allentown and forty from Reading. $40-50.

BELLEVILLE

Hickory Grove B&B

RD 1, Box 281
Belleville, PA, 17004
(717) 935-5289

NOTES: Credit cards accepted: A Master Card; B Visa; C American Express; D Discover Card; E Diners Club; F Other: 2 Personal checks accepted: 3 Lunch available: 4 Dinner available: 5 Open all year

Hickory Grove is nestled among the foothills of Stone Valley, in the heart of Big Valley, with many area attractions, including crafts, antiques, flea markets, and quilt shops in Amish country. Homemade baked goods served with breakfast.

Hosts: Caleb & Bertha Peachey
Rooms: 5 (2 PB; 3 SB) From $45
Continental Breakfast
Credit Cards: No
Notes: 2, 5, 7 (outdoors), 10

BERNVILLE

Sunday's Mill Farm

B&B of Southeast Pennsylvania
146 W. Philadelphia Avenue
Boyertown, PA, 19512
(215) 367-4688

An 1852 farmhouse that has been decorated with quilts, antiques, and original art. A queen room with powder room on the second floor shares a bath with a double room. An 1820 stone grist mill is on the property. Lush, fenced pastures and water available for people traveling with horses. Near Hawk Mountain, antique shops, Amish Country the Appalachian Trail, outlets, and skiing. Resident dog. $35-55.

BERWYN

Bed & Breakfast Connections 212

P.O. Box 21
Devon, PA, 19333
(800) 448-3619

A warm welcome awaits you in this suburban townhouse decorated with a contemporary flair. Dramatic king suite with private attached bath. Luxuriate in the Jacuzzi or relax on the private patio. Delicious full breakfast on weekends and continental on weekdays. Within walking distance of the train, convenient to Main Line universities and Valley Forge Park. Smoking on patio only; resident dog. $75.

B&B Connections 243

P.O. Box 21
Devon, PA, 19333
(800) 448-3619; (215) 687-3565

A charming 1770 fieldstone farmhouse near the universities, the Brandywine Valley, and Valley Forge Park. Two second-floor guest rooms with a shared bath are located in the old part of the house. A working fireplace in one room, plus back stairs leading down to the comfortable den with TV. A second room boasts a wood-burning stove and private bath. Full breakfast, resident dog, no smoking. $85-95.

BETHLEHEM

Bethlehem Inn

B&B of Southeast Pennsylvania
146 W. Philadelphia Avenue
Boyertown, PA, 19512
(215) 367-4688

This completely restored inn is conveniently located near Moravian College and the historic Moravian tour sites, as well as Lehigh University, the Bach Festival, Musikfest, and Bethlehem Christmas activities. The house has two rooms with queen beds and private baths, as well as a suite available for up to four people with its own private bath and queen beds. $75-120.

The Gaslight House

B&B of Southeast Pennsylvania
146 W. Philadelphia Avenue
Boyertown, PA, 19512
(215) 367-4688

Within the walking tour of historic Bethlehem, this air conditioned townhouse is in a quiet area for exploring the unique city. One double room with private bath on the second floor. Children over ten are welcome to sleep on a cot. $40-50.

BIRD-IN-HAND

Greystone Manor B&B

2658 Old Philadelphia Pike, Box 270
Bird-in-Hand, PA, 17505
(717) 393-4233

Greystone Manor is a lovely old French Victorian mansion and carriage house with Victorian furnishings, decorative windows and doors. Surrounded by Amish farms. Minutes from Lancaster, Intercourse, Strasburg, outlet malls, farmers' market, and local craft shops. Quilt shop in mansion basement.

Hosts: Sally & Ed Davis
Rooms: 13 (PB) $48.76-89.04
Continental Breakfast
Credit Cards: A, B
Notes: 2, 5, 7 (limited), 8, 9, 10, 12, 14

Greystone Manor B&B

BLUE BELL

Lone Star Inn

B&B of Southeast Pennsylvania
146 W. Philadelphia Avenue
Boyertown, PA, 19512
(215) 367-4688

A 200-year-old stone house tucked away near modern business campuses and malls yet away from the hustle and bustle. The first floor has a cheerful dining room for breakfast and two sitting rooms for guests. Two suites on the second floor, one with a queen bed and working fireplace. The second has a double bed and large bath-sitting room with Jacuzzi tub. Three additional rooms with private baths, one with a working fireplace. In-ground pool and tennis court for guests' use. Children over twelve are welcome. $85-100.

BRACKNEY

Indian Mountain Inn B&B

RD 1, Box 68
Brackney, PA, 18812
(717) 663-2645

A true country inn nestled in the Endless Mountains near Binghamton, New York. Full restaurant, spa, liquor license. Surrounded by rolling mountain acres; ideal for all outdoor activities year round. Cozy sitting room with wood stoves. The inn is newly refurbished, and the innkeepers live on the premises. Packages available.

Hosts: Howard, Deborah & Henrietta Frierman
Rooms: 8 (PB) $63.60
Continental Breakfast
Credit Cards: A, B, D
Notes: 2 (as deposit), 4, 5, 7 (limited), 8, 9, 13 (XC), 14

CANADENSIS

Brookview Manor B&B Inn

RR 1, Box 365
Canadensis, PA, 18325
(717) 595-2451

Situated on 4 picturesque acres in the Pocono Mountains, Brookview Manor offers eight guest rooms and suites uniquely appointed with country and antique furnishings. Enjoy the wraparound porch, hiking trails, fishing, and nearby skiing, golf, tennis, boating, and antiquing. A delicious full breakfast, afternoon refreshments, and warm hospitality are all included.

Hosts: Patty & David DeMaria
Rooms: 8 (6 PB; 2 SB) $55-160
Full Breakfast
Credit Cards: A, B
Notes: 2, 5, 6, 8 (over 12), 9, 10, 11, 12, 13, 14

Dreamy Acres

Box 7, Canadensis, PA, 18325
(717) 595-7115

Dreamy Acres is situated in the heart of the Pocono Mountain vacationland on 3 acres of land with a stream flowing into a small pond. The house is 500 feet back from the highway, giving a pleasing, quiet atmosphere.

Hosts: Esther & Bill Pickett
Rooms: 6 (4 PB; 2 SB) $34-50 plus tax
Continental Breakfast May-Oct.
Minimum stay weekends: 2; holidays, 3
Closed Christmas
Credit Cards: No
Notes: 7, 8 (over 12), 9, 10, 11, 12, 13

Nearbrook B&B

RD 1, Box 630
Canadensis, PA, 18325
(717) 595-3152

Surrounded by roses and rock gardens, woods and stream, Nearbrook boasts the tiniest arched bridge in the Poconos. Dick cooks a hearty breakfast which is served out on the porch in the fresh mountain air during the summers.

Hosts: Barbara & Dick Robinson
Rooms: 3 (1 PB; 2 SB) $45
Full Breakfast
Credit Cards: No
Notes: 2, 5, 8, 10, 11, 12, 13

Old Village Inn

North Skytop Road
Canadensis, PA, 18325
(717) 595-2120

A turn-of-the-century, recently restored, full-service Victorian country inn with contemporary comforts and amenities. Featuring a delightful sixty-seat restaurant, lounge/bar, and beautiful antique-filled rooms and suites with TV and air-conditioning. Located near Promised Land State Park, Lake Wallenpaupack, Alpine Mountain, and Camelback Mountain for skiing. Close to Buck Hill and Skytop resorts.

Hosts: Otto & Vera Lissfeld
Rooms: 8 (PB) $62-110
Full Breakfast/MAP available
Credit Cards: A, B, C, D, E
Notes: 2, 4, 5, 9, 10, 11, 12, 13, 14

The Pine Knob Inn

Box 275
Canadensis, PA, 18325
(717) 595-2532

Step back into yesteryear. Experience the atmosphere of years gone by in our 1840s inn situated on 15 acres abounding with antiques and art. Enjoy gourmet dining. Guests gather on the veranda on summer evenings or by the fireplace after a day on the slopes. Daily rate includes breakfast and dinner.

Hosts: Ann & Scott Frankel
Rooms: 27 (21 PB; 6 SB) $140
Full Breakfast
Credit Cards: A, B
Notes: 2, 4, 5, 7, 8 (over 5), 9, 10, 11, 12, 13

Pump House Inn

Skytop Road
Canadensis, PA, 18325
(717) 595-7501

High in the Poconos, the Pump House Inn dates from 1842. Antiques, books, and distinctive furnishings grace this friendly country inn. Sophisticated dining is the mainstay at the Pump House, where the chef emphasizes French continental cuisine.

Host: John Keeney
Rooms: 10 $65-100

Continental Breakfast
Credit Cards: A, B, C, E, F
Closed January
Notes: 2, 4, 5, 7, 8, 9, 10, 11, 12, 13

CHESTER SPRINGS

B&B Connections 213

P.O. Box 21
Devon, PA, 19333
(800) 448-3619; (215) 687-3565

High on a ridge overlooking the countryside, this c. 1850 historically registered farmhouse is decorated with family heirlooms and antiques. The bedroom boasts an authentic country Victorian king bed; private hall bath. An adjoining fireside living room completes the private suite. Continental-plus breakfast; resident cat. $60.

B&B Connections 216

P.O. Box 21
Devon, PA, 19333
(800) 448-3619; (215) 687-3565

Complimentary wine or sparkling water await your arrival at this lovely 1830s farmhouse with classic features. Located in the country, this home is the perfect spot for the history buff. Two guest rooms: one with double bed and one with an antique bed slightly less than double size. Shared bath. Relax by the stream on this quiet 10-acre country retreat. A continental-plus breakfast is served in front of the original dining room fireplace and beehive oven. No smoking; resident cat. $65.

CHURCHTOWN

B&B Connections 309

P.O. Box 21
Devon, PA, 19333
(800) 448-3619; (215) 687-3565

This inviting 1919 house is located in Lancaster County. Two guest rooms: one offers a double bed and single spool bed. Second room has a double four-poster and an additional three-quarter-size bed. Shared bath. Continental breakfast during the week, with home-baked goods. On weekends a full breakfast is served. Restricted smoking. $55.

Churchtown Inn B&B

Mail to: 2100 Main Street
Narvon, PA, 17555
(215) 445-7794

Lovely eighteenth-century stone mansion, restored and filled with charm and history. Located in the heart of Pennsylvania Dutch country, near all tourist attractions, antique markets, and outlets. Dine at an Amish home by prior arrangement. Air-conditioned, private baths. Lovely glass garden room. Ask about special-event weekends and holiday packages. Musical innkeeper.

Hosts: Hermine & Stuart Smith & Jim Kent
Rooms: 8 (6 PB; 2 SB) $49-95
Full Breakfast
Credit Cards: A, B
Notes: 2, 5, 8 (12 and up), 9, 10, 11, 12, 13, 14

CONCORDVILLE

West-Trimble House

B&B of Southeast Pennsylvania
146 W. Philadelphia Avenue
Boyertown, PA, 19512
(215) 367-4688

The original part of this house was built in 1728 and added to in the middle of the nineteenth century. It is listed on the National Historic Register, and the property can be traced back to land grants given by William Penn. Two guest rooms share a bath. One has a queen four-poster bed, and the other twin beds. Children over six are welcome; resident cats. Wilmington, Delaware is a short distance away, as are Longwood Gardens, Winterthur, and West Chester State University. $57-70.

COOKSBURG

Clarion River Lodge

River Road, Cook Forest
Cooksburg, PA, 16217
(800) 648-6743

A once-private estate along the gentle Clarion River adjacent to Cook Forest State Park. Full menu fine dining and wine. Twenty rooms, all with private baths, air-conditioning, and TV. Spectacular natural setting. Canoeing, bicycling, hiking, cross-country skiing.

Host: Skip Williams
Rooms: 20 (PB) $57-99
Full Breakfast weekends; continental weekdays
Credit Cards: A, B, C
Notes: 3, 4, 5, 7, 9, 10, 11, 12, 13, 14

CRESCO

LaAnna Guest House

RD 2, Box 1051
Cresco, PA, 18326
(717) 676-4225

Built in the 1870s, this Victorian home welcomes guests with large rooms that are furnished in Empire and Victorian antiques. Located in a quiet mountain village with waterfalls, mountain views, and outdoor activities.

Hosts: Kay Swingle & Julie Wilson
Rooms: 2 (1 PB; 1 SB) $25-30
Continental Breakfast
Credit Cards: No
Notes: 2, 5, 7, 8, 9, 10, 11, 12, 13 (XC), 14

DUSHORE

Cherry Mills Lodge

RR 1, Box 1270
Dushore, PA, 18614
(717) 928-8978

Lazy ambience with numerous activities available. We welcome you year-round to simply relax with reading, fishing at our own little creek, country walks, or passive therapy in our outdoor surroundings. For the hard-core fitness minded, mountain biking, trail hiking, acres of training roads, cross-country skiing, plus nearby hunting are available.

Hosts: Florence & Julio
Rooms: 8 (1 PB; 7 SB) $50
Full Breakfast
Credit Cards: A, B
Notes: 2, 3, 4, 5, 7, 8, 9, 11, 13 (XC)

Bechtel Mansion Inn

EAST BERLIN

Bechtel Mansion Inn

400 West King Street
East Berlin, PA, 17316
(717) 259-7760

Magnificent restored Victorian mansion with quality period furnishings and handmade quilts. Perfect setting for honeymoons and special occasions! Guest rooms are air-conditioned, with private baths. The mansion is on the western frontier of the Pennsylvania Dutch country. Excellent restaurants, golf courses, and antiques nearby. Convenient to York, Gettysburg, and Lancaster County. Located in a national historic district approximately 100 miles from both Washington, DC, and Philadelphia.

Hosts: Ruth Spangler, Charles & Mariam Bechtel
Rooms: 7 (PB) $82.25-106
Suites: 2 (PB) $116.75-132.50
Continental-plus Breakfast
Minimum stay Oct. weekends & holidays: 2
Credit Cards: A, B, C, D
Notes: 2, 5, 7 (limited), 8, 9, 10, 12, 13 (18 miles), 14

EAST GREENVILLE

Country Pond Farm

B&B of Southeast Pennsylvania
146 W. Philadelphia Avenue
Boyertown, PA, 19512
(215) 367-4688

This home has been in the same family since 1734, when they received the grant from William Penn. A guest room on the second floor shares a bath. Full breakfast every day but Sunday, which is continental. $40-45.

The Old Grist Mill

B&B of Southeast Pennsylvania
146 W. Philadelphia Avenue
Boyertown, PA, 19512
(215) 367-4688

A lovely Victorian home furnished with antiques on a famous trout stream. Two double rooms, each with a private bath, plus a single room for a child sharing parents' bath. On the third floor there are three rooms with two single beds each and shared bath. Resident dog. $40-50.

EAST STROUDSBURG

The Inn at Meadowbrook

RD 7, Box 7651
East Stroudsburg, PA, 18301
(717) 629-0296

A quiet country inn on 43 acres of rolling hills and meadows in the heart of the Poconos. Fishing lake, tennis courts, and a large outdoor swimming pool. Enjoy the beauty of a peaceful rural location.

Hosts: Bob & Kathy Overman
Rooms: 16 (10 PB; 6 SB) $50-85
Continental Breakfast
Credit Cards: A, B, C
Notes: 2, 4, 5, 7, 8 (12 and over), 9, 10, 11, 12, 13

ELIZABETHTOWN

Hershey Bed & Breakfast 16

P.O. Box 208
Hershey, PA, 17033
(717) 533-2928

A luxurious getaway at a beautiful country estate home. Hobby farm with horses, angus, two fishing ponds, tennis court, and swimming pool. Full breakfast, private and shared baths. $65-75.

ELM

Elm Country Inn

Box 37, Elm, PA, 17521
(717) 664-3623

Located in a small country village in beautiful Lancaster County, we are near the Amish country. The house was built in 1860 and has been refurbished, keeping most of the old character intact. Hosts are knowledgeable about the area and will help guests plan their sight-seeing.

Hosts: Berry & Melvin Meck
Rooms: 2 (1 PB; 1 SB) $45-55
Full Breakfast
Credit Cards: A, B
Notes: 5, 8, 9, 10, 11, 12, 14

EPHRATA

Gerhart House B&B

287 Duke Street
Ephrata, PA, 17522
(717) 733-0263

Built in 1926, when quality and aesthetics were considered in building. Parlor is trimmed in native chestnut woodwork. Beds have handmade Mennonite quilts and freshly ironed linens. Full breakfast at individual tables. We are in the heart of Amish country, near Ephrata Cloister, outlet shopping, antique markets, and fine restaurants.

Hosts: Richard & Judith Lawson
Rooms: 5 (3 PB; 2 SB) $45-75
Full Breakfast
Credit Cards: A, B
Closed Christmas Eve & Christmas
Notes: 2, 5, 7, 8, 9, 11

The Guesthouse and the 1777 House at Doneckers

318-324 North State Street
Ephrata, PA, 17522
(717) 733-8696

Experience the Doneckers' warm hospitality in the picturesque setting of historic Lancaster County. Let us pamper you with country elegance, fine antiques, folk art, hand-stenciled walls, and designer linens. Jacuzzi baths and fireplaces in some rooms. Restaurant and fashion stores, and artists' studios and galleries.

Host: H. William Donecker
Rooms: 29 (27 PB; 2 SB) $59-175 + tax
Buffet Breakfast
Credit Cards: All
Closed Christmas Day
Notes: 2, 3, 5, 4, 7, 8, 9, 10, 11, 12

The Historic Smithton Inn

900 West Main Street
Ephrata, PA, 17522
(717) 733-6094

A romantic 1763 stone inn with fireplaces in every room, canopy beds, easy chairs, quilts, candles, down pillows, nightshirts, flowers, chamber music, and feather beds. Parlor, library, and gardens for guests to enjoy. In Lancaster County, an antique and crafts area settled by the Pennsylvania Dutch, Mennonite, and Amish peoples.

Host: Dorothy Graybill
Rooms: 8 (PB) $65-115
Full Breakfast
Credit Cards: A, B, C
Notes: 2, 5, 6, 8, 9, 10, 11, 12

Springwoods

B&B of Southeast Pennsylvania
146 W. Philadelphia Avenue
Boyertown, PA, 19512
(215) 367-4688

A Civil War frame farmhouse which has been added to and tastefully restored. Three guest rooms: one double with private bath, one with a double bed, and the third with twin brass beds and a queen sofabed. All rooms share a guest sitting room with TV. Two cats and a small dog in residence. The house is five minutes away from a golf course open to the public. Near Amish Country and the antique emporiums of Adamstown. $65.

The Guesthouse and the 1777 House at Doneckers

ERWINNA

Evermay on-the-Delaware

River Road
Erwinna, PA, 18920
(215) 294-9100

Lodging in manor house and carriage house. Liquor license. Parlor with fireplace. A significant, distinguished country retreat located on 25 acres of gardens, woodland paths, and pastures between the Delaware

River and Canal. Dinner served Friday, Saturday, Sunday, and holidays.

Hosts: Ron Strouse & Fred Cresson
Rooms: 15 (PB) $70-125
Continental-plus Breakfast
Minimum stay weekends: 2
Credit Cards: A, B
Closed Dec. 24
Notes: 2, 7, 8 (over 12), 9, 10, 11, 12

Golden Pheasant Inn

Golden Pheasant Inn

River Road
Erwinna, PA, 18920
(215) 294-9595

This 1857 fieldstone inn is situated between the Delaware River and the Pennsylvania Canal. Five romantic rooms are furnished with an incredible blend of antiques. Three dining rooms, including a candlelit greenhouse. Masterful classical French cuisine by chef/owner Michel Faure. Extensive wine selections. Dinner Tues.-Sun. from 5:30.

Hosts: Michel & Barbara Faure
Rooms: 5 (1 PB; 4 SB) $95-125
Continental Breakfast
Minimum stay weekends: 2; holidays: 3
Credit Cards: A, B
Notes: 2, 4, 5, 7, 9, 10, 11, 12, 13

EXTON

B&B Connections 204

P.O. Box 21
Devon, PA, 19333
(800) 448-3619; (215) 687-3565

This cozy townhouse, in a quiet wooded setting, offers a warm and friendly atmosphere. Twin room with an adjoining den for listening to music or watching TV, private bath, queen hideabed. Take a dip in the pool or enjoy the patio overlooking the countryside. Continental breakfast weekdays; full on weekends. No smoking. $55.

Duling Kurtz House & Country Inn

146 South Whitford Road
Exton, PA, 19341
(215) 524-1830

Charming 1830s stone house and barn, elegantly furnished with period reproduction furniture. Fourteen guest rooms, including four suites, all with private bath. Fine restaurant serves lunch Monday through Friday and dinner Monday through Saturday.

Host: Blair McClain
Rooms: 14 (PB) From $49.95
Continental Breakfast
Credit Cards: A, B, C, E
Notes: 2, 3, 4, 5, 7, 8, 9, 10, 12, 14

FOGELSVILLE

Glasbern

B&B of Southeast Pennsylvania
146 W. Philadelphia Avenue
Boyertown, PA, 19512
(215) 367-4688

Within two miles of the intersection of I-78/22 and Route 100, amid hills and orchards. Twelve rooms and one suite in the barn, each with queen bed and private bath, TV, telephone, and climate control. Conference room available for ten. Breakfast is served in the converted hayloft, now the living/dining area, which has a large open fireplace. Three self-contained suites are available in the old farmhouse, and four suites are available in the carriage house. $125-200.

GERMANTOWN

B&B Connections 303

P.O. Box 21
Devon, PA, 19333
(800) 448-3619; (215) 687-3565

Rhododendron line the long drive up to this Quaker-built 1870s home. The lovely front porch overlooks the garden. Two large, comfortable guest rooms on the second floor, one with a double bed and the other with twins. Shared bath, full breakfast. Resident dog; no smoking. $30-35.

B&B Connections 318

P.O. Box 21
Devon, PA, 19333
(800) 448-3619; (215) 687-3565

This large Victorian home dates back 120 years and offers two bedrooms and a third-floor apartment. A sitting room with TV is available. Shared bath with antique tub. The three-room apartment offers one double and three twin beds, full kitchen, and bath. A full breakfast is provided. Resident dog; no smoking. $35-50.

Bed & Breakfast Connections 330

P.O. Box 21
Devon, PA, 19333
(800) 448-3619

This large turn-of-the-century home offers a delightful second-floor guest room furnished with antiques. French doors lead to your private adjoining bath. A continental breakfast is served in your room. Smoking outside on the porch; resident cat. $42.50.

B&B Connections 331

P.O. Box 21
Devon, PA, 19333
(800) 448-3619; (215) 687-3565

Circa 1885, this home offers two second-floor guest rooms with connecting bath; one with a single canopied bed and the other with two twins. A continental-plus breakfast is served in the dining room. An ideal location for visiting Historic Germantown or the interesting shops of Chestnut Hill. An eighteen-minute train ride from the heart of Philadelphia. No smoking; resident dog. $35.

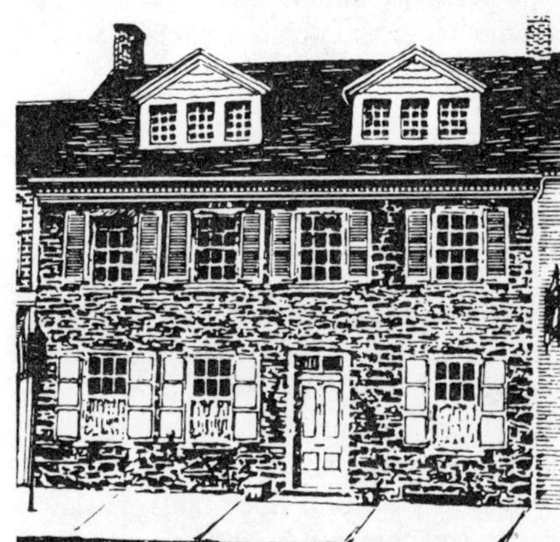

The Brafferton Inn

GETTYSBURG

The Brafferton Inn

44 York Street
Gettysburg, PA, 17325
(717) 337-3423

This 1786 stone home is listed on the National Register of Historic Places. Enjoy our colonial antiques, stenciled decor, and full breakfast served near a primitive mural. Experience Gettysburg in the first house built in town. Featured in the February 1988 issue of *Country Living* magazine.

Hosts: Mimi & Jim Agard
Rooms: 10 (6 PB; 4 SB) $55-95
Full Breakfast
Credit Cards: A, B
Notes: 2, 4, 5, 7 (limited), 8 (over 7), 9, 10, 11, 12, 13, 14

Hershey Bed & Breakfast 9

P.O. Box 208
Hershey, PA, 17033
(717) 533-2928

A large, comfortable home built in the mid 1800s with four guest rooms and shared bath. This dwelling has a traditional setting surrounded by history. Many well-known landmarks are within walking distance. Air-conditioning, continental breakfast. $65-75.

Hickory Bridge Farm

231 Hickory Bridge Road
Gettysburg, PA, 17353
(717) 642-5261

Quietly located at the edge of the mountains just eight miles west of Gettysburg. Country cottages in a wooded location by a pure mountain stream. Dinners are offered Friday, Saturday, and Sunday in a restored barn furnished with fine antiques. Family owned and operated for fifteen years.

Hosts: Mary Lynn & Robert Martin, Dr. & Mrs. James Hammett
Rooms: 4 (PB) $45-79
Full Breakfast
Minimum stay weekends: 2
Credit Cards: A, B
Notes: 2, 4, 5, 7, 8, 9, 11, 12, 13

Keystone Inn

231 Hanover Street
Gettysburg, PA, 17325
(717) 337-3888

Keystone Inn is a large late-Victorian brick house, filled with lots of natural woodwork. The guest rooms are bright, cheerful, and air-conditioned. The soft pastels and ruffles give you a warm welcome. Each room has a reading nook and writing desk. Choose a breakfast to suit your mood from our full breakfast menu.

Hosts: Wilmer & Doris Martin
Rooms: 4 (2 PB; 2 SB) $60-70
Full Breakfast
Credit Cards: A, B
Notes: 2, 4 (Nov.-March), 8, 9, 10, 11, 12, 13

The Old Appleford Inn

218 Carlisle Street
Gettysburg, PA, 17325
(717) 337-1711

This three-story Victorian mansion, built in 1867 by Judge Robt. McCurdy, has a piano and fireplace in the antique-filled living room, a library with fireplace, apple stenciling in the dining room. Twelve elegant bedrooms, each uniquely decorated, all with private baths. There's a plant-filled sun room with white wicker, and a large, open front porch. Complimentary sherry and full breakfast. Surrounded by Gettysburg College, the battlefield, a nearby ski area, and places to shop for antiques.

Hosts: Maribeth & Frank Skradski
Rooms: 12 (PB) $78-98 + tax
Full Breakfast
Credit Cards: A, B, C
Notes: 2, 5, 8 (over 14), 9, 12, 13, 14

GORDONVILLE

The Osceola Mill House

313 Osceola Mill Road
Gordonville, PA, 17529
(717) 768-3758

The Osceola Mill House is located in scenic Lancaster County, surrounded by Amish farms in a quaint, historic setting. Antiques and reproductions, poster beds, fireplaces, and Amish quilts. Close to restaurants, craft and antique shops.

Hosts: Robin & Sterling Schoen
Rooms: 4 (SB) $85
Full Breakfast
Minimum stay holidays: 2
Credit Cards: No
Closed Dec. 24-Jan. 2 & Easter
Notes: 2, 8 (over 12), 9

Beechmont Inn

HANOVER

Beechmont Inn

315 Broadway
Hanover, PA, 17331
(717) 632-3013

An elegant 1834 Federal inn with antiques, fireplace, air-conditioning. Enjoy a gourmet breakfast in your room, the dining room, or outdoors under the vine-covered trellis. Enjoy great antiquing in nearby New Oxford. Located thirteen miles from Gettysburg; Pennsylvania Dutch country nearby.

Hosts: Terry & Monna Hormel
Doubles: 7 (PB) $67.84-100.70
Full Breakfast
Credit Cards: A, B
Notes: 2, 5, 7 (restricted), 8 (over 12), 9, 10, 11, 12, 13 (XC)

HARRISBURG

Hershey Bed & Breakfast 6

P.O. Box 208
Hershey, PA, 17033
(717) 533-2928

A comfortable home offering two B&B rooms and shared bath. Pool, air conditioning, full breakfast. Smokers welcome. $55.

Hershey Bed & Breakfast 7

P.O. Box 208
Hershey, PA, 17033
(717) 533-2928

This country home offers you a king-sized waterbed, private bath, air-conditioning, and full breakfast. Minutes from Hershey Park. Resident dog and cat. $55-65.

Academy Street B&B

HAWLEY

Academy Street B&B

528 Academy Street
Hawley, PA, 18428
(717) 226-3430
Winter phone: (201) 316-8148

Outstanding historic 1863 Italianate Victorian built by Civil War hero, the first sheriff of Wayne County. Near largest and most

6 Pets welcome: 7 Smoking allowed: 8 Children welcome: 9 Social drinking allowed: 10 Tennis available: 11 Swimming available: 12 Golf available: 13 Skiing available: 14 May be booked through travel agents

beautiful recreational lake in state, with all activities. Convenient to I-84. Lovely furnished inn; full gourmet breakfast and afternoon tea. Large bright, airy, air-conditioned rooms.

Host: Judith Lazan
Rooms: 7 (3 PB; 4 SB) $65-75
Full Breakfast
Credit Cards: A, B
Closed Nov.-April
Notes: 7, 9, 10, 11, 12

The Settlers Inn

4 Main Street
Hawley, PA, 18428
(717) 226-2993

A grand Tudor-style hotel beside the park in the village of Hawley. Near Lake Wallenpaupack and many recreational activities. Elegant dining featuring a creative regional menu. Complimentary afternoon tea is served by the fireplace or on the spacious front porch. Enjoy specialty shopping, antiquing, museums, and summer theaters.

Hosts: Grant & Jeanne Genzlinger
Rooms: 18 (PB) $60-80
Full Breakfast
Credit Cards: A, B, C
Notes: 2, 3, 4, 5, 7, 8, 9, 10, 11, 12, 13, 14

HERSHEY

Hershey Bed & Breakfast 1

P.O. Box 208
Hershey, PA, 17033
(717) 533-2928

Lovely home near the Hershey Medical Center. One B&B room with private bath, full or continental breakfast, air conditioning. Resident dog; no smoking. $50.

Hershey Bed & Breakfast 2

P.O. Box 208
Hershey, PA, 17033
(717) 533-2928

Formerly the Milton Hershey Boys School, this large, comfortable brick home is located just north of town. Convenient to Hershey museums, park, rose gardens, Chocolate World, sports arena and stadium, theater, and outdoor recreation. Twelve guest rooms; one with private bath, others share four baths. Continental breakfast. Resident cat, handicapped accessibility, air-conditioning, no smoking. $50-55.

Hershey Bed & Breakfast 3

P.O. Box 208
Hershey, PA, 17033
(717) 533-2928

1700 log home on a lovely horse farm. Country roads for walking or biking, and field and woods for hiking. One guest room with private half-bath and sitting room. Resident pets. No smoking, continental breakfast. Children over six are welcome at a charge of $10. $65.

Hershey Bed & Breakfast 4

P.O. Box 208
Hershey, PA, 17033
(717) 533-2928

Countryside home with one guest room and private bath. No smoking. Resident cat and dog. A full breakfast is served on weekends; continental during the week. $55.

Hershey Bed & Breakfast 5

P.O. Box 208
Hershey, PA, 17033
(717) 533-2928

This home near the Hershey Motor Lodge offers three B&B rooms, shared bath, full breakfast. Children are welcome. $55-60.

HESSTON

Aunt Susie's Country Vacations

RD 1, Box 225
Hesston, PA, 16647
(814) 658-3638

Experience country living in a warm, friendly atmosphere in a Victorian parsonage or a renovated country store and post office. All rooms are nicely furnished with antiques and oil paintings. Raystown Lake is nearby for recreation; boating, swimming, and fishing are within three miles. Bring your family to the country.

Hosts: Joan, John, and Susan
Rooms: 8 (2 PB; 6 SB) $45-50
Continental-plus Breakfast
Credit Cards: No
Notes: 2, 5, 8, 9, 10, 11, 12

HICKORY

Shady Elms Farm B&B

RD 1, Box 188
Hickory, PA, 15340
(412) 356-7755

Restored early 1800 colonial mansion on 140 acre working farm. Furnished with antiques. Swimming and fishing pond. Winter sledding, skiing, and ice skating. Seven miles from intersection of I-70 and I-79. Close to Washington and Jefferson, Bethany, and West Liberty colleges.

Hosts: Marjorie & Connie Curran
Rooms: 3 (2 PB; 1 SB) $45-50
Full Breakfast
Credit Cards: No
Notes: 2, 5, 6, 7, 8, 9, 10, 11, 12

HILLSGROVE

The Tannery House

Box 99, Route 87
Hillsgrove, PA, 18619
(717) 924-3505

Located in picturesque Sullivan County, in the village of Hillsgrove, our country home has an old-fashioned wraparound porch. Summer breakfasts are served in the gazebo. Furnishings are antiques and collectibles, and there is a Victorian parlor with player piano. We are surrounded by state forest where you can enjoy cross-country skiing, hunting, fly-fishing, canoeing, and hiking.

Hosts: Linda & Dennis Renninger
Singles: 3 (SB) $21.15
Rooms: 4 (1 PB; 3 SB) $42.29-53
Continental Breakfast
Credit Cards: A, B (surcharge)
Notes: 2 (2 weeks in advance), 5, 7 (limited), 8, 9, 13 (XC)

HOLICONG

Ash Mill Farm

Box 202
Holicong, PA, 18928
(215) 794-5373

Ten sheep-filled bucolic acres in Bucks County. Enjoy your country breakfast and afternoon tea with Mozart, Bach, and Vivaldi. Six antique-filled rooms just minutes from New Hope.

Hosts: Patricia & Jim Auslander
Rooms: 6 (4 PB; 2 SB) $75-125
Full Breakfast
Credit Cards: A, B
Notes: 2, 5, 8 (over 15), 9, 10, 11, 12, 13 (XC)

HOLTWOOD

Country Cottage

B&B of Southeast Pennsylvania
146 W. Philadelphia Avenue
Boyertown, PA, 19512
(215) 367-4688

In Amish country, this house sits on top of a hill. There are two decks for sitting and a ramp for a wheel chair. A small bedroom with double bed has a private bath. The living room with sofabed has a large stone fireplace. In an alcove off the dining room is a complete kitchen. Accommodations are possible for up to ten people in one party. $65.

JERSEY SHORE

Sommerville Farms B&B

RD 4, Box 22
Jersey Shore, PA, 17740
(717) 398-2368

A Victorian farmhouse, comfortably furnished with antiques, located on a 200-acre working farm. Historic area along the West Branch of the Susquehanna River and scenic Pine Creek Valley. Fishing, cross-country skiing, boating, hiking the Appalachian Trail, antique auctions and shops, Penn State football games.

Hosts: Bill & Jane Williams
Rooms: 6 (SB) $42.40
Full Breakfast
Minimum stay during foliage weekends: 2
Credit Cards: A, B
Notes: 2, 5, 8, 9, 11, 12, 13

Kane Manor B&B

JIM THORPE

The Harry Packer Mansion

Packer Hill
Jim Thorpe, PA, 18229
(717) 325-8566

This 1874 Second Empire mansion features original appointments and ultra-Victorian decor. Completely restored for tours, B&B, fabulous Mystery Weekends, and a host of other activities. The adjoining carriage house is elegantly decorated in a hunt motif.

Hosts: Bob & Patricia Handwerk
Rooms: 13 (8 PB; 5 SB) $75-110
Full Breakfast
Credit Cards: A, B
Notes: 2, 5, 9, 10, 11, 12, 13, 14

KANE

Kane Manor B&B

230 Clay Street
Kane, PA, 16735
(814) 837-6522

We are one of the best-kept secrets in the Alleghenies. Come and discover for yourself the feeling of being surrounded by the Allegheny National Forest. Step inside the inn and you'll find yourself surrounded by history. All ten guest rooms are decorated differently, and all have their own personality. Hiking, boating, swimming, golfing, cross-country skiing. Gathering Room, Gift Shoppe, and Cellar Pub.

Host: Laurie Anne Dalton
Rooms: 10 (6 PB; 4 SB) $69-89
Continental Breakfast weekdays; full on weekends
Minimum stay during Sept.-Oct. and Jan.-Feb. weekends: 2
Credit Cards: A, B, C
Notes: 2, 5, 7, 8, 9, 10, 11, 12, 13, 14

KENNETT SQUARE

Meadow Spring Farm

201 East Street Road
Kennett Square, PA, 19348
(215) 444-3903

This B&B, located on a working farm in the Brandywine with cows, pigs, lambs, and horses, has a pool, hot tub, and solarium, Amish quilts, Laura Ashley linens, and a game room for your enjoyment. Dinner is available with advance notice. Some of the available activities in the area include canoeing and tubing, museums, tennis, bicycling, hot-air balloon rides. Five minutes from Longwood Gardens and minutes away from other Brandywine Valley attractions.

Host: Anne Hicks
Rooms: 6 (3 PB; 3 SB) $55-70
Full Breakfast
Credit Cards: No
Notes: 2, 4, 5, 7, 8, 9, 11, 12, 14

Meadow Spring Farm

KING OF PRUSSIA

B&B Connections 207

P.O. Box 21
Devon, PA, 19333
(800) 448-3619; (215) 687-3565

A lovely modern home nestled among tall shade trees and convenient to Villanova University, Bryn Mawr College, Valley Forge Park, and the Valley Forge Convention Center. Ground-floor room with a queen bed adjoins the family room with TV and fireplace. The sofa converts for sleeping extra family members. Private bath, full breakfast. Resident cats; no smoking. $55.

KINZERS

Sycamore Haven Farm

35 South Kinzer Road
Kinzers, PA, 17535
(717) 442-4901

We are a dairy farm located fifteen miles east of Lancaster, right in Pennsylvania Dutch country. Our rooms are newly papered and painted, and we have a porch in the back of the house with a lovely swing. We also have a balcony with lounge chairs and forty dairy cows that we milk morning and evening. The children will really enjoy our many kittens and pet sheep, who like a lot of attention.

Hosts: Charles & Janet Groff
Rooms: 3 (SB) $30
Continental Breakfast
Credit Cards: No
Notes: 2, 5, 6, 8, 10

KULPSVILLE

Pool House

B&B of Southeast Pennsylvania
146 W. Philadelphia Avenue
Boyertown, PA, 19512
(215) 367-4688

Located less than a mile from the exit of the northeast extension of the Pennsylvania Turnpike, this converted carriage house overlooks the in-ground pool. Guests may take a quick dip at the convenience of the hosts. The cottage has a large living room with queen sofabed, a small corner kitchen, dining area, and private courtyard. Close to Skippack Village. $75.

KUTZTOWN

Crystal Cottage

B&B of Southeast Pennsylvania
146 W. Philadelphia Avenue
Boyertown, PA, 19512
(215) 367-4688

Separate from the main house on 20 acres, four miles north of Kutztown, the old summer kitchen of this farm has been turned into a self-contained suite. Breakfast is brought from the main house, but there is a kitchen in the cottage. $50-60.

Roebling Delaware Inn

LACKAWAXEN

Roebling Delaware Inn

Scenic Drive
Lackawaxen, PA, 18435
(717) 685-7900

Classic inn on the majestic upper Delaware River, where Zane Grey wrote "Riders of the Purple Sage" and where Roebling built the forerunner of the Brooklyn Bridge. Endless mountains surround. Old World charm plus private baths, TV, air-conditioning, queen beds. Canoeing, rafting, fishing, tennis, and skiing nearby. Midweek specials.

Hosts: Donald & JoAnn Jahn
Rooms: 5 (PB) $49-75
Full Breakfast
Minimum stay holidays: 2
Credit Cards: A, B, C
Closed Christmas
Notes: 2, 5, 7 (restricted), 8, 9, 10, 11, 12, 13, 14

LAHASKA

Golden Plough Inn

Route 202 & Street Road
Lahaska, PA, 18931
(215) 794-4002; (215) 794-4003; FAX (215) 794-4001

Each of the 45 elegant guest rooms reflects the charm of eighteenth-century American country style: cherry wood, exquisite fabrics, Jacuzzis, balconies, fireplaces. All have private baths, dressing areas, refrigerators, air conditioning, TV. Adjacent to Peddler's Village, six restaurants, dinner theater, and eighty specialty shops. Gardens, festivals, antiques, and New Hope galleries nearby. Washington's Crossing, vineyards, and the canals along the Delaware River are handy.

Hosts: Earl Jamison & Robert Cassidy
Rooms: 45 (PB) $85-200 (suites)
Continental Breakfast
Credit Cards: A, B, C, E, F
Notes: 2, 3, 4, 5, 7, 8, 9, 10, 11, 12, 13, 14

Golden Plough Inn

LAMPETER

The Walkabout Inn

837 Village Road
Lampeter, PA, 17537
(717) 464-0707

The Walkabout Inn is an authentic British style B&B in the heart of the Amish country, convenient to all major attractions. The house is a 22-room brick 1925 Mennonite farmhouse with wraparound porches. Australian-born Richard and his wife, Maggie, serve a full five-course candlelight breakfast. Guest rooms have antiques and cable TV. Restaurant guides and coupons are available, and Richard will plot your day with exciting things to do and see. Anniversay/honeymoon specials.

Hosts: Richard & Margaret Mason
Rooms: 5 (3 PB; 2 SB) $45-75
Full Breakfast
Credit Cards: A, B, C
Notes: 2, 4, 5, 7, 8, 9, 10, 11, 12, 14

LANCASTER

Buona Notte B&B

2020 Marietta Avenue
Lancaster, PA, 17603
(717) 295-2597

Turn-of-the-century home with large, comfortable rooms, wraparound porch, large backyard and picnic table. Hershey Park, Gettysburg area and Pennsylvania Dutch country are all nearby. Breakfast includes homemade breads, muffins, coffee cakes, and jams. French and Italian are spoken here. Franklin & Marshall College is two miles away.

Hosts: Joe & Anna Predoti
Rooms: 3 (1 PB; 2 SB) $45-50
Continental Breakfast
Credit Cards: No
Notes: 5, 8, 10, 12

Hershey Bed & Breakfast 12

P.O. Box 208
Hershey, PA, 17033
(717) 533-2928

Country farmhouse, c. 1817, situated on a working dairy farm near Hershey, Lancaster, and Harrisburg, at Exit 20. Two guest rooms with shared bath, plus a cottage that sleeps four with private bath. Full breakfast; no smoking. $55.

Hershey Bed & Breakfast 13

P.O. Box 208
Hershey, PA, 17033
(717) 533-2928

Farmhouse inn, c. 1738, nestled on 12 acres of farmland in Lancaster County. Located just off Route 283 between Lancaster and Harrisburg. Three guest rooms with private or shared bath. Continental breakfast. No smokers; resident cat. $65-75.

Hershey Bed & Breakfast 14

P.O. Box 208
Hershey, PA, 17033
(717) 533-2928

Historic Civil War brick house located near Routes 30 and 501. Seven guest rooms, including family suites, with private or shared bath. Continental breakfast. No smoking. $65-95.

Hollinger House B&B

2336 Hollinger Road
Lancaster, PA, 17602-4728
(717) 464-3050

This Adams-style house, built in 1870, offers large rooms, high ceilings, wraparound porch, and 5.5 acres of manicured grounds. Close to good restaurants, Amish country, historic and family attractions. Mennonite owned and operated. German spoken.

Host: Jean M. Thomas
Rooms: 5 (1 PB; 4 SB) $35-55
Full Breakfast
Credit Cards: No
Notes: 2, 5, 8, 9, 10, 11, 12

Meadowview Guest House

2169 New Holland Pike, Route 23
Lancaster, PA, 17601
(717) 299-4017

Located in the heart of the Pennsylvania Dutch area, close to historic sites, antiques, farmers and flea markets, and excellent restaurants. Large air-conditioned rooms, guest kitchen with coffee and tea. To help you enjoy our beautiful county, personalized maps will be provided.

Hosts: Ed & Sheila Christie
Rooms: 3 (1 PB; 2 SB) $25-40
Continental Breakfast
Credit Cards: No
Closed Dec. 1 - March 14
Notes: 2, 8 (over 6), 9, 10, 11, 12

Witmer's Tavern

Witmer's Tavern—Historic 1725 Inn

2014 Old Philadelphia Pike
Lancaster, PA, 17602
(717) 299-5305

Sole survivor of the sixty-two inns that once lined the nation's first turnpike between Philadelphia and Lancaster, Witmer's Tavern still operates as a lodging facility. The four-story blue limestone inn, with its individual room fireplaces, early iron door hinges and latches, nine-over-six bubbly windows, and early woodwork, served to provision early settlers on their way west. Today's guests enjoy fresh flowers, antiques, quilts, fireplaces, and the romance of the old inn.

Host: Brant Hartung
Rooms: 7 (2 PB; 5 SB) $55-125
Continental Breakfast
Credit Cards: No
Notes: 2, 5, 7, 9, 10, 11, 12, 13, 14

LANCASTER/STRASBURG

Limestone Inn B&B—Circa 1786

33 East Main Street
Strasburg, PA, 17579
(717) 687-8392

Enjoy life in the slow lane at one of the most photographed homes in Lancaster County. In Strasburg's historic district, this 204+-year-old home is listed on the National Register of Historic Places. The Baltimore and Washingtonian magazines' "Great Getaways" recommend our accommodation when visiting the Amish country.

Hosts: Jan & Dick Kennell
Rooms: 4 (2 PB; 2 SB) $65-80 + tax
Full Breakfast
Minimum stay weekends & holidays: 2
Credit Cards: C
Notes: 2, 5, 7 (restricted), 8 (over 12), 9, 10, 11, 12

Limestone Inn B&B

LANDIS STORE

Cottage at the Quiltery

B&B of Southeast Pennsylvania
146 W. Philadelphia Avenue
Boyertown, PA, 19512
(215) 367-4688

This cottage has been skillfully decorated with antiques, handmade furniture, and quilts. The living room has a wood-burning stove and bay window. Hand-hewn stairs lead to a bedroom with a double bed and private bath. Breakfast is served in the main house. Good restaurants and antique shops are in the area. $70.

LIBERTY

Hill-Top Haven

RD 1, Box 5-C
Liberty, PA, 16930
(717) 324-2608

This comfortable rambling ranch home is located 29 miles north of Williamsport, in a rural mountain area, surrounded by fields, woods, and flower beds. The house is filled with handmade crafts and many antiques. State parks, tennis, skiing, golf, biking, and snowmobile trails are close by.

Hosts: Richard & Betty Landis
Rooms: 2 (SB) $30-35
Continental Breakfast
Credit Cards: No
Notes: 5, 8, 10, 11

LITITZ

Alden House

62 East Main Street
Lititz, PA, 17543
(717) 627-3363

Circa 1850 pre-Civil War townhouse, located in the center of the historic district of Lititz, a charming Moravian community. Walk to quaint shops, restaurants, and museums. Ten minutes to Lancaster and the Amish attractions. Three large porches to relax on at day's end.

Host: Gloria Adams
Rooms: 7 (5 PB; 2 SB) $68.90-100.70
Continental-plus Breakfast
Minimum stay weekends & holidays: 2
Credit Cards: A, B
Notes: 2, 5, 7, 8, 9

Swiss Woods B&B

500 Blantz Road
Lititz, PA, 17543
(717) 627-3358

A visit to Swiss Woods, nestled on the edge of the woods overlooking Speedwell Forge Lake, is reminiscent of a trip to one of Switzerland's guest houses. Located in beautiful Lancaster County, home of the Pennsylvania Dutch, Swiss Woods was designed with comfort and atmosphere in mind. The gardens are landscaped with a unique variety of flowering perennials and annuals. Enjoy breakfast in our "Ankerstube" dominated by a sandstone fireplace with lots of natural woodwork and large, sunny windows. Our rooms feature queen beds and private baths, two with whirlpool baths, patios, or balconies.

Hosts: Debrah & Werner Mosimann
Rooms: 7 (PB) $65-100
Full Breakfast
Credit Cards: A, B
Notes: 2, 5, 8, 9, 14

LOGANVILLE

Country Spun Farm B&B

Box 117, Loganville, PA, 17342
(717) 428-1162

Delightful countryside accommodations with private baths on a working sheep farm afford the visitor a beautiful setting, individually planned day trips, extensive gardens, and hospitality-plus. A full breakfast is served in the country kitchen or by the garden. Central to York, Lancaster, Gettysburg, and Hershey; one mile from I-83, Exit 3.

Hosts: Greg & Martha Lau
Rooms: 2 (PB) $55-65
Full Breakfast
Credit Cards: A, B, D
Notes: 2, 5, 8 (12 and over), 9, 10, 11, 12, 14

MACUNGIE

Victorian Retreat

B&B of Southeast Pennsylvania
146 W. Philadelphia Avenue
Boyertown, PA, 19512
(215) 367-4688

Two rooms on the second floor, one with a king waterbed and full private bath. Off the bedroom is an enclosed porch. The second room has a queen bed and private bath with shower. Guests are welcome on Friday, Saturday, and Sunday only. Resident cat. $50-55.

MALVERN

Bed & Breakfast Connections 215

P.O. Box 21
Devon, PA, 19333
(800) 448-3619

Since 1745 this elegant country inn has been a premier stop for hungry travelers. Located along the Main Line and convenient to the Brandywine Valley, Valley Forge Park, and suburban universities, the inn offers eight suites with four-poster beds. The inn also serves lunch and dinner; continental breakfast is included in the rate. $110-165.

MANHEIM

Herr Farmhouse Inn

2256 Huber Drive
Manheim, PA, 17545
(717) 653-9852

Historic circa 1738 stone farmhouse nestled on 11.5 scenic acres of farmland. The inn has been tastefully restored, retaining original pine floors, moldings, and six working fireplaces. The perfect retreat, with Lancaster County attractions and fine restaurants nearby.

Host: Barry Herr
Rooms: 3 (1 PB; 2 SB) $68.90-90.10
Suite: 1 (PB)
Continental-plus Breakfast
Minimum stay weekends & holidays: 2
Credit Cards: A, B
Notes: 2, 5, 7, 8 (over 5), 9

MERCER

Magoffin Inn

129 South Pitt
Mercer, PA, 16137
(412) 662-4611

When visiting the Magoffin Inn, one is reminded of a gentler, quieter era. The house, a brick Queen Anne Victorian, was built in 1884 by Dr. Montrose Magoffin as a home. The Magoffin Inn has nine guest rooms for weary travelers, completely furnished in antiques. Other amenities include clock radios and TV.

Hosts: Jacque McClellann & Gene Slagle
Rooms: 9 (7 PB; 2 SB) $50-90
Full Breakfast
Credit Cards: A, B, C
Closed Christmas & Thanksgiving
Notes: 2, 3 (Mon.-Sat.), 4 (Tues.-Sat.), 8, 9, 10, 11, 12, 14

The Stranahan House B&B

117 East Market Street
Mercer, PA, 16137
(412) 662-4516

Enjoy a peaceful night's rest and a delicious breakfast amid antiques and cherished family heirlooms. The 150-year-old Colonial Empire red brick home is near the center of town and the county courthouse. Close to the historical society, antique shops, Amish country, forges, and colleges. Five minutes from I-79 and I-80.

Hosts: Jim & Ann
Rooms: 2 (1 PB; 1 SB) $50-60
Full Breakfast
Credit Cards: No
Notes: 2, 5, 8, 9, 10, 11, 12, 14

MERION STATION

B&B Connections 211

P.O. Box 21
Devon, PA, 19333
(800) 448-3619; (215) 687-3565

Private back stairs lead to the guest rooms in this comfortable suburban home centrally located to suburban or Center City universities and historic attractions. Sitting room with TV, bedroom with a double bed and adjoining private bath. Wholesome breakfast of natural foods; no smoking. $50.

MERTZTOWN

Longswamp B&B

RD 2, Box 26
Mertztown, PA, 19539
(215) 682-6197

This 200-year-old-home, furnished with antiques and every comfort, is set in gorgeous countryside, yet is close to Reading, Kutztown, Allentown, and Amish country. Delicious bountiful breakfasts draw raves from guests.

Hosts: Elsa & Dean Dimick
Rooms: 9 (5 PB; 4 SB) $53-68.90
Full Breakfast
Credit Cards: A, B
Notes: 2, 5, 8, 9, 10, 11, 12, 13

Mansard Mansion

B&B of Southeast Pennsylvania
146 West Philadelphia Avenue
Boyertown, PA, 19512
(215) 367-4688

Located in a hidden valley, this B&B offers two suites, each consisting of two bedrooms with queen beds and private bath. On the second floor there are two rooms with private bath. There is a sitting room with wood-burning fireplace. Guests are welcome to use the basketball court in the barn, and children are welcome. A separate building once used to hide runaway slaves is now refurbished as a hideaway room, with a queen bed, working fireplace, and private bath. Off the courtyard is a three-room country-style private suite for two couples or a family. Each bedroom there has its own bath. A bedroom on the first floor has a fireplace and two single beds. Off the sitting room and up a small flight of stairs is the second bedroom, with twin beds and private bath. $70-150.

MIDDLETOWN

Hershey Bed & Breakfast 10

P.O. Box 208
Hershey, PA, 17033
(717) 533-2928

Gracious home set on 9 acres of land with a deck facing the woods. Ten minutes from Hershey Park and local attractions. Two rooms, shared bath, full breakfast. No smoking. $45.

MILFORD

Black Walnut B&B Inn

RD 2, Box 9285
Firetower Road
Milford, PA, 18337
(717) 296-6322

Tudor-style stone house with historic marble fireplace, twelve charming guest rooms with antiques and brass beds. A 160-acre estate, quiet and peaceful, conveniently located near horseback riding, antiquing, golf, skiing, rafting, and canoeing on the Delaware River.

Host: Hermien Ankersmit
Rooms: 12 (8 PB; 4 SB) $50-100
Full Breakfast
Credit Cards: A, B, C
Notes: 2, 5, 9, 11, 12, 13

Cliff Park Inn

RR 2, Box 8562
Milford, PA, 18337
(717) 296-6491; (800) 225-6535

A Mobil three-star-rated golfers' country inn with gourmet restaurant. Cliff Park is surrounded by an established regulation nine-hole golf course edged by deep woods.

Come enjoy gracious hospitality in historic surroundings.

Host: Harry Buchanan
Rooms: 18 (PB) $90-135
Full Breakfast
Credit Cards: A, B, C, D, E
Notes: 2, 3, 4, 5, 7, 8, 9, 10, 11, 12, 13, 14

MILLERSVILLE

Walnut Hill B&B

80 Walnut Hill Road
Millersville, PA, 17551
(717) 872-2283

Come and enjoy the quiet country living in our 1815 stone farmhouse. Relax on our screened porch or in your air-conditioned room. Close to attractions, but not in the mainstream. Near Millersville University.

Hosts: Melvin & Kathryn Shertzer
Rooms: 3 (SB) $40
Full Breakfast
Credit Cards: No
Notes: 2, 5, 7, 8, 10, 11, 12

MT. AIRY

B&B Connections 315

P.O. Box 21
Devon, PA, 19333
(800) 448-3619; (215) 687-3565

This 42-room English country manor was recently placed on the National Register of Historic Homes. Accommodations range from a twin-bedded room with a shared bath to a lovely suite with fireplace. Full breakfast is served on fresh linens, with fine silver. $69-75.

Bed & Breakfast Connections 321

P.O. Box 21
Devon, PA, 19333
(800) 448-3619

The quaint shops and restaurants of Chestnut Hill are only a short walk away from this twelve-room stone home. One large double room. A second room offers twin beds and a comfortable sitting area. The bath is shared. On weekends, a full gourmet breakfast is served; continental-plus on weekdays. No smoking; resident cats. $55-60.

B&B Connections 348

P.O. Box 21
Devon, PA, 19333
(800) 448-3619; (215) 687-3565

A lovely 1920s stone colonial on a tree-lined suburban street convenient to Chestnut Hill, historic Germantown, the Medical College of Pennsylvania, and the train the Philadelphia. Two cozy third-floor guest rooms, shared bath. Informal continental breakfast; no smoking; resident cat. $40.

MOUNT GRETNA

Hershey Bed & Breakfast 11

P.O. Box 208
Hershey, PA, 17033
(717) 533-2928

This inn offers a tranquil place where time seems to stand still. Eight guest rooms, private baths, continental breakfast. Adults only. $65-95.

MOUNT JOY

Cedar Hill Farm

305 Longenecker Road
Mount Joy, PA, 17552
(717) 653-4655

This 1817 stone farmhouse sits in a quiet area overlooking a stream. The host was born on this working farm. The charming bedrooms have private baths and are centrally air-conditioned. The farm is located near Amish farms and Hershey. Other attractions are nearby farmers' markets, antique shops, and interesting country villages.

Hosts: Russel & Gladys Swarr
Rooms: 4 (PB) $45-55
Continental-plus Breakfast
Credit Cards: A, B, C
Notes: 2, 5, 8, 9, 10, 11, 12, 13

Cedar Hill Farm

MOUNTVILLE

Mountville Antiques and B&B

407 East Main Street, Box 19
Mountville, PA, 17554
(717) 285-7200; 285-5956

Five miles west of Lancaster, PA. Six rooms furnished with antiques, four with private baths and queen beds, two with shared bath and double beds. Herb and flower garden surround the relaxing patio. Near all PA Dutch attractions, quilt shops, markets, and auctions. Chocolate World, Hershey, PA, and Gettysburg all within easy driving distance. Advance reservations preferred.

Hosts: Sam & Pat Reno
Rooms: 6 (4 PB; 2 SB) $55-65
Full Breakfast
Credit Cards: A, B
Notes: 8 (12 and over), 9, 10, 12, 13

MUNCY

The Bodine House

307 South Main Street
Muncy, PA, 17756
(717) 546-8949

Built in 1805 and located in the National Historic District of Muncy, the Bodine House offers guests the opportunity to enjoy the atmosphere of an earlier age. The comfortable rooms are furnished with antiques, and candlelight is used in the living room by the fireplace, where guests enjoy complimentary wine and cheese. Three blocks from town center, movies, restaurants, library, and shops.

Hosts: David & Marie Louise Smith
Rooms: 4 (3 PB; 1 SB) $50-60 + tax
Full Breakfast
Credit Cards: A, B, C
Notes: 2, 5, 8 (over 6), 9, 10, 11, 12, 13, 14

NEW CUMBERLAND

Hershey Bed & Breakfast 15

P.O. Box 208
Hershey, PA, 17033
(717) 533-2928

An eleven-room limestone farmhouse that sits on 3 acres high on a hill overlooking a creek. Legend has it that this house was part of the Underground Railroad. Each guest room has a double bed and comfortable seating with good lighting. One room has a private bath; two share a bath. Two rooms have large porches to enjoy in good weather. Furnishings throughout are antiques. Full breakfast. $70.

NEWFOUNDLAND

White Cloud

RD 1, Box 215
Newfoundland, PA, 18445
(717) 676-3162

We're located three miles south of Newfoundland on Route 447 and are a meatless, natural-foods inn and restaurant with 45 acres of wooded land, a tennis court, pool, library, and meditation room.

Hosts: George & Judy Wilkinson
Rooms: 20 (7 PB; 13 SB) $38.50-54
Full Breakfast
Credit Cards: A, B
Closed December 25
Notes: 2, 3, 4, 5, 6, 8, 9, 10, 11, 12, 13, 14

NEW HOPE

Backstreet Inn of New Hope

144 Old York Road
New Hope, PA, 18938
(215) 862-9571

The Backstreet Inn of New Hope offers the comfort and serenity of a small inn in the town of New Hope, Bucks County, Pennsylvania. We are located in a quiet, tucked-away street, yet within walking distance of the center of town.

Hosts: Bob Puccio & John Hein
Rooms: 7 (5 PB; 2 SB) $85-125
Full Breakfast
Credit Cards: A, B
Minimum stay weekends:2; holidays: 3
Notes: 2, 5, 7, 8, 10, 11, 12, 13, 14

Backstreet Inn of New Hope

Centre Bridge Inn

River Road
New Hope, PA, 18938
(215) 862-9139

A romantic country inn overlooking the Delaware River in historic Bucks County, featuring canopy beds and river views. Fine restaurant serving French-Continental cuisine and spirits in an old-world-style dining room with fireplace, or alfresco dining in season.

Host: Stephen R. Dugan
Rooms: 9 (PB) $80-125
Continental Breakfast
Minimum stay weekends: 2; holidays: 3
Credit Cards: A, B, C
Notes: 2, 4, 5, 7, 8 (over 8), 9, 10, 11, 12

Wedgwood Inn of New Hope

111 West Bridge Street
New Hope, PA, 18938
(215) 862-2570

Voted "Inn of the Year" by readers of inn guidebooks, this historic inn, situated on 2 acres of landscaped grounds, is steps from the village center. Antiques, fresh flowers, and Wedgwood china are the rule at the inn, where all house guests are treated like royalty.

Hosts: Carl A. Glassman & Nadine Silnutzer
Rooms: 12 (10 PB; 2 SB) $70-160
Continental-plus Breakfast
Minimum stay weekends: 2 ; holidays: 3
Credit Cards: No
Notes: 2, 5, 8, 9, 10, 11, 12, 13, 14

The Whitehall Inn

RD 2, Box 250
New Hope, PA, 18938
(215) 598-7945

Experience a 1794 estate with fireplaced rooms, heirloom sterling, European crystal and china. Afternoon high tea, chamber music, velour robes, chocolate truffles.

Swimming pool on premises, dressage horses, roses, and our legendary four-course candlelight breakfast featured in *Bon Appetit, Gourmet,* and *Food and Wine.* A very special inn!

Hosts: Mike & Suella Wass
Rooms: 6 (4 PB; 2 SB) $110-160
Full Breakfast
Minimum stay weekends: 2; holidays: 3
Credit Cards: A, B, C, D, E, F
Notes: 2, 5, 8 (over 12), 9, 10, 11, 12, 13, 14 (weekdays)

NEWTOWN SQUARE

Bed & Breakfast Connections 217

P.O. Box 21
Devon, PA, 19333
(800) 448-3619

A lovely suburban home centrally located to historic Philadelphia, the Brandywine Valley, and Valley Forge Park. A charming fieldstone colonial on the edge of a woods overlooking a pond and 5 acres of rolling hunt country. Three second-floor guest rooms, each with private bath. $75.

NORTH WALES

Joseph Ambler Inn

1005 Horsham Road
North Wales, PA, 19454
(215) 362-7500

Spend the evening in the original stone farmhouse, dating back to 1734, or in the newly converted 1820 stone bank barn also housing the restaurant, or the Corybeck tenant farmer's cottage. All rooms have private baths, telephones, and television, and each is uniquely decorated with antiques and reproductions.

Hosts: Steve & Terry Kratz
Rooms: 28 (PB) $92-149.80
Full Breakfast
Credit Cards: A, B, C, D, F
Notes: 2, 4, 5, 7, 8 (over 12), 9, 10, 11, 12

ORBISONIA

Salvino's Guest House

Route 522, Box 116
Orbisonia, PA, 17243
(814) 447-5616

Victorian home located in a small town in central Pennsylvania. There is a quilt shop next door; one-half mile from E.B.T. Steam RR and trolley museum. One hour from Lake Raystown, Old Bedrod Village, Belleville Amish country, flea market, and Cowans Gap State Park. Resident dogs.

Hosts: Elaine & Joe Salvino
Rooms: 5 (SB) $30-40
Continental Breakfast
Credit Cards: A, B
Notes: 2, 5, 6, 8

OXFORD

Hershey's Log House Inn B&B

15250 Limestone Road
Oxford, PA, 19363
(215) 932-9257

In a country setting with homey hospitality, quiet, and peace. Log house in a wooded area, with trails, animals, and birds to enjoy; recreational activities in the barn: roller skating, Ping-Pong, bicycling. Many attractive sights, Longwood Gardens, and museums. Near Philadelphia, Baltimore, Wilmington, and the Amish country in Lancaster.

Hosts: Ephraim & Arlene E. Hershey
Room: $40
Continental Breakfast
Notes: 5

PAOLI

Bed & Breakfast Connections 209

P.O. Box 21
Devon, PA, 19333
(800) 448-3619

Pleasant Grove Farm

A seasoned innkeeper at the New Jersey shore, this hostess is now opening her own home during the winter months. Located on a quiet cul-de-sac, it is convenient to suburban colleges and Valley Forge Park. The double room offers a bath shared with the hostess. There is also a TV den available. Continental breakfast is served in the country kitchen. No smoking. $45.

PALM/EAST GREENVILLE

Summerfield Farm

B&B of Southeast Pennsylvania
146 West Philadelphia Avenue
Boyertown, PA, 19512
(215) 367-4688

In a tiny Berks County village, this beautiful stone house is more than 200 years old. Hosts are antique dealers who have a shop in the large Pennsylvania Dutch barn behind the house. Two bedrooms, each with a double bed and antiques. The bath is shared if both rooms are occupied. Breakfast is served in the dining area of the kitchen. An in-ground pool is located near the barn if guest want to take a quick dip. No children; no smoking. $75.

PARADISE

Maple Lane Guest House

505 Paradise Lane
Paradise, PA, 17562
(717) 687-7479

We have clean, comfortable, air-conditioned rooms with canopy and poster beds, handmade quilts, hand stenciling, and antiques. This is a large dairy farm with winding stream and woodland in real Amish country, close to all the Pennsylvania Dutch attractions of Lancaster County.

Hosts: Edwin & Marion Rohrer
Rooms: 4 (2 PB; 2 SB) $45-58
Continental Breakfast
Minimum stay weekends: 2; holidays, 3
Credit Cards: No
Notes: 2, 5, 8, 10, 11, 12

PEACH BOTTOM

Pleasant Grove Farm

368 Pilottown Road
Peach Bottom, PA, 17563
(717) 548-3100

Come and enjoy our large, 175-year-old, Federal-style stone home. At one time a country store and post office. Century Farm Award. Watch the cows being milked or feed the pigs. Full country breakfast.

Hosts: Charles & Labertha Tindall
Rooms: 4 (SB) $37.10-42.40
Full Breakfast
Minimum stay weekdays & weekends: 2; holidays: 3
Credit Cards: No
Dinner available by prior arrangement
Notes: 2, 4, 5, 8, 11, 12

PENNSBURG

Chesterfield Farm II

B&B of Southeast Pennsylvania
146 West Philadelphia Avenue
Boyertown, PA, 19512
(215) 367-4688

Set in the middle of parkland, this old stone farmhouse has been refurbished with collectibles and antiques. On the second floor there are two guest rooms that share a bath. Children over ten are welcome, and infants. There is fishing and boat rental within a mile, and horseback riding and swimming within two miles. Smoking is restricted. One dog and two cats in residence. $60.

PHILADELPHIA

B&B Connections 102

P.O. Box 21
Devon, PA, 19333
(800) 448-3619; (215) 687-3565

Independence Square is one-half mile away from this townhouse. Your hosts are very knowledgeable about the city and will be happy to assist you in making sight-seeing plans. Your guest room with two twin beds is on the second floor with private bath. Continental-plus breakfast. $40.

B&B Connections 104

P.O. Box 21
Devon, PA, 19333
(800) 448-3619; (215) 687-3565

On the Pennsylvania Registry of Historic Homes, this three-story colonial townhouse is only five blocks from Independence Hall. Two third-floor guest rooms are decorated with antiques. One offers twin beds and the other a double. Shared connecting bath, TV, and small refrigerator for guests. A full breakfast is served in the dining room. $65.

B&B Connections 108

P.O. Box 21
Devon, PA, 19333
(800) 448-3619; (215) 687-3565

This charming townhouse is located just off Rittenhouse Square. The focal point of its guest room is the massive walnut antique double bed, floral drapes, and bookcases lining the wall. Private adjoining bath, private entrance. Gourmet continental breakfast is served in your room. No smoking; resident cats. $75.

Bed & Breakfast Connections 110

P.O. Box 21
Devon, PA, 19333
(800) 448-3619

This Victorian townhouse is walking distance to Children's Hospital and the University of Pennsylvania. Two second-floor guest rooms offer a queen bed with sitting area, couch, TV, and adjoining private bath. The second room is for the single traveler and shares a bath with the hostess. Full breakfast. $45.

Bed & Breakfast Connections 111

P.O. Box 21
Devon, PA, 19333
(800) 448-3619

This historically registered row home provides generous third-floor guest quarters and is near the University of Pennsylvania, Drexel University, the Civic Center, and Children's Hospital. One room has two twin beds and a double. Private bath. Continental-plus breakfast; laundry facilities, and refrigerator space. Resident smoker. $50.

Bed & Breakfast Connections 114

P.O. Box 21
Devon, PA, 19333
(800) 448-3619

This 1811 registered townhouse with a Society Hill address is right in the hub of historic Philadelphia and close to the attractions of New Market Square and South Street. A large third-floor room has a double bed, settee, and comfortable chairs to pull up to the fireplace. Private adjoining bath. A second-floor room provides a double bed and private bath. A full gourmet breakfast is served in the kitchen. No smoking. $60.

B&B Connections 120

P.O. Box 21
Devon, PA, 19333
(800) 448-3619; (215) 687-3565

A wrought-iron fence surrounds the cluster of unique brick townhouses designed by I.M. Pei and located just one block from Independence Park. Pei's trademark spiral staircase leads to the elegant second-floor sitting room with grand piano. On the third floor is a guest room with two twin beds and TV. Private bath. A continental breakfast is served on the massive antique dining room table downstairs or on the back patio. No smoking, resident dog. Two-night minimum stay. $55.

B&B Connections 122

P.O. Box 21
Devon, PA, 19333
(800) 448-3619; (215) 687-3565

Complete privacy awaits the guest in this townhouse located along Antique Row and within walking distance of the historic district. The guest room is bright and inviting, with double bed, TV, and phone. Sliding glass doors lead to a deck where you can relax and enjoy the city skyline. With private adjoining bath and full breakfast, this house is perfect for the business traveler. Resident cats. $55.

Bed & Breakfast Connections 126

P.O. Box 21
Devon, PA, 19333
(800) 448-3619

Located near the Italian Market in South Philly, this charming little street is still easily accessible to the historic area. Private third-floor accommodations are available with twin beds, sitting room, private bath. Full breakfast. Fluent Italian is spoken. No smoking. $40.

B&B Connections 128

P.O. Box 21
Devon, PA, 19333
(800) 448-3619; (215) 687-3565

This lovely Society Hill townhouse dates back to 1791 and is ideally located to all historic attractions. The first guest room is 2.5 floors above the elegant living room. The original random-width flooring has been preserved throughout the house. This room has a private adjoining bath. Two third-floor rooms share a connecting bath. A continental breakfast is served in the kitchen. Resident pipe smoker. $70.

Bed & Breakfast Connections 136

P.O. Box 21
Devon, PA, 19333
(800) 448-3619

Dating back to the 1830s, this brick townhouse has been restored. Located just one block from Washington Square and 1.5 blocks from Independence Hall. A twin room and double room are available on the third floor; shared bath. A second-floor living room offers a Franklin stove, TV, and stereo. Full breakfast; resident dog; smoking on the patio. $60.

Bed & Breakfast Connections 147

P.O. Box 21
Devon, PA, 19333
(800) 448-3619

Built between 1805 and 1810 and redone after the Civil War in the Federal style, this Society Hill townhouse saw further renovation when its current owners purchased it. Three guest rooms, one on the second floor with private bath and two on the third with private baths. Resident smoker. Two-night minimum on weekends. $75-80.

B&B Connections 148

P.O. Box 21
Devon, PA, 19333
(800) 448-3619; (215) 687-3565

Located within walking distance of the historic district, this historically certified building has recently been redone. Guests have a private entrance on the fourth floor, antique double bead, and beamed ceiling. Private adjoining bath and individually controlled thermostat. A continental breakfast is provided. No smoking. $65.

Germantown B&B

5925 Wayne Avenue
Philadelphia, PA, 19144
(215) 848-1375

Your 1900s oak bedroom in a 100-year-old house has cable TV and a private bath. This is a homestay with a family with three children. Twenty minutes to Independence Hall; walk to other historic sites, restaurants, and conveniences.

Hosts: Molly & Jeff Smith
Rooms: 1 (PB) $37.50
Continental Breakfast
Credit Cards: No
Notes: 2, 5, 8, 9, 11

La Reserve

1804 Pine Street
Philadelphia, PA, 19103
(215) 735-1137

La Reserve, *grande dame* of Philadelphia B&Bs, is a well-preserved 140-year-old private mansion in the Victorian Rittenhouse Square section of center city, which is the cultural soul of the city. Friendly black lab in residence. *Bienvenue a La Reserve.*

Host: John T. Lynagh
Rooms: 8 (2 PB; 6 SB) $40-75
Continental Breakfast
Credit Cards: No
Notes: 2, 5, 7, 8, 9, 10, 11, 12, 14

Cole's Log Cabin B&B

PINE BANK

Cole's Log Cabin B&B

RD 1, Box 98
Pine Bank, PA, 15354
(412) 451-8521

The Log Cabin B&B is made up of two colonial log homes, circa 1820s, joined together to form one large house. We are located in the extreme southwestern part of Pennsylvania, in a very rural farming area. Our major activities are hiking, bird watching, antiquing, and relaxing. We now have a very secluded, fully equipped lodge available for families or groups.

Hosts: Jane & Terry R. Cole
Rooms: 3 (1 PB; 2 SB) $50
Continental Breakfast
Credit Cards: No
Closed July 5-Aug. 15
Notes: 2, 7, 9, 11, 12, 14

POINT PLEASANT

Tattersall Inn

Box 569
Point Pleasant, PA, 18950
(215) 297-8233

Overlooking a river village, this manor house dates to the eighteenth century and features broad porches for relaxation and a walk-in fireplace for cool evenings. Enjoy our antique-furnished rooms and collection of vintage phonographs.

Hosts: Gerry & Herb Moss
Rooms: 7 (PB) $75-95
Continental Breakfast
Credit Cards: A, B, C
Notes: 2, 5, 7, 8, 9, 10, 11, 14

POTTSTOWN

Foxhill

B&B of Southeast Pennsylvania
146 West Philadelphia Avenue
Boyertown, PA, 19512
(215) 367-4688

The original owner of Foxhill obtained his land grant from William Penn, and the first house was built in 1750 with two additions in 1800 and 1840. The hosts' interests include photography, restoring antiques, and arranging dried flowers. They offer a double room with private bath on the second floor, up some very steep stairs. Smoking outside only; resident dog. Children are welcome. $45.

QUAKERTOWN

Sign of the Sorrel Horse

Box 243, Old Bethlehem Road
Quakertown, PA, 18951
(215) 536-4651

Built in 1749 of stone, near Lake Nockamixon, as a stagecoach stop. Secluded on 5 manicured acres. A gracious country inn with five antique-filled rooms, all with

Tattersall Inn

private baths. Includes sherry and fruits in the common area and fine gourmet dining. Swimming pool. AAA three-star rated.

Hosts: Monique Gaumont, Janvin & Jon Atkin
Rooms: 5 (PB) $85-125
Continental Breakfast
Credit Cards: A, B
Notes: 4, 5, 6, 9, 10, 11, 12, 13, 14

READING

Gallery Guest House

B&B of Southeast Pennsylvania
146 West Philadelphia Avenue
Boyertown, PA, 19512
(215) 367-4688

Located on the west side of Reading, this house offers a gallery featuring the work of a local sculptor. On this quiet, tree-lined street, the hostess offers a twin room with full bath. There is also a double and a single room which would share a bath if both were occupied. All guest rooms are on the second floor. Resident dog; no smoking. $50.

The House on the Old Canal

B&B of Southeast Pennsylvania
146 West Philadelphia Avenue
Boyertown, PA, 19512
(215) 367-4688

Within the sound of a 50-foot waterfall on the Schuykill River, this 180-year-old stone farmhouse has a wide porch and a view of the river. Your hostess prepares her own bread, relishes, and jellies. Two rooms on the second floor, one with a double bed and the other with a queen. A sitting room with TV and bath are shared by the guests. Breakfast will be served on the porch in summer and in the dining room at other times. A boat is available for fishing, and bicycles may be borrowed. Children are welcome with their own sleeping bags. Smoking is permitted in the sitting room. $60.

Hunter House

118 South Fifth Street
Reading, PA, 19602
(215) 374-6608

Located in historic downtown, this elegant circa 1840 restoration offers spacious rooms/suites with private bath and kitchens. Convenient to Reading's world-famous outlets, commercial center, antique markets, Amish country, state parks, and more. A casual and friendly atmosphere amid period

The Inn at Centre Park

furnishings and antiques creates a unique and sheltered urban experience.

Hosts: Norma & Ray Staron
Rooms: 4 (2 PB; 2 SB) $60-70
Full Breakfast
Credit Cards: A, B
Notes: 2, 5, 7, 8, 9, 10, 11, 12, 13

The Inn at Centre Park

730 Centre Avenue
Reading, PA, 19601
(215) 374-8557

Our mansion and carriage house, built in the late 1800s, are beautifully preserved examples of Victorian elegance. Original leaded glass, ornate plaster, paneled and carved woods. We have furnished the inn with consideration of your comfort and enjoyment. If you are traveling on business, your needs for FAX, phone service, and meeting space will be met. If your stay is strictly for pleasure, you will find our beautiful suites, large porches, and many fireplaces enchanting. We are located in the center of the city, a short drive from local antique markets and minutes from outlet shopping.

Rooms: 4 (PB) $130-190
Full Breakfast
Credit Cards: A, B, C
Notes: 2, 3, 4, 5, 7 (restricted), 8 (limited), 9, 10, 12

New Barn House

B&B of Southeast Pennsylvania
146 West Philadelphia Avenue
Boyertown, PA, 19512
(215) 367-4688

On a quiet side street convenient for the outlets and the antique and flea markets in Adamstown. The hostess, who is a quilter, has furnished the two second-floor guest rooms with her work. One room has a king bed with a sitting area. The second room has a queen bed and a double bed. Each room has a color TV. The bath, with an antique footed tub, is shared by the guests. Breakfast is served in the dining area of the kitchen. Three cats live with the hosts and their son. Smoking outside only. $50.

The Studio Guest House

B&B of Southeast Pennsylvania
146 West Philadelphia Avenue
Boyertown, PA, 19512
(215) 367-4688

Located in a residential section, near the Reading Museum, and convenient to the outlets. The hosts, who are world travelers, have an extensive collection of contemporary art. The hostess is a potter, and has a studio in the house. The guest room has a double bed and full private bath across the hall. There is another room with a double sofabed for additional family members. A sauna is available, and children are welcome. Breakfast is served on the outside deck in the summer and in the dining room the rest of the year. Smoking is permitted in the sitting area. $55.

Windy Hill

B&B of Southeast Pennsylvania
146 West Philadelphia Avenue
Boyertown, PA, 19512
(215) 367-4688

A manor house on 12 acres 8 miles south of the city. The original farmhouse (dated 1785) was enlarged in the early 1900s to support an elegant life-style. On the second floor are two guest rooms, one with twin beds and private bath. The second has a queen bed and private bath down the hall. Children over six are welcome. There are two small dogs and one cat, but not in the guest quarters. There is a second-floor screened porch, and the paneled living room with fireplace is available for guests. Smoking outside only. $65.

REHRERSBURG

Kurr House

B&B of Southeast Pennsylvania
146 West Philadelphia Avenue
Boyertown, PA, 19512
(215) 367-4688

This is a log house on the historic register in an area settled by Germans who trekked the 300 miles from Schoharie, New York, in 1721. The hosts live a few doors down the street. There are two small sitting rooms, one of which has a TV and radio. Hidden stairs off the kitchen lead to two bedrooms, the first with an antique double rope bed and the second with a single rope bed and a double. The hostess provides a continental breakfast. No smoking; no children under fifteen. $65.

SCENERY HILL

Century Inn

Route 40
Scenery Hill, PA, 15360
(412) 945-6600

Stagecoach stop built in 1794, the oldest inn in continuing existence on the National Pike. Furnished in antiques, with tennis courts, croquet, a huge gazebo, and 25 acres. Good antiquing and specialty shopping.

Host: Megin Harrington
Rooms: 9 (PB) $75-125
Full Breakfast
Credit Cards: No
Closed Dec. 23-Feb. 9
Notes: 2, 3, 4, 7, 8, 9, 10, 11, 12

SKIPPACK

Highpoint

B&B of Southeast Pennsylvania
146 West Philadelphia Avenue
Boyertown, PA, 19512
(215) 367-4688

Four miles from the village, which is famous for its antique shops, restaurants, and gift shops. This large, restored Victorian is surrounded by fields and ideal for a getaway. The young hosts have kept the authentic features but allowed light and air to fill the rooms. On the second floor there are three rooms, each with a double bed. A suite can be made with a fourth room for a third family member. Two baths are shared. There is a sitting room where smoking is permitted. Breakfast is served in the dining room. English sheepdog in residence. Children over twelve are welcome. Two-night minimum. $60.

SMOKETOWN

Homestead Lodging

184 East Brook Road
Smoketown, PA, 17576
(717) 393-6927

Come to our beautiful Lancaster County setting, where you hear the clippity-clop of the Amish buggies go by and can experience the sights and freshness of our farmlands. We are located within walking distance of restaurants and outlets, and within minutes of farmers' markets, quilt shops, antiques, auctions, and craft shops.

Hosts: Robert & Lori Kepiro
Rooms: 5 (PB) $26-49
Complimentary coffee
Credit Cards: A, B
Notes: 5, 7, 8, 9, 10, 11, 12

SPRINGTOWN

Wildernest

B&B of Southeast Pennsylvania
146 West Philadelphia Avenue
Boyertown, PA, 19512
(215) 367-4688

Wildernest is on 12 acres of meadow and woods bordering Cooks Creek. A spectacular cedar contemporary home with country ambience, Wildernest features an orchid solarium with Jacuzzi, wraparound deck where guests may sunbathe or relax with refreshments, and a twenty-foot bridge connecting upper levels. Three double rooms; one with private bath and two that share a bath if both rooms are occupied. Located in Bucks County. Five minutes to Delaware River and Canal and Lake Nockomixon. $75.

STARLIGHT

The Inn at Starlight Lake

Box 27
Starlight, PA, 18461
(717) 798-2519

A classic country inn since 1909 on a clear lake in the rolling hills of northeast Pennsylvania, with activities for all seasons, from swimming to cross-country skiing. Near the Delaware River for canoeing and fishing. Excellent food and spirits, convivial atmosphere.

Hosts: Jack & Judy McMahon
Rooms: 26 (20 PB; 6 SB) $110-140 MAP
Full Breakfast
Credit Cards: A, B
Closed first 2 weeks of April
Notes: 2, 3, 4, 7 (limited), 8, 9, 10, 11, 12, 13, 14

The Inn at Starlight Lake

STARRUCCA

The Nethercott Inn

1 Main Street
Starrucca, PA, 18462
(717) 727-2211

A lovely Victorian home built around 1893, nestled in the Endless Mountains in the quaint borough of Starrucca. Downhill skiing, cross-country skiing, snowmobiling, hunting, fishing.

Hosts: Ned & Ginny Nethercott
Rooms: 5 (3 PB; 2 SB) $40-65 + tax
Continental-plus Breakfast

Credit Cards: A, B, C
Notes: 2, 5, 8, 9, 10, 12, 13 (XC)

STRASBURG

The Decoy

958 Eisenberger Road
Strasburg, PA, 17579
(717) 687-8585

Spectacular view, quiet rural location in Amish farm country. Former Amish home, near local attractions. Bicycle tours available with advance reservations. Two cats in residence.

Hosts: Debby & Hap Joy
Rooms: 4 (PB) $31.80-53
Full Breakfast
Credit Cards: No
Notes: 2, 5, 8

Limestone Inn B&B

33 East Main Street
Strasburg, PA, 17579
(717) 687-8392

Situated in Strasburg's historic district and the heartland of Amish country, this 205-year-old home is listed in the National Register of Historic Places. A visit to the Limestone promises to be a warm reflection of times past.

Hosts: Jan & Dick Kennell
Rooms: 6 (2 PB; 4 SB) $65-80
Full Breakfast
Credit Cards: C
Notes: 2, 5, 7 (restricted), 8 (over 12), 9

SUMNEYTOWN

Kaufman B&B

B&B of Southeast Pennsylvania
146 West Philadelphia Avenue
Boyertown, PA, 19512
(215) 367-4688

The innkeeper offers four double rooms on the third floor and two shared baths. Each room has its own personality. "The Elevator Room" is named for the machinery still visible in the corner of the ceiling, dating back to the time when the building was used as a cigar factory. It has a four-poster bed. "The Brass and Wicker Room" is self-explanatory. "The East Room" has a tall Victorian bed and matching furniture in the sitting area. The fourth room, "Country Room," is smaller, with a four-poster canopy bed. Two of the rooms have working gas fireplaces; air-conditioned. A full country breakfast is served downstairs in one of the four dining rooms. There is also a country bar. $60-80.

THORNTON

Pace One Restaurant & Country Inn

Box 108
Thornton, PA, 19373
(215) 459-3702

Pace One is a renovated 250-year-old stone barn with rooms on the upper three levels. The ground floor is a restaurant and bar. Beautiful stone, hand-hewn wood beans, old wood floors, and deep-set windows establish a charming rustic atmosphere.

Host: Ted Pace
Rooms: 7 (PB) $65-75
Continental Breakfast
Credit Cards: A, B, C, E
Notes: 2, 3, 4, 5, 7, 8, 9, 10, 11, 12

TOWANDA

Victorian Guest House

118 York Avenue
Towanda, PA, 18848
(717) 265-6972

A charming Victorian guest house, circa 1897, complete with tower rooms, arched windows, and wraparound porches. High-ceilinged guest rooms are furnished in Victorian and turn-of-the-century antiques. Guests are welcome to share the parlor.

Hosts: Tom & Nancy Taylor
Rooms: 12 (6 PB; 6 SB) $40-55
Continental Breakfast
Credit Cards: A, B, C, E
Notes: 2, 5, 7, 8

TROY

Silver Oak Leaf B&B

196 Canton Street
Troy, PA, 16947
(717) 297-4315

Silver Oak Leaf B&B is in the heart of the Endless Mountains. The house is a 90-year-old Victorian that has great charm. There is a great deal to do and see: antiques, fishing, auctions, hunting, or just relaxing. Gourmet breakfasts; wine served in the evening.

Hosts: Steve & June Bahr
Rooms: 4 (SB) $42.40
Full Breakfast
Credit Cards: No
Notes: 2, 5, 8, 9, 10, 11, 12, 13

VALLEY FORGE

Bed & Breakfast Connections 201

P.O. Box 21
Devon, PA, 19333
(800) 448-3619

This stone colonial is an ageless beauty on 4 acres of wooded land. The original part of the house was built sometime before 1700; two additions are each over 200 years old. Two third-floor rooms. One has a view of the stream and woods, an antique cast-iron double bed, and private adjoining bath. The second room has a beamed ceiling, queen bed with canopy, and private bath. Both rooms have a twin bed for other family members. A large second-floor room has a shared bath. Full English breakfast is served in front of the old fireplace with eight-foot hearth. Resident dog; resident smoker. $70.

Bed & Breakfast Connections 203

P.O. Box 21
Devon, PA, 19333
(800) 448-3619

Just minutes from Valley Forge Park, this comfortable old stone home offers four second-floor rooms. Two have double beds; the third a four-poster bed. A smaller room with antique brass bed is available for the single traveler. Three baths serve these rooms. Continental breakfast; no smoking. $55-65.

Valley Forge B&B

Box 562
Valley Forge, PA, 19481
(215) 783-7838

Convenient to Philadelphia, Lancaster County, and the Brandywine Valley. A large French colonial on 3 wooded acres with a guest parlor with fireplace, central air-conditioning, full breakfast, TV and VCR. Your host is a musician, equestrian, needlepointer, and epicure.

Host: Carolyn Williams
Rooms: 3 (PB) $45-65
Full Breakfast
Credit Cards: A, B, C, E
Notes: 2, 3, 5, 6, 7, 8, 9, 10, 11, 12, 13, 14

WASHINGTON CROSSING

Woodhill Farms Inn

150 Glenwood Drive
Washington Crossing, PA, 18977
(215) 493-1974

Ideally situated on 10 wooded acres in historic Washington Crossing, Bucks County. Just eleven years old, our European six-bedroom inn offers quiet seclusion. Guest rooms are tastefully furnished, all have private baths, color TV, individual thermostats, and central air-conditioning. Send for a free brochure.

Hosts: Don & Mary Lou Spagnuolo
Rooms: 6 (PB) $74.20-116.60
Continental Breakfast weekdays; Full weekends
Credit Cards: A, B
Notes: 2, 5, 7 (limited), 8 (under 1 or over 6), 9, 10, 12

WAYNE

Bed & Breakfast Connections 214

P.O. Box 21
Devon, PA, 19333
(800) 448-3619

A turn-of-the-century carriage house located within walking distance of the train station, shops, and restaurants in the village. The first-floor guest wing features a large room with antique four-poster bed, private hall bath. A small twin room can be used by additional family members. Continental breakfast; no smoking. $60.

WEST CHESTER

Bed & Breakfast Connections 302

P.O. Box 21
Devon, PA, 19333
(800) 448-3619

Enjoy the country charm of this 200-year-old "Bankhouse." A private entrance from a large second-floor porch leads to the guest rooms. One is a double, the second a twin room. A sitting room adjoins the two. Shared bath. A full country breakfast is served; smoking outside only. $55.

The Barn

1131 Grove Road
West Chester, PA, 19380
(215) 436-4544

The Barn is a beautifully converted 1800s stone barn with the stones dramatically exposed on the interior walls. Wide-width pine floors and old beams are a lovely setting for simple furniture, special antiques, and a growing art collection. Right off Route 100, an easy drive to Brandywine attractions and Pennsylvania Dutch country.

Hosts: Susan D. Hager and son
Rooms: 2 (PB) $55
Full Breakfast
Credit Cards: C
Notes: 2, 5, 6, 7, 8, 9, 10, 14

The Crooked Windsor

409 South Church Street
West Chester, PA, 19382
(215) 692-4896

Charming Victorian home centrally located in historic West Chester, within short driving distance of Longwood Gardens, Brandywine Museum, Winterthur, Valley Forge, and other points of interest. Completely furnished with fine antiques. Pool and garden.

Host: Winifred Rupp
Rooms: 4 (S2B) $65
Full Breakfast
Credit Cards: C
Notes: 2, 5, 9, 10, 11, 12, 14

WEST LAWN

Bed & Breakfast Connections 323

P.O. Box 21
Devon, PA, 19333
(800) 448-3619

A colonial home on a quiet street convenient to outlet shopping in Reading, antiquing in Adamstown, and the folk festival in Kutztown. Two spacious second-floor guest rooms, one with a queen and double bed. The second room has a king bed and crib. Shared bath. Full breakfast on weekends; continental on weekdays. Resident cat and dog; no smoking. $50.

WILLOW STREET

The Apple Binn Inn B&B

2835 Willow Street Pike
Willow Street, PA, 17584
(717) 464-5881; (800) 338-4296

As a village B&B, the Apple Bin Inn offers distinctive colonial charm with a country touch. Built in the 1860s, this home established its roots in the mainstream of southern Lancaster Country. Drive through the beautiful countryside, learn of the Amish, browse antique and craft shops and outlets. Comfortable guest rooms feature posted beds, wing chairs, love seats, color cable TV, air conditioning, and more.

Hosts: Barry & Debbie Hershey
Rooms: 5 (2 PB; 3 SB) $45-70
Full Breakfast
Credit Cards: A, B, C
Notes: 2, 3, 5, 9, 10, 11, 12

Green Gables B&B

2532 Willow Street Pike
Willow Street, PA, 17584
(717) 464-5546

Located three miles south of Lancaster, on Route 222N, Green Gables B&B is a 1907 Victorian home with original oak woodwork and stained-glass windows. Be our guest while visiting and touring Lancaster County.

Hosts: Karen & Mike Chiodo
Rooms: 3 (SB) $50
Continental-plus Breakfast
Credit Cards: No
Notes: 2, 5, 8, 10, 11, 12

WOMELSDORF

Hiwwelhaus

B&B of Southeast Pennsylvania
146 West Philadelphia Avenue
Boyertown, PA, 19512
(215) 367-4688

Hiwwelhaus means "log house," and although this is a new one, the charm and convenience are evident. Two rooms, each with a king bed and private bath. One is on the first floor, and the other on the second. Guests have the use of the living room and the large front porch on the first floor. This is an ideal family base, since it is only sixteen miles from the Reading outlets, twenty from Hershey, and thirty from Lancaster County. $55.

YELLOW HOUSE

The Crossroads Inn

B&B of Southeast Pennsylvania
146 West Philadelphia Avenue
Boyertown, PA, 19512
(215) 367-4688

The Crossroads Inn dates back to 1801 and is furnished with charm and elegance. On the second floor are five guest rooms, each with a private bath. One room also has a daybed that can be made up as a single. The fifth room has twin beds and a private bath across the hall. Guest sitting room. The first floor is a restaurant that serves lunch and dinner daily. Breakfast is served in the small dining room. $67.

Rhode Island

BLOCK ISLAND

The Barrington Inn

Beach & Ocean Avenue
Box 397
Block Island, RI, 02807
(401) 466-5510

Recently renovated, century-old farmhouse turned inn on beautiful picturesque Block Island, located just twelve miles off the coast of Rhode Island. A warm, friendly atmosphere; bright cheerful rooms; indescribable views and breathtaking sunsets await your visit. Brochure available.

Hosts: Joan & Howard Ballard
Rooms: 6 (PB) $85-125. Off-season rates
Continental-plus Breakfast
Credit Cards: A, B
Closed Nov. 20-March
Notes: 2, 7, 8 (over 12), 9, 10, 11

The Blue Dory Inn

Box 488
Block Island, RI, 02807
(401) 466-5891

The Victorian age is alive and well at the Blue Dory. Located on Crescent Beach, this delightful year-round inn offers an opportunity to revisit a period of time that has long since gone by. The inn is filled with antiques and turn-of-the-century decor, yet has all the modern comforts.

Innkeepers: Ann & Ed Loedy; Manager: Vin Mc-Aloon
Rooms: 14 (PB) $55-245
Continental-plus Breakfast
Credit Cards: A, B, C, F
Notes: 2, 5, 8, 9, 10, 11

Hotel Manisses

Spring Street
Block Island, RI, 02807
(401) 466-2421; (401) 466-2063

Block Island is a most scenic vacation spot. Biking, beaches, sailing, and just relaxing are right at hand. The Hotel Manisses is a restored Victorian Inn with period furnishings: marble-top bureaus, wooden beds, and elegant paintings. Our restaurant serves all fresh seafood and flaming coffees.

Hosts: The Abrams Family
Rooms: 17 (PB) $65-300
Full Breakfast
Credit Cards: A, B, C
Notes: 2, 4, 5, 7, 8 (over 10), 9, 10, 11, 14

Rose Farm Inn

Roslyn Road, Box E
Block Island, RI, 02807
(401) 466-2021

Sea and country setting, convenient to downtown and beaches. Comfortable rooms with ocean view, furnished with antiques, queen or king beds. Great stone porch and sun deck cooled by sea breezes. Light buffet breakfast is served on the porch.

Hosts: Robert & Judith Rose
Rooms: 10 (8 PB; 2 SB) $85-150
Continental Breakfast
Credit Cards: A, B, C
Closed Nov.-April
Notes: 2, 7, 8 (over 12), 9, 10, 11, 14

The Sheffield House

High Street
Block Island, RI, 02807
(401) 466-2494

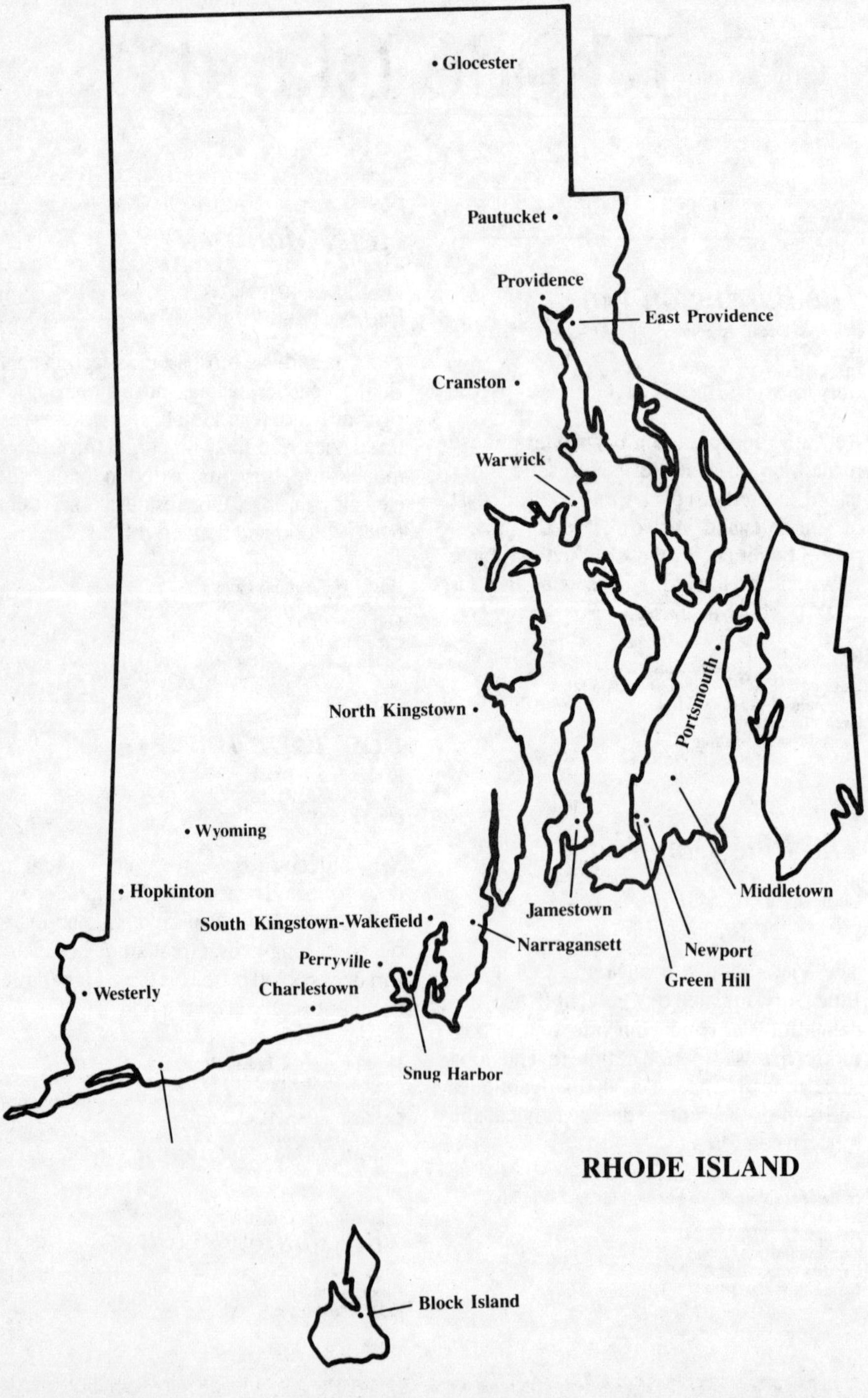

Glocester
Pautucket
Providence
East Providence
Cranston
Warwick
North Kingstown
Portsmouth
Wyoming
Hopkinton
South Kingstown-Wakefield
Jamestown
Middletown
Narragansett
Newport
Perryville
Green Hill
Westerly
Charlestown
Snug Harbor
Block Island

RHODE ISLAND

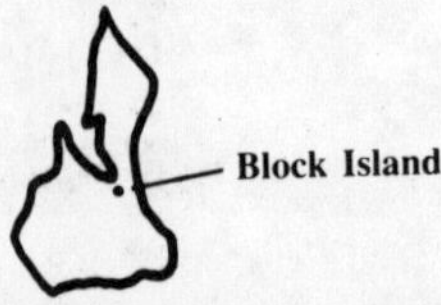

An 1888 Victorian house in the historic district. A quiet location just two blocks from beaches, restaurants, and shops. Individually decorated guest rooms, parlor, country kitchen, porch, gardens, and friendly, knowledgeable hosts.

Hosts: Steve & Claire McQueeny
Rooms: 7 (5 PB; 2 SB) $60-150
Continental Breakfast
Credit Cards: A, B, C
Notes: 2, 5, 7, 9, 10, 11

1661 Inn and Guest House

Spring Street
Block Island, RI, 02807
(401) 466-2421; (401) 466-2063

The 1661 Inn has nine guest rooms, all with private baths, and is open May 4 through October 8. The 1661 Inn Guest House has ten rooms; five with private baths, and is open year-round. Full breakfast is served, and children are welcome.

Hosts: Joan & Justin Abrams, Steve & Rita Draper
Rooms: 19 (14 PB; 5 SB) $65-300
Full Breakfast
Credit Cards: A, B, C
Notes: 2, 8

The White House

Spring Street, Box 447
Block Island, RI, 02807-0447
(401) 466-2653

Spacious thirteen-room New England mansion furnished with French Provincial antiques. Collection of rare presidential signatures and documents in the Presidents' Room. Balcony wraps around The Captain's Quarters and Oriental Bedroom overlooking the old harbor and ocean. Three-minute walk to shops, boutiques, eateries, and ferry slips. Station wagon service (free) to and from airport and ferries.

Hosts: Joseph J. & Violette Connolly
Rooms: 5 (1 PB; 4 SB) $100-120; less off-season
Full Breakfast
Credit Cards: A, B, C
Notes: 2, 5, 6, 7, 9, 10, 11

CHARLESTOWN

B&B Affiliates RI-291

P.O. Box 3291
Newport, RI, 02840
(401) 849-1298

This split-level ranch in rural surroundings is only two miles from magnificent white sandy beaches and close to wildlife refuges. Two guest rooms on the main floor are across the hall from the bath. A third room is on the ground floor. Children over two are welcome; cat in residence; outdoor smoking only. $55.

General Stanton Inn

4115A Old Post Road
Box 222
Charlestown, RI, 02813
(401) 364-8888

We are near the beach and one-half hour from Newport and Mystic, Conn. We have a flea market on the grounds from March through October every Sunday and Monday holidays.

Hosts: Janice & Angelo Falcone
Rooms: 15 (13 PB; 2 SB) $72.80-106.40
Full Breakfast
Minimum stay holidays: 3
Credit Cards: A, B, C
Notes: 2, 4, 7, 8, 9, 10, 11, 12

One Willow by the Sea

1 Willow Road
Charlestown, RI, 02813
(401) 364-0802

Enjoy warm, year-round hospitality in a peaceful, rural home. South County shoreline community. Guest comfort is our priority. Wake to birds, sunshine, and a delicious breakfast that is often served on the sun deck. Explore our local 27 miles of pristine sandy beaches, salt ponds, wildlife refuges. We have fine restaurants, theaters, live music, craft fairs, antique shows, historic

New England landmarks, and a wealth of other activities nearby. Providence, Newport, and Mystic are a short drive. French is spoken. We'll pamper you.

Host: Denise Dillon Fuge
Rooms: 4 (SB) $55
Full Breakfast
Credit Cards: No
Notes: 2, 5, 8, 11, 12, 14

CRANSTON

B&B Affiliates RI-247

P.O. Box 3291
Newport, RI, 02840
(401) 849-1298

This is a classic 1798 Federal house with center chimney, gable roof, five-bay facade, and ornate pedimented fanlight doorway. The 6-acre farm has been owned by an old Rhode Island family since the eighteenth century. It is located in an area once known as Hope Furnace, where cannon balls were made for the Revolutionary War. The sitting room has pegged wide-board pine floors; behind the fireplace is an old smoke house that opens onto a screened-in porch. Pool, English rose and herb gardens, orchard, blacksmith shop, and two classic barns. Three guest rooms, each with its own fireplace and shared baths. Three cats in residence. $65.

B&B Affiliates RI-280

P.O. Box 3291
Newport, RI, 02840
(401) 849-1298

Come pick your own blueberries for breakfast in July and August, and in November and December view the cutting of Christmas trees. This lovely Garrison colonial offers the delights of rural living, yet is just a twenty-minute drive from Providence College and Brown University. One room on the ground level with Ethan Allen beds and comfortable chairs, private bath. $60.

EAST PROVIDENCE

B&B Affiliates RI177

P.O. Box 3291
Newport, RI, 02840
(401) 849-1298

This lovely Federal home is located just across the street from the waterfront. Guests arriving by boat can dock at one of four marinas within walking distance. All guests can enjoy the private harborside beach, nearby bike paths, and Crescent Park Carousel. Four rooms with shared baths, continental breakfast, dog in residence, children over ten or infants are welcome, and smoking is permitted. $55-60.

GLOCESTER

B&B Affiliates RI-156

P.O. Box 3291
Newport, RI, 02840
(401) 849-1298

When you visit this 3-acre farm, you can help feed the turkeys and sheep or go fishing and swimming in the nearby lake. Near hiking, golf, cross-country skiing, and snowmobiling. The 150-year-old farmhouse is on a quiet road in a rural area. Two guest rooms share a bath down the stairs. A sitting room offers a piano and organ, and guests join the hosts for a full breakfast in the kitchen. Pets are welcome but must be kept on a leash; children welcome. Smoking on the first floor only. $38.

GREEN HILL

Fairfield-By-The-Sea B&B

527 Green Hill Beach Road
Green Hill, RI, 02879-5703
(401) 789-4717

An artist's contemporary home in a secluded country area. Twenty miles east of Mystic and twenty-five miles west of Newport. Day trips to Plymouth and Block Island. Biking and birding are favorites. Large fireplace and good library for guests. Fine restaurants abound. An informal and relaxed ambience.

Host: Jeanne Lewis
Rooms: 2 (SB) $40-55
Continental-plus Breakfast
Minimum stay summer weekends: 2; holidays: 3
Credit Cards: No
Notes: 2, 5, 7, 8, 9, 10, 11, 12, 13

HOPKINTON

B&B Affiliates RI-145

P.O. Box 3291
Newport, RI, 02840
(401) 849-1298

Set in a semirural area, this turn-of-the-century home is close to golf and tennis. Just seven miles from Watch Hill beach, and less than a mile from I-95, it is an easy drive to either Mystic Seaport or Newport. Inground swimming pool and brick patio. The two second-floor guest rooms are furnished with country accents. Continental breakfast is served in the dining room that overlooks the outdoor lounge area. Resident cat; children welcome, restricted smoking. $50.

B&B Affiliates RI-165

P.O. Box 3291
Newport, RI, 02840
(401) 849-1298

This 1763 colonial mansion was owned by the same family for 187 years. It is located in the center of a small New England village of eighteenth- and nineteenth-century homes; a place where you can mail a letter at the post office and have lunch for under three dollars. Seven guest rooms with nonworking fireplaces, rough-hewn beamed ceilings, wide plank floors. Guests have two sitting rooms to enjoy. Full country breakfast; children over ten welcome; outdoor smoking only; no pets. $50-60.

JAMESTOWN

B&B Affiliates RI-205

P.O. Box 3291
Newport, RI, 02840
(401) 849-1298

Expansive grounds, an old-fashioned veranda, and comfortable rooms beckon you to unwind in this twin-turreted Victorian home. Large sleeping rooms feature antique or period furnishings. A hearty continental breakfast is served in the dining room or on the breezy veranda. Children are welcome; two resident dogs; smokers in residence. $50.

B&B Affiliates RI-217

P.O. Box 3291
Newport, RI, 02840
(401) 849-1298

A newer colonial home with antiques, paintings, and 1830s working grandfather clock. Breakfast is served at a nineteenth-century walnut table in the dining room. Open from May-October. Three rooms with shared baths; full breakfast; cat in residence; smoking allowed. $50-60.

MIDDLETOWN

B&B Affiliates RI192

P.O. Box 3291
Newport, RI, 02840
(401) 849-1298

Whimsical touches in every room create a special setting in this 1915 gable-roofed house. Catch a quiet moment just outside your room in a small alcove with an ocean view or in the large sitting room with its plant-filled sun room. One ocean beach is just a five-minute walk, and another is a two-minute drive. Three rooms, shared baths. Continental breakfast; cat in residence; children over sixteen welcome; smoking outside only. $60-70.

NARRAGANSETT

B&B Affiliates RI111

P.O. Box 3291
Newport, RI, 02840
(401) 849-1298

This 1896 home has been furnished with cherished antiques and lots of Victorian touches. Enjoy the buffet breakfast in the quaint dining room at an intimate table for two. Relax in a wicker rocker on the front porch or in the Victorian parlor. The beach, shopping, and restaurants are all just a short walk away. Four rooms, two with private baths; children welcome; restricted smoking. $50-65.

B&B Affiliates RI245

P.O. Box 3291
Newport, RI, 02840
(401) 849-1298

This magnificent Victorian summer estate sits right on the ocean. Beautiful English antiques adorn the lovely entry hall. The parlor offers TV, a player piano, regulation pool table, and binoculars for watching boats at sea. An enclosed porch overlooks the ocean. Ten rooms, shared and private baths. Full country breakfast; dog in residence; children over ten are welcome; smoking outdoors. $55-114.

B&B Affiliates RI257

P.O. Box 3291
Newport, RI, 02840
(401) 849-1298

This classic Victorian is just one-half block from the beach. Bicycles, fishing gear, croquet, horseshoes, darts and more are available, or enjoy the old-fashioned porch and large yard. Three rooms with shared baths. Hearty continental breakfast; children welcome; no smoking. $45-60.

B&B Affiliates RI269

P.O. Box 3291
Newport, RI, 02840
(401) 849-1298

Originally built as a summer residence in 1894, this comfortable Victorian has been lovingly restored. It is situated on a residential street just one block from the ocean. Three rooms with shared bath, full breakfast. Children over seven are welcome; restricted smoking. $65-75.

The House of Snee

The House of Snee

191 Ocean Road
Narragansett, RI, 02882
(401) 783-9494

Turn-of-the-century Dutch colonial with a magnificent view from the front porch, within easy walking distance to the beach. Breakfast is served in the family dining room daily; there's a guest reading room on the second floor and TV in the living room. The house has five fireplaces.

Host: Mildred Snee
Rooms: 3 (SB) $50

NOTES: Credit cards accepted: A Master Card; B Visa; C American Express; D Discover Card; E Diners Club; F Other: 2 Personal checks accepted: 3 Lunch available: 4 Dinner available: 5 Open all year

Full Breakfast
Credit Cards: No
Notes: 2, 5, 8, 9, 10, 11, 12

Ilverthorpe Cottage

41 Robinson Street
Narragansett, RI, 02882
(401) 789-2392

Lacy touches, hand-carved moldings, stenciled walls are found throughout this 1896 Victorian "cottage." A convenient three blocks from the beach, so you don't even need a car. Travel to Newport for a day of mansion touring, sailing, and shopping, or take the ferry to nearby Block Island. Whatever your pleasure, you'll enjoy the sumptuous gourmet breakfast each morning.

Hosts: Chris & Jill Raggio
Rooms: 4 (2 PB; 2 SB) $70-75
Full Breakfast
Credit Cards: No
Notes: 2, 5, 7 (restricted), 8, 9, 10, 11, 12, 14

Mon Rêve

41 Gibson Avenue
Narragansett, RI, 02882
(401) 783-2846

Victorian home (c. 1890) on 2 quiet acres near the beach. Fine restaurants in the area. Newport is a thirty-minute drive; three blocks to Ocean Boulevard. Bikes for guests. Breakfast is beautifully served in the enclosed sun porch. Free parking. The home is on the National Register in the historic district. French and Italian are spoken here. This is our eleventh year in business.

Hosts: Eva & James Doran
Rooms: 2 (PB) $50-75
Full Breakfast
Credit Cards: No
Notes: 2, 5, 6, 7 (restricted), 10, 11, 12

Murphy's B&B

43 South Pier Road
Narragansett, RI, 02882
(401) 789-1824

Charming 1894 Victorian restored with care by the owners. Situated on a tree-lined residential street one block from the ocean, this makes a perfect base for enjoying our beautiful beaches, historic Newport and Providence, Block Island, the area's many antique shops, art galleries, and fine restaurants. We are known for our gracious ambience and fabulous breakfasts.

Hosts: Kevin & Martha Murphy
Rooms: 3 (SB) $50-65
Full Breakfast
Credit Cards: No
Closed Nov. 15-April 30
Notes: 2, 3, 4, 7 (outside), 8 (over 10), 9, 10, 11, 12

The Richards

144 Gibson Avenue
Narragansett, RI, 02882
(401) 789-7746

Gracious accommodations in an 1884 historic manse. Relax by the fire in the library or your fireplaced guest room. Enjoy a leisurely full breakfast with homemade muffins, strudels, blintzes. Nancy's many special touches will spoil you — down comforters, canopy beds, flowers from the gardens, etc.

Hosts: Steven & Nancy Richards
Rooms: 4 (2 PB; 2 SB) $50-75
Full Breakfast
Minimum stay weekends: 2; holidays: 3
Credit Cards: No
Notes: 2, 5, 8 (over 12), 9

NEWPORT

B&B Affiliates RI113

P.O. Box 3291
Newport, RI, 02840
(401) 849-1298

This Queen Anne Victorian is richly appointed with fine carved oak woodwork, plenty of fireplaces, a parlor grand piano. Enjoy a water view from your sleeping room and relax on the large lawn. Four rooms and four apartments, with private and shared baths. Light continental breakfast; children welcome; smoking permitted. $65-125.

B&B Affiliates RI127

P.O. Box 3291
Newport, RI, 02840
(401) 849-1298

This 1950 home is filled with fresh flowers and peaceful mauves and blues. Breakfast is served in the delightful dining room or outside on the patio. Two rooms, one with private bath. Two dogs in residence; no children; smoking permitted. $70-75.

B&B Affiliates RI195

P.O. Box 3291
Newport, RI, 02840
(401) 849-1298

An idyllic setting on this nation's first gas-lit street makes this renovated 1915 inn the perfect getaway. A literal stone's throw from famed Bannister's and Bowen's wharves, with ample off-street parking. Nine rooms with private and shared baths. Elegant continental breakfast; children over twelve are welcome; restricted smoking. $75-145.

B&B Affiliates RI224

P.O. Box 3291
Newport, RI, 02840
(401) 849-1298

Thorough and meticulous restoration has brought back the original graciousness of this 1751 Georgian Colonial. This house was used as British headquarters during the American Revolution. Sleeping rooms all have working fireplaces, private baths, lovely antiques, and many period pieces. Nine rooms. Full breakfast; restricted smoking. $80-125.

B&B Affiliates RI241

P.O. Box 3291
Newport, RI, 02840
(401) 849-1298

This 1880s Victorian home was once the gardener's cottage for the Astor estate. Within walking distance of Hazard's Beach and central Newport. Three rooms with shared baths. Continental breakfast, resident dog; children over twelve welcome. Smoking outdoors only. $60-70.

B&B Affiliates RI244

P.O. Box 3291
Newport, RI, 02840
(401) 849-1298

The central location and homey atmosphere of this 1870s Victorian inn make it ideal for guests who want to be close to attractions. Old-fashioned Empire style, brass, or four-poster beds, antiques, braided rugs. Breakfast is served family style at the large pine table in front of the dining room fireplace. Eight rooms, private and shared baths. Children are welcome; no smoking. $45-95.

B&B Affiliates RI251

P.O. Box 3291
Newport, RI, 02840
(401) 849-1298

This early 1900s home has an enclosed front porch overlooking the quiet residential street. Breakfast is served in the country kitchen, where a yellow canary sings accompaniment. One room with shared bath. There is an extra room for other party members. Light continental breakfast; children welcome; smoking permitted. $60.

B&B Affiliates RI252

P.O. Box 3291
Newport, RI, 02840
(401) 849-1298

Tucked into a quiet side street on Historic Hill, this colonial is convenient for walking to all downtown attractions. The parlor is filled with antiques, and a continental breakfast is served in the dining room on a beautiful harvest table. One room with twin beds and attached private bath. Children over twelve are welcome. Restricted smoking. $65.

B&B Affiliates RI260

P.O. Box 3291
Newport, RI, 02840
(401) 849-1298

This lovely French-style carriage house offers a private entrance to a quiet haven over the garage located just minutes from the Newport mansions and Bailey's beach. Help-yourself continental breakfast; children welcome. One suite with king or twin beds plus futon, private bath. $95.

B&B Affiliates RI270

P.O. Box 3291
Newport, RI, 02840
(401) 849-1298

This magnificent house was built in 1869, a spectacular example of the opulence of Newport's grandest age. The grand staircase and entrance hall rises thirty-five feet with projecting balconies at various levels. Located on the harborfront, this home has four guest rooms with water views. One room has a private bath. Continental breakfast; dog in residence; restricted smoking; children welcome. $55-165.

B&B Affiliates RI287

P.O. Box 3291
Newport, RI, 02840
(401) 849-1298

The spectacular view from this oceanfront home is matched by the sound of waves rolling up against the rocky shore. One very private room is located over the garage, with a splendid view of the water. A second room in the main house has large windows and TV. Both have private baths. A full breakfast is served; smoking is permitted; and children over sixteen are welcome. Two-night minimum in the summer. $75-95.

B&B Affiliates RI289

P.O. Box 3291
Newport, RI, 02840
(401) 849-1298

This turn-of-the-century Victorian is conveniently located close to most attractions. Off-street parking is provided. Three rooms with shared bath, continental breakfast. children over ten are welcome, and smoking is permitted outdoors. $65.

B&B Affiliates RI292

P.O. Box 3291
Newport, RI, 02840
(401) 849-1298

This lovely 100-year-old home offers original moldings and fireplace mantle, beautiful stained-glass windows, large front porch. Two suites have skylights, cable TV, telephone, small refrigerator, and microwave ovens. A full breakfast is served; dog in residence; no children; restricted smoking. $85-95.

Bellevue House

14 Catherine Street
Newport, RI, 02840
(401) 847-1828

Originally built in 1774, Bellevue House was converted into the first summer hotel in Newport in 1828. We are on top of Historic Hill, off the famous Bellevue Avenue, three blocks from the harbor. We retain a combination of ideal location, colonial history, nautical atmosphere, and Victorian charm.

Hosts: Joan & Vic Farmer
Rooms: 8 (6 PB; 2 SB) $70-90 + tax
Continental Breakfast
Credit Cards: No
Closed Nov.-April
Notes: 2, 8 (over 10), 9, 10, 11, 12, 14

Brinley Victorian Inn

23 Brinley Street
Newport, RI, 02840
(401) 849-7645

Romantic all year long, the inn becomes a Victorian Christmas dream come true. Comfortable antiques and fresh flowers fill every room. Friendly, unpretentious service and attention to detail will make this inn your haven in Newport. Park and walk everywhere. AAA approved.

Hosts: Peter Carlisle & Claire Boslem
Rooms: 17 (13 PB; 4 SB) $55-130
Continental Breakfast
Minimum stay weekends: 2; holidays: 3
Credit Cards: A, B
Notes: 2, 5, 7, 8 (over 12), 9 10, 11, 12, 14

Cliffside Inn

2 Seaview Avenue
Newport, RI, 02840
(401) 847-1811

This gracious 1880 Victorian inn has such charm that visitors return year after year. Set in a peaceful, quiet neighborhood, close to attractions, with the beach a five-minute walk and the famous Cliff Walk a block down the street.

Host: Annette King
Rooms: 11 (PB) $75-175
Full Breakfast

Cliff View Guest House

4 Cliff Terrace
Newport, RI, 02840
(401) 846-0885

Two-story Victorian (c. 1890) on quiet dead-end street leading to the famous Cliff Walk, a three-mile path bordering the ocean. Five-minute walk to the beach; ten to fifteen to the downtown harbor area. Ten-room house has four guest rooms; two share a bath and have a view of the ocean. The other two have private baths but no ocean view.

Hosts: Pauline & John Shea
Rooms: 4 (2 PB; 2 SB) $55-65 + tax
Continental Breakfast
Credit Cards: A, B
Closed Nov. 1-May 1
Notes: 2, 7, 9, 10, 11, 12

Clover Hill Guest House

32 Cranston Avenue
Newport, RI, 02840
(401) 847-7094

Clover Hill is a gracious Victorian home built c. 1891. Within walking distance are the wharf area with its shops, restaurants, and the harbor, filled with magnificent yachts. Minutes away are Bellevue Avenue and the famous Newport mansions, the Cliff Walk, Ten Mile Ocean Drive, and beaches. Pets in residence.

Hosts: June & Audrey Gallon
Rooms: 2 (SB) $65-80
Full Breakfast
Credit Cards: No
Notes: 2, 5, 8, 10, 11, 12, 14

Elm Tree Cottage

336 Gibbs Avenue
Newport, RI, 02840
(401) 849-1610

Designed by renowned New England architect William Ralph Emerson, this shingle-style mansion exemplifies Newport's elegant summer "cottages." Built in 1882, situated on an acre of land in a quiet neighborhood with views of Easton's Pond and First Beach. Just two blocks from Cliff Walk and a short distance from Newport's outstanding restaurants, mansions, wharf, and shopping area. Most rooms have fireplaces; all have private baths.

Harborside Inn

Hosts: Priscilla & Thomas Malone
Rooms: 5 (PB) $135-160
Full Breakfast
Credit Cards: A, B
Closed Thanksgiving & Christmas
Notes: 2, 8, 9, 10, 11

Francis Malbone House

392 Thames Street
Newport, RI, 02840
(401) 846-0392

Our colonial inn was built in 1760 and reflects the graciousness and elegance of another age. The beautifully appointed rooms indicate attention to detail and all have private baths. Cozy library, landscaped courtyard, and convenient harbor-front location. Continental breakfast; off-street parking. $80-200.

Halidon Hill Guest House

Halidon Avenue
Newport, RI, 02840
(401) 847-8318

Modern, spacious rooms, ample on-site parking, in-ground pool and deck area. Just minutes from beaches, shopping areas, local restaurants, and mansions.

Hosts: Helen & Paul Burke
Rooms: 2 (SB); 2 apartments $55-125
Continental Breakfast
Credit Cards: A, B
Notes: 2, 5, 7, 8, 9, 10, 11, 12, 14

Harborside Inn

Christie's Landing
Newport, RI, 02840
(401) 846-6600

The Harborside Inn blends the charm of colonial Newport with the hustle and bustle of Newport's active waterfront. Each suite provides a view of the harbor and features a wet bar, refrigerator, cable TV, sleeping loft, and balcony. A short walk to quaint specialty shops, colonial homes and churches, restaurants and antique shops.

Host: Mary Comforti
Rooms: 14 (PB) $55-190 + tax
Continental Breakfast
Credit Cards: A, B, C
Notes: 2, 5, 7, 8, 9, 10, 11, 12

Hydrangea House

16 Bellevue Avenue
Newport, RI, 02840
(401) 846-4435

A small European style inn providing you with cozy comfort, homespun hospitality, and stylized service you deserve. Breakfast is enjoyed in the art and antique gallery or on the veranda with flowers and plants. Easy walking access to the harbor, beaches, and mansions. Airport shuttle available; off-street parking. AAA approved.

Hosts: Dennis Blair & Grant Edmondson
Rooms: (PB) $60-125
Notes: 5, 10, 11, 12, 14

The Inn at Old Beach

19 Old Beach Road
Newport, RI, 02840
(401) 849-3479

This elegant Victorian inn was built in 1879 and is listed on the Rhode Island Historic Register. Located in one of the most prestigious neighborhoods, it is within walking distance of mansions, beaches, shops, restaurants, and cliffwalk. Romantic guest rooms, fireplaces, gazebo, and garden will add to a delightful stay.

Hosts: Cynthia & Luke Murray
Rooms: 5 (PB) $60-115
Continental Breakfast
Credit Cards: A, B, C
Notes: 2, 5, 8 (over 12), 9, 10, 11, 12

The Inntowne

6 Mary Street
Newport, RI, 02840
(401) 846-9200

An elegant, reconstructed 26-room inn with colonial reproduction furniture, private baths, telephones, air conditioning. Continental breakfast and afternoon tea is served in the antique breakfast room. The perfect location for easy walking to all Newport's shops and restaurants.

Hosts: Betty & Paul McEnroe
Rooms: 26 (PB) $60.50-165
Continental Breakfast
Credit Cards: A, B, C
Notes: 2, 5, 7, 8 (over 12), 9, 10, 11, 12

Jailhouse Inn

13 Marlborough Street
Newport, RI, 02840
(401) 847-4638

Built in 1772, the Newport Jail functioned for over 200 years. Now transformed into an inn, the Jail House maintains the nostalgic flavor of the past with modern conveniences and cheerfulness. A stone's throw to restaurants, shops, and the harbor, each room features a refrigerator, telephone, cable TV, private bath, and air-conditioning. Experience the many faces of this quaint and lively town while staying in an authentic piece of its history.

Host: Beth Hoban
Rooms: 22 (PB) $45-125
Continental Breakfast
Credit Cards: A, B, C
Notes: 2, 5, 7, 8, 9, 10, 11, 12

Jenkins Guest House

Jenkins Guest House

206 South Rhode Island Avenue
Newport, RI, 02840
(401) 847-6801

We built this house when we were married on a quiet side street in a residential area of Newport. Some special features are: three-minute walk to the beach; fifteen from downtown. Yachting activities, boutiques,

NOTES: Credit cards accepted: A Master Card; B Visa; C American Express; D Discover Card; E Diners Club; F Other: 2 Personal checks accepted: 3 Lunch available: 4 Dinner available: 5 Open all year

and shopping; ten-minute walk to mansions. Plenty of parking on grounds.

Hosts: David & Sally Jenkins
Rooms: 2 (SB) $60
Continental Breakfast
Credit Cards: No
Open April 1-Nov. 1
Notes: 2, 8, 9, 10, 11, 12

La Forge Cottage

96 Pelham Street
Newport, RI, 02840
(401) 847-4400

La Forge Cottage is a Victorian B&B located in the heart of Newport's Historic Hill area. Close to beaches and downtown. All rooms have private baths, TV, phone, air conditioning, refrigerators, and full breakfast room service. French and German spoken. Reservations suggested.

Hosts: Louis & Margot Droual
Rooms: 6 (PB) $67.20-106.40
Suites: 4 (PB) $106.40-140
Full Breakfast
Credit Cards: A, B, C
Minimum stay weekends: 2; holidays: 3
Notes: 2, 5, 7, 8, 9, 10, 11, 12, 14

The Melville House

The Melville House

39 Clarke Street
Newport, RI, 02840
(401) 847-0640

Step back into the past and stay at a colonial inn built circa 1750, located in the heart of Newport's historic district and on the National Register of Historic Places. Homemade breakfast, complimentary sherry hour, off-street parking. Walk to wharfs, shops, restaurants, historic buildings.

Hosts: Rita & Sam Rogers
Rooms: 7 (5 PB; 2 SB) $44.80-106.40
Continental-plus Breakfast
Minimum stay weekends: 2; holidays: 3
Credit Cards: A, B, C
Closed Jan. & Feb.
Notes: 2, 7, 8 (over 12), 9, 10, 11, 12

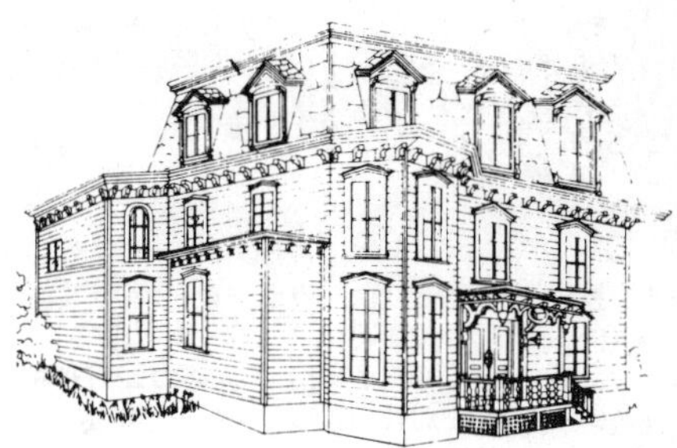

Pilgrim House Inn

Pilgrim House Inn

123 Spring Street
Newport, RI, 02840
(401) 846-0040; (800) 525-8373

This Victorian inn, with its comforts and elegance, is located two blocks from the harbor in the midst of the historic district. A fireplaced living room, immaculate rooms, and wonderful atmosphere await you. Breakfast on our deck overlooking Newport's harbor. Just outside our door are the mansions, shops, and restaurants.

Hosts: Pam & Bruce Bayuk
Rooms: 10 (8 PB; 2 SB) $49.50-137.50
Continental Breakfast
Credit Cards: A, B
Closed January
Notes: 2, 8 (over 12), 9, 10, 11, 12

Queen Anne Inn

16 Clarke Street
Newport, RI, 02840
(401) 846-5676

Come and be welcome at the inn, a bright restored Victorian townhouse hidden in the heart of the historic district two blocks from the harbor. Enjoy breakfast in the garden or comfortable sitting room before walking or sailing tours of the city, wharves, or antique shops. Open April-November.

Host: Peg McCabe
Rooms: 14 (S7B) $50-75
Continental Breakfast

Spring Street Inn

353 Spring Street
Newport, RI, 02840
(401) 847-4767

Empire Victorian, c. 1858, with five double rooms and one apartment, all with private baths. Guest sitting room. Walk to all Newport highlights. Off-street parking; free bus nearby. Harbor view suite with balcony sleeps two to four people. Extensive continental breakfast.

Host: Parvine Latimore
Rooms: 6 (PB) $55-95
Continental Breakfast
Credit Cards: A, B
Notes: 2, 3, 4, 5, 7, 8 (12 and over), 9, 10, 11, 12, 14

Wayside

406 Bellevue Avenue
Newport, RI, 02840
(401) 847-0302

Our 1890s Georgian-style house is within walking distance of mansions, the Tennis Hall of Fame, shops, and restaurants. Relax in attractive bed/sitting rooms; utilize our barbecue facilities and heated in-ground pool. This area is popular with walkers, joggers, and bicyclists because it is safe and scenic. Enjoy Newport year-round.

Hosts: The Posts
Rooms: 8 (PB) $95
Continental Breakfast
Credit Cards: No
Notes: 2, 5, 7, 8, 9, 10, 11, 12

The Willows

8 Willow Street
Newport, RI, 02840
(401) 846-5486

In the historic point of Newport, the Willows pampers you with secluded gardens, solid brass canopy beds, fresh flowers in rooms, mints on pillows, champagne glasses and silver ice buckets, lights on dim. Breakfast in bed on bone china and silver services. Three blocks from downtown and the waterfront.

Host: Patricia Murphy
Rooms: 5 (PB) $68-125
Continental Breakfast
Credit Cards: No
Closed Jan.
Notes: 2, 7 (restricted), 9, 10, 11, 12, 14

NEWPORT/MIDDLETOWN

Lindsey's Guest House

6 James Street
Middletown, RI
(401) 846-9386

One mile to Newport's famous mansions, Cliff Walk, Tennis Hall of Fame. Lindsey's is a split-level home with large yard, deck, and off-street parking. Ten-minute walk to beaches and Norman Bird Sanctuary.

Hosts: Anne & Dave
Rooms: 3 (1 PB; 2 SB) $40-60
Continental Breakfast
Credit Cards: A, B
Notes: 2, 5, 8, 9, 10, 11, 12, 14

NORTH KINGSTOWN

B&B Affiliates RI-121

P.O. Box 3291
Newport, RI, 02840
(401) 849-1298

Tasteful country charm characterizes each room of this nineteenth-century colonial. Once a dairy farm, this home is located on 2.5 acres surrounded by a picket fence, stone walls, and barns. Convenient to Newport, Narragansett, and Providence. Three rooms, shared bath; hearty continental breakfast. Dog in residence; children are welcome; smoking outdoors only. $45-55.

B&B Affiliates RI-151

P.O. Box 3291
Newport, RI, 02840
(401) 849-1298

Built in 1745 by a grandson of the founder of Wickford, the house was confiscated by the patriots during the Revolutionary War because its owner was a Tory. The second-floor guest area includes two rooms, a sitting room, bath, and outside deck overlooking Wickford Harbor and Narragansett Bay. Sun yourself on the small private beach, stroll the ground, or take a short walk to the town dock or village center. Cat in residence; children welcome; limited smoking. $65.

B&B Affiliates RI246

P.O. Box 3291
Newport, RI, 02840
(401) 849-1298

Nestled along a country road, this 1920 colonial manor house was built on a seventeenth-century stone foundation and is surrounded by ancient stone walls. The 6-acre holly farm has walking paths to enjoy. One room with double bed and private bath, plus a cottage with a double sofabed and private bath. A hearty continental breakfast is served. $60.

B&B Affiliates RI264

P.O. Box 3291
Newport, RI, 02840
(401) 849-1298

This lovely home dates back to the mid-1800s, when the surrounding fields and meadows were a celery farm. Extensive renovations and restoration have resulted in an opulence that is reminiscent of the Victorian age. Five rooms with shared baths. Full breakfast; children over twelve are welcome. Restricted smoking. $60.

B&B Affiliates RI279

P.O. Box 3291
Newport, RI, 02840
(401) 849-1298

Bright, airy rooms and tasteful decor make this mid-1700s colonial farmhouse a special delight. The large screened porch has plenty of lounge furniture for relaxing in. Two second-floor guest rooms have bordered wallpaper and antique furnishings, shared bath. A hearty continental breakfast is served. No children. $50-60.

B&B Affiliates RI290

P.O. Box 3291
Newport, RI, 02840
(401) 849-1298

A five-minute stroll from this 1809 colonial puts you in the center of historic Wickford Village, where you can shop in unique boutiques, antique and gift shops. Breakfast is served in the dining room or on the brick patio. Three rooms with private baths, continental breakfast. Air-conditioned. Cat in residence; children welcome; restricted smoking. $75.

PAWTUCKET

B&B Affiliates RI-130

P.O. Box 3291
Newport, RI, 02840
(401) 849-1298

The architect who built this home for himself in 1932 added many features—detailed moldings and fireplace mantles, bull's eye glass windows, and corner display cupboards. Relax in the formal living room or informal den, both with working fireplaces. A lovely porch overlooks the yard. A hearty continental breakfast is served in the dining room or on the porch in the summer. Two rooms, one with shared bath, one with a private half-bath. No children or pets; limited smoking. $55.

PERRYVILLE

B&B Affiliates RI-273

P.O. Box 3291
Newport, RI, 02840
(401) 849-1298

This thirteen-room house is a charming vestige of colonial days. The lovely 1732 farmhouse sits on acres of beautiful grounds with formal gardens, apple trees, and raspberry bushes. The hosts collect and display antiques. A full breakfast is served in the sun room. Three guest rooms; two with private bath. Two dogs and one cat in residence; children welcome; limited smoking; smoker in residence. $55.

PORTSMOUTH

B&B Affiliates RI-186

P.O. Box 3291
Newport, RI, 02840
(401) 849-1298

Old-fashioned country charm abounds in this new colonial-style home. The home is located in a quiet hilltop neighborhood with a beautiful view of the distant bay from several rooms. The outdoor deck overlooks the spacious backyard. Two guest rooms share a bath. Continental breakfast, children are welcome; smoking on the deck only. $50-60.

B&B Affiliates RI-286

P.O. Box 3291
Newport, RI, 02840
(401) 849-1298

This house offers a private suite attached to a ranch house, with its own entrance and deck. Screened French doors lead to the private deck and backyard. A continental breakfast is left outside your door in the morning, to be enjoyed at your leisure. One double bed, private bath with shower. Children over twelve are welcome. Smoking permitted outside only; smoker in residence. $55-65.

PROVIDENCE

B&B Affiliates RI118

P.O. Box 3291
Newport, RI, 02840
(401) 849-1298

The hostess, a preservation consultant, has created a showplace of the Federal period in her own home, with authentic antiques in every room. Located on historic East Side, within walking distance of Brown University and the Rhode Island School of Design. One suite with double bed and private bath, plus a room with two twin beds. Continental breakfast; air-conditioning; children welcome; no smoking. $80.

B&B Affiliates RI119

P.O. Box 3291
Newport, RI, 02840
(401) 849-1298

An interesting blend of modern and traditional styles in a 1849 Greek Revival home. There is a commanding view of Brown University and the surrounding city. One suite with two twins and a daybed, private bath. Continental breakfast, air-conditioning, dog in residence. Children are welcome. No smoking. $75.

B&B Affiliates RI122

P.O. Box 3291
Newport, RI, 02840
(401) 849-1298

Graciousness is a way of life in this lovely century-old Victorian with two sitting rooms. Breakfast is served on a lace-covered table in the formal dining room. Two rooms with private baths. Full breakfast. Three cats in residence; children welcome; smoking outdoors only. $55-65.

B&B Affiliates RI184

P.O. Box 3291
Newport, RI, 02840
(401) 849-1298

This 1930s home is located near Brown University and Rhode Island School of Design. The second-floor guest rooms have been appointed with rattan and wicker furniture. Three rooms with shared bath, hearty continental breakfast. Cat in residence; children welcome; smoking on porch only. $65.

B&B Affiliates RI208

P.O. Box 3291
Newport, RI, 02840
(401) 849-1298

This beautiful 1860 Italianate home is located in the historic East Side in an area known for outstanding architecture. Wide plank floors, marble fireplaces, and tasteful Oriental antiques, carpets, and exquisite paintings. A private third-floor suite includes a sleeping room and large sitting room, private bath. Continental breakfast, air conditioning; cat in residence. $75.

B&B Affiliates RI211

P.O. Box 3291
Newport, RI, 02840
(401) 849-1298

Two hundred years ago, the Federal part of this colonial stood on a large farm, which is now the historic East Side. The guest suite includes two sleeping rooms and a private bath. An 1830s four-poster bed, pre-Revolutionary Windsor chair, fireplace, and collection of antique teapots are just part of what makes the room special. An adjoining room features a 1795 single canopy bed. Continental breakfast; older children allowed; outdoor smoking only. $75.

B&B Affiliates RI232

P.O. Box 3291
Newport, RI, 02840
(401) 849-1298

This 1846 colonial is located on a quiet street within walking distance of Brown University. Two second-floor rooms, one with a king bed and private bath. Hearty continental or full breakfast; no children; nonsmokers preferred. $60.

B&B Affiliates RI234

P.O. Box 3291
Newport, RI, 02840
(401) 849-1298

This turn-of-the-century home is conveniently located on the East Side close to Wayland Square and Brown. The guest rooms has one twin bed and shared bath. Full breakfast, cat in residence; no children; restricted smoking. $45.

B&B Affiliates RI242

P.O. Box 3291
Newport, RI, 02840
(401) 849-1298

All rooms of this 1850s Greek Revival have a magnificent view of the domed State House. Breakfast is served in the kitchen on a huge oak table, or on the second-floor porch in summer. Two rooms have double beds and a shared bath. Breakfast is a hearty continental during the week and full on weekends. Children are welcome; smoking on porch only. $65.

B&B Affiliates RI250

P.O. Box 3291
Newport, RI, 02840
(401) 849-1298

Just a mile from Brown and two blocks from the bus line, this lovely 1905 home combines the advantages of a quiet neighborhood and proximity to East Side attractions. Three guest rooms with shared bath, continental breakfast. Children are welcome; no smoking. $65.

B&B Affiliates RI256

P.O. Box 3291
Newport, RI, 02840
(401) 849-1298

This quaint 1812 colonial is set back from the street and surrounded by beautiful gardens. Located just two blocks from Benefit Street and the Brown campus. The wide pine floors and exposed beams lend a feeling of history that is carried out in the second-floor guest rooms, one of which has a four-poster bed and Hitchcock chair. Two rooms with double beds and shared bath; one room has a fireplace. Continental breakfast, air-conditioning; children over five welcome; no smoking. $65.

The Old Court B&B

144 Benefit Street
Providence, RI, 02903
(401) 751-2002

In the heart of Providence's historic Benefit Street area, you'll find the Old Court, where tradition is combined with contemporary standards of luxury. The Old Court was built in 1863 and reflects early Victorian styles. In rooms that overlook downtown Providence and Brown University, you'll feel as if you've entered a more gracious era.

Host: Nicole Cini
Rooms: 10 (PB) $105-115
Continental Breakfast
Credit Cards: A, B, C
Notes: 2, 5, 7, 10, 11, 12, 14

SNUG HARBOR

"Almost Heaven" in Snug Harbor

49 West Street
Wakefield, RI, 02879
(401) 783-9272

Located around the corner from Rhode Island's beautiful saltwater beaches, marinas, and famous seafood restaurants, "Almost Heaven" offers the traveler easy access to everything. Newport, 30 minutes; Mystic, 40 minutes. Fishing, swimming, summer theater nearby. Peaceful and quiet. Accommodations are ideal for a family of four or two couples.

Host: Deloris Simpson
Rooms: 2 (SB) $47-62
Full Breakfast
Credit Cards: No
Notes: 2, 5, 7 (on deck), 8, 9, 10, 11, 12

SOUTH KINGSTOWN

Admiral Dewey Inn

668 Matunuck Beach Drive
South Kingstown, RI, 02879
(401) 783-2090; (401) 783-8298

Nestled in the small beach village of Matunuck, this Victorian B&B first opened for guests in 1898. Now on the National Historic Register, the Admiral Dewey has been completely restored and is decorated entirely with Victoriana. There are rockers on the wraparound porch, a large breakfast room with tiled fireplace. Near the Theatre-by-the-Sea, the Trustom Pond Wildlife

Refuge, Matunuck and Moonstone Beaches, and antique shops. Shuttle service to the Block Island ferry and local airports. Polish and French spoken.

Hosts: Joan & Hardy LeBel
Rooms: 10 (8 PB; 2 SB) $80-120
Continental Breakfast
Credit Cards: A, B
Notes: 2, 5, 9, 11, 12, 14

B&B Affiliates RI109

P.O. Box 3291
Newport, RI, 02840
(401) 849-1298

This contemporary home is a veritable gallery of artwork. Spiral stairs lead to the balcony overlooking the cathedral-ceiling sitting room, where a corner fireplace blazes during cool weather. Located on 3.5 acres near a salt pond and within walking distance of an uncrowded ocean beach. Two rooms, shared bath. Hearty continental breakfast; dog in residence; children over five welcome. $62.

B&B Affiliates RI112

P.O. Box 3291
Newport, RI, 02840
(401) 849-1298

This shuttered Cape is located on a quiet road within a mile of town. The surrounding woods offer privacy as you lounge in the backyard. Guests have a private entrance and are invited to relax in the parlor or enclosed porch. Two rooms with shared bath, full country breakfast. Cat in residence; children welcome; restricted smoking. $50-55.

B&B Affiliates RI235

P.O. Box 3291
Newport, RI, 02840
(401) 849-1298

This 1930s colonial is located in the historic village of Kingston, close to the University of Rhode Island. Spacious grounds include a lounge area, gardens, vine-covered arbor, and tennis court. Four rooms with semi-private baths, full breakfast. Children are welcome, smoking is restricted. $50-60.

B&B Affiliates RI237

P.O. Box 3291
Newport, RI, 02840
(401) 849-1298

This exquisite 1818 Federal home has all the New England charm you could want. It is one of the oldest houses in Wakefield and was once the home of a state governor. There is a game room, TV, library, and in-ground swimming pool. Two double rooms with private bath. One room has an attached single room for family groups. Full country breakfast; children over twelve welcome; no smoking. $65-75.

B&B Affiliates RI255

P.O. Box 3291
Newport, RI, 02840
(401) 849-1298

This quiet farmhouse borders a reservation originating from an Indian outpost dating back to 1675. Nestled on the shores of Worden's Pond, it offers peaceful surroundings with the convenience of major highways nearby. Bring your own canoe to enjoy the pond. One room with shared bath, color TV. Rollaways available. Full breakfast; pets and farm animals on premises; pets welcome if restrained. $35-40.

WAKEFIELD

Blueberry Bush B&B

128 South Road
Wakefield, RI, 02879
(401) 783-0907

Blueberry Bush B&B

Oversized Cape Cod with a large backyard containing cooking facilities for families. Central location for Mystic Village and Seaport, Newport, Block Island, and all the "South County" beaches in Rhode Island. Hosts for nine years.

Hosts: June & Peter Nielsen
Rooms: 2 (SB) $55
Full Breakfast
Credit Cards: No
Notes: 2, 5, 7 (limited), 11, 12, 14

WARWICK

B&B Affiliates RI283

P.O. Box 3291
Newport, RI, 02840
(401) 849-1298

Located in historic Pawtuxet Village, this beautifully refinished Victorian features a wraparound porch, spacious sitting room with antiques, dining room with fireplace, and spacious yard. Two rooms with shared bath on the second floor. Hearty continental breakfast; dog in residence; smoking outdoors. $55.

WESTERLY

B&B Affiliates RI141

P.O. Box 3291
Newport, RI, 02840
(401) 849-1298

Located on 20 acres in a country setting, but just two miles from the ocean, the home is situated on a hilltop and surrounded by rolling fields and informal gardens. Three rooms with shared baths, hearty continental breakfast. Children are welcome; two cats in residence; outdoor smoking only. $50-60.

B&B Affiliates RI172

P.O. Box 3291
Newport, RI, 02840
(401) 849-1298

This 1835 classic Greek Revival is in the heart of the city's cultural center. Wilcox Park is just across the street, with 12 acres of gardens, a gazebo, walking paths, and fountains. Three rooms with shared bath on the second floor, hearty continental breakfast.

Children are welcome; restricted smoking. $60-65.

B&B Affiliates RI180

P.O. Box 3291
Newport, RI, 02840
(401) 849-1298

This lovely early twentieth-century home has an expansive wraparound stone porch and magnificent view of the ocean across the salt ponds. Two golf courses and one tennis club within walking distance. Misquamicut Beach and Watch Hill are minutes away, and Mystic is just a short drive. Twelve rooms, shared and private baths. Hearty continental breakfast; no children; restricted smoking. $45-85.

Pineapple Hospitality RI235

P.O. Box F821
New Bedford, MA, 02742-0821
(508) 990-1696

A 1920s Gustave Stickley summer cottage located on the ocean marshes five minutes from town beaches. Two bedrooms, one with water view. Two double beds or one canopy double; private bath. Continental breakfast. No smoking; children over three are welcome. $95.

Shelter Harbor Inn

10 Wagner Road
Westerly, RI, 02891
(401) 322-8883

This early nineteenth-century farm, transformed into a delightful country inn serving breakfast, lunch, and dinner daily year-round, is ideally located between Mystic and Newport. Twenty-four guest rooms with private baths. Paddle tennis and croquet—hot tub and private beach. Public golf and tennis nearby.

Hosts: Jim & Debbye Dey
Rooms: 24 (PB) $78-102
Full Breakfast
Credit Cards: A, B, C, E
Notes: 2, 3, 4, 5, 7, 8, 9, 10, 11, 12, 14

Woody Hill Guest House B&B

330 Woody Hill Road
Westerly, RI, 02891
(401) 322-0452

Your hostess, a high-school English teacher, invites you to share her reproduction colonial home with antiques and gardens. You may snuggle under quilts, relax on the porch swing, visit nearby Newport and Mystic, or swim at beautiful ocean beaches. Westerly has it all!

Host: Dr. Ellen L. Madison
Rooms: 3 (1 PB; 2 SB) $55-65
Full Breakfast
Credit Cards: No
Closed one week in Feb.
Notes: 2, 5, 8, 9, 10, 11, 12

WESTERLY/HAVERSHAM

Covered Bridge 1 RI

P.O. Box 447A
Norfolk, CT, 06058
(203) 542-5944

1920s beach house overlooking a saltwater pond, beautifully decorated by the architect-artist owner. There are two guest rooms with private baths, one with a deck, in the main house. There are also two cottages on the grounds. The public beach is close by, and it is an easy drive to Mystic or Newport. Continental-plus breakfast. $95-110.

WYOMING

B&B Affiliates RI-278

P.O. Box 3291
Newport, RI, 02840
(401) 849-1298

A peaceful country setting on a quiet road. Country decor and antiques give this recently built saltbox home a feeling of yesteryear. Cathedral ceiling with large windows; two guest rooms just off the second-floor gallery that overlooks the sitting room. A continental breakfast is served in a sunny alcove just off the kitchen. Shared bath; children welcome; limited smoking. $35-55.

The Way Stop

161 New London Turnpike
Wyoming, RI, 02898
(401) 539-7233

A 1757 post-and-beam farmhouse located on 50 acres of fields, woods, and pond for hiking, swimming, canoeing, or paddle boating. Providence, beaches, historic sites, Mystic, and outlet shopping are a short distance away. Fireplaces, a screened porch, patios, many antiques, and "eclectic stuff" abound for relaxing.

Host: Billie Stetson
Rooms: 2 (SB) $50 + tax
Continental Breakfast
Credit Cards: No
Open April-Oct.
Notes: 6, 7, 8, 9, 10, 11, 12, 14

South Carolina

ABBEVILLE

The Belmont Inn

106 East Pickens Street
Abbeyville, SC, 29620
(803) 459-9625

The Belmont Inn has its own special ambience and provides its guests the finest in intimacy and privacy. Your stay will be marked by graceful personal service and attention to detail in an atmosphere of Southern elegance. Full dining, lounge, and meeting rooms. Listed in the National Register of Historic Places.

Rooms: 24 (PB) $50-65
Continental Breakfast
Credit Cards: A, B, C
Notes: 2, 3, 4, 5, 7, 8, 9, 10, 11, 12, 14

AIKEN

The Willcox Inn

100 Colleton Avenue
Aiken, SC, 29801
(803) 649-1377; (800) 288-6754

Beautiful, spacious rooms that have been occupied by Winston Churchill, President Roosevelt, and Elizabeth Arden. Our dining room is known for its fine cuisine, including pheasant in whiskey sauce, rack of lamb, etc. Beautiful town with a lot to offer: golf, polo matches, antique shopping, and more.

Host: Stig Jorgensen
Rooms: 30 (PB) $93-113
Full Breakfast
Credit Cards: A, B, C
Notes: 3, 4, 5, 7, 8, 9, 10, 12, 14

ANDERSON

Evergreen Inn

1103 South Main Street
Anderson, SC, 29621
(803) 225-1109

Two historic mansions on the National Register, with on-premises restaurant. The inn has seven guest rooms, six baths, and eight fireplaces; there is also a honeymoon suite done in pink and rose velvet with satin and lace. Twenty minutes away from three lakes, each with over 1,000 miles of shoreline and public parks. Antique shops and the downtown area are within walking distance. Located halfway between Charlotte and Atlanta, the inn is an excellent stopping place for a quiet dinner and enjoyable stay.

Hosts: Peter & Myrna Ryter
Rooms: 7 (6 PB; 2 SB) $65
Continental Breakfast
Credit Cards: A, B, C, E
Notes: 2, 4, 5, 7, 9, 10, 11, 12

BEAUFORT

Bay Street Inn

601 Bay Street
Beaufort, SC, 29902
(803) 524-7720

Fourteen-room Sams Mansion on the inland waterway, once a planter's townhouse and now on the National Register. Five bedrooms with water views; gardens, library, golf, tennis, beach, bikes available. Featured in the movie "The Prince of Tides."

Hosts: Gene & Kathleen Roe
Rooms: 5 (PB) $70-80

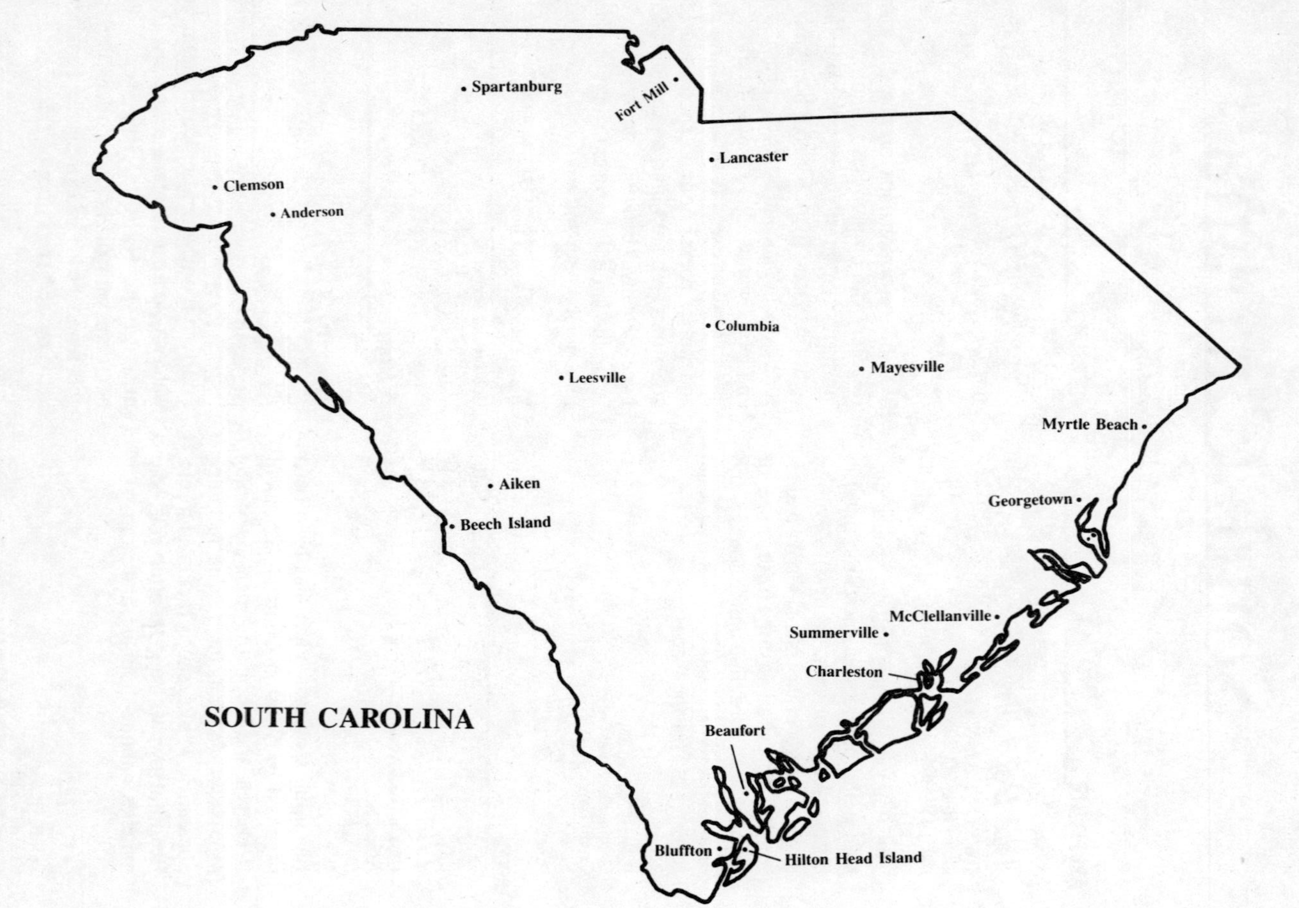
SOUTH CAROLINA
Spartanburg
Fort Mill
Lancaster
Clemson
Anderson
Columbia
Mayesville
Leesville
Myrtle Beach
Aiken
Beech Island
Georgetown
McClellanville
Summerville
Charleston
Beaufort
Bluffton
Hilton Head Island

Full Breakfast
Credit Cards: A, B
Notes: 2, 5, 7, 8, 9, 10, 11, 12

The Rhett House Inn

1009 Craven Street
Beaufort, SC, 29902
(803) 524-9030

All the guest rooms have been created for your comfort and convenience. They are authentically furnished with homespun quilts and freshly cut flowers, adding to their warmth and individuality. Our inn beautifully recreates the feeling of the Old South. You'll fall in love with the warmth and graciousness of an earlier way of life.

Hosts: Marianne & Steve Harrison
Rooms: 8 (PB) $85.60-131
Full Breakfast
Minimum stay weekends & holidays: 2
Credit Cards: A, B
Notes: 2, 5, 8 (over 5), 9, 10, 11, 12, 14

The Cedars B&B Inn

BEECH ISLAND

The Cedars B&B Inn

1325 Williston Road, Box 117
Beech Island, SC, 29841
(803) 827-0248

An 1820s country manor house on 12 parklike acres, six miles east of Augusta, Ga. Beautifully decorated with antiques and reproductions; modern baths. Close by are Redcliffe Plantation State Park, fine dining, antique shops, and historic districts.

Hosts: Ralph & Maggie Zieger
Rooms: 4 (3 PB; 1 SB) $44-50
Continental-plus Breakfast
Credit Cards: A, B
Notes: 2, 5, 7, 8 (over 12), 9, 12, 14

BLUFFTON

The Fripp House Inn

Box 857, Bluffton, SC, 29910
(803) 757-2139

Built in 1835, Fripp House is a landmark of this historic village on the May River. Private gardens with pool and fountains; spacious home with warm hospitality and hearty breakfast. Five minutes from Hilton Head Island.

Hosts: Grant & Dana Tuttle
Rooms: 3 (PB) $46-81
Full Breakfast
Minimum stay holidays: 2
Credit Cards: A, B
Notes: 2, 5, 8, 9, 10, 11, 12, 14

CHARLESTON

Anne Harper's B&B

56 Smith Street
Charleston, SC, 29401
(803) 723-3947

This circa 1870 home is located in Charleston's historic district. Two connecting rooms with connecting bath and sitting area with TV. The owner is a retired medical technologist and enjoys serving a full breakfast.

Host: Ann D. Harper
Rooms: 2 (PB) $60
Full Breakfast
Minimum stay: 2
Credit Cards: No
Notes: 2, 5, 7 (limited), 8 (over 10), 9, 10, 11, 12

Ansonborough Inn

21 Hasell Street
Charleston, SC, 29401
(803) 723-1655; (800) 522-2073

Turn-of-the-century warehouse that has been converted into a 37-suite inn located in the historic district. Each suite has a sitting area, bedroom(s), private bath, and kitchen facilities. Off-street parking, morning newspaper, continental breakfast, and afternoon wine service are included in the rate. Meeting facilities are available.

Hosts: Buck & Frankie Limehouse
Rooms: 37 (PB) $89-158
Continental Breakfast
Credit Cards: A, B, C
Notes: 2, 5, 7, 8, 9, 12, 14

Barksdale House Inn

27 George Street
Charleston, SC, 29401
(803) 577-4800

One of Charleston's most luxurious ten-room inns. A 200-year-old home featuring individually designed rooms, some with whirlpool tubs and fireplaces. Flowers, daily newspaper, wine, tea, sherry, turndown service with chocolates, fountain in the courtyard, and parking. Transportation to and from the airport is available with advance notice.

Hosts: George & Peggy Sloan
Rooms: 20 (PB) $75-150
Continental Breakfast
Credit Cards: A, B
Closed Dec. 24-25
Notes: 2 (deposit), 5, 7, 8 (over 12), 9, 10, 11, 12, 14

The Belvedere

40 Rutledge Avenue
Charleston, SC, 29401
(803) 722-0973

Beautiful colonial 1900 mansion on the exterior with an 1800 Georgian interior. Located in the downtown historic section, on Colonial Lake, within short walking distance of all historic points of interest, restaurants, and shopping. Continental breakfast and use of public areas and piazzas in this romantic, beautifully restored and furnished mansion.

Hosts: David S. Spell & Rick Zender
Rooms: 3 (PB) $95-110
Continental Breakfast
Credit Cards: No
Closed Dec 1-Feb. 15
Notes: 2, 9, 10, 11, 12, 14

Brewton House

Historic Charleston B&B
43 Legare Street
Charleston, SC, 29401
(803) 722-6606

This carriage house has a first-floor living room, dining room, kitchen, washer-dryer. On the second floor are two bedrooms—one queen four-poster and one twin—full bath. Garden and patio. Nonsmokers preferred. $115.

Cannonboro Inn

Cannonboro Inn

184 Ashley Avenue
Charleston, SC, 29403
(803) 723-8572

NOTES: Credit cards accepted: A Master Card; B Visa; C American Express; D Discover Card; E Diners Club; F Other: 2 Personal checks accepted: 3 Lunch available: 4 Dinner available: 5 Open all year

Traditional B&B inn recognized by the City of Charleston as an architecturally significant structure. Guests enjoy a full American breakfast in the formal dining room or on the columned piazza overlooking a Low Country garden. Located within the historic district.

Hosts: Robert Warley & James Hare
Rooms: 6 (PB) $59-79
Full Breakfast
Credit Cards: A, B
Notes: 2, 5, 8, 9, 12, 14

Country Victorian B&B

Country Victorian B&B

105 Tradd Street
Charleston, SC, 29401-2422
(803) 577-0682

Rooms have private entrances and contain antique iron and brass beds, old quilts, oak and wicker antique furniture, and braided rugs over heart of pine floors. Homemade cookies will be waiting. The house, built in 1820, is within walking distance of restaurants, antique shops, churches, art galleries, museums, and all historic points of interest. Parking and bicycles are available. Many extras.

Host: Diane Deardurff Weed
Rooms: 2 (PB) $65-85
Continental-plus Breakfast
Credit Cards: No
Notes: 2, 5, 8, 9, 10, 11, 12, 14

1837 Bed & Breakfast

126 Wentworth Street
Charleston, SC, 29401
(803) 723-7166

Accommodations in a wealthy cotton planter's home and brick carriage house. Centrally located in the historic district, within walking distance of boat tours, Old Market, antique shops, restaurants, and main attractions. Full gourmet breakfast is served in the formal dining room.

Hosts: Richard Dunn & Sherri Weaver
Rooms: 8 (PB) $49-85
Full Breakfast
Credit Cards: A, B, C
Notes: 2, 5, 9, 10, 11, 12

Elliot House Inn

78 Queen Street
Charleston, SC, 29401
(800) 729-1855

Twenty-six beautifully appointed guest rooms graced with elegant period-style furniture and Oriental rugs. Secluded courtyard with heated Jacuzzi for year-round enjoyment. Within walking distance of fine restaurants, horse-drawn carriage tours, and the best shopping.

Host: Louise Doyle
Rooms: 26 (PB) $100-130
Continental Breakfast
Credit Cards: A, B, C
Notes: 2, 3, 4, 5, 6, 7, 8, 9, 10, 11, 12, 14

Greely House

Historic Charleston B&B
43 Legare Street
Charleston, SC, 29401
(803) 722-6606

A carriage house with two separate units. The first floor bedroom has twin beds and a full bath. On the second floor there are two bedrooms with an adjoining bath. One room has twin beds, the other a double. These two rooms are rented only to the same party. $60.

The Hayne House

30 King Street
Charleston, SC, 29412
(803) 577-2633

Circa 1755 with 1820 addition, one of the city's oldest B&Bs, on the National Register. Located one block from the Battery, within the heart of the historic district. Walking distance from shopping, restaurants, Waterfront Park. Nice back porch with rockers and a swing. Furnished in antiques. Sitting room, piano, no TV, but lots of good books. Bicycles; complimentary tea; continental-plus breakfast.

Host: Ben Chapman
Rooms: 4 (PB) $55-80
Continental-plus Breakfast
Minimum stay weekends & holidays: 2
Credit Cards: B
Notes: 2, 5, 7, 8, 9, 10, 11, 12

Historic Charleston B&B 2

43 Legare Street
Charleston, SC, 29401
(803) 722-6606

On Tradd Street, this house offers a bedroom with twin beds, full bath, lovely garden, off-street parking, small refrigerator. $55.

Historic Charleston B&B 4

43 Legare Street
Charleston, SC, 29401
(803) 722-6606

A Rutledge Avenue carriage house with living room, fireplace, patio, and sleeper bed. On the second floor is a double room, bath, and study. $85.

Historic Charleston B&B 5

43 Legare Street
Charleston, SC, 29401
(803) 722-6606

Two units on Legare Street. The carriage house has a living room, kitchen, and half bath. The second-floor has a bedroom with twins, dressing room, and full bath. There is also an efficiency with fireplace, seating area, double bed, bath, small kitchen. $65-80.

Historic Charleston B&B 6

43 Legare Street
Charleston, SC, 29401
(803) 722-6606

On Gibbes Street. Bedroom with queen canopy bed, full bath, small refrigerator. $75.

Historic Charleston B&B 7

43 Legare Street
Charleston, SC, 29401
(803) 722-6606

Four units in a carriage house on Broad Street. One has twin beds, bath, and kitchen. The second has twin beds with full bath. The third, a double bed with full bath. The last offers a queen bed with fireplace and bath. No smoking. $70-80.

Historic Charleston B&B 8

43 Legare Street
Charleston, SC, 29401
(803) 722-6606

On Tradd Street. Living room with fireplace, bedroom with twin beds, full bath, and off-street parking. $70.

Historic Charleston B&B 9

43 Legare Street
Charleston, SC, 29401
(803) 722-6606

Large bedroom with queen bed, seating area, and full bath. Patio, small refrigerator, off-street parking. $80.

Historic Charleston B&B 10

43 Legare Street
Charleston, SC, 29401
(803) 722-6606

Limehouse Street. Carriage house with living room and fireplace, kitchen. Second floor has a double bed, full bath. Off-street parking. $90.

Historic Charleston B&B 10A

43 Legare Street
Charleston, SC, 29401
(803) 722-6606

Wentworth Street. Carriage house. First floor includes a small kitchen, full bath, spiral stairs leading to loft with queen poster bed. Off-street parking; nonsmokers preferred. $85.

Historic Charleston B&B 11

43 Legare Street
Charleston, SC, 29401
(803) 722-6606

Orange Street carriage house. On the first floor is a living room, efficiency kitchen. The second floor has a large bedroom with a double bed and single bed, full bath. $85.

Historic Charleston B&B 12

43 Legare Street
Charleston, SC, 29401
(803) 722-6606

Orange Street. Bedroom with queen canopy bed, bath, lovely walled Charleston garden. Small refrigerator and microwave available. Nonsmokers preferred. $70.

Historic Charleston B&B 14

43 Legare Street
Charleston, SC, 29401
(803) 722-6606

On Tradd Street. Sitting room, bedroom with twin beds, bath, off-street parking. No smoking. $70.

Historic Charleston B&B 15

43 Legare Street
Charleston, SC, 29401
(803) 722-6606

Broad Street. Large bedroom with queen bed, full bath with Jacuzzi tub. Off-street parking. Nonsmokers preferred. $85.

Historic Charleston B&B 16

43 Legare Street
Charleston, SC, 29401
(803) 722-6606

Hassell Street carriage house. Large bedroom with a queen canopy bed, kitchen, full bath, off-street parking. Nonsmokers. $80.

Historic Charleston B&B 17

43 Legare Street
Charleston, SC, 29401
(803) 722-6606

Two units on Tradd Street. The first is a large room with twin beds, sitting area, breakfast area, full bath. The second is a suite with living room, small kitchen, breakfast area, bedroom with queen bed. $80-90.

Historic Charleston B&B 18

43 Legare Street
Charleston, SC, 29401
(803) 722-6606

Two units on Tradd Street. The first has a first-floor bedroom with double bed and full bath. The second is a bedroom with twin beds and full bath. Off-street parking; no smoking. $65.

Historic Charleston B&B 19

43 Legare Street
Charleston, SC, 29401
(803) 722-6606

Anson Street room with queen bed, trundle sofa, kitchenette, bath, and patio. No smoking. $75.

Historic Charleston B&B 20

43 Legare Street
Charleston, SC, 29401
(803) 722-6606

Tradd Street room with king bed, full bath, off-street parking. No smoking. $75.

Historic Charleston B&B 22

43 Legare Street
Charleston, SC, 29401
(803) 722-6606

Broad Street room with queen bed, sitting room with sofa, full bath, off-street parking. $80.

Historic Charleston B&B 23

43 Legare Street
Charleston, SC, 29401
(803) 722-6606

King Street carriage house. On the first floor is a large living room with sleeper sofa, fireplace, and efficiency kitchen. The second floor has a bedroom with twin beds, full bath, washer/dryer. $100.

Historic Charleston B&B 24

43 Legare Street
Charleston, SC, 29401
(803) 722-6606

George Street carriage house. Two units, each with a living room with sleeper sofa and full kitchen. Bedroom with queen bed and full bath. Both units have porches, cable TV, and off-street parking. $85.

Historic Charleston B&B 25

43 Legare Street
Charleston, SC, 29401
(803) 722-6606

Lenwood Street. On the first floor is a living room with sleeper sofa, full kitchen, and half bath. On the second floor, the bedroom has a double canopy bed and cable TV. Off-street parking. $80.

Historic Charleston B&B 2A

43 Legare Street
Charleston, SC, 29401
(803) 722-6606

Wentworth Street. On the first floor is a living room with fireplace, dining room, kitchen, and private patio. On the second are two bedrooms and a full bath. Off-street parking. $75.

Historic Charleston B&B 3A

43 Legare Street
Charleston, SC, 29401
(803) 722-6606

Tradd Street. On the first floor is a living room with fireplace. On the second, two bedrooms, full bath. Off-street parking. $75.

Historic Charleston B&B 4A

43 Legare Street
Charleston, SC, 29401
(803) 722-6606

Meeting Street. Two units. The first has a living room with fireplace, daybed, kitchen, bedroom with double canopy bed, and bath. The second has a large living room with fireplace, kitchen, bedroom with queen canopy bed, full bath, daybed, porches. Off-street parking. $95.

Historic Charleston B&B 6A

43 Legare Street
Charleston, SC, 29401
(803) 722-6606

Tradd Street kitchen house. On the first floor is a living room with fireplace. The second floor includes two bedrooms, full bath. Garden and patio. Nonsmokers preferred. $125.

Historic Charleston B&B 7A

43 Legare Street
Charleston, SC, 29401
(803) 722-6606

Rutledge Avenue carriage house. The first floor has a living room with fireplace and double sleeper sofa, plus kitchen with fireplace and washer/dryer. The second floor has two bedrooms, bath. Bikes available, off-street parking available. No smoking. $80.

Historic Charleston B&B 8A

43 Legare Street
Charleston, SC, 29401
(803) 722-6606

Wentworth Street. Two bedrooms (one king and the other double canopy), bath. Full breakfast is served. Off-street parking is available. No smoking. $85.

Historic Charleston B&B 9A

43 Legare Street
Charleston, SC, 29401
(803) 722-6606

Broad Street carriage house. On the first floor is a living room with fireplace, kitchen, and bath. The second has two bedrooms, full bath. Off-street parking. $95.

Historic Charleston B&B 10A

43 Legare Street
Charleston, SC, 29401
(803) 722-6606

Church Street carriage house. The first floor includes living/dining room with fireplace and full kitchen, half bath, and laundry room. Second floor includes two bedrooms with double beds and full bath. Off-street parking. $85.

Historic Charleston B&B 11A

43 Legare Street
Charleston, SC, 29401
(803) 722-6606

George Street. Living room with working fireplace, kitchen, two bedrooms, and full bath. Grand piano, cable TV, and off-street parking. $95.

Historic Charleston B&B 12A

43 Legare Street
Charleston, SC, 29401
(803) 722-6606

First floor includes living room with fireplace, full kitchen, and patio. Second floor has two bedrooms, one queen and one double, full bath, washer/dryer. $95.

Historic Charleston B&B 13A

43 Legare Street
Charleston, SC, 29401
(803) 722-6606

Wentworth Street carriage house with two units. The first has a large room with queen poster bed, full bath, refrigerator, and separate sink in room. Large patio.The second unit offers two rooms, fireplace, bath. $80-90.

Historic Charleston B&B 1B

43 Legare Street
Charleston, SC, 29401
(803) 722-6606

Wentworth Street. Second floor. One unit las a large bedroom with full bath. Two others have queen canopy beds with adjoining bath. No smoking. $85.

Historic Charleston B&B 3B

43 Legare Street
Charleston, SC, 29401
(803) 722-6606

King Street bedroom with double canopy bed. Also one single room with full bath. Three other rooms, two with private baths. $55-75.

Historic Charleston B&B 5B

43 Legare Street
Charleston, SC, 29401
(803) 722-6606

Beaufain Street. Two suites. The first has a large bedroom with king bed and a room with single bed, full bath, small refrigerator, private piazza with hammock, and a delightful view of Colonial Lake. The second has a large bedroom with queen bed and another room with a single bed, small refrigerator, piazza overlooking the lake. No smoking. $95.

Historic Charleston B&B 7B

43 Legare Street
Charleston, SC, 29401
(803) 722-6606

South Battery. Small sitting room, three bedrooms, full bath. $55.

Indigo Inn

1 Maiden Lane
Charleston, SC, 29401
(803) 577-5900; (800) 845-7639

Located in the heart of Charleston's historic district, the Indigo Inn is renown for its Southern hospitality. All rooms are appointed in eighteenth-century antiques and antique reproductions. The complimentary Hunt Breakfast is best enjoyed in our intimate courtyard. Private parking, complimentary newspaper, and afternoon wine service.

Hosts: Buck & Frankie Limehouse
Rooms: 40 (PB) $110-140
Continental Breakfast
Credit Cards: A, B, C
Notes: 2, 5, 6, 7, 8, 9, 12, 14

Jasmine House

64 Hasell Street
Charleston, SC, 29401
(803) 577-5900; (800) 845-7639

Elegant 1840s Greek Revival mansion and carriage house, completely restored and furnished with fine antiques. Traditional Charleston courtyard (with Jacuzzi), continental breakfast, and afternoon wine service. Located in the historic district, two blocks from market.

Hosts: Buck & Frankie Limehouse
Rooms: 8 (PB) $125-195
Continental Breakfast
Credit Cards: A, B, C
Notes: 2, 5, 7, 8, 9, 12, 14

John Rutledge House Inn

116 Broad Street
Charleston, SC, 29401
(803) 723-7999; (800) 476-9741

This National Landmark was built in 1763 by John Rutledge, coauthor and signer of the U.S. Constitution. Large rooms and suites located in the main and carriage houses offer the ambience of historic Charleston. Rates include wine and sherry upon arrival, turndown service with brandy and chocolate, and breakfast with newspaper delivered to your room.

Host: Richard Widman
Rooms: 19 (PB) $100-220
Continental Breakfast
Credit Cards: A, B, C
Notes: 2, 5, 7, 8, 9, 10, 11, 12, 14

Kerrison Mansion

Historic Charleston B&B
43 Legare Street
Charleston, SC, 29401
(803) 722-6606

A gazebo garden house with living room, kitchen, spiral stairs to a hexagonal bedroom with queen bed. Private bath with shower; patio. No smoking. $85.

Kings Courtyard Inn

198 King Street
Charleston, SC, 29401
(803) 723-7000; (800) 845-6119

Kings Courtyard Inn, circa 1853, is located in the heart of the antique and historic district. Convenient to attractions, shops, and restaurants. Rate includes continental breakfast and newspaper, wine and sherry served in the lobby. Turndown service with chocolate and brandy. AAA four diamond.

Host: Laura Fox
Doubles: 34 (PB) $130
Type of Beds: 10 Double;10 Queen; 14 King
Continental Breakfast
Credit Cards: A, B, C
Notes: 2, 5, 7, 8, 9, 10, 11, 12, 14

Maison DuPre

East Bay & George Streets
Charleston, SC, 29401
(803) 723-8691; (800) 662-INNS

Three restored Charleston "single houses" and two carriage houses comprise Maison DuPre, originally built in 1804. The inn features period furniture and antiques and is ideally located in the historic Ansonborough district. Complimentary continental breakfast and a "Low-Country Tea Party" are served. "Maison DuPre with its faded stucco, pink brick and gray shutters is one of the city's best-looking small inns" — *New York Times.*

Hosts: Lucille, Bob & Mark Mulholland
Doubles: 15 (PB) $98-200
Type of Beds: 2 Twin; 13 Queen
Continental Breakfast
Credit Cards: A, B, C
Notes: 2, 5, 8, 9, 10, 11, 12

Middleton Inn

Ashley River Road
Mail to: Limehouse Properties
8 Cumberland Street
Charleston, SC, 29401
(803) 556-0500; (800) 571-7277

Located along the Ashley River in the historic plantation district. Each room features fireplace, Italian tile bathroom, and beautiful paneling. On-premises swimming, tennis, nature walks. Golf nearby. Historic market area is fifteen minutes away. Rate includes a continental breakfast, parking, newspaper, and recreation.

Hosts: Buck & Frankie Limehouse
Rooms: 52 (PB) $79-124
Continental Breakfast
Credit Cards: A, B, C
Notes: 2, 5, 6, 7, 8, 9, 10, 11, 12, 14

The Palmer Home

5 East Battery
Charleston, SC, 29401
(803) 722-4325

Magnificent antebellum mansion overlooking Fort Sumter (where the Civil War began) and Charleston Harbor. Located in the heart of the historic district. Swimming pool on premises.

Host: Dr. Olivia Palmer
Rooms: 3 (PB) $95
Continental Breakfast
Credit Cards: No
Notes: 2, 5, 10, 11, 14

Rutledge Victorian Guest House

114 Rutledge Avenue
Charleston, SC, 29401
(803) 722-7551

A century-old Victorian house in Charleston's historic district—quaint but elegant, with a beautiful decorative porch. Inside the house are twelve-foot ceilings, eight-to-ten-foot doors and windows, and fireplaces everywhere. Ten- to twenty-minute walk to boat tours, shopping, dining, historic sights. Air conditioning, parking, TV, and help with tours and sight-seeing are available.

Hosts: Jean, BJ, & Mike
Rooms: 8-11 (5 PB; 3-6 SB) $45-85
Continental Breakfast
Credit Cards: A, B
Notes: 2, 5, 7 (outside), 8, 9, 10, 11, 12, 14

Shealy House

Historic Charleston B&B
43 Legare Street
Charleston, SC, 29401
(803) 722-6606

One bedroom with queen canopy bed, efficiency kitchen, sitting area with a trundle sofa, full bath, portacrib, bicycles, and off-street parking. No smoking. $85.

Villa de La Fontaine B&B

138 Wentworth Street
Charleston, SC, 29401
(803) 577-7709

Villa de La Fontaine is a columned Greek Revival mansion in the heart of the historic district. It was built in 1838, and boasts a three-quarter-acre garden with fountain and terraces. It has been restored to impeccable condition and furnished with museum-quality furniture and accessories. Your hosts are retired A.S.I.D. interior designers and have decorated the rooms with eighteenth-century American antiques. Several of the rooms feature canopy beds. Breakfast is prepared by a master chef who prides himself on serving a different menu every day. Off-street parking.

Hosts: William Fontaine & Aubrey Hancock
Rooms: 4 (PB) $85
Suites: 2 (PB) $135
Full Breakfast
Minimum stay weekends 2; holidays: 3; Spoleto: 3
Credit Cards: A, B, C
Notes: 2, 5, 8 (12 and over), 9, 10, 11, 12, 14

Webb House

Historic Charleston B&B
43 Legare Street
Charleston, SC, 29401
(803) 722-6606

Two bedrooms, one with a queen canopy bed, one with a double canopy bed. Full bath, screened porch, and off-street parking. $75.

NOTES: Credit cards accepted: A Master Card; B Visa; C American Express; D Discover Card; E Diners Club; F Other: 2 Personal checks accepted: 3 Lunch available: 4 Dinner available: 5 Open all year

CLEMSON

Nord-Lac

Box 1111
Clemson, SC, 29633
(803) 639-2939

Located in a rural setting in the Smoky Mountain foothills, this B&B has two structures. One is a fairly modern home with three exquisitely antique-furnished rooms; the other is an 1826 log cabin that sleeps four. Tennis, billiards, and an antique museum are on the premises.

Hosts: Elaine & Jim Chisman
Rooms: 4 (2 PB; 2 SB) $40-100
Full Breakfast
Credit Cards: No
Notes: 2, 5, 8, 9, 10, 11, 12, 14

COLUMBIA

Claussen's Inn

2003 Greene Street
Columbia, SC, 29205
(803) 765-0440; (800) 622-3382

Restored bakery, c. 1928, listed in the historic register and located within walking distance of shopping, restaurants, and entertainment. Luxurious rooms with private baths, outdoor Jacuzzi, and four-poster beds. Rates include a continental breakfast delivered to the guest room, complimentary wine and sherry, turndown service with chocolates and brandy, and a newspaper.

Host: Dan O. Vance
Rooms: 29 (PB) $75-100
Continental Breakfast
Credit Cards: A, B, C
Notes: 5, 7, 8, 9, 10, 12, 14

FORT MILL

Pleasant Valley B&B Inn

160 East at Blackwelder Road
P.O. Box 446
Fort Mill, SC, 29715
(803) 548-5671

Nestled in the beautiful Old English District, the inn is located in the wooded, peaceful countryside. Built in 1874, it has been restored and furnished with some antiques. Each of the guest rooms has its own bath and TV. After breakfast, take a stroll in the shade of 100-year-old oaks. Equipped with facilities for the disabled. The house is convenient to Carowinds Theme Park, Rock Hill, Lancaster, SC, and Charlotte, NC. Ten percent senior citizen discount.

Hosts: Mr. and Mrs. Bob Lawrence
Rooms: 5 (PB) $45
Continental Breakfast
Credit Cards: No
Closed Dec. 15-Jan. 1
Notes: 2, 8, 10, 11, 12, 14

GEORGETOWN

Five Thirty Prince Street

530 Prince Street
Georgetown, SC, 29440
(803) 527-1114

Innovatively decorated, light, airy 75-year-old home nestled in a charming c. 1725 national register historic district. High ceilings, fans, seven fireplaces, full gourmet breakfasts. Stroll to shops, excellent restaurants, and the Harborwalk. Short drive to nearby beaches, golf. Boat, tram, and walking tours available. Enjoy the Low Country's finest. One hour to Charleston and Myrtle Beach.

Host: Nancy Bazemore
Rooms: 2 (PB) $60
Full Breakfast
Credit Cards: No
Notes: 2, 5, 6, 7, 8, 9, 10, 11, 12, 14

The Shaw House

8 Cypress Court
Georgetown, SC, 29440
(803) 546-9663

Lovely view overlooking Willowbank Marsh; wonderful bird watching. Many antiques throughout the house; rocking chairs on porch. Within walking distance of the historical district and many wonderful restaurants. Fresh fruits and Southern breakfast. One hour drive to Myrtle Beach or Charleston.

Hosts: Mary & Joe Shaw
Rooms: 3 (PB) $45
Full Breakfast
Credit Cards: No
Notes: 2, 5, 7, 8, 9, 10, 11, 12, 14

HILTON HEAD ISLAND

Ambiance

8 Wren Drive
Hilton Head Island, SC, 29928
(803) 671-4981

Marny welcomes you to sunny Hilton Head Island. Her cypress home, nestled in subtropical surroundings, is located in Sea Pines Plantation. Ambiance reflects the hostess's interior decorating business by the same name. All of the amenities of Hilton Head are offered in a contemporary, congenial atmosphere. The climate is favorable year-round for all sports. Ambiance is across the street from a beautiful beach and the Atlantic Ocean.

Host: Marny Kridel Daubenspeck
Rooms: 2 (PB) $60-70
Continental Breakfast
Credit Cards: No
Notes: 2, 5, 7, 8 (over 12), 9, 10, 11, 12

Halcyon

Shipyard Plantation Harbour Master 604
Hilton Head Island, SC, 29928
(803) 785-7912

Living room, dining room, music room, and sun deck are all available to our guests. Halcyon House is close to the pool, bike trails, beach, and bird-watching sites. Transportation and historic tours of Charleston, Savannah, and Beaufort may be arranged on request.

Host: Maybelle Wayburn
Double: 1 (PB) $65
Type of Beds: 1 Double
Continental Breakfast
Credit Cards: No
Notes: 2, 4, 7, 9, 10, 11, 12

LEESVILLE

Able House Inn

244 West Church Street
Leesville, SC, 29072
(803) 532-2763

Chateau estate, ten miles from I-20 on Route 1, thirty minutes from Columbia. Choose from five guest rooms, each with private bath. Living room, sun room, swimming pool, and patio are available to guests. Fresh popcorn and soft drinks each evening.

Hosts: Annabelle & Jack Wright
Rooms: 5 (PB) From $45-52
Continental Breakfast
Credit Cards: A, B
Notes: 2, 5, 7 (restricted), 8, 11, 12

Windsong

MAYESVILLE

Windsong

Route 1, Box 300
Mayesville, SC, 29104
(803) 453-5004

Situated in open farmland, this large house has balconies and porches, plus an open fireplace in the large den. Private entrance. A quail hunting preserve is operated by your host. An excellent place to stop over, whether you're traveling north or south.

Hosts: Lynda & Billy Dabbs
Rooms: 2 (PB) $40-50
Full Breakfast
Credit Cards: No
Notes: 2, 4, 5, 7, 8, 9

McCLELLANVILLE

Laurel Hill Plantation

8913 North Highway 17, Box 190
McClellanville, SC, 29458
(803) 887-3708

Laurel Hill faces the Intracoastal Waterway and the Atlantic Ocean. Porches provide a scenic view of marshes and creeks. The house is furnished in country and primitive antiques that reflect the Low Country lifestyle. Thirty miles north of Charleston.

Hosts: Jackie & Lee Morrison
Rooms: 4 (SB) $65
Full Breakfast
Credit Cards: No
Notes: 2, 4, 5, 7, 8, 9

MYRTLE BEACH

Serendipity

407-71 Avenue N
Myrtle Beach, SC, 29577
(803) 449-5268

Award-winning Mission-style inn, one and one-half blocks from the beach. Pool, Jacuzzi, shuffleboard, Ping-Pong. Near sixty golf courses, tennis, pier, and deep-sea fishing. Air conditioning, color TV, refrigerator, private baths in all rooms. Historic Charleston 90 miles; great shopping, restaurants are nearby.

Hosts: Cos & Ellen Ficarra
Rooms: 2 (PB) $50-65
Efficiencies: 4 (PB) $60-72
Suites: 4 (PB) $65-82
Continental-plus Breakfast
Credit Cards: A, B, C
Closed Dec.-Jan.
Notes: 7, 8, 9, 10, 11, 12, 14

SPARTANBURG

The Nicholls-Crook Plantation House

Box 5812
Spartanburg, SC, 29304
(803) 583-7337

A circa 1793 Georgian-style, up-country plantation house with period antiques. Listed on the National Register of Historic Places. Restful rural setting with easy access from Interstates 26 and 85. Gourmet breakfast in the tavern room.

Hosts: Suzanne & Jim Brown
Rooms: 3 (1 PB; 2 SB) $65-85
Full Breakfast
Closed Christmas
Credit Cards: No
Notes: 2, 8 (over 12), 9, 14

The Nicholls-Crook Plantation House

SUMMERVILLE

B&B of Summerville

304 South Hampton Street
Summerville, SC, 29483
(803) 871-5275

Slaves' quarters of a restored 1865 house on the Register of Historic Places in a quiet setting. Weather permitting, breakfast can be served in the greenhouse, gazebo, by the pool, or self-prepared from a stocked refrigerator. Wine, soft drinks, fruit, bikes, charcoal grill are available.

Hosts: Dusty & Emmagene Rhodes
Rooms: 1 (PB) $45
Continental Breakfast
Credit Cards: No
Notes: 2, 5, 7, 8 (12 or over), 9, 10, 11, 12

South Dakota

CANOVA

Skoglund Farm

Route 1, Box 45
Canova, SD, 57321
(605) 247-3445

Enjoy yourself on the S.D. prairie: cattle, fowl, peacocks, horses, home-cooked evening meal, and full breakfast. Visit nearby attractions: "Little House on the Prairie," "Corn Palace," "Doll House," "Prairie Village," or just relax, hike, and enjoy a family farm. Rate includes evening meal and breakfast.

Hosts: Alden & Delores Skoglund
Rooms: 5 (SB) $60
Full Breakfast
Credit Cards: No
Notes: 2, 3, 4, 5, 6, 7, 8, 9, 10, 11, 12, 14

HILL CITY

Bed & Breakfast Heart of the Hills

517 Main Street
Hill City, SD, 57745
(605) 574-2704

Within walking distance of the 1880 train, gift shops, and restaurants. Mt. Rushmore and the Crazy Horse Memorial are just minutes away. Queen bed, large sitting room with a studio couch that makes into a double bed; private bath, private entrance. Breakfast is served on the deck by the water fountain or in the dining room.

Hosts: Carol & Wes Shafer
Rooms: 2 (PB) $30-40
Full Breakfast
Credit Cards: No
Notes: 2, 5, 7, 8, 9, 12, 13

MILESVILLE

Old West & Badlands B&B 3227

P.O. Box 728
Philip, SD, 57567
(605) 859-2120

Located 3 miles south of Milesville. Western farm home. The hostess quilts and weaves on a floor loom. Two baths, full breakfast. Joggers and walkers welcome. $40.

OKATON

Old West & Badlands B&B 2529

P.O. Box 728
Philip, SD, 57567
(605) 859-2120

Guest rooms are in a separate house on this farm that features farm animals, including a horse for experienced riders. Your hosts have six children and offer guide service and baby-sitting. $40.

PHILIP

Old West & Badlands B&B 2065

P.O. Box 728
Philip, SD, 57567
(605) 859-2120

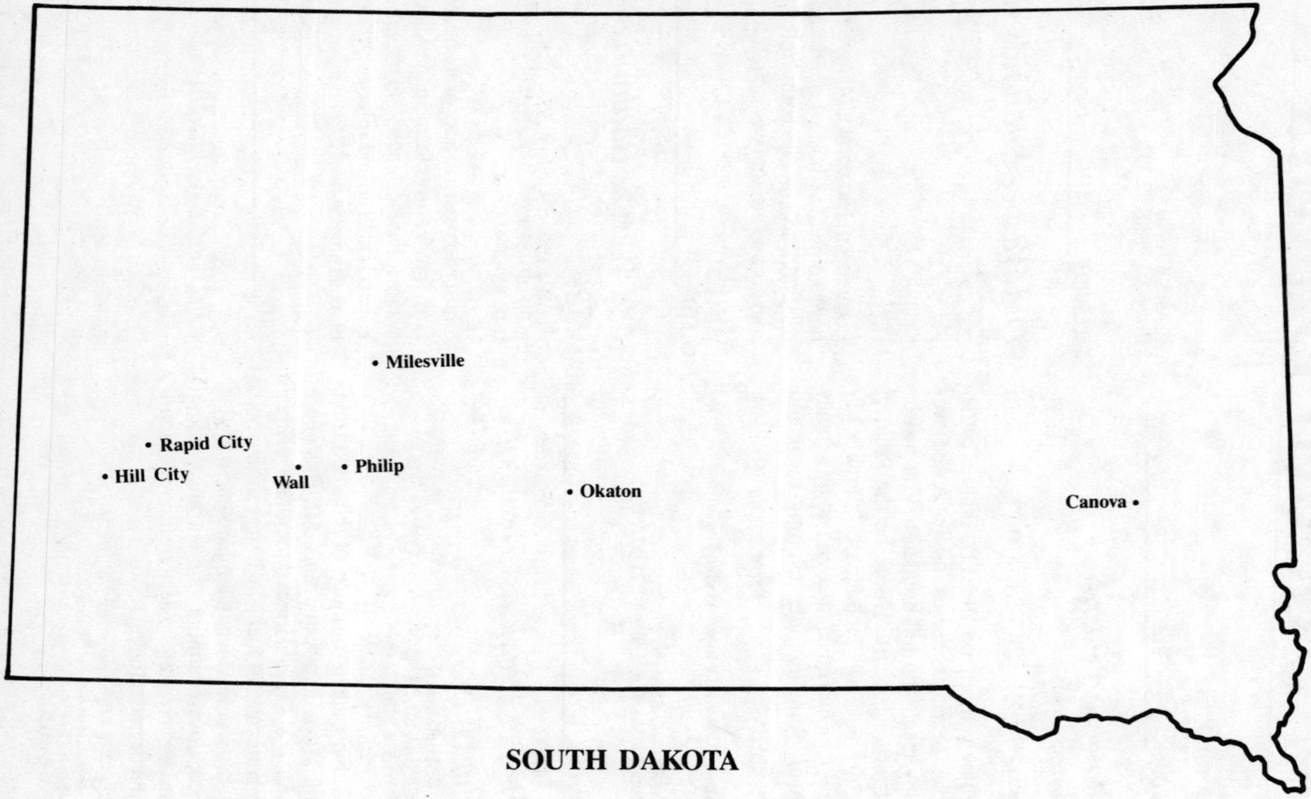

Milesville
Rapid City
Hill City
Wall
Philip
Okaton
Canova

SOUTH DAKOTA

Located 2.5 miles north of Philip on Highway 73. Enjoy a quiet stay in a new subterranean home heated by passive solar heat. On Lake Waggoner, with great fishing and bird watching. Located thirty minutes from the Badlands. $40.

Old West & Badlands B&B 2112

P.O. Box 728
Philip, SD, 57567
(605) 859-2120

Located 23 miles north of Philip, this family operation raises grain and livestock: wheat, sheep, pigs, and chickens are the main endeavors. $40.

Old West & Badlands B&B 2117

P.O. Box 728
Philip, SD, 57567
(605) 859-2120

Located 8 miles northwest of Philip. Enjoy a peaceful walk by the creek, volleyball, badminton, or horseshoes. Family room with piano. Located at the end of the road—quiet. Only thirty minutes from the Badlands. $40.

Old West & Badlands B&B 2120

P.O. Box 728
Philip, SD, 57567
(605) 859-2120

Located 12 miles north of Highway 14, between Philip and Wall. Near historic Old Deadwood Trail. Watch farm operations and breathe the fresh air. Set your own pace away from traffic and noise. Walk a country mile. No smoking. $40.

Old West & Badlands B&B 2135

P.O. Box 728
Philip, SD, 57567
(605) 859-2120

Located 2.5 miles north of Philip, an ideal stop on your way to the Black Hills. Stay in a new ranch-style home situated next to Lake Waggoner, a lake with plentiful game fish. Golf course one mile away. Private cable TV and HBO. Pets allowed. $40.

Old West & Badlands B&B 2157

P.O. Box 728
Philip, SD, 57567
(605) 859-2120

Located 23 miles north of Philip. Large, newer home with private bath and family room, pool table. This is a working farm with pigs, sheep, and wheat. Corrals available for livestock. The home is air-conditioned. Three rooms, lots of camper space. Outdoor bathroom facilities. $40.

Old West & Badlands B&B 2579

P.O. Box 728
Philip, SD, 57567
(605) 859-2120

Located 2 miles north of Philip on Highway 73. A modern ranch-style home designed to harmonize with its surroundings. Scenery includes grain fields, a meandering creek, grazing livestock, and fishing lake. Wildlife is frequently seen from the house; golf course and large vegetable farm within walking distance. Two rooms with private bath and family room. Two extra rooms are also available. $40.

RAPID CITY

Audrie's Cranbury Corner B & B

RR 8, Box 2400
Rapid City, SD, 57702
(605) 342-7788

Spacious rooms are furnished in comfortable European antiques, each room featuring a private entrance, private bath, fireplace, patio, hot tub, and full breakfast served in your room. Secluded Black Hills setting only seven miles west of Rapid City. Your door opens to Rapid Creek for fishing and scenic hiking trails.

Hosts: Hank & Audry Kuhnhauser
Rooms: 3 (PB) $70.72-81.12
Full Breakfast
Notes: 2, 5, 9, 10, 11, 12

The Carriage House

721 West Blvd.
Rapid City, SD, 57701
(605) 343-6415

The stately three-story pillared colonial house resides on the historic, tree-lined boulevard of Rapid City. The English country decor creates an ambience of elegance, refinement, and relaxing charm. Gourmet breakfasts are served in the formal dining room. Scenic Mt. Rushmore is only 26 miles away.

Hosts: Betty & Joel King
Rooms: 5 (2 PB; 3 SB) $59-89
Full Breakfast
Credit Cards: A, B
Notes: 2, 5, 10, 12

WALL

Old West & Badlands B&B 2198

P.O. Box 728
Philip, SD, 57567
(605) 859-2120

Located 9 miles north of Wall. Ranch-style home with recreation room with trampoline. Breakfast indoors or out; beautiful view. Or stay in the guest house. Box stalls and corrals for livestock. Extended vacations could include daily ranch chores, brandings, covered wagon and trail rides to the Badlands and Indian reservation. Private entrance, private bath available. $40.

Tennessee

CHATTANOOGA

B&B Hospitality, Tennessee CH1

P.O. Box 110227
Nashville, TN, 37222-0227
(800) 458-2421; (615) 331-5244

Hilltop country Victorian, surrounded with porches, with an excellent view of Lookout Mountain. Near Chickamauga, Pigeon Mountains, Rock City, and other attractions. Four guest rooms, three baths, continental breakfast. $50.

B&B Hospitality, Tennessee CH6

P.O. Box 110227
Nashville, TN, 37222-0227
(800) 458-2421; (615) 331-5244

Restored museum house fifteen minutes from Chattanooga, near Chickamauga Battlefield Park. An antebellum plantation house with four rooms and three baths. Also available is a suite of two bedrooms, bath, and kitchen. Continental breakfast. $65-110.

B&B Hospitality, Tennessee CH7

P.O. Box 110227
Nashville, TN, 37222-0227
(800) 458-2421; (615) 331-5244

Signal Mountain beauty. A master suite, separate Jacuzzi room, small balcony porch, king bed. Also a double room with private bath. Heated pool, woodsy setting, near Lookout Mountain, Signal Point. $65-75.

COLUMBIA

B&B Hospitality, Tennessee C01

P.O. Box 110227
Nashville, TN, 37222-0227
(800) 458-2421; (615) 331-5244

Country home with a suite featuring a large double room, private bath, private entrance, large sitting room with TV and wood-burning stove. One twin room with private half-bath. Continental breakfast. $40-50.

CROSSVILLE

B&B Hospitality, Tennessee CR2

P.O. Box 110227
Nashville, TN, 37222-0227
(800) 458-2421; (615) 331-5244

A country French home with three double rooms, private baths, and two powder rooms. Six miles from I-40 on the Cumberland Plateau. $60.

GATLINBURG

Buckhorn Inn

Route 3, Box 393
Gatlinburg, TN, 37738
(615) 436-4668

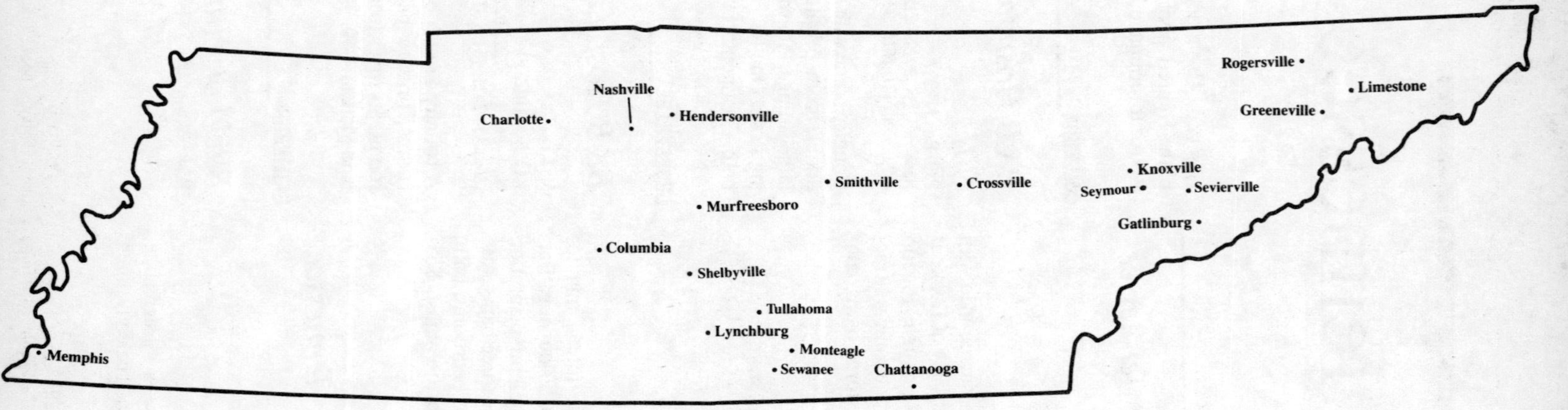
Rogersville
Limestone
Greeneville
Nashville
Charlotte
Hendersonville
Knoxville
Smithville
Crossville
Seymour
Sevierville
Murfreesboro
Gatlinburg
Columbia
Shelbyville
Tullahoma
Lynchburg
Monteagle
Memphis
Sewanee
Chattanooga

TENNESSEE

A truly unique country inn offering peaceful seclusion with the feeling and tradition of early Gatlinburg. Established in 1938, Buckhorn Inn was built on a hillside facing magnificent views of Mt. Leconte and includes 40 acres of woodland, meadows, and quiet walkways. Located just six miles northeast of Gatlinburg, near the Greenbrier entrance to the Great Smoky Mountains National Park.

Hosts: John & Connie Burns
Rooms: 11 (PB) $65-114
Full Breakfast
Credit Cards: No
Closed Christmas Eve and Day
Notes: 2, 4, 5, 7 (restricted), 9, 10, 11, 12, 13

Buckhorn Inn

Hippensteal Inn

P.O. Box 707
Gatlinburg, TN, 37738
(615) 436-5761

Hippensteal Inn, an artist's retreat, offers the Southern hospitality Gatlinburg is famous for. We stress comfort: queen beds, fireplaces and whirlpool tubs in each guest room, a large lobby, and private meeting room. Enjoy our breathtaking view of the Smokies and relax on our wraparound porches. Quiet and peaceful.

Hosts: Lisa & Vern Hippensteal
Rooms: 8 (PB) $90
Full Breakfast
Credit Cards: A, B, C, D
Notes: 2, 5, 8, 9, 10, 11, 12, 13

GREENEVILLE

Big Spring Inn

315 North Main Street
Greeneville, TN, 37743
(615) 638-2917

A three-story circa 1905 manor house in the historic district that includes homes built from 1783 to 1900 and the home of President Andrew Johnson. The inn has nearly 2 acres of trees and gardens, and a pool. We love to cook, and our breakfast is definitely a treat. Near the Smokies, white-water rafting, hiking, riding, and antiques.

Hosts: Jeanne Driese & Cheryl Van Dyck
Rooms: 5 (3 PB; 2 SB) $57-79
Full Breakfast
Credit Cards: A, B, C
Notes: 2, 4, 5, 7 (limited), 9, 10, 11, 12, 14

HENDERSONVILLE

Monthaven

1154 Main Street West
Hendersonville, TN, 37075.
(615) 824-6319

On the National Register of Historic Places, Monthaven offers both a heritage of nearly 200 years and a 75-acre estate for the enjoyment of visitors to Nashville and middle Tennessee. The main house served as a field hospital during the Civil War. Afternoon tea and evening cookies are served. Log cabin available.

Host: Hugh Waddell
Rooms: 3 (PB) $75
Log Cabin (PB) $85
Suite: $75
Continental-plus Breakfast
Credit Cards: Major
Notes: 2, 3, 4, 5, 6, 7, 8, 9, 10, 11, 12, 14

Monthaven

JOHNSON CITY

B&B Hospitality, Tennessee J1

P.O. Box 110227
Nashville, TN, 37222-0227
(800) 458-2421; (615) 331-5244

Near East Tennessee University, this lovely two-story home has two double rooms with private baths and one king room with private bath. $55-60.

KNOXVILLE

B&B Hospitality, Tennessee K1

P.O. Box 110227
Nashville, TN, 37222-0227
(800) 458-2421; (615) 331-5244

Eighteenth-century luxury hotel. Some units with Jacuzzi. Near the University of Tennessee and downtown. Walk to good restaurants. Concierge service. $65.

B&B Hospitality, Tennessee K2

P.O. Box 110227
Nashville, TN, 37222-0227
(800) 458-2421; (615) 331-5244

Swimming pool in season. Hostess has one king room with private bath and one double room with crib. Located in a residential area. Continental breakfast. $45-50.

B&B Hospitality, Tennessee K3

P.O. Box 110227
Nashville, TN, 37222-0227
(800) 458-2421; (615) 331-5244

Caterer and her husband have a charming home in a wooded area. Hot tub. One suite with private bath. Lake privileges. An intimate gourmet dinner will be served by appointment for an extra charge. This house has stained-glass windows, cathedral ceilings, a boat dock, and canoe access. $70.

LIMESTONE

Snapp Inn B&B

Route 3, Box 102
Limestone, TN, 37681
(615) 257-2482

Your hosts will welcome you into this gracious 1815 Federal home furnished with antiques and set in farm country. Enjoy the mountain view from the full back porch or play a game of pool or horseshoes. Close to Davy Crockett Birthplace Park; fifteen-minute drive to historic Jonesborough or Greeneville.

Hosts: Dan & Ruth Dorgan
Rooms: 2 (SB) $40-50
Full Breakfast
Credit Cards: No
Notes: 2, 5, 6, 8, 9, 11, 12, 14

Snapp Inn B&B

LYNCHBURG

Lynchburg B&B

Box 34
Lynchburg, TN, 37352
(615) 759-7158

This nineteenth-century home is located within walking distance of the Jack Daniel distillery. Each spacious room features carefully selected antiques. Formerly the home of the first Moore County sheriff (1877).

Host: Virginia and Mike Tipps
Rooms: 2 (PB) $42-45
Continental Breakfast
Credit Cards: A, B
Notes: 5, 8, 10, 12

MEMPHIS

B&B Hospitality, Tennessee M1

P.O. Box 110227
Nashville, TN, 37222-0227
(800) 458-2421; (615) 331-5244

This restored 1901 mansion is on the National Registry of Homes. Three large rooms with private baths. All rooms have period furniture and share a bright sitting room. $60.

B&B Hospitality, Tennessee M6

P.O. Box 110227
Nashville, TN, 37222-0227
(800) 458-2421; (615) 331-5244

Quiet elegance in the center of town. This 1911 Indiana stone home is near the downtown area and other attractions. Two double rooms with private baths and two with a shared bath. Victorian decor. $50.

B&B Hospitality, Tennessee M7

P.O. Box 110227
Nashville, TN, 37222-0227
(800) 458-2421; (615) 331-5244

One hour from Memphis, this charming restored mansion offers five rooms, private baths, TV, antiques. Dinner is served Monday through Saturday at extra charge. $70.

Lowenstein-Long House

217 North Waldran
Memphis, TN, 38105
(901) 527-7174

A beautifully restored Victorian mansion near downtown, listed on the National Registry of Historic Places. Convenient to all major tourist attractions: Mississippi River, Graceland, Beale Street, the Memphis Zoo, Brooks Museum, and Victorian Village. Free off-street parking.

Hosts: Walter & Samantha Long
Rooms: 4 (PB) $50
Continental-plus Breakfast
Credit Cards: A, B, C
Notes: 2, 5, 7 (limited), 8, 9, 10, 11, 12

MONTEAGLE

Edgeworth Inn

Box 340 Monteagle Assembly
Monteagle, TN, 37356
(615) 924-2669; (615) 924-2476

A friendly nine-room 1896 mountaintop inn in the Monteagle Assembly National Historic District, the southern Chautaugua. Enjoy rope hammocks, wicker rockers, and gingerbread porches; delve into plentiful books and magazines by the cheerful library fire, or experience the refreshing waterfalls and pools along the many nearby trails. The University of the South at Sewanee is six miles away.

Host: Merrily Teasley
Rooms: 9 (PB) $65-85
Continental-plus Breakfast
Credit Cards: A, B
Notes: 2, 5, 7, 8 (call), 9, 10, 11, 12, 14

MURFREESBORO

Clardy's Guest House

435 East Main Street
Murfreesboro, TN, 37130
(615) 893-6030

Located in the historic district, this twenty-room Victorian Romanesque home is filled with antiques and features ornate woodwork and fireplaces. An eight-by-eight-foot stained-glass window overlooks the magnificent staircase. The area has much to offer history buffs and antique shoppers. Clardy's Guest House is thirty miles from Nashville, just two miles off I-24.

Hosts: Robert & Barbara Deaton
Rooms: 4 (2 PB; 2 SB) $30-40
Continental Breakfast
Credit Cards: No
Notes: 2, 5, 7, 8, 9, 10, 11, 12

NASHVILLE

B&B Hospitality Tennessee 1

P.O. Box 110227
Nashville, TN, 37222
(615) 331-5244; (800) 678-3625

This retired couple offers one king room with TV and one double room, private bath. Near bus and shopping; three miles to Opryland. Continental breakfast. $45.

B&B Hospitality, Tennessee 2

P.O. Box 110227
Nashville, TN, 37222-0227
(800) 458-2421; (615) 331-5244

Built in the mid-1800s on the site of Indian camping grounds, this beautiful Greek Revival with Victorian decorative elements served as a hospital during the Civil War. Fifteen minutes from Nashville. Both the log guest house and main house are furnished in antiques. Continental breakfast. $65-75.

B&B Hospitality Tennessee 3

P.O. Box 110227
Nashville, TN, 37222
(615) 331-5244; (800) 678-3625

Twin room with private bath, sitting room with two sofas. No smoking. This suite has TV, a fireplace, pool table. Rocking chairs on porch. Upstairs is a queen room with private bath. $45-50.

B&B Hospitality, Tennessee 5

P.O. Box 110227
Nashville, TN, 37222-0227
(800) 458-2421; (615) 331-5244

Located twenty minutes from downtown Nashville. Within thirty minutes of many historic sites, educational facilities, and country music points of interest. The house is decorated with family antiques, Oriental rugs, weavings and woodcrafts by the hosts. Continental breakfast. $50.

B&B Hospitality, Tennessee 7

P.O. Box 110227
Nashville, TN, 37222-0227
(800) 458-2421; (615) 331-5244

Conveniently located near the airport, this house offers one twin room, one double, and one queen, private or shared bath. Swimming pool. There is also a suite with a double room, sitting area, private entrance, private bath, Jacuzzi and swimming pool. $40-55.

B&B Hospitality, Tennessee 11

P.O. Box 110227
Nashville, TN, 37222-0227
(800) 458-2421; (615) 331-5244

The only house in downtown Nashville. Built in 1859, with twelve-foot ceilings and fireplaces. First floor tea room where guests have a continental breakfast. Rooms furnished in antiques; private and shared baths. One block from Convention Center and fifteen minutes from Opryland. $65.

B&B Hospitality, Tennessee 12

P.O. Box 110227
Nashville, TN, 37222-0227
(800) 458-2421; (615) 331-5244

Historic district of Nashville. This restored Victorian was built in 1902 and has recently been restored. The bedroom is filled with antiques and has a huge adjoining bath. Continental breakfast. $50.

B&B Hospitality Tennessee 13

P.O. Box 110227
Nashville, TN, 37222
(615) 331-5244; (800) 678-3625

A restored 1900 home near downtown on the east side of the Cumberland River. Double room filled with antiques; adjoining bath has a clawfoot tub. There is also a double room upstairs with private bath. $50-60.

B&B Hospitality Tennessee 14

P.O. Box 110227
Nashville, TN, 37222
(615) 331-5244; (800) 678-3625

Near Vanderbilt, Belle Meade Shopping Center, Belle Meade Mansion, and Cheekwood. This home offers a large double room with sitting area, dressing room, and private bath. A large upstairs room has a private bath. $50.

B&B Hospitality, Tennessee 17

P.O. Box 110227
Nashville, TN, 37222-0227
(800) 458-2421; (615) 331-5244

Interesting artist studio suite with antique bed, private bath, and sitting room overlooking a formal English garden. Private entrance. Antiques, art and book collections. Wheel chair access to all rooms on the first floor. $60-70.

B&B Hospitality, Tennessee 19

P.O. Box 110227
Nashville, TN, 37222-0227
(800) 458-2421; (615) 331-5244

One block from David Lipscomb campus and very well located. This recording artist and counselor enjoy people and are interested in country music. Two double rooms with private baths. $45.

B&B Hospitality Tennessee 24

P.O. Box 110227
Nashville, TN, 37222
(615) 331-5244; (800) 678-3625

A quiet, secluded poolside guest house with twin beds and private bath. Located close to I-40, eight miles from downtown, near golf, fishing. $60.

B&B Hospitality, Tennessee 25

P.O. Box 110227
Nashville, TN, 37222-0227
(800) 458-2421; (615) 331-5244

Chalet-style house with a two-story deck overlooking a babbling brook. Nestled in a forest of weeping willows, lush greenery, and gardens. One double and one twin room with a shared bath. Near Belle Meade Mansion, Cheekwood; thirty minutes from the airport and Opryland. Swimming pool, playground, and tennis. No pets, no smoking. Children over two are welcome. $60.

B&B Hospitality Tennessee 30

P.O. Box 110227
Nashville, TN, 37222
(615) 331-5244; (800) 678-3625

Two bedrooms with private/shared bath with a hostess who loves people. Near all major interstates, airport; six minutes to downtown. Bus nearby. Patio. Continental breakfast. $45.

B&B Hospitality Tennessee 31

P.O. Box 110227
Nashville, TN, 37222
(615) 331-5244; (800) 678-3625

Separate unit with kitchen, den with fireplace, bedroom, and bath. Private entrance, covered patio with grill. Continental breakfast. $75.

Hachland Hill Inn

5396 Rawlings Road
Nashville, TN, 37222
(615) 255-1727

A secluded dining inn 15 minutes from downtown Nashville. A perfect executive retreat or for family reunions or honeymooners. Each day, renowned author and chef Phila Hach will provide you with unforgettable cuisine from the grand old South. Accommodations are in a historic log house brimming with museum antiques.

Host: Phila Hach
Rooms: 25 (PB) $55-65
Full Breakfast
Credit Cards: C
Notes: 2, 4, 5, 6, 7, 8, 9, 14

Hachland Hill Inn

Lockeland Springs B&B

340 21st Avenue North
Nashville, TN, 37203
(615) 320-7914

Eclectic Victorian house in an historic district. Beautifully done with antiques, Oriental rugs, art collection. Beautiful yard and gardens.

Host: Brooks Parker
Rooms: 2 (PB) $50-65
Continental-plus Breakfast
Credit Cards: No
Notes: 5, 6, 7, 10, 11, 14

Miss Anne's B&B

3033 Windemere Circle
Nashville, TN, 37214
(615) 885-1899

Miss Anne's is a cozy little place filled with antiques and collectibles. Breakfast includes home-baked goodies and Southern cooking. We are located one and one-half miles from Opryland and are convenient to all other Nashville attractions.

Hosts: Robin & Ann Cowell
Rooms: 4 (SB) $35-40
Full Breakfast
Credit Cards: No
Notes: 2, 5, 9, 11, 12

ROGERSVILLE

Hale Springs Inn

110 West Main Street
Rogersville, TN, 37857
(615) 272-5171

Elegant, three-story Federal brick building built in 1824; the oldest continuously run inn of Tennessee. Beautifully furnished with antiques from the period. Some of the rooms feature four-poster canopy beds, and all rooms have working fireplaces. Air-conditioning. Bring your own wine. Candlelight dining.

Host: Ed Pace
Rooms: 9 (PB) $45-75
Continental Breakfast
Credit Cards: A, B, C
Notes: 4, 5, 7, 8, 9, 10, 11, 12

Hale Springs Inn

SEVIERVILLE

Blue Mountain Mist Country Inn

Route 3, Box 490
Sevierville, TN, 37862
(615) 428-2335

Our inn is a new Victorian-style farmhouse with a big wraparound porch overlooking rolling hills, with the Smoky Mountains as a backdrop. Furnished with country antiques, grandmother's quilts, and old photographs, our inn provides a homey atmosphere. We are minutes from the Great Smoky Mountains National Park, Gatlinburg, and Dollywood.

Hosts: Norman & Sarah Ball
Rooms: 12 (PB) $69-105
Full Breakfast
Credit Cards: A, B
Notes: 2, 5, 8, 9, 10, 11, 12, 14

Blue Mountain Mist Country Inn

SEWANEE

B&B Hospitality, Tennessee SW1

P.O. Box 110227
Nashville, TN, 37222-0227
(800) 458-2421; (615) 331-5244

Overlooking Lost Cove. Gourmet fare and luxurious accommodations, continental croquet, table tennis, informal skeet shooting, stables, and kennels. King suite with Jacuzzi tub, one queen room with antiques, and one twin room. No smoking. $75.

B&B Hospitality, Tennessee SW2

P.O. Box 110227
Nashville, TN, 37222-0227
(800) 458-2421; (615) 331-5244

Restored home has two double rooms, one canopy bed with antiques, and a double with antiques and shared bath. Children ten and over are welcome. A full breakfast is served at 7:30 A.M. $50.

SEYMONS

The Country Inn

701 Chris-Haven Drive
Seymons, TN, 37865
(615) 573-7496

The inn is in a quiet country setting on a golf course, with tennis courts and a swimming pool. We are located very near an excellent steakhouse for dinner. Very near Pigeon Forge, Gatlinburg, and the national park.

Host: Annette Christenberry
Rooms: 12 (PB) $45
Continental Breakfast
Credit Cards: No
Closed Dec.-Feb.
Notes: 2, 3, 7, 8, 9, 10, 11, 12, 13, 14

SHELBYVILLE

B&B Hospitality, Tennessee SH1

P.O. Box 110227
Nashville, TN, 37222-0227
(800) 458-2421; (615) 331-5244

Guest house with one king, one double, and one twin room, shared bath. The main house has a double with private bath. $40-45.

County Line B&B

Route 6 Box 126
Shelbyville, TN, 37160
(615) 759-4639

Two-story house, c. 1908, located on a horse farm. Approximately 4.5 miles from the Jack Daniel distillery, Lynchburg, and Miss Mary Bobo's Boarding House. Relaxed country atmosphere. Continental breakfast includes fresh-baked muffins and breads. Brochure available; reservations encouraged.

Hosts: Jim & Harriet Rothfeldt
Rooms: 3 (1 PB; 2 SB) $38
Continental Breakfast
Credit Cards: A, B
Notes: 2, 5, 7, 8 (over 3), 9, 10

SMITHVILLE

B&B Hospitality, Tennessee SM1

P.O. Box 110227
Nashville, TN, 37222-0227
(800) 458-2421; (615) 331-5244

Near Center Hill Lake, this spacious guest house has a patio and fully furnished kitchen. Wood-burning stove, two double rooms, and bath. The main house has one twin room, crib, and bath. $40-50.

TULLAHOMA

B&B Hospitality, Tennessee T1

P.O. Box 110227
Nashville, TN, 37222-0227
(800) 458-2421; (615) 331-5244

Near Tullahoma and Winchester, on the shores of Tims Ford Lake one hour from Nashville, Huntsville, and Chattanooga. Hosts like woodworking and hand weaving. One queen room and one single. $50.

County Line B&B

WARTRACE

Ledford Mill

R2, Box 152
Wartrace, TN, 37183
(615) 455-2546

A private hideaway where you are the only guests in our cozy, open suite with kitchenette. Spend the night in a nineteenth-century grist mill, listening to the waterfalls and murmuring waters of Shippmans Creek.

Hosts: Norma & Bill Rigler
Suite: 1 (PB) $60
Continental Breakfast
Credit Cards: A, B, C
Notes: 2, 5, 6, 7, 8, 9, 10, 11

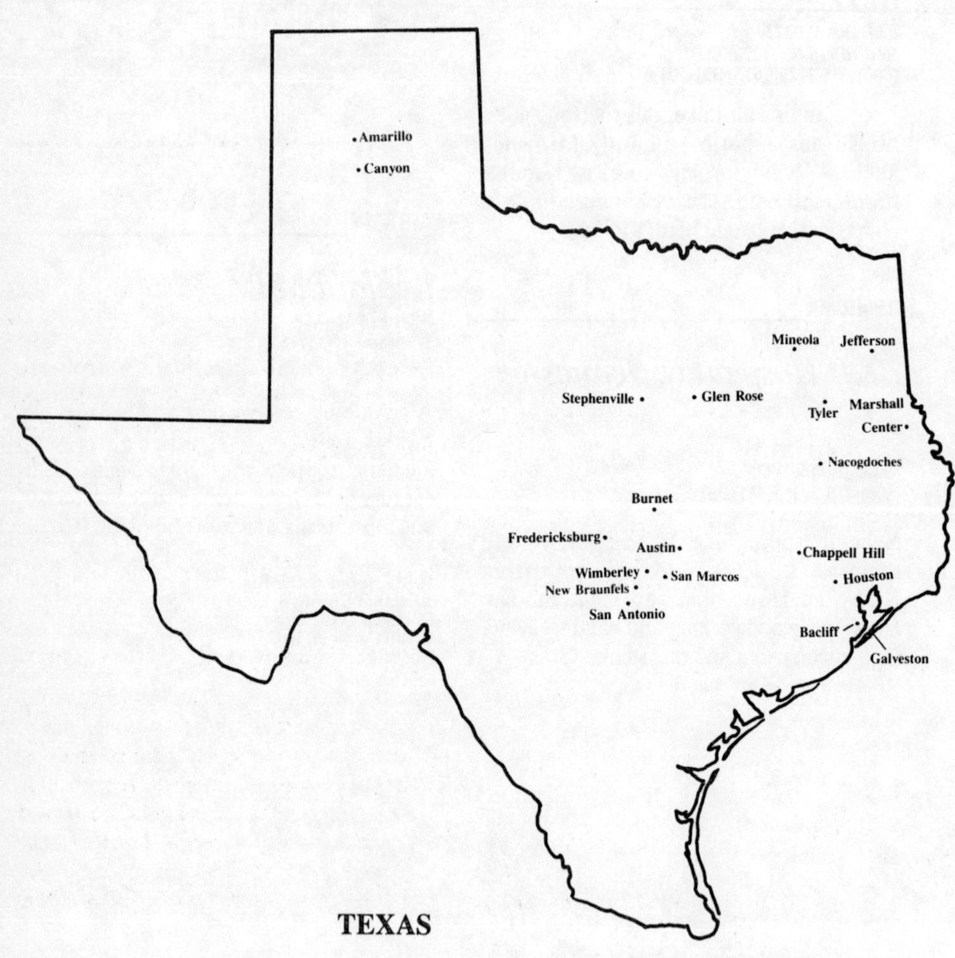
Amarillo
Canyon
Mineola
Jefferson
Stephenville
Glen Rose
Tyler
Marshall
Center
Nacogdoches
Burnet
Fredericksburg
Austin
Chappell Hill
Wimberley
San Marcos
Houston
New Braunfels
San Antonio
Bacliff
Galveston
TEXAS

Texas

AMARILLO

Parkview House

1311 South Jefferson
Amarillo, TX, 79101
(806) 373-9464

This turn-of-the-century Prairie Victorian located in the heart of the Texas Panhandle has been lovingly restored by the present owners to capture its original charm. Furnished with antiques and comfortably updated, it has a large family TV room and parlor for reading or listening to music. Convenient to a park, biking, jogging, hiking, and the prize-winning musical drama, "Texas" in Pale Duro State Park. Near the Panhandle Historical Museum and Lake Meredith.

Hosts: Nabil & Carol Dia
Rooms: 4 (2 PB; 2 SB) $50-60
Suite: 1 (PB) $75
Continental-plus Breakfast
Credit Cards: A, B
Notes: 2, 5, 8, 9, 10, 11, 12, 14

Parkview House

AUSTIN

B&B Scottsdale & The West 100

P.O. Box 3999
Prescott, AZ, 86302
(602) 776-1102

Refurbished 1920s mini-estate with artwork and antiques located close to the University of Texas and state capitol. Five rooms, shared baths, continental breakfast. Pets in home. $49-54.

The Brook House

609 West 33rd
Austin, TX, 78705
(512) 459-0534

The Brook House is a 1920s estate featuring large, airy rooms with ten-foot ceilings, private baths, and lovely period decor in romantic, antique-filled guest rooms. Our sumptuous gourmet breakfasts are served on our plant-lined veranda. Located near dining, shopping, historic homes, the Capitol, and the University of Texas. Come let us pamper you.

Hosts: Jan Mahaffey, Gary & Maggie Guseman
Rooms: 5 (PB) $59-89
Full Breakfast
Credit Cards: A, B, C
Notes: 2, 5, 6, 8, 9, 10, 11, 12, 14

The McCallum House

613 West 32nd Street
Austin, TX, 78705
(512) 451-6744

The historic McCallum House, an Austin landmark, is ten blocks north of the University of Texas, twenty blocks north of the Texas Capitol. All rooms have period furnishings and telephones. Four have private porches; all have kitchen facilities; one is a large, three-room apartment.

Hosts: Nancy & Roger Danley
Rooms: 5 (PB) $60-70
Full Breakfast
Minimum stay holidays: 2
Credit Cards: No
Notes: 2, 5, 8, 9, 10, 11, 12

Southard-House

908 Blanco Street
Austin, TX, 78703
(512) 474-4731

Charming 1890 Greek Revival home located in a quiet neighborhood twelve blocks from the Capitol and two from the unique West End shopping district. Restaurants are within a safe walking distance of five to fifteen minutes. We look forward to making your stay very enjoyable.

Hosts: Jerry & Rejina Southard
Rooms: 5 (PB) $52-99
Full Breakfast weekends; continental weekdays
Credit Cards: A, B, C, D, E
Notes: 2, 5, 7, 8, 9, 10, 11, 14

BACLIFF

Small Inn

4815 West Bayshore
Bacliff, TX, 77518
(713) 339-3489

See ocean freighters, sailboats, and pelicans from poolside while enjoying your breakfast, then fish from our private pier, spend the day touring NASA, the Astrodome in Houston, or head for Galveston and Victorian homes, a railroad museum, or the beach. Boat rental, jet skiing, and parasailing are all minutes away. This home welcomes families. Located between Houston and Galveston.

Hosts: George & Harriet Small
Rooms: 1 (PB) $50
Full Breakfast
Credit Cards: No
Notes: 3, 4, 5, 7, 8, 9, 10, 11, 12, 14

BURNET

Rocky Rest B&B

404 South Water Street
P.O. Box 130
Burnet, TX, 78611
(512) 756-2600

Rocky Rest is a two-story rock house built by Adam R. Johnson in 1860. Located in Burnet, the heart of the Texas hill country. In the area you can enjoy boating, fishing, water skiing, and hunting. Burnet is located ninety miles north of San Antonio and fifty miles northwest of Austin. Enjoy wild flowers in the spring and the breathtaking sight of a bald eagle in the fall.

Host: Fannie Shepperd
Rooms: 3 (1 PB; 2 SB) $55-60
Full Breakfast
Credit Cards: No
Closed Dec.
Notes: 2, 3, 4, 6, 8, 11, 12

CANYON

Hudspeth House

1905 Fourth Avenue
Canyon, TX, 79015
(806) 655-9800

Our historic B&B is located only twelve minutes away from Palo Duro Canyon, home of the famous "Texas" musical drama. Our facilities offer beautiful accommodations, gourmet breakfasts, and a health spa. Take a stroll to the Panhandle Plains museum or just relax and enjoy our warm hospitality.

Hosts: Dave & Sally Haynie
Rooms: 8 (5 PB; 3 SB) $45-110

Full Breakfast
Credit Cards: A, B
Notes: 2, 5, 7 (limited), 8, 9, 10, 11, 12, 14

CENTER

Pine Colony Inn

500 Shelbyville Street
Center, TX, 75935
(409) 598-7700

This gracious old hotel is located a few short miles from the Texas State Railroad between Rusk and Palestine. The Pine Colony Inn has enough room to house a B&B convention, with twelve guest rooms, each with unique decor, antiques, collectibles, and lace curtains.

Hosts: Regina Wright & Marcille Hughes
Rooms: 12 (1 PB; 11 SB) $27-55
Full Breakfast
Credit Cards: A, B
Notes: 5, 8, 9, 10, 11, 12

Pine Colony Inn

CHAPPELL HILL

The Browning Plantation

Route 1, Box 8
Chappell Hill, TX, 77426
(409) 836-6144

This three-story antebellum home on a 220-acre working plantation is in the National Register. All antique furnishings, pool, and model railroad. The area is known for its antiques, horse farms, and historical significance. Sixty miles northwest of Houston on Highway 290.

Hosts: Dick & Mildred Ganchan
Rooms: 6 (2 PB; 4 SB) $75-110
Full Breakfast
Credit Cards: No
Notes: 2, 5, 8 (over 12), 9, 10, 11, 12, 14

The Browning Plantation

FREDERICKSBURG

Country Cottage Inn

405 East Main
Fredericksburg, TX, 78624
(512) 997-8549

Romance and charm in a lovingly restored Texas frontier home (circa 1850). Two-foot-thick stone walls, exposed hand-cut beams, high ceilings, period Texas antiques, porch swings, Laura Ashley linens, bathrobes, whirlpool tubs, fireplace, and complimentary wine insure your comfort.

Host: Jeffery Webb
Rooms: 5 (PB) $65-95
Continental Breakfast
Credit Cards: A, B
No smoking
Notes: 2, 5, 8, 9, 10, 11, 12

J Bar K Ranch B&B

HC-10, Box 53-A
Fredericksburg, TX, 78624
(512) 669-2471

Relax and enjoy your visit to a Texas Hill Country ranch in our large German rock home with antiques and a historic marker. Enjoy a full country breakfast, native wildlife, Texas hospitality, and a tour of the ranch. Next to a small active country church. Located just fifteen minutes northwest of Fredericksburg, with its German heritage and architecture, many quaint shops, and excellent restaurants.

Hosts: Kermit & Naomi Kothe
Rooms: 3 (2 PB; 1 SB) $65 (extra person $20)
Full Breakfast
Credit Cards: A, B (surcharge)
Closed Jan. & Feb.
Notes: 2, 7, 8 (10 and over), 9

Schmidt Barn

501 West Main Street
Fredericksburg, TX, 78624
(512) 997-5612

This guest house B&B is a renovated 130-year-old rock barn located 1.5 miles from historic Fredericksburg, next door to the hosts' home. A loft bedroom with queen bed overlooks the living room below. Small kitchen and bath. All decorated in antiques. Featured in *Country Living* magazine.

Hosts: Charles & Loretta Schmidt
Barn: 1 (PB) $65 + tax
Continental Breakfast
Credit Cards: A, B, C, D
Notes: 2, 5, 7, 8, 9, 10, 11, 12, 14

GALVESTON

The Gilded Thistle

1805 Broadway
Galveston, TX, 77550
(409) 763-0194

An 1893 Victorian home in historic Galveston, known throughout the country for its wealth of Victorian homes. Why not stay for a day or weekend in elegant accommodations? Sip coffee on a veranda, watch the moon come up. Snack tray, coffee, and juice at door. Enter a wonderland of fanciful ambience with down-home elegance and superb service.

Host: Helen Hanemann
Rooms: 3 (1 PB; 2 SB) $115-135
Full Breakfast
Credit Cards: A, B
Notes: 2, 5, 8, 10, 11, 12

Hazlewood House

1127 Church Street
Galveston, TX, 77550
(409) 762-1668

Romantic Victorian home with three rooms to choose from with private baths. Antique furnishings, Oriental carpets, and fine tapestries throughout. Wine and cheese on arrival, morning coffee, and a hearty continental breakfast served on fine china, crystal, and silver. Near the beach, historical tours, musicals, museums, and trolley.

Host: Pat Hazlewood
Rooms: 3 (PB) $55-125
Continental Breakfast
Credit Cards: No
Notes: 2, 5, 9, 10, 11, 12, 13, 14

The Victorian Inn

511 Seventeenth Street
Galveston, TX, 77550
(409) 762-3235

Massive Italian villa built in 1899. Spacious guest rooms are romantically decorated with king beds and antiques. The four rooms on the second floor have balconies. Third-floor suite has a private bath and two bedrooms. The inn is within walking distance of Historic Strand: restaurants, shops, boats. Less than one mile to the beach.

Hosts: Janice & Bob Hellbusch
Rooms: 6 (2 PB; 4 SB) $80-150
Continental Breakfast

Credit Cards: A, B, C
Notes: 2, 5, 7 (restricted), 8 (over 12), 9, 10, 11, 12, 13, 14

GLEN ROSE

Inn on the River

209 SW Barnard Street
Glen Rose, TX, 76043
(817) 897-2101

This 1860 inn on the Paluxy River near the town square is a designated Historic Texas Landmark. The 21 rooms and 3 suites are individually designed, and all have private baths. This area of Texas is noted for its scenic hills, rivers, Dinosaus Valley State Park, and Fossil Rim Wildlife Conservation Ranch.

Hosts: Steve & Peggy Allman
Rooms: 25 (PB) $80-125
Full Breakfast
Credit Cards: A, B, C
Notes: 2, 10, 11, 12, 14

The Victorian Inn

HOUSTON

Durham House B&B

921 Heights Blvd.
Houston, TX, 77008
(713) 868-4654

Durham House is a faithfully restored Queen Anne Victorian on the National Register of Historic Places. Located in central Houston, just ten minutes from downtown, Durham House is convenient for business travelers and tourists. Guests may use the backyard gazebo, the player piano, the screened back porch. Walk and jog on the boulevard.

Host: Marguerite Swanson
Rooms: 5 (4 PB; 1 SB) $55-60
Full Breakfast
Credit Cards: A, B
Notes: 2, 5, 8, 10, 11, 12, 14

Sara's B&B Inn

941 Heights Blvd.
Houston, TX, 77008
(713) 868-1130; (800) 593-1130

This Queen Anne Victorian is located in the Houston Heights, a neighborhood of historic homes, many of which are on the National Register. Each bedroom is uniquely furnished, having either single, double, queen or king beds. The Balcony Suite consists of two bedrooms, two baths, kitchen, living area, and a fine view overlooking the deck. The sights and sounds of downtown are only four miles away.

Hosts: Donna & Tillman Arledge
Rooms: 12 (3 PB; 9 SB) $46-96
Continental Breakfast
Credit Cards: A, B, C, E, F
Notes: 2, 5, 8, 9, 10, 11

JEFFERSON

McKay House B&B Inn

306 East Delta Street
Jefferson, TX, 75657
(214) 665-7322; (214) 348-1929 (Dallas)

Jefferson is a river-port town from the frontier days of the Republic of Texas. It has historic mule-drawn tours, thirty antique shops, boat rides on the river, and a narrow-gauge train. The McKay House, a recently restored 1851 Greek Revival cottage, offers period furnishings, cool lemonade, porch swings, fireplaces, and a full gentleman's breakfast. Hospitality abounds, and Victorian nightclothes are provided.

Host: Peggy Taylor
Rooms: 7 (PB) $70-125
Full Breakfast
Credit Cards: A, B
Notes: 2, 5, 9, 12, 14

Pride House

409 Broadway
Jefferson, TX, 75657
(214) 665-2675

A gingerbread Victorian (1889) with high ceilings, stained-glass windows in every room, porches for rocking, and sun-dried linens. Breakfast may include Richard II's eggs, meats, poached pears, creme fraiche with praline sauce, served in the breakfast room, a sunny porch, or the privacy of your own room.

Host: Ruthmary Jordan
Rooms: 10 (PB) $70-90
Full Breakfast
Credit Cards: A, B
Notes: 2, 5, 6, 7, 8, 9, 11, 12, 14

Wise Manor

Wise Manor

312 Houston Street
Jefferson, TX, 75657
(214) 665-2386

A gem of a Victorian home that looks as if it has just stepped out of a fairy tale. The little two-story cottage is painted in salmon tones with crisp, white gingerbread trim. Surrounded by large pecan trees, it peers out from behind a wrought-iron fence. It is furnished in Victorian pieces with marble-top tables and ruffled curtains at the windows. Antique white bedspreads and folded appliqued quilts adorn the ornate walnut beds.

Host: Katherine Ramsay Wise
Rooms: 3 (2 PB; 1 SB) $30-55
Credit Cards: A, B, C
Notes: 2, 5, 7, 8, 9

MARBLE FALLS

La Casita

1908 Redwood Drive
Marble Falls, TX, 78654
(512) 598-6443

Nestled fifty feet behind the main house, this private cottage is rustic and Texan on the outside yet thoroughly modern inside. Native Texan hosts can suggest wineries, parks, and river cruises. However, relaxing in a country setting is the main attraction here. Guests choose their entree with a full breakfast.

Hosts: Joanne & Roger Scarborough
Rooms: 1 (PB) $55
Full Breakfast
Credit Cards: No
Notes: 2, 5, 7 (outside), 8, 9, 11, 12, 14

MARSHALL

Three Oaks B & B

609 N. Washington Avenue
Marshall, TX, 75670
(214) 938-6123

Victorian home built in 1895, located in a national historic district. One private suite, offering almost 2,000 square feet, including formal areas furnished with antiques. Popular as a honeymoon retreat, for anniversaries or birthdays. Breakfast is wheeled to the guest room on a tea cart adorned with vintage linens, silver, china, and crystal.

Hosts: Sandra & Bob McCoy
Suite: 1 (PB) $85
Type of Beds: 1 Double; 1 Queen
Full Breakfast
Credit Cards: No
Closed Jan.-March
Notes: 2, 9, 10, 11, 12

Wood Boone Norrell House

215 East Rusk Street
Marshall, TX, 75670
(214) 935-1800; (800) 423-1356

Restored 1884 Queen Anne with verandas and a large balcony. Each room is decorated with turn-of-the-century antiques. All rooms have private baths with showers. Nestled in the piney wood of East Texas, just minutes from antique shopping and fishing.

Hosts: Michael & Patsy Norrell
Rooms: 5 (PB) $65
Full Breakfast
Credit Cards: A, B
Notes: 2, 5, 6, 8, 14

MINEOLA

Munzesheimer Manor B&B Inn

202 North Newsom
Mineola, TX, 75773
(903) 569-6634

A romantic getaway "where time stands still" in an 1898 Victorian home. Extensively restored, including central air-conditioning, private baths, ceiling fans. Fresh flowers; seven fireplaces; Victorian gowns and nightshirts create a special mood. Many area lakes, festivals. Near Canton First Monday Trade Days, Christmas tree farms, antique and craft shops.

Hosts: Bob & Sherry Murray
Rooms: 6 (PB) $59-79
Full Breakfast
Credit Cards: A, B, C
Notes: 2, 5, 10, 11, 12, 14

Wood Boone Norrell House

NACOGDOCHES

Haden Edwards Inn

106 North Lanana Street
Nacogdoches, TX, 75961
(409) 564-9999

Located in the oldest town in Texas, within walking distance of downtown and several historic sites, including Oak Grove Cemetery, where Haden Edwards is buried. The present inn has been completely restored with all modern conveniences, including central air-conditioning, private baths, ceiling fans. A full homemade buffet breakfast is served in the main dining room.

Host: Jean Barnhart
Rooms: 5 (PB) $65-90
Full Breakfast
Credit Cards: A, B
Notes: 2, 5, 7 (restricted), 8 (over 12), 9, 10, 11, 12, 14

NEW BRAUNFELS

Hill Country Haven

227 South Academy
New Braunfels, TX, 78130
(512) 629-6727

Each of the three guest rooms is decorated with a charming selection of antiques and has its own private bath. Garden-fresh flowers, bedtime mints, and fine English soaps. Breakfast is served in your room, the garden, or the formal dining room. New Braunfels is noted for its German architecture, historic landmarks, quaint shops and antique stores. Nearby you will find tubing, rafting, canoeing, hiking, golf, tennis, sailing and fishing. Near the Guadalupe River, Canyon Lake, and Landa Park's 300 acres.

Host: Amanda Case
Rooms: 3 (PB) $45-75 + tax
Continental-plus Breakfast
Credit Cards: A, B
Notes: 2, 3 (picnic), 5, 7, 8 (over 12), 9, 10, 11, 12, 14

SAN ANTONIO

Bullis House Inn

621 Pierce Street
P.O. Box 8059
San Antonio, TX, 78208
(512) 223-9426

Lovely historic white-columned mansion with wide veranda, swimming pool, spacious guest rooms with fireplaces. Downstairs parlors have decorative fourteen-foot plaster ceilings, marble fireplaces, lovely patterned wood floors, and more. Weekend and honeymoon packages available.

Hosts: Steve & Alma Cross
Rooms: 8 (2 PB; 6 SB) $29-89
Continental Breakfast
Credit Cards: A, B, C, D
Notes: 5, 7, 8, 9, 10, 11, 14

SAN MARCOS

Crystal River Inn

326 West Hopkins Street
San Marcos, TX, 78666
(512) 396-3739

Romantic, luxurious Victorian mansion that captures the matchless spirit of Texas hill country. Close to headwaters of crystal-clear San Marcos River. Antiques, fireplaces, and fresh flowers adorn the rooms. Wicker-strewn veranda and fountain courtyard offer hours of peaceful rest and relaxation. Enjoy sumptuous brunches including gourmet items such as stuffed French toast and bananas Foster crepes.

Hosts: Mike & Cathy Dillon
Rooms: 8 (6 PB; 2 SB) $50-90
Full Breakfast
Credit Cards: A, B, C
Notes: 2, 5, 10, 11, 12, 14

The Oxford House

STEPHENVILLE

The Oxford House

563 North Graham Street
Stephenville, TX, 76401
(817) 965-6885

Stephenville is the northern tip of the beautiful Texas hill country. Located on Highway 67 west of Lake Granbury and east of Proctor Lake. Tarleton State University is located in town. The Oxford House was built in 1898 by Judge W.J. Oxford, Sr., and the completely restored two-story Victorian, presently owned by the grandson of the judge, has antique furnishings. Enjoy a quiet, peaceful atmosphere, home-cooked country breakfast, and shopping within walking distance.

Hosts: Bill & Paula Oxford
Rooms: 5 (4 PB; 1 SB) $65-72
Country Breakfast
Credit Cards: A, B
Notes: 2, 4, 5, 7 (restricted), 8 (over 10), 9, 14

TYLER

Rosevine Inn B&B

415 South Vine
Tyler, TX, 75702
(903) 592-2221

Rosevine Inn is located on a historical "brick street" area of Tyler. There are several shops within walking distance. We have a lovely courtyard and a hot tub for guests to enjoy. We serve wine and cheese on arrival and a wonderful formal-style breakfast in the dining room. The innkeepers love visiting with the guests and welcoming them to Tyler, the "Rose Capital of the World."

Hosts: Bert & Rebecca Powell
Rooms: 5 (PB) $62.21-73.20
Full Breakfast
Credit Cards: A, B, E
Notes: 2, 5, 8 (over 12), 9, 10, 12, 14

WICHITA FALLS

Guest House Bed & Breakfast

2209 Miramar Street
Wichita Falls, TX, 76308
(817) 322-7252

This is a separate three-room guest house located on the grounds of our colonial home. Decorated in Early American and Victorian antiques, the rooms feature unusual touches such as antique doll furniture. We serve afternoon refreshments. There are twelve public tennis courts within a half mile and golf within one mile.

Hosts: Mr. & Mrs. Robert Vinson
Cottage: 1 (PB) $45-60
Full Breakfast
Credit Cards: No
Notes: 2, 5, 8, 9, 10, 11, 12

WIMBERLEY

The Chalet

B&B of Wimberley
P.O. Box 589
Wimberley, TX, 78676
(512) 847-9666

A large paneled living room overlooks the deck. Amenities include a spacious bedroom, attractive bath with whirlpool tub, fireplace, kitchenette, TV, and air-conditioning. Complimentary wine; continental breakfast. $85.

Leveritt Loop Lodge

B&B of Wimberley
P.O. Box 589
Wimberley, TX, 78676
(512) 847-9666

Quiet and private; near town, yet very secluded. Walk to the river. King bed, modern bath, air-conditioned and heated. Coffee bar, refrigerator, and two-burner range for light cooking. Continental breakfast. $55.

The Ranch Room

B&B of Wimberley
P.O. Box 589
Wimberley, TX, 78676
(512) 847-9666

Large sitting room/bedroom/kitchenette combined. Cozy dining area. All decks and grounds of the estate are available to guests. Sleeps four; continental breakfast. $65.

The Tree House

B&B of Wimberley
P.O. Box 589
Wimberley, TX, 78676
(512) 847-9666

High up, with a private entrance, an attractive bedroom, sitting room, and kitchen. Full bath and private deck; continental breakfast. $75.

Utah

CEDAR CITY

Meadeau View Lodge

P.O. Box 356
Cedar City, UT, 84720
(801) 682-2495

Located in the triangle reaching from Cedar Breaks to Bryce Canyon to Zion Park. Hiking, fishing, bicycling, snowmobiling, cross-country skiing, or just relaxing. Quiet, homey atmosphere. Nine rooms with private baths; families welcome. Located 29 miles east of Cedar City on Highway 14; 10 miles west of Highway 89.

Hosts: Val & Harris Torbenson
Rooms: 9 (PB) $50-60 + tax
Full Breakfast
Credit Cards: A, B
Notes: 2, 3, 4, 5, 6, 7 (restricted), 8, 13, 14

Paxman Summer House

170 North 400 West
Cedar City, UT, 84720
(801) 586-3755

The Paxman Summer House is a turn-of-the-century Victorian on a quiet street two blocks from the Shakespearean Festival. Tastefully decorated with antiques. A short drive to Cedar Mountain, Brian Head Ski Resort, Zion National Park, and Bryce Canyon National Park. Local golf course, pool, and tennis courts are nearby.

Host: Karlene Paxman
Rooms: 4 (PB) $55-59
Continental-plus Breakfast
Credit Cards: A, B
Reservations suggested
Notes: 5, 7 (outside), 10, 11, 12, 13, 14

HENEFER

Dearden B&B Inn

20 West 100 North
Henefer, UT, 84033
(801) 336-5698

The Dearden B&B Inn is nestled in the foothills of the Wasatch Mountains. Beautiful scenery. All sports are within thirty minutes to one hour. Henefer is the only town on the Mormon Pioneer Trail, and offers a warm, friendly atmosphere.

Host: Wilhelmina Dearden
Rooms: 8 (SB) $27.25
Continental-plus Breakfast
Credit Cards: B
Notes: 2, 5, 6, 7, 8, 10, 12

HURRICANE

Pah Tempe Hot Springs Resort B&B

825 North 800 East 35-4
Hurricane, UT, 84737
(801) 635-2879

This peaceful resort is located in a grove on an ancient Painte Indian healing ground in the Virgin River Canyon. One swimming pool and soaking pools up to 107 degrees F. Paiute medicine man, Clifford Jake, rededicated the property to its original healing purposes. No use of drugs, alcohol, or tobacco is part of the concept.

Host: Ken Anderson
Rooms: 9 (3 PB; 6 SB) $40-90
Full Breakfast
Credit Cards: A, B
Notes: 2, 3, 4, 5, 8, 10, 11, 12, 14

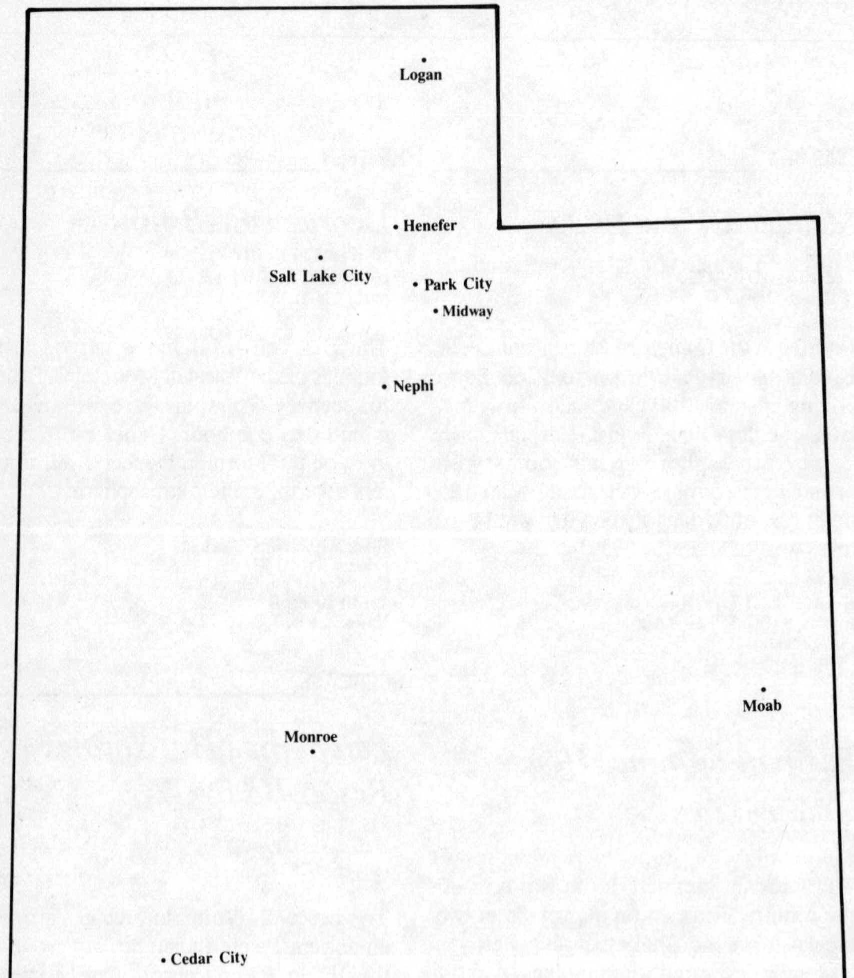

Logan

Henefer

Salt Lake City

Park City

Midway

Nephi

Moab

Monroe

Cedar City

Hurricane

St. George

UTAH

LOGAN

Center Street B&B Inn

169 East Center Street
Logan, UT, 84321
(801) 752-3443

Our inn, a step into the past and the unusual, features fantasy rooms: the Jungle Bungalow, the Arabian Nights Suite, Aphrodite's Court, Garden Suite, Victorian Suite, and the Pirate's Paradise. They have exotic decor such as waterfalls, wild animals, Grecian statues, stars, huge acquariums, etc. Also Jacuzzis, free movies, and private breakfasts. Skiing, hiking, boating, theater, and entertainment are nearby.

Hosts: Clyne & Ann Long
Rooms: 6 (PB) $25-95
Continental-plus Breakfast
Credit Cards: A, B, C
Notes: 2, 5, 8 (infants only), 9, 10, 11, 12, 13, 14

MIDWAY

Schneitter Family Hotel at The Homestead

700 North Homestead Drive
Midway, UT, 84049
(800) 327-7220; (801) 654-1102

The original Schneitter Family Hotel at the historic Homestead Resort. Eight Victorian rooms individually appointed with antiques, linens, and special amenities. Adjacent solarium and whirlpool. Nonsmoking, adults only. The AAA four-diamond resort offers golf, swimming, horseback riding, tennis, elegant dining, sleigh rides, cross-country skiing, snowmobiling, and complete meeting facilities.

Hosts: Britt Mathwich
Rooms: 8 (PB) $85
Continental Breakfast
Credit Cards: A, B, C
Notes: 2, 3, 4, 5, 9, 10, 11, 12, 13, 14

MOAB

Castle Valley Inn

CVSR Box 2602, 424 Amber Lane
Moab, UT, 84532
(801) 259-6012

The seven-room "western" inn is situated on 11 acres of orchard, lawn, and fields. Relax in the Grandview hot tub and enjoy striking red-rock scenery in every direction. Guests feast on a variety of fresh, healthy meals. A generous Canyonlands breakfast is included. Close to national parks.

Hosts: Eric & Lynn Thomson
Rooms: 8 (5 PB; 3 SB) $40-70
Full Breakfast
Credit Cards: A, B
Notes: 2, 3, 4, 5, 7 (limited), 9, 11, 12, 13, 14

MONROE

Petersons B&B

Box 142
Monroe, UT, 84754
(801) 527-4830

Halfway between Denver and Los Angeles. King-size feather bed room has a private entrance, bath, refrigerator stocked with cold drinks, and color TV. There's a suite with twin beds, and a canopy double-bed room. Near five national parks and four national forests. Seven blocks to restaurant.

Host: Mary Ann Peterson
Rooms: 3 (2 PB; 1 SB) $40
Full Breakfast
Credit Cards: No
Notes: 4, 5, 8, 10, 11, 12, 14

NEPHI

The Whitmore Mansion B&B Inn

110 South Main Street
Nephi, UT, 84648
(801) 623-2047

This Queen Anne Victorian mansion, built in 1898, represents the warmth and charm of days past. A visit to the mansion is truly a memorable experience. Easy access from I-15; just 85 miles south of Salt Lake City.

Hosts: Bob & Dorothy Gliske
Rooms: 6 (PB) $49.05-70.85
Full Breakfast
Credit Cards: A, B
Notes: 2, 4, 5, 8, 9, 11, 12, 14

The Whitmore Mansion B&B Inn

PARK CITY

The Old Miners' Lodge

615 Woodside Avenue, Box 2639
Park City, UT, 84060
(801) 645-8068; (800) 648-8068

A restored 1893 miners' boarding house in the national historic district of Park City, with ten individually decorated rooms filled with antiques and older pieces. Close to historic Main Street, with the Park City ski area in its backyard, the lodge is "more like staying with friends than at a hotel!" A nonsmoking inn.

Hosts: Hugh Daniels, Jeff Sadowsky, Susan Wynne
Rooms: 10 (PB) $40-175
Full Breakfast
Minimum stay, Christmas: 4-6; US Film, 4; Art, 2
Credit Cards: A, B, C, D
Notes: 2, 5, 8, 9, 10, 11, 12, 13, 14

The Old Miners' Lodge

Washington School Inn

P.O. Box 536
Park City, UT, 84060
(800) 824-1672; (801) 649-3800

Historical restoration of an old schoolhouse, decorated with modified Victorian. Hot tub and sauna on the property. Located in downtown historic Park City, close to Salt Lake area airport (45 minutes) and some of the best skiing in the world.

Hosts: Nancy Beaufait & Delphine Covington
Rooms: 15 (PB) $75-225
Full Breakfast; continental in summer
Credit Cards: A, B, C, D, F
Notes: 5, 8 (over 12), 9, 10, 11, 12, 13, 14

ST. GEORGE

Greene Gate Village

76 West Tabernacle Street
St. George, UT, 84770
(801) 628-6999

Eight comfortable homes, all dating back to the time of the pioneers, each lovingly restored with attention to detail. Greene Gate Village can cater parties, receptions, conventions, and family reunions. Close to Zion, Bryce, and Grand Canyon national parks, nine golf courses. Skiing in the area. Mild climate year round.

Hosts: Mark & Barbara Greene
Rooms: 11 (PB) $40-74
Full Breakfast
Credit Cards: A, B, C
Notes: 2, 3, 4, 5, 6, 8, 9, 10, 11, 12, 14

Seven Wives Inn

Seven Wives Inn

217 North 100 West
St. George, UT, 84770
(801) 628-3737

The inn consists of two adjacent pioneer adobe homes with massive hand-grained moldings framing windows and doors. Bedrooms are furnished in period antiques and handmade quilts. Some rooms have fireplaces; one has a whirlpool tub. Swimming pool on premises.

Hosts: Donna & Jay Curtis, Alison & Jon Bowcutt
Rooms: 13 (PB) $40-75
Full Breakfast
Credit Cards: A, B, C, E
Notes: 2, 5, 8, 9, 10, 11, 12, 14

SALT LAKE CITY

Brigham Street Inn

1135 East South Temple
Salt Lake City, UT, 84102
(801) 364-4461

Brigham Street Inn is a Victorian mansion built in 1898, done in both traditional and contemporary design. Minutes away from Temple Square, downtown, and the University of Utah. Also minutes away from all outdoor activities: hiking, skiing, tennis, and golf.

Hosts: John & Nancy Pace
Rooms: 9 (PB) $65-140
Continental Breakfast
Credit Cards: A, B, C
Notes: 2, 5, 7, 8, 9, 10, 11, 12, 14

Historic Manor House

B&B Rocky Mountains 34
P.O. Box 804
Colorado Springs, CO, 80901
(719) 630-3422

You'll feel right at home in this historic five-bedroom manor house. Large cut-glass windows let in sunlight from east and west, keeping the rooms bright all day. Full breakfast is served buffet style. No smoking, no pets. Children welcome. $49-69.

Suite Victorian

B&B Rocky Mountains 103
P.O. Box 804
Colorado Springs, CO, 80901

Enjoy this B&B built in 1903 and surrounded by a small quarter-horse breeding and training farm. Lots of wildlife in the area, as well as shopping, restaurants, and ski resorts. The inn has four suites furnished with folk art and southwestern touches. Suites, doubles, queens, and twins are available; one room has a Jacuzzi tub. All have phone, TV, and private bath. Children are welcome; no pets, no smoking. $50-85 seasonal.

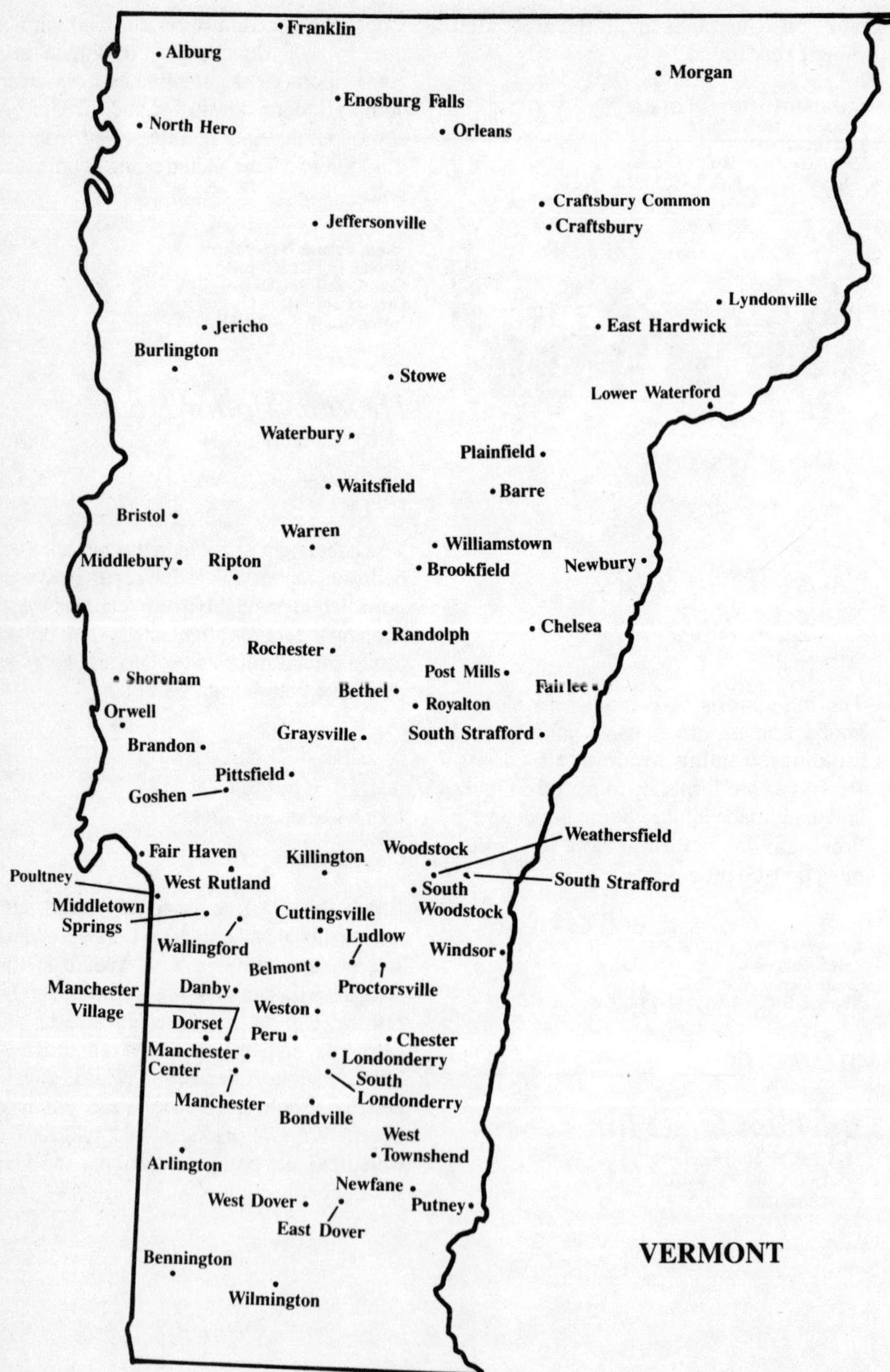
Franklin
Alburg
Morgan
Enosburg Falls
North Hero
Orleans
Craftsbury Common
Jeffersonville
Craftsbury
Lyndonville
Jericho
East Hardwick
Burlington
Stowe
Lower Waterford
Waterbury
Plainfield
Waitsfield
Barre
Bristol
Warren
Williamstown
Middlebury
Ripton
Brookfield
Newbury
Chelsea
Randolph
Rochester
Post Mills
Shoreham
Bethel
Fairlee
Orwell
Royalton
Graysville
South Strafford
Brandon
Pittsfield
Goshen
Weathersfield
Fair Haven
Killington
Woodstock
Poultney
West Rutland
South Strafford
South
Woodstock
Middletown
Springs
Cuttingsville
Ludlow
Wallingford
Windsor
Belmont
Proctorsville
Manchester
Village
Danby
Weston
Dorset
Peru
Chester
Manchester
Center
Londonderry
South
Londonderry
Manchester
Bondville
West
Townshend
Arlington
Newfane
West Dover
Putney
East Dover
Bennington
Wilmington
VERMONT

Vermont

ALBURG

Auberge Alburg

RD 1, Box 3
Alburg, VT, 05440
(802) 796-3169

A cozy turn-of-the-century house overlooking Lake Champlain, plus a renovated barn with newly built garden suite or loft room for utter privacy. Cosmopolitan atmosphere: eight languages spoken, books, grand piano, authentic Russian Gypsy entertainment. Espresso coffee on porch. Mini-conference facilities and space for summer theater. Montreal tours and lodging are also available. Very informal. Dormitory facilities; group packages.

Hosts: Gabrielle Tynauer & Charles Stastny
Rooms: 6 (1 PB; 5 SB) $40-75
Continental-plus Breakfast
Credit Cards: No
Notes: 2, 3, 4, 5, 6 (call), 7 (restricted), 8, 9, 10, 11, 12, 13

ARLINGTON

The Arlington Inn

Historic Route 7A
Arlington, VT, 05250
(802) 375-6532; (800) 443-9442

An elegant Victorian inn with antique-filled guest rooms in one of Vermont's finest Greek Revival homes. Candlelight dining on creative American cuisine that has been awarded numerous Taste of Vermont Awards as well as the Travel Holiday Dining Award.

Hosts: Paul & Madeline Kruzel
Rooms: 13 (PB) $60-150
Continental Breakfast
Minimum stay weekends: 2; holidays: 3
Credit Cards: A, B, C
Notes: 2, 4, 5, 7, 8, 9, 10, 11, 12, 13, 14

The Evergreen Inn

Sandgate Road, Box 2480
Arlington, VT, 05250
(802) 375-2272

Old-fashioned colonial country inn in the Green River Valley and Green Mountains. Off the beaten path, casual, relaxed atmosphere. Family owned and operated for over fifty years. Close to art centers, summer theaters, antiques, auctions, fairs, golf courses. Home cooking and baking.

Host: Mathilda Kenny
Rooms: 19 (PB and SB) $50-60
Full Breakfast
Credit Cards: No
Closed Oct. 15-May 15
Notes: 2, 3 (July & Aug.), 4, 6, 7, 8, 9, 10, 11, 12

Hill Farm Inn

Hill Farm Inn

RR 2, Box 2015
Arlington, VT, 05250
(802) 375-2269; (800) 882-2545

Visit one of Vermont's original farmsteads that has also been an inn since 1905. Stay in a 1790 or 1830 farmhouse and enjoy hearty home cooking and homegrown vegetables, plus a jar of homemade jam to take home. Nestled at the foot of Mt. Equinox and surrounded by 50 acres of farmland with the Battenkill River bordering the lower pasture.

Hosts: George & Joanne Hardy
Rooms: 13 (8 PB; 5 SB) $60-90
Full Breakfast
Minimum stay weekends: 2; Holidays: 3
Credit Cards: A, B, C, D
Notes: 2, 4, 5, 7 (restricted), 8, 9, 10, 11, 12, 14

The Inn at Sunderland

Route 7A
Arlington, VT, 05250
(802) 362-4213

The inn is a restored Victorian farmhouse built in 1840, with chestnut trim and doors, eleven-foot ceilings, a polished walnut staircase, six working fireplaces, and a two-level porch overlooking the pack pasture and the Green Mountains. Located midway between Arlington and Manchester, at the foot of Mt. Equinox, the inn is on the Battenkill River, one of America's premier trout streams.

Hosts: Tom & Peggy Wall
Rooms: 10 (8 PB; 2 SB) $65-95
Full Breakfast
Credit Cards: A, B, C
Closed April
Notes: 2, 7, 8, 9, 10, 11, 12, 13, 14

Ira Allen House

RD 2, Box 2485
Arlington, VT, 05250
(802) 362-2284

Vermont state historic site, home of Ira Allen (Ethan's brother, who lived here with him). Norman Rockwell Museum, Hildene, hiking, canoeing, biking, skiing, antiques. Enjoy the experience of a relaxing stay at our historic inn and a bountiful homecooked breakfast.

Hosts: Rowland & Sally Bryant
Rooms: 9 (4 PB; 5 SB) $55-70
Full Breakfast
Credit Cards: A, B, C
Closed April
Dinner available on winter Saturdays
Notes: 2, 8 (over 10), 9, 10, 11, 12, 13

Ira Allen House

Shenandoah Farm

Arlington, VT, 05250
(802) 375-6372

This colonial home near the Battenkill River is located five miles from Rt. 7A on Rt. 313. Close to Norman Rockwell museum and recreational activities. Five antique-filled guest rooms are offered with private or shared baths.

Hosts: Woody & Diana Masterson
Rooms: 5 (1 PB; 4 SB) $60-65
Full Breakfast
Minimum stay holidays: 2
Credit Cards: No
Notes: 2, 5, 7, 8, 9, 10, 11, 12, 13

BARRE

Woodruff House

13 East Street
Barre, VT, 05641
(802) 476-7745; (802) 479-9381

Large Victorian 1883 home located on a quiet park close to downtown shops and restaurants. Barre is the "Granite Center of the World." Great scenery, fantastic fall foliage. Halfway between Boston and Montreal, off I-89. Friendly and warm, like coming home to Grandma's.

Hosts: Robert & Terry Somaini & Katie
Rooms: 2 (PB) $55-65
Full Breakfast
Credit Cards: No
Notes: 2, 5, 8 (12 and over), 12, 13

The Leslie Place

BELMONT

The Leslie Place

P.O. Box 62
Belmont, VT, 05730
(802) 259-2903

Peacefully set on 100 acres near Weston, this restored 1840 farmhouse is close to major ski areas, restaurants, theater, and shops. While surrounded by mountain views and meadows, guests will find comfortably spacious room creating a welcome retreat. Brochure available.

Host: Mary K. Gorman
Rooms: 4 (PB) $55-65
Full Breakfast
Credit Cards: A, B
Notes: 2, 5, 9, 10, 11, 12, 13

BENNINGTON

American Country Collection 41

984 Gloucester Place
Schenectady, NY, 12309
(518) 370-4948

This Victorian is situated one mile from the center of Bennington, with a stream in the backyard and a large front porch for rocking. Each room is highlighted with antiques and country touches. Near Bennington College, Southern Vermont College, and skiing at Prospect Mountain. Six rooms with private baths. A full breakfast is served, and children twelve and over are welcome. $60-90 + gratuity.

BETHEL

Poplar Manor

RD 2, Box 136
Bethel, VT, 05032
(802) 234-5426

Circa 1810 Federal house with beamed ceilings in a beautiful setting in central Vermont. Furnished with antiques and collectibles; country kitchen; large rooms. All sports nearby, including swimming holes and skiing at Killington and Woodstock. Near national fish hatchery and Vermont Law School. Many restaurants nearby, including one within walking distance. The White River runs at the edge of our property.

Hosts: Bob & Carmen Jaynes
Rooms: 4 (SB) $33-35
Continental-plus Breakfast

Credit Cards: No
Notes: 2, 5, 6 (call), 7, 8, 9, 10, 11, 12, 13, 14

BONDVILLE

Alpenrose Inn

Winhall Hollow Road
Bondville, VT, 05340
(802) 297-2750

Small country inn on a quiet road. All rooms are furnished with antiques, some with canopy beds. Cozy lounge with large fireplace. Free tennis to house guests, golf, horseback riding, fishing are within minutes. Near ski lifts and the Appalachian Trail.

Host: Rosemarie Strine
Rooms: 7 (PB) $75-98
Full Breakfast
Credit Cards: No
Closed April 1-June 15; Oct. 23-Nov. 22
Notes: 2, 7 (limited), 9, 10, 11, 12, 13

BRANDON

The Arches Country Inn

53 Park Street
Brandon, VT, 05733
(802) 247-8200

A stately colonial mansion located in the heart of Brandon on Route 73. Homey atmosphere. Outdoor pool. Downhill and cross-country skiing, canoeing, hiking, fishing, bicycling, golf, tennis, antiques, covered bridges, museums nearby. Dining rooms are open to the public (restaurant closed Tuesdays).

Hosts: Jack & Ellen Scheffey
Rooms: 7 (PB) $70-95
Full Breakfast
Credit Cards: A, B, C, D
Notes: 3, 4, 5, 7, 8, 9, 10, 12, 13, 14

The Brandon Inn

On the Village Green
Brandon, VT, 05733
(802) 247-5766

Restored 1786 inn on the village green in Brandon, a typical Vermont village. Individually decorated guest rooms have private baths. Relax in the beautifully appointed, spacious public rooms or around the large, secluded pool. Fine dining, outside terrace. Chef owned and operated.

Hosts: Sarah & Louis Pattis
Rooms: 28 (PB) $90-125
Full Breakfast
Minimum stay some weekends: 2
Credit Cards: A, B, C
Notes: 2, 3, 4, 5, 7, 8, 9, 10, 11, 12, 13, 14

The Brandon Inn

Old Mill Inn

Stone Mill Dam Road
Brandon, VT, 05733
(802) 247-8002

The Old Mill Inn is a restored 1786 farmhouse on 10 acres with horses, chickens, ducks, and pigs, bordering a country club golf course. All rooms are decorated with antiques and handmade quilts. A country breakfast is served, and activities such as hiking, biking, fishing, and cross-country and downhill skiing are minutes away.

Hosts: Karl & Annemarie Schreiber
Rooms: 6 (PB) $75-85
Full Breakfast
Credit Cards: No
Notes: 2, 4 (by arrangement), 8, 9, 10, 11, 12, 13, 14

BRISTOL

Long Run Inn

RD 1, Box 560
Bristol, VT, 05443
(802) 453-3233

Antique-filled country inn built in 1799 near the base of Mount Abraham in Lincoln. A wraparound rocking-chair porch overlooks a peaceful trout stream. Various cuisines are represented in menus developed and prepared by the innkeepers. Cross-country skiing, fishing, swimming, and hiking available. Close to Middlebury and Burlington attractions.

Hosts: Mike & Bev Conway
Rooms: 8 (SB) $66-76
Full Breakfast
Credit Cards: No
Closed mid-March to mid-May; Nov.-Dec. 30
Notes: 2, 4, 7 (restricted), 8 (over 10), 9, 10, 11, 13

BROOKFIELD

Green Trails Country Inn

By the Floating Bridge
Brookfield, VT, 05036
(802) 276-3412

Cozy, relaxing, informal, "Like going home to Grandma's." Home-cooked meals at hearthside, guest rooms decorated with quilts and antiques. Hiking and biking, with serene vistas. In winter, enjoy horse-drawn sleigh rides, cross-country skiing (34 km tracked trails), and fireside friendship. "The epitome of a country inn" — NBC's "Today." B&B or MAP available.

Hosts: Pat & Peter Simpson
Rooms: 15 (9 PB; 6 SB) $68-80
Full Breakfast
Credit Cards: No
Closed April
Notes: 2, 4, 8, 9, 10, 11, 12, 13, 14

Green Trails Country Inn

BURLINGTON

American Country Collection 73

984 Gloucester Place
Schenectady, NY, 12309
(518) 370-4948

Located just a few miles from the center of Burlington, this turn-of-the-century farmhouse is on 10 acres of locust and maple trees, gardens, woods, and pastures. Pillars and three porches emphasize the Victorian structure of the house. Guests have a private entrance, dining room, living room with fireplace, TV, VCR, and stereo. Three guest rooms, one with private bath, have double beds. Children over sixteen welcome. Dog, cat, and fifteen sheep on premises. Continental-plus breakfast. $50-85.

CHELSEA

Shire Inn

8 Main Street
Chelsea, VT, 05038
(802) 685-3031

An 1832 historic brick Federal, "Very Vermont," inn. Eighteenth-century accommodations with twentieth-century bathrooms. Small & intimate, some rooms have working fireplaces. Chef-owned and operated, with five-course dining available. Centrally located: thirty miles north of Woodstock/Queeche, thirty-four miles to Hanover/Dartmouth, thirty miles south of Montpelier.

Hosts: James & Mary Lee Papa
Rooms: 6 (PB) $70-$95
Minimum stay weekends & holidays: 2
Full Breakfast
Credit Cards: A, B
Notes: 2, 4, 5, 8 (over 6), 9, 10, 11, 13

Shire Inn

CHESTER

The "Chester House"

P.O. Box 708, Main Street
Chester, VT, 05143
(802) 875-2205

A village B&B inn of extraordinary charm and hospitality. Located on the village green, the home was built in 1780 and is in the National Registry of Historic Places. Easy access to skiing, hiking, cycling, antiquing, golf, and just enjoying the beautiful Green Mountains of Vermont.

Hosts: Irene & Norm Wright
Rooms: 4 (PB) $50-75
Full Breakfast
Credit Cards: No
Notes: 2, 5, 9, 10, 11, 12, 13, 14

Greenleaf Inn

Depot Street, Box 188
Chester, VT, 05143
(802) 875-3171

Lovely 1880s home, now a comfortable village inn facing an expansive lawn. Just five charming rooms, each with private bath. Art gallery on premises features Vermont scenes — browse or buy. Walk to antiques, village green attractions. Bicycle tourists welcome. Full breakfast in our sunny dining room.

Hosts: Elizabeth & Dan Duffield
Rooms: 5 (PB) $70-80
Full Breakfast
Credit Cards: A, B
Notes: 2, 4, 5, 7, 8 (over 6), 9, 10, 11, 12, 13, 14

The Hugging Bear Inn & Shoppe

Main Street
Chester, VT, 05143
(802) 875-2412

Charming Victorian home on the village green. The shop has over 3,500 bears, and guests may "adopt" a bear for the night as long as he's back to work in the shop by 9:00 the next morning. Puppet show often performed at breakfast; breakfast music provided by an 1890 music box. Thanksgiving and Christmas dinners available. Two lovable cats in residence.

Hosts: The Thomases
Rooms: 6 (PB) $75-95
Full Breakfast
Minimum stay weekends: 2; holidays: 2-3
Credit Cards: A, B, C, D
Notes: 2, 5, 6, 8, 9, 10, 11, 12, 13

The Stone Hearth Inn

Route 11 West
Chester, VT, 05143
(802) 875-2525

The "Chester House"

Built in 1810, The Stone Hearth Inn is widely know for its old-fashioned, informal hospitality. All of the guest rooms retain the romance of the period with antique furnishings, exposed beams, and wide pine floors. Fully licensed pub, dining room, library, and recreation room with whirlpool spa. Gift shop.

Hosts: Janet & Don Strohmeyer
Rooms: 10 (PB) $48-120
Full Breakfast
Credit Cards: A, B, D
Notes: 2, 4, 5, 7, 8, 9, 10, 11, 12, 13

The Craftsbury Inn

CRAFTSBURY

The Craftsbury Inn

Main Street
Craftsbury, VT, 05826
(802) 586-2848

An 1850 country inn located in Vermont's unique Northeast Kingdom. The ten guest rooms have custom quilts. We offer excellent cuisine. In summer and fall one may canoe, fish, bike, hike, swim, sail, and play tennis or golf. Winter offers the finest and most consistent cross-country skiing in the East.

Hosts: Blake & Rebecca Gleason
Rooms: 10 (6 PB; 4 SB) $55-90
Full Breakfast
Credit Cards: A, B
Closed April & Nov.
Notes: 2, 4, 7, 8, 9, 10, 11, 12, 13, 14

CRAFTSBURY COMMON

The Inn on the Common

Main Street
Craftsbury Common, VT, 05827
(802) 586-9619; (800) 521-2233

With luxuriously appointed bedrooms in three historically designated buildings, the inn is a wonderful destination. Swimming pool, clay tennis court, walking trails, bike rentals, and 110 km of ski trails for the active; film and book libraries for the contemplative. Magnificent gardens, great views, serene surroundings, superb cuisine, excellent wines.

Hosts: Michael & Penny Schmitt
Rooms: 16 (PB) $170-190
Full Breakfast
Credit Cards: A, B
Notes: 2, 4, 5, 6, 7, 8, 9, 10, 11, 12, 13, 14

CUTTINGSVILLE

Buckmaster Inn

Lincoln Hill Road, Box 118
Shrewsbury, VT, 05738
(802) 492-3485

Country charm in a picturesque Green Mountain village overlooking a farm. Wide board floors show off family antiques. Homemade baked goodies served each morning in the dining room or on the porch in the summer. Wood-burning stone fireplaces. In a rural setting, this 1801 stagecoach stop is eight miles southeast of Rutland.

Hosts: Sam & Grace Husselman
Rooms: 4 (1 PB; 3 SB) $50-60
Full Breakfast
Credit Cards: No
Notes: 5, 8, 10, 11, 12, 13, 14

Maple Crest Farm

Lincoln Hill Road, Box 120
Cuttingsville, VT, 05738
(802) 492-3367

Located high in the Green Mountains, ten miles south of Rutland and twelve miles north of Ludlow, this 1808 twenty-seven-room historic home has been lovingly preserved for five generations. Cross-country skiing and hiking are offered on the farm. Close to major ski areas, Rutland, and places of historic interest. A real taste of true old Vermont hospitality. Maple syrup made on premises.

Hosts: William & Donna Smith
Rooms: 6 (1 PB; 5 SB) $50
Full Breakfast
Credit Cards: No
Closed Jan., Feb.
Notes: 2, 7, 9, 10, 11, 12, 13

DANBY

Quails Nest B&B Inn

Box 221
Danby, VT, 05739
(802) 293-5099

Nestled in a quiet mountain village, the inn offers its guests friendly conversation around the fireplace, rooms filled with cozy quilts and antiques, tips about local attractions, and a hearty, home-cooked breakfast in the morning.

Hosts: Anharad & Chip Edson
Rooms: 5 (3 PB; 2 SB) $50-65
Full Breakfast
Credit Cards: A, B
Notes: 2, 5, 7, 8 (over 6), 9, 10, 11, 12, 13

Silas Griffith Inn

South Main Street
Danby, VT, 05739
(802) 293-5567

Built in 1891 by Vermont's first millionaire, a now lovingly restored Victorian mansion and carriage house. Relax in antique-filled guest rooms with spectacular Green Mountain views. Dinner available.

Hosts: Paul & Lois Dansereau
Rooms: 17 (11 PB; 6 SB) $71.02-86.92
Full Breakfast
Minimum stay holidays: 2
Credit Cards: A, B, C
Notes: 2, 4, 5, 7 (limited), 8, 9, 11, 14

DORSET

Marble West Inn

Dorset West Road
Dorset, VT, 05251
(802) 867-4155

Marble West Inn is a Greek Revival home built in the 1840s. The house remained in

Inwood Manor

the family of Helen "Honey" West until she sold it to be an inn in 1985. Listed in the National Register of Historic Places, the inn features marble-columned porches overlooking the surrounding hills. Maple and white birch trees provide shade, and a little pond reflects the dark woodlands. The interior decor features beautiful stenciling that can be seen in the main hallway, polished hardwood floors covered with Oriental carpets, and displays of local artwork.

Hosts: Bill & Diane Coleman
Rooms: 8 (PB) $75-150
Full Breakfast
Credit Cards: A, B, C
Notes: 2, 5, 9, 11, 12, 13, 14

EAST BARNET

Inwood Manor

Lower Waterford Road
East Barnet, VT, 05821
(802) 633-4047

"Creating" a country inn before it became chic and approaching it as a life-style, not a business, has helped keep Ron and Peter going for ten years in rural northeast Vermont. An abandoned building before they bought it, Inwood Manor was restored from its boardinghouse/stage-coach-stop past to a charming, comfortable, old-style country inn on 20 private acres with a pond for swimming and ice skating.

Hosts: Ron Kaczor & Peter Embarrato
Rooms: 9 (SB) $45-65
Full Breakfast
Credit Cards: A, B
Notes: 2, 4, 5, 9, 11, 12, 13, 14

EAST DOVER

Cooper Hill Inn

Cooper Hill Road, Box 146
East Dover, VT, 05341
(802) 348-6333

Informal and cozy hilltop inn with "one of the most spectacular mountain panoramas in all New England." Quiet country-road location. Hearty home-cooked meals are a tradition here. Double rooms and family suites all feature private baths. Dinner and breakfast included in the daily rate.

Hosts: Pat & Marilyn Hunt
Rooms: 7 (PB) $85.60-117.70 MAP

Suites: 3 (PB) $96.30-128.40 MAP
Full Breakfast
Credit Cards: No
Closed for 1 week in April & November
Notes: 2, 4, 7, 8, 9, 10, 11, 12, 13, 14

EAST HARDWICK

Brick House Guests

Box 128, 2 Brick House Road
East Hardwick, VT, 05836
(802) 472-5512

Federal brick house with comfortable Victorian furnishings, sitting on the edge of a small village with open farmland and woods nearby. Beautiful gardens, perennial flowers, and herb nursery. The area is unspoiled, hilly and rural. Nearby you'll find tennis and golf, horseback riding, swimming in clear lakes, canoeing, and good local restaurants.

Hosts: Thomas & Judith Kane
Rooms: 3 (1 PB; 2 SB) $50-65
Full Breakfast
Credit Cards: A, B
Closed Dec. 24-26
Notes: 2, 5, 6, 7, 8, 9, 10, 11, 12, 13 (XC)

ENOSBURG FALLS

Berkson Farms

RD 1, Route 108
Enosburg Falls, VT, 05450
(802) 933-2522

Homey, relaxed atmosphere in a century-old restored farmhouse situated on a 600-acre working dairy farm, surrounded by a large variety of animals and all the simple, wonderful joys of nature and life itself. Warm hospitality and country home cooking.

Hosts: Bob & Shayne Lutz
Rooms: 4 (1 PB; 3 SB) $37.45-58.85
Full Breakfast
Credit Cards: No
Notes: 2, 4, 5, 6, 7, 8, 9, 10, 11, 12, 13

FAIR HAVEN

Maplewood Inn

Route 22A South
Fair Haven, VT, 05743
(802) 265-8039

This beautifully restored 1843 Greek Revival inn has exquisitely appointed rooms and suites and common areas that include a TV room with fireplace, BYOB tavern, gathering room with books and games furnished in various period styles and antiques. Many extras; near lakes, shops, and restaurants.

Host: Cindy Soder
Rooms: 5 (4 PB; 1 SB) $65-95 (suites)
Full Breakfast
Credit Cards: A, B, C
Notes: 2, 5, 7, 8 (over 5, call), 9, 10, 11, 12, 13, 14

FAIRLEE

Silver Maple Lodge

Route 5, Fairlee, VT, 05045
(802) 333-4326; (800) 666-1946

Historic B&B country inn. Cozy rooms with antiques, or knotty pine cottages. Enjoy beach, boating, fishing, and swimming at Lake Morey, one mile away. Golf, tennis, skiing, and hot-air balloon rides nearby. Dartmouth College, seventeen miles. Walk to restaurant.

Hosts: Scott & Sharon Wright
Rooms: 15 (8 PB; 7 SB) $38-58
Continental Breakfast
Minimum stay holidays: 2
Credit Cards: A, B, C
Closed Christmas Eve
Notes: 2, 8, 9, 10, 11, 12, 13, 14

FRANKLIN

Fair Meadow Farm B&B

Box 430, Route 235
Franklin, VT, 05457
(802) 285-2132

In the family since 1853, Fair Meadows is nestled in the northwest corner of Vermont. Peace, quiet, and comfort. When guests arrive, they are invited to "make themselves at home." North of Burlington, sixty-five miles south of Montreal.

Hosts: Terry & Philip Pierce
Rooms: 5 (SB) $45
Full Breakfast
Credit Cards: No
Notes: 2, 5, 6, 7, 8, 9, 13, 14

GAYESVILLE

Cobble House Inn

Box 49, Gayesville, VT, 05746
(802) 234-5458

The inn sits secluded on a hilltop overlooking the Green Mountains. The White River flows along our boundary, offering swimming and fishing. Each room is decorated in antiques and country furnishings, and we have a dining room that features Northern Italian cuisine prepared by our chef/owners. Complimentary afternoon hors d'oeuvres are served.

Hosts: Beau, Phil & Sam Benson
Rooms: 6 (PB) $75-95
Full Breakfast
Credit Cards: A, B
Notes: 2 (for deposit), 4, 5, 8 (over 5), 9, 10, 11, 12, 13, 14

GOSHEN

Blueberry Hill Inn

RD 3, Goshen, VT, 05733
(802) 247-6735; Reservations (800) 448-0707

Nestled in the Green Mountain National Forest, Blueberry Hill offers the ultimate country inn experience. Seventy-five kilometers of cross-country and hiking trails, gourmet cuisine, and antique-filled rooms make this an unforgettable stop. Homemade goodies and fine Vermont handcrafts.

Host: Tony Clark
Rooms: 12 (PB) $136-192
Full Breakfast
Credit Cards: A, B
Notes: 2, 4, 5, 8, 9, 10, 11, 12, 13, 14

JEFFERSONVILLE

Windridge Inn

P.O. Box 426
Jeffersonville, VT, 05464
(802) 644-5556

A village inn listed on the National Historic Register. Pine paneling, slate and wide board floors, stenciling. Furnished with period antiques. Pool and indoor/outdoor tennis on premises. Skiing, canoeing, hiking, and stables are nearby.

Hosts: Carole & Yves Labbe
Rooms: 4 (PB) $55-65
Full Breakfast
Credit Cards: A, B, C
Notes: 4, 5, 7, 8 (over 8), 9, 10, 11, 12, 13, 14

JERICHO

Eaton House B&B

Box 139, Brown's Trace
Jericho, VT, 05465
(802) 899-2354

Eaton House is a wonderfully designed saltbox offering mountain views from a splendid pastoral setting. Weather permitting, breakfast is served in the rock garden. Winter offers a wonderful area to curl up by the fire. Grand piano, TV, library, and refreshments available.

Hosts: Sue & Dave Eaton
Rooms: 3 (1 PB; 2 SB) $50-70
Full Breakfast
Credit Cards: No
Notes: 2, 5, 8, 9, 10, 11, 12, 13(XC)

KILLINGTON

Grey Bonnet Inn

Route 100N
Killington, VT, 05751
(802) 775-2537

Romantic, antique-filled mountain lodge on 25 acres with indoor and outdoor pools, whirlpool, sauna, game and exercise rooms. Library and cozy pub. Relax in front of the fire in our living room. All rooms have private bath, color TV, phone. Award-winning dining, piano entertainment, ski movies. Cross-country skiing out our back door. AAA and Mobil three-star rated.

Hosts: Barbara & Bill Flohr
Rooms: 40 (PB) $59-125 + tax
Full Breakfast
Credit Cards: A, B, C
Closed April 15-June 1 & Oct. 22-Thanksgiving
Notes: 2, 4, 7, 8, 9, 10, 11, 12, 13, 14

The Inn at Long Trail

Route 4, Sherburne Pass
Box 267
Killington, VT, 05751
(802) 775-7181; (800) 325-2540

Historic country inn, high in the ski country of Vermont, located at the junction of the historic Appalachian & Long Trails, for excellent hiking in the mountains. Irish pub, wood-paneled public rooms, and fireplace suites. Hot tub. Ideal for hiking and skiing. Open summer, fall, and winter.

Hosts: Kyran, Murray & Rosemary McGrath
Singles: 4 (PB)
Rooms: 22 (PB)
Seasonal rates
Minimum stay weekends: 2; holidays: 3
Full Breakfast
Credit Cards: A, B
Closed April 15-June 30
Notes: 2 (with CC) 4, 7, 8, 9, 10, 11, 12, 13, 14

Mountain Meadows Lodge

Thundering Brook Road
RR1, Box 4080
Killington, VT, 05751
(802) 775-1010

Would you like a nice place on a lake in the mountains of Vermont? Mountain Meadows is a friendly country inn, in a beautiful lakeside setting, with home-style cooking, swimming pool. Hiking, boating, fishing, scenic aerial gondola, alpine slide, and excellent playhouse are nearby. Tennis, golf, and many attractions. Or just relax and enjoy Vermont's scenery.

Hosts: The Stevens Family
Rooms: 18 (15 PB; 3 SB) $86-96 + tax
Full Breakfast
Credit Cards: A, B
Closed April 1-June 1; Oct. 15-Nov. 20
Notes: 2, 4, 8, 9, 10, 11, 12, 13, 14

The Vermont Inn

Route 4
Killington, VT, 05751
(802) 775-0708; (800) 541-7795

A small country inn built as a farmhouse in 1840. Country charm, warm atmosphere, and gourmet dining on a 5-acre mountain setting. Dining room, open to public, has a three-diamond award from AAA. Package plans are available.

Hosts: Susan & Judd Levy
Rooms: 17 (13 PB; 4 SB) $90-190 MAP
Full Breakfast
Minimum stay weekends: 2
Credit Cards: A, B, C
Closed April 15-May 25
Notes: 2, 4, 7, 8 (over 6), 9, 10, 11, 12, 13, 14

LONDONDERRY

Blue Gentian Lodge

Magic Mountain Road
Londonderry, VT, 05148
(802) 824-5908

Walk to the ski lifts of Magic Mountain. Lounge/library with fireplace. Full country breakfast. All large rooms have private bath, color TV. Fire walls separate rooms. Game rooms, BYOB, ice machine, soda machine, outdoor pool. Near excellent hiking, shopping, antiquing.

Host: June Kidde
Rooms: 14 (PB) $29.95-55
Continental Breakfast
Credit Cards: C
Notes: 2, 4, 5, 7, 8 (over 9), 9, 10, 11, 12, 13

The Highland House

Route 100
Londonderry, VT, 05148
(802) 824-3019

An 1842 inn, with swimming pool and tennis court, set on 32 acres. Seventeen rooms, fifteen with private baths. Classic candlelight dining with homemade soups, breads, and desserts. Within minutes to skiing, hiking, horseback riding, shopping, and points of interest.

Hosts: Bill & Judy Raffaele
Rooms: 17 (15 PB; 2 SB) $63-93
Full Breakfast
Minimum stay weekends: 2; holidays: 3
Credit Cards: A, B, C
Closed one week in Nov., three in April
Notes: 2, 4, 7, 8 (over 5), 9, 10, 11, 12, 13

The Village Inn at Landgrove

RFD Box 215
Londonderry, VT, 05148
(802) 824-6673

This renovated farmstead is featured in *Country Inns and Back Roads.* Rooms and meals, pool, tennis courts, pitch-and-putt golf. Families welcome.

Hosts: Else & Don Snyder
Rooms: 18 (16 PB; 2 SB) $45-75
Full Breakfast
Credit Cards: A, B, D
Closed April 1-May 26 & Oct. 30-Dec. 15
Notes: 2, 4, 7 (limited), 8, 9, 10, 11, 12, 13, 14

Rabbit Hill Inn

LOWER WATERFORD

Rabbit Hill Inn

Route 18
Lower Waterford, VT, 05848
(800) 76-BUNNY; (802) 748-5168

You are invited home to a New England classic, est. 1795. Set on 15 acres above the Connecticut River, the inn is a hideaway in a tiny historic district. This romantic inn is award-winning and features antiques, many canopied beds, fireplaces. The exceptional detail, cuisine, decor, and service have been featured by both national and international media. Guests enjoy a sense of fantasy, whimsy, and charm.

Hosts: John & Maureen Magee
Rooms: 18 (PB) $78-150
Full Breakfast
Credit Cards: A, B
Notes: 2, 4, 5, 9, 11, 12, 13, 14

LUDLOW

The Andrie Rose Inn

13 Pleasant Street
Ludlow, VT, 05149
(802) 228-4846

Casual but elegant c. 1829 country village inn nestled at the base of Okemo Mountain ski resort. Enjoy fireside cocktails with complimentary hors d'oeuvres. Lavishly appointed guest rooms, all with private baths and down comforters, some with cathedral ceilings, whirlpool tubs, and skylights. Spoil yourself with thick terry towels and almond scented toiletries. Savor delectable breakfasts and epicurean dinners, both by candlelight. Use inn bikes to tour back roads. Minutes from lakes, theater, golf, tennis, hiking, and shopping. And, of course, only .5 mile from downhill and cross-country skiing. Dinner available for $45/couple.

Hosts: Rick & Carolyn Bentzinger
Rooms: 8 (PB) $95-105
Full Breakfast

Credit Cards: A, B, C
Notes: 2, 4, 5, 9, 10, 11, 12, 13, 14

The Combes Family Inn

RFD 1, Box 275
Ludlow, VT, 05149
(802) 228-8799

Bring your family home to visit ours at The Combes Family Inn. Located on a quiet country back road with 50 acres of meadows to explore. Luke, reported to be the friendliest Lab around, shares the farm with lots of equally friendly cats, dogs, innkeepers, and guests. Homey atmosphere and country cooking.

Hosts: Ruth & Bill Combes
Rooms: 12 (10 PB; 2 SB) $74-86
Full Breakfast
Minimum stay, fall & winter weekends: 2; holidays: 4
Credit Cards: A, B, C
Closed April 15-May 15
Notes: 2, 4, 6, 7, 8, 9, 10, 11, 12, 13, 14

Echo Lake Inn

Echo Lake Inn

Box 154
Ludlow, VT, 05149
(800) 356-6844

Surrounded by Echo Lake, the Black River, and the mountains, near the birthplace of President Coolidge, the inn offers a pool, tennis, boating, fishing, hiking, and cycling. Porch dining. Minutes to Killington and Okemo ski centers; short distance from Woodstock, Weston, and Manchester.

Hosts: Phil & Kathy Cocco
Rooms: 26 (14 PB; 12 SB) $50-70
Full Breakfast & Dinner
Credit Cards: A, B
Closed April
Notes: 2, 4, 8, 9, 10, 11, 12, 13, 14

The Governor's Inn

The Governor's Inn

86 Main Street
Ludlow, VT, 05149
(802) 228-8830

An extraordinary reputation for excellence surrounds this premier eight guest room Victorian country house. Snuggle in a century-old brass four-poster, wake up to a wonderful English breakfast. Enjoy Vermont all day, then come home to Mozart, afternoon tea, and a crackling fire. Gather for hors d'oeuvres and a six-course dinner.

Sip brandy in the late evening. Judged one of the nation's ten best inns for the second year. Rates include breakfast, tea, and dinner.

Hosts: Charlie & Deedy Marble
Rooms: 8 (PB) $130
Full Breakfast
Credit Cards: A, B
Notes: 2, 3 (picnic basket), 4, 5, 9, 10, 11, 12, 13, 14

The Okemo Inn

RFD 1, Box 133
Ludlow, VT, 05149
(802) 228-8834

Eleven cozy guest rooms with private baths. King-size sauna, in-ground pool, fireside cocktail lounge, TV room and library. Candlelight dinners and hearty breakfasts featuring delicious country cuisine. Rent bicycles or stroll a quiet country lane. Golf, tennis horseback riding, skiing, summer theaters and evening concerts, country stores and antique emporiums all nearby.

Hosts: Ron & Toni Parry
Rooms: 11 (PB) $82
Full Breakfast
Credit Cards: A, B, C, D
Closed 2 weeks in April and Nov.
Notes: 2, 4, 7, 8 (over 6), 9, 10, 11, 12, 13, 14

LYNDONVILLE

The Wildflower Inn

Darling Hill Road
Lyndonville, VT, 05851
(800) 627-8310

Nestled on 500 acres in Vermont's Northeast Kingdom, The Wildflower Inn is a special place for all ages to enjoy the country. Each season captures the beauty of Burke Mountain and Lake Willoughby. A moonlit sleigh ride, the luxury of a spa, or refreshments by the pool will capture your heart.

Hosts: Jim & Mary O'Reilly
Rooms: 20 (16 PB; 4 SB) $64-125
Full Breakfast
Credit Cards: A, B
Notes: 2, 4, 5, 8, 9, 10, 11, 12, 13, 14

MANCHESTER

Birch Hill Inn

P.O. Box 346
Manchester, VT, 05254
(802) 362-2761

Quiet country inn away from busy streets. Panoramic views, swimming pool, trout pond, and walking trails on premises. Golf, antiquing, biking, tennis, and hiking nearby. Selected for The Innkeepers Register.

Hosts: Jim & Pat Lee
Rooms: 6 (PB) $98-148
Full Breakfast
Credit Cards: A, B
Closed Nov.1-Dec. 26, April 5-Memorial Day
Notes: 2, 4, 7 (restricted), 10, 11, 12, 13, 14

The Inn at Manchester

Box 41, Manchester, VT, 05254
(802) 362-1793

Beautifully restored turn-of-the-century Victorian set on 4 acres in the picture-book village of Manchester. Elegant rooms with bay windows, brass beds, antiques, and an extensive art collection. Luscious full country breakfast. Secluded pool, skiing, shops, theater in the area. Come for peace, pancakes, and pampering.

Hosts: Stan & Harriet Rosenberg
Rooms: 20 (13 PB; 7 SB) $70-105
Full Breakfast
Credit Cards: A, B, C
Notes: 2, 5, 8 (over 8), 9, 10, 11, 12, 13, 14

MANCHESTER CENTER

Brook-N-Hearth Inn

SR 11 & 30, Box 508
Manchester Center, VT, 05255
(802) 362-3604

Homey colonial-style inn 2.5 miles east of the town center on Routes 11 and 30. Features full breakfast, cozy rooms, private baths, family suite, cable TV, lounge, BYOB, recreation rooms, outdoor heated swimming pool, cross-country and walking trails by brook.

Hosts: Larry & Terry Greene
Rooms: 3 (PB) $50-70
Full Breakfast
Minimum stay holidays: 2
Credit Cards: A, B, C
Closed early Nov. & early May
Notes: 2, 7, 8, 9, 10, 11, 12, 13

Manchester Highlands Inn

Box 1754
Manchester Center, VT, 05255
(802) 362-4565

Discover Manchester's best-kept secret, a graceful Queen Anne Victorian inn on a hilltop overlooking town. Front porch with rocking chairs, large outdoor pool, game room, and pub with stone fireplace. Rooms individually decorated with feather beds, down comforters, and lace curtains. Gourmet country breakfast and afternoon snacks are served.

Hosts: Robert & Patricia Eichorn
Rooms: 15 (12 PB; 3 SB) $80-105
Full Breakfast
Credit Cards: A, B, C, D
Notes: 2, 5, 7 (limited), 8, 9, 10, 11, 12, 13, 14

Manchester Highlands Inn

MANCHESTER VILLAGE

1811 House

Manchester Village, VT, 05254
(802) 362-1811

This classic Vermont inn offers you the warmth and comfort of your own home. Built in the 1770s, the house has operated as an inn since 1811 except for one brief period when it was the residence of Abraham Lincoln's granddaughter. All guest rooms have private baths; some have fireplaces, Oriental rugs, fine paintings, and canopied beds. The inn sits on more than 3 acres of lawn containing flower gardens and trout pond, and offers an exceptional view of the Green Mountains. Within walking distance of golf and tennis; near skiing, fishing, canoeing, and all sports.

Hosts: Marnie & Bruce Duff
Rooms: 14 (PB) $100-170
Full Breakfast
Credit Cards: A, B, C
Notes: 2, 5, 7 (limited), 8 (over 16), 9, 10, 11, 12, 13, 14

Village Country Inn

Historic Route 7A
Manchester Village, VT, 05254
(802) 362-1792

A French country inn decorated in shades of mauve, celery, and ecru. Long porch with chintz rockers, wicker, and flowers. Elegant candlelight dining and cocktails are available in our tavern. Guest rooms are a fantasy of ice-cream colors, each one different. Swimming pool; tennis court. Breakfast and dinner included in daily rates.

Hosts: Anne & Jay Megen
Rooms: 30 (PB) $135-185
Full Breakfast
Credit Cards: A, B, C
Notes: 2, 4, 5, 7, 9, 10, 11, 12, 13, 14

MIDDLEBURY

Brookside Meadows

RD 3, Box 2460
Middlebury, VT, 05753-8751
(802) 388-6429

Attractive farmhouse built in 1979. Quiet rural setting, but only three miles from village center and Middlebury College. Spacious lawns and perennial gardens. Best downhill and cross-country skiing. All rooms with private bath. Special two-bedroom suite has living room with wood stove and private entrance. Green Mountain view and country sounds. Near Shelburne Museum.

Hosts: Linda & Roger Cole
Rooms: 3 (PB) $69.55-85
Suite (4 people) $128.40-144.40
Full Breakfast
Credit Cards: A, B
Notes: 2, 5, 8 (over 5), 9, 10, 11, 12, 13, 14

Brookside Meadows

The Middlebury Inn

Courthouse Square
Middlebury, VT, 05753
(802) 388-4961; (800) 842-4666

Elegantly restored 1827 village inn located in the historic district of a lovely college town. Guest rooms have private baths, telephone, color TV. Formal or informal dining; afternoon tea served daily. Museums, unique shops, historic sites to explore. Swimming, golf, hiking, boating, downhill and cross-country skiing are nearby. Special packages are available.

Hosts: Frank & Jane Emanuel
Rooms: 75 (PB) $88-132
Credit Cards: A, B, C
Notes: 2, 3, 4, 5, 6 (restricted), 7, 8, 9, 10, 11, 12, 13, 14

Swift House Inn

Route 7, Middlebury, VT, 05753
(802) 388-9925

A warm and gracious Federal-style estate with window seats overlooking the formal gardens, fireplaces in ten of the rooms, and whirlpool tubs. Relax in our cozy pub room and then enjoy award-winning cuisine in our elegant cherry-paneled dining room. Walking distance to shopping and Middlebury College; just a short drive to skiing, golf, and swimming.

Hosts: John & Andrea Nelson
Rooms: 20 (PB) $65-140
Full Breakfast
Credit Cards: A, B, C, D, E
Notes: 2, 4, 5, 7, 8, 9, 10, 11, 12, 13, 14

Middletown Springs Inn

MIDDLETOWN SPRINGS

Middletown Springs Inn

Box 1068
Middletown Springs, VT, 05757
(802) 235-2198

An 1879 Victorian mansion in a Vermont village in a national historic district. Ten guest rooms and five large common rooms are decorated in Victorian style and furnished in antiques. Experience rural Vermont and an exceptional country inn. The food, the hospitality, and the area offer everything you hope for.

Hosts: Jane & Steve Sax
Rooms: 10 (8 PB; 2 SB) $70-110
Full Breakfast
Credit Cards: A, B
Notes: 2, 4, 5, 7 (limited), 8 (over 6), 9, 10, 11, 12, 13 (XC), 14

MORGAN

Hunt's Hideaway

RR 1, Box 570
West Charleston, VT, 05872
(802) 895-4432; (802) 334-8322

Our B&B was started in 1981 after the hosts stayed in B&Bs in Europe during their many years of traveling. Contemporary split level on 100 acres; brook, pond, in-ground pool. Located in Morgan, six miles from I-91 near Canadian border.

Host: Pat Hunt
Rooms: 3 (SB) $25-35 plus tax
Full Breakfast
Credit Cards: No
Kitchen Privileges
Notes: 2, 5, 6, 7, 8, 9, 10, 11, 12, 13

NEWBURY

A Century Past

Box 186, Route 5
Newbury, VT, 05051
(802) 866-3358

A charming historic house dating back to 1790, nestled in the tranquility of a quaint Vermont village. A cozy sitting room with fireplace: chat with newfound friends or curl up with a good book. Wake up to fresh baked muffins, hot coffee or tea, great French toast — all served in a comfortable dining room.

Host: Patricia Smith
Rooms: 4 (2 S1B) $55
Full Breakfast
Credit Cards: A, B
Closed Christmas
Notes: 2, 8 (over 12), 9, 10, 11, 12, 13

NEWFANE

West River Lodge

RR 1, Box 693
Newfane, VT, 05345
(802) 365-7745

West River Lodge is a small country inn with farmhouse charm, furnished with antiques. Located in the Green Mountains close to various country pastimes: hiking, swimming, skiing, English riding, trail riding. Riding clinic held in May; watercolor workshop in July. Close to flea markets and antique centers. MAP plan available at extra charge.

Hosts: Jack & Gill Winner
Rooms: 5 (2 PB; 3 SB) $45-75
Full Breakfast
Credit Cards: No
Notes: 2, 3, 4, 5, 7 (limited), 8, 9, 10, 11, 12, 13, 14

NORTH HERO

American Country Collection 47

984 Gloucester Place
Schenectady, NY, 12309
(518) 370-4948

A quiet, secluded estate on 50 acres with views of the Green Mountains and a half-mile of private lakefront on Lake Champlain. The four rooms in the restored 100-year-old farmhouse and carriage house function as a B&B only in the winter and spring. $50-60.

ORLEANS

Valley House Inn

4 Memorial Square
Orleans, VT, 05860
(802) 754-6665

NOTES: Credit cards accepted: A Master Card; B Visa; C American Express; D Discover Card; E Diners Club; F Other: 2 Personal checks accepted: 3 Lunch available: 4 Dinner available: 5 Open all year

One-quarter mile from Exit 26 off I-91. An 1800s country inn located in the center of the Northeast Kingdom's lakes region. One mile from top eighteen-hole golf course. Easy access to scenic hiking, biking, hunting, and ice, lake, and river fishing. Skiing at Jay Peak and Burke Mountains, just thirty minutes away.

Hosts: David & Louise Bolduc
Rooms: 22 (PB) $35-60
Continental Breakfast
Credit Cards: A, B, C
Notes: 2, 3, 4, 5, 7, 8, 9, 11, 12, 13, 14

ORWELL

Historic Brookside Farms

Route 22A, Orwell, VT, 05760
(802) 948-2727

In 1989, we celebrated the 200th anniversary of Brookside Farms, a 300-acre estate with its Greek Revival mansion. All rooms are furnished with antiques, which, as part of our antique shop, are for sale. On the premises are cross-country skiing and hiking; golf and tennis are nearby.

Rooms: 8 (4 PB; 4 SB) $65-152
Full Breakfast
Credit Cards: No
Notes: 2, 3, 4, 5, 7, 8, 9, 13, 14

PERU

Johnny Seesaw's

Route 11, Bromley Mt.
Peru, VT, 05152
(802) 824-5533

The essential Vermont Experience. This unique log lodge features cozy rooms, charming cottages with fireplaces, game room, casual, candlelit country cuisine, all in the beautiful Green Mountains.

Hosts: Nancy & Gary Okun
Rooms: 25 (PB) $66
Full Breakfast
Minimum stay weekends: 2; holidays: 5
Credit Cards: A, B, C
Closed April, May, Nov.
Notes: 2, 4, 6, 7, 8, 9, 10, 11, 12, 13

PITTSFIELD

The Inn at Pittsfield

Route 100, Box 675
Pittsfield, VT, 05762
(802) 746-8943

Hospitality, warmth, and good food have been a watchword at our inn since 1830. We are dedicated to continuing the tradition. Our central location on Vermont's most scenic highway makes us convenient to four-season activities. Hiking, biking, fishing, antiquing, skiing, or just plain relaxing. We have it all.

Hosts: Vikki Budasi & Barbara Morris
Rooms: 9 (PB) $59-79
Full Breakfast
Credit Cards: A, B, C
Notes: 2, 4, 5, 7 (limited), 8, 10, 11, 12, 13, 14

PLAINFIELD

Yankees' Northview B&B

RD 2, Box 1000
Plainfield, VT, 05667
(802) 454-7191

Roomy colonial located on a quiet country road in picturesque Calais. Antique-filled rooms, quilts, stenciled walls, sitting room with fireplace. Enjoy your breakfast on the garden patio with mountain views. Museums, antiques, quaking bog, and year-round recreation are nearby. Cross-country ski rentals available. Picnic area with fireplace for guest use.

Hosts: Joani & Glen Yankee
Rooms: 3 (SB) $35-50
Full Breakfast
Credit Cards: No
Notes: 2, 5, 8, 9, 10, 11, 12, 13 (XC)

POST MILLS

The Lake House Inn

P.O. Box 65
Post Mills, VT, 05058
(802) 333-4025

One of northern New England's most enduring traditions has been the warm hospitality of its country inns. The Lake House, in the village of Post Mills in Thetford, VT, has twelve comfortable, homelike guest rooms with shared and private baths. Breakfast features home-baked muffins and breads. Near restaurants, Dartmouth College, flea markets, antique stores, golf, tennis, swimming.

Host: Betty Pemberton
Rooms: 12 (2 PB; 10 SB) $79-89
Full Breakfast
Credit Cards: No
Notes: 2, 3, 4, 5, 8, 9, 10, 11, 12, 13, 14

POULTNEY

Lake St. Catherine Inn

Cones Point Road
Poultney, VT, 05764
(802) 287-9347

Rural country resort on crystal-clear Lake St. Catherine. Relaxation and wholesome dining. Families welcome. AAA and Mobil Travel Guide approved. Rates include free use of aluminum boats, canoes, paddle boats, and sailboats. Breakfast and dinner included in the daily rate.

Hosts: Patricia & Raymond Endlich
Rooms: 35 (PB) $102-150 MAP
Full Breakfast
Credit Cards: No
Open mid-May-mid-Oct.
Notes: 2, 4, 7, 8, 9, 10, 11, 12, 14

PROCTORSVILLE

The Golden Stage Inn

Box 218
Proctorsville, VT, 05153
(802) 226-7744

The tradition of hospitality continues in our 200-year-old stagecoach stop. The warmth of grandmother's quilts, antiques, greenery, favorite books, and a blazing fire comfort you while Marcel prepares silken sauces and Kirsten bakes delectable chocolate desserts. The pool and gardens provide summertime delights, and the cookie jar is always full.

Hosts: Kirsten Murphy & Marcel Perret
Rooms: 10 (6 PB; 4 SB) $135-155
Full Breakfast
Credit Cards: A, B
Closed April & November
Notes: 2, 4, 7, 8 (over 8), 9, 10, 11, 12, 13, 14

Hickory Ridge House

PUTNEY

Hickory Ridge House

RR 3, Box 1410
Putney, VT, 05346
(802) 387-5709

Gracious 1808 Federal brick manor surrounded by fields and woods on a quiet country road near Putney. Connecticut River and I-91 convenient. Six working fireplaces, high ceilings, original tamarack floors, antique furnishings throughout. Area offers fine crafts and music, hiking, cross-country skiing, boating, and swimming. Handicapped accessible.

Hosts: Jacquie Walker & Steve Anderson
Rooms: 7 (3 PB; 4 SB) $45-80
Full Breakfast

Credit Cards: A, B
Notes: 2, 5, 8, 13

RANDOLPH

Placidia Farm B&B

RD 1, Box 275
Randolph, VT, 05060
(802) 728-9883

Six miles north of Randolph on 81 acres with mountain views, pond, and brook. Lovely hand-hewn log home with private apartment for B&B guests. Large deck for enjoying the view; TV, hi-fi, books, and games.

Host: Viola A. Frost
Apartment: 1 (PB) $75-80
Full Breakfast
Credit Cards: No
Notes: 2, 5, 8, 9, 10, 11, 12, 13

RIPTON

The Chipman Inn

Route 125
Ripton, VT, 05766
(802) 388-2390

A traditional Vermont inn built in 1828, situated in the Green Mountain National Forest. Fine food, wine, and spirits for guests. Nine rooms, all with private bath. Fully licensed bar and large fireplace.

Hosts: Joyce Henderson & Bill Pierce
Rooms: 9 (PB) $63.60-103.88
Full Breakfast
Credit Cards: A, B, C
Closed Nov. 15-Dec. 26 & Apr. 1-May 15
Notes: 2, 4, 7, 8 (over 12), 9, 12, 13

ROCHESTER

Harvey's Mountain View Inn

Rochester North Hollow
Rochester, VT, 05767
(802) 767-4273

One of eleven choices by *Family Circle,* September 26, 1989 issue, under farm and ranch categories, "Family Resorts of the Year." Accommodates twenty visitors. Heated swimming pool, duck/trout pond, special animal area at the inn. Farm one mile across the valley view. Fireplace room, modern bedrooms, many antiques, hayrides, picnics, pony rides.

Hosts: Don & Maggie Harvey
Rooms: 9 (2 PB; 7 SB) $90-104
Full Breakfast and Dinner
Credit Cards: No
Notes: 2, 3, 4, 5, 7 (restricted), 8, 9, 10, 11, 12, 13

Liberty Hill Farm

Liberty Hill Road
Rochester, VT, 05767
(802) 767-3926

Working dairy farm nestled between the White River and Green Mountain National Forest, with year-round activities. The 1820 farmhouse, where hearty home-cooking is served family style at dinner and breakfast, has eighteen rooms of old-fashioned charm. Families are always welcome to visit the barn. Breakfast and dinner included in the daily rate.

Hosts: Bob & Beth Kennett
Rooms: 7 (SB) $90 MAP
Full Breakfast
Credit Cards: No
Notes: 2, 4, 5, 7, 8, 9, 10, 11, 12, 13, 14

ROYALTON

Fox Stand Inn

Route 14
Royalton, VT, 05068
(802) 763-8437

Built in 1818 as a stagecoach stop. Our dining room and tavern are open to the public and offer fresh seafood, choice meats, and international creations. The inn's second floor has five comfortably furnished guest rooms. Swimming, canoeing, tubing, bicycling, hiking, or fishing are readily at hand.

Hosts: Jean & Gary Curbery
Rooms: 5 (S2B) $50-60
Full Breakfast
Credit Cards: A, B
Notes: 2, 4, 5, 7, 8, 9, 10, 11, 12, 13, 14

Shoreham Inn & Country Store

SHOREHAM VILLAGE

Shoreham Inn & Country Store

Main Street
Shoreham Village, VT, 05770
(802) 897-5081; (800) 255-5081

The Shoreham Inn is a small, family-run inn dating back to the late 1790s, located on the green in the historic village of Shoreham. In the heart of the Champlain Valley and Vermont's famous apple country, the inn is five miles east of Fort Ticonderoga and twelve miles southwest of Middlebury, VT. Adjacent to the inn is the country store, dating back to 1828 and offering a selection of gifts, wine, beer, cheese, Vermont crafts, and groceries.

Hosts: Cleo & Fred Alter
Rooms: 11 (S7B) $70
Full Breakfast
Credit Cards: No
Closed Nov. 1-20
Notes: 2, 4, 7 (limited), 8, 9, 10, 11, 12, 13, 14

SOUTH LONDONDERRY

The Londonderry Inn

Route 100, Box 301-70
South Londonderry, VT, 05155
(802) 824-5226

An 1826 homestead that has been welcoming guests for nearly fifty years. Special family accommodations. Huge living room, billiards and Ping-Pong rooms, and cozy tavern. Well-known dining room with dinner menu that changes nightly. May we send you our brochure?

Hosts: Jim & Jean Cavanagh
Rooms: 23 (18 PB; 5 SB) $32.86-79.50
Continental-plus Breakfast
Credit Cards: No
Notes: 2, 4, 5, 7, 8, 9, 10, 11, 12, 13, 14

SOUTH STRAFFORD

Watercourse Way B&B

Route 132
South Strafford, VT, 05070
(802) 765-4314

An 1850 country guest house on the banks of the Ompompanoosuc River. Angora goats, Christmas trees, brook trout, vegetable and flower gardens, fireside breakfast, warm atmosphere. Fine dining, shopping in Hanover, NH, and Woodstock, VT. Skiing, hiking, riding, swimming nearby. Simple satisfaction.

Hosts: Lincoln and Anna Alden
Rooms: 3 (SB) $60; $50 off-season
Full Breakfast
Credit Cards: A, B, C
Closed Thanksgiving and Christmas
Notes: 2, 7 (limited), 8, 9, 10, 11, 13, 14

SOUTH WOODSTOCK

Kedron Valley Inn

Route 106
South Woodstock, VT, 05071
(802) 457-1473

Our 1800s inn is scenically located, yet we're near much fun, including sleigh rides and trail rides. We're known for our queen canopy beds, fireplaces in the rooms, luscious food, and a large heirloom quilt collection. Featured in *Country Living, Good Housekeeping,* and *Yankee.*

Hosts: Max & Merrily Comins
Rooms: 28 (PB) $90-155
Full Breakfast
Minimum stay weekends & holidays: 2
Credit Cards: A, B
Closed April
Notes: 2, 4, 6, 7, 8, 9, 10, 11, 12, 13, 14

STOWE

Andersen Lodge — An Austrian Inn

RD 1, Box 1450
Stowe, VT, 05672
(802) 253-7336

A small, friendly Tyrolean inn in a quiet setting. Heated swimming pool, tennis court, living rooms with fireplaces, TV, and air-conditioning. Near a major ski area, eighteen-hole golf course, riding, hiking, fishing. Rec path close by. Sauna and Jacuzzi.

Hosts: Dietmar & Trude Heiss
Rooms: 78 (PB) $78
Full Breakfast
Credit Cards: A, B, C
Closed April 10-June 1; Oct. 25-Dec. 10
Notes: 2, 4, 9, 12, 13

Bittersweet Inn

RR 2, Box 2900
Stowe, VT, 05672
(802) 253-7787

Bittersweet Inn is a brick Cape with a converted carriage house dating back to 1835. The house is on 9 acres overlooking Camel's Hump Mountain, just a half mile to the center of town and minutes to ski lifts and cross-country touring. A good-sized swimming pool is located out back with plenty of room for just taking it easy.

Hosts: Barbara & Paul Hansel
Rooms: 8 (PB and SB) $54-76
Continental Breakfast
Credit Cards: A, B, C
Closed April 9-22 & Nov. 19-27
Notes: 2, 6, 7, 8, 9, 10, 11, 12, 13, 14

Butternut Inn at Stowe

Mountain Road #1
P.O. Box 950
Stowe, VT, 05672
(800) 3BU-TTER

Award-winning nonsmoking inn, adults preferred. Eight acres of beautiful landscaped grounds by a mountain stream. Cottage gardens, pool, antiques, afternoon tea, collectibles. All rooms with private baths. Close to sleigh rides, downhill skiing, cross-country skiing, summer hiking, golf, tennis, horseback riding.

Hosts: Jim & Deborah Wimberly
Rooms: 18 (PB) $90-140
Full Breakfast
Credit Cards: A, B
Notes: 9, 10, 11, 12, 13, 14

The 1860 House

The 1860 House

School Street
P.O. Box 276
Stowe, VT, 05672
(802) 253-7351; (800) 248-1860

National Historic Register inn with exceptional center-village accommodations. King/queen beds with private baths. Enjoy the lovely flower gardens, the warm fire in the living room, and friendly conversations on the deck. Rent the whole inn for your private group, or ask about our photography workshops and bike tours.

Hosts: Richard M. Hubbard & Rose Marie Matulionis
Rooms: 5 (PB) $75-115
Full Breakfast
Credit Cards: A, B
Notes: 2, 5, 8, 9, 10, 11, 12, 13, 14

The Gables Inn

Mountain Road
RR 1, Box 570
Stowe, VT, 05672
(802) 253-7730

Classic country inn with thirteen beautifully appointed rooms in an 1860s farmhouse. New carriage house suites have queen beds, fireplaces, Jacuzzis, and TV. Outdoor hot tub and pool, sitting room, and den. Hearty country breakfasts and candlelight family-style dinners. Minutes from seasonal attractions and Stowe village. Smoke-free bedrooms and dining room.

Hosts: Sol & Lynn Baumrind
Rooms: 17 (PB) $75-115 summer; $110-180 MAP winter
Full Breakfast
Credit Cards: A, B, C
Notes: 2, 4 (winter), 8, 9, 10, 11, 12, 13, 14

Golden Kitz Lodge

RD #3, Box 2980
Route 108, Mountain Road
Stowe, VT, 05672
(802) 253-4217; (800) KITS-LOV

Share legendary Old World eclectic antique family treasures in cozy, caring comfort with warm hugs and Teddy bears. Fireside soup and wine. Piano, guitar, and more for fun. Yummy, chummy 1747 International Room breakfasts. Front porch wicker rockers. Art studio, too. Romantic riverside path for walking, biking, skating, or cross-country skiing to shops, theater, dining, and dancing. Family members are writers, artists, potters, skiers, bikers, dancers and world-traveling adventurers.

Hosts: Sam, Annette, Alyce & Margie MacElwee Jones
Rooms: 16 (8 PB; 8 SB) $40-80
Ala Carte Breakfast
Minimum stay holidays: 2
Credit Cards: A, B, C, D, E, F
Notes: 2, 5, 6, 7 (restricted), 8, 9, 10, 11, 12, 13, 14

Guest House Christel Horman

RR 1, Box 1635
Mountain Road
Stowe, VT, 05672
(802) 253-4846

Small, cozy B&B with eight large double rooms with full private baths. Guest living room with color TV, VCR, Hearthstone fireplace, and many books and magazines. Rates include a full country breakfast. One and one-half miles to downhill and cross-country skiing. Skiweek rate available.

Hosts: Christel & Jim Horman
Rooms: 8 (PB) $56-60
Full Breakfast
Credit Cards: A, B
Notes: 2, 5, 7, 8 (10 and over), 9, 10, 11, 12, 13, 14

Logwood Inn & Chalets

Route 1, Box 2290
Stowe, VT, 05672
(800) 426-6697

Handsome main lodge with fifteen guest rooms; two separate, fully equipped, chalets. Large, quiet living room with large fieldstone fireplace, library, TV room with cable, heated swimming pool, clay tennis court. Spacious lawns with flowers and white birches. Near major ski area, eighteen-hole golf course, riding, hiking, and fishing.

Hosts: Sam & Melanie Kerr
Rooms: 25 (PB) #60-120
Full Breakfast
Credit Cards: A, B
Notes: 2, 4 (winter), 5, 7, 8, 9, 10, 11, 13, 14

The Raspberry Patch

RR 2, Box 1915
Randolph Road
Stowe, VT, 05672
(802) 253-4145

Country elegance, breathtaking views, and a warm, cheery welcome invite you to come and enjoy the peaceful, friendly atmosphere. Rooms are beautifully decorated with down comforters and antiques. A great breakfast is served when you want up—until 11:00 A.M. Sitting room with TV, games, and fireplace. Central air-conditioning. Minutes to fine restaurants.

Host: Linda Jones
Rooms: 4 (3 PB; 1 SB) $50-100
Full Breakfast
Credit Cards: A, B
Notes: 2, 5, 6, 7 (restricted), 8, 9, 10, 11, 12, 13, 14

The Siebeness

Mountain Road, Box 1490
Stowe, VT, 05672
(802) 253-8942; (800) 426-9001

A warm welcome awaits you at our charming country inn. Antiques, private baths, homemade quilts, air conditioning. Fireplace lounge, BYOB bar, hot tub, pool with beautiful mountain views. Famous for outstanding food. Near skiing and golf. Packages available.

Hosts: Nils & Sue Andersen
Rooms: 10 (PB) $60-95
Full Breakfast
Credit Cards: A, B, C, D, E, F
Notes: 2, 4 (winter), 5, 7, 8, 9, 10, 11, 12, 13, 14

Ski Inn

Route 108
Stowe, VT, 05672
(802) 253-4050

This comfortable inn, noted for good food and good conversation, is a great gathering place for interesting people. Guests enjoy themselves and one another. Nearest lodge to all Stowe ski lifts. Cool and quiet in the summer.

Hosts: Larry & Harriet Heyer
Rooms: 10 (5 PB; 5 SB) $70
Continental Breakfast; full breakfast and dinner in winter
Minimum stay holidays: 2-3
Credit Cards: No
Notes: 2, 4 (winter), 5, 7, 8, 9, 10, 11, 12, 13

Stowehof Inn and The Farm at Stowehof

Edson Hill Road
Stowe, VT, 05672
(802) 253-9722; (800) 422-9722

Elegant country estate with exceptional views. Uniquely decorated rooms with fireplaces, antiques, and sauna. Award-winning dining in our critically acclaimed dining room, The Seasons. Music on the Steinway. Romantic sleigh rides in winter and surrey rides with gourmet picnic in summer. Supersaver ski week and equestrian packages available. Heated pool, all-weather tennis courts, and golf available.

Host: William O'Neil
Rooms: 52 (PB) $124-184
Full Breakfast
Credit Cards: A, B, C
Notes: 2, 3, 4, 5, 7, 8, 9, 10, 11, 12, 13, 14

Timberhölm Inn

Cottage Club Road
RR 1, Box 810
Stowe, VT, 05672
(802) 253-7603

Nestled in a quiet location in the woods, the Timberhölm Inn welcomes guests from all over the world. Warm up after a day of skiing with a complimentary cup of soup by a large fieldstone fireplace and enjoy the spectacular mountain views from the deck. Rooms finely appointed with antiques and quilts.

Hosts: Kay & Richard Hildebrand
Rooms: 8 (PB) $60-100

Suites: 2 (PB)
Buffet Breakfast
Credit Cards: A, B
Notes: 2, 5, 7 (restricted), 8, 9, 10, 11, 12, 13

Ye Olde England Inne

The Mountain Road, Box 320B
Stowe, VT, 05672
(802) 253-7558; (800) 477-3771

As filmed in "Lifestyles of the Rich and Famous." Laura Ashley rooms and cottages, four-posters, fireplaces and Jacuzzis. Classic English luxury amid beams, brass, copper, and stone, plus Mr. Pickwick's Polo Pub with rare ales, malts, cognacs, and vintage ports. Copperfields for superb gourmet cuisine. AAA, three-diamond Mobil rated.

Hosts: Christopher & Linda Francis
Rooms: 18 (18 PB; 8 w/Jacuzzi) $69-125
Cottages: 3 (PB)
Minimum stay weekends: 2
Full Breakfast
Credit Cards: A, B
Notes: 2, 3, 4, 5, 6, 7, 8, 9, 10, 11, 12, 13, 14

WAITSFIELD

Hyde Away

RR 1, Box 65
Waitsfield, VT, 05673
(802) 496-2322; (800) 777-4933

One of the oldest (c. 1820) and most comfortable inns in the valley. Centrally located less than five minutes from Sugarbush, Mad River Glen, Mt. Ellen, historic Waitsfield, the Long and Catamount trails. Full public restaurant and rustic tavern; hearty country meals. Families and children are welcome. Hiking, biking, swimming, fishing, tennis, and golf nearby. Mountain bike touring center.

Host: Bruce Hyde
Rooms: 15 (SB) $70
Full Breakfast
Credit Cards: A, B, C
Notes: 2, 4, 5, 7, 8, 9, 10, 11, 12, 13, 14

Knoll Farm Country Inn

RFD 1 Box 179, Bragg Hill
Waitsfield, VT, 05673
(802) 496-3939

A unique combination of farm and inn, with spectacular views, pastures, pond, farm animals, and 150 acres. Breakfast and dinner are served family style; food is home grown. Four cozy guest rooms, large kitchen, well-stocked library, piano, old-fashioned organ. A return to basic nineteenth-century living, where guests experience fellowship together and inner spiritual renewal.

Hosts: Ann Day, Harvey & Ethel Horner
Rooms: 4 (SB) $70-100
Full Breakfast and Dinner
Credit Cards: No
Closed April & Nov.
Notes: 2, 4, 8 (over 7), 10, 11, 12, 13, 14

Mountain View Inn

Lareau Farm Country Inn

Box 563, Route 100
Waitsfield, VT, 05673
(802) 496-4949

Nestled in an open meadow beside the Mad River, this 1832 Greek Revival farmhouse is only minutes from skiing, shopping, dining, soaring, and golf. Sleigh rides, cross-country skiing, and swimming are on the premises. When you come, you feel at home and relaxed. Hospitality is our specialty.

Hosts: Dan & Susan Easley
Rooms: 14 (10 PB; 4 S2B) $75-110

Newtons' 1824 House Inn

Full Breakfast
Credit Cards: A, B, C
Notes: 2, 5, 8 (over 6), 9, 10, 11, 12, 13, 14

Mad River Barn

Route 17, Box 88
Waitsfield, VT, 05673
(802) 496-3310

Family owned, friendly lodge on the edge of the Long Trail in the Green Mountains. Swimming, walking trails, gardens on the premises. Hiking, biking, golf nearby. Modern rooms, some with TV; most can sleep four. Children under ten free in room with parents. Adjacent to cross-country and downhill skiing.

Host: Betsy Pratt
Rooms: 15 (PB) $60-75
Full Breakfast
Credit Cards: A, B, C
Notes: 2, 5, 7, 8, 9, 10, 11, 12, 13, 14

Millbrook Inn

Route 17, RFD, Box 62
Waitsfield, VT, 05673
(802) 496-2405

Relax in the friendly, unhurried atmosphere of our cozy 1850s inn. Seven guest rooms are decorated with hand stenciling, antique bedsteads, and handmade quilts. Breakfast and dinner included in daily rate. Dine in our romantic small restaurant that features hand-rolled pasta, fresh fish, veal, shrimp, and homemade desserts from our varied menu.

Hosts: Joan & Thom Gorman
Rooms: 7 (4 PB; 3 SB) $50-130
Full Breakfast
Minimum stay weekends: 2; holidays: 3
Closed April 10-June 10; Oct. 25-Thanksgiving
Credit Cards: A, B, C, E
Notes: 2, 4, 7, 8 (over 10), 9, 10, 11, 12, 13

Mountain View Inn

RFD, Box 69, Route 17
Waitsfield, VT, 05673
(802) 496-2426

Mountain View Inn, a small country inn, circa 1826, has seven guest rooms, each with private bath, accommodating two people. The rooms are decorated with stenciling, quilts, braided rugs, and antique furniture. Meals are served family style around an antique harvest table. Good fellowship is enjoyed around the wood-burning fire in the living room.

Hosts: Fred & Susan Spencer
Rooms: 7 (PB) $58.85-69.55
Full Breakfast
Minimum stay weekends: 2
Credit Cards: No
Notes: 2, 4, 5, 7 (restricted), 8, 9, 10, 11, 12, 13, 14

Newtons' 1824 House Inn

Route 100, Box 159
Waitsfield, VT, 05673
(802) 496-7555

Enjoy relaxed elegance in a perfect country setting. Six guest rooms, all with private baths. Classical music, Oriental rugs, fireplaces, sun porch. Gourmet breakfast with souffles, fresh orange juice. Located on 52 acres on the Mad River, with a private swimming hole. Featured in the *Los Angeles Times* and *Glamour* Magazine.

Hosts: Nick & Joyce Newton
Rooms: 6 (PB) $75-95
Full Breakfast
Credit Cards: A, B, C
Notes: 2, 5, 9, 10, 11, 12, 13, 14

White Rocks Inn

Tucker Hill Lodge

RD 1, Box 147
Waitsfield, VT, 05673
(800) 543-7841

Tucker Hill Lodge is nestled on a wooded hillside overlooking Route 17 in the Mad River Valley in north central Vermont, one of the East's most beautiful resort areas. Bike, fish, golf, ride. Tennis and swimming on the premises.

Rooms: 22 (16 PB; 6 SB) $55-98
Full Breakfast
Credit Cards: A, B, C, D, E, F
Notes: 2, 4, 5, 7, 8, 11, 12

Valley Inn

RR 1, Box 8
Waitsfield, VT, 05673
(802) 496-3450; (800) 638-8466

Our recipe for a great Vermont vacation: take an exceptional country inn in a lovely Vermont village, add cozy bedrooms with private baths, stir in some conversation around a warm fire, add great meals, a sauna and hot tub, and mix in nice people like you.

Hosts: The Stinson Family
Rooms: 20 (PB) $70-180 MAP
Full Breakfast
Credit Cards: A, B, C
Notes: 2, 4 (winter), 5, 7 (limited), 8, 9, 10, 11, 12, 13, 14

WALLINGFORD

Wallingford Inn

North Main Street, Box 404
Wallingford, VT, 05773
(802) 446-2849

Charming 1876 Victorian mansion offers ten elegantly appointed rooms, eight with private bath, two with connecting bath. Antiques, oak woodwork, and polished wood floors. Enjoy candlelight dining. Full-service bar.

Hosts: Kathleen & Joseph Lombardo
Rooms: 10 (8 PB; 2 SB) $53.50-74.90
Full Breakfast
Credit Cards: A, B
Notes: 4, 5, 7, 8 (over 5), 9, 10, 11, 13

White Rocks Inn

RR 1, Box 297
Wallingford, VT, 05773
(802) 446-2077

Circa 1840s farmhouse inn, listed on the National Register of Historic Places, beautifully furnished with antiques, Oriental rugs, canopy beds. All rooms have private baths. Close to four major ski areas, hiking, horseback riding, canoeing, summer theater, and good restaurants. Nonsmokers only.

NOTES: Credit cards accepted: A Master Card; B Visa; C American Express; D Discover Card; E Diners Club; F Other: 2 Personal checks accepted: 3 Lunch available: 4 Dinner available: 5 Open all year

Hosts: June & Alfred Matthews
Rooms: 5 (PB) $60-90
Full Breakfast
Minimum stay weekends: 2; holidays: 2-3
Credit Cards: A, B
Closed November
Notes: 2 (for deposit), 8 (over 10), 9, 10, 11, 12, 13

WARREN

Beaver Pond Farm Inn

RD Box 306, Golf Course Road
Warren, VT, 05674
(802) 583-2861

Beaver Pond Farm is an elegantly restored Vermont farmhouse located on a quiet country meadow with spectacular views of the nearby Green Mountains. It is located adjacent to the Sugarbush Golf Course and 40 km of groomed cross-country ski trails. One mile from downhill trails of Sugarbush. Hearty breakfasts, snacks, hors d'oeuvres, and setups. Prix fixe dinners are available three times a week during the winter season. Package plans are available, including skiing in winter and golf in summer.

Hosts: Bob & Betty Hansen
Rooms: 6 (4 PB; 2 SB) $32-65
Full Breakfast
Credit Cards: A, B, C
Closed April 10-May 25
Notes: 2, 4, 7, 8 (7 and over), 9, 10, 11, 12, 13, 14

Sugartree Inn

RR Box 38
Warren, VT, 05674
(802) 583-3211; (800) 666-8907

An intimate mountainside country inn featuring handmade quilts atop canopy, brass, and antique beds. Oil lamps, original art, antiques, stained glass, and country curtains. Full country breakfast. Enchanting gazebo amid myriad flowers in summer, blazing foliage in fall, and downhill skiing in winter.

Hosts: Howard & Janice Chapman
Rooms: 10 (PB) $75-120
Minimum stay holidays: 2
Full Breakfast
Credit Cards: A, B, C, D
Closed the last two weeks in April
Notes: 2, 7, 8 (over 6), 9, 10, 11, 12, 13, 14

Sugartree Inn

WATERBURY

Grünberg Haus B&B

RR 2, Box 1595
Waterbury, VT, 05676
(802) 244-7726

Hand-built Tyrolean chalet on 10 wooded acres. Huge fireplace, library, pub, sauna Jacuzzi, grand piano, tennis court, chickens, trails. Breakfast specialties in the mountains. Cozy chalet guest rooms feature antiques and balconies. Stowe, Sugarbush, covered bridges, cross-country ski centers, shops, antiques, galleries, mountain peaks nearby. Guests write, "One of the highlights of our trip!"

Hosts: Mark Frohman & Christopher Sellers
Rooms: 10 (SB) $55-70
Full Breakfast
Credit Cards: A, B, C
Notes: 2, 5, 9, 10, 11, 12, 13, 14

Inn at Blush Hill

Blush Hill Road, Box 1266
Waterbury, VT, 05676
(802) 244-7529; (800) 736-7522

A circa 1790 restored Cape on five acres with beautiful mountain views. The inn has four fireplaces, a large sitting room, and lots of antiques. It is located across from a golf course, and all summer sports are nearby. Enjoy skiing at Stowe, Sugarbush, and Bolton Valley, only minutes away. Packages available.

Hosts: Gary & Pam Gosselin
Rooms: 6 (2 PB; 4 SB) $60-100
Full Breakfast
Minimum stay holidays: 3
Credit Cards: A, B, C
Notes: 2, 5, 8, 9, 10, 11, 12, 13, 14

Thatcher Brook Inn

RD 2, Box 62, Route 100 N
Waterbury, VT, 05676
(802) 244-5911; (800) 292-5911

A faithfully restored Victorian Mansion on the Vermont Register of Historic Buildings. Our guest rooms all have private baths; some have fireplaces, and others whirlpool tubs. Enjoy our gourmet restaurant and Baileys Fireside Tavern. Near Ben and Jerry's ice cream factory, Cold Hollow Cider Mill, and Shelburne Museum.

Hosts: Kelly & Peter Varty
Rooms: 24 (PB) $75-160
Continental-plus Breakfast
Credit Cards: A, B, D, E
Notes: 2, 4, 5, 7 (limited), 8, 9, 10, 11, 12, 13, 14

WEATHERSFIELD

The Inn at Weathersfield

Route 106, Box 165
Weathersfield, VT, 05151
(802) 263-9217

An eighteenth-century stagecoach stop offering bedrooms with private baths, most with working fireplaces. The inn serves American nouvelle cuisine dinners, has a full bar and extensive wine cellar, and features live piano music nightly. Dinner, high tea, and full breakfast are included in the room rate. On the 21-acre premises is a pond, an outdoor recreation area, horse-drawn sleigh or carriage rides, box stall, and paddock facilities. An indoor recreation room features a sauna, aerobics equipment, and a pool table. Nearby is alpine and cross-country skiing, golf, tennis, hiking, and many points of interest.

Hosts: Mary Louise & Ron Thorburn
Rooms: 12 (PB) $160-200 MAP
Full Breakfast
Credit Cards: A, B, C, D
Notes: 2, 4, 5, 7, 8 (8 and over), 9, 10, 11, 12, 13, 14

WEST DOVER

Doveberry Inn

HCR 63, Box 9, Route 100
West Dover, VT, 05386
(802) 464-5652

A small country inn with eight rooms, run by two sisters who are graduates of the New England Culinary Institute. There is a living room with fireplace, books, games, and VCR for guest use. All rooms have private baths, cable TV, and VCRs. Full liquor license.

Host: Patricia Rossi
Rooms: 8 (PB) $75-120
Full Breakfast
Credit Cards: A, B, C
Notes: 4, 7 (restricted), 8 (over 8), 9, 10, 11, 12, 13

WESTON

1830 Inn on the Green

Route 100
Weston, VT, 05161
(802) 824-6789

Colonial building built in 1830 as a blacksmith/wheelwright shop, located in the center of town overlooking the delightful village green. Parlor with fireplace, slate terrace overlooking the gardens and pond. Furnished with traditional and family antiques.

Hosts: Sandy & Dave Granger
Rooms: 4 (PB) $60-80
Full Breakfast

The Inn at Weston

Credit Cards: A, B
Notes: 2, 5, 9, 10, 11, 12, 13, 14

The Inn at Weston

Box 56, Weston, VT, 05161
(802) 824-5804

Enjoy beautifully appointed guest rooms and continental cuisine in this country inn nestled in the Green Mountains in the picturebook village of Weston. Take a pleasant walk to the Weston Playhouse for professional summer theater or visit the nearby Benedictine Priory. Cross-country skiing from the door and four downhill ski areas within twenty minutes.

Hosts: Jeanne & Bob Wilder
Rooms: 19 (12 PB; 7 SB) $64-98
Full Breakfast
Credit Cards: A, B
Notes: 2, 4, 5, 7, 8 (over 6), 9, 10, 11, 12, 13

The Wilder Homestead Inn & 1827 Craft Shoppe

RR 1, Box 106D
Weston, VT, 05161
(802) 824-8172

An 1827 brick home listed on the National Register of Historic Places. Walk to shops, museums, summer theater. Crackling fires in common rooms, canopy beds, down comforters. Rooms have original Moses Eaton stenciling and are furnished with antiques and reproductions. Weston Priory nearby.

Hosts: Peggy & Roy Varner
Rooms: 7 (5 PB; 2 SB) $60-85
Full Breakfast
Minimum stay weekends: 2; holidays: 2-3
Credit Cards: A, B
Notes: 2, 5, 7 (restricted), 8 (over 6), 9, 10, 11, 12, 13, 14

The Wilder Homestead Inn

WEST RUTLAND

The Silver Fox Inn

RFD 1, Box 1222, Route 133
West Rutland, VT, 05777
(802) 438-5555

A 1768 country inn on 3 acres bordering the Clarendon River. Spacious, individually decorated guest rooms and suites. Original wide-board floors, four-post cherry beds, antiques, quilted bedspreads. Two-course country breakfast and four-course candlelit dinners are available; bar on premises. Fishing, biking, cross-country skiing. Twenty minutes to Killington-Pico downhill skiing.

Hosts: Pam & Gerry Bliss
Rooms: 7 (PB) $76-160
Full Breakfast
Minimum stay weekends, foliage, and holidays: 2
Credit Cards: A, B, C
Closed April
Notes: 2, 4, 7 (restricted), 8 (12 and over), 9, 10, 11, 12, 13, 14

WEST TOWNSHEND

American Country Collection 93

984 Gloucester Place
Schenectady, NY, 12309
(518) 370-4948

This 1769 farmhouse is reputed to be the oldest standing house in West River Valley. The house retains its somewhat rustic atmosphere with old wooden beams, original wainscoting, pegged raised paneling, a few slightly tipsy door frames. Three guest rooms with private baths, continental or full breakfast. Near skiing, covered bridges, flea markets, hiking, lakes. Children nine and over are welcome. $55-60.

Windham Hill Inn

RR 1, Box 44
West Townshend, VT, 05359
(802) 874-4080

Circa 1825 farmhouse and barn located at the end of a dirt road high in the mountains on 150 acres. Spectacular views, hiking trails, cross-country ski-learning center. Summer concerts are given in the barn. Fifteen guest chambers—antiques, quilts, old-fashioned shoe collection. Wonderful candlelit dinners with six courses on fine china and antique silverware. Warm, caring innkeepers. A true country experience; judged one of the ten best inns in the country, 1988 and 1989.

Hosts: Ken & Linda Busteed
Rooms: 15 (PB) $175 MAP
Full Breakfast
Credit Cards: A, B, C
Closed April 1-May 15 & Nov. 1-Thanksgiving
Notes: 2, 4, 8 (over 12), 9, 10, 11, 12, 13, 14

WILLIAMSTOWN

Rosewood Inn B&B

Box 31, Williamstown, VT, 05679
(802) 433-5822

Charmingly gracious Victorian, centrally located in a quiet Vermont village. Spacious antique-filled rooms, elegant wraparound porches. All seasonal activities are nearby. We feature a full gourmet breakfast.

Hosts: John & Elaine Laveroni
Rooms: 4 (PB and SB) $50-80
Full Breakfast
Credit Cards: A, B, C
Notes: 2, 5, 7, 11, 12, 13

WILMINGTON

Misty Mountain Lodge

Stowe Hill Road, Box 114
Wilmington, VT, 05363
(802) 464-3961

A small family inn built in 1803, with a beautiful view of the Green Mountains. We accommodate twenty people; home cooked meals prepared by the owners. Our cozy living room has a large fireplace where guests gather to visit, read, or join in a hearty singalong with your host. Summer walking trails. Close to several major southern Vermont ski areas and Marlboro Music for summer enjoyment.

Hosts: Buzz & Elizabeth Cole
Rooms: 9 (S4B) $44-56
Full Breakfast
Credit Cards: No
Notes: 2, 4, 5, 7, 8, 9, 10, 11, 12, 13, 14

Nordic Hills Lodge

179 Coldbrook Road
Wilmington, VT, 05363
(802) 464-5130; (800) 326-5130

Come let yourself be spoiled at our family-operated lodge that offers the nostalgia of a country inn with all the modern conveniences. Skiing, championship golf, tennis, and horseback riding are within minutes. Immaculate rooms with in-room TV, sauna, game room, BYOB bar, outdoor heated pool, and Jacuzzi complete your stay.

Hosts: George & Sandra Molner & Marianne Coppola
Rooms: 27 (PB) $48-130
Full Breakfast
Credit Cards: A, B, C, E
Notes: 2, 4 (winter), 5, 7, 8, 9, 10, 11, 12, 13

Trail's End

Smith Road
Wilmington, VT, 05363
(802) 464-2727

Tucked along a country road, Trail's End offers traditional New England hospitality in a secluded, tranquil setting. The inn provides a warm, cozy atmosphere with a mix of antiques and family pieces. The rooms vary in size and have been decorated with oak dressers, brass headboards, and fluffy comforters.

Hosts: Bill & Mary Kilburn
Rooms: 18 (PB) $65-150
Full Breakfast
Credit Cards: A, B
Closed April 3-May 25; Nov. 1-Nov. 21
Notes: 2, 7, 8, 9, 10, 11, 12, 13

The White House of Wilmington

Route 9
Wilmington, VT, 05363
(802) 464-2135

Turn-of-the-century mansion set high on a rolling hill features elegant accommodations, award-winning continental cuisine, outdoor pool, sauna, indoor pool, and whirlpool. Complete cross-country ski touring center. Three-star Mobil rating. Rate includes breakfast and dinner.

Host: Robert B. Grinold
Rooms: 12 (PB) $109-212
Full Breakfast
Minimum stay weekends and holidays
Credit Cards: A, B, C, E (5% service fee)
Notes: 2, 4, 5, 7, 8 (over 10), 9, 10, 11, 12

Juniper Hill Inn

WINDSOR

Juniper Hill Inn

RR 1, Box 79
Windsor, VT, 05089
(802) 674-5273

Lavish yourself in our elegant but informal inn with antique-furnished guest rooms, all with private baths and some with working fireplaces. We serve sumptuous dinners by candlelight and hearty, full breakfasts. Cool off in our outdoor pool or visit antique shops, covered bridges, museums, and craft shops. Central to Woodstock and Quechee in Vermont and Hanover, New Hampshire. A perfectly romantic inn.

Hosts: Jim & Krisha Pennino
Rooms: 15 (PB) $80-115
Full Breakfast
Credit Cards: A, B, C
Closed Nov. 1-Dec. 15 & mid-March-April 30
Notes: 2, 4, 9, 10, 11, 12, 13, 14

WOODSTOCK

Canterbury House

43 Pleasant Street
Woodstock, VT, 05091
(802) 457-3077

Lovely 100-year-old village home just four blocks east of the village green. Furnished with authentic Victorian antiques. Comfortable rooms with private baths; within walking distance of shops and restaurants.

Hosts: Barbara & Bill Hough
Rooms: 7 (PB) $90-115
Full Breakfast
Credit Cards: A, B
Notes: 2, 8 (9 and over), 9, 10, 11, 12, 13

The Charleston House

21 Pleasant Street
Woodstock, VT, 05091
(802) 457-3843

This circa 1835 Greek Revival home has been authentically restored. Listed in the National Register of Historic Homes. Furnished with antiques combined with a hospitality reminiscent of a family homecoming. Located in the picturesque village of Woodstock—"one of the most beautiful villages in America."

Hosts: Barb, Bill & John Hough
Rooms: 7 (PB) $100-135
Full Breakfast
Credit Cards: A, B
Notes: 2, 5, 8 (over 9), 9, 10, 11, 12, 13, 14

Village Inn of Woodstock

41 Pleasant Street
Woodstock, VT, 05091
(802) 457-1255

Walk to shops and galleries. Restored Victorian mansion, circa 1899, has working fireplaces, tin ceilings, oak and chestnut woodwork, stained glass. Candlelight dining on premises; chef-owned inn. Cocktail lounge; warm, friendly staff.

Hosts: Kevin & Anita Clark
Rooms: 8 (6 PB; 2 SB) $53-106
Full Breakfast
Minimum stay Sept. 20-Oct. 20 weekdays: 2; weekends & holidays: 2
Credit Cards: A, B
Notes: 2, 4, 5, 8, 9, 10, 11, 12, 13

Virginia

ABINGDON

Summerfield Inn

101 West Valley Street
Abingdon, VA, 24210
(703) 628-5905

Summerfield Inn is located in the Abingdon historic district, just two blocks from world-famous Barter Theatre. We're near the Appalachian Trail, Mount Rogers National Recreation Area, South Holston Lake, the Blue Ridge Parkway, Virginia Creeper Trail, excellent restaurants, and marvelous shops. Just off I-81 at Exit 8.

Hosts: Champe & Don Hyatt
Rooms: 4 (PB) $55-75 + tax
Continental Breakfast
Credit Cards: A, B
Notes: 2, 7 (limited), 8 (over 12), 9, 10, 12

ALEXANDRIA

The Little House

719 Gibbon Street
Alexandria, VA, 22314
(703) 548-9654

The entire antique-filled, two-bedroom Victorian townhouse is rented to guests. A Jacuzzi, washer and dryer, and stocked kitchen is available. Privacy is assured, but should guest need help with reservations or sight-seeing, the off-premises manager will provide these services.

Host: Jean Hughes
Rooms: 2 (PB) $200
Stocked refrigerator
Credit Cards: No
Notes: 2, 5, 6, 7, 8, 9

The Little House

Morrison House

116 South Alfred Street
Alexandria, VA, 22314
(703) 838-8000; FAX (703) 684-6283

Located in the midst of Alexandria's historic Old Town, Morrison House combines the elegance of a Federal Period inn with the intimacy and charm of a small European hotel. Our elegant rooms, English butlers, and New American cuisine grill provide for a memorable experience.

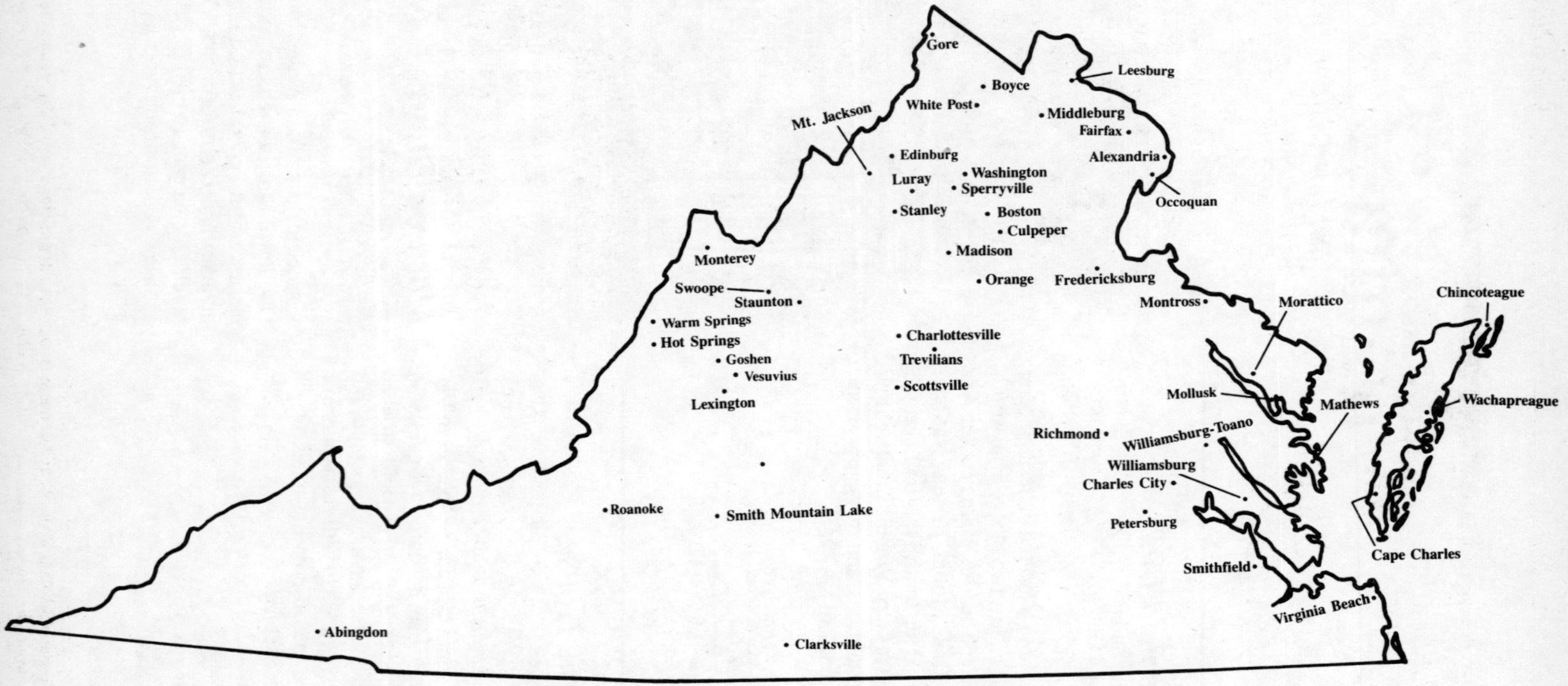

Gore
Leesburg
Boyce
White Post
Mt. Jackson
Middleburg
Fairfax
Edinburg
Alexandria
Luray
Washington
Sperryville
Occoquan
Stanley
Boston
Culpeper
Monterey
Madison
Orange
Fredericksburg
Swoope
Staunton
Montross
Moratticco
Chincoteague
Warm Springs
Charlottesville
Hot Springs
Trevilians
Goshen
Vesuvius
Scottsville
Lexington
Mollusk
Mathews
Wachapreague
Richmond
Williamsburg-Toano
Williamsburg
Charles City
Roanoke
Smith Mountain Lake
Petersburg
Cape Charles
Smithfield
Virginia Beach
Abingdon
Clarksville

VIRGINIA

Hosts: Robert & Rosemary Morrison
Rooms: 42 (PB) $125-195
Suites: 3 (PB) $250-385
Full Breakfast and free parking in weekend packages
Credit Cards: A, B, C, E, F
Notes: 2, 3, 4, 5, 7, 8, 9, 10, 11, 12, 14

BOSTON

Thistle Hill B&B

Route 1, Box 291
Boston, VA, 22713
(703) 987-9142

Situated in Rappahannock County just 1.5 hours west of Washington, DC. Guests enjoy cozy antique-furnished rooms. Relax and stroll through tree-filled acreage. Many seasonal activities. Located near the Blue Ridge Mountains, midway between Culpeper and Sperryville on Rt. 522.

Hosts: Charles & Marianne Wilson
Rooms: 4 (PB) $75-115
Full Breakfast
Minimum stay holidays & Oct. weekends: 2
Credit Cards: A, B
Closed March
Notes: 2, 4, 8 (12 and over), 9, 11, 12, 14

BOYCE

The River House

Route 2, Box 135
Boyce, VA, 22620
(703) 837-1476

A rural getaway on the Shenandoah River, built in 1780 and 1820. Convenient to scenic, historic, and recreational areas, we also offer special features and programs for house parties, small workshops, and family reunions. Accommodations are available for small, two- or three-day business conferences and executive retreats during the week. Relaxing, book-filled bed/sitting rooms have fireplaces, air conditioning, and private baths.

Host: Cornelia S. Niemann
Rooms: 5 (PB) $70-85
Full Breakfast/Brunch
Credit Cards: A, B
Closed Christmas Day
Notes: 2 (by arrangement), 3 (on request), 4 (by arrangement), 5, 6, 7, 8, 9, 10, 11, 12

CAPE CHARLES

Nottingham Ridge B&B

P.O. Box 97-B
Cape Charles, VA, 23310
(804) 331-1010

A picturesque country retreat high atop the sand dunes, with the Chesapeake Bay as a backdrop. Sun, sand, and serenity are the main attractions. Our private beach affords our guests many hours of leisure. Chartered fishing boats leave from the nearby village daily. We offer wine, cheese, and a breathtaking view of the sun setting over the water. Located approximately 3.5 miles north of the Chesapeake Bay Bridge Tunnel, twenty-five minutes from Norfolk/Virginia Beach area, and one hour from historic Williamsburg.

Host: Bonnie Nottingham
Rooms: 3 (PB) $65-85
Full Breakfast
Credit Cards: No
Notes: 2, 5, 7 (restricted), 8 (over 8), 9, 10, 11, 14

Pickett's Harbor

Pickett's Harbor

Box 97AA
Cape Charles, VA, 23310
(804) 331-2212

The perfect place for rest and relaxation! A colonial home in a secluded wooded setting, with all rooms overlooking 17 acres of private wide beach on Chesapeake Bay. The home is decorated with antiques and reproductions, and natural flora and fauna abound on Virginia's Eastern Shore. Central air-conditioning.

Hosts: Sara & Cooke Goffigon
Doubles: 5 (2 PB; 3 SB) $65-75
Full Breakfast
Credit Cards: No
Notes: 2, 5, 8 (over 6), 9, 10, 11, 12, 14

CHARLES CITY

Edgewood Plantation

RD Box 490
Charles City, VA, 23030
(804) 829-2962

A unique national landmark Gothic with fourteen rooms, ten fireplaces, old canopy beds, period clothes, antiques, and candlelight breakfast. Refreshments are served, and the house has a swimming pool and hot tub. Many historic attractions are nearby. Located between Richmond and Williamsburg, in plantation country. Featured in *Discerning Traveler,* May 1990. An Antique collector's delight.

Host: Dot Boulware
Rooms: 4 (2 PB; 2SB) $130
Full Breakfast
Credit Cards: A, B
Notes: 5, 9, 10, 11, 12, 13, 14

North Bend Plantation

Route 1, Box 13A
Charles City, VA, 23030
(804) 829-5176

James River plantation, c. 1819, on the National Register of Historic Places. Located twenty-five minutes west of Williamsburg, in Virginia plantation country. Nature walks, horseshoes, croquet, volleyball, badminton, and pool on premises. Excellent restaurants, antique shops, and shopping nearby. Private and peaceful, surrounded by 250 acres of farmland.

Hosts: George & Ridgely Copland
Rooms: 3 (1 PB; 2 SB) $75-95
Full Breakfast
Credit Cards: No
Notes: 2, 5, 9, 10, 14

CHARLOTTESVILLE

Afton House

Guesthouses B&B
P.O. Box 5737
Charlottesville, VA, 22905
(804) 979-7264

A mountain retreat with panoramic views to the east, this spacious home is on the old road up the mountain pass. There are four spacious rooms, mostly furnished in antiques. One has a private bath, and three share two hall baths. Full breakfast. Antique shop on the premises, and others in the village. $65-75.

Alderman House

Guesthouses
P.O. Box 5737
Charlottesville, VA, 22905
(804) 979-7264

Pictured in several magazine articles, this large formal Georgian home is authentic in style and elegant in decor. It was built in the early 1900s and is located about one mile from the University of Virginia. Guests may choose a room with a four-poster bed or one with twins, each with adjoining private bath and air- conditioning. No smoking. $64-80.

Bellaire

Guesthouses B&B
P.O. Box 5737
Charlottesville, VA, 22905
(804) 979-7264

In one of Charlottesville's loveliest neighborhoods, convenient to the town and university, this comfortable guest suite adjoins the host home by a breezeway. There is a sitting area with fireplace, twin beds, and a large dressing room/bath. Full or continental breakfast is served in the dining room or on the terrace. Air-conditioned. $56-64.

Ben-Coolyn

Guesthouses
P.O. Box 5737
Charlottesville, VA, 22905
(804) 979-7264

Ben-Coolyn is a beautiful home on a small hill surrounded by oaks and old English boxwood. One guest room has a queen bed and private bath. A second has a double and a 3/4 bed, and the third has two twins, shared bath. Each room has a fireplace, twelve-foot ceilings, and large windows with original glass with views of the mountains and Monticello. A first-floor sitting room and sun room are available for guests. Continental breakfast. No smoking, no air-conditioning. $64-80.

Bollingwood

Guesthouses B&B
P.O. Box 5737
Charlottesville, VA, 22905
(804) 979-7264

A lovely home in a convenient neighborhood with a private city garden, this guest house is within walking distance of the university, shops, and restaurants. The house has been furnished with antiques throughout. One guest room with twin canopy beds has a hall bath. The second, with two antique 3/4 beds, has an adjacent bath. Air conditioning. $56-64.

Brookwood

Guesthouses B&B
P.O. Box 5737
Charlottesville, VA, 22905
(804) 979-7264

Originally a turn-of-the-century farmhouse just a few miles from the university, this lovely brick manor house was embellished in the 1930s by Hunter Perry. Two guest rooms, one with a double bed and one with twin beds, each have an adjoining bath. Air conditioning and ceiling fans. Downstairs there are two twin rooms with a shared bath. Full breakfast. $64-80.

Burnley

Guesthouses B&B
P.O. Box 5737
Charlottesville, VA, 22905
(804) 979-7264

A charming early twentieth-century white frame house in a pleasant, tree-shaded yard within walking distance of the university. One room with twin beds has a lovely sitting area with pull-out sofabed and TV. A second room is a single with its own lavatory and shares the full hall bath with the twin room. There is also a double room with private bath. Air-conditioning. $64-80.

Cathill

Guesthouses
P.O. Box 5737
Charlottesville, VA, 22905
(804) 979-7264

A country house in a rural setting only a few minutes' drive from Charlottesville and the University of Virginia. Accommodations consist of a large paneled room with fireplace and sofa bed in the sitting area and a queen bed and adjoining bath. During the summer, visitors may enjoy the pool and informal gardens. No smoking in the house. $64-80.

Chester

Guesthouses
P.O. Box 5737
Charlottesville, VA, 22905
(804) 979-7264

This charming country home in Scottsville, twenty-five minutes south of Charlottesville, was built from 1825 through 1875. Five guest rooms: one with twin beds, two with doubles, one with an antique 3/4 bed, and one with a queen. Several porches provide pleasant sitting in the evening. Full breakfast is served; dinner is available by arrangement. $55-70.

Clifton — The Country Inn

Route 9, Box 412
Charlottesville, VA, 22901
(804) 971-1800

A Virginia historic landmark, Clifton is among the few remaining large plantation properties in Albemarle County. On 45 secluded acres with walking trails, private lake, small pool, tennis court, and croquet pitch. All rooms feature wood-burning fireplaces, private bath, large sitting areas, canopy or four-poster beds. Five minutes to Charlottesville.

Host: Sue Putalik
Rooms: 9 (PB) $115-165
Full Breakfast
Credit Cards: A, B
Notes: 2, 4 (by arrangement), 5, 8, 9, 10, 11, 12, 13, 14

Clover Green Farm

Guesthouses B&B
P.O. Box 5737
Charlottesville, VA, 22905
(804) 979-7264

Situated in beautiful rolling country in the foothills of the Blue Ridge. The house sits atop a hill, and guests are welcome to sit by the fire in the living room or enjoy the spectacular views from the spacious sun room. The first-floor guest room with a double bed is a large, sunny room with adjoining private bath. Smokers welcome. $64-80.

Copps Hill Farm

Guesthouses B&B
P.O. Box 5737
Charlottesville, VA, 22905
(804) 979-7264

This immaculately kept ranch home is located on a small horse farm seven miles northwest of Charlottesville. Guests may enter the private lower-level entrance where they have their own suite, a family room with TV, double sofabed, and two bedrooms with adjoining bath. Full farm breakfast is served in the dining room or on the sun porch overlooking rolling pastures. $56-64.

Clifton--The Country Inn

Farmington Heights

Guesthouses B&B
P.O. Box 5737
Charlottesville, VA, 22905
(804) 979-7264

Gracious living just off the Farmington Country Club back nine. This lovely home has wonderful views of pasture and hills. One guest room has a queen bed and adjoining bath. A second room offers twin beds and private bath. Guests may enjoy the pool. Air-conditioned. $64-80.

Fox View

Guesthouses B&B
P.O. Box 5737
Charlottesville, VA, 22905
(804) 979-7264

This traditional home has spectacular views of hills, fields, and mountains. The guest facilities consist of a separate suite upstairs with a large sitting room, double bedroom with adjoining bath, twin room, and single room that share a larger bath. Air- conditioned. $56-64.

Grove Road

Guesthouses B&B
P.O. Box 5737
Charlottesville, VA, 22905
(804) 979-7264

A lovely traditional home in a quiet neighborhood. The home is attractively furnished, and the guest room offers a double bed with private hall bath. Choice of continental or full breakfast. $56-64.

Hobbit Hill

Guesthouses
P.O. Box 5737
Charlottesville, VA, 22905
(804) 979-7264

In a country setting a few miles west of the city, Hobbit Hill is surrounded by dogwoods, azaleas, and rhododendron. Three lovely rooms and two baths. Two rooms have double beds, one with an adjoining bath. A third room has two antique 3/4 beds and shares the hall bath with one of the double rooms. $56-64.

Home Tract

Guesthouses
P.O. Box 5737
Charlottesville, VA, 22905
(804) 979-7264

Located five miles west of Charlottesville, in Ivy, Home Tract is an old Virginia farmhouse painstakingly restored to its former charm. The original section was built c. 1800. The second-floor guest room with a double bed has a private bath. No air- conditioning. $56-64.

Ingleside

Guesthouses B&B
P.O. Box 5737
Charlottesville, VA, 22905
(804) 979-7264

This farm has been in the same family for several generations and is located on 1250 acres of rolling pasture backed by steep, wooded mountains. The house was built around 1840 of bricks made from the farm's red clay, and has magnificent views in all directions. The furniture is mostly English antique. Accommodations consist of a large double room with fireplace and adjacent bath. A tennis court is available. $56-64.

The Inn at the Crossroads

Guesthouses B&B
P.O. Box 5737
Charlottesville, VA, 22905
(804) 979-7264

Built as a tavern in 1820, the inn is a four-story brick structure with timber framing and an English kitchen on the lower level. A fifteen-minute drive from Charlottesville, the inn is on spacious grounds with boxwood, well, and outbuildings. Each of the five newly renovated guest rooms has a different theme. One room has twin beds, three have double beds, and one has a king bed. Two shared baths. $49-59.

Longhouse

Guesthouses
P.O. Box 5737
Charlottesville, VA, 22905
(804) 979-7264

Built sometime between 1812 and 1845 to serve as a stagecoach tavern, this two-story gray clapboard house twenty minutes west of Charlottesville blends stateliness of outline with a snug interior and warm atmosphere. The downstairs guest wing offers a smaller room with double bed; a large room has a queen bed, single bed, and private bath. There is a creek for wading. No smoking inside. Air-conditioned. $56-64.

Maho-Nayama

Guesthouses
P.O. Box 5737
Charlottesville, VA, 22905
(804) 979-7264

Attention to detail is evident in the landscaping and furnishings of this beautiful Japanese-style home. The large master bedroom has a king bed and master bath with a sunken tub. Two double rooms share a connecting bath. A private tennis court is available with advance notice (and $5 fee). The house is located in a rural wooded area six miles northeast of town. Air-conditioned. $64-80.

Meadowbrook

Guesthouses B&B
P.O. Box 5737
Charlottesville, VA, 22905
(804) 979-7264

A beautifully appointed colonial clapboard home just north of the Route 250 bypass in a quiet residential neighborhood. Two guest rooms are decorated with antiques. One has a double bed and one has twins. They have private half-baths and share a tub/shower. $64-80.

Meadow Run

Guesthouses B&B
P.O. Box 5737
Charlottesville, VA, 22905
(804) 979-7264

Enjoy relaxed rural living in this new contemporary home six miles from Charlottesville. There is a double room and a twin room, with shared bath between. Many windows allow you bucolic vistas of the Southwest Range. Fireplaces in the kitchen and living room add to the homey, friendly feel of Meadow Run. Air conditioned. $56-64.

Meander Inn

Guesthouses B&B
P.O. Box 5737
Charlottesville, VA, 22905
(804) 979-7264

A 75-year-old Victorian farmhouse on 50 acres of pasture and woods. The inn offers five queen or twin rooms, some with private bath. In winter, guests may enjoy the outdoor hot tub after skiing, or just relax around the woodstove and listen to the old player piano. In summer, the deck or front porch are perfect for reading or enjoying the views. A full country breakfast is served. $65-75.

Millsteam

Guesthouses
P.O. Box 5737
Charlottesville, VA, 22905
(804) 979-7264

A lovely large house about twenty minutes north of Charlottesville. The house was built before the Civil War and enlarged in 1866. Two large guest rooms have private baths. Guests are welcome to enjoy the fireplace in the library or the mountain views from the living room. A full breakfast is served in the kitchen with hand-hewn exposed beams. $64-80.

Northfields

Guesthouses B&B
P.O. Box 5737
Charlottesville, VA, 22905
(804) 979-7264

This gracious host and hostess enjoy having guest in their lovely home on the north edge of the city. The large guest room is furnished with twin beds. A second room has a double four-poster bed and private hall bath. Full gourmet breakfast; no smoking. $52-56.

North Garden

Guesthouses B&B
P.O. Box 5737
Charlottesville, VA, 22905
(804) 979-7264

This 110-year-old meticulously restored farmhouse is situated on a small farm in a pastoral setting with beautiful views. In the summer, the yard is full of flowers. The guest room is sunny and bright, with three large windows, bright cheery colors, double bed, and private bath. Located twenty minutes south of Charlottesville and thirty minutes to Wintergreen. $56-64.

Northwood

Guesthouses B&B
P.O. Box 5737
Charlottesville, VA, 22905
(804) 979-7264

A 1920s city house, convenient to the historic downtown area of Charlottesville. Only a few blocks from Thomas Jefferson's courthouse and the attractive pedestrian mall with many shops and restaurants. The guest quarters have a double bed and adjoining bath. There is a comfortable sitting room with TV adjacent to the bedroom. $52-56.

Polaris Farm

Guesthouses
P.O. Box 5737
Charlottesville, VA, 22905
(804) 979-7264

In the middle of rolling farmland dotted with horses and cattle, this lovely architect-designed brick home offers a twin room with adjoining bath on the first floor and two upstairs twin rooms that share a bath. There are gardens and terraces where one can view the Blue Ridge Mountains, a spring-fed pond for swimming, boating, and fishing, and miles of trails for walking or horseback riding. Air conditioned. $64-80.

Recoletta

Guesthouses B&B
P.O. Box 5737
Charlottesville, VA, 22905
(804) 979-7264

An older Mediterranean-style house built with flair and imagination. The red tile roof, walled gardens with fountain, and tasteful, artistic design create the impression of a secluded Italian villa within walking distance of the university, shopping, and restaurants. The guest room has a beautiful brass double bed and private hall bath with show. Air conditioned. $56-64.

Rolling Acres Farm

Guesthouses B&B
P.O. Box 5737
Charlottesville, VA, 22905
(804) 979-7264

A lovely brick colonial home in a wooded setting on a small farm, this guest house has two guest rooms with a hall bath upstairs. One has a double bed, and the other has twins. The house is furnished with many Victorian pieces. A short, beautiful drive west of town. No smoking; air conditioned. $56-64.

Silver Thatch Inn

3001 Hollymead Drive
Charlottesville, VA, 22901
(804) 978-4686

Silver Thatch Inn is a rambling white clapboard home that dates from 1780. With three dining rooms and seven guest rooms, Silver Thatch Inn is a sophisticated retreat on the outskirts of Charlottesville. Silver Thatch's Modern American Cuisine uses the freshest of ingredients, and all sauces are prepared with fruits and vegetables. The menu features grilled meats, poultry, and game in season; and there are always vegetarian selections. Silver Thatch Inn provides a wonderful respite for the sophisticated traveler who enjoys fine food and a quiet, caring atmosphere.

Hosts: Joe & Mickey Geller
Rooms: 7 (PB) $115-135
Continental-plus Breakfast
Credit Cards: A, B
Closed Dec. 23-26; first two weeks in Jan.; first 2 weeks Aug.
Notes: 2, 4, 8, 9, 10, 11, 12

Silver Thatch Inn

Tunlaw

Guesthouses B&B
P.O. Box 5737
Charlottesville, VA, 22905
(804) 979-7264

Your interesting, much-traveled host lives in a modest cottage hidden away on a side street near the University of Virginia. Her guest room has a double bed and private adjoining bath. Continental breakfast with homemade breads. $52-56.

200 South Street Inn

200 South Street
Charlottesville, VA, 22901
(804) 979-0200

Lovely restored inn, garden terrace, sweeping veranda, located in historic downtown Charlottesville, with English and Belgian antiques, six Jacuzzi tubs, eleven fireplaces, canopy and four-poster beds. Revolving art exhibit. Continental breakfast and afternoon tea (with wine) and canapes. Near Monticello and Ash Lawn.

Host: Donna Deibert
Rooms: 20 (PB) $92-172.50
Continental Breakfast
Credit Cards: A, B, C
Notes: 2, 4, 7, 8, 9, 10, 11, 12, 13, 14

Wayside

Guesthouses B&B
P.O. Box 5737
Charlottesville, VA, 22905
(804) 979-7264

A one-story brick Colonial furnished in Early American antiques, this home is located on an elegant private street near the university. There is a single or double room with hall bath, plus a twin room with adjoining bath and private entrance. Air conditioning and ceiling fans. $56-64.

Winston

Guesthouses
P.O. Box 5737
Charlottesville, VA, 22905
(804) 979-7264

This quaint Cape Cod brick home is located on a quiet side street near the University of Virginia. The private upstairs guest room offers twin beds and an adjoining bath. Delicious home-style breakfast. Air-conditioned. $52-56.

Winton on Pantops

Guesthouses B&B
P.O. Box 5737
Charlottesville, VA, 22905
(804) 979-7264

A brick colonial east of town on Pantops Mountain overlooking Charlottesville. The home is furnished with many antiques and offers two double rooms. One room also has a single bed. Shared bath, full breakfast, resident cats. $52-56.

Woodstock Hall

Route 3, Box 40
Charlottesville, VA, 22901
(804) 293-8977

A faithfully restored 1757 inn on the Historic National Register. Located off I-64, close to the University of Virginia, Monticello, and other historic landmarks. Experience all the eighteenth-century charm of a fine inn, including gourmet breakfast; yet be provided with the modern conveniences demanded by today's discriminating traveler.

Hosts: Jean Wheby & Mary Ann Elder
Rooms: 4 (PB) $95-130 + tax
Full Breakfast
Credit Cards: No
Notes: 2, 5, 8 (over 10), 9, 10, 11, 12, 13 (18 miles)

Miss Molly's Inn

CHINCOTEAGUE

Miss Molly's Inn

113 North Main Street
Chincoteague, VA, 23336
(804) 336-6686

A charming Victorian inn on the bay two miles from Chincoteague National Wildlife Refuge and Assateague National Seashore. All rooms are air-conditioned and furnished with period antiques. Room rate includes breakfast and afternoon tea. Marguerite Henry stayed here while writing *Misty of Chincoteague.*

Hosts: Dr. & Mrs. James Stam
Rooms: 13 (PB and SB) $55-105
Full Breakfast
Credit Cards: No
Closed Dec. 1-March 30
Notes: 2, 7 (limited), 8 (over 12), 9, 10, 11, 12, 14

Year of the Horse Inn

600 South Main Street
Chincoteague, VA, 23336
(804) 336-3221

Three guest rooms with private bath and balcony, right on the water, plus a two-bedroom apartment that sleeps six. One-hundred-foot pier for fishing or crabbing. Located just ten minutes from the ocean beach, wildlife refuge, and wild ponies of Chincoteague.

Host: Carlton Bond
Rooms: 5 (PB) $70-90
Continental Breakfast
Credit Cards: A, B
Closed Dec. & Jan.
Notes: 2, 7, 8, 9, 10, 11, 12, 14

CLARKSVILLE

Needmoor Inn

801 Virginia Avenue
P.O. Box 629
Clarksville, VA, 23927
(804) 374-2866

Needmoor Inn, c. 1889. A Victorian B&B in the heart of beautiful Kerr Lake, stands amid 1.25 acres of stately shade and fruit trees and a large herb garden. Enjoy comfortable antiques, private baths, gourmet breakfasts, complimentary bicycles, and therapeutic massage. Area activities include all water sports, excellent bass fishing, Occoneechee State Park, and Prestwould Plantation.

Hosts: Lucy & Buddy Hairston
Rooms: 3 (PB) $45-65
Full Breakfast
Credit Cards: No
Notes: 2, 5, 8, 9, 10, 11, 12

CULPEPER

Fountain Hall B&B

609 South East Street
Culpeper, VA, 22701
(703) 825-8200; (800) 476-2944

Built in 1859, this grand B&B is within walking distance of historic downtown Culpeper. The inn is furnished with antiques and warmly welcomes business and leisure travelers. Area activities and attractions include wineries, historic battlefields, antique shops, the Skyline Drive, tennis, swimming, golf, and more.

Hosts: Steve & Kathi Walker
Rooms: 5 (PB) $55-85
Continental-plus Breakfast
Credit Cards: A, B, C
Notes: 2, 5, 9, 10, 11, 12, 14

EDINBURG

Mary's Country Inn

218 South Main Street
Route 2, Box 4
Edinburg, VA, 22824
(703) 984-8286

Our Victorian inn is situated in the heart of the Shenandoah Valley on the edge of town next to Stoney Creek and the Edinburg Mill Restaurant. We are close to a vineyard, antique shops, hiking, fishing, caverns, and other points of interest. We are reminiscent of Grandma's country home, complete with a bountiful breakfast buffet.

Hosts: Mary & Jim Clark
Rooms: 5 (3 PB; 2 SB) $55-60
Full Breakfast
Credit Cards: A, B
Closed January
Notes: 2, 7 (limited), 8, 9, 13, 14

Mary's Country Inn

FAIRFAX

The Bailiwick Inn

4023 Chain Bridge Road
Fairfax, VA, 22030
(703) 691-2266

Located in the historic city of Fairfax, only fifteen miles west of the nation's capital and minutes from Civil War battlefields and George Mason University. A choice of rooms with fireplaces, Jacuzzi tubs, and even a bridal suite. Afternoon tea is served in the brick-walled garden. Featherbeds complement the colonial furnishings, recreating the ambience of famous Virginians' mansions.

Hosts: Anne & Ray Smith
Rooms: 14 (PB) $95-175
Full Breakfast
Credit Cards: A, B
Notes: 2, 5, 8, 9, 10, 11, 12, 14

The Bailiwick Inn

FREDERICKSBURG

Fredericksburg Colonial Inn

1707 Princess Anne Street
Fredericksburg, VA, 22401
(703) 371-5666

Lodging at the Fredericksburg Colonial Inn offers a romantic inn with thirty suites of Civil War era history. Great for conferences or getaways. Private baths, canopy beds, Victorian antiques, TV, morning coffee. Civil War museum and videos. Walk to battlefields, town attractions, antique and craft shops, taverns and restaurants. One hour from Washington, DC.

Rooms: 30 (PB) $50-65
Continental Breakfast
Credit Cards: A, B, C
Notes: 2, 5, 6, 7, 8, 9, 10, 11, 12, 14

Kenmore Inn

1200 Princess Anne Street
Fredericksburg, VA, 22401
(703) 371-7622

Elegant inn built in the late 1700s. On the historical walking tour, near shops and the river. Grand dining and a relaxing pub for your enjoyment. Serving lunch and dinner daily.

Hosts: Ed & Alice Bannan
Rooms: 13 (PB) $78-99
Continental Breakfast
Credit Cards: A, B, C
Closed Jan. 3-13
Notes: 2, 3, 4, 5, 7, 9, 10, 11, 12, 14

Lavista Plantation

4420 Guinea Station Road
Fredericksburg, VA, 22401
(703) 898-8444

Classical Revival circa 1838 manor house located on 10 quiet country acres. Surrounded by farm fields and mature trees. Stocked pond, six fireplaces, antiques, rich Civil War past, radio, phone, TV, bicycles, nearby historic attractions. Fresh eggs and homemade jams; air-conditioned.

Hosts: Edward & Michele Schiesser
Rooms: 1 (PB) $58.58-74.55
Suite: 1 (PB)
Full Breakfast
Credit Cards: A, B
Notes: 5, 7, 8, 9

Richard Johnston Inn

711 Caroline Street
Fredericksburg, VA, 22401
(703) 899-7606

In the downtown historic district, near many antique shops, Civil War battlefield, and the homes of George Washington and Robert E. Lee. Close to Amtrak and hiking.

Hosts: Dennis & Libby Gowin
Rooms: 9 (5 PB; 4 SB) $55-120
Continental Breakfast
Credit Cards: A, B, C
Notes: 2, 5, 14

GORE

Rainbow's End

Route 1, Box 335
Gore, VA, 22637
(703) 858-2808

Enjoy your stay at this comfortable country home on Timber Ridge in the Appalachian Mountains. Nearby Winchester provides quaint shops, historic attractions, antiquing, and fairs. The area provides hiking, fishing, and hunting in season. Every season has much to offer in this quiet apple country.

Hosts: Thom & Eleanor McKay
Rooms: 2 (SB) $40
Type of Beds: 1 Double; 1 King
Continental Breakfast
Credit Cards: No
Notes: 2, 5, 9

GOSHEN

The Rose Hummingbird Inn

Country Lane, P.O. Box 70
Goshen, VA, 24439
(703) 997-9065

Nestled in mountain splendor, this country Victorian mansion in the historic Shenandoah Valley offers antique furnishings, wraparound first- and second-floor verandas, fireplaces in many rooms, including the sitting room and library. Visit nearby historic sites, Lexington, Virginia Horse Center, Natural Bridge, and the Blue Ridge Parkway. Enjoy family-style Southern cooking.

Hosts: Bill & Bonnie Saunders
Rooms: 7 (PB) $60
Full Breakfast
Credit Cards: A, B, C, D
Notes: 2, 3 (private groups w/res.), 4 (w/res.), 5, 7 (limited), 8 (over 8), 9, 10, 11, 12, 13, 14

HOT SPRINGS

Vine Cottage Inn

U.S. Route 220
Hot Springs, VA, 24445
(703) 839-2422

A rambling and charming country inn situated in a mountain spa resort village. Twelve uniquely decorated rooms with large, inviting pedestal tub baths. Spacious and comfortable sitting room with fireplace, reading/writing alcove, and large TV.

Hosts: Pat & Wendell Lucas
Rooms: 12 (9 PB; 3 SB) $70
Continental Breakfast
Credit Cards: A, B
Notes: 2, 4, 5, 7, 8, 9, 10, 11, 12, 13

LEESBURG

Fleetwood Farm B&B

Route 1, Box 306-A
Leesburg, VA, 22075
(703) 327-4325

Beautiful 1745 plantation manor house, a Virginia Historic Landmark on the National Register of Historic Places. Fireplaces, air-conditioning, private baths (one with large Jacuzzi), cookout facilities, horseshoes, croquet, canoe and fishing equipment. Lovely gardens. Near Middleburg, Manassas Battlefield, Harpers Ferry, and Wolftrap. Forty miles to Washington, DC.

Hosts: Carol & Bill Chamberlin
Rooms: 2 (PB) $95-120
Full Breakfast
Credit Cards: No
Notes: 2, 7 (outside), 8 (over 12), 9, 10, 11, 12, 14

LEXINGTON

Fassifern B&B

Route 5, Box 87
Lexington, VA, 24450
(703) 463-1013

Cozy 1867 antique-filled manor house on 3.5 park-like acres near quaint, historic Lexington in the beautiful Shenandoah Valley. Convenient to I-81 and I-64 on Scenic Byway 39. Adjacent to the Virginia Horse Center. For travelers with discriminating taste.

Hosts: Ann Carol & Arthur Perry
Rooms: 5 (PB) $65-75 + tax
Continental-plus Breakfast
Credit Cards: A, B, C
Notes: 2, 5, 9, 10, 11

Irish Gap Inns

Route 1, Box 40
Vesuvius, VA, 24483
(804) 922-7701

Situated on 285 mountaintop acres bordering the Blue Ridge Parkway, The Bee Skep Inn and the Gatehouse B&B offer old-world charm with modern comfort. Hiking, fishing, swimming, wild flowers, and farm animals. Handicap facilities. Send for brochure.

Hosts: Dillard Saunders & Martha Shewey
Rooms: 7 (6 PB; 1 SB) $68-98
Full Breakfast
Credit Cards: A, B
Notes: 2, 4 (with reservations), 5, 6, 7, 8, 9, 11

Llewellyn Lodge at Lexington

603 South Main Street
Lexington, VA, 24450
(703) 463-3235

A warm and friendly atmosphere awaits guests to this lovely brick colonial. Upon arrival, guests are welcomed with refreshments. A hearty gourmet breakfast is served that includes omelets, Belgian waffles, sausage, bacon, and homemade muffins. The decor combines traditional and antique furnishing. Within walking distance of the Lee Chapel, Stonewall Jackson House, Washington and Lee University, and Virginia Military Institute.

Hosts: Ellen & John Roberts
Rooms: 6 (PB) $50-75
Full Breakfast
Credit Cards: A, B, C
Notes: 2, 5, 7, 8, 9, 10, 11, 12, 14

LURAY

Boxwood Place

120 High Street
Luray, VA, 22835
(703) 743-4748

1876 manor house at the foot of the Blue Ridge Mountains. Decorated with primitive antiques, handmade reproductions, folk art, wooden toys, and counted cross-stitch. Large country breakfast. Close to beautiful Skyline Drive, Luray Caverns, and the Shenandoah River.

Hosts: Bernie & Stan Wells
Rooms: 2 (SB) $60
Full Breakfast
Credit Cards: No
Notes: 2, 5, 10, 11, 12, 14

Shenandoah Countryside

Guesthouses B&B
P.O. Box 5737
Charlottesville, VA, 22905
(804) 979-7264

This brick farmhouse has a panoramic view of the Shenandoah Valley. Two upstairs guest rooms, one with twin beds and dressing room and one with an antique brass double bed and private balcony. Shared bath. A double room with private bath is available on the first floor. Finnish sauna bath on lower level. $56-80.

Shenandoah River Roost

Route 3, Box 566
Luray, VA, 22835
(703) 743-3467

Country log home facing the Shenandoah River. Three miles from famous Luray Caverns, ten minutes from the Skyline Drive, fishing, swimming, tubing, and hiking. Close to two golf courses and horseback riding.

Hosts: Gerry and Rubin McNab
Rooms: 2 (SB) $55 + tax
Full Country Breakfast
Credit Cards: No
Closed Nov. 1st-May 1st
Notes: 2, 6, 7, 8 (over 12), 9, 10, 11, 12

MADISON

Shenandoah Springs Country Inn

HC 6, Box 122
Madison, VA, 22727
(703) 923-4300

On Shenandoah Springs estate you will enjoy swimming, canoeing, fishing, and horseback riding. You may rent one of our cottages or stay at the Inn.

Hosts: Anne & Douglas Farmer
Rooms: 7 (2PB; 5SB) $75-100
Full Breakfast
Credit Cards: No
Notes: 2, 4, 5, 8 (over 6), 10, 11, 13

MATHEWS

Ravenswood Inn

Box 250
Mathews, VA, 23109-0250
(804) 725-7272

Secluded estate on Chesapeake Bay's East River offers unique opportunity for relaxation and enjoyment of quiet country atmosphere, romantic candlelight dinner, and fine wine. Large magnolia-shaded deck, hot tub, bicycles, sailboat, and massage therapist to help you relax.

Hosts: Marshall & Linda Warner, Peter & Sally Preston
Rooms: 5 (PB) $150/couple, MAP
Full Breakfast and Dinner
Credit Cards: No
Closed Jan.
Notes: 2, 4, 9, 10, 14

RiverFront House B&B

Route 14 East, Box 310
Mathews, VA, 23109
(804) 725-9975

Waterfront setting and Williamsburg, too (55-minute trip). Nineteenth-century house on 10 acres in Chesapeake Country , the perfect place to laze around, use as a base for exploring, for day cruises across the Bay or down river. Biking, craft and antique shops, berry picking.

Host: Annette Waldman Goldreyer
Rooms: 8 (PB) $50-70
Full Breakfast
Credit Cards: No
Closed Thanksgiving - April 1
Notes: 2, 3, 7, 8 (over 4), 9, 10, 14

Red Fox Inn & Mosby's Tavern

MIDDLEBURG

Red Fox Inn & Mosby's Tavern

Box 385, Middleburg, VA, 22117
(800) 223-1728

Built in 1728 as Chinn's Ordinary, the inn was a popular stopping place for travelers between Winchester and Alexandria. The inn's nineteen guest rooms are decorated with period reproductions; most have canopied beds; some have working fireplaces; all have color TV, private baths, telephones, thick cotton bathrobes, bedside sweets, and fresh flowers. Complimentary breakfast is offered in the room or dining room, with a complimentary copy of the Washington morning paper.

Hosts: Turner & Dana Reuter
Rooms: 19 (PB) $125-225
Continental Breakfast
Credit Cards: A, B, C
Notes: 2, 5, 7, 8, 9

Welbourne

Middleburg, VA, 22117
(703) 687-3201

A seven-generation antebellum plantation home in the middle of Virginia's fox-hunting country. On a 600-acre working farm. Full Southern breakfasts, working fireplaces, cottages. On the National Register of Historic Places.

Hosts: Nat & Sherry Morison
Rooms: 11 (PB) $58-94
Full Breakfast
Credit Cards: No
Notes: 2, 5, 6, 7, 8, 9

MOLLUSK

Greenvale Manor

Route 354, Box 70
Mollusk, VA, 22517
(804) 462-5995

1840 waterfront plantation house on 13 acres, located on the Rappahannock River with private beach, dock, pool, spacious lawns, large antique-filled rooms with private baths and air- conditioning. Enjoy sunsets and sweeping water views from the veranda and relax in a tranquil setting.

Hosts: Pam & Walt Smith
Rooms: 9 (7 PB; 2 SB) $65-100
Full Breakfast
Credit Cards: No
Notes: 2, 5, 7, 9, 10, 11, 12, 14

The Inn at Montross

Highland Inn

MONTEREY

Highland Inn

Main Street
Monterey, VA, 24465
(703) 468-2143

Gracious lodging and dining in a classic Victorian inn listed on the National Register of Historic Places. Scenic mountain setting with many nearby attractions.

Hosts: Michael Strand & Cynthia Peel
Rooms: 18 (PB) $43-59
Continental Breakfast
Minimum stay holidays: 2
Credit Cards: A, B
Notes: 2, 4, 5, 7, 8, 9, 11, 12, 14

MONTROSS

The Inn at Montross

Courthouse Square
Montross, VA, 22520
(804) 493-9097

On the site of a seventeenth-century tavern, this house has been in continuous use for over three hundred years. Guest rooms feature four-poster beds (some with canopies) and antiques. A restaurant featuring fine dining, pub room, and English tavern are on the premises. Historic area near Washington's birthplace and Stratford Hall.

Hosts: Eileen & Michael Longman
Rooms: 6 (PB) $65-125
Continental Breakfast
Credit Cards: A, B, D
Notes: 2, 3, 4, 5, 6, 7, 9, 10, 11, 12, 14

MORATTICO

Holly Point

Box 64
Morattico, VA, 22523
(804) 462-7759

Besides the many historical sites in the area, Holly Point has 120 acres of pine forest and looks out on a lovely view of the Rappahannock River. There are many land and water activities: hiking, biking, swimming, boating, water skiing, fishing, and crabbing.

Host: Mary Chilton Graham
Rooms: 4 (1 PB; 3 SB) $30-35
Continental Breakfast
Credit Cards: No
Closed Nov.1-May 1
Notes: 2, 6, 7, 8, 9, 11

MT. JACKSON

The Widow Kip's Shenandoah Inn

Route 1, Box 117
Mt. Jackson, VA, 22842
(703) 477-2400

A stately 1830 colonial on 7 rural acres in the Shenandoah Valley overlooking the mountains. Friendly rooms filled with family photographs, bric-a-brac, and antiques (all for sale). Each bedroom has a working fireplace, canopy, sleigh, or Lincoln bed. Two cozy cottages are also available. Pool, nearby battlefields to explore, caverns, canoeing, hiking, or downhill skiing. Bicycles, picnics, grill available.

Host: Rosemary Kip
Rooms: 7 (PB) $60-80 (suite)
Full Breakfast
Minimum stay holidays: 2
Credit Cards: A, B
Notes: 2, 5, 6, 10, 11, 12, 13

OCCOQUAN

Rockledge Mansion

410 Mill Street
Occoquan, VA, 22125
(703) 690-3377

Stone National Historic Landmark built in 1758, located less than a mile from I-95, thirty minutes to Washington, DC. Working fireplaces, antiques, oversized Jacuzzis, plus kitchenette in accessory building suites. Walk to the river, shops, art galleries, restaurants. Very quiet and private, on 2 acres.

Hosts: Joy & Ron Houghton
Suites: 3 (PB) 75-120
Continental Breakfast
Credit Cards: No
Notes: 2, 5, 8, 9, 10, 11, 14

Hidden Inn

ORANGE

Hidden Inn

249 Caroline Street
Orange, VA, 22960
(703) 672-3625

A romantic Victorian featuring nine guest rooms, all with private bath. Jacuzzi tubs, working fireplaces, and private verandas are available. Wicker and rocking chairs on the wraparound verandas, hand-made quilts and canopied beds enhance the Victorian flavor. Full country breakfast, afternoon tea, and gourmet dinners are served. Located minutes from Monticello, Montpelier, and Virginia wineries.

Hosts: Ray & Barbara Lonick
Rooms: 9 (PB) $79-149
Full Breakfast
Credit Cards: A, B
Notes: 2, 4, 5, 8, 9, 10, 14

Mayhurst Inn

US 15 South, Box 707
Orange, VA, 22960
(703) 672-5597

Mayhurst is a fanciful Italianate Victorian plantation home on 36 acres in historic Orange County. Some rooms have fireplaces, and the inn is air conditioned. Fishing pond, fields for strolling, and an antique shop. Dinner is available on Saturday evenings.

Hosts: Stephen & Shirley Ramsey
Rooms: 7 (PB) $95-150
Full Breakfast
Credit Cards: A, B
Notes: 2, 4 (Sat.), 5, 8 (12 and over), 9, 14

The Shadows

Route 1, Box 535
Orange, VA, 22960
(703) 672-5057

A restored 1913 stone house on 44 acres, featuring a large stone fireplace, guest rooms and cottages filled with antiques, flowers and lace. Romantic getaway in a country Victorian setting.

Hosts: Barbara & Pat Loffredo
Rooms: 6 (PB) $85.20-117.15
Full Breakfast
Credit Cards: No
Notes: 2, 5, 8 (over 12), 14

PETERSBURG

Mayfield Inn

3348 West Washington Street
P.O. Box 2265
Petersburg, VA, 23804
(804) 733-0866; (804) 861-6775

Mayfield Inn is a 1750 manor house listed on the National Register of Historic Places. It was authentically restored in 1986. Guest accommodations are luxuriously appointed with Oriental carpets, pine floors, antiques, period reproductions, and private baths. Situated on 4 acres of grounds, with a forty-foot outdoor swimming pool.

Hosts: Jamie & Dot Caudle
Rooms: 4 (PB) $60-80
Full Breakfast
Credit Cards: A, B
Notes: 2, 5, 7, 8, 9, 10, 11, 12, 14

Abbie Hill B&B

RICHMOND

Abbie Hill B&B

Box 4503
Richmond, VA, 23220
(804) 355-5855; FAX (804) 353-4656

Desirable for tourists and corporate travelers alike, this elegant 1907 Colonial

Revival townhouse, located in Richmond's most prestigious historic district, is near convention and corporate centers, museums, restaurants, shopping, historic sites. Enjoy exquisite period decor, hearty Virginia breakfasts by the fire. Laundry facilities available, TV in rooms, afternoon tea available.

Hosts: Barbara & Bill Fleming
Rooms: 3 (PB) $65-85
Full Breakfast
Credit Cards ($150 minimum): A, B
Notes: 2, 5, 8 (over 12), 9, 14

B&B on the Hill

2304 East Broad Street
Richmond, VA, 23223
(804) 780-3746

Choose from accommodations in two beautifully restored inns or a number of private homes. Extensive battlefield parks, colonial plantations, Thomas Jefferson's famous Virginia Capitol, and the Edgar Allan Poe Museum are nearby. $72.50-140.

Church Hill

Bensonhouse of Richmond & Williamsburg
2036 Monument
Richmond, VA, 23220
(804) 353-6900

This 1870s Victorian with working fireplaces, exposed wood and brick walls, and skylights contains baskets and other craft pieces from all over the world, especially from Brazil. The home offers an antique quilt-covered double bed with private half-bath and courtyard off the guest room. The upstairs bath is shared with the owner for showering. $65.

The Emmanuel-Hutzler House

2036 Monument Avenue
Richmond, VA, 23220
(804) 353-6900

Typical of several houses on Monument Avenue, the interior of this house has a classical, early Renaissance appearance, with natural mahogany raised paneling, leaded glass windows, and coffered ceilings with dropped beams. There is an elevator to the second-floor guest rooms, each of which has a private bath (two have fireplaces, one has a 4x6 Jacuzzi).

Hosts: Lyn M. Benson & John Richardson
Rooms: 4 (PB) $85-110
Full Breakfast
Credit Cards: A, B, C
Notes: 2, 5, 8 (over 12), 9, 10, 11, 12, 14

Fan District

Bensonhouse of Richmond & Williamsburg
2036 Monument
Richmond, VA, 23220
(804) 353-6900

This wonderful Fan townhouse is located on one of Richmond's most charming streets. Built in 1900, it was totally renovated. The exposed brick wall and skylight in the foyer, bay window in the front parlor, custom-made bookshelves in the library, leaded glass transoms, and marbled fireplaces give a fresh feeling in this traditional home. There is a deck. Choose a twin room with fireplace and private bath with shower or an antique 3/4 rope bed with private bath. No smoking. $68-75.

Summerhouse

Bensonhouse of Richmond & Williamsburg
2036 Monument
Richmond, VA, 23220
(804) 353-6900

This large, gracious 1908 house sparkles with new life because of restoration. This home, which was featured on the 1986 Fan Christmas Tour, offers adjoining third-floor twin and queen rooms with private bath, wet bar, and beautiful views of the city. The second-floor queen room and private bath has an optional adjoining suite with fireplace. No smoking; resident dog. $95-105.

ROANOKE

The Mary Bladon House

381 Washington Avenue SW
Roanoke, VA, 24016
(703) 344-5361

A lovely 1890s Victorian house in the historic "Old Southwest" neighborhood of Roanoke. Spacious rooms, tastefully decorated with crafts and period antiques to capture the charm of a time when elegant comfort was a way of life. A step back in time for the young and the young at heart.

Hosts: Bill & Sheri Bestpitch
Rooms: 2 (PB) $70
Suite: (PB) $95
Full Breakfast
Credit Cards: A, B, D
Notes: 2, 4, 5, 8, 9, 10, 11, 12, 14

High Meadows--Virginia's Vineyard Inn

SCOTTSVILLE

Chester B&B

Route 4, Box 57
Scottsville, VA, 24590
(804) 286-3960

An 1847 Greek Revival estate on 7 acres abounding with shaded lawns, century-old boxwood, antiques, and Oriental rugs. Four guest rooms have fireplaces, as do the living room, dining room, and library. Monticello, Ash Lawn, Montpelier, the University of Virginia, Appomattox, and the Blue Ridge Mountains are all within an easy hour's drive of historic Scottsville.

Hosts: Gordon Anderson & Dick Shaffer
Rooms: 5 (1 PB; 4 SB) $65-90
Full Breakfast
Credit Cards: C
Notes: 2, 4, 5, 6, 7, 9, 11, 14

High Meadows — Virginia's Vineyard Inn

Route 4, Box 6
Scottsville, VA, 24590
(804) 286-2218

Enchanting nineteenth-century European-style auberge with tastefully appointed, spacious guest rooms, private baths, period antiques. Several common rooms, fireplaces, and tranquility. Pastoral setting on 23 acres. Privacy, relaxing walks, gourmet picnics. Virginia wine tasting and weekend candlelight dining.

Hosts: Peter & Mary Jae Abbitt Sushka
Rooms: 7 (PB) $90.52-101.17
Full Breakfast
Minimum stay weekends & holidays: 2
Credit Cards: No
Closed Dec. 24-25
Notes: 2, 4, 5, 6, 8 (over 8), 9, 10, 11, 14

SMITHFIELD

Isle of Wight Inn

1607 South Church Street
Smithfield, VA, 23430
(804) 357-3176

Luxurious colonial B&B inn located in a delightful, historic river port. Several suites feature fireplaces and Jacuzzis. Antique shop, featuring tallcase clocks and period furniture. Over sixty old homes in town dating from 1750. Thirty minutes and a ferry ride from Williamsburg and Jamestown; less than one hour from James River plantations, Norfolk, Hampton, and Virginia Beach.

Hosts: Marcella Hoffman, Sam Earl & Robert Hart
Rooms: 12 (PB) $49-79
Continental-plus Breakfast
Credit Cards: A, B, C
Notes: 2, 5, 7, 8, 9, 10, 11, 12, 14

SMITH MOUNTAIN LAKE

Holland-Duncan House

Route 5, Box 681
Smith Mountain Lake, VA, 24121
(703) 721-8510

Historic 1820 Blue Ridge plantation home on 28 acres with a log summer kitchen and smokehouse renovated with large fireplaces for guests. Two lovely rooms in the Federal house are tastefully furnished with antiques. Centrally located to all recreation at beautiful Smith Mountain Lake.

Hosts: Kathryn & Clint Shay
Rooms: 4 (2 PB; 2 SB) $45-65
Full Breakfast
Credit Cards: A, B
Closed Dec. & Jan.
Notes: 2, 6 (cabins), 8, 9, 10, 11, 12

The Manor at Taylor's Store

Rt. 1, Box 533
Smith Mountain Lake, VA, 24184
(703) 721-3951

Circa 1799, 120-acre estate near Smith Mountain Lake, Roanoke, and the Blue Ridge Parkway. On-premises hiking, fishing, canoeing, swimming, hot tub. Warm hospitality amid antique splendor.

Hosts: Lee & Mary Lynn Tucker
Rooms: 6 (4 PB; 2 SB) $60-85
Cottage sleeping 6-8 available
Full Breakfast
Credit Cards: A, B
Notes: 2, 5, 8 (in cottages), 9, 10, 11, 12, 13, 14

SPERRYVILLE

The Conyers House

Box 157, Route 707
Sperryville, VA, 22740
(703) 987-8025

Nestled in the foothills of the Blue Ridge Mountains, The Conyers House is in the middle of Virginia's most beautiful hunt country. The hostess is an avid fox hunter who will encourage you to ride cross country. The host collects old cars and is an old film buff. An elegant candlelight fireside five-course dinner may be ordered at extra charge. Innkeeping seminars are offered for those thinking of becoming hosts.

Rooms: 8 (4 PB; 4 SB) $90-185
Full Breakfast
Credit Cards: No
Notes: 2, 4, 5, 6 (call), 7 (limited), 8 (weekdays), 9, 10, 11, 13

STANLEY

Jordan Hollow Farm Inn

Route 2, Box 375
Stanley, VA, 22851
(703) 778-2209; (703) 778-2285

A restored colonial horse farm, Twenty-two rooms with private baths, several with fireplaces and whirlpool baths; one suite. Full-service restaurant and pub. Horseback riding, English and Western. In the Shenandoah Valley just ten miles from Skyline Drive and six miles from Luray Caverns.

Hosts: Jetze & Marley Beers
Rooms: 22 (PB) $75-125
Full Breakfast, box lunch, full dinner
Credit Cards: A, B, D, E
Notes: 2, 3, 4, 5, 6, 7, 8, 9, 10, 11, 12, 13, 14

STAUNTON

Frederick House

18 East Frederick Street
Staunton, VA, 24401
(703) 885-4220

An historic townhouse hotel in the European tradition. Large, comfortable rooms or suites, private baths, cable television, air-conditioning, telephones, and antique furnishings. Convenient to fine restaurants, shopping, museums, and the Blue Ridge Mountains.

Hosts: Joe & Evy Harman
Rooms: 14 (PB) $40-70
Full Breakfast
Credit Cards: A, B, C, D, E
Notes: 2, 4, 5, 8, 9, 10, 11, 12, 14

SWOOPE

Lambsgate B&B

Route 1, Box 63
Swoope, VA, 24479
(703) 337-6929

Six miles west of Staunton on Routes 254 and 833. Restored 1816 farmhouse and working sheep farm in the historic Shenandoah Valley. Relaxing country setting with hiking and biking nearby. Central for visiting historic sites, national park, and forests.

Hosts: Dan & Elizabeth Fannon
Rooms: 3 (SB) $36.58
Full Breakfast
Minimum stay July 4: 2
Credit Cards: No
Notes: 2, 5, 8, 9

TREVILIANS

Prospect Hill

Route 3, Box 430
Trevilians, VA, 23093
(703) 967-0844; (800) 277-0844

Prospect Hill is a 1732 plantation just fifteen miles east of Charlottesville. Lodgings are in the manor house and renovated outbuildings featuring working fireplaces, Jacuzzis, and breakfast in bed. Candlelight dinners are served every evening by reservation.

Hosts: Michael & Bill Sheehan
Rooms: 12 (PB) $120-170
Full Breakfast
Credit Cards: A, B
Closed Dec. 24 & 25
Notes: 2, 4, 5, 7, 8, 14

VESUVIUS

Sugar Tree Inn

Highway 56
Vesuvius, VA, 24483
(703) 377-2197

Historic log buildings with a beautiful main lodge containing a living room, dining room, breakfast room, library, and three bedrooms. Log guest cottage has four rooms. All rooms have stone fireplaces, antique furnishings, and original art. Excellent dinners served. One-half mile from the Blue Ridge Parkway. Enjoy hiking, antiquing, sight-seeing.

Hosts: The Schroeder Family
Rooms: 9 (7 PB; 2 SB) $120 + tax
Continental Breakfast
Credit Cards: No
Closed Oct.-April
Notes: 2, 4, 7, 8, 9, 11, 12

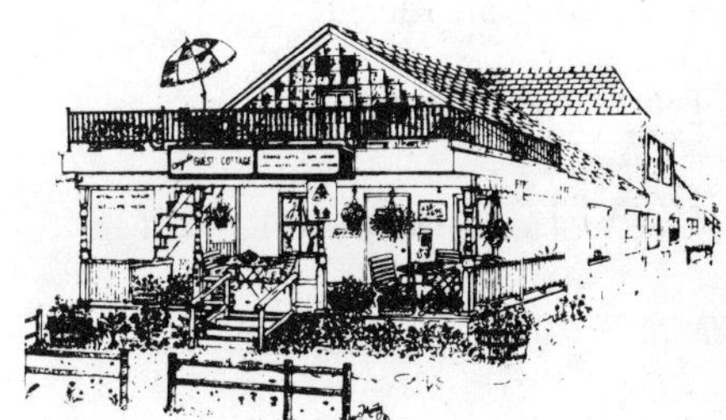

Angie's Guest Cottage

VIRGINIA BEACH

Angie's Guest Cottage

302 24th Street
Virginia Beach, VA, 23451
(804) 428-4690

Located in the heart of the resort area, one block from the ocean. Large beach house that former guest describes as "cute, clean, comfortable, and convenient." All rooms are air-conditioned; some have small refrigerators and private entrances. Breakfast is served on the front porch, and there is also a sun deck, barbecue pit, picnic tables,

Host: Barbara G. Yates
Rooms: 6 (1 PB; 5 SB) $47.96-65.40
Continental-plus Breakfast
Minimum stay in season: 2
Credit Cards: No
Closed Oct. 1-April 1
Notes: 7 (limited), 8, 9, 10, 11, 12

WACHAPREAGUE

The Burton House

11 Brooklyn Street
Wachapreague, VA, 23480
(804) 787-4560

Recently restored 1883 Victorian overlooking the Barrier Islands. Spacious rooms with period furnishings. Gazebo porch. Fully air-conditioned when needed. Bikes to ride; rental boats available. Complimentary home-cooked breakfast and evening refreshments are served.

Hosts: Pat, Tom, and Mike Hart
Rooms: 7 (PB) $53.25-63.90
Full Breakfast
Credit Cards: No
Notes: 2, 5, 7 (on porches) 8 (over 12), 10, 11, 12

WARM SPRINGS

The Inn at Gristmill Square

Box 359
Warm Springs, VA, 24484
(703) 839-2231

The inn is an unusual restoration of five buildings. An old gristmill is now the inn's restaurant. The country store was once a blacksmith shop, and three other buildings house the fourteen guest rooms. Located in Virginia spa country, the inn is noted for its food.

Hosts: The McWilliams Family
Rooms: 14 (PB) $88-110
Continental Breakfast
Credit Cards: A, B
Notes: 2, 4, 5, 6, 7, 8, 9, 10, 11, 12, 14

WASHINGTON

Caledonia Farm B&B

Route 1, Box 2080
Flint Hill, VA, 22627
(703) 675-3693

Beautifully restored 1812 stone home and romantic guest house on farm adjacent to Shenandoah National Park. Splendor for all seasons in Virginia's Blue Ridge Mountains. Skyline Drive, wineries, caves, historic sites, superb dining. Fireplaces, air-conditioning, bicycles. Only 68 miles to Washington, DC.

Host: Phil Irwin
Rooms: 3 (1 PB; 2 SB) $70-100 + tax
Full Breakfast
Credit Cards: A, B (for confirmation only)
Dinner available by reservation weekdays
Notes: 2, 3, 4, 5, 8 (over 12,) 9, 10, 11, 12, 13, 14

The Foster-Harris House

Main Street, Box 333
Washington, VA, 22747
(703) 675-3757

A charming farmhouse Victorian in a tiny historic village just sixty-five miles from Washington, DC. World-acclaimed five-star restaurant three blocks away. Antiques, fresh flowers, outstanding views of the Blue Ridge Mountains. Fireplace stoves in some rooms. Near Skyline Drive and Luray Caverns. Fully air-conditioned.

Hosts: Brendan McCarthy & Amy Harrison
Rooms: 4 (3 PB; 1 SB) $74.90-133.75
Full Breakfast
Credit Cards: A, B
Notes: 2, 5, 6, 7, 8, 9, 10, 11, 12, 14

WHITE POST

L'Auberge Provencale

P.O. Box 119
White Post, VA, 22663
(703) 837-1375; FAX: (703) 837-2004

Luxury overnight accommodations, elegant romantic dining, and the "breakfast of one's dreams." L'Auberge Provencale offers the perfect getaway for pleasure or business. Superb French "Cuisine Moderne" is created by Master Chef Alain. Country charm, city sophistication. Dating to the c. 1753 "Mt. Airy" recreated as an inn of the South of France.

Hosts: Alain & Celeste Borel
Rooms: 9 (PB) $115-200
Full Breakfast
Credit Cards: A, B
Closed Jan. 1-Feb. 10
Notes: 2, 4, 7, 8 (over 10), 9, 10, 11, 12, 13, 14

WILLIAMSBURG

For Cant Hill Guest Home

4 Canterbury Lane
Williamsburg, VA, 23185
(804) 229-6623

Our home is only six to eight blocks from the restored area of Williamsburg, yet very secluded and quiet in a lovely wooded setting overlooking a lake that joins the College of William and Mary campus. The rooms are beautifully decorated, and the hosts are happy to make dinner reservations for you and provide helpful information on the many area attractions.

Hosts: Martha & Hugh Easler
Rooms: 2 (PB) $55
Continental Breakfast
Credit Cards: No
Notes: 2, 5, 8 (10 and over), 9, 10, 11, 12

Fox Grape

701 Monumental Avenue
Williamsburg, VA, 23185
(804) 229-6914; (800) 292-3699

Warm hospitality awaits you just a seven-minute walk north of Virginia's restored colonial capital. Furnishings include counted cross stitch, antiques, stained glass, stenciled walls, duck decoys, and a cup plate collection. Pat enjoys doing counted cross stitch. Bob carves walking sticks and makes stained-glass windows.

Hosts: Bob & Pat Orendorff
Rooms: 4 (2 PB; 2 SB) $45-55
Continental Breakfast
Credit Cards: A, B
Notes: 2, 5, 7, 8, 9, 10, 11, 12, 14

Himmel-Bed & Breakfast

706 Richmond Road
Williamsburg, VA, 23185
(804) 229-6421

This cozy country Cape Cod looks as though it jumped off of the pages of *Country Living* magazine, with its unique collection of country antiques, stencil walls, and canopied beds. Full country breakfast, central air conditioning, complimentary bikes. Within walking distance of restored area. No smoking.

Host: Mary Peters
Rooms: 3 (PB) $70-85
Full Breakfast
Credit Cards: Yes
Notes: 2, 5, 8, 9, 10, 12, 14

Legacy of Williamsburg Tavern

930 Jamestown Road
Williamsburg, VA, 23185
(800) WMBGSBB

An eighteenth-century style B&B inn with authentic furnishings. Step through our doors and step back two hundred years in time. Suites or rooms with canopy beds, fireplaces, private baths, bathrobes, bikes, and mouth-watering breakfasts that include homemade Belgium waffles, breads, and muffins.

Hosts: Mary Ann & Ed Lucas
Rooms: 4 (PB) $75-125
Full Breakfast
Credit Cards: A, B
Notes: 2, 5, 9, 10, 11, 12, 14

Liberty Rose

1022 Jamestown Road
Williamsburg, VA, 23185
(804) 253-1260

Liberty Rose sits atop an acre of great old trees. Be delighted with unique private baths, luxurious bedchambers, wonderful antiques, and scrumptious breakfasts. Reserve the room of your choice from "Rose Victoria," "Magnolia Peach," "Savannah Lace," or "Sweet Caroline."

Hosts: Brad & Sandi Hirz
Rooms: 4 (PB) $80-125
Full Breakfast
Credit Cards: A, B
Notes: 2, 5, 10, 12

Sheldon's Ordinary

Sheldon's Ordinary

Bensonhouse of Richmond & Williamsburg
2036 Monument
Richmond, VA, 23220
(804) 353-6900

This home is a copy of the eighteenth-century Sheldon's Tavern in Litchfield, Connecticut. Built in 1983, it is located one mile from Colonial Williamsburg and adjacent to the College of William and Mary, in a quiet wooded area. There is a third-floor guest room with queen bed and private bath overlooking the boxwood garden below. A queen room has a fireplace and TV. A continental-plus breakfast is served. No smoking; resident dog and cat. $85-90.

The Travel Tree 9

P.O. Box 838
Williamsburg, VA, 23187
(804) 253-1571

Treat your family to an elegant two-bedroom suite near Busch Gardens. The convenience of your own bath, breakfast nook, sitting area, and private entrance assures your privacy. Four miles from restored area; no smoking. $70-120.

The Travel Tree 10

P.O. Box 838
Williamsburg, VA, 23187
(804) 253-1571

Rest safe and secure, tucked under the eaves of a story-and-a-half cottage in a charming, wooded setting. Sleep upstairs in a queen brass bed; relax downstairs in the sitting room with Pullman kitchen. Shared baths. One mile from restored area; no smoking. $90-126.

The Travel Tree 133

P.O. Box 838
Williamsburg, VA, 23187
(804) 253-1571

Luxuriate in a spacious room with king bed, dining alcove, private bath, and private entrance. Or enjoy a pleasant twin room furnished with Oriental accents and an adjacent private bath. Three miles from the restored area; no smoking. $50-65.

The Travel Tree 139

P.O. Box 838
Williamsburg, VA, 23187
(804) 253-1571

Relax in an airy, inviting room with private entrance, private bath, kitchenette, and patio doors leading to the lawn. Or choose the gracious suite furnished with eighteenth- and nineteenth-century antiques, a four-poster double bed, sitting area with fireplace, breakfast room, and private bath. One mile from restored area. No smoking. $65-85.

The Travel Tree 501

P.O. Box 838
Williamsburg, VA, 23187
(804) 253-1571

Bike the lovely streets of Williamsburg, returning in time for afternoon tea and wine in the parlor. Choose from five rooms, each furnished in the colonial style with canopy or four-poster beds and private baths. Family suite available. Four blocks from restored area. Limited smoking. $80-145.

The Travel Tree 605

P.O. Box 838
Williamsburg, VA, 23187
(804) 253-1571

Walk to the historic area. The colonial guest rooms will charm you, from the first-floor suite with fireplace to the quaint third-floor dormered room. All have queen beds and private baths. No smoking. Five blocks from the restored area. $65-95.

The Travel Tree 710

P.O. Box 838
Williamsburg, VA, 23187
(804) 253-1571

Savor the colonial atmosphere in a replica of an eighteenth-century home. Each bedroom is furnished with both a queen and a twin canopy bed and has a private bath. Breakfast is served in the formal dining room. No smoking. Five blocks from the restored area. $85.

War Hill Inn

4560 Long Hill Road
Williamsburg, VA, 23185
(804) 565-0248

Eighteenth-century home on 32-acre farm three miles off Rt. 60. Close to Colonial Williamsburg, William & Mary College, Busch Gardens, shopping outlets. Seven antique-furnished guest rooms with private baths.

Hosts: Shirley, Bill, Cherie & Will Lee
Rooms: 7 (PB) $45-75
Cottage: $90
Suite: 2 (PB)
Full Breakfast
Credit Cards: A, B, C
Notes: 2, 5, 8, 9

Williamsburg Sampler B&B

Williamsburg Sampler B&B

922 Jamestown Road
Williamsburg, VA, 23185
(804) 253-0398; (800) 722-1169

Richly furnished, stately, six-bedroom brick colonial home with collections of pewter, antiques, and samplers. Located in the heart of Williamsburg and within walking distance of Colonial Williamsburg. Parallels the College of William and Mary. Short drive to the Yorktown Battlefields, Jamestown Settlement, James River plantations, and Busch Gardens.

Hosts: Helen & Ike Sisane
Rooms: 4 (PB) $75-100
Full Breakfast
Credit Cards: No
Notes: 2, 5, 8, 9, 10, 11, 12, 14

WILLIAMSBURG-TOANO

Blue Bird Haven

8691 Barhamsville Road
Toano, VA, 23168
(804) 566-0177

Nine miles from Colonial Williamsburg, five minutes to Williamsburg Pottery. Friendly, at-home atmosphere, "inside tips" for visitors. Comfortable, traditionally furnished guest rooms with handmade quilts, spreads, rugs, wall hangings, in private wing. Homemade buffet breakfasts feature granola, quiche, stradas, blueberry pancakes, Virginia ham, muffins, spoonbread, cheese grits.

Hosts: June & Ed Cottle
Rooms: 4 (PB) $48-58
Full Breakfast
Minimum stay holidays: 2
Credit Cards: No
Notes: 2, 4, 5, 6, 7, 8 (over 6), 9, 10, 11, 12

Washington

ANACORTES

Channel House B&B

2902 Oakes Avenue
Anacortes, WA, 98221
(206) 293-9382

A classic island home built in 1902, the Channel House offers large, comfortable rooms, two with fireplaces, and lovely water and island views. The outdoor hot tub is a treat after a busy day of hiking or biking on the islands. Pat's oatmeal-raisin cookies are baked fresh every day. Anacortes is the beginning of the San Juan Island and Sydney, B.C., ferry routes and a center for chartering of sail and power boats for wonderful vacation trips.

Hosts: Dennis & Patricia McIntyre
Rooms: 6 (4 PB; 2 SB) $65-85
Full Breakfast
Credit Cards: A, B
Notes: 2, 5, 8 (over 12), 9, 10, 11, 12, 14

Channel House B&B

Dutch Treat House

1220 31st Street
Anacortes, WA, 98221
(206) 293-8154

Established in 1986, this 1930 Dutch Colonial house has four large, bright corner guest rooms. The decor is country; two rooms have a view of Mt. Baker. Located next to a park; families are welcome. Full breakfast includes fresh seasonal fruit, daily baked muffins, and a hot entree. Your hosts gladly recommend fine local restaurants and vantage points for viewing the natural beauty of Washington.

Hosts: Mike & Melanie Coyne
Rooms: 4 (SB) $55
Full Breakfast
Credit Cards: A, B
Notes: 2, 5, 8, 9, 10, 11, 12

Old Brook Inn

530 Old Brook Lane
Anacortes, WA, 98221
(206) 293-4768

This four-bedroom Cape Cod with cedar shingle siding welcomes families with children.

Host: Dick Ash
Rooms: 2 (PB) $60-65
Continental Breakfast
Credit Cards: A, B
Notes: 2, 5, 6, 7, 8, 9, 10, 11, 12, 14

ASHFORD

Growly Bear B&B

37311 SR 706
Ashford, WA, 98304
(206) 569-2339

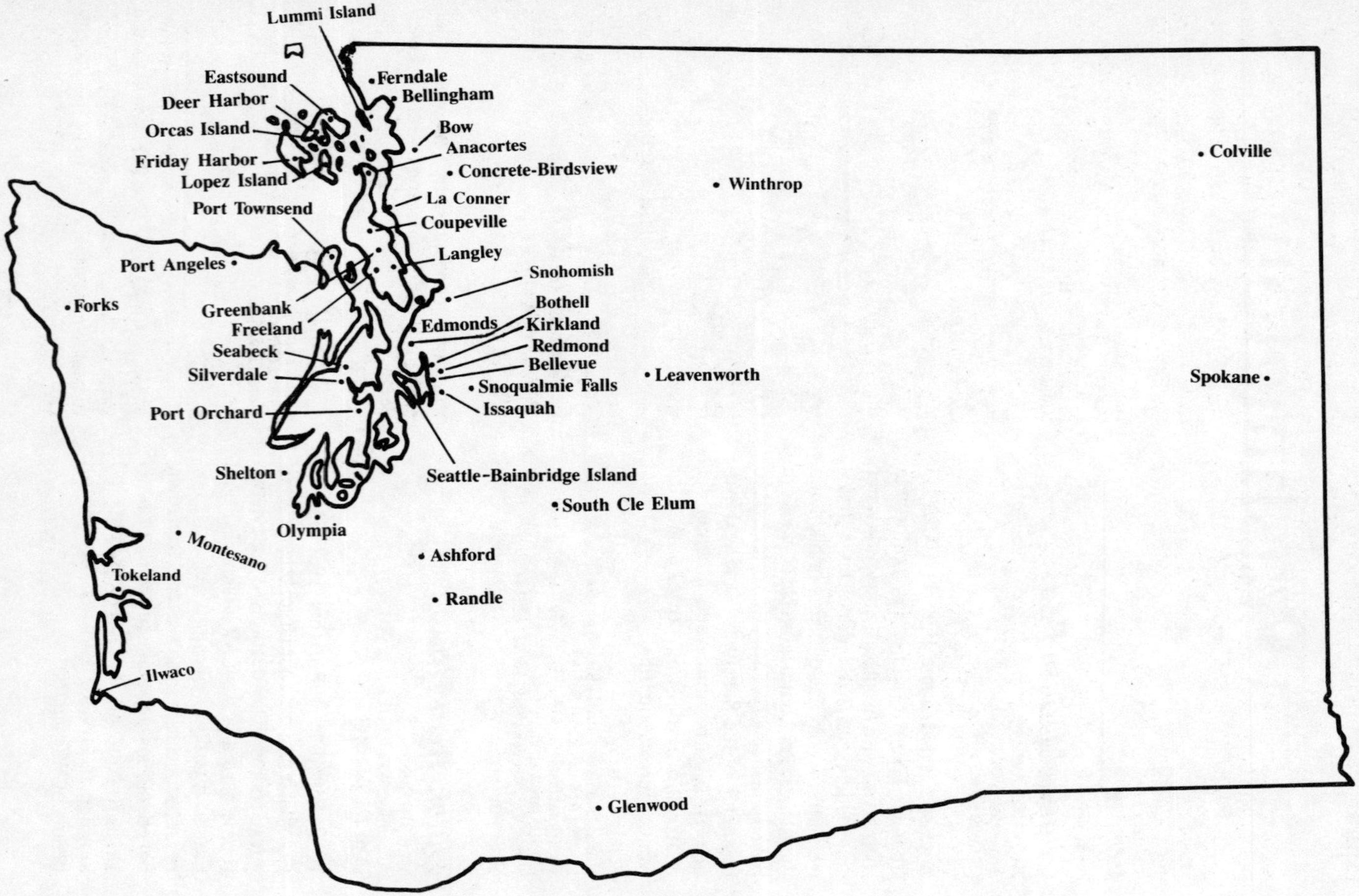

Lummi Island
Eastsound
Ferndale
Bellingham
Deer Harbor
Orcas Island
Bow
Anacortes
Friday Harbor
Lopez Island
Concrete-Birdsview
Colville
Winthrop
La Conner
Port Townsend
Coupeville
Langley
Port Angeles
Snohomish
Forks
Greenbank
Bothell
Freeland
Edmonds
Kirkland
Redmond
Seabeck
Bellevue
Silverdale
Snoqualmie Falls
Leavenworth
Spokane
Port Orchard
Issaquah
Shelton
Seattle-Bainbridge Island
South Cle Elum
Olympia
Montesano
Ashford
Tokeland
Randle
Ilwaco
Glenwood

WASHINGTON

Experience a bit of history and enjoy your mountain stay at a rustic homestead house built in 1890. Secluded location near Mt. Rainier National Park. Listen to Goat Creek just outside your window; indulge in fresh pastries from the Growly Bear Bakery.

Host: Susan Jenny
Rooms: 2 (1 PB; 1 SB) $50-80
Full Breakfast
Credit Cards: A, B, C
Notes: 2, 5, 7 (restricted), 13, 14

Growly Bear B&B

Mountain Meadows Inn

28912 SR 706 East
Ashford, WA, 98304
(206) 569-2788

Gracious hospitality, unique, quiet country atmosphere. Relax while absorbing nature's colors and sounds from our full porch overlooking the pond. Evening campfires. Nearby Mt. Rainier National Park offers all-season recreation.

Hosts: Chad Darrah
Rooms: 3 (PB) $60.23-82.13
Full Breakfast
Minimum stay holidays: 2
Credit Cards: A, B
Notes: 2, 5, 8 (over 10), 9, 13, 14

BAINBRIDGE ISLAND

Bombay House

8490 Beck Road
Bainbridge Island, WA, 98110
(206) 842-3926

The Bombay House is a spectacular 35-minute ferry ride from downtown Seattle. The house was built in 1907 and sits high on a hillside in the country overlooking Rich Passage. Widow's walk, rustic, rough-cedar gazebo, masses of gardens exploding with seasonal color. Watch the ferry pass and see the lights of Bremerton in the distance. Just a few blocks from the beach, a country theater, and fine dining. A great spot for the visiting Seattle business traveler or vacationer.

Hosts: Bunny Cameron & Roger Kanchuk
Rooms: 5 (3 PB; 2 SB) $55-93
Continental Breakfast
Credit Cards: A, B, C
Notes: 2, 5, 9, 10, 11, 12, 14

BELLEVUE

The Lions B&B

803 92nd Avenue NE
Bellevue, WA, 98004
(206) 455-1018

Serene, quiet, yet in the heart of the city. Private quarters with equipped kitchen and two bedrooms. Also large room with private bath in main house. Scandinavian hostess. Within walking distance of dining, shopping, parks, water. Fifteen minutes from downtown Seattle. Bus service.

Host: Ruth Svenasen
Rooms: 3 (1 PB; 2 SB) $60
Full Breakfast
Credit Cards: No
Notes: 2, 5, 8, 9, 10, 11, 12, 13, 14

Petersen B&B

10228 SE Eighth
Bellevue, WA, 98004
(206) 454-9334

Petersen B&B is located in a well-established neighborhood five minutes from the Bellevue Shopping Square and twenty minutes from Seattle. It offers two rooms, one with a queen waterbed, and a spa on the deck off the atrium kitchen. Homestyle breakfast; airport pick-up can be arranged.

Hosts: Eunice & Carl Petersen
Rooms: 2 (SB) $40-45
Full Breakfast
Credit Cards: No
Notes: 2, 5, 7 (outside), 8, 9, 10, 11

BELLINGHAM

Bellingham's DeCann House B&B

2610 Eldridge Avenue
Bellingham, WA, 98225
(206) 734-9172

A Victorian B&B that combines the best of European hospitality and American convenience. Featuring family heirlooms, private baths, and a billiard room for mingling. Ask us about excursions to Vancouver, the San Juan Islands, or the Alaska ferry. Our breakfast will start your day with a smile.

Hosts: Van & Barbara Hudson
Rooms: 2 (PB) $40-65
Full Breakfast
Credit Cards: No
Notes: 2, 5, 8 (over 12), 9, 10, 11, 12

The Castle B&B

1103 Fifteenth Street
Bellingham, WA, 98225
(206) 676-0974

This 101-year-old house overlooks the San Juan Islands, Bellingham Bay, and historic Fairhaven in America's fourth corner, NW Washington. Gorgeous scenery, boating, hiking, skiing, special shopping areas, and restaurants. Collections of early electric lamps, castle furnishings. Highly unusual castle atmosphere and healthful food.

Hosts: Larry & Gloria Harriman
Rooms: 3 (1 PB; 2 SB) $45-85
Full Breakfast
Credit Cards: A, B
Notes: 2, 5, 9, 10, 11, 12, 14

North Garden Inn

1014 North Garden
Bellingham, WA, 98225
(206) 671-7828

North Garden Inn is an 1897 Queen Anne Victorian on the National Register. Many of the guest rooms have splendid views of Bellingham Bay. The inn features two studio grand pianos in performance condition and is located close to shopping, fine dining, and Western Washington University.

Hosts: Frank & Barbara De Freytas
Rooms: 6-10 (1 PB; 5 SB) $42.04-52.82
Full Breakfast
Credit Cards: A, B
Notes: 2, 5, 8, 9, 14

Schnauzer Crossing

4421 Lakeway Drive
Bellingham, WA, 98226
(206) 733-0055; (206) 734-2808

Schnauzer Crossing is a luxury B&B located between Seattle and Vancouver, B.C. Enjoy this destination B&B, with its lakeside beauty, swimming, canoeing, outdoor hot tub, and tennis, its master suite with fireplace and Jacuzzi tub. Sail in the San Juan Islands or climb 10,000-foot Mt. Baker. Experience Washington State!

Hosts: Vermont & Donna McAllister
Rooms: 2 (PB) $90-125
Full Breakfast
Credit Cards: A, B
Notes: 2, 5, 6 (outdoors), 7 (outside), 8, 9, 10, 11

BOTHELL

NW Bed & Breakfast 161

610 SW Broadway
Portland, OR, 97205
(503) 243-7616

Very attractive contemporary home in a wooded setting above Lake Washington. Thirty to forty-five minutes from downtown Seattle. Fireplace in the living room, pool outside the guest bedroom, private garden.

One cat in residence. Smoking allowed. One room with twin beds share 1.5 baths with hosts. $40.

BOW

Alice Bay B&B

982 Scott Road, Samish Island
Bow, WA, 98232
(206) 766-6396

Samish Island is a refuge for wildlife, and Alice Bay shelters a blue heron rookery. A restful room overlooks the bay, and a hot tub soaks the day away. In the morning, you'll be served food from the *Alice Bay Cookbook* in our summer kitchen, which is warmed by a southern exposure.

Hosts: Terry & Julie Rousseau
Rooms: 1 (PB) $65
Continental-plus Breakfast
Credit Cards: No
Notes: 2, 5, 8, 9, 10, 11

COLVILLE

Lakeside Manor B&B

2425 Pend Oreille Lakes
Colville, WA, 99114
(509) 684-8741

The mansion is on a tiny peninsula with one lake at the front door and another at the back. Large indoor Jacuzzi, fireplace, panoramic views of the lakes and mountains. Centered in the Colville National Forest in northeast Washington.

Host: Pat Thomas
Rooms: 2 (SB) $65
Continental Breakfast
Credit Cards: No
Notes: 2, 5, 9, 11, 12, 13, 14

CONCRETE-BIRDSVIEW

Cascade Mountain Inn

3840 Pioneer Lane
Concrete, WA, 98237
(206) 826-4333; (800) 826-0015

The inn is located close to the Skagit River, Baker Lake, and the North Cascades National Park, just off Highway 20 in a pastoral setting. Easy access to hiking, fishing, and sight-seeing in one of the nation's most scenic mountain areas. Full cooked country breakfast.

Hosts: Ingrid & Gerhard Meyer
Rooms: 6 (PB) $80-84
Full Breakfast
Credit Cards: A, B
Notes: 2, 5, 8 (over 10), 9, 14

COUPEVILLE

The Inn at Penn Cove

702 North Main Street
Coupeville, WA, 98239
(206) 678-8000

The elegance of two 100-year-old restored Victorians, with all the comforts of today, welcome you like a visit to Grandma's. Soak in clawfoot tubs or spas. Located in the historic seaport village of Coupeville on beautiful Whidbey Island, a twenty-minute ferry ride away. Complete breakfast; handicapped accessible; executive retreat/meetings.

Hosts: Jim & Barbara Cinney
Rooms: 6 (PB) $75-125
Full Breakfast
Credit Cards: A, B, D
Notes: 2, 5, 8, 9, 10, 11, 12, 14

DEER HARBOR

Palmer's Chart House

Box 51
Deer Harbor, WA, 98243
(206) 376-4231

The first B&B on Orcas Island (since 1975), with a magnificent water view. The 33-foot private yacht *Amante* is available for a minimal fee with Skipper Don. Low-key, private, personal attention makes this B&B unique and attractive. Well-traveled hosts speak Spanish.

Hosts: Majean & Donald Palmer
Rooms: 2 (PB) $45-60
Full Breakfast
Credit Cards: No
Notes: 2, 4 (by arrangement), 5, 8 (over 10), 9, 10, 11, 12, 14

EASTSOUND

Kangaroo House

Box 334
Eastsound, WA, 98245
(206) 376-2175

Restful 1907 home on Orcas Island, gem of the San Juans. Period furnishings, extensive lawns and flower gardens. Gourmet breakfasts. Walk to village shops, galleries, and restaurants. Panoramic view of the islands from Moran State Park.

Hosts: Jan & Mike Russillo
Rooms: 5 (2 PB; 3 SB) $65-100
Full Breakfast
Credit Cards: A, B
Notes: 2, 5, 8, 9, 10, 11, 12

EATONVILLE

Old Mill House B&B

116 Oak Street, Box 543
Eatonville, WA, 98328
(206) 832-6506

Your passport to the twenties! Indulge in spacious guest rooms complete with costumes and memorabilia, a shower with seven heads, a library leading to a secret prohibition bar and dance room. On the National Historic Register.

Hosts: Catharine & Michael Gallagher
Rooms: 4 (1 PB; 3 SB) $55-70
Full Breakfast
Credit Cards: A, B
Notes: 2, 5, 8, 9, 11, 13, 14

EDMONDS

Harrison House

210 Sunset Avenue
Edmonds, WA, 98020
(206) 776-4748

New waterfront home with sweeping view of Puget Sound and the Olympic Mountains. Many fine restaurants within walking distance. Your spacious room has a private bath, private deck, TV, wet bar, telephone, and king-size bed. University of Washington is nearby.

Hosts: Jody & Harve Harrison
Rooms: 2 (PB) $40-50
Continental Breakfast
Credit Cards: No
Notes: 2, 5, 9, 10, 11, 12, 13

NW Bed & Breakfast 189

610 SW Broadway
Portland, OR, 97205
(503) 243-7616

Delightful lakefront home. The specialty of the house is sour-dough waffles cooked over an outdoor fire, weather permitting. Handmade quilts on beds. Five miles from the ferry to the Olympic Peninsula. Hosts will take guests on a barge cruise around Lake Ballinger. Very convenient for Seattle. Two rooms with double beds and one room with twins. Guest bath and stall shower. $50.

FERNDALE

Hill Top B&B

5832 Church Road
Ferndale, WA, 98248
(206) 384-3619

Large, comfortable rooms with sitting areas, one with fireplace. Beds and walls warmed with an array of quilts made by your hostess. Private entry and patio, hearty breakfast, panoramic mountain view. Piano, cable TV.

Hosts: Paul & Doris Matz
Rooms: 3 (1 PB; 2 SB) $44-49
Full Breakfast
Credit Cards: A, B
Closed Christmas
Notes: 2, 5, 8, 9, 10, 11, 12

FORKS

Miller Tree Inn

Box 953
Forks, WA, 98331
(206) 374-6806

Comfortable 1917 farmhouse offers warm hospitality, choice of breakfast, and quiet country atmosphere. It's the Olympic Peninsula's best location for hiking, beach combing, and fishing. Located near the Hoh Rain Forest, or Rialto Beach. Hot tub.

Hosts: Ted & Prue Miller
Rooms: 6 (2 PB; 4 SB) $40-55
Full Breakfast
Credit Cards: A, B
Notes: 2, 5, 6, 8 (over 4), 9

FREELAND

Cliff House

5440 Windmill Road
Freeland, WA, 98249
(206) 321-1566

On Whidbey Island. Daringly different! In a private world of luxury, this stunning home is yours alone. Secluded in a forest on the very edge of Puget Sound, the views are breathtaking! Stone fireplace, spa, beach. King-sized feather bed, gourmet kitchen. Also, cozy and charming Seacliff cottage.

Hosts: Peggy Moore & Walter O'Toole
Rooms: 2 (PB) $135-265
Continental-plus Breakfast
Minimum stay: 2
Credit Cards: No
Closed Christmas
Notes: 2, 9, 12

Pillars by the Sea

1367 East Bayview Avenue
Freeland, WA, 98249
(206) 221-7738

Turn-of-the-century home, restored to its beautiful original condition. Rooms have queen beds with private baths. This historic home overlooks beautiful Holmes Harbor. You can hike, beach walk, relax. Tennis, golf, horseback riding, bicycling. Restaurants nearby. Hosts speak French, Spanish, and German.

Hosts: Richard & Andree Ploss
Rooms: 2 (PB) $70-80
Full Breakfast
Credit Cards: A, B
Closed Jan.
Notes: 2, 9, 10, 11, 12

FRIDAY HARBOR

Tucker House B&B

260 "B" Street
Friday Harbor, WA, 98250
(206) 378-2783

Located on San Juan Island, Tucker House offers three private cottages, three rooms in the main house, and a hot tub. Walking distance to ferry, shops, restaurants, galleries, marina, and whale museum. One of the rooms accommodates four people. Children welcome in cottages.

Hosts: John & Evelyn Lackey & Mitzi Stack
Rooms: 6 (3 PB; 3 SB) $69.88-96.75
Full Breakfast
Credit Cards: A, B
Notes: 2, 5, 7, 8, 14

GLENWOOD

Flying L Ranch

25 Flying L Lane
Glenwood, WA, 98619
(509) 364-3488

Built in 1945 by the Lloyds and operated as a B&B since 1960. On 160 beautiful acres with trails, wildflowers, wildlife, pond, in a tranquil, secluded valley at the base of 12,276-foot Mt. Adams. Intimate lodge, guest house with views, fireplaces, common kitchens, cabin, spa. Restaurant nearby.

Hosts: Darvel & Ilse Lloyd
Rooms: 12 (8 PB; 4 SB) $49-69
Full Breakfast
Minimum stay certain weekends & holidays: 2

Credit Cards: A, B, C, E
Notes: 2, 5, 9, 13, 14

GREENBANK

Guest House Cottages

835 East Christenson Road
Greenbank, WA, 98253
(206) 678-3115

Luxurious couples' retreat on Whidbey Island. Beautiful log lodge for 2; four cozy cottages; Wildflower Suite in 1920s farmhouse. Each accommodates two adults. Outdoor pool, hot tub, exercise room, in-room Jacuzzis in all accommodations, wildlife pond, and 25 acres of land. All cottages have kitchens, VCRs, complimentary movies, fireplaces, and country antiques.

Hosts: The Creger Family
Rooms: 6 (PB) $85-225 + tax
Continental-plus Breakfast
Minimum stay weekends: 2; holidays: 2-3
Credit Cards: A, B, C, D
Notes: 2, 5, 9, 11, 14

Guest House Cottages

ILWACO

Inn at Ilwaco

120 Williams Street NE
Ilwaco, WA, 98624-0922
(206) 642-8686

A year-round nine-room country inn; seven rooms have private baths. Gourmet breakfast. Quiet, in-town location, near charter fishing, ocean beaches, golf, lighthouses, kite flying, bicycling, historic sights. Renovated 1928 Presbyterian church with New England style and a 120-seat performing arts theater.

Host: Bruce Siau
Rooms: 9 (7 PB; 2 SB) $55-75
Full Breakfast
Credit Cards: A, B
Closed Jan. 12-Feb. 1
Notes: 2, 8, 9, 10, 11, 12, 14

ISSAQUAH

Wildflower B&B Inn

25237 SE Issaquah-Fall City Road
Issaquah, WA, 98027
(206) 392-1196

Quiet country charm in a small, delightful suburb of Seattle. Two-story log home nestled in acres of evergreens offers the comfort of spacious rooms, antique furnishings, home-cooked breakfasts. Nearby are Gilman Shopping Village, a small theater, and excellent restaurants. Close to state and county recreational parks; thirty-five minutes from skiing.

Host: Laureita Caldwell
Rooms: 4 (2 PB; 2 SB) $45-50
Full Breakfast
Notes: 2, 5, 8 (over 11), 10, 11, 12

KIRKLAND

Shumway Mansion

11410 99th Place NE
Kirkland, WA, 98033
(206) 823-2303

Overlook Lake Washington from this award-winning 1909, twenty-three-room mansion. Seven individually decorated guest rooms with private baths. Variety-filled breakfast. Complimentary use of athletic club. Short distance to all forms of shopping; twenty minutes to downtown Seattle. Water and snow recreation close at hand.

Hosts: Richard & Salli Harris
Rooms: 7 (PB) $65-95
Full Breakfast
Credit Cards: A, B, C
Notes: 2, 5, 8 (over 12), 9, 10, 11, 14

LA CONNER

Heather House

505 Maple Street
La Conner, WA, 98257
(206) 466-4675

Three bedroom, two bath Cape Cod home in downtown La Conner. Easy walk to shopping and dining. Hosts live next door, so guests can enjoy freedom and privacy. View of farm, Cascade Mountains, and Mount Baker. Halfway between Seattle and Vancouver, B.C. Near ferry to the San Juan Islands.

Hosts: Wayne & Bev Everton
Rooms: 3 (SB) $45-65
Continental Breakfast
Credit Cards: A, B
Notes: 2, 5, 9, 10, 11, 12, 14

The White Swan Guest House

The White Swan Guest House

1388 Moore Road
Mt. Vernon, WA, 98273
(206) 445-6805

The White Swan is a very special "storybook" farmhouse six miles from the historic waterfront town of La Conner. Fine restaurants, great antiquing, and interesting shops in Washington's favorite artist community. Just one hour north of Seattle and ninety miles south of Vancouver. Separate honeymoon cottage on premises.

Host: Peter Goldfarb
Rooms: 4 (1 PB; 3S2B) $65-95
Continental Breakfast
Credit Cards: A, B
Notes: 2, 5

LANGLEY

Country Cottage of Langley

215 Sixth Street
Langley, WA, 98260
(206) 221-8709

Old-fashioned hospitality in country elegance. Remodeled 1926 farmhouse on 3 acres of manicured lawn with a view of Puget Sound and the Cascades Mountains. Five rooms or suites with private baths, full breakfast. Two blocks to the water and downtown Langley, the art capital of Whidbey Island. Bicycling, strolling wooded parks, and water sports are all island activities.

Hosts: Trudy & Whitey Martin
Rooms: 5 (PB) $75-85
Full Breakfast
Credit Cards: A, B
Notes: 2, 5, 9, 10, 11, 12, 14

Eagles Nest Inn

3236 East Saratoga Road
Langley, WA, 98260
(206) 321-5331

Country Cottage of Langley

The inn's rural setting on Whidbey Island offers a sweeping view of Saratoga Passage and Mount Baker. Casual elegance abounds. Relax and enjoy the wood stove fireplace, spa, library, and bottomless chocolate chip cookie jar. Write or call for brochure. Canoeing and horseback riding available.

Hosts: Nancy & Dale Bowman
Rooms: 4 (PB) $85-105
Full Breakfast
Minimum stay holiday weekends: 2
Credit Cards: A, B
Notes: 2, 5, 10

Log Castle

3273 East Saratoga Road
Langley, WA, 98260
(206) 321-5483

Located on Whidbey Island, thirty miles north of Seattle. Log lodge on secluded beach. Big stone fireplace, turret bedrooms, panoramic views of Puget Sound and the Cascade Mountains. Norma's breakfast is a legend. Watch for bald eagles and Orca whales from our widow's walk.

Hosts: Senator Jack & Norma Metcalf
Rooms: 4 (PB) $70-90
Full Breakfast
Minimum stay holidays: 2
Credit Cards: A, B
Notes: 2, 5, 8 (over 11), 10

Lone Lake Cottages & Breakfast

5206 South Bayview Road
Langley, WA, 98260
(206) 321-5325

Whidbeys' Shangri-la. Enjoy total privacy in our waterfront cottages or in a sternwheel houseboat. All are decorated with touches of the Orient. Sweeping view, fireplace, kitchen, TV/VCR, Jacuzzi tubs, canoes, fishing, and bicycles.

Host: Dolores Meeks
Rooms: 3 (PB) $95
Continental-plus Breakfast
Credit Cards: No
Notes: 2, 5, 9, 10, 11, 12

LEAVENWORTH

Run of the River B&B

9308 East Leavenworth Road
Leavenworth, WA, 98826
(509) 548-7171

Run of the River, a log B&B inn located on the Ieicle River, is surrounded on two sides by a wildlife and bird refuge. All rooms have hand-hewn log furniture, high cathedral pine ceilings, and private baths. From the decks you can enjoy our spectacular Cascade panorama.

Hosts: Monty & Karen Turner
Rooms: 4 (PB) $75-105
Full Breakfast
Credit Cards: A, B, C
Notes: 2, 5, 9, 10, 11, 12, 13, 14

LOPEZ ISLAND

Inn at Swifts Bay

Route 2, Box 3402
Lopez Island, WA, 98261
(206) 468-3636

On Lopez Island, in the San Juans of Washington State, the Inn at Swifts Bay is situated on 3 wooded acres. Four guest rooms, two with private bath. Fireplaces in common areas, hot tub on deck, private beach, award-winning breakfasts. A designated "Northwest Best Place."

Hosts: Robert Herrmann & Christopher Brandmeir
Rooms: 4 (2 PB; 2 SB) $75-115
Full Breakfast
Credit Cards: A, B
Notes: 2, 5, 9, 10, 11, 12, 14

MacKaye Harbor Inn

Route 1, Box 1940
Lopez Island, WA, 98261
(206) 468-2253

The ideal waterfront getaway! Lopez's only B&B on the beach, this Victorian home is full of charm and nostalgia. Beautiful grounds, beach-combing, biking, rowing, and kayaking. Eagles, deer, seals, and otters frequent the area. Full gourmet breakfasts.

Hosts: Sharon & Gary Emmick
Rooms: 5 (PB and SB) $59-85
Full Breakfast
Credit Cards: A, B
Notes: 2, 5, 9, 10, 11, 12, 14

LUMMI ISLAND

West Shore Farm B&B

2781 West Shore Drive
Lummi Island, WA, 98262
(206) 758-2600

Unique octagonal owner-built home with 180-degree view of islands, passing boats, sunsets, eagles, seals, and Canadian mountains on the northern horizon. Our quiet natural beach, farm animals, garden, orchard, resident poultry, stock of books, maps, bicycles and natural gourmet food are rejuvenating.

Hosts: Carl & Polly Hanson
Rooms: 2 (PB) $75
Full Breakfast
Credit Cards: A, B
Notes: 2, 3, 4, 5, 8, 9, 10, 14

MONTESANO

Sylvan Haus—Murphy B&B

417 Wilder Hill Drive
P.O. Box 416
Montesano, WA, 98563
(206) 249-3453

A gracious three-story family home surrounded by towering evergreens at the top of Wilder Hill Drive. Watch the changing seasons while breakfasting at the old round oak dining table. Near Grays Harbor, Sea-Tac Airport, Olympic Peninsula; thirty minutes to ocean beaches.

Hosts: Mike & JoAnne Murphy
Rooms: 3 (1 PB; 2 SB) $50 + tax
Full Breakfast
Credit Cards: No
Notes: 2, 5, 8 (over 14), 11, 12

OLYMPIA

Harbinger Inn

1136 East Bay Drive
Olympia, WA, 98506
(206) 754-0389

Completely restored National Historic Landmark. View of East Bay Marina, Capitol, and Olympic Mountains. Ideally located for boating, bicycling, jogging, fine dining, and business ventures. A "Northwest Best Place."

Hosts: Marisa & Terrell Williams
Rooms: 4 (1 PB; 3 SB) $50-75
Continental Breakfast
Credit Cards: A, B, C
Notes: 2, 5, 8 (over 12), 9

ORCAS ISLAND

NW Bed & Breakfast 129

610 SW Broadway
Portland, OR, 97205
(503) 243-7616

A three-story Victorian inn built in the early 1900s overlooking water and other San Juan islands. Extensively restored in 1985. Local activities include sailing, bicycling, hiking, golf, and horseback riding. Moran State Park, with huge trees, freshwater lake, and views of all 172 San Juan islands, is nearby. Bicycle and moped rentals available. Continental breakfast; dinner is available with reservations. Seventeen rooms, private and shared baths. Two-night minimum stay required. $48-125.

Turtleback Farm

Route 1, Box 650, Eastsound
Orcas Island, WA, 98245
(206) 376-4914

A meticulously restored farmhouse set on 80 acres in Crow Valley on Orcas Island in the San Juan Islands. Seven antique-filled guest rooms, each with a private bath. An award-winning full breakfast is served.

Hosts: William & Susan C. Fletcher
Rooms: 7 (PB) $65-145
Full Breakfast
Credit Cards: A, B
Notes: 2, 5, 9, 12, 14

PORT ANGELES

Tudor Inn

1108 South Oak
Port Angeles, WA, 98362
(206) 452-3138

Located between the mountains and the sea, this half-timbered Tudor home was built by an Englishman in 1910 and has been tastefully restored and furnished with European antiques and an English garden. Tea is served in the lounge or the library.

Hosts: Jane & Jerry Glass
Rooms: 5 (1 PB; 4 S2B) $55-85
Full Breakfast
Minimum stay weekends & holidays: 2
Credit Cards: A, B
Notes: 2, 5, 8 (over 10), 9, 10, 11, 12, 13, 14

Tudor Inn

PORT ORCHARD

Ogle's Bed & Breakfast

1307 Dogwood Hill SW
Port Orchard, WA, 98366
(206) 876-9170

Secluded hillside home overlooking Puget Sound. View anchored navy ships. Secure off-street parking. Charming Port Orchard is a gateway to the beautiful Olympic Peninsula. Excellent restaurants, antique shops, large marinas nearby. Quiet, restful setting.

Hosts: Quentin & Louise Ogle
Rooms: 2 (SB) $48.50
Full Breakfast
Credit Cards: A, B
Notes: 5, 7 (restricted), 8 (over 12), 9, 10, 11, 12

PORT TOWNSEND

Heritage House

305 Pierce Street
Port Townsend, WA, 98368-8131
(206) 385-6800

Featuring the finest collection of Victorian antiques on the Olympic Peninsula, this National Historic Landmark (c. 1880) offers spectacular water and mountain views from atop the bluff. Warm hospitality and comfort, and marvelous breakfasts, too.

Hosts: Pat & Jim Broughton, Carolyn & Bob Ellis
Rooms: 6 (4 PB; 2 SB) $55-89
Full Breakfast
Credit Cards: A, B, C
Notes: 2, 5, 8 (12 and over), 9, 10, 11, 12, 14

The James House

1238 Washington Street
Port Townsend, WA, 98368
(206) 385-1238

A grand Victorian mansion built by Francis James in 1889, the James House became the first B&B in the Northwest in 1973. Its fine tradition of warmth and hospitality continues in this splendid seaport setting.

Hosts: Carol McGough & Anne Tiernan
Rooms: 12 (4 PB; 8 SB) $47-120
Continental Breakfast
Credit Cards: A, B
Notes: 2, 5, 9, 10, 11, 12

The Lincoln Inn

538 Lincoln Street
Port Townsend, WA, 98368
(206) 385-6677

An 1888 historic inn located in the West Coast's famous Victorian seaport of Port Townsend. Antique-filled rooms, water views, private baths (some with Jacuzzis), full sumptuous breakfast, and gourmet dining available at night.

Hosts: Robert & Joan Allen
Rooms: 6 (PB) $60-70
Full Breakfast
Credit Cards: A, B
Notes: 2 (in advance), 4, 5, 9, 10, 12

Lizzie's Victorian B&B

731 Pierce Street
Port Townsend, WA, 98368
(206) 385-4168

An 1888 Victorian mansion within walking distance of shops and restaurants. The inn is decorated in antiques and some original wallpaper. Parlors are comfortable retreats for reading or conversation. Gateway to the Olympic Mountains, San Juan Islands, and Victoria.

Hosts: Bill & Patti Wickline
Rooms: 8 (5 PB; 3 SB) $50-89
Full Breakfast
Credit Cards: A, B
Notes: 2, 5, 8 (over 10), 9, 10, 11, 12

Starrett Mansion B&B Inn

744 Clay Street
Port Townsend, WA, 98368
(206) 385-3205

Situated on a bluff overlooking the Olympic Mountains, the Cascades, Puget Sound, and historic Port Townsend. The house is renowned for its Victorian architecture, free-hung staircase, frescoed domed ceiling with a solar calendar, and sumptuous breakfasts.

Hosts: Edel & Bob Sokol
Rooms: $65-125
Full Breakfast
Credit Cards: A, B
Notes: 2, 5, 9, 10, 11, 12

RANDLE

Hampton House B&B

409 Silverbrook Road
Randle, WA, 98377
(206) 497-2907

Country charm in a restored 1906 local landmark on 1.5 acres. Near Mt. St. Helens and Mt. Rainier. Two large bedrooms with queen beds. Friendly hosts help you plan sight-seeing in the area. Full breakfast features N.W. fruit and berries in season. Two-hour drive from either Seattle or Portland airports.

Hosts: Sylvia & Jack Wasson
Rooms: 4 (SB) $55
Full Breakfast
Credit Cards: No
Oct. 15-Apr. 15, reservations only
Notes: 2, 5, 12, 13

REDMOND

Cedarym — A Colonial B&B

1011 - 240th Avenue N.E.
Redmond, WA, 98053
(206) 868-4159

"... a few minutes and a couple centuries away" from Seattle, this authentic colonial reproduction home is situated on over 2 acres of landscaped grounds. Enjoy the gazebo-covered spa, walk in the woods, and breakfast by candlelight.

Hosts: Mary Ellen & Walt Brown
Rooms: 2 (SB) $48.65
Full Breakfast
Credit Cards: A, B
Notes: 2, 5, 9, 10, 11, 12, 14

SEABECK

Summer Song

Box 82
Seabeck, WA, 98380
(206) 830-5089

The majestic Olympic Mountains reflecting on Hood Canal provide a quiet, spectacular setting for this private waterfront cottage with its gentle touch of country comfort. The cottage will accommodate up to four guests and features a bedroom, living room, kitchen, bath, fireplace, TV, and VCR. A perfect place to relax, swim, boat, fish, or hike.

Hosts: Ron & Sharon Barney
Cottage: 1 (PB) $55-65
Full Breakfast
Credit Cards: A, B
Notes: 2, 5, 7, 9, 11, 14

SEATTLE

Capital Hill House

2215 East Prospect
Seattle, WA, 98112
(206) 322-1752

Elegantly furnished traditional brick house on a tree-lined street in an exclusive residential neighborhood. Near the University of Washington, Seattle Art Museum, Seattle Convention Center, and city center. Three hours from Canada. Hostess has traveled extensively in Europe, Canada, the US, and Mexico.

Host: Mary A. Wolf
Rooms: 3 (1 PB; 2 SB) $55
Full Breakfast
Credit Cards: No
Notes: 2, 5, 8, 9, 10, 11, 12, 14

Chambered Nautilus

5005 22nd Avenue NE
Seattle, WA, 98105
(206) 522-2536

A gracious 1915 Georgian colonial nestled high on a hill, furnished with a mixture of American and English antiques and reproductions. Offers excellent access to Seattle's theaters, restaurants, public transportation, shopping, bike and jogging trails, and the University of Washington campus.

Hosts: Bunny & Bill Hagemeyer
Rooms: 6 (4 PB; 2 SB) $59-95
Full Gourmet Breakfast
Credit Cards: A, B, C, E, F
Notes: 2, 5, 7, 9, 10, 11, 12, 14

Chelsea Station B&B Inn

4915 Linden Avenue North
Seattle, WA, 98103
(206) 547-6077

For a quiet, comfortable, and private accommodation, nothing beats Chelsea Station. With Seattle's rose gardens at our doorstep, you can breathe in the restorative calm. Walk Greenlake's exceptional wooded pathways, then try a soothing cup of tea or a nap in the afternoon. That's our style, and we welcome you to it. Member, ASTA, WBBG, SBBA.

Hosts: Dick & Marylou Jones
Rooms: 5 (PB) $69-89
Full Breakfast
Minimum stay holidays: 3
Credit Cards: A, B, C, D, E, F
Notes: 2, 5, 8 (over 11), 9, 10, 11, 12, 14

Galer Place B&B

Galer Place B&B

318 West Galer
Seattle, WA, 98119
(206) 282-5339

Quiet, cozy 1906 Victorian, close to downtown and Seattle center. Delicious full breakfasts. Four guest rooms, all furnished with antiques and private baths. Peace and tranquility within the city.

Hosts: Chris & Terry Giles
Rooms: 4 (PB) $80-90
Full Breakfast
Minimum stay weekends: 2
Credit Cards: A, B, C, E
Notes: 2, 5, 6, 7 (limited), 8 (over 12), 9, 10, 11, 12

Marit's B&B

6208 Palatine Avenue North
Seattle, WA, 98103
(206) 782-7900

Marit's is a charming ivy-covered, brick Tudor home in a quiet residential neighborhood. You will enjoy Scandinavian hospitality, elegant breakfasts served on fine china, and view of Puget Sound and the Olympic Mountains. Close to city and the University of Washington. Walk to Woodland Park Zoo and Green Lake.

Hosts: Carl & Marit Nelson
Rooms: 2 (SB) $55
Full Breakfast
Credit Cards: No
Notes: 2, 5, 8, 9, 10, 11, 12, 14

Mildred's B&B

1202 Fifteenth Avenue East
Seattle, WA, 98112
(206) 325-6072

A traditional 1890 Victorian gem in an elegant style. Old-fashioned hospitality awaits: red carpets, lace curtains, fireplace, grand piano, and wraparound porch. Across the street is the Seattle Art Museum, Flower Conservatory, and historic 44-acre Volunteer Park. Electric trolley at the front door. Minutes to city center, freeways, and all points of interest.

Host: Mildred Sarver
Rooms: 3 (SB) $55-66
Full Breakfast
Credit Cards: A, B, C
Notes: 2, 5, 8, 9, 10, 11, 12, 14

Mildred's B&B

NW Bed & Breakfast 180A

610 SW Broadway
Portland, OR, 97205
(503) 243-7616

Handsome turn-of-the-century home on a quiet street in the Capitol Hill area. One of many lovely older homes that have recently been restored in this neighborhood. Short ride and direct bus to downtown and the University of Washington. Near Volunteer Park, Seattle Art Museum. Walk to restaurants, cafes, and shops. Two-night minimum stay. Two rooms with double beds, private baths. $50.

NW Bed & Breakfast 165A

610 SW Broadway
Portland, OR, 97205
(503) 243-7616

Georgian brick, c. 1926, minutes to downtown by bus. Near the university and hospitals on First Hill. Walk two blocks to Volunteer Park, Seattle Art Museum, and many fine restaurants, boutiques, and theater. Sunny deck and garden for your enjoyment. Restricted smoking; resident dog. Two queen rooms, one room with a queen and a single, and one room with twin beds. Private or shared baths. $50-60.

Roberta's B&B Inn

1147 Sixteenth Avenue East
Seattle, WA, 98112
(206) 329-3326

A classic turn-of-the-century home nestled on a quiet tree-lined street in Seattle's historic Capitol Hill neighborhood. Five minutes from downtown, the University of Washington, two lakes, and public transportation. The hosts will gladly fill you in on all the local attractions, restaurants, and available activities.

Host: Roberta C. Barry
Rooms: 5 (4 PB; 1 SB) $75-95
Full Breakfast; early morning coffee
Minimum stay holidays: 2
Credit Cards: A, B, C, E
Notes: 2, 5, 8 (over 12), 9, 10, 11, 12

Roberta's B&B Inn

Salisbury House

750 Sixteenth Avenue East
Seattle, WA, 98112
(206) 328-8682

An elegant turn-of-the-century home on Capitol Hill, just minutes from Seattle's cultural and business activities. The spacious library, living room, and wraparound porch invite relaxation. Two blocks from a park and the Seattle Art Museum.

Hosts: Mary & Cathryn Wiese
Rooms: 4 (S2B) $60-70
Full Breakfast
Credit Cards: A, B, C, D, E
Notes: 2, 5, 8 (over 12), 9, 10, 11, 12, 14

Tugboat Challenger

Tugboat Challenger

809 Fairview Place North
Seattle, WA, 98109
(206) 340-1201

Restored 1944 tugboat in downtown Seattle. Carpeted, granite fireplace; bar; laundry. Refrigerators, TV, phone, VCR, sinks, sprinkler system, private entrance for each room. Restaurants, bars, classic and modern sailboats, powerboats, rowboats, and kayak rentals. Swimming. Featured in *Travel & Leisure, Cosmopolitan,* and many major papers.

Host: Jerry Brown
Rooms: 7 (4 PB; 3 SB) $50-110
Full Breakfast
Credit Cards: A, B, C
Notes: 2, 5, 7, 8, 9, 11, 14

Williams House B&B

1505 Fourth Avenue North
Seattle, WA, 98109
(206) 285-0810

A family B&B in an Edwardian home with much of the original woodwork and original gas-light fixtures. Decorated with antiques, most guest rooms have views of Seattle, the mountains, or the water. A sunny enclosed porch is shared by all. Close to downtown, the Space Needle, Public Market. Public transportation available.

Hosts: Susan, Doug & Daughters
Rooms: 5 (1 PB; 4 SB) $65-90
Full Breakfast
Credit Cards: A, B, C, E
Notes: 2, 5, 7 (limited to porches), 8 (by prior arrangement), 10, 11, 12

SEAVIEW

Shelburne Country Inn

Box 250
Seaview, WA, 98644
(206) 642-2442

Washington's oldest country inn, nestled between the Columbia River and Pacific Ocean. We'll pamper you with great food, friendly innkeepers, and exquisite furnishings. Restaurant on the premises. "One of the West Coast's premier country inns"—*Christian Science Monitor.*

Hosts: Laurie Anderson & David Campiche
Rooms: 16 (13 PB; 3 SB) $69-140
Gourmet Breakfast
Credit Cards: A, B, C
Notes: 2, 4, 5, 8, 9, 14

SEQUIM

Margie's B&B

120 Forrest Road
Sequim, WA, 98382
(206) 683-3565

A spacious contemporary ranch home on beautiful Sequim Bay. The fantastic water view is enhanced by year-round lush green surroundings, and the peace and quiet of country life. View of Mt. Baker.

Rooms: 6 (1 PB; 5 SB) $60-80
Full Breakfast

Seabreeze Beach Cottage

Credit Cards: A, B
Notes: 2, 8 (over 12), 9, 10, 12

SHELTON

Twin River Ranch B&B

E5730 Highway 3
Shelton, WA, 98584
(206) 426-1023

Grand old farmhouse with stone fireplace, beamed ceilings, rooms tucked under eaves. Salmon stream right outside. This 140-acre Angus ranch borders a saltwater bay just five miles north of Shelton. Southern Olympic Peninsula, Olympic National Park, Hood Canal, hiking all nearby.

Hosts: Bjorn & Phlorence Rohde
Rooms: 2 (SB) $40-50
Full Breakfast
Credit Cards: No
Notes: 2, 7 (limited), 9 (limited), 10, 11, 12

SILVERDALE

Seabreeze Beach Cottage

16609 Olympic View Road NW
Silverdale, WA, 98383
(206) 692-4648

Challenged by lapping waves at high tide, this private retreat will awaken your five senses with the smell of salty air, a taste of fresh oysters and clams, views of the Olympic Mountains, and the exhilaration of sun, surf, and sand. Spa at water's edge.

Host: Dennis Fulton
Rooms: 2 (PB) $119-149
Continental Breakfast
Credit Cards: A, B
Notes: 2, 5, 6, 8, 9, 11, 12, 14

SNOHOMISH

Countryman B&B

119 Cedar Street
Snohomish, WA, 98290
(206) 568-9622

An 1896 landmark Queen Anne Victorian near 250 antique shops. Library, art gallery, private parking, private airport nearby. Free limousine tour of the historic district offered.

Hosts: Larry & Sandy Countryman
Rooms: 3 (PB) $60
Full Breakfast
Credit Cards: A, B, C
Notes: 2, 5, 6, 8, 10, 11, 12, 14

NOTES: Credit cards accepted: A Master Card; B Visa; C American Express; D Discover Card; E Diners Club; F Other: 2 Personal checks accepted: 3 Lunch available: 4 Dinner available: 5 Open all year

SNOQUALMIE FALLS

The Old Honey Farm Country Inn

8910 384th Avenue SE
Snoqualmie Falls, WA, 98065
(206) 888-9399

Lovely ten-room New England style country inn. Beautiful rural setting with Cascade Mountains view. Gracious dining open to the public for breakfast, lunch, and dinner. Service bar. Snoqualmie Falls, winery, historic railroad, herb farm, shopping, golf, and hiking nearby. No smoking.

Hosts: Conrad & Mary Jean Potter & Marilyn Potter
Rooms: 10 (PB)
Full Breakfast
Credit Cards: A, B, D
Notes: 2 (in advance), 3, 4, 5, 8 (over 14), 9, 12, 13

SOUTH CLE ELUM

The Moore House Country B&B

526 Marie Street, Box 2861
South Cle Elum, WA, 98943
(509) 674-5939

The Moore House offers ten bright and airy rooms in a renovated railroad-crew hotel recently placed on the Historic Register. Accommodations range from economical to exquisite, including one that is a real caboose. They each capture the essence of the bygone era of railroading. Old print wallpaper, oak antiques, artifacts combine with the peaceful language of nature to create an ideal romantic interlude. Adjacent to Iron Horse Trail State Park.

Hosts: Connie & Monty Moore
Rooms: 10 (5 PB; 5 SB) $30-95
Full Breakfast
Minimum stay winter weekends & holidays: 2
Credit Cards: A, B, C
Notes: 2, 5, 8, 9, 12, 13, 14

SPOKANE

Luckey's Residence

West 828 28th Avenue
Spokane, WA, 99203
(509) 747-5774

This house, which resembles an English cottage, was built in the 1930s on the South Hill, among pine trees and volcanic rock. Two miles from downtown; two blocks from a scenic drive overlooking a canyon; two blocks to public swimming pool, tennis court, and children's play area. City bus one block.

Hosts: Royden & Patricia Luckey
Rooms: 4 (SB) $35
Full Breakfast
Credit Cards: No
Notes: 2, 5, 8, 10, 11, 12

Whispering Pines B&B

East 7504 44th Avenue
Spokane, WA, 99223
(509) 448-1433

Nestled in the pines of South Spokane, offering a panoramic view of the valley below. King and queen beds, private and shared baths, separate entrance to guests' TV sitting room, full breakfast, and air-conditioning. Kitchen and laundry facilities available. Minutes from town, and surrounded by woodland serenity and wildlife.

Hosts: The Campbells
Rooms: 3 (1 PB; 2 SB) From $48
Full Breakfast
Credit Cards: A, B
Notes: 2, 5, 9, 10, 11, 12, 14

TOKELAND

Tokeland Hotel

100 Hotel Road
Tokeland, WA, 98590
(206) 267-7006

A national historic landmark, the Tokeland Hotel is located on a peninsula bordering

Washington's Willapa Bay and the Pacific Ocean.

Host: Marlys Kemmish
Rooms: 18 (SB) $55-60
Full Breakfast
Credit Cards: A, B, C
Notes: 2, 3, 4, 5, 6, 7 (restricted), 8, 9, 11, 14

WINTHROP

Dammann's B&B

716 Highway 20 E
Winthrop, WA, 98862-0536
(509) 996-2484

Antique-filled guest rooms and sitting room, rec room, piano, and outdoor hot tub. This is a nonsmoking B&B. Located on the Methow River. The valley is a recreation paradise, with photography, seasonal hunting, fishing, hiking, and skiing.

Hosts: Hank & Jean Dammann
Rooms: 2 (1 PB; 1 SB) $45
Continental Breakfast
Credit Cards: No
Notes: 2, 5, 8, 9, 10, 11, 12, 13

West Virginia

BERKELEY SPRINGS

Highlawn Inn

304 Market Street
Berkeley Springs, WV, 25411
(304) 258-5700

Highlawn Inn, a restored Victorian, is located in a quaint mountain town famous for its historic mineral baths. Only two hours from Washington, DC, we specialize in romantic getaways for adults only. Antiques, decorator linens, private baths, color TVs, and air conditioning in all rooms. All kinds of recreation nearby.

Host: Sandra M. Kauffman
Rooms: 6 (PB) $70-90
Full Breakfast
Credit Cards: A, B
Notes: 2, 4 (some holidays & weekends), 5, 7, 9, 10, 11, 12

Highlawn Inn

BRAMWELL

Three Oaks & A Quilt

Box 84, Bramwell, WV, 24715
(304) 248-8316

Visitors to historic Bramwell come to view a most unique town of mansions built by bituminous coal operators in the early 1900s. Three Oaks & A Quilt is a delightfully relaxing Victorian experience. Quilts are artfully displayed; a "Whig Rose" hangs on the front porch wall. Reservations, please.

Host: B. J. Kahle
Rooms: 2 (PB and SB) $55
Full Breakfast
Credit Cards: No
Notes: 2, 5, 7 (limited), 8 (12 and over), 9, 10, 11, 12

CAIRO

Bias Farm B&B

Route 1, Box 284A
Cairo, WV, 26337
(304) 643-4517

Take a step into the past and spend some time in a restored log house built in the 1800s, nestled in a private valley. Enjoy miles of walking trails, catch and release fishing in two spring-fed lakes. Owners live in separate dwelling.

Hosts: Doris & Richard Bias
Rooms: 2 (SB) $45
Full Breakfast
Credit Cards: No
Notes: 2, 5, 9, 10, 11, 12

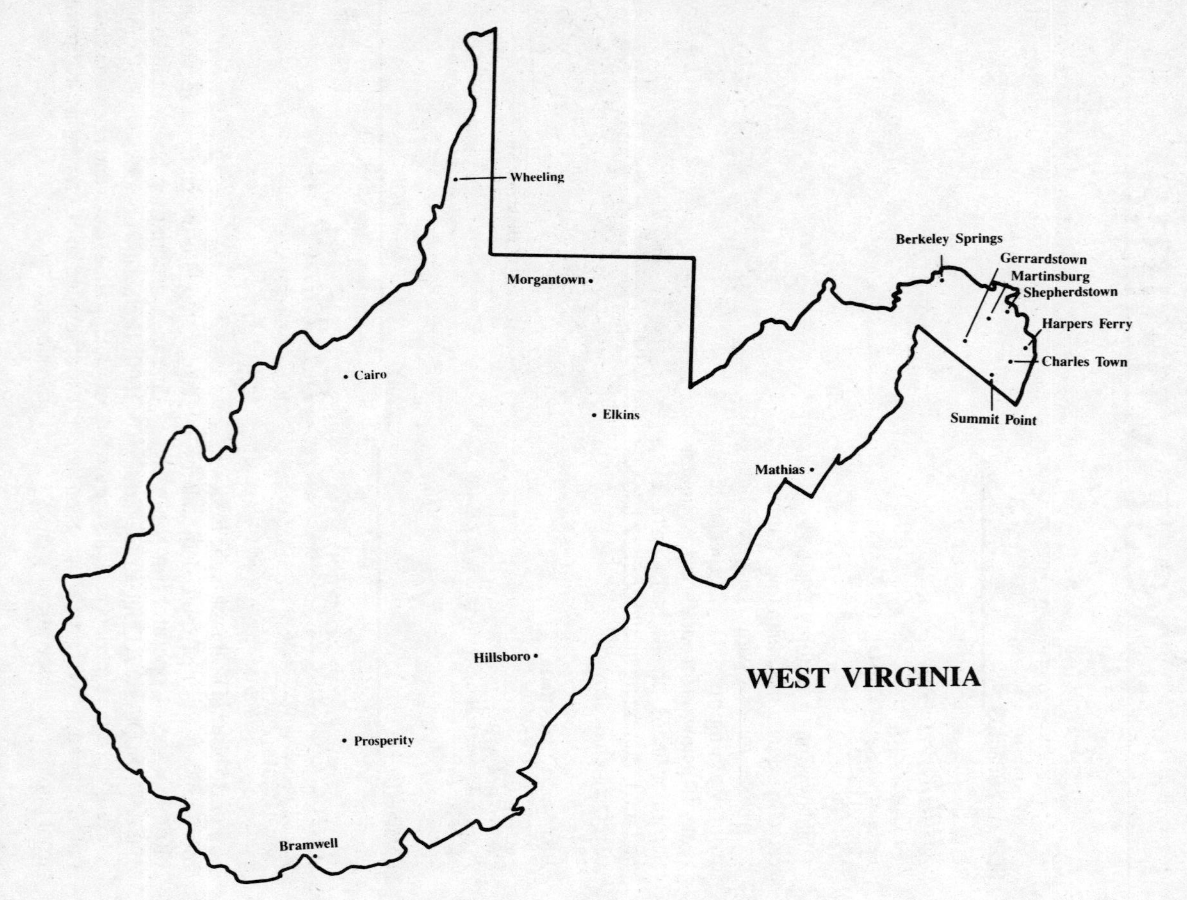
Wheeling
Morgantown
Berkeley Springs
Gerrardstown
Martinsburg
Shepherdstown
Harpers Ferry
Charles Town
Summit Point
Cairo
Elkins
Mathias
Hillsboro
Prosperity
Bramwell
WEST VIRGINIA

CHARLES TOWN

The Carriage Inn

417 East Washington Street
Charles Town, WV, 25414
(304) 728-8003

Each of the five bedrooms is large and airy, with its own private bath and queen canopy bed, and four of the rooms have working fireplaces. Charles Town is the home of the Charles Town races, the Jefferson County Museum, Old Oprah House, and the site of the John Brown Gallows. The inn is located eight miles from Harpers Ferry.

Hosts: Bob & Virginia Kaetzel
Rooms: 5 (PB) $65-95
Full Breakfast
Credit Cards: A, B
Notes: 2, 5, 9, 10, 11, 12

Cottonwood Inn

Route 2, Box 61-S
Kabletown Road & Mill Lane
Charles Town, WV, 25414
(304) 725-3371

The Cottonwood Inn offers B&B accommodations in a restored Georgian farmhouse (circa 1800). The inn is located on Bullskin Run in the historic Shenandoah Valley, near Harpers Ferry and Charles Town, and is furnished in antiques and period reproductions. Fireplaces in the dining room, parlor/library, and one guest room. We invite you to join us and enjoy the inn's peaceful secluded acres, memorable country breakfasts, and warm hospitality.

Hosts: Colin & Eleanor Simpson
Rooms: 7 (PB) $70-92
Full Breakfast
Credit Cards: A, B
Notes: 2, 5, 7, 8, 9, 10, 11, 12, 13 (XC), 14

Gilbert House B&B

Box 1104
Charles Town, WV, 25414
(304) 725-0637

Comfort, hospitality, and elegance describe this grand historic home, a magnificent greystone (circa 1760) on the National Register. Located in a quaint village near Harpers Ferry, Antietam battlefield, and I-81. Large rooms with private baths and fireplaces; tasteful antiques. Honeymoon suite available. Stream, wooden bridge, and gazebo nearby. Village ghost.

Hosts: Jean & Bernie Heiler
Rooms: 3 (PB) $85-130
Full Breakfast
Minimum stay weekends & holidays: 2
Credit Cards: A, B, F
Notes: 2, 5, 7, 9, 10, 11, 12

The Retreat at Buffalo Run

ELKINS

The Retreat at Buffalo Run

214 Harpertown Road
Elkins, WV, 26241
(304) 636-2960

Ideal location for exploring mountains, forests, and rivers of West Virginia. Secluded setting near Davis and Elkins College and Summer Augusta Festival, one mile from downtown Elkins and ten minutes from the commuter airport. Turn-of-the-century home on a 1-acre lot with tall oaks, hemlock, rhododendron groves, flower and vegetable gardens. Seven comfortable guest rooms and 3.5 baths. Hardy breakfast with homemade goods.

Hosts: The Rhoads
Rooms: 7 (S3.5B) $39
Continental Breakfast
Credit Cards: No
Notes: 2, 5, 8, 9, 10, 11, 13

Prospect Hill Farm

GERRARDSTOWN

Prospect Hill Farm

Box 135
Gerrardstown, WV, 25420
(304) 229-3346

Prospect Hill is a Georgian mansion set on 225 acres and listed on the National Register of Historic Places. Once a well-to-do gentleman's home, it has a permanent Franklin fireplace, antiques, and a hall mural depicting life in the early Republic. Guests may choose one of the beautifully appointed rooms in the main house or the former slave quarters, where rooms are complete with country kitchen and fireplace. There is much to do on this working farm near Harpers Ferry, Martinsburg, and Winchester.

Hosts: Charles & Hazel Hudock
Cottage: $85-95
Rooms: (PB) $75-85
Full Breakfast
Credit Cards: A, B
Notes: 2, 5, 7, 8 (in cottage), 9, 10, 11, 12, 14

HARPERS FERRY

Fillmore Street B&B

Fillmore Street
Harpers Ferry, WV, 25425
(301) 321-5634; (304) 535-2619

Mountain view, antique-furnished Victorian home known for its hospitality, service, and gourmet breakfast. Private accommodations and baths, in-room television, air-conditioning, complimentary sherry and tea, and a blazing fire on cool mornings.

Hosts: Alden & James Addy
Rooms: 2 (PB) $65-72
Full Breakfast
Credit Cards: No
Closed Thanksgiving, Christmas, and New Year's Day
Notes: 2, 7, 8 (over 12), 9

HILLSBORO

The Current

HC 64, Box 135
Hillsboro, WV, 24946
(304) 653-4722

A country home surrounded by a Morgan horse farm just a short walk from the Greenbrier River and a 75-mile trail. Near state parks, national forest, Cranberry Wilderness, and the Pearl S. Buck home. Mountain biking, cross-country skiing, golf trips arranged. Large deck with outdoor hot tub; antiques and quilts.

Hosts: Leslee McCarty & John Walkup
Rooms: 3 (SB) $30-45
Full Breakfast
Credit Cards: A, B
Notes: 2, 5, 8, 9, 10, 11, 12, 13

LEWISBURG

Lynn's Inn B&B

Route 4, Box 40
Lewisburg, WV, 24901
(304) 645-2003

A comfortable home in a farm setting with full country breakfast. Downtown historic

Lewisburg is 3 miles away; the state fair, 4.5 miles. Green Brier Hotel, 10 miles. Within easy driving distance to some of the best hiking, fishing, hunting, golf, spelunking, white water, and skiing places in the East.

Hosts: Richard & Lynn McLaughlin
Rooms: 3 (PB) $40-50
Full Breakfast
Credit Cards: No
Notes: 2, 5, 8, 9, 10, 11, 12

MARTINSBURG

Boydville, The Inn at Martinsburg

601 South Queen Street
Martinsburg, WV, 25401
(304) 263-1448

This historic manor house on 10 acres still contains the original wallpaper and woodwork. Described by *Travel & Leisure* as "a country inn as stupendous as any Relais and Chateaux lodging on the other side of the Atlantic." Only 1.5 hours from downtown Washington, in the heart of Civil War country.

Hosts: Owen Sullivan & Ripley Hotch
Rooms: 6 (PB) $100-115
Full Breakfast
Credit Cards: A, B, C
Notes: 2, 5, 9, 10, 11, 12, 14

Dunn Country Inn

Route 3, Box 33 J
Martinsburg, WV, 25401
(304) 263-8646

The Dunn Country Inn is surrounded by acres of rolling pasture and woodlands, providing a tranquil setting. Large native stone home built in 1805, with an addition in 1873, offers diversity in design and decor. Near Harpers Ferry National Historic Park, white-water rafting, canoeing, horseback riding, race track, and sixty-store outlet mall.

Hosts: Prince & Dianna Dunn
Rooms: 5 (1 PB; 4 SB) $75-100
Full Breakfast
Credit Cards: A, B
Notes: 2, 5, 10, 11, 12

MATHIAS

Valley View Farm

Route 1, Box 467
Mathias, WV, 26812
(304) 897-5229

National Geographic's America's Great Hideaways calls Valley View Farm "Your home away from home." This cattle and sheep farm of 250 acres specializes in excellent food and friendly hosts. Near Lost River State Park; horseback riding and other recreation available in season. Craft shops.

Hosts: Ernest & Edna Shipe
Rooms: 4 (SB) $40
Full Breakfast
Credit Cards: No
Notes: 2, 4, 5, 6, 7, 8, 9, 10, 11

MORGANTOWN

Chestnut Ridge School

1000 Stewartstown Road
Morgantown, WV, 26505
(304) 598-2262

A restored 1920s elementary school welcomes you with warm hospitality. We are surrounded by outstanding scenic attractions and recreational areas. Come "back to school," and enjoy personal attention, our special muffins, and beautiful sunsets.

Hosts: Sam & Nancy Bonasso
Rooms: 4 (PB) $52.32-58.86
Continental Breakfast
Minimum stay football weekends: 2
Credit Cards: No
Notes: 2, 5, 8, 9, 10, 11, 12

PROSPERITY

Prosperity Farmhouse B&B

Box 393
Prosperity, WV, 25909
(304) 255-4245

Thomas Shepherd Inn

Our B&B is situated in rural West Virginia; however, it is just six miles from Beckley, which offers all the attractions of a small city of 20,000. We work the 80-acre farm by raising cattle, chickens, goats, horses, a huge garden, feed corn, and hay. The building itself is not part of the house; it sits thirty feet behind it. Totally private. Upstairs includes bedroom that sleeps four. Downstairs there is a great room with kitchenette, bath, and dining area that sleeps two. Near white-water rafting, Winterplace Ski Resort, state parks, New River Gorge, theater.

Hosts: John & Tara Wooton
Rooms: 2 (SB)
Full Breakfast
Credit Cards: A, B
Notes: 2, 7, 8, 9, 10, 11, 12, 13, 14

SHEPHERDSTOWN

Shang-Ra-La Vacation Farm

Terrapin Neck, Route 1, Box 156
Shepherdstown, WV, 25443
(304) 876-2391

Enjoy the farm and wildlife preserve on the Potomac River in the beautiful and peaceful Shenandoah Valley. Four duplex efficiency cottages. Prepare your own meals or eat in our dining room. Walk the nature trails or sight-see in Shepherdstown, the oldest town in the state, or Harpers Ferry. Sixty-five miles from Washington, DC or Baltimore.

Hosts: Richard & Sandy Hessenauer
Cabin: $50/night; $200/week; $400/month
Full Breakfast extra
Minimum stay holidays: 2
Credit Cards:-A, B
Notes: 2, 4, 5, 7, 8, 9, 10, 11, 12

Thomas Shepherd Inn

Box 1162
Shepherdstown, WV, 25443
(304) 876-3715

Small, charming inn in a quaint, historic Civil War town that offers that special hospitality of the past. Guests find fresh flowers at their bedsides, fluffy towels and special soaps in their baths, complimentary beverage by the fireside, memorable breakfasts. Bicycles, picnics available.

Hosts: Margaret Perry
Rooms: 6 (4 PB; 2 SB) $75-90
Full Breakfast
Credit Cards: A, B
Notes: 2, 5, 7 (limited), 8 (over 12), 9, 10, 11, 12

SUMMIT POINT

Countryside

P.O. Box 57
Summit Point, WV, 25446
(304) 725-2614

Countryside is located in a charming village near historic Harpers Ferry and is decorated with items old and new: quilts, baskets, books, and collectibles. Guests are welcomed with a cheerful room, bath, and breakfast amid lovely rural scenery.

Hosts: Lisa & Daniel Hileman
Rooms: 2 (PB) $53-63.60
Continental Breakfast
Credit Cards: A, B
Notes: 2, 5, 8, 9, 10, 11, 12

WHEELING

Stratford Springs

355 Oglebay Drive
Wheeling, WV, 26003
(304) 233-5100

An historic inn nestled on 30 acres of rolling wooded hills in the Mountain State's historic Ohio Valley, ten minutes from I-70. Elegant large rooms and suites, casual to fine dining, unique gift shoppes, swimming, tennis, golf, and athletic center. Adjacent to Oglebay Park and near other points of interest.

Host: Jeannette Fore
Rooms: 6 (PB) $85-150
Continental Breakfast
Credit Cards: A, B, C
Notes: 2, 3, 4, 5, 7, 8, 9, 10, 11, 12, 13, 14

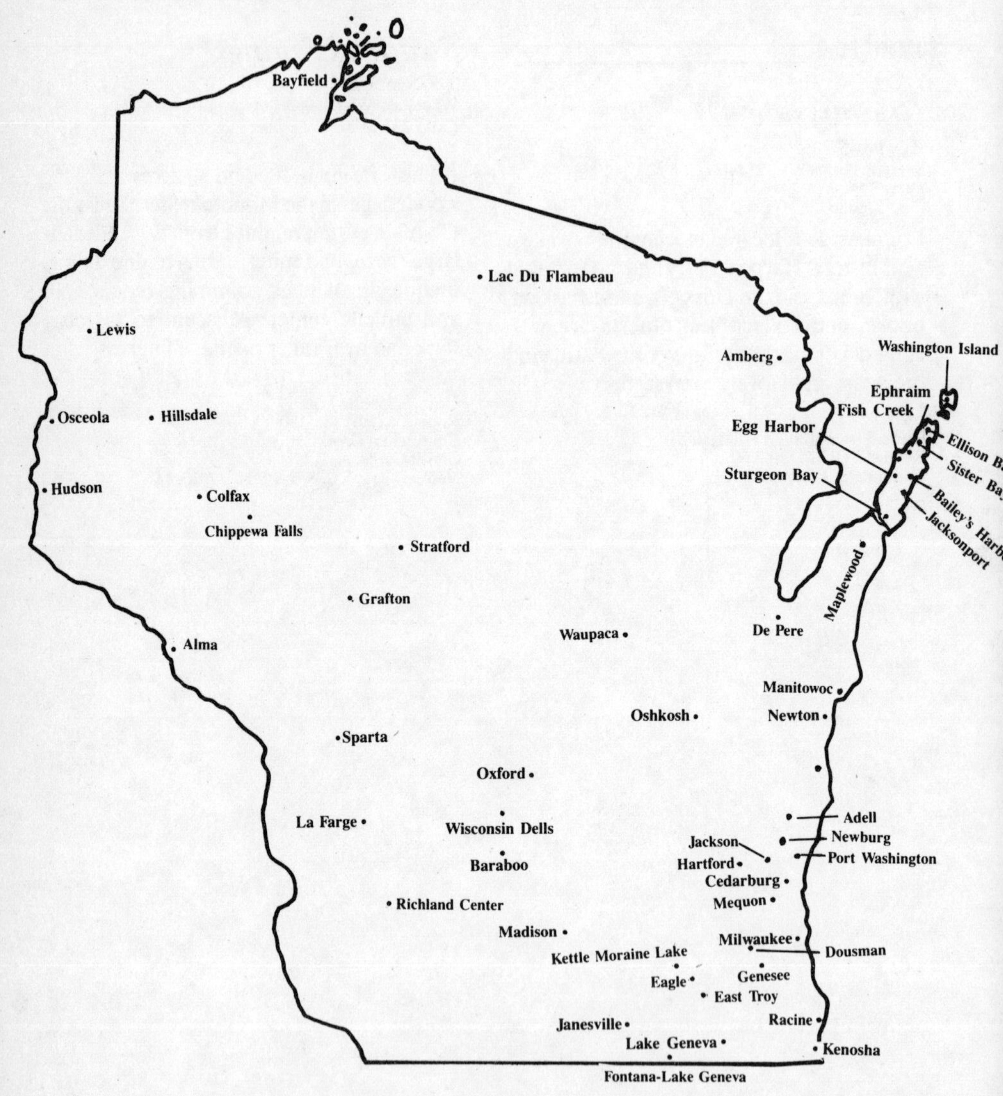

Bayfield
Lac Du Flambeau
Lewis
Amberg
Washington Island
Ephraim
Fish Creek
Egg Harbor
Osceola
Hillsdale
Hudson
Colfax
Chippewa Falls
Sturgeon Bay
Stratford
Maplewood
Grafton
Waupaca
De Pere
Alma
Manitowoc
Oshkosh
Newton
Sparta
Oxford
La Farge
Wisconsin Dells
Baraboo
Adell
Jackson
Newburg
Hartford
Port Washington
Cedarburg
Mequon
Richland Center
Madison
Milwaukee
Kettle Moraine Lake
Dousman
Genesee
Eagle
East Troy
Racine
Janesville
Lake Geneva
Kenosha
Fontana-Lake Geneva

WISCONSIN

Wisconsin

ADELL

Hillside Contemporary

B&B Guest Homes
Route 2, Algoma, WI, 54201
(414) 743-9742

Private guest area is in the spacious lower level of this multi-level contemporary on the side of a hill. Separate outside entrance, beautiful views of the yard through full-length windows. Full breakfast; no smoking; children welcome. $42.

ALMA

The Gallery House

215 North Main Street
Alma, WI, 54610
(608) 685-4975

A traditional B&B in a historic 1861 mercantile building. Three guest rooms, full breakfast. John Runions watercolor gallery and the Spice Shop, with herbs, spices, teas, and gifts.

Hosts: John & Joan Runions
Rooms: 3 (SB) $40
Full Breakfast
Credit Cards: No
Notes: 2, 5, 9, 10, 11, 12

AMBERG

Northwoods Log Lodge

B&B Guest Homes
Route 2, Algoma, WI, 54201
(414) 743-9742

Secluded home on the shore of a lake. 120 acres available for exploring or cross-country skiing. Two-night minimum; no smoking; generous continental breakfast. $115.

BAILEYS HARBOR

Kangaroo Lake Home

B&B Guest Homes
Route 2, Algoma, WI, 54201
(414) 743-9742

Comfortable family home surrounded by gardens on a large lot invites relaxing on the lakeshore or in the yard. Quiet setting, yet close to Door peninsula activities. Continental breakfast; no smoking or children. $55.

BARABOO

The Barrister's House

226 Ninth Avenue
Baraboo, WI, 53913
(608) 356-3344

Colonial charm and simple elegance in a parklike setting. Unique guest rooms; library with fireplace; sitting room with game table, piano and fireplace; screened porch, veranda, and terrace. Gracious continental breakfast. Located in the heart of the Baraboo/Wisconsin Dells/Devils Lake vacationland.

Hosts: Glen & Mary Schulz
Rooms: 4 (PB) $50-60
Continental Breakfast
Credit Cards: No
Notes: 2, 5, 8 (over 6), 9, 10, 11, 12, 13

The Washington House Inn

BAYFIELD

Old Rittenhouse Inn

Box 584
Bayfield, WI, 54814
(715) 779-5111

Our inn is a beautiful Victorian mansion built in 1890 overlooking Lake Superior. Guest rooms are furnished with antiques and working fireplaces. Dinner, offered nightly by reservation, features fine formal service.

Hosts: Jerry & Mary Phillips
Rooms: 20 (PB) $69-159
Continental Breakfast (full available at extra charge)
Minimum stay May-Oct. weekends: 2
Credit Cards: A, B
Notes: 2, 5, 8, 9, 10, 11, 12, 13

CEDARBURG

Stagecoach Inn

West 61 North 520, Washington Avenue
Cedarburg, WI, 53012
(414) 375-0208

The Stagecoach Inn is a historic restored 1853 stone building of Greek Revival style. Twelve cozy rooms offer stenciled walls and Laura Ashley comforters, central air conditioning, and private baths. Suites with large whirlpool baths are available. Located in the heart of historic Cedarburg, the inn also features an on-premises pub with a 100-year-old bar and a chocolate shop.

Hosts: Liz & Brook Brown
Rooms: 12 (PB) $55-85
Continental Breakfast
Credit Cards: A, B, C
Notes: 2, 5, 9, 10, 11, 12, 13, 14

The Washington House Inn

West 62 North 573 Washington Avenue
Cedarburg, WI, 53012
(414) 375-3550; (800) 369-4088

Built in 1884 and listed on the National Registry, The Washington House Inn is located in the heart of the Cedarburg historic district. Rooms feature antique furnishings, whirlpool baths, fireplaces. Walking distance to Cedar Creek Settlement antique shops and fine dining.

Host: Wendy Porterfield
Rooms: 29 (PB) $61.95-145.95
Continental Buffet Breakfast
Credit Cards: A, B, C, D, E, F
Notes: 2, 5, 7, 8, 9, 10, 11, 12, 13

The Willson House

CHIPPEWA FALLS

The Willson House

320 Superior Street
P.O. Box 532
Chippewa Falls, WI, 54729
(715) 723-0055

NOTES: Credit cards accepted: A Master Card; B Visa; C American Express; D Discover Card; E Diners Club; F Other: 2 Personal checks accepted: 3 Lunch available: 4 Dinner available: 5 Open all year

The Willson House is a 103-year-old Queen Anne Victorian that has been renovated and furnished with antiques. There are rooms available with fireplaces and sitting porches. Chippewa Falls is the home of Leinenkugel's Brewery, which offers tours. The Cook-Rutledge Mansion is one block away. Tours are given May-October. There are two large scenic parks and Lake Wissota nearby; tandem bike available.

Hosts: Tom & Barb Knowlton
Rooms: 4 (1.5 PB; 2.5 SB) $45-65
Full Breakfast
Credit Cards: No
Closed Christmas Eve & Day
Notes: 2, 5, 7 (restricted), 8 (over 12), 9, 10, 11, 12, 13

COLFAX

Son-Ne-Vale Farm

Route 1, Box 132
Colfax, WI, 54730
(715) 962-4342

Enjoy staying in the large farmhouse or one of the two duplex cottages available. Nearby bowling, golf, fishing, restaurants, historical sites, and museums. Tainter Lake is only fourteen miles away for boating and fishing.

Host: Lillian Sonnenberg
Rooms: 4 (2 PB; 2 SB) $45
Full Breakfast
Credit Cards: No
Closed Oct. 15-April 15
Notes: 2, 4, 6, 7, 8, 9, 11, 12

DE PERE

Colonial Homestead

B&B Guest Homes
Route 2, Algoma, WI, 54201
(414) 743-9742

Just ten minutes to downtown Green Bay and close to Highway 41. Summertime guests can enjoy the lovely garden and large pool. Continental breakfast; no smoking or children. $45-65.

DOUSMAN

B&B of Milwaukee I1

1916 West Donges Bay Road
Mequon, WI, 53092
(414) 242-9680

Located on 3.5 acres of rolling countryside. Double bed with private bath. Guests may use hosts' bicycles or swim in the inground pool. Located near many lakes, golf courses, cross-country ski trails, and fine restaurants. $40-50.

EAGLE

Eagle Centre House B&B

W370 S9590 Hwy. 67
Eagle, WI, 53119
(414) 363-4700

Replicated 1850s Greek Revival stagecoach inn decorated with antiques on 16 secluded acres in the southern Kettle Moraine Forest. Four large chambers with private baths; two with whirlpools. Near "Old World Wisconsin," the State of Wisconsin's Outdoor Living History Museum. Ski, bike, hike, shop, golf, fish, swim, or horseback ride.

Hosts: Riene & Dean Herriges
Rooms: 4 (PB) $69-99 + tax
Full Breakfast weekends; Continental weekdays
Credit Cards: A, B, C
Notes: 2, 5, 8 (limited), 9, 11, 12, 13

EAST TROY

Greystone Farms B&B

770 Adam's Church Road
East Troy, WI, 53120
(414) 495-8485

105-year-old farm home on a quiet country road, beautifully decorated in semi-Victorian fashion. Comfortable and friendly, with an excellent full breakfast. Near Kettle Moraine State Forest, Old World Wisconsin, hiking, skiing, bicycling. Small farm animals.

Hosts: The Leibners
Rooms: 4 (SB) $45-55
Full Breakfast
Credit Cards: A, B
Notes: 2, 5, 7, 8, 9, 10, 11, 12, 13

EGG HARBOR

Country Gardens B&B

6421 Highway 42
Egg Harbor, WI, 54209
(414) 743-7434

Enjoy the fields and forests of this 160-acre Door County fruit and grain farm. This 1900s home radiates warmth and comfort. Four bedrooms share two baths. Balcony; full breakfast in striking country kitchen varies daily. Preferred Host Award in 1988 and 1989. Located close to the many and varied activities that Door County is famous for. Brochure available; reservations preferred.

Hosts: Jim & Crystal Barnard
Rooms: 4 (S2B) $55-85
Full Breakfast
Credit Cards: A, B
Notes: 2, 5, 8, 9, 10, 11, 12, 13, 14

ELLISON BAY

Europe Lake Hide-a-Way

B&B Guest Homes
Route 2, Algoma, WI, 54201
(414) 743-9742

Hidden away near the tip of Door County, this home has a large deck where breakfast is served in warm weather. Just a few minutes from Newport State Park, so guests can easily enjoy beautiful sand beaches and trails. Cross-country ski out the door in winter. $50-65.

EPHRAIM

Eagle Harbor Inn

9914 Water Street, Box 72
Ephraim, WI, 54211
(414) 854-2121

Nestled in the heart of historic Ephraim, Eagle Harbor is a gracious, antique-filled country inn. Centrally located, across from the lake, and close to the boat ramp, golf course, park, beach, and cross-country ski trails.

Hosts: Ronald & Barbara Schultz
Rooms: 9 (PB) $67-98
Full Breakfast
Credit Cards: A, B
Notes: 2, 5, 9, 10, 11, 12, 13, 14

Hillside Hotel of Ephraim

P.O. Box 17
Ephraim, WI, 54211
(800) 423-7023; (414) 854-2417

Hillside is a restored country Victorian inn on Eagle Harbor, Ephraim, in beautiful Door County. Well-known for full specialty breakfasts and gourmet dining, Hillside features original furnishings, a 96-foot veranda, and a large private beach. Located near shops, galleries, restaurants, and cultural events. Complimentary brochure.

Hosts: The McNeils
Rooms: 12 (SB) $65
Full Breakfast
Credit Cards: A, B, C, D
Notes: 2, 4, 5, 8, 9, 10, 11, 12, 13, 14

FISH CREEK

Thorp House Inn

Box 490
Fish Creek, WI, 54212
(414) 868-2444

A turn-of-the-century historic home with a bay view. Four romantic guest rooms, parlor with stone fireplace, and cozy library, all furnished in fine antiques and lots of authentic detail. Fireplace cottages done in country antiques also available.

Hosts: Christine & Sverre Falck-Pedersen
Rooms: 4 (SB) $55.92-69.63
Continental Breakfast
Credit Cards: No

Closed winter, except for weekends
Notes: 2, 9, 10, 11, 12, 13

Thorp House Inn

FONTANA-LAKE GENEVA

B&B of Milwaukee I4

1916 West Donges Bay Road
Mequon, WI, 53092
(414) 242-9680

Lovingly decorated ranch home perched on a hill with beautiful views, front and back. Stenciling, wicker, and seamstress touches. Crepes are a specialty at breakfast. Queen bed, private bath. $60.

GENESEE

B&B of Milwaukee I2

1916 West Donges Bay Road
Mequon, WI, 53092
(414) 242-9680

Located southwest of Waukesha, close to many lakes, ski trails, and golf courses. Spacious contemporary with manicured grounds, spa, exercise room, and fire pit. Guest room on the upper level has a double bed and private bath. $45-55.

GRANTON

Artist's Home

B&B Guest Homes
Route 2
Algoma, WI, 54201
(414) 743-9742

Near Neillsville and thirty minutes from Marshfield Clinic, set in a picturesque village in central Wisconsin Amish country. Rooms have semi-private entrance and are near hostess's art studio. Excellent hunting and fishing in the area. Full breakfast; no smoking; children welcome. $40-45.

HARTFORD

B&B of Milwaukee J2

1916 West Donges Bay Road
Mequon, WI, 53092
(414) 242-9680

A pleasant 45-minute drive from downtown Milwaukee to this Victorian inn with period antiques. Close to Holy Hill, Pike Lake, cross-country and downhill skiing. Four rooms, three with shared bath. $40-60.

HILLSDALE

Country Setting

B&B Guest Homes
Route 2
Algoma, WI, 54201
(414) 743-9742

A secluded home in the woods with antiques galore. Excellent golf just three miles away. Ski or snowmobile from the front door.

Many lakes in the area. Full breakfast; children over 4 welcome. $45-50.

HUDSON

Jefferson-Day House

1109 3rd Street
Hudson, WI, 54016
(715) 386-7111

This 1857 home offers antique collections, air-conditioned rooms, and three-course fireside breakfasts. The pleasing decor and friendly atmosphere will relax you, while the nearby St. Croix River, Octagon House Museum, and Phipps Theatre for the Arts will bring you enjoyment. Two rooms have double whirlpools.

Hosts: Sharon, Wally, and Marjorie Miller
Rooms: 3 (PB) $75-135
Full Breakfast weekends, continental weekdays
Credit Cards: No
Notes: 2, 5, 8 (over 9), 9, 11, 12, 13, 14

JACKSON

B&B of Milwaukee J1

1916 West Donges Bay Road
Mequon, WI, 53092
(414) 242-9680

An 1844 log home, with a twenty-foot-high fieldstone fireplace, on 4 acres. Near ski trails and slopes, West Bend, and shops in Cedarburg. Eleven rooms. $32-56.

JACKSONPORT

Country Home in the Woods

B&B Guest Homes
Route 2
Algoma, WI, 54201
(414) 743-9742

Set in 31 acres of woods just two miles from Whitefish Dunes State Park, this large ranch home has a snowmobile trail and various hiking opportunities. Convenient to all the joys of Door County. Full breakfast; smoking allowed; children welcome. $55.

JANESVILLE

Jackson Street Inn B&B

210 South Jackson Street
Janesville, WI, 53545
(608) 754-7250; (800) 222-3209

Comfortable Victorian air-conditioned home. Leaded-glass windows and cushioned window seats in the spacious, cheerful sleeping rooms. Sitting room with books, games, magazines, and menus from nearby restaurants. Marble fireplaces, intricate oak paneling, coffered ceilings in the dining and TV rooms. Putting green, shuffleboard court, attractive landscaped lawn and gardens. Near I-90 on Highway 11. Off-street parking.

Hosts: Ilah & Bob Sessler
Rooms: 4 (2 PB; 2 SB) $50-60
Full Breakfast
Credit Cards: A, B
Notes: 2, 5, 7, 8, 9, 10, 11, 12, 13 (XC), 14

KENOSHA

The Manor House

6536 Third Avenue
Kenosha, WI, 53143
(414) 658-0014

Romantic, breath-taking stately brick Georgian mansion overlooking Lake Michigan in the heart of Kenosha's lakeshore historic district. Listed on the National Register of Historic Places. Furnished with carefully selected antiques and surrounded by beautifully landscaped grounds. Midway between Chicago and Milwaukee. Meeting rooms available. Weekday discounts and corporate rates.

Hosts: Janice & Cecil Nichols
Rooms: 4 (PB) $99.90-144.30
Continental Breakfast

Credit Cards: A, B, C
Notes: 2, 5, 7 (restricted), 8 (12 and over), 9, 10, 11, 12, 13, 14

KETTLE MORAINE LAKE

B&B of Milwaukee J7

1916 West Donges Bay Road
Mequon, WI, 53092
(414) 242-9680

Treat yourself to a quality lakeside getaway. The private farmhouse suite has three rooms with a convenient kitchen, bath, and sitting room with wood-burning stove. Furnished with handmade quilts, braided rugs, and lots of atmosphere. Accommodates up to six people. Also on the property is an authentic 1800 log home that has been expertly restored. Two bedrooms with private baths, kitchen area with microwave. TV and wood-burning stove/fireplace. Accommodates up to six people. $55-75.

LAC DU FLAMBEAU

Ty-Bach B&B

3104 Simpson Lane
Lac du Flambeau, WI, 54538
(715) 588-7851

For a relaxing getaway anytime of the year, share our modern home on the shore of a tranquil northwoods lake. Guest quarters include a large living area and a deck overlooking our "Golden Pond." Eighty acres of woods to explore, Native American cultural attractions; listen to the loons!

Hosts: Janet & Kermit Bekkum
Rooms: 2 (PB) $45-50
Full Breakfast
Credit Cards: No
Notes: 2, 5, 6, 9, 11, 13 (XC)

LA FARGE

Trillium

Route 2, Box 121
La Farge, WI, 54639
(608) 625-4492

Your own private cottage located on our farm amid 85 acres of fields and woods, near a tree-lined brook. Situated in a thriving Amish farming community just thirty-five miles southeast of La Crosse.

Host: Rosanne Boyett
Cottage: 1 (PB) $52.50-63
Type of Beds: 2 Twin; 2 Double
Full Breakfast
Children under 12 stay without charge
Credit Cards: No
Notes: 2, 5, 7, 8, 9, 10, 11, 12, 13

Trillium

LAKE GENEVA

B&B of Milwaukee I5

1916 West Donges Bay Road
Mequon, WI, 53092
(414) 242-9680

Lovely turn-of-the-century home with many antiques. Five rooms, private baths, lake view, private dock. Full breakfast. Adjacent cottage with kitchen and lounge area and four rooms on property. Call for rates.

Eleven Gables Inn on the Lake

493 Wrigley Drive
Lake Geneva, WI, 53147
(414) 248-8393; (414) 248-6096

Nestled in evergreens, guarded by giant oaks, this quaint carpenter's gothic, located in the Edgewater Historical District 1.5 blocks from downtown, offers rooms, suites, bridal chamber, and 2-3 bedroom country cottages. Fireplaces, wet bars, down comforters, balconies, courtyards, private pier, bicycles, watercraft. Prime all-season resort area.

Host: Audrey Milliette
Rooms: 12 (7 PB; 5 SB) $79-135
Cottages: 2
Full Breakfast
Credit Cards: A, B, C
Notes: 2 (in advance), 5, 6, 7 (restricted), 8, 9, 10, 11, 12, 13, 14

Elizabethian Inn

463 Wrigley Drive
Lake Geneva, WI, 53147
(414) 248-9131

The inn, on the lakefront of Lake Geneva, has its own pier for swimming, sunbathing, boating, and fishing. Enjoy the comfortable, warm atmosphere of an old New England inn with high poster beds, beautiful old quilts, and antique furniture.

Host: Elizabeth Farrell
Rooms: 10 (PB) $85-95
Full Breakfast
Minimum stay weekends & holidays: 2
Credit Cards: A, B
Notes: 2, 5, 8 (over 12), 9, 10, 11, 12, 13

LAKE MICHIGAN

B&B of Milwaukee J4

1916 West Donges Bay Road
Mequon, WI, 53092
(414) 242-9680

Beautiful home on Lake Michigan with a beach just beyond the sun porch door. Paddle-boat and beach hiking. Large room with queen hideabed, private bath, private entrance, and separate spa room. Near Kohler and Sheboygan. Full breakfast. Dogs and cats in residence. $90.

LEWIS

7 Pines Lodge

Box 4
Lewis, WI, 54851
(715) 653-2323

Rustic elegance and country warmth await you at this historic lodge set on 57 acres amid virgin white pines, a private trout stream, and bountiful nature. Come rejuvenate with us.

Host: Joan Simpson
Rooms: 8 (5 PB; 3 SB) $63-98
Continental or Full Breakfast
Minimum stay weekends: 2
Credit Cards: A, B
Notes: 2, 4, 5, 8, 9, 10, 11, 12, 13(XC)

MADISON

The Collins House

704 East Gorham Street
Madison, WI, 53703
(608) 255-4230

On the shores of Lake Mendota in downtown Madison, this restored home of the Prairie School of Architecture is listed on the National Register of Historic Places.

Hosts: Barb & Mike Pratzel
Rooms: 4 (PB) $66.08-95.20
Full Breakfast weekends; Continental weekdays
Minimum stay holidays: 2
Credit Cards: A, B
Notes: 2, 5, 6 (restricted), 7 (restricted), 8, 9 (restricted), 10, 11, 12, 13

Mansion Hill Inn

424 North Pinckney Street
Madison, WI, 53703
(608) 255-3999

Eleven luxurious rooms, each with private bath. Whirlpool tubs, fireplaces, stereo systems, remote cable television, and mini-bars. Private wine cellar. VCRs and access to athletic club available on request. Refreshments served daily in the parlour.

Host: Polly Elder
Rooms: 11 (PB) $112-280
Continental Breakfast
Credit Cards: A, B, C
Notes: 2, 4 (with notice), 5, 7, 9, 14

MANITOWOC

Country Estate

B&B Guest Homes
Route 2
Algoma, WI, 54201
(414) 743-9742

A restored 1885 German-style brick farm home. Two rebuilt grand pianos grace the living room. Host will accompany musicians or play duo piano numbers. No TV to distract guests. Excellent fishing, hunting, and skiing are nearby. Children welcome; full breakfast; no smoking. $45.

MAPLEWOOD

Guest's Delight

B&B Guest Homes
Route 2
Algoma, WI, 54201
(414) 743-9742

A large, tastefully decorated colonial home adjacent to Annaphee State Trail. Slightly south of Sturgeon Bay, in beautiful Door County. Easy drive to swimming, boating, fishing waters, and the rest of the Door peninsula. Full farm breakfast; children welcome. $49.

MEQUON

Historic Country Home

B&B Guest Homes
Route 2
Algoma, WI, 54201
(414) 743-9742

This large stone farmhouse on the historic register is a veteran of house tours. Set on spacious hidden grounds, the home is decorated in Early American antiques and fine reproductions. Well-known artist and her husband have their studio and shop on the grounds. Generous continental breakfast; no smoking. $55-60.

MILWAUKEE

B&B of Milwaukee A1

1916 West Donges Bay Road
Mequon, WI, 53092
(414) 242-9680

Ideal location within walking distance to all major attractions. Turn-of-the-century Victorian, renovated in 1982 with a beautiful, serene, contemporary interior. Guests may use the entire first floor: sitting room, meeting room, kitchen, and dining room. Bedroom with queen bed and private bath. Lower level has queen bed, private bath, and sitting room. Air-conditioning; resident cat. $70.

B&B of Milwaukee B1

1916 West Donges Bay Road
Mequon, WI, 53092
(414) 242-9680

Lovely Tudor home in the city featuring leaded glass windows and natural woodwork. British hosts offer their special touch of traditional B&B. The host is a language professor at a nearby university. Second-floor guest room with twin beds and private bath. $40-45.

B&B of Milwaukee B2

1916 West Donges Bay Road
Mequon, WI, 53092
(414) 242-9680

Historic Register home with two rooms on the second floor, both with queen beds. The master bedroom has an adjacent sitting alcove, canopy bed, and decorative fireplace. Both rooms have private baths. Breakfast is served on heirloom china in the dining room. Smoking is allowed. $65-75.

B&B of Milwaukee B4

1916 West Donges Bay Road
Mequon, WI, 53092
(414) 242-9680

Tudor home with a mammoth third-floor suite, beautifully decorated with stained and beveled glass and oak woodwork. Skylights. The bedroom has a double bed. Sitting area has stereo and TV. Private bath with whirlpool. Children welcome; full breakfast. $70-80.

B&B of Milwaukee B5

1916 West Donges Bay Road
Mequon, WI, 53092
(414) 242-9680

This comfortable first-floor apartment suite has two double rooms, a living room, full bath, kitchen, and third room with a double futon. Very near the University of Wisconsin and Columbia Hospital. $45-65. Family rates available.

B&B of Milwaukee C2

1916 West Donges Bay Road
Mequon, WI, 53092
(414) 242-9680

Well-decorated, two-story colonial located in a pleasant suburb fifteen minutes from downtown or Cedarburg and five minutes to Cardinal Stritch College. The host teaches at a local university. Double bed, private bath, private phone, TV. A second room with hideaway bed is also available. $45-55.

B&B of Milwaukee D1

1916 West Donges Bay Road
Mequon, WI, 53092
(414) 242-9680

Exclusive suburb, fifteen minutes from the heart of the city, just off I-43. Beautifully decorated ranch in secluded location. Enjoy a full breakfast on the large sun porch that overlooks a lovely deck and flower gardens. One twin room with private bath and private entrance. $69-79.

B&B of Milwaukee D2

1916 West Donges Bay Road
Mequon, WI, 53092
(414) 242-9680

A pleasant 1878 farmhouse located twenty minutes from downtown Milwaukee, close to Cedarburg. Easy access to I-43. Heavily wooded two-acre lot with pond. The house has many antiques throughout and a sun room furnished with wicker. Two bedrooms on the second floor, one with a queen, the second with twin beds. Shared or private bath, full breakfast, resident sheep dog. $50-55.

B&B of Milwaukee D4

1916 West Donges Bay Road
Mequon, WI, 53092
(414) 242-9680

Large Dutch colonial home with a beautiful country setting on a main road close to I-43. Large acreage, trails, pond, and tennis court. Four bedrooms, two with twin beds, and one private suite with queen bed, sitting room, and wet bar. Common sitting area with fireplace for guests. Hostess is an avid quilter. $60-90.

B&B of Milwaukee D5

1916 West Donges Bay Road
Mequon, WI, 53092
(414) 242-9680

Germantown area. This fieldstone home on 5 acres dates to the 1840s. Downstairs is a lovely living room with fireplace, Oriental rugs, and a variety of antiques. Breakfast is served in the dining room. Three guest rooms, shared or private bath. $45-65.

B&B of Milwaukee E2

1916 West Donges Bay Road
Mequon, WI, 53092
(414) 242-9680

Affluent western suburb. Newer colonial, completely redecorated with new sun room and screened porch. Country bedroom has a queen bed with private bath. Near many shops, zoo, stadium, state fairgrounds, Medical College of Wisconsin, and Mt. Mary College. Full breakfast, air-conditioning. $45-55.

B&B of Milwaukee E4

1916 West Donges Bay Road
Mequon, WI, 53092
(414) 242-9680

This home is in the State Fair Park area, close to the city, I-94, and hospital. Two comfortable rooms with shared bath. Full breakfast. $35-40.

B&B of Milwaukee E5

1916 West Donges Bay Road
Mequon, WI, 53092
(414) 242-9680

Ranch home in a quiet residential neighborhood close to many west-side activities including the zoo and State Fair Park. The guest room has a king bed with private bath. Full breakfast. $50-60.

B&B of Milwaukee F1

1916 West Donges Bay Road
Mequon, WI, 53092
(414) 242-9680

Suburban home close to Boerner Botanical Gardens, shopping center, cross-country skiing, and golf courses. Two-acre natural wooded lot. Guests may enjoy the "quiet" room with books, fireplace, and chess set. The two bedrooms are graced with original artwork and fresh wildflowers in season. The master has a king bed and adjoining bath, the other has double bed and shared or private bath. Two cats and a dog in residence. $45-60.

B&B of Milwaukee F2

1916 West Donges Bay Road
Mequon, WI, 53092
(414) 242-9680

Pleasant ranch with one twin room. Lovely Florida room overlooking large yard. Private half bath and shared shower. Full breakfast. $45-50.

B&B of Milwaukee G1

1916 West Donges Bay Road
Mequon, WI, 53092
(414) 242-9680

South Milwaukee. Newly restored white frame Victorian with lovely antiques throughout. Close to Louth Lake Drive and near bus lines. Grant Park is nearby for hiking, cross-country skiing, and biking. Large backyard adjoins a wooded parkway. Full breakfast. Three bedrooms: two double, one single; shared bath. $35-55.

B&B of Milwaukee G2

1916 West Donges Bay Road
Mequon, WI, 53092
(414) 242-9680

This restored Victorian is located in the historic and ethnic community of Bay View. The home dates to 1896 and is decorated with antiques and the host's artistic touches. On bus line and less than ten minutes from downtown. Four rooms, shared bath. Full gourmet breakfast, air-conditioning, portacrib, parking. Resident cats isolated from guests. $45-55.

Ogden House

2237 North Lake Drive
Milwaukee, WI, 53202
(414) 272-2740

Located just two blocks from Lake Michigan and one mile north of downtown, Ogden House is in the historic district of Milwaukee's early mansions. We offer the charm of fireplaces, high canopy beds, and old-fashioned hospitality. Our home is your home.

Hosts: Mary Jane & John Moss
Rooms: 2(PB) $68.25-78.75
Continental-plus Breakfast
Credit Cards: No
Notes: 2, 5, 7, 9, 14

NEWBURG

B&B of Milwaukee J6

1916 West Donges Bay Road
Mequon, WI, 53092
(414) 242-9680

Large split-level home on 30 acres. Barn with upper level has ample space for workshops; lower level has fireplace and lounge. Call for fees.

NEWTON

Rambling Hills Tree Farm

8825 Willever Lane
Newton, WI, 53063
(414) 726-4388

Enjoy the serenity of country living in a comfortable modern home with panoramic views of 50 acres of rolling hills, small fishing lake, swimming pond, marsh, meadows, and forest with a network of trails and boardwalks to hike or ski. Three miles from Lake Michigan.

Hosts: Pete & Judie Stuntz
Rooms: 4 (SB) $42
Full Breakfast
Credit Cards: No
Notes: 2, 5, 7, 8, 9, 11, 13

NORTH KETTLE MORAINE

B&B of Milwaukee J3

1916 West Donges Bay Road
Mequon, WI, 53092
(414) 242-9680

Discover a lovely 1891 home in the Queen Anne style. Enjoy the small-town atmosphere, or take part in year-round outdoor activities in nearby state parks. Close to Wade House, golf, Road America. Four rooms, two with double beds, one with twins, and one with a 3/4 bed. Shared baths. $42-54.

OCONOMOWOC

The Inn at Pine Terrace

351 East Lisbon Road
Oconomowoc, WI, 53066
(414) 567-7463; (800) 421-4667

This thirteen-room inn is furnished to reflect the opulent graciousness of a highly decorative arts period. Modern amenities such as double whirlpool baths, cable TV, telephones, and a new swimming pool have been blended into the period setting. Pine Terrace overlooks Fowler Lake and is a short walk or bike ride to the downtown area's shops and restaurants. There are historic walking tours around the lake, boating, sailing, fishing, biking, skiing, and community events to enjoy. All rooms have double whirlpool baths.

Hosts: Tim & Sandy Glynn
Rooms: 13 (PB) $59-109.50
Full Breakfast
Credit Cards: A, B, C
Notes: 2, 5, 6, 7, 8, 9, 11, 12, 13, 14

NOTES: Credit cards accepted: A Master Card; B Visa; C American Express; D Discover Card; E Diners Club; F Other: 2 Personal checks accepted: 3 Lunch available: 4 Dinner available: 5 Open all year

OSCEOLA

St. Croix River Inn

305 River Street
Osceola, WI, 54020
(715) 294-4248

A meticulously restored eighty-year-old stone home nestled in one of the region's finest recreational areas. Ski at Wild Mountain or Trollhaugen. Canoe or fish in the lovely St. Croix River. Then relax in your suite , some with fireplaces, all with Jacuzzi whirlpool baths.

Host: Vickie Farnham
Rooms: 7 (PB) $75-150
Full Breakfast
Credit Cards: A, B, C
Notes: 2, 5, 7 (limited), 9, 10, 11, 12, 13, 14

OSHKOSH

The Tiffany Inn

206 Algoma Blvd.
Oshkosh, WI, 54901
(414) 893-0552

The inn is named after the famous American art glass creator Louis Comfort Tiffany. The inn has eleven rooms with cable TV and is within walking distance of the University of Wisconsin, the Aircraft Association Museum, paddlewheel lake cruises, Oshkosh clothing outlets, the Paine Art Center and Arboretum, plus many fine restaurants. All rooms with double whirlpool baths.

Hosts: Mary & Tom Rossow
Rooms: 11 (PB) $49.50-75.50
Full Breakfast
Credit Cards: A, B, C
Notes: 2, 5, 6, 7, 8, 9, 10, 11, 12, 13, 14

OXFORD

Halfway House B&B

Route 2, Box 80
Oxford, WI, 53952
(608) 586-5489

Our house was a stopping place for travelers on an old logging road and has been called Halfway House since the 1800s. In a quiet, rural setting with a large lawn, flower beds, birds, and game. The hosts, a veterinarian and his wife, have traveled to Africa and Europe. Skiing within twenty-five miles.

Hosts: Dr. & Genevieve Hines
Rooms: 4 (SB) $29.40-44.10
Full Breakfast
Credit Cards: No
Notes: 2, 5, 9, 12

PLYMOUTH

52 Stafford, An Irish Guest House

52 Stafford Street
Plymouth, WI, 53073
(414) 893-0552

Listed on the National Register of Historic Places, this inn has twenty rooms, seventeen of which have whirlpool baths and cable TV. 52 Stafford features one of the most beautiful pubs in America, which serves lunch and dinner. There are 35,000 acres of public recreation land nearby, cross-country skiing, hiking, biking, sports fishing, boating, swimming, golf. Crystal-clear lakes and beautiful fall colors.

Host: Sean O'Dwanny
Rooms: 20 (PB) $69.50-99.50
Full Breakfast
Credit Cards: A, B, C, D, E
Notes: 2, 3, 4, 5, 6, 7, 8, 9, 10, 11, 12, 13, 14

PORT WASHINGTON

B&B of Milwaukee J5

1916 West Donges Bay Road
Mequon, WI, 53092
(414) 242-9680

Refurbished stately Victorian with two large rooms with queen beds, private baths, and two-person whirlpools. Guest parlor with fireplace. Near marina and lake activities. Air-conditioned; adults only. $69-89.

RACINE

B&B of Milwaukee H1

1916 West Donges Bay Road
Mequon, WI, 53092
(414) 242-9680

On Lake Michigan, this three-story historic home dates from 1867. Just 2.5 blocks from the marina, tennis courts, Festival Park, and restaurants. A short drive from Lake Geneva. Third-floor suite consists of a large bed/sitting room with double canopy bed, love seats, desk, and provincial decor; ample room for four people. Bath with tub, kitchen for breakfast and snacks. Views through the trees of Lake Michigan. $80-100.

RICHLAND CENTER

The Mansion

323 South Church Street
Richland Center, WI, 53581
(608) 647-2808

Nineteen-room brick mansion built in the early 1900s by a lumberman. Located just around the corner from Frank Lloyd Wright Warehouse/Museum in this city of Wright's birth. Quarter-sawn oak woodwork and parquet floors of oak, walnut, and maple. Quietly elegant, but affordable. Air conditioned, but no TV.

Hosts: Beth Caulkins & Harvey Glanzer
Rooms: 4 (S2B) $45-55
Continental-plus Breakfast
Credit Cards: No
Notes: 2, 5, 6 (inquire), 7, 8 (over 12), 10, 11, 13 (XC)

SHEBOYGEN FALLS

The Rochester Inn

504 Water Street
Sheboygen Falls, WI, 53085
(414) 467-3123

The Rochester Inn is listed on the National Register of Historic Places. The region features a championship golf course, excellent restaurants and shops, hiking, cross-country skiing in Northern Kettle Morraine State Park, and Greak Lakes sport fishing centers. All rooms have double whirlpool baths.

Hosts: Dan & Ruth Stenz
Rooms: 5 (PB) $69.50-99.50
Full Breakfast
Credit Cards: A, B, C, D
Notes: 2, 5, 6, 7, 8, 9, 10, 11, 12, 13, 14

SISTER BAY

Blufftop Home

B&B Guest Homes
Route 2
Algoma, WI, 54201
(414) 743-9742

Remodeled ranch home that overlooks the bay and the beautiful sunsets of Door County. Bath and a half is shared by the two rooms; large solarium for your relaxing pleasure. Children welcome; generous continental breakfast; no smoking. $55.

SOUTH KETTLE MORAINE

B&B of Milwaukee I3

1916 West Donges Bay Road
Mequon, WI, 53092
(414) 242-9680

An 1848 farmhouse filled with antiques and collectibles. Bike, hike, or ski in this nature wonderland, or drive twenty minutes to Lake Geneva. Prearrange dinner with your professional chef hostess. Six country bedrooms with two shared baths. $54-72.

SPARTA

Just-N-Trails B&B

Route 1, Box 274
Sparta, WI, 54656
(608) 269-4522

Unwind in a 1920 farmhouse on a working dairy farm. Five bedrooms — tthree private and two shared baths. Laura Ashley linens; full breakfast. Near the safe, scenic Elroy-Sparta Bike Trail and Amish community. New "Little House on the Prairie" log cabin with bath. "The Granary," whirlpool and fireplace.

Hosts: Don & Donna Justin
Rooms: 6 (4 PB; 2 SB) $40-60
Full Breakfast
Credit Cards: A, B
Notes: 2, 5, 8, 9, 10, 11, 12, 13, 14

STEVENS POINT

Victorian Swan on Water

1716 Water Street
Stevens Point, WI, 54481
(715) 345-0595

Explore this romantic, historic house at the gateway to Wisconsin vacationland. Cozy nooks, fireplace, bountiful breakfasts in the plant-filled sun room. There is also a TV room, and meeting rooms are available. River walkways, forest preserves, scenic cross-country ski trails, golf, tennis close. Air-conditioned.

Host: Joan Ouellette
Rooms: 4 (PB) $45-60 + tax
Full Breakfast
Credit Cards: A, B, C, D
Notes: 2, 5, 9, 10, 12, 13, 14

STRATFORD

Family Dairy Farm

B&B Guest Homes
Route 2
Algoma, WI, 54201
(414) 743-9742

Large, modern operating dairy farm about thirteen miles north of Marshfield. Hosts are Mennonites who can speak Pennsylvania Dutch and some German. Fishing, boating, skiing, snowmobiling are nearby. Guests are welcome to participate in farm activities. No smoking; full farm breakfast; children and pets are welcome. $45.

STURGEON BAY

The Gray Goose B&B

4258 Bay Shore Drive
Sturgeon Bay, WI, 54235
(414) 743-9100

Enjoy warm hospitality in our Civil War home in Door County. Authentic antique furnishings. Four large, comfortable rooms share two baths. Guest sitting room with a water/sunset view to remember. Beautiful dining room. Full porch with wicker and swing. Quiet, wooded site north of town. Brochure and gift certificates available.

Hosts: Jack & Jessie Burkhardt
Rooms: 4 (S2B) $52.75-73.85
Full Breakfast
Minimum stay holidays: 2
Credit Cards: A, B, C
Notes: 2, 5, 7, 8 (over 16), 9, 10, 11, 12, 13

The Gray Goose B&B

White Lace Inn

16 North Fifth Avenue
Sturgeon Bay, WI, 54235
(414) 743-1105

The White Lace Inn is a romantic getaway featuring three restored turn-of-the-century houses brought together by a winding garden pathway. The fifteen elegant guest rooms are furnished in fine antiques. Three rooms have double whirlpool tubs, six have fireplaces, and four have both fireplace and whirlpool.

Hosts: Dennis & Bonnie Statz
Rooms: 15 (PB) $62-135
Continental Breakfast
Credit Cards: A, B
Notes: 2, 5, 9, 10, 11, 12, 13

WASHINGTON ISLAND

Island Home

B&B Guest Homes
Route 2
Algoma, WI, 54201
(414) 743-9742

An unusual style home hand-built by one man many years ago. The present owners have filled it with antiques and reminders of their trips to Scandinavian countries. They speak Swedish and Norwegian. Full breakfast. $65.

WAUPACA

Crystal River B&B

East 1369 Rural Road
Waupaca, WI, 54981
(715) 258-5333

Beautiful 1853 home on the bank of Crystal River in the historic district of Rural features country comfort of luxurious down comforters on queen antique brass or iron beds. Four romantic rooms feature views of the river, wildwood garden, woods, and riverfront Victorian gazebo. Main floor includes the River Room, library, Morning Room, TV Room, fireplace, and parlor. A mile from the famous Chain O'Lakes.

Hosts: Gene & Lois Sorenson
Rooms: 5 (2 PB; 3 SB) $40-75
Full Breakfast
Credit Cards: A, B
Notes: 2, 5, 8 (over 12), 9, 10, 11, 12, 13

WHITEWATER

The Greene House B&B & Guitar Gallery

Route 2, Box 214
Whitewater, WI, 53190
(414) 495-8771; (800) 468-1959

Put your feet up and relax in an authentic 1850s farmhouse or enjoy one of the many available activities. Superb cross-country skiing, hiking, horseback riding, bicycling, antiquing, outdoor music theater. Fifteen minutes north of Lake Geneva; a short drive from Chicago, Milwaukee, or Madison.

Hosts: Lynn & Mayner Greene
Rooms: 6 (SB) $49-75
Full Breakfast
Credit Cards: A, B, C
Notes: 2, 4, 5, 8, 9, 10, 11, 12, 13 (XC), 14

WISCONSIN DELLS

Historic Bennett House B&B

825 Oak Street
Wisconsin Dells, WI, 53965
(608) 254-2500

A pioneer photographer's gracious 1863 home on the National Historic Register. Elegantly decorated with lace, antiques, crystal. Romantic guest rooms, luscious fireside breakfasts. Relax at sunset on the porch. Enjoy Greyhound Racetrack, antiquing, scenic tours, biking, hiking, bird watching, museums, golf, state parks, attractions, water sports. Gift certificates.

Hosts: Gail & Rich Obermeyer
Rooms: 3 (1 PB; 2 SB) $59.13-86
Full Breakfast
Credit Cards: No
Notes: 2, 5, 9, 10, 11, 12, 13, 14

Wyoming

BIG HORN

Spahn's Bighorn Mountain B&B

Box 579
Big Horn, WY, 82833
(307) 674-8150

Towering log home and secluded guest cabins on the mountainside in whispering pines. Borders one million acres of public forest with deer and moose. Gracious mountain breakfast served on the deck with binoculars to enjoy the 100-mile view. Owner was a Yellowstone Ranger. Fifteen minutes from Sheridan and I-90.

Hosts: Ron & Bobbie Spahn
Rooms: 4 (PB) $45-80
Full Breakfast
Credit Cards: A, B
Notes: 3, 4, 5, 6 (call), 8, 9, 13 (XC), 14

South Fork Inn

BUFFALO

South Fork Inn

Box 854
Buffalo, WY, 82834
(307) 684-9609

Located in the Big Horn National Forest, South Fork Inn is a rustic mountain lodge. We have ten guest cabins and a main lodge with our dining room and game room. Activities include horseback riding, fishing, hiking, biking, skiing, and many others.

Hosts: Ken & Patty Reid
Rooms: 10 (3 PB; 7 SB) $25-45
Full Breakfast
Credit Cards: E
Notes: 2, 3, 4, 6, 7, 8, 13

CASPER

B&B Western Adventure 245

P.O. Box 20972
Billings, MT, 59104
(406) 259-7993

The picture windows of this ranch-style home look out over a scenic view of the North Platte River. One can always see a variety of wildlife, from ducks and geese in winter, bald and golden eagles in early spring, and pelicans and herons in summer. A herd of deer are in residence year round. Two large bedrooms with private entrance have private baths. Guests are encouraged to roam the 7 acres, the large lawn, and lounge in the lawn furniture. Float trips, fishing trips, skiing, and snowmobiling are all

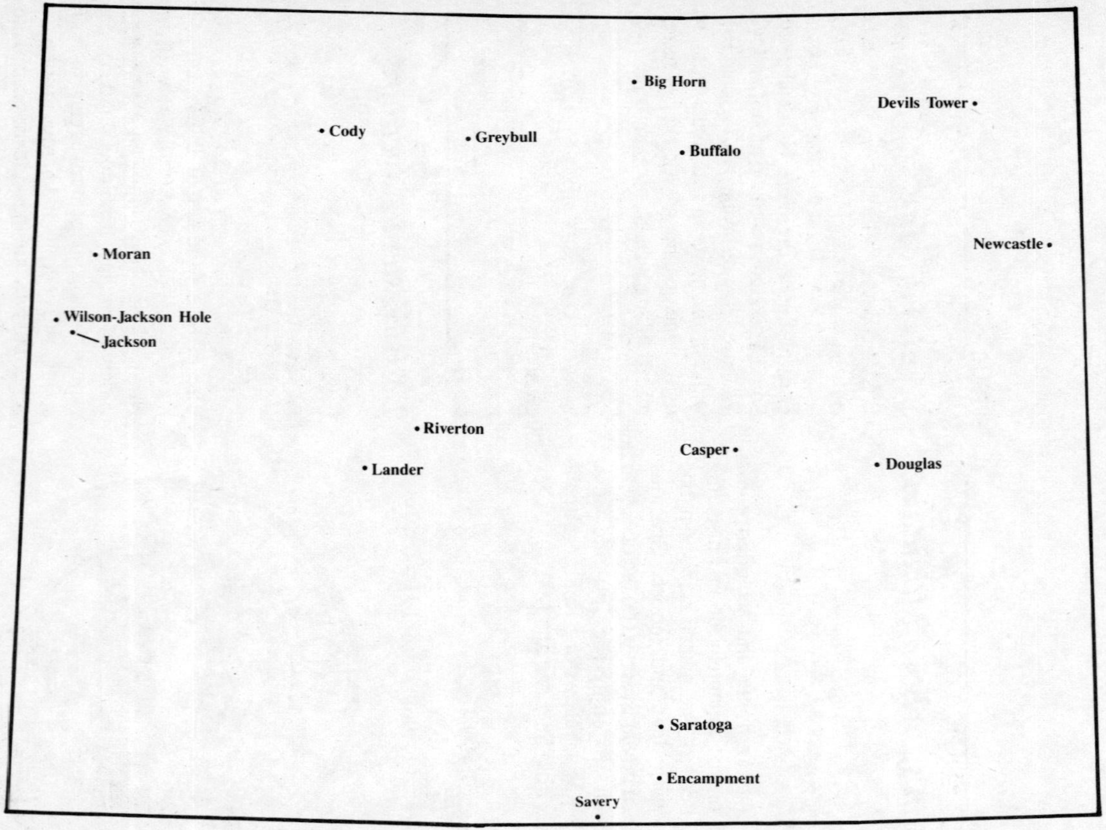

Big Horn
Devils Tower
Cody
Greybull
Buffalo
Newcastle
Moran
Wilson-Jackson Hole
Jackson
Riverton
Casper
Lander
Douglas
Saratoga
Encampment
Savery

WYOMING

available. Hosts will accompany you to the river as guides. Full breakfast from 7:00-8:00 A.M.; continental for those who want to sleep in. No smoking or pets in the house. $35-45.

CHEYENNE

B&B Western Adventure 242

P.O. Box 20972
Billings, MT, 59104
(406) 259-7993

Secluded, with a view of distant mountains to the west, this modern rustic home is on 10 country acres near I-25 and I-80. Near antelope, deer, and elk hunting, and fishing. Three bedrooms, one with a queen bed and semi-private bath. On the lower level are two rooms that share a bath and sitting room. Full ranch breakfast served at 6:30 weekdays; continental for late risers. $40.

CODY

Hunter Peak Ranch

Box 1731, Painter Rt.
Cody, WY, 82414
(307) 587-3711

Hunter Peak Ranch, at 6,700-feet elevation, is located in the Shoshone National Forest, with access to North Absaroka and Beartooth Wilderness Areas and Yellowstone. Come enjoy the area's photographic opportunities, hiking, horseback riding, and pack trips.

Hosts: Louis & Shelley Cary
Rooms: 8 (PB) $50
Full Breakfast
Minimum stay: 3
Credit Cards: C
Closed Dec. 15-May 15
Notes: 2 (deposit), 3, 4, 6, 7, 8, 9, 11, 14

DEVIL'S TOWER

B&B Western Adventure 241

P.O. Box 20972
Billings, MT, 59104
(406) 259-7993

Country home at the foot of Devil's Tower, with a majestic view of America's first national monument. Unique bedroom with king bed, private shower, private entrance and deck. Located in the northeast corner of Wyoming in the Black Hills area about thirty minutes off I-90. Within walking distance of the ranger-guided nature walk, climbing demonstration, and visitor center. There are free evening campfire programs, abundant wildlife, cross-country skiing, and hunting during the fall season. No pets; smoking outside only; children over sixteen are welcome. $45-52.

DOUGLAS

Deer Forks Ranch

1200 Poison Lake Road
Douglas, WY, 82633
(307) 358-2033

Working cattle and sheep ranch 25 miles southwest of Douglas and I-25. Daily horseback riding; participation in ranch activities, fishing, big game hunting, prairie dog hunting, hiking on 5,900 acres. Large housekeeping guest houses are fully furnished and equipped for cooking. In business for 27 years; state of Wyoming licensed for big game outfitting, B&B, and ranch recreation. Weekly rates available.

Hosts: Benny & Pauline Middleton
Rooms: 3 (PB) $70
Full Breakfast
Credit Cards: C
Closed Dec.-April
Notes: 2, 3, 4, 6, 7, 8, 9, 14

ENCAMPMENT

Platt's Rustic Mountain Lodge

Star Route 49
Encampment, WY, 82325
(307) 327-5539

A peaceful mountain view and wholesome country atmosphere with lots of western hospitality, horseback riding, fishing, hiking, rock hounding; fully guided tours available to ranch recreational activities and scenic mountain areas. Enjoy the flora and fauna, historic trails, old mining camps, plus snowmobiling and cross-country skiing in the winter. By reservation only.

Hosts: Mayvon & Ron Platt
Rooms: 3 (SB) $35
Continental or Full Breakfast
Minimum stay: 2
Credit Cards: No
Closed Thanksgiving & Christmas
Notes: 8, 9, 13

GREYBULL

B&B Western Adventure 240

P.O. Box 20972
Billings, MT, 59104
(406) 259-7993

Located between Sheridan and Cody and two hours from Yellowstone, this authentic cattle and horse ranch sits on the western slope of the Big Horn Mountains in breathtaking Shell Canyon. The hosts are licensed outfitters and know the habits of the abundant wildlife in the area. Spacious bunkhouse with two rooms and private baths, a common family room with TV, games, and laundry facilities. There are also two rooms available in the main house. Horseback riding and fall hunting trips can be arranged. Full ranch breakfast; continental for late risers. No smoking in the home; children over twelve are welcome. $30-40.

JACKSON

Sundance Inn

135 West Broadway
Jackson, WY, 83001
(307) 733-3444

Conveniently located just one and one-half blocks from the town square, the Sundance Inn offers cozy, friendly lodging to travelers visiting to explore the western town of Jackson and its surrounding area. Amy and Casey Morton and their staff are happy to recommend a variety of outings to satisfy the interests of their guests.

Hosts: Amy & Casey Morton
Rooms: 26 (PB) $44-77
Continental Breakfast
Credit Cards: A, B, C, D
Closed April 10-April 30
Notes: 6, 7, 8, 9, 10, 11, 12, 13, 14

JACKSON HOLE

B&B Western Adventure 50

P.O. Box 20972
Billings, MT, 59104
(406) 259-7993

A snug, new home with fabulous views of the Jackson Hole Valley below. This four-story home has a two-story living-dining room with fireplace. Six guest rooms all have private showers. Located eight miles from the town of Jackson and eight miles from Teton Village. Breakfast features homemade breads, muffins, and granola. No smoking in the house; may not be appropriate for the physically handicapped. $75-95.

B&B Western Adventure 80

P.O. Box 20972
Billings, MT, 59104
(406) 259-7993

Two-story modern log home bordering the national forest in a secluded area where wildlife is abundant. The guest room looks out over bighorn sheep, deer, or elk in the spacious backyard. Two rooms with private baths. River access to a trout stream; guided fishing trips can be arranged. $50-60.

B&B Western Adventure 205

P.O. Box 20972
Billings, MT, 59104
(406) 259-7993

Two bedrooms on the second level share a bath and family room with redwood deck that overlooks the spectacular Teton Mountain Range. Located four miles from Teton Village ski resort and five from Jackson Hole. Fine restaurants, tennis, swimming, and fishing guides are within a mile. Full breakfast. $50-70.

LANDER

Black Mountain Ranch

548 North Fork Road
Lander, WY, 82520
(307) 332-6442

Discover the treasures and country comfort of Black Mountain Ranch. The ranch is nestled along the Popo Agie River in the foothills of the Wind River Mountains, on the way to Yellowstone. Trout fishing, horseback riding, hiking, llama picnics, and interesting local tours available.

Hosts: Dan & Rosie Ratigan
Rooms: 6 (2 PB; 4 SB) $46-56
Full Breakfast
Credit Cards: A, B
Closed Oct. 1-April 30
Notes: 2, 4, 8, 9, 14

LARAMIE

Annie Moore's Guest House

819 University
Laramie, WY, 82070
(307) 721-4177

Six individually decorated guest rooms, four with sink. Large, sunny common living rooms, second-story sun deck. Across the street from the University of Wyoming; two blocks from the Laramie Plains Museum; six blocks from downtown. Fifteen to thirty minutes from skiing, hiking, camping, fishing, uncrowded wilderness area.

Host: Diana Kopulos
Rooms: 6 (SB) $45-55
Continental Breakfast
Credit Cards: A, B, C
Closed Thanksgiving & Christmas
Notes: 2, 8 (over 4), 9, 14

B&B Western Adventure 30

P.O. Box 20972
Billings, MT, 59104
(406) 259-7993

This old three-story Queen Anne home has been beautifully restored. There are six guest rooms furnished with antiques; three shared baths. Located across from the University of Wyoming in downtown Laramie. Continental-plus breakfast; no pets or smoking; children over fourteen are welcome. $42-52.

MORAN

Box K Ranch

Box 110
Moran, WY, 83013
(307) 543-2407

Located in the beautiful Buffalo Valley, surrounded by national forest, with Grand Teton Park outside our front door and a short drive to Yellowstone. Horseback riding, float trips, hiking, fishing — all with great Western hospitality.

Host: Walter M. Korn
Rooms: 3 (1 PB; 2 SB) $60
Full Breakfast
Credit Cards: Yes
Closed Nov.-April
Notes: 3, 4, 8, 9

NEWCASTLE

4W Ranch Recreation

1162 Lynch Road
Newcastle, WY, 82701
(307) 746-2815

Looking for the unbeaten path? Spend a few days on our working cattle ranch with 20,000 acres of diversified rangeland to explore at your leisure. Rates include three meals a day.

Hosts: Bob & Jean Harshbarger
Rooms: 2 (SB) $60 for 1; $100 for 2 AP
Full Breakfast
Credit Cards: B
Notes: 2, 3, 4, 5, 7, 8, 9

RIVERTON

B&B Western Adventure 218

P.O. Box 20972
Billings, MT, 59104
(406) 259-7993

This working ranch is surrounded by the Wind River Reservation, home of the Shoshone and Arapaho tribes. Three rooms on the second floor share a bath. There is excellent fishing, hunting, and snowmobiling nearby, as well as ranch living to be experienced. $35-40.

SARATOGA

Hotel Wolf

101 East Bridge Street
Box 1298
Saratoga, WY, 82331
(307) 326-5525

The Hotel Wolf, built in 1893, served as a stagecoach stop. During its early years, the hotel was the hub of the community and noted for its fine food and convivial atmosphere. The same holds true today. The dining room is acclaimed as one of the finest in the region. Nearby is a mineral hot springs.

Hosts: Doug & Kathleen Campbell
Rooms: 11 (7 PB; 4 SB) $21-75
Continental Breakfast
Credit Cards: A, B, C, E
Notes: 2, 3, 4, 5, 7, 8, 9, 10, 11, 12

SAVERY

Savery Creek Thoroughbred Ranch

Box 24
Savery, WY, 82332
(307) 383-7840

Remote, but easily reached, horse ranch in beautiful location. Furnished with antiques, unspoiled, and low-key. Riding is featured. Ask about special riding packages that include all meals.

Host: Joyce B. Saer
Rooms: 4 (1 PB; 3 SB) $55
Full Breakfast
Credit Cards: C
Notes: 2, 3, 4, 5, 6, 8, 9, 11, 13 (XC), 14

SHERIDAN

B&B Western Adventure 250

P.O. Box 20972
Billings, MT, 59104
(406) 259-7993

This gracious log home ihas hiking trails leading directly to the adjacent Big Horn National Forest. With a 100-mile view, breakfast is served on the deck so you can watch the abundant wildlife.. Two rooms with private baths, plus a secluded cabin that sleeps six. The hosts will take you gold panning or Jeeping in the wilderness. $45-75.

Kilbourne Kastle

320 South Main Street
Sheridan, WY, 82801
(307) 674-8716

On Sheridan's historic district walking tour, Kilbourne Kastle is near a golf course and good fishing areas. A convenient stopover on your way to Cody, Yellowstone, and Glacier national parks. One block from downtown Sheridan.

Hosts: Jack & Pat Roush
Rooms: 3 (SB) From $30
Continental Breakfast
Credit Cards: A, B
Notes: 2, 5, 8, 9, 10, 11, 12

WILSON-JACKSON HOLE

Teton Tree House

Box 550
Wilson, WY, 83014
(307) 733-3233

Helpful, longtime mountain and river guides offer a special four-story, open-beam home on a forested mountainside. Large, rustic, but elegant rooms have exceptional views of the Jackson Hole Valley and mountains beyond. Generous, tasty, healthy breakfasts.

Hosts: Chris & Denny Becker
Rooms: 5 (PB) $90.85-112.35
Full Breakfast (low cholesterol)
Credit Cards: A, B, D
Notes: 5, 8 (no infants), 9, 10, 11, 12, 13, 14

Hotel Wolf

Teton View Bed and Breakfast

2136 Coyote Loop, Box 652
Wilson, WY, 83014
(307) 733-7954

Rooms all have mountain views, cozy country decor, own entrance, private deck overlooking Teton Mountain range, and comfortable lounge area with books and refrigerator. Homemade pastries, fresh fruit, and fresh-ground coffee is served in the family dining room with views of the mountains.

Hosts: Jane and Tom Neil
Rooms: 3(1 PB; 2 SB) $48.15-96.95
Continental Breakfast
Credit Cards: A, B
Notes: 2, 5, 6, 8, 9, 10, 11, 12, 13, 14

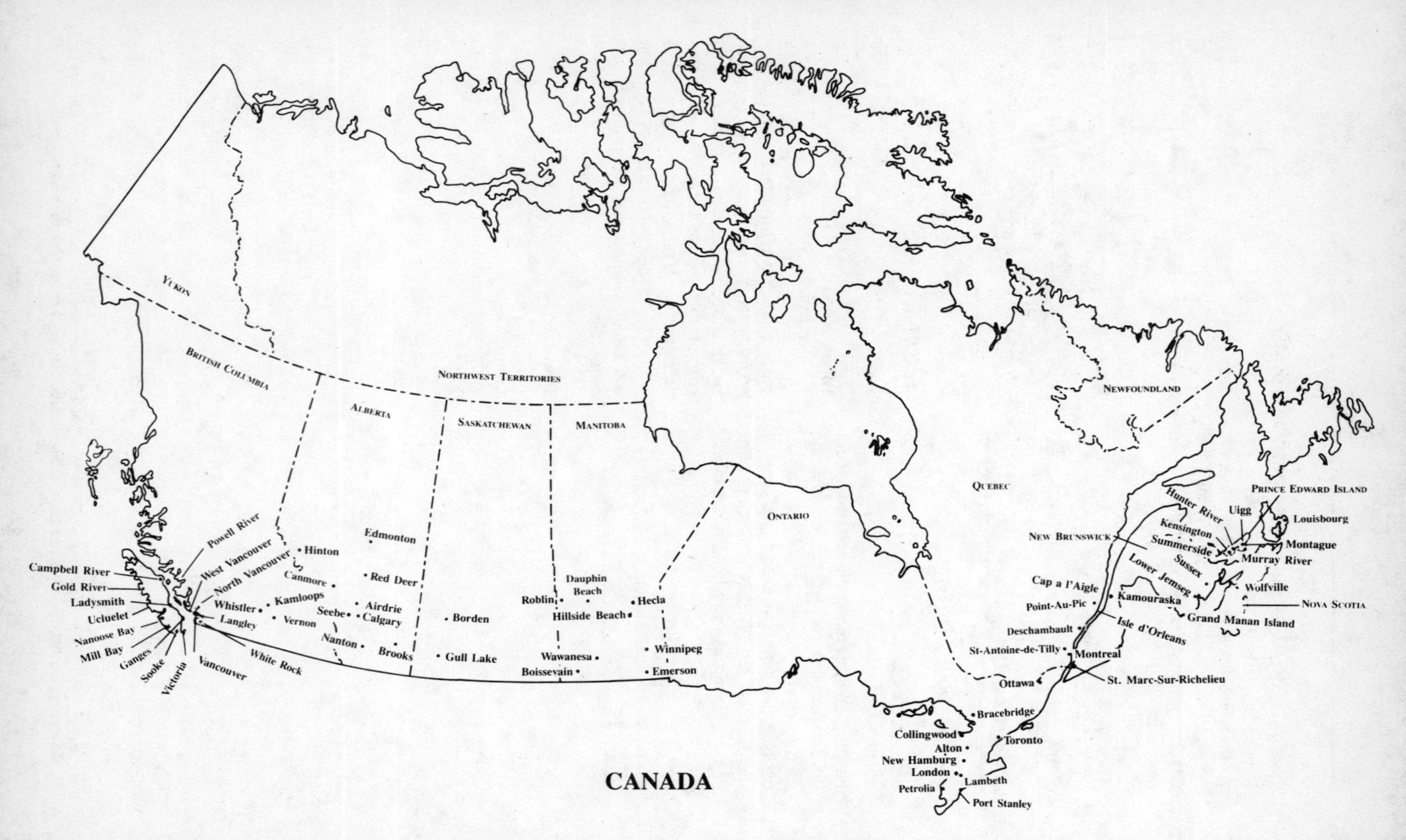

Yukon
British Columbia
Northwest Territories
Alberta
Saskatchewan
Manitoba
Ontario
Quebec
Newfoundland
New Brunswick
Prince Edward Island
Nova Scotia
Campbell River
Gold River
Ladysmith
Ucluelet
Nanoose Bay
Mill Bay
Ganges
Sooke
Victoria
Vancouver
White Rock
Langley
Whistler
North Vancouver
West Vancouver
Powell River
Kamloops
Vernon
Hinton
Canmore
Seebe
Airdrie
Calgary
Nanton
Brooks
Edmonton
Red Deer
Borden
Gull Lake
Roblin
Dauphin Beach
Hillside Beach
Hecla
Wawanesa
Boissevain
Winnipeg
Emerson
Ottawa
Bracebridge
Collingwood
Toronto
Alton
New Hamburg
London
Lambeth
Petrolia
Port Stanley
St-Antoine-de-Tilly
Montreal
St. Marc-Sur-Richelieu
Deschambault
Point-Au-Pic
Cap a l'Aigle
Kamouraska
Isle d'Orleans
Lower Jemseg
Grand Manan Island
Sussex
Summerside
Kensington
Hunter River
Uigg
Louisbourg
Montague
Murray River
Wolfville
CANADA

Alberta

AIRDRIE

Alberta B&B 4

P.O. Box 15477, MPO
Vancouver, BC, V6B 5B2
(604) 944-1793

In a country setting, this home is a ten-minute drive from the outskirts of Calgary, or an hour's drive to Banff. A five-level home with one guest room and shared bath.

BROOKS

Alberta B&B 3

P.O. Box 15477, MPO
Vancouver, BC, V6B 5B2
(604) 944-1793

A country inn offers four double rooms, each with private bath, air-conditioned throughout. A full country breakfast is served in the solarium. The "Gathering Room" with fireplace is for guests' use. Pets are welcome to stay in the heated kennels. Sportsmen have on-site facilities for cleaning their catch, with freezer storage.

CALGARY

Alberta B&B 1

P.O. Box 15477, MPO
Vancouver, BC, V6B 5B2
(604) 944-1793

Multilevel home with a family room with fireplace and cedar-lined hot tub that guests are welcome to use. The guest room has a double bed and private bath.

CANMORE

Haus Alpenrose

629 Tenth Street
P.O. Box 723
Canmore, ALB, T0L 0M0
(403) 678-4134

Haus Alpenrose is a small, rustic, comfortable lodge in the very heart of the Canadian Rockies, at the foot of the Three Sisters and Chinaman's Peak. We have private rooms, family rooms with bunk beds, and dorms. Kitchen, lounge with stone fireplace, sauna. Separate bathroom facilities for men and women. Near Banff, hiking, climbing, cross-country and downhill skiing, golf, and fishing.

Hosts: Ottmar & Ulrike Setzer
Rooms: 10 (SB) $40-50
Full Breakfast
Credit Cards: A, B
Closed Oct. 1-Nov. 15
Notes: 8, 9, 10, 11, 12, 13, 14

Cougar Creek Inn

P.O. Box 1162
Canmore, ALB, T0L 0M0
(403) 678-4751

Cougar Creek Inn is nestled in a quiet area of town and flanked with spectacular mountain views. The rooms are quiet; the setting is rustic. Guests have their own sitting area with fireplace, color TV, games, and a small library. Breakfasts are homemade, wholesome, and hearty. The area offers numerous outdoor activities, including skiing, hiking, biking, golf, fishing, and tennis.

Host: Mrs. Patricia Doucette
Rooms: 4 (SB) $60 Canadian
Full Breakfast
Credit Cards: No
Notes: 2 (for deposit), 3, 5, 7 (restricted), 8, 9, 10, 11, 12, 13

EDMONTON

Alberta B&B 2

P.O. Box 15477, MPO
Vancouver, BC, V6B 5B2
(604) 944-1793

Beautiful red brick home designated as an historic home, owned by hosts who are professional musicians with the Edmonton Symphony. Accommodation is one upstairs guest room with double bed and private bath. Two cats in residence.

HINTON

Black Cat Guest Ranch

Box 6267
Hinton, ALB, T7V 1X6
(403) 865-3084

Wilderness guest ranch with sixteen comfortably equipped rooms. Guided trail rides, hiking, cross-country ski trails. Great home-cooked meals. Hot tub with mountain view, central room with fireplace, piano, lots of books, dart boards. Near Jasper.

Hosts: Mary & Jerry Bond
Rooms: 16 (PB) $92 + tax
Full Breakfast
Credit Cards: A, B
Notes: 2, 3, 4, 5, 7, 9, 13 (XC), 14

NANTON

Alberta B&B 5

P.O. Box 15477, MPO
Vancouver, BC, V6B 5B2
(604) 944-1793

A small ranch in the beautiful foothills of the Canadian Rockies. The hosts keep cattle, horses, and sheep. Two guest rooms and shared bath. Horseback riding is available, as well as fishing in nearby lake and mountain streams.

RED DEER

Alberta B&B 6

P.O. Box 15477, MPO
Vancouver, BC, V6B 5B2
(604) 944-1793

Situated approximately midway between Edmonton and Calgary, this home offers a bungalow with upstairs guest room, downstairs guest room with adjacent sitting room, and one guest bath.

SEEBE

Brewster's Kananaskis Guest Ranch

General Delivery
Seebe, ALB, T0L 1X0
(403) 673-3737

Relax in the old Brewster family homestead forty-five minutes west of Calgary, just off the Trans-Canada Highway. Ride to the ridge of Yamnuska Mountain, explore the Bow River, soak in our whirlpool, or tee off on one of the four golf courses that are minutes from the ranch.

Hosts: The Brewster Family
Rooms: 27 (PB) $68-88
Full Breakfast
Credit Cards: A, B
Closed Oct. 15-April 30
Notes: 4, 7, 8, 10, 11, 12, 14

British Columbia

CAMPBELL RIVER

April Point Lodge and Fishing Resort

Box 1, Campbell River
BC, V9W 4Z1
(604) 285-2222; FAX: (604) 285-2411

April Point Lodge is located on Quadra Island, approximately 100 miles north of Vancouver. April Point features world-class salmon fishing and outstanding dining in a pristine natural setting. The lodge is easily reached by plane or car.

Hosts: The Petersons
Rooms: 38 (SB) $99-199
Full Breakfast
Credit Cards: A, B, C, E
Closed Nov. 1-March 31
Notes: 2, 3, 4, 6, 7, 8, 9, 10, 11, 12, 14

Campbell River Lodge & Fishing Resort

1760 Island Highway
Campbell River, BC, V9W 2E7
(604) 287-7446

Campbell River's oldest fishing lodge, located on the banks of the famous Campbell River. Experienced guides for salt-water salmon fishing; dining room, Olde English-style pub; squash court; sauna, and whirlpool (seasonal).

Hosts: Ted & Sharon Arbour
Rooms: 30 (PB) $79-89 + tax
Continental Breakfast
Credit Cards: A, B
Closed Christmas Day
Notes: 4, 6, 7, 8, 9

GANGES

Applecroft B&B

Town & Country B&B
Box 46544, Station G
Vancouver, BC, V6R 4G6
(604) 731-5942

Fine country hospitality on an 1893 family farm two miles north of Ganges, next to a golf course and tennis courts. Minutes away from lakes, ocean beaches, restaurants, and ferries. There is a secluded, self-contained cottage, or stay in guest rooms in the main house, all with private baths. Full farm breakfast. No pets, no smoking. $50-65.

Applecroft B&B

KAMLOOPS

Alberta B&B 7

P.O. Box 15477, MPO
Vancouver, BC, V6B 5B2
(604) 944-1793

A lovely home on the South Thompson River. Weather permitting, breakfast will be served on the patio overlooking the swimming pool and private dock with canoe. Children are most welcome. Three guest rooms share two baths.

LADYSMITH

Manana Lodge & Marina

RR 1, 4760 Brenton Page Road
Ladysmith, BC, V0R 2E0
(604) 245-2312

Located on a secluded bay in Ladysmith Harbor. Licensed dining room, gift shop, marina, store, overnight moorage, marine fuel, laundry facilities. Complimentary use of canoe and mountain bikes. Fishing and sailing charters can be arranged in advance.

Hosts: Jim & Ruth Bangay, Don & Gail Kanelakos
Rooms: 4 (PB) $45-65
Full Breakfast
Credit Cards: A, B
Notes: 4, 5, 8, 9, 10, 11, 12, 14

Yellow Point Lodge

RR 3, Ladysmith
BC, V0R 2E0
(604) 245-7422

Set on 180 acres of private natural forest land surrounded by the Gulf Islands, the lodge and cottages have been a rustic favorite for fifty years. No phones or TV. All meals and recreational activities included in the daily rate.

Hosts: Richard Hill & Millie Hogg
Rooms: 55 (25 PB; 30 SB) $84-149
Full Breakfast
Credit Cards: A, B
Notes: 2, 3, 4, 7, 8 (16 and over), 9, 10, 11

LANGLEY

The Willoughby Inn B&B

Town & Country B&B
Box 46544, Station G
Vancouver, BC, V6R 4G6
(604) 731-5942

A traditional Tudor home with hardwood floors and a great B&B ambience. All guest rooms are separate from the rest of the house for privacy. Three rooms, private baths. Full breakfast. Located on 2.5 acres in Langley Township, forty minutes east of downtown Vancouver. $55.

The Willoughby Inn B&B

MILL BAY

Pine Lodge Farm

3191 Mutter Road
Mill Bay, BC, V0R 2P0
(604) 743-4083

An antique-filled pine lodge built on a 30-acre farm overlooking the ocean, with majestic arbutus trees and breathtaking views of the sea and islands. Walking trails, fields, and farm animals add to the paradise-like setting. Located in historic Mill Bay. No smoking.

Hosts: Barbara & Cliff Clarke
Rooms: 7 (PB) $65-75 Canadian
Honeymoon Cottage $95
Full Breakfast
Credit Cards: A, B
Notes: 2, 5, 8, 9, 12, 13

NANOOSE BAY

The Lookout

3381 Dolphin Drive, RR 2
Nanoose Bay, BC, V0R 2R0
(604) 468-9796

Situated halfway between Victoria and Tofino, our cedar home is set in tall evergreens and is quiet and peaceful, with 180-degree view of Georgia Strait and the majestic mountains beyond. Relax on our wraparound deck and enjoy the passing boats, Alaskan cruise ships, eagles, and whales. Fairwinds Golf Course, Schooner Cove Marina and resort are within a half mile. Hearty breakfast on the deck—what you want, when you want it.

Hosts: Marj & Herb Wilkie
Rooms: 3 (1 PB; 2 SB) $50-70 Canadian
Full Breakfast
Credit Cards: No
Closed Dec. 1 to April 1
Notes: 2, 8 (over 10), 9, 10, 11, 12, 14

NORTH VANCOUVER

Helen's B&B

302 East Fifth Street
North Vancouver
BC, V7L 1L1
(604) 985-4869

Welcome to our old Victorian home, its charm and comfort enhanced by antiques, wonderful views, and color cable TV in each room. Five blocks to the Pacific; twenty minutes to the Horseshoe Bay Ferries; minutes to Grouse Mountain, Whister Sea-Bus, restaurants, and shopping. Gourmet breakfast served in elegant dining room. Ten percent senior discount; ten percent discount from Nov.-April.

Host: Helen Boire
Rooms: 3 (2 PB; 1 SB) $60-70
Full Breakfast
Credit Cards: No
Closed Christmas
Notes: 7, 8, 9, 10, 11, 12, 13

Jane's Gourmet B&B

Town & Country B&B
Box 46544, Station G
Vancouver, BC, V6R 4G6
(604) 731-5942

Private garden-level suite furnished with two double and one single bed, full bath, fireplace, cable TV, fine antiques, and stereo. Only twenty-five minutes from downtown Vancouver, ten to the beach or golf. Gourmet breakfasts are served every day, plus fresh-baked cookies in the afternoon. No smoking, no pets. $85-90.

Laburnum Cottage B&B

Town & Country B&B
Box 46544, Station G
Vancouver, BC, V6R 4G6
(604) 731-5942

This charming home, with a Victorian air and antiques, is set on a half acre of award-winning English garden and surrounded by virgin forest. Only fifteen minutes from downtown Vancouver and Horseshoe Bay. Guest rooms have private baths, or stay in the "Summerhouse Cottage" in the garden. Relax on the patio or in the cool of the garden. German and French are spoken; wheel chair accessible. No smoking. $75-110.

The Nelsons'

470 West St. James Road
North Vancouver, BC, V7N 2P5
(604) 985-1178

Tastefully appointed home on a quiet residential street, with a restful patio and sun deck overlooking the heated pool, in a garden setting. Full breakfast menu offers various choices of home-cooked food. Minutes from Vancouver's many attractions. Sorry, no smoking or pets. Cats in residence.

Hosts: Roy & Charlotte Nelson
Rooms: 3 (PB) $55
Full Breakfast
Credit Cards: No
Closed Nov.-March
Notes: 2, 8 (over 6), 10, 11, 12, 13

Old English B&B 1

P.O. Box 86818
North Vancouver, BC, V7L 4L3
(604) 986-5069

Waterfront, wilderness, and a great view are all at your fingertips at this outstanding B&B. Private one-bedroom suite with fireplace, TV, private entrance. The suite is decorated with a mixture of antiques and modern furniture. Breakfast is served in the dining room or on the sun deck. Good hiking and scuba diving in the area; artists' colony nearby. $95.

Old English B&B 2

P.O. Box 86818
North Vancouver, BC, V7L 4L3
(604) 986-5069

This spacious home is decorated with Indian artwork, pottery, and weaving. Three rooms are offered: a double with private bath and Jacuzzi tub; a large bed/sitting room with king and queen beds and private patio; a third room with twins and its own patio. The last two rooms share a bath.

Old English B&B 3

P.O. Box 86818
North Vancouver, BC, V7L 4L3
(604) 986-5069

This home is convenient to buses to downtown. Three guest rooms share a two-room bath. Two rooms have twin beds that can be made into kings. The third room is a queen. Private entrance and sitting room with TV; heated pool with patio. $60.

Old English B&B 4

P.O. Box 86818
North Vancouver
BC, V7L 4L3
(604) 986-5069

Within easy reach of the University of British Colombia and downtown Vancouver. Queen room with private bath, TV, and sitting area. A second room has either a king bed or two twins, private bath. $65-70.

The Platt's B&B

4393 Quinton Place
North Vancouver
BC, V7R-4A8
(604) 987-4100

Fifteen to twenty minutes to the heart of town and famous Stanley Park. Close to the Capilano suspension bridge, fish hatchery, and the Cleveland dam. Quiet parklike area, ideal for cycling. Homemade bread and jams featured at breakfast.

Hosts: Nancy & Elwood Platt
Rooms: 2 (PB) $50 US
Full Breakfast
Credit Cards: No
Notes: 2, 5, 8 (over 10), 9, 10, 11, 12

Sue's Victorian B&B

152 East Third Street
North Vancouver, BC, V7L 1E6
(604) 985-1523

This restored 1904 home is four blocks from the harbor, Lonsdale Quay, and the Seabus terminus. Even closer are restaurants and shops. Nonsmoking. Long-term rates available. Guest refrigerator. Choice of full, continental, or no breakfast in busy season. Two cats live here. Please bring your slippers.

Host: Sue Chalmers
Rooms: 4 (2 PB; 2 SB) $45-55 Canadian
Continental Breakfast
Minimum stay: 2
Credit Cards: No
Notes: 2, 5, 8, 10, 11, 12, 13

POWELL RIVER

Ocean View B&B

4024 Dorval Avenue
Powell River, BC, V8A 3G2
(604) 485-6880

Our lovely home overlooks Malaspina Strait across to Vancouver Island. Comfortable beds, TV lounge, patio, and a full breakfast await you. Centrally located: shopping, dining, beaches, nature trails, recreation complex, and Vancouver Island ferry terminal are all within a five minute drive. Plane and bus pickup can be arranged.

Hosts: Chuck & Doreen Meredith
Rooms: 4 (2 PB; 2 SB) $40
Full Breakfast
Credit Cards: No
Notes: 5, 7 (restricted), 8, 9, 10, 11, 12, 14

SOOKE

Ocean Wilderness

P.O. Box 1203
Sooke, BC, V0S 1N0
(604) 646-2116

Thirty miles from Victoria on the west coast of Vancouver Island. Five acres with ocean beach, marine life, forest trails. Watch for seals, sea lions, whales, eagles. Explore hiking trails and wild west-coast beaches. Seven miles to friendly Sooke village. Spacious guest rooms are tastefully decorated with canopied beds and antiques.

Hosts: Bill & Marion Paine
Rooms: 6 (PB) $125-160 Canadian
Full Breakfast
Credit Cards: A, B
Notes: 2, 3, 4, 5, 8, 9, 10, 11, 12, 14

UCLUELET

Burley's Lodge

1078 Helen Road, Box 550
Ucluelet, BC, V0R 3A0
(604) 726-4444

A waterfront home/lodge on a small drive-on island at the harbor mouth in friendly Ucluelet. Watch ducks and birds play, heron and kingfisher work, and eagles soar. Trollers, draggers, and seiners, sail and sport boats in the harbor. There's a view from every window, a large living room, decks, fireplace, rec room with pool table. Enjoy the open ocean, sandy beaches, lighthouse lookout, nature walks, charter fishing, diving, whale watching, and sightseeing cruises.

Hosts: Ron Burley & Micheline Riley
Rooms: 6 (S4B) $30-50
Continental Breakfast
Credit Cards: A, B
Closed Dec. 15-Jan. 15
Notes: 9, 10, 11, 12

VANCOUVER

Diana's Luxury B&B

1019 East 38th Avenue
Vancouver, BC, U5W 1J4
(604) 321-2855

Our B&B is close to downtown in a quiet neighborhood. We are close to Stanley Park, shopping, skiing, the old Expo 86 site, and many more attractions.

Rooms: 7 (3 PB; 4 SB) $60 US
Continental Breakfast
Credit Cards: B
Notes: 5, 7, 8, 9, 10, 11, 12, 13, 14

NW Bed & Breakfast 902

610 SW Broadway
Portland, OR, 97205
(503) 243-7616

Traditional colonial built in the 1920s, with a sun deck, garden, den, breakfast and dining room. On a beautiful tree-lined street in the finest west-side area. Near many attractions, located ten minutes from city center, the airport, and the University of British Columbia. One twin room and one double room share a bath. $50-55.

NW Bed & Breakfast 904A

610 SW Broadway
Portland, OR, 97205
(503) 243-7616

Wonderfully convenient location for sightseers and business travelers. The spacious home is furnished in traditional style with Spanish and period pieces. Hospitable hosts are fluent in German. Guests are welcome to enjoy the heated pool. Guest quarters are on a separate level with private entrance. Two rooms with king beds share a bath. $45.

West End Guest House

NW Bed & Breakfast 967

610 SW Broadway
Portland, OR, 97205
(503) 243-7616

New contemporary townhouse in Fairview Heights, a residential district. Short walk to False Creek and minutes from public transportation, Granville Island, downtown, and beaches. Continental breakfast. No smoking. Two cats and one dog in residence. One queen room with private bath and Jacuzzi. Another single room shares the hosts' bath. $55.

West End Guest House

1362 Haro Street
Vancouver, BC, V6E 1G2
(604) 681-2889

Also known as "The Pink Victorian," this 1906 historic home boasts the perfect location, just a few blocks from Stanley Park, English Bay Beach, and downtown. Robsonstrasse is just one block away. Guests enjoy special amenities such as brass feather beds, remote TV, phones, private baths, Casablanca ceiling fans or opening skylights, nighttime sherry, and a full gourmet breakfast.

Host: Madeleine Prevost
Rooms: 7 (PB) $84-150 Canadian
Type of Beds: 2 Twin; 1 Double; 5 Queen
Full Breakfast
Credit Cards: A, B
Notes: 5, 9, 10, 11, 12, 13

VERNON

The Windmill House

5672 Learmouth Road
S19A, C2, RR 1
Vernon, BC, V1T 6L4
(604) 549-2804

Set in the pastoral Coldstream Valley, we are ideally situated for fishing, beaches, orchards, skiing, hot springs, gold panning, trail riding, golf, sailing, and cycling. Excellent mid-point stopover between Vancouver and Calgary. Easy access to Banff and the Rockies.

Hosts: Linda & Jeremy Dyde
Rooms: 4 (1 PB; 3 SB) $35-50 Canadian
Full Breakfast
Credit Cards: No
Notes: 2, 5, 6, 8, 9, 10, 11, 12, 13

VICTORIA

Battery Street Guesthouse

670 Battery Street
Victoria, BC, V8V 1E5
(604) 385-4632

Guesthouse (1898) in downtown Victoria. Within walking distance of town and sites. Park and ocean are one block away. Quiet, comfortable, and centrally located. Hostess speaks Dutch.

Host: Mrs. Pamela Verduyn
Rooms: 7 (SB) $55-65 Canadian
Full Breakfast
Credit Cards: No
Notes: 2, 5, 10, 11, 12

Cadboro Bay B&B

Town & Country B&B
Box 46544, Station G
Vancouver, BC, V6R 4G6
(604) 731-5942

Two guest rooms share one bath; generous gourmet breakfast. Guests are welcome to use the living room and secluded patio. Located near a sandy beach, tennis, and the University of Victoria. Downtown is fifteen minutes by car. In the village a block away are two restaurants, a neighborhood pub, and various shops. $50-55.

Camelia House

All Season B&B Agency
Box 5511, Station B
Victoria, BC, V8R 6S4
(604) 595-2337

Tucked away in a quiet residential area close to Oak Bay Village shopping, recreation center, and ocean walks, Camelia House offers a relaxing atmosphere, original 1913 charm, and convenient access to downtown. $45-55.

Cedar House

All Season B&B Agency
Box 5511, Station B
Victoria, BC, V8R 6S4
(604) 595-2337

An architecturally designed home located in the picturesque Rockland district, one block from Government House and Craigdarroch Castle. Two cats in residence. $45-60.

Craigmyle

1037 Craigdarroch Road
Victoria, BC, V8S 2A5
(604) 595-5411; FAX: (604) 370-5276

The Craigmyle is situated in the residential area of Victoria known as Rockland, directly in front of Craigdarroch Castle and only one mile from city center. Walk downtown along Antique Rowe, or we are directly on the city bus route. We are only one block from the Victoria Art Gallery. Breakfast consists of hot or cold cereal, eggs, bacon, and fried tomato, plus Jim's homemade jams. Five-day cancellation policy.

Hosts: Jim & Cathy Pace
Rooms: 19 (PB) $65-85
Full Breakfast
Credit Cards: A, B
Notes: 8, 9, 10, 11, 12, 14

Elk Lake Lodge

Elk Lake Lodge

5259 Patricia Bay Highway
Victoria, BC, V8Y 1S8
(604) 658-8879

Originally built in 1910 as a country chapel, Elk Lake Lodge has been beautifully restored. Four individually decorated guest rooms, a magnificent lounge, and outdoor hot tub are available for guests. Just steps to the lake for trout fishing, sailing, and wind surfing.

Host: Marie McQuade
Rooms: 4 (2 PB; 2 SB) $60-75 Canadian, + tax
Full Breakfast
Credit Cards: A, B
Notes: 5, 6, 7 (restricted), 8 (over 5), 9, 11

Garden City B&B A2

660 Jones Terrace
Victoria, BC, V8Z 2L7
(604) 479-9999

Perfect for large groups. Outdoor pool with hot tub and weights area. Well located near the airport and ferry. Five rooms ranging from $65 per couple. Reservations are a must. With notice, we can accommodate children.

Garden City B&B F3

660 Jones Terrace
Victoria, BC, V8Z 2L7
(604) 479-9999

Spectacular view of sea and the Olympic mountains. All rooms with private bath and entrance. $80 Canadian.

Garden City B&B F5

660 Jones Terrace
Victoria, BC, V8Z 2L7
(604) 479-9999

Edwardian home built in 1911 features exceptional cultured marble Jacuzzi, sitting room, antiques. Honeymoon suite, queen rooms, each with fireplace and special view. $75-150.

Garden City B&B F10

660 Jones Terrace
Victoria, BC, V8Z 2L7
(604) 479-9999

Tudor home with a top-floor suite suited to two couples, plus queen room and double room. Close to town, with a lovely garden. $50-80.

Garden City B&B I1

660 Jones Terrace
Victoria, BC, V8Z 2L7
(604) 479-9999

Great for honeymooners: quiet and peaceful, located on an inlet with beautifully decorated rooms, each with private bath. Some rooms have water views, others have garden views. $80-95.

Garden City B&B L2

660 Jones Terrace
Victoria, BC, V8Z 2L7
(604) 479-9999

Garden Farm B&B is a delight at any time of the year. A trout pond in front of the dining room, woodland trails, peace and quiet, and most unique home. $60-80.

Garden City B&B O6

660 Jones Terrace
Victoria, BC, V8Z 2L7
(604) 479-9999

Luxurious country farm with outdoor solar-heated pool. Horses, sheep, one dog, one cat. Only fifteen minutes away from town. $70-85.

Great-Snoring-On-Sea

10858 Madrona Drive, RR 1
Sidney, Victoria
BC, V8L 3R9
(604) 656-9549

Let us spoil you in our luxurious English-antique furnished villa perched high on a cliff overlooking the sea. Lie in bed and watch the sea-lions, bald eagles, and Orca whales.

Beautiful Butchard Gardens, Empress Hotel tea, and ferries are nearby.

Hosts: Sharon & Bill Flavelle
Rooms: 2 (PB) $85-155 US
Gourmet Breakfast
Credit Cards: No
Notes: 2, 7 (limited), 8 (call), 9, 10, 11, 12, 14

Heritage House B&B

3808 Heritage Lane
Victoria, BC, V82 7A7
(604) 479-0892

A beautiful 1910 Character home on three-quarters of an acre in a country setting. Quiet and secluded, with lounging veranda. Large rooms, guest parlor with fireplace, and library/den with additional fireplace. Continental or full breakfast. Afternoon hot tea and crumpets with evening snacks. TV and video, as well as old-time radio programs. Private parking. Convenient to ferries, downtown, and all highways.

Hosts: Larry & Sandra Gray
Rooms: 8 (SB) $50-59
Full or Continental Breakfast
Credit Cards: A, B
Notes: 5, 12, 13

Laird House

All Season B&B Agency
Box 5511, Station B
Victoria, B.C., V8R 6S4
(604) 595-2337

Come enjoy the warmth and gracious hospitality of Laird House, a charming 1912 heritage-style home in the quiet, peaceful setting of James Bay. The three charmingly furnished rooms, one with fireplace and balcony, share two guest baths. Resident dog. $45-65.

Mikker's

All Season B&B Agency
Box 5511, Station B
Victoria, BC, V8R 6S4
(604) 595-2337

Spacious new home overlooking quiet farmland with a great view of Mount Baker. Island View Beach is just a short drive away. One room with Jacuzzi, one with fireplace. Dutch and German spoken. $45-60.

Oak Bay Guest House

1052 Newport Avenue
Victoria, BC, V8S 5E3
(604) 598-3812

A classic 1912 B&B inn, situated in a quiet residential area. Guest rooms have private baths. Beaches, restaurants, marina, pub, golf, and shopping all within easy walking distance. Minutes from downtown; city bus at door. Guest lounge with TV overlooking manicured gardens. Full breakfast served. Adult oriented; no pets.

Hosts: Michael Dahlgrin & Neil Boucher
Rooms: 12 (10 PB; 2 SB) $59-99
Full Breakfast
Credit Cards: A, B
Notes: 5, 7 (restricted), 9, 10, 11, 12

The Pines

All Season B&B Agency
Box 5511, Station B
Victoria, BC, V8R 6S4
(604) 595-2337

Feel at home as you enjoy breakfast in the country-style kitchen. Advance reservations for self-contained suite with private entrance, bath, queen and hideaway beds. On good bus route and within walking distance of restaurants. $40-65.

Portage Inlet B&B

993 Portage Road
Victoria, BC, V8Z 1K9
(604) 479-4594

Located on an acre of waterfront three miles from city center. We specialize in organic food, and what we do not grow, we purchase from local farmers who are organically inclined. Since we do not spray with any pesticides, we have a myriad of birds and animals that live on and adjacent to our "acre of paradise."

Hosts: Jim & Pat Baillie
Rooms: 4 (3 PB; 1 SB) $65-95 Canadian
Full Breakfast
Credit Cards: A, B
Notes: 5, 8, 9, 10, 11, 12, 14

Scholefield House

All Season B&B Agency
Box 5511, Station B
Victoria, BC, V8R 6S4
(604) 595-2337

A c. 1892 Victorian Italianate offering the warmth and comforts of home. The rooms are furnished with charm and delicate taste. Four rooms share two baths. A full gourmet breakfast is served in the dining room. Two resident cats. $45-65.

The Sea Rose

All Season B&B Agency
Box 5511, Station B
Victoria, BC, V8R 6S4
(604) 595-2337

Enjoy the tranquility of the ocean and mountains. The Sea Rose is located along Victoria's scenic marine drive. Guests are invited to relax in the panoramic sea view sun room or in their private suites. $80-110.

Shirewood

All Season B&B Agency
Box 5511, Station B
Victoria, BC, V8R 6S4
(604) 595-2337

Large English Tudor home nestled in 4 acres with space to roam and relax. Discover B&B in "our little bit of Olde England." Two suites with private entrances, each with large bed/sitting rooms. Resident dog and cat. $55-75.

Silver Lace Cottage

All Season B&B Agency
Box 5511, Station B
Victoria, BC, V8R 6S4
(604) 595-2337

This quality character home with a lovely orchard garden is situated in a quiet residential area close to town, parks, and the ocean. Enjoy the private guest studio with a view of the back garden, or the two rooms in the main house. Breakfast is a healthy gourmet experience. Resident dog. $50-70.

Springfarm

All Season B&B Agency
Box 5511, Station B
Victoria, BC, V8R 6S4
(604) 595-2337

Are you looking for a quiet retreat by the sea, a place only a few minutes from downtown, yet far removed from its tension, a place close to a park with beach access, somewhere to relax on a sun deck overlooking the San Juan Islands with your morning coffee or breakfast? Come see us. $40-65.

Twin Willows

All Season B&B Agency
Box 5511, Station B
Victoria, BC, V8R 6S4
(604) 595-2337

Olivia and Joe welcome you to stay at their comfortable older residence. Relax in the shade of the two willow trees in the secluded backyard. Easy to find and close to all amenities. $40-50.

WEST VANCOUVER

Beachside B&B

4208 Evergreen Avenue
West Vancouver, BC, V7V 1H1
(604) 922-7773; FAX (604) 926-8073

Quiet, beautiful waterfront home in one of the finest areas in Vancouver. A lovely sand beach is at the doorstep. Minutes from downtown and Stanley Park, the house's southern exposure affords a panoramic view of the city, harbor, and Alaska cruise ships from the beachside Jacuzzi and dining room. Antique stained glass, old brick, and hanging baskets. Fishing, sailing, wilderness hiking, skiing, antiques, shopping, and excellent restaurants within ten minutes.

Beachside B&B

Hosts: Gordon & Joan Gibbs
Rooms: 3 (PB) $85-125
Full Breakfast
Credit Cards: A, B
Notes: 2, 5, 8, 9, 10, 11, 12, 13, 14

WHISTLER

Alberta B&B 11

P.O. Box 15477, MPO
Vancouver, BC, V6B 5B2
(604) 944-1793

European hospitality is offered at the chalet by the French and German hosts. Guest sitting room with wood stove, sun deck with a view of Whistler and the Blackcomb Mountains. Delicious continental breakfast with home-baked croissants and rolls. Horseback riding, swimming, golf, tennis, canoeing, fishing, skiing. Six guest rooms with down comforters, each with private bath.

WHITE ROCK

Alberta B&B 12

P.O. Box 15477, MPO
Vancouver, BC, V6B 5B2
(604) 944-1793

This home offers a private guest lounge with fireplace, TV, stereo, piano, library, and refrigerator. Hearty full breakfasts. It is located three minutes from the U.S. border; forty minutes from downtown Vancouver; thirty from the airport; and twenty minutes from the Victoria ferries. Close to sailing, fishing, riding, and golf. Three guest rooms with private baths.

Manitoba

BOISSEVAIN

Dueck's Cedar Chalet

B&B of Manitoba
93 Healy Crescent
Winnipeg, MAN, R2N 2S2
(204) 256-6151

Large, all-cedar bedroom with private in-room Jacuzzi. Close to Turtle Mountain Provincial Park, International Peace Gardens, good beaches, the U.S. border. Private baths. $50.

Neufelds

B&B of Manitoba
93 Healy Crescent
Winnipeg, MAN, R2N 2S2
(204) 256-6151

Two-story rooms with private entrance on a grain farm in the rolling countryside of Turtle Mountain. Near good beaches, cross-country ski trails, good hunting. $35.

DAUPHIN BEACH

Bide Awhile

B&B of Manitoba
93 Healy Crescent
Winnipeg, MAN, R2N 2S2
(204) 256-6151

Ten miles east of Dauphin, this house has rustic charm by the water's edge. Wake to the sound of waves and birds singing. Three-minute walk along the beach to a golf course and clubhouse with food service and bar. Hearty prairie breakfast is served in the dining room facing the lake. Restricted smoking. Bikes and canoe available. Pets welcome; only open summers. $44.

EMERSON

Tanglewood

B&B of Manitoba
93 Healy Crescent
Winnipeg, MAN, R2N 2S2
(204) 256-6151

Relax in this peaceful neighborhood town on the U.S. border. Located in a country-like setting with flowers and fruit trees on the banks of the Red River. Historic 1881 home. $35.

HECLA

Solmundson Gesta Hus

B&B of Manitoba
93 Healy Crescent
Winnipeg, MAN, R2N 2S2
(204) 256-6151

Four generations of the Solmundson family were born and raised on Hecla Island. Their guest house offers luxurious B&B accommodations. The house overlooks Lake Winnipeg and the historic Icelandic village of Hecla. Hecla Provincial Park features beaches, hiking trails, an a golf course. In the winter, enjoy cross-country skiing, ice fishing, and skidooing. $55-69.

HILLSIDE BEACH

Hillside Beach Resort

B&B of Manitoba
93 Healy Crescent

Winnipeg, MAN, R2N 2S2
(204) 256-6151

Located on Lake Winnipeg, a beautiful resort for getting away from it all in summer or winter. Come for the weekend and cross-country ski, water ski, boat, fish, cycle, or just relax. $40.

ROBLIN

Andres

B&B of Manitoba
93 Healy Crescent
Winnipeg, MAN, R2N 2S2
(204) 256-6151

Relax on the huge deck or in the luxurious sitting lounge overlooking beautiful Shell Valley. Enjoy the game room, hiking, cross-country skiing, fishing. Special German homemade sausage. $38.

WAWANESA

Pletts

B&B of Manitoba
93 Healy Crescent
Winnipeg, MAN, R2N 2S2
(204) 256-6151

This farm is in a beautiful area near the junction of the Souris and Assiniboine rivers. Attractions within a half-hour include Spruce Woods Provincial Park, Souris Swinging Bridge. Relax in the beautifully landscaped backyard with patio, sun deck, firepit, and childrens' play area. Delicious home-cooked meals. $35.

WINNIPEG

Alexanders

B&B of Manitoba
93 Healy Crescent
Winnipeg, MAN, R2N 2S2
(204) 256-6151

Luxurious home just off north bypass 101. Private facilities, delicious muffins. Quick access to Birds Hill Park, popular beaches, Rainbow Stage, Kildonan Park, and Kildonan Place Mall. $35-40.

Algeos

B&B of Manitoba
93 Healy Crescent
Winnipeg, MAN, R2N 2S2
(204) 256-6151

Enjoy this modern home and large, shaded lot. Take a walk in Fraser Grove Park on the Red River. Excellent bus service, restaurants, and shopping. Hosts will give tours and pickup service for an extra charge. $35.

Bannerman East

B&B of Manitoba
93 Healy Crescent
Winnipeg, MAN, R2N 2S2
(204) 256-6151

Come and enjoy our lovely Georgian home, evening tea, quiet walks in St. Johns Park or along the Red River. Close to Seven Oaks Museum, Planetarium Concert Hall, Rainbow Stage. $35.

Belangers

B&B of Manitoba
93 Healy Crescent
Winnipeg, MAN, R2N 2S2
(204) 256-6151

Enjoy the relaxing atmosphere in this special home built in 1900. Sitting room adjacent to guest bedroom. Can accommodate a family of four. $35.

Fillions

B&B of Manitoba
93 Healy Crescent
Winnipeg, MAN, R2N 2S2
(204) 256-6151

Located in a nice community setting close to the Trans-Canada Highway city route. Nearby attractions include the mint, St. Vital Mall, Fun Mountain Waterslide, Tinkertown, outdoor pool, bicycle path. $32.

Hawchuks

B&B of Manitoba
93 Healy Crescent
Winnipeg, MAN, R2N 2S2
(204) 256-6151

Located on the banks of the Red River, this beautiful Tudor home has English gardens and a riverbank walkway. Top off the day with a paddlewheel boat dinner cruise. English, German, and French spoken. For an additional charge, a full course dinner is available. $59.

Hillmans

B&B of Manitoba
93 Healy Crescent
Winnipeg, MAN, R2N 2S2
(204) 256-6151

Cozy private sitting room, full breakfast of your choice. Located downtown, close to bus route, airport, Polo Park, planetarium, concert hall. $40.

Klassens

B&B of Manitoba
93 Healy Crescent
Winnipeg, MAN, R2N 2S2
(204) 256-6151

Your hosts speak English and German and are interested in antiques. Home baking, strawberries and raspberries in season. Relax with tea on the deck. City tours available at additional charge. Within walking distance of the University of Manitoba, Assiniboia Downs Racetrack, and the Prairie Living Museum. Children are welcome. $35.

Lobreaus

137 Woodlawn Avenue
Winnipeg, MAN, R2M 2P5
(204) 256-9789

Our four-level split home, which is located on a half acre of parklike grounds near the Red River, features spacious guest rooms. Located in the south of Winnipeg, with quick and easy access to downtown. We are near the University of Manitoba, The Mint, St. Boniface attractions, a shopping mall, park, and good restaurants.

Hosts: Francis & Anya Lobreau
Rooms: 3 (1 PB; 2 SB) $34-38
Full Breakfast
Credit Cards: No
Notes: 5, 8, 10, 11, 12

Southern Rose Guest House

533 Sprague Street
Winnipeg, MAN, R3G 2R9
(204) 775-3484; (204) 786-3105

Experience the charm of decades past with a touch of Southern hospitality. Enjoy morning breakfast and the newspaper in the formal dining room or on the wraparound cedar sun deck. Play horseshoes or relax in the redwood hot tub. Close to Polo Park Mall, restaurants, zoo, airport.

Host: Ray Antymis
Rooms: 3 (SB) $35-45
Full Breakfast
Credit Cards: B
Notes: 5, 8, 9, 10, 11, 12

New Brunswick

GRAND MANAN ISLAND

Shorecrest Lodge

North Head, Grand Manan Island
NB, E0G 2M0
(506) 662-3216

A charming country inn overlooking the sea. We cater to nature lovers on an island blessed with an abundance of birds, whales, and wildflowers. Grand Manan has a reputation as the best natural-history destination in Maritime Canada. Whale watching arranged.

Hosts: Andrew & Cynthia Normandeau
Rooms: 16 (2 PB; 14 SB) $60
Continental Breakfast
Credit Cards: B
Notes: 2, 3, 4, 7, 8, 9, 10, 11, 12

LOWER JEMSEG

Oakley House

Lower Jemseg
NB, E0E 1S0
(506) 488-3113; FAX: (506) 488-2785

Enjoy a warm stay in a graciously rebuilt home in the peaceful lower Saint John River valley. Organic food; eclectic library, music; canoeing, swimming, bird watching, cycling. The area is rich in loyalist history. Lovely fully furnished suite available by the week. French and Spanish spoken. No smoking.

Hosts: Max M. & Willi Evans Wolfe
Rooms: 3 (SB) $45-50 Canadian
Full Breakfast
Credit Cards: B
Notes: 2, 5, 9, 11, 13

ST. ANDREWS

Pansy Patch

59 Carelton Street
St. Andrews, NB, E0G 2X0
(506) 529-3834; (203) 354-4181 (winter)

A very unique house with turret housing a four-room B&B and a lovely antique and book shop. All rooms overlook the water and a beautiful garden where you are welcome to stroll or sit in the shade reading and relaxing.

Hosts: Michael & Kathleen Lazare
Rooms: 4 (SB) $90 Canadian
Full Breakfast
Credit Cards: A, B, C
Notes: 2, 6, 9, 10, 11, 12, 14

SUSSEX

Anderson Country Vacation Farm

RR 2, Sussex
NB, E0E 1P0
(506) 433-3786

A working farm of 200 acres with sheep and beef cattle, a wide variety of fowl, colorful pheasants and peacocks, wild Canadian geese, swans, ducks, donkey, goat, and friendly dog. Pond stocked with native trout and nature trail on premises. Fundy National Park is one hour away, as are the reversing falls at Saint John and the magnetic hill at Moncton.

Hosts: Tom & Laura Anderson
Rooms: 3 (SB) $25-30
Full Breakfast
Credit Cards: No
Notes: 5, 8, 11, 12

Nova Scotia

ANNAPOLIS ROYAL

Garrison House Inn

350 St. George Street
Annapolis Royal, NS, B0S 1A0
(902) 532-5750

An historic 1854 roadside inn located opposite Fort Anne in the heart of Annapolis Royal, Canada's oldest town (1605). Our three intimate dining rooms offer fresh local fare from the sea and the fertile Annapolis Valley, served and prepared with verve and imagination to our guests and the traveling public.

Host: Patrick Redgrave
Rooms: 7 (5 PB; 2 SB) $58-68
Full Breakfast
Credit Cards: A, B, C
Notes: 3, 4, 7, 8, 9, 10, 11, 12, 13, 14

LOUISBOURG

Greta Cross B&B

81 Pepperell Street
Louisbourg, NS, B0A 1M0
(902) 733-2833

An older home, situated on a hill overlooking the harbor and the fortress of Louisbourg. In a quiet area. Homemade breads, muffins, jams, etc. Snack on arrival and at bedtime if desired. Many interesting spots to visit. Smoking on request in lounge only.

Host: Mrs. Greta Cross
Rooms: 3 (S2B) $30
Full Breakfast
Credit Cards: No
Open April 1-Nov. 1
Notes: 2, 3, 6, 7 (restricted), 8, 9, 10, 11, 14

WOLFVILLE

Blomidon Inn

127 Main Street
Wolfville, NS, B0P 1X0
(902) 542-2291

Offering the gracious comforts of a nineteenth-century sea captain's mansion, with a reputation for elegant accommodations and hospitable country cuisine—a reputation that extends far beyond the province of Nova Scotia.

Hosts: Jim & Donna Laceby
Rooms: 27 (25 PB; 2 SB) $42.90-97.90
Continental Breakfast
Credit Cards: A, B, C, F
Notes: 3, 4, 5, 7, 8, 9, 10, 14

Ontario

ALTON

Cataract Inn

RR 2, Alton
ONT, L0N 1A0
(519) 927-3033

Antiques and cotton prints suited to the 130-year-old inn abound, but the mattresses are strictly modern and comfortable. Terry cloth gowns hang behind the door, coverups as you make the short walk down the hall to the spacious bathrooms. Imagine waking from a sound sleep . . . the sun pouring in your window . . . the birds singing or the trees shining crystalline with frost. Smell the coffee and homemade muffins? Late riser? No hurry—we'll wait for you.

Hosts: Rodney & Jennifer Hough
Rooms: 5 (S2B) $75-125
Continental Breakfast
Credit Cards: A, B, C
Closed Christmas
Notes: 3, 4, 8 (over 5), 11, 12, 13

Inn at the Falls

BRACEBRIDGE

Inn at the Falls

17 Dominion Street
Bracebridge, ONT, P0B 1C0
(705) 645-2245

Located in a wooded small-town setting overlooking the Muskoka River and falls, this restored Victorian inn exudes traditional old-fashioned hospitality. Eighteen tastefully decorated rooms with private bath, TV, and phones, fireplaces. Fine dining, outdoor heated pool, authentic English pub, entertainment, patio.

Hosts: Jan & Peter Rickard
Rooms: 18 (PB) $96
Full Breakfast
Credit Cards: A, B, C
Notes: 2, 3, 4, 5, 7, 8, 9, 10, 11, 12, 13, 14

LAMBETH

Twin Pines

7 Scott Place
Lambeth, ONT, N0l 1S0
(519) 652-2706

New two-story house on a quiet cul-de-sac in Lambeth Park estates. Offers beautifully furnished rooms, central air, use of backyard deck and recreation room. No smoking. $28-38.

LONDON

Annigan's

194 Elmwood Avenue East
London, ONT, N6C 1K2
(519) 439-9196

Owned by an interior designer, this turn-of-the-century house features a turret, fireplace, and fine architectural details. Two double and one twin rooms; full bath, powder room, smoking lounge. Downtown, Grand Theatre, U.W.O. bus routes, and antique stores are close by. $35-50.

Chiron House

398 Piccadilly Street
London, ONT, N6A 1S7
(519) 673-6878

Recall the comfort and elegance of an earlier time in our turn-of-the-century home lovingly maintained and furnished in period with modern amenities. Located centrally within walking distance of theater, restaurants, and shopping. Convenient for UWO and airport. Suite with whirlpool available; free parking. $44-55.

Clermont Place

679 Clermont Avenue
London, ONT, N5X 1N3
(519) 672-0767

Air-conditioned home in a parklike setting with recreational facilities nearby. Close to Highway 22 and 126 in Northeast London. Each room has a double bed; one has a water bed. Gourmet meals, served by a cozy fireside, are available on request. $40-45.

Corsaut

RR 3, Ilderton
London, ONT, N0M 2A0
(519) 666-1876

Quiet, tree-shaded farm located just six miles north of London offers two attractive rooms, one with double bed and one with a single. Guests may enjoy the ponies and see our antique John Deere tractors. Nonsmokers preferred. Air-conditioned. $25-30.

Cozy Corners

87 Askin Street
London, ONT, N6C 1E5
(519) 673-4598

Our 1871 Victorian home is in the core area of London. We have lovingly restored it to maintain the warm glow of wood and stained glass. Three bedrooms, kitchenette, and bath. English and French spoken. Full breakfast is served between 7:30-9:00 only. $30-40. Children under 10: $10.

Dillon's Place

56 Gerrard Street
London, ONT, N6C 4C7
(519) 439-9666

Air-conditioned old home in South London has comfortable people and a large, friendly Labrador. Guest rooms with double or twin beds and bath nearby. Very close to downtown, Wellington Road, Victoria Hospital, and bus service. Nonsmoking adults preferred. $25-35.

Eileen's

433 Hyde Park Road
London, ONT, N6H 3R9
(519) 471-1107

Comfortable Cape Cod home on an acre of land with trees. One double, one twin, and one single bedroom. Five minutes to Thames Valley golf course and Springbank Park. Ten minutes to downtown, theaters, shopping and U.W.O. Bus service. Lots of parking; use of swimming pool; central air-conditioning. $25-40.

Ferndale West

53 Longbow Road
London, ONT, N6G 1Y5
(519) 471-8038

Ferndale West offers central air, extra-large rooms, two with queen beds, one of which is a two-room suite; other is a twin. Very close to the university, cross-country skiing, and there is a nature walk at the end of the street. Use of swimming pool. $32-47.

Hindhope

RR 2, Lucan
London, ONT, N0M 2J0
(519) 227-4514

Century-old country home twenty minutes from London on Highway 7. Thirty-minute drive to Lake Huron and Grand Bend. Children and pets welcome; no smoking in bedrooms. Additional meals on request. $25-30.

Johnson B&B

308 Princess Avenue
London, ONT, N6B 2A6
(519) 672-2394

Lovely old home offering a room with double beds and nearby bath. Also a suite of rooms with private bath and kitchenette. Nonsmokers, please. $30-45.

Lambert House

231 Cathcart Street
London, ONT, N6C 3M8
(519) 672-8996 (after 6:00 P.M.)

Quiet turn-of-the-century home in the heart of Old South London. Close to downtown, parks, golf, and six antique shops. Guests are served welcome snacks. Afternoon tea and champagne with breakfast on weekends. No pets; adults preferred. $30-40.

McLellan Place

880 Farnham Road
London, ONT, N6K 1R9
(519) 473-3709

Lovely trilevel home with air-conditioning, three bedrooms, two baths. Breakfast in formal dining room or on the back patio. Near Westmount shopping mall, Wally World, minigolf. No smoking. Visa and Mastercard accepted. $30-40.

Overdale

2 Normandy Gardens
London, ONT, N6H 4A9
(519) 641-0236

Air-conditioned home in mature, residential West London. Near parks and golf courses; easily accessible to U.W.O. and downtown. Guest floor has three bedrooms with full bath. Separate suite with bath and kitchen. Twin, double, or king beds. Only open April 1-Dec. 31. $40-45.

Rolling Ridge Farm

RR 1, Arva
London, ONT, N0M 1C0
(519) 666-0896

Unwind in our big old country home ten miles northwest of London and five miles west of Arva. Two double bedrooms, one with a private bath. See our maple-syrup making and products. Use of swimming pool; hayloft fun. No pets. $25-35.

The Rose House

526 Dufferin Avenue
London, ONT, N6B 2A2
(519) 433-9978

Welcome to London's finest B&B home, located in a quiet, exclusive residential area of century-old homes in the downtown area. London is midway between Detroit and Toronto and is a theatre, medical, and shopping center for southwest Ontario.

Hosts: Betty & Doug Rose
Rooms: 3 (1 PB; 2 SB) $35-45
Full Breakfast

Credit Cards: No
Notes: 5, 9, 10, 11, 12, 13

Serena's Place

720 Headley Drive
London, ONT, N6H 3V6
(519) 471-6228

Air-conditioned home in the prestigious residential area of West London. Three bedrooms and full bath. Sun room for relaxation. Near Springbank Park and Thames Valley Golf Course. Ten minutes from Theatre London. Bus service at the door. $25-40

Trillium

71 Trillium Crescent
London, ONT, N5Y 4T3
(519) 453-3801

Restful, modern, air-conditioned home offers two guest rooms — one with queen bed, one with twins — on a quiet crescent just off highway 126. Close to U.W.O., hospitals, airport, Fanshaw Pioneer Village, golf course, bus routes, and shopping. No smoking, please. Home-cooked meals on request. $30-45.

Tudor Lane

141 Windsor Crescent
London, ONT, N6K 1V9
(519) 439-9984

Tudor-style home in South London offers three guest rooms; one with two-piece bath. Close to 401; near downtown area. Children and pets welcome. $25-35.

NEW HAMBURG

The Waterlot Rest

17 Huron Street
New Hamburg, ONT, N0B 2G0
(519) 662-2020

Two large and very comfortably appointed rooms and one suite. Marble shower, bidet, sink and sitting area. Fine dining on the premises.

Host: Gord Elkeer
Rooms: 3 (1 PB; 2 SB) $75-100
Continental Breakfast
Credit Cards: A, B, E
Notes: 2, 3, 4, 5, 9, 10, 11, 12, 13

OTTAWA

Albert House

478 Albert Street
Ottawa, ONT, K1R 5B5
(613) 236-4479

Gracious Victorian home built in 1875 by renowned Canadian architect. Each room is individually decorated and has a private bath, telephone, TV, and air conditioning. Lounge with fireplace. Parking is available, but we are within walking distance to most attractions. There are two large but friendly dogs in the house.

Hosts: John & Cathy Delroy
Rooms: 17 (PB) $65-90 Canadian
Full Breakfast
Credit Cards: A, B, C, E
Notes: 5, 7, 9, 11, 12, 13

Auberge McGee's Inn

185 Daly Avenue
Ottawa, ONT, K1N 6E8
(613) 237-6089

Welcome to McGees! A handsomely restored Victorian mansion, centrally located and within walking distance of all downtown attractions. Featuring rooms with private bath, telephone, cable TV, fireplaces, Jacuzzi suites. Free parking. Recommended by *Country Inns,* Frommer's, AAA/CAA, OHMA. 1990 Noel Kerr award for hospitality.

Hosts: Anne Schutte & Mary Unger
Rooms: 14 (10 PB; 4 SB) $68-108
Full Breakfast

Credit Cards: A, B
Notes: 5, 8 (over 5), 11, 12, 13

Australis Guest House

35 Marlborough Avenue
Ottawa, ONT, K1N 8E6
(613) 235-8461

Our sixty-year-old home is a classic residence with fireplaces and leaded windows in a lovely part of downtown Ottawa. Near parks, embassies, and the river. Our breakfasts are hearty and friendly and famous for their conversation. Oldest established B&B in Ottawa. Winner of the Ottawa Hospitality Award in 1989.

Hosts: Brian & Carol Waters
Rooms: 3 (1 PB; 2 SB) $40 Canadian
Full Breakfast
Credit Cards: No
Notes: 5, 7, 8

Beatrice Lyon Guest House

479 Slater Street
Ottawa, ONT, K1R 5C2
(613) 236-3904

One-hundred-year-old family home, five minutes from the Parliament Buildings, National Archives, National Arts Center. Thirty minutes from museums, National Art Gallery, Byward Market, and Rideau Shopping Center.

Host: Beatrice Lyon
Rooms: 3 (SB) $40
Full Breakfast
Credit Cards: No
Notes: 2, 5, 7, 8, 9, 10, 11, 12, 13

Cartier House Inn

46 Cartier Street, Ottawa
ONT, K2P 1J3
(613) 236-4667

Eleven exquisite rooms/suites with antique furniture, rich draperies, carefully selected works of art in a restored turn-of-the-century mansion. Jacuzzis in suites; turn-down service; morning newspaper. On a quiet street within walking distance of Parliament buildings, National Arts Center, shopping, and restaurants. Member of European-based chain of inns: Relais du Silence.

Host: Noreen Spanier
Rooms: 11 (PB) $103.95-145.95 Canadian
Continental Breakfast
Credit Cards: A, B, C, E, F
Notes: 2, 5, 7 (limited), 8 (8 and over), 9, 10, 11, 12, 13, 14

Auberge McGee's Inn

Constance House

62 Sweetland Avenue
Ottawa, ONT, K1N 7T6
(613) 235-8888

A heritage home (1895) in downtown Ottawa that boasts antique chandeliers and original maple wood staircase. Year-round comfort with air-conditioning and fireplace. Each room has its own sink, terry robes, hair dryer. Suite available for extended visits.

Host: Esther M. Peterson
Rooms: 5 (1 PB; 4 SB) $48-54
Suite: $80-88
Full Breakfast
Minimum stay holidays: 2
Credit Cards: A, B, C
Notes: 2, 5, 8, 9, 10, 11, 12, 13, 14

Gasthaus Switzerland Inn

89 Daly Avenue
Ottawa, ONT, K1N 6E6
(613) 237-0335

We are located in the heart of Ottawa, within walking distance to Parliament Hill, the old market, the Rideau Center, Congress Center, Ottawa University, and the Rideau Canal.

Hosts: Sabine & Josef Sauter
Rooms: 25 (21 PB; 4 SB) $52-88
Full Swiss Country Breakfast
Credit Cards: A, B
Notes: 5, 8 (over 12), 10, 11, 12, 13

O'Connor House Downtown

O'Connor House Downtown

172 O'Connor Street
Ottawa, ONT, K2P 1T5
(613) 236-4221; FAX: (613) 236-4232

The most centrally located B&B in Ottawa. A short walk to Parliament buildings, Rideau Canal, National Gallery, bicycle paths, and shopping. Less than one-half hour to beaches, lakes, and ski resorts. Enjoy friendly, comfortable accommodation; full Canadian buffet breakfast, guest lounge with TV and snack area, free use of bicycles or ice skates, air-conditioning, and parking.

Host: Donna Bradley
Rooms: 34 (SB) $49-62 Canadian
Full Breakfast
Credit Cards: A, B, C, E, F
Notes: 2, 5, 7, 8, 10, 11, 12, 13, 14

Robert's B&B

488 Cooper Street
Ottawa, ONT, K1R 5H9
(613) 563-0161

Robert's Bed & Breakfast is a large and most comfortable home over 100 years old. Furnished with a pleasant blend of Canadian and American pieces. Large suite with queen bed, bathroom, sitting room, balcony. Within walking distance of Parliament buildings and museums.

Host: Robert Rivoire
Rooms: 4 (SB) $50 Canadian
Suite: 1 (PB) $64 Canadian
Full or Continental Breakfast
Credit Cards: No
Notes: 2, 5, 9, 10, 11, 12, 13, 14

PETROLIA

Rebecca's B&B

4058 Petrolia Street
P.O. Box 1028
Petrolia, ONT, N0N 1R0
(519) 882-0118; (519) 882-0244

Original Petrolia oil-boom home, 100 years old, furnished with some antiques, including a restored player piano. Baby-sitting available with adequate notice. Guest rooms are on the third floor with shared bath. Ten minute walk from downtown, unique library, craft and antique shops, year-round theater.

Hosts: John & Becky MacLachlan
Rooms: 3 (SB) $35-40
Continental Breakfast
Credit Cards: No
Notes: 5, 7 (restricted), 8, 9, 10, 11, 12, 13

PORT STANLEY

Great Lakes Farms' Guest House

RR 1, Union
ONT, N0L 2L0
(519) 633-2390

NOTES: Credit cards accepted: A Master Card; B Visa; C American Express; D Discover Card; E Diners Club; F Other: 2 Personal checks accepted: 3 Lunch available: 4 Dinner available: 5 Open all year

A separate century farm home on 250 scenic acres with pool table, Jacuzzi bath, glassed-in veranda. Antique furniture and polished pine floors. Close to Port Stanley (Lake Erie) beach, restaurants, Quaker village of Sparta, Hawk Cliff, the Elgin Hiking Trail, or the bright lights of London and Stratford Shakespearean Theater.

Hosts: Bob & Marge Thomas
Rooms: 3 (SB) $40-50
Continental Breakfast
Credit Cards: No
Notes: 2, 3, 4, 5, 8, 9, 10, 11, 12, 13 (XC)

TORONTO

Burken Guest House

322 Palmerston Blvd.
Tononto, ONT, M6G 2N6
(416) 920-7842

Splendidly situated in a chamring residential neighborhood adjacent to downtown. Eight tastefully appointed rooms with shared bathrooms. Limited parking on premises; public transportation nearby. Friendly, capable service in a relacxed, Old World atmosphere.

Hosts: Burke & Ken
Rooms: 8 (SB) $63-68
Continental Breakfast
Credit Cards: A, B
Notes: 5, 8, 9, 14

Oppenheims

153 Huron Street
Tononto, ONT, M5T 2B6
(416) 598-4562

Oppenheims is now beginning its tenth year of operation. The four eclectic rooms and "special" breakfasts have been featured on national TV, CNN Travel News, and over twenty-five magazines and newspapers. The house, built in 1890, features four pianos, a turn-of-the-century general store, and huge kitchen. It is downtown, halfway between the art gallery and the Royal Ontario Museum. No smoking. One dog in residence.

Host: Susan Oppenheim
Rooms: 4 (SB) $50-55
Full Breakfast
Minimum stay: 3
Notes: 2)deposit only), 5, 8 (over 12), 9, 10, 11, 12, 14

Burken Guest House

6 Pets welcome: 7 Smoking allowed: 8 Children welcome: 9 Social drinking allowed: 10 Tennis available: 11 Swimming available: 12 Golf available: 13 Skiing available: 14 May be booked through travel agents

Prince Edward Island

HUNTER RIVER

Chez Le Clair Tourist Home

RR 2, Hunter River
PEI, C0A 1N0
(902) 963-2267

Our home is over one hundred years old and is situated on the north shore of Prince Edward Island, three miles from Cavendish Beach and two from North Rustico Beach. Both beaches are within the National Park on PEI. Lobster suppers, horseback riding within three miles.

Hosts: Joyce & Fred LeClair
Rooms: 5 (SB) $30
Continental Breakfast
Credit Cards: No
Closed Oct. 1-May 31
Notes: 2, 7, 8, 9, 10, 11, 12, 14

KENSINGTON

Sherwood Acres Guest Home

RR 1, Kensington
PEI, C0B 1M0
(902) 836-5430

Fourteen Km. north of Kensington on Route 20, on a family-operated potato and grain farm. Enjoy a quiet, relaxing holiday in this modern home with well-appointed rooms. Near beautiful sandy beach. Barbecue and picnic tables are available. Breakfast includes homemade breads, jams, and muffins. Hospitality award winners.

Hosts: Erma & James Hickey
Rooms: 5 (S3B) $40
Full Breakfast
Credit Cards: No
Notes: 2, 5, 8, 9, 10, 11

MONTAGUE

Partridge's

Panmure Island RR 2
Montague, PEI, C0A 1R0
(902) 838-4687

Partridge's B&B, surrounded by sandy beaches, is near Panmure Island Provincial Park, where well-trained lifeguards patrol one of the most beautiful beaches on PEI. A leisurely walk through the woods to our beach offers quiet relaxation. Wild strawberries and raspberries can be picked, clams can be dug, and Graham's Lobster Factory is nearby. Baby-sitting, as well as cribs and kitchen privileges, are available. Bicycles, canoe, and rowboat are a few of the other added attractions. Hostess has two cats, and pets are permitted.

Host: Mrs. Gertude Partridge
Rooms: 7 (5 PB; 2 SB) $40 + tax
Full Breakfast
Credit Cards: B
Notes: 2, 5, 6, 8, 9, 10, 11, 12, 13 (XC), 14

MURRAY RIVER

Bayberry Cliff Inn B&B

RR 4, Little Sands
PEI, C0A 1W0
(902) 962-3395

Situated on the edge of a 40-foot cliff, the inn consists of two converted post-and-beam barns decorated with antiques and marine

NOTES: Credit cards accepted: A Master Card; B Visa; C American Express; D Discover Card; E Diners Club; F Other: 2 Personal checks accepted: 3 Lunch available: 4 Dinner available: 5 Open all year

art. Stairs to the shore. Seals, restaurants, craft shops nearby.

Hosts: Don & Nancy Perkins
Rooms: 7 (SB) $35-65
Full Breakfast
Credit Cards: A, B
Closed Oct. 1-May 15
Notes: 8, 9, 11

SOUTH RUSTICO

Barachois Inn

P.O. Box 1022
Charlottetown, PEI, C1A 7M4
(902) 963-2194

The Barachois Inn is located on Route 243 in South Rustico, which is only 6 Km. from two national parks. We have a 15-room Victorian home in a beautiful and historic community that boasts a museum and the oldest Catholic Church on Prince Edward Island. The inn has been totally restored with artwork and antiques. We offer a view of the bay and surrounding countryside.

Hosts: Judy & Gary MacDonald
Rooms: 6 (1 PB; 5 SB) $45-60
Full Breakfast
Credit Cards: No
Notes: 2, 8, 9, 11, 12, 14

SUMMERSIDE

Faye & Eric's B&B

380 MacEwen Road
Summerside, PEI, C1N 4X8
(902) 436-6847

All rooms tastefully decorated. Two suites available—one with Jacuzzi and whirlpool bath. Housekeeping unit sleeps four and has private entrance and bath. Private kitchen for guests, patio, and barbecue. Beach about three miles away; restaurant and shopping within walking distance.

Hosts: Jo Ann Acorn & Ian Doughart
Rooms: 8 (3 PB; 5 S4B) $35-85
Continental Breakfast
Credit Cards: B
Notes: 7, 9, 12

Silver Fox Inn

61 Granville Street
Summerside, PEI
C1N 2Z3
(902) 436-4033

For nearly a century, proud owners have carefully preserved the beauty of the spacious rooms with their fireplaces and fine woodwork. Combining modern comfort with the cherished past, the Silver Fox Inn offers accommodation for twelve guests. Its six bedrooms, each with private bath, feature period furnishings.

Host: Julie Simmons
Rooms: 6 (PB) $55-60
Continental Breakfast
Credit Cards: A, B, C
Closed Christmas
Notes: 5, 7, 8 (over 10), 9, 10, 11, 12, 13

UIGG

MacLeod's Farm B&B

Vernon Post Office
Uigg, PEI, C0A 2E0
(902) 651-2303

Mixed farm, centrally located on Route 24, three Km. off Route 1 or Route 3 in the quiet, scenic community of Uigg. Large play area, hay rides, kittens, bunnies, and Newfoundland dog for guests' enjoyment. Beaches and music festival twenty minutes away. Home-baked breads and homemade jams.

Hosts: Malcom & Margie MacLeod
Rooms: 3 (SB) $35-38
Full Breakfast
Credit Cards: B
Notes: 2, 8, 9, 11, 12, 13

Quebec

CAP A L'AIGLE

La Pinsonniere

124 St. Raphael
Cap a L'Aigle
QUE, G0T 1B0
(418) 665-4431; FAX: (418) 665-7156

A small deluxe inn located in Charlevoix, a haven for artists and dreamers. This beautiful country stretches from Quebec City to Baie Ste-Catherine along the St-Laurent River, and offers a world of discoveries, from exquisite cuisine to whale watching.

Hosts: Janine & Jean Authier
Rooms: 28 (PB) $195-350, dinner included
Full Breakfast
Minimum stay weekends: 2; holidays: 3
Credit Cards: A, B
Closed Oct. 1-Feb. 20
Notes: 3, 4, 7, 8, 10, 11, 12, 13, 14

DESCHAMBAULT

L'Auberge du Roy

106 rue St-Laurent
Deschamabault, QUE, G0A 1S0
(418) 286-6958

Old Victorian building in a charming countryside location offering luxury, comfort, elegance, and relaxation. Tennis court, badminton court, outdoor terrace. The inn boasts a three-star restaurant with French cuisine.

Hosts: Isabelle & Jean-Claude Lisita
Rooms: 6 (4 PB; 2 SB) $55-125
Full Breakfast
Credit Cards: A, B
Notes: 3, 4, 5, 7, 8, 9, 10, 11, 12, 13

ISLE D'ORLEANS

Le Vigie du Pilote

170, Chemin Marie-Carreau, St.-Jean
Isle D'Orleans, QUE, G0A 3W0
(418) 829-2613

Come and enjoy the peaceful and relaxed atmosphere of the river pilot's home. A luxurious house on beautiful Orleans Island, only thirty-five minutes from Quebec. Quiet country surroundings with magnificent views over the St. Lawrence River. Nonsmokers only.

Hosts: John & Lorraine Godolphin
Rooms: 3 (PB) $60-75 Canadian
Full Breakfast
Closed Nov. 1-April 30
Credit Cards: No
Notes: 2, 8, 9, 11, 12

KAMOURASKA

Gite du Passant

81 Avenue Morel, C. P. 174
Kamouraska, QUE, G0L 1M0
(418) 492-2921

Nineteenth-century home situated on a patch of land on the south shore of the St. Lawrence River. Watch the glorious sunsets. Very quiet.

Host: Mariette Le Blanc
Rooms: 4 (1 PB; 3 SB) $30
Full Breakfast
Maximum stay: 3
Credit Cards: No
Closed Nov. 1-April 30
Notes: 8, 9, 11

NOTES: Credit cards accepted: A Master Card; B Visa; C American Express; D Discover Card; E Diners Club; F Other: 2 Personal checks accepted: 3 Lunch available: 4 Dinner available: 5 Open all year

MONTREAL

A B&B Downtown Network 1

3458 Laval Avenue
Montreal, QUE, H2X 3C8
(514) 289-9749

Downtown Sherbrook Street. Sylvie offers a double in her attractive and uniquely designed split-level duplex. Only a few minutes' walk to Old Montreal and fascinating St. Denis Street. In the summer, enjoy Sylvie's homemade rhubarb-strawberry preserves with your croissants. Be her guest at the health club. One room, shared bath, full breakfast. $55.

A B&B Downtown Network 2

3458 Laval Avenue
Montreal, QUE, H2X 3C8
(514) 289-9749

Downtown, in the heart of the Latin Quarter. Enjoy the superb location of this restored traditional Quebecoise home. Your host, active in the restaurant business, offers two sunlit doubles and one triple with a bay window opening onto a typical Montreal scene. The privacy of this tastefully furnished home is perfect for first or second honeymoons. Shared bath, full breakfast. $55-75.

A B&B Downtown Network 3

3458 Laval Avenue
Montreal, QUE, H2X 3C8
(514) 289-9749

When traveling to Quebec City, stop at this listed landmark home built in 1671, which faces the beautiful St. Lawrence River. Your hostess, a blue-ribbon chef, offers guest a memorable breakfast featuring "Quiche Floriane." Experience the warmth and hospitality of a typical Quebecoise home. Two rooms, shared bath, full breakfast. $55.

A B&B Downtown Network 4

3458 Laval Avenue
Montreal, QUE, H2X 3C8
(514) 289-9749

Downtown double off Sherbrooke Street. This antique-filled apartment on Drummond Street is tastefully decorated and only two minutes to the Museum of Fine Arts and all shopping. Mount Royal Park is nearby, and McGill University is just two blocks. Your hosts will pamper you with a gourmet breakfast and invite you to join them for a sherry in the evening. One double room, shared bath. $55.

A B&B Downtown Network 5

3458 Laval Avenue
Montreal, QUE, H2X 3C8
(514) 289-9749

Downtown, near St. Denis Street. Be in the heart of everything. The big bay window of this ninety-year-old restored home overlooks the city's most historic park. Original woodwork and detail add to the charm of this home. The neighborhood is famous for its excellent "bring your own wine" restaurants, and your host knows them all. Two double rooms and two triples, shared baths, full breakfast. $55-75.

A B&B Downtown Network 6

3458 Laval Avenue
Montreal, QUE, H2X 3C8
(514) 289-9749

Old Montreal. Your hosts spoil their guests with Quebecoise hospitality. As a city councillor, the host was instrumental in the preservation of the Latin Quarter. They'll be glad to suggest one of the city's sensational restaurants and have personal knowledge of the antique district. One double room, private bath, full breakfast. $75.

A B&B Downtown Network 7

3458 Laval Avenue
Montreal, QUE, H2X 3C8
(514) 289-9749

Downtown, turn-of-the-century home. This restored Victorian features a marble fireplace, original hardwood floors, and a skylight. Your host offers two charmingly decorated singles and two doubles (one with a brass bed), and grandma's quilt in the winter. You can bird watch on the balcony or have a challenging game of Scruples in the evening. Shared baths, full breakfast. $40-55.

B&B à Montréal B1

P.O. Box 575, Snowdon Station
Montréal, QUE, H3X 3T8
(514) 738-9410

Your hostess's love of art and antiques is obvious in her fabulous three-story townhouse. Fireplace, cozy living room, and a view of the city's most historic park all add to the charm of this home. One double with brass bed and private bath. $50-70 (Can).

B&B à Montréal B2

P.O. Box 575, Snowdon Station
Montréal, QUE, H3X 3T8
(514) 738-9410

Just one block from Montreal's theater complex, this condo apartment offers a delightful double room. For your convenience, she provides a secretary table stocked with stamps and cards. $50-70 (Can).

B&B à Montréal B3

P.O. Box 575, Snowdon Station
Montréal, QUE, H3X 3T8
(514) 738-9410

From this house you can walk to the hockey arena or the city's most elegant shopping complex. Stencilled glass windows, original woodwork and detail, and smart period furnishings are just some of the features of this home. $50-70 (Can).

B&B à Montréal B4

P.O. Box 575, Snowdon Station
Montréal, QUE, H3X 3T8
(514) 738-9410

Joggers and nature lovers—this is for you. A luxury apartment in one of Montreal's architectural gems offers a panorama of the city and the beauty of the park at the doorstep. Elegant furnishings, fireplace, and a gracious hostess. One double room. $50-70 (Can).

B&B à Montréal B5

P.O. Box 575, Snowdon Station
Montréal, QUE, H3X 3T8
(514) 738-9410

A delightful plant-filled townhouse featuring a grand piano. Relax in the master bedroom with a king bed. Enjoy browsing in the nearby antique shops and at the Atwater Market. $50-70 (Can).

Manoir Ambrose

3422 Stanley
Montreal, QUE, H3A 1R8
(514) 288-6922; FAX (514) 288-5757

Situated on the quiet and restful slope of beautiful Mount-Royal, within walking distance of Montreal's restaurants, theatres, shopping districts, metro system.

Host: Lucie Seguin
Rooms: 37 (23 PB; 14 SB) $45-70
Continental Breakfast
Credit Cards: A, B
Notes: 5, 6, 7, 8, 9, 14

POINT-AU-PIC

Auberge Donohue

145 Principal, CP 211
Point-au-Pic, QUE, G0T 1M0
(418) 665-4377

Situated right by the St. Lawrence River. All rooms with view of the river; some with fireplace, balcony, queen bed. Very large living room for our guests; private outdoor pool.

Host: Orval Aumont
Rooms: 17 (PB) $85-135
Continental Breakfast
Credit Cards: A, B
Notes: 2, 5, 7, 8, 9, 10, 11, 12, 13, 14

PORTNEUF

Edale Place

Edale Place
Portneuf, QUE, G0A 2Y0
(418) 286-3168

A family home of the Victorian era, quiet and comfortable, in open countryside only forty-five minutes from downtown Quebec. Flowers in summer, clean snow in winter.

Hosts: Mary & Tam Farnsworth
Rooms: 4 (SB) $50
Full Breakfast
Credit Cards: No
Notes: 5, 7, 8, 9, 11, 12, 13

ST-ANTOINE-DE-TILLY

Manoir De Tilly

3854 De Tilly Road
QUE, G0S 2C0
(418) 886-2407

Come taste typical Quebec cuisine in the warm atmosphere of a two-century-old manor. Located on the south shore of the St. Lawrence River, in one of the most beautiful villages of Quebec.

Hosts: Jocelyne & Majella Gagnon
Rooms: 32 (PB) $75-150
Full Breakfast
Credit Cards: A, B, C
Notes: 3, 4, 5, 7, 8, 9, 10, 11, 12, 14

ST-MARC-SUR-RICHELIEU

Auberge Handfield

555 Chemin du Prince
St-Marc-sur-Richelieu
QUE, J0L 2E0
(514) 584-2226

The Handfield Inn is a family business that stresses genuine hospitality. In 1984, major renovations enabled us to maintain efficiency and comfort without sacrificing the originality of this home, which was built more than 160 years ago.

Host: Mr. Conrad Handfield
Rooms: 50 (PB) $42-105
Continental Breakfast
Credit Cards: A, B, E, F
Notes: 4, 5, 7, 8, 9, 10, 11, 12, 13

Hostellerie Les Trois Tilleuls

290 rue Richelieu
St-Marc-sur-Richeliu
QUE, J0l 2E0
(514) 584-2231

The Hostellerie Les Trois Tilleuls is a charming inn on the banks of the Richelieu River, a short thirty minutes from Montreal. Twenty-five rooms with balconies overlooking the Richelieu River. The dining room features authentic French cuisine with an extensive wine list of exceptional vintages.

Host: Mr. Michel Aubriot
Rooms: 25 (PB) $81
Full Breakfast
Credit Cards: All
Notes: 4, 5, 7, 8, 9, 10, 11, 12, 13

SILLERY

Fernlea

2156 Rue Dickson
Sillery, QUE, G1T 1C9
(418) 683-3847

Beautiful home with an English garden in a quiet residential neighborhood. One minute to the bus taking you to Quebec's historic downtown area, the Plains of Abraham, museums, your choice of fine restaurants. Ten-minute walk to large shopping malls. Cross-country and downhill skiing in winter. Tours beginning at the house for the Isle of Orleans and other points of interest.

Host: Joyce Butler-Coutts
Rooms: 4 (S2B) $50-60
Continental-plus Breakfast
Credit Cards: No
Notes: 5, 8 (over 8), 9, 10, 11, 12, 13, 14

Puerto Rico

CEIBA

Ceiba Country Inn

P.O. Box 1067
Ceiba, Puerto Rico, 00635
(809) 885-0471

In the hills on the east coast, in a pastoral setting with a view of the sea. Quiet, serene atmosphere with a cozy cocktail lounge. Centrally located for trips to El Yunque, Luquillo, San Juan, Vieques, Culebra, and St. Thomas.

Hosts: Don Bingham & Nicki Treat
Rooms: 9 (PB) $55
Continental Breakfast
Credit Cards: A, B, C, E
Notes: 3, 5, 7, 8, 9, 11, 14

OCEAN PARK

Ocean Walk Guest House

Atlantic Place #1
Ocean Park, Puerto Rico, 00911
(809) 728-0855

Oceanfront guest house with a sun deck, swimming pool, cable TV in most rooms, open grill, and bar.

Host: Karl Walder
Rooms: 20 (14 PB; 6 SB) $40-100
Continental Breakfast
Credit Cards: A, B, C
Notes: 3, 5, 7, 8, 9, 10, 11, 14

SAN JUAN

El Canario Inn

1317 Ashford Avenue, Condado
San Juan, Puerto Rico, 00907
(809) 722-3861

San Juan's most historic and unique B&B. All guest rooms are air-conditioned, with private bath and telephone. Cable TV and Jacuzzi. Beautiful tropical patio areas for relaxation. Only one block to beautiful Condado Beach, casinos, boutiques, and many fine restaurants. El Canario is perhaps the best deal for your vacation dollar in the Caribbean.

Hosts: Jude & Keith Olson
Rooms: 25 (PB) $50-85
Continental Breakfast
Credit Cards: A, B, C, D, E
Notes: 5, 7, 8, 9, 10, 11, 12, 14

El Prado Inn

1350 Calle Luchetti
Condado, San Juan
Puerto Rico, 00907
(800) 468-4521; (809) 728-5925

Located in the most elegant section of San Juan, near beaches, casinos, restaurants, and major hotels.

Host: Anna Maria Lambdy
Rooms: 22 (PB)
Continental Breakfast
Credit Cards: All major
Notes: 2, 5, 6, 7, 8, 9, 10, 12, 14

Tres Palmas Guest House

2212 Park Blvd., San Juan
Puerto Rico, 00913
(809) 727-5434; (809) 727-4617

We provide a home away from home in a tropical setting where your days begin with fresh Puerto Rican coffee and friendly conversation. We are known as the best bar-

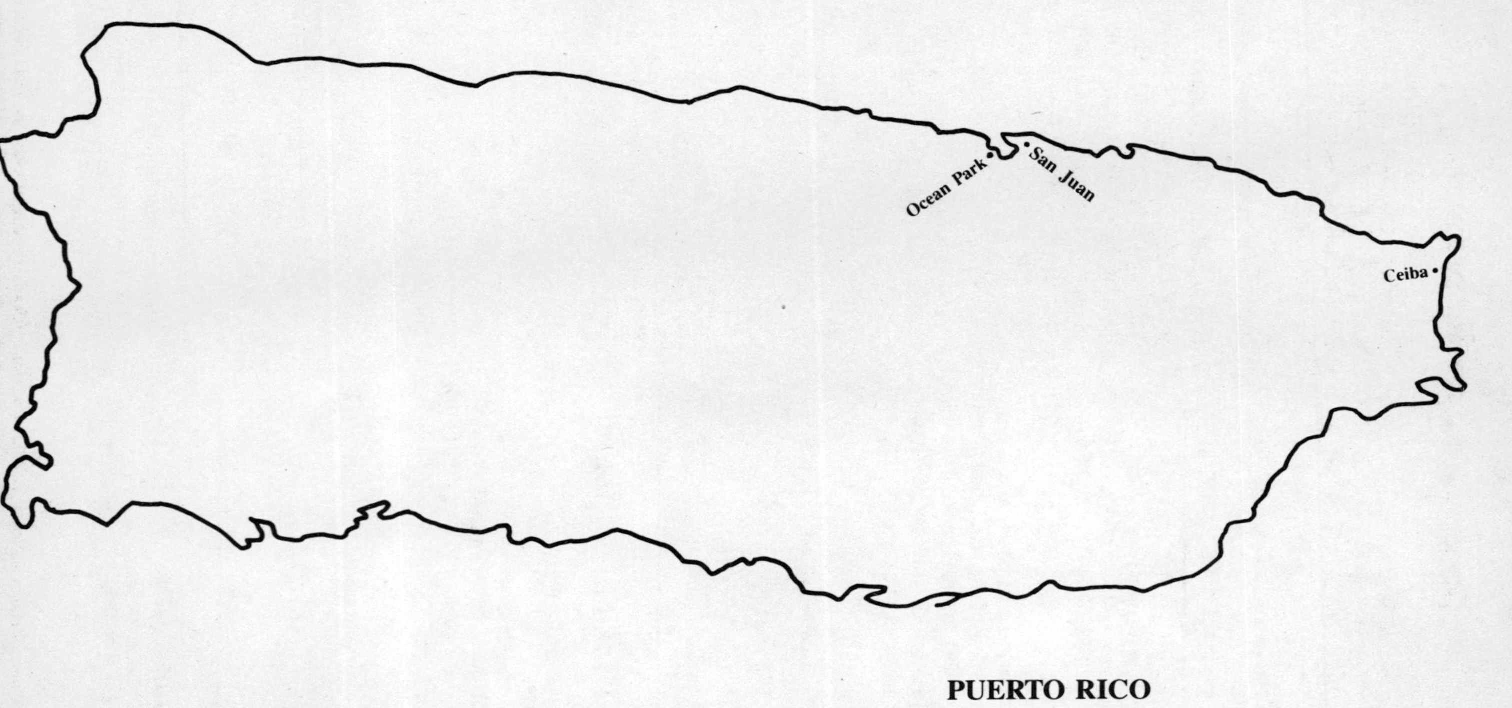

PUERTO RICO

gain on the island! Ocean front with sun roof and Jacuzzi-type pool.

Hosts: Jeannette & Elvin Torres
Rooms: 7 (5 PB; 2 SB) $40.10-87.80
Continental Breakfast
Credit Cards: A, B, C
Notes: 5, 7, 8 (12 and over), 9, 10, 11, 12, 14

SANTURCE

La Condesa Inn

Cacique 2071 Ocean Park
Santurce, Puerto Rico, 00911
(809) 727-3698; (809) 727-3900

This establishment is a four-star facility featuring a variety of well-appointed rooms and suites. One block from the ocean, with its own pool and dining area with bar. There are innumerable opportunities for visiting historical and recreational areas. Shopping and excellent dining nearby. Color cable TV and hot-spring spa.

Hosts: Luis and Eric Cintron
Rooms: 16 (PB) $55
Continental Breakfast, light lunch
Credit Cards: A, B, C
Notes: 3, 5, 6, 7, 8, 9, 10, 11, 14

Virgin Islands

ST. THOMAS

Danish Chalet Inn

Box 4319, St. Thomas
US Virgin Islands, 00803
(800) 635-1531; (809) 774-5764

Family-operated inn overlooking Charlotte Amalie Harbor. Five minute walk to duty-free shopping, boutiques, and waterfront activities. Ten minutes to the airport; ten to fifteen minutes to beaches. In-room phones, honor bar, sun deck, Jacuzzi, cool harbor and mountain breezes, congenial atmosphere.

Hosts: Frank & Mary Davis
Rooms: 13 (5 PB; 8 SB) $55-85
Continental Breakfast
Credit Cards: A, B
Checks 30 days in advance
Notes: 5, 7, 9, 14

Galleon House

P.O. Box 6577
St. Thomas
US Virgin Islands, 00804
(800) 524-2052; (809) 774-6952

Lovely fourteen-room small hotel in a historic district, one block from town. Fantastic harbor view. Warm, hospitable inn with delightful home-cooked breakfast. Fresh-water pool, easy walk to shopping and restaurants. Air-conditioned rooms with private balconies, cable TV, telephones, and guest refrigerators. Write or call for color brochure.

Hosts: Donna & John Slone
Rooms: 14 (12 PB; 2 SB) $45-115
Continental-plus Breakfast
Credit Cards: A, B, C
Notes: 5, 7, 8, 9, 10, 11, 12, 14

Inn at Mandahl

Box 2483, Charlotte Amalie
St. Thomas, US Virgin Islands, 00803
(809) 775-2100

Eight large rooms with private terraces and chaise lounges. All rooms face the ocean, giving a view of fourteen American and British islands from their perch on a hillside 200 feet above our beach. Quiet isolation on 15 acres adjacent to an eighteen-hole golf course on St. Thomas's cool north side. Complimentary continental breakfasts; pool; refrigerators in all rooms. Unsurpassable ambience.

Hosts: John & Deena Palmer
Rooms: 8 (PB) $61-118 seasonal
Continental Breakfast
Credit Cards: A, B, C
Notes: 2, 4, 5, 7, 8, 9, 10, 11, 12, 14

Island View Guest House

Box 1903, St. Thomas
US Virgin Islands, 00803
(800) 524-2023; (809) 774-4270

With a spectacular view of St. Thomas harbor, Island View is relaxed and low tempo. Telephone in every room. Air-conditioning and kitchens available on request. Cable TV on premises. Laundry facilities. Five minutes to town and beach. Our twenty-eighth year in business.

Hosts: Norman Leader & Barbara Cooper
Rooms: 15 (13 PB; 2 SB) $45-90
Continental Breakfast (full available)
Credit Cards: No
Notes: 5, 7, 8 (14 and over), 9, 11

Mafolie Hotel

P.O. Box 1506
St. Thomas, US Virgin Islands, 00804
(809) 774-2790; (800) 225-7035

Home of the "World Famous View" 800 feet above the town and harbor. Continental breakfast, free beach transportation to Magen's Bay. Fresh-water pool and large deck for sunning. Activities arranged at pool bar.

Hosts: Tony & Lyn Eden
Rooms: 23 (PB) $56-115
Continental Breakfast
Credit Cards: A, B
Notes: 2, 3, 4, 5, 7, 8, 9, 10, 11, 12, 14

6 Pets welcome: 7 Smoking allowed: 8 Children welcome: 9 Social drinking allowed: 10 Tennis available: 11 Swimming available: 12 Golf available: 13 Skiing available: 14 May be booked through travel agents